A HISTORY OF SOUTH-EAST ASIA

A HISTORY OF
SOUTH-EAST ASIA

BY

D. G. E. HALL

Professor Emeritus of the History of South-East Asia
University of London

THIRD EDITION

St. Martin's Press   New York

First edition 1955
Reprinted 1958, 1960, 1961
Second edition 1964
Reprinted 1964, 1965, 1966
Third edition 1968
Reprinted 1970 (twice), 1975, 1976

CONTENTS

PART I

TO THE BEGINNING OF THE SIXTEENTH CENTURY

PART II

SOUTH-EAST ASIA DURING THE EARLIER PHASE OF EUROPEAN EXPANSION

PART III

THE PERIOD OF EUROPEAN TERRITORIAL EXPANSION

PART IV
NATIONALISM AND THE CHALLENGE TO EUROPEAN DOMINATION

LIST OF ILLUSTRATIONS

ix

LIST OF MAPS

PREFACE TO THE THIRD EDITION

In introducing the new edition of his pioneer work, *Les États hindouisés d'Indochine et d'Indonésie*, in 1964 George Cœdès explained that since the publication of the previous edition in 1948 so much progress had been made by research that it had become necessary to rewrite much of the book to bring it up to date. And he went on to predict that within another fifteen years that edition also would become out of date. My own book, of course, covers a much wider area and a much longer period than *Les États*, and this would to some extent explain the need for radical revisions of parts of it within so much less a space of time. But, having said that, I realize that some further explanation is called for of the nature of the advance of knowledge in the field of South-East Asian history that has been responsible for the addition, among other things, of some four hundred titles to the previous bibliography. Some of them, it must be confessed, related to inadequacies in my own knowledge when writing the text of earlier editions. Others represent the results of the strong upsurge of interest, especially in America, in very recent history and current events. Most of them, however, are the outcome of the historian's interest in history for its own sake. They constitute attempts to improve upon the existing record by the discovery of new sources and/or the reinterpretation of existing ones.

Since the earliest edition of this book appeared in 1955 the study of the first fifteen centuries has been enriched by pioneer labours in several fields. In Burma's case Gordon Luce and his disciples Bohmu Ba Shin and Dr. Than Tun have used new epigraphical and archaeological discoveries for radical revisions of the chronicle stories. Some of them are summed up in Luce's paper, 'The Career of Htilaing Min (Kyanzittha), the Uniter of Burma, A.D. 1084–1113', read to the Royal Asiatic Society in 1966 on the occasion of his presentation with the Society's Triennial Gold Medal. His long-awaited *magnum opus* on Burma's history in the eleventh and twelfth centuries was in the press when these words were written.

In the Indonesian field also superb work has been done in exploring and interpreting epigraphical sources by J. G. de Casparis and the late L. Ch. Damais.[1] Three important works by leading Dutch archaeo-

[1] See Dr. Buchari's article, 'Epigraphy and Indonesian Historiography' in Soedjatmoko *et al.* (eds.), *An Introduction to Indonesian Historiography*, Ithaca (N.Y., 1965).

logists, W. F. Stutterheim,[2] F. D. K. Bosch[2] and H. R. van Heekeren,[3] have appeared in English translations, including Bosch's masterly assessment of the respective roles of Indians and Indonesians in the development of Indonesia's pre-Islamic culture. Notable use of Chinese sources has been made by Professor Wang Gung-wu of the University of Malaya in his illuminating study of the early history of Chinese trade with the South China Sea,[4] by Paul Wheatley in valuable studies of the historical geography of the Malay Peninsula and its environment before 1500,[5] and by O. W. Wolters in producing the first authentic account of early Sumatran commerce with the outside world.[6] Among other things Wolters describes the part played by Sumatran Malays in the development of east-west sea communications via the Malay Archipelago, thereby exploding the myth of the predominance of Indian maritime énterprise in that field.

Archaeological studies of the delta of the Mekong by Louis Malleret have helped to fill out our previously sketchy knowledge of Funan [7] while similar work by B. P. Groslier on the Angkor regior [8] has provided an introduction to the economic data without which it had previously been impossible to form realistic notions of the material basis of its civilization as well as of much of its political thought. These studies, together with Luce's work on the Pagan inscriptions [9] and van Naerssen's upon those of the Śailendra period in Java,[10] have demonstrated the fact that archaeology and epigraphy can provide essential source material for an understanding of social and economic life, and free the historian from dependence upon the jejune record of dynastic events, wars and supernatural portents provided by court chronicles and similar writings.

In 1955, when the first edition of this book appeared, students of the early history of Indonesia were much concerned with the questions raised by Professor C. C. Berg regarding the historical value of the masterpieces of Javanese literature, the *Arjunavivaha*, the *Pararaton*,

[1] *Studies in Indonesian Archaeology* (The Hague, 1956).
[2] *Selected Studies in Indonesian Archaeology* (The Hague, 1961).
[3] *The Stone Age of Indonesia* ('s Gravenhage, 1957).
[4] 'The Nanhai Trade; A Study of the Early History of Chinese Trade in the South China Sea.' JRASMB, vol. xxxi, part 2 (1958), pp. 1–135.
[5] *The Golden Khersonese; Studies in the Historical Geography of the Malay Peninsula before A.D. 1500* (Kuala Lumpur, 1961).
[6] *Early Indonesian Commerce; A Study of the Origins of Śrivijaya* (Ithaca, New York, 1967).
[7] *L'Archéologie du delta du Mékong*, 4 vols (Paris, 1959–63).
[8] *Angkor et le Cambodge au XVIe siècle d'après les sources portugaises et espagnoles* (Paris, 1958).
[9] 'The Economic Life of the Early Burman', JBRS, xxiii (1933), pp. 120–7.
[10] 'Some Aspects of the Hindu-Javanese Kraton', *Journal of the Oriental Society of Australia*, vol. ii, no. 1 (1963).

the *Nagarakertagama* and the *Babad Tanah Jawi*. His own interpretations of them stirred up much controversy, and pertinent criticisms of them have been published by F. D. K. Bosch,[1] J. G. de Casparis,[2] and P. J. Zoetmulder[3] in particular. The non-expert in Old Javanese literature, which is a very big field, is at a great disadvantage in trying to assess the chief issues involved; but it would seem to be begging the question for Damais, followed by Cœdès, to dismiss Berg's approach as 'far too theoretical' without any discussion. Cœdès, indeed, devoted a mere footnote in *Les États* (on pp. 337–8) to Berg's work. The most judicious estimate of it is by de Casparis in his paper contributed to *Historians of South-East Asia*. After pointing out the weaknesses in Berg's use of his own method he writes: 'In spite of these objections, I think that not only Berg's principles (if moderately and carefully applied), but also a number of his results will greatly assist progress on the difficult road towards a new conception of the older history of Indonesia.'[4]

The most weighty general criticism of Berg's method is by Father Zoetmulder, himself, like Berg, a lifelong student of Javanese literature. His main argument is that the use of the concept 'culture-pattern' is dangerous in the case of an extinct culture with no possibility of verification; for it means that in order to interpret the meaning of writings belonging to it one has to use those same writings as the key to understanding the culture itself, yet with a most inadequate knowledge of the language involved. Nevertheless, he declares, Berg's work is proof of the significance of cultural history for Indonesian historiography, for without these disciplines it would be 'simply impossible'. He sums up with the penetrating comment that Berg is far more interested in explaining the character of his Javanese sources than in writing new history.

In his slim volume, *Les Peuples de la Péninsule indochinoise*[5] Cœdès has made some challenging statements of much interest to every student of South-East Asian history. In the first place he complains—with reason—that writers of South-East Asian history—myself included—have attributed far too much importance to the period from Albuquerque's conquest of Malacca in 1511 onwards, and to European

[1] 'C. C. Berg and Ancient Javanese History', *Bijdr. Kon. Inst.* (1965), cxii.
[2] 'Historical Writing on Indonesia (Early Period)' in D. G. E. Hall (ed.), *Historians of South-East Asia*, pp. 121–63.
[3] 'The Significance of the Study of Culture and Religion for Indonesian Historiography' in Soedjatmoko, *An Introduction to Indonesian Historiography*, pp. 326–43.
[4] Pp. 161–2.
[5] Paris, 1962. The English translation (Berkeley and Los Angeles, 1966) bears the strangely inappropriate title *The Making of Southeast Asia*. It does not deal with Malaya or the island world of Indonesia and the Philippines.

activities in particular. They have tended, he says, to treat the first
fifteen centuries as merely a preamble to the five following ones, and
to consider these latter from a European rather than an Asian or national
point of view. And he goes on to declare that the repercussions of the
Western impact were more important upon European international
relationships than upon the political and cultural history of the Indo-
Chinese peninsula itself, particularly before the colonial period beginning in the nineteenth century. This last point, of course, is strikingly
true of the mainland area he is dealing with; he does well to emphasize
how very short was the duration of the European (French and British,
to be precise) empires there. The social and cultural effects of the
impact hardly show themselves in any real way before the end of the
century. But while deeply sympathizing with his dissatisfaction over the
disparity in the treatment of the earlier period compared with the later
one, I see no justification for reducing the scale of treatment of the
later period so as to make it conform more closely to that of the earlier,
as he does in his book. The plain fact is that the sources for the study
of the last five centuries are many, many times more numerous than
those for the earlier period. Moreover, the *apparatus scholasticus*
required by the researcher into the earlier period takes a lifetime to
acquire, so that the number of workers in the field is extremely limited;
and, if that were not enough, the difficulties imposed by the nature of
the material, and its lacunae, are often wellnigh insuperable. Nevertheless, let it be emphasized as strongly as possible that the early history
of the South-East Asian peoples is of special value to the student, and
not only because of its intrinsic interest, great and rewarding though it
is. It is vital to an understanding of their later history: one neglects it
at one's peril.

In striving to ascribe South-East Asians their proper place in their
own history Cœdès propounds a further thesis: that the real turning-
point in Indo-China's history came in the thirteenth century, long
before the coming of the Portuguese. It shows itself, he thinks, in the
decline of Sanskrit culture, the spread of Theravada Buddhism, and in
the Mongol invasions with the changes in political geography which
they caused, directly or indirectly. The centrepiece of his book is the
section entitled 'The crisis of the thirteenth century and the decline
of Indian civilization'. The thirteenth century was indeed a watershed
in the history of South-East Asia. Nevertheless, when one finds him in
the 1964 edition of *Les États hindouisés* describing the two subsequent
periods up to 1511 as 'The Decline of the Hindu Kingdoms' and 'The
End of the Hindu Kingdoms' one questions whether the use of such

terms betrays a failure to observe the real nature of the political and cultural developments of the fourteenth and fifteenth centuries, namely, the fact that the leading peoples, not only of the Indo-Chinese Peninsula, but in Indonesia also, were developing their own highly individual political systems and cultures. Their languages had long been used in inscriptions—a vast corpus—and had become the vehicles for literatures of no mean level. Indeed, what might look like an Indian superstructure was a mere façade. They were absorbing into their cultures various extraneous elements, Chinese and Indian, but at the same time adjusting them to their own requirements and outlook. If it is true, as I wrote in the Preface to the first edition, that South-East Asia's history cannot be safely viewed from any other perspective until seen from its own, something like this is equally true of its culture. For whatever foreign cultural elements the South-East Asian peoples have adopted, they have made uniquely their own.

Some of the most notable advances in knowledge have been made in the field of economic and social history, especially in the case of Indonesia. The publication in English of three works of outstanding importance, J. C. van Leur's *Indonesian Trade and Society* (The Hague, 1955), B. Schrieke's *Indonesian Sociological Studies* (2 vols, The Hague, 1955, 1957) and W. F. Wertheim's *Indonesian Society in Transition* (The Hague, 1956, 2nd ed. 1964), has considerably influenced historical thought. In addition, three authoritative research monographs, Mrs. M. A. Meilink-Roelofsz's *Asian Trade and European Influence in the Indonesian Archipelago between 1500 and about 1630* (The Hague, 1962), Kristof Glamann's *Dutch Asiatic Trade, 1620–1740* (The Hague, 1958) and G. C. Allen and Audrey G. Donnithorne's *Western Enterprise in Indonesia and Malaya: A Study in Economic Development* (London, 1957), have provided the student with a large body of information not available before, and expert guidance in its interpretation. One must also acknowledge such valuable studies as John S. Bastin's *The Native Policies of Sir Stamford Raffles in Java and Sumatra* (London, 1957), J. A. M. Caldwell's masterly essay, 'Indonesian Export and Production from the Decline of the Culture System to the First World War' (in C. D. Cowan (ed.) *The Economic Development of South-East Asia*, London, 1964), Ruth T. McVey's *The Rise of Indonesian Communism* (Ithaca, New York, 1965) and Clifford Geertz's *The Religion of Java* (Glencoe, Ill., 1960). For the neighbouring area of Malaya Dr. Wong Lin-Ken has added much to our knowledge with his *The Trade of Singapore, 1819–69* (JRASMB, vol. xxxiii, part 4) and *The Malayan Tin Industry to 1914* (Tucson, Arizona, 1965), the latter of which will long remain the definitive work on its subject. For other areas valuable additions to knowledge have been made by Father de la Costa's *The Jesuits in the Philippines, 1581–1768* (Cambridge, Mass., 1961), Frank H. Golay's *The Philippines, Public Policy and National Economic Development* (Ithaca, New York, 1961), Hugh Tinker's *The Union of Burma* (London, 1957), D. E. Smith's *Religion and Politics in Burma* (New Jersey, 1965), Winston L. King's *A Thousand Lives Away, Buddhism in Contemporary Burma* (Oxford and London, 1964) and Louis J. Walinsky's *Economic Development in Burma, 1951–1960* (New York, 1962). Besides these, but with more emphasis upon political history, other noteworthy monographs that have made their mark are Le Thanh Khoi's *Le Vietnam, Histoire et Civilisation* (Paris, 1955), John F. Cady's *History of Modern Burma* (Ithaca, New York, 1958), C. Northcote Parkinson's *British Intervention in Malaya, 1867–1877* (Singapore, 1960) and C. D. Cowan's *Nineteenth-Century Malaya, The Origins of British Political Control* (London, 1961).

Some extremely interesting publications of the historian's basic materials must be noted. The G. Th. Pigeaud has provided us with a lavish English edition of Prapanca's Old Javanese masterpiece, the *Nagarakertagama* (*Java in the Fourteenth Century*, 5 vols, The Hague, 1960–3). A welcome new printing of Pe Maung Tin and G. H. Luce's translation of the early portions of the Burmese *Glass Palace Chronicle* has been issued by Rangoon University Press (1960). From the Dutch records have come two huge volumes of Snouck Hurgronje's *Ambtelijke Adviezen, 1889–1936* (The Hague, 1957, 1959) and Dr. W. Ph. Coolhaas's selection of the Dutch East India Company's *Generale Missieven* for the years 1610–38 (The Hague, 1960). Also in the Indonesian field is C. Skinner's fine English edition of the *Sja'ir Perang Mengkasir* (The Rhymed Chronicle of the Macassar War, The Hague, 1963) and A. H. Johns's 'Malay Sufism' (JRASMB, xxx, part 2, 1957), an edited translation of eighteen Sufi tracts composed at Acheh in the seventeenth century. From the India Office records in London have come two edited collections of original documents, Alastair Lamb's *British Missions to Cochin China: 1778–1822* (JRASMB, xxxiv, parts 3 and 4, 1961) and my own *Michael Symes: Journal of His Second Embassy to the Court of Ava in 1802* (London, 1955).

Finally, three further features of the advance in South-East Asian historical studies must be briefly mentioned. Interest in the great achievements of South-East Asian art in the past has been much stimulated by the publication of a number of superbly illustrated volumes by such experts as B. P. Groslier (Indo-China), Frits A. Wagner

(Indonesia), A. J. Bernet Kempers (Ancient Indonesia), Alexander Griswold (Burma) and Louis Frédéric. In the second place there has been a marked upsurge of interest in South-East Asian historiography, as, of course, is only to be expected when one realizes how great has been the expansion in the study of South-East Asian history itself. The South-East Asia section of the Conference on Historical Writings on the Peoples of Asia, held at the London School of Oriental and African Studies in 1956, produced and discussed a wide range of papers dealing with historiography, and these were subsequently published under the title *Historians of South-East Asia* (London, 1961). A further symposium entitled *An Introduction to Indonesian Historiography*, edited by Soedjatmoko and three associates, was issued by Cornell University Press in 1965. The two volumes contain a wealth of information. Then in the third place the number of general histories has been increased by John F. Cady's *Southeast Asia; its historical Development* (New York, 1964), B. R. Pearn's *Outline of South-East Asian History* (Kuala Lumpur, 1963) and Nicholas Tarling's *Concise History of South-East Asia* (New York, 1966).

All the developments so briefly chronicled in this Preface indicate tremendous vitality in the study of our subject, especially in the realm of original research. There is much pioneering in which the discovery and absorption of new material are the important tasks. Moreover, with the establishment of centres and programmes students of different disciplines are coming together in co-operative effort and money is being found for more and more field-work. How vitally necessary this is can only be understood by anyone familiar with the work that was carried on in the days of the colonial régimes.

ACKNOWLEDGMENT

My sincere thanks go to Miss Patricia Herbert, my research assistant during a spell of teaching at the University of Michigan, Ann Arbor, for taking over much of the burden of preparing the Bibliography in this volume.

PREFACE TO THE FIRST EDITION

THE present work, large and detailed though it may appear to the reader unfamiliar with the subject, is a bare outline, perilously compressed and oversimplified in many parts. As an introduction to South-East Asian history, designed as much for the non-specialist reader as for the student intending to pursue the subject further, its story is told with as few distracting footnotes as possible. Special care, however, has been bestowed upon the selection and arrangement of titles for the bibliography. The available literature, it may be remarked, is immense, running to many thousands of books, articles and collections of printed documents. For the earlier periods there are thousands of inscriptions and a great mass of local chronicles still inadequately explored. For the later periods the contemporary accounts, documents and memoirs listed in Section III of the bibliography are of quite unusual interest.

So much research work is in progress, by European scholars and, happily, an ever-increasing number of Asian ones, that it is difficult to keep pace with the progress of discovery and interpretation over the whole field. Hence the treatment of many subjects, especially in the very important pre-European period, must be regarded as provisional only. For instance, Burma's wealth of inscriptions—and she is incomparably richer in this respect than any other region of South-East Asia—is likely soon to yield results of no little importance as a result of the devoted labours of Gordon Luce over many years. These will certainly lead to modifications in the account of the Pagan period given here. Then, also, research by both Dutch and Indonesian scholars during the past twenty years or so is likely to lead to considerable revision of N. J. Krom's version of Old Javanese history. An attempt has been made here to indicate the importance of C. C. Berg's recent series of attacks upon accepted notions regarding the story of Airlangga's division of his kingdom, the reign of Kertanagara and the early Majapahit period. A final pronouncement on these matters is at present impossible, and it is well to take into account the prudent assessment of the situation by J. G. de Casparis in his valuable 'Twintig jaar studie van de oudere geschiedenis van Indonesië'.[1]

[1] *Orientatie*, no. 46, 1954, pp. 638–41.

The early chapters of this book owe much to George Cœdès's *Les États hindouisés d'Indochine et d'Indonésie*, to which the highest tribute must be paid, not only as a work of rare scholarship but also for presenting for the first time the early history of South-East Asia as a whole. Previously the history of the individual states had been treated so much in isolation that the significance of their many parallel developments was hardly realized. The attention drawn to them by Cœdès has been immensely stimulating to thought and research.

The work that has been done by European scholars in the discovery of South-East Asian history is beyond praise. Krom's monumental *Hindoe-Javaansche Geschiedenis*, indeed, takes its place among the great works of pioneer research. There are, however, today signs of dissatisfaction on the part of European scholars themselves with their previous approach to the subject, which, it is felt, has been too much influenced by certain preconceptions inherent in their own training and outlook. De Casparis applies the epithet 'Europe-centric' to this approach, and contends that it shows itself clearly in F. W. Stapel's ponderous five-volume *Geschiedenis van Nederlandsch Indië*, in which the 'Hindu period' of Indonesian history is treated as if it were a sort of prelude or introduction to the history of Dutch activities. Similarly, Indian writers, who largely through the work of the French and the Dutch have come to discover 'Greater India', may be accused of an India-centric approach. The revolutionary change that has come over South-East Asia since the Second World War has inevitably led to much re-examination of the older conceptions of its history, and to attempts at a reorientation of outlook.

It is in this respect that Berg's work assumes special significance. For not only has he made a lifelong study of Indonesian historical literature, but he has laid down also a method of approach to its interpretation which, though admittedly imposing a heavy task on the historian, is the only one which he believes is capable of giving trustworthy results. He explains it as the need to see a people's history-writing as an element in its culture pattern, which is not isolated, either structurally or in its evolutionary and dynamic aspect, from the remainder. The literatures of the peoples of South-East Asia abound in writings which are either in chronicle form or connected with historical events. Their number is legion; some are of great length. Relatively few have as yet been used by historical writers. The great majority still await exploration and comparative study. The significance of Berg's challenge therefore extends far beyond his own field of research.

This book is in the main based upon lecture courses delivered to university classes in London, Rangoon and Singapore. Parts of it have been used in lectures delivered in the University of Indonesia at Djakarta and the Chulalongkorn University at Bangkok. It was as a result of the experience gained while conducting these classes, and through contacts with students and teachers in South-East Asia, that the author came to realize the need for some such book as the present one. It represents, therefore, a survey of work already published in one form or another. He has, however, incorporated in several chapters—those dealing with Arakan, the background to Singapore and the reign of Bodawpaya of Burma—the results of his own recent researches, not as yet published.

The completely objective history has never been produced, nor are one man's knowledge and judgement adequate for a fully satisfactory treatment of so vast a subject as the present one. What is attempted here is first and foremost to present South-East Asia historically as an area worthy of consideration in its own right, and not merely when brought into contact with China, India or the West. Its history cannot be safely viewed from any other perspective until seen from its own. With the available literature for its present study this is not at all easy, particularly in the case of the period after 1511, the history of which in European writings tends to be rather that of European activities in South-East Asia than of South-East Asia itself. To many of them—though not all[1]—de Casparis's epithet 'Europe-centric' applies with special force.

The extent to which this book manages to achieve its declared object is a matter over which opinions may differ, but the writer hopes that the sources of its inspiration—the delight he has had in his long association with South-East Asian students, and the friendship and kindness they have always shown him—have made it possible for him to treat the history of their peoples with sympathy and understanding, and to convey some sense of the intellectual stimulus and illumination to be derived from its study.

The spelling of proper names has presented many problems. Various systems of romanization have been used by European writers. These are discussed on pages 99–104 of the author's section on South-East Asia in C. H. Philips's *Handbook of Oriental History* (Royal Hist. Soc., 1951). Writers of history have tended to vary these according to taste, and usually with the object of avoiding the excessive use of

---

[1] Notable exceptions are the histories of Burma by A. P. Phayre and G. E. Harvey respectively, and W. A. R. Wood's *History of Siam*.

diacritical signs. Moreover, there is no uniformity of practice as between the different states today, so that in a work such as this absolute consistency in the representation of sounds is impossible. Here the method followed has been to simplify spellings and avoid inconsistencies wherever possible. The result may not please the language scholar, but it has seemed the best way out of the difficulty. The following points are a useful guide to pronunciation:

(i) Vowels have Italian values; consonants generally English ones.

(ii) In Burmese words a consonant is aspirated by placing 'h' *before* it; in Tai words by placing the 'h' *after* it. But since this may cause confusion in the cases of 't' and 'p', the method used here is to show the aspirated forms by the use of an apostrophe after these letters, except in the case of the word 'Thailand', which is the form officially adopted by that country.

(iii) Special cases:
'g' is hard, but the Burmese 'gy' is pronounced 'j';
initial 'ky' is pronounced 'ch';
final 'n' in Burmese represents a nazalization of the preceding vowel;
initial 'ng' is pronounced like the final 'ng' in 'sing';
'ś' in Sanskrit words, e.g. Śrivijaya, is pronounced 'sh';
'ou' is normally pronounced 'oo', but in 'Toungoo', an older form of spelling, it represents 'ow' as in 'plow'.

ACKNOWLEDGMENTS

My special thanks are due to Professor W. Ph. Coolhaas, Professor C. H. Philips, Mr. A. H. Christie and Mr. C. D. Cowan, who read portions of my script before it went to the press, and to Mr. H. R. Klieneberger of the Library staff of the School of Oriental and African Studies for checking the entries in the bibliography. Dr. Coolhaas's detailed notes on my treatment of Dutch activities were of much help, and if we were unable to agree on a number of matters, I am none the less deeply grateful to him for his help.

I must also thank the various institutions and individuals who have kindly allowed me to reproduce illustrations of which they hold the copyright. Their names are recorded in the list of illustrations on pp. ix–xi. To Mr. A. H. Christie I am specially indebted for permission to use his map of the Prehistory of Eastern Asia, and much help in the preparation of other maps.

My wife has given unstinted help in the preparation of the typescript, and in proof-reading and indexing; and even more in the patience she has shown during many months when all my spare time was devoted to the writing of this book.

D.G.E.H.

PREFACE TO THE SECOND EDITION

MY very grateful thanks must be expressed to Dr. J. G. de Casparis, Professor C. D. Cowan and Dr. O. W. Wolters for the valuable help they have given me in preparing the new material for this edition. The exciting reconstruction of the early history of Sumatra provided by Dr. Wolters comes from his as yet unpublished work *Early Indonesian Commerce and the Origins of Śrivijaya*, which throws entirely fresh light upon South-East Asian proto-history.

D.G.E.H.

ABBREVIATIONS

BEFEO	Bulletin de l'Ecole Française d'Extrême Orient (Hanoi).
BKI	Bijdragen van het Koninklijk Instituut voor de Taal-Land-en Volkenkunde ('s-Gravenhage).
BSEI	Bulletin de la Société des Etudes Indochinoises de Saigon.
BSOAS	Bulletin of the School of Oriental and African Studies (London).
CEFEO	Cahiers de l'Ecole Française d'Extrême Orient (Hanoi).
DNB	Dictionary of National Biography (London).
FEQ	Far Eastern Quarterly (Ithaca, N.Y.).
FES	Far Eastern Survey (New York).
HRAF	Human Relations Area Files
JA	Journal Asiatique.
J.Am.O.Soc.	Journal of the American Oriental Society (Newhaven, Conn.)
JBRS	Journal of the Burma Research Society (Rangoon).
JGIS	Journal of the Greater India Society (Calcutta).
JRAS	Journal of the Royal Asiatic Society (London).
JRASMB	Journal of the Royal Asiatic Society, Malayan Branch. (Singapore).
JSS	Journal of the Siam Society (Bangkok).
RAA	Revue des Arts Asiatiques (Paris).
TBG	Tijdschrift van het Bataviaasch Genootschap van Kunsten en Wetenschappen (Batavia, now Jakarta).

PART I
TO THE BEGINNING OF THE SIXTEENTH CENTURY

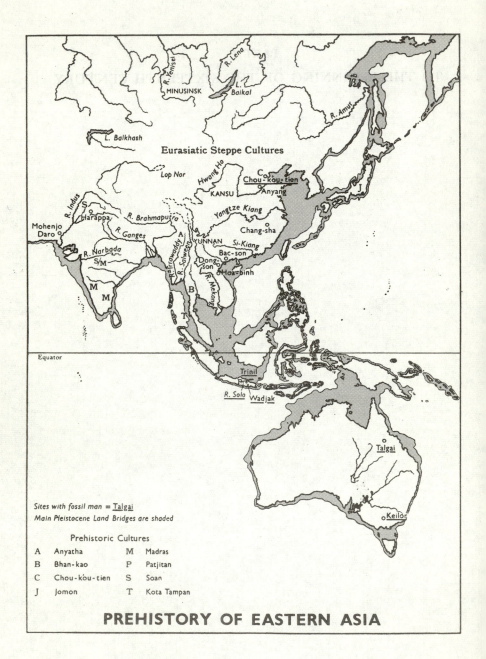

Eurasiatic Steppe Cultures

Sites with fossil man = <u>Talgai</u>
Main Pleistocene Land Bridges are shaded

Prehistoric Cultures

A	Anyatha	M	Madras
B	Bhan-kao	P	Patjitan
C	Chou-kou-tien	S	Soan
J	Jomon	T	Kota Tampan

PREHISTORY OF EASTERN ASIA

CHAPTER I

THE PEOPLING OF SOUTH-EAST ASIA

SOUTH-EAST ASIA is a term which came into general use during the Second World War to describe the territories of the eastern Asiatic mainland forming the Indo-Chinese peninsula and the immense archipelago which includes Indonesia and the Philippines. In using the term American writers have standardized the form 'Southeast' and have been followed by Victor Purcell[1] and E. H. G. Dobby.[2] But there seems to be no valid reason for coining a new form in preference to either 'South-East' or 'South East', both of which have the sanction of long usage. The Royal Navy uses the hyphen. During the war SEAC used the unhyphenated form, but the Mountbatten Report[3] reverts to the use of the hyphen. Like all terms applied to a large area for the sake of convenience, it is open to a number of objections. Discussion of these here is unnecessary, since our use of the term is dictated solely by convenience.

The area with which the present work is concerned includes the mainland states of Burma, Thailand, Laos, Cambodia, North and South Vietnam and Malaya together with the two great island groups comprised in the Republic of Indonesia and the Republic of the Philippines. The Philippines, however, do not come clearly into South-East Asian history until their conquest by Spain late in the sixteenth century. And as Spain linked them up closely with Mexico, and the United States of America acquired them at the end of the nineteenth century, their part in South-East Asian history was slight, especially after the middle of the seventeenth century, when Dutch efforts to wrest them from Spain finally broke down. The rest of this vast area is one upon which from very early times Chinese and Indian influences have been brought to bear, and in one part of which, Annam and Cochin China, there was for many centuries an intense struggle between them for supremacy. Its cultural history is of marked interest, therefore, especially during the period of the Middle Ages in Europe, when, under the stimulus

[1] *The Chinese in Southeast Asia*, 1951.
[2] *Southeast Asia*, 1950.
[3] *Report to the Combined Chiefs of Staff by the Supreme Allied Commander South-East Asia*, 1951.

of Indian influences, art and architecture developed to a pitch which bears comparison with anything the rest of the world can show.

By the end of the Middle Ages, when the Portuguese appeared on the scene, South-East Asia was divided into two main cultural areas: one called by the French scholars *l'Inde extérieure*, where Indian influences predominated, and the other, consisting of Tongking, Annam and Cochin China, where, with the fall of the 'Hinduized' kingdom of Champa in the fifteenth century, Chinese influences had the mastery.

The reader must be warned, however, against the insidious tendency to overstress the part played by the imported cultures and to under-rate the importance of the indigenous ones of the area. The use of such terms as 'Further India', 'Greater India' or 'Little China' is to be highly deprecated. Even such well-worn terms as 'Indo-China' and 'Indonesia' are open to serious objections, since they obscure the fact that the areas involved are not mere cultural appendages of India or China but have their own strongly-marked individuality. The art and architecture which blossomed so gorgeously in Angkor, Pagan, central Java and the old kingdom of Champa are strangely different from that of Hindu and Buddhist India. For the real key to its under-standing one has to study the indigenous cultures of the peoples who produced it. And all of them, it must be realized, have developed on markedly individualistic lines.

Indian influence, which, unlike Chinese, had no political implica-tions, was, in the process of absorption by the native societies in South-East Asia, transformed just as much as, for example, that of ancient Greece was in its impact upon western Europe. For the peoples who felt the stimulus of Indian culture were, as George Cœdès puts it,[1] not 'wild men' but communities with a relatively high civilization of their own. And even the Vietnamese, who were under Chinese rule from 111 B.C. to A.D. 939, and under the Han were subjected to inten-sive sinization, developed a culture which, while owing an immense amount to China, nevertheless preserved its own identity, with its roots going back to a pre-Chinese past.

The main reason for this failure to pay due regard to the indigenous culture of the peoples of our region is easy to see. Both politically and culturally, South-East Asia has been overshadowed by India and China, which were great powers with established civilizations long before her own historical period begins. And it was only through the fertilizing impact of their cultures that her own began to develop and

[1] *Les États hindouisés d'Indochine et d'Indonésie*, 1948, p. 27.

achieve greatness. For obvious reasons also, when European scholars became aware of it their attention was concentrated upon rulers, Courts and temples, where the external influences were strongest, while their approach had necessarily to be made in the first instance through Chinese or Sanskrit writings.

The evidence of the life of the common people has been much harder to come by, and so far all too little has been discovered. What does exist, however, points indubitably to the fact that in the so-called 'Hinduized' states the great mass of the people was for long either untouched by Indian culture or in absorbing it changed it by bringing it into line with indigenous ideas and practices. Thus the structure of society was largely unaffected by Indian influences. The caste system, which is fundamental to Hinduism, has had notably little influence, and woman has largely maintained the high place accorded her before the earliest impact of Indian culture, a far higher one than she has ever occupied in India during recorded history. Moreover, after the introduction of Hinduism and Buddhism the religious ideas and practices of earlier times persisted with immense vitality, and in coming to terms with them both religions were profoundly changed.

South-East Asia today is an anthropologist's paradise. In its mountains and jungles live the remnants of a great variety of peoples representing early stages of its ethnological history: pigmy Negritos living as primitive nomads, peoples akin to the Australian aborigines, and others that would appear to be Indonesians in more backward stages of development. There has obviously been a great deal of intermixture between the earlier inhabitants and later comers. The whole area, indeed, has been described as a chaos of races and languages.

Traces of extremely early human types have been discovered in Java. Eugéne Dubois's *Pithecanthropus erectus* and von Koenigswald's even earlier *Homo modjokertensis* belong to the early pleistocene age, and were once thought to form a race apart in human history. The late pleistocene age has yielded eleven skulls, found at Ngandong in the Solo valley, which are of a more advanced human type, but with a reasonably close affinity to the pithecanthropoid type. Then there are the Wadjak skulls of late pleistocene or post-pleistocene age, which appear to be related to proto-australoid man.

Homo modjokertensis and *Pithecanthropus erectus* have been shown to be closely related with *Sinanthropus* or Peking Man, and their artefacts, like his, are akin to those of the Soan culture of north-west India and the Anyathian of Burma. On the basis of the evidence so far examined two hypotheses of outstanding interest have been formulated:

(*a*) that the mongoloid peoples are ultimately derived from this stem, and (*b*) that a clear line may be traced linking *Pithecanthropus erectus* through *Homo soloensis* (i.e. the Ngandong skulls) with *Homo australicus*. If this should turn out to be true, (*a*) the mongoloid features that are so widespread today over our area were not, as was once thought, introduced for the first time by neolithic or bronze-age immigrants; (*b*) a branch of *Homo sapiens* must have evolved in South-East Asia, since there is no evidence of its having done so in Australia; and (*c*) the theory that the mesolithic Veddoid peoples were the original inhabitants of South-East Asia is exploded.

The traces of a mesolithic culture are widespread. It has been named Bacsono-Hoabinhian from the regions where the greatest number of its artefacts has been found, the provinces of Bacson and Hoabinh in Tongking. The distinguishing feature of its stone implements is that they are worked on one side only. With them have been found bone utensils and pottery. The human remains have been interpreted to indicate a dark-skinned race of small stature and of Australoid-Veddoid type. Traces of a Melanesoid type have been found in Indo-China. Artefacts of these peoples have been found in northern Annam, Luang Prabang, Siam, Malaya, and on the east coast of Sumatra. Anthropologists have classified these people as Veddoid after the Vedda tribes of Ceylon, and assign to this group the Senoi and Sakai hill-tribes of Malaya, and other backward peoples of south Celebes and on the Engano and Mentawei Islands off the west coast of Sumatra.

They practised ritual cannibalism. The men were hunters, fishermen and collectors; the women in some cases used a primitive mattock for cultivating the soil. Canoes made out of hollowed-out tree trunks were in use. There has been much speculation as to the possible connection of this culture with the neolithic, which succeeded it. Von Heine-Geldern, for instance, has ventured the theory, challenged by other scholars, that the neolithic oval-axe culture found in northern Burma, among the Nagas of Assam, in Cambodia and in the eastern islands of the Archipelago, is connected with the use of a plank-built canoe, and that both represent a development of mesolithic culture.

Two other forms of celt come from the neolithic period: the shouldered axe found in many places from the Ganges to Japan, but not south of a line drawn through the middle of the Malay Peninsula, and, most widespread of all, the rectangular axe, found in the river valleys of the Hoang-Ho, Yangtse, Mekong, Salween, Irrawaddy and Brahmaputra, as well as throughout Indonesia. As it is found in its purest form on the Malay Peninsula and in middle and south Sumatra, this has been taken to have been the route by which it reached Indonesia.

Discussion has centred round the possible relationship between the shouldered axe and the rectangular axe, and the connection of both with the spread of the Austro-Asiatic languages. Von Heine-Geldern identifies the shouldered axe with the culture of the Mon-Khmer peoples of the mainland, and thinks that the neolithic peoples who brought the rectangular axe culture spread also the Austronesian languages. Van Heekeren, on the other hand, rightly warns against identifying culture waves or migrations with the spread of a language, and points to the lack of archaeological confirmation for von Heine-Geldern's theories.[1]

The distribution of the rectangular axe culture does coincide roughly with that of the Austronesian languages, and it is noteworthy that its influences are found not only throughout Indonesia but also in places as far apart as Madagascar in the west and Easter Island in the east. It is of great interest also because of the great developments in the arts achieved by the immigrants bringing it. They were Malays, or Indo-nesians, as some scholars prefer to call them. Both terms are open to objection; 'Indonesian' suggests the boundaries of the present Republic, while to many readers 'Malay' suggests the population of Malaya or the coastal Malays in many parts of the Archipelago. Actually, however, ever since F. and P. E. Sarasin made their study of the racial composition of Indonesia[2] the word 'Malay' has had a wide ethnic significance. Their migration into South-East Asia occupied several centuries before the beginning of the Christian era, and although opinion today does not favour the Sarasins' theory of two main waves, the first, of 'Proto-Malays' bringing an advanced neolithic culture, and the second, of 'Deutero-Malays' bringing a bronze-iron one, it is still impossible to be precise about what happened. Hendrik Kern, the pioneer of research into the origin of the Indonesian languages, thought that the liguistic evidence pointed to the region of Champa, Cochin-China and Cambodia as the birthplace of the neolithic culture. Von Heine-Geldern traces the original home of the people, who introduced it, farther back to the region in western China where the great rivers of east and south-east Asia have their origin. Their tools show them to have been excellent wood-workers. They decorated their wooden houses with beautiful carving, produced pottery and are thought to have made woven fabrics.

[1] H. R. van Heekeren, *The Stone Age of Indonesia*, 1957, p. 131.
[2] P. E. Sarasin, *Reisen in Celebes*, 1905.

There seems to be evidence also that prior to their arrival in the islands they knew how to cultivate rice.[1]

There is no evidence in support of the theory that metal-culture was introduced by a new wave of immigrants. Duyvendak, indeed, not only denies categorically that there were two migrations of Malay peoples into South-East Asia, but asserts that a knowledge of metals was brought to elements of the coastal population through trading contacts with foreigners. The culture originated in China and Tong-king in about 300 B.C., and in the Chinese *Ch'ien Han Shu* there is authentic evidence of the coastal barter through which it came to the lands to the south.[2]

This culture cannot be strictly characterized as bronze since iron was also worked at the same time. The name Dong-Son has been applied to it from the village in Tongking where the most striking evidence of it has been found. Bronze work of a very high order was produced, a notable feature of which were the kettle-drums of various types and sizes used for ritual purposes throughout the whole area of South-East Asia.[3] The peoples of this culture developed high skill in navigation and boat-building; they were hardy seafarers with some knowledge of astronomy. They travelled far and wide as merchants, and it is interesting to note that some of their trade names for weights and measures are still used in India and China.

Another marked characteristic was the association of megaliths with their religion. These monuments comprise images, usually of ancestors, grinding stones with a magical significance, troughs in which skulls were preserved, menhirs which may have been phallic symbols, dolmens at burial places, burial chambers of long flat stones and terrace graves. Von Heine-Geldern thinks that, while most of this culture belongs to the bronze-iron age, some goes back to the neolithic period. The earlier he characterizes as monumental and symbolic, the later as more graphic and ornamental. Van Heekeren, however, has pointed out that while neolithic megaliths of this kind occur in eastern Polynesia none has yet been discovered in Indonesia or the Indo-Chinese peninsula.[4]

Thus when South-East Asia felt the earliest impact of Indian culture, it possessed a civilization of its own. Cœdès[5] sums up its

---

[1] van Heekeren, *op. cit.*, p. 131.
[2] J. Ph. Duyvendak, *Inleiding tot de Ethnologie van de Indonesische Archipel*, 1946.
[3] H. R. van Heekeren, 'Bronzen Keteltrommen', *Orientatie*, no. 46, Jan. 1954, pp. 615–25. *See also* Bibliography, iv, s.v. Goloubew, von Heine-Geldern, van der Hoop, Lévy, Mansuy, and Tweedie.
[4] *The Stone Age of Indonesia*, p. 131.
[5] *Op. cit.*, pp. 25–6.

characteristics thus: on the material side (i) the cultivation of irrigated ricefields, (ii) the domestication of the ox and buffalo, (iii) a rudimentary use of metals, and (iv) skill in navigation; on its social side (i) the importance of woman and of descent by the maternal line, and (ii) the organization resulting from irrigated cultivation; on its religious side (i) animism, (ii) the worship of ancestors and of the god of the soil, (iii) the location of shrines on high places, (iv) burial in jars or at dolmens, and (v) a mythology imbued with a cosmological dualism of mountain *versus* sea, winged beings *versus* water beings, men of the mountain *versus* men of the sea-coast. Furthermore, its separate languages have shown a remarkable faculty for derivation by way of prefixes, suffixes and infixes. Peoples more or less impregnated with this culture, though of much racial diversity, were to be found over most of the area, living mainly in coastal districts and along river valleys. Further inland, and in the mountains, were others, in various degrees of backwardness.

Krom, from his study of Javanese civilization before the coming of Indian influence, adds to the list given by Cœdès (i) the *wayang*, or puppet shadow theatre, (ii) the *gamelan* orchestra, and (iii) *batik* work.[1] In such a vast area there were naturally local diversities of culture. It is significant, however, that the Chinese would seem to have had some idea of the cultural unity of the region when they applied to its various peoples and languages the name K'un-lun, if, indeed, those scholars are correct who attribute so wide a meaning to the term.[2] It may be of some significance that I Tsing, writing in the late seventh century, says that the term was applied to the people from the south who first came to Tongking and Canton, presumably as traders. Thus it was probably originally used for the maritime peoples of the coast of Indo-China, and later extended to the population of Indonesia, i.e. all the Malay-type peoples.

There has been much scholarly discussion about the possible relationship between this culture and that of pre-Aryan India in attempts to explain the evidence of tools and language indicating cultural elements common to both regions. One theory is of ethnic waves, originating in Indo-China or the islands, flowing into India before the arrival of the Aryans. Another is of an exodus of aboriginal inhabitants from India to South-East Asia resulting from the arrival of either the Dravidians or the Aryans. They are, of course, purely speculative. Pater Schmidt applied the term 'Austric' to the two great groups of

[1] *Hindoe-Javaansch Geschiedenis*, pp. 47–8.
[2] Cœdès, *op. cit.*, pp. 26–7, discusses this point.

Austro-Asiatic and Austronesian languages found in the area stretching from the Himalayas to Easter Island and from Madagascar to Hawaii when attempting to demonstrate their underlying unity. Their relations with the pre-Dravidian Munda languages of India, now for the most part lost, were first traced by the Austrian philologist Franz Felix Adalbert Kuhn, who died in 1886. Then Schmidt, having shown the lexicographic relationship between the Austric and the Munda groups, went on to formulate the theory that the peoples speaking them were mutually related, culturally and anthropologically. So far, however, solid evidence of this is completely lacking, and the tendency today is to view with suspicion any attempt to identify culture waves or migrations of peoples with the spread of a language. One must bear in mind that in the greater part of India as in South-East Asia, the monsoons have exerted a dominant influence over human life: one would expect to find many features common to the way of life in both areas. It may well be that the East Asian background of the early South-East Asian cultures is the more important.

When Indian culture began to exert its influence the great prehistoric migrations had ended. In the islands the Indonesians, who had established themselves there in neolithic times, formed the basis of the populations. They were of two kinds: first of all those who had preserved to some extent purity of race, such as the Bataks of Sumatra, the Dyaks of Borneo, and the Alfurs of Celebes and the Moluccas; and in the second place the Malays of the coasts, of many varieties and mixtures, Malays of Sumatra, Sundanese, Javanese, Madurese and Balinese, peoples impregnated more or less with Austro-Asiatic culture, and referred to by the Chinese as K'un-lun and by the Indians as Dvipantara, the 'people of the islands'.

On the mainland there were the Chams in what is today central and southern Annam, the Khmers in the Mekong delta, Cambodia and the middle Mekong region, the Mons, closely related to the Khmers, in the Menam valley and what is now called Lower Burma, the Pyus, possibly the advance guard of the Tibeto-Burmans, in the Irrawaddy and Sittang basins, and the Malays of the Peninsula. Thus many, but not all, of the principal ethnic groups occupied to a large extent their present habitat.

The chief historical changes were to take place on the mainland. Thus we shall see the Chams ousted from central Annam by the Vietnamese, the Mons of the Menam overcome by the T'ais and those of the Irrawaddy by the Burmese. The Pyus disappear completely. The 'push to the south' which characterizes the prehistoric period is to be seen again in the historic period. It explains the actual grouping in Indo-China and to some extent in the islands today. Generally speaking, though there are notable exceptions, the migrations proceed by the narrow valleys of the rivers starting from China and the borders of Tibet, drawn on by the attraction of deltas and the sea.

But they are not migrations in the usually accepted meaning of the term. They are very slow, long-drawn-out movements, with much assimilation of conquerors and conquered, in the course of which the older inhabitants adopt the language and customs of the immigrants. There is rarely annihilation or eviction, hardly ever the displacement of a great mass of people. Thus the basic element of the population of the Indo-Chinese mainland today remains Indonesian. The history of the T'ais in late historical times offers an excellent example of what took place elsewhere in other periods. As Cœdès puts it: 'a warlike aristocracy succeeded in imposing its language which made oil-stains among the other ethnic groups'.[1]

[1] *Op. cit.*, p. 30.

SOUTH-EAST ASIAN PROTO-HISTORY

(a) The spread of Indian influence

THE term 'Hinduization' has been generally applied by scholars to the impact of Indian culture upon South-East Asia. Cœdès goes so far as to term the states which developed under its influence *les états hindouisés*, in spite of the fact that Buddhism played an important role in the movement, and Theravada Buddhism[1] ultimately became the dominant faith of Burma and Arakan, the Tai states and Cambodia. And whereas Hinduism disappeared before Islam in the Malay Peninsula and Indonesia at the end of the European Middle Ages, Buddhism continued to receive the staunch allegiance of the countries it had conquered.

The application of so extended a meaning to the word 'Hindu' is not without its dangers, since in the ordinary use of the terms 'Hindu' and 'Buddhist' there is a clear distinction based upon real points of difference. In the history of the two religions in South-East Asia, however, it is not always easy to draw a clear dividing line between them, especially in the case of Tantrayana Buddhism, which showed marked Hindu features, and even at times, as in the cult of Śiva-Buddha in thirteenth-century Java, defies exact classification. Moreover, even in states where Hinayana Buddhism[1] prevailed, Brahmans played an important ceremonial part, especially at Court, and still do so in Burma, Siam and Cambodia, though themselves strikingly different from their counterparts in India. In the present survey some equivocation in the use of the term 'Hindu' may be unavoidable. The context, however, will, it is hoped, prevent any confusion of meaning.

Relations between the western ports of South-East Asia and India may go back well into the prehistoric period. Traders and shippers from both sides were involved; and, as we find at a much later date, groups of traders from particular places would reappear annually at the ports with which regular relations had been built up and would reside there during the trading season dictated by the monsoons. We

[1] These peoples today object to the term 'Hinayana' (Little Vehicle); they call their Buddhism 'Theravada', the Buddhism of the *Theras* (Teachers).

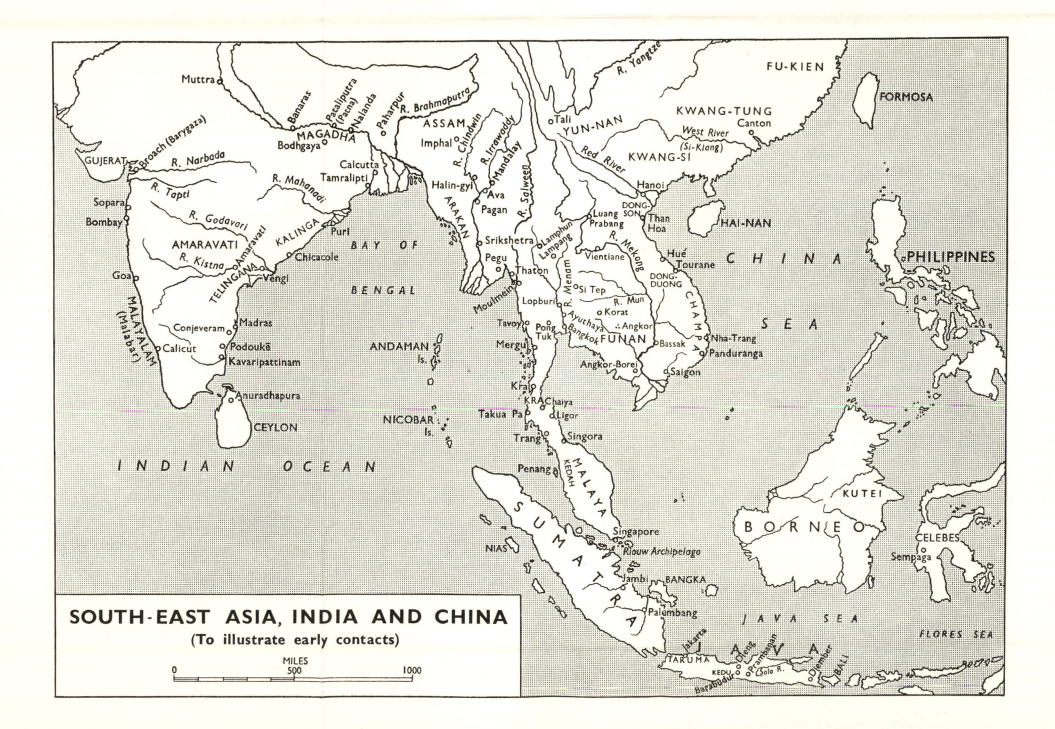

SOUTH-EAST ASIA, INDIA AND CHINA

(To illustrate early contacts)

MILES

0   500   1000

must, however, beware of using the term 'colonies' to describe these settlements, or reading backwards the conditions of a later age when there is evidence that at certain emporia a nucleus of traders would remain behind during the wet monsoon to act as agents for the others and particularly to collect local produce pending the return of the trading fleets. Furthermore, since the myth has grown up that the trading relations in the first instance, and the import of Indian culture in the second, have to be explained in terms of Indian enterprise alone, the point must be clearly made that the Malays (Indonesians) were *par excellence* a sea-going people, and indications are not wanting that they resorted to the ports of India and Ceylon every bit as much as the shipmen of India and Ceylon to the ports of South-East Asia.

Exact information about the lands to the east of the Indian Ocean is conspicuously absent from Indian literature. There are purely incidental allusions, almost impossible to interpret, in Sanskrit classical verse and Tamil court poetry.[1] The *Rāmāyana*, for instance, speaks of *Yavadvipa*, the island of gold and silver, and the *Vayu Purana*, while spelling the word *Yamadvipa*, mentions *Malayadvipa* also. Sir Roland Braddell, one of the most penetrating students of the historical geography of the area, equates *Malayadvipa* with Sumatra, while *Yavadvipa* is interpreted by scholars as a regional name for Java-cum-Sumatra.[2] The point of special interest here lies in the prominence given to Sumatra, for in the light of the much ampler early Chinese accounts of South-East Asia it would seem that the earliest developments in Indian-Indonesian trade were with Sumatra, whose south-eastern ports also pioneered the earliest trading voyages direct to China across the South China Sea.

Other early place-names applied in the *Rāmāyana* to parts of South-East Asia were *Suvarnadvipa*, Golden Island or Peninsula, and *Suvarnabhumi*, Land of Gold. The Buddhist *Jātakas*, or birth-stories of the Buddha, which enshrine folk tales of early India, often tell of voyages to *Suvarnabhumi*. The name also appears in other texts, together with a few other names applied by Indians to places in South-East Asia; but the only information to be drawn from all these references put together is that in India there was a vague idea of an eldorado eastwards across the ocean. They tell us precisely nothing about the spread of Indian culture in that direction. A statement in Kautilya's *Arthaśāstra*, recommending a king to people an old or a new country by seizing the territory of another or deporting the surplus population of his own, has been taken to indicate an early wave of Indian immigrants to

[1] Paul Wheatley, *The Golden Khersonese*, Kuala Lumpur, 1961, chap. III, pp. 176–84.
[2] *Ibid.*, pp. 178–9.

South-East Asia before the Christian era. But so imaginative an interpretation looks like a flight of nationalistic fancy rather than sober historical thinking; for if one thing is certain it is that Indian culture was not brought to South-East Asia by waves of immigrants.[1]

Indigenous South-East Asian writings dealing with this early period can provide little help: those extant are recent recensions, none of which is more than two hundred years old. They tell us what dynasties of a much later period wanted people to believe about ancient times, and in particular about their own splendid ancestry. Chinese sources, while invaluable for the light they shed upon the political geography and trade of our area, even though extremely difficult to interpret, contain disappointingly slight information about the spread of Indian influence. They do indeed give us our earliest glimpse of a Hindu court, that of Funan the precursor of Cambodia, and they mention the story of the Brahman Kaundinya, whose arrival on the scene they place in the first century A.D. They also mention states in the Malay Peninsula with apparently Sanskrit names. But before the appearance of the earliest Sanskrit inscriptions at the end of the fourth century or later the Indian contact with the countries of South-East Asia is hidden in dense mist.[2]

Geographical texts of European classical antiquity have been searched for evidence on the subject. They come from the period when the growth of wealth and luxury in the Roman Empire was leading to increasing demands for oriental products. The disturbed conditions on its Parthian frontier in the first century B.C. caused Rome to encourage voyages of discovery in the Erythraean Sea (Indian Ocean), and in due course words such as *Chryse* (gold) and *Argyre* (silver) began to be applied to the lands beyond India. But it was a long time before writers knew anything of the countries beyond the Ganges and the island of Ceylon. The *Periplus of the Erythraean Sea*, compiled in about A.D. 70–1, is the earliest text to mention trade between Indian ports and the countries further east. It is a manual of Graeco-Egyptian trade and navigation in the Indian Ocean of anonymous authorship. The compiler had not personally been further east than the Malabar Coast, but had picked up a little information from eastern traders he met there. After mentioning three great ports in western India—Broach, Cranganore, and Porakad—to which Greek ships made voyages, the author says that native ships go from these to three more on the eastern side beyond the Gulf of Manaar—namely Kaveripatnam, Pondicherry, and

---

[1] The passage is today generally taken to refer to settlements in uncultivated areas of India.

[2] In Funan, however, the earliest case may possibly be attributed to the third century.

one that he calls 'Sopatma', which Indian research identifies with Markānum. From these in turn great ships called *kolandia* trade with the territories at the mouth of the Ganges, and among others with the island of Chrysê, which produces tortoise-shell. Farther east than this they do not go. Chrysê, 'gold land', was a name later applied to a part of Burma, and as 'gold island' to Sumatra. And as tortoise-shell was a product of the Archipelago, Dutch scholars are inclined to think that this may be a vague reference to the trade of that region. Dionysius Periegetes, a second-century Greek writer, mentions the 'gold island' but adds nothing new to the *Periplus*.

What appears at first to be more definite information comes from the *Geographia* of the Alexandrine geographer Ptolemy, who wrote in A.D. 165 or possibly earlier, and certainly used much earlier sources. Recent research, however, surveyed by Paul Wheatley,[1] shows that in its present form the work was compiled by a Byzantine author of the tenth or eleventh century on principles laid down by Ptolemy, and incorporated parts only of the original book. The extant manuscript maps, Wheatley tells us, were not drawn until the latter end of the thirteenth century.[2] Book VII of the work deals with the 'Golden Khersonese', once identified with Lower Burma, but now with the Malay Peninsula. The map of Trans-Gangetic India that can be drawn from the data contained in the Ptolemaic tables of Latitudes and Longitudes shows the major features of mainland South-East Asia in a clearly recognizable form, and Wheatley is convinced that in drawing his own map 'Ptolemy' used authentic information.[3] But the question is, to which period of historical geography does his account apply? And Wheatley's answer is, to a very much later period than the second century, so far as the Malay Peninsula is concerned. There are equal difficulties when one attempts to make sense of his account of the Archipelago. One has therefore to admit that for evidence concerning the diffusion of Indian culture in South-East Asia these works of early European geographers provide very little more substance than Indian classical writings.

In the late nineteenth century, when European scholars began the intensive study of the antiquities of South-East Asia and began to realize the extent of the influence of Sanskrit culture upon the religion, art and architecture of the area, the tendency was to regard these things as the results of a movement of Indian expansion eastwards. Attempts therefore were directed towards explaining it in terms of Indian

---

[1] *Op. cit.*, chap. x and appendices 1, 2, and 3.
[2] *Ibid.*, p. 138.   [3] *Ibid.*, p. 145.

conditions; South-East Asia was at the receiving end and played a passive role. In due course Indian scholars joined in the fascinating chase for information, and made important contributions to the literature of the subject. Their work shows an enthusiasm which partly reflects the excitement of the quest, but largely also the nationalistic ardour that was sweeping through the educated classes of India as the twentieth century dawned and proceeded upon its troubled way. Radhakumud Mookerji's *Indian Shipping: A History of Seaborne Trade and Maritime Activity of the Indians from the Earliest Times*, published in 1912, illustrates to what flights of fantasy the enthusiast could ascend. In his address before the University of Leiden in March 1946 entitled 'The Problem of the Hindu Colonization of Indonesia' Professor F. D. K. Bosch referred to Mookerji's vision of huge fleets of Indian adventurers, like Drakes and Cavendishes, crossing the sea to Farther India and Indonesia, founding kingdoms, establishing colonies, expanding the trade of their mother-country, and in due course bringing over talented artists from Bengal, Kalinga and Gujerat to erect matchless monuments.[1]

One interesting feature of India's national movement was the foundation in 1926 of the Greater India Society, whose name is a sufficient indication of the nature of its approach to South-East Asian studies. Its members saw the countries of South-East Asia as 'ancient Indian colonies'; indeed, R. C. Majumdar used the term in the titles of scholarly works on the early history of Champa and Java, and described the art and architecture of Java and Cambodia as derived from India and fostered by the Indian rulers of these colonies. The Society has indeed stimulated a great deal of scholarly research work, but it has also created much misunderstanding; and the unhistorical myths to which it has given wide currency have shown an amazing power of persistence. Even Siam is claimed as an Indian colony by Phanindra Nath Bose,[2] and in the Preface to his book he comments on 'the extent and greatness of that *Greater India*, which had been established outside India by the brave and adventurous sons of India in the days of yore. In a Foreword to the Book Dr P. C. Bagchi writes, 'The history of the Indian colonization of Indo-China and the Malay Peninsula forms a glorious chapter to the history of India.'

When, however, Indian history was searched for an explanation of this wave of emigration the theories put forward were sadly out of tune with a glorious movement of expansion. Two were based upon the

[1] *Selected Studies in Indonesian Archaeology*, 1961, p. 5.
[2] *The Indian Colony of Siam*, Lahore, 1927.

assumption that it arose out of disturbed conditions in India, which caused large numbers of refugees to seek new homes across the sea. The one attributed it to the bloody conquest of Kalinga by the Maurya emperor Asoka in the third century B.C., which, it was suggested, might have provoked such an exodus. But there is no evidence of such a movement, and Indian influence does not begin to show itself in South-East Asia until several centuries later. The other attributed it to the pressure of the Kushana invasions of India in the first century A.D. The Yueh-chi nomads, who gained control over Bactria shortly after 100 B.C.,[1] began some time later to expand southwards under Kushan control. In A.D. 50 there was a Kushan king in the Kabul valley. Soon afterwards they dominated the Punjab and were pressing towards Gujerat and the Gangetic plain. Their leader became the Emperor Kanishka in A.D. 78, and from his capital at Peshawar ruled much of north India. Were there any evidence to prove that his conquests caused an emigration of Indians overseas, there would be no difficulty on the score of the time factor. But there is none whatever. Others again have assumed an exodus of Indians in consequence of the campaigns of Samudragupta, which, though unlikely, falls in the period of earliest Indian influence in South-East Asia.

In *Les États hindouisés* Cœdès has formulated an ingenious hypothesis to explain what he thinks took place.[2] The spread of Indian culture, he believes, came as a result of an intensification of Indian trade with South-East Asia early in the Christian era. He does not support the theory of a mass emigration of fugitives from India, but sees Indian trading settlements arising in South-East Asian ports, through which the arrival was facilitated of more cultivated elements, priests and literati, able to disseminate Indian culture. The contact between the Mediterranean world and India, he explains, followed by the foundation of the Maurya and Kushan empires on the one hand, and the rise of the Seleucid and Roman empires on the other, led to an important trade in luxury articles between East and West. During the two centuries preceding the Christian era India lost her principal source for the import of the precious metals when the movements of the nomads cut the Bactrian route to Siberia. Hence in the first century A.D. she sought to import them from the Roman Empire. But the grave effects of this upon the imperial economy caused the Emperor Vespasian (69–79) to stop the flight of precious metals, and Indians had to seek for them elsewhere. They turned, Cœdès thinks, to the Golden

---

[1] Before 100 B.C. if A.D. 78 is the date of Kanishka's accession.

[2] *Op. cit.*, pp. 41–4. In *Les peuples de la Péninsule Indochinoise*, 1962, chap. ii, Cœdès has elaborated and corrected his views.

Khersonese, and the Sanskrit names, such as *Suvarnabhumi* and *Suvarnadvipa*, which they gave to parts of South-East Asia, indicate that to Indians they were famous chiefly for gold.

This theory, like those previously mentioned, suffers from the defect of being based upon the assumption that the initiative in establishing relations between India and South-East Asia was taken by Indians, and not by South-East Asians. On this point van Leur's scornful comment, 'To what extent Indonesian shipping played an active role is a question never raised!'[1] is highly apposite; indeed, as we shall see later in this chapter it was the Sumatran Malays who blazed the trail in developing the all-sea trade-route to China, and such evidence as we have suggests that Malay seamen and ships played every bit as important a part as Indian in the trade of South-East Asia with India and Ceylon.[2] And the same is true of the diffusion of Indian culture. Van Leur also rejected the notion that trade and the trader were disseminators of culture: most traders, he said, belonged to the lower social groups, and ships' crews were often composed of African negroes and slaves. Such people, he argues, could not have been 'administrators of ritual, magical consecration and disseminators of rationalistic, bureaucratic written scholarship and wisdom'.[3] That was the work of Brahmans. Nevertheless, it was through the operation of trade that the vital contacts were made, he points out; but they were made at court level and arose out of the dominant position rulers and nobles held in foreign trade. The Brahmanization of South India, he reminds us, was going on at the beginning of the Christian era, and South India was, more than any other part of the subcontinent, the trading region for Indonesia. Thus the princes of Indonesia were aware of what was happening, and copied those of Dravidian India by inviting the Brahman priesthood to their courts. The transmission was at court level and was the work of Brahmans.

Here we come to the very heart of the matter, the nature of the cultural elements transmitted from India to South-East Asia. Cœdès enumerates four: (*a*) a conception of royalty characterized by Hindu or Buddhist cults, (*b*) literary expression by means of the Sanskrit language, (*c*) a mythology taken from the *Rāmāyana* and *Mahābhārata*, the *Purānas* and other Sanskrit texts containing a nucleus of royal tradition and the traditional genealogies of royal families of the Ganges region, and (*d*) the observance of the *Dharmasastras*, the sacred law of Hinduism, and in particular the *Manava Dharmasastra* or 'Laws of Manu'.[4] It is thus something to do with rulers and courts, not peoples;

---

[1] J. C. van Leur, *Indonesian Trade and Society*, The Hague, Bandung, 1955, p. 92.
[2] *Ibid.*, pp. 98–9.   [3] *Ibid.*, p. 99.   [4] *Les États hindouisés*, p. 36.

the Indian transmitters were court functionaries, not missionaries. More often than not it was a case of an ambitious ruler, anxious to copy the grander style of the Indian courts, employing Brahmans to consecrate him as a god-king in accordance with the ideas and ritual of the Indian classics. It was essential, when forcing other rulers into a state of vassalage, to have consecration of this sort whereby the worship was established of a linga as the king's sacred personality and he himself was identified with Śiva.

Van Leur's brilliant refutation of the Indian colonization theory was of special value on its positive side for the emphasis he laid upon the role of the Brahman. The most thorough examination, however, of the whole question of the transmission of Indian culture was made by Bosch in the Leiden address already referred to. Both men were confining their survey to Indonesia, but much of what they say applies equally to the other 'hinduized' states of South-East Asia. Bosch gives careful consideration to the two immigration theories propounded by Dutch scholars; he labels them respectively the 'ksatriya-hypothesis' and the 'vaisya-hypothesis'. The former, which was propounded by Professor C. C. Berg, saw Indian culture introduced as a result of the activities of Indian warrior immigrants, who played the part of the robber barons described in the Javanese Panji cycle of narratives, marrying native women and breeding a kraton society of mixed blood. And Moens took the idea a stage further by seeking to link the accession of new Indonesian dynasties with the fall of dynasties in India followed by the (hypothetical) emigration of their scions to the Archipelago. The latter, expounded by Professor N. J. Krom, was to the effect that Indian penetration was peaceful, and that it began with traders who settled and married native women, thereby introducing Indian culture. In this way, he suggested, the Indonesians voluntarily accepted the higher Hindu civilization.

Bosch's criticisms of these hypotheses may be tabulated as follows: (a) A conquering prince would have mentioned his success in an inscription, or, if not, one of his descendants would have done so. (b) There is no sign of Dravidian mixture in the population of Java or Bali. (c) The borrowed words of Indian origin in the Indonesian languages show the pure Sanskrit form, indicating that they came from a literary, learned court circle; whereas settlers would have used either a Dravidian dialect or a vernacular of Aryan origin. (d) Indonesian social structure followed Indian theory, not practice; for while some acquaintance with the four primary divisions of Hindu society is to be found, there is not the slightest indication of the introduction of the real castes with all their special rules and ritual as in India. (e) The design and detail of Indonesian art and architecture show that they were not created by Indians but by Indonesians; for instance, the similarities with Indian models in the case of the monuments of central Java would be accounted for by the fact that the Javanese architects were acquainted with the *śilpaśastras*, the classical Indian compendia of technical information about architecture and sculpture. (f) If merchants had played a part in the transmission of culture, the early centres of Hindu civilization would be found at the coastal emporia, whereas they are found at royal residencies in the interior, and, in the case of Java, in 'the almost inaccessible plains' of Kedu and Prambanan. (g) Commercial contacts are inadequate for the transmission of the higher civilization of one people to another. For example, the Chinese in Indonesia have had no influence upon the local culture, and this must also have been true of the Indians.[1]

Bosch's conclusion therefore is that it was at the royal residence that the new culture was to be found with its blending of Indonesian and Hindu elements. It was, he explains, reminiscent of such things as the learned manuscript, the code of law, the cell of the recluse and the monastery; it belonged to the sphere of religion, and its practitioners were, like the scribes and scholastics of mediaeval Europe, 'clerks'.[2]

So far this discussion has centred almost entirely upon Brahmanism. Buddhism, however, played a very important part; indeed, Cœdès seems to suggest that it blazed the trail and appeared in South-East Asia before Brahmanism. Certainly the number of images of Buddha of the Amaravati school that are associated with the earliest archaeological sites showing Indian influence are significant. Amaravati, on the river Kistna about eighty miles from the east coast of India, was the home of a great school of Buddhist sculpture which flourished especially during the century from A.D. 150 to 250. Bosch describes the role of the many Buddhist pilgrims who flocked eastwards to propagate the Buddha-ideal. Unlike Brahmans they were missionaries. They would appear at Indonesian courts, preach the law, convert the ruler and his family, and found an order of monks. This stream of devotees from India, he then goes on to say, would stimulate a much stronger countercurrent towards India of native *bhiksus* bound for the holy land of the Buddha and famous Indian monasteries, where they would often make lengthy stays.

The Nalanda monastery near Rajagriha, in the old kingdom of

[1] Bosch, *op. cit.*, pp. 8–10.   [2] *Ibid.*, p. 11.

Magadha, attracted vast numbers of pilgrims from abroad. For a time it was the largest and most important Buddhist centre of the Mahayana School. They went in search of sacred manuscripts, relics and images. Indonesian pilgrims were so numerous that a monastery was founded there for them, and a famous inscription there dating from about 860, and referred to by students of epigraphy as 'Balaputra's Charter' records the donation of villages for its upkeep by a Pāla king.[1] These were the people, says Bosch, who conveyed Buddhist art to their homeland, where it took root 'miraculously', causing architecture, sculpture, painting and poetry to flourish.[2] Buddhism, he thinks, had a far greater popular appeal than Hinduism, which was 'an esoteric doctrine transmitted from *guru* to pupil' and confined to the Brahman caste.[3] But if Buddhism blazed the trail, Hinduism made a big impact when it revived in India under Gupta protection between the fourth and sixth centuries. When the Chinese pilgrim Fa Hsien, on his way homewards after visiting India, found heresy and Brahmanism flourishing in Java, Hinduism, Bosch thinks, was new to Indonesia, and it was brought there by gurus of the Śaiva-Siddhanta sect, who made a big impact upon the ruling class at the kraton because of the supernatural powers with which they claimed to be invested. Through the Brahman Siva could enter the king, conferring immortality upon him; through the Brahman divine omnipotence could be invoked to maintain world order; and consecration by the Brahman gave a higher sanctity to all the festivals of the popular religion. There was therefore a demand for Siddhanta initiates in the Archipelago; rulers sent messengers to India to invite them, and on arrival they were given influential offices at the kratons.[4] In a subsequent essay entitled '"Local Genius" en Oud-Javaanse Kunst', published in 1952, Bosch came down even more strongly against the theory of Indian expansion into Indonesia.[5] The evidence showed, he claimed, that Indian influence spread there mainly through Indonesian initiative in assimilating such elements of Indian culture as attracted them rather than as a result of an Indian effort at cultural expansion. It came about through the great number of Indonesians going to visit Indian sacred places and studying under Indian teachers.

Some years ago in an article contributed to *Cahiers d'histoire mondiale* Cœdès described the old civilization of Cambodia and Java as an Indian superstructure upon an indigenous substratum.[6] Bosch, however, comes nearer to the truth when he describes the old Hindu-Indonesian

---

[1] *Infra*, p. 45.   [2] *Op. cit.*, p. 14.   [3] *Ibid.*, p. 17.   [4] *Ibid.*, p. 19.
[5] *Mededelingen Koninklijke Akademie van Wetenschappen*, Afd. Lett., n.r. xv, i, 1952.
[6] Vol. i, no. 2, Oct. 1953, pp. 368–77. But see also *Les Peuples de la Péninsule Indochinoise*, chap. ii.

culture as the product of the fecundation of the 'living matter' of Indonesian society by the Indian spirit, and goes on to explain that a new life was procreated which was to develop into an independent organism.[1] But we must be very careful to distinguish between the court culture and that of the people, for it was to be a very long time before Indian cultural elements were in any real way absorbed by the mass of the people themselves. Their traditional culture continued to prevail. What really happened was that the South-East Asian peoples over a long period of their early history absorbed into their traditional culture patterns imported Buddhist and Hindu elements, which they adjusted to their own peculiar requirements and outlook. It was not until from the thirteenth century onwards Theravada Buddhism, and somewhat later Islam, began to be propagated as popular religions, that external influences began to make any real impact upon the ordinary villager; and even then it was a much slower process than in-digenous writings, reflecting the outlook of court or monastery, would give one to understand: a process still incomplete. Moreover, in coming to terms with the indigenous cultures the imported religions were forced to change their character to a marked degree. And in the case of the Theravada countries the propagation of the faith was carried out by South-East Asians, notably Mon monks, who went to Ceylon to study, to collect canonical texts, and to receive orthodox ordination.

In the absence of historical documents showing from what parts of India the cultural influences flowed into South-East Asia, the evidence has to be sought for in much the same way as in the case of the origin and date of the movement itself. It is significant that modern Indian writers who have pronounced upon the subject have been tempted to stress rather too much the claims of their own localities. Thus, as Cœdès puts it, Madras claims for the Tamils, and Bengal for the Bengalis, the honour of having colonized 'Greater India'.

The script used in the earliest inscriptions has also been examined for light on the problem. The great difficulty here arises from the fact that in their earliest forms the various types of Indian writing show their fewest divergencies. Hence, while R. C. Majumdar thinks that the oldest Sanskrit inscription in Funan uses Kushana script from north India, K. A. Nilakanta Sastri argues that all the alphabets used in South-East Asia have a south Indian origin, and that Pallava script has a predominant influence. Cœdès, however, points out that the employment of a pre-Nagari script for a short time at the end of the

[1] *Selected Studies in Indonesian Archaeology*, p. 20.

eighth and the beginning of the ninth centuries is evidence of a wave of Bengali influence.[1]

The plastic arts and architecture afford little help, since their earliest examples do not appear until long after the first impact of Indian culture and show a diversity of influences. Of the architecture Parmentier ventures the considered opinion that, shorn of its images and inscriptions, it is so different from its Indian prototypes that the connection is by no means obvious.

So far the sea alone has figured in this discussion as the way by which Indian influence came into South-East Asia. It was the obvious way of travel between India and the Archipelago; indeed the voyage from the Coromandel Coast to the Straits of Malacca was a comparatively short one, and at the right time of the year was easy and safe even for small vessels. There was, however, a northerly land route from India to China through Assam, Upper Burma and Yunnan. Historical evidence shows it to have been in use as early as 128 B.C. when Chang Ch'ien discovered the products of Szechwan in Bactria. Steps were taken to develop it, and in A.D. 69, for its better control and protection, China founded the prefecture of Yung-ch'ang across the upper Mekong with its headquarters east of the Salween, about sixty miles from the present Burma frontier. Along this route in A.D. 97 travelled envoys from the eastern part of the Roman empire to Yung-ch'ang. The Buddhist pilgrim I-tsing tells us that it was used at the end of the third century by twenty Chinese monks, who went to the Court of Śri Gupta.

In the fourth century China relaxed her hold on the Burma frontier to such a degree that in 342 the Yung-ch'ang prefecture was abolished. Thereafter the route was apparently closed until Ko-lo-feng (748–79) of Nanchao reopened it, and thereby promoted much economic development in northern Burma and contacts between the Pyu of Burma and the T'ang Court in China. Evidence discovered in Pyu sites tends to show that some Indian influence penetrated overland into Upper Burma. By the same route it came also to the T'ai kingdom of Nanchao. But the usual way of communication between India and Burma was by sea.

To reach the countries in the eastern parts of the Indo-Chinese mainland ships had to pass through either the Malacca or the Sunda Straits. Owing to the prevalence of piracy in these narrow waters travellers sought to avoid them by using a number of short cuts overland. Archaeological discoveries along these overland routes attest

[1] *Les États hindouisés*, p. 59.

their importance, not only in the early days of Indian penetration, but later also when the empire of Śrivijaya maintained strict control over the straits and forced all ships to put in at one or other of its ports.

The favourite short cut was across the narrow Isthmus of Kra, from Takua Pa on the western side to Ch'aiya on the eastern, or from Kedah to Singora. Farther north there was a route from Tavoy over the Three Pagodas Pass and thence by the Kanburi river to the valley of the Menam. Two ancient sites, P'ong Tuk and P'ra Pathom, lie on this route. Further still to the north lay a route to the Menam region by Moulmein and the Raheng pass. Later on these last two routes were used by the Burmese in their invasions of Siam, notably in the sixteenth and eighteenth centuries. More recently they were used by the Japanese to invade Burma during the Second World War. There was yet another overland route used by early travellers. It led from the Menam to the Mekong and passed over the K'orat plateau via Si T'ep to the Bassak region, which was the cradle of the Khmer kingdom of Cambodia.

(b) The earliest states; Funan, the Lin-yi

So far as historical evidence goes, the first signs of states formed in the manner that has been described in the preceding section show that they were in existence by the end of the second century A.D. They appear in three regions: (a) that of the lower Mekong and its delta, (b) north of Hué in modern Annam, and (c) the northern part of the Malay Peninsula. They probably existed elsewhere, say in Arakan and Lower Burma, but the evidence is lacking. In the absence of archaeological and epigraphical material earlier than the fifth century, our sole sources of information for the earlier period are the place-names in the *Niddesa* and Ptolemy's *Geographica*, and the references in the Chinese dynastic histories to relations with the states of South-East Asia. The latter are invaluable, for without them the earliest history of the important states of Funan and Champa would be completely unknown. But their geographical particulars are vague and their transcriptions of Sanskrit names difficult to recognize.

Funan represents the modern Chinese pronunciation of two characters once pronounced *B'iu-nam*, the name by which they knew the pre-Khmer kingdom, whose original settlements were along the Mekong between Chaudoc and Phnom Penh. This was not its real name, which is unknown, but the title assumed by its rulers. It is the modern Khmer word *phnom*, 'mountain', in Old Khmer *bnam*, and the full title was *kurung bnam*, 'king of the mountain', the vernacular equivalent of the Sanskrit *śailaraja*, itself reminiscent of the title borne by the Pallava Kings of Conjeveram in south India.

Funan's capital city was for some time Vyadhapura, 'the city of hunters', which lay near the hill Ba Phnom and the village of Banam in the present Cambodian province of Prei Veng. The Chinese say that it was 120 miles from the sea. Oc Eo, its port, on the maritime fringe of the Mekong delta bordering the Gulf of Siam some three miles from the sea has been the subject of excavations by a French archaeologist.[1] It was an immense urban agglomeration of houses on piles intersected by a network of little canals, part of an irrigation system extending for over 200 kilometres, which had been constructed, with wonderful skill, to drain what had previously been 'a cesspool of soft mud barely held together by mangrove trees',[2] and to irrigate rice fields for the support of a large population mainly concentrated in lake-cities. These were linked up with each other and with the sea by canals large enough to take sea-going ships, so that it was possible for Chinese travellers to talk about 'sailing across Funan' on their way to the Malay Peninsula. Oc Eo was a centre of industry and trade: its site bears evidence of maritime relations with the coast of the Gulf of Siam, Malaya, Indonesia, India, Persia and, indeed, directly or indirectly with the Mediterranean. It was situated on what was in its day the great maritime highway between China and the West. The Funanese were of Malay[3] race, and still in the tribal state at the dawn of history. The culture of Oc Eo itself is characterized by M. Malleret as half-indigenous, half-foreign; its foreign affinities, he says, were almost entirely with India.

The earliest Chinese reference to the kingdom comes from the pen of K'ang T'ai, who together with Chu Ying was sent thither on a mission in the middle of the third century. He tells the story of the foundation of the kingdom by Kaundinya, whose name he transliterates Hun-t'ien. According to his account this ruler was a foreigner, who came from a place which may be India, the Malay Peninsula, or even the southern islands. He was guided to his future kingdom by a dream, in which he was vouchsafed a divine revelation of his destiny. On arrival he defeated an attempt by the queen of the country, Liu-yeh, 'Willow Leaf', to seize his ship by transfixing her boat with an arrow from his magic bow. Then he married her and founded the dynasty which ruled after him for a century and a half.

[1] Louis Malleret, 'Les Fouilles d'Oc-Éo (1944)', BEFEO, xvi, i, 1951.
[2] B. P. Groslier, *Angkor, Art and Civilization*, p. 17.
[3] The word is used here in its widest ethnic sense.

The story is apparently a local adaptation of the Indian legend of the Brahman Kaundinya and the Nagi Soma, the daughter of the King of the Nagas. The correct account of the Indian legend is given in an inscription found at Misön in Champa. This tells how the Brahman Kaundinya received a sacred javelin from Aśvattharman, the son of Drona, and threw it in order to mark the site of his future capital. He then married Soma, the daughter of the naga king, and founded a line of kings. The descendants of the Pallava rulers of Conjeveram used a similar legend to explain their own origin. At a later date the legend was adopted by the Khmers and the naga became the sacred symbol of their origin. A mystic union between the Khmer king and a naga princess had a prominent place in the Court ceremonial of Angkor; he was required to maintain the well-being of his realm through consummation of a union with a nine-headed naga. The nine-headed cobra indeed became the dominant theme of Khmer iconography.

The *Liang History* asserts that one of Kaundinya's descendants, Hun P'an-h'uang, died at the age of over ninety and was succeeded by his second son P'an-p'an, who handed over the conduct of affairs to his great general Fan Man. Attempts have been made to explain the title *Fan* as a Chinese transliteration of the Sanskrit suffix *varman*, used by certain rulers in South India and later adopted by a number of South-East Asian dynasties; but there can be no doubt that it is a clan name of native origin.[1] According to the *Southern Ch'i History* Fan Man's full name was Fan Shih-man, and on the death of P'an-p'an after a reign of only three years he was chosen king by popular acclamation. His accession may be placed early in the third century.

Fan Shih-man was a great conqueror. He extended his power so widely that he took the title of Great King. He also built a fleet which dominated the seas. The *Liang History* says that he attacked ten kingdoms, and names four of them. There is some difficulty in identifying these, but his vassal states probably included the lower valleys of the Mekong and Tonle Sap and parts of the delta. He is thought also to have reduced the coastal strip from the Mekong-Donnai delta to Camranh Bay. One of his conquests has been identified with Ptolemy's Kattigara, which Paul Lévy places in Cochin China. Another, *Tun-sun*,[2] described by the *Liang History* as 'the mart where East and West meet together', i.e. a place on one of the land routes across the Malay Peninsula, was probably the confederacy of small Mon states in the lower Meklong valley, with which the sites of P'ong-Tük and

[1] Cœdès, *op. cit.*, p. 71, n. 1.
[2] The name seems to be of Mon origin, indicating that there were five states.

P'ra Pat'om, yielding Buddhist remains of the second to the sixth century A.D., were connected.[1]

The Chinese assert that Fan Shih-man died while conducting an expedition against a state called Chin-lin, 'Frontier of Gold'. This has been identified with either Suvarnabhumi, 'Land of Gold', or Suvarnakudya, 'Wall of Gold', and might be placed in either Lower Burma or the Malay Peninsula. Cœdès is of opinion that he is the king referred to as Śri Mara in a Sanskrit inscription of Vo-canh in the region of Nha-trang, now in southern Annam, but at one time in the kingdom of Champa. The inscription shows that he was a patron of Buddhism and used Sanskrit as the official language of his Court. Finot, however, thinks that Sri Mara was a vassal of Funan.

So far it has been impossible to assign exact dates to any of the rulers or events in the early history of Funan. According to the calculation of Cœdès, the events giving rise to the legend of Kaundinya must have occurred not later than the first century A.D. During the reign of Fan Shih-man's successor, Fan Chan, through the relations of Funan with India and China, certain apparently well-attested dates do at last emerge. Fan Chan was a nephew of the Great King, who killed the legitimate heir, usurped the throne and reigned some twenty years before dying at the hands of a brother of the man he had removed from his path. His reign falls somewhere between 225 and 250. He received a visit from a native of India, who so charmed him by his account of that country that he sent an embassy, which after embarking at the port of Chü-li in the Malay Peninsula went by sea and up the Ganges to a Court identified by Sylvain Lévi as that of the Murundas. This embassy belongs to the years 240–5.

Meanwhile, according to the *History of the Three Kingdoms*, he sent in 243 a mission to China with a present of musicians and products of his country. Somewhere between 245 and 250 his successor, Fan Hsun, received a return mission from China, which met an envoy of the Murundas at his Court. K'ang T'ai, who recorded the first extant account of the kingdom of Funan, was a member of this mission. Funan, he wrote, had walled cities containing palaces and dwelling-houses. The people were ugly, black, frizzy-haired and went naked. Their manners were simple, but they were not given to theft. They practised a primitive kind of agriculture. They enjoyed using the chisel and engraved ornaments. Many of their eating utensils were made of silver. Taxes were paid in gold, silver, pearls and perfumes. They had also books and depositories of archives. Their writing

[1] Wheatley, *op. cit.*, pp. 10, 15–21, 286.

resembled that of the Hu; a central Asian people using an Indian script.

K'ang T'ai seems to have persuaded Fan Hsun to issue a decree ordering the men to wear clothing, and they adopted the piece of cloth wrapped round the waist which is now the Cambodian sampot. Such is his story. Kaundinya is said to have introduced the custom of clothing for women. According to the legend, Soma wore no clothes when he arrived in the country. He therefore dressed her in a fold of cloth with a hole through which she passed her head. He also made her do her hair in a knot. Such was the fabled origin of clothing and hairdressing in Cambodia.

The relations with China, cemented by these missions, remained close throughout Fan Hsun's reign, which lasted until at least 287. The *Chin History* mentions a series of missions from him covering the period 268–87. But relations were not invariably good, for he appears to have made an alliance with Fan Hsiung, who came to the throne of Lin-yi (Champa) in 270, and to have joined his ally in a ten-years war against Chiao-chi (Tongking). When the first emperor of the Chin dynasty came to the throne in 280, the Governor of Tongking addressed a memorial to him complaining of the raids of the Lin-yi, aided by friendly bands from Funan, upon the commandery of Je-nan. The *Chin History*, in recording this incident, says that the state to which the Lin-yi raiders belonged had been founded about a century earlier by a native official, Ch'u Lien, who had taken advantage of the weakness of the Han dynasty (206 B.C.–A.D. 221) to carve out a kingdom for himself at the expense of Je-nan in the year A.D. 192. The Chinese name for his kingdom was Hsiang-lin, which was in fact the name of their sub-prefecture in which the independence movement took place. It coincided almost exactly with the present Annamite province of Thua-thien, in which the city of Hué is situated.

Thus does the state later to be known as Champa first appear in history. Archaeological evidence shows that the centre of its power lay just to the south of the Hué region, in the modern Annamite province of Quang-nam, which is so rich in archaeological sites that it was evidently the sacred territory of Champa. But, although the famous sites of Tra-kieu, Misön and Dong-duong have yielded specimens of Amaravati art, no evidence exists, as in the case of neighbouring Funan, of the dynastic traditions of the Kings of Champa or of the coming of Indian influence. Not till the beginning of the seventh century does the name Champa first appear in epigraphy, though as the name of the kingdom of the Chams it was probably in existence before that date. It is, however, by the Chinese name of Lin-yi that they are known during the first phase of their long struggle to expand northwards into the lands under Chinese control.

The narrow coastal strip from the Porte d'Annam to the Col des Nuages, which they coveted, was probably at this time inhabited by wild tribes in a backward state. Their own territory stretched down the coast from the Col des Nuages to the Bay of Camranh, but they had settlements also in the Mekong valley, the valleys of the Sesan and Song-ba, and the neighbouring hills. They held the western slopes of the Annamite Chain up to the Mekong valley from Stung Treng to the river Mun. They belonged to the Indonesian group of peoples. Later the Indonesian settlements round the Bay of Nhatrang were to form their southern province of Panduranga, now Phan-rang, but this formed part of the empire of Funan when we first hear of the Lin-yi. The people of this region were related to the Funanese rather than to the Chams. They appear to have received Indian influence as early as the beginning of the first century A.D. According to Parmentier, their earliest art and architecture is Khmer rather than Cham. Their region continued to form part of Funan until the Chenla conquest of that country in the latter part of the sixth century.

The Governor of Tongking's complaint is not the earliest mention of the Lin-yi in the Chinese annals. Somewhere between 220 and 230 a mission was sent by one of the descendants of K'iu-lien to the Governor of Kwangtong and Tongking. It is in the record of this that the names 'Lin-yi' and 'Funan' appear for the first time. In 248 the Lin-yi are said to have pillaged the towns of the north, and to have fought a big battle with the Chinese in the region of Badon on the Song Giang. The Fan Hsiung, who came to the throne in 270 and began another series of attacks upon Tongking in alliance with Funan, as we have seen above, is said to have been a grandson of K'iu-lien. When, after a lengthy struggle, these were beaten off, another king of the Lin-yi, Fan Yi, sent in 284 the first official embassy from that kingdom to the Imperial Court of China.

Fan Yi reigned for more than fifty years. His chief minister, Wen, who is said to have been of Chinese origin, succeeded to the throne in 336. Four years later, when the Chinese emperor refused to recognize his northern boundary at the Porte d'Annam, he took possession of the territory involved, and at his death in 349 was carrying his arms still farther northwards. Wen's son and successor, Fan Fo, however, was forced to restore all that his father had conquered. The Chinese record embassies from him in 372 and 377.

Of the earliest states in the Malay Peninsula mentioned by the Chinese, some, as we have seen, are identified with conquests of Fan Shih-man of Funan. The earliest written description of them was in the accounts given by K'ang T'ai and Chu Ying of their visit to Funan in the middle of the third century.[1] They have been lost, but much of the information in them has survived in quotations made by later writers. The evidence itself as well as the efforts of modern scholars to interpret it have been surveyed by Professor Paul Wheatley in his *Golden Khersonese*,[2] which offers the most up-to-date study of the early historical geography of the Malay Peninsula. What is said here, there-fore, is based entirely upon his findings.

The states in the lists of Fan Shih-man's conquests that can with certitude be placed on the Peninsula are *Tun-sun*, which has been des-cribed above, *Ch'ü-tu-k'un* (or *Tu-k'un*), which cannot be located with exactitude, and *Chiu-chih* (*Chü-li*), a trans-isthmian state used by travellers from China to India and some way to the south of *Tun-sun*. The seventh century *Liang-shu* mentions a kingdom of *Lang-ya-hsiu*, which, it shows, was founded in the second century A.D. This is easily recognized as the Langkasuka of the Malay and Javanese chronicles. An immense amount of effort has been expended by scholars to fix its precise location, and their interpretation of the evidence has differed considerably. Wheatley places it in the Patani region. Later, after a period of eclipse, presumably the result of conquest by Funan, it was to become a kingdom of some importance until the sixteenth century.[3] Later Chinese writers also mention a *Tan-Ma-Ling*, which Wheatley places in the Ligor district, i.e. north of Langkasuka.[4] *Chü-li*, the port of embarkation of the Funan mission of A.D. 240 to the Murunda Court, has been thought to have been the Takola of Ptolemy's *Geo-graphia*, but this now seems very doubtful. That there was such a port there is ample evidence in Indian sources, and that Indian traders frequented it probably as early as the third century A.D. Wheatley accepts Sir Roland Braddell's suggestion that it was in the neighbour-hood of Trang.[5]

(c) The period of the earliest inscriptions

So far as our present knowledge goes, it is impossible to give a connected narrative of the early history of the states mentioned in the previous section. The Chinese, for instance, have nothing to say

---

[1] *Supra*, p. 24.   [2] pp. 14–24.   [3] Wheatley, *op. cit.*, pp. 252–7.   [4] *Ibid.*, pp. 66–7.
[5] *Ibid.*, chap. xvii, pp. 268–72, is devoted to a discussion of the evidence regarding this place.

about Funan between 287 and 357, and we have no other evidence to draw upon for this period. When once again light begins to penetrate the darkness inscriptions appear in Funan, Champa, Borneo and Java, and we enter upon a new period in which much stronger cultural influences are evident.

In recording the receipt of tribute from a King of Funan named Chan-t'an the Chinese describe him as a Hindu. Chan-t'an is the Chinese transcription of Chandan, the royal title of the Kushanas of Kaniskha's line, with which Funan is thought to have established contact in the middle of the third century. Hence the theory has been put forward that this king may have been a scion of that house who fled to Funan as a result of the conquest of north India by Samudra-gupta (c. 335–c. 375), the second ruler of the Gupta dynasty.

The subsequent conquest of much of south India by this king resulted in the submission of the Pallava sovereign and his viceroys and caused such grave disturbances that it is feasible to imagine the flight of princes, Brahmans and literati to seek new homes beyond the sea in lands where Indian culture already existed. This may account for the strong Pallava influence which is found in Cambodia, Champa and the Malay Peninsula, as well as for the fact that the inscriptions of the new period are in Pallava characters. But it is only a supposition.

The date 357 is the only one known of Chandan's reign. If, as is supposed, he was an Indo-Scythian, his reign may account for the Iranian influence in early Khmer statuary, and for the fact that when the Khmers conquered Funan their new kingdom had the name of Kamboja, which, it has been suggested, may indicate some relationship with the Iranian Kambojas. The cabochon with a Sassanide effigy found at Oc Eo seems to be a further pointer to a possible connection.

The *Liang History* asserts that one of Chandan's successors was a Brahman from India named Kiao-chen-ju, whom a supernatural voice bade go and rule over Funan. According to this account he was well received by the people, who chose him as their king. He then changed all the rules in accordance with Indian methods. His name is thought to be a Chinese rendering of 'Kaundinya', and the story would thus indicate the restoration of the Hindu element in the ruling family against the indigenous clan of the Fan, under whose rule Indian influence had tended to be weakened by contact with the local culture. No date is assigned to the reign of this second Kaundinya, but one of his successors, with a name which may stand for Śreshthavarman, is reported to have sent an embassy to the Emperor Wen (424–53). The

Liu Sung History mentions further embassies in 434, 435 and 438, and says that this king refused to help the Lin-yi in an attack on Tongking.

The greatest king of the later history of Funan was Jayavarman, or Kaundinya Jayavarman, who died in 514. The date of the beginning of his reign is unknown. He sent merchants to trade at Canton. On their return journey they were wrecked off the coast of Champa, and a monk, Nagasena, who was with them made his way back to the capital overland. In 484 Jayavarman sent him to China to ask for aid against the Lin-yi; but this was refused. Jayavarman's letter to the Chinese emperor shows that the official religion of Funan was Śaivite, but that Buddhism was also practised.

This story comes from the *Southern Ch'i History*, which also contains an account of the kingdom as it was in Jayavarman's day. It is a picture of a seafaring people, carrying on both trade and piracy, and constantly preying upon their neighbours. The king lives in a palace with a tiered roof, while the houses of the common people are built on piles and have bamboo leaves as a covering for their roofs. The people fortify their settlements with wooden palisades. The national dress is a piece of cloth tied round the waist. The national sport is cock-fighting and pig-fighting. Trial is by ordeal. The king rides about in public on an elephant.

A later text, the *Liang History*, adds that not only the king but the whole Court, and the concubines as well, ride on elephants. The deities of the sky are worshipped. These are represented by bronze images; some with two faces and four arms, others with four faces and eight arms—evidently a reference to the cult of Harihara. The dead are disposed of in four ways: by throwing the corpse into the current of a river, by burning it to ashes, by burial in a trench, and by exposure to the birds. This account also refers to a custom of washing still found in Cambodia and known as the *trapeang*, the use of a common bathing tank by a number of families.

On the occasion of the reception of an embassy from Jayavarman in 503, the Imperial Court recognized his greatness by conferring upon him the title of 'General of the Pacified South, King of Funan'. No inscriptions set up by him have been discovered, but his chief queen and a son named Gunavarman each left a Sanskrit one. Both display Vaisnavite inspiration. The prince's, at Thap-muoi in the Plaine des Joncs, commemorates the foundation of a sanctuary containing a footprint of Vishnu called Chakratirthasvamin. It is reminiscent of Purnavarman's sanctuary in Java with his footprints likened to those of

Vishnu. Gunavarman's inscription records the reclamation of marsh-land. Purnavarman was famous for irrigation works. The footprints of Vishnu signify the reconquest of territory—in both cases, it would seem, by peaceful means.

Rudravarman, who succeeded his father Jayavarman in 514, is des-cribed by the *Liang History* as a usurper, born of a concubine, who on his father's death murdered the rightful heir, presumably Guna-varman, and seized the throne. Between 517 and 539 he despatched a number of missions to China. When he died, presumably in about 550, a movement occurred in the middle Mekong region under the leadership of two brothers, Bhavavarman and Chitrasena, and under somewhat mysterious circumstances the power of Funan was over-thrown. Rudravarman's embassy of 539 seems to have been the last that Funan as an independent state sent to the Imperial Court. Early .in the next century, when the Chinese record the next embassy from the Funan region, the *New T'ang History* explains that the 'City of Hunters', the old capital of Funan, has been conquered by Chenla, and its king forced to emigrate to a place in the south.

Funan was the first great power in South-East Asian history. Like Rome in European history, its prestige lived on long after its fall. Its traditions, notably the cults of the sacred mountain and the naga princess, were adopted by the Khmer Kings of Cambodia. And although its architecture has disappeared completely, there is every reason to believe that some of its characteristics are preserved in a number of Cambodian buildings of the pre-Angkor period which still exist, and that the Gupta-style Buddhas, the mitred Vishnus and the Hariharas of that period convey some idea of the way in which the Funan sculptors fashioned the human form.

Champa's earliest inscriptions are associated with a King Bhadra-varman. They are found in Quang-nam and Phu-yen. The older generation of French scholars identified Bhadravarman with Fan Huta, the son and successor of Fan Fo, who was driven back by the Chinese from the Porte d'Annam frontier, and dated the inscriptions *c*. 400. The distinguished Dutch scholar Vogel, however, attributes them to Fan Fo's reign. In both cases, however, the king's name bears not the slightest resemblance to 'Bhadravarman', and Stein has suggested that the kings with Sanskrit names who reigned in Quang-nam were not the same as the Lin-yi rulers of the Hué region whose doings ᵃre chronicled in the Chinese histories. He thinks that there were two separate states, and that the southern one was later conquered by the Lin-yi.

Bhadravarman, whoever he may have been, founded the first sanctuary to be built in the Misön area and dedicated it to Śiva-Bhadreśvara. Such linking of a royal founder's name with that of Śiva became a widespread custom later on in states where Śaivite traditions of kingship prevailed. One of Bhadravarman's rock inscriptions is of particular interest, since it contains the oldest extant text in any Indonesian language. It enjoins respect for the 'king's naga', which seems to be a divinity guarding a water-spring. These inscriptions indicate clearly that the Court religion was Śiva-worship; the god Śiva-Bhadreśvara was represented by a linga, which is the earliest example of its kind in South-East Asia.

No contemporary Chinese account of the customs of the Lin-yi exists, but the thirteenth-century traveller Ma Tuan-lin has described them, presumably from earlier sources. He says that they were reputed to be the same as those of Funan and all the kingdoms beyond. He stresses the importance of woman, saying that marriages all take place in the eighth month and that the women choose their husbands. He also mentions the custom of urn burial. Seven days after death, he tells us, the king's body is ceremoniously conducted to the seashore, where it is burnt on a pyre. The bones are then placed in a gold vase and thrown into the sea.

The fall of the Chin dynasty at the beginning of the fifth century led to such a spate of Cham attacks on Tongking that the Chinese governor was forced to appeal to the Imperial Court for help. In 431 the Chinese made a sea attack on Champa, but were driven off. It was in consequence of this threat that King Yang Mah tried, without success, as we have seen, to obtain the help of Funan in an attack on Tongking. In 446 a new Governor of Tongking, T'an Ho-ch'u, decided to teach the Lin-yi a severe lesson. He swooped down on their capital in the Hué region, plundered it and retired with a booty estimated at 100,000 lb. of pure gold. China, it is to be noted, made no attempt permanently to occupy and annex Lin-yi territory. Her aim was simply to keep her frontier region quiet by administering a dose of frightfulness to the 'barbarians' beyond it. After this there was a long period of peace during which the customary embassies were sent to China.

In 529 a new dynasty, the fourth in Cham history according to Maspero's reckoning, came to the throne. Rudravarman, its first king, was granted investiture by China, and in 534 sent an embassy. Nine years later he was tempted to send a raiding force into Tongking. The opportunity seemed a good one, for the Vietnamese leader, Li

Bon, had revolted against China and was endeavouring to assert his independence. Rudravarman's raiders, however, were defeated by Li Bon's general, Phaum Tu. In 547 Li Bon's revolt itself was suppressed by China. It was not long, however, before the weakness of the Southern Ch'en dynasty (557–89) again tempted the Chams to renew their raids; but only for a brief spell. For the conquests of Yang Chien, the founder of the Swei dynasty, caused King Sambhuvarman to change his policy and present tribute in 595.

Ten years later the Chinese decided to administer another dose of the same medicine as in 446. Their armies invaded Champa, took its capital, and again carried away a vast amount of booty. For a while Sambhuvarman was submissive. Then, as a sign of his recovery, he began to neglect to send the customary tribute. But the accession of the T'ang dynasty in 618 led him to decide that discretion was the better part of valour. So Cham missions were once more sent dutifully to the Imperial Court at Ch'ang-an, and a long lull began in Cham aggression.

From their proximity to India it would naturally be inferred that the valleys of the Irrawaddy and the Menam must have been penetrated by Indian influence both earlier and more profoundly than Funan and Champa. Unfortunately there is practically no archaeological evidence from these regions before the middle of the sixth century, and Chinese sources do not refer to them. The absence of such evidence does not, however, prove very much either way, but merely that the Chinese had no intercourse with these countries so early. They do indeed mention a Buddhist kingdom of Lin-yang in their story of Fan Chih-man's attempt to conquer the Chin-lin in the third century, and in such a way as to suggest that it lay in central Burma.

If, as seems likely, they made their earliest contact via Yunnan with the Pyu kingdom in the same century, the assumption may not be far-fetched that Lin-yang was the Pyu kingdom whose capital, bearing the legendary name of Śrikshetra, was at Hmawza, near Prome in central Burma. The earliest fragments of inscriptions found there go back to c. 500. Local chronicles give long lists of legendary kings beginning from the time of the Buddha, but there is no means of verification.

The legends of the Mon people of Burma centre around the city of Thaton (Sudhammavati), which may have had some connection with Orissa. There seems no reason to doubt that the Burmese name for a Mon, 'Talaing', takes its derivation from Telingana, and indicates the region in India whence their culture came. Legend asserts that

Buddhaghosa, the father of Sinhalese Buddhism of the fifth century, was a Mon monk of Thaton, that he brought the Pali scriptures to his native city in 403, and later died there. No archaeological evidence exists concerning this subject. The earliest Mon sites are those of Si T'ep, P'ra Pathom and P'ong Tük in the Menam basin, and date from before 550. In their early days they were under Funan, but nothing is known of them during this period. In the seventh century they formed part of the Mon kingdom of Dvaravati, but whether this existed as early as the fifth or sixth centuries is also unknown.

The earliest epigraphical evidence regarding the kingdom of Arakan has been interpreted as showing a Candra dynasty reigning there from the middle of the fourth century. Its capital, near later Mrohaung in northern Arakan, was called by the Indian name of Vaisali. The names of thirteen kings whose reigns covered a period of 230 years have been preserved, but only one of them can be equated with a name in the Arakanese chronicles. He is Candrodaya, who may be Sandasurya of the chronicles, but his date of accession is given in them as the equivalent of A.D. 146.

In the Malay Peninsula Cherok Tekun, on the mainland opposite Penang, has yielded some fragments of rock inscriptions in Sanskrit that have been attributed to the fourth century. A slightly later one comes from near Bukit Meriam in Kedah. It is on a slate slab found in a ruined brick house which may have been the cell of a Buddhist monk. It consists of two Buddhist verses in Sanskrit inscribed in the characters of the oldest Pallava alphabet. The second runs: 'Karma accumulates through lack of knowledge. Karma is the cause of rebirth. Through knowledge it comes about that no karma is effected, and through absence of karma there is no rebirth.'

The late neolithic site of Kuala Selinsing in Perak has yielded a fifth-century cornelian seal inscribed with the name of Śri Vishnuvarman. But the most interesting find dating from this period comes from the north of the present Province Wellesley. It is an inscribed slate slab on a stupa surmounted by a *chattravali*, or seven-tiered 'umbrella'. The Sanskrit text consists of the Buddhist verse quoted above and a prayer for the success of a voyage projected by one Buddhagupta, the master of a junk, who is said to reside in the 'Red Land'. The Red Earth Land, known to the Chinese as *Ch'ih-t'u*, is described in a text containing the report of a Chinese mission there early in the seventh century. The very considerable discussion on the subject of its location that has so far been published, has been examined by Wheatley, who is of the opinion that it was in the region of the Kelantan River rather than the P'at'alung region of the Gulf of Siam favoured by Cœdès.[1] This inscription also is in Pallava script. Thus Mahayana Buddhism was in Malaya at this time, and had apparently been brought there from South India.

The same period shows the establishment of relations between some of the peninsular states and China. In 515 a King of Lankasuka called Bhagadatta is mentioned in this connection. The *Liang History* describes his people as wearing their hair loose and sleeveless cotton garments. The king, as usual, rides upon an elephant under a canopy, preceded by drums and flags and surrounded by a fierce-looking body-guard. North of Lankasuka was the state of P'an-p'an, which ran along the Gulf of Siam. Its earliest missions to China date from the period 424–53. From this state the second Kaundinya was said to have made his way to restore Hinduism in Funan.

The history of Indonesia in these early centuries is much less distinct than that of Funan or Lin-yi. The earliest indigenous records from Borneo are in the form of seven inscriptions found in the Kutei region in the east of the island at a sanctuary whose religious cult has not been identified with certainty. They are said to come from c. 400 and emanate from a King Mulavarman, who mentions his father Asvavarman and his grandfather Kundunga. The father is said to have been the founder of the dynasty. Kundunga is not a Sanskrit word, and seems to point to the Indonesian origin of the family. In the valleys of the rivers Kapuhas, Mahakam and Rata in western Borneo other signs of Indian influence have shown themselves in the form of Brahmanical and Buddhist images in the Gupta style.

Java's earliest inscriptions come from the hinterland of Djakarta, the capital of the Republic of Indonesia. At the foot of the mountains near Bogor—previously Buitenzorg—three rock inscriptions dating from c. 450, or perhaps a century later, have been found. A fourth belonging to the same period was found east of Tandjong Priok, the port of Djakarta. The author was a King Purnavarman of Taruma, who observed Brahmanical rites and promoted irrigation works, the earliest known in Java. Two of the inscriptions reproduce his footprints, and one those of his elephant. He is described as a great warrior, and these are the usual marks of the occupation of a country after conquest. Stutterheim, however, has suggested that his most important conquest was the peaceful one recorded in one of the inscriptions wherein he claims to have dug a canal some fifteen kilometres in length in the short

[1] *Golden Khersonese*, chap. iii, pp. 26–36; *Les États hindouisés*, p. 89.

space of twenty days.[1] Further inscriptions of this kingdom have been found near the coast at the extreme west of the island, and it would seem that Taruma was, in its day, an extensive kingdom.

These Indonesian inscriptions, valuable as they are, however, are not readily susceptible to explanation in the light of Chinese evidence about Indonesia in the same centuries. The chronological outline of rulers and events, which has illuminated both Funanese and Lin-yi history before the seventh century, is lacking in respect of Indonesia, and the historian has been unable to do more than eke out his narrative with a catalogue of such scraps of evidence as seem to fill the picture. An attempt has recently been made by Dr O. W. Wolters to suggest a few of the broad outlines of Indonesian proto-history which are reflected in the development of early Indonesian commerce with the outside world up to the emergence of the maritime empire of Śrivijaya in south-eastern Sumatra in the second half of the seventh century.[2] His main findings, briefly summarized below, are of special significance.

While up to the early third century A.D. there is in fact no evidence of direct sailing and commercial communication between (western) Indonesia and (southern) China, the Chinese in the first half of that century knew indirectly of an important commercial centre apparently somewhere on the south-eastern coast of Sumatra, which they called *Ko-ying*. Its importance lay merely in its trade connections with India. At that time the main route of international trade through South-East Asia ran across the northern end of the Malay Peninsula through the Mon state of *Tun-sun*.[3] *Ko-ying's* trading contacts with China would therefore have been through *Tun-sun* or one of the other Isthmian states of the peninsula, or possibly through Funan.

By the beginning of the fifth century this situation has changed decisively. There is clear evidence, represented by pilgrim intineraries, of direct communication across the South China Sea between Indonesia and southern China. There was Fa Hsien, the earliest of the pilgrims whose writings are still extant, who made his way homewards to China from the homeland of the Buddha in 413–14, and wrote sad comments on the predominance of pagans and heretics in the kingdom of *Ye-p'o-ti*, i.e. 'Java'. There was also the missionary monk Gunavarman, a prince of Kashmir, who ten years later made the direct crossing on his way to China from *Shê-p'o*, from whose kingdom of *Ho-lo-tan* the Chinese record embassies from 430 to 452. Thus between the early third century

---

[1] *Het Hind” isme in de Archipel*, p. 94.
[2] O. W. Wolters, *Early Indonesian Commerce and the Origins of Śrivijaya*, an unpublished thesis presented in 1962 for the degree of Ph.D. in the University of London.
[3] Wheatley, *op. cit.*, p. 286.

and the beginning of the fifth conditions of Indonesian commerce had changed radically.

What had happened to bring this about? In the first place the barbarian invasions of northern China early in the fourth century caused a massive flight of Chinese southwards, and, towards the end of the century and increasingly thereafter, the southern Chinese dynasties, denied their traditional trade-route across central Asia based on Kansu, seem to have become more and more dependent upon maritime communications for their luxury imports from western Asia.[1] The *Liu Sung shu* referring to the first half of the fifth century comments: 'Precious things come from the mountains and seas by this way . . . thousands of varieties all of which the rulers coveted. Therefore ships came in a continuous stream, and merchants and envoys jostled with each other.'[2] In the second place the coastal Malays of south-east Sumatra, were now making an increasingly important contribution to this commerce by providing shipping facilities between Indonesia and China, and probably from India and Ceylon.

The evidence adduced by Dr Wolters of this development of Indonesian commerce suggests that while the Indonesian shippers at first handled 'Persian',[3] i.e. western Asian, produce destined for the Chinese market, they subsequently proceeded to foist upon the trade Indonesian pine resin and benzoin as deliberate substitutes for 'Persian' frankincense and myrrh, and that by about 500 these products of the Sumatran jungle had come to be accepted by the Chinese as 'Persian-type' goods. Moreover, by that date the 'Barus' camphor of Sumatra was also known to the Chinese. The importance of the Malay role in all this must be emphasized. When the substitute transaction was achieved, there is no evidence that shipping from the Persian Gulf had yet begun to sail direct to China; according to Byzantine writers in the first half of the sixth century it went no farther east than Ceylon.[4] Indian ships may have been sailing to China, but it is a striking fact that Chinese sources mention only *K'un-lun*, or South-East Asian, ships as bringing the luxury goods from the *Nan hai*, 'the southern ocean', to the south Chinese ports. Funanese ships are unlikely to have handled the 'Persian' trade with its Indonesian connections, and in fact in the later fifth century we hear of Funanese communications with Tongking being interrupted by Cham pirates.[5]

There is, however, evidence of two western Indonesian kingdoms

---

[1] Wolters, *op. cit.*, pp. 145–6.   [2] *Ibid.*, p. 148.
[3] *Po-ssu* (Persia), the general name applied by the Chinese to the produce of western Asia.
[4] *Ibid.*, pp. 307–9.   [5] *Ibid.*, p. 325.

which were trading with China in these years. In 430 *Ho-lo-t'o* (or *Ho-lo-tan*) is mentioned by the Chinese as sending envoys to seek protection from its neighbours and also to ask for the removal of trading restrictions on its merchants.[1] This kingdom is more likely to have been in western Java than anywhere else. Then in 502 the Chinese say that the ruler of *Kan-t'o-li* sent envoys to the new Liang dynasty because he had been advised in a dream that, if he paid tribute, merchants would multiply in his kingdom.[2] An analysis of the Chinese geographical evidence of the fifth, sixth and seventh centuries indicates that *Kan-t'o-li* was, as the *Ming History* states, on the same coast where Śrivijaya later flourished. *Kan-t'o-li*, with its tributary record from 441 to 563, appears therefore in history as the successor of *Ko-ying* and the predecessor of Śrivijaya as the overlord of the south-east Sumatra coast.[3]

Other kingdoms, such as *P'o-li* and *Tan-tan*, were also sending tribute in the fifth and sixth centuries. They seem to have been in Java, but there is no evidence that they had an important share in the new trade with China. The explanation for their missions may well be that they were demonstrating their political importance as regional overlords. China was still unfamiliar to the Indonesians, and the emperors were probably invested with a certain amount of glamour and felt to be a new and important factor in the affairs of the region. A ruler might also, as was the founder of Malacca centuries later, be attempting to safeguard himself against attack.

Thus by the beginning of the seventh century the outlines of Indonesian history are beginning to become apparent. A harbour-kingdom was well established on the south-east coast of Sumatra, and there were several important kingdoms on the island of Java. Expanding Indonesian communications with the outside world were bringing wealth and new ideas to that region. It is not surprising that the following centuries were to see the rise of substantial empires and a flowering civilization in western Indonesia.

---

[1] Wolters, *op. cit.*, p. 322.   [2] *Ibid.*, p. 344.   [3] *Ibid.*, pp. 455–7.

CHAPTER 3

THE ISLAND EMPIRES (1)

(a) The emergence of Śrivijaya; the Śailendras

THE FALL OF FUNAN, with its powerful fleet and commercial ramifications, was followed by the rise of a new maritime empire at the western end of Indonesia. The earliest historical evidence of the new state is fragmentary, the lacunae are baffling in the extreme, and the picture that emerges is often far from clear. But since George Cœdès published the first study of the history of Śrivijaya in 1918[1] much progress has been made in clarification and amplification. On some important points, however, there are still wide divergencies of opinion among scholars.

Śrivijaya, although it has seemed to emerge suddenly and perhaps inexplicably into the light of history, mainly because of the paucity of the available evidence, must be seen against the Indonesian historical background that has been sketched in the previous chapter. The development of the direct sea route to China by the beginning of the fifth century A.D. brought new importance to the south-east coast of Sumatra, which had long traded with India and Ceylon. Dr Wolters calls it the 'favoured coast' of early Indonesian commerce, and it was from here that the voyage across the South China Sea was pioneered. From as early as 441 Kan-t'o-li, its chief port, had adopted the policy of sending tribute to China. The evidence does not show whether it was situated at either Jambi or Palembang, but he is convinced that it alone of the 'tributary' kingdoms of Indonesia during the fifth and sixth centuries was the predecessor of Śrivijaya as overlord of the 'favoured coast', attracting to its service the roaming Malay shippers of this coast and of the offshore islands. The international communications, leading to and from it, sustained its maritime trade with China. Thus Śrivijaya can be seen as growing up on a coast whose commercial assets, primarily its seamen and their ships, had already seen over 200 years of development.

The political lay-out in Java and Sumatra in the middle of the seventh century is indicated by the Chinese record of missions coming

[1] G. Cœdès, 'Le royaume de Çrivijaya', BEFEO, xviii (1918), no. 6, 1–36.

from states there. Two states in Sumatra are mentioned: 'Mo-lo-yeou' on the east coast, which has been identified as Malayu, now Jambi, on the river Batang, and somewhat farther south 'Che-li-fo-che', the Chinese form of the Sanskrit Śrivijaya, at what is today Palembang. Java seems to have been divided between three kingdoms: in the extreme west Purnavarman's Taruma with a changed name, in the centre 'Ho-ling', or Kalinga, and in eastern Java a kingdom with its capital somewhat south of modern Surabaya.

The two Sumatran states were visited in 671 by the famous Chinese Buddhist pilgrim I-tsing while on his way to India. At Śrivijaya, he tells us, there were over a thousand Buddhist monks, and their rules and ceremonies were the same as in India. The fact that he spent six months there studying Sanskrit grammar before going on to India is evidence of Śrivijaya's importance as a centre of Mahayanist learning.

In 685, after a long period of study at the Buddhist 'university' of Nalanda in Bengal, I-tsing returned to Śrivijaya and spent some four years there translating Buddhist texts from Sanskrit into Chinese. In 689, being in urgent need of writing materials and helpers, he made a brief visit to Canton, then returned to Śrivijaya with four collaborators and settled down to complete his two memoirs on the Buddhist religion in his own time. These were completed and despatched to China in 692; he himself followed in 695.

In the second of his books I-tsing makes the intriguing statement that Malayu (Jambi), where he had stayed for two months after leaving Śrivijaya on his way to India, had since then become a part of Śrivijaya. What exactly his words signified was only established by the discovery of a series of Old Malay inscriptions dating from 683 to 686. Two of them were found near to Palembang, the third at Karang Brahi on the upper reaches of the river Batang, and the fourth on the island of Banka. Together with the Cham inscriptions mentioned earlier they form the earliest examples of the Malay-Polynesian group of languages so far discovered.

These valuable records, taken together, attest the existence at Palembang of a Buddhist kingdom which had just conquered the hinterland of Malayu and was about to attack Java. The oldest one, which comes from the Palembang region, records that, on a date that can be fixed as 13 April 683, a king, who is unnamed, embarked with a force of 20,000 men to seek the magic power, and as a result conferred victory, power and riches on Śrivijaya. The second commemorates the foundation in 684 of a public park, called Śrikṣetra, by order of a King Jayanasa (or Jayanaga) as an act of Buddhist merit. The third and fourth, dated 686, call down curses upon the inhabitants of the Batang river region and the island of Banka respectively, should they be disobedient to the king or his officers, and the Banka one mentions that the army of Śrivijaya is about to depart on an expedition against Java.

Thus does Śrivijaya emerge to view as an expanding power, stretching out her tentacles towards the Straits of Malacca on the one side and those of Sunda on the other. Palembang, almost equidistant from both, was exceptionally well placed for the task of maintaining a commercial hegemony over Indonesia by controlling the two channels through which all traffic must pass between India and China. The developments of Arab navigation, and of trade between India and China, combined to give a new significance to the straits, and Palembang was the normal port which ships from China would make for during the north-east monsoon. It seems to have had at this time a flourishing commerce and mercantile marine, and to have maintained its own regular communications with both India and China. I-tsing tells us that he travelled from China to Śrivijaya on a ship belonging to a Persian merchant. His voyage onwards to India was made in one belonging to the King of Śrivijaya. The hypothesis therefore seems to be a reasonable one that the inscriptions of 683–6 point to certain important stages in the career of King Jayanasa (or Jayanaga), the conqueror of Malayu, and presumably of Taruma also, and the originator of the policy that was to make Palembang until the thirteenth century the centre of a powerful maritime empire of the islands.

Palembang seems to have had a hard struggle to become, and remain, powerful. The *Hsin T'ang shu* says that it had fourteen cities under its sway. Were these its conquered rivals?[1] It is not difficult to imagine it sending out naval expeditions to occupy strategic points on the main trade routes, and forcing its vassals to trade with the 'favoured coast' alone. A few, for instance Kedah on the mainland, which was under Śrivijayan control by 695 at the latest, would be nominated ports of call on the voyage between the Bay of Bengal and south-east Sumatra, and Dr Wolters has suggested that it was to destroy the beginning of competition in the China trade from harbours on the Straits of Malacca that the navy of Śrivijaya moved into the Straits early in its recorded history. To conquer and hold together such an empire must have involved endless campaigning, as indeed the inscriptions of 683–6 bear eloquent witness.

The obvious importance of Palembang as a Buddhist centre at the time of I-tsing's pilgrimages is one of those tantalizing facts which

---

[1] Wolters, *op. cit.*, p. 520.

emerges from a background so indistinct as to leave much to surmise. The early history of Buddhism in the Archipelago is unknown save for a few stray references of this sort. If I-tsing is right, Hinayana Buddhism was widespread there before the end of the seventh century. That Śrivijaya's Buddhism was mainly Mahayanist, however, has been confirmed by the discovery of Bodhisattvas there, though there is also evidence of the existence of some Hinayana Buddhism of the Sanskrit canon. The differences between the two forms were then far less distinct than they became later, particularly in thirteenth-century South-East Asia.

It would be interesting to know what part Śrivijaya played in the Mahayanist movement of expansion throughout South-East Asia, which has been described as one of the dominating facts of the latter half of the eighth century. It coincides with the accession of the Pala dynasty in Bengal and Magadha in the middle of the century, and has been attributed to their influence and that of Nalanda. It exhibits the same mixture of Buddhist and Hindu cults, and the tendency to Tantric mysticism, as in Bengal. Its spread also coincides with the appearance in Java of the Buddhist Śailendra dynasty bearing the imperial title of Maharaja. With this dynasty was to be linked an important phase in the history of Śrivijaya.

For the next half-century after the four Old Malay inscriptions the only references to Śrivijaya come from the Chinese record of embassies. These cover the period from 695 to 742, but tell us very little. Princes of Śrivijaya bring presents of dwarfs, musicians and multicóloured parrots, and the emperor in acknowledgment confers titles of honour on the king. Then there is a complete blank until 775, when the much-discussed Ligor stele, discovered at the Wat Sema-muang, takes up the story.

The stele has two faces, both containing inscriptions. Face A contains ten Sanskrit verses commemorating the foundation of a Mahayanist sanctuary by a King of Śrivijaya and bears the Saka date corresponding to 15 April 775. It thus indicates the expansion of the empire of Śrivijaya and also of Mahayana Buddhism to the Malay Peninsula. Face B bears what Cœdès and Krom describe as an unfinished inscription celebrating a victorious king, who bears the title of Śri Maharaja because he is of Śailendra family. Krom and a number of other scholars identified the King of Śrivijaya on face A with the Śailendra monarch mentioned on face B, and hence inferred that a Śailendra was ruling over Śrivijaya in 775. And, as it was already established that a Śailendra, vouched for by inscriptions at Kalasan and Kelurak, was ruling in central Java also at the same time, Krom concluded that Java was then under the supremacy of the Sumatran kingdom. The assumption, therefore, was that the Śailendras were a Śrivijaya dynasty which had conquered parts of Java.

The discovery of the stele led the Indian scholar R. C. Majumdar in 1933 to ask whether it was not possible for the Śrivijayan capital to have been located on the Malay Peninsula rather than in south-east Sumatra. Then in 1935 Dr Quaritch Wales put forward the claims of Chaiya on the east coast as a more likely place. But, leaving aside the details of what has proved a barren discussion, it may be simply stated that the evidence pointing to Palembang remains unshaken.[1] Equally barren has been the attempt to ascribe an Indian origin to the Śailendra dynasty. R. C. Majumdar's supposition that it was in some way connected with the Śailodbhava kings of Kalinga has been rejected. K. A. Nilakanta Sastri in 1935 suggested that since the title Śailendra, 'King of the Mountain', was often applied to Śiva, and the Pandyas of South India claimed descent from the god and assumed the title 'Minankita Śailendra', the Śailendras might have had a South Indian origin. In his more recent work, *The History of Sri Vijaya* (1949), however, he has abandoned the theory, though still unable to align himself with Przyluski and Cœdès, who ascribe to them a purely Javanese origin. But this does not imply, as Stutterheim once tried to argue,[2] that it was Śrivijaya that came under Javanese domination, and not the other way round.

The question has been asked whether the ruler of Śrivijaya mentioned in face A of the Ligor inscription was indeed the Śailendra ruler referred to on face B. Assuming that they were different persons, the suggestion has been made that the latter was Balaputradeva, a Śrivijayan king, the son of a Javanese Śailendra ruler, who, according to an inscription at Nalanda, now dated about 860,[3] founded a monastery for Indonesian pilgrims going there to study, to which King Devapala assigned the revenues of a number of villages.[4] But the

[1] For further study of this question see G. Ferrand, 'L'empire sumatranaise de Çrivijaya' in JA, 1922; Quaritch Wales, 'A Newly-explored Route of Ancient Indian Cultural Expansion' in *Indian Art and Letters*, new Series IX (1935), i, p. 155; Nilakanta Śastri, 'Śrivijaya, Candrabhanu and Vira-Pandya' in TBG, lxxvii (1937), 2, pp. 251–68; J. L. Moens, 'Çrivijaya, Yava en Kataha', *ibid.*, lxxvii (1937), 3, pp. 317–487.
[2] W. F. Stutterheim, *A Javanese Period in Sumatra's history*, Surakarta, 1929. For the literature regarding the origin of the Śailendras the reader is referred to R. C. Majumdar, 'Les rois Śailendra de Suvarnadvipa' in BEFEO, I, xxxiii (1933), pp. 121–42; G. Cœdès, 'On the Origin of the Śailendra of Indonesia' in JGIS, I (1934), 2, p. 61; K. A. N. Sastri, 'Origin of the Śailendras' in TBG, lxxv (1935), 4; J. Przyluski, 'The Śailendravamsa' in JGIS, ii (1935), 1, p. 25.
[3] J. G. de Casparis, *Prasasti Indonesia*, II, Bandung, 1956, pp. 260, 297.
[4] Cœdès, *Les États hindouisés*, pp. 159–60, 184–6.

accumulating evidence regarding Balaputradeva, as will be shown in due course, makes it quite clear that, whatever his claims to Java may have been, he had no authority there whatever. Moreover, the script on both faces of the Ligor inscription appears to be identical, and suggests that both were inscribed at roughly the same period. The full explanation of this challenging document has yet to be established.[1]

Java itself possesses hardly any epigraphical document between Purnavarman's fifth-century inscriptions and a Sanskrit inscription of 732 in a Saivite sanctuary at Changgal, south-east of the Borobudur. This records the erection of a linga by a King Sanjaya of Mataram in Kunjarakunja in the island of Java 'rich in grain and gold mines'. As Java produced no gold, attempts have been made to identify the name Kunjarakunja with some place in the Malay Peninsula, but Stutterheim has proved that it was in fact the name of the district in which Sanjaya erected his sanctuary. Sanjaya, king of Mataram, also appears in a much later inscription discovered by Stutterheim at Kedu in central Java. This valuable record is dated 907 and gives a list of the predecessors of the then reigning king, Maharaja Balitung, beginning with Sanjaya. The remaining eight rulers all bear the title Sri Maharaja. Sanjaya's immediate successor, Rakryān Panangkaran, who was reigning in 778, is described as 'ornament of the Sailendra dynasty'[2] in an inscription at Chandi Kalasan, east of Jogjakarta, which commemorates the foundation of the chandi as a shrine to the Buddhist goddess Tara.

Now the old kingdom of Mataram was in central Java, and King Sanjaya, though credited with sensational conquests in Bali, Sumatra and even in Cambodia up to the borders of China in a Javanese work of much later date, is nowhere in any contemporary or near-contemporary source referred to as either Maharaja or a Sailendra. Moreover, he was a Saivite, not a Buddhist. Hence the list of rulers beginning with him that is found in Balitung's inscription of 907 has presented historians with very difficult problems. The fact that a Chinese account records that between 742 and 755 the capital of *Ho-ling* (i.e. Central Java) was transferred farther eastwards by a King *Ki-yen*, identified with Gajayana, founder of a sanctuary of Agastya at Dinaya in East Java in 760, has led to the theory that the Buddhist Sailendras drove out the dynasty of Sanjaya from central Java, and with it the Saivite religion; and the suggestion has accordingly been put forward that

---

[1] For further discussion see Cœdès in *Oriens Extremus*, 6, 1, 1959, pp. 42–8 and de Casparis, *op. cit.*, II, p. 260, n. 77.
[2] He was a feudatory of the Sailendra house.

Balitung's list is not a dynastic one but a list of rulers of Central Java arranged in chronological order.

The emergence of Sanjaya must be seen against a background of struggle between the forces of unity and disunity in Java. Among a host of petty rulers one would from time to time build up his power by forcing the 'rakryāns' ruling the neighbouring localities to render him obedience and tribute. When, from time to time, such a ruler was able to extend his power over a wide area, he would proceed to demonstrate his greatness by building a 'chandi', or monumental tomb, dedicated to the deity with whom he chose to be identified in life and united in death. Sanjaya, as 'rakryān' of the district of Mataram, gave its name to the kingdom that he carved out for himself. The chandi bearing the Śaivite symbol of the linga, which he erected in 732, was the outward sign and manifestation of his claims to overlordship.

The evidence about him and his successors, however, is tantalizingly scrappy; and, while its monumental remains, among the most magnificent in South-East Asia, are still with us, and we have at our disposal an immense body of scholarly work concerning them, the political history of old Mataram is little known. Until recently nothing was known for certain as to the identity of the Śailendras. Of the dynasty of 'kings of the mountain', responsible for the erection of the glorious Buddhist monuments of the late eighth and early ninth centuries in Central Java, the questing historian could find a vast amount of theory and disappointingly little fact. On the other hand Dutch archaeologists have made notable contributions to our knowledge of the monuments themselves.

The Borobudur, which represents the highest expression of the artistic genius of the Śailendra period, is utterly unlike any other Javanese monument. It is not a temple with an interior, but an immense stupa in the form of stone terraces covering the upper part of a natural hill, on the flattened top of which stands the central stupa. Its height is 150 feet. To traverse the whole distance through the galleries up to the summit involves a walk of over three miles. The walls of the galleries on both sides are adorned with bas-relief sculptures illustrating Mahayanist texts. They run to thousands. In addition there are 400 statues of the Buddha. The base has a series of reliefs depicting the effects of good and evil deeds in daily life producing karma. But these are now covered up by a broad casement of stonework. The Japanese, during their occupation of Java from 1942 to 1945, showed enough interest in the monument to have a small part of the casement removed and some of the reliefs of the original base excavated. The stones have not been replaced, and it is now possible to see the uncovered reliefs.

From the religious point of view the sanctuary as a whole forms an impressive and convincing textbook of Buddhism as taught by the Nalanda school. The style of sculpture follows the classic models of Gupta India, but the reliefs are not Indian, they are Javanese. They provide a wonderful picture of Javanese life and customs. The Javanese artists in adopting Indian models had already changed them in conformity with their own traditions.[1] Even the conventionalized figures are often given a vitality that seems to break through formalism, and there are many human touches.

Architecture was the supreme achievement of the Śailendras. Most of them are mere names in a list, but their glorious shrines are still to be seen on the Kedu plain near to Jogjakarta. Not far from the Borobudur is the splendid Chandi Mendut containing three original stone statues of huge size, representing a preaching Buddha between two Bodhisattvas. Thanks to careful restoration by the Dutch, it is in excellent condition today. Other outstanding examples of the same period are Chandi Sari, a single vihara; Chandi Plaosan, consisting of two central squares, each with a vihara, surrounded by a belt of shrines and two belts of stupas; and the unfinished Chandi Sevu, consisting of a large vihara surrounded by four square belts of small shrines said to number 240.

In basic principles of construction and decoration these products of the Śailendra period differ little from the more sober Śaivite temples on the Dieng plateau nearby, which bear witness to the prosperity of the seventh century and the period of Sanjaya, but the vast scale on which they were planned, their more highly-developed technique and more imaginative use of ornamentation show an artistic expansion which must have come from a new impulse of great vitality. The idea once held was that they were the products of a wave of immigration from India. But there is no evidence of one, and Stutterheim has shown that these monuments were not only built by Javanese stonemasons and sculptors but also were associated with indigenous religious ideas and practices par excellence. A chandi was in no sense an Indian temple. The outstanding feature of the culture of the Sailendra period is the vitality and potency of the Indonesian element. In literature this tendency is already to be seen in the Old Javanese translation of the Sanskrit work *Amaramala*, which was produced under the patronage of a Sailendra prince whose name, given at the beginning of the work, was Jitendra.

---

[1] W. F. Stutterheim, *Het Hinduïsme in de Archipel*, p. 25.

Some of the mystery concerning the founders of these monuments, and the monuments themselves, has recently been cleared up by the publication in Bandung, Java, of new epigraphical material, translated and edited for Dinas Purbakala, the Indonesian Department of Archaeology, by Dr J. G. de Casparis. It is contained in two volumes with the general title *Prasasti Indonesia*, the first of which, *Inscripties uit de Çailendra-tijd*, appeared in 1950, and the second, *Selected Inscriptions from the seventh to the ninth century A.D.*, in 1956. In his first study Dr de Casparis is able to make a clear distinction between the real Śailendra dynasty and the list of rulers given in Balitung's inscription of 907, which Cœdès interpreted as containing a mixture of Śailendras and non-Śailendras. The inscriptions, de Casparis tells us, contain the names of three Śailendra kings and a princess belonging to the period 775–842. They are additional to Balitung's list, none of the kings of which, according to de Casparis's showing, was a Śailendra: all were indeed the lineal descendants of Sanjaya. During this period, therefore, there were not one but two reigning dynasties in central Java, the kings of the Sanjaya line being until 832 subordinate to the Śailendras. On this showing, which accords with Vogel's interpretation of the Kalasan inscription, Pañcapana, the Rakryān Panangkaran, was not a Śailendra but a vassal of the Śailendra king Vishnu. The table of the two dynasties runs thus:

Sanjaya's line (Saivite)	The Śailendras (Buddhist)
Sanjaya (732–*c.* 760)	. . . .
R. Panangkaran (*c.* 760–*c.* 780)	? (Bhanu, 752)
R. Panungalan (*c.* 780–*c.* 800)	Vishnu (Dharmatunga) (before 775–82)
R. Warak (*c.* 800–before 819)	Indra (Sangramadhanamjaya) (782–?812)
R. Garung (?R. Patapan) (before 819–?838)	Samaratunga (=Tara) (?812–?832)
R. Pikatan (?838–?851)	Balaputra =Pramodavardhani (Princess)
R. Kayuwani (?851–after 882)	

In 832 Rakryān Patapan, whom de Casparis equates with Rakryān Garung of the Sanjaya line, erected an inscription proclaiming his authority over most of central Java. This would imply the end of Śailendra rule in Java. Exactly what happened the evidence does not show. De Casparis offers the following explanation. He presumes the death of the Śailendra Samaratunga in that year. Balaputra, his infant son, was too young to come to the throne. Pramodavardhani, his daughter, is shown by the epigraphical evidence to have married into the Sanjaya house. Her husband was Rakryān Pikatan, the son of Rakryān Patapan, the author of the inscription of 832. Ten years later, in an inscription of 842 recording the dedication of ricefields to the upkeep of the Borobudur, she is described as queen. Her husband probably succeeded his father in 838.

Thus did the hegemony over central Java pass out of Śailendra hands. The young prince Balaputra, it is surmised, fled to Sumatra, married a Śrivijaya princess, and ultimately became the ruler of his adopted state. In Java Rakryān Pikatan and his Śailendra consort were the parents of Kayuwani, who came to the throne in the middle of the ninth century. 'Later Javanese princes from Kayuwani to Balitung,' writes de Casparis, 'and probably his predecessors, considered themselves as belonging to the dynasty founded by Sanjaya in 732, but their titles show that they indirectly also belong to the Çailendra dynasty.'[1]

In his second study much light is thrown upon Prince Balaputradeva, the failure of the Śailendras in Central Java and the supplanting of Buddhism by Śaivism as the court religion. Three Sanskrit inscriptions from the Ratubaka Plateau a little to the south of Prambanan deal with the erection of lingas there by a prince, with a name composed of synonyms for the sage Agastya, to celebrate a victory in the year 856 over an unknown enemy.[2] The evidence, as de Casparis indicates,[3] links him up with the founder of a Śiva temple Bhadraloka at Pereng, which is recorded in an inscription, dated 863, partly written in Sanskrit verse and partly in Old Javanese prose, which Krom interpreted as the first clear proof of the cessation of Sailendra hegemony in Java. Dr de Casparis's conclusion is that the victory of 856 marked the culmination of a long struggle for dominance between the Sanjaya house and the Sailendras, and that while Rakryān Patapan's 832 inscription

---

[1] *Op. cit.*, p. 202.
[2] *Prasasti*, II, p. 256. De Casparis thinks that the unknown enemy were probably Malay-speaking invaders seeking to establish claims by marrying into the then powerless Śailendra family.
[3] *Ibid.*, pp. 249, 258.

shows that a prince of the Sanjaya house has made himself independent of the Śailendras and established a Śaivite centre in northern Central Java, the Śailendras themselves probably continued to reign in southern Central Java and to strive to reassert their ascendancy.

How that struggle ended is made clear by an Old Javanese inscription of unknown site, dated 856,[1] the year of the victory recorded in the Ratubaka inscriptions. It mentions Balaputradeva in connection with the struggle in the preceding period, and indicates that after defeat in the open country he retired to a stronghold, described as constructed with hundreds of stones, where he was attacked and defeated by Kumbhayoni, the founder of the Ratubaka lingas and of the Pereng temple. The lingas thus indicate that the final victory for the Sanjaya-vamsa was won on the Ratubaka Plateau.

The Old Javanese inscription of 856 mentions a King Jatiningrat, who after defeating Balaputra resigned his throne and handed over the symbols of power to one Dyah Lokapala, whom de Casparis identifies with Kayuwani. He, it will be remembered, was the son of Pikatan of the Sanjaya line and the Śailendra princess Pramodavardhani, who as Queen Sri Kahulunnan issued the edicts recorded in the inscription of 842, mentioned above, dedicating rice-fields for the upkeep of the Borobudur and also participated in the foundation of Chandi Plaosan. The story of the king, who on retiring from the throne to devote himself to a spiritual life, and acquire merit by religious foundations, takes a new name, is of special significance,[2] for there is a close parallel with that of King Airlangga of later Indonesian history. He retired to a hermitage in 1045 and also adopted the name Jatiningrat. Moreover, the parallel between the two rulers, de Casparis points out, extends over their careers as a whole. The three linga inscriptions show that Kumbhayoni's (alias R. Pikatan, alias Jatiningrat) life was divided into a sequence of four periods, one of asceticism, then one of fierce battles, then one of complete victory, and finally one of resignation. The life of Airlangga similarly is divided into this same sequence of periods, and de Casparis's suggestion is that when he resigned the throne, adopted the name Jatiningrat and became a hermit, he was inspired by the example of King Kumbhayoni, so powerful was the influence of tradition in early Indonesian history.

The Ratubaka Plateau would seem to have been an ideal place for Balaputradeva's last stronghold. A Śailendra foundation of the eighth century was situated there, and Buddhist statues together with a silver plate bearing on it the abbreviated form of the Buddhist creed have

---

[1] *Ibid.*, pp. 260, 280–99.   [2] *Ibid.*, p. 291.

been discovered there and a Sailendra inscription in north Indian script dated 792. It had special associations with the Śailendra house. This would explain why Kumbhayoni after his victory made a special point of erecting lingas there, and transformed the place into a Śaivite centre. But de Casparis warns us that in explaining this struggle religious factors must not be stressed.[1] It was not a case of religious fanaticism, but rather a struggle for dominance between two rival families, and it may be that popular support went to the Sanjaya champion because of the tremendous burden the huge Śailendra foundations laid on the people.

When Balaputradeva was finally chased from his strong position, he must have escaped to Sumatra, and in a way still unknown became king of Śrivijaya. Various suggestions aimed at explaining this have been made. It has been thought that he may have had a claim to the Śrivijayan throne through his mother. Krom thought it likely that Dharmasetu, who is mentioned in the Nalanda inscription as Balaputradeva's maternal grandfather, was a king of Śrivijaya, that his daughter married the Śailendra Samaragravira and became the mother of the defeated prince.[2] A much earlier family relationship has been suggested by Cœdès in a study of face B of the Ligor inscription published in 1950.[3] He thinks that two kings, father and son, are mentioned, the father being identical with the ruler of Śrivijaya mentioned on face A, and the son becoming the first Śailendra after marriage with a princess descending from the 'Kings of the Mountain' of Funan. While not committing himself to so precise a statement de Casparis has pointed out that the two inscriptions—i.e. A and B—can be interpreted in such a way as to suggest a close relationship between the Śrivijaya kings of Palembang and the Śailendra kings of Central Java;[4] but he warns us that family relations are not the full explanation of Balaputradeva's succession to the Śrivijayan throne.[5] There may have been several candidates with claims based upon family relationship; he, however, possessed the considerable advantage of bringing with him important territorial claims. It is significant that in the Nalanda inscription the fact is stressed that his father and grandfather were kings of Java. Even if he himself were unable to recover his inheritance, his claims would pass to his successors. Thus Krom's suggestion that the shift of the Javanese capital from Central to East Java in the first

[1] *Op. cit.*, I, p. 294.

[2] In the Nalanda inscription Balaputradeva is called king of Sumatra and a descendant of the Śailendra kings of Java. His father's title is shown as Samaragravira, 'foremost hero in battle', and his grandfather is described as the 'Śailendra slayer of enemy heroes'.

[3] 'Le Çailendra Tueur des Heros ennemis' in *Bingkisan Budi*, pp. 58–70.

[4] *Op. cit.*, I, pp. 99–100.   [5] *Op. cit.*, II, p. 296, n. 66.

half of the tenth century was due to fear of a Śrivijayan attack may hold the key to that mystery.[1] Equally, suggests de Casparis, Balaputra-deva's defeat in Java may have induced him to send his mission to the Pala king in *c.* 860 through anxiety to cultivate friendly relations with what was then the greatest Buddhist power in the West in view of a possible threat to his eastern flank.[2]

Thus some of the mystery of the Śailendras in Central Java, and of their disappearance from there and simultaneous appearance in Sumatra, has been cleared up through the patient and penetrating work of de Casparis. He has some equally penetrating things to say about their artistic monuments.

He insists that the Buddhist foundations of the Śailendras must be examined in the light of ancestor-worship, and shows that the nine Bodhisattvas sculptured on the outside of Chandi Mendut, close to the Borobudur, may be interpreted as representing the ancestors of King Indra, its founder. If so, the Śailendra dynasty, which, it has been generally assumed, had its origin not long before the date of its earliest inscriptions, may have been founded as early as the first half of the seventh century. Thus the view, long held by Cœdès, that the Java 'Kings of the Mountain' were in some way connected with the Funan monarchy bearing the same title no longer appears to be ruled out by the time factor, since the end of Funan may have coincided with the foundation of the Śailendra dynasty in Java. And indeed de Casparis has found in two Śailendra inscriptions, at Kelurak and Plaosan, allusions pointing to the name of the last capital of Funan, Naravaranagara.

His interpretation of the 'hidden meaning' of the Borobudur is of special interest. Mention has already been made of the stone casement covering the reliefs around the foot of the monument. Guesses have been hazarded as to the reason for sculpturing the reliefs only to cover them up afterwards. From an inscription of 842 de Casparis infers that the full name of the monument was Bhumisambarabhudhara, 'the Mountain of Accumulation of Virtue on the ten Stages of the Bodhisattva'. Its foot would thus represent the first stage. The covering of this, he tells us, is not to be explained in terms of Mahayanism, but rather in those of ancestor-worship. The first stage of the Bodhisattvabhumi must be seen as the one which the Śailendra king Indra would occupy when he reached the status of a Bodhisattva. It was covered up by way of reservation. In a sense it was dead, and only upon his becoming a Bodhisattva could the reliefs surrounding it be uncovered and brought to life again.[3]

[1] *Infra*, p. 59.   [2] *Prasasti Indonesia*, II, p. 297.   [3] *Ibid.*, p. 184.

CHANDI MENDUT

CHANDI MENDUT (interior)

In order to see things in their proper setting it is necessary to treat the complex Chandi Mendut-Chandi Pawon-Chandi Borobudur as one whole, capable of analysis from the double standpoint of Mahayana Buddhism and ancestor-worship. From the one standpoint it represents the Path leading to Buddhahood, with the 'Temple of the Bamboo Grove' (Chandi Mendut) as the first preparatory stage. The word *gotra*, however, used in this connection to indicate the fundamental element of Buddhahood, awakened at this stage, also signifies in a non-Buddhist sense a line of ancestors. From this latter standpoint, therefore, the chandi demonstrates King Indra's realization that he followed a line of ancestors, represented, as already indicated, by the nine Bodhisattvas sculptured on its outside.

Chandi Pawon, the name of which, according to de Casparis, refers to a royal cremation, represents the last worldly stage giving entrance to the supramundane stages in the progress of the Bodhisattva. These latter are represented in the Borobudur itself. The covered-up foot of the monument, as we have seen, symbolizes the first. The open terraces above it account for the remainder, culminating in the tenth and topmost. Again it is the 'hidden meaning' which carries the greater significance, for according to de Casparis's interpretation it implies a representation of the nine preceding Sailendra princes, each in his proper place on the road leading to Buddhahood, with the first ancestor, 'the "root" (*mula*) of the dynasty, the Çailendra, "Lord of the Mountain", at the final momentary meditation before obtaining Buddhahood'.

(b) The greatness and decline of Śrivijaya

Definite evidence is lacking concerning both the origin of the Sailendras and the disappearance of their power in central Java. So far as history is concerned, unheralded they come and unheralded they go. Moreover, they, who bequeathed to Java so glorious a heritage of religious architecture and art, built no enduring monuments either in Sumatra or anywhere else in their empire when they became the ruling dynasty of Śrivijaya. Internal evidence of Śrivijaya's history under their rule is conspicuous by its absence. May the lack of it in the tenth century be attributed to the destruction caused by the great Chola raid of 1025? Or does the explanation lie in the fact, noted by Cœdès, that she was a 'great economic power which neglected the spiritual values'? Her sovereigns, he suggests, were too busy controlling the traffic of the straits to waste time on such matters.[1]

[1] *Op. cit.*, p. 221.

It is intriguing to find that at about the time when the Śailendra power disappears from Java the Chinese begin to employ a different name for Śrivijaya. Instead of Che-li-fo-che they call it San-fo-ts'i. The new name appears first in the record of an embassy of 904–5, and continues to be used until the end of the fourteenth century. No explanation of this change in nomenclature has been suggested. And the transliteration itself presents a difficulty, for while *fo-ts'i* stands for *vijaya*, *śri* should. be rendered by the Chinese characters for *che-li*.

From the middle of the ninth century a new external source, the writings of Arabic-Persian geographers, becomes important. They extol the riches and power of the Maharaja of 'Zabag', who is the 'king of the isles of the eastern sea'. They mention in particular that he rules over the maritime country of 'Kalah' and the island of 'Sribuza'. 'Kalah' stands for Kra, now the name of a region of the Malay Peninsula, but then applied by the writers to the whole Peninsula. 'Sribuza' is a rendering of Śrivijaya and is applied to both Palembang and the island of Sumatra.

The Arab Mas'udi, writing in 955, speaks in exaggerated terms of the enormous population and innumerable armies of the kingdom of the maharaja. As Krom has pointed out, the defence of a privileged position such as Śrivijaya assumed involved perpetual recourse to force. The empire, like that of the Dutch in the seventeenth century, was a vast trading monopoly, and rivals had to be reduced to subjection or neutralized. Its territories, wrote the Arabs, produced camphor, aloes, cloves, sandalwood, nutmeg, cardamum, cubeb and much else. Its trade was far-reaching. The Nalanda inscription recording Balaputra's foundation of a vihara there is evidence of established relations with Bengal, which was presumably one of its sources of piece-goods. There is evidence also of intercourse with the Coromandel Coast.

When in 971 the Chinese opened an agency at Canton for the management of sea-borne commerce the merchants of Śrivijaya are mentioned in the list of foreigners resorting there. The *History of the Sung* records the arrival of a merchant of Śrivijaya in 980 at Swatow, and five years later that of a purely commercial mission. The restoration of order by the Sung dynasty led to much intercourse with Śrivijaya. The Chinese record the arrival of embassies in 960, 962, 971, 972, 974, 975, 980, 983, and 988. In some cases the king's name is mentioned, but it has not been possible to transliterate the Chinese into Sanskrit with certainty. Regular intercourse between the two

Courts went on until 1178, when the Chinese emperor, finding the expense of receiving these embassies somewhat too heavy, directed that in future they should proceed no farther than Chuan-Chu in Fukien province, but trade there in the ordinary way.

The Śrivijaya ambassador, who appeared at the Imperial Court in 988 and left for home in 990, heard on reaching Canton that his country was being attacked by the Javanese. After waiting for a year at Canton he sailed homewards, but on arrival in Champa heard such bad news that he returned to China to ask for the issue of a decree placing his country under the imperial protection. That was in 992. In the same year Javanese envoys appeared before the emperor to complain of continual war with San-fo-ts'i. The war was provoked by Dharmavamsa (c. 985-c. 1006), King of East Java, who aimed at destroying Srivijaya and substituting Javanese supremacy over the islands. Little is known of the actual struggle, though it would appear that for some years the Javanese attacks placed Palembang in dire peril. They were, however, beaten off. Then, it is thought, Śrivijaya, aided by its vassals from the Malay Peninsula, organized a great counter-attack and burnt Dharmavamsa's kraton. He himself was killed and his empire collapsed.

Śrivijaya's success in the long struggle with Dharmavamsa came partly through cultivating friendly relations with China on the one hand and with the Cholas in India on the other. Had either supported the Javanese attack the result might have been very different. In sending the customary tribute to China in 1003 the King of Śrivijaya announced that he had erected a Buddhist temple for the offering of prayers for the life of the emperor. This time the Chinese version of the king's name is recognizable as Śri Chulamanivarmadeva.

About two years later this same king emulated Balaputra's example by building at Negapatam on the Coromandel Coast a Buddhist temple, named after him the Chulamanivarmadeva Vihara. The Chola king Rajaraja granted the revenues of a large village for its upkeep. Like the earlier Nalanda endowment, the Negapatam one was established to provide a place where the merchants of Śrivijaya could resort for worship in accordance with their own religious tenets. It witnesses to the importance of the trading connection between Palembang and the Coromandel Coast, which drove a flourishing trade in Indian piece-goods with South-East Asia.

In Rajaraja's grant of revenues to the Negapatam vihara it is stated that the King of Śrivijaya belonged to the Śailendra family. In his reign the empire stood at the height of its power and prestige. Unhappily none of its records has survived, and all that is known of it, even the names of its kings, comes solely from external sources. Thus the Chinese record a mission received in 1008 from Chulamanivarmadeva's son Maravijayottungavarma, but there is no mention of the date of the father's death. From another external source also comes the interesting information that Śrivijaya was still a famous Buddhist centre. The renowned Atiśa, who reformed Tibetan Buddhism, is said to have studied there from 1011 to 1023 under Dharmakirti, the head of the Buddhist clergy in Sumatra. The Tibetan biography of Atiśa calls Sumatra the chief centre of Buddhism and Dharmakirti the greatest scholar of his time.

The good relations cultivated by Śri Chulamanivarmadeva with the Cholas did not last long. An expanding sea power like that of the Cholas was bound to resent the methods used by the old empire of the islands to maintain its commercial monopoly. In 1017 the Chinese record the reception of a mission from yet another King of Śrivijaya, Haji Sumatrabhumi by name. It was in his reign that his empire sustained at Chola hands a staggering blow, from which it never fully recovered. In 1007 the Cholas had begun to raid eastwards, and Rajaraja boasted that in that year he conquered 12,000 islands. This exaggerated claim has been taken to refer to an expedition against the Maldives. His son and successor, Rajendra, has been credited with an attempted raid on the possessions of Śrivijaya in the Malay Peninsula; but there is some doubt as to whether this actually took place. Rajaraja died in 1014, and Rajendra seems to have remained for some years on friendly terms with Śrivijaya, and even to have confirmed the grant made by his father to the Negapatam vihara.

The great raid which crippled the Malay empire occurred in 1025. Details of it were recorded by Rajendra in an inscription at Tanjore dated 1030-1. Nilakanta Sastri's translation runs thus: '[Rajendra] having despatched many ships in the midst of the rolling sea and having caught Sangrama-Vijayottungavarman, the King of Kadaram, together with the elephants in his glorious army, [took] the large heap of treasures, which [that king] had rightfully accumulated; captured with noise the [arch called] Vidyadharatorana at the war-gate of his extensive capital, Śrivijaya, with the jewelled wicket-gate adorned with great splendour and the gate of large jewels; Pannai with water in its bathing ghats; the ancient Malaiyur with the strong mountain for its rampart; Mayirudingam, surrounded by the deep sea [as] by a moat; Ilangasoka undaunted [in] fierce battles; Mappapalam having abundant [deep] water as defence; Mevilimbangam guarded by beautiful walls;

Valaippanduru possessed of Vilaippanduru [?]; Talaittakkolam praised by great men [versed in] the sciences; the great Tamralinga [capable of] strong action in dangerous battles; Ilamuri-deam, whose fierce strength rose in war; the great Nakkavaram, in whose extensive gardens honey was collected; and Kadaram of fierce strength, which was protected by the deep sea.'[1]

Most of these places were situated in either Sumatra or the Malay Peninsula, but several of the names have not been identified. Those that can be identified with certainty are Palembang, Malayur (Jambi), and Pané, on the east coast of Sumatra; Lankasuka (Ligor), Takola, and Kedah, on the Malayan mainland; Tumasik, the old name for Singapore Island, Acheh at the northern tip of Sumatra, and the Nicobar Islands. It is interesting to see that Sangrama Vijayottungavarman, the King of Śrivijaya, was known to the Tamils as King of Kedah, although the chief seat of his power lay in Sumatra. Allowing for the obscurity of several of the names, the extent of the empire of Śrivijaya corresponds fairly closely with the contemporary Arab accounts of the empire of Zabag.

Krom is of opinion that the attacks began with Palembang, followed by the occupation of important places on the east coast of Sumatra. Then the Malay Peninsula was dealt with. On the way home Acheh and the Nicobars were raided. No attempt was made at conquest in the real sense. Indeed the only political result of the raid of which there is any record was the accession of a new Śailendra king, Śri Deva, in place of the captured one. His embassy to China in 1028 was accorded more than the usual honours.

The weakness of Śrivijaya after the raid enabled Airlangga of Java (1019–42) to reconquer the patrimony lost by his father Dharmavamsa in 1006. In face of the Chola threat the two Indonesian states buried the hatchet, and in 1030 Airlangga married a daughter of Sangrama Vijayottungavarman. From 1030 until 1064 nothing is known of the history of Śrivijaya. An inscription dated 1064 on the image of a makara found at Solok, to the west of Jambi, mentions a certain Dharmavira, but nothing is known of him. The image bears traces of Javanese artistic influence. After the raid Śrivijaya seems to have re-established its authority over Sumatra but never to have recovered its old power. With Airlangga it achieved a *modus vivendi* which left it supreme over the west of the Archipelago and Java over the east. But there is evidence of Java's commercial relations with the west.

There is a brief record of a Chola raid on the Malay Peninsula about

[1] *History of Śri Vijaya*, p. 80.

1068, when King Virarajendra is said to have conquered Kidaram on behalf of Śrivijaya and to have handed it over to the king, who had sought Chola aid and protection. This seems to have later given the Chinese the erroneous impression that it was the Chola king who was the vassal of Śrivijaya, and not the other way round. Whatever may be the meaning of this stray and obscure reference, there are clear indications that during Virarajendra's reign friendly relations again existed between the two powers, and no little commercial intercourse. An inscription in Tamil dated 1088, found near Baros on the west coast of Sumatra, mentions an important south Indian corporation. In 1090, at the request of Śrivijaya, the Chola king Kulottunga I granted a new charter to the Negapatam vihara.

In 1077, and not in 1067 as was once believed, Śrivijaya had sent a mission to China. In 1079, however, the Chinese received missions from both Jambi and Śrivijaya, a curious circumstance that suggests rivalry between Palembang, the capital of the Malay empire, and its neighbour. In 1082 only Jambi was in official communication with China, and it is likely that in the 1079–82 period Jambi was able to supplant Palembang as the capital of Śrivijaya.

During the twelfth century there is little to report. The Chinese record a few embassies, and the commercial importance of Śrivijaya is suggested by the fact that one of its envoys in 1157 had long been resident in China and had been made a Chinese official; in 1157 his rank was raised. Obviously Śrivijaya was able to employ experienced agents in China. Yet this must have been a period of slow decline. The development of the kingdom of Kediri in east Java as a naval and commercial power stimulated economic progress in the Archipelago, and Śrivijaya is thought to have benefited thereby. But in 1178 the Chinese writer Chou K'u-fei relegated her to the third place among wealthy foreign states; she was surpassed by the Arab lands and Java. Her methods too seem to have become more and more piratical. Every passing ship was attacked if it failed to put in to one of her harbours.

Nevertheless at the beginning of the thirteenth century Śrivijaya must still have been a great power. She is described as such in 1225 by Chao Ju-kua, the Chinese inspector of foreign trade at Ch'uan-chou in his *Chu-fan-chi*, 'Record of Foreign Nations'. He lists no less than fifteen vassal states, covering the whole of the Malay Peninsula south of the Bay of Bandon and all western Indonesia, including the state of Sunda in West Java. Nilakanta Sastri thinks that there is reason to suspect that his political information was not as up-to-date as his commercial data. But there can be no doubt that Śrivijaya still controlled both sides of the Straits of Malacca and Sunda. Not until that control was broken did her power vanish.

Chao Ju-kua's account of her capital shows it to have been a typical water city full of creeks, with people living in boats or houses built on rafts, like Mrohaung, the old capital of Arakan, modern Bangkok and many older cities back to the days of Funan. One gathers, however, that Palembang no longer exerted so tight a control over its vassal states as once it had done. Aru, on the east coast of Sumatra, had set up its own king. Chao Ju-kua's list of dependencies is not absolutely reliable: Ceylon, for instance, is included in it. The list also includes Palembang, but we have seen that there are reasons for believing that Jambi was now the capital, though the Chinese preferred to call the empire by the familiar name of *San-fo-ch'i*. Chinese officials were never very interested in political events in Sumatra, provided that there was no interruption in trade. It is not surprising that Kertanagara's expedition to Sumatra had Malayu—i.e. Jambi—as its objective, and according to the *Pararaton* was planned as early as 1275. In 1281 the Śrivijaya embassy to China went from Malayu, and Marco Polo mentions Malayu as the foremost state in Sumatra when he visited the island in 1292. During this period the name Śrivijaya drops out of use.

One sign of the coming breakdown comes from the year 1230, when Dharmaraja Chandrabanu of Tambralinga (Ligor) erected an inscription at Ch'aiya, in which he assumes the style of an independent ruler. He makes no reference to Śrivijaya. In 1247 and again in 1270 he interfered in Ceylon. The defeat of his second expedition was so severe that it is thought to have been the cause of Ligor's inability to withstand the T'ai onslaught which came some twenty years later. There is reason to think that Dharmaraja Chandrabanu developed very friendly relations with the rising T'ai state of Sukhodaya (Suk-'ot'ai) on the Menam. Cœdès suggests that the explanation of this, and also of Tambralinga's attempt to interfere in Ceylon, lies in its adherence to Hinayana Buddhism of the Pali canon. The T'ai also were Buddhists of the same school, and Ceylon was not only the foremost centre of this form of Buddhism but claimed to possess two of the most prized relics of the Buddha, his begging-bowl and the famous Kandy tooth. Tambralinga's relations with her suzerain may have been complicated by a growing antagonism between Hinayana and Mahayana Buddhists.

Not much is known of Śrivijaya's decline bar its symptoms. Dr. O. W. Wolters has recently attempted to interpret the evidence by means of what is known of the changing patterns of Asian trade, and

especially the growing importance of Chinese overseas voyages.[1] Dr.
Wolters observes that, until the end of the eleventh century, China was
dependent upon foreign ships in her commerce with the Nanyang.
Trade had to be carried on according to the 'tributary' system laid
down by the imperial court in its dealings with individual foreign
states. That is to say, trade with China was not open and free to all
merchants, Chinese or foreign. It was restricted to the 'tribute'
missions sent to the emperor by his 'vassal' barbarian rulers, or, at
least, to the so-called 'vassals'. From the seventh century until the
leadership passed from Palembang to Malayu (Jambi) at the end of
the eleventh century, Palembang, with a well-governed port, and at
the head of a loosely knit empire of trading ports, provided just the
sort of entrepôt needed by merchants trading to and from China. Its
rulers became fabulously rich through this system of trade, and one
can imagine that the maharaja's immense wealth enabled him to
reward his loyal followers with bounteous dispensations of patronage.
With his fleet, which included quotas of ships supplied by his vassals,
he policed the seas, making them safe for the peaceful trader.

All this changed during the period of the Southern Sung (1127–
1278). Their dependence upon seaborne trade led them to open
the trade with the Nanyang to Chinese vessels.[2] There was a great
expansion of the Chinese mercantile marine, and Chinese vessels
began to trade directly with South-East Asian ports. Chau Ju-kua,
for instance, mentions in 1225 that Chinese merchants were visiting
Java, while another source mentions that they were visiting the ports
of the Gulf of Siam. Others followed their example, and we hear of
Tamil and Cairo merchants trading directly to north Sumatra for
camphor. During the Mongol period (1278–1367) things got worse for
Śrivijaya. By 1330 Chinese merchants were handling much of the
freight of the Indian Ocean, while the north Sumatran harbours, Aru,
Samudra, Lamuri and Perlac, were becoming independent centres of
trade. Thus Palembang and Malayu ceased to be needed as entrepôts
by Asian traders, and Chinese reports significantly mention that *San-
fo-ch'i* was using force to compel ships to visit its harbours. In such
a way, and for reasons outside the control of the maharajas, did
Śrivijaya's system of commerce break down; its imperial power
dwindled, and foreign accounts of the twelfth, thirteenth and early
fourteenth centuries speak of piracy.

Political factors in addition to economic decay further contributed
to Śrivijaya's decline. In the latter half of the thirteenth century her

[1] *The Fall of Śrivijaya in Malay History. Asia Major* Supplementum, 1968.

[2] On this subject see Lo Jung-pang, *China as a Sea Power, 1127–1368*, Ph.D. thesis
(Berkeley, Calif., 1957).

authority was assailed from two opposite sides, by the T'ai of the Menam valley and by the East Javanese kingdom of Singosari under the leadership of the empire-building Kertanagara. The T'ai kingdom of Sukhot'ai struck a decisive blow at Śrivijaya's power on the mainland, according to the Mon chronicles, by expanding its control, from about 1280, over her northern possessions in the Malay Peninsula. An inscription, set up by Rama Khamheng at Sukhot'ai in 1292, claims that the Ligor kingdom had come under his sway. The *Yuan History*, in referring to a mission received from Rama Khamheng in 1295, says that the people of Siam and those of *Ma-li-yu-eul* (Malayu) had been killing each other for a long time, but the latter had now submitted.

Java under Kertanagara (1368–92) claimed overlordship over southeast Sumatra, and, as will be shown in the following chapter, sent the much-discussed Pamalayu expedition to enforce it. According to the *Nagarakertagama*, the kingdom of Sunda and parts of the Malay Peninsula also had to recognize his suzerainty. After his death his claims passed to the rulers of Majapahit, and in 1365 the *Nagarakertagama* included Sumatra within the empire of Hayam Wuruk. By that time Malayu had become part of the Minangkabau kingdom founded by Adityavarman. Thus Śrivijaya was no longer the focus of Malay activities.

Then came the Ming victory in China. The Hung-wu Emperor, T'ai-tsu (1368–98), the founder of the dynasty, issued the order that henceforth only China's 'vassals' might sell goods to Chinese, and only when they brought 'tribute' to China. An elaborate set of regulations was put into effect. Canton was made the sole port for South-East Asian trade. Trading superintendents were appointed at China's ports to suppress illegal practices. And the periodicity of missions from 'distant' countries was laid down. There was an immediate revival of trade in the harbours of south-east Sumatra, and the Chinese record no less than six missions from *San-fo-ch'i* between 1371 and 1377, all but one from Malayu. Knowing apparently nothing about Majapahit's claims to overlordship, China in 1370 sent an imperial envoy to Malayu, and in 1374 even Palembang was emboldened to send its own mission to China. Other Malay ports also followed its example, Lampung in 1376 and Pahang in 1378.

The Javanese retaliation for China's disregard of their suzerain rights was probably savage. Their envoys were in China in 1377 when the decision was taken to grant investiture to Malayu. They reported this to their ruler, who promptly enticed to Java the imperial envoys bearing investiture to Malayu, and had them assassinated. The

Chinese record says that the emperor would not punish Java. Nevertheless, two Javanese missions arriving late in 1379 were given an unfriendly reception and their members detained; in the following year the emperor rejected the tribute offered by the Javanese ruler, and again detained his envoys. Javanese sources are silent about the affair, while Chinese sources merely state that *San-fo-ch'i* became increasingly weak and ceased to send missions. The promising Malay trade of the 1370's languished, and, with it, the prospects for revived Malay maritime power in Sumatra. China herself proceeded to tighten up her anti-foreign regulations still further, instituting a system of passes to prevent unauthorized people from coming in to trade, and issuing many edicts against private trade. The result was a shortage of the goods usually coming from South-East Asia, and an increase in clandestine trade and piracy. Thus the Malays were, as Krom put it, 'left in the lurch', and Śrivijaya's brief revival ended in complete collapse.

But worse was to follow. In 1397 the Emperor T'ai-tsu, irked by the cessation of trade with the Sumatran ports, ordered his 'vassal', the king of Ayut'ia, to inform the king of Majapahit of his displeasure at the breakdown of trade, and to request him to remedy the situation. The result was far from what the emperor intended, or expected, for Majapahit thereupon announced the annexation of Śrivijaya and, in the words of the Chinese, 'destroyed the country'. Palembang is here indicated. It had long been known as the 'Old Harbour'. Majapahit appointed a small chief to rule what was left of it when the Javanese fleet had done its work. But the local Chinese elected the Nan-hai merchant, Liang Tao-ming headman, and under his leadership the place soon began to recover. Early in the reign of the Yung-lo emperor an imperial guard commander visited South-East Asia and met Liang's son, who was taken to China, arriving in February 1405. As a result a special mission went from the emperor to Palembang and brought Liang himself back with it in December 1405. And the Chinese record that he was given presents by the emperor.

Nevertheless, the old capital of Śrivijaya never rose again from its ashes, for long before Liang's election the Malay leaders had left the city to found a new centre elsewhere. Both Tomé Pires and Albuquerque's son speak of an evacuation of Palembang. Tomé Pires seems to sum up pretty accurately what happened when he writes that a prince of Palembang threw off allegiance to Java, incurred thereby a brutal invasion of his city, and escaped with a small following to Singapore and, eventually, to Malacca.

CHAPTER 4

THE ISLAND EMPIRES (2)

(a) *Java to the Mongol invasion of 1293*

THE dominance of the Buddhist Śailendras over central Java in the eighth century caused Śaivism to seek a refuge in the eastern parts of the island. There is evidence of the existence of an independent kingdom there in the latter half of the century, with its centre somewhere in the neighbourhood of Malang. It was thus a forerunner of the much later kingdom of Singosari. Its monuments were similar in style to the ones that the Śailendras were erecting at the same time in central Java, but were dedicated to the cult of Agastya, the sage who Hinduized south India. The rulers of the state were the guardians of a royal linga representing much the same politico-religious ideas as were to be found in contemporary Champa and Jayavarman II's Cambodia. The oldest dated document coming from East Java belongs to this period. It is a Sanskrit inscription dated 760 recording the foundation at Dinaya of a sanctuary of Agastya by a king named Gajayana.

During the second half of the ninth century the return of Śaivism to central Java has been taken as an indication of the decline of Śailendra power there. Balitung (898–910), whose inscriptions are the first to mention the kingdom of Mataram, was the first of four Śaivite kings who left inscriptions in the Kedu plain near Prambanan and represent a dynasty which had come from East Java, and was presumably the one to which Gajayana belonged. Very little is known of them.

Balitung's successor, Daksa (910–?919), probably built the majestic monuments of the Prambanan group, a vast complex of 156 shrines ranged around a central cluster of eight major temples, with the temple of Śiva as its dominating feature. Just as the Borobudur with its galleries of reliefs forms a textbook of Mahayana Buddhism, so on a smaller scale is the Śiva temple, with its galleries of reliefs illustrating the stories in the *Ramayana*, one of Hinduism. In one of the other temples of the central group is the lovely statue of Durga, Śiva's consort, known locally as Lara Djonggrang, 'slender maiden'. The complex forms a mausoleum housing the bodily remains of the king, the royal family and the magnates of the realm, each identified with the deity to which his or her shrine was dedicated, the royal personages in the major temples with the deities of the Hindu pantheon, the magnates in the smaller shrines with the protecting deities of the districts with which in life they were associated. The whole must have afforded an indescribable impression of magnificence and splendour.

Daksa's successor, Tulodong, reigned from 919 to 921. The last of the four was Wawa, whose dates, according to Krom, were 924-8. He was the last king to maintain his capital in central Java. Traces of it have been discovered close by Prambanan. The great aim of these kings seems to have been to restore the Śaivite tradition which the Buddhist Śailendras had interrupted. After Wawa's brief reign central

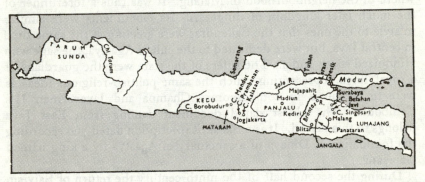

Mediaeval Java

Java for some undiscovered reason sank into the background. An earthquake or pestilence has been suggested as the cause of the sudden transfer of the capital to East Java, but it seems most unlikely, since there is no evidence of such an occurrence. The king who made the move was Sindok (929-47), who is regarded as the founder of a new dynasty which reigned in East Java until 1222. It is possible that one reason for his move was the fear that Śrivijaya might attempt to revive the Śailendra claims to central Java. Like all these early kings, Sindok is only a name. All that is known of him personally is that he ruled jointly with his chief queen, who was the daughter of a high official, the Rakaryan Bawang. This is one of many examples in Old Javanese history of the importance of woman in the community. On his death he was succeeded by his daughter Śri Iśanatunggavijaya, who ruled as queen. Her husband, a Javanese nobleman, held the position of prince-consort.

The period from 929 to 1222 was one of great importance in Java's cultural development. The transfer of the seat of power to the valley of the river Brantas led to a weakening of Hindu influence on government, religion and art and a corresponding increase in the importance of the native Javanese element. Notwithstanding the allegiance of the earlier rulers of East Java to the Śaivite tradition, Indian influence had always been weaker there than in central Java. Under the cloak of Śiva the old indigenous cults flourished, as indeed they did in Cambodia and Champa as well. Sindok's reign provides a series of Old Javanese inscriptions which are a valuable source for the study of the institutions of the country. They show clearly that its civilization was Indonesian, not Indian.

In the days when it was usual to think in terms of 'waves' of Indian 'immigration', one explanation of the growing predominance of the Javanese element was that from the ninth century onwards Java received no more of them. But the question that poses itself is whether she had ever received any. Waves of immigration have been too easily assumed on extremely tenuous evidence, and this assumption has militated against seeing the development of Javanese culture in its proper perspective. And, it may be remarked, this is equally true in the cases of Burma, Siam, Cambodia and Champa.

The rise of the East Javanese kingdom had important economic consequences for that region. The untilled swamps of the coastal areas and the delta were brought under intensive cultivation. The rulers of the new period began to develop an interest in overseas trade. Commercial connections were made with the Moluccas on one hand and with Sumatra and the Malay Peninsula on the other. Bali also for the first time began to play a part in Javanese history. Late in the tenth century a Balinese ruler married a daughter of Sindok's grandson, and thus opened the way for the introduction of Javanese culture into the island.

The best known of Sindok's descendants is Dharmavamsa (c.985–c.1006), who has been described as the first historical person of whom we have more than a dim vision. He ordered a codification of Javanese law and encouraged the translation of Sanskrit texts into Javanese. Among other works parts of the *Mahabharata* were translated into Javanese prose with the Sanskrit verses interpolated. Thus arose the oldest prose literature in the language.

His greatest enterprise was directed against the powerful empire of Śrivijaya. His attacks upon Palembang during the last decade of the tenth century, as we have seen, placed Śrivijaya in imminent danger, until in 1006 the great Sumatran counter-attack resulted in the

BURIAL IMAGE OF KING AIRLANGGA FROM BELAHAN

(now in Mojokerto Museum, Java)

destruction of his kraton and his own death. The East Javanese kingdom temporarily disappeared. Its place was taken by a number of warring chiefs, each supreme in his own district.

Dharmavamsa had designated as his successor his son-in-law Airlangga, the son of a Javanese princess, the great-granddaughter of Śindok, who had married the Balinese prince Dharmodayana. He was in Java at the time of the disaster of 1006, but managed to escape with his faithful servant Narottama and took refuge at a cloister of hermits at Wonogiri. There he remained for some years waiting for an opportunity to claim his throne. In 1019 he left his hiding-place and received official consecration as king. But his sway extended over only a fragment of the kingdom, and at first he dared not make any attempt to recover the remainder through fear of intervention by Śrivijaya. There are indications that in 1022 he may have succeeded his father in Bali.

Three years later fortune favoured him in a quite unexpected manner. Śrivijaya was temporarily crippled by the great Chola raid, and its threat to the East Javanese kingdom disappeared. Airlangga thereupon began the task of reducing to obedience the various local magnates who had divided the kingdom among themselves. It was a long struggle, but by about 1030 he had made such progress that Śrivijaya recognized him, and its king gave him a daughter in marriage. A *modus vivendi* was established between the two powers, which recognized Śrivijaya's supremacy over the west of the Archipelago and Java's over the east. Java, which the Cholas had presumably considered a commercial backwater not worth raiding, began rapidly to rise in importance as a trading centre. Airlangga's ports in the bay of Surabaya and at Tuban traded not only with the 'Great East' but were also the resort of merchants from the west—Tamils, Sinhalese, Malabaris, Chams, Mons, Khmers and Achinese.

Such were the external signs of the new vigour infused into East Java by this fine statesman. Internally he did much to improve cultivation. But his reign has been celebrated by later ages chiefly for its literary activity. Its most famous product is the *Arjunavivaha*, composed by the Court poet Mpu Kanwa, probably in honour of Airlangga's marriage with the Sumatran princess. The *Mahabharata* story of the ascetic Arjuna is used as an allegorical representation of Airlangga's own story. A version of it was adapted for presentation by the Javanese theatre and has become one of the most popular themes of the *wayang*, or shadow drama. In the poem itself and in the *wayang* adaptation the setting is entirely Javanese.

The inscriptions of the reign mention three religious sects: Śaivites, Mahayana Buddhists, and Rishi, or ascetics. The return of Śaivite rule to central Java had brought no antagonism between Buddhists and Hindus; their mutual relations everywhere were excellent. This symbiosis of the two religions was to be found in contemporary Cambodia also. The Mahayana, especially in its Tantric form, was becoming a secret sect, to which the highest in the land belonged. Śaivism was the first stage on the way to enlightenment; after passing through it the believer was ready to be inculcated with the higher Buddhistic knowledge. Both priesthoods were so powerful that Airlangga deemed it prudent to bring them under royal control. He himself claimed to be an incarnation of Vishnu. His mausoleum at Belahan contained a remarkable portrait statue of him as Vishnu riding on the man-eagle Garuda.[1] It was the common practice for the kings of his line to be worshipped after death in the form of Vishnu. Ancestor-worship was a special task laid upon a king. At certain set times he had to establish ritual contact with his ancestors in order to strengthen his position by the receipt of new magical powers from them. Hence the many chandis scattered about East Java celebrating a dead ruler in the guise of Śiva, Vishnu or the Bodhisattva Avalokitesvara were all centres of ancestor-worship and, although outwardly Hindu or Buddhist, represented a cultus that was a survival from the pre-Hindu past.

Some four years before his death in 1049 Airlangga retired to a cloister to become a Rishi. Before doing so, he is said to have performed an act strangely at variance with the policy he had pursued throughout his reign; he divided his kingdom between his two sons. Both were the children of concubines; he had no son born in royal wedlock. As their claims were equal, it may be that he feared that to prefer one at the expense of the other would bring on civil war and worse disunity than would result from peaceful partition. The Javanese kingship, it must be remembered, was not a central power administering the whole kingdom. It was a case of a maharaja controlling countless little lordships. The king received the homage and tribute of the higher chieftains, who managed their own affairs. Mediaeval Javanese history, like that of Europe, shows a constant struggle in progress between the centripetal and the centrifugal tendencies. Kings maintained their power only by repeated punitive expeditions.

The river Brantas was the dividing line between the two kingdoms.

---

[1] Now in the museum at Modjokerto, East Java.

The eastern one, called Janggala, was of little importance; it was soon absorbed by the western one, called Panjalu at first, but better known to history as Kediri. The union came about peacefully through the marriage of Bamesvara (1182–94) of Kediri with the Princess Kirana of Janggala.[1]

For many years after Airlangga's death Javanese history is almost a blank. There are many inscriptions, but they contain little historical substance. Chinese sources mention Kediri as a powerful well-organized state. Ten kings are mentioned up to 1222, but most are mere names. Kamesvara is known through his marriage and Dharmaja's poem *Smaradahana*, in which he is associated with the god Kama and his wife with the goddess Rati, Kama's wife. Jayabhaya (1135–57) is Airlangga's best-remembered successor. Javanese tradition asserts that he prophesied the downfall of his country and its rise once more to greatness. He is the hero of a poem by Mpu Panuluh entitled *Harivamsa*. Little is known of his reign, though in local legend it figures as a time of romantic chivalry. Its real fame rests on the fact that it produced another great masterpiece of Old Javanese literature, the *Bharatayuddha*, an adaptation of the story of the great battle between the Pandavas and Kauravas from the *Mahabharata*. The Kediri period indeed witnessed an unparalleled flowering of literature.

It was also a time of much commercial development throughout Indonesia. The Moluccas, the home of the clove and nutmeg, began to be politically as well as commercially important. Ternate was a vassal state of Kediri. There are accounts of extensive Arab trade with the whole Archipelago. They came to buy pepper, spices and precious woods. They were Mahomedans, but at this time had not attempted proselytizing activities in these regions. Many merchants came also from Cambay in Gujerat with Indian piece-goods to sell. To this city Persians had brought the faith of the Prophet, and before the end of the thirteenth century merchants of Gujerat were to make a start with the conversion of the Malay world.

Kediri fell in 1222, and a new state, Singosari, took its place as the ruling power in Java. The story is told in the Javanese Chronicle, the *Pararaton* or 'Book of Kings'. The central figure of the drama was Ken Angrok, 'he who upsets everything'. By exploiting the dissatisfaction of Janggala with its subordination to Kediri, he managed, after a career of crime, to dethrone Kertajaya, the last king of Airlangga's

---

[1] But see C. C. Berg's *Herkomst, Vorm en Functie der Middeljavaanse Rijksdelingstheorie*, 1953, in which the story of Airlangga's division of his realm is shown to be unhistorical.

line, and found a new state. There was indeed so much dissatisfaction in Janggala that many people were migrating to the neighbouring region of Tumapel in the Malang district. Ken Angrok, a man of low origin, murdered the Regent of Tumapel and usurped his place by marrying his widow Ken Dedes. He then availed himself of a quarrel between Kertajaya and his clergy to attack Kediri. In 1222 he defeated the king at the battle of Ganter. Then as King Rajasa he built his kraton at Kutaraja, later known as Singosari.

No further facts of his reign are given in the Javanese Chronicle until his death in 1227, and there is so much legend in his story that it is impossible to distinguish between fact and fiction. Rajasa was himself murdered by Anusapati, a son of Ken Dedes by her former husband. After a reign of just over twenty years the murderer himself fell a victim to his half-brother Tohjaya, a son of Rajasa, who seized the throne in 1248. The latter, however, soon died and was succeeded by a son of Anusapati, who reigned as King Vishnuvardhana (1248-68).

The story of the early years of Singosari is completely lacking in details, save for the sordid list of murders through which one king was replaced by another. Archaeology, however, has revealed two developments of much interest during this period. In architecture and art the purely Javanese element has come into its own fully. In religion the symbiosis of Śaivism and Buddhism has become a marriage; and although outwardly in the sculptures their Hindu or Buddhist characters are distinguishable, their real significance must be sought in native folklore and legend. They personify the divine and magic powers worshipped by the people. When King Vishnuvardhana (1248-68) died his ashes were divided between two shrines. At Chandi Mleri he was worshipped as an incarnation of Śiva, while at Chandi Djago as the Bodhisattva Amoghapaśa. The latter in its terraces and walks contains a wealth of sculptured reliefs representing the *jataka* stories of the Old Javanese Tantri.

The last King of Singosari, Kertanagara, who succeeded his father Vishnuvardhana in 1268, completed the process of religious unification by practising the cult of the Śiva-Buddha. As a king initiated in the secret Tantric knowledge necessary for the welfare of his realm, it was his duty to combat the demoniac powers that were rampant in the world. To accomplish this, ecstasy must be cultivated through alcohol and sexual excesses. His orgies shocked the compiler of the *Pararaton*, who dismisses him as a drunkard brought to ruin by inordinate indulgence in lust. On the other hand, in the poem *Nagarakertagama*, composed in 1365 by Prapanca, the head of the Buddhist clergy, he is

described as a saint and ascetic, free from all passion. Professor
C. C. Berg of Leiden, who has published a recent study of his reign,
is convinced that for a proper understanding of his policy this latter
estimate must be taken seriously.[1]

Kertanagara believed that in order to defeat the centrifugal tendencies in Java he must combat the curse of division and strife laid
upon the country by the action of the ascetic Bharada, who was
believed to have carried out the partition of Airlangga's kingdom.
Hence he erected his own statue in the guise of Aksobhya, a medit-
ative Buddha, on the spot where Bharada had lived. It now adorns
the Krusenperk at Surabaya, where it is popularly referred to as
Djaka Dolog, 'Daddy fatty'. His brand of Tantric Buddhism, known
as *kalachakra*, had developed in Bengal towards the end of the Pala
dynasty. Thence it had spread to Tibet and Nepal, and also to
Indonesia, where it found in the Javanese ancestor-cult a system to
which it adapted itself with remarkable ease. Śiva-Buddha was thus
an Indian cloak sheltering a native cult of great antiquity and power.

The different versions of Kertanagara's reign, provided by the
Pararaton and the *Nagarakertagama* respectively, represent more
than differences of opinion regarding the personality of the king
himself; for the former gives him a short and inconspicuous reign,
while the latter gives him a much longer one, lasting until 1292 and
full of brilliant achievement. Krom, in his monumental *Hindoe-
Javaansch Geschiedenis* (1931), compiled the account of the reign that
has been generally accepted by modern historical scholarship, subject
to the modifications in his original views which he incorporated in
his contribution to the first volume of Stapel's *Geschiedenis van
Nederlandsch Indië*. He accepted the longer reign attributed to the king
by the *Nagarakertagama* and showed him as an empire-builder whose
greatest aim was the conquest of Sumatra. In 1275, according to
Krom, he sent a great expedition, known as the Pamalayu, to begin
the subjugation of the island, from which it did not return until
1293, the year after his death. By 1286 the conquest had gone so well
that he sent a replica of the image of his father Vishnuvardhana at
Chandi Djago to be solemnly installed at Dharmasraya in the kingdom
of Malayu in order to ensure contact between that kingdom, as his
vassal state, and his dynasty through the cult of ancestor-worship.

This version of the reign, generally accepted until recently, has

---

[1] 'Kertanagara de miskende empirebuilder' in *Orientatie*, no. 34, July 1950, pp. 3–32.
See also his section of F. W. Stapel's *Geschiedenis van Nederlandsch Indië*, ii, pp. 7–148,
in which he discusses Old Javanese historical writings.

been subjected to drastic revision by Professor Berg. In 'Kertanagara de miskende empirebuilder' he attempts a reconstruction of the story based primarily upon a reconsideration of the date of the attack on Sumatra. He shows that there is no evidence that Kertanagara sent the Pamalayu in 1275. Not only was he not in a position to do so as early as 1275, but the *Nagarakertagama* passage that has been taken as an assertion that he did has been misinterpreted. What it really says is that, as a result of the king's assumption of divinity earlier in that year, the order was issued for Malayu to be conquered. This must be interpreted to mean that in that year he was specially consecrated for the pursuit of an imperialist programme, the crowning achievement of which was ultimately to be the conquest of Śrivijaya. From an exhaustive analysis of the available evidence Berg formulates the hypothesis that the expedition did not actually leave Java until seventeen years later, in 1292, the year of Kertanagara's death.

This involves a reinterpretation of what, in Krom's view, was the most important direct evidence of an earlier conquest, namely the image of Vishnuvardhana which Kertanagara sent to Sumatra in 1286, according to the inscription of that date found in the heart of the island on the river Batang. It was an image of Buddha Amoghapasa-lokesvara, the inscription tells us, and was conveyed to Sumatra by four Javanese state officials on Kertanagara's orders and erected at Dharmasraya. There it was the joy of all the subjects of the land of Malayu, from the maharaja himself downwards. Berg's theory is that, so far from testifying to a successful military campaign, it is evidence of a friendly policy which sought to draw Malayu into an Indonesian confederacy headed by Singosari. It bears witness to the fact that up to that date no warlike expedition had been sent against Sumatra.

On the basis of this hypothesis he proceeds to reconstruct the development of Kertanagara's policy of expansion according to a sequence of events which is logical and convincing if one accepts his interpretation of the passage in the *Nagarakertagama* regarding the dedication ceremony of 1275. After the king's accession in 1268, he says, he planned to make his kingdom a great Indonesian power. His father's chief minister, Raganatha, who objected to this on the grounds that it was too hazardous an undertaking, was given another appointment, and in his place two supporters of the new policy, Kebo Tengah and Aragani, became the king's principal advisers and were entrusted with the necessary measures for his assumption of divinity as a Buddha-Bhairava. This, the necessary preliminary to setting in motion his ambitious scheme, took place in 1275.

Berg insists that the king's policy can only be properly understood in the light of what he believes to be the fundamental significance of this act of consecration. He dismisses the idea that the king's imperialism may be attributed to caprice. Equally, he discounts any attempt to interpret it as a revival of an earlier Javanese imperialism. He thinks that the stories of Sanjaya's conquests, of the Javanese action against Śrivijaya shortly before A.D. 1000, and of the imperialist expansion of the kingdom of Kediri outside Java in the twelfth century are without real historical foundation. The imperialism of Singosari, he contends, was due to an external cause: it was one of the repercussions of the Mongol invasion of eastern Asia. He accepts the theory, originally propounded by Moens in 1924,[1] that Kertanagara's Bhairava-dedication was a consequence of Kublai Khan's dedication as a Jina-Buddha in 1264, and again in 1269, which signalized his adoption of a programme of further Mongol conquests. Fear of the Mongols, Berg suggests, was the mainspring of Kertanagara's policy. Hence in 1275, under the guise of a Bhairava-dedication ceremony, he committed himself to a far-reaching imperialistic programme which aimed at uniting Indonesia against a possible threat from China. By imitation of Kublai Khan's dedication he hoped to develop similar powers. His plan was to build up a sacred Indonesian confederacy and mobilize its strength against the Mongols by means of his magical powers as a Bhairava-Buddha. Thus it is significant that one of his early acts was to establish friendly relations with Champa, which itself was threatened by the Mongols. And his presentation of the Amoghapasa image to Sumatra in 1286 represented an export of his own *sakti* to a territory also threatened by Mongol imperialist expansion.

After the ceremony of 1275 Kertanagara proceeded systematically to carry out a planned programme. In 1280, according to the *Nagarakertagama*, he exterminated the malignant Mahishi-Rangkah. The precise meaning of this is obscure, but it would seem to refer to the steps he had to take in order to establish his authority firmly in his own kingdom before any movement of expansion was possible. The indications are that this was a very serious outbreak of opposition to his policy. Throughout his reign the centrifugal forces were barely held in check.

The next step, according to Berg, was the annexation of the island of Madura lying opposite to his principal port of Tuban. The task of preserving its loyalty was entrusted to Banjak Wide, an officer high in

[1] J. L. Moens, 'Het Buddhism op Java en Sumatra in zijn laatste bloeiperiode' in TBG, lxiv (1924).

the king's confidence, who was given the title of Arya Viraraja. The previously accepted story was that Viraraja was banished there because the king suspected his loyalty. Berg, however, rejects the banishment theory on the grounds that the post of Governor of Madura was one of key importance in view of the need to secure his eastern flank while pursuing a policy of expansion in the west.

This was followed by the conquest of Bali, for which, Prapanca tells us, the order was given in 1284. He also speaks of other acts of hostility on the part of Kertanagara against his neighbours, but the absence of precise details in his statements poses very difficult problems. If, as Berg attemps to demonstrate in his 'misunderstood empire-builder' article, Kertanagara carried through a carefully integrated programme of military conquests leading up to the final objective of the subjugation of Malayu, his next necessary step, after securing his eastern flank, would have been to reduce the kingdom of Sunda on his western flank, and thereby effect the unification of the whole island. Prapanca asserts that Sunda was in Kertanagara's empire, but offers no clue as to how or when it was acquired. Berg, in working out a logical sequence of events in the king's aggressive programme, places its conquest in 1289 or early 1290.

It is unnecessary, however, to pursue his highly ingenious argument, since in two subsequent articles[1] he has offered an entirely new interpretation of the nature of the Pamalayu, involving a radical change of view regarding Kertanagara's 'conquests'. The word should be translated 'agreement with Malayu', he thinks; no military action was taken against Malayu. The conquests mentioned by Prapanca were spiritual ones: Kertanagara was building up a sacred confederacy of Indonesian states to meet the Mongol menace. His method was to establish spiritual ties with each. Bali and Sunda were not conquered by force of arms: they were brought into a holy alliance. Such was the nature and object of the Pamalayu.

That this is a mistaken view of Kertanagara's policy has been shown by J. G. de Casparis in an article entitled 'Writings on Indonesian History (Early Period)' published in 1961.[2] The evidence he adduces comes from a fragmentary inscription on the back of the famous demoniac Camunda statue announcing that military action was about to be taken against a territory named Sadeng, which Berg in a much-discussed paper[3] identified with Bali, interpreting the inscription as a

---

[1] 'De Geschiedenis van Pril Majapahit', *Indonesië*, iv, pp. 481–520; v, pp. 198–202.

[2] In D. G. E. Hall (ed.), *Historians of South-East Asia* (1961), pp. 160–1, footnote 223.

[3] 'De Sadeng-oorlog en de Mythe van Groot-Majapahit', *Indonesië* (1951), v, pp. 385–422.

reference to Gaja Mada's war with the Balinese in the next century. A missing fragment of the inscription, however, discovered in 1940, has been deciphered to show that the word is not Sadeng. Moreover, Damais has calculated the date mentioned in the inscription as the equivalent of 17 April 1292, i.e. some months before Kertanagara's murder at the hands of Jayakatwang. If the date is correct, and according to Casparis there is good reason to accept it, the enigmatic Kerta-nagara is displayed as a ruler capable of using the utmost repression to stamp out rebellion, one whose policy was, as de Casparis puts it, one of *parcere subjectis et debellare superbos*. It may indeed throw light upon the despatch of the Pamalayu, if Berg is correct in assigning the date 1292 to it.

While Kertanagara was engaged in building up, by one or the other method, an anti-Mongol defence front, the danger from the north, which earlier had been no larger than a man's hand, began to assume threatening proportions. Kublai Khan was sending envoys to the states of South-East Asia, which had been in the habit of recognizing the overlordship of China, to demand tokens of submission. It soon became clear that he was asking not for the usual declarations of respect accompanied by presents of representative products of each country, but for actual obedience, and where this was refused was prepared to back his demands by military action. At first Kertanagara maintained a watchful, non-committal attitude. It may be that he was playing for time in order to weigh up the actual risks involved in refusal.

If so, the disaster which befell the Mongol expedition against Japan in 1281, and the subsequent failure of Kublai's forces in Tongking and Champa in 1285, may have influenced him in staging his rash act of defiance in 1289. For he arrested the whole Mongol deputation which appeared in his capital in that year and sent the envoys back, as the Chinese record puts it, with disfigured faces. This has been held to indicate that he cut off their noses, or at least that of the leader of the deputation, Meng K'i. Duyvendak, however, insists that the statement must not be taken literally, but as signifying that Peking was deeply hurt by the king's rude rejection of the mission.

However that may be, Kublai Khan prepared a great fleet and army with which to punish the recalcitrant ruler, and Kertanagara seems to have been aware, when launching his Pamalayu expedition in 1292, that real danger was to be expected from China. Presumably he gambled on the expedition completing its task successfully before the arrival of the Mongol reprisal force.

But what was its task? The *Nagarakertagama* asserts that the expedition of 1292 went not only to Malayu but also to the west coast of Borneo and the Malay Peninsula. It claims that Kertanagara acquired Bakulapura—i.e. Tanjungpuri—in Borneo, and Pahang, the name applied to the whole of the southern part of Malaya in Prapanca's day. It does not say exactly when they were occupied, but scholars are agreed that it must have been at the time of the Pamalayu expedition. It looks as if, being aware of the impending Mongol attack, Kertanagara hoped to ward it off by seizing strategic points on its route. Berg argues that his expeditionary force narrowly missed intercepting the Mongol armada off the coast of Borneo. In the absence of conclusive evidence as to the part the Pamalayu was intended to play in the general plan for dealing with the Mongol threat, speculation is all too easy. If its ultimate object was to mobilize real resistance to an expected attack, it was ineffective, for it failed to prevent the Mongol force from landing in Java.

Before that happened, however, an internal movement in Java against Kertanagara's authority brought about the total collapse of his plans. The despatch of a powerful expedition abroad left Singosari dangerously weakened. Discontented vassals were presented with an excellent opportunity to rebel, and the king's policy had many opponents. Kediri was the obvious centre for such a movement, since its ruling family had never forgotten its humiliation at the hands of Ken Angrok. Jayakatwang, the Prince of Kediri, became the leader of a formidable rebellion which threatened the capital. He skilfully drew off the royal army by a diversionary attack from the north. Then, on the day when the king and his circle were busy with the orgies prescribed by the cult of the Śiva-Buddha, he made a surprise attack on the capital from the west, captured it, and put to death Kertanagara, his chief minister and the other members of the circle while, in the words of the *Pararaton*, they were drinking palm wine.

Thus when the Mongol armada under Admiral Yi-k'o-mu-su arrived at Tuban shortly afterwards, in 1293, the king whose power it had come to break had disappeared from the scene and his throne was occupied by Jayakatwang of Kediri. Its arrival presented Kertanagara's son-in-law, the previous Crown Prince Vijaya, with a heaven-sent opportunity to overthrow the usurper. When Singosari was captured he had fled to Madura. On the advice of Viraraja, however, he had returned to Java and made his submission to Jayakatwang, who had rewarded him with the governorship of a district in the lower Brantas valley.

He now sought the assistance of the Mongols in overthrowing

Jayakatwang and promised in return to recognize Kublai Khan's overlordship over Java. His proposal was accepted, and the combined forces easily defeated the usurper and captured his capital. Then, when the Mongols were off their guard and their troops were split up into small detachments engaged in the task of pacification, Vijaya began a series of surprise attacks upon them. Successful in these, he cleverly manoeuvred the remainder into so unfavourable a position that Admiral Yi-k'o-mu-su abandoned the campaign and sailed away homewards, leaving him in command of the situation.

Vijaya now became king with the title of Kertarajasa Jayavarddhana. He built his kraton at Majapahit, the seat of his headquarters in the lower Brantas valley at the time of the Mongol arrival, and was the founder of the last great dynasty in Javanese history which maintained the Hindu tradition.

Krom's estimate of the situation when the Mongol fleet sailed away was that the empire built up by Kertanagara had been weakened, but not broken, by his death. Kublai Khan's expedition had completely failed, and in effect had brought Java profit through assisting in the continuation of the Singosari-Majapahit dynasty. Against that Berg points out that as a result of the Chinese invasion of Java Kertanagara's great expedition of 1292 had to return home in the following year, and that in fact all the results of his efforts were lost. For Jayakatwang's action caused Singosari's attempt to unite *nusantara*, the island empire outside Java, under her leadership to miss its mark. The work had to be undertaken afresh by Majapahit, and in his view failed to achieve the results that were within Kertanagara's reach at the time of his death. His conclusion is that under slightly more favourable circumstances Kertanagara might have become a national hero rather than a 'misunderstood empire-builder'.

(b) Majapahit, 1293–c. 1520

The elimination of Jayakatwang gave Prince Vijaya the opportunity to save his face, says Professor Berg, by transferring attention from Java's defeat by the Mongols to his own victory over the usurper. As a result of his successful manoeuvres in forcing the Chinese to give up their enterprise and return home, he put over the appearance of victory with great success. Three inscriptions of his reign, dated respectively 1294, 1296 and 1305, convey the impression that he enjoyed unchallenged power as the son-in-law and lawful successor of Kertanagara and was recognized by all the chiefs who had been the latter's vassals. This is echoed by Prapanca, 'the kraton His Master's Voice', as Berg dubs him. Thus the *Nagarakertagama* states that all Java was overjoyed at the accession of Kertarajasa Jayavarddhana and his fourfold marriage with the daughters of Kertanagara.

Kertanagara left no son; and although as a descendant of the great Rajasa (Angrok) Prince Vijaya had a perfectly good claim to the throne, the *Nagarakertagama* lays such emphasis upon his marriage with the four daughters of Kertanagara, and upon their great influence as to suggest that this constituted his real claim to be his father-in-law's successor. Krom and Stutterheim took it for granted that the four ladies in question were indeed Kertanagara's daughters. The inscription of 1305, however, indicates that the marriages constituted a mystical union with the territories 'conquered' by Kertanagara as a result of his dedication as a Bhairava Buddha in 1275. The four wives represented Bali, Malayu, Madura and Tanjungpura. Berg has posed the hypothesis that not one of them was a natural daughter of Kertanagara.[1] His explanation of the situation is that just as Kertanagara had won *nusantara* by yoga, so Kertarajasa Jayavarddhana created four 'daughters of Kertanagara' by means of Bhairava ritual, and in uniting himself with them established a special relationship with the island empire brought into being by Kertanagara. Thus by sexual union with them as *yoginis* he developed new magical power for carrying on Kertanagara's programme to a further stage.

Apparently the marriages were not made simultaneously, nor were all of them permanent. The names of only the first and the fourth are known. The first, who is described as the paramesvari, or chief queen, was Dara Petak, the Sumatran princess brought back to Java by Kertanagara's Pamalayu expedition. She became the mother of Kertarajasa's son Jayanagara, who succeeded him in 1309. The fourth, who is said to have been the king's favourite wife, was a Cham princess named Gayatri, who became the mother of two daughters, the elder of whom succeeded Jayanagara in 1328 as ruler of Majapahit. She was brought to Java by the mission despatched to Champa by Kertanagara in 1291 or early 1292 with a Javanese princess for Jayasimhavarman III, and arrived after the departure of the Mongol armada for home.

The name of the Javanese princess was Tapasi. Berg notes that the word signifies *yogini* and is of opinion that her despatch to Champa was connected with Kertanagara's Bhairava rites. She represented an export of his *sakti* to a territory exposed to the Mongol threat. The

[1] 'De Geschiedenis van Pril Majapahit' (1. Het mysterie van de vier dochters van Krtanagara), *Indonesië*, iv, pp. 481–520.

other two 'daughters of Kertanagara' are vague figures; their marriages
with Kertarajasa appear to have been merely temporary and ritual
unions. The *Nagarakertagama* and the inscriptions ascribe children
to Dara Petak and Gayatri only.

The validity of this argument has
been challenged by Father P. J.
Zoetmulder in his paper 'The Significance of the Study of Culture and
Religion for Indonesian Historiography'.[1] He contends that our
knowledge of Indonesian tantrism
is inadequate to justify a claim that
'daughters of Kertanagara' were
actually created by circle rites. We
are dealing with a particular form
of Tantrism, for an understanding of
which a general knowledge of its component parts—Buddhism, Saivism
and Vaisnavism—is inadequate.
Moreover, what is found in India
does not necessarily apply to Indonesia, so that in the absence of
Indonesian data we must not attribute the characteristics of Kalachakra
Buddhism to Indonesia. Thus, while
it is true that circle rites played a
dominant role, very little is known
of such rites in Indonesia. Where
is the evidence, he asks, of a ritual involving sexual union between the
Lord of the Circle and yoginis? It
was possible, he admits, to create
'daughters of Kertanagara' by such
ritual, but the secrets of Tantric

BURIAL IMAGE OF KERTANAGARA

rituals were so closely guarded that only the initiated could furnish
the answer. We cannot.

The *Nagarakertagama* asserts that the reign of Kertarajasa was
peaceful and the whole land obedient. This was until recently the
accepted view. It was assumed that the *Pararaton*, which lists a whole

[1] Contributed to Soedjatmoko (ed), *An Introduction to Indonesian Historiography*
(Cornell University Press, 1965).

series of rebellions beginning with one led by Rangga-Lawe in 1295, wrongly places the early ones in Kertarajasa's reign. Krom, for instance, places Rangga-Lawe's in 1309, the first year of Jaya-nagara's reign.[1] The reign, he explains, was one of constant rebellions, all of which were fomented by old companions of Prince Vijaya who had helped him to obtain the crown and were disappointed with their rewards. The fact that he was able, as King Kertarajasa Jayavarddhana, to keep these ambitious people under his thumb serves to show how strong he must have been.

Stutterheim, on the other hand, while attributing the revolts to the same cause as Krom, accepts the dates given in the *Pararaton*.[2] Berg[3] agrees with Stutterheim in the matter of the dates. He shows that there is reason to believe that the passages telling the story of the revolts belong to a 'proto-Pararaton', probably written about 1330, which contains trustworthy material. As far as their cause is concerned, however, his analysis of the evidence leads him to a conclusion that differs radically from Krom's. Their origin, he demonstrates quite convincingly, lay in a conflict between two parties: those in favour of Kertanagara's holy confederacy and those opposed to it, the pan-Indonesian party and the anti-foreign party. Thus Rangga-Lawe's rebellion began because in 1295 Jayanagara, the infant son of the Sumatran paramesvari Dara Petak, was given the title of Prince of Kediri, the Javanese equivalent of the English 'Prince of Wales'. The son of a Malay mother was thus given official recognition as the future ruler of Java. Moreover, in that same year the king began to suffer from a lingering illness, and Dara Petak came into prominence as the mother of a child who might soon become the titular ruler of Maja-pahit while still a minor. The rebellion was thus a sign of Javanese antipathy against a foreign queen and her Sumatran entourage.

Such is the explanation of a long list of conflicts—nine in all, according to the *Pararaton*—which disturbed the reigns of Kert-arajasa and his son Jayanagara from 1295 until shortly before the latter's death in 1328. Besides Rangga-Lawe's, which was quickly suppressed, three of the rebellions, associated respectively with leaders named Sora, Nambi and Kuti, were of special importance. Sora's was a formidable one which lasted from 1298 to 1300. Nambi stirred up national sentiment in East Java against the half-Sumatran Jayanagara. He was the son of the great Viraraja, whose

[1] *Hindoe-Javaansch Geschiedenis*, chap. x, pp. 346–82.
[2] *Cultuurgeschiedenis van Indonesië*, ii, pp. 72–3.
[3] *Loc. cit.* See also de Casparis, 'Twintig jaar studie', *Orientatie*, no. 46, pp. 636–40, where the Dara Petak story is examined.

personal estates were in the Lumajang district of East Java. Apparently Viraraja disliked the tendency of Kertarajasa's policy and obtained permission to retire to his East Javanese home. There, after a time, he began to neglect his duties as a vassal and failed to appear at Court to pay his annual homage.

His son Nambi, who was chief minister at Majapahit, found his position too difficult under the circumstances, and on the grounds that his father was ill, he obtained permission to leave the capital and visit him. The two of them then began to fortify themselves in the stronghold. When Kertarajasa died in 1309 they had broken off all contact with Majapahit. Viraraja died in 1311, and as Nambi still continued to defy the royal authority Jayanagara had finally to go to war with him. An expedition was sent against him in 1316, and according to the *Nagarakertagama* his stronghold at Padjarakan was captured, and he himself killed. Berg, however, shows that he maintained the struggle for another ten years before being finally disposed of.

In 1319 Jayanagara was threatened by the most dangerous of all these rebellions. Kuti, its leader, was a Javanese nobleman, who gained possession of the capital itself. The king fled to Badander, accompanied by part of his bodyguard under a young officer named Gaja Mada. The young man saved the situation by a daring stratagem. Returning in disguise to the capital to find out how the land lay, he announced that the King had been killed by Kuti. The reception of this news by the populace showed that Kuti was unpopular. Gaja Mada therefore was able to raise a successful insurrection against him and restore the king. For this courageous act he was rewarded by appointment as Patih of Kahuripan. A few years later he became Patih of Kediri. He was to rise to a still more important position.

Between the Kuti affair and the death of Jayanagara in 1328 no important events are recorded. The circumstances of the king's death are interesting. He was foolish enough to take possession of Gaja Mada's wife. The injured husband instigated the Court physician, in performing an operation upon the king, to allow the knife to penetrate farther than was necessary, and immediately afterwards had his unfortunate agent executed. As Jayanagara left no successor, the throne should now, according to Krom, have devolved upon Gayatri. She had retired to a nunnery and for this reason is represented as having voluntarily stood down in favour of her elder daughter Tribhuvana, whom it has been customary to describe as the regent. But this assumes that Gayatri was a natural daughter of

Kertanagara, whereas, on Berg's hypothesis, she was a Cham princess. Her Cham origin would seem to be the explanation of her renunciation of the world. She cannot have renounced the throne, he contends, since she had no claim to it.

Tribhuvana was married to a Javanese nobleman, who as prince-consort took the title of Kertavarddhana and was created Prince of Singosari, but had no share in the royal authority. Her reign, which lasted until 1350, when she resigned the crown to her son Hayam Wuruk, saw the rise of Gaja Mada to a position of power and influence never previously held by a minister in Javanese history. In 1330 he was appointed *mapatih*, or chief minister, of Majapahit. Thenceforward until his death in 1364 he was the real ruler of the kingdom.

The part played by Gaja Mada in suppressing Kuti's rebellion shows him in his early days as a supporter of the pan-Indonesian policy. This probably explains why his appointment as *mapatih* caused a rebellion in East Java. In 1331, when he returned to Majapahit after suppressing it, he is said to have taken an oath before the council of ministers never again to enjoy *palapa* until *nusantara* had been subdued. That he was announcing the adoption of a new policy of imperialist expansion is clear, but the word *palapa* has caused much speculation among scholars. Krom suggested that it might connote either his personal revenues or leave of absence from duty. Stutterheim could offer no explanation of its meaning.[1] Berg, however, claims to have solved the riddle.[2] The word, he explains, means the exercise of mortification and was used to describe the Bhairava Buddhist rite involving the enjoyment of sexual intercourse with a *yogini*. The announcement therefore indicated the suspension of the policy based upon Bhairava rites, or, in other words, the substitution of a policy of military conquest, involving the imposition of Javanese domination over *nusantara*, for Kertanagara's plan of a pan-Indonesian confederacy maintained through a system of yoga.

Two objections to this view raise doubts as to the validity of Berg's interpretation of Gaja Mada's policy. In the first place Father Zoetmulder in the paper referred to above[3] comments upon the uncertainties in the translation of older Javanese texts, and, using Berg's rendering of *amukti palapa* as an example, expresses the opinion that while one cannot specifically deny its validity, yet without additional evidence it is too speculative to assert that it refers to the performance of circle

---

[1] *Op. cit.*, pp. 76–7.
[2] 'De Geschiedenis van Pril Majapahit', *Indonesië*, v, pp. 198–202.
[3] In Soedjatmoko, *op. cit.*

rites. We are, he warns, dealing with an extinct culture, which from its very nature precludes the possibility of verification. The other objection is of a more positive kind. It follows from de Casparis's rejection of Berg's interpretation of the evidence of the Camunda inscription, also noted above.[1] He points out that if one sees Kertanagara as a military conqueror, and not as the architect of a pan-Indonesian confederacy based upon a system of yoga-relationships, Berg's theory of a period of 'interdict' between 1331 and 1351, involving the substitution of a military policy for Kertanagara's supposed policy of holy alliance, falls to the ground. According to de Casparis the change of policy announced by Gaja Mada in 1331 in the form of a programme of military action to impose Majapahit's domination over *nusantara* must be seen as a resumption of Kertanagara's policy of conquest after an interruption of forty years during which Majapahit had been paralysed by internal weakness and revolts.

The record states that the ministers present at this famous council-meeting derided Gaja Mada's oath. They were soon to be disillusioned. Some were removed from office. For the next thirty years and more Gaja Mada was to be the effective ruler of Majapahit and director of its policy. The reduction of the island of Bali, which had reverted to independence when Kertanagara's confederation fell to pieces with his death, became Gaja Mada's main objective. Other places were mentioned by him when he took his epoch-making oath—Gurun, Seran, Tanjungpura, Aru, Pahang, Dompo, Sunda, Palembang and Tumasik, the old name for Singapore. These places and others also, it has been assumed, were brought under Majapahit's control during the period from 1331 to 1351. But only in Bali's case can one speak with certainty. Its conquest began in 1331 and was apparently completed in 1343. It was in Bali that the old Javanese culture made its greatest impact outside Java itself. The island, however, was never wholly Javanized: it continued to develop its own individual type of 'Hinduized' culture, which, unlike Java's, was able to maintain its integrity against the assaults of Islam.

Evidence of Javanese cultural influence, dating from this period, it is thought, is to be found also in Dompo, Sumbawa and some other places which tradition has assigned to the empire of Majapahit. Her dependent states are enumerated in the *Nagarakertagama*. They comprise all of Sumatra, a group of names from the Malay Peninsula, Mendawai, Brunei and Tanjungpuri in Borneo, and a long list of

[1] 'Historical Writing on Indonesia (Early Period)' in D. G. E. Hall (ed.), *Historians of South-East Asia*.

places eastwards of Java, beginning with Bali and including Makassar, the Bandas and the Moluccas. Many of the names can only be identified by guesswork. We are given a picture of an empire as extensive as present-day Indonesia plus much of Malaya. Krom, Stutterheim and the many writers who have followed them have accepted it as substantially true. Vlekke, for instance, has given a graphic description of a mighty empire maintained by overwhelming sea-power. After its fall, he says, nothing as great was achieved again 'until the Netherlanders completed their conquest'.[1]

BALINESE TEMPLE

Did Prapanca's Great Majapahit ever exist as a reality? The question has been posed by Professor C. C. Berg in another of his attacks upon the orthodox interpretation of mediaeval Javanese history as set forth in Krom's *Hindoe-Javaansch Geschiedenis*.[2] And his unequivocal answer is that the *Nagarakertagama* list of the dependencies of Majapahit is of great value as a statement of an important historical myth and a reflection of the geographical knowledge of Gaja Mada's own day, but for the student of political history it is 'worth-

[1] *Nusantara*, p. 53.

[2] 'De Sadeng-oorlog en de Mytfie van Groot-Majapahit', *Indonesië*, v (1951). pp. 385–422

less'. It is based upon totally inadequate evidence. On the other hand Krom, while accepting Prapanca's list of Majapahit's dependencies, made it clear in his view they represented rather a sphere of influence than a territorial empire.[1] Java, he writes, did not rule the whole of Sumatra, the Peninsula, Borneo and the East, but was firmly established only in certain parts of them. Within this sphere no other foreign influence was permitted. Her subjects paid her tribute or some other token of recognition of her supremacy. The looseness of the connection must be emphasized: the subordinate states were internally self-governing.[2] Thus the picture that seems to emerge is that of a sea-empire similar to that of Srivijaya in its earlier heyday, maintained by naval power, and effective for as long as the Javanese fleet maintained control over the seas. But on the question of the extent of the empire Dr. Pigeaud in his monumental study of the *Nagarakertagama*[3] appears to be as sceptical as Berg regarding the acceptability of Prapanca's list of tributaries. He thinks it doubtful whether Majapahit's authority at any time counted for much in the countries mentioned. He describes the poet's geographical knowledge as 'chaotic'. It was picked up, he suggests, from court officials who had been in contact with foreign merchants and Javanese traders trading with the islands. So far as the ascertainable facts go, the state of Majapahit was limited to East Java, Madura and Bali.

The relations between Sumatra and Majapahit during the period from the return of Kertanagara's *Pamalayu* expedition are as obscure as during the previous one. At the end of the eleventh century the Srivi-jayan leadership had passed from Palembang to Malayu (Jambi), and the next period had seen a serious decline in the power and activities of the Malay commercial empire. The expansion of Java's sea-power and imperial pretensions in the thirteenth century had naturally led to Kertanagara's attempt to assert his supremacy over a weakened Srivijaya; for that is how the despatch of first the Amoghapasa statue and then the *Pamalayu* expedition must be seen. King Maulivar-madeva, who was on the throne at this time, sent two princesses to Majapahit with the returning Pamalayu fleet. One of them, Dara Petak, as we have already seen, married Kertarajasa Jayavardhana and became the mother of Jayanagara. The other, whose name was Dara Jingga, was, according to Stutterheim, married to a member of the Javanese royal house and bore a son who succeeded Maulivarma-deva as King of Malayu. Berg, however, suggests that she went

[1] *Hindoe-Javaansche Geschiedenis*, p. 415.   [2] *Ibid.*, p. 338.
[3] Th. Pigeaud, *Java in the Fourteenth Century* (The Hague, 1962), vol. iv, p. 69.

through a Bhairava-ritual 'marriage' with Kertarajasa, after which she was sent back to Malayu to be married to Visvarupakumara, the son and successor of Maulivarmadeva. If one may accept his version of the story, their son was the Adityavarman who later ruled over much of Sumatra, and by virtue of his mother's double marriage was regarded as at the same time the eldest son of his Sumatran father and the youngest 'son' of Kertarajasa. He was brought up at the Majapahit kraton and served as commander of the Javanese forces which overcame Bali. In 1343 he dedicated at Chandi Jago a statue of Manjuśri, the Bodhisattva who combats ignorance. Stutterheim has interpreted this as an allusion to his early years of tutelage at the Court.

Soon afterwards he was ruling in Malayu, where, presumably, he succeeded his father. There he made no attempt to revive the sea-power once wielded by Śrivijaya, but concerned himself solely with the expansion of his dominion over the inland parts of Sumatra.

He extended his power over the Menangkabau mountain districts and became the ruler of an inland state, based upon them, that was to all intents and purposes independent. In 1347 he erected an inscription in which no sign of dependence on Java appears. Ruins in Sumatra dating from his reign show the prevalence of strong Tantric Buddhism with Śaivite elements. Its days, however, were numbered. Already Islam had begun to make progress in the northern coastal regions of the island. Ibn Batuta, who visited Samudra in 1345–6, wrote that it had been Muslim for nearly a century.

The accession of Hayam Wuruk in 1350 brought no change in the policy of Majapahit. Gaja Mada remained in control until his death in 1364. The young king was apparently quite content to leave the direction of affairs in his hands. In 1351, however, one of the most dramatic incidents in the early history of Java took place. Historians refer to it as the 'Bubat bloodbath'. It was the final, culminating event of the period during which Chandi Javi was closed and the policy of blood and iron pursued.

The story goes that soon after ascending the throne Hayam Wuruk asked the King of Sunda for a daughter in marriage. His proposal was accepted, and the king himself, with a splendid retinue, brought the princess to Bubat, north of the city of Majapahit, where the ceremony was to take place. At the last moment Gaja Mada intervened with the stipulation that the bride should be handed over in the manner of a formal act of tribute from a vassal to his overlord. The King of Sunda realized that he had been neatly trapped. Rather than surrender his kingdom's independence, he attempted to fight his way out. But he and all his retinue were overpowered and slain. From the existing evidence it is not clear whether the marriage actually took place or whether the princess committed suicide beside her father's dead body. If it did take place she died soon afterwards. After the affair Sunda seems to have acknowledged the overlordship of Majapahit for a time, but ultimately recovered her independence.

An inscription dated with the year of the 'Bubat bloodbath' mentions the foundation of a temple dedicated as a memorial to those who lost their lives along with King Kertanagara at the Tantric ritual celebration at which he was murdered in 1292. It is known today as Chandi Singasari. It seems to have been Gaja Mada's tribute to the man whose empire he had sought to revive. Also, under his patronage, Prapanca began the composition of the *Nagarakertagama* in which, in cantos 42 and 43, he extols Kertanagara's statecraft and wisdom, and points to his religious perfection as the cause of his descendants' glory as divine kings and reuniters of the realm. It was a compliment to Hayam Wuruk, Kertanagara's great-grandson, to whom the poem is dedicated.

In addition to the list of Majapahit's dependencies Prapanca gives the names of states with which she maintained friendly relations. They include Siam, Burma, Cambodia, Champa and 'Yavana',—i.e. Vietnam—besides more distant countries such as China, the Carnatic and Bengal, with which she had commercial intercourse. Chinese sources record Javanese embassies at the time of the accession of the Ming dynasty, mentioning dates from 1369 to 1382. During the same period Palembang also sent embassies to China asking for support against Java. In 1377 the emperor sent a letter of recognition to a King of Palembang. Before it arrived a Majapahit force occupied the city and the Chinese envoys were put to death. Palembang was going rapidly downhill. At about this time a Chinese pirate, Leang Taoming, at the head of some thousands of his compatriots, established control over the city. Java apparently did nothing to interfere, and Krom suggests that she pursued a deliberate policy of neglect. But this assumes the existence of 'Great Majapahit' with its far-flung Indonesian empire, which Berg has relegated to the realm of mythology. The kingdom founded by Adityavarman, it may be remarked, had no external interests.

Gaja Mada's attention was concentrated so much upon imperial affairs, that it is not easy to discover what part he played in the direction of internal policy. Prapanca gives an excellent account of Javanese administration in his own day, and shows that members of the royal family exercised important functions. The king's father dealt with justice, taxation and the classification of the population. His uncle supervised agrarian affairs and the upkeep of the roads and bridges. There was a survey of all desas and sacred lands; police duties were laid down and families numbered; fixed occupations were assigned to various classes of the population; regulations were issued concerning gifts to officials and pious foundations, the maintenance of the army, the protection of cultivating and landholding, the payment of the royal revenues, the assessment of taxation and the enforcement of the various forms of labour services.

Most of these regulations, it is thought, must be ascribed to Gaja Mada himself. The range of his activities was so great that when he died a state council decreed that it was impossible to appoint a successor, and divided his functions among four ministers. Possibly the decision was a polite method of indicating that the council considered it unwise to place so much power again in one man's hands.

Gaja Mada's name is associated with a law-book which was compiled under his instructions. It seems to have supplanted the *Kutaramanava*, an adaptation of the Laws of Manu, which had been the chief written source of Javanese law before the Majapahit period. But the form in which both works have come down to modern times was the product of a later period. A judgement of Rajasanagara's reign, inscribed on copper, shows how judges were instructed to work in civil cases. They had to take into account the law as laid down in the law-book, local customs, precedent and the opinions of spiritual teachers and of the aged. They must also question impartial neighbours before finally reaching their decision.

Of the king as a ruler very little is said. Presumably after Gaja Mada's death he found the task of co-ordinating and directing the the work of the four ministers appointed to supervise the administration too arduous, for a few years later he again appointed a prime minister with general control over the whole range of state business. Prapanca's picture of the life of a great potentate conveys the impression that amid the distractions of living royally he can have had little energy left for the conduct of affairs. 'Truly King Hayam Wuruk is a great potentate. He is without cares and worries. He indulges in all pleasures. All beautiful maidens in Janggala and Kediri are selected for him, as many as possible, and of those who are captured in foreign countries the prettiest girls are brought into his harem'[1].

Hayam Wuruk left no son by a principal queen. By his chief wife he had only a daughter. She married her nearest relative, the king's

[1] B. H. M. Vlekke, *Nusantara*, p. 62.

nephew Vikramavarddhana, Prince of Mataram, who became heir-apparent. There was a son, Virabumi, by a lesser wife. The king was anxious to make special provision for him. He was accordingly

JAVANESE WAYANG PUPPET

appointed ruler of East Java and married to the heir-apparent's sister. Such an arrangement was bound to cause trouble after the king's death. Indeed there is evidence that even before that event Virabumi was ruling his appanage as an independent kingdom.

The reign of Vikramavarddhana (1389–1429) was a period of rapid decline. The civil war which developed in consequence of Virabumi's refusal to recognize the authority of Majapahit was the chief cause of failure, for it fatally weakened Majapahit's control over her subject states. Thus was the way opened for the rise of a new state, Malacca, whose expansion was further facilitated by the vacuum created by the fall of Srivijaya and the concentration of Malayu upon inland affairs. Moreover, the spread of Islam added a powerful religious factor to the political opposition and lent new strength to the centrifugal tendencies always present in Java itself. For some years good relations were maintained between Vikramavarddhana and his brother-in-law. In 1399, however, when the king's only son by his chief queen died, troubles began. Civil war broke out in 1401. In 1406 Virabumi was assassinated and his head brought to Majapahit in token of the restoration of unity to the kingdom.

The Chinese had recognized both kings. When Virabumi's capital was taken some members of the suite of the Chinese envoy were killed there. The emperor demanded an immensely large sum of money by way of compensation. Vikramavarddhana sent one-sixth of the amount as a token payment. This satisfied the emperor, and he remitted the remainder of the debt.

The embassy sent to Java on this occasion was the first of a long series, for the Ming emperor Yung-lo wished to revive China's prestige and make her once more the great centre of the eastern world. Most of them were led by the famous eunuch admiral Cheng-ho, who made a remarkable series of voyages between 1405 and 1433, visiting Champa, Java, Sumatra, India and Ceylon, and even Arabia and East Africa. His Muslim secretary Ma Huan wrote a valuable account of three of the voyages, the *Ying-yai Sheng lan*, originally compiled in 1416, later improved and expanded in 1451.

The Chinese pirate-ruler of Palembang attempted to rob Cheng-Ho in 1407, but the admiral, warned in time by Che Tsing-k'ing a Chinese of the city, arrested the pirate chief and appointed Che Tsing-k'ing in his place. It is significant that in dealing with this matter Cheng-Ho regarded himself as acting on behalf of Majapahit, and the new chief was nominally subject to Vikramavarddhana. Malacca, which had received its first Chinese mission in 1403, claimed Palembang. The emperor, however, found its claims unacceptable and decided in favour of Majapahit.

The revival of Chinese interest in the Archipelago was thus in no way directed against Majapahit. Evidently China did not feel called upon to pursue the policy of 'fragmentation'; Ma Huan's account of his travels shows that already Java's overseas empire was no more than a name, if even that. To maintain authority over such an empire required nothing less than a Gaja Mada, and after his death Majapahit produced no one of his stature. The weakening of political ties, however, made little, if any, difference to Java's commerce. For instance, when in the fifteenth century the ports of Borneo, which had previously paid tribute to Majapahit, demonstrated their independence by developing relations with China, their trading relations with Java remained unaffected. And Chinese trade with the Moluccas was conducted mainly through Java.

Very little is known of the last century of Majapahit's history after the death of Vikramavarddhana's death in 1429. He was succeeded by his daughter Queen Suhita (1429–47), in whose reign a rebellion occurred under a leader named Bhre Daha. The next ruler was her brother Bhre Tumapel, who became King Kertavijaya (1447–51). After him there is no mention of any further sovereigns of the old royal house.

The next ruler, Bhre Pamotan, held his Court at Keling Kahuripan and reigned as Rajasavarddhana (1451–3). Then after a kingless period of three years a certain Hyang Purvaviśesa reigned from 1456 to 1466. In 1460 his ambassadors caused a scandal in China by killing six priests of another mission in a drunken brawl. Bhre Pandan Salas, who reigned from 1466 to c. 1478 with the title of Singhavikrama-varddhana, abandoned the kraton at Majapahit in 1468. Javanese tradition asserts that in 1478 Majapahit was conquered by a coalition of Mahommedan states. This, however, is impossible, since there is clear evidence that a 'Hindu' king, Ranavijaya, was reigning in 1486.

The end of Majapahit is shrouded in darkness. Krom's last king is Pateudra, who was in occupation of the throne in 1516. He is mentioned by Barbosa as the heathen king of a heathen people to whom Albuquerque sent an embassy after the conquest of Malacca in 1511. The name 'Pateudra' is presumably the Portuguese rendering of Pati Udara. Barbosa writes that the coastal havens were Mahommedan and at times rebelled against the 'King of Java', but were suppressed. A report sent in January 1514 to the King of Portugal by de Brito, the Governor of Malacca, adds just a little to this picture. He says that Java has two 'kaffir-rulers', the King of Sunda and the King of Java, but the Moors control the coastal regions.

CHAPTER 5

THE KHMERS AND ANGKOR

(a) The Khmer kingdom of Cambodia to 1001

THE disappearance of the empire of Funan in the middle of the sixth century came, according to the Chinese account, through the rebellion of a feudatory state named Chenla. The *History of the Sui* describes the occurrence thus: 'the kingdom of Chenla is on the south-west of Lin-yi. It was originally a vassal kingdom of Funan. The family name of the king was Ch'a-li and his personal name Che-to-sseu-na. His predecessors had gradually increased the power of the country. Che-to-sseu-na attacked Funan and conquered it.' Lin-yi is, of course, Champa, Ch'a-li stands for Kshatriya, and Che-to-sseu-na for Chitrasena. No explanation of the name 'Chenla' has yet been found; it cannot be related to any Sanskrit or Khmer word.

Funan proper stretched over southern Cambodia and Cochin China of modern times. Chenla was to the north of it; it occupied the lower and middle Mekong from Stung Treng northwards, and its original centre was in the region of Bassak just below the mouth of the Mun river. It thus covered what is now northern Cambodia and the southern part of the kingdom of the Laos. According to the *History of the Sui*, before the subjugation of Funan the Chenla capital was situated near a mountain called 'Ling-kia-po-p'o'—i.e. Lingaparvata—on which was a temple consecrated to the god 'P'o-to-li'— i.e. Bhadresvara—to whom the king annually offered a human sacrifice during the night.

A Khmer legend recorded on a tenth-century inscription ascribes the origin of the royal family to the marriage of a hermit, Kambu Svayambhuva, with the celestial nymph Mera given him by the god Śiva. This story, which is obviously quite different from that of Kaundinya and the naga princess, seems to have been invented to explain the name 'Kambuja', which the Khmers adopted as a result of Indianization.

Bhavavarman, 'Protégé of Siva', the elder of the two brothers who led the revolt against Funan, had become King of Chenla through marriage with Princess Lakshmi of the Kambu-Mera dynasty, which

had had about a century and a half of history before that event. His
father Viravarman is mentioned in inscriptions as a vassal of Funan.
His grandfather is called 'Sarvabhauma', and if, as is thought, Rudravarman, the last King of Funan, is indicated by this title, he himself
belonged to the Lunar dynasty founded by Kaundinya and Soma.
His marriage was of great significance in the development of Khmer
royal traditions, since it was used to explain how the later Cambodian
monarchs claimed to trace their descent from both the Lunar and the
Solar lines with their entirely unrelated dynastic legends.

What exactly took place when Rudravarman of Funan disappeared
from the scene is not known. Cœdès thinks that an attempt was made
to restore the legitimate line, and that this provoked the brothers
Bhavavarman and Chitrasena to place themselves at the head of a
movement to vindicate their own rights as grandsons of the last reigning king. The picture is complicated by the fact that, although Rudravarman presumably died somewhere about 550, Funan was still sending missions to China at the beginning of the next century, though
from a capital farther to the south, since the old capital of Vyadhapura
had been captured by the Chenla brothers. Briggs thinks that the
evidence points to the fact that Bhavavarman did not annex Funan,
but that it enjoyed autonomy until 627, when it was incorporated with
Chenla in the reign of Iśanavarman. He points out that the hereditary
line of ministers which had served Rudravarman continued in office
at the old capital as the servants of Bhavavarman, though he never
moved his capital from Chenla.[1]

The exact site of his capital is uncertain. It may have been near
Vat Phu or possibly at Stung Treng. In any case it was to Chenla
that the sovereignty over Funan was transferred; and even if Briggs's
view is correct that a 'wise policy of conciliation' was pursued towards
the conquered state, Bhavavarman's long reign seems to have been a
period of warfare, during which his brother Chitrasena, who commanded his armies, was kept constantly busy. The empire of Funan
had included peoples and vassal states stretching from Champa in the
east to the Bay of Bengal in the west, and including most of the Malay
Peninsula. Of these only Funan proper seems to have acknowledged
the suzerainty of Chenla. The Malay states known to the Chinese as
Lang-ya-hsiu, P'an-P'an and Ch'ih-t'u seem to have opened diplomatic relations with China, as also did the Mon state of Dvaravati on
the Menam.

The exact length of Bhavavarman's reign is unknown. The date of

[1] Lawrence Palmer Briggs, *The Ancient Khmer Empire*, p. 42.

his sole inscription, commemorating the foundation of a linga, is 598. Chitrasena succeeded him in *c.* 600 and took the regnal name of Mahendravarman, 'Protégé of the Great Indra'. The dates of his reign are unknown, but it was a short one, since he was getting on in years when he became king. All accounts of him, Cham, Chinese and his own inscriptions, describe him as a hero and a conqueror. During his own reign he conquered the lower Mun valley. He celebrated his conquests by establishing lingas dedicated to 'Girisa', the 'Lord of the Mountain'. His inscriptions have been found along the Mekong near Kratié and Stung Treng, and to the west as far as Buriram and Surin.

His son Isanavarman, who succeeded him in *c.* 611, was credited by the Chinese with the completion of the conquest of Funan. From the date given in the *T'ang History* this must have taken place in, or shortly after, 627. Its separate existence as a vassal state was terminated and its territory annexed. The Chinese record that it continued to send embassies even after its annexation. Briggs suggests that these were missions of protest sent by the deposed dynasty.[1]

Isanavarman I also extended his power westwards towards the region that was later to become the centre of the Angkor monarchy. A prince named Baladitya, apparently a scion of the Kaundinya-Soma line which had ruled over Funan, had established an independent state in the valley of the Stung Sen, a tributary of the Tonlé Sap river running parallel to the Mekong. His kingdom seems at first to have been known by the name of Baladityapura, though it is better known by its later name of Aninditapura. This was conquered by Isanavarman, who thereupon built himself a new capital on the Stung Sen. The new city was called Isanapura. Its site was apparently about twelve miles north of the present city of Kompong Thom and is marked by the most impressive group of ruins of pre-Angkor Cambodia so far discovered. The reason for the transfer seems to have been that with a policy of westwards expansion in view his old capital on the Mekong was too near to his eastern frontier. Thereafter he extended his sway over three states of north-west Cambodia: Cakrankapura, Amoghapura, and Bhimapura. In the south also he conquered territories which brought his dominions as far to the west as the modern city of Chantabun and up to the borders of the Mon kingdom of Dvaravati. It is significant that both he and his father, in order to facilitate their policy of conquest, cultivated friendly relations with Champa. Isanavarman himself married a Cham princess.

According to Chinese sources, Iśanavarman I reigned until 635, though his latest inscription is dated 628–9. His successor was Bhavavarman II, whose relationship to him is unknown, as also are the dates of his reign. Briggs suggests that he may have been 'a son of the mysterious son of his namesake who disappeared so completely from history'.[1] Only one of his inscriptions can be dated; Cœdès attributes it to 639. He was succeeded by Jayavarman I, who, according to Cœdès, was his son, but Briggs denies this.[2] He thinks that Jayavarman probably belonged to the dynasty of Iśanavarman. The earliest date of his reign is an inscription dated 657, but it is thought that he came to the throne some years earlier. He reigned for possibly forty years, and though no building can be assigned to him he was the author of many inscriptions. One of them calls him 'glorious lion of kings, the victorious Jayavarman'. He conquered central and upper Laos up to the borders of the kingdom of Nanchao. But his large dominions were never peaceful, and the civil wars which split the Chenla empire asunder after his death had their origin much earlier. He himself was able to maintain his hold over the Mekong region, but Baladityapura seems to have been the centre of a rival power controlling the west, and it is doubtful whether he controlled the south of Iśanavarman's far-flung dominions. He left no heir, and for more than a century after his death Cambodia passed through a very troubled period. From an inscription of 713 it would appear that his widow Jayadevi reigned after him, but failed to check the separatist movements that challenged his authority during his lifetime.

Up to the reign of Jayavarman I the Khmers had progressively consolidated their power over the lower Mekong region and around the Tonlé Sap. They left behind much that is of archaeological interest today. There are brick towers, single or in groups, statuary showing a likeness to Hindu prototypes but also strongly-marked local traits, and rich decorative sculpture of the sort which developed with such exuberance during the Angkor period. Administration was well organized, but from the epigraphical sources at our disposal it is impossible to present an integrated picture of its functioning.

The inscriptions are all connected with religious shrines, and evidence is plentiful regarding the state religion. Buddhism no longer held a favoured position as it had done under Funan. Hinduism was predominant, and in particular the linga cult of Śiva was the essence of the Court religion. The principal Śaivite and Vaiśnavite sects found in India are mentioned. The worship of Harihara, or Śiva and Vishnu

[1] *Op. cit.*, p. 52.   [2] *Ibid.*, p. 53.

united in a single body, which is said to have first appeared on the rocks of Badami and Mahavellipur in the Pallava country some time before A.D. 450, was a marked feature of the period.

Most of the inscriptions are in Sanskrit, but there were some already in the Khmer language. An inscription at Ak Yom in the Mun valley, which may possibly be dated 609, is the oldest so far discovered in the Khmer language. Literary culture was based upon the Sanskrit classics, and much use was made of the mythology of the *Ramayana*, the *Mahabharata* and the *Puranas*. But all this was the culture of the Court; how far it affected the outlook of the ordinary people we are not told. That the old pre-Hindu culture still persisted strongly cannot be doubted, and it is interesting to find in the inscriptions confirmation of the importance of the matrilineal constitution of the family.

So far as the material culture of this period is concerned, the *History of the Sui* gives some account of it as it was in the reign of Iśanavarman. Most of the space, however, is devoted to the king and his Court. The only industry mentioned is agriculture, and it is dismissed in one cursory sentence: 'in this kingdom rice, rye, a little millet and some coarse millet are cultivated.' And from the fact that Ma Tuan-lin in the thirteenth century incorporated the whole passage in his *Ethnography of the Peoples Outside China* one is left with the impression that no great social or economic changes had taken place during the intervening centuries, and that upon the basis of an economy of small peasant agriculturists the architectural and artistic wonders of Angkor were achieved. Up to the present research has for obvious reasons been concentrated upon the temple and the Court, and unfortunately outside them history has little to tell in the case of Cambodia.

The *History of the T'ang* asserts that shortly after 706 the country split up into two separate parts, which it names the Land Chenla and the Water Chenla. The names signify a northern and a southern half, which may conveniently be referred to as Upper and Lower Chenla. Jayavarman I's successors were in nominal control of both as 'Adhirajas', or Supreme Rulers, but in fact power was in the hands of a group of petty kinglets. So great was the confusion, and so scanty is the evidence, that it is impossible to tell a coherent story. Ever since the appearance of Aymonier's classic *Le Cambodge* in 1900 theory after theory has been formulated regarding the sites of the capitals of the two divisions mentioned by the Chinese.[1] In his *Deux Itinéraires*[2]

---

[1] Briggs discusses this question in detail in *op. cit.*, pp. 58–9.
[2] BEFEO, iv 1904, pp. 131–385.

Paul Pelliot advanced the theory that Vyadhapura was the capital of Lower Chenla, and Sambhupura (Sambor) the seat of Upper Chenla. For some time this was generally accepted. But it has been challenged by Henri Maspero, Cœdès and Pierre Dupont. The last named believes that for the location of Upper Chenla one must look to the old homeland of the Khmers, which he places well to the north in the Bassak-Paksé region and the lower part of the river Mun. Lower Chenla, he thinks, comprised Sambhupura, Vyadhapura and Baladityapura. On this showing Lower Chenla would have been the true successor of the kingdom of Jayavarman I.

All that is known of Upper Chenla comes from the Chinese record of embassies. They called it Wen Tan, and its territories seem to have extended northwards to Yunnan, with a population of Khas and possibly of T'ais on the Nanchao border. Its first embassy arrived in China in 717. In 722 it joined in a war against the Chinese Governor of Chiao-chou (Tongking), but was defeated. Another embassy was recorded in 750, but from which Chenla is uncertain. The Crown Prince of Wen Tan went to the Court of China in 753 and received the title of 'Protector Firm and Persevering'. China was then at war with Nanchao, whose king, Kolofeng, had allied with Tibet. The crown prince accompanied the Chinese army, which was utterly defeated by Nanchao. The last record of an envoy from Wen Tan is in 799. All that can be said of its history during this period is that, compared with Lower Chenla, it maintained a reasonably stable existence.

In Lower Chenla in the period immediately following the death of Jayavarman I two dynasties strove for supremacy: the Lunar dynasty of Aninditapura under Iśvara (lords) of Baladitya's family, and the newly formed Solar dynasty of Sambhupura. The old kingdom of Baladityapura, which had been conquered by Iśanavarman, was restored by Nripatindravarman, who ruled as king and acquired a strip of delta territory extending to the sea at the old Funanese port of Oc Eo. Its capital is thought to have been at Angkor Borei. Sambhupura, near the present Sambor and Kratié, broke off from Chenla under Jayavarman I. Many inscriptions and monuments date from the period 681–716. A princess of this state, thought to have been a daughter of its founder, married Pushkaraksha, a son of Nripatindravarman of Aninditapura, and her husband became King of Sambhupura. Thus both kingdoms came under monarchs claiming to belong to the Kaundinya-Soma dynasty.

After this period information about Lower Chenla is very slight

and raises more questions than it answers. There is no record of
embassies to China, and only a few inscriptions. The last inscription
of Queen Jayadevi, dated 713, speaks of misfortunes. A door-
inscription of Preah Theat Kvan Pir in the province of Kratié, dated
716, runs: 'Pushkara had the god Pushkaresa erected by munis and
the most eminent of Brahmans.' Presumably Pushkaraksha of Sambhupura was its author. This is claimed to be the first example in
Cambodian history of the apotheosis of a king.[1] Four inscriptions of
the period 770–81 mention a King Jayavarman who had not been
included in the previously accepted list of Cambodian kings. In order
to prevent confusion, therefore, Cœdès calls him Jayavarman I *bis*.
All come from the territory of the kingdom of Sambhupura.

The family of Nripatindravarman of Aninditapura seems to have
made itself supreme over the whole delta region. Cœdès suggests that
the marriage of Pushkaraksha with the heiress of Sambhupura was a
conquest in disguise. The Adhirajas of Vyadhapura apparently controlled only a short strip of territory along the Mekong in the vicinity
of Jayavarman I's old capital. A son of Pushkaraksha married the
heiress to its throne, and as King Sambhuvarman united the whole of
Lower Chenla. His son Rajendravarman, who reigned in the second
half of the eighth century, is therefore generally accepted as Rajendravarman I among the Kings of Cambodia. He was succeeded by
his son Mahipativarman. It is thought that the capital of these kings
was also at Angkor Borei.

During the latter part of the century Lower Chenla was attacked
by Malay pirates from 'Java'. The term may refer to Java itself, to
Sumatra or the Malay Peninsula, or even to all three. They seized
the islands of Pulo Condor and used them as a base for raids which
extended as far north as Tongking. In 774 and 787 they raided
Champa. Cambodia was also attacked, but the inscriptions do not say
precisely what happened. A Javanese inscription claims that the
country was conquered by King Sanjaya. An early tenth-century
Arab writer, Abu Zaid Hasan, tells the story of the travels of a merchant named Sulayman, who travelled in these regions in 851 and
picked up an account of a Javanese expedition against Chenla in the
closing years of the eighth century. Although legendary, it seems to
throw some light on the conditions prevailing at the time.

A young Khmer king rashly expressed a desire to see before him
the head of the Maharaja of 'Zabag' (i.e. Śrivijaya) on a dish. The
story reached the ears of the maharaja, who made a surprise attack

[1] Briggs, *op. cit.*, p. 60.

upon the Khmer king's capital, seized him and cut off his head. Taking it home with him, he had it embalmed, and sent it back in an urn as a warning to the king's successor. A Khmer inscription of a later date asserts that Jayavarman II, before his accession to the throne of Cambodia, visited Java. Apparently he was taken to the Śailendra Court to pay homage as the successor of the beheaded king. Historians are inclined to think that there is much truth in the Arab story, since when Jayavarman II had gained control over his kingdom he staged a special ceremony at which he made an express declaration of his independence. Briggs therefore suggests that he was the successor of Mahipativarman, and that the latter was the Khmer king who was beheaded by the Śailendra maharaja.[1]

Notwithstanding the lack of historical evidence, the eighth century provides interesting examples of pre-Angkorian art and architecture. The chronology and classification of Khmer art have been radically changed since 1937, when Philippe Stern published his challenging *Le Bayon d'Angkor et l'évolution de l'art Khmer*. He stimulated a new crop of researches into the subject by Parmentier, Madame de Coral Rémusat, Pierre Dupont and other scholars. In 1940 the results were incorporated by Madame de Coral Rémusat in a work of great importance, *L'art Khmer, les grandes étapes de son évolution*, which places the major monuments in their historical setting with something like exactitude, and among other things gives a new significance to the long period of development before the establishment of Angkor as the capital and artistic centre of the Khmer realm.[2]

Jayavarman II was the founder of the Angkor kingdom, though not of the actual city. Briggs assumes that he was chosen by the ministers of Mahipativarman in accordance with the instructions of the Javanese maharaja of the Arab story.[3] He did not belong to the line of Rajendravarman I. Later inscriptions make him a great-grandson of Nripatindravarman of Aninditapura, but a successful claimant to a throne could always be provided with a suitable genealogy. Nothing is known of his father. That he himself came from Java to assume the crown is certain. The suggestion has been made that his family may have settled there during the time of troubles, and that he had been held as a hostage at the Śailendra Court. He left behind no inscription, so far as is known, and his importance in Khmer history has only comparatively recently been recognized.

[1] *Op. cit.*, p. 69.
[2] An excellent summary of Khmer art and architecture *c.* 550–790 is given by Briggs in *ibid.*, pp. 69–80.
[3] *Ibid.*, p. 69.

The chief facts of his reign are given in an eleventh-century inscription, the Sdok Kak Thom stele, which was translated by Louis Finot in 1915. He began his long reign by planting his capital, which he named Indrapura, at a place which has been identified with the archaeological site of Banteay Prei Nokor, east of Kompong Cham on the lower Mekong. There he took into his service a Brahman, Sivakaivalya, who became the first priest of the new cult which he established as the official religion. It was that of the Deva-raja, the god-king, a form of Śaivism which centred on the worship of a linga as the king's sacred personality transmitted to him by Śiva through the medium of his Brahman chaplain. The prosperity of the kingdom was considered to be bound up with the welfare of the royal linga. Its sanctuary was at the summit of a temple-mountain, natural or artificial, which was at the centre of the capital and was regarded as the axis of the universe.

This conception of a temple-mountain is of much earlier origin than Śiva-worship itself. It goes back to an ancient Mesopotamian practice, and from thence had come to ancient India, where a number of Hindu dynasties had their sacred mountains. Funan, as we have seen, had its sacred hill of Ba Phnom, and in Java the Śailendras were 'Kings of the Mountain'. The adoption of the cult by Jayavarman was a gesture of independence, a sign that he recognized no superior on earth. More than that, it signified his claim to be a Chakravartin, a universal monarch, and bore for him and his successors much the same meaning as the white elephant was to have for the monarchs who were Buddhists of the Theravada school. From his time onwards for several centuries it was the duty of every Khmer king to raise his temple-mountain for the preservation of the royal linga, which enshrined his 'sacred ego'. Thus arose the great temples which were the glory of the Angkor region.

Indrapura, however, was only the first of a number of capitals founded by Jayavarman II. He was apparently anxious to find a site which, while providing a suitable eminence for his temple, would be more easily defensible against both external attacks by Malays and internal enemies. His next move was into the region of the Great Lake, whose bountiful supplies of fish combined with the high yield of rice from its flood-plain to enable it to sustain a large population. Here he planted his second capital at Hariharalaya, 'the abode of Harihara', south-east of modern Siemreap. Its site is today marked by the group of ruins called Roluos. Later he founded a third capital, named Amarendrapura, at a site which is still uncertain. Finally he moved to Phnom Kulen in the Kulen hills, some thirty miles north-east of Angkor, where he built Mahendraparvata. Excavations on the summit of Phnom Kulen have revealed a number of temples, including his great pyramid-temple and its linga. His buildings, which were completely hidden by thick forest, were largely excavated by Philippe Stern and Henri Marchal. They are in a style that is obviously transitional, linking up the 'pre-Angkorian' with the style which predominated during the early days of Angkor. There are signs of both Javanese and Cham influences; the former explained by the king's early connection with Java, the latter as yet inexplicable in terms of historical facts. It is thought that this final move marked the completion of the conquest of his heritage, and that his previous capitals must have been connected with stages in his campaigns. But of these no historical evidence has so far come to light.

Cœdès places his accession in the year 802. Against this Briggs points out that that is the date on which the inscriptions say that he established his capital on Mount Mahendra (Phnom Kulen).[1] Its significance lies in the fact that it is the year in which he instituted a new era by a formal declaration of Cambodian independence and by the establishment of the ritual for the worship of the Deva-raja. The date of his return from Java and the length of time he resided at each of his earlier capitals are unknown.

Mahendraparvata was not his final residence, for ultimately he returned to Hariharalaya and remained there until his death in 850. In northern Cambodia his authority did not extend beyond the region of the Great Lake. He may have chosen this area as the centre of his power partly because of its proximity to the sandstone quarries of Phnom Kulen and to the passes giving access to the Korat plateau and the Menam basin. It was an excellent base from which to launch the policy of expansion imposed by the Chakravartin title upon its holders.

Jayavarman II's reign made a great impression upon his kingdom. He was the founder of its greatness, and especially of the far-reaching claims of its ruling authority. From his reign the pyramid-sanctuary marked the centre of the royal city. At its summit, which was the centre of the universe, the Deva-raja entered into relationship with the divine world. He himself was the god to whom in his own lifetime the temple was dedicated. At his death it became his mausoleum.

For some time after Jayavarman II's death his successors continued to reside at Hariharalaya. His son Jayavarman III (850–77) was famous

[1] *Ibid.*, p. 88.

THE BUDDHA WITH SNAKE BACKGROUND TO HEAD, ANGKOR

as a hunter of elephants. Several foundations in the neighbourhood of Angkor date from his reign, but no inscriptions. He was succeeded in 877 by a cousin, who became Indravarman I and made his mark upon Khmer history. A tenth-century inscription describes him as a nephew of Jayavarman II's queen. The importance of matrilineal descent is clearly indicated by the matrilineal genealogies given in inscriptions. Indravarman's queen traced her descent back to the royal families of Chenla and Funan. Through her he acquired rights over Sambhupura, which had not been exercised by his predecessors. He was the first Khmer king to undertake irrigation works in the Angkor region. When he constructed a huge artificial lake north of his capital for the storage of water needed for irrigation during the dry season, he was doing something of supreme importance to the subsequent development of the Khmer monarchy. The priority he gave to irrigation set a fashion followed by his successors.

His Bakong temple, built to house the royal linga, Indresvara, was also a new departure in Khmer history: it was the first stone pyramid to be constructed, being composed of five superimposed graded terraces with the shrine at the top. Archaeologists have noted a strong resemblance between it and the Borobudur, and the question has been asked whether Indravarman hoped to rival the achievements of the Sailendras. In 879 he dedicated statues of his parents, his maternal grandparents and of Jayavarman II and his queen to the Preah Ko, a collection of six towers on a single terrace. These two monuments together with the temple of Lolei built by his successor at the time of Indravarman's death form the 'Roluos group' which is considered to mark the beginning of classical Khmer art. They exemplify the Khmer form of ancestor-worship; the identification of the human being with a god is indicated by the use of the first part of the name plus *-esvara* for a man or *-devi* for a woman. Indravarman I's few inscriptions are the earliest long ones. In one he is called 'Lion among kings'.

Indravarman I's son and successor, Yasovarman I, began his reign with the construction of a vast reservoir measuring seven kilometres by two, into which the waters of the Siemreap River were made to flow by changing its course. It came to be known as the Eastern Baray. In the second year of his reign he laid out a new capital, named after him Yasodharapura, the first city of Angkor. It was built around a natural hill, Phnom Bakheng, and enclosed an area of about sixteen square miles. A moat 200 metres wide enclosed it. Within this enclosure was an agglomeration of villages and markets interspersed with paddy fields. No less than 800 artificial water pools have been discovered within this enclosure arranged in a geometric pattern around the base of Phnom Bakheng. The 'Mountain of Yaśovarman' was a hill of five terraces faced with masonry. On its summit were five square sandstone towers forming a quincunx, the central one housing the royal linga, Yasodharesvara. Like other dynastic temples it was conceived as a model of Mount Meru with the Siemreap River as its sacred Ganges. Yaśovarman's city and its successor, Jayavarman VII's Angkor Thom, built late in the twelfth century, overlap. But the Phnom Bakheng is just outside the southern wall of Angkor Thom.

Yaśovarman's passion for building led him to crown nearly every hill near his capital with a shrine. His best-known foundation today is Preah Vihear, which has been the subject of bitter controversy between Thailand and Cambodia. It crowns a triangular promontory in the Dangrek Mountains nearly 1600 feet above the plain, and is one of the great achievements of Khmer architecture. He had about a hundred monasteries built throughout his kingdom for Saivite, Vaishnavite and Buddhist sects. These 'Yaśodharashrama' were of wood, and each included a royal pavilion for the king's use when touring the kingdom. Twelve of them have been discovered in recent times.

Little is known of the political history of these reigns, or of those that follow up to the end of the tenth century. Yaśovarman's inscriptions pay him the most fulsome tributes as a warrior. If the inscription of 947 at Baksei Chamrong is reliable, his dominions extended as widely as those of Funan in her greatest days. If he reigned for only eleven years, and carried out so vast a building programme, it is difficult to believe that he had the time and the means to acquire a far-flung empire extending to China in the north, Champa on the east and the Indian Ocean on the west, with the northern part of the Malay Peninsula as far as P'an-P'an (Grahi) included. Briggs suggests that even if he was not responsible for the expansion represented by these boundaries, the territories included in them acknowledged his overlordship. Doubt has been thrown on 900 as the real year of his death. On the available evidence he could have reigned until nearly 910, it is thought. His inscriptions cover only the area between southern Laos and the Gulf of Siam, and not farther west than Chantabun. Champa on the east of his kingdom and the Mon states of the Menam valley were certainly independent. Briggs expresses the opinion that 'more misinformation has probably been written about Yaśovarman than about any other king of Cambodian history' and that much that has been attributed to him belongs to a later period. One example of this

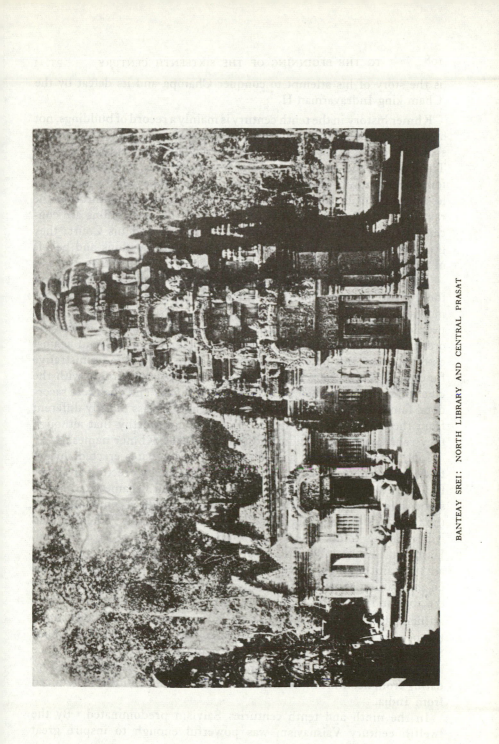

BANTEAY SREI: NORTH LIBRARY AND CENTRAL PRASAT

is the story of his attempt to conquer Champa and its defeat by the Cham king Indravarman II.

Khmer history in the tenth century is mainly a record of buildings, not of political events. It was a period of splendour when civilization took shape. It corresponds to a period of anarchy in China at the end of the T'ang period and during that of the Five Dynasties. Historians therefore have to rely almost entirely upon inscriptions; all documents of less durable materials, such as palmleaf, have perished through the ravages of mildew, white ants or fire. And the inscriptions are concerned solely with the affairs of the Deva-raja and his Court; they give hardly any clue to the material civilization, customs and beliefs of the people.

The king as head of the state occupied so exalted a position in theory, and was committed to a life involving so much religious ceremonial, that he can have had little, if any, personal contact with his people. As the source of all authority he was the guardian of law and order, the protector of religion, and the defender of his land against external foes. But he can have performed hardly any administrative functions. These were in the hands of a narrow oligarchy, with the chief offices held by members of the royal family and the great sacerdotal families. They intermarried and formed a class racially different from the rest of the population. But it is noteworthy that although they represented the Hindu tradition they used Khmer names.

Like the king, only in a smaller way, the magnates erected shrines to their own personal cults. The belief was that by erecting an image the 'sacred ego' of the person to be worshipped became fixed in the stone, and the shrine would contain an inscription recommending to the founder's descendants the continuance of the cult. When he died it became his tomb. Thus the innumerable statues of Śiva, Vishnu, Harihara, Lakshmi, Parvati and of Bodhisattvas found on temple sites are portraits of kings, queens and magnates, while their names, carved on the statues, show a fusion of their personal titles with the names of the gods and goddesses, with whom they are united. Each statue was an artificial body with magic properties conferring immortality upon the person it represented. The practice was widespread throughout South-East Asia. It is found in Champa and was of special importance in Java and Bali. It exhibits a blending of the cult of ancestor-worship, dating from neolithic times, with Hindu and Buddhist ideas introduced from India.

In the ninth and tenth centuries Śaivism predominated. By the twelfth century Vaiṣṇavism was powerful enough to inspire great foundations, of which the outstanding example was to be the Angkor Wat itself. But Buddhism always had its followers, and as all these religions were foreign importations they found it essential to preserve mutual tolerance. Moreover, there was much syncretism, for the old cults of animism and ancestor-worship continued to be the real religion of the mass of the people. In social life also, while the Laws of Manu and other Brahmanical codes were officially recognized by the Court, the deciding factor in most matters was immemorial custom.

Six kings reigned during the course of the tenth century. Their reigns are mainly a record of buildings. Two only are noteworthy in connection with political changes. Jayavarman IV (928–42) was a usurper who conquered Yaśodharapura (Angkor) and was either driven out or abandoned it to establish a new capital at Koh Ker, away to the north-east. Rajendravarman II (944–68) dethroned the usurper's son Harshavarman II and transferred the capital back to Angkor, which remained the capital city of the Khmers thenceforward until its final abandonment in 1432. The return to Yasodharapura involved a great task of reconstruction, and the king is praised in an inscription for rendering it 'superb and charming by erecting there houses ornamented with shining gold, palaces glittering with precious stones, like the palace of Mahendra on earth'. He was responsible for the invasion of Champa in 945–6, and a Cham inscription credits him with carrying away the gold image of Bhagavati from the temple of Po Nagar. Although he himself was a Śaivite, his inscriptions display a great variety of religious practices and extreme toleration. Buddhism in particular seems to have flourished during his reign. Ancestor-worship too became more closely identified with the great temples than ever before.

Jayavarman V's long reign (968–1001) was an age of learning and of brilliant ministers. He was very young at his accession, and his long minority enabled the great Brahman families to take the lead. No Cambodian reign was more distinguished for learning. 'From all directions brahmans celebrated for their wisdom . . . who possess the essence of the science of Vedanta . . . faithful to their duty . . . and profoundly versed in the Vedas and Vedantas, have saluted him . . .' runs an inscription. Women held high positions at court. There was Prana, chief of confidential secretaries, Indralakshmi, Jayavarman's younger sister, married to Divakara, a Brahman from northern India, and praised in inscriptions, and Jahnavi, famous for her religious foundations. The Chinese reported that the women of the royal family held high political posts and praised their knowledge of astrology and government. At the beginning of Jayavarman's reign the Banteay Srei, considered the most beautiful of all the Khmer temples, was dedicated. It was the first to be restored by French archaeologists by anastylosis, a method first exploited by the Dutch in Java. Its central sanctuaries are small, compared with most major Khmer monuments, and for some unknown reason it has come to be known as the 'Citadel of the Women'. It is not only beautiful architecturally but it contains some of the most beautiful mural decorations in Khmer art.

(b) From 1001 to the abandonment of Angkor in 1432

The first half of the eleventh century is notable for the reign of another of the great kings of Khmer history, Suryavarman I (1002-50). He succeeded 'a phantom king who flitted across the throne', as Finot describes Udayadityavarman I (1001-2), the successor of Jayavarman V. There is no evidence regarding either the disappearance of Udayadityavarman I or the accession of Suryavarman I. The latter is said to have been a son of a King of Tambralinga, and to have claimed the throne by virtue of descent through his mother from the maternal line of Indravarman I. The indications are that he landed in eastern Cambodia in 1001, and after a long civil war was ultimately installed at Angkor in c. 1010. Later inscriptions date his reign from 1002, when Udayadityavarman I disappeared. His chief rival after 1002 was a certain Jayaviravarman, who held parts of Cambodia until 1007, or possible 1011. Suryavarman's claim was a weak one. He is described in one inscription as having gained the throne by his sword, which 'broke the circle of his enemies'.

Suryavarman's buildings have attracted much attention. The two that are best known, the Phimeanakas ('celestial palace') and the Ta Keo, had been begun in the reign of Jayavarman V. The Ta Keo was the first of the Khmer temples to be built of sandstone. Like the earlier Bakheng and the later Angkor Wat, its central feature is a platform surmounted by five towers. The Phimeanakas, on the other hand, is in pyramidal style with one central tower only. Legend has it that it was a palace, but Khmer palaces were always in wood, and its plan is quite unlike the traditional palace layout. Chou Ta-kuan, who visited Angkor at the end of the thirteenth century, records the popular belief that the Khmer king spent the first watch of every night in the tower with the mythical naga in the form of a beautiful woman, and that upon this ceremonial consummation depended the welfare of the kingdom. The towers of these two temples are gilded, and the fashion is first mentioned in Suryavarman's reign. It was a contemporary Mon custom, which the Khmers are thought to have copied.

The Chiengmai Chronicle of a much later date describes Khmer expansion in the Menam valley during his reign. An inscription at Lopburi dating from this period claims that his empire included both the Mon kingdom of Dvaravati and the Malay kingdom of Tambralinga, later Ligor. Local chronicles credit him with the occupation of the Mekong valley as far north as Chiengsen, but archaeology shows no traces of it beyond Luang Prabang. In contrast with the many campaigns waged on other fronts, his eastern frontier seems to have remained at peace throughout his reign.

The eleventh century was indeed a period of increasing warfare for the Khmers. Suryavarman's son and successor Udayadityavarman II (1050–66) was busy dealing with revolts throughout his reign. The first broke out in the far south and seems to have been caused by Cham interference from the region of Panduranga. That region, which had been in a state of revolt for some time, was thoroughly subdued by King Jaya Paramesvaravarman, whose forces also made an incursion into Cambodian territory and sacked Sambhupura. The revolt which ensued was led by a chief who is described as a master in the science of archery. He may have been a Cham. At first he achieved no little success and defeated more than one Cambodian army. When he was finally crushed by the famous Cambodian general Sangrama, who celebrated each of his victories with a pious foundation, he took refuge in Champa.

During Udayadityavarman's reign King Anawrahta of Pagan reduced the Mon peoples of southern Burma and took Thaton, their capital. T'ai tradition asserts that he extended his conquests as far as Lopburi and Dvaravati, and that the Khmers had to recognize Burmese suzerainty over the conquered territories as the price of receiving back Lopburi. Gordon Luce has shown that Suryavarman I's armies attacked the Mon states of Burma, and that they were decisively defeated by Anawrahta's general Kyanzittha. The Burmese, however, attempted no conquests east of the Thaton kingdom.

Two further revolts took place during Udayadityavarman II's reign. One was in the north-west and was led by a royal general, Kamvau, who actually threatened the capital, but was defeated by Sangrama. The other, in the east, was also crushed by him. The suggestion has been made that they may have been the result of the king's hostility to Buddhism. His father, coming from a Buddhist state, had shown special favour to the religion, though maintaining the cult of the god-king. Udayadityavarman built only Saivite sanctuaries. In the most magnificent of them all, the gilded Baphuon, he installed a gold linga. It was the largest temple built up to that time in Cambodia. Parmentier describes it as 'one of the most perfect of Khmer art'. Chou Ta-kuan, who saw it in its full glory, writes that it was 'really impressive'.

Harshavarman III (1066–80), Udayadityavarman II's younger brother, tried to repair the damage and loss caused by the warfare of

RELIEF FROM THE BANTEAY SREI

the previous reign. He was a peace-loving king, but the times were against him. He was dethroned by a revolt led by a prince named Jayavarman, not of the royal family, but apparently the son of a vassal ruler—or provincial governor—of a city named Mahidharapura, the site of which has not yet been identified.

Jayavarman VI, who founded a new dynasty, had a troubled reign. Members of the family of Harshavarman III raised the south against him, and continued the struggle until the accession of Suryavarman II in 1113. Cœdès thinks it is doubtful whether he ever reigned at Angkor, though an inscription of a century later asserts that he was

ANGKOR WAT

consecrated there. Mahidharapura, somewhere in the north, seems to have been the headquarters from which he directed operations.

He was succeeded by his elder brother Dharanindravarman I (1107–13), a man of advanced age who had retired to a monastery. Although an inscription records that he 'governed with prudence', he was quite unable to cope with the rebellion which had lasted throughout his brother's reign. That task was performed by his grandnephew on the maternal side, a young man of boundless ambition, who crushed the house of Harshavarman III, deposed the feeble Dharanindravarman I, and was consecrated king as Suryavarman II.

Suryavarman II (1113–50) became the most powerful king of Khmer history. Cœdès comments: 'His accession coincides with the deaths of Jaya Indravarman II of Champa and Kyanzittha of Pagan. A better knowledge of the relations between these countries might show a connection of cause and effect between the disappearance of two powerful kings and the seizure of power by an ambitious Khmer king able to strike both east and west.'[1] His armies went farther afield than ever before in Khmer history. The inscriptions of his reign are, however, strangely silent regarding his campaigns against Champa and Annam, as well as against the Mons and T'ais of the Menam valley. Most of them are found in the north, where he apparently spent much of his time and founded a number of temples.

Suryavarman II's conquest of Champa has been dealt with elsewhere. It was provoked by the Cham attitude towards his attempts to coerce them as allies in his operations against the Annamite kingdom of Dai-Viet. All his attempts to invade Annam by the overland route from Savannakhet to Nghe-an failed, as also did his effort to hold Champa in subjection.

Little is known about his western campaigns. The T'ais had begun to infiltrate into the Menam valley and had settled in the state of Lavo (Lopburi). According to the T'ai chronicles, his campaigns against that state and the Mon kingdom of Haripunjaya (Lamp'un) failed. But Khmer influence upon the contemporary architecture of Lopburi was so strong that doubt is thrown on their veracity. The *Sung History* shows a considerable expansion of Khmer sovereignty. It describes the Cambodian frontiers as the southern border of Champa, the sea in the south, the borders of Pagan in the west, and Grahi on the east coast of the Malay Peninsula.

Suryavarman II was the first King of Cambodia since Jayavarman II to enter into diplomatic relations with China. His first embassy

[1] *Les États Hindouisés d'Indochine et d'Indonésie*, p. 269.

was received in China in 1116. A second appeared in 1120. When, eight years later, a third arrived the emperor conferred high titles upon the 'King of Chenla'. Between 1136 and 1147 discussions took place regarding commercial difficulties, which were peaceably settled.

Suryavarman was as famous as a builder as he was as a warrior, since he was the founder of the Angkor Wat. With the possible exception of the Banteay Chhmar, at the foot of the Dangkrek mountains about a hundred miles north-west of Angkor, and now a heap of ruins, it is the largest religious building in the world. Of all the Khmer monuments it is the best preserved. The central sanctuary, 130 feet high, stands on a square terrace 40 feet high and 750 feet square. At the corners rise four towers connected by galleries and communicating with the central shrine by covered passages. Around this immense central building is a lofty wall of galleries, with towers at its four corners. This in turn is enclosed by an outer square of colonnades. Beyond this there is a further enclosure measuring 850 by 1,000 metres and surrounded by a wall of laterite and sandstone. The whole was originally surrounded by a moat 200 metres wide enclosing a total area of nearly a square mile.

The legend was that the Wat was not built by human hands but by Indra, the Lord of Heaven, who sailed down to earth for the purpose. Originally all nine great pinnacles were plated with gold, while the sculptures of incredible richness, covering the walls in high and low relief, were ablaze with colour. The central shrine contained a gold statue of Vishnu mounted on a garuda, which was taken out of its sanctuary on festival occasions. It was of course, a representation of the king deified as Vishnu, and the majestic shrine was erected in order to become his mausoleum when he died. The enthusiasm for Vaiṣṇavism which it manifests was to be found at the same time in Java, where the Kings of Kediri, like Suryavarman, were incarnations of Vishnu. But Śaivism was still important, as the many Śaivite scenes depicted on the walls bear witness. The total effect is of a blending of the two cults, with the emphasis on Vaiṣṇavism.

The exact date of Suryavarman's death is unknown. Cham inscriptions show that he was still reigning in 1149. Cœdès thinks that he probably sent the Cambodian expedition against Tongking which met with disaster in 1150, and that he must have died in that year. His vast building programme, coupled with his rash and largely unsuccessful foreign policy, plunged his country into a sea of misfortunes, from which she was only rescued by Jayavarman VII.

The period from his death to the accession of Jayavarman VII is

very obscure. There are no contemporary inscriptions, and information concerning it has to be gleaned from those of the ensuing period
and foreign sources. Dharanindravarman II, his cousin on the female
side, who succeeded him in 1150, was a Buddhist who broke the long
tradition of Hinduism. In 1160 he was succeeded by Yaśovarman II,
who is thought to have been one of his sons, but not the legitimate
heir to the throne. His eldest son, Jayavarman, who should have
succeeded, went into voluntary exile in Champa, so the story goes,
because as a good Buddhist he shrank from causing civil war by
pressing his claim.

Yaśovarman's short reign, which ended in 1165 or 1166, saw two
rebellions. The first, referred to as the revolt of the *Rahus*, seems to
have been a peasants' revolt, presumably against the harsh conditions
they suffered as a result of Suryavarman's extravagance. The second,
led by a chief called Tribhuvanadityavarman, cost Yaśovarman his
throne and his life. The rebel leader is described in an inscription as
'a servant ambitious to arrive at the royal power'. When Jayavarman
heard of the insurrection he hurried back home to help his brother,
or mayhap to seize the throne for himself. An inscription at the
Phimeanakas runs: 'Seeing the moment come, he rose to save the
land heavy with crime.' But he was too late. He found Yaśovarman
dead and the usurper on the throne, and he retired again into obscurity.

In 1167 Jaya Indravarman IV of Champa, also a usurper, began a
long series of attacks upon Cambodia. His sole object seems to have
been plunder. At first the campaigns were limited to border fighting,
in which the Chams won some success as a result of training their
cavalry in the use of the crossbow. In 1177, however, having failed
to obtain the necessary number of horses for a raid on the grand scale,
they resorted to a surprise attack by sea, which resulted in the capture
and sack of Angkor. The old city of Yaśodharapura was defended by
wooden palisades, which proved inadequate to meet the sudden
attack launched by a well-prepared enemy. King Tribhuvanadityavarman lost his life when the capital was taken. The central government
collapsed and anarchy became widespread.

It was now Jayavarman's turn to deal with the situation. He dealt
first with the Chams. The great naval fight in which he routed them
is represented almost identically on the walls of the Bayon, his own
funerary monument, and those of the Banteay Chhmar. His next
task was to reduce the country to obedience. By 1181 he had established his power firmly enough to celebrate his coronation at Angkor.
Almost immediately afterwards, however, he was faced by a serious

rising in the dependent kingdom of Malyang, in the southern part of what is now the province of Battambang. His army, which quelled the rebels, was led by a young Cham prince, Śri Vidyananda, who was a refugee from his own country, though for what reason is unknown. He displayed such ability as a commander that Jayavarman VII marked him out for a still greater enterprise which he was preparing secretly against Champa.

The conquest of Champa was the greatest military achievement of Jayavarman's reign. The patience and care which he bestowed upon preparing his great act of vengeance were notable. He even sent an embassy with presents to the King of Dai-viet so as to ensure Annamite neutrality. The story, which belongs rather to the history of Champa than that of Cambodia, is told in Chapter 7. That he envisaged the permanent reduction of Champa to the position of a vassal state is shown not only by his appointment of the Cham prince Vidyanandana as commander-in-chief of the invading force but also by the fact that when Champa fell a second time to the Khmer armies, in 1203, its administration was entrusted to another Cham, Ong Dhamapatigrama, who had spent some time at the Court of Angkor. It is also significant, in quite a different connection, that the Cham viceroy, who was created Yuvaraja in 1207, employed the Khmer troops at his disposal mainly in attacks upon Annam. They were led by another Cham prince, Ong Ansaraja, a son of Jaya Harshavarman II (1162–3) and heir to the throne of Champa.

Under Jayavarman VII the sway of Angkor extended possibly even more widely than under Suryavarman II. An inscription dated 1186 at Say Fong, on the Mekong close to Vien Chang (Vientiane), indicates its farthest extension northwards. Chinese sources show that it exercised at least nominal suzerainty over part of the Malay Peninsula. They also assert that the kingdom of Pagan was a dependency of Cambodia at this time. Attempts have been made to explain that in their ignorance of the geography of Burma they confused Pegu, the capital of the Mon country, with Pagan. But even this suggestion is unacceptable. Burmese and Mon sources are completely silent on the subject, and the rule of Pagan under Narapatisithu (1172–1210) was too firmly established to admit of Cambodian suzerainty over any part of the country.

One interesting development in Burma during this king's reign was destined to have important effects upon Cambodia by the middle of the next century. Among the companions of the Mon monk Chapata, who in 1190 established a chapter of Theravada Buddhism after the

Sinhalese pattern in Burma, was a Khmer prince whom Cœdès suspects to have been a son of Jayavarman VII. The teachings of the new sect were brought by missionary monks to the states of the Menam valley, and ultimately to Cambodia itself, with revolutionary effects. For unlike Saivism, Vaiśnavism, and Mahayana Buddhism, which were imposed from above, the new doctrines were preached to the people, and stimulated a popular movement which carried the Khmers as a whole into the Hinayana fold, which they have never deserted.

Jayavarman VII's internal work shows a building programme of the most extravagant order. It was unparalleled alike in its immensity and in the haste and carelessness with which it was carried out. In the first place, with the lessons of the Cham invasion in view, he set himself to build an impregnable city. The result was Angkor Thom, which was planned on a much smaller scale than Yaśodharapura. While it was under construction the king resided in a temporary capital, Nagara Jayaśri, which was erected just outside the north-east corner of the new one.

Angkor Thom was enclosed by a wide moat some eight miles in circumference and a formidable laterite wall, supported on the inside by an enormous earth embankment. Five stone causeways crossed the moat and gave access to the city through five monumental gates, each with towers surmounted by gigantic heads with four human faces. The causeways themselves were flanked on each side by balustrades formed by rows of giants holding on their knees a naga, whose seven heads rose fanwise at each end of the causeway.

At the centre of the city rose the strangest monument ever erected by a Khmer king, the Bayon, next to the Angkor Wat the largest temple of the Angkor group.[1] It was a pyramidal temple with its central mass crowned by a tower of gold bearing four gigantic human faces. Around it from an inner and an outer gallery arose many smaller four-faced towers, the number of which has been estimated at fifty. It was built in such a hurry that stone was piled upon stone without any form of cement. Its decorations were among the finest in Khmer architecture, its architectural motif one of the most striking in the world, but it is now in a worse state of ruin than almost any of the other great Angkor temples. The myriad faces which so impressively and disconcertingly confront the observer are portraits of Jayavarman himself in the guise of the Mahayanist Bodhisattva Avalokitesvara, usually referred to in South-East Asia as Lokesvara.

Like his father Dharanindravarman II, he was a Buddhist, and

[1] Cœdès, *Pour mieux comprendre Angkor*, chap. vi, 'Le mystère du Bayon', pp. 121–50.

under him Mahayanism became for a time the dominant religion in Cambodia. Suryavarman II had blended Vaiśnavism with Śaivism in such a way as to substitute a Vishnuraja for a Devaraja at the Angkor Wat. Jayavarman VII took the blending process a further stage by the substitution of a Buddharaja cult with its centre at the Bayon. In 1933 the French archaeologist Trouvé discovered a huge statue of the Buddha in a pit under the central tower of the Bayon.

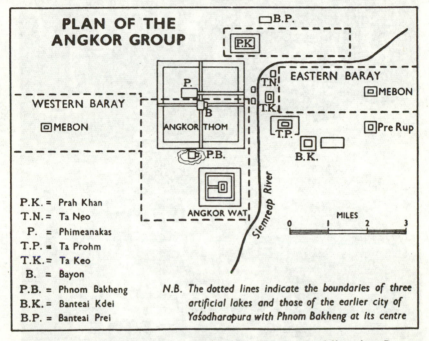

PLAN OF THE ANGKOR GROUP

B.P.
P.K.

EASTERN BARAY

WESTERN BARAY

MEBON

MEBON

Pre Rup

ANGKOR THOM

P.B.

B.K.

Siemreap River

ANGKOR WAT

MILES
0   1   2   3

P.K. = Prah Khan
T.N. = Ta Neo
P.   = Phimeanakas
T.P. = Ta Prohm
T.K. = Ta Keo
B.   = Bayon
P.B. = Phnom Bakheng
B.K. = Banteai Kdei
B.P. = Banteai Prei

N.B. The dotted lines indicate the boundaries of three artificial lakes and those of the earlier city of Yaśodharapura with Phnom Bakheng at its centre

This must have been the representation of the Buddharaja. It was apparently buried there during the violent Hindu reaction after Jayavarman's death, when the Bayon became a Śaivite shrine and the linga cult replaced that of Lokesvara.

Śaivism, however, did not disappear during Jayavarman's reign. No great Śaivite monument was erected, but among the smaller shrines as many were dedicated to Śiva as to Lokesvara. Needless to say, the mass of the people remained largely untouched by these developments in the official cult. They interpreted its various forms in terms of their own animism and ancestor-worship.

Jayavarman VII's building programme included much more than his two great monuments, Angkor Thom and the Bayon. Among other things he claimed also to have built no less than 121 rest-houses

under him Mahayanism became for a time the dominant religion in

ANGKOR THOM: THE PINNACLES OF THE BAYON

the two great monuments, Angkor Thom and the Bayon. Among
other things he is said also to have built no less than 13,500 houses

at intervals along the roads radiating from the capital. His chief queen Jayarajadevi, we are told, 'filled the earth with a shower of magnificent gifts'. On her death he raised her elder sister Indradevi to the position she had occupied. Indradevi had been a distinguished teacher of the Buddhist doctrine in three monastic schools. Besides erecting 'numerous images of Jayarajadevi with images of the king and herself in all the cities', she composed in perfect Sanskrit the famous inscription on the Phimeanakas which gives her husband's biography.

A programme such as this was far too heavy for a people already crushed by the burden of wars and the buildings of Suryavarman II. Thousands of villages were assigned for the upkeep of the great temples, while tens of thousands of officiants and hundreds of dancers were employed in their service, not to mention the army of labourers, masons, sculptors and decorators required for the constructional work. Jayavarman VII may have been the greatest of all the Khmer monarchs, and it may be claimed that his reign represented the apogee of Cambodia, but he impoverished his people with heavy taxation and insatiable demands for forced labour and military service. Cœdès poses the question whether he is not rather to be seen as 'a megalomaniac whose foolish prodigality was one of the causes of the decadence of his country'.[1] There can be no doubt as to the answer.

Up to the present no definite evidence regarding the date of Jayavarman VII's death has come to light. At one time it was supposed to have been in 1201. Now Cœdès places it in 1218. The increase in the length of the reign attributed to him illustrates the growth of knowledge concerning him during the past fifty years. In 1900 little more than his name was known. The programme of conquest and buildings with which he is now credited would certainly demand a reign ending not earlier than 1215. Moreover, the date of his birth also has been altered. Cœdès, who at one time placed it shortly before 1130, now favours a date not later than 1125. This would make him well over ninety at the time of his death.[2]

The details of Khmer history during the remainder of the thirteenth century are hard to find. There are no important contemporary inscriptions, and the Chinese dynastic histories have nothing to say about the period. The chief sources of information are Cham and T'ai inscriptions, and later Cambodian ones. No great ruler arose after Jayavarman VII. Much of his work perished soon after his death.

[1] Op. cit. sup., chap. viii, pp. 176–210.
[2] Les États Hindouisés, pp. 286, 291.

TEN-ARMED BODHISATTAVA, ANGKOR

Champa was evacuated and a Hindu reaction swept away the cult of the Buddharaja. Everywhere lingas replaced Lokesvaras.

The evacuation of Champa was the first step in the dissolution of the empire. There is reason to think that it was followed soon afterwards by the independence of Tambralinga, though quite what happened is by no means clear. The T'ai also were strengthening their hold on the upper Menam valley at the expense of the Khmer power. In Cambodia itself, however, there were no signs of collapse, and only a few of decay, so that at the end of the century it was possible for the Chinese observer Chou Ta-kuan to describe a magnificent city and a prosperous country, notwithstanding the ravages of T'ai raiders.

Five more Kings of Angkor are mentioned before the inscriptions come to an end and the official Cambodian Chronicle begins. One of them, Jayavarman VIII (1243–95), had the longest reign in Khmer history, but achieved no distinction either as statesman or builder. The great age of Khmer architecture had come to an abrupt end with the passing of Jayavarman VII. Jayavarman VIII was largely responsible for the acts of vandalism on the Buddhist images erected by his predecessor. Under him Brahman dominance was re-established.

He was quite unable to curb the T'ai. It was during his reign that they gained control over most of what is today the kingdom of Thailand or Siam. A big step in this direction was taken when a T'ai chieftain who had married a daughter of Jayavarman VII defeated the Khmer governor of the upper Menam valley and established the kingdom of Sukhot'ai. Rama Khamheng, who ascended its throne in 1270, expanded his power far and wide at the expense of the Khmer empire. Farther north another T'ai prince, Mangrai, conquered the old Mon kingdom of Haripunjaya in the Meping valley and built the city of Chiengmai as his capital. Both he and Rama Khamheng established close relations with Kublai Khan, who had conquered the old T'ai kingdom of Tali, or Nanchao, in 1253. Their attacks upon the Khmer were made with his encouragement. Jayavarman VIII asked for trouble by stolidly turning a deaf ear to Mongol demands for homage, and even went so far as to imprison Kublai's envoy. Had Marshal Sögatu succeeded in subduing Champa, doubtless Cambodia's turn would have come next. But his attempt ended in disaster. Hence Kublai found the T'ai all the more useful as a means of weakening the proud Angkor regime.

The early conquests of the T'ai caused such serious losses both of revenue and of man power for forced labour that they alone would account for the sudden stop in the erection of great monuments of art. Otherwise, however, the life of Cambodia went on much as before, and for a time may have become somewhat easier for the oppressed masses, whose main task was to labour for the greedy gods. At the top of the scale the abandonment of great enterprises, whether of erecting temples or of foreign conquest, promoted a new zest for learning. As Louis Finot puts it: 'Sanskrit verse was still written. Wise men abounded there, and foreign savants came, drawn by the reputation of this kingdom of high culture. Nowhere was knowledge more in honour. Scholars occupied the first charges of the State; they were on terms of familiarity with kings. Their daughters were queens. They themselves were royal preceptors, grand judges, ministers. There was a "King of Professors".'[1]

But it was at the other end of the scale that the great change was in progress which was to be the most potent factor in causing the collapse of the old culture, upon which the greatness of Angkor had been based. This was the conversion of the people to the Buddhism of the Sinhalese Mahavihara sect. We have seen how the new teaching had been introduced into Burma at the end of the twelfth century by Mon monks. Thence it had spread to the Mon peoples of the Menam valley, where Hinayana Buddhism had already centuries of existence behind it. By the middle of the thirteenth century it was spreading northwards to the T'ai and eastwards to the Khmers.

It was simple and needed no priesthood for the maintenance of expensive temples and elaborate ceremonial. Its missionaries were monks who prescribed austerity, solitude and meditation, and were devoted to a life of poverty and self-abnegation. Unlike the hierarchy at the capital, they were in direct contact with the people, and they undermined completely the old state religion and all that went with it. 'From the day when the sovereign ceased to be Śiva descended to earth,' writes Cœdès,[2] 'or the living Buddha, as Jayavarman VII had been, the royal dynasty failed any longer to inspire the people with the religious respect which enabled it to accomplish great enterprises. Under the threat of the anarchical spirit of Sinhalese Buddhism his prestige diminished, his temporal power crumbled away, and the god-king was thrown down from his altar.'

When Chou Ta-kuan arrived in Angkor with the Chinese embassy of 1296–7 a new king, Indravarman III, was on the throne. He was a soldier who had married Jayavarman VIII's daughter and seized the

[1] In G. Maspero, L'Indochine, i, p. 108.
[2] Pour mieux comprendre Angkor, p. 66.

royal power by deposing his father-in-law and imprisoning the legitimate claimant. He tried to infuse new energy into the kingship; and whereas his predecessor had never shown himself in public, Indravarman appeared often in the streets. His reception of a Chinese mission was a sign of a change of attitude, if not of policy. Jayavarman VIII had imprisoned the members of the sole Chinese mission on record to his Court; this one was accorded an honourable reception. It was sent by Timur Khan, Kublai's grandson and successor, and Chou Ta-kuan asserts that homage was paid by Indravarman III to the new emperor. But there is no sign of the usual official relations subsequently, and Pelliot, in his edition of Chou Ta-kuan's *Memoirs on the Customs of Cambodia*,[1] quotes a Chinese author of 1520 to the effect that Cambodia never did pay homage to China.

Still, Indravarman must have done enough to placate the Imperial Court. Moreover, he was able to hold the T'ai attacks, and the danger from their direction lessened. In 1317 Rama K'amheng died and the power of Sukhot'ai declined. Chou Ta-kuan mentions that before Indravarman's accession Cambodia proper had been subjected to Siamese raids. From his time until the foundation of Ayut'ia in 1350 she seems to have been in no great danger.

There is reason to suspect that in religion also Indravarman III reversed the policy of Jayavarman VIII. He would appear to have made no change in the official state ceremonial, which had become Śaivite again after Jayavarman VII's death. But there are records of his benefactions to a Buddhist monastery and shrine at the close of his reign. An inscription dated 1309, recording a gift of revenues made by him to the monastery, shows that he had abdicated in the previous year.[2] Did he do so, as Cœdès suggests, in order to become a monk and devote himself to the study and practice of the new Hinayana doctrine? That Hinayana Buddhism had become the predominant religion of the people by the end of Jayavarman VIII's reign is abundantly evident from Chou Ta-kuan's account of the religions of Angkor. Everybody, he says, worshipped the Buddha, and his description of the *chu-ku* (Siamese *chao-ku*='sir'), the name he applies to the Buddhist monks, who 'shave the head, wear yellow clothing and leave the right shoulder uncovered', leaves no doubt that they were Hinayanist.

Little is known of the reigns of Indravarman's two immediate

---

[1] BEFEO, ii, (1902), pp. 123–77.
[2] Until recently he was thought to have died in 1307. On this point see Briggs, *Ancient Khmer Empire*, p. 252.

successors, Indrajayavarman (1308–27) and Jayavarman Paramesvara (1327–?). The latter is the last Cambodian king to be mentioned by the inscriptions. Not only is the date of the end of his reign unknown, but also his connection with the earliest kings of the Cambodian Chronicle, who begin in c. 1340 with a posthumous name, Mahanippean. The Sanskrit inscriptions end abruptly in the reign of Jayavarman Paramesvara; there is no decline in their style or in the skill of the lapidists who executed them. The only explanation would seem to be that the king and his Court became converts to Hinayana Buddhism, and the official language thus became Pali. With the passing of the *deva-raja* passed also the habit of celebrating his achievements in conventional Sanskrit verse exquisitely carved in stone. Was Jayavarman Paramesvara the king under whom this important change took place?

Briggs[1] shows that there is good reason to suppose that he had a long reign, that he was the Khmer king who helped the exiled Laos prince Phi-Fa and his son Fa-Ngum to found the independent kingdom of Lan Chang with its capital at Muang Swa in 1353, that Fa Ngum married his daughter, and that largely through her efforts the Laotians were converted to Hinayanism. Jayavarman Paramesvara is said to have exhorted his son-in-law, soon after his accession, to obey the teaching of the Buddha in his relations with his subjects.

The Cambodian Chronicle, on the other hand, places a series of four kings, beginning with Nippean Bat (Nirvanapada), on the throne of Angkor between 1340 and 1353. It also asserts that in the latter year the king of Ayut'ia, Rama Thibodi I, captured the city and held it for four years, during which time the Khmer king took refuge at the Court of Laos. Briggs, however, in his article 'Siamese Attacks on Angkor before 1430'[2] has propounded the hypothesis that they, together with the Siamese capture of Angkor, belong to a much later period. 'Those who prepared the Chronicles', he complains,[3] 'apparently set back the dates of the reigns and events, interjected kings and otherwise distorted and misrepresented the facts.' His thesis is that the account in the Chronicles of a Siamese conquest of Angkor in 1353, and of a further one in 1394, when they are said to have placed a Siamese prince on the throne, and to have held the city until driven out in 1401, is false, for Angkor did not fall until 1431. The accession of Nippean Bat he places in 1405, thus leaving an indeterminate gap to be filled between the death of Jayavarman VIII

[1] *Ibid.*, pp. 253–5.   [2] FEQ, viii (1948), pp. 3–33.
[3] *The Ancient Khmer Empire*, p. 254.

and that date. For light on this subject he adduces the references to Cambodia in the *Ming History*. The accession of the Ming Dynasty in 1368 brought Cambodia once more into relationship with China, and its records list missions between the two countries and their dates. The Hung Wu Emperor (1368–98), for instance, sent four missions to Cambodia, and the Yung-lo Emperor (1403–24) three. The *Ming History* records the reception of ten embassies from 'Chenla' between 1371 and 1403, and mentions the names of three kings. The third of these, *Phing-ya*, according to Briggs's reckoning, should be Nippean Bat.

Save for the few references to Cambodia found in the Ming records, the Khmer Chronicles are our sole source of information for the period from the middle of the fourteenth century to the end of the fifteenth. Those extant today were produced in the nineteenth century, with the exception of a fragment presented to Rama I of Siam in 1796 by the Khmer king Ang Eng, who had been a refugee at Bangkok before his restoration in 1795. They have been used by French writers of Cambodian history from the eighteen-sixties onwards. The most important is Nong's *Royal Chronicle of Cambodia*, compiled because an earlier one had been lost, and completed in about 1818. It was translated into French in 1865–6 at the request of Doudart de Lagrée and edited by Francis Garnier.[1] Later recensions formed the basis of the histories compiled respectively by Jean Moura[2] and Adhemar Leclère.[3] So far as their treatment of events is concerned, all pretty well agree; but they differ considerably in chronology. Moura's chronology has been followed by Étienne Aymonier[4] and Georges Maspero[5] among others. Recently M. Bernard Philippe Groslier in the first chapter of his *Angkor et le Cambodge au XVIᵉ Siècle d'après les Sources portugaises et espagnoles*[6] has submitted the Cambodian sources, and the French accounts based on them, to careful scrutiny, and has attempted a reconstruction of the dynastic chronology up to the end of the sixteenth century. The Cambodian sources, it must be emphasized, are mere dynastic records in the narrowest sense of the term, and the problems they pose are almost entirely those of chronology. Among these the date(s) of the Siamese conquest(s) of Angkor and of the city's abandonment as a royal capital are of special interest. M. Groslier

[1] 'Chronique royale du Cambodge', *Journal Asiatique*, sixth series, vol. xviii, pp. 336–85, and vol. xx, pp. 112–44.
[2] *Le Royaume du Cambodge*, 2 vols (Paris, 1883).
[3] *Histoire du Cambodge* (Paris, 1914).
[4] *Le Cambodge*, 3 vols (Paris, 1900–4).
[5] *L'Empire Khmer* (Phnom Penh, 1904).   [6] Paris, 1958.

accepts Briggs's revision of the list of kings in the Cambodian Chronicle, but not his contention that Angkor did not fall to the Siamese before 1431. Now, however, the Briggs revision itself has been challenged by Dr. O. W. Wolters in a study entitled 'The Khmer king at Basan (1371–73) and the restoration of the Khmer chronology during the 14th and 15th centuries'.[1] In it from a re-examination of the Ming accounts of relations with Cambodia, and of certain key statements of chronology in Khmer writings in terms of the twelve-year animal cycle, he has put forward his own reconstruction of Cambodian dynastic history from roughly the middle of the fourteenth century until the beginning of the sixteenth. It is impossible here to follow in detail Dr. Wolters's analysis of the source material; but it can be confidently asserted that, even if in the light of further discovery not all his findings are sustained, Briggs's theories regarding the dates of the kings of the Cambodian Chronicle and of the fall of Angkor are shown to be wholly untenable. The remainder of this section therefore is devoted to an exposition of his views.

The early Ming records mention five Khmer kings between 1371 and 1405, when *P'ing-ya* reported his father's death and his own accession to the throne. The first, *Hu-erh-na*, sent 'tribute' which was presented to the emperor on 14 December 1371. The record shows that he was not ruling at Angkor, but at Basan in the province of Srei Santhor on the eastern side of the Mekong. He sent a second mission, which was received in November 1373. After an interval of a little over four years another king, Samdach Kambujadhiraja presented 'tribute' in January 1378; and from his style of 'Supreme Ruler of Kambuja' it may be inferred that Angkor was his capital. He sent further missions up to 1383. Late in 1386 a new king, Samdach *Pao-p'i-yeh* Kambuja, received Chinese envoys at his court, and subsequently despatched missions to China, that were received in September 1387 and October 1388. Further Khmer missions were received in 1389 (three) and in 1390, but the king's name is not mentioned. A new king, *P'o-p'i-ya*, sent a mission in 1404 in reply to the Yung-lo Emperor's mission of 1403 to announce his accession to the imperial throne. Then in August 1405 *P'ing-ya's* envoys reported his father's death. His last mission went to China in 1419.

For dating important events the Cambodian Chronicles use the twelve-year animal cycle, and this seems to have been a guiding factor in the compilation of the recensions. The dates had to be made to conform to the animal years traditionally associated with certain

[1] *Asia Major*, xii, 1 (1966), pp. 48–89.

events. These animal years, Dr. Wolters believes, can rarely be taken as authentic, for he claims that the compilers of the nineteenth-century recensions have been led astray by preconceived notions about the dating of certain events. Thus, the notion that the first Siamese capture of Angkor came early in the reign of Ramadhipati, the first king of Ayut'ia, has led them to date it 1353. The Ang Eng fragment, however, claims that it took place in the 'year of the cock', and Dr. Wolters suggests that the 'year of the cock' 1369, the last year of Ramadhipati's reign, is the appropriate date. It would, he points out, fit in with the Ming references to Cambodia, which show *Hu-erh-na* ruling at Basan, far away from Angkor, between 1371 and 1373. If one accepts this date, and if Nong's Chronicle is right in saying that Nippean Bat came to the throne eight years before the Siamese capture of Angkor, his reign must be placed in the thirteen-sixties, and not in the first decade of the fifteenth century, as Briggs argues.

According to the unanimous testimony of the chronicles Angkor was under Siamese rule for six years. The Ang Eng fragment asserts that a King Kalamegha ruled elsewhere than at Angkor, and that after reigning three years he was succeeded by his nephew Gamkat, who fought the Siamese and recaptured the city. On this showing Kala-megha would be the *Hu-erh-na* of the Ming records, and Gamkat the Samdach Kambujadhiraja who sent missions to China from Angkor in 1377, 1380 and 1383.

All the Cambodian sources agree that Gamkat's successor, Dhar-masokaraja, reigned three years. Dr. Wolters identifies him with the king called *Pao-p'i-yeh* by the Chinese, who sent missions in 1387 and 1388. The emperor, we are told, conferred a seal of office upon him, and his second mission went to offer his thanks for the honour. The Chinese accounts furnish evidence of disturbed conditions in Cambodia during his reign. His 'tribute' consisted of 59 elephants and 60,000 catties of incense, and in May 1388 the emperor rebuked the re-doubtable Cham king, Che Bong Nga, for seizing some elephants en route for China. Was the Cham monarch, Dr. Wolters asks, fighting Khmers as well as Vietnamese? He would accept Boisselier's con-tention that the Bien Hoa inscription, commemorating a Cham victory in what has been accepted as the year 1421, really refers to this earlier period.[1] The severe struggle that raged continually between the Khmers and the Siamese in the provinces of Chantabun and Jolburi, with raiding and counter-raiding, and deportations of thousands of

---

[1] J. Boisselier, *La Statuaire du Champa* (Paris, 1963), pp. 360–1. A. Cabaton, 'L'inscription chame de Bien-Hoa', BEFEO, iv, p. 687.

hapless peasants, might well have tempted the Chams to join in. There is sound evidence, says Dr. Wolters, of bad relations between Chams and Khmers during the period 1387–1400.

Three Khmer missions were received by China during the year 1389. This fact points to it as a year of crisis, the year of the second fall of Angkor to the Thai, Dr. Wolters thinks. They must have attacked during the dry season of 1388–9. The Khmer chronicles say that the city fell after a siege of seven months, and by treachery, not through weakness. They tell us that King Dharmasoka (*Pao-p'i-yeh*) died during the siege, and his death was followed by the defection of two mandarins and two leading Buddhist monks to the enemy. It was in consequence of this that the city fell. As on the previous occasion, the Siamese stripped Angkor of all they could carry away and deported thousands of prisoners. A Siamese vassal prince was placed in control. His career was short. Dharmasoka's successor, whom Dr. Wolters identifies with the Chinese *P'o-p'i-ya*, escaped, and within a short time procured the assassination of the usurper and recovered the throne. Thus 1389 was a year of rapid changes, and these would account for the three Khmer missions sent to China in such quick succession. The first, suggests Dr. Wolters, was sent to inform the emperor of the new king's accession, the second to report his recovery of Angkor, and the third to assert his right to recognition as lawful ruler of Cambodia. He identifies him with Paramarajadhiraja Ramadhipati Sri Darmi-karaja of the Ang Eng fragment, the Prea Reach Angka Prea Barom Reachea Thireach in the 'Chronological List of the Kings of Cambodia' made for Doudart de Lagrée at the same time as the French translation of Nong's *Royal Chronicle*. He is the ruler known to historians as Ponhea Yat, whom Briggs places upon the throne after the supposed fall of Angkor in 1431. Dr. Wolters and Briggs agree on one point, namely that Ponhea Yat came to the throne after the fall of Angkor. But according to the former this occurred after the second fall of the city in 1389; it did not fall to the Thai a third time during this period.

Ponhea Yat, according to this reckoning, reigned from 1389 to 1404. He did not establish his court at Basan, as Moura thought, but at 'Caturmukha' 'the city of the four faces', i.e. Phnom Penh. His son, Prince Gamkat, who succeeded him, transferred his capital back to Angkor. Cambodian sources accord him the title Narayana Ramadhi-pati, or Prea Noreay Reamea Thyphdey. He is the *Ping-ya* of the Chinese records. The Ang Eng fragment gives him an uneventful reign of twenty-five years; by Cambodian reckoning, therefore, which counts the first and last years of the reign as two, he must have died in 1428. He sent his last mission to China in 1419. According to Briggs[1] Khmer envoys to China in 1414 complained that Cham raids had on several occasions prevented the despatch of embassies to the Imperial Court. The emperor, he tells us, sent a letter of warning to the Cham king; but this did not restrain the latter from carrying out a large-scale invasion of the Mekong delta region, whence his forces were not expelled until about 1426.

When Narayana Dhipati died, the Ang Eng fragment tells us, great dissensions arose within the royal family. His brothers, Sri Raja and Tieraraja, fought for the crown. The latter won, killed his brother, and reigned with the title Sri Sodaiya at 'Muan Nagara Hlvan', i.e. Angkor. He is also known as Srey. Trouble broke out between him and his son Dharmaraja, who rebelled and dethroned him. According to the fragment, Prince Dharmaraja's grandmother, the mother of Srey, was a Siamese princess whom Ponhea Yat had married. She had warned him (Dharmaraja) that his father did not trust him, and had designs on his life. So he fled to Korat, raised an army and drove his father out of Angkor, whence he escaped first to Lovek and afterwards to Ayut'ia. The victorious prince then proclaimed himself king with the title of Dharmarajadhiraja. Meanwhile, however, Narayana Ramadhipati's widow had taken refuge at Pursat and proclaimed her son, Chau Ba, king. He resisted all Dharmaraja's attacks, and the fragment ends with the two kings reigning simultaneously in their respective capitals.

Dr. Wolters accepts this account as reliable. It is interesting to contrast it with Moura's version of the story, compiled from a much later, and apparently rather more anti-Siamese, recension of the Cambodian Chronicle. According to it King Srei, ruling at Phnom Penh, sent his younger brother, Thommo Reachea (Dharmaraja), to Angkor as governor. In the year after his accession, 1473 according to this account, Srei had to deal with a rebellion led by his nephew, Soryotei, a son of Preah Noreay (Narayana), supported by the Siamese, who apparently gained possession of the Cambodian provinces of Chantabun, Korat and Angkor. They followed this up by capturing King Srei himself, and deported him and the rebel Soryotei to Siam. Dharmaraja thereupon assumed the leadership in the fight for liberation, and ultimately, after a three years' struggle, drove out the Siamese and was crowned king.

If with Dr. Wolters one accepts the earlier recensions of the

[1] *The Ancient Khmer Empire*, p. 255.

chronicles, namely the Ang Eng fragment of 1796 and Nong's *Royal Chronicle* of 1818, as the more trustworthy accounts, the question of dating has still to be faced. The fragment gives no dates whatever. Nong and the 'Chronological List' both date Dharmarajadhiraja's seizure of the throne 1468, and the former adds that in 1476 at his request Siam sent an expedition which conquered the Pursat ruler, and deported him and his brother to Ayut'ia. But, as against these dates, we now have the evidence of some Khmer-language inscriptions recently discovered in Tenasserim.[1] They show that a Cambodian king and his brother lived there in Siamese territory from 1462 to 1465. The 'king' must have been the Pursat ruler. Hence, in view of a statement in the Ang Eng fragment that Dharmarajadhiraja was born in the 'year of the hare' and was twenty-one at his accession, Dr. Wolters would place his birth in the 'year of the hare' 1423, and consequently his accession to the throne in 1444. At this rate the capture of the Pursat ruler could have taken place in 1452, the year of a mission from a Khmer recorded by the Chinese. The *capture* of the rival prince would have been an appropriate occasion for a mission to China.

With Srey's deposition Angkor ceased to be the royal capital, for Dharmarajadhiraja made Phnom Penh his capital. Thus, according to Dr. Wolters's reckoning, Angkor was abandoned, not in 1432 as Briggs supposed, and not as a result of its capture and sack by the Siamese, but some time after 1444, i.e. about half a century after the second Siamese sack. And its abandonment was immediately due to feuds within the royal family stimulated by Siam, which caused a civil war involving regional divisions, rival capitals, and such a wasteful consumption of manpower that, according to the record, 'primitives' participated in the fighting. Worse still, rival candidates for the throne sought outside allies, Ayut'ia in particular. Thus a vicious process began, which more than anything else spelt ruin to the kingdom, especially after the middle of the seventeenth century, when the Vietnamese joined in the game of colonizing and annexing Khmer lands; and finally in the nineteenth century, when the Hué monarchy vied with the Bangkok monarchy for control over the mere rump of a once-great empire.

[1] G. Cœdès, 'Documents épigraphiques provenant de Tenasserim' in *Felicitation Volumes . . . presented to his Highness Prince Dhaninivat Kromamun Bidyalath* (Bangkok, 1965), ii, pp. 203–9.

(c) The economic basis of Khmer civilization

The economic factors, which made possible so great an outburst of glorious art and architecture in the Angkor region from the tenth to the thirteenth centuries, have only recently been investigated. For many years archaeologists were so busily engaged upon the study of what was above the ground and visible that the examination of the sub-soil was neglected. Recently, however, M. Bernard Philippe Groslier has been engaged upon this task, and with the aid of aerial photography has made discoveries which not only answer the questions, which had long perplexed students of Khmer antiquities, but also indicate the lines along which future research into other South-East Asian civilizations might profitably proceed. In 1958 he summed up his results in a section of his book dealing with Portuguese and Spanish accounts of Cambodia in the sixteenth century.[1] It is a brief statement, but it provides for the first time the essential facts for lack of which it had hitherto been impossible to present a rounded picture of Khmer civilization. The basic question, which had worried the minds of students, was: how could an agricultural community, 'une civilisation du vegetal', have become rich enough to produce a range of monuments, which, as M. Groslier sees it, is incomparable for number, size and perfection. It was, he tells us, a matter of agricultural hydraulics. The Khmers, who had inherited methods of irrigation from Funan, found the Angkor region ideal for the purpose of constructing a system of water utilization that would cause the soil to yield its utmost in the service of man. It was a system designed to solve the problem posed by too much and too heavy monsoon rain within too short a time. What they did was to construct a vast *réseau hydraulique*, which ensured that as much water as possible was conserved during the rains so that during the dry season it could be used rationally for both human consumption and the permanent irrigation of the paddy-fields. Aerial photography has enabled the plan of this remarkable system to be plotted. It depended upon the construction of immense storage tanks, the *barays*, one of which had a capacity of 30 million cubic metres, supplied with an ingenious apparatus for carrying off the water as and when it was needed. The whole region, running to some twelve and a half million acres, was minutely divided into square paddy fields, capable of yielding three, and even four, harvests a year. The complex net of waterways

---

[1] *Angkor et le Cambodge au XVIe siècle d'après les sources portugaises et espagnoles,* Paris, 1958, pp. 107–21.

served other purposes also. It protected the soil from diluvial erosion through uncontrolled flooding in the rainy season. It seems to have controlled the annual inundation of the great Tonle Sap lake. Moreover, it provided an efficient means of travel and transport at any season of the year; even the moats of the chief monuments formed an integral part of it, enabling materials from the quarries to be brought direct to the building sites.

The city itself, so far from being an urban agglomeration, was rather a collection of waterworks stretching far and wide beyond the palace and its immediate temples, with a considerable population densely settled along its causeways and canals, and much of its land cut up into cultivated holdings. In this connection modern research has established the significant fact that each Khmer king, upon taking office, was expected to carry out works 'of public interest', particularly works of irrigation, before starting upon his own temple-mountain. Indeed, M. Groslier goes so far as to say that the labour bestowed upon the ever-developing irrigation system is 'far more impressive than the building of temples, which were merely chapels crowning a cyclopean undertaking'.[1]

We have seen the Khmer king as the *deva-raja*, the intermediary between men and the divine powers, the upholder of the established order (dharma) handed down by his ancestors, the intercessor with the spirit world for the fertility of his realm, and his city as the image of the universe interpreted in terms of the Hindu Mount Meru. It is now obvious that he must also be seen as the creator and director of the public works designed to ensure prosperity. Thus the religious and economic systems were intimately bound up with each other, and hark back to a condition of society anterior to any impact of Indian influence. As M. Groslier expresses it, 'La religion fondamentale de la société khmère, sous son brillant manteau indien, fut le culte des eaux et du sol.'[2] The ubiquitous naga of Khmer art, the water spirit, was the central figure of the popular religion.

The Angkor economy, and the organization of society which it entailed, depended upon a system of water utilization so highly complex and artificial, that any interference with it could have extremely serious consequences. So long as rulers were public-spirited and people were content to play the part assigned to them in keeping the vast mechanism going, Angkor prospered; and from 802 until far into the twelfth century the heartland of the Khmer kingdom enjoyed quite

[1] *Angkor, Art and Civilization*, London, 1957, p. 30.
[2] *Angkor et le Cambodge au XVIe siècle*, p. 116.

exceptional tranquillity. But royal megalomania, showing itself in increasing extravagance in building and in wasteful wars of aggression undermined the economy, and bred discontent with the established order. And when the machine was already beginning to show signs of strain, the persistent T'ai raids deep into the metropolitan area ultimately wrecked it beyond repair.

(d) Cambodia from 1444 to the Siamese conquest in 1594

Cambodian history during the long period from the abandonment of Angkor to the Siamese conquest in 1594 is almost as obscure as during the preceding period after the reign of Jayavarman VIII. The records, however, are slightly ampler, and, from the reign of Dharmarajadhiraja the ages of kings at the time of important events are given. The Khmers never forgot the challenge of Ayut'ia, and their traditions conceal nothing of the wars with the Thai. The latter remained the enemy for long after the period of their two occupations of Angkor. Dr. Wolters[1] makes the pertinent suggestion that the Khmer rulers may have regarded the struggle rather as a civil war than one between two independent kingdoms; there is no reference to it in Ming records, no Khmer complaint of Siamese aggression.

Nong and the 'Chronological List' assert that Dharmarajadhiraja was succeeded by his eldest son, Srei Sukonthor, in 1504. Dr. Wolters, however, asks whether the royal funeral rites of the year 1486, described by Nong, were for Dharmarajadhiraja. This was also the year of the birth of his son Ang Chan, who was to become a great figure in Cambodian history. Nong records that in 1512 Srei Sukonthor was murdered by his brother-in-law, Kan, who seized the throne. Ang Chan with other members of the royal family escaped to Pursat, where he is said to have rallied his partisans. In due course, when he was strong enough to make a bid for the throne, he invaded Angkor province, and ultimately defeated and killed Kan. Nong, on the other hand, makes him flee to Ayut'ia, whence in 1516 he returned to Cambodia, rallied the people against Kan, and defeated him in that same year. Dr. Wolters accepts Nong's dates for both the murder of Srei Sukonthor and the accession of Ang Chan.

Ang Chan became the most powerful monarch Cambodia was to produce after the fall of Angkor. During his long reign of fifty years he was able to turn the tables on Siam and regain for his country some at least of her former prestige. The Siamese chronicles mention a

[1] 'The Khmer King at Basan (1371–3)', *Asia Major*, vol. xii, pt. 1, p. 85.

Cambodian raid on the Prachim province in 1531. A Siamese counter-attack by land and sea during the dry season of 1532-3 was led by Chau Pnhea Ang, a son of the exiled king Preah Srei, who had died in Siam. There is much disagreement between the chronicles on each side as to what took place. One version of the Siamese chronicles claims victory for Siam, while the Cambodian chronicle makes Ang Chan the winner, and asserts that Chau Pnhea Ang was killed near Pursat in 1534. One version of the Siamese chronicles appears to confirm this: it states that the Siamese forces were dispersed by bad weather and that Chau Pnhea Ang died in Cambodia. Garnier assigns the date 1555 to this event, and it seems probable that these raids and counter-raids are related to that date rather than the earlier one, for Siam was then passing through a period of dynastic troubles which offered Cambodia an excellent opportunity to weaken her rival. The Burmese had taken advantage of the situation to lay siege to Ayut'ia in 1548-9, and although they had had to abandon it and go home, the accession of the warlike Bayinnaung to the Burmese throne in 1551 was followed by an all-out attempt by Burma to subjugate all the Tai states within her reach, the Shan States, Chiengmai, the Laos Kingdom and Siam herself.[1] W. A. R. Wood in his *History of Siam* places the Cambodian raid on Prachim in 1549 during the Burmese siege of Ayut'ia,[2] and Chau Pnhea Ang's defeat and death in 1556. 'The kings of Cambodia,' he comments, 'filled with regard to Siam a similar role to that filled by the kings of Scotland with regard to England in the Middle Ages.' From 1559 onwards Ang Chan unceasingly raided Siamese territory. In 1564 his armies advanced to the walls of Ayut'ia, but returned empty-handed, for the city had fallen into Burmese hands in February of that year, and there was a Burmese army of occupation.

When Ang Chan died, presumably in 1566,[3] and was succeeded by his only son Barom Reachea I, the contest with Siam continued with such vigour that in 1570 the new king established his headquarters in the Angkor region and his armies occupied the Korat province. But according to M. Groslier, he and his successors were 'sorry figures',[4] and the struggle produced no decisive results, though causing appalling suffering through widespread devastation and wholesale deportations of people.

Under Barom Reachea's son and successor Satha (1576-?1594) the tide turned decisively against Cambodia. The death of Bayinnaung in

---

[1] *Infra*, chap. 14.
[2] Page 115. He calls Ang Chan 'Chandaraja' and Chau Pnhea Ang 'P'ya Ong'.
[3] Groslier, *op. cit.*, p. 15.
[4] *Ibid., loc. cit.*

1581 weakened Burma's hold on Siam, and a new Siamese leader of magnetic personality, Pra Naret, began rapidly to build up his country's powers of resistance, not only to the Burmese, but also to the Cambodian raids.[1] The Cambodian Chronicle mentions a successful expedition against Siam in 1580, but the evidence of the Siamese chronicles makes this doubtful. Three years later Pra Naret invaded Cambodia, it would seem, and according to the Siamese gained an important success, which some modern writers have construed as indicating the capture of Lovek.[2] There is, however, no evidence of a Siamese capture of the Cambodian capital until 1594, notwithstanding an inscription at An Lok, mentioned by M. Groslier, which talks of the 'fall' of Lovek in 1587. On the other hand, Wood's circumstantial story of Siamese relations with Cambodia at this crucial period has the ring of probability.[3] King Satha, he writes, decided to help Siam against the Burmese, and in 1585 concluded a treaty to this effect with Pra Naret. Under its terms he sent an army under the command of his brother Srisup'anma[4] which in the following year co-operated with the Siamese in defeating a Laotian invasion led by the Burmese governor of Chiengmai. A subsequent quarrel, however, between Pra Naret and the Cambodian prince, broke up the alliance, and when in the early months of 1587 Ayut'ia was again besieged by the Burmese, Satha himself invaded Siam and seized Prachin. The result was that when the Burmese were forced to abandon the siege through lack of supplies, Pra Naret was baulked of a decisive victory over their retreating forces through having to turn and deal with the Cambodians. He pursued them deeply into their own country, capturing Battambang and Pursat, but Lovek he failed to take for the same reason that the Burmese had failed to take Ayut'ia a few months earlier.

During the next few years Burmese pressure was too great for Pra Naret (King Naresuen, as he became in 1590) to attempt to clinch matters with Cambodia, but he awaited only the right moment. King Satha on the other hand began anxiously—but fruitlessly—to seek Spanish and Portuguese help. In 1593, when the Burmese attempts to restore their hold over Siam had been brought to a final halt, three Siamese armies simultaneously invaded Cambodia and, after capturing Siemreap and Bassac in the north and Battambang and Pursat farther south, converged upon Lovek. King Satha fled to Srei Santhor leaving his younger brother Soryopor to defend the capital, which, according

---

[1] *Infra*, pp. 271–2.   [2] *Op. cit.*, p. 19.
[3] *History of Siam*, pp. 133–7.
[4] Wood's version of the name.

to the Siamese accounts, put up a strong resistance, but was ultimately carried by assault, in January 1594 according to Groslier,[1] in the following July according to Wood.[2] The captured city was placed under a Siamese military governor. At Srei Santhor the defeated king was deposed by a relative, Reamea Chung Prei, and with his two elder sons fled to Luang Prabang, where he died in 1596.

With Satha's reign Cambodian history enters upon a much better known period. Two new sources yield useful material, stone inscriptions at the Angkor Wat and Spanish and Portuguese writings. The deliberate destruction of reservoirs and other hydraulic works by the Siamese between 1350 and 1431 had made the Angkor Thom area almost uninhabitable. On the other hand the great temples seem to have remained accessible, and the country to the south and west, which had not depended upon the city's vast hydraulic system, continued to be inhabited and cultivated. And even if there is good reason to disbelieve the stories of a return to Angkor by certain rulers in the fifteenth century, there is equally good reason to think that from time to time in the course of their struggles with Siam Cambodian kings made their headquarters in the Angkor neighbourhood.

Various European accounts[3] mention the 'rediscovery' of a city, obviously Angkor Thom, in the second half of the sixteenth century. The most striking of these, by Diogo do Couto, is in an unpublished chapter of his *Deçadas da Asia* giving a remarkably good description of Angkor itself and its irrigation system.[4] He writes that the city was discovered in 1550 or 1551 by a Cambodian king hunting in the area, who was so attracted by the fertility of the region that he established his court there. This would make Ang Chan the city's discoverer. It is noteworthy that from this time inscriptions begin to reappear there. Groslier suggests, however, that it is improbable that he established his court there. The reoccupation of the old city, he thinks, and the repopulation of the region might possibly have been carried out by Barom Reachea I round about 1570, though this is uncertain. What is certain is that Satha installed his court at or near Angkor and restored the Wat 'before or after 1576'.[5] A stone inscription of July 1577 mentions his restoration of 'Brah Bisnuloka', i.e. the Angkor Wat. Another of 1579 relates how for the glorification of Buddhism he had repaired the great towers of the Wat, built new summits to them, re-

[1] *Op. cit.*, p. 19.   [2] *Op. cit.*, p. 147.
[3] Groslier, *op. cit.*, pp. 21–3.
[4] Discovered by Professor C. R. Boxer and reproduced in a French translation by Groslier in *op. cit.*, pp. 68–74.
[5] Groslier, *op. cit.*, p. 17.

covered them with gold, and consecrated a reliquary to his ancestors and his deceased father. The inscription also commemorates the birth of a son[1] to him, and records the consecration of the child to Buddha at the Wat, 'this great domain . . . of powerful spirits and of the companies of his ancestors'.[2] How long Satha held his court there is unknown. There is evidence that Catholic missionaries at his invitation visited the ruins somewhere between 1583 and 1589. They were responsible for giving the West its earliest information about Angkor. An inscription at the Wat dated 1587, and recording the erection of images of the Buddha and repairs to 'the towers with four faces', by a court dignitary, suggests that the king himself was no longer there. It was the year of the great Siamese invasion which nearly succeeded in capturing Lovek.

[1] Later Barom Reachea II.
[2] Groslier, *loc. cit. sup.*

CHAPTER 6

BURMA AND ARAKAN

(a) The pre-Pagan period

THE earliest historical evidence touching the land of Burma relates to the old overland route between China and the West, which crossed the northern region of the country. The first reference to its use is in 128 B.C., when Chang Ch'ien discovered the products of the Chinese province of Szechwan in Bactria. Steps were taken to develop it, but only in A.D. 69 did China found the prefecture of Yung-ch'ang across the Mekong with its headquarters east of the Salween, some sixty miles from the present Burma frontier. The peoples who submitted were called the Ai-lao, who were said to be under the rule of seventy-seven 'district princes'. They bored their noses and loaded their ears. Shortly after the foundation of the prefecture they revolted. With the suppression of their rebellion there ensued a century of peace, during which the peoples beyond them, called by the Chinese the Tun-jen-i and the Lu-lei, sent embassies. They are thought to have been settled in northern Burma.

In A.D. 97 ambassadors coming from the Tan or Shan in the Roman empire arrived in Yung-ch'ang by the northern land route. They may have come from Tanis, east of the Nile delta. Other travellers between the Roman empire and China used the sea route and made the short overland journey across Tenasserim. Thus in 131–2 Tan envoys on their way to Tongking, then in Chinese hands, are said to have used this route, as also a trade delegation from the Roman empire to China in 166, and the merchant Ch'in Lun in 226.

Burmese Buddhist legends tell of Indian influence coming to Lower Burma by sea. In the *Jatakas* the region is referred to as Suvarnabhumi, the Golden Land. A favourite Burmese story is of the two brothers, Tapusa and Palikat, who are said to have been given eight hairs of his head by Gautama. These they brought by sea to the Golden Land and enshrined under the Shwe Dagon Pagoda, which adorns modern Rangoon. The Mon chronicles contain a legend which tells how Sona and Uttara, two Buddhist monks, were deputed to the Golden Land by the Third Buddhist Synod at Pataliputra in c. 241

140

B.C. So far as historical evidence is concerned, however, there is no trace of the penetration of Indian influence earlier than the fragments of the Pali canon found at Hmawza (Śrikshetra or Old Prome) dating from *c.* A.D. 500.

Ptolemy's *Geographia* shows a coastline roughly approximating to that of Arakan and Burma as far as the Gulf of 'Sabara' (? Martaban). His Argyra fits the situation of Arakan, and he mentions Chrysé as its neighbour. He mentions a race of cannibals who occupy a river mouth thought by scholars to be in the Moulmein region. It may be of some significance that their name corresponds to Vesunga, a port named in the *Jatakas*.

In connection with the conquests of Fan Shih-man, the Great King of Funan, mention has been made in an earlier chapter[1] of the Buddhist kingdom of Lin-yang, which, it has been suggested, may have been situated in central Burma. If so, whence came its Buddhism? Was it from India by the northern land route? Chinese works from the fourth century onwards refer to the wild and troublesome tribes south-west of Yung-ch'ang, and especially the P'u, who tattooed, used bows and arrows, and some of whom were cannibals and went naked. Beyond them some 3,000 li south-west of Yung-ch'ang was a civilized people, the P'iao, who as the Pyu are the earliest inhabitants of Burma of whom local memory survives.

Their capital, Śrikshetra, is mentioned in the seventh century by the Chinese pilgrims Hsuan-tsang and I-tsing. Legends of this people come from the area between Halin, in Shwebo district, and Prome. Inscriptions at both these places are of seventh-century or earlier origin. Urn inscriptions, deciphered by the late Otto Blagden, show a Vikrama dynasty reigning at Prome from at least 673 to 718. Three kings are mentioned:

Suryavikrama, who died in 688 aged 64.
Harivikrama, who died in 695 aged 41.
Sihavikrama, who died in 718 aged 44.

The dates are provisional, since the era is not stated. If, as is thought, it is the 'Burmese Era', which begins in A.D. 638, this may have originated as a Pyu era under this dynasty. Inscriptions have also been found with the name of a Varman dynasty, but where it reigned has not been discovered. The name indicates the possibility of Pallava influence from Conjeveram.

[1] Chap. 2, (b).

Śrikshetra, now Hmawza, the only Pyu site searched with thoroughness, has provided archaeologists with much valuable material. There are traces of a massive city wall, embracing an area larger than that of Pagan or Mandalay, and with impressive internal and external moats. The importance of the city is shown by the fact that Mon inscriptions as late as Kyanzittha's reign (1084-1112) still referred to it as the capital. Close to it are three large Buddhist stupas, one 150 feet high. It has also a number of small vaulted chapels, which are prototypes of the later Pagan temples. There are large stone sculptures in relief in the Gupta style, small images in the round, silver coins, probably symbolical, with curious designs of the sun, moon and stars, and terra-cotta votive plaques with Sanskrit legends in Nagari characters.

The religious remains are mixed and syncretist. There are numerous stone sculptures of Vishnu, bronze statuettes of Avalokitesvara and other Mahayanist Bodhisattvas, besides statuary and Pali inscriptions showing that Hinayana Buddhism flourished there from an early date. The dead were burnt and their ashes stored in urns within pagoda precincts, or in extensive cemeteries on brick platforms covered with earth. Mention has been made earlier of the Candra dynasty of Vaisali, the first Arakanese rulers to be attested by epigraphy. The same source shows a second dynasty, founded in the eighth century by Śri Dharmavijaya, whose grandson is said to have married a daughter of a Pyu King of Śrikshetra.

In the eighth and ninth centuries the T'ai state of Nanchao dominated Upper, and much of Lower, Burma. Kolofeng, its ruler, (748-79) built a fortress to control the upper Irrawaddy and enlisted local tribesmen in his armies. He had relations with the Pyu, whom he may have subdued, since Pyu soldiers served with the Nanchao force which captured Hanoi in 863. His campaigns opened the old road to India across Upper Burma. One of the routes passed through the Pyu capital—presumably this was Halin—whence it proceeded up the Chindwin to the borders of Manipur. There are signs that northern Burma in this period saw much development. Contemporary writers refer to the production of gold, amber, salt, horses, long-horned cattle, elephants for ploughing, and much else.

I-mou-hsün, Kolofeng's grandson and successor, sent a present of Pyu musicians to the T'ang Court in 800. In 801-2 a Pyu king sent a formal embassy, accompanied by thirty-five musicians, to China via Nanchao. Chinese interest in the Pyu was stimulated, and the *T'ang History* contains a graphic account of the Pyu capital. The Chinese also state that in 832 'Man rebels' (?Nanchao) plundered the Pyu capital and deported 3,000 captives to Yunnanfu.

Was this the end of the Pyu kingdom? It is the last we hear of it. Were the Pyu the advance-guard of the Burmese? Their language belongs to the Tibeto-Burman group. The Pyu face of the Myazedi inscription of 1113 shows that speakers of the language still existed then. As a people they have completely disappeared. Presumably they merged with the Burmese when the latter became the dominant people in Burma.

The Pyu claimed suzerainty over eighteen subject states, mainly in Lower Burma. One of them, Mi-chen, whose king secured recognition from China in 805, was in 835 destroyed by Nanchao. Among them also were the K'un-lun states near a port, Mo-ti-po, from which Palembang and Java could be reached. These were Mon states. The Mons in Burma were mainly to the eastward of the Irrawaddy, and their settlements spread as far south as Tavoy. The basin of the Menam Chao P'ya was, however, their political and cultural centre. There their Buddhist kingdom of Dvaravati flourished from the sixth century onwards. Its earliest known capital was at Nakorn Pat'om, thirty miles west of modern Bangkok. Here a Mon inscription of c. 600 has been discovered; it is the earliest so far known to archaeologists. Later Lopburi, away to the north, was to be its capital; eighth-century Mon inscriptions have been found there. A further Mon state centred around Haripunjaya in the Meping valley, and was said to have been founded by a queen of Lopburi. The Mons had a high culture; they were pioneers in the cultivation of rice and beans in Burma, and were the creators of the irrigation system at Kyaukse, in the dry zone of central Burma, which made it of vital strategic importance again and again in Burmese history.

The Arab geographers refer to Lower Burma by the name Ramañña-desa, 'the Mon country'. The word is an adaptation of the old Mon word *Rmen* from which the modern 'Mon' derives. The Burmese called them Talaings, a word which some have derived from Telingana, signifying south-east India, whence came their Hindu-Buddhist culture. Certainly the script of the early Mon inscriptions resembles Pallava script, but nothing is known for certain of the etymology of the word.

The Mons had not only to sustain the attacks of the Nanchao invaders after the destruction of the Pyu capital, but later in the ninth century to lose control over the Kyaukse area to the incoming Burmans. The traditional date of the foundation of the Mon capital Hamsavati, now Pegu, is 825. Pagan, the Burmese capital, may possibly have been founded in 849, the traditional date of the construction of its walls by

Pyinpya. It is said to have been formed by the union of nineteen villages. If the date is correct, the depopulation of the Pyu capital in the north may have caused a movement of refugees downstream which led to the formation of a new centre at Pagan. The Burmese chronicles push its foundation back to the second century A.D., but there are insuperable difficulties in the way of accepting this hypothesis.

Between 849 and the foundation of the Pagan kingship in 1044 by Anawrahta there is almost a complete blank so far as reliable historical sources are concerned. This is all the more tantalizing, since it was during this period that the main body of the Burmese people entered Burma and settled down. G. H. Luce has attempted to trace their history before they began, in the middle of the ninth century, to come down from the hills in what are now the Northern Shan States and penetrate into the Kyaukse district south of modern Mandalay. The earliest known home of the Tibeto-Burman-speaking peoples was somewhere between the Gobi Desert and north-east Tibet, possibly Kansu. The earliest Chinese written records mention the Ch'iang, who were tribes of shepherds and goatherds to the west of the Chinese. The ancestors of the Burmese, Luce thinks, were to be found among the Ch'iang. The Chinese constantly raided them to obtain victims for human sacrifice. From these raids the Ch'iang took refuge in north-east Tibet. In the first millennium B.C. the Chinese rulers of T'sin pursued them, and many fled southwards.

The Burmese were on the eastern edge of the migration, and some centuries later with the rise of Nanchao they came under its dominance. From their overlords they learnt the arts of war, the use of the bow, horsemanship, the terracing of hill slopes for cultivation, wet rice cultivation on the plains, and much else. The desire for independence, which has been such a strong feature of their mentality throughout history, led them to escape from Nanchao, and they made for the hot arid plains of Upper Burma.

They entered Burma through the region between the N'mai Hka and the Salween, and it was shortly after the destruction of the Pyu kingdom in 832 by Nanchao that they are found in the 'Eleven Villages' of Myittha in the Kyaukse district. There they took over an already existing irrigation system, which, according to Luce, must have been originally developed by the Mons. By their sudden movement down from the hills they drove a wedge into the Mons, leaving some in the north separated from the main body in the south.

They fanned out to cross the Irrawaddy. Some went beyond it to the Pondaung range, the Chin hills and the Akyab region of Arakan.

Others went to found a second home in Minbu district west of the
Irrawaddy, where in the Salin-Sagu region they entered another
irrigated system, older than that of Kyauksè, and presumably the
work of Sgaw Karens and Palaungs. Further migrations took them
down the Irrawaddy to the Taungdwingyi rice-lands and Prome, up
the Chindwin to a number of places whose names have not been
identified, and up the Mu valley northwards to Shwebo, Tabayin and
Myedu, where they mixed with other tribes.

According to Luce's most recent pronouncement on the subject,[1] the
'Mranma', as they called themselves, formed their first kingdom by a
loose federation of the tribes settled in the Kyaukse and Minbu areas.
They called it *Tambadipa*, 'the copper country', a name which continued to be incorporated in the royal title until the end of the Burmese
monarchy in 1885. The foundation of the Pagan kingship imposed a
unified command over Tambadipa, and under the leadership of Anawrahta (1044–77) and Kyanzittha (1084–1113) the original kingdom,
stretching for about a hundred miles down the Irrawaddy, became an
empire over a thousand miles from north to south, i.e. from north of
Bhamo to below the Isthmus of Kra, with some control across the Salween to the east, and contacts with Arakan and East Bengal on the west.
The Burmese chronicles, which place the foundation of Pagan in A.D.
108, give a list of forty kings reigning there before the accession of
Anawrahta, but these are unknown to history. Before his time only one
Burmese monarch is mentioned in the inscriptions. He is Saw Rahan,
an eleventh-century ruler who built a Buddhist shrine on Mount Turan,
eight miles from Pagan. The earliest historical reference to the city
itself is in a Cham inscription dating from some time before 1050. The
earliest mention of the 'Mranma' is in a Mon inscription of 1102, in
which they are called the 'Mirma'. Mien, the name by which the
Chinese knew them and their country, only appears in 1273, when the
Mongols had started the conquest of the kingdom of Pagan.

(b) The empire of Pagan, 1044–1287

It was Anawrahta (1044–77) who first united Burma politically and
founded the greatness of Pagan. He is, however, rather a majestic
legendary figure than a historical personage. Moreover, not a single
authentic inscription dates from his reign, save for votive tablets
briefly inscribed. His achievements were real enough and left a
permanent impress upon his country and people. He united under

---

[1] 'The Career of Htilaing Min (Kyanzittha)', JRAS (1966), parts 1 & 2, p. 54.

THE SORABA GATE IN OLD PAGAN

his sway most of what may be termed Burma proper, together with northern Arakan and Lower Burma, the Mon country. Eastwards he made expeditions into the Shan country, but not with the intention of adding it to his kingdom, since he built a line of forty-three outposts along the eastern foothills to restrain the Shans from attempting to push into the plains. The Siamese chronicles assert that he attacked Cambodia and ruled over most of what is now Siam, obtaining the Hinayana Buddhism, which he established as the official religion of Pagan, from Nakorn Pat'om. But there would seem to be no historical basis for such assumptions.

His most important achievement was the conquest of the Mon kingdom of Thaton. Tradition asserts that he took a Mon monk, Shin Arahan, into his service and charged him with the task of converting the Burmese to Hinayana Buddhism. This entailed a struggle with a priesthood known as the Ari, who dominated Upper Burma. They were Mahayanist and practised Tantric and other erotic rites. To obtain copies of the Pali canon, the Tripitaka, for the proper instruction of the people, he conquered Thaton, which possessed thirty complete sets, deported to Pagan its king, Makuta, and its entire population of 30,000 souls. Such is the story told by the nineteenth century Burmese chronicle, the *Hmannan Yazawin*. According to Gordon Luce,[1] however, Anawrahta's campaign must be seen against the background of the westward expansion of Angkor. The conquest of Lopburi by Suryavarman I (*supra* p. 105) had caused a great influx of Mon refugees into the states of Pegu and Thaton. These in their turn were then invaded by the Khmers, whereupon Anawrahta intervened, allied with Pegu and conquered Thaton. Thus was the first Union of Burma formed by a champion of Buddhism against invaders whose king was identified with Śiva.

The Khmer invasion must have been launched before 1050, the date of Suryavarman's death. Anawrahta was then extending his power southwards. He occupied the old Pyu capital of Sri Ksetra and pushed on to the moated city of Khabin, then the capital of the coastal region. He may have received a call for help from Pegu while building the Maung Di[2] pagoda there. Both the Burmese and the Mon chronicles mention Kyanzittha as the victorious Burmese leader. The *Glass Palace Chronicle* tells with gusto the story of the Khmer rout. Afterwards many of them settled at a place west of the mouth of the Rangoon River that came to be known as 'Cambodia Bazaar'.

Gordon Luce questions further items in the traditional story told by the chroniclers. The influence of Shin Arahan, he demonstrates,[3] was probably, as was claimed, the chief agent in the changeover of the Pagan court from Tantric Mahayanism to Theravada Buddhism, but the real change took place in Kyanzittha's reign rather than Anawrahta's. The evidence shows, he says, that Shin Arahan was Kyanzittha's 'right-hand man', not Anawrahta's. And the capture of Thaton in 1057 cannot have been undertaken because King Makuta rejected Anawrahta's demand for copies of the Tripitaka, for there were none to be had in Thaton, only a Jataka commentary. Moreover Anawrahta, though a champion of Buddhism, was a Mahayanist rather than a Theravadin. Thus while the capture of the place and Makuta's deportation to Pagan are historical facts, the reason for the campaign is not clear, save in terms of the king's main political objects, namely the opening of a door to the sea and the sealing off of his kingdom's frontiers from external invasion.

What the chronicles do not say is that Anawrahta and his son, Sawlu,

---

[1] G. H. Luce, 'Mons of the Pagan Dynasty' in JBRS, XXXVI, Part I, August 1953, pp. 1–19.

[2] Twelve miles east of modern Rangoon.   [3] JRAS, *loc. cit. supra*, p. 57.

went on to conquer territories far to the south of Thaton. This is confirmed by inscriptions found at Mergui, by a dedication on the part of Sawlu in Maunglaw district, and by votive tablets relating to Kyanzittha at Mokti pagoda south of Tavoy. It may be, Luce suggests, that King Parakramabahu's invasion of Burma a century later in 1165 was undertaken partly in order to oust the Burmans from the Isthmus of Kra.

The defeated conquered their conquerors: Mon culture became supreme at the court of Pagan. Pali became its sacred language and the Mon alphabet was ultimately adopted for the literary expression of the Burmese language. King Makuta went into honourable confinement at Myinkaba just south of Pagan, building there the Nanpaya, an exquisite example of Mon architecture. The Buddhism that was brought from Thaton, however, was by no means the pure milk of the Theravada gospel. The evidence of epigraphy and archaeology shows clearly that Pagan Buddhism, in Luce's words, 'was mixed up with Mahayanism, and towards the end of the dynasty at least with Tantrism. It rested doubtless on a deep bed of Naga and Nat worship.' And in King Makuta's throne-room at the Nanpaya the bas-reliefs of Hindu deities show how closely the two religions were interwoven. Furthermore, in spite of the tradition that Buddhaghosa brought Pali Buddhism to Thaton in 403 from Ceylon, the evidence goes to show that the real influence upon Thaton's Buddhism was not Ceylon but Conjeveram, which had become a famous centre in the fifth century under the great commentator Dhammapala.

The contact with Ceylon, which had such momentous consequences for Buddhism in Burma, is mentioned in both the Burmese and the Sinhalese chronicles. It arose out of Vijaya Bahu I's struggle to drive out the Cholas. At a critical moment shortly before 1067, when he was short of funds to pay his troops, he sent an urgent appeal to Anawrahta, who responded by sending him 'many ships' laden with merchandise. The Sinhalese king ultimately recovered both his capitals and crushed the invaders. When, however, in 1073-4 he came to celebrate his *abhiseka* (coronation), there was no chapter of monks in his country able to confer valid ordination, after fifty years of Chola (i.e. Hindu) rule. Again he turned to Anawrahta, who sent him 'learned and virtuous theras' to assist in the purification of the Buddhist Order. They went to work with their Sinhalese colleagues in discovering and copying the Pali Tripitaka. Copies were presented to the Burmese delegation, and in due course—during the reign of Sawlu (1077-84), Luce thinks—the manuscripts reached Pagan and their gist was speedily translated. The impact of the new study can be seen today on the walls of the Pahtothamya temple, which Luce ascribes to Sawlu's reign.[1] They contain hundreds of paintings, with Mon glosses, illustrating the Pali scriptures. Here we have the earliest evidence in Burma of the great access of Tripitaka knowledge that was in time to bring her fully into the Theravada fold. Theravada Buddhism was to become the most powerful influence in her national life.

The splendid temples of Pagan were not built until after Anawrahta's reign. He built only solid pagodas. The Shwezigon Pagoda was ascribed to him by tradition, and he is said to have enshrined beneath it a miraculously produced replica of the Kandy Tooth presented to him by the grateful Vijaya Bahu I. Archaeologists today, however, attribute it to the reign of Kyanzittha. It is significant that one of its notable features is a set of shrines to the Thirty-seven Nats. Nat-worship, Burma's own form of animism, so important an ingredient in the basic culture of all South-East Asia, continued to hold sway with scarcely abated force over men's minds, from the highest downwards. The Pali scriptures, setting forth the Buddhist ethic, came ultimately to exert sufficient moral force to liberate them from the worst of their animistic practices. But Buddhism had to come to terms with the old religion, and in so doing became highly syncretistic. Nat-worship continued to exist in two forms: one closely interwoven with Buddhism, and the other having no connection with it, and frowned on by the monkhood.

Kyanzittha served Anawrahta as a general many years; but they quarrelled and the quarrel was never made up. Kyanzittha was expelled from Pagan and went to live on his appanage, Htilaing in Kyaukse district. There he had been brought up and, though a Burman, had come to love the Mons and admire their culture. Luce rejects the story that he was a son of Anawrahta, although this was vouched for by two Ava inscriptions some three hundred years later, and the other stories of his birth in the *Glass Palace Chronicle*. His accession to the throne came through Sawlu's failure to crush a rebellion led by the governor of Pegu, who captured the king and murdered him. Kyanzittha allied with the family of Makuta, the ex-king of Thaton, who were also in revolt, and with their aid crushed the main rebellion. The price of Mon support, however, was the marriage of Kyanzittha's daughter to Makuta's grandson with the promise that their son should inherit the kingdom after his death. The Soraba Gate at Pagan had been damaged during the siege of the city by the rebels. It is thought that one of Kyanzittha's first acts on becoming king was to repair it.

[1] Alexander Griswold in *Burma, Korea, Tibet* (Art of the World), Methuen, 1964, p. 28, attributes it to Kyanzittha's reign.

Kyanzittha raised the Burmese kingship to a higher level, celebrating a splendid coronation in 1086 with Brahmanical ritual, building a grander palace, and erecting a series of inscriptions, mostly in the Mon language, which rank as literature. In them he claims that a prophecy of the Buddha foretold that in the year of Gautama's entry into Nirvana he (Kyanzittha) would found Sri Ksetra, that he would succeed to the throne of Pagan in 1084, and that he would one day attain to Buddhahood. One wonders if this was the first time such messianic claims had been made in Burma. They were an important feature of the politico-religious propaganda associated with the last Burmese dynasty in the eighteenth and nineteenth centuries. They still are not without their influence in certain Burmese circles today.

Kyanzittha devoted his life to the ideal of establishing a real partnership between the Burman and Mon peoples. His enthusiasm for Mon culture was intense. With him Pagan's great age of temple-building began. All his temples are Mon in style. The lovely Ananda temple was his masterpiece. The story goes that he entertained eight monks who had fled from persecution in India, and whose description of the cave temple of Ananta in the Udayagiri hills of Orissa kindled in him the desire to build one in imitation. Compared with its exterior loveliness of form and proportion, its dim interior is at first somewhat disappointing. The building is a solid mass pierced by lofty vaulted corridors leading to four central chambers, in each of which stands a gigantic statue of the Buddha with its head and shoulders lit by natural light from outside in such a way as to produce a dazzling effect as the spectator emerges from the dim corridor. Before the western image are two life-size kneeling statues of Kyanzittha and Shin Arahan. Luce has drawn attention to the temple's educational function.[1] 'Each of the four large halls', he writes, 'contained the same series of sixteen key sculptures so that monks or guides could lecture to four large audiences simultaneously. Then, entering the outer corridor, they could follow the famous series of 80 stone reliefs, illustrating step by step the progress of Gotama up to the Enlightenment. . . . The temple contains altogether over 1600 stone sculptures and 1400 terracottas.'

But, he claims, the king's main contribution to his country's history was the collection and purification of the Tripitaka. The orthodox Pali texts of the Sinhalese Mahavihara monastery were reaching Pagan from 1075 onwards. Kyanzittha built a stone library for their study. His son Rajakumar, who would have succeeded him but for his treaty with the Thaton royal family, worked there with a band of monkly

[1] 'The Career of Htilaing Min (Kyanzittha)', p. 66.

scholars, and the progress of their studies is illustrated in the Pagan temples. Rajakumar's own temple, the Kubyaukgyi, which was being built when Kyanzittha died, is dubbed by Luce 'an encyclopaedia of human history as known to the Theravadin'.[1] He was the author of the famous inscription which has been called the Rosetta Stone of Burma, because the same text appears on its four faces in Pyu, Mon, Burmese and Pali respectively. It has been associated by archaeologists with the Myazedi Pagoda, south of Pegu. It tells the story of the reign, and records the prince's presentation of a gold image of the Buddha to his father on his deathbed as a token of his acceptance of the succession of his half-Mon nephew. The discovery of this epigraph in 1911 provided a key not only to the Pyu language but also to the dates of the early kings of Pagan.

Kyanzittha sent missions to China in 1103 and 1106. They were a new departure in Burmese policy. The suggestion has been made that they represented an attempt to facilitate overland trade with the Tali kingdom, the successor of old Nanchao, subdued by China in the ninth century. Such evidence as there is shows that Tali was raiding northern Burma, and it looks as if Kyanzittha's missions to the Northern Sung at their capital, K'ai-feng, aimed at enlisting imperial support to restrain their unruly vassal. But the Sung were too busy with northern invaders to take action on the Yunnan frontier. Burma had to deal with the matter alone. An early Ava inscription, Luce says,[2] mentions an invasion from the China side in the year 1111, and claims that Kyanzittha's grandson, and heir, was victorious over it.

There has been much speculation about the visit of a Chola prince to Kyanzittha. The king is said to have converted him to Buddhism and to have given him a daughter in marriage. The Cholas from the Coromandel Coast had raided Srivijaya in 1025, subdued Kedah in 1068–9, were developing extensive trading contacts with South-East Asia and sending missions to China. But the inscription mentioning the visit is tantalizingly fragmentary; and although there is further evidence of Kyanzittha's relations with this enterprising Tamil people, it is too vague even for the exercise of hopeful guesswork. The suggestion has been made that the prince was the ruler of a Tamil colony in the Delta region of Lower Burma; but it has yet to be shown that there ever was such a colony in Burma. Is it another example of the Indian colonization myth? There could well have been a Chola trading 'colony' at a Delta port.

Anawrahta's conquest of the Mons had disastrous consequences for

[1] *Ibid.*, p. 65.   [2] *Ibid.*, p. 63.

that people. It rang up the curtain on the tragedy of Burmese relations with them that by the nineteenth century had seen the final failure of their struggles to maintain their political and cultural identity and almost —but not quite—their elimination as a people. Kyanzittha's policy of developing a partnership between the two peoples failed: Burmese national sentiment was against granting equality to the Mons. During the long reign of his grandson, the half-Mon Alaungsithu (1113–65) there was a sharp decline in Mon cultural influence at Pagan. It was to suffer total eclipse during the following period.

The reign of Alaungsithu shows two distinct pictures in striking contrast. One, much played up by the chronicles, is that of the ideal Buddhist king, travelling far and wide throughout his dominions engaged upon building works of Buddhist merit, and composing inscriptions reflecting a deep sense of other-worldliness expressed in poetry unsurpassed in the literature of his country. His finest building, the Thatpinnyu temple, was consecrated in 1144. Its style resembles closely that of the Ananda, but the main mass rises much higher before the tapering process begins. The spirit which inspired Alaungsithu in his pious works reaches its perfect expression in his Pali prayer inscribed at the Shwegu Pagoda. *Mutatis mutandis*, it suggests the aspiration of the mediaeval saint in Christendom. Here is a short passage in Luce's glowing English:

> But I would build a causeway sheer athwart
> The river of Samsara, and all folk would speed
> Across, until they reach the Blessed City.
> I myself would cross
> And drag the drowning over . . .
> Ay, myself tamed, I would tame the wilful;
> Comforted, comfort the timid;
> Wakened, wake the asleep;
> Cool, cool the burning;
> Freed, set free the bound.
> Tranquil and led by the good doctrines
> I would hatred calm.[1]

The other picture is of revolts and disorder. The king's early years were spent quelling revolts in Tenasserim and northern Arakan. An inscription at Buddhagaya commemorates the repairs executed there at Alaungsithu's request by a ruler of Arakan in token of gratitude for

[1] Translation by G. H. Luce and Pe Maung Tin in *Burma Research Society* Fiftieth Anniversary Publications, no. 2 (Rangoon, 1960), pp. 382–4.

ANANDA TEMPLE, PAGAN

help in driving out a usurper. The chronicles say that he was murdered by his son Narathu, but this is not confirmed by the inscriptions. The probable date of his death is 1165.

Narathu, known in the inscriptions as Imtaw Syan, 'Lord of the Royal House', has the nickname in popular history of Kalagya, 'the king killed by Indians'. The Indians, however, seem to have been Sinhalese, if the *Chulavamsa* account of what happened is to be trusted. According to it the Burmese king interfered with Ceylon's trade with Cambodia via the Malay Peninsula, seized a Sinhalese princess on her way to Cambodia, and placed an embargo upon the Burmese elephant trade with Ceylon. King Parakkama Bahu I accordingly sent an armada which devastated the Bassein area, while a Sinhalese force made its way up the Irrawaddy, took the city of Pagan by surprise and killed the king. Burmese sources make no mention of this incursion, but Dr Than Tun, a modern Burmese scholar who has made Pagan his special study, is inclined to accept it.[1] That was in 1165, it was followed by an interregnum of nine years at Pagan until the accession of Narapatisithu in 1174. This was a dividing-line in Burmese history. From a period in which Mon is the chief language of the inscriptions we pass to one in which Burmese predominates. For the remainder of the Pagan period Mon as a literary expression disappears completely. The same change shows itself also in architectural style: the great temples of the new period, the Sulamani, Htilominlo and Gawdawpalin, are built in a distinctive Burmese style with large doorways to let in the light, brighter interior colours and an exterior design which aims at conveying a sense of height. Even more important in the long run was the effect upon Burmese Buddhism of the contacts with Ceylon stimulated by this encounter. A religious movement began in Burma which was to substitute the Sinhalese form of Theravada teachings for the Conjeveram form brought from Thaton in Anawrahta's reign.

The story, as given in the *Hmannan Yazawin* ('Glass Palace Chronicle'), tells how during the disorders of Narathu's reign Shin Arahan's successor, the primate Panthagu, retired to Ceylon. After Narapatisithu's accession he returned, but soon died. His successor, a Mon monk named Uttarajiva, followed his example in 1180 by going there, and on his return received the title of 'First Pilgrim of Ceylon'. One of his monks, Chapata, also a Mon, remained behind in Ceylon for ten years. On his return in 1190 he became the 'Second Pilgrim of Ceylon'. He brought with him four foreign monks, one of whom,

[1] Than Tun, 'History of Burma down to the end of the thirteenth century' in *New Burma Weekly*, 29 Nov. 1958, pp. 83-4.

Tamalinda, must have been, according to Cœdès, a son of Jayavarman VII of Angkor.

At Nyaung-u they formed a chapter for ordination according to Mahavihara principles and built a pagoda of Sinhalese pattern. This caused a schism in Burmese Buddhism between those who followed the new leaders and those who remained loyal to the Thaton form. The king gave his support to the reformers, but the Former Order, as the Thaton school was called, continued to exist for another two centuries. The reformers set about their task with missionary ardour. Large numbers of monks went to Ceylon for ordination, and Buddhism became for the first time in the Indo-Chinese peninsula a truly popular movement, not something imposed by the Court. As such it spread far and wide beyond the confines of Burma, embracing the T'ai peoples, the Laos states and Cambodia. The results were of permanent importance; for while during the subsequent period Islam became the religion of the peoples of Malaya and Indonesia, it made no headway in the Buddhist countries. The various cults of Śaivism, Vaiśnavism, Sanskrit Hinayana and Mahayana Buddhism were Court religions, whose main function was the deification of kings and ruling classes. They made no real impression upon the mass of the people. States, where they were established, were easily won over to Islam.

Narapatisithu's reign was the longest in the Pagan period. In 1211 he was succeeded by his son Natonmya (wrongly named Nantaungmya in the chronicles),[1] popularly known as Htilominlo, 'he whom the royal umbrella designated as king', from a legend that the royal umbrella had miraculously indicated him as the rightful claimant to the throne. During his reign were built the last two temples in the grand style, the Mahabodi, an imitation of the famous temple at Buddhagaya, and the Htilominlo. The chronicles show Natonmya devoting his time so fully to pious works that he left the management of the realm to his four half-brothers, who ruled jointly, meeting together at a building called the Hlutdaw, 'Place of Release'. This has been claimed as the origin of the Hlutdaw of modern times, the Burmese Supreme Royal Council, composed of the four highest ministers of state, the Wungyis. Dr. Than Tun, however, has disposed of this myth. Epigraphic evidence, he says, shows that Natonmya had five ministers of state, none of whom was his half-brother; and there is no mention of the Hlutdaw in the inscriptions.

The inscriptions show that in 1231(?) Natonmya was succeeded by his son Naratheinhka who was dethroned by his younger brother Kyazwa

[1] Than Tun, op. cit., in New Burma Weekly, 3 Jan. 1959, pp. 23–5.

in 1235.[1] Kyazwa was the ablest of the later Pagan monarchs, and ruled with vigour. A long edict, issued by him in 1249, is extant; it describes in gruesome detail the various punishments to be inflicted for various types of crime, and seems to indicate that he made a great effort to stamp out dacoity, which always became prevalent when the central government was weak. He lost a struggle with the Buddhist church over lands which he had confiscated because he was worried about the vast amount of property dedicated to the upkeep of monasteries and temples. His reign is notable for a Buddhist mission which went to study in Ceylon and on its return instituted a further purification movement. The austere puritanism of Ceylon's Buddhism appealed powerfully to the reformers in Burma's monastic order, but the hold of traditional ideas and practices upon the great mass of both clergy and people was so strong that they must have made very slow headway.

When the Pagan kingdom was founded, one of Anawrahta's campaigns aimed at extending Burmese control northwards. But although he occupied Tagaung, the capital of the Kadu people then supreme in northern Burma, he failed to hold it. Later kings were more successful, and in 1196 Narapatisithu claimed that his dominions included not only Tagaung, but stretched also as far as Ngasaunggyan further north. In 1236 Kaungzin is mentioned as the administrative headquarters of the Burmese in that area. Dr. Than Tun places it just opposite to Bhamo on the Irrawaddy, with the Ngasaunggyan fort four miles to the north guarding the frontier. This pressure northwards was to have disastrous results for Burma in the reign of Narathihapate (1256–87). A brutal despot who showed no zeal for religion, he built the Mingalazedi Pagoda and commemorated its dedication by a hyperbolic inscription, in which he described himself as the 'supreme commander of a vast army of 36 million soldiers, the swallower of 300 dishes of curry daily'. He boasted also of possessing 3,000 concubines. His pagoda, which took six years to build, inspired the Burmese proverb: 'The pagoda is finished and the great country ruined.' The Burmese chronicles refer to him as the Tarokpyemin, 'the king who ran away from the Chinese'.

During his reign the Mongol conquest of China was completed by Kublai Khan. When the conqueror had established himself at Peking he sent out missions to demand tokens of submission from all the states recorded in the imperial archives as tributaries of the Middle Kingdom. In 1271 his viceroy in Yunnan was instructed to send

---

[1] See tables on p. 917.

envoys to Pagan to request the payment of tribute. Narathihapate proudly refused to receive them. Two years later the demand was renewed by an imperial envoy, who was the bearer of a letter from Kublai Khan himself. This time the rash king seized the ambassador and his retinue and summarily executed them.

Kublai, with many irons in the fire, had to postpone action, and Narathihapate carried his defiance further by attacking the little state of Kaungai on the Taping river because its chief had submitted to China. Thereupon Kublai ordered the local authorities to punish the Burmese, and the Governor of Tali sent a Tartar force, which defeated them at the battle of Ngasaunggyan and drove them back into their own country (1277). The battle was made famous by the graphic account of it written by the Venetian traveller Marco Polo from eye-witness stories.

A second Tartar force under Nasr-uddin, the Viceroy of Yunnan, advanced into the Bhamo district, and after destroying some Burmese stockades retired homewards because of the excessive heat. The Burmese thereupon recovered their self-confidence and renewed their raids on the Yunnan frontier. In 1283, therefore, the Tartars invaded again by the same route, defeated the Burmese at Kaungsin, and planted garrisons in the upper Irrawaddy valley. Narathihapate, believing that his capital was about to be attacked, abandoned it in panic and fled to Bassein in the delta region.

This precipitate act sealed the fate of his kingdom. The central authority vanished, northern Arakan proclaimed its independence, and the Mons of the south rose in rebellion under a leader Tarabya, assisted by a Shan adventurer, Wareru, who is said to have absconded from Sukhot'ai. Too late Narathihapate sent his submission to Yunnan and attempted to return to his capital. In 1287 on his way northwards he was murdered by one of his sons, who was holding Prome.

At about the same time Prince Ye-su Timur, Kublai's grandson, fought his way down the Irrawaddy to occupy Pagan, whence he sent out detachments to enforce the submission of the provinces. A Tartar occupation of the kingdom was not at first envisaged. The campaign had been a costly one, and the original plan was to organize northern and central Burma into two provinces of the Tartar empire and permit a member of the royal family to return to Pagan and rule over central Burma. When, therefore, after a bloodbath of the royal princes in the south, the sole survivor, Kyawswa, returned to Pagan, he was accorded official recognition. So for a few years Pagan was a provincial capital. Its very existence, however, was threatened by three Shan chiefs who had made themselves masters of the vital Kyauksè region, from which it drew all its supplies of rice. In 1299 they murdered Kyawswa and burnt his city.

(c) From the Mongol conquest of Pagan (1287) to the Shan sack of Ava (1527)

The Mongol invasions of Burma gave the Shans the opportunity to play a dominant role in that unhappy country. This proved to be more than the Mongols had bargained for. They had begun to organize northern and central Burma into two provinces. In 1283, when they had taken Tagaung, they had made it the centre of a new province of Chieng-mien. Similarly, in 1287, when Pagan fell, they set about organizing central Burma into a province named Mienchung. These arrangements were upset by the Shans.

The story of Shan penetration into Upper Burma has long been obscure, but recently Gordon Luce has thrown much light upon the subject from his researches into Old Tai inscriptions in northern Siam, east Burma and Laos, and information contained in the *Yuan-shih* and the *Ming-shih*. We now have a much clearer outline of the situation when Pagan fell.[1] The *Yuan History* applies the name *Pai-i* to the North and North-West Shans, and places them in 1278 on the Sino-Burmese frontier between the Irrawaddy and the Salween. It was the Mongol conquest of Yunnan which had caused them to cluster there, but Pagan's power and prestige in northern Burma had prevented them from making any further move westward. When in 1271 the Yunnan viceroy had demanded the submission of Pagan, the initial suggestion had come to him from a Pai-i chieftain. The Mongol victory at Kaung-zin in December 1283 'opened the floodgates', as Luce puts it. The Shans descended from the hills to cover both banks of the Irrawaddy, and also drove the Chins out of the Chindwin valley into the western hills. During the Mongol invasions the 'Three Shan Brothers', as they are called in the Burmese chronicles, made themselves masters of three principalities in the Kyauksè area. Athinkaya, the eldest, became Chief of Myinsaing; Yazathinkyan, the second, Chief of Mekkaya; and Thihathu, the youngest, Chief of Pinle. King Kyawswa, on returning to Pagan as the vassal of the Mongols, confirmed them in the possession of these principalities. So say the chronicles. In other sources they make their first appearance in February 1289, when they dedicated a pagoda in their area.

[1] G. H. Luce, 'The Early Syam in Burma's History', JSS, XLVI, 2 Nov. 1958.

Ten years later the province of Mien-chung disappears. An inscription set up by Athinkaya in 1293 claims that he and his brothers, having defeated the *Taruk* (i.e. Mongol) army, now rule the whole of Burma. Luce suggests that they tried to rule through Kyawswa, but his subservience to the Mongols became obnoxious to them. In 1297 he sent his eldest son to Peking, and the emperor gave the king official recognition and conferred decorations on the crown prince and the Shan Brothers. They, however, refused to accept their decorations. During March/April 1298 rebellion flared up and Pagan was besieged, but the Buddhist monks persuaded the combatants to make peace. A couple of months later, however, the Shan Brothers seized Pagan, imprisoned the king and his two sons for submitting to China, and placed upon the throne Sawhnit, a bastard son of the king. The new king sent reports of the affair calculated to deceive the Chinese at Tagaung and the Viceroy of Yunnan, and in 1299 the Brothers allowed the captive crown prince to head another embassy to Peking, presumably to present their version of the matter to the emperor. On his return he, his father and his captive brother were then callously done to death.

Another son of Kyawzwa, however, escaped to Yunnan, and the story he had to tell caused the imperial commissary to espouse his cause. Thus came about the last Mongol invasion, sent to punish the Shan Brothers. But the strength of the resistance, both Burmese and Shan, to the Mongols was underestimated, and the expeditionary force was too small for its task. It began the siege of Myinzaing in January 1301. But the defenders beat off all attacks, and after the failure of a grand assault on 28 February negotiations opened. The Burmese account asserts that the Mongol commander accepted a heavy bribe to lead his forces home. The retreat began early in April. The Mongols had to fight their way out and suffered severe casualties. The Yunnan authorities executed the commander and his chief-of-staff. To soften the blow the Shan Brothers sent envoys to Peking with tribute. It was accepted, and during the next few years five more tribute missions from the Shan Brothers are recorded, as well as one Mongol mission to 'Mien' in 1308. In April 1303 the emperor formally abolished the Chieng-mien province.

The repulse of the Mongols was a victory for the Shans, and they now carried all before them. Myinsaing, however, was too far away from the Irrawaddy to become the capital of an Upper Burma kingdom. Pagan also was no longer suitable. Shorn of its Mon provinces the kingdom lay almost entirely in the dry zone. Hence it had become necessary to remove its capital to some place near the junction of the

Myitnge with the Irrawaddy, whence the paddy traffic from the Kyauksè ricelands could be controlled. Ava, the obvious place, was for some reason declared unpropitious by the Brahmans. Finally in 1312 Thihathura, the sole survivor of the Shan brothers, fixed his capital at Pinya close by. Later inscriptions attribute the discomfiture of the Mongols to him and refer to him as the 'Tarok Kan Mingyi', 'the king who defeated the Chinese'. In 1315 one of his sons, after a family quarrel, crossed the river and founded another principality at Sagaing.

The Mongol abandonment of Upper Burma and the weakening of their power in Yunnan opened the way for a great increase in Shan activity in the far north of Burma, and for the foundation of a new kingdom with its capital at Che-lan and with ambitions of expanding its authority southwards. In Burma proper there was anarchy and disorder. The Shan rulers of Pinya and Sagaing quarrelled incessantly, and one of them, Narathu of Pinya, in 1364 called in the Maw Shans to attack Sagaing. The population stampeded into the jungle. The Maws then turned and sacked Pinya as well. Thereupon a stepson of the chief of Sagaing, Thadominbya, founded a new capital at Ava and set about reducing the country to obedience.

Ava, a corruption of In-wa, 'the entrance to the lake', was founded in 1364 or 1365. As the capital of Upper Burma, and, after 1634, of the whole of Burma, its name became so closely associated with the country itself that Europeans came to refer to Upper Burma as the 'land of Ava', and to the government as the 'Court of Ava', even when the capital was at Amarapura or Mandalay. The striking thing about Ava was that it was Burmese, not Shan. The royal city followed the pattern of Pagan. Its founder sought to conciliate Burmese national sentiment by tracing his descent from the legendary kings of Tagaung. From its foundation its inscriptions were in excellent Burmese. Thadominbya's efforts to establish his rule were directed to the Burmese districts to the southwards, which were unaffected by Shan infiltration. In 1368 he died of smallpox while attacking Sagu. His successor, Mingyi Swasawke (1368–1401), significantly laid stress on his descent from the Pagan dynasty.

The Shan penetration into Upper Burma led to the formation of a new Burmese centre on the Sittang river, where in 1280 a village had been fortified on a hill spur (taungngu) as an outpost against slave-raids from the nearby Karen states. The fall of Pagan led numbers of Burmese families to escape from Shan rule by trekking off and settling there. Its early development was almost unhampered, and by the middle of the fourteenth century it had become strong enough for its chief, Thinhkaba (1347–58), to assert his independence by assuming the royal title and building himself a palace in traditional style. During the reign of his son Pyanchi (1358–77) the liquidation of Sagaing and Pinya brought a fresh wave of Burmese immigrants to Toungoo. Pyanchi erected an inscription at Pagan, in which he recorded a visit he paid to make offerings to the temples there and stated that he and his wife had welcomed refugees from the Shan terror. The new state had a chequered existence; both Ava and Pegu tried to quench its independence. But its rulers were destined to play an important part in Burmese history later on.

Mingyi Swasawke was anxious to revive the traditional Burmese policy of subduing the Mons of the south. In the early part of his reign, however, the threat from the Shans on his northern and northwestern frontiers was too serious for him to embark on any adventures in Lower Burma. Moreover, Pyanchi of Toungoo was friendly with the Mons. He was forced, therefore, to pursue a peaceable policy, and in 1371 he had a conference with King Binnya U of Pegu, at which the frontier between Burma and the Mon country was delimited.

From the first he trod delicately in his relations with the powerful and quarrelsome Shan states. In 1371 he refused to intervene in a struggle that was in progress between the Sawbwas of Kale in the upper Chindwin valley and Mohnyin in the Katha district. In 1373, however, Mohnyin raided Myedu in the Shwebo district. By this time the Mongol dynasty, after a period of rapid decline, had been supplanted by the Mings, and until Ming rule was firmly established in Yunnan, where the Mongols were making a last stand, the Shan states in and around northern Burma went in no fear of the strong hand of Peking. The Myedu raid was the beginning of a long series of attacks from Mohnyin, and in 1383, two years after the last Mongol resistance had been stamped out in Yunnan, the harassed King of Ava sent an embassy to the Ming viceroy there asking for help.

The Chinese, who were now for the first time in contact with the Maw Shans, were as anxious as Mingyi Swasawke to restrain their lawlessness. Hence he was accorded official recognition as 'Governor' of Ava, and the viceroy ordered Mohnyin to keep the peace. For some years the order seems to have been effective, but in 1393 a further Mohnyin raid penetrated to Sagaing. The king's brother-in-law, Thilawa, Chief of Yamethin, inflicted so severe a defeat upon the marauders that for some years afterwards all the neighbouring Shan sawbwas treated Ava with respect.

The support obtained from China in 1383 enabled Mingyi Swasawke to turn his attention at last to the project of gaining control over the Irrawaddy waterway down to the sea. In 1377 he had procured the murder of the pro-Mon Pyanchi of Toungoo. In 1385, therefore, when Razadarit succeeded Binnya U to the throne of Pegu and a traitorous uncle wrote offering to hold Pegu as his vassal in return for support in a rebellion against his nephew, Mingyi Swasawke saw a golden opportunity for extinguishing Mon independence.

But the Mons proved a tougher proposition than he had bargained for; and although he took Prome and carried the fighting again and again into the heart of the Mon country, he failed to capture Pegu. The Mon chronicles mention contingents of Shans from the mountains in his forces, and sometimes refer to the invaders as Shans. But the struggle was essentially one of Burmese against Mons. It was not a Shan migration that the Mons held up, but a Burmese push towards the Irrawaddy delta. All the Upper Burma inscriptions of the period are in Burmese; and before the long period of the warfare ended, Burmese vernacular literature was born.

Mingyi Swasawke's successor, Minhkaung, who ruled energetically from 1401 to 1422, made tremendous efforts to bring the struggle to a successful issue, and nearly succeeded. But Razadarit was an able opponent who weakened the Burmese striking power by obtaining Arakanese help and fomenting discord between Ava and the Shan states of the north. In 1374 Mingyi Swasawke had placed an uncle on the throne of Arakan. On the latter's death in 1381 he sent his own son to rule there, but the prince was soon driven out. In 1404, as punishment for an Arakanese raid on the Pakokku district, he sent an expedition which occupied the capital, while the king fled to Bengal and his son escaped into the Mon country. This time he placed a son-in-law on the throne. But the Arakanese prince returned with Mon support and killed the Burmese puppet king. The Burmese replied by sending another expedition, and so began a ding-dong struggle between the two sides which lasted until 1430, when the exiled king, Narameikhla, returned, and with help from Bengal regained his throne.

In 1406, after some years of peace with the Shans, Minhkaung was tempted to interfere in the feud which had again broken out between Kale and Mohnyin. According to the Chinese account, he sent a force under 'Nolota' (Nawrahta), his 'Senior Comforter' (Wungyi), who robbed the land and killed the Sawbwa of Mohnyin and his son. The emperor sent his 'Governor' of Ava a severe reprimand, and the latter withdrew his troops and sent a propitiatory embassy. But so thoroughly had the Burmese commander performed the task entrusted to him that it was not until 1416 that the sawbwaship of Mohnyin was revived, the dead sawbwa's nephew and heir having fled and taken refuge in Nan-tien.

In due course the Sawbwa of Hsenwi took upon himself to avenge the ravaging of Mohnyin. In 1413 he raided some Ava villages and sent some of the prisoners to Peking. But the Burmese followed him up and defeated his force at Wetwin, near the present Maymyo. In the following year, at the instigation of Razadarit of Pegu, he raided again, while at the same time the Shan Chiefs of Mawke and Mawdon attacked Myedu. This time they were driven off, but in 1415, while the Burmese forces were campaigning in the delta, the two chiefs attacked again and threatened Ava itself. Minhkaung's son by a Maw Shan princess, Minrekyawswa, was at the time almost within sight of decisive victory over the Mons. Only Pegu and Martaban were left to Razadarit. But he had to be recalled in haste to Ava to deal with the Shan threat, and victory over the Mons slipped from the Burmese grasp. Two years later the prince was killed while on another campaign in the delta. That was the end of the struggle with the Mons. The Shan pressure had become so insistent that further campaigning in the delta involved too much risk.

Hsinbyushin Thihathu succeeded his father as King of Ava in 1422, and as husband of the Maw Shan princess. He attacked the Shans, but through the treachery of his wife was ambushed by the Sawbwa of Onbaung (Hsipaw) in 1426 and killed. The sawbwa then placed his own nominee, Kalekyetaungnyo, upon the throne. But he was driven out, together with the Onbaung Shans, by a Burmese chief, Mohnyinthado, who seized the crown for himself. Mohnyinthado reigned from 1427 to 1440. The country was in disorder. The feudal chiefs were independent, and were supported against the king by the Sawbwas of Onbaung and Yawnghwe. There were times when he even lost control over the vital Kyauksè area. The Onbaung raids forced him to abandon Ava temporarily. He was kept so busy with the efforts to stave off complete disaster that when, in 1430, the exiled King of Arakan returned home and began to build a new capital at Mrohaung he had no power to interfere. Arakan began a long period of independence.

Under Mohnyinthado's sons, Minrekyawswa (1440-3) and Narapati (1443-69), the Ava kingship revived considerably. The chief factor in this was the Chinese attack on the Maw Shans. With the passing of Kublai Khan's dynasty in 1368 China lost control over the route across Asia to the West. In their search for new outlets for trade the Mings, with their eyes upon the Irrawaddy, decided that the Maw Shans must be subdued. The result was a long struggle lasting from 1438 to 1465. There was added reason for the Chinese move in view of the fact that an ambitious Maw Shan chieftain, Thonganbwa ('Ssu-jen-fa'), was attempting to revive the old Nanchao empire. In 1441 Wang Chi, the President of the Board of War, was appointed to lead a strong army, which drove the Shans out of Luch'uan. Some of them fled to Hsenwi, but the majority, under Thonganbwa, crossed the Irrawaddy and took refuge in Mohnyin. The story of Wang Chi's campaigns is told in the *Ming shih*, which states that the emperor offered 'Ssu-jen-fa's' land to whoever should succeed in arresting him. An inscription at the Tupayon Pagoda, erected by Narapati at Sagaing, relates how Thonganbwa, fleeing before Wang Chi to Mohnyin and Kale, was captured by the Burmese and presented to their king on his coronation day.

Wang Chi's forces in due course conquered Mohnyin, and he demanded the surrender of the fugitive. When Narapati refused his demand the Chinese proceeded to invade Burmese territory. A battle was fought near Tagaung in which, according to the *Hmannan Yazawin*, the Chinese general was killed and his army badly mauled (1445). In the following year the Chinese invaded in greater strength and appeared before the walls of Ava. Narapati thereupon agreed to their demand. Thonganbwa, however, committed suicide, and only his dead body could be surrendered. Narapati also formally accepted Chinese overlordship. In return the Yunnan forces assisted him to subdue the rebellious Chief of Yamethin. In 1451 he received from China a gold seal of appointment as 'Comforter of Ava', and three years later a slice of Mohnyin territory.

While the Shans felt the impact of China's chastising hand the Ava king managed to maintain some semblance of authority. But it was very delicately poised, for the constant state of friction between the Shan states—a major cause of Burma's survival—always threatened to involve the king in some dispute or other, or give his vassals an excuse to rebel. Thihathura (1469-81) was the last of the Ava kings in whose reign revolts and disorder were not the normal state of affairs. During this brief interval of relative calm the Ava kings established relations with the famous centre of Theravada Buddhism at Kandy in Ceylon. In 1456 Narapati bought land there for the maintenance of Burmese monks visiting the Temple of the Tooth.

In 1474 Thihathura and his queen sent brooms made from the hair of their heads as an offering.

Much future trouble might have been prevented had China agreed to Thihathura's request in 1472 for the cession of Mohnyin. Instead, however, China contented herself with warning the sawbwa against obstructing the route between Burma and Yunnan. The trouble was that, although from time to time she would administer a dose of frightfulness and send them scattering in all directions, China failed to administer the Shans. And her policy of fragmentation aimed at preventing the development of any powerful state within the areas from which she claimed allegiance. Hence, when her control weakened even for a short time, Upper Burma and the regions to the north and east became, as Harvey puts it, 'a bedlam of snarling Shan states'.

That is what happened after Thihathura's death in 1481. Two kings, Minhkaung (1481-1502), and Shwenankyawshin (1502-27), completely failed to stem the disorders. Mohnyin became so strong and threatening that in 1507 Ava resorted to appeasement by ceding territory in order to gain time. So serious became the situation that in 1520 the Chinese pushed across the Salween and moved their advanced base to Tengyueh. Unfortunately this had not the slightest effect. In 1527 Mohnyin's chronic attacks culminated in the capture and sack of Ava, the death of Shwenankyawshin, and his replacement by the sawbwa's son Thohanbwa, a 'full-blooded savage', says Harvey, who pillaged pagodas, massacred monks, and made bonfires of the precious contents of monastic libraries. The remaining rulers of Ava, from 1527 until its absorption in 1555 into the reunited kingdom of Burma created by Bayinnaung, were all Shan chiefs.

The force that reunited Burma in the middle of the sixteenth century, and finally delivered the Ava region from the Shan terror, was built up unostentatiously at Toungoo in the Sittang valley, away from the main centres of disturbance. During the long struggle between Ava and the Mons the little state barely maintained its existence, with each of the combatants from time to time attempting to bring it to an end. No ruling family held power for long. But a turning point came under King Minkyinyo (1486-1531), when the chaos in Ava offered an able ruler an excellent opportunity for expanding his domains. His most important acquisition was the Kyauksè area. In 1527, when the Sawbwa of Mohnyin sacked Ava, so many Burmese chiefs fled to take service under him that he became the most powerful ruler in Burma.

With this addition to his strength he turned his attention southwards and began to make preparations for an attack upon the rich and cultivated Mon kingdom of Pegu. The various Shan sawbwas to the northwards of his territory were so deeply engaged in quarrelling among themselves that he gambled on their congenital incapacity for combined action and determined on a bid to acquire the fabulous riches of Pegu as a basis for further conquests. In 1531, however, while in the midst of his preparations he died, and it fell to his brilliant son Tabinshwehti to carry through his cherished project.

The Mon kingdom which Anawrahta of Pagan had conquered in the middle of the eleventh century and incorporated in his dominions had regained its independence during the Mongol invasions which brought about the downfall of the great Buddhist state in 1287. The initial movement of severance came in 1281, when Wareru, or Mogado, captain of the guard to King Rama Khamheng of Sukhot'ai, eloped with one of the king's daughters, so the story runs, and seized the port of Martaban. At Donwun in Thaton district, his birthplace, he is said to have started his career as a pedlar. After establishing himself at Martaban he joined with a Mon rebel leader, Tarabya, in expelling the Burmese from Pegu. By 1287 they had gained control over all the country south of Prome and Toungoo. Then they quarrelled, and Wareru murdered Tarabya.

Siamese sources assert that Wareru held his new kingdom as the vassal of Rama Khamheng who conferred on him the title of Chao Fa Rua. This, however, did not prevent him from obtaining recognition of China and ruling as an independent sovereign. Martaban was his capital, and remained the capital of the Mon kingdom until 1363. Southwards his territory stretched down the Peninsula as far as Mergui. But the kingdom of Ayut'ia, after its foundation in 1350, claimed all the territory from Martaban southwards, and ultimately acquired most of it. Wareru is said to have beaten off an attack by the three Shan Brothers. His chief monument today is the law-book known as the *Wagaru Dhammathat*, a digest of the Laws of Manu, compiled at his behest by monks from the writings of earlier scholars preserved in Mon monasteries. It is the earliest law-book in Burma still extant.

After Wareru's death in 1296 the Mon kingdom passed through a time of internal troubles and succession disputes which lasted many years, and might have had disastrous results had the Shans or the Siamese been in a position to intervene. When, however, they did at last attack, a strong king, Binnya U (1353–85), was on the throne; and though forced to yield territory, he managed to save his kingdom. The attacks came from both Chiengmai and Ayut'ia. The Chiengmai forces burnt Taikkola, Sittaung and Donwun, but were driven off in 1356. In 1363 the Siamese forced Binnya U to abandon Martaban and pressed their attacks upon the provinces of Moulmein and Tenasserim. Binnya U transferred his capital temporarily to Donwun, and finally in 1369 established it at Pegu, which remained the capital of the Mon kingdom until Tabinshwehti extinguished its independence in 1539. In 1362 he repaired the Shwe Dagon Pagoda and raised its height to 66 feet. It was a famous resort of pilgrims, standing just outside the small fishing village of Dagon, named after it, and centuries later renamed Rangoon by Alaungpaya (1755).

Binnya U's reign was a troubled one, full of wars and strife. The Siamese held Martaban and Tenasserim and were constantly threatening. His eldest son Razadarit (1385–1423) had to deal not only with raids from Chiengmai, Kampengp'et and Ayut'ia, but also, as we have seen, with a long succession of attacks from Ava. Against them all he defended his realm with success. Only the preoccupation of Ayut'ia with her attempts to subdue Cambodia, Sukhot'ai and Chiengmai saved the Mon country from becoming a bone of contention between Ava and Siam. Razadarit was not only a statesman who played his cards with consummate skill; he has also a great name in Burmese and Mon tradition as an administrator. The Burmese say that he divided the 'Three Talaing Countries', Pegu, Myaungmya, and Bassein, into thirty-two provinces each. Presumably the area indicated was what British administrators called a 'circle', under a *myothugyi* or *taikthugyi*.

With the cessation of the Burmese wars shortly before Razadarit's death, the Mon kingdom passed into a long period of peace and prosperity. Its capital became a great centre of commerce and the resort of foreign merchants. Its three busy ports of Martaban, recovered from Siam; Syriam, just below Dagon; and Bassein, in the delta, carried on regular trade with India, Malacca, and the Malay Archipelago. In 1435 Nicolo di Conti of Venice, the first recorded European to visit Burma, stayed four months at Pegu, then ruled by Binnyaran I (1426–46).

The fifteenth-century Kings of Pegu were deeply interested in religion. Binnyakyan (1450–53) raised the height of the Shwe Dagon Pagoda to 302 feet. His successor, Queen Shinsawbu (1453–72), a daughter of Razadarit, constructed additions to the precincts of the pagoda which made it very much as it is today. Missions were again sent to Ceylon, and, like those of an earlier period, stimulated a new religious revival which affected the whole of Burma and caused the rulers of Ava also to seek direct contact with the source of Theravada teaching.

The centre of the movement was the Kalyani *thein* near Pegu, which took its name from the river in Ceylon where the monks who founded it had been ordained. Kalyani ordination became the standard form for the whole country. The story of the reforms is told in the inscriptions erected at the *thein* by Shin Sawbu's successor Dammazedi (1472–92). He was a monk chosen for the succession by the devout queen, and accordingly made to leave his cloister and marry her daughter. He became a Buddhist ruler of the best type, famous for his wisdom. A collection of his rulings, the Dammazedi *pyatton*, is still extant. Under him mildness prevailed and a gracious civilization flourished. Friendly intercourse was maintained with China, and missions were again sent to Buddhagaya. When he died he was honoured as a saint, and a pagoda was erected over his bones.

His son Binnyaran II (1492–1526) received two more European prospectors, both Italians. The first was Hieronomo de' Santo Stefano, who in 1496 sold him a valuable stock of merchandise and was kept waiting for payment much longer than he had bargained for. The second was Ludovico di Varthema, who wrote with enthusiasm about the splendour of the king and his capital, and the abundance of elephants in the country. He listed shellac, sandalwood, cotton, silk, and rubies as the main articles of trade from which the king drew his revenue.

Binnyaran also received in 1512 a European prospector of a different sort. He was Ruy Nunez d'Acunha, deputed by Affonso de Albuquerque after the capture of Malacca to report on conditions at Tenasserim, Martaban, and Pegu. As a result of his visit a Portuguese trading station was opened in 1519 at Martaban. It was a sign of a new age that was dawning. Another, the gathering of a Burmese nationalist revival at Toungoo, was hardly as yet visible during Binnyaran's reign. The pent-up avalanche broke suddenly upon his successor Takayutpi (1526–39) when Tabinshwehti fell upon the delta region in 1535. Within a very short period the Burmese leader had reduced the whole of the Mon kingdom to submission, captured Pegu by stratagem, and brought the rule of Wareru's line to an end.

CHAPTER 7

THE T'AIS AND THE KINGDOM OF AYUT'IA

THE Shans, the Laotians and the Siamese are all descended from a parent racial group, cognate to the Chinese, which is thought to have made its first historical appearance in the sixth century B.C. From that time onwards Chinese records make frequent references to them as the 'barbarians' south of the Yang-tse-kiang. They came under Chinese suzerainty early in the Christian era, but made many attempts to assert their independence. In order to escape subjection to China many of them emigrated to the region now occupied by the Northern Shan States of Burma. There the Chinese knew them as the Ailao. The warlike kingdom of Nanchao in west and north-west Yunnan had a T'ai population, but rulers of a different race. Between 757 and 763, under Ko-lo-feng, Nanchao conquered the valley of the upper Irrawaddy. In 791 I-mou-hsün, his grandson and successor, accepted Chinese overlordship, and through him the earliest relations were established between the Pyu of Burma and the Chinese.

I-mou-hsün was a conqueror who expanded his control over neighbouring states and tribes. His successors in the ninth century pursued the same policy. Not only did they destroy the Pyu capital in 832 and carry their conquests as far as the delta region of the Irrawaddy, but they twice invaded China and besieged Chengtu. They raided Tongking and Annam, then under Chinese rule. Before the end of the century, however, they made their peace with China and settled down as a vassal kingdom. Thenceforward for a considerable period little mention is made of them by the Chinese dynastic histories.

But the T'ai never ceased to be on the move, slowly, very slowly, infiltrating along the rivers and in the valleys of central Indo-China. Small groups of them settled among the Khmers, the Mons, and the Burmese. T'ai mercenaries appear on the bas-reliefs of the Angkor Wat. Long before that they had been crossing into the Menam valley from those of the Salween and Mekong. North of Raheng, at the junction of the Mep'ing and the Mewang rivers, the small independent T'ai state of P'ayao came into existence as early as 1096. Early in the twelfth century their *muongs* in the upper Menam valley

KHMER TOWERS AT LOPBURI, SIAM—THE PHRA PRANG SAM YOT

began to form tiny states under chieftains called *chaos* and *sawbwas*.[1] In the thirteenth century what had been a movement so slow as to be scarcely observable became what has been described by Cœdès as an 'effervescence', showing itself on the southern confines of Yunnan. Possibly it was a result of the weakening of Khmer power in that region towards the end of Jayavarman VII's reign through his concentration upon holding Champa in subjection. In 1215 the T'ai state of Mogaung, north of Bhamo in Upper Burma, came into existence. In 1223 Moné or Muong Nai, another powerful Shan state, was founded. The year 1229 is the traditional date of the establishment of the Ahom kingdom of Assam, also a T'ai achievement.

At about the same time the T'ai chiefs of Chieng Rung and Chieng Sen on the upper Mekong made a marriage alliance. To this period also the legendary mass migration of T'ais along the Nam U river to the site of the present Luang Prabang may possibly be ascribed. In 1238 two T'ai chiefs attacked and defeated the Khmer commander at Sukhot'ai, then the capital of the north-western part of the Angkor empire, and established there the centre of a T'ai kingdom which was

[1] *Sawbwa* is the Burmese rendering of the T'ai *Chao P'ya*.

to become a mighty state under Rama Khamheng in the latter half of the century.

Kublai Khan's conquest of the kingdom of Nanchao in 1253 caused an even stronger 'effervescence' among the T'ais. Cœdès thinks that the prodigious epic of the Mongol conquests struck their imagination and inspired them to great achievements. Whether this be so or not, the Mongols adopted the traditional Chinese policy of 'fragmentation' and favoured the establishment of a series of T'ai states at the expense of the older states. And what happened was not a mass displacement of population in the areas affected but the seizure of power by a T'ai governing class.

The fall of Pagan in 1287 resulted in the division of much of its territory under T'ai rulers. In the upper Menam valley Mangrai, the T'ai Chief of Chieng Rai, conquered the old Mon state of Haripunjaya, or Lampun, in 1290-2 and founded the kingdom of Chiengmai. Between 1283 and 1287 Rama Khamheng of Sukhot'ai conquered the Mons of the Menam valley and substituted T'ai rule for Khmer over an area which included much of the upper Mekong region as well. In 1287 Mangrai, Rama Khamheng and Ngam Muong, the Chief of P'ayao, met together and concluded a firm pact of friendship. The year was significantly that of the Mongol conquest of Pagan. The decline of Khmer power on the one side and the disappearance of a strong Burma on the other provided the T'ais with an unrivalled opportunity for expansion, provided they kept the peace among themselves.

Rama Khamheng, or 'Rama the Brave' (1283-c.1317), had proved himself a redoubtable warrior before he succeeded his father Sri Indraditya as king of Sukhot'ai. He became a renowned statesman, under whom the T'ais absorbed the best elements of the civilizations with which they came into contact. Indeed, Sukhot'ai during this period has been called the 'cradle of Siamese civilization'. The T'ais possessed a social organization of a feudal type, vestigial remains of which still persist in the Shan and Laos states and the Muongs of Tongking and Thanh-hoa. Through long contact with China they had a relatively advanced civilization. They were as remarkable as assimilators as the Normans in Europe. By the trade route through Assam, joining China and India, they had made contact with the Buddhism of northern India, and the influence of Buddhist and Sena art upon their own in the extreme north of the Menam basin is easily recognizable.

Under Rama Khamheng, in expanding down the Menam valley and into the Malay Peninsula, they conquered an area that had been Mon

since before the dawn of the historical period. It was the home of a
fine civilization with deep roots. In the seventh century, when the
strong hand of Funan was removed, the Buddhist kingdom of Dvaravati
had arisen there. Of its history unfortunately very little is known.
While the Khmers conquered large parts of what is now eastern and
north-eastern Thailand, Dvaravati maintained its independence up to
the reign of Suryavarman I (1011–50), when what was then called
Lavo, namely the region of the Menam valley, came under Khmer
rule.

In the thirteenth century, when the western parts of the Khmer
empire were coming under T'ai control, Lavo regained its independence and sent embassies to China. Thus it was not absorbed into
Rama Khamheng's kingdom, though in the middle of the next century
it came under a T'ai ruler. Nevertheless the majority of Rama Khamheng's subjects must have been Mons and Khmers, and from them
he adopted the script which he used for reducing the T'ai language
to writing in 1283. His aim was to establish an official language that
could be used also by his Mon-Khmer-speaking subjects. In his
celebrated inscription of 1292 at Sukhot'ai he employed the new
characters for the first time, and this inscription is the oldest extant
specimen of the T'ai language. His alphabet, the Sukodaya script,
was adopted throughout Siam. It had a strong influence also upon
the development of writing in the Laos states.

Sukhot'ai's geographical situation helps to explain its role as the
cradle of Siamese civilization. It lay on the dividing-line between the
spheres of influence of the Khmers on the one hand and of the Mons
and Burmese on the other. Moreover, it had easy communication
with Lower Burma, through which it could maintain relations with
the metropolis of its Buddhism, Ceylon. Through all these contacts
it absorbed important cultural elements and incorporated them in the
civilization of Siam. To quote Cœdès: 'From Cambodia the Siamese
assimilated its political organization, material civilization, writing and
a considerable number of words. Siamese artists learnt from Khmer
artists and transformed Khmer art according to their own genius,
and above all under the influence of their contact with their western
neighbours, the Mons and Burmese. From these latter the Siamese
received their juristic traditions, of Indian origin, and above all
Sinhalese Buddhism and its artistic traditions.'[1]

A postscript to Rama Khamheng's inscription, of later date, sets
forth the details of his conquests. It runs: 'Rama Khamheng is

---

[1] *Les États hindouisés*, p. 370, translated.

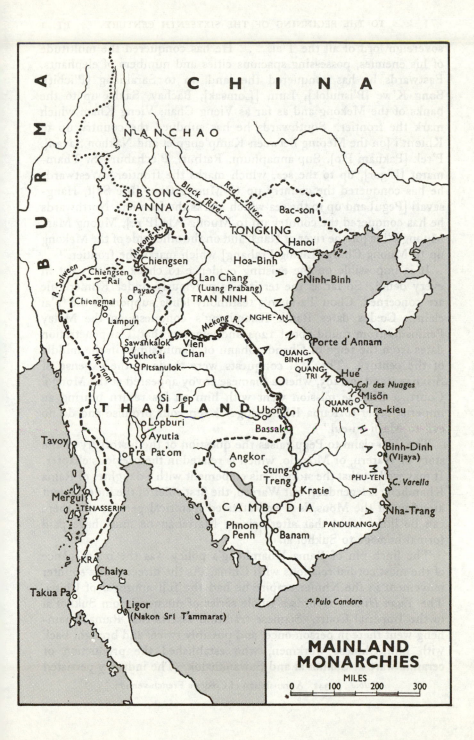

CHINA

N A N C H A O

BURMA

SIBSONG
PANNA

Black River

Red River

Bac-son

TONGKING

Hanoi

Ninh-Binh

Chiengsen

Hoa-Binh

R. Salween

Mekong R.

Chiengsen
Rai

Payao

Lan Chang
(Luang Prabang)
TRAN NINH

Chiengmai

Lampun

NGHE-AN

Mekong R.

Porte d'Annam

Sawankalok

Vien
Chan

QUANG-
BINH

Me-nam

Sukhot'ai

Pitsanulok

QUANG-
TRI

Hué

Col des Nuages

Si Tep

Ubon

Misön

QUANG
NAM

Tra-kieu

THAILAND

Lopburi

Bassak

Binh-Dinh
(Vijaya)

Tavoy

Ayutia

P'ra Pat'om

Angkor

Stung-
Treng

PHU-YEN

C. Varella

Mergui

TENASSERIM

Kratie

CAMBODIA

Nha-Trang

PANDURANGA

Phnom
Penh

Banam

KRA

Chaiya

Takua Pa

Pulo Condore

Ligor
(Nakon Sri T'ammarat)

CHAMPA

LAOS

ANNAM

**MAINLAND
MONARCHIES**

MILES

0   100   200   300

sovereign lord of all the T'ais . . . He has conquered the multitude of his enemies, possessing spacious cities and numbers of elephants. Eastwards he has conquered the land up to Saraluang [P'ichit], Song K'we [P'isnulok], Lum [Lomsak], Bachay, Sakha up to the banks of the Mekong and as far as Vieng Chan, Vieng Kham which mark the frontier. Southwards he has subdued the country up to Khiont'i [on the Meping between Kamp'engp'et and Nakhon Savan], P'rek [Paknam P'o], Sup'annaphum, Ratburi, P'echaburi, Si Thammarat [Ligor], up to the sea, which marks the frontier. Westwards he has conquered the country up to Muong Chot [Me So]t, Hangsavati [Pegu] and up to the sea which marks the frontier. Northwards he has conquered the country up to Muong P'le [P're], Muong Man, Muong P'lua [on the river of Nan], and on the other side of the Mekong up to Muong Chava [Luang Prabang] which marks the frontier.'[1]

It is impossible on the existing evidence to check up this list in every detail. So far as the territories previously under Khmer rule are concerned, Chou Ta-kuan's testimony lends support to the T'ai claim. Cœdès dates Rama Khamheng's conquests in the Malay Peninsula from round about 1294 and suggests that T'ai penetration dates from the reign of Chandrabhanu of Tambralinga in the middle of the century. The T'ai conquests were made at the expense of Śrivijaya, and in 1295, when a Siamese envoy appeared at the Mongol Court, a Chinese mission went with him on his return bearing an imperial order to Rama Khamheng: 'Keep your promise and do no evil to Ma-li-yu-eul.'

The T'ai claim to Pegu raises the question of the historicity of the story of Wareru, or Mogado, which is related in the previous chapter. It may well be that the story of his elopement with a daughter of Rama Khamheng is legendary, but Wareru, the first ruler of the independent kingdom of the Mons, is a well-attested historical person, and there can be little doubt that after seizing Martaban he must have paid formal homage to Sukhot'ai.

The linch-pin of Rama Khamheng's policy was the maintenance of the most cordial relations with China. As the director of a splinter movement in the Khmer empire he had the full approval of China. The *Yuan History* records a whole series of missions from Sukhot'ai to the Imperial Court. Siamese tradition asserts that Rama Khamheng went there in person once, and possibly twice, and brought back with him Chinese workmen, who established the production of ceramic ware at Sukhot'ai and Sawankhalok. The industry persisted

---

[1] *Ibid.*, p. 342. A translation of Cœdès's French version.

down to the middle of the eighteenth century. The sites of the old kilns with their huge heaps of celadon refuse are a striking testimony to the importance of the industry at certain periods.

Rama Khamheng's great inscription paints a picture of a prosperous state governed with justice and magnanimity, and with Pali Buddhism of the Sinhalese orthodox pattern as its official religion. The king, we are told, with his Court and all his magnates, practises the religion of the Buddha with devotion. For all this, however, it is not surprising to learn that on the south side of the city there is a hill (Khao Luang) on which dwelt the most important of all the spirits in the country, P'ra Khap'ung, and that the ruler of Sukhot'ai made regular ritual offerings at his shrine in order to ensure the prosperity of the realm.

The Chinese applied the name 'Sien' to the kingdom of Sukhot'ai. 'Syam' was the name used by the Khmers for the 'savages' from the middle Menam depicted on the south gallery of the Angkor Wat. The earliest use of the word so far discovered is in a Cham epigraph of the eleventh century, which mentions Siamese in a list of prisoners of war. The name seems to be a variant of the word 'Shan', applied by the Burmese to the wedge of hill states running southwards from Mogaung and Mohnyin in the far north. Its etymology is unknown. After the foundation of Ayut'ia in 1350 the territory that owed obedience to its monarchs became known as Siam. Europeans often called the city itself 'the city of Siam'.

Rama Khamheng ceased to reign shortly before 1318; tradition asserts that he disappeared in the rapids of the river at Sawankhalok. Under his son Lo T'ai (?1317–?1347) the power of Sukhot'ai declined almost as rapidly as it had arisen. A false reading of his name has caused him to be celebrated in some writings as Sua T'ai, the 'tiger of the T'ais'. Far from being a tiger he was interested chiefly in works of Buddhist merit and founded a number of *Buddhapada*, or foot-prints of the Buddha, in imitation of the one on Adam's Peak in Ceylon. His religious devotion earned him the title of Dharmaraja.

Lo T'ai's son Lu T'ai, who succeeded him in ?1347, was a scholar who was completely preoccupied with religion, and eventually resigned his crown in 1361 to enter a monastery. In 1345 he had composed a large treatise on Buddhist cosmology, the *Traibhumikatha*, which is still extant under the name *Traiphum P'a Ruang*. An inscription describes him thus: 'This king observed the ten royal precepts. He showed mercy towards all his subjects. When he saw another man's rice he did not covet it, and when he saw another's wealth he did not behave unworthily. . . . If he arrested people guilty of cheating or insolence, those who put poison in his food so as to cause him illness or death, he never killed or beat them, but forgave those who behaved evilly towards him. The reason why he repressed his heart and restrained his temper, and did not give way to anger when he might have done, was that he desired to become a Buddha and to take every creature beyond the ocean of the affliction of transmigration.'[1]

The way was thus left open for an ambitious T'ai prince to found a new state in the south. According to tradition, he belonged to the Chiengsen house, from which Mangrai, the founder of Chiengmai, had sprung. He married a daughter of the Mon ruler of U T''ong and eventually succeeded him. Having made himself master of much of the old kingdom of Lavo, he forced the pious Lu T'ai to acknowledge his suzerainty. Then, when an epidemic of cholera forced him to evacuate his own city, he went fifty miles to the southward and founded a new capital, Dvaravati Sri Ayudhya, on an island in the Menam. In 1350 he was crowned with the title of Ramadhipati. He is regarded as the first King of Siam.

Three years after his accession another T'ai chieftain, Fa Ngum, united all the small Laos states to the north, in the region of the upper Mekong, to found the kingdom of Lang Chang, later known as Luang Prabang. Here also Khmer influence was felt, for Fa Ngum had been brought up at the Court of Angkor and was married to a Khmer princess.

The new kingdom of Ayut'ia was a strong one which soon began to make its power felt. It gained control over the middle and lower Menam, and of much of the Malay Peninsula,[2] including Tenasserim and Tavoy in what is now Burma, and exercised suzerainty over Sukhot'ai. Whether a strong China would have permitted so powerful a state to arise without let or hindrance is highly doubtful. Kublai Khan and his successors had encouraged the T'ais to dismember the Khmer empire in accordance with the traditional Chinese policy of fragmentation pursued towards the 'southern barbarians', but it was the weakness of the Mongol power in the middle of the fourteenth century that made possible the creation of so strong a kingdom as Ayut'ia became. As soon as the Mongols were supplanted by the Mings the situation changed radically. The Siamese kings seem to have been aware of this, for they sent frequent embassies to Nanking,

[1] A translation of Cœdès's French version in *Les États hindouisés*, pp. 368–9, and his *Receuil des inscriptions du Siam*, i, p. 107.
[2] Wood's story in his *History of Siam*, p. 64, that Ramadhipati extended his conquests to Malacca must not be taken literally, since Malacca was not founded until 1403 or thereabouts.

the Ming capital, and sedulously cultivated friendly relations. As diplomatists the T'ais have never been surpassed.

The transference of the main centre of T'ai power in the Menam valley from Sukhot'ai southwards to Ayut'ia spelt danger for Cambodia, for her capital, Angkor, was now within range of attack. As soon as he had founded his new capital, Ramadhipati began to make sustained efforts to subdue Cambodia. This date, as we have seen, was challenged by Lawrence Palmer Briggs, who believed that there was no conquest of Angkor until 1431. Dr. O. W. Wolters, however, in his suggested reconstruction of Khmer chronology accepts the hypothesis that Angkor was taken by the T'ais during Ramadhipati's reign; but he places the date in 1369, the year of the king's death. The Siamese held Angkor for six years, but were driven out by King Gamkat. Khmer resentment at the rule of the foreigner would largely account for this; but Dr. Wolters draws attention to the fact that Ramadhipati's brother-in-law Boromoraja, who came to the throne in 1370, was more interested in establishing Ayut'ia's hegemony over the T'ai kingdoms of Sukhot'ai and Chiengmai than in pursuing the traditional struggle against the Khmers.[1]

Ramadhipati I promulgated the first system of law on record in Thailand. It embodies much ancient T'ai custom going back to the Nanchao period. Modified as it was subsequently by assimilation with the Laws of Manu, it provided the basic principles of Siamese law for centuries up to the reign of Chulalongkorn, and has not been entirely superseded by modern legislation. For all his importance in Siamese history, practically nothing is known of Ramadhipati personally. When he died in 1369 he was succeeded by his son Prince Ramesuen, who was Governor of Lopburi. He, however, was unpopular, and in face of disturbances which he was unable to quell he abdicated in 1370 in favour of an uncle, who became Boromoraja I.

During the early part of his reign the new king had to devote his whole attention to the task of re-establishing authority over the upper Menam valley. Sukhot'ai was bent upon reviving its independence. In 1371 Boromoraja led an invasion of the northern kingdom and succeeded in capturing several towns. This was the first of a series of annual invasions culminating in 1378 in the submission of King T'ammaraja II of Sukhot'ai, and the cession to Ayut'ia of its western districts, including Kamp'engp'et. The king, who transferred his capital to P'itsanulok, was allowed to reign over the remainder as the vassal of Siam.

[1] 'The Khmer King at Basan (1371–3)', *Asia Major*, vol. xii, pt. 1, p. 81.

The extension of Ayut'ia's power so far northwards brought trouble with Chiengmai, and just before Boromoraja's death a struggle began which was to last off and on for several centuries. Like so many of these wars, it arose out of a disputed succession. In 1387 Sen Muang Ma, a boy of fourteen, succeeded to the Chiengmai throne, and an uncle at once sought to dispossess him by summoning Siamese aid. The Siamese invading force, however, was defeated at the village of Sen Sanuk, close to Chiengmai. The battle became famous in local history through the exploit of the princess Nang Muang, who, although far advanced in pregnancy, took part in the fighting dressed as a man riding on an elephant.

In the following year Boromoraja I died and was succeeded by his son, a boy of fifteen. He was immediately dethroned and put to death by the ex-king Ramesuen, who seized power and reigned until 1395. Ramesuen revived his father's policy of expansion into the Khmer lands, and in 1389, according to Dr. Wolters's reckoning, after a siege of seven months, Angkor fell a second time to the T'ai armies. This time, however, they were soon driven out. The Siamese chronicle, the *P'ongsawardan*, credits Ramesuen also with the capture of Chiengmai, and relates how he battered down its walls with large cannon. According to Wood the story is apocryphal. What actually happened was that the King of Chiengmai, on the pretext of helping Sukhot'ai to make another bid for independence, led an army there. But King T'ammaraja, realizing that Chiengmai's real aim was to gain control over his kingdom and use it as a base from which to attack Ayut'ia, defeated the Laos army and drove it out of his territories. The Siamese took no part in the struggle.

The period 1395–1408 is a blank in Siamese history. A phantom king, Ram Raja, a son of Ramesuen, occupied the throne, but nothing is recorded of his reign. In 1408 he was deposed through a palace revolt led by a son of Boromoraja I, who succeeded to the throne as Int'araja (1408–24). The only noteworthy events in his reign occurred in the north, where there were two succession disputes.

The first was in Sukhot'ai, where the Siamese intervened and imposed a settlement in 1410. The other occurred in the following year in Chiengmai and resulted from the death of Sen Muang Ma. A Siamese force commanded by T'ammaraja III of Sukhot'ai was sent to place one of the claimants on the throne. Instead of proceeding directly to Chiengmai it attacked the city of P'ayao, once an independent T'ai state, away to the north-west. Here, according to the Chiengmai Chronicle, cannon were used by both sides. The resistance of the city was so stubborn that the Siamese abandoned the siege and went on to Chiengrai to recruit their strength for an attack on Chiengmai. The capital, however, resisted all attempts to take it, and finally the Siamese moved off again to Chiengrai, captured it after some resistance, and deported large numbers of prisoners to Ayut'ia.

When in 1424 Int'araja died he left three sons. A struggle for the throne at once broke out between the two elder ones. An attempt to settle it by personal combat on elephants resulted in both combatants being thrown from their mounts and killed. The youngest brother was thereupon proclaimed king as Boromoraja II (1424-48). He was the conqueror of Angkor, though from what has been said in the previous chapter the word 'conqueror' can only be applied in this case with a somewhat restricted meaning; for his attempt to impose a Siamese puppet king upon Cambodia was an immediate failure, and in effect his campaign was little more than a successful raid on a big scale. Its objective, to make Cambodia a vassal state, was not realized. The Cambodian Chronicle mentions further fighting after a brief interval, and it is significant that the T'ais obtained no territory as a result of the struggle of 1431-2. In the subsequent fighting the initiative was by no means always with the T'ais.

In 1438 an important step was taken in the consolidation of the kingdom of Siam. Boromoraja II appointed his eldest son, Ramesuen, to be Governor of P'itsanulok, thereby incorporating what was left of the old kingdom of Sukhot'ai as a province of Siam. Shortly afterwards, in 1442, another succession struggle in Chiengmai afforded an opportunity for Siamese intervention. Again it was unsuccessful. The Chiengmai army inflicted a severe defeat upon the Siamese. The king was taken ill during the campaign and the expedition was abandoned. When in 1448 he died he was conducting a further abortive campaign against the arch-enemy.

Prince Ramesuen, who succeeded him as Boromo Trailokanat (1448-88), usually shortened to Trailok, has left his mark upon the administrative history of his country. His measures aimed at the creation of a centralized system of administration. Up to his time the various provincial governments had been subject to very little central control. The provinces indeed had functioned much in the same way as the great fiefs of mediaeval France and Germany. In order to control them the central administration was reorganized on a departmental basis and the rank of its principal officers raised. A distinction was made between the five great civil departments and the military administration. The civil departments were the Ministry of the

Interior, at the head of which was the chief minister; the Ministry of Local Government, which dealt with the city and province of Ayut'ia; the Ministry of Finance, which also dealt with foreign trade; the Ministry of Agriculture, which was concerned with cultivation and land tenure; and the Ministry of the Royal Household, which had charge of palace affairs and justice.

The military administration under the Kalahom was also divided into departments, whose heads had ministerial rank. This remained largely the structure of the central government until the nineteenth century. In its distribution of functions it was ahead of all the other governments of South-East Asia. Siam's neighbour Burma, for instance, never achieved more than a mere rudimentary differentiation of functions at the highest level. Its supreme body of ministers composing the Hlutdaw maintained, in theory, joint control over the whole field of administration until the abolition of the monarchy in 1886.

Another notable measure of Trailok's reign was the regulation of the Sakdi Na grades. From the earliest times under the T'ai social system every man might possess an amount of land varying according to his status. Trailok overhauled the whole system, laying down definite rules regarding the status of the different classes of people and assigning amounts of land to each. The amounts varied from the equivalent of 4,000 acres for a Chao P'ya down to that of 10 acres in the case of the lowest class. The system, which survived until recent times, supplied more than a framework to society. For officials, before the introduction of salaries in the second half of the nineteenth century, it determined their emoluments; each received the amount of land prescribed by the Sakdi Na and was expected to live on the revenue received therefrom. In the courts the amount of the fine which could be imposed was determined by a man's Sakdi Na grade; so too was the compensation to be paid for his murder. For the lowest grades, seeing that there was plenty of land for all and in monsoon Asia nature is beneficent, it meant that no one need starve.

The Kot Mont'ien Ban, or 'Palace Law', of 1450 was a further lengthy and detailed enactment of this Siamese Edward I, and like the English monarch's work was definitive rather than novel. It was a codification and clarification of existing custom. It enumerated the tributary states and the form of their tribute, defined the relative rank of all classes at Court from queens and royal princes downwards, regulated ceremonies, prescribed functions of officials, and fixed punishments. Thus it laid down the procedure to be followed when a member of the royal family was to be beaten to death with a sandalwood club.

Trailok's reign was one of almost incessant war with Chiengmai. This time it was the northern kingdom which started the trouble. The war arose out of the dissatisfaction felt in Sukhot'ai at its incorporation in the Siamese kingdom. Matters came to a head in 1451 when the Governor of Sawankhalok offered to become a tributary of Chiengmai in return for support in a rebellion against Ayut'ia. The King of Chiengmai at once despatched a force, which attacked Sukhot'ai but was repulsed. A second force, sent against Kamp'eng-p'et, captured the city. But an invasion of the Chiengmai dominions by the King of Luang Prabang caused the whole campaign to be called off, and for some years no further move was made.

Trailok was in no position to take advantage of the Luang Prabang diversion by seeking to deal a decisive blow at Chiengmai, for his attention was concentrated upon developments in the Malay Peninsula. He was handicapped also by an alarming outbreak of smallpox throughout his kingdom. Exactly what happened in Malaya is not clear. Wood asserts that Malacca rebelled, that the Siamese captured the city in 1455, but failed to make their control effective for long. Apparently the rapid rise of the power of Malacca during the first half of the fifteenth century was achieved only in face of the chronic hostility of Siam, which during the sudden decline of the Javanese power after the death of Hayam Wuruk had sought to extend her suzerainty over the whole of the Malay Peninsula.

Krom's account of the reign of Mudhafar Shah, better known as Raja Kasim (1446–59), causes one to suspect the veracity of the Siamese record. He writes that the greatest expansion of Malacca's power occurred under this ruler, whose name is associated with his success in beating off Siamese attacks. Winstedt in his *History of Malaya* is silent on the subject of the supposed Siamese capture of Malacca, but records that Raja Kasim defeated a Siamese fleet off Batu Pahat. The story of the Siamese attacks on Malacca, as recorded in the *Sejarah Melayu*, or 'Malay Annals', shows two as having been made during Raja Kasim's reign, the first by land and the second by sea. Both were defeated, and the Malay account of the former expressly states that the city was not taken.[1] The second was defeated before it reached its objective. Afterwards, according to the *Sejarah Melayu*, Sultan Muzaffar Shah and the King of Siam exchanged envoys and presents and made peace.[2]

[1] Translated by C. C. Brown in *Journal of the Malayan Branch of the R.A.S.*, xxv, parts 2 and 3, 1952–3, p. 66.
[2] *Ibid.*, pp. 70–2.

Tomé Pires, who resided at Malacca soon after its capture by the Portuguese in 1511, and in his *Suma Oriental* presents a picture of the East that is remarkable for its trustworthiness, mentions an alliance between Malacca and Siam in the reign of 'Modafarxa'. He says that this ruler fought successfully with the Rajas of Pahang, Trengganu and Patani, and also against the states of Kampar and Indragiri in Sumatra, and that his success was due to his alliances with the Javanese, the Chinese and the Siamese. As in 1456 China accorded Raja Kasim the title of 'sultan' in recognition of his importance, this may have affected Siam's attitude towards him. She was usually very heedful of the wishes of the Mings.

In 1460 the clouds gathered again in the upper Menam region. The Governor of Sawankhalok fled to Chiengmai and stirred up its king once more to invade Siam. In the next year the Chiengmai forces captured Sukhot'ai and besieged P'itsanulok. An invasion from Yunnan forced them to retire to defend their own territories, and in 1462 the Siamese recaptured Sukhot'ai. Sawankhalok, however, remained in Chiengmai's possession. The threat from Chiengmai caused Trailok to transfer his headquarters from Ayut'ia to P'itsanulok in 1463, and that city became for all practical purposes his capital for the remainder of his reign. Soon afterwards Chiengmai made the third attack of his reign on Sukhot'ai. It was severely repulsed, and the Siamese chased the retreating enemy as far as Doi Ba. There, however, they turned and made a stand. In a battle fought by moonlight the Siamese were checked and retreated homewards. After this there was peace for some years.

In the interval Trailok received tonsure as a monk and entered a monastery for a time. He then sought to weaken Chiengmai by occult means. In 1467 he sent a Burmese monk to sow dissension at the Court of Chiengmai. In the next year he followed this up by sending an embassy, headed by a Brahman, bent on the same object. Much trouble was indeed caused by these emissaries, for their slanders led to the execution of the king's eldest son and a faithful minister on false charges. But the Brahman's actions caused suspicion, the plot was discovered, and both he and the Burman were thrown into the river with stones tied to their necks. The war was resumed in 1494, and went on intermittently and without result for the next quarter of a century.

Shortly before his death in 1488 Trailok took the important step of creating his son, Prince Jett'a, Maha Uparat—i.e. Second King or Vice-King. This is the first mention of an office which lasted until

the second half of the nineteenth century. The Maha Uparat was
given some of the appurtenances of kingship and ten times the amount
of land granted to the highest official in the government. In the early
days the dignity was usually conferred upon the king's eldest son.
As Jai Jett'a, however, was not his eldest son, it has been suggested
that his intention was to divide the administration of the kingdom
between the two capitals of P'itsanulok and Ayut'ia. He died before
this could be arranged, and was succeeded by his eldest son Boromoraja III (1488–91). Ayut'ia became again the capital, but Jai
Jett'a, as Maha Uparat, remained at P'itsanulok as its governor.

When Boromoraja III died Jai Jett'a succeeded him as Rama
T'ibodi II (1491–1529). With his reign we enter a new period in the
history of South-East Asia. He received the first envoy of the Portuguese conqueror of Malacca, Duarte Fernandez, who came to
announce the victory to the Court of Ayut'ia. Siam still claimed
suzerainty over the whole of the Malay Peninsula, but Rama T'ibodi's
attention was concentrated upon Chiengmai, and he was not in a
position to create difficulties over the Portuguese possession of Malacca.
He therefore consented to treaties permitting them to trade at Ayut'ia,
Nakhon Sritammarat, Patani, Tenasserim and Mergui.

Trouble with Chiengmai had flared up early in the reign because
one of the Siamese royal princes, who had taken the yellow robe there,
smuggled away a white crystal image of the Buddha to Ayut'ia. The
King of Chiengmai thereupon invaded Siamese territory and Rama
T'ibodi restored the image. A second incident occurred in 1508,
when an attack by Chiengmai on Sukhot'ai led to a Siamese invasion
of Chiengmai. It failed, as also did a further one in 1510. When
Duarte Fernandez arrived in Ayut'ia the war was in full swing. In
1513 the Chiengmai forces raided Sukhot'ai and returned home with
a haul of prisoners and booty. Two years later they took Sukhot'ai
and Kamp'engp'et, but a large Siamese army under the king himself
drove them back into their own territory and inflicted on them a
decisive defeat on the banks of the Me Wang river near Nakhon
Lamp'ang.

The Siamese did not follow up this victory, but it is significant
that Rama T'ibodi set about to reorganize the whole military system
upon the basis of compulsory service. The kingdom was divided up
into military divisions and subdivisions, and all men of eighteen and
over were enrolled for call-up, if and when required. Boromoraja IV
(1529–34) made a treaty of peace with Chiengmai, and for a few years
there was a breathing space in the interminable struggle.

In 1545, however, another succession dispute at Chiengmai offered Siam an opportunity for intervention, which she seized. But this story must be deferred to another chapter, since it was no longer a simple struggle between Ayut'ia and Chiengmai. The Laos kingdom of Lan Chang (Luang Prabang) was also involved, as well as the newly united kingdom of Burma, created by the victories of Tabin-shwehti, and ambitious to establish its authority over all the T'ai states.

CHAPTER 8

THE KINGDOM OF CHAMPA

THE foundation and early history of the Cham kingdom has been dealt with in a previous chapter. The story is now taken up from the early part of the seventh century, when the accession of the T'ang dynasty in China brought a lull in Cham aggression which for various reasons lasted until the beginning of the ninth century. The seventh century saw the beginnings of artistic developments, chiefly at Mison and Tra-kieu, close to Amaravati (Quang-nam) just south of modern Tourane and the Col des Nuages. Some of the Mison monuments are still to be seen, but at Tra-kieu only the bases remain, since the city was later destroyed. Most of them belong to the long and peaceful reign of Prakasadharma, who on coming to the throne in 653 adopted the regnal title of Vikrantavarman. They are closely Indian in style. Several are dedicated to Vishnu, whose cult appears for the first time in Champa during his reign. Both he and his successor, Vikrantavarman II (?686–731), sent numerous missions to China. A rock inscription of Prakasadharma, found to the north of Nha-trang, shows that his sway extended well to the south of the modern Cap Varella.

In the middle of the eighth century the Chinese cease to mention the Lin-yi; they refer to the Chams by the name Huan-wang. This change synchronizes with a transference of the centre of gravity in the kingdom southwards from Quang-nam to Panduranga (Phan-rang) and Kauthara (Nha-trang). A new dynasty—the fifth, according to Georges Maspero's reckoning—reigns there from 758 to 859 and begins to use posthumous names indicating the god with whom the dead king has united himself. More stress is laid on state Śaivism, and the cult of the linga becomes more important even than in Cambodia. It imposes itself upon the ancient indigenous worship of upright stones symbolizing the god of the soil. There are many examples of the use of the *moukhalinga*, an Indian form of the cult, in which the stone has a metal covering decorated with one or more human faces, symbolizing, as in the case of the Khmer Devaraja, the identification of the king with Siva. It is an interesting case of

CHAM DANCER,
c. seventh century

symbiosis, whereby the imported and the traditional cults were united in an attempt to broaden the basis of the state religion.

The second half of the eighth century was a critical time for Champa. Like Cambodia, it had to sustain a number of heavy Javanese attacks. One in 774 destroyed the old sanctuary of Po Nagar at Nha-trang. Three years later another destroyed a temple near the capital, Virapura, which occupied a site not far from modern Phanrang. But the Javanese peril passed away, and early in the ninth century Champa herself again went over to the offensive. Under Harivarman I she renewed her attacks on the Chinese provinces to the north, with varying success. There were also Cham attacks on Cambodia early in the reign of Jayavarman II, the founder of the Angkor dynasty. It used to be thought that Yaśovarman, the founder of the city of Angkor, replied to these by an invasion of Champa which was repelled by Indravarman II. But it is now known that the record of the Khmer invasion refers to a much later one.

Under Indravarman II (854–93) the north again became the centre of gravity; he founded a new capital, Indrapura, in Quang-nam province. He restored good relations with China, and in his reign Chinese historians begin to refer to Champa by a third name, Changcheng—i.e. the city of Chan, or, in its Sanskrit form, Champapura. His reign was a peaceful one, notable for a great Buddhist foundation, a monastery, the ruins of which have been located at Dong-duong, south-east of Mison. This is the first evidence of the existence of Mahayana Buddhism in Champa.

Indravarman II founded the sixth dynasty in Champa's history. The kings of his line were more active than any of their predecessors in their interest in the religious life of the country. Not only did they build new sanctuaries but they protected religious foundations against pirates and restored them after desecration. They erected inscriptions describing in detail their donations to temples and monasteries. During the reign of Indravarman's successor, Jaya Simhavarman I, relations with Java were close and friendly. A relative of his queen went to Java on a pilgrimage and returned to hold high office under a number of kings. This contact is thought to explain the Javanese influence on Cham art which shows itself in the tenth century.

During the tenth century events of great importance for the future of Champa took place beyond her northern borders. In 907 the T'ang dynasty fell in China, and the Annamites took advantage of the situation to stage a struggle for independence which resulted in the foundation of the kingdom of Dai-co-viet (Annam and Tongking) in 939. This happened during the reign of the Cham king Indravarman III (c. 918–59). At first the change seems to have had little effect upon Champa, unless the friendly relations cultivated by Indravarman III's successor, Jaya Indravarman I, with the first Sung emperor may be taken to indicate the likelihood of trouble arising between Champa and the new kingdom.

Trouble indeed did arise under the next king, Paramesvaravarman. He was persuaded by a refugee Annamite claimant in 979 to espouse his cause and sent an expedition by sea against Hoa-lu, the capital of the Dinh dynasty. It came to grief, however, in a storm. Then in the following year, when Le Hoan seized the throne from the Dinh and sent a mission to Champa to announce his accession, Paramesvaravarman was foolish enough to clap the envoy into prison. The result was an Annamite invasion which destroyed Indrapura and killed the Cham king. His successor, Indravarman IV, had to take refuge in the south while appealing in vain for Chinese help. Such was the disorder in northern Champa that an Annamite named Luu Ky-Tong seized power and successfully resisted an attempt by Le Hoan to depose him. When in 986 Indravarman IV died Luu Ky-Tong even proclaimed himself King of Champa and sought Chinese recognition.

In 988 a Cham resistance movement came to a head under a native leader, who was proclaimed king at Vijaya (Binh-dinh). His task was rendered easier by the death of Luu Ky-Tong in 989, but he had to beat off a renewed Annamite attack in the following year. He took the title of Harivarman II and was the founder of the seventh dynasty in

Cham history. After a short period of peace, during which he secured recognition by China and restored the capital to Indrapura, he launched a series of counter-attacks upon Annam. Thus began the long struggle which was to end only with the extinction of the Cham kingdom. Annamite pressure upon the northern Cham provinces became so acute that as early as the year 1000 Harivarman II's successor, who is known by the incomplete name of Yang Pu Ku Vijaya Sri—, was forced to abandon Indrapura and transfer his capital to the less exposed Vijaya.

The eleventh century was one of disaster, when the Chams lost their northern provinces to Annam. They sent frequent missions to China, and in 1030 made an alliance with Suryavarman I of Angkor. But all hopes of help from these quarters were illusory, and in 1044 a long series of Annamite attacks culminated in another great Cham disaster. Their capital, Vijaya, was taken and King Jayasimhavarman II beheaded. A new dynasty, the eighth, was founded by a war leader belonging to one of the noble families. He took the title of Jaya Paramesvaravarman I and set himself to revive the kingdom. He repressed revolts in the southern provinces and made every effort to develop good relations with both Annam and China by means of frequent missions.

Rudravarman III, however, who came to the throne in 1061, while seeking to lull Annamite suspicions by continuing to send frequent missions, went ahead with preparations to attack the arch-enemy. When he launched his attack, late in the year 1068, it was a fiasco. It brought the inevitable Annamite counter-invasion in 1069. Li Thanh-Ton speedily obtained possession of the capital and captured the fugitive king, after pursuing him into Cambodian territory. Then the victor celebrated his triumph with a great ceremonial banquet in the royal palace and made a holocaust of the capital. His wretched captive, Rudravarman III, was taken away to Tongking, and only liberated on making a formal surrender of the three northern provinces of his country, corresponding to modern Quang-binh and Quang-tri. On arrival home, however, he was quite unable to restore his authority, and with his death in 1074 his short-lived dynasty came to an end.

A prince named Thang founded the ninth dynasty. He took the title of Harivarman IV and was soon displaying the greatest energy repairing the damage caused by the invaders and reviving the fortunes of his country, enfeebled as it was through the loss of its northern provinces. Champa's recovery seems to have been remarkably rapid, for not only did Harivarman drive off a further Annamite attack but he also defeated a Khmer one, and followed this up by sending a raiding force which penetrated Cambodia as far as Sambor on the Mekong, where it destroyed all the religious sanctuaries.

Harivarman IV's policy was to cultivate better relations with the Annamites. Hence it was with some reluctance that in 1076 he allowed himself to be drawn into a coalition organized by China for an attack on Annam. When it failed he took care to ward off Annamite anger by sending propitiatory offerings. After this regular tribute was sent to Annam until the end of the century. In 1103, however, his son Jaya Indravarman II was persuaded by an Annamite refugee into making a vain attempt to recover the three lost northern provinces. But this was only a passing interlude in a long period of peaceable relations with Annam which lasted until the middle of the thirteenth century. Not that the Chams acquiesced in the permanent loss of the disputed territory; on the contrary, they were forced to live at peace with Annam because they had to concentrate all their efforts upon defending their independence against the Khmers.

This new struggle was precipitated by the warlike Suryavarman II of Angkor, who made a determined attempt to impose Khmer rule upon Champa. His ambition to become a world conqueror was favoured by the circumstances of his time. Because of the struggle between the Sung and the Kin, China was unable to exercise a restraining hand on the 'southern barbarians'. Annam also, as a result of the long minority of Li Anh-Ton, was weakened by faction struggles among the magnates. The Khmers began by raiding Champa. Then, when refugees sought safety by crossing over into Annamite territory, Suryavarman invaded the province of Nghe-an and pillaged the coastal districts of Thanh-hoa. In 1132 he persuaded, or forced, Jaya Indravarman III to join with him in an attack which failed. The Cham king thereupon made his peace with Annam, and when some years later Suryavarman renewed the attack he refused to co-operate with the Khmers.

In revenge for this, Suryavarman in 1145 invaded Champa, took the capital, Vijaya, and made himself master of the kingdom. Jaya Indravarman III disappeared during the struggle; what happened to him is unknown. The northern part of Champa remained under Khmer rule until 1149, but in the southern region of Panduranga a new Cham king, Jaya Harivarman I, arose in 1147. In the next year, having driven off a Khmer invading force, he went over to the offensive, and in 1149 recovered Vijaya and reunited the kingdom. But he was not yet master in his own house. A pretender, Vamsaraja, collected a large force of savage peoples from the mountains, and when this was routed escaped to Annam. There he was allowed to recruit another large force, with which he invaded Champa. He was again defeated, in late 1150 or early 1151, and both he and his Annamite commander lost their lives.

Jaya Harivarman I's troubles were still not over. In 1155 the district of Panduranga rose in rebellion, and it was not until 1160 that the revolt was finally crushed. Notwithstanding all these disturbances his reign was a period of recuperation. He repaired the damage of war, devoted part of the booty to the restoration of temples, and erected new ones. He sent embassies to China and appeased Annam by regular payments of tribute. A rupture was nearly caused by the lawless behaviour of the Cham envoy bearing presents to Thein To in 1166. An Annamite force actually crossed the frontier in 1167, but by that time Jaya Harivarman I was dead, and his successor, Jaya Indravarman IV, sent a rich present to Thein To, who recalled his troops.

Jaya Indravarman IV was a clever adventurer who had seized the throne from Jaya Harivarman I's son. His great desire was to turn the tables on Cambodia in revenge for Suryavarman II's invasions of Champa. His first attack, made in 1170 after assuring himself of Annam's neutrality, went by land and failed. In 1177, however, he sent an expedition by sea to the Mekong delta, whence it sailed up the river and took Angkor by surprise. The city was pillaged, and the Cham force then retired with immense booty. This daring act caused the deepest hatred between Champa and Cambodia for many years.

In 1190 after long preparation Jayavarman VII, the builder of Angkor Thom, launched a great attack on Champa under the leadership of a Cham prince, Sri Vidyanandana, who had been educated at Angkor. Once more the Cham kingdom fell to the Cambodian invaders. Jaya Indravarman IV was sent a captive to Angkor, and the son of Jayavarman VII, Prince In, was proclaimed king in his stead at Vijaya. The realm was again split into two, and the Cham Sri Vidyanandana became ruler of Panduranga as the vassal of Cambodia and with the title of Suryavarman.

Rebellions arose everywhere against the new régime. Prince In was chased out of Vijaya in 1191 by a Cham leader, who proclaimed himself king as Jaya Indravarman V. Jayavarman VII thereupon sent the captive Jaya Indravarman IV with an army to regain his throne. The latter called upon Suryavarman, who had crushed his own rebels, for aid. Suryavarman led a force to Vijaya, captured the city and killed Jaya Indravarman V. He then turned on the unlucky Jaya Indravarman IV, whom he defeated and killed in 1192. Having reunited Champa by these successes, he threw off his allegiance to Cambodia. He now had to meet a whole succession of Khmer attacks. For some years he was successful. He sent embassies to Annam and China, and in 1199 secured an edict of investiture from the Emperor Long Can.

In 1203, however, the Khmer armies drove him out. After attempting unsuccessfully to shelter in Annam, whither he had fled by sea, he evaded an Annamite attempt to arrest him and sailed away, and, writes Maspero, 'history does not tell us what became of him'. For seventeen years, 1203–1220, Champa was under Khmer domination. Then, for some reason about which the records are silent, the Khmer army of occupation evacuated the country. It was a voluntary withdrawal, and a Cham prince of the old royal line took over the reins of government peaceably and assumed the difficult task of reconstruction.

There has been much speculation among historians as to the cause of the Khmer evacuation. Maspero's conclusion, accepted by Cœdès, is that T'ai pressure upon the Khmer empire had become so acute that Angkor was forced to abandon the idea of holding Champa in subjection. Her century-long feud with Cambodia left Champa very weak, and her recovery was slow. Throughout the period she had had to forego all attempts to regain her three northerly provinces from Annam. But it was a case of postponement only: she was implacable in her resolve never finally to acquiesce in their abandonment. And as Annam was equally determined to keep them, there could be only one end to the contest: the total extinction of one or other of the contending parties.

The resumption of the struggle took place during the reign of Jaya Paramesvaravarman II, the king who came to the throne when the Khmers left. According to the *Annamite Annals* the Chams took advantage of the weakness of the Li dynasty to commit a series of piratical raids upon the coastal districts of Annam. In 1225 a new dynasty, the Tran, succeeded the Li, and in due course an Annamite envoy was sent to complain that the Cham tribute had not been paid regularly. Jaya Paramesvaravarman II replied by demanding the return of the lost provinces. The result was a fresh Annamite invasion led by King Tran Thai-Ton in person. Cham resistance was fierce. Jaya Paramesvaravarman II seems to have been killed during the struggle, presumably in 1252. He was succeeded by his younger brother, Jaya Indravarman VI, a man of peace. And although the Annamites had won no spectacular success, they were glad to call off the struggle, for they themselves were now threatened by a new danger from the north.

The victories of the Mongols in China were the cause of this sudden cessation in the Cham-Annamite war. Only five years later, in 1257, a Mongol army pillaged Hanoi, but retired before strong Annamite resistance. In 1260 Kublai Khan succeeded to the Mongol leadership, and, while continuing the conquest of the Sung empire, began to demand tokens of obedience from the states which had previously recognized Chinese overlordship. Envoys were sent to Annam, Cambodia and Champa ordering their kings to proceed to his headquarters and pay homage in person. All made excuses and sought to temporize by sending envoys and presents.

In Champa's case matters came to a head in 1281, when Kublai's patience was exhausted and he sent Marshal Sögatü to impose Mongol administration upon the country. The appearance of the Mongols caused a nation-wide movement of resistance in Champa. Sögatü soon found his task too great for his resources, and he was unable to deal a knock-out blow to the Cham army, for Indravarman V retired with it into the mountains. When Kublai sent reinforcements Annam refused them passage by land. In 1285 Kublai's son Togan, while trying to force his way through Tongking, was defeated and driven back into China by the Annamites, while Sögatü, on attempting to go to his aid, was defeated and driven back into Champa, where he was killed by the Chams.

Indravarman V, in the hope of avoiding further trouble, at once sent an envoy with tribute, which was accepted. Kublai had too many irons in the fire to risk another adventure in Champa. Three years later, when Marco Polo visited the country, a new king, Jaya Sinhavarman III (1288–1307), was reigning peaceably. He was determined, however, to make no concessions to China and to take no chances, for in 1292, when the Mongol fleet sailed down his coast on its famous punitive expedition against Java, the Cham fleet shadowed it to see that it made no attempt to land in Champa.

Jaya Sinhavarman III was disposed to ally with Annam. In 1301 he received a visit from Tran Nhon-Ton, who had abdicated in favour of his son Tran Anh-Ton and was ostensibly seeking merit by a round of pilgrimages to sacred shrines in neighbouring countries. On leaving, the ex-king professed himself so gratified at the warmth of his reception that he promised the Cham monarch one of his daughters in marriage. Jaya Sinhavarman III, who was partial to foreign marriages and already had a Javanese wife, weakly swallowed the bait. In the negotiations, which led up to a marriage alliance in 1306, he was cajoled into·surrendering two of the Cham provinces north of the Col des Nuages as the price for the hand of a sister of Tran Anh-Ton.

He died in the following year, and his son Che Chi, who succeeded him as Jaya Sinhavarman IV, had to bear the consequences of this stupid act. For the ceded provinces, renamed Thuan-chau and Hoa-chau by. Annam, were so rebellious that they made life unbearable for their Annamite administrators, who naturally attributed all their troubles to Cham support of the rebellious elements. In 1312 Annam, unable to put up with this condition of affairs any longer, invaded Champa, dethroned Jaya Sinhavarman IV and took him away a prisoner, having replaced him by his younger brother Che Nang.

Champa now became a province of Annam and its ruler was designated a 'feudatory prince of the second rank'. In the following year, when troops of the T'ai ruler, Rama Khamheng of Sukhot'ai, crossed Cambodian territory and raided Champa, Annam faithfully carried out the task of a suzerain by driving them off. Che Nang, however, was a loyal Cham and unwilling to submit to Annamite domination. In 1314 he rebelled and made an attempt to recover the two provinces ceded by his father. Success favoured him at first, but in 1318 he was so badly defeated that he disbanded his army and fled to Java, his mother's home.

He was succeeded by a viceroy, Che Anan, installed by the victorious Annamite commander. In 1323 he in turn threw off his allegiance to Annam. He managed to beat off every Annamite attempt to depose him, but made no attempt to recover the ceded provinces. After 1326 he was left to reign in peace until his death in 1342. The Franciscan friar Odoric of Pordenone, who travelled in these regions during his reign, placed on record that the King of Champa had no less than 200 children, and a very fine country with rich fishing grounds off its coast. He was the founder of the twelfth dynasty in Cham history, which held power until 1390.

In 1353 his successor, Tra Hoa, made a further attempt to recover the lost provinces, but failed. This, however, was the prelude to a period of amazing Cham recovery. It began in 1360 with the accession of Che Bong Nga, the last king of the short-lived dynasty, and a military adventurer of immense daring and resource. So great was his success that Maspero calls his reign the 'apogee' of Cham power. Cœdès, however, challenges this appraisal and prefers to regard it as 'the last ray of the setting sun'.[1] Che Bong Nga took advantage of the establishment of the Ming dynasty in China to begin a series of successful attacks on Annam, which culminated in 1371 with the sack of Hanoi. When the first Ming emperor ordered him to stop his campaigns he proceeded to attack pirates at sea and send the booty to China, while under cover of this he continued his war with Annam. That country was kept in a constant state of terror until in 1390 the indomitable Cham king was killed in a sea fight.

His successor was soon forced to abandon all his conquests, but owing to revolutions in Annam, which caused a temporary loss of power by the Tran dynasty, Annam's counter-attack did not come until 1402. Then Champa lost the province of Indrapura (Quangnam), and would have been forced to yield much more to her northern neighbour had not China intervened in 1407 and driven off the Annamite fleet, which was attacking Vijaya.

The tables were then turned on the Annamites in the most dramatic way. For the Chinese proceeded to conquer and annex Annam, which they held until 1428. The Chams on their part recovered the territory they had lost in 1402. Moreover, they were soon so aggressive that they turned their arms upon the enfeebled kingdom of Cambodia, which was forced to appeal to the Ming for protection. And when in 1428 Le Lo'i, the Annamite national leader, expelled the Chinese and regained his country's independence his successors for some years were glad to maintain peaceable relations with Champa.

In 1441 the long reign of Jaya Sinhavarman V came to an end and Champa became a prey to civil war. The Annamites were presented with an unrivalled opportunity once and for all to break the power of their troublesome neighbour. In 1446 they took Vijaya, but the Chams recovered the city. In 1471, however, the final conquest was achieved. No less than 60,000 people are said to have lost their lives in this last struggle, while the royal family and 30,000 prisoners were carried away into captivity.

Annam annexed the whole of Champa down to Cap Varella. Beyond it in the far south a diminutive Cham state continued to exist for some centuries. A succession of kings was recognized by China until 1543. A Cham Court existed in this region until 1720, when the last king fled with most of his people before Annamite pressure into Cambodian territory. His last descendant died early in the present century.

[1] Maspero, *Le Royaume de Champa*, pp. 199–218; Cœdès, *Les Etats hindouisés*, p. 395.

CHAPTER 9

ANNAM AND TONGKING

THE Vietnamese, as they now prefer to be called, are today the most numerous of the peoples of the Indo-Chinese peninsula. They occupy the valleys of the Red and Black rivers of Tongking, the coastal belt of Annam and the Mekong delta region of Cochin China. At the beginning of the Christian era they occupied Tongking and northern Annam only. They pushed southwards at the expense of the Chams, whose kingdom they conquered in the fifteenth century. Under the leadership of the Nguyen of Hué the last remaining independent Cham districts were absorbed during the seventeenth century. In the same century the Vietnamese began to plant colonies in the Mekong delta region in what was then Cambodian territory, and from that time onwards their steady penetration into Cochin China has been continuous.

Their origin has been much debated. They are thought to have been the result of intermarriage between local tribes already settled in Tongking and a mongoloid people, who may represent the third prehistoric migration to reach Indo-China—in their case via the Yangtse valley and what are now the Chinese provinces of Chekiang, Fukien, Kwang-tong and Kwang-si. Their language has predominantly T'ai affinities, but contains so many Mon-Khmer elements that some theorists have attempted to place it in the Mon-Khmer group. ·

The earliest archaeological evidence, chiefly from the sites of Thanh-hoa and Dong-son, shows their culture as a Mongol-Indonesian mixture already profoundly influenced by China. Chinese culture spread over the Chekiang, Fukien, Kwang-tong and Kwang-si area during the period from the ninth to the fourth centuries before the Christian era. In the third century B.C. it began to affect the region that is now Tongking and northern Annam. Under Shih Huang Ti (246–209), the 'First Emperor' of the Ch'in dynasty, General Chao T'o conquered the two Kwangs and they were annexed to China. Their population at the time was non-Chinese; it was made up of peoples related to the T'ais and the Annamites. Chinese colonization of the area began from about 214 B.C., when three forts were established as the centres of the commanderies of Nan-hai (Canton), Kuei-lin (Siun-chou) and Siang (Nan-ning). Modern Tongking and Annam remained for the time being outside the Chinese empire. The Red River delta was then under the rule of Lo princes, its territorial divisions being administered in feudal style by hereditary chieftains. In 208 B.C., when the Ch'in Dynasty was tottering to its fall, the Governor of the Yuë country proclaimed his independence. His son Chao T'o, who succeeded him, expanded his power southwards over the Red River delta and the lands to the south of it that now form the Vietnamese provinces of Thanh-hoa, Nghe-an and Ha-tinh. In 207 he called his kingdom Nan-yuë (Nam Viet), the kingdom of the southern people. The Han Dynasty (202 B.C.–A.D. 220) accorded Chao T'o its recognition in 196 B.C. when he accepted Chinese suzerainty. The Canton dynasty, founded by him, confined its direct rule to Kwangtung and Quang-si, leaving the south under its own native administration. But the incorporation of this area in the Nan-yuë kingdom must have increased the Yuë (Viet) element in the delta area. 'If one knew for certain to which ethno-linguistic group the Lo belonged', writes Cœdès,[1] 'and to which the Yuë, the problem of the formation of the Vietnamese people might *ipso facto* find its solution.'

In 112 B.C. the Chao dynasty threw off its allegiance to China; but in the following year the Emperor Wu Ti (140–87 B.C.), the creator of Chinese imperialism in Asia, annexed the Canton kingdom, and organized it as nine commanderies. Three of these, Chiao Chih, Chiu Chen and Jenan, covered modern Tongking and northern Annam as far southwards as the Col des Nuages. Nan-yuë was not integrated in the imperial administration: its commanderies were treated as commanderies for Chinese settlement. The indigenous feudal lords functioned under the general supervision of the Chinese prefect. Si Kuang (Tich Quang), prefect of Chiao Chih from A.D. 1 to 25, carried out a more intense Sinization, and during his term of office large numbers of Chinese immigrants entered Tongking. Many were officials with their families, and Chinese literati seeking a refuge from the rule of the usurper Wang Mang, whom Si Kuang refused to recognize. The recruitment of a militia of Chinese type and the creation of a subordinate civil service of indigenous officials threatened the traditional feudal structure of society, and in A.D. 40 the local lords rebelled. They were led by the sisters Trung, one of whom, Trung Trac, was elected queen. But they met disaster at the hands of a Chinese army, and in consequence Chinese administration and institutions were imposed.

---

[1] *Les Peuples de la Péninsule Indochinoise*, p. 45.

The country was administered as an imperial province, Chinese immigration was stepped up, and the policy of assimilation was adopted. Chinese studies were organized, and indigenous scholars sat for the Chinese examinations leading to the mandarinate. Chinese became the official language and the language of the Vietnamese intellectual *élite*. There was also some miscegenation between the indigenes and the Chinese. Thus a mixed aristocracy arose, and it was from their ranks that the later national leaders Li Bon and Li-phat-Tu sprang.

As time progressed, the Vietnamese of Tongking and northern Annam developed an increasing self-consciousness which showed itself in hostility to foreign rule. The third century A.D. saw a number of revolts against China. It saw also the beginnings of conflict with the Chams, which, with breaks, was to go on until the fifteenth century. This complicated the Chinese issue, for China's help was needed to repel the Chams. The sixth century witnessed another series of Vietnamese struggles for independence. The first, which began in 541, was a movement against the tyranny of the Chinese governor Siao Tseu. At the outset it was successful, and in 544 its leader Li Bon proclaimed himself king of Nam Viet. But in 547 he was defeated and his movement collapsed. The second, which occurred in 590, was an attempt to take advantage of the situation in China at the fall of the Ch'en Dynasty. The third, which began in 600, was led by another member of the Li family, Li-phat-Tu, and was crushed in 602, by General Lieu Fang, who subsequently proceeded to punish the Cham king Sambhuvarman for his encroachments upon the Jenan commandery. The revolts all failed, but through them national consciousness began to be aroused.

In 622 the new Tang Dynasty established the Protectorate General of Ngannan, 'The Pacified South'. Such was the derivation of the regional name Annam. The mountainous regions were separated from the lowlands and were administered according to the imperial system for lands inhabited by barbarian tribes. The Red River delta area was divided into four *chau* or prefectures, of which Giao-chau was the most important. In it was situated the capital of the whole area, Tong-binh. Tang domination was firm and efficient: it gave the country the peace which promoted prosperity, and there were few internal revolts. The most notable one, according to the *Annals*, was that of the 'Black Emperor', Mai Thuc Loan, who in 722 captured the capital and proclaimed himself emperor. He was in alliance with the Lin Yi (Chams) and the Land Chen La (Khmers), but failed to establish his rule. Traces of his citadel may still be seen near a temple dedicated to his memory. In 767 Tongking was invaded by marauders described in the *Annals* as coming from Java and the southern islands. The Chinese Imperial Commissioner, Chang Po-yi, drove them back to the sea, and they thereafter turned their attention to the coasts of Champa and Chen-la. The Chams themselves were pirates, with the king himself sharing the profits of their forays. The Tang, however, effectively restrained them, and during this period of Vietnamese prosperity they are said to have played some part in the maritime commerce between China and the Nanyang, though perhaps not to the extent that Le Thanh Khoi would have us believe when he asserts that they controlled the traffic in spices and silks from the seventh to the tenth century. He does not appear to be aware of the activities of the Malays of Sumatra's 'favoured coast' in this field.

A further Vietnamese revolt took place in 791 when Phung Hung, Lord of Son-Tay, seized control of the capital. He died soon afterwards, but his son Phung An succeeded him and ruled well for a few years until forced to surrender by a new Chinese Protector. The Chams under Harivarman I took advantage of his rebellion to occupy the two provinces they had long claimed. But in 808 Protector Chang Chou defeated them and drove them out of the disputed territory. Their defeat ushered in a long period of frontier peace.

In the middle of the ninth century a series of invasions took place from an entirely new quarter. The Kingdom of Nanchao had been founded early in the previous century in the west and north-west of what came to be known later as Yunnan. Its aid was sought in the middle of the ninth century by the T'o and Man mountain tribes between it and the Red River valley in resisting what they considered to be the excessive exactions of the Chinese. According to Le Thanh Khoi the Nanchao raiders made their first incursion in 846.[1] After an interval of some years they returned to attack the Vietnamese forts in the delta in 858,[2] but were driven off. There was a further attack in 862; then in the next year they overran the whole country and captured the capital. The T'ang general Kao P'ien took the field against them in 864 with a considerable force, and during the next two years administered severe defeats on them, finally clearing them out of Vietnam. Nanchao was crushed, the victorious Kao P'ien was appointed Imperial Commissioner, garrisons were established on the frontiers, and a citadel, Dai-la-thanh, was built to the north-west of modern Hanoi. Its name is associated with the first period of Vietnamese art,[3] represented today by fragments of Buddhist sculpture.

[1] *Le Vietnam, Histoire et Civilisation* (Paris, 1955), p. 126.
[2] Or 860, according to Le Thanh Khoi, *ibid.*
[3] B. P. Groslier, *The Art of Indochina* (London, 1962), p. 149.

It is distinguished by its individuality: later on Vietnamese art became increasingly subordinated to Chinese styles.

Dhyana Buddhism, a Mahayana form, had been brought to Tongking from China at the end of the sixth century. The T'ang became its patrons. The Vietnamese sangha attracted the attention of notable Buddhist pilgrims, I-Tsing among them, and Buddhist studies throve. Dhyana taught that truth was to be found, not in the study of the scriptures, but in deep meditation. By complete absorption the practitioner comes to enjoy absolute tranquility, and ultimately achieves absolute blessedness. The cultural development inspired by Buddhism became a feature of the national consciousness, which had grown up through the centuries of struggle against China's political control. The opportunity to assert independence came when the T'ang fell in 907, for China's political fragmentation during the period of the Five Dynasties caused her to lose effective power over her southern provinces. During the shortlived dynasty of the Later Liang (907–923) an indigenous chieftain, Khuc Thua Du, was accorded imperial recognition as governor of Tongking. His son, who succeeded him, sent his own son on a mission to a ruler of the Southern Han dynasty, who decided to reduce Vietnam to obedience. But it was in vain, for a former general of Khuc Thua Du became the leader of a successful resistance movement and made himself the effective governor of the country. In 937 he was assassinated by one of his officers, who had espoused the Chinese cause. But the movement for independence could not be halted. A new leader, Ngo Quyen, soon liquidated the traitor and in 938 decisively defeated the Chinese. Then in 939 he secured his acceptance by his countrymen as king of the independent kingdom of Nam Viet and established his capital at Co-loa. Vietnamese independence was at last launched.

French scholars distinguish fifteen dynasties during the whole period of Annamite history. Four held power for brief periods before 939 during intervals in Chinese domination. The first three after 939 had very short careers, numbering in all only eight kings and covering the period up to 1009. With one exception, the later ones had longer careers, each of which marks a distinct development in the country's history. At first the independent kingdom comprised only Tongking and the three northern Annamite provinces of Thanh-hoa, Nghe-an and Ha-tinh. South of these the kingdom of Champa held sway.

The Ngo dynasty was unable to control the local chieftains and never secured recognition from China. The Dinh dynasty (968–79) was even more ephemeral. The earlier Le dynasty (979–1009) started off with a flourish. Its first king, Le Hoan, invaded Champa in 982, killed its king, sacked its capital Indrapura, and retired home with vast booty. His successor, however, was dethroned in 1009 to make way for the Li dynasty, which lasted for over two centuries. Between 968 and 1009 important developments in the sphere of religion took place. Tien-Hoang of the Dinh dynasty established the official religious organization by incorporating Taoists and Buddhists in an administrative hierarchy. The second Le king imported classical texts of Mahayana Buddhism from China and made an effort to induce his people to accept Buddhism in place of the indigenous cults of animism and ancestor-worship. In effect Buddhism became grafted on to the indigenous cults, which continued to exist as strongly as ever. The scholars, however, remained for the most part Taoist or Confucian.

The Li dynasty (1009–1225) began the long fight to recover the Annamite provinces from Champa, which in its cultural aspect represented a struggle between Chinese and Indian influence. In the eleventh century Annamite pressure forced the Chams to abandon their northern provinces. After the sack of Indrapura by Le Hoan in 982 the Chams transferred their capital farther south to Vijaya (Binh Dinh). But in 1044 Vijaya itself was sacked by the Annamites and its king beheaded. It was taken a second time in 1069. Its king, Rudravarman III, was chased into Cambodian territory and taken prisoner. Then, after a grand ceremonial banquet held by Li Thanh-Ton in the captured city, he and his family were deported to Annam. In the following year he regained his liberty by the formal cession of the three northern provinces to Annam.

The Chams made tremendous efforts to recover the lost provinces, but in the twelfth century the attacks launched by the great Cambodian warrior Suryavarman II reduced them to impotence, so far as their struggle with Annam was concerned. The Cambodian wars, which ended in 1220, left the three northern provinces firmly in Cambodian hands.

In 1225 the Li dynasty was supplanted by the Tran. Champa was then beginning slowly to recover after her long contest with Cambodia. But the lost provinces remained an eternal bone of contention, and in the middle of the thirteenth century the duel showed signs of beginning again. This time, however, it had hardly got going when a truce was imposed on both sides by the Mongol threat. In 1257 a Mongol army sacked Hanoi (Thanh-long), but was forced to retire before growing Annamite resistance. Kublai Khan, who became emperor in 1260, sent envoys to all the states of the Indo-Chinese peninsula demanding tokens of obedience. The danger caused Champa to attempt a rapprochement with Annam, but nothing came of it. Nevertheless when Marshal Sögatü was sent by Kublai in 1281 to impose Mongol rule on Champa, Annam found herself forced to fight as the ally of the Chams, for in striving to overcome the extremely effective Cham resistance Kublai tried to send an army through Annamite territory, and the Annamites, realizing that their own independence was at stake, resisted. In 1285 a Mongol army fought its way to Hanoi through Lang-son and Bac-ninh. But again Annamite resistance was too strong and it had to retire. Another Mongol army under Kublai's son Togan was defeated when attempting to enter Tongking from the north, and Marshal Sögatü, in trying to come to his aid, was defeated and killed by the Chams. In 1287 Hanoi was occupied by the Mongols for the third time, but again the Annamites forced them to evacuate the country, and Tran Nho'n-Ton (1278–93) re-entered his capital in triumph.

Together Champa and Annam had successfully repelled all the Mongol attempts to subjugate them. To cement the friendship thus achieved, the King of Champa was persuaded to ask for an Annamite princess in marriage. When in 1306, after long negotiations, Tran Anh-Ton consented to bestow his sister upon the Cham monarch, the price demanded, and strangely enough accepted, was the cession to Annam of the provinces of Quang-tri and Thu'a-thien (Hué). But Jaya Sinhavarman died soon after the marriage, and the Chams at once started to recover the two provinces. Then in 1312 Tran Anh-Ton invaded Champa, crushed its resistance and took its king a prisoner to Tongking. The conquered kingdom was thereupon reduced to the rank of a feudatory state of Annam.

In 1326, after several rebellions and an appeal to China, Champa regained her independence. But it was the leadership of Che Anan, and not the injunction issued by Peking in 1324 ordering the Annamites to respect Champa, that caused them to relinquish their prey. In 1353 the Chams made an effort to regain the Hué region but failed. Then the Cham hero Che Bong Nga (1360–90) began a series of attacks which kept Annam in a constant state of terror during his reign. In 1371 he even sacked Hanoi. In 1377 Tran Due-Ton staged a counterattack and managed to penetrate as far as Vijaya, but he was ambushed outside the city and perished with the whole of his force. Che Bong Nga reoccupied all the territories previously taken from Champa by her rival. As soon as he was dead, however, the Annamites recovered all the territory they had lost to him as far as Tourane, and in 1398, in order the better to direct their efforts to complete the conquest of Champa, moved their capital southwards from Hanoi to Thanh-hoa.

Then came a sudden and unexpected halt in their progress. In 1400 a general named Le-Qui-Li deposed the Tran monarch and seized the throne. The partisans of the Tran dynasty thereupon called in Chinese aid, and in 1407 the Ming emperor Yung-lo sent an army to Tongking which occupied Hanoi and seized the usurper. The Chinese had come to stay, and had they not made the mistake of attempting to denationalize the country by forcing their language and customs upon the people they might have added Annam to their empire as a vassal state. As it was, however, the discontented people found a leader in a Thanh-hoa chieftain named Le Lo'i, who in 1418 began guerrilla operations against the Chinese with marked success. In 1427 he penned them up in Hanoi. The emperor sent an army to relieve the city, but Le Lo'i defeated it before it could make contact with the beleaguered garrison, and in 1428 the city capitulated. Le Lo'i then proclaimed himself King of Annam and became the founder of a second Le dynasty. He adroitly warded off the wrath of the Ming emperor by sending an embassy with tokens of his submission to Chinese overlordship, and Peking deemed it wise to let well alone and accord him formal recognition.

The Chams had taken advantage of the troubles in Annam to recover their lost provinces to the north of the Col des Nuages. At first the new Annamite dynasty maintained peaceful relations with its southern neighbour, but in 1441 a new series of Cham attacks began. In 1446 the Annamites, taking advantage of civil war in Champa, reoccupied Vijaya, but not for long, for the Chams soon recovered it. It was left to Le Thanh-Ton (1460-97), the greatest of the Le rulers, to deal the death-blow to the Cham kingdom in 1471. He transformed Champa into a circle of his dominions.

The political independence wrested by Le Lo'i from the Ming proved to be real and durable. But while throwing off Chinese domination the Annamites conserved the culture which in the course of the centuries they had absorbed from China. Le Thanh-Ton divided his empire into thirteen circles and gave it the strong administrative system which it maintained long after his time. His successors, however, were weaklings. Between 1497 and 1527 no less than ten kings came to the throne, four of them usurpers. Their ineptitude encouraged the ambition of the great mandarin families. The Court became a centre of intrigue, while central control over the feudal magnates practically lapsed. In 1527 an ambitious mandarin Mac

Dang-Dung, who had made and unmade kings since 1519, ordered the reigning monarch Le Hoang-De Xuan to commit suicide and usurped the throne. In 1529 he abdicated in favour of his son Mac Dang-doanh, but retained control until his death in 1541.

In 1533, however, through the powerful Nguyen family, the Le dynasty was restored. Nguyen Kim drove the Mac out of the Annamite provinces of Nghe-an and Thanh-hoa, but when he was poised for the conquest of Tongking in 1545 he was assassinated, and his sons were too young to take up his task. The Mac therefore remained in control of Tongking, and China, appealed to by both sides, authorized them to govern the parts they occupied as hereditary lordships under her suzerainty. The Mac dynasty ruled Tongking until 1592. Annam proper in the south was nominally under the Le dynasty, but as they were *rois fainéants* actual power was wielded by Nguyen Kim's successors as mayors of the palace. His immediate successor was his able son-in-law Trinh Kiem, who died in 1570.

When Nguyen Kim's two sons grew up, bitter rivalry developed between them and the Trinh. Trinh Kiem procured the murder of the elder, but the younger, Nguyen Hoang, escaped death by feigning madness, and Trinh Kiem sent him to govern the southern provinces that had once been the Cham kingdom. He calculated that in such a dangerous area the young man would not long survive. In this he was mistaken, for Nguyen Hoang, throwing off the cloak of madness, won the affection of the people of the south and before long was beginning to build up his military strength.

In 1570, when Trinh Kiem died, the Annamite dominions were divided between three authorities. The Mac were masters of Tongking, with Hanoi as their capital. The Trinh, as mayors of the palace for the Le sovereigns, ruled Thanh-hoa, Nghe-an and Ha-tinh, with Tay-do as their capital. The Nguyen, also acting on behalf of the Le, ruled the southern provinces, with Quang-tri as their centre. In 1592 Trinh-tong, Trinh Kiem's successor, captured Hanoi and obtained control over most of Tongking. The Mac fled to Cao-bang on the Chinese frontier, where they managed to hold out with the support of Peking until 1677. As China refused for many years to recognize the authority of the Le over Tongking, the Mac at Cao-bang, though without effective power, were always a potential danger. Not until the Mings were supplanted by the Manchus at Peking was Chinese recognition withdrawn from them and transferred to the Le. Nevertheless from 1592 onwards the Trinh were the lords of the north, and in 1593 they moved their capital, and the puppet Le sovereign, from Tay-do to Hanoi.

From time to time Nguyen Hoang appeared at Court. He still hoped that an opportunity would arise for him to regain the position held by his father. By the end of the century, however, it was obvious that the power of the Trinh was too well established to be shaken. In 1600 therefore, when a revolt occurred in Ninh Binh, and Nguyen Hoang went to quell it, he severed his connection permanently with the Court of Hanoi. Thenceforward the two rival families, each supreme in its own sphere, began to prepare for the inevitable war, which broke out in 1620.

CHAPTER 10

MALACCA AND THE SPREAD OF ISLAM

LONG before the days of the Prophet the Arabs had made settlements along the trade route between the Red Sea and China. Islam gave a new impetus to their shipping. In the eighth century they were sufficiently numerous in south China to sack Canton (758). In the ninth century there were small communities of Mahommedan merchants in several ports on the route to China. In the eleventh century they are mentioned as having existed in Champa for some time. They married native women but kept themselves socially apart from the non-Mahommedan communities. There is no evidence of Arab settlements of any importance in the Indonesian archipelago. Much of it, including Java and the Spice Islands, lay well away from the trade route to China.

The reports of the early Arab geographers concerning South-East Asia are vague and fantastic, and much of their information is second-hand. An Arabic-inscribed gravestone of a young woman at Leran, near Gresik, has been taken as the earliest evidence of the presence of Muslims in Java. The date may be 1082 or 1102, but there is a strong suspicion that the stone was brought there at a later period. Even if the date is genuine, the inscription does no more than indicate the presence of an Arab, or Persian, there in about 1100. There is no evidence of the spread of Islam to that area until long afterwards.

In 1292 the Polos, on their way home from China, visited Sumatra. 'Ferlec', the first port they entered, has been identified as Perlak. According to Marco's story, it was visited by so many Muslim traders that they had converted the natives of the place to the Law of the Prophet. From what he has to say further it is obvious that the conversion of Sumatra had only just begun. His is the earliest report we have of Islamic proselytizing activities in South-East Asia.

From Perlak the Polos went on to Samudra, where their ship was delayed for five months by the monsoon. In its immediate vicinity have been found the oldest relics, in the form of tombstones, of the Mahommedan sultanate of Samudra. Marco writes that at the time of his visit it was not Mahommedan. Its conversion must have come soon afterwards, since the tombstone of Sultan Malik al Saleh, its first Muslim ruler, is dated 1297. The stone came from Cambay in Gujerat.

The spread of Islam to Gujerat was one of the results of the conquests of Mohammed of Ghor in north India and the Ganges valley nearly a century earlier. In the latter half a struggle for dominance over Gujerat was decided in favour of the Mahommedans. Cambay fell into their hands in 1298, and although the majority of the Gujeratis remained Hindu the Court and ruling class became Muslim. In the thirteenth century Cambay already had a long history behind it as an emporium. Arab and Persian merchants had been settled there from the ninth century. Its trading connection with Indonesia was also of long standing. The conversion to Islam of many of its native merchants added the stimulus of missionary ardour to their trade with Indonesia. Hence it can have been no mere coincidence that the evidence of the presence of Islam in the northern ports of Sumatra bears witness to a Cambay origin.

Ibn Batuta, who was twice at Samudra on his way to and from China in 1345–6, tells us that the sultan followed the rite of Shafi'i, the form of Islam which all Indonesian believers profess today. On his showing also the country around was still non-Muslim. On the opposite bank of the river to the town of Samudra a Mahommedan grave dated 1421 has been found. This is thought to have been the site of Pasé, mentioned in the *Malay Annals* as Pasai, which Diogo Lopes de Sequeira visited in 1509. It was apparently the first important diffusion-centre of the new faith in South-East Asia.

So far as the Peninsula is concerned, the earliest Islamic document is a stone inscription at Trengganu with its date defaced. It is somewhere between 1303 and 1387. Blagden, whose authority commands respect, favours the earlier date. The stone may have been a boundary mark between the territory of Islam and the 'territory of the war', and shows by its wording that the new faith had not been accepted by the local people. Against the early date suggested by Blagden stands the testimony of Ibn Batuta that in 1345–6 the ruler of the Malay Peninsula was an infidel. Does he refer to the King of Kedah? The *Nagarakertagama* of 1365 claims the region as a dependency of Majapahit. Actually there is little evidence suggesting the spread of Islam to the Peninsula before the fifteenth century.

It was the rise of Malacca that gave the real impetus to the conversion of the Peninsula. There has been much divergence of view regarding the date of the city's foundation. Against the arguments

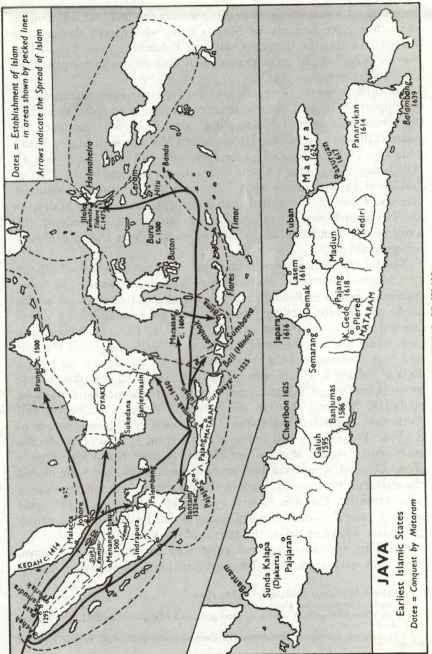

Dates = Establishment of Islam in areas shown by pecked lines

Arrows indicate the Spread of Islam

THE SPREAD OF ISLAM

JAVA

Earliest Islamic States

Dates = Conquest by Mataram

in favour of a date earlier than 1400 stands the fact that no mention of such a place is made by Marco Polo, who passed through the Straits in 1292; the Blessed Odoric of Pordenone, who passed that way in 1323; Ibn Batuta in 1345–6; and Prapanca, who composed the *Nagarakertagama* in 1365.

In 1918, however, Ferrand[1] put forward an ingenious argument in support of Gaspar Correa's statement in *Lendas da India*[2] that when the Portuguese arrived Malacca had already been in existence for more than seven centuries. He identified Malacca with Marco Polo's 'Malayur', which he placed on the Peninsula, and with 'Ma-li-yu-eul', which, according to the Chinese account, was attacked by the T'ais of Sukhot'ai in and before 1295. In 1921 G. P. Rouffaer attacked Ferrand's thesis.[3] He argued that both names referred to Malayu— i.e. Jambi in Sumatra—and on the available evidence built up the story of the foundation of the city by Paramesvara that is generally accepted today.

The founder, whose name means 'prince-consort', was the husband of a Majapahit princess. According to Sumatran tradition, he was a Śailendra prince of Palembang. During the war of secession which broke out in 1401 between Virabumi of East Java and King Vikramavarddhana of Majapahit he took refuge in Tumasik (Singapore), then under a chief who owed allegiance to Siam. He killed his host and took possession of the town. In 1402 he was driven out by the Raja of Pahang or Patani, also a vassal of Siam, and according to one account brother of the murdered chief. After some wanderings he settled at Malacca, then an insignificant village of sea-rovers and fishermen. A place of that name is mentioned in a Siamese source in *c.* 1360. Tomé Pires, who was in Malacca from 1512 to 1515, tells the story with a wealth of detail not elsewhere available in his valuable *Suma Oriental*, which was discovered as recently as 1937.[4] He placed the arrival of 'Paramjcura' there in about 1400. D'Albuquerque's son, who wrote his *Commentaries* in 1557, gives substantially the same story. So also does de Barros in *Decada* II, but he dates the foundation of the city 250 years before the arrival of the Portuguese.

Aided by the sea-rovers and reinforced by numbers of Malays, who came over from Palembang to join him, Paramesvara rapidly

---

[1] 'Malacca, le Malayu et Malayur' in JA, 1918.
[2] Composed between 1512 and 1561.
[3] 'Was Malaka emporium voor A.D. 1400 genaamd Malajoer?' in BKI, The Hague, 1921, deel 77, part 1.
[4] The English translation by Armando Cortesão was published by the Hakluyt Society in 1944.

built up a large settlement. It began as a market for irregular goods, a pirate centre. Then, by forcing all vessels passing through the Straits to put into its harbour for passes, it developed at the expense of Samudra and Singapore. Both Siam and Majapahit claimed suzerainty over the Peninsula, but Siam alone could enforce it. Hence when in 1403 Malacca was visited by a Chinese envoy, the eunuch Yin-k'ing, Paramesvara seized the opportunity to apply for recognition by the Ming emperor and support against Siam. In 1405 he sent an embassy to China and promptly received recognition. Ming policy, as we have seen, aimed at restoring Chinese control over the states of South-East Asia. Ambassadors were sent from port to port to explain Chinese policy and were followed by a war fleet to enforce it where necessary. The mission which appeared at Malacca in 1403 was sent by the third Ming emperor Ch'eng-tsu (Yung-lo). It was the one which went to Java and found two kings there. It was followed by a war fleet under Cheng Ho, whose series of voyages began in 1405.

Paramesvara maintained the closest possible relations with China. In 1409 Cheng Ho visited Malacca, and in 1411 the king returned the compliment by going personally to Peking to pay his respects to the emperor. In the following year he sent his nephew. R. A. Kern states that in 1414 his son Mohammed Iskander Shah went to China to announce his father's death.[1] This would appear to be a mistake, which, as Sir Richard Winstedt points out,[2] was due to the fact that the Chinese failed to realize that Paramesvara had become a Muslim and changed his name to Megat Iskandar Shah. His conversion seems to have been the result of his marriage to a daughter of the Sultan of Pasé, who himself was a recent convert to Islam. According to Cœdès, he paid a further visit to China in 1419 to ask for support against Siam.

Malacca's expansion was particularly rapid. Its position was more favourable than Palembang's or Jambi's for controlling shipping passing through the Straits. It thus became the heir to the commercial power once wielded by Śrivijaya. It became an emporium, whereas the Sumatran ports were merely places for the export of pepper. It thrust itself into the trade route in spices (cloves, nutmeg and mace) from the Moluccas to India. Previously the route had been from the Moluccas to East Java and thence to India. Now ships leaving East

---

[1] In Stapel, *Geschiedenis van Nederlandsch-Indië*, I, p. 322.
[2] *History of Malaya*, pp. 41–3, expresses the view held by Kern. In *The Malays, a Cultural History* he quotes the account given by Tomé Pires of Paramesvara's conversion to Islam and consequent change of name. See also on this point Cœdès, *Les États hindouisés*, p. 410, f.n. 2.

Java had to put in at Malacca before proceeding onwards to India. The rising state, which at first had paid tribute to Siam to escape destruction, soon ceased to consider itself a dependency of Ayut'ia, especially after Cheng Ho in 1409 had presented Paramesvara with a silver seal, a cap, and official robes 'and declared him king'.[1] Indeed, Paramesvara so far forgot his humble beginnings as to demand the submission of Palembang, and the Emperor Yung-lo had to intervene in order to maintain the status quo. This was one of the objects of Cheng Ho's third voyage in 1415.

Megat Iskandar Shah, who, according to Tomé Pires, embraced Islam at the age of seventy-two, died in 1424. His son, who succeeded him, significantly took the old Śrivijaya title of Śri Maharaja. He went at once to China for recognition, taking his son with him. In the Chinese record of his visit he appears as Si-la Ma-ha-la. Fear of trouble from Siam led him to send regular embassies to China throughout his reign, which lasted until 1444. Winstedt tells us that in some recensions of the *Malay Annals* he is credited with the organization of the elaborate palace etiquette which still obtains in Perak.[2] He also received a visit from Cheng Ho.

His son Raja Ibrahim, who succeeded him, assumed the title of Śri Paramesvara Deva Shah. Winstedt thinks that his assumption of this hybrid Hindu-Muslim title may indicate a reaction against the new faith. He sent a mission to China in 1445, but in the following year was dethroned and murdered as a result of a coup d'état by Tamil Muslims led by his elder brother Raja Kasim, whose mother was the daughter of a rich Tamil or half-Tamil merchant from Pasé.

Raja Kasim assumed the title of Muzaffar Shah. The Portuguese writers refer to him as Modafaixa or Malafar Sha. He reigned until 1459. His reign saw the emergence of a famous figure in Malaccan history, Tun Perak, the brother of Tun Kudu, a wife of Muzaffar Shah. In the *Malay Annals* he is celebrated as the victorious hero of campaigns against the Siamese, Pahang and Pasé. Winstedt calls him 'the brain of Malacca's imperialist policy in Malaya and Sumatra for more than three reigns'.[1] The story goes that the king's Tamil uncle, who had been mainly instrumental in placing him on the throne, received thereby so much power that the bendahara, the father of Tun Perak and Tun Kudu, committed suicide. The Tamil Tun Ali then became bendahara. This caused so bitter a feud between him and Tun Perak that the king to end it offered Tun Ali any bride he might choose as the price of his resignation. His price was the hand of Tun Kudu,

---

[1] Winstedt, *History of Malaya*, p. 41.   [2] *Ibid.*, p. 44.   [3] *Ibid.*, p. 46.

and with her brother's acquiescence the king handed her over. Tun Perak himself then became bendahara. The lady seems to have accepted the change of husband with complacency.

Tun Perak was responsible for the defeat of the Siamese attacks on Malacca that have been dealt with in Chapter 7, and for a great extension of Malacca's territorial dominion. Tomé Pires speaks of successful campaigns against Pahang, Trengganu and Patani in the Peninsula, and Kampar and Indragiri in Sumatra. He also brought about the resumption, in 1456, of relations with China, which had been interrupted by the coup d'état and subsequent Tamil régime. The emperor conferred on Muzaffar Shah the title of sultan and sent him 'a cap of leather, a dress, a daily dress of red silk gauze, a girdle adorned with rhinoceros horn and cap of gauze'.[1]

When he died in 1459 Muzaffar Shah was succeeded by his son Raja Abdullah, who assumed the title of Mansur Shah. In the first year of his reign the new ruler sent an embassy to China. The return mission sent by the emperor was shipwrecked, but two years later another was despatched which arrived safely. During Mansur Shah's reign Tun Perak further extended Malacca's sway. A great expedition against Pahang deposed Maharaja Deva Sura, a vassal of Siam, and placed a Malaccan prince on its throne. This was by way of revenge for the Siamese attacks on Malacca during the previous reign. Afterwards peace was patched up with Siam. Before the end of the reign the empire of Malacca included Kedah, famous for its tin, Trengganu, Pahang, Johore, Jambi, Kampar, Bengkalis, the Carimon Islands and Bintang. Pasé might have been included in the list, for Tun Perak led an expedition which crushed a rebellion there and restored its sultan to his throne, in return for his promise to accept Malaccan suzerainty. But he broke his promise, and his state ultimately became part of the dominions of Acheh.[2]

Malacca was now a political power of the first rank, able to withstand Siam. She was also the most important commercial centre in South-East Asia as well as the main diffusion-centre of Islam. Two more sultans sat on the throne before Albuquerque's conquest in 1511: Ala'uddin Riayat Shah (1477–88), a son of Sultan Mansur Shah, and Mahmud (1488–1511), a brother of Ala'uddin Riayat Shah. In Mahmud's reign Malacca was at the height of her wealth and prestige. Tun Perak, the great bendahara, whose name is associated with

---

[1] Part of the inscription on his grandson's tombstone, *ibid.*, p. 46.
[2] The English name for this place was Achin, the Dutch Atjeh. The Indonesian republic has adopted the latter, the English spelling of which is given here.

her greatest triumphs, died in *c.* 1498, but his successors continued to be the real rulers. Mahmud himself was little more than a figure-head. He is said by the Portuguese to have been an opium addict. His main interest was in religion and mysticism.

War broke out again with Siam over the Siamese claim to over-lordship, which Mahmud refused to recognize, saying that his only suzerain was the Emperor of China. Siamese attacks were beaten off and their fleet was defeated off Pulo Pisang. Malacca also helped Pahang to drive off an attack by Siam's vassal Ligor. This state of war only ended with the Portuguese conquest.

Malacca has been described as not a trading city in the accepted sense, but rather the site of a vast fair, where during the season the products of China and the Far East were exchanged for those of western Asia and Europe. Tomé Pires, who arrived there as secretary and accountant of the Portuguese factory in the year following Albuquerque's conquest of the city wrote in his invaluable *Suma Oriental* a detailed account of its commerce and administration under its sultans such as is found in no other source. 'Men cannot estimate the worth of Malacca on account of its greatness and profit', he writes. Where other ports had one Shabandar to take charge of all ships coming into the port, Malacca had no less than four. The most important was the one who dealt with the ships from Gujerat. Another was in charge of merchants from the Coromandel Coast, Bengal, the Mon kingdom of Lower Burma, and Pasai in north Sumatra; a third in charge of those from Palembang, Java, the Moluccas and the Bandas, Borneo and the Philippines; and a fourth in charge of the Chinese and merchants from the eastern ports of the Indo-Chinese Peninsula.

Gujerat's importance lay largely in the fact that its chief port Cambay was the main rendezvous for merchants travelling to Malacca from Cairo, Mecca, Aden and the ports of the Persian Gulf. Their practice, Pires tells us, was, after trading in Gujerat, to 'take up their companies for their cargo' and 'embark in March for Malacca sailing there direct'. Piece-goods formed by far the biggest item in the cargoes they took there. 'The principal merchandise brought back', he writes, 'is cloves, mace, nutmeg, sandalwood, seed-pearls, some porcelain, a little musk; they carry enormous quantities of apothecary's lignaloes, and finally some benzoin, for they load up with these spices, and for the rest they take a moderate amount.' 'The rest' consisted of gold, tin, large quantities of white silk and white damask, coloured silks and birds from the Banda islands much prized for their plumage. Herein lay the secret of Malacca's quite exceptionally rapid rise to a position of world importance at the end of the fifteenth century, a position, be it noted, that it was never to hold again after its conquest by the Portuguese in 1511. It became the focus of an expanding east–west trade movement in which Muslim trade from the ports of north-west India played a dominant role. 'Malacca cannot live without Cambay, nor Cambay without Malacca, if they are to be very rich and very prosperous,' was Tomé Pires's comment when his countrymen had already cut the lifeline between the two ports, and Muslim merchants were beginning to transfer their custom to other centres in Sumatra and Java.

Malacca gave a new impetus to the propagation of Islam in South-East Asia. The first Muslim ruler of Pahang was a son of the Sultan of Malacca. When he died in 1475 his grave was marked by a stone inscribed in classical Arabic similar to that of the first Sultan of Samudra. Both were imported from Cambay. Vast numbers of these inscribed tombstones, with blank spaces left for the insertion of names, were brought to Malacca by Gujerati merchants; so many, in fact, that later on the Portuguese found them handy material in building their first fort there. Trengganu officially adopted Islam on becoming a vassal state of Malacca. Patani was converted from Malacca; Kelantan as Patani's vassal. A Muslim prince is mentioned as ruler of Kedah in 1474. Across the straits Rokan entered the Islamic fold in the first half of the century, Kampar, Indragiri and Siak later. Brunei also, the first Muslim state to appear in Borneo, came to accept Islam through its trading connection with Malacca. The Malaccan dynasty saw in Islam a political instrument of great potential value; by adopting the religion officially it secured admittance to what Van Leur has described as 'the unity of Islam' with its assurance of powerful allies, and its expansive ardour. Thus, as Malacca established overlordship over the states of the Peninsula and of the east coast of Sumatra across the straits, so Islam penetrated them. It was a political weapon against Buddhist Siam; still more it supplied the Malaccan empire with a cohesive force which enabled it to hold together after the Portuguese capture of Malacca itself.

R. A. Kern makes the striking claim that 'Java was converted in Malacca'.[1] It is, of course, very far from true, but it does serve as a useful pointer to the way in which Islam made its first impact upon Java, namely through the very close connection which grew up between Malacca and the ports of northern Java, notably Tuban and Gresik. Malacca received not only its spices but also its vital food supply

---

[1] In F. W. Stapel (ed.), *Geschiedenis van Nederlandsch Indie*, vol. i, p. 328.

through the east Javanese ports. The trade was in Javanese hands, and by the beginning of the sixteenth century they formed the most important element in Malacca's population. Its army was Javanese; most of its shipwrights were Javanese; and the great Javanese aristocratic families who ran the trade between eastern Indonesia and Malacca were represented there. One Javanese merchant-prince is said to have maintained his own force of 6,000 slave troops. In this way was Islam introduced into the coastal districts of Java, which were asserting their independence of the declining empire of Majapahit, to become a potent weapon in their struggle against the Hindu-Buddhist central authority. Of these merchant-princes themselves Tomé Pires tells us that they were 'not Javanese of long standing in the country', but were descended from Chinese, Persians and Tamils who had settled there some seventy years earlier.[1]

The tradition of a Muslim conquest of Java, referred to on p. 89 above, comes from the story in the *Babad Tanah Jawi* of the overthrow of the *kraton* of Majapahit by a disowned son of its last king Bra Vijaya, who at the moment of defeat is shown as ascending the lofty look-out tower and thence floating up to heaven. The son, Raden Patah, is said to have founded Demak as an Islamic centre and to have conquered Majapahit at the head of an alliance of north Javanese Muslim states, thereupon becoming the first Muslim king of Java. Its most important effect upon historical thinking comes from the idea which it conveys of a sudden break in Javanese history, bringing with it what C. C. Berg has described as a cleavage in Javanese cultural life through the substitution of Islamic for Hindu-Javanese culture, to use Krom's term. Berg claims that by ending his *Hindoe-Javaansche Geschiedenis* at the fall of Majapahit Krom conveyed the impression that it ushered in a cultural change of fundamental importance.

Such a notion, however, is quite untenable. It has been attacked by the sociologists on the one hand who see the elements of Javanese culture today as the products of a process of continual evolution. Berg sums up their point of view aptly by denying that Java was ever *converted* to Islam: what really happened was that her pattern of culture gradually absorbed elements of Islam, just as earlier it had absorbed elements of Hinduism and Buddhism, and was later to absorb elements of European civilization.[2] Moreover, the political advance of Islam was very slow. Dr H. J. de Graaf represents the empire of Majapahit as gradually disintegrating through its vassal states embracing

---

[1] Cortesão, *op. cit.*, vol. i, p. 182.
[2] 'The Islamization of Java', *Studia Islamica*, iv, Paris, 1955, p. 137.

Islam and declaring their independence.[1] Schrieke thinks that the *coup de grâce* was administered by the ruler of Demak at the head of a combination of Muslim coastal lords probably in the year 1514,[2] but points out that when the Dutch first arrived in 1597 much of the interior was still 'infidel'. In East Java the Hindu-Buddhist state of Panarukan maintained its independence until 1614. Balambangan in the farthest east of the island successfully resisted a *jihad* launched against it by Sultan Agung of Mataram in 1639 and did not go over finally to Islam until late in the eighteenth century. The 'infidel' kingdom of Pajajaran in West Java, with its capital at Pakuan near modern Bogor, continued to exist until the fifteen-seventies, although cut off from the sea through the capture of its port, Sunda Kalapa, by Muslim Bantam half a century earlier. It fell when Panembahan Yusup, the second sultan of Bantam, captured Pakuan, slaughtered the whole royal family and forcibly converted the magnates to Islam. What we see then is a series of what were essentially political changes occupying a long period of time; and, as van Leur has emphasized, what took place was mainly an affair of rulers and aristocracies.[3] Mass conversion was unlikely, for at this stage missionary activities were not directed at the masses of the people.

One of van Leur's most interesting theories was that the propagation of Islam in Indonesia received its strongest impetus from the appearance of the Portuguese in the Indian Ocean in 1497.[4] This point was taken up by Schrieke in an essay entitled 'The Penetration of Islam in the Archipelago', which was unpublished at his death in 1945 and has since been issued in an English translation of his writings.[5] 'The race with Christianity', as he terms it, had actually begun before the arrival of the Portuguese in the East. The close coherence of the Muslim powers, he points out, found expression in their annual meeting at Mecca, and through this medium rumours of the Christian struggle against Islam in the Iberian Peninsula reached Indonesia ahead of the Portuguese. Hence by the time of their arrival the Muslim powers were already pressing on to extend Islam's influence as widely as possible. When Malacca fell in 1511 to the Portuguese, and became a strategic centre for their attack upon Islam and the Islamic trade in the vast island world of South-East Asia, the Crescent was already a move or two ahead of the Cross. It never lost its lead. The Muslim

---

[1] *Geschiedenis van Indonesië.*
[2] B. Schrieke, *Indonesian Sociological Studies*, Part II, *Ruler and Realm in Early Java*, pp. 65–9.
[3] *Indonesian Trade and Society*, p. 115.
[4] *Ibid.*, p. 113.   [5] *Op. cit.*, pp. 232–7.

traders, driven out of Malacca, settled in the rising north Sumatran state of Acheh, which by the middle of the sixteenth century became the most important entrepôt for the trade of the Indian and West Asian Muslims with the Archipelago, and, like Malacca and its predecessor Pasai, a centre of Islamic studies.

In Java, as we have seen, Muslim operations were first concentrated upon securing the immensely important ports of the northern coast, thus cutting off the Portuguese from contact with their potential allies the Hindu-Buddhist states of the interior. For instance in 1522 a Portuguese ship visited Sunda Kalapa, the port of the Sundanese kingdom of Pajajaran, and made a treaty with its Regent permitting the establishment of a factory there. But when five years later a Portuguese expedition arrived there for the purpose of planting the factory, the place was in Muslim hands. It is noteworthy also that from the northern Javanese ports, and Demak in particular, Islam spread to southern Borneo and the Moluccas ahead of the Portuguese. This start, as we shall see in Chapter 12, enabled it without much difficulty to win the race in the east of the Archipelago. How far the policies of religious imperialism pursued in their respective regions by Acheh, Bantam and Demak, represented a reaction to the Portuguese threat to Islam it would be hard to say: other compelling motives undoubtedly played their part, and, unfortunately, the historical evidence is extremely defective. The general picture of Islam's progress in Indonesia, however, makes the race theory a very attractive one; the subject calls for a definitive study.

The case of Celebes seems to have been exceptional. Notwithstanding long trading contracts with Muslim ports in Indonesia, its rulers did not begin to go over to Islam until the end of the sixteenth century, when Portuguese power was visibly waning. The interesting suggestion has been made that the strong loyalty of its peoples to their *adat* (customary law) was the cause of the delay.[1] When in 1603 Macassar officially adopted Islam, the motive of political aggrandizement was uppermost; in setting out to extend its power over its neighbour states it calculated that as a Muslim state it stood a better chance of success by swimming with the advancing tide of Islam. The conversion of its ruler was thus the prelude to a series of expeditions against the states to the north, who were forced to accept Islam as well as his overlordship. The various mountain tribes of the island were never converted. Elsewhere there were also notable cases of resistance. Bali successfully repulsed all attempts to introduce the religion of the

[1] J. Noorduyn, 'De Islamisering van Makasar' in *Bijdragen*, Deel 112, 1956, p. 250.

Prophet, even when a holy war was proclaimed against its princes and people by Sultan Agung of Mataram in the sixteen-thirties. It maintained close connections with the last Hindu-Buddhist states of East Java and became a storehouse of Old Javanese literature when the advance of Islam caused it to disappear from Java itself.

If our knowledge of the spread of Islam in South-East Asia as a political force is far from adequate, even more so is the picture that can be presented of its progress as a missionary movement. Scholars are generally agreed that the trader was the most common missionary. Throughout the areas where Islam spread the ruler was the chief merchant; he controlled all external trade and traders, for he directed and controlled all supplies of the basic commodities required by them, rice on Java and in Macassar to exchange for spices in the Spice Islands, pepper at Bantam and the ports of south-east and south-west Sumatra, pepper also and especially gold at Acheh. He had the first choice of all the goods brought to his country, bought them wholesale at his own prices, and fixed the prices at which they were to be sold in the common market. His most important official in dealing with foreign merchants was the Shahbandar ('Ruler of the port'), who by reason of his duties was in most cases a foreigner.

Schrieke has drawn attention to the important fact that when trade with the Red Sea ports via Cambay and Aden had got into the hands of Muslim merchants, after the end of the thirteenth century, foreign Muslims tended to become shahbandars in the ports of both India and the Archipelago.[1] He suggests that it was through them that Islam extended its influence at court level: they were able to indicate 'what was considered good form' at the great Mohammedan courts abroad, to warn of the danger of Portuguese expansion, and to recommend the adoption of Islam as a means of extending the ruler's own power. They also introduced Muslim scholars and holy men to stimulate his religious zeal and establish centres in his country for Islamic propaganda. The courts became to a greater or less degree centres of Islamic learning, producing a not inconsiderable literature much of which is still extant. The local centres of Muslim *walis*, or saints, came into being in order to counteract the influence of the hermits, who for many centuries had been the teachers and mentors of the common people. It was a contest in supernatural powers, and in Sumatra and Java brotherhoods of Sufi mystics from India, organized in trade guilds, became an important element in society. Sufism, as Sir Richard Winstedt has shown,[2] had a powerful influence in Malacca

[1] *Op. cit.*, p. 238.   [2] *The Malays; a Cultural History*, pp. 33–44.

also, and later, after its fall, when Acheh took the lead, two Sumatran mystics, Hamzah of Barus and Shams al-din of Pasai, disseminated doctrines which had their effects upon the whole Malay world. The appeal of Sufism was assisted by the deep-seated popular mysticism of Malaya and Indonesia with its roots in animism and its inclination towards a pantheism 'that finds Him closer than the veins of one's neck'.[1] Moreover, as Sir Hamilton Gibb has shown, the Sufi brotherhoods succeeded in spreading Islam because of their tendency to tolerate popular usages and beliefs not in accordance with the strict practice of Muslim orthodoxy.[2] So far as Java was concerned, C. C. Berg sums up what happened as Islamization, not conversion.[3] Most significant of all, perhaps, is the fact that Muslim law has not the same sanction in Malaya and Indonesia as in other Muslim countries: their own *adat* law has maintained its position.

The Muslim scholars and holy men played an important part in political as well as religious affairs at the various courts which received them. They both gave impetus to the political expansion of Islam and also strove to promote a sense of unity among the Muslim communities of the Peninsula and Archipelago in opposing the advance of Portuguese and, later, Dutch power. The *Babad Tanah Jawi* mentions many by name and provides vivid pictures of their activities, which with their mixture of fact and fable are reminiscent of Bede's *Ecclesiastical History of England*. Schrieke describes their influence upon the courts of Bantam and Acheh.[4] At the former, he says, it showed itself in punishments for using tobacco and opium similar to those established at the same time by Aurangzeb in Mughal India, in anti-European propaganda throughout the Archipelago, in stimulating an interest in Mecca and the pilgrimage, and in spreading a knowledge of Arabic literary works, often by means of translations. At Acheh during the sixteenth and seventeenth centuries a vast number of Malay writings on Islamic doctrines were produced. Their authors were in every case foreign scholars, many of whom were members of brotherhoods of mystics.

Acheh's greatness, like that of its predecessors, Malacca and Pasai, was based upon its commerce and maritime power. Like them, its market was almost entirely in the hands of Gujerati merchants. For a time it was a serious threat to the Portuguese in Malacca. Achinese ships sailed to India, Ceylon and the Red Sea. Achinese rulers maintained contacts with the Sultan of Turkey, the Great Mughal and the

---

[1] *Ibid.*, p. 38.   [2] H. A. R. Gibb, *Modern Trends in Islam*, 1945, p. 25.
[3] It is the theme of his article quoted above.   [4] *Op. cit.*, pp. 241–67.

rulers of Western India, the Coromandel Coast, Bengal and Ceylon. Its suzerainty extended over the west coast states of Sumatra, some of the east coast ones and several of the Malay states of the Peninsula. Even more important were its pre-eminence throughout the Malay world as the 'Gate to the Holy Land', the point of departure for the pilgrimage to Mecca, and its renown as a centre of religious study. Indian, Persian and Arab scholars stayed and worked there, as well as Malay and Javanese scholars on their way home after completing their pilgrimage. In his account of Mecca Snouck Hurgronje mentions the large number of religious foundations there for students from the Archipelago at the time of his visit and says that those for the Achinese were among the best known.[1] And Schrieke comments that there is no reason to assume that they did not exist in earlier times as well, for the rulers of Acheh, Bantam, Mataram, Palembang and Banjermasin, who are recorded to have received titles, holy flags and consecrated garments from Mecca, all sent rich contributions towards the maintenance of its activities.

Through Acheh also the influence of Mughal India passed to the Muslim courts of Malaya and the Archipelago. Its rulers copied Mughal architecture, gardens, court dress and ceremonial, and even adopted Mughal titles for some of its administrative officers.

[1] *Mekka in the Latter Part of the Nineteenth Century*, a translation of Volume II of Snouck Hurgronje's *Mekka* by J. H. Monahan, p. 255.

THE ECONOMY OF SOUTH-EAST ASIA
BEFORE THE BEGINNING OF THE EUROPEAN IMPACT

IT is impossible to present a completely integrated picture of the old economy of South-East Asia before the sixteenth century when the writings of European visitors begin to provide valuable information not available in indigenous sources themselves. The abundant chronicle writings are concerned only with dynastic happenings. Chinese writings are more helpful in matters of commerce and commercial products; but they need expert interpretation, and there are many gaps in their evidence. Nevertheless, recent work by Paul Wheatley and O. W. Wolters demonstrates how valuable they are for the solution of some of the most intractable problems faced by the historian of the early period. For the internal economies and social systems of the most advanced societies inscriptions provide source material; but the equipment, linguistic and otherwise, required for their study is such that few workers are attracted into their field. Their usefulness to the economic historian has been indicated by Gordon Luce for the Pagan period in Burmese history and by F. H. van Naerssen for the Śailendra period in Javanese; but a vast amount of work remains still to be done. Finally, as Louis Malleret has shown in the case of Funan, and Bernard Philippe Groslier in the case of Angkor, archaeology can be of great assistance in providing evidence unavailable in written records. Nevertheless, the picture is at best a blurred one. The account lacks precise data, notably statistical evidence. And there are large blank spaces.

Basic features of the old economy still survive. About ninety per cent of the peoples of South-East Asia live in the rural areas, and among them traditional methods of food production and many traditional handicrafts still survive. Various scattered groups of backward peoples are still food gatherers. They include the Negrito Semang and the Senoi-Temiar of the Malay Peninsula, the Kubu of Sumatra, the Toala of Celebes, the Punan of Borneo and small groups in New Guinea. Their total number today is very small, probably only a few hundred thousand. One would be inclined to think that there has been little change in their habitat and numbers during historical times.

As today, two systems of land cultivation prevailed; shifting cultivation characterized by the term 'slash and burn' and settled cultivation using methods of irrigation. The former, for which there are several local names, is found not only in the interior uplands of South-East Asia, but also under similar conditions in other tropical regions of the world. The method used is to clear a patch of forest or jungle by felling and burning, and to raise on it tubers or yams followed by hill rice, millet or maize; then, after two years at most, to move on to another area and treat it in the same way. Given enough land in proportion to population, so that an adequate period of fallow is provided before the rotation starts again, the fertility of the soil is maintained and erosion avoided. But such conditions demand a very low population density, and, because of the large area covered by a particular group, the village itself might have to be moved from time to time. The whole village community probably lived in one house with a matrilineal form of social organization. The 'longhouses' found today among the Dyaks of Borneo, the Toradja of Celebes and the Sakai in the Malay Peninsula offer examples of this kind of society.

The more advanced peoples, living under settled conditions in river valleys or deltas, developed irrigation systems for the conservation and utilization of the monsoon rain. These were created and maintained by the organized labour of villages, usually of single-family houses. The land was embanked to conserve the water in the rice-fields and regulate its distribution from field to field. It was a highly developed type of agriculture, and is found at the beginning of the historical period among the peoples with the highest levels of civilization. It entailed, to begin with, heavy tasks such as clearing away dense tropical jungle, draining swamps and, in some cases, terracing hillsides. One of the most spectacular achievements of the method was its application to mountainous areas, as in Bali, parts of Java, and what is now the Shan State in the Union of Burma.

In a recent paper read to the Siam Society[1] Gordon Luce has called irrigated rice 'the prime product of South-East Asia', and 'one of the great economic discoveries in the history of humanity'. The Rubicon between dry and wet rice, he claims, was crossed by the more advanced Mon-Khmer-speaking peoples of the Indo-Chinese Peninsula. They pioneered its cultivation in the delta of the Red River of Tongking. Their efforts, he thinks, caused a population explosion. This in turn led to migrations to other delta areas, and the foundation of new centres

[1] 'Rice and Religion: a Study of Old Mon-Khmer Evolution and Culture', JSS, liii, 2 (July 1965), p. 141.

of wet-rice cultivation near the mouths of the Mekong, the Menam and the Irrawaddy.

To complete Luce's over-all picture, he thinks that when the Tong-king plain was overrun by the Vietnamese, the majority of the wet-rice cultivators still living there went up the Red River to Yunnan. Then, escaping westwards from the cold, high plateau of central Yunnan, they followed the Red River to its source south of Tali, made their way across northern Burma to Khasi in the plains of east Assam, where they established a new centre. The main body, however, moved on into the plain of the Ganges, whence Aryan penetration drove them into the hills of central and eastern India. Here their descendants are met with today as speakers of the Munda languages, and number some four million souls.

The Mons were the pioneers of wet-rice cultivation in Burma before the arrival of the Burmese, and in Siam before the arrival of the Thai. In the central dry zone of Burma they constructed the Kyauksè irriga-tion system which came to be of vital strategic importance to the successive Burmese capitals of Pagān and Ava. In Java the spread of irrigation in the plains between Japara and Gresik was a key factor in the successive development of the powerful kingdoms of Kediri, Singosari and Majapahit. The construction and maintenance of highly intensive systems of irrigation in the cases of Funan and Angkor has been noted in earlier chapters. Angkor city has been described as an island in a flooded plain. It was not an urban agglomeration so much as a col-lection of waterworks, whose function was to irrigate its neighbourhood. Initially, however, the individual village must have been the prime factor in the irrigation process: it was a communal effort of mutual self-help. Lordship came to play a role—e.g. in the case of Śailendra central Java—when neighbouring communities became involved in utilizing the waters of a particular river and its tributaries. Despotism was respons-ible for the highly intensive systems. But beyond them how far did its writ run? The largely self-contained and self-supporting village com-munity was the normal social unit, using the domestic buffalo for ploughing, cultivating also clumps of bamboo and a variety of palm and fruit trees, and supplementing its food supply by fishing. This civiliza-tion of buffalo, bamboo and boat was in existence long before the historical period opens.

The capital was also a collecting-centre of produce, since the royal revenue was paid almost entirely in kind. It thus became a com-mercial centre, attracting foreign merchants, with the ruler himself as chief merchant. The typical early capital city was to be found up a

river well away from the coast, yet accessible to shipping. One has only
to think of Palembang, Angkor, Pegu the Mon capital, Pagan, Ayut'ia
and Mrohaung, the capital of old Arakan. They were intersected by
canals, much of the population lived on house-boats and traffic was
mainly by water.

In the earliest communities, of which we have evidence, land ownership was communal. The individual's right to cultivate certain fields
for his livelihood was subject to the superior right of the community as
a whole to dispose of the land in the common interest. Dr. F. H. van
Naerssen, a pioneer in the study of early Javanese social conditions,
has shown that in central Java during the Śailendra period the cultivator
owned not the land itself but the harvest derived from it by his labours.
In Vietnam there was a periodical re-allocation of rice-fields belonging
to the commune among its peasant members, who, however, possessed
individual plots in addition. In the Philippines there was no notion
of landed property until the Spaniards introduced it by recognizing the
chief as the owner of the land of the community, able to dispose of it
by sale. Everywhere population was sparse, land was plentiful, and
labour was at a premium. Early Java's case is probably typical: the
rights of the lord of a particular locality were to (a) a share of the harvest
produced by individual cultivators and to (b) certain labour services.
In Burma right up to British times the *myothugyi* enjoyed similar rights.

Though by far the most important crop, rice was not the only one.
In the drier zones, notably central Burma, un-irrigated crops such as
millet (for fodder), cotton, groundnuts, beans, lentils and sesamum (for
cooking oil) were produced. Garden crops were of vital importance,
with palm trees the chief. Their juice was used for sweetening and to
make toddy; the leaves of the dhani palm were used for roofing the
bamboo-built houses and also for the production of manuscripts.
Coconut plantations were a feature of every village. Also prominent
among the cultivated fruit trees were the banana, the papaya and the
mango. The pineapple grew wild in the lush jungle. The clove was
indigenous to the Moluccas, the nutmeg to the Bandas. Pepper was
produced in western Java and southern Sumatra. These became
important articles of international commerce. Also in such a list were
forest products such as 'Barus' camphor of northern Sumatra, known
to the Chinese in the third century A.D., and Sumatran pine resin and
benzoin, which, as we have seen,[1] came to be substituted for 'Persian'
frankincense and myrrh by Indonesian shippers trading to China.

Villages were largely self-sufficient, with house-building a co-

---

[1] *Supra*, p. 39.

operative effort and simple carpentry, spinning and weaving normal household industries. Inside the village community some specialization existed in pottery, the making of parasols and of household and agricultural tools. There were also villages of specialists, tin and silver miners, gold-washers, metal-workers, knife and weapon makers, ivory-workers and, in the Buddhist countries, carvers of images of the Buddha. There were villages of boat and ship builders. Yenangyaung in central Burma was a place of oil-drillers with, close by, Nyaung U, where the large earthenware pots for the carriage of 'earth oil' by boat were made.

Distribution was carried on through periodical bazaars held locally and the fairs held at festival times at some religious centre. In many parts of the mainland a bazaar was held every five days. The religious festivals attracted buyers and sellers from far and wide as well as purveyors of entertainment like their counterparts at European fairs, dramatic performances, puppet-shows, dancing and music. Trade was mostly by barter, but at the more important centres uncoined metal lumps were used by weight as currency, with an official assayer to supervise the transaction. At such centres there would be brokers, grain-measurers and weighmen appointed by the ruler. Their charges were fixed by custom. The ruler himself was chief merchant, with powers of pre-emption upon all goods brought in by foreign merchants. Ports and capital cities were the natural collecting-centres of local products, and hence the resort of foreign merchants. Valuable woods, spices and pepper, rubies and other precious stones, gold, ivory, coral, gums and resins and camphor were sought by the foreigner, who was also attracted to ports visited by Chinese junks bringing porcelain and silk. There was a big local demand for Indian textiles; but it was a trade which only the expert could carry on successfully, for each area had its own preference in the matter of patterns and designs, and rejected anything different from the customary ones. There was a vast number of different varieties in the trade.

Staple ports such as Funan's Oc Eo, Srivijaya's Palembang, Malacca and East Java's Tuban developed widespread commercial connections. The Malay Peninsula and Indonesia were from early times a transition area for trade, a meeting ground for merchants coming from the east and the west. The monsoons of the Indian Ocean and the trade winds of the South China Sea obliged ships to wait in their harbours for favourable winds, thus fostering trade. In the north was the narrow neck of the peninsula across which goods were transhipped so that the pirate-infested straits could be avoided. Beyond the straits to the south was the south-east coast of Sumatra, from which, as O. W. Wolters has shown, Malay shippers early on pioneered the direct sea route to China, long before the rise of Śrivijaya. The Chinese mention *Ko-ying* and *Kan-to-li*, ports which seem to have been predecessors of Srivijaya. The 'favoured coast', as Wolters calls it, had trade connections with India and Ceylon as well as with China.

Later the east Javanese powers Kediri, Singosari and Majapahit developed formidable naval power. Their northern ports had reached an advanced stage in the development of shipping long before the Portuguese appeared on the scene. When Śrivijaya became weak after the great Chola raid of 1025, Kediri seized the opportunity to establish her naval and commercial power; she seems to have come to an understanding with Palembang regarding their respective trading spheres. The Javanese empires of the thirteenth and fourteenth centuries, however, asserted their supremacy over the Sumatran ports for reasons discussed in Chapter 4. 'Great Majapahit' must have existed, though not as the vast territorial empire of legend. Like Śrivijaya it was an empire of sea ports maintained by overwhelming naval power; though, unlike Śrivijaya, it had a solid territorial basis, in the rich food-producing lands of the Brantas area. Tuban was its staple port for the receipt of tribute. Its naval power was used to control vassals. Śrivijaya used its naval power to curb piracy: to make the seas safe for the peaceful trader. The loyalty and co-operation of its vassals brought rich rewards from the suzerain; disloyalty brought severe punishment.

Foreign traders lived in their separate communities in the trading quarters of the ports or capitals they visited. Each community had its head who represented its members in the local courts of justice and in all dealings with the authorities; it lived under its own regulations. This method of procedure was prescribed by local rulers. The word 'extraterritoriality' with its derogatory significance had not been invented then. In any case the ruler had the whip hand. All trade was solely by his permission. As chief merchant he had the right of pre-emption of all imported goods. Sales and purchases could be conducted only through his officials. Food and water for the return voyage could be obtained only with his consent. His port officer, the *shahbandar*, supervised foreign shipping, market-places used by foreigners, assigned them *godowns* (i.e. warehouses), kept check on weights, measures and coinage, and adjudicated in disputes involving ships' captains or merchants. As in the case of the ports of mediaeval England, France and Flanders, there was a body of well-known maritime custom which was applied in the ports of South-East Asia; and under the aegis of a great commercial power trade was normally carried on peacefully and prosperously.

Through the well-informed writing of Tomé Pires fifteenth-century Malacca provides the best example extant of a great international emporium. The general picture he gives probably applies equally to Śrivijaya. There was a regular scale of 'gifts' to the ruler and his officers, which in Malacca's case amounted to one or two per cent of the goods imported. Prices were decided on by consultation with the prospective buyers as a group. There were two main methods of trading. In one the owner of the goods rented cargo space and either accompanied his goods to their destined market, or deputed an agent to do so. In the other case a *nakoda* (skipper) acted as agent for a merchant who provided him with goods and money for trading. Rulers of states traded in this way, maintaining their factors at the foreign port with which they had trading relations. We also hear of guilds of Indian traders importing piece-goods into South-East Asia, of Sufi trade guilds playing a part in the conversion of Indonesians to Islam; but little is known of their economic activities. Palembang in its great days and late fifteenth-century Malacca provided special facilities for the transhipment of goods. Each in its turn dominated the narrow straights and hence the shipping passing through them; but they offered also very real services to ships and merchants.

The trade in spices and pepper gave South-East Asia special importance. Little is known as yet about its early developments or their connection with the growth of Java's naval power. Well before the rise of Malacca, however, these commodities together with South-East Asia's drugs, camphor and pine resins, its precious stones and valuable woods, were in great demand in China and Japan, on the one hand, and in the West, on the other. In Malacca's time they were carried via the Gujerati ports of western India to the ports of the Red Sea and Persian Gulf. Persians and Arabs played their part in this trade. Long before the tenth century they were trading by the sea route to China, though almost certainly not in the same ships for the entire voyage. On this subject there are many questions and few answers as yet. From China, in return for its 'tribute', and through clandestine voyages of Chinese merchants evading the Ming prohibition of private foreign trade, Malacca received such commodities as raw and woven silk in great quantities, expensive fabrics such as damask, satin and brocade, and enormous quantities of porcelain and pottery. Indian cotton textiles in great abundance and variety came to Malacca from the ports of Gujerat, the Coromandel Coast and Bengal. The Coromandel Coast was famous for its 'painted' fabrics, the chintzes of later European trade. The white cotton fabrics of Bengal were equally sought after. Bengal also exported to Malacca unlimited quantities of food in the form of rice, sugar-cane, dried and salted meat, preserved vegetables, candied fruits such as ginger, and oranges and lemons. Malacca had to rely entirely on imported food. A further source of this was the then independent Mon kingdom of Pegu in Lower Burma. In its ports teak-wood junks were built and sailed to Malacca laden with rice and sugar-cane to be sold on the spot along with their cargoes. Tomé Pires tells us that every year fifteen or sixteen three- or four-masted junks were sent to Malacca to be sold in this way, besides twenty to thirty ships of shallow draft. The Gujeratis, who were second to none in their knowledge of the Indian Ocean, built ships specially designed for its sailing conditions. Their planks were lashed together with coconut fibre; no iron was used. They were not built to stand up to heavy seas: their movements were determined by the sailing seasons imposed by the monsoons. Their chief peril lay in getting becalmed so that their crews ran out of water. European ships had later to observe these same seasons.

Malacca itself had no industries save shipbuilding, woodwork, the forging of arms and the drying and salting of fish. Its shipbuilding was for war purposes only; its war vessels were small, light and fast. The shipbuilding yards of the north Javanese ports and Pegu supplied it with its commercial vessels. Its merchant fleets visited the Coromandel Coast, Ceylon, Bengal, Pegu and even China. The Javanese were good shipbuilders, and the north Javanese ports played an important part in Malacca's economy; for not only did their ships bring the spices of the Moluccas, but, through the abundant crops of their hinterland, Demak, Japara, Tegal, Semarang and Cheribon provided a third vital source of food for Malacca, along with Bengal and Pegu. Japara built large junks able to carry no less than 400 tons of rice. Malacca's own Javanese shipwrights were so famous that after its conquest Albuquerque took away with him sixty of them to Goa.

CHAPTER 12

THE COMING OF THE EUROPEAN

MEDIAEVAL Europe had no recorded contacts with South-East Asia until late in the thirteenth century, when the Polos, returning from the Court of Kublai Khan by the sea route, passed down the coast of Champa, rounded the southern extremity of the Malay Peninsula, and were held up for five months by monsoon conditions in northern Sumatra before passing on their way across the Indian Ocean. They had crossed Asia by the overland caravan route to China, where in 1275 they had been received by Kublai in the 'Upper Court' at Shangtu. During their seventeen years' sojourn in China Marco was employed as an intelligence officer by the Imperial Court and was sent on distant journeys. On one of these, a four-months journey from Peking to the west, he went via the land of the 'gold-teeth' people, with its capital at Yung-ch'ang, between the Mekong and the Salween, by an itinerary which it is impossible to trace, to a town in northern Burma, which he calls 'Mien'. What impressed him most were two stone towers fifty feet in height, one covered with gold and the other with silver, and both hung round with bells which tinkled in the wind. If his claim to have actually entered Burma is true, and much doubt has been thrown upon it, he may have reached Tagaung. He refers to 'Mien' as the capital of Burma, but it is not recognizably Pagan, nor could he have travelled so far within the time at his disposal.

Of greater interest is his account of the Great Khan's war with the King of 'Mien and Bangala'. His description of the battle of Ngasaunggyan, fought in the Namti valley in 1277, wherein the Tartar archers won a victory by causing panic among the Burmese elephants, must have been derived from eye-witnesses. But he erroneously attributes the leadership of the Mongol forces to Nasr ed-Din, who was the commander of the later expedition which captured Kaungsin, the Burmese stronghold commanding the defile of Bhamo.

He gives a brief glimpse into one of the semi-independent Laos states on the Yunnan border. The king has 300 wives; there is abundance of gold and elephants and many kinds of spices; wine made from rice is drunk, and both men and women tattoo their bodies all over with figures of beasts and birds in black colouring stuff. How much of this was mere hearsay it is impossible to determine. His information certainly contains much that is inaccurate, as is shown by his reference to 'Bangala' as a part of the dominions of the King of Burma. The word can only refer to Bengal; apparently Polo confused the deltas of the Ganges and the Irrawaddy. It is significant that Fra Mauro's map, based upon the information in his book, makes a similar error.

Marco's account of his homeward voyage, which began early in 1292, contains interesting material on South-East Asia. Kublai's great-nephew Arghun, Tartar lord of Persia, had requested a Mongol princess of China in marriage. The Great Khan selected the Lady Kukachin for this purpose and committed her to the special care of the Polos, who had begged him to allow them to return to their native land. Marco's description of the Chinese junk in which they made the voyage tallies exactly with those of such fourteenth-century travelogues as the Blessed Odoric, Ibn Batuta and Fra Jordanus. He says that 'Chamba'—i.e. Champa—is a very rich region ruled by a king who pays an annual tribute of elephants to the Great Khan. He writes in extravagant terms of the Mongol 'victory' over Champa in 1281, but is silent on the subject of the final disaster which befell Marshal Sögatü's army there four years later.

Java he calls the 'Great Island of Java' as distinct from 'Java the Less', his name for Sumatra. Java, he tells us, was reputed among mariners to be the largest island in the world and was more than 3,000 miles in circumference.[1] His extravagant notion of its size reflects an idea that was current among Arab seamen, whose knowledge was confined to the few ports on its north coast which they frequented. The island, he says, produces black pepper, nutmegs, spikenard, galingale, cubebs, cloves and all other kinds of spices. In point of fact, though the island was a great mart for spices, it produced none. He does not seem to have visited it but to have relied entirely on seamen's gossip for his account of it. His statement that Java had never fallen into the Great Khan's possession is intriguing in view of the great armada which Kublai despatched against Kertanagara of Singosari not so very long after Marco's departure from China.

Among other islands, some of which are very difficult to identify, he mentions Pulo Condore, lying opposite to the Mekong delta, the strategic possibilities of which were to be much debated by the English

[1] Pauthier's text gives 5,000 miles.

and the French in the seventeenth and eighteenth centuries, and Bintang at the east end of the Straits of Malacca, where the Sultan of Malacca settled after Albuquerque captured his city in 1511. The identity of 'Malaiur', which he describes as a fine and noble city with its own king, great trade, and abundance of spices, has been the subject of a certain amount of debate, as we have seen in the previous chapter. It must obviously be Jambi, and it is perhaps of some significance that he makes no mention of a Javanese conquest. Equally significant is the fact that he makes no mention of Malacca.

In striking contrast to his inaccurate account of Java is his better-informed description of Sumatra. His estimate of its compass at 2,000 miles is not far from the truth. His reference to the recent conversion to Islam of 'Ferlec' by Saracen merchants is a piece of valuable historical evidence. He personally visited six Sumatran 'kingdoms'; and although he credited the island with only eight states, there is much that rings true in his account, even if he was credulous enough to record the story that one of them was peopled by men with tails about a palm in length and of the thickness of a dog's, though without a hair on them.

In the year before the Polos began their homeward journey from China a Franciscan friar, John of Monte Corvino, set out for Peking in the hope of converting Kublai Khan to Christianity. He and his little company reached India via Ormuz and the Persian Gulf. Then, after a stay of over a year on the Coromandel Coast, they proceeded onwards by the sea route through the Archipelago, reaching their destination before Kublai's death in 1294. This was the beginning of half a century of Latin missions to the Mongol Court. And as several of the missionaries either went or returned by the sea route, South-East Asia received further attention in books of travel.

The best, and indeed the only one worthy of serious consideration, was by the Franciscan Odoric of Pordenone, who left Europe in 1316 and returned early in 1330. His route, after leaving the Coromandel Coast, was via Sumatra, Java, Borneo and Champa to Canton. His *Description of the East*, written after his arrival home, is characterized by Sir Raymond Beazley as 'the fullest, most graphic, and the most amusing picture of Asia left by any religious traveller of this age'.[1] Notwithstanding a good many inaccuracies, it does to some extent supplement Marco Polo's picture of South-East Asia. His knowledge of Sumatra compares unfavourably with Polo's. He mentions only three kingdoms, and he does not give the island a name. But his

[1] *Dawn of Modern Geography*, iii, p. 253.

'Lamori', at the extreme north-west, is undoubtedly Polo's 'Lambri', and his 'Sumolchra', where people branded their faces with hot iron, corresponds to the Venetian's 'Samara', the place from which the island was ultimately to take its name. He was horrified by the customs of the island, such as communal marriage and cannibalism. Children, he credulously asserts, were brought in by foreign merchants and sold for slaughter as food.

His account of Java is fuller than Polo's, though he repeats some of the latter's inaccuracies. While Polo has nothing to say about the government of the island, Odoric speaks of a great king who rules over seven under-kings and lives in a magnificent palace. The Great Khan of Cathay, he writes, has often taken the field against this King of Java, but never with success. When due allowance is made for the exaggeration, the statement is not entirely wide of the mark. The Great Khan, of course, did not command in person the sole expedition he sent against Kertanagara.

He mentions 'Patem' or 'Talamasim', presumably a region in Borneo, as lying near to Java, and bordered on the south by a dead sea whose waters run only in a southwards direction, so that if a man drifts into them he is never seen again. Here he meets the sago palm and watches the process of sago-preparation, though not with complete understanding.

His account of Champa[1] has striking similarities with Polo's, but he does not mention the Mongol invasions. The king, he says, is polygamous and has 200 children. He has also 14,000 tame elephants. Vast shoals of fish come ashore in Champa at certain times of the year and allow themselves to be caught, 'doing homage to the emperor', according to the local saying. He mentions the prevalence of suttee and professes having seen a huge tortoise larger than the dome of St. Anthony of Padua.

His chapter on 'Nicuveran'—i.e. the Nicobar Islands—is full of legendary nonsense, and disconcertingly so, for he implies that he had visited 'it'. He describes 'Nicuveran' as a great island 2,000 miles in circuit, remarkable for naked, dog-headed, ox-worshipping cannibals.

Two other friars of this period wrote of South-East Asia, Jordanus and John Marignolli. Jordanus, whose work is entitled *The Wonders of the East*, went to India in 1330, but no farther eastwards. He describes the spice trade, 'Java' (=Sumatra) and Champa, and repeats

---

[1] Sir Raymond Beazley is wrong in giving Cochin China as the equivalent of Polo's and Odoric's Champa. It was the old kingdom of Champa with its centre just south of modern Hué to which they referred.

what had become the traditional yarns of Arab seamen. 'There is also', he writes, 'another exceeding great island, which is called Jaua, which is in circuit more than seven [thousand?] miles as I have heard, and wherein are many world's wonders. Among which, besides the finest aromatic spices, this is one, to wit, that there be found pygmy men, of the size of a boy of three or four years old, all shaggy like a he goat. They dwell in the woods and few are found.' In 'Java', he also tells us, 'they delight to eat white and fat men when they can get them'. Franciscan friars, presumably.

John Marignolli of Florence, who arrived in China by the overland route in 1342 and left for home in December 1346, travelled homewards through South-East Asia. He describes 'Saba' (Java or Sumatra) as a remote and matchless isle, where women have the mastery in all things and the queens are descended from Semiramis. The queen, he says, honoured him with banquets and presents, and he rode on an elephant from the royal stables. Was he by any chance referring to the Minangkabau districts of Sumatra? On the island's sacred mountain, he was told, the Magi first saw the star which led them to Bethlehem. His account of his travels is, strangely enough, introduced into his Latin *Annals of Bohemia*, which he compiled as domestic chaplain to the Holy Roman Emperor Charles IV. It contains graphic descriptions of personal experiences mingled with fantastic hearsay.

Whence came all these fantastic tales? 'One must notice', writes Sir Henry Yule of Jordanus,[1] 'the frequent extraordinary coincidences of statement, and almost of expression, between this and other travellers of the same age, especially Marco Polo. At first one would think that Jordanus had Polo's book. But he certainly had not Ibn Batuta's, and the coincidences with him are sometimes almost as striking. Had these ancient worthies, then, a Murray from whom they pilfered experiences, as modern travellers do? I think they had; but *their* Murray lay in the traditional yarns of the Arab sailors with whom they voyaged, some of which seem to have been handed down steadily from the time of Ptolemy—peradventure of Herodotus—almost to our own day.'

Soon after the middle of the fourteenth century the Mongol dynasty made way for the Mings, and Western intercourse with China ceased. The next European to travel in South-East Asia was not a missionary but a trading prospector, a Venetian of noble family, Nicolo de' Conti, who spent twenty-five years wandering about the East and returned

[1] *Cathay and the Way Thither*, Preface, p. xvii.

home in 1444. As a young man he was a merchant in Damascus. Then he passed through Persia, sailed along the Malabar Coast, visited parts of the interior of India, went on to Ceylon and thence to South-East Asia. There he visited Sumatra, Java, Tenasserim, Arakan and Burma. He is thought to have gone also as far as southern China. He returned home via the Red Sea and Cairo. On arrival he confessed that to save his life he had been forced to renounce the Christian religion and become a Muslim. Pope Eugenius IV granted him absolution on condition that he related his adventures to the papal secretary, Poggio Bracciolini, who wrote the account of them that we now possess.

Conti calls Sumatra 'Taprobana', a name applied by Europeans in early days to Ceylon. This curious error appears in both the Catalan Map of 1375 and Fra Mauro's of 1458. He says, however, that among the natives it is known as 'Sciamuthera'. Although he remained there a year, he has little of real interest to say about it. Its chief products were pepper, camphor and gold, but the people were cruel, and in parts of the island there was cannibalism and head-hunting.

He mentions also an island named 'Andamania', 'which means the island of gold'. It is 800 miles in circumference, he says, but the inhabitants are cannibals and travellers avoid it. Tenasserim abounds in elephants and a species of thrush. Presumably he refers to the mina bird. From Tenasserim he went to Bengal, where he stayed for some months. Then he took ship down to Arakan and travelled overland to Ava, the capital of the Upper Burma kingdom, going by the route across the Yomas to the Irrawaddy, which he thought larger than the Ganges. Ava was then in its heyday and the chief centre of Burmese culture. He estimated its circumference at fifteen miles and considered it a noble city. He describes the Burmese method of catching elephants and their use of them in battle. The king, he tells us, rides upon a white elephant. He is nearer the truth when describing the universal practice of tattooing, the 'frightful serpents without feet, as thick as a man, and six cubits in length', and the universal belief that rhinoceros horn was an antidote against poison.

He travelled down the Irrawaddy and made his way through the creeks to 'a very populous city called Panconia'—i.e. Pegu, the capital of the Mon kingdom. But although he stayed there four months he tells us little about it. Equally disappointing is his account of Java. He describes the process of running amuck and says that the chief amusement is cock-fighting. The inhabitants he considers inhuman, since they ate dogs, cats, mice and unclean animals.

In 1496 another Italian, a Genoese merchant, Hieronomo de Santo Stefano, crossed from the Coromandel Coast to Burma and reached Pegu, which he calls by its correct name. He was a trading prospector making his way round the East from one commercial centre to another, doing what trade he could at each. He was unable to go to Ava because there was war between the two states. He had, therefore, to sell his valuable stock to the King of Pegu, who kept him waiting eighteen months for payment. While there his companion, Messer Hieronomo Adorno, died. He buried him in what he took to be a ruined church, 'frequented by none'.

On leaving Pegu he set sail for Malacca, but was driven by stress of weather to Sumatra, 'where grows pepper in considerable quantities, silk, long pepper, benzoin, white sandal wood, and many other articles'. There he was plundered of his rubies and much else by the Mahommedan ruler of a port which he does not name. He decided, therefore, that it was 'not a desirable place to stay in' and took ship for Cambay on the west coast of India.

Santo Stefano was followed shortly afterwards by a Bolognese traveller, Ludovico di Varthema, who left Europe towards the end of 1502 and travelled through Egypt, Syria, Arabia, Persia, India to South-East Asia, returning to Lisbon after an absence of some five years. Very little is known of him. He had the instinct of the geographer, an insatiable desire to visit foreign countries and learn about them. He was the first European on record to visit the holy places of Islam. He did so by becoming a Muslim and attaching himself to a company of Mamelukes at Damascus.

His account of Tenasserim is, with the exception of Conti's few remarks, the first authentic account written by a European. The city of 'Ternassari', he tells us, was situated at the mouth of a river of the same name. Large two-masted junks (*giunchi*) were built there for trade with Malacca. Its importance, it is to be noted, lay in the fact that much of the Malay Peninsula was under Siam, and it served one of the best short cuts between the Indian Ocean and the Gulf of Siam.

Varthema describes Pegu as a great city, west of a beautiful river, containing 'good houses and palaces built of stone with lime', and enclosed with a wall. When he arrived there the king was absent on an expedition against the King of Ava. On his return he granted the visitor an audience. Varthema was much impressed by the vast number of rubies worn by the king, as also by his affability. 'He is so humane and domestic', he writes, 'that an infant might speak to him.' He sold the king some coral in return for rubies.

Varthema was the first to make Europe acquainted with Malacca. He mentions the great commerce carried on at the port, and especially its spice trade. More ships arrived there, he tells us, than at any other place in the world. The majority of the inhabitants of the city were 'Giavai'—i.e. Javanese. There were also the 'men of the sea', who did not care to reside on land, and set the local authorities at defiance. These were the 'Orang-laut' of the Malays, the 'Cellates', or 'men of the straits', of Tomé Pires and de Barros, the 'sea-gipsies' of Crawfurd, whose headquarters were the narrow straits of the Johore Archipelago. They lived by the produce of the sea or by robbery. The natives of Malacca, he says, were a bad race, the worst ever created, and foreigners slept on board their ships to avoid assassination. The most marketable commodities to be obtained were spices and silks.

In Sumatra Varthema visited the flourishing port of Pedir, near Acheh. Every year, he tells us, eighteen to twenty ships were laden with pepper for China. It also produced an immense quantity of silk and much benzoin. So extensive was its trade, and so great the number of merchants resorting there, that one of its streets contained about 500 money-changers. Stamped money of gold, silver and tin was in use there, with a devil stamped on one side and something resembling a chariot drawn by elephants on the other. He was much impressed by the strict administration of justice there. Three-masted junks with two rudders were built there. He also makes the interesting statement that the natives excelled in the art of making fireworks. This is corroborated by Crawfurd,[1] who mentions that the more advanced Malay peoples already used firearms when the Portuguese first arrived in the Archipelago.

He visited the island of Banda, where nutmegs and mace grew, but the people were without understanding; the Moluccas, where the people were worse than those of Banda; Borneo; and the 'beautiful island of Giava', which was divided up into many kingdoms all subject to a pagan king, who resided inland. But he heard so many hair-raising stories of the cannibalism there that he left as soon as possible for fear of being carried off and eaten. Crawfurd dubs his description of the island false and worthless.[2] From Java he returned to Malacca, and after a stay of only three days took ship for the 'City of Cioromandel'.[3]

[1] *Descriptive Dictionary of the Indian Islands*, p. 23.
[2] *Ibid.*, pp. 165–6.
[3] Badger in his edition of *The Travels of Ludovico Di Varthema* (Hak. Soc., 1863) suggests Negapatam.

Varthema's work was first published in 1510 in Rome. His description of men, countries and scenes which he had himself seen at once attracted attention, and translations of it were issued in Latin, German, Spanish, French, Dutch and English. After him we pass from the age of mediaeval wanderers to that of the Portuguese filibusters.

PART II

SOUTH-EAST ASIA DURING THE EARLIER PHASE OF EUROPEAN EXPANSION

CHAPTER 13

THE PORTUGUESE AND SPANIARDS IN SOUTH-EAST ASIA

(a) The Portuguese

AT the end of the Middle Ages the Portuguese were well fitted for the leadership of a European effort to exploit the trade of the Indian Ocean. Their position on the Atlantic made them a race of mariners able to cope with the risks of the sea. In their long crusade against the Moors they had built up a formidable naval power. They employed skilled Genoese seamen. They were ahead of other powers in the construction of 'great ships' able to accommodate large numbers of men for long ocean voyages. Their chief ports, Lisbon and Oporto, had trading connections with both the Mediterranean and northern Europe. When, under the leadership of Vasco da Gama, they made their first appearance in the Indian Ocean they had behind them the experience of a long series of explorations and the urge of a fervent nationalism, which impelled them to destroy Islam.

In the eastern seas they excelled the Moors in both fighting and navigating their ships, and the ships themselves were in every way superior to those of the Arabs, which were built for sailing only under favourable monsoon conditions. Lest the crusading motive be overstressed, let it be stated that long before they first rounded the Cape of Bona Esperanza the economic motive had begun to compete with the religious; and as the ideas of commerce and colonization gained ground, so the mediaeval crusading ideal weakened. In the light of the experience gained at Calicut, the chief emporium of Arab trade on the Malabar Coast, the enormous profits of the spice trade and the desire to wrest the trade monopoly from the Moors became overriding considerations. Happily it was possible to serve God and Mammon at the same time, for by striking at Arab trade in the Indian Ocean Portugal aimed a blow at the Ottoman empire, which drew the major part of its revenues from the spice monopoly.

Against the strong opposition of the Arabs and other Muslim traders the Portuguese rapidly expanded their power and influence.

Cochin, their first settlement and a centre of the pepper trade, became the headquarters of their first viceroy, Francisco de Almeida, whose policy was to gain the mastery over the trade of the Malabar Coast, while at the same time resisting the pressure to extend Portuguese influence into the Red Sea or the Straits of Malacca, since in his view such a course was calculated to weaken their position. His successor, Don Affonse de Albuquerque, however, decided that such limited aims would fail to achieve the desired result. To gain commercial supremacy over the Indian Ocean it was necessary to seize and control the main strategic points and drive a trade which should provide a revenue adequate for the maintenance of irresistible power.

The capture of Goa in 1510 gave him a centre from which to develop control over the Indian trade, but Muslim vessels could still collect the produce of Bengal, Burma, Sumatra, the Spice Islands, Siam and China at the great emporium of Malacca. He proposed to stop this trade by holding the mouth of the Red Sea and at the same time striking at its very headquarters. Moreover, since Malacca under a Muslim ruler was the chief diffusion-centre of Islam in Indonesia, by capturing it he would be carrying out the obligation laid on the Portuguese by the bull of Alexander VI. Thus the conquest of Malacca in 1511 was one of the most important features of an over-all strategic plan, and not an act of revenge for the treachery of the sultan in his dealings with Diogo Lopez de Sequeira when he attempted to establish a factory there in 1509. The *Malay Annals* state that Sequeira abused the sultan's hospitality by beginning to build a fort from which to menace the city. There can be no doubt that he was sent there with the deliberate intention of manufacturing a *casus belli*.

From Malacca Albuquerque sent ambassadors to Siam and Burma. Duarte Fernandez, who went to Siam, was the first European to visit Ayut'ia. From Malacca Albuquerque also sent an expedition to the Moluccas. Its leader, Antonio d'Abreu, had strict instructions to refrain from filibustering, to do everything possible to establish friendly relations with the islands, and to observe the customs of the people. Ternate, Tidore and Halmahera and a number of small islands were the original home of the clove tree. Nutmeg and mace were the principal products of Amboina and the Banda Islands. Malacca, the chief distribution centre for these spices, received its supplies from Javanese traders, who collected them from the islands themselves. Supplies were so abundant and cheap that if the Portuguese were to keep the prices high in Europe it was essential for them to establish a monopoly and restrict export. This entailed driving out the Javanese traders and policing the sea-routes between Indonesia and Arabia. The chief difficulty lay in the fact that shortly before the arrival of the Portuguese the Spice Islands had been converted to Islam.

A more pressing danger at first, however, lay in the state of affairs at Malacca itself. There the Portuguese were on the defensive. The neighbouring country was unsubdued, the Muslim sultans of Indonesia were hostile, and Sultan Mahmud of Malacca, who escaped when his city fell, made the island of Bintang in the Straits of Singapore his headquarters and used his powerful fleet in an attempt to cut off Malacca from all trade with the Archipelago. In 1517 he took the offensive, stockaded himself on the Muar river close to the city, and was not driven out until 1520. In the following year, assisted by the forces of Acheh, whose sultan was expanding his power over northern Sumatra, he returned. But the Portuguese stormed his fortified position after twelve days of heavy fighting. In 1526 a Portuguese counter-attack upon his capital on Bintang was successful. But his son and successor established himself on the southern tip of the mainland at Johore and continued the struggle by harassing Portuguese shipping. And Muslim merchants, in order to avoid Malacca, transferred their headquarters to Brunei on the southern coast of Borneo, which became a new centre for the spread of Islam.

After 1526, however, Acheh became the leader of the opposition to the Portuguese. The increased demand for pepper brought its sultan a corresponding increase in power, and between 1529 and 1587 the Achinese made attempt after attempt to capture Malacca. The biggest of these occurred in 1558, when an armada of 300 war-boats, with 15,000 troops and 400 artillerymen from Turkey, besieged the city for a month. The years 1570 to 1575 were a critical period, when, in addition to three major Achinese attacks, the city had to meet a dangerous attack launched in 1574 by the Javanese state of Japara. It was saved only by the timely arrival of reinforcements from Goa. In 1587 a period of easier relations began, when a new Sultan of Acheh, Ala'uddin Riayat, in difficulties with the rebellious chiefs of his dependent states, was glad to make peace with the Portuguese. Notwithstanding all the threats and dangers of the years before 1587, Portuguese Malacca prospered exceedingly; its trade continued to expand and showed vast profits.

Abreu's expedition, which left Malacca for the Spice Islands in December 1511, met with little success. He lost two of his three ships; and although he procured a cargo of cloves and nutmeg from the Bandanese, he was unable to make Ternate and Tidore, the chief clove

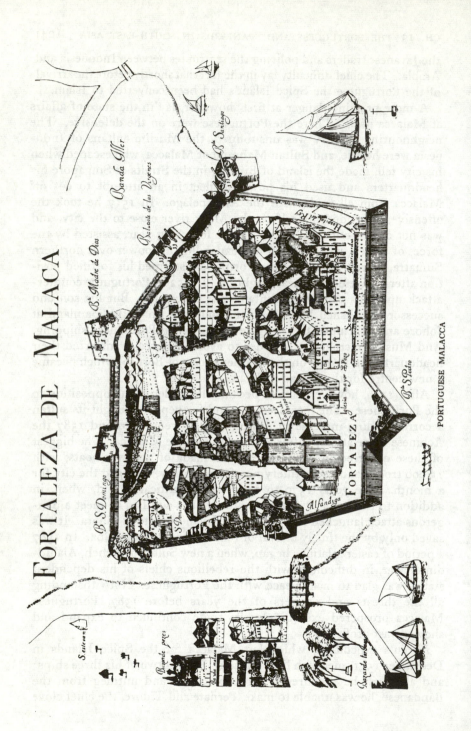

FORTALEZA DE MALACA

Banda Mer

B.ª Madre de Dios

Baluarte de las Virgens

Hosp.ª del Rey

S.ª Paula Cajero

S. Agostin

Misericordia

Snada

Sg. Pag

Iglesia mayor

Casa del Domin.

S. Domingo

Alfandiga

B.ª S. Domingo

S.ª Santiago

FORTALEZA

B.ª S. Pedro

Settewan

Barande pres

Barade la vila

PORTUGUESE MALACCA

islands. A second expedition in 1513 was more successful. The Sultans of Ternate and Tidore provided a large cargo of cloves, and each granted permission for a factory to be established on his island. These two chiefs were the heads of opposing island confederacies, and both played for Portuguese support. The situation was complicated in 1521 by the arrival of Magellan's ship the *Victoria* on her homeward voyage. This Spanish intrusion into their preserve led the Portuguese to seek to strengthen their position by concluding a treaty with Ternate giving them the monopoly of its clove trade.

At the same time Portugal protested to Spain that the appearance of a Spanish ship in the Spice Islands constituted an infringement of the Treaty of Tordesillas, concluded between the two states in 1494. The papal bull of 1493 had separated their respective spheres of interest by a line drawn from the North to the South Pole 100 miles to the west and south of the Azores and the Cape Verde Islands. The treaty had improved on this by laying down the dividing line 370 miles west of the Cape Verde Islands. Nothing, however, had been done towards demarcating the respective spheres of the two powers on the far side of the newly discovered continent.

In consequence of the Portuguese protest a conference of experts met in 1524, but failed to agree on the exact location of the Moluccas, since the computations of each side differed by no less than forty-six degrees. Spain thereupon sent a fleet of seven ships by way of the Straits of Magellan to assert her claim to the islands. Only one ship reached them. It was welcomed by Tidore, and a struggle then began between the Portuguese allied with Ternate and the Spanish allied with Tidore. Fortune favoured the Portuguese, for the Spanish were dependent for help upon Cortez in Mexico, and when it failed to arrive in time were forced to come to terms with their opponents. In Europe also the Portuguese managed to carry their point. In 1529 by a new treaty the Spanish agreed to halt their explorations seventeen degrees east of the Moluccas. This, however, did not prevent them, later in the century, from sailing to the Philippines and founding Manila in 1570.

The Portuguese voyages to the Spice Islands brought the question of Java to the fore. The normal route from Malacca followed the southern coast of Borneo, crossed the Java Sea to Gresik near Surabaya, and proceeded thence via the south of Celebes to the Moluccas. The hostility of the Java Muslims made this way unsafe. Hence an attempt was made to establish connections with the Hindu states, and in 1522 a ship was sent to Sunda Kalapa, later to become the Dutch port of Batavia. The Hindu raja granted facilities for building a fort, but when the Portuguese returned in 1527 they found that the town had been conquered by the Muslim state of Bantam and renamed Jacatra.

The rapid spread of Islam constituted a serious setback to their plans. The Bandanese and Amboinese maintained close connections with the Muslim sultans of Java. The Portuguese failed to obtain permission to build forts on the Banda Islands or to monopolize the nutmeg trade. Amboina was less difficult, and for their supply of nutmeg they had to rely upon cultivating friendly relations with its chiefs. By 1535 the whole of the north coast of Java had become Muslim; only in the extreme east of the island did Hinduism[1] hold out. Under the circumstances, therefore, it was decided to make a great effort to convert the non-Muslim peoples so as to prevent the further spread of Islam. Where Islam had already penetrated, Catholic missions had no hope of success.

Missionary enterprise was first directed to those parts of East Java which had not yet embraced the faith of the Prophet. But it came just too late, for except in the extreme east, in which they had no interest, Hindu rule was already tottering before Muslim penetration. Parts of Amboina had not yet accepted Islam, and the Catholic missionaries gained a foothold there, as also in the northern part of Halmahera. The Portuguese ally, the Sultan of Ternate, was, however, the enemy of Christianity, and for commercial reasons they dared not support the missionaries against him.

Moreover, in the Moluccas they had gained a bad reputation for rapacity. Only one Portuguese governor, Antonio Galvão (1536–40), behaved in such a way as to gain the respect and regard of the native peoples. The saintly Jesuit St. Francis Xavier, who arrived in Amboina in 1546, wrote that the knowledge of the Portuguese in the Moluccas was restricted to the conjugation of the verb *rapio*, in which they showed 'an amazing capacity for inventing new tenses and participles'. Amboina and its neighbouring islands were thought to be ripe for Christianity, and as they were independent of both Ternate and Tidore, and the Portuguese needed a second base in the Spice Islands, the decision was taken to concentrate upon their conversion. St. Francis, who spent a year and a half in the 'Islands of Divine Hope', as he called the Moluccas, found the Christian communities too ignorant and the population too barbarous for his liking. After a tour of all the places where Christian communities existed he decided

[1] The word is used relatively. The existing religion was mainly a mixture of ancestor worship and other traditional cults. It had a Hindu-Buddhist façade.

that he could do better work in China and returned to Malacca.

In practice the fortunes of Christianity depended almost entirely upon the military strength of the Portuguese. Most of their converts fell away when threatened by the Muslims. Sultan Hairun of Ternate became their determined enemy, and he was powerful enough to defy them. He attacked the Christian communities, and by 1565 had practically ruined the whole mission. Goa then sent a fleet to restore the situation, a fortress was built on Amboina, and Christianity began to revive. But not for long, for the Portuguese quarrelled with Hairun, who accused them of depriving him of his legal share of the spice profits. Then, to make matters worse, they made a solemn agreement with him and immediately afterwards treacherously murdered him (1570).

The result was disastrous. Ternate rose in revolt, led by its new sultan Baabullah. For nearly five years the Portuguese fortress on the island was besieged. Neither Goa nor Malacca could send help, and when in 1574 the fortress fell the Christian communities were doomed. Amboina, however, was saved by Vasconcellos, its governor, who rallied the native Christians there and built a new fort. The hostility of Baabullah drove the Portuguese to turn to Tidore, where in 1578 they were permitted to build a fort. No sooner were they installed there than Francis Drake appeared at Ternate, and the vengeful Baabullah offered him a treaty and a lading of spice. His return home from his voyage of circumnavigation (1577–80) aroused English interest in the possibility of voyages direct to the Spice Islands, and in 1586 Cavendish crossed the Archipelago from north to south through the Straits of Macassar and Bali.

The extension of Portuguese commercial activity in South-East Asia, notwithstanding the constant threats to their position at Malacca and in the Moluccas, was indeed remarkable. After 1545 they managed to obtain a share in the trade of Bantam, which had become the chief pepper port for the supply of both India and China, and through which it has been estimated that $3\frac{1}{2}$ million pounds of pepper passed annually. To avoid the southern passage to the Moluccas via East Java they made treaties with the Sultan of Brunei which enabled them to use a northern one through the Sulu Archipelago and the Celebes Sea. It was through their application of the name of his kingdom to the whole of the island that its corrupt form 'Borneo' came into general use. By both routes they touched at the island of Celebes, but never realized the different parts were those of a single island and not a group of separate ones; hence the name by which they knew them— 'the Celebes'.

In their relations with the more powerful kingdoms of the Indo-Chinese mainland the Portuguese had to be content to play a humbler role than at Malacca and in the Spice Islands. Many of them served as mercenaries in the armies of the various monarchs and often proved a source of embarrassment to their employers. Under commercial treaties with Siam they were permitted to trade at Ayut'ia the capital, at Mergui and Tenasserim in the Bay of Bengal, and at Patani and Nakon Srit'ammarat on the eastern coast of the Malay Peninsula. Both Ayut'ia and Patani did a considerable Chinese trade, and the Portuguese factories at both places flourished. The Siamese ports were also useful as places where Portuguese ships bound for China could shelter during the north-east monsoon, when the China Sea was difficult to navigate. They remained well established there until ousted by the Dutch in about 1630. Their missionaries and traders settled also in Cambodia, and it would appear that a Portuguese friar was in 1570 the first European to see the Great Lake and the ruins of Angkor.

In Burma and Arakan Portuguese mercenaries and adventurers were more in evidence than missionaries and traders. Diogo Soarez de Mello played an important part in the wars of Tabinshwehti and Bayinnaung and helped the latter to gain his crown in 1551. In Siam the Portuguese never attempted to gain territorial possessions; the king was too powerful. So it was in Burma until the end of the sixteenth century. But in 1599, when Pegu was captured and its booty shared between a rebellious prince of Toungoo and the King of Arakan, and the country laid waste by Siamese invaders, Philip de Brito, a *feringi* leader in the service of Arakan, seized its chief port, Syriam, and tried to gain the mastery over Lower Burma. But after an adventurous career of fourteen years he fell before the revived power of the house of Bayinnaung.

At almost the same time another *feringi* leader, Gonsalves Tibão of Dianga, made himself 'king' of the island of Sandwip, lying below the eastern arm of the Ganges delta, and maintained himself there from 1609 to 1617. In 1615 with the help of Goa he even attacked Mrohaung, the capital of Arakan, but was driven off. From the middle of the sixteenth century Portuguese freebooters settled in large numbers at Dianga, close by Chittagong, then in the dominions of Arakan. They made the place a notorious centre of piracy, whence they sailed up the creeks of the Sunderbunds to bring back thousands of slaves, whom they sold to the King of Arakan. Their forays went on until 1666, when the Mughal Viceroy of Bengal, Shayista Khan, wiped out their pirate nest and annexed the Chittagong district to the empire of Aurungzeb.

The decline of Portuguese power in the East set in early, though in South-East Asia, through their tenacious hold on Malacca, there were few signs of it before the appearance of the English and the Dutch as competitors for the control of the spice trade. The Portuguese have been described by Sir Hugh Clifford as swarming into Asia in a spirit of open brigandage.[1] Against the Muslim peoples their crusading zeal stimulated rather than restrained their cruel and capricious behaviour. Even their own historians were ashamed at their crimes in the Moluccas, where the natives were driven into resistance by the injustice of their trading methods. And although priests and monks multiplied in their dominions, they were ineffectual missionaries because of the misdeeds of traders and freebooters. That indeed seems to have been the theme of Mendes Pinto's *Peregrinaçam*, which for all its questionable accuracy of detail gives a remarkably authentic picture of Portuguese activities in the middle of the sixteenth century. Moreover, the cost of their military and ecclesiastical establishments was more than the profits of their commercial enterprise could bear.

'Look at the Portuguese,' wrote Sir Thomas Roe, the English ambassador to the Mughal Court in 1613. 'In spite of all their fine settlements they are beggared by the maintenance of military forces; and even their garrisons are only mediocre.' Albuquerque's policy of erecting forts and establishing domination over native rulers has been held to have been one of the chief causes of their downfall. They behaved as conquerors rather than merchants, and when internal disorganization and lack of discipline began to appear, as they did before the middle of the sixteenth century, general corruption resulted. There were too many potential de Britos and Tibãos, all anxious to make their fortunes and get home while the going was good.

The union of Spain and Portugal, if not the main cause of their downfall, had serious consequences for the Portuguese, for the enemies of Spain became their enemies, and in their attacks on them were aided by native rulers and peoples who had learnt from bitter experience to detest them. One has also to realize that the Dutch and English had made so much progress in developing their sea-power during the century before they appeared in the East that in sea fights with the Portuguese they could both sail and fight their ships better than their opponents. Yet when all has been said regarding the moribund state of the Portuguese empire at the end of the sixteenth century, the fact remains that, like Charles II, it took an unconscionable time in dying.

[1] *Further India*, London, 1904, p. 48.

(b) The Spaniards in the Philippines

The Treaty of Saragossa, concluded between Spain and Portugal in 1529, drew a line seventeen degrees east of the Moluccas as the boundary between the Spanish and Portuguese spheres of interest. This placed the island group, discovered by Magellan in 1521, and named by him San Lazaro, clearly within the Portuguese sphere. Spain, however, was determined to have a share in the spice trade, and with that object sent a further expedition to the western Pacific in 1542. In February of that year Ruy Lopez de Villalobos sailed from Mexico with 5 ships and 370 men on a reconnoitring expedition of the archipelago. His expedition achieved practically nothing, but he it was who named the islands the Philippines in honour of the Emperor Charles V's son Philip, the heir to the Spanish throne; and in spite of strong Portuguese protests Spain claimed them. For twenty years she made no attempt to establish her claim. Then, late in 1564, Miguel Lopez de Legaspi, with a force hardly any larger than Villalobos's, put out from Mexico to attempt the permanent occupation of the islands, and in the following April landed on Cebu and planted the first Spanish settlement there. Before his death in 1572 he had extended Spanish control over the islands of Cebu, Leyte, Panay, Mindoro and the fertile central plain of Luzon. He had crowned this achievement in May 1571 by taking possession of the town of Manila and making it the capital of the new dominion he had acquired for King Philip II.

The Spanish occupation of the Philippines was relatively bloodless. For one thing Philip II was much concerned that the bloody conquests of Mexico and Peru should not be repeated in the Philippines; for another, save among the Moros of Mindanao there was nothing of the nature of a political power to deal with. The only political unit, the *barangay*, was a relatively small kinship group; hence armed resistance was only on a local scale. Even more important, however, was the fact that Philip II had named as joint commander with Legaspi an Augustinian friar Andres de Urdaneta, who before taking orders had commanded a ship in Villalobos's expedition. He and his fellow missionaries, believing that Spanish dominion over the peoples of their newly-acquired territories should be guided rather by the papal injunction to convert them to Christianity than by the crusading notion of subjugating infidels, showed themselves more effectual than the military in the work of conquest, and zealous in protecting their flocks from exploitation by the colonists.

Luckily for the Catholic missionaries, Islam, which had begun to spread to the southern Philippines during the latter part of the fifteenth century, had had very little impact upon the central and northern parts of the archipelago by the time of their arrival, and they found their task relatively easy. The Filipinos were animists and nature worshippers. They had no temples or religious buildings, and no organized priesthood, and as the Catholic missionaries were always in short supply, they had to be content for the most part with outward ritual and formalism. The old magic and animism remained unshaken; indeed, the acceptance of Christianity by the ordinary people was not a little furthered by their belief in the magic property of baptism, and with the extension of the Church the Spanish clergy incurred the danger of themselves coming under the influence of the popular superstitions of their flocks. After the conquest Church and State remained entirely interdependent, with the State supporting the Church and ecclesiastical advance aiding the consolidation of political control.

In colonizing the Philippines Spain had three clear objectives: to gain a share in the spice trade, to make contacts with China and Japan in order to pave the way for their conversion, and to Christianize the Filipinos themselves. She succeeded only in the third. The Philippines produced no spices, and while the Portuguese dominated the Moluccas the Spaniards could do nothing there. Indeed, the Portuguese made two determined attempts, in 1568 and 1570, to drive Legaspi out of the Philippines. It was only after the union of the crowns of Spain and Portugal in 1580, when the Portuguese hold on the Moluccas was threatened by the hostility of the Sultan of Ternate and the appearance of Francis Drake there, that Spanish intervention began. In 1582 the first of a series of expeditions—nearly all fruitless—was launched by Manila against the sultan. It failed through disease. In 1585 a much larger one consisting of twenty-four ships led by Juan Morones came no nearer success, although reinforced by the Portuguese from Tidore. In 1593 Governor Dasmarinas sent a powerful expedition of 100 vessels against Ternate, but off Surphur Point, Batangas in South Luzon its Chinese rowers mutinied and massacred the Spaniards. In 1603 in response to an appeal from the Portuguese Governor of the Moluccas because of the arrival of the Dutch upon the scene Juan de Gallinato was sent to co-operate with admiral Hurtado de Mendoza against Ternate. Dutch help to the Ternateans, however, enabled them to repulse the attack. Two years later with Dutch help Sultan Zaide of Ternate expelled the Portuguese from their fort on his island and also from Tidore. This brought an immediate riposte from Manila, and in the following year Governor Acuna himself led an expedition, which defeated Zaide and his Dutch allies and left a strong Spanish-Filipino garrison in Ternate. But Dutch pressure was steadily mounting, and the truce of 1609 with Spain brought no relaxation to the struggle in the eastern seas. And the Dutch were now no longer concerned merely with the elimination of Hispano-Portuguese power in the pepper and spice producing areas of Malaysia, but were going all out for the conquest of the Philippines.

The conversion of China and Japan to Christianity was in any case a chimera. In Japan, where Spanish missionaries operated for a time, the intense friction which developed between them and the Portuguese, especially when the Spanish Franciscans set out to break the religious monopoly of the Jesuits, led to the expulsion of both nations between 1614 and 1624. The Shogun Ieyasu, anxious to make Yedo a great commercial centre, granted the Spaniards free trade, and sent an embassy to Manila to ask for mining instructors. But the attempts of the Catholic missionaries to evade the expulsion order of 1614 led to a severe persecution, and in 1624, when Manila sent an envoy, the Shogun Iemitsu (1623–51) refused him audience and ordered all Spaniards to leave the country.

With neither spices nor gold and silver, trade with China and Japan was essential to make the Philippine colony even pay its way. When Portuguese hostility—all the stronger after the union of the crowns in 1580—barred Spanish traders from eastern Asia, the authorities at Manila pursued the policy of attracting Asian traders to their city. In this they were successful: Manila became the resort of traders from China, Japan, Siam, Cambodia and the Spice Islands. Before the end of the sixteenth century the China trade was prospering. Spanish galleons from the Mexican port of Acapulco brought to Manila cargoes of silver dollars and bullion with which to purchase Chinese silks, velvets, porcelain, bronzes and jade, and the Mexican dollar went in such quantities to the Chinese commercial ports of Canton, Amoy and Ningpo, that it became the medium of exchange in the international trade of the Far East.

The Manila galleon became the economic life-line of the colony. It enabled Manila, with its excellent harbour close to the 'rice basket' of central Luzon, to maintain its position as the metropolis of the archipelago. There was considerable Chinese immigration. They occupied a separate quarter at Manila, where they were useful not only for their contribution to the colonial economy, but also as the scapegoats for the economic hardships that from time to time aroused discontent with Spanish rule. Anti-Chinese riots, which in 1603, 1639, 1662 and

1782 led to frightful massacres, served as a safety-valve for Filipino resentment. Mutual hostility was the normal state of affairs between the Spaniards and the Chinese. The colonial government produced an annual deficit which had to be made up with silver bullion from the treasury of Mexico, and most of this subvention found its way into Chinese hands. Nevertheless, the overriding fact of the interdependence of the two peoples normally prevented bloodshed. Moreover, massacres of Chinese had extremely serious effects upon the trade of Manila, and as most of the agriculture in the islands remained primitive, and the Spaniards took no steps to discover the economic resources of their colony, the Chinese were indispensable. The drain on the Mexican treasury, and the fears of mercantile interests in Spain lest their monopolies in Mexico and Peru be threatened by the import of Chinese textiles, led from time to time to proposals to abandon the Philippines. But the opposition of the missionaries, who argued that the islands would relapse into paganism or be taken over by the Protestant Dutch, always carried the day.

In taking over the rapidly-conquered areas of his island-empire Legaspi divided up the population into *encomiendas* under the control of Spanish colonists. The object was to steer a middle course between safeguarding native rights and ensuring the profits of the colonists. The *encomendero* had the right to collect tribute from the five hundred to a thousand Filipinos on his estate. In return he was pledged to rule and protect his people and ensure their conversion to Christianity. The tribute could take the form of labour services, and here abuses soon showed themselves, for the subsistence type of Philippine agriculture was quite inadequate to meet the demands of Spanish rule. The missionaries headed by Domingo de Salazar, first Bishop of Manila, whose authority was almost equal to that of the Governor, thundered against the illegal exactions by the *encomenderos*. In 1595 the Audiencia began to take the matter in hand by laying down a standard computation of payments, the *tasacion*; later it adopted the plan of gradually liquidating private *encomiendas*.

The most powerful factor in lightening the pressure upon the Filipinos was the improvement in the production of rice. But not for long, for early in the seventeenth century the gathering strength of the Dutch in the Malay archipelago threatened the Spanish hold on the Philippines. The Spaniards, as we have seen, used the Philippines as a base for an offensive against the Spice Islands, which the Dutch foiled. They in their turn tried to wrest the Philippines from Spain: they wanted Manila as an emporium of spices and silks. But though the Spaniards lost the 'war of cloves' they managed to hold on to the Philippines until the Treaty of Munster (1648) removed the threat of Dutch conquest. The struggle, however, severely strained the Philippine economy, and it was naturally the labourer who suffered most. Two methods of exploitation, introduced through stress of war, hit him hard. Under the *polo* system all except chieftains and their eldest sons had to serve in the labour pool. This was hard enough, but working conditions were appalling, wages were rarely paid, and only the rice supplied monthly by the village treasuries kept the labourer alive. Even worse was the *vandala*, the compulsory sale of products to the government in return for token payments or promissory notes. Starvation and disease took so heavy a toll in lives that the population under Spanish control declined appreciably. When peace returned, however, the pressure on the Filipino was relaxed, and the population curve began to move upwards.

In taking over the islands the Spaniards left the existing system of food production unchanged and made few alterations in the indigenous labour systems. An increased food supply was of course necessary, but the measures taken to ensure it brought no fundamental changes, though they involved forcing the Filipinos to grow a surplus. A fair price for their produce would have easily overcome this difficulty. The Spaniards did, however, introduce important changes in the land system, which were responsible for the growth of landlordism on a large scale, that was to become so prominent a feature of Filipino society in the nineteenth century. In the first place they introduced the notion of ownership: the chieftains assumed the ownership of the *barangay* lands which their dependents cultivated. Previously all landowning had been communal in character with the title vested in the *barangay*. In the second place under Spanish law all lands owned neither communally nor privately belonged to the royal domain, and could be assigned to Filipino chieftains as real estate. Little is known of the early history of these forms of landowning—the subject awaits the researcher—but certain facts can be stated: (*a*) the religious orders acquired their estates by purchasing lands, once communally owned, from local chieftains; (*b*) the ecclesiastical estates became the largest item of the Spanish-owned *latifundia*, but represented only a small fraction of the total land under cultivation, and (*c*) the bulk of all cultivated lands remained in the possession of the Filipinos. There were very few individual Spanish landlords: the exploitation of the Filipinos was exercised by their own chieftains and by the clergy, against whom there was no effective protection.

Spain treated the Filipinos as a segregated community with its own laws and magistrates. On to this were grafted Spanish political institutions transplanted from Mexico. The *barangay* became the basic unit of local government under a *cabeza* (head) with the privileges of a hidalgo. For some two centuries the office was hereditary, but a law passed in 1786 introduced the elective principle. The *cabeza* was responsible for the collection of taxes, and had duties in connection with the *polo* and *vandala* which were a source of graft and power to him. Higher up in the scale the *pueblo* (township) with its parish church and outlying clusters of population (*vistas* or *barrios*) was a principal settlement under a *gobernadorcillo*. It was an extensive territorial unit. The *gobernadorcillo* was appointed annually by a process of democratic nomination with Spanish officialdom having the final voice. The 'little governor', usually dubbed *capitan*, was assisted by a number of officials, and these and the *cabezas* formed a local oligarchy with considerable power. It has been estimated that the power wielded by these 'bosses' in the field of local government—'caciquism'—proved the major obstacle to democratic growth in modern times. An important institution, already referred to, was the community treasury (*caja de comunidad*), supervised by treasury officials and under the judicial protection of the Audiencia. Every Filipino, when paying his tribute, deposited half a bushel of rice in the treasury. The object was to build up a surplus against famine, but lavish expenditure upon local fiestas prevented the accumulation of a substantial surplus. A few large *pueblos* were organized as cities with a government similar to that of cities in Spain and Spanish America. By the end of the seventeenth century six of these had been created, with Manila at their head.

The biggest unit of internal administration was the province (*alcaldia*). Confined at first to the pacified regions of Luzon and the Visayas, the provinces numbered fifteen by the end of the sixteenth century. Each was under an *alcalde-mayor* appointed by, and responsible to, the governor-general. The salary was very low, but the *alcalde-mayor* was permitted the privilege of personal trade, a source of scandalous corruption which made his office highly lucrative. The unpacified regions throughout the archipelago were divided into districts called *corregimientos* under politico-military officers (corregidores).

At the head of the central government in the Philippines was the governor and captain-general, who was appointed and removed from office by the king. Not only did he exercise great powers in the executive, military, judicial and religious fields as the king's representative, but because of the great distance of the Philippines from Spain he conducted the foreign relations of the colony with Asian rulers, receiving embassies, concluding treaties, declaring war and making peace. His powers, however, were subject to various checks. In the first place there was the Royal Audiencia, first created in 1583, a supreme court of almost omnicompetence, through which much of his power had to be exercised. In cases of vacancy due to death or absence the Audiencia exercised the gubernatorial powers; its special task was to protect the Filipino from abuse of official powers. In the second place each governor, upon relinquishing office, had his acts examined by a court (*residentia*) presided over by his successor. It was possible also for the king to appoint a special investigator (*visitador*) to look into colonial affairs. But internally the biggest check upon the governor's powers was exercised by the Church, whose priests and friars learned the indigenous languages and developed a closer association with the Filipinos than anyone else, and were able to make complaints either directly to the king or through the powerful religious orders to which many of them belonged.

The system of justice was based upon the recognition of Filipino customary law where it did not violate Spanish Catholic morality. In cases not covered by customary law Hispano-Roman law was applied. The *gobernadorcillo* could try petty civil cases. The *alcalde-mayor* heard appeals from these and exercised a wide criminal and civil jurisdiction. The Audiencia heard appeals from his court. In theory the Council of the Indies in Spain was the highest court of appeal, but cases from the Philippines were seldom referred to it. The clergy, it is interesting to note, opposed and criticized the application of Spanish legal procedure to the Filipinos, fearing that the spread of Roman ideas of law would reduce their own influence.

The Spanish arrival in the Philippines was only just in time to halt the advance of Islam into the centre and north of the archipelago. Islam had, however, taken a firm hold upon Mindanao, Sulu and the other islands of the south, and when the Spaniards attempted to conquer them for the Cross they stirred up such fierce resistance that not only did the 'Moros' maintain their independence, but their counter-attacks upon Christian communities and Spanish-held territory inflicted frightful bloodshed and damage. It was not only a matter of the Cross and the Crescent, though that was how the Spaniards saw it, but a struggle for independence by a people just as brave and adventurous as the Spaniards themselves, and with long traditions of sea-roving. The preliminary skirmishes began during Legaspi's régime. Then in 1578 the Spaniards made their first serious invasion of Moro territory.

They captured the city of Jolo[1] in the Sulu archipelago but failed to hold it in face of the deadly hatred of the population. In 1596 Captain Esteban Rodriguez de Figueroa led an expedition to Mindanao in an effort to plant a colony there. It failed miserably; worse still, it provoked a whole series of appalling raids upon towns and villages in Luzon and the Visayas. The Visayas suffered horribly and the Jesuit missions on Leyte, Samar, Cebu and Bohol were heavily damaged. The Spanish efforts to defend their exposed southern territories from bases at Iloilo and Cebu proved inadequate, and all their punitive expeditions failed. Moreover, when the Dutch appeared upon the scene they found useful allies among the Moros. Hence, after insistent appeals from the Jesuit missionaries, it was decided to establish a military base upon the Mindanao coast. Accordingly in 1635 Zamboanga was seized, and under the expert direction of the Jesuit missionary-engineer Father Melchor de Vera a powerful fortress was erected, which restrained Moro depredations and enabled the Spaniards to take the offensive against the Moro bases at Jolo and on Lake Lanao in northern Mindanao. Neither side, however, could win an outright victory, and when the Chinese leader Koxinga, having ousted the Dutch from Formosa in 1661, went on to threaten Manila in the following year, Zamboanga was evacuated by the Spaniards and their hopes of conquering the Moros were abandoned for the time being. The Moros too had gained little from their alliance with the Dutch, so tenacious had been Spanish resistance to their attacks. Thus by the middle of the seventeenth century a position of stalemate had been reached.

(c) Spanish intervention in Cambodia

Cambodia, a minor political power in the sixteenth century, away from the great maritime highways and with little to offer of commercial value in the eyes of the European trader, was somewhat late in attracting Western notice compared with other parts of South-East Asia. The Portuguese Dominican Gaspar da Cruz, the first Christian missionary known to have worked there, was at Lovek in 1555, but stayed only a short time because of the opposition of the Buddhist clergy. Two more Portuguese Dominicans, Lopo Cardoso and João Madeira, arrived there in 1583 or 1584,[2] but met with the same reception as their predecessor. King Satha, however, for commercial reasons was anxious for contacts with Malacca. Hence, although they and others who arrived in 1584

[1] The Spanish rendering of the word 'Sulu'.
[2] 1570 has been the usually accepted date. For C. R. Boxer's note on its inadmissibility see Groslier, *Angkor et le Cambodge au XVIᵉ siècle*, pp. 29–30.

soon left, a few stayed on, relying on the king's favour. One of these, the Dominican Sylvestre d'Azevedo, who learnt the Khmer language, was in charge of a small Christian community of Chams, Malays, Japanese and some Portuguese merchants at the capital.

At about the same time Portuguese and Spanish soldiers of fortune began to arrive in the country. Under the leadership of the Portuguese Diogo Veloso, whom, according to the Cambodian Chronicle, Satha 'adopted' as his 'son', they formed a pretorian guard, and the king was induced to write to Malacca inviting missionaries to come to his kingdom. His real object by so doing was to obtain Portuguese help in his struggle against Pra Naret of Siam, but in this he was unsuccessful: Malacca could spare neither men nor money. He turned therefore to the Philippines where Manila, since the union of the crowns of Spain and Portugal in 1580, had become in theory the centre of power in the Far East—Far West in Spanish eyes—in place of Malacca.

The Spaniards were looking for an opportunity to intervene on the mainland. Hence in 1593 two Spanish adventurers, Blas Ruiz de Hernan Gonzales and Gregorio Vargas Machuca, left Manila for Cambodia, and after extraordinary adventures on the way arrived at Sattha's court shortly before the great Siamese attack on Lovek was launched.[1] The king at once sent Veloso and Vargas to the Spanish governor of the Philippines, Gomez Perez Dasmarinas, bearing a royal letter inscribed on gold leaf asking for help against Siam and offering in return freedom for missionaries and a number of commercial privileges. Manila sent a non-committal reply by Veloso; but when he arrived with it he found the Cambodian capital in Siamese hands. He himself was taken prisoner and with a number of missionaries and other Europeans was deported to Ayut'ia.

There Velloso found King Naresuen anxious to conciliate the Spaniards, for his situation was far from easy, with Cambodia to hold down on the one side and Burma to deal with on the other. Thus it came about that he was soon on his way back to Manila as interpreter to a Siamese mission accredited to the Spanish governor. He arrived there in June 1595 to be reunited with his former associates Vargas and Blas Ruiz, the latter of whom had been captured by the Siamese at Lovek, but had managed to escape by seizing the junk on which he and others of his compatriots were being taken to Siam, landing the Siamese crew and sailing it to Manila. The project now was to obtain aid for King Satha, of whose flight to Laos no news had reached

---

[1] The latest, and most complete, version of the story is by Bernard P. Groslier in *op. cit.*, chap. ii, pp. 27–62.

Manila. The ecclesiastics were all for intervention; they overcame the opposition of the acting-governor, Don Luiz Dasmarinas, the son of Governor Gomez Perez Dasmarinas, who had been murdered while leading an expedition bound for the Moluccas, and in August 1595 Veloso and Vargas, styling themselves Satha's ambassadors, signed capitulations with the Manila government providing for the establishment of Spanish suzerainty over Cambodia and of a Spanish garrison there, and the conversion of the king and queen to Christianity.

There followed one of those highly romantic episodes in the story of European activities in the East of which this particular period provides such amazing examples. One has only to think of the exploits of 'king' Gonsalves Tibao of Sandwip and Philip de Brito at Syriam. In January 1596 an expeditionary force consisting of a frigate and two junks bearing 120 soldiers under the command of General Juan Xuares Gallinato and a number of Dominican friars left Manila bound for Cambodia. A storm dispersed it and the only vessel to reach its destination was one of the junks commanded by Blas Ruiz. The other, with Veloso in command, was stranded south of the Mekong delta, but her people were able to make their way on foot to Phnom Penh. Gallinato's frigate was blown far down into the Singapore straits and it was not until the following May that he was able to reach Cambodia.

Meanwhile Blas Ruiz and Veloso on arrival at Phnom Penh had found that King Satha had disappeared from the scene, the Cambodians had driven the Siamese garrison out of Lovek, and the royal power had been seized by a usurper, Chung Prei, whose headquarters were at Srei Santhor. He was supported by an army of Chams and Malays, which Satha had recruited for the defence of Lovek against the Siamese, but which had arrived only after the city's fall. Chung Prei ordered the Spaniards to remain in the foreign quarter at Phnom Penh. There trouble flared up between them and the Chinese, and on 12 April the Spaniards ran amuk in the Chinese quarter and pillaged their junks in the harbour. Chung Prei ordered them to make restitution, but was unable to enforce his order because at the time his army was away from the capital. Several weeks of negotiations then ensued until suddenly, on the night of the 11–12 May or the next one, the Cambodians, who sympathized with the Chinese, rose against the Spaniards. In the fighting which followed Veloso and Blas Ruiz attacked the palace at Srei Santhor, killed Chung Prei and one of his sons, blew up the magazine, set the fortifications ablaze, and finally regained their ships. On the day after this bloody affray Gallinato unexpectedly arrived on the scene. The court was in a state of complete panic, and according to some accounts a section of the magnates offered him the crown. He decided, however, that the whole project must be abandoned and the expeditionary force must return to Manila. Accordingly he restored the goods seized from the Chinese, promised reparation for the misdeeds of the Spaniards at Srei Santhor, and early in July sailed homewards.

This, however, was far from the end of the affair. On the homeward voyage Veloso and Ruiz persuaded Gallinato to drop them off at the Vietnamese port of Faifo so that they might make their way to the Laos kingdom in search of King Satha. In October 1596 they arrived at Vientiane to find that he and his eldest son Chestha were both dead, but that his second son Chau Pnhea Ton and other members of the royal family were still there. The arrival of the two trouble-makers at Vientiane was soon reported at Srei Santhor, where a son of Chung Prei had been placed on the throne by the magnates. The news caused such alarm that the new king promptly fled and the magnates thereupon invited the exiled Chau Pnhea Ton to return and assume the crown. He reached Srei Santhor in May 1597 together with Veloso and Blas Ruiz and was proclaimed king with the title of Barom Reachea II.

The new ruler was completely under the control of the two adventurers supported by the growing number of Spanish volunteers who gradually appeared on the scene. But there was disorder throughout the country; the magnates rebelled; and urgent appeals for help were sent to both Manila and Malacca. The king himself was persuaded to write to the heads of the three religious bodies in Malacca, the Franciscans, the Dominicans and the Jesuits, as well as to Manila and Goa, offering complete freedom to preach in his kingdom. For a time Veloso and Blas Ruiz were able to hold down parts of the country, but against the increasing opposition their position became hazardous in the extreme. In Manila the enthusiasm of the missionaries rose to fever heat: they pressed for a holy war. And Don Luiz Dasmarinas, who had handed over control on the arrival of Don Francisco Tello de Guzman as governor, offered personally to finance a new expedition provided he were guaranteed the governorship of Cambodia in the event of its annexation by Spain. It was sheer madness: there was not even a gambler's chance of success. Nevertheless, in September 1598 a small expedition under the command of Dasmarinas left Manila for Cambodia. Of his three ships one was totally lost in a storm, one was driven back to the Philippines, but after refitting managed to make Phnom Penh in October; his own was wrecked on the China coast and the survivors eventually reached the Portuguese settlement of Macao.

In Cambodia the royal family and the magnates were planning to depose Barom Reachea II in favour of Satha's exiled brother Soryopor; the deposed son of Chung Prei was canvassing support in the provinces. Moreover, Siam was becoming worried by the new signs of Spanish intervention. The forces at the command of Veloso and Blas Ruiz were totally inadequate to maintain their puppet on his throne; yet in this desperate situation with sublime self-assurance they were trying to persuade the king to accept a Spanish protectorate over his kingdom. It needed only an appropriate incident to trigger off a showdown.

This was provided by the Laksamana of the Malays, who stirred up an attack upon Luiz Ortez, one of the Spanish leaders, and when the Spaniards in revenge started to sack the Malay camp, laid siege in turn to theirs with his Malays and the exasperated Cambodians. The Spaniards, overwhelmed by numbers, were massacred almost to a man, Veloso and Blas Ruiz, who hearing of the trouble rushed to the support of their compatriots, were also killed. Only a few refugees escaped by boat.

The massacre took place in about the middle of the year 1599. It ended all hope of Spanish influence in Cambodia. A few months later the Laksamana had Barom Reachea II assassinated. The magnates then raised Pnhea An, a younger brother of Satha and Soryopor, to the throne as Barom Reachea III. He lasted only a few months (early-late 1600) before assassination—this time by an outraged husband—removed him also, but not before he had got rid of his overmighty Cham and Malay mercenaries and made a new approach to Manila through a Spanish soldier who had escaped the massacre. His successor Chau Pnhea Nhom, a son of Satha, who seized power and held on to it until the middle of 1603, welcomed some Dominican missionaries to Phnom Penh and made discreet enquiries of the Governor of the Philippines regarding possible Spanish aid. But the opposition in Cambodia was too great: Spanish 'protection' was too high a price to pay for independence of Siam. So in 1603, with the connivance of the royal family and the magnates, the exiled Prince Soryopor with armed Siamese support seized the throne from Nhom and became Barom Reachea IV. With him a new period of Cambodian history begins: Cambodia is a vassal state of Siam.

CHAPTER 14

BURMA AND THE T'AI KINGDOMS IN THE SIXTEENTH CENTURY

(a) To 1570

THREE years after the foundation of Ayut'ia in 1350 another T'ai kingdom, later known as the kingdom of Laos or Luang Prabang, was founded in the upper Mekong valley. It came into existence through the union of a number of small Laos states under the leadership of a chief of Muong Swa named Fa Ngum, who had been brought up at the Court of Angkor and was married to a Khmer princess. The origin of the Laos states on the Mekong is obscure and legendary. The T'ai seem to have settled there in the second half of the thirteenth century, and to have been first under the suzerainty of Angkor and later under that of Sukhot'ai. Through such channels they came into contact with Indian culture. Under Fa Ngum they were converted to Hinayana Buddhism. His father-in-law sent him a mission of monks bearing with them the Pali scriptures and a famous statue of the Buddha, which had been sent much earlier by a King of Ceylon as a present to Cambodia and was called the Prabang. It was installed at Lang Chang, Fa Ngum's capital, in a temple specially built for it, and at a later date the city came to be named after it.

Fa Ngum's military prowess earned him the title of 'the Conqueror'. The kingdom which he acquired and consolidated extended from the borders of the Sibsong Pannas along the valley of the Mekong down to the northern confines of Cambodia. On the west it touched the borders of the T'ai states of Chiengmai, Sukhot'ai and Ayut'ia, while on the east its neighbours were Annam and Champa. Though sparsely populated, it was one of the largest states in Indo-China. Fa Ngum's reign was one of constant campaigns and aggression, and both Annam and Ayut'ia felt the impact of his power. But to his peace-loving, easygoing subjects his autocratic rule, and the exhaustion caused by his wars, became increasingly unpalatable, until in 1373 his ministers united to drive him into exile, and placed on the throne his son Oun Hueun, a young man of seventeen.

P'aya Sam Sène T'ai, as he is known in the official chronicle, earned
his title of 'Lord of 300,000 T'ais' from the census of males which he
carried out in 1376. His reign was a period of consolidation and
administrative development. He was married to a Siamese princess
of Ayut'ia, and in carrying out the organization of his kingdom was
much influenced by Siamese methods. He also built temples and
founded monastic schools for the study of Buddhism. Economically,
Lang Chang was well placed. It had easy communications with both
Annam and Siam, and it soon became an important centre of trade,
with its gumlac and benzoin much in demand by the Siamese.

Prosperity depended upon the maintainance of good relations with
these two powerful neighbours. In the latter half of the fifteenth
century, however, Lang Chang was nearly brought to ruin through the
hostility of Annam. This was aroused by an incident which occurred
in the reign of Lan-Kham-Dèng (1416–28). He had offered assistance
to the Annamites when they were invaded by the Chinese in 1421, but
the force he sent had gone over to the Chinese and had eventually
been driven back into its own country by the exasperated Annamites.
During the subsequent period they were too deeply involved in their
final struggle with Champa to take their revenge. But as soon as Le
Than Ton had completed the reduction of Champa in 1471, he began
to prepare to attack Lang Chang. In 1478 he delivered his blow,
storming the city of Lang Chang itself and driving its king, P'aya Sai
Tiakap'at (1438–79), into exile. His success, however, was shortlived.
A son of the fugitive king, T'ène Kham, rallied the Laos forces and
drove out the Annamites. He then succeeded to the throne and set
himself to re-establish his country's prosperity by cultivating better
relations with her eastern neighbour.

The struggle with Annam was followed by a long period of peace
during which, as a result of the development of closer commercial
relations with the Menam valley cities, the kingdom prospered. King
P'ot'isarat (1520–47), the builder of Wat Visoun, was a devoted
Buddhist who strove to stamp out the popular animism and witch-
craft, but failed. He was the first of the Laos kings to take up his
residence at the city of Vien Chang (Vientiane), which, lying much
farther down the Mekong, occupied a central position in his long-
strung territories and was better placed than Lang Chang for trade
with Siam and Annam.

The period of comparative calm ended in 1545, when P'ot'isarat
was tempted to intervene in an acute succession dispute in the much-
troubled kingdom of Chiengmai. In 1538 Muang Kesa, the fifteenth

9

king since the foundation of the state, had been deposed by his son
T'ai Sai Kham. The latter's cruelty and misgovernment, however, led
to his assassination in 1543, and with him the direct male line became
extinct. P'ot'isarat thereupon claimed the throne through his mother,
a Chiengmai princess, and sent a strong force which rapidly defeated
the various rival claimants who had come upon the scene, and caused
a deputation to be sent to him with an offer of the crown. He accepted
it for his son Sett'at'irat, a boy of twelve. Pending the boy's arrival
the notables of the kingdom met and appointed a princess, Maha
Tewi, as regent.

The news of Sett'at'irat's accession to the throne of Chiengmai
brought a Siamese army on the scene, led by King P'rajai himself.
Apparently his excuse for intervention was the punishment of Muang
Kesa's murderer. But as this had already been carried out before his
arrival, and Siam's real aims were well known, and likely to be stoutly
resisted, he was persuaded by Princess Maha Tewi, a woman of
immense ability in the exercise of statecraft, to return home. In 1547
King P'ot'isarat was killed in a hunting accident, and Sett'at'irat had
to return to Lang Chang in order to deal with an attempt by his
younger brothers to partition the kingdom. As soon as his back was
turned another crop of pretenders arose to dispute the Chiengmai
succession, and once again King P'rajai invaded the kingdom. This
time Princess Maha Tewi resisted. The Siamese were repulsed before
the walls of Chiengmai. While retreating they were defeated in a series
of engagements by the pursuing Laos army and completely routed.

The story of the campaign is graphically told by Fernão Mendes
Pinto, who of course claims to have accompanied the expedition. He
tells us also that on arrival home King P'rajai was poisoned by T'ao
Sri Suda Chan, one of his four senior non-royal consorts. She was
pregnant by a lover, whom she had taken during the king's absence
on campaign. Her own son, a boy of nine, succeeded his father as
king, but she soon had him put out of the way. Then after a blood-
bath of her opponents she placed her lover on the throne. Two months
later they were both assassinated at a royal banquet.

Pinto cannot have accompanied P'rajai's army, since he represents
the campaign as a victorious one against an invading force from Chiengmai. His account seems to be a hotch-potch of stories picked up
probably from Portuguese soldiers-of-fortune who had served in the
Siamese army. His story of T'ao Sri Suda Chan's coup d'état is
nearer the mark, though the Siamese version accepted by Wood[1]

[1] *History of Siam*, p. 111.

represents the assassination of her and her lover as taking place while they were in the royal barge on their way to an elephant hunt. Pinto's dates do not fit in with what is known of the story. But in any case the Siamese records for this period are so conflicting and obscure that it is almost impossible to check his details.

The leaders in the assassination plot placed Prince T'ien, a younger brother of P'rajai, on the throne with the title of Maha Chakrap'at. Wood assigns this event to the year 1549,[1] but there is good reason for placing it a year earlier, since that would accord with the date ascribed by the Burmese chronicles[2] to Tabinshwehti's invasion of Siam, which took place towards the end of the year of Maha Chakrap'at's accession, and the Burmese sources for this period are more reliable than the Siamese in the matter of dates.

Tabinshwehti (1531-50) of the Toungoo dynasty, whose rise has been recorded in Chapter 6, § c, aimed at reuniting the whole of Burma under one ruler. His first step, for which his father had been in the midst of preparations when he died, was to conquer the richer and more urbane kingdom of Pegu. Such was the chaos in the Ava kingdom after the conquest of its capital by the Shans in 1527 that he took the risk of leaving his rear undefended while he concentrated upon his southern objectives. His first campaign in 1535 gave him possession of the Irrawaddy delta and its chief town Bassein. Pegu, however, was strongly defended, and only fell by stratagem in 1539 after four years' resistance. The Mon king, Takayutpi, fled northwards to Prome, where Tabinshwehti's attack was foiled by reinforcements sent down from Ava by its Shan ruler.

But Takayutpi died, and many of the Mon chiefs offered their allegiance to the Burmese king, seeing in him the only leader capable of giving their land settled government. Moreover, he wisely showed respect for their customs and institutions and accorded Mons equality of treatment with his Burmese. In 1541, with an army reinforced by Mon levies and a contingent of Portuguese mercenaries under João Cayeyro, he captured the port of Martaban. It had put up a magnificent resistance, but was finally taken by storm and sacked without mercy. Pinto, who again claims to have been present, gives a vivid eye-witness account of the horrible massacre systematically carried out by the conqueror. Moulmein, cowed by the treatment of Martaban, surrendered, and the whole of the Mon kingdom down to the

---

[1] *Ibid.*, p. 112.
[2] According to Phayre's reading in his *History of Burma*, p. 100. But see Harvey's note in his *History of Burma*, p. 343.

Siamese frontier at Tavoy fell into Burmese hands. Then as a thank-offering for victory Tabinshwehti placed new spires on the chief Mon pagodas. The most renowned of them all, the Shwe Dagon, received a special offering of ten viss (36.5 lb.) of pure gold.

In the following year Prome was starved into submission after a five-months siege and treated with the same cruelty as Martaban. Its capture opened the way to central Burma. But before Tabinshwehti was in a position to take the offensive he had to meet a powerful counter-attack launched against Prome by the Shan ruler of Ava in league with the sawbwas of six of the Shan states. With the help of his Portuguese gunners he won a decisive victory, which he followed up by occupying all the country as far as the districts of Minbu and Myingyan. At Pagan he was crowned with ancient ceremonial. But he did not go on to attack Ava. He returned southwards and in 1546 staged a second coronation at Pegu, using both Burmese and Mon rites.

Neither Toungoo nor Pagan was to be his capital, but Pegu with its historic Mon associations. The explanation, so often given, that he was pro-Mon in his sympathies is inadequate. It is true that he did everything possible to conciliate the Mons, even to adopting their hair-style. But a pro-Mon king would hardly have permitted the atrocities perpetrated at Martaban and Prome. His real reason seems to have been that he planned to attack Ayut'ia and needed the Mon country as a base. He sought to become a Chakravartin, the world conqueror of the Buddhist white elephant myth. The King of Siam possessed a number of these precious animals, and he was determined to have them.

Actually, however, his first great enterprise after his coronation was an invasion of Arakan. This move does not seem to have formed part of any over-all plan but to have been purely opportunist. A discontented Arakanese prince appeared at his Court and offered to become his vassal if he would place him on the throne at Mrohaung. But the city's fortifications were too powerful for him, and he was glad of an excuse to abandon the expedition. The excuse was the news of a Siamese raid on the Tavoy region. Wood, however, rightly points out that the violent revolutions that had been taking place at the Court of Ayut'ia led him to believe that the moment was ripe for an invasion. His preparations were on a great scale, and the force he led into Siam when the campaigning season began with the end of the wet monsoon of 1548 was indeed formidable. Nevertheless it failed to break through the defences of Ayut'ia, and on returning homewards nearly came to grief before the incessant attacks of the Siamese.

After two major reverses Tabinshwehti, though only thirty-six years old, completely lost his morale. He became a debauchee and left the conduct of affairs to others. The Mons, who had borne the brunt of his wars, rose in revolt under Smim Htaw, a minor prince of the old dynasty. While Tabinshwehti's brother-in-law and alter ego Bayinnaung was absent dealing with this rebellion another member of the Mon royal family, Smim Sawhtut, procured the king's murder (1550). Pegu opened its gates to him with joy. For the moment Tabinshwehti's kingdom was in hopeless chaos. A Mon leader ruled as king in Pegu. Another was gathering strength at Martaban. And the Burmese chiefs of Toungoo and Prome refused to recognize the authority of Bayinnaung, who aimed at succeeding the murdered king.

First of all, however, Smim Htaw marched on Pegu and eliminated his rival Smim Sawhtut. Then Bayinnaung seized Toungoo and was crowned king. His next move was to gain control over central Burma as far northwards as Pagan. He considered the feasibility of an attack on Ava, but decided to reconquer the Mon kingdom first. In 1551, with a mixed force of Burmese and Mons, and a Portuguese detachment led by Diogo Soarez de Mello, he defeated Smim Htaw in a battle fought outside the walls of Pegu. Mon resistance thereupon collapsed everywhere. Smim Htaw himself was hunted through the delta, managed to escape in an open boat to Martaban, but was finally caught in the hills around Sittaung and cruelly done to death. His gallant struggle caught the popular imagination, and many local traditions of him still survive.

Bayinnaung was crowned at Pegu with the grandest ceremonial. He began to build a magnificent palace-city for himself and his Court. His next military enterprise, the subjugation of northern Burma and the Shan states, was on a far more ambitious scale than the two campaigns whereby he had restored the kingdom created by Tabinshwehti. In 1553 he sent an army of observation up the Irrawaddy, but its advance caused the Shan chiefs to set aside their mutual quarrels and unite against the threatened invasion. He therefore raised the largest force he could possibly muster, and late in 1554 launched a two-pronged attack against Ava from Toungoo and Pagan respectively. In March 1555 the city fell, and he then pushed his conquests to Bangyi in Monyua district and Myedu in Shwebo district, beyond which in those days the authority of the Ava rulers did not extend.

Next he turned on the Shans. In 1556 he subdued Hsipaw and Moné while on his way to conquer Chiengmai. This state was now ruled by a Shan prince named Mekut'i, who had been accepted as their king by the local chieftains when Sett'at'irat, having secured the throne of Luang Prabang, refused to return to Chiengmai. Mekut'i surrendered without resistance, swore allegiance to Bayinnaung, and agreed to pay an annual tribute of elephants, horses, silk and other products of his country. This expedition had a profound effect upon the Shan chiefs on the borderland between Burma and China; all hastened to pay homage to the new conqueror.

As soon as the Burmese army left Chiengmai, however, forces from Luang Prabang moved in. In 1558 they defeated Mekut'i and would have deposed him had not Bayinnaung reappeared on the scene and driven them out. He then proclaimed the deposition of Sett'at'irat from the throne of Luang Prabang. Sett'at'irat in reply formed a large coalition of Shan states and advanced to Chiengsen at the head of their combined forces. Bayinnaung, however, by occupying the territories of his allies, forced him to retire, and the confederation broke up (1559).

In the following year Bayinnaung returned to Pegu, and Sett'at'irat, taking advantage of the lull, made a formal alliance with Ayut'ia. In 1563, in order to maintain closer contact with the Siamese and avoid a surprise attack by the Burmese, he removed his capital to Vien Chang and strongly fortified the city. He also built there a shrine for the famous Emerald Buddha (Pra Keo), which he had carried off from Chiengmai when he had returned to Luang Prabang after his father's death. His greatest architectural work in his new capital was the pyramidal structure known as the That Luong, which is today the finest example of Laotian architecture, though severely damaged in 1873 by bandits from Yunnan.

Bayinnaung's assumption of suzerainty over the Shan states was a new departure in Burmese history. It was the inevitable result of the successful resistance of the Burmese to the Shan attempts to dominate Burma, which had gone on ever since the fall of Pagan in 1287 and had brought the ruin of the Ava kingdom. Henceforward there was to be no longer any question of the Shans recovering control over Upper Burma; the shoe was now firmly on the other foot.

The Burmese champion's control over Chiengmai was of even greater immediate importance, since it vastly facilitated an attack upon Ayut'ia. And it was Bayinnaung's dearest ambition to force the most powerful of all the T'ai states to submit to his authority. Sett'at'irat's alliance with King Chakrap'at and Siam's rapid recovery after Tabinshwehti's invasion hastened his decision to strike as soon as possible.

His demand for a couple of white elephants and Chakrap'at's refusal, much discussed as the cause of the war, must surely be regarded merely as formalities preceding hostilities, like the solemn throwing down of the gauntlet in mediaeval Europe.

The invasion began after the close of the wet monsoon of 1563. The Burmese forces crossed from the Sittang valley to Chiengmai. They then proceeded by way of Kamp'engp'et and Sukhot'ai to Ayut'ia, which surrendered in February 1564 after slight resistance. The king and most of the royal family were carried off to Burma as hostages, while a son of Chakrap'at was left behind as vassal ruler with a Burmese garrison to control him. As soon as he had settled the new régime at Ayut'ia, Bayinnaung planned to lead a punitive expedition against the King of Chiengmai, whose attitude had been unsatisfactory when the Burmese army had passed through his state. News came, however, of a serious Mon rebellion, and he had to hurry off to Pegu, leaving his son, the heir-apparent, to command the force marching against Chiengmai.

On arrival home Bayinnaung found that the rebels, aided by Shan and Siamese prisoners settled in the neighbourhood, had burnt Pegu together with his own palace and even some of the older buildings dating from Dammazedi's reign. With characteristic energy he crushed the outbreak, rounded up the rebels, and was only dissuaded by the intervention of the Buddhist clergy from burning several thousands of them in huge bamboo cages. He at once began to build an even more magnificent palace-city than the one that had been destroyed. The Venetian Caesar Fredericke and the Englishman Ralph Fitch, who saw it in its full glory, have recorded their wonder at its size and richness. In some parts, they said, its roofs were covered with plates of gold.

Meanwhile the heir-apparent's expedition against Chiengmai had met with general resistance and King Mekut'i had taken refuge in Vien Chang. The Burmese therefore invaded the kingdom of Luang Prabang and prepared to attack Sett'at'irat in his capital. On the appearance of their flotilla before Vien Chang the king fled. They occupied the city, capturing the queen and Oupahat, or heir-apparent, as well as the fugitive Mekut'i. When, however, they tried to follow up Sett'at'irat his harassing tactics were too much for them and they had to give up the attempt. In October 1565 they arrived back in Burma with their prisoners. Mekut'i was placed in safe custody at Pegu while Princess Maha Tewi was installed a second time as regent at Chiengmai, this time with a Burmese garrison.

In Siam Prince Mahin, who had been established as regent by Bayin-naung, functioned under the control of the pro-Burmese Raja of P'itsanulok. Sett'at'irat's successful defiance of the Burmese caused Mahin to turn to him for assistance in throwing off the yoke of Bayin-naung. In 1566 the two of them attacked P'itsanulok, but the arrival of a Burmese army forced them to abandon the enterprise. In the hope of preventing further trouble, Bayinnaung in the following year permitted the captive king Chakrap'at, who had become a monk, to return to Siam on a pilgrimage. His generosity was misplaced, for on arrival home the king threw off the yellow robe and joined Prince Mahin in another attack on P'itsanulok.

Bayinnaung therefore had to stage a second invasion of Siam. In 1568 he set out from Martaban and made for P'itsanulok, which he relieved. Then he passed on to Ayut'ia. This time the city put up a desperate defence and defied all his efforts to storm it. Sett'at'irat sent a force to the assistance of his ally, but the Burmese ambushed it and drove it off. The siege lasted until August 1569, when the city fell through treachery. King Chakrap'at had died during the siege. Prince Mahin died a prisoner on his way to Pegu. Maha T'ammaraja, the pro-Burmese Raja of P'itsanulok, was installed as the next vassal ruler of Ayut'ia, and Bayinnaung prepared to lead his victorious army to punish the King of Vien Chang. He had gorged his men with the plunder of Ayut'ia. The city's defences were dismantled and vast numbers of its population deported to Lower Burma.

For the second time the Burmese invasion of the Laos kingdom was a failure. Vien Chang defied all Bayinnaung's attempts to take it, and in April 1570, with his troops exhausted by famine and disease, he beat a hasty retreat so as to reach home before the onset of the wet monsoon. Siam, on the other hand, remained under Burmese control for the next fifteen years. One interesting result of this was the adoption by Siam of the Burmese Era beginning in A.D. 638. It became known as the Chula Sakarat to distinguish it from the Maha Sakarat beginning in A.D. 78, which it displaced. It remained in official use until 1887, when Chulalongkorn adopted the European calendar. According to Wood, the Burmese *dhammathat*, based on the Laws of Manu, was introduced at the same time and grafted on to Siamese law.

(b) From 1570 to 1599

Bayinnaung's career has been aptly described as 'the greatest explosion of human energy ever seen in Burma'. 'The king of Pegu', wrote the Venetian Caesar Fredericke, who visited his capital in 1569, 'hath not any army or power by sea, but in the land, for people, dominions, gold and silver, he far exceeds the power of the Great Turk in treasure and strength.' The bare record of the events of his reign shows him everlastingly hastening somewhere to assert his authority: it is a catalogue of campaigns.

There is, however, another side to his story, though it is of minor importance. Strange as it may seem in one who was responsible for so much human bloodshed, he strove to be a model Buddhist king, building pagodas wherever he went, distributing copies of the Pali scriptures, feeding monks, and promoting the collection and study of the *dhammathats*. The costly offerings he made to pagodas at Pegu on his return from Vien Chang in 1570 give the impression of being acts of atonement for the demerit incurred through the deaths of so many thousands of human beings. He probably explained away his own responsibility in much the same terms as, two centuries later, King Naungdawgyi used when rejecting the British demand for compensation for the massacre of Negrais (1759). The victims, he said, were fated to die in such a way.

But if Bayinnaung had no strong feelings about human slaughter, he had conscientious scruples against animal sacrifices such as the Muslim practice of killing goats in celebration of Bakr Id or the offering of white animals to the Mahagiri spirit on Mount Popa. Such practices he prohibited, as also the killing of slaves, elephants and horses at the death of a Shan sawbwa for burial along with his body.

In his zeal for the enhancement of his reputation as a Buddhist king throughout Indo-China he sent offerings on several occasions to the famous Tooth of the Buddha at Kandy in Ceylon, providing lights to burn at its shrine, craftsmen to beautify the building, and brooms, made from his own and his chief queen's hair, for use there. In 1560 the Viceroy of Goa, Dom Constantino de Braganza, led an expedition to punish the Raja of Jafna for the persecution of Catholic converts made there by St. Francis Xavier. In sacking the place a tooth, reputed to be the Kandy one, was seized and taken to Goa. Bayinnaung sent envoys with the offer of a large sum of money for it. But the archbishop intervened and referred the matter to the Inquisition, which condemned it to be destroyed as a dangerous idol. The sentence was carried out before a great concourse of people, among whom were the scandalized Burmese envoys.

Some years later Bayinnaung asked Raja Dharmapala of Colombo for a daughter in marriage. Having no daughter, but being anxious to please the king, that ruler palmed off on him the daughter of one of his ministers as his own. He also sent with the bride a tooth, which he claimed was the genuine one. The Raja of Jafna, he said, had palmed off a monkey's tooth on the Viceroy of Goa. Both the 'princess' and the tooth were received in Burma with the highest honour, and the Raja of Colombo received so munificent a present in return that the King of Kandy offered a princess and a tooth, both of which should be genuine. But it was useless for him to protest that the real tooth had never left its temple at Kandy and that the Raja of Colombo had no daughter. Bayinnaung was far too shrewd to permit any doubt as to the authenticity of the raja's gifts. The tooth he had deposited in a jewelled casket beneath the Mahazedi Pagoda.

In 1571 died Sett'at'irat of Vien Chang, the chieftain who had never bent the knee to the king of kings. His brother the Oupahat had been a hostage in Burma since 1565, and Bayinnaung sent envoys to Vien Chang to negotiate his return as a vassal ruler. But the Laotians had bitter memories of Burmese invasions, and they murdered the envoys. In revenge Bayinnaung sent Binnya Dala, his Mon commander-in-chief, with an army composed of levies drawn from Chiengmai and Siam to attack Vien Chang. It was defeated, and Bayinnaung either put his general to death or exiled him to a place where he soon died. Then in the dry season of 1574-5 he personally led an expedition which drove the regent, General Séne Soulint'a, out of the capital and placed the Oupahat on the throne.

As soon as his back was turned his puppet's power began to dwindle. In 1579 he sent another army to deal with the general disorder, which his vassal was unable to quell. But no sooner had it completed its task and left for home than the unhappy king was driven out of his capital and died while fleeing to safety. Bayinnaung thereupon sought to solve the problem by placing Séne Soulint'a himself on the throne. But he was an old man and only survived for two years. He was succeeded by his son Nakone Noi, who soon found his task impossible. Revolts broke out everywhere. In the confusion the new king was dethroned and anarchy reigned supreme. There was no longer any fear of Burmese intervention; Bayinnaung had died in 1581 and his son Nanda Bayin had other things to attend to.

For several years no solution could be found. Sett'at'irat's only son had been born at the time of his death in 1571. When he had placed the Oupahat on the throne in 1575 Bayinnaung had carried off the young prince as a hostage to Burma. In 1591 the abbots of the leading monasteries met and decided that the only cure for the country's ills was to recall the legitimate heir from captivity. The moment was propitious, since King Nanda Bayin was so hard pressed by the gathering strength of a Siamese national movement against Burmese dominance led by Pra Naret that he willingly released the prince. In 1592 Prince Nokeo Koumane gained possession of Luang Prabang and was accepted as king. His first act after establishing control over his kingdom was publicly to proclaim its independence of Burma.

When Bayinnaung died in 1581 he was poised for an attempt to deliver a knock-out blow to the kingdom of Arakan. The Burmese chronicles assert that shortly before his death he deputed a mission to the Mughal emperor Akbar. As Bengal had been conquered by the Mughal armies in 1576, and there is no mention of a Burmese mission to Fatehpur Sikri in the Mughal records, it seems more probable that the mission went to the Viceroy of Bengal. Its object seems to have been to sound him regarding his attitude towards a Burmese attack upon Arakan. But the blow was never delivered, and when the two states did in fact come to war, in 1596, it was the Arakanese who were the aggressors, joining in the general scramble for loot which occurred when Nanda Bayin's armies were driven out of Siam and Pra Naret's counter-offensive was making serious inroads into Burma.

Bayinnaung had sown the wind; his son reaped the whirlwind. Not that Nanda Bayin was lacking in either ability or determination, but sooner or later the reaction against his father's extravagance and megalomania must come. The Mons in particular were driven to desperation by the unceasing demands upon them for military service and the famine and exhaustion which resulted from their inability to cultivate their lands. For uncultivated delta lands relapse quickly into impenetrable jungle, and the task of clearing them is heart-breaking.

The Siamese might have attempted to regain their independence earlier had not Boromoraja of Cambodia seized the opportunity presented by their weakness to pay off old scores. In the year after the second fall of Ayut'ia he invaded Siam, and, though driven out with heavy loss, kept up the pressure until after Bayinnaung's death. The threat to Ayut'ia made it necessary to restore the fortifications which had been dismantled, and the Burmese had to permit the strengthening of the city's defences. The Siamese also found a new leader in Pra Naret, the 'Black Prince', later to be King Naresuen, the elder son of T'ammaraja, who had been taken as a hostage to Burma when his father became vassal king of Ayut'ia. In 1571 as a lad of sixteen he had been allowed to return home as a result of the marriage of one of his sisters to Bayinnaung. His courage and resourcefulness against the invading Cambodians made him the hope of the patriots.

Nanda Bayin's accession was the signal for a dangerous attempt to break up the united kingdom. Bayinnaung's brother Thadominsaw, the Viceroy of Ava, tried to draw the Viceroys of Prome and Toungoo into a movement for independence. They, however, forwarded his letters to the Court, and Nanda Bayin, suspecting that some of his ministers were involved, arrested them and had them burned to death together with their wives and families. Gaspero Balbi, a Venetian jeweller, who witnessed the appalling scene, describes it in his account of his travels, an English translation of which was published by Richard Hakluyt in his *Principall Voyages*. In 1584 Nanda Bayin led an army against his uncle and defeated him in a battle in which the two leaders, in traditional style, fought a duel on elephants.

Pra Naret had been summoned to bring a contingent from Siam to support his overlord against the Ava rebels. According to Wood, Nanda Bayin planned to have him murdered, but the Mon chiefs entrusted with the task disclosed the plan to the prince. Instead of marching on Ava, therefore, he appeared before Pegu and threatened an attack. On learning of Nanda Bayin's victory over the Ava forces, however, he retreated to Martaban, collected a large number of Siamese prisoners, who had been deported to Lower Burma during Bayinnaung's wars, and led them back to their own country. Nanda Bayin sent a force in pursuit of him, but he turned and defeated it in the Menam valley. Shortly afterwards another Burmese force, chasing some Shan prisoners who were fleeing from Burma to P'it-sanulok, was also defeated and driven back over the frontier. The die was now cast. Siam was asserting her independence. The Governors of Sawankhalok and P'ijai, fearing Burmese vengeance, rebelled against Pra Naret, but he stormed Sawankhalok and executed them both.

In December 1584 Nanda Bayin invaded Siam through the Three Pagodas Pass, midway between Moulmein and Tavoy. He was to to join up with the Chiengmai army before Ayut'ia, but Pra Naret defeated each force separately. In November 1586 three Burmese armies began a converging movement upon Ayut'ia, and from January to June 1587 the city was besieged. But the administrative arrangements for such a large-scale effort were defective, and the invasion ended in disaster. Things might have gone even worse with the Burmese had not King Satt'a of Cambodia invaded Siam while the siege was in progress, so that as soon as the Burmese retired Pra Naret had to concentrate upon driving out the Cambodians instead of seeking to deliver a knock-out blow at Nanda Bayin's disorganized and disheartened forces. On the other hand, his pursuit of the Cambodians was so relentless that he nearly succeeded in capturing their capital Lovek. Outside its walls, however, lack of supplies forced him to abandon the enterprise and return home.

From this moment the independence of Siam was assured. But the stubborn Burmese king refused to give up the futile struggle and thereby accomplished his own doom. He could have held his own country together had he been wise enough to evacuate Siam. In his desperate attempts to raise and equip new armies his demands fell most heavily upon the Mons, already alienated by the treatment they had received over many years. Many tried to evade the press-gang by taking the yellow robe and becoming monks. But the king had them unfrocked. Many abandoned their villages and took to the jungle. Bassein rebelled, without success, and all the captured rebels were tortured to death. Many fled to Arakan and Siam.

In 1587 Ralph Fitch, the first recorded Englishman to set foot in Burma, arrived at Bassein from Bengal. He had left England with three companions in 1583 and had travelled to India. There he had parted with his companions and pursued his way farther eastwards alone. On his journey through the creeks from Bassein to Pegu he noted the houses built on 'great high postes' for fear of the many tigers, he supposed. In his account, which Hakluyt included in the second edition of his *Principall Navigations*, and Purchas printed also in his *Pilgrimes*, he indicates no signs of the coming collapse. He describes the country as 'very fruitful' and was much impressed by the king's majesty and riches. Unfortunately he kept no diary or notes for fear of being arrested as a spy by the Portuguese on his way home, as indeed he had been on his way out. Hence in writing his account of Burma he made extensive use of Thomas Hickock's translation of Caesar Fredericke's story of his own visit to the country in 1569, when he saw Bayinnaung in his glory. This also was published by Hakluyt.

Caesar Fredericke wrote what might be described as a guide for commercial prospectors, and as such it is invaluable, full of useful information about trade, conditions of travel, and currency and exchange. Ralph Fitch also was a merchant, seeking knowledge that would be of possible commercial value. He obviously could not improve on the Venetian's account, and he was a modest man with no pretensions to literary skill. He does, however, add a few independent touches which show that he could be interested in things other than trade. Here is his description of the Shwe Dagon Pagoda:

'About two dayes journey from Pegu there is a Varelle or Pagode, which is the pilgrimage of the Pegues: it is called Dogonne, and is of a wonderfull bignesse, and all gilded from the foot to the toppe. It is the fairest place, as I suppose, that is in the world: it standeth very high, and there are foure ways to it, which all along are set with trees of fruits, in such wise that a man may go in the shade above two miles in length.'

His account of the Buddhist monkhood is equally apt:

'The Tallipoies go very strangely apparelled with one camboline or thinne cloth next to their body of a brown colour, another of yellow doubled many times upon their shoulder: and those two be girded to them with a broad girdle: and they have a skinne of leather hanging on a string about their necks, whereupon they sit, bareheaded and barefooted: for none of them weareth shoes; with their right armes bare and a great broad sombrero or shadow in their hand to defend them in the Summer from the Sunne, and in the Winter from the rain. They keepe their feasts by the Moone: and when it is new Moone they keepe their greatest feaste: and then the people send rice and other things to that kiack or church of which they be; and there all the Tallipoies doe meete which be of that Churche, and eate the victuals which are sent them. When the Tallipoies do preach, many of the people carry them gifts into the pulpit where they sit and preach. And there is one that sitteth by them to take that which the people bring. It is divided among them. They have none other ceremonies nor service that I could see, but onely preaching.'

In 1590 T'ammaraja died and Pra Naret became king, in name as well as in fact. In the list of Kings of Siam he is known as Naresuen. By 1593 Nanda Bayin had failed in five full-scale invasions of Siam. In the last, which was launched at the end of 1592, the Burmese heir-apparent was defeated and killed at Nong Sa Rai before he reached Ayut'ia. The ruins of a pagoda erected on the spot where he was killed—in personal combat with Naresuen, according to the Siamese—are still to be seen. From this time onwards it was the turn of the Siamese to invade Burma.

But first it was necessary to deal with Cambodia, so that there should be no danger of a stab in the back when Naresuen's attention was concentrated upon Burma. Immediately after the Burmese defeat of February 1593 Naresuen began a campaign against Cambodia. It was long and severe. Eventually in July 1594 Lovek was taken and the king fled to Luang Prabang. No attempt was made to annex the kingdom; it was enough to paralyse it so that Naresuen should be free to deal with the arch-enemy. Thousands of prisoners were deported to Siam to be settled in her depopulated northern provinces; many Siamese previously carried off by King Satt'a's raids were brought back.

Naresuen's first moves in taking the offensive against Burma show a statesmanlike regard for the needs of his kingdom. He did not seek to inflict a knock-out blow, which would merely have brought plunder and might have involved him in an exhausting attempt to hold the turbulent Burmese in subjection. Siam was a trading state and had urgent need of ports on the Indian Ocean. Southern Burma had useful ones within comparatively easy reach of Ayut'ia. It was on these that Naresuen first concentrated his attention. In 1593 the Siamese made themselves masters of Tavoy and Tenasserim. Thereupon the Mon Governor of Moulmein, sick of the massacres of his people, rose in rebellion and called on Siam for help. In response Naresuen led a force which not only drove off the Burmese from besieging Moulmein but also took Martaban.

Nanda Bayin's next loss was Chiengmai. The old Princess Maha Tewi, whom Bayinnaung in 1564 had made regent for the second time, had died in 1578. With the object of strengthening his position vis-à-vis Luang Prabang, Bayinnaung had next placed his son Tharrawaddy Min on the throne of Chiengmai. When things began to go badly with Nanda Bayin, Nokeo Koumane of Luang Prabang declared war on Chiengmai, and Tharrawaddy, unable to obtain help from his brother, was in such dire straits that he appealed to King Naresuen. It was a heaven-sent opportunity for the King of Ayut'ia. In 1595, in return for reinforcements which saved his kingdom, Tharrawaddy had to place the much-coveted Chiengmai under Siamese suzerainty.

In that same year the Siamese threatened the city of Pegu. But a Burmese force came down from Toungoo and forced Naresuen to withdraw. Then, with the writing on the wall, a family quarrel broke out which made disaster inevitable. Prome, Toungoo and Ava were all governed by brothers of Nanda Bayin. When the Toungoo Min went to the assistance of Pegu against Naresuen, his brother the Pyi[1] Min took advantage of his absence to attack Toungoo. The king was helpless to deal with the situation and a general revolt began. The Toungoo Min invited the Arakanese to join with him in an attack on Pegu. In 1599 a powerful Arakanese fleet seized the port of Syriam and conveyed a land force to effect a junction with the Toungoo army besieging Pegu. Then Naresuen realized what was afoot and attempted to join in. He was just too late, for when he arrived in Burma Nanda Bayin was a prisoner on his way to Toungoo, and Pegu lay in ashes. The confederates had divided the booty. Toungoo received the king and the Tooth of Buddha, Arakan a princess and the royal white elephant. The Arakanese on leaving set fire to the city. They deported thousands of Mon households. They also maintained a foothold in the country by retaining Syriam, which was placed under one of their Portuguese mercenaries, Philip de Brito.

Naresuen, in an effort to gain possession of Nanda Bayin, marched northwards to attack Toungoo. But he was so heavily defeated that he had to return home. Nanda Bayin was murdered soon after reaching Toungoo. With the fall of Pegu all semblance of a central government disappeared. Siam held Lower Burma from Martaban southwards. A parcel of warring chiefs divided the remainder of the country between them, while Philip de Brito, with Syriam as his base, began to play a game of high stakes.

[1] The Burmese name for Prome

CHAPTER 15

INDONESIA FROM THE PASSING OF MAJAPAHIT TO THE RISE OF MATARAM

(a) The Indonesian states

WHEN the Hindu-Buddhist empire of Majapahit disappeared from the scene, Muslim Demak, which, Schrieke thinks, administered the *coup de grâce* and did so because the Portuguese of Malacca were seeking to establish contact with its ruler, became the leading state in Java. Members of the old dynasty held out for a century and more at Pasuruan, Panarukan and Balambangan in the eastern parts of the island, but Raden Patah of Demak gained possession of the Majapahit regalia. Later accounts of this period ascribed to him a Majapahit origin, besides telling the dramatic story of his conquest of the city at the head of a Muslim army. Both stories are apocryphal. Dr de Graaf thinks he probably came to Demak from Palembang, and had Chinese blood in him. His kingdom owed its importance to two main factors, its control over the northern rice-growing plains stretching from Japara to Gresik and the extensive trade of those two ports. Through Japara the rice of Java was exported to Malacca; Gresik conducted a flourishing trade with the Spice Islands.

Raden Patah's reign extended from *c.* 1500 to 1518. His son Pangeran Sabrang Lor, also known as Pati Eunus, who succeeded him, had led an abortive attack in 1512 on the Portuguese at Malacca. He reigned only three years. His brother Tranggana, who succeeded him in 1521, raised the state to its highest pitch of prosperity and influence, and assumed the title of sultan. Closely associated with Demak's power was the theologian, statesman and soldier, Sunan Gunung Jati— called 'Falatehan' by the Portuguese—who came from Pasei, having made the pilgrimage to Mecca, and married Tranggana's sister. As Demak's representative he extended his control westwards over the coastal region of Java. At the same time Javanese Muslim colonists settled in the ports of Cheribon and Bantam, then under the rule of the Hindu-Buddhist Sundanese kingdom of Pajajaran with its centre near present-day Bogor. Sunan Gunung Jati gained control over both ports and turned them into orthodox Muslim states. He established his son Pangeran Pasarean at Cheribon, while he himself ruled Bantam. When this son died in 1552, Sunan Gunung Jati transferred his own residence to Cheribon leaving another son, Hassan Udin, in charge of Bantam. Under this ruler Bantam became an independent state: he founded a kraton there and extended his power deeply into the interior at the expense of Pajajaran. He also gained control over the Lampongs and cultivated relations with the southern states of Sumatra. He married a princess of Indragiri who brought him as dowry the pepper port of Silebar.

Much earlier on, Sunan Gunung Jati's activities had caused Pajajaran to lose the harbour of Sunda Kalapa (now Djakarta) which served its capital Pakuan. As in Majapahit's case, if Schrieke is right, it came about through the Portuguese seeking to establish contact with the 'infidel' kingdom. In 1522 a Portuguese ship had come to Sunda Kalapa and its Sundanese regent had made a treaty permitting the establishment of a Portuguese trading settlement at the mouth of the river Chiliwung. The Portuguese did nothing towards carrying the treaty into effect until 1527. When, however, they returned, they found that Sunda Kalapa had been captured by Bantam and renamed Djakarta; and instead of opening a factory there, they had to purchase their pepper in the bazaar. It was Hassan Udin's son Panembahan Yusup (1570–80) who, as mentioned above,[1] slaughtered the whole royal family of Pajajaran at Pakuan and forcibly converted the Sundanese magnates to Islam. Long before the end of the century Bantam had become one of the principal pepper ports of Indonesia and the 'southern staple port of Chinese trade', as van Leur describes it. Its great bazaar to the east of the city outside the gates was a centre for trade, both local and international, wholesale and retail, very similar to that of Malacca in the days of its sultans. There were to be seen, once more to quote van Leur, 'all sorts of foodstuffs (of which rice and salt, for example, came from overseas, and may perhaps have been vended by the Javanese who had transported them), pots, pans, pepper bags, spices, Gujerati and Bengali with painted articles and trinkets, Persians and Arabs with jewels, rows of Chinese shops . . . with all their expensive goods: damask, velvet, satin, silk, gold thread, cloth of gold, porcelain, lacquered work, copperwork, woodwork, medicinal products and the like'.[2] It was an aristocratic city with wealthy nobles who maintained their armed retinues of warriors and slaves, and a patriciate of wholesale traders, among whom Chinese merchants formed probably the most influential group.

---

[1] Page 215.   [2] *Indonesian Trade and Society*, p. 140.

Demak's sea power seems to have enabled her to control the ports of the south coast of Borneo, but the evidence of this is uncertain. The island of Lombok came under her rule and was 'Islamized'. To the south and south-east the expansion of her control over the interior of Java was extensive; in particular she subdued the Hindu-Buddhist realm of Supit Urang with its capital at Malang. But her attempts to conquer the eastern territories of the former Majapahit empire were less successful, and ultimately ended in disaster. Sultan Tranggana's attack upon Panarukan was defeated with immense loss in 1546, and he himself was killed. His empire thereupon disintegrated so suddenly that his son and successor Sultan Prawata had no power outside the city of Demak itself.

The Portuguese possession of Malacca became a serious threat to the trading states of the north Javanese coast. The monopoly over the spice trade, that the Portuguese were able to enforce through their establishments on Ternate and Amboina, crippled the regular traffic of the Javanese harbours so that with the failure on the one hand of the attempts of Acheh and her Javanese allies to regain Malacca for Islam, and on the other of those of the local rulers, with Javanese help, to break Portuguese power in the Moluccas, the prosperity and military power of the coastal states declined. At the same time their relations with the inland regions deteriorated, and we now find the states to the south of central Java beginning to play a bigger part in history. Some time before the break-up of Demak's empire we begin to hear of the little kingdom of Pengging. A prince of this state, Jaka Tingkir, was sent to Demak for his education. He rose to become the head of the sultan's bodyguard, received a daughter in marriage with Pajang (now Surakarta) as an appanage, and took the title of Pangeran Adivijaya. During the struggles which followed the death of Sultan Tranggana he was able to increase his power to such an extent that in about 1568 he became sultan of Pajang. The Portuguese referred to him as 'emperor'; the Banjermasin chronicle calls him Sultan Surya Alam, 'Sun of the World'. For a few years—less than twenty according to de Graaf—he was pre-eminent among the rulers of Java. Javanese sources say that his most feared rival was Pangeran Aria Penangsang, the ruler of Jipang, who had striven to attain to supreme power in Java by the assassination of all possible rivals. Among those who fell by the krisses of his murder gangs had been Sultan Prawata himself in *c.* 1550. When ultimately, and inevitably, war arose between Aria Penangsang and Adivijaya, so the story goes, the latter promised the district of Mataram as the prize for anyone killing his rival. It was won by a certain Kjai Gede Pamanahan, who in personal combat with Aria Penangsang caused his stallion to throw him. Kjai Gede, upon receiving his fief, proceeded to build his capital at the present Kota Gede, and soon settlers were coming in to occupy his vacant lands. He died in *c.* 1575 and was succeeded by his son, known to history as Senapati ('general') from the title conferred upon him by his overlord Sultan Adivijaya of Pajang.

Panembahan Senapati Ingalaga was, according to the seventeenth century *babads,* or dynastic panegyrics composed by official court poets, the founder of the Mataram dynasty, which achieved the greatest sway of any ruling family after the fall of Majapahit, and produced Sultan Agung (1613–45), one of the outstanding characters of Indonesian history. Unfortunately, the Javanese accounts of Senapati's career contain so much myth and miracle, reminiscent of stories in the earlier *Pararaton* and *Nagarakertagama,* that it is almost impossible to sift out the little that can be accepted as historical from the clogging mass of allegory and poetic fiction, since these sources are practically all there are at the disposal of the historian. Nevertheless, in his *Geschiedenis van Indonesie,*[1] and in much greater detail in his monograph *The Reign of Panembahan Senapati Ingalaga,*[2] Dr de Graaf has essayed this difficult task, and constructed an account of the political history of central and east Java during the last quarter of the sixteenth century in which he sets out what in his opinion are the acceptable facts.

Dr de Graaf rejects out of hand the genealogy 'invented' by the *babad*-writers connecting Senapati with the more famous dynasties of earlier Java, notably that of Majapahit, and presents him as a man of comparatively low origin. He divides the reign into a series of phases. The first sees Senapati allying with the western regencies and stealing their allegiance from Pajang. The second shows him fortifying his capital with a stone wall while relations with Pajang deteriorate to the point of war. A great attack by Pajang, however, fails because of an eruption of Mount Merapi. The next phase is concerned with Demak. After the death of Sultan Adivijaya of Pajang in 1586, his successor Pangeran Benawa obtains Senapati's help against the raids of the Adipati of Demak. Demak is defeated and Benawa offers the over-lordship of Pajang to Senapati, who, however, refuses it. The fourth and last phase sees Senapati's attempts to expand his power eastwards. The first is directed at Surabaya, strong through overseas trade and proud of its Majapahit traditions. He fails to conquer it, but at Jipang

[1] 's-Gravenhage, 1949.
[2] Verhandelingen van het Koningklijk Instituut voor Taal-, Land- en Volkenkunde, Deel 13, 's-Gravenhage, 1954.

(modern Mojokerto) envoys of the priest-ruler of Giri arrange an understanding by which Surabaya recognizes Mataram's overlordship. Next
he proceeds to deal with Madiun, which at the instigation of Surabaya
had made an alliance with Panaraga against Mataram. His third attack
is against the Hindu-Buddhist state of Pasuruan. Its general, Adipati
Kaniten, is defeated in the field and its ruler then pays homage. His
last move is in support of the rights of the legitimate claimant to the
regency of Kediri, which had been denied to him by his overlord
Surabaya. It brings a double attack by the Surabayans and their allies
upon Mataram through Madiun. Senapati is victorious but dies soon
after, in 1601. He had made his power felt from Cheribon to Pasuruan,
but the coastal states, notably Surabaya, remained practically independent, otherwise the great attack on Mataram at the end of the reign
would have been impossible. It is noteworthy, says Dr de Graaf, that
the Dutch, who appeared in Java during Senapati's last years, hardly
mention him, but accord the title 'king' to coastal potentates such as
the rulers of Tuban and Surabaya. The Adipati of Pati, according to
the Javanese accounts, long defied Senapati, and finally led an invasion
into the heart of Mataram, reaching as far as Prambanan. Senapati's
cavalry, however, defeated him, and his extensive territory came under
Mataram's (nominal?) sway.

The picture of Senapati drawn by Dr de Graaf is that of a tyrant,
not a king: a lucky soldier who founded a dynasty but did nothing
constructive. His son and successor, Panembahan Krapyak (1601-13),
was busy throughout his short reign dealing with rebellions and striving
—with little success—to hold his inheritance together. The first, and
most dangerous, revolt was raised by his elder brother, Pangeran Puger
of Demak, Senapati's second son. With the aid of Dutchmen captured
from Jacob van Heemskerck's squadron, whence they had gone ashore
at Japara to open trade, he beat off the first attack by the Mataram
forces. Finally in 1604 Krapyak himself took the field and defeated his
brother. Some time later another brother, Pangeran Jayaraga of
Panaraga, made an attempt to seize the throne. Little, however, is
known of this rebellion, since, unlike Puger's, there is no foreign source
with which to check the Javanese accounts. It seems to have been
speedily suppressed.

The remainder of the reign was taken up with hostilities against
Surabaya. The powerful city-state, which had been the chief opponent
of Senapati's Mataram, was ever ready to help the enemies of Krapyak.
The war took the form of chronic raiding and counter-raiding. The
city itself behind its massive walls and ramparts, five miles in

circumference, with regular bastions in the Chinese style half a cannon-shot away from each other, according to the description of the Dutchman Artus Gijsels, could defy all attempts to storm it, and Krapyak made none. The Javanese accounts of the war are unsatisfactory: as Dr de Graaf puts it, they arouse more thirst for information than they assuage.[1]

Panembahan Krapyak's death is mentioned in a letter of 1 January 1614 by Jan Peterszoon Coen.[2] His eldest son Rangsang, later to be known as Sultan Agung, who succeeded him, was the first Javanese ruler of whom there is a personal description by a European; and the events of whose reign can be satisfactorily checked up by comparing indigenous and European sources. Agung's career is of the greatest interest, not only for what he did, or tried to do, but also for the views of Javanese history that it caused to be propagated. He aimed to become an empire-builder in the grand manner, and his court-poets invoked and embroidered the traditions of a Majapahit greater than the reality, weaving a new web of mythology to substantiate his claims to universal allegiance.

The products of their imaginative labours have been devastatingly analysed by Professor C. C. Berg, who has singled out Dr de Graaf's account of Senapati for special attention.[3] He points out that according to the *Babad Tanah Jawi* story Senapati accomplished in general the same warlike deeds as his grandson Agung, and that while it is quite possible that Senapati's gains were lost and the work had to be done all over again by Agung, there is also the possibility to be reckoned with that because the compiler of the *Babad Tanah Jawi* has ascribed to Agung forefathers who are certainly fictitious, Senapati himself may be in the same category; that the deeds ascribed to Senapati may be interpreted as a projection into the past of Agung's conquering expeditions, which are historical; and that the court poet ascribed adversity to Senapati during the latter part of his life in order the more to exaggerate the story of Agung's conquests. According to this theory Agung himself, not Senapati, was the *novus homo*, the founder of the dynasty, and as such according to Javanese ideas his power had to be legitimated through the recognition of suitable ancestors ultimately tracing back 'to a well-known ruler in an unverifiable past'.[4] Agung's court poet, Berg points

---

[1] *De Regering van Sultan Agung, Vorst van Mataram (1613–45) en die van zijn Voorganger Panembahan Seda-ing-Krapjak (1601–13)*, 's-Gravenhage, 1958, p. 22.
[2] *Ibid.*, p. 25.
[3] Notably in 'Twee Nieuwe Publicaties betreffende de Geschiedenis en de Geschiedsschrijving van Mataram', *Indonesie*, viii, pp. 97–128. See also 'Javanese Historiography —a Synopsis of its Evolution' in D. G. E. Hall (ed.), *Historians of South-East Asia*, London, 1961, pp. 13–23.   [4] *Indonesie*, viii, p. 111, my translation.

out, would have been well aware that this sort of thing had been done twice before in Java, namely in the case of the Airlangga-poem, i.e. Mpu Kanwa's *Arjunavivaha*,[1] and that of Propanca's *Nagarakertagama*,[2] and his interest in 'events' was that of the high priest in tradition, not that of the historian in history.

Whatever we may think about the historicity of the Senapati story, there can be no doubt that long before Agung appeared upon the scene Mataram was a power to be reckoned with in the politics of Java. At the outset of his reign Agung was able to take the offensive with success against the allies of Surabaya. In 1614 there were raids into east Java followed by a counter-attack by Surabaya and her allies—a contemporary Dutch source lists them as Tuban, Lasem, Gresik and Pasuruan—which came to grief against the Mataram forces in a battle at the river Brantas near Kediri. In the next year Agung conquered a regency called Vira-Saba in the Javanese accounts, which apparently stretched from the neighbourhood of Mojokerto to the mouth of the Brantas. It was an area of strategic importance from which one could command the overland way into the Brantas delta as well as communications between the delta and the eastern end of Java. His success led to another counter-attack by Surabaya and her allies, this time aimed at the heart of the Mataram state; but they were again defeated in a battle fought near the present Surakarta (Solo). A few months later in quick succession Lasem and Pasuruan fell. In 1617 Pajang, which was foolish enough to rebel, became Agung's next victim, and for her presumption was horribly devastated.

In 1619 the great port of Tuban was conquered and the dominance at sea of the eastern regencies came to an end. Thereafter the Mataram war fleet became appreciably stronger, and Agung was able to threaten Surabaya so seriously with sea blockade that in May 1620 Jan Peterszoon Coen wrote to the Dutch governor-general expressing his doubts about the city's further powers of resistance. Actually they were greater than he anticipated; not until 1625, after a five-year struggle, did Agung at last gain his objective. Blockade proved extremely difficult: it was impossible to surround the city effectively for the neighbourhood was swampy and very unhealthy, and part of the city itself was situated on an island. Assault was out of the question because of its strong fortifications. Attrition was the chief method employed: every year after harvest the Mataram forces systematically ravaged the surrounding country. But even then the city capitulated only when Agung dammed up the Kali Mas river and cut off its water supply.

---

[1] *Supra*, p. 69.   [2] *Supra*, pp. 72 et sqq.

During the siege expeditions were sent to Borneo, in 1622, which forced Banjermasin and Sukadana to acknowledge Agung's suzerainty. In 1624 the conquest of the island of Madura was undertaken. The western part was easily subdued but there was a bloody struggle for the eastern. Agung placed the Adipati of Sampang over the whole island and gave him one of his sisters in marriage. To defeated Surabaya Agung behaved magnanimously, placing the defeated ruler's son Pangeran Pekik in charge as vassal-ruler and giving him also a sister in marriage.

Surabaya's fall was Agung's greatest achievement; only Balambangan in east Java, closely linked with Bali, and western Java, dominated by Bantam did not recognize his suzerainty. Cheribon, which offered homage and a princess in marriage in 1625, represented the farthest extension westwards of his influence. In 1624 he had assumed the title *susuhunan*, 'royal foot' (i.e. placed upon the head of a vassal paying homage), which the Dutch appropriately translated as 'emperor'.

(b) The Anglo-Dutch assault on the 'ring fence'

That the English made so late a start in exploiting the Cape route to the Indian Ocean and beyond was in no way due to lack of interest in Eastern trade. The voyages of John Cabot from Bristol in the reign of Henry VII were undertaken with the object of reaching the great spice and silk markets of eastern Asia. The discovery of America resulted in the postponement of the achievement of this aim for something like a century. But the many attempts to discover a northern passage either round America or round Russia and Siberia show that the original object of intrusion into the trade of Asia was kept constantly in mind. The failure of the Muscovy Company to open up the North-East Passage led to Anthony Jenkinson's attempts to find a way to the Far East overland through Russia. But the sole result was a short-lived trading connection with Persia. And when the London merchants sought to develop a route to the East through Syria, though they managed to establish a prosperous trade with the eastern Mediterranean, it was useless as a gateway to India and the lands beyond. Individual prospectors such as John Newbery and Ralph Fitch did indeed make their way via the Levant to India, and in Fitch's case to South-East Asia; but Newbery disappeared on his way home, and Fitch's experiences showed clearly the impracticability of the route he used for large-scale commerce. Hence as the sixteenth century drew towards its close the London merchants came to realize that the only practicable route was round the Cape of Good Hope.

The difficulties which for so long deterred the English from exploiting the Cape route must be realized if their appearance in South-East Asia as competitors with the Portuguese and the Dutch is to be seen in its true perspective. In the first place there is no evidence that they deliberately refrained from poaching in the Portuguese preserves out of respect for the papal award of 1492. During the first half of the sixteenth century their lack of knowledge concerning the trade and navigation of the Indian Ocean was a sufficient deterrent. The Portuguese took the greatest pains to maintain secrecy regarding their operations in the East. No Portuguese navigator would serve on an English ship, nor would they permit an Englishman to sail on one of their eastbound ships if he were of sufficient education to learn their secrets.

During the second half of the century English geographical knowledge improved immensely as a result of the work of such scholars as Dr. John Dee, Richard Eden and the two Hakluyts. But there were still immense difficulties to be overcome. England produced practically no goods that were saleable in tropical countries. Her greatest need was to sell her woollen cloth, and for this a northern approach seemed to be essential. Moreover, not until the end of the century did her merchants dispose of enough fluid capital to risk on an all-round voyage of 16,000 miles for a cargo of spices. Expeditions involving long voyages were indeed sent out, but they went westwards in search of Spanish treasure ships.

There was also a further difficulty involved in long trading voyages. Ships required large crews in proportion to their size, and the longer the voyage the more space was required for their provisions, so that the problem was to find enough space for a profitable cargo. The Portuguese solved it by building large carracks of 1,200–1,500 tons which required proportionately fewer men to handle them than the 200-ton merchantmen which constituted the largest type normally employed by English shippers. The war with Spain led to the construction of larger ships by private enterprise, but not until sufficient headway had been made in meeting this difficulty were the English in a position to compete with the Portuguese in the trade of the Indian Ocean.

When Philip II of Spain acquired the crown of Portugal in 1580 he in effect invited the enemies of Spain to invade the Portuguese empire. In that same year Drake returned from his voyage round the world bringing with him, besides the precious metals he had looted from the Spaniards, a small cargo of cloves he had acquired at Ternate after crossing the Pacific. He reported that he had made a trade treaty with the king of the island, who was anxious for help in a struggle he was engaged in against the Portuguese. His exploit stimulated much interest in the East Indies, and six years later Thomas Cavendish left on a voyage which took him through the Magellan Straits, across the Pacific to the Philippines and on to the south-west coast of Java, where he refitted for his voyage home. He reported that trade might be carried on freely with the Moluccas and, moreover, that he had heard in Java that if the Portuguese pretender, Don Antonio, whose cause England supported, were to go to the East Indies they would be at his disposal. There were two schools of thought in England regarding the question of the Portuguese empire. Drake and the Devon men believed that England's best plan for obtaining access to the trade of the Indian Ocean would be by helping Portugal to gain her independence. Then, they argued, she could expect to be rewarded by a share in the Portuguese monopoly.

The London merchants, however, favoured a direct attack upon the monopoly, and after the defeat of the Armada in 1588 they began to petition the queen to encourage trade via the Cape route. Drake's capture in 1587 of the Portuguese *San Filippe* off the Azores with a cargo of spices worth £108,000 led them to suggest that the proposed venture could be financed by the plunder of Portuguese ships. And they pointed out that trade could be opened with places between south India and the Philippines without going near any Portuguese or Spanish stronghold. To their original petition, presented in October 1589, there is no answer on record. But the project was revived in the following year and resulted in the despatch in 1591 of an expedition of three ships from Plymouth under George Raymond and James Lancaster bound for the East Indies by the Cape route. It is significant that both Cornelis de Houtman, whom the Dutch Amsterdam merchants chose to lead their first expedition to the East Indies, and Lancaster were men who had spent part of their early life in Lisbon.

The expedition would have been successful had it not been for the appalling mortality among the crews. On the way to the Cape it became so serious that one ship had to be sent home from Table Bay with the sick men. After leaving the Cape Raymond's ship was lost at sea. Lancaster, however, reached north-west Sumatra and passed on to Penang, whence he carried on commerce-raiding activities against Portuguese shipping passing through the Straits of Malacca. But he lost so many men by disease that he was unable to work his ship home; for when, after leaving St. Helena, he was delayed by calms he had to run across to the West Indies for provisions, and while collecting them he was marooned on Mona through his ship drifting away with only six men on board to San Domingo, where she surrendered to the Spaniards. He himself and eighteen men were taken by a French privateer to Dieppe, whence he reached England on 24 May 1594. The venture had come to grief, but the fact that an English ship had roamed the Indian Ocean, preying with impunity upon Portuguese commerce, aroused some compensating enthusiasm. And while Lancaster was away another carrack, with an even richer cargo than Drake's prize of 1587, had been taken.

The London merchants, however, hesitated to send a further expedition by the direct route. There was a deepening trade depression and much opposition from the merchants engaged in the Levant trade. In 1596 Dudley was able to obtain support for a voyage to China via the Magellan Straits, and Benjamin Wood's disastrous expedition was despatched. The original plan was abandoned and his squadron of three ships entered the Indian Ocean by the Cape route. After reaching the Malay Peninsula they were all lost, and the sole survivor, a Frenchman, was in 1601 picked up by a Dutch ship from Mauritius, where he was living in Robinson Crusoe style.

The news of Houtman's voyage to Bantam (1595–7) caused opinion to veer once more in favour of the Cape-route approach: the Dutch intrusion into the field was seen as a threat to the Levant trade. When, therefore, in 1599 van Neck's four ships returned to Holland not only with rich cargoes but also in record time, a large subscription began to be raised in the London market for a further voyage to the East. The appearance in 1598 of an English translation of Linschoten's *Itinerario*, providing first-rate information regarding the trade and navigation of the Indian Ocean, had already aroused considerable interest, and, together with the reports of van Neck's success, clinched opinion in favour of the formation of a company to trade to the East Indies by the Cape route.

But there were still great difficulties to be overcome. Elizabeth's government was in financial straits; there was the Irish rebellion and the war with Spain. The project was held up by the queen's negotiations with Spain. When, however, these broke down in July 1600, the Privy Council tipped the promoters of the company to go ahead, with the assurance that an application for a royal charter would be successful. On 31 December of that same year the East India Company began its official existence. Stow's *Chronicle* attributes its creation to a Dutch corner in pepper, and the story has often been quoted, though entirely legendary.

Under its royal charter the Company, which consisted of a governor and twenty-four 'committees' appointed to organize a trading expedition to the East Indies, was granted a monopoly of trade in the region between the Cape of Good Hope and the Magellan Straits for a period of fifteen years. For its first voyage it raised a capital of £68,000. Four ships were specially purchased at a cost of £41,000, £6,860 was spent on goods for trading, and specially coined 'rials of eight' to the value of £21,742 were put on board for the purchase of return cargoes. Lancaster, who had assisted in fitting out the fleet, was placed in charge of the expedition, with John Davis as pilot-major. He had occupied a similar position in Cornelis de Houtman's fleet on his second voyage in 1598–1600.

Lancaster's fleet left in February 1601 and reached Acheh on 5 June 1602. It sailed on to Bantam, where permission was obtained to build a factory. Then it set out for home with full cargoes of spices. It brought back so much pepper that there was a glut in the market and the shareholders had to receive part payment of the proceeds of the voyage in pepper. Lancaster had met with no opposition from the Dutch, who were already well established in the East Indian trade, and had received active assistance from the King of Acheh in keeping Malacca ignorant of his arrival in its neighbourhood. Bantam was the most suitable site for the first English factory, since it was not only a flourishing centre for local commerce but was the port to which the Chinese junks came for their pepper. It continued to be the head-quarters of English trade in the Archipelago until 1682.

When Lancaster founded the first English factory in the East Indies the Dutch had already put in four years of the most intensive efforts to capture the markets hitherto dominated by the Portuguese. Before the end of 1601 no less than fifteen fleets, comprising in all sixty-five ships, had sailed to the Indian Ocean either round the Cape or through the Magellan Straits. Philip II's decree of 1594 closing the port of Lisbon to Dutch and English traders has usually been given as the cause of this truly remarkable onslaught upon the Portuguese 'ring fence'. Recently, however, Dutch scholars have been inclined to ascribe less importance to it, and to point out that long before 1594 the Dutch were dissatisfied with their position as middlemen between Lisbon and the rest of Europe and were anxious to make the voyage direct to the East for their own profit. The decree, it is claimed, hastened this new development of Dutch enterprise, but did not cause it.

When the Dutch assumed the task of wresting the spice trade from the Portuguese they possessed certain advantages which placed them well ahead of the English or any other likely competitors. Their extensive fishing trade was an excellent nursery for seamanship. Their function as the waggoners and factors of Europe, in which they were competing successfully with the Hanseatic cities, gave them experience as middlemen which few could rival. Moreover, their financial methods were the most up-to-date in Europe, and they had at their disposal an amount of fluid capital which from the start gave them an immense superiority over the English East India Company. Their chief reasons for hesitation in attempting to develop the Cape route were, as in the case of the English, the lack of knowledge concerning the navigation of the Indian Ocean and their long concentration upon attempts to discover a North-East Passage.

In 1592, however, Jan Huygen van Linschoten of Haarlem, who had spent four years in Portugal and subsequently five years in Goa as secretary to its archbishop, arrived back in his native country with an immense fund of knowledge regarding the trade and navigation of the Indian Ocean, which he at once placed at the disposal of the leading geographers and cartographers. His *Reysgeschrift van de Navigatiën der Portugaloysers in Orienten*, published in 1595, and *Itinerario, Voyagie ofte Schipvaert van Jan Huygen van Linschoten naar Oost— ofte Portugaels Indien*, which appeared a year later, contained exactly the practical information that had hitherto been lacking. Perhaps more important still, he showed that the Portuguese power in the East was rotten and that their relations with the native peoples were so bad that other traders had a splendid opportunity to enter into competition. And he pointed to Java as an excellent centre for establishing trade, since the Portuguese rarely went there.

In 1595 the first Dutch expedition set out to the East Indies by the Cape route. It was financed by a syndicate known as the Compagnie van Verre, which came into existence as a result of the failure to make headway with the discovery of the North-East Passage. The expedition was under the leadership of Cornelis de Houtman, who had spent some years as a merchant in Lisbon. How much he actually learnt from Linschoten before his departure is uncertain, but it is significant that his course was plotted by Linschoten's close friend and colleague, the cartographer Plancius, and he used the *Reysgeschrift*. He himself was a bad commander, a boaster and ruffian, who nearly brought the expedition to grief through his 'preposterous' conduct. The fact that on the outward journey alone 145 of his 249 men

THE LINSCHOTEN MAP, 1599

died has been attributed to his deficiencies as a commander, but, in view of Lancaster's losses in men during his first voyage, must probably with more justice be put down to lack of experience.

With his small squadron of four ships he reached Bantam in June 1596. He was well received, but his behaviour was so outrageous that he and some of his men were thrown into prison. The Dutch ships thereupon bombarded the town. A month later de Houtman was ransomed. After sailing off eastwards to Jacatra and other north Javanese ports as far as the island of Bali, de Houtman's officers forced him to make for home, though inadequate cargoes had been procured and he was anxious to visit the Moluccas. In August 1597 he returned to the Texel with three out of his four ships and eighty-nine men. Notwithstanding the disappointingly small cargoes which he brought back with him, there was great jubilation in Holland at his return. His voyage had demonstrated that with better organization and leadership successful trade with the Indies was possible. And preparations were at once put in hand for further expeditions.

The rejoicing of the Dutch was equalled by the consternation of the Portuguese at de Houtman's exploit. The Viceroy of Goa equipped a fleet to prevent further Dutch voyages. The King of Bantam was strictly forbidden to receive further foreign European merchants and reprisals were taken against his shipping. But the Javanese resistance was so determined that the Portuguese fleet had to retreat on Malacca.

In 1598 no less than five expeditions, numbering in all twenty-two ships, left Holland for the East Indies. Of these, thirteen went via the Cape and nine via the Magellan Straits. Oliver van Noort, in one of the westward-bound ships, returned via the Cape and became the first Dutch commander to circumnavigate the globe. The biggest single expedition was sent by the Compagnie van Verre from Amsterdam under Jacob van Neck, with van Warwijck and van Heemskerck next in command. On the outward voyage the island of Mauritius was discovered by van Warwijck and named after Maurice of Nassau. Van Neck reached Bantam in six months from leaving home. The Bantammers, having had to fight off a Portuguese fleet, traded willingly, and with four ships fully laden with pepper he sailed for home, whither he arrived less than fourteen months after his departure. His treatment of the natives had been so tactful that he brought with him for presentation to Prince Maurice a gold cup from the young sultan and a letter from his chief minister. The remaining four ships of van Neck's squadron sailed along the north coast of Java, touching at

Jacatra, Tuban and Gresik. Van Heemskerck and van Warwijck then went on to Amboina, whence the former was sent on to the Banda Islands. He established a factory on Lonthor and returned to Holland in 1599. Van Warwijck went on to Ternate and returned home late in 1600. The cargoes brought back by van Neck yielded a profit of 100 per cent on the outlay for the whole expedition. When the remaining ships returned home and the accounts were closed a total profit of 400 per cent was declared.

Other ships of the fleets sent out in 1598 visited Sumatra, Borneo, Siam, Manila, Canton and Japan. But none of the other expeditions made such staggering profits as van Neck's. The two expeditions through the Magellan Straits failed badly to the tune of half a million guilders, and one of those via the Cape brought heavy losses to its promoters. But the significant fact is that, notwithstanding their struggle for independence against Spain, these losses, which would have brought a crisis in London, neither crippled nor even cramped the Dutch effort. Several more companies were formed and more ships than ever before were despatched to the East. There were so many companies competing with each other in sending out ships that the period up to the formation of the United East India Company in 1602 goes by the name of the *wilde vaart*, or the period of indiscriminate voyaging. So far as South-East Asia was concerned there was hardly a port of any importance that was not visited by Dutch ships. Everywhere almost without exception they were received with friendliness and their help was sought against the Portuguese. The most striking exception was the murder of Cornelis de Houtman at Acheh in 1599 and the imprisonment of his brother Frederick there for two years, during which he composed the earliest Malay-Dutch dictionary and Malay translations of a number of Christian prayers.

In 1600 Steven van der Haghen concluded the first important treaty with a native ruler. It was with a chief of Amboina, who besides permitting the Dutch to establish the 'Kasteel van Verre' on his territory promised them the exclusive delivery of all the cloves produced there. It was the first of many similar agreements whereby the Dutch sought not merely to oust the Portuguese but to monopolize the trade against all comers from Europe. Before the ever-increasing number of Dutch ships that poured into their preserves the Portuguese were at a great disadvantage. At home Lisbon could send no help. Philip III's use of the port for his naval preparations against England and the Netherlands in 1599 caused the English to blockade it, and in any case the extravagance and inefficiency of Spanish policy had reduced it to a mere shadow of its former greatness. Goa therefore had to manage with such naval forces as it could muster in the Eastern seas. In 1601 Furtado de Mendoza put out from Malacca with a fleet of thirty vessels to attack Bantam, but Wolphert Harmensz with five ships of the Compagnie van Verre drove him off. But while the Dutch ships were scattered collecting cloves among the islands of the Moluccas the Portuguese commander succeeded in an effort to regain control of Amboina. He followed this up with an attack upon Ternate in co-operation with the Spaniards from Manila. But this failed and he returned with his exhausted troops to Malacca. The Portuguese were also foiled by a Dutch squadron in an attack upon their old enemy the Sultan of Johore.

The failure of the Portuguese attempt to drive the Dutch out of the Archipelago provided the latter with an excellent opportunity for a general counter-offensive, but one which under the existing conditions of trade they were not in a position to seize. It had become urgently necessary to bring the *wilde vaart* to an end. Prices were rising steeply as a result of the competition between the merchants of different companies to procure cargoes, and in some cases they had even come to blows. A movement towards amalgamation began in 1600. The formation of the English East India Company convinced the Dutch that only by a united national effort could they consolidate and preserve what they had gained in the enthusiasm of their first push to the East. Such were the factors which brought into being the United East India Company or the V.O.C. (Vereenigde Oostindische Compagnie).

The constitution of the Company was laid down by the *octrooi* of the States General of 20 March 1602 which brought it into being. It was granted the monopoly of trade in the regions between the Cape of Good Hope and the Magellan Straits for an initial period of twenty-one years, together with power to make treaties, build forts, maintain armed forces and install officers of justice. In each city where amalgamating companies were established, namely Amsterdam, Middelburg, Delft, Rotterdam, Hoorn and Enkhuizen, there was to be a V.O.C. Chamber, while the governors of these companies, numbering seventy-six were to form its directors, with the provision that vacancies were to remain unfilled until the number had declined to sixty. The actual management of day-to-day affairs was entrusted to a body of seventeen, referred to as the *Heeren XVII*, the *Directeuren* or the *Majores*. On this body the Amsterdam Chamber was to have eight seats. An initial capital of 6½ million guilders was subscribed, of which Amsterdam's share amounted to 3,675,000 guilders. Each Chamber was to fit out ships independently, but profit and loss were to be shared by all. Finally the Company was to take over all the factories established in the East by its predecessors, namely at Ternate in the Moluccas, Banda, Bantam and Gresik on the north coast of Java, Patani and Johore on the Malay Peninsula, and Acheh at the north-western tip of Sumatra. It was a truly remarkable piece of amalgamation, in which local interests and central direction were harmonized in such a way as to provide for the utmost concentration of the national effort. And it is noteworthy that the capital with which it commenced operations was practically ten times as large as the English Company's.

Wybrand van Warwijck commanded the first fleet of fifteen ships sent out by the Company, and within three years thirty-eight ships had been equipped and despatched to the East. They went out in powerful, heavily armed fleets designed to attack the Portuguese, and while new factories were being established in Java, Celebes (at Macassar) and on the mainland of India (at Surat, Masulipatam and Petapoli) relations were established with Ceylon, where the Portuguese monopolized the cinnamon trade, and preparations were made to trade directly to China and Japan.

The counter-attack upon the Portuguese had only mixed success. With their backs to the wall they showed unexpected powers of resistance, and they received valuable assistance from the Spaniards at Manila. A Portuguese fleet was defeated off Johore in 1603. Two years later notable successes were gained in the Spice Islands: the Portuguese fortresses on Amboina and in the Moluccas came under the suzerainty of the Netherlands. But in 1606 the Dutch attack on Malacca was beaten off by the Portuguese, while a Spanish fleet from the Philippines conquered their trading posts in the Moluccas. And although in 1607 they recovered eastern Ternate from the Spaniards, their attacks on Mozambique and Goa in the next year completely failed, and they wasted their resources in fruitless efforts to capture Manila.

In 1609 the situation showed clear signs of improvement. By the occupation of the island of Banda-Neira and the establishment of Fort Nassau the Dutch regained the upper hand in the Spice Islands, while by the Twelve Years' Truce signed with Spain at Antwerp they obtained a breathing-space from the long struggle in Europe together with the right to hold all the conquests they had made from Spain and Portugal. In that same year they took a far-reaching and much-needed step in the consolidation of their power in the East by the appointment of Pieter Both as Governor-General of the Indies with control over all 'forts, places, factories, persons and business of the United Company'. With him was associated a 'Council of India' consisting of four members. His instructions laid down that the possession of the Spice Islands was of the highest importance to the Company and that all competitors must be excluded from them. Before these instructions were drawn up there had already been trouble between the Dutch and the English in both the Moluccas and the Bandas. It was soon to develop into a serious quarrel.

(c) The Anglo-Dutch struggle for the spice trade

'From the beginning of the century the English, though far inferior in strength, had been following the Dutch around the archipelago, pursuing them like gadflies,' writes J. S. Furnivall.[1] And Bernard Vlekke writes in the same vein: 'The merchants of London followed their more powerful neighbours wherever they went, hoping to profit from the pioneer work of others. The expenses of the war against Spain, by which Indonesian trade was made safe for the northern nations, were left graciously to the Netherlanders, and wherever the Dutch Company founded a trading post the English were sure to follow: at Patani, at Djambi, at Jacatra, and in many other places.'[2] And he proceeds to quote Furnivall's statement in support of his own.

Now, though plausible, neither statement will bear detailed examination. Far more authoritative accounts of this period, based upon research into the original manuscript sources, are to be found in the works of Sir William Foster[3] and W. H. Moreland[4] on the East India Company's activities on the one hand, and those of H.T. Colenbrander[5] and F. W. Stapel[6] on the VOC's on the other. But those of the latter two are available in Dutch only. Hence the 'gadfly' legend of English attempts to trade with South-East Asian ports is widely accepted. In any case it is difficult for a Dutchman to write dispassionately

[1] *Netherlands India*, Cambridge, 1939 and 1944, pp. 26–7.
[2] *Nusantara, A History of the East Indian Archipelago*, Harvard Univ. Press, Cambridge, Mass., 1945, p. 111.
[3] See particularly *England's Quest of Eastern Trade* (1933), *The Voyages of Sir James Lancaster* (1940), *The Voyage of Sir Henry Middleton to the Moluccas* (1943) and *The Journal of John Jourdain* (1905).
[4] *Peter Floris, His Voyage to the East Indies in the Globe* (1934), *The Relations of Golconda* (1931).
[5] *Koloniale Geschiedenis* (3 vols., 1925) and his monumental *Jan Pieterszoon Coen* (5 vols., 1919).
[6] *Geschiedenis van Nederlandsch Indië*, vol. iii.

TERNATE IN THE SEVENTEENTH CENTURY

of this period. Dutch expansion to the East formed a major item in their eighty years' struggle for independence and was undertaken as much for political and strategic as for economic reasons. Their East India Company conducted a concentrated national offensive against Portugal and Spain, and they bitterly resented the intrusion of the English into the spice trade, since the latter had lost much of their Elizabethan hatred of Spain and would gladly have made peace with the Portuguese on a basis of live and let live in the East.

Moreover, from their experience as middle-men the Dutch realized, in a way that the English could not, that the market for spices in Europe was limited, and that competition, by forcing up the purchase price in the East and causing a glut in the West, would dangerously reduce the possibilities of profitable trade. They therefore concentrated upon establishing a monopoly, and were prepared, by fair means or foul, to exclude all competitors. And the English, who had sympathized with and helped the Dutch in their struggle against Philip II of Spain, were at first surprised, and subsequently deeply indignant, at their treatment by the people whom they regarded as their natural allies in Europe.

The trouble began during what is known as the Second Voyage of the English Company, which was intended to open up direct relations with Amboina and the Banda Islands. Its commander, Henry Middleton, on arrival at Bantam in December 1604 found there a powerful Dutch fleet under Steven van der Haghen, which had been sent out to attack the Portuguese. The Dutch attitude was friendly, and he learnt from the English factors who had been left behind by the First Voyage that after Lancaster's departure for home the attitude of the natives had become so difficult that but for the backing of the Dutch factors the English factory might have been exterminated. Middleton arrived at Amboina before the Dutch and began to negotiate with the Portuguese for permission to trade. But the Dutch fleet, following on, forced the Portuguese to capitulate and prevented him from carrying on trade. He went on to Tidore, where by chance he saved the Sultan of Ternate and three Dutch merchants, who were fleeing from the place. He was again followed up by the Dutch fleet, now bent on the capture of Tidore, which fell to it in May 1605. He managed to obtain a cargo of cloves at Ternate, and one of his ships collected a fair quantity of mace and nutmegs in the Bandas; but Dutch hostility forced him to return to Bantam without planting a factory.

The commanders of the Third Voyage had much the same experience as Middleton's. David Middleton, his brother, arrived in the

Moluccas in January 1608 to find a struggle in progress between the Dutch and the Spaniards, who had come to the help of the Portuguese and inflicted a severe reverse on the Dutch and their ally the Sultan of Ternate. As he refused to join in an attack upon the Dutch, he was refused permission to trade. William Keeling, who arrived in the Bandas in February of the following year, found the Dutch factors friendly and began to collect a cargo of spices. But in the following month Admiral Verhoeff arrived there in command of a powerful fleet with special orders to enforce the monopoly. Having overcome all resistance, the Dutch then forced the local chiefs to sign treaties granting them a monopoly of the spice trade and ordered Keeling to depart. In 1610 David Middleton, in charge of the Company's Fifth Voyage, arrived at Banda Neira only to be ordered away by the Dutch governor. When he adopted a defiant attitude, saying that the English had a right to be there since their nations were friends in Europe, the Dutch threatened force. He also made a show of force and got away to the island of Wai, which was not under Dutch control. There he secured a good lading and left behind two factors to collect more.

As incident after incident of this sort followed one another, the English merchants came to realize that they were up against a resolute Dutch move to monopolize the commerce of the Archipelago; and the East India Company decided to invoke the support of the government. In November 1611 it complained to Lord Treasurer Salisbury of the 'uncivil and inhuman wrongs' committed by the Dutch against its servants and begged him to take the matter up with the States General. The English ambassador at The Hague, who was instructed to make representations on the subject, warned Salisbury that the V.O.C. was so powerful that it was quite likely to flout the orders of the States General if these were contrary to its own interests. The only result of his intervention was the production by the Dutch of a long list of counter-charges against the English. He suggested, therefore, that pressure should be brought to bear upon both companies by their respective governments to negotiate an agreement for joint trade.

Neither side, however, was willing to come to such an arrangement; so that although, under pressure from both governments, two conferences were held—one in London in 1613 and the other at The Hague in 1615—nothing came of them. The Dutch took their stand upon the treaties they had concluded with native rulers, though the manner in which they had secured some of them would not bear investigation, and complained that the English expected to share free of cost the commerce which they had wrested from Spain and Portugal at immense cost. The English contended that they had traded in the Moluccas long before the Dutch had appeared on the scene, and that as a friendly nation they should not be debarred from trading there on the pretext of Dutch hostilities with other powers. They refused outright to pay any share of the expenditure already incurred by the Dutch in fighting the Spaniards and the Portuguese, or to join with them in further acts of war. In this they were supported by James I, who was most assiduously cultivating friendly relations with Philip III.

Meanwhile the English were busily engaged in broadening the scope of their trade. They had discovered that the best way to obtain spices was to lade cotton goods and opium in India for sale in the spice ports of the Archipelago. One result of this was that in 1609 they began to cultivate relations with the Mughal emperor Jehangir and at the same time, against fierce Portuguese resistance, to force their way into the textile trade of western India. Another was the despatch of the *Globe* in 1611 to engage in trade in the Bay of Bengal and the Gulf of Siam. The Dutch had already pushed their way with considerable success into the textile trade between the Coromandel Coast and the countries on the opposite side of the bay; and in 1610 the committee entrusted with the preparation of the English Company's Seventh Voyage obtained the services of two Dutchmen, Pieter Willemszoon Floris and Lucas Antheuniszoon (always referred to in the English records as Peter Floris and Lucas Antheunis), both of whom had had practical experience in the Dutch Coromandel factories, to take charge of the enterprise.

The voyage of the *Globe* opened a new chapter in the history of the East India Company, for it not only resulted in the establishment of an English factory at Masulipatam on the Coromandel Coast but also directly in the opening of commercial relations with Siam and indirectly with Burma. In Siam factories were planted at Patani, a Malay state under Siamese suzerainty, and at Ayut'ia, the capital. Both Patani and Ayut'ia were important for their trade with China, whence came supplies of silk and porcelain, and Japan. The merchants of the two countries went to Ayut'ia principally to buy hides and skins, and to Patani for spices imported there from the Archipelago. The dye-wood known as 'brazil', aloes-wood, benzoin and tin could also be obtained in the local markets. The Dutch were already established at both places and the rulers welcomed competition from other Europeans. From Ayut'ia two factors were sent up to Chiengmai to open trade with the Laos states. While they were there King Anaukpetlun of Burma besieged the city. One of them got away before it fell; the other, Thomas Samuel, was captured and taken to Pegu with his unsold goods. There he died, and the East India Company's first relations with Burma were opened when the Masulipatam factory sent two of its assistants to Pegu to claim his goods.

While the *Globe* was engaged upon this enterprise further developments were taking place in Sumatra, Java, Borneo and Celebes. Captain Thomas Best, after establishing English trade at Surat in 1612 (in the teeth of Portuguese opposition), went on to Acheh in April 1613 to exploit the pepper trade. Two years later, against strong Dutch opposition, factories were planted at Acheh, Priaman and Jambi. In 1617 the English at Bantam planted factories at Jacatra and Japara on the north coast of Java. The Dutch destroyed the factory at Japara in the course of a war with Mataram, but it was re-established in 1619. In 1611 or 1612 Bantam had also planted a factory at Succadana on the south-west coast of Borneo. This was in consequence of a report that the Dutch were obtaining gold and diamonds there; but Dutch competition prevented it from making headway, and when in 1622 the town was sacked by a Javanese force both Dutch and English sustained heavy losses and withdrew.

The factory at Macassar in Celebes was founded by John Jourdain in 1613. This tough Devon seaman, whom Jan Pieterszoon Coen considered the 'most guilty' of all his English opponents,[1] became the leading protagonist of the struggle against the Dutch when in that year he was entrusted by Sir Henry Middleton with the task of planting a factory in the Moluccas. He went first to Hitu on the northern coast of Amboina, where the Dutch refused him permission to buy cloves. He thereupon sailed across to Luhu on the western end of Ceram, where the Dutch had become unpopular through using their monopoly agreement to beat down the price of cloves by almost 50 per cent. When the natives explained that they would willingly supply him with cloves were it not for their fear of the Dutch, he went up to the Dutch factory to expostulate. There he was confronted by an indignant young man who was none other than the future governor-general himself.

In the interview that took place each struck sparks off the other's armour. Coen, 'in a choleric manner', said that if Jourdain bought cloves without Dutch consent 'it was so much stolen from them, and therefore they would prevent it, if by any means they might'. Jourdain replied that the country was free for the English as for the Dutch, and when Coen refused his challenge to put the matter to a meeting of the

---

[1] H. Terpstra, *De Factorij der Oostindische Compagnie te Patani*, p. 216.

chiefs he went off to an assembly of the natives and told them what had passed between himself and Coen. The natives accordingly demanded the attendance of the Dutch, and in their presence re-affirmed their desire to trade with the English. But it was all to no purpose; for though Jourdain contemptuously refused to be deterred by Dutch threats to use force, he failed to persuade the natives to disobey their masters and sailed away to Kambelu, on the opposite coast of Ceram, in response to a message that he might take delivery of a quantity of cloves there. He obtained a small supply, but the chief was too frightened of the Dutch to grant his request to plant a factory.

There was nothing for it but to return to Bantam with his mission unaccomplished. On the way he called at Macassar; and although the Dutch had settled there, the king was on bad terms with them and gladly permitted him to establish a factory. It proved to be of considerable importance, for Macassar was a halfway house between Java and the Spice Islands. Its connection with the latter was important, for it sent them gold and much-needed rice in return for spices. For many years it was to be a thorn in the side of the Dutch, stoutly maintaining its independence and defying all their attempts to prevent a large leakage in their spice monopoly, until at last they conquered it in 1667.

So far as the Moluccas were concerned, the English persevered in attempts to carry on trade despite Dutch opposition. Cloves fetched more than three times the price of pepper in the London market, and there was a demand for the finer spices all over the East. In every way it was the most lucrative trade in the East, and, writes Foster, our countrymen can scarcely be blamed for struggling hard against the attempt to exclude them from all share in this commerce'.[1] They were, however, too weak to undertake anything more than sporadic efforts, in which they encouraged the natives to break their contracts with the Dutch in the hope of English support. When, in face of the determined attitude of the Dutch, these efforts petered out, as they did in the case of the attempts of the *Concord* and the *Thomasine* to trade with Ceram in 1615, the unfortunate natives were left in the lurch.

It was in the Bandas that the great struggle took place which more than anything else brought matters to a head. It began with the expedition in 1615 of George Ball and George Cokayne in the *Concord* and *Speedwell* to the islands. On arrival at Neira in March they found

[1] *England's Quest of Eastern Trade*, p. 261.

a strong Dutch squadron there under the command of no less a person
than the governor-general himself, Gerard Reynst (1614–15). What
had happened was that the Dutch, in view of persistent English
attempts to trade with the islands, had decided that the only effective
method of maintaining their monopoly was that of outright conquest.
Reynst not only forbade the English to trade but sent ships to shadow
them in their endeavours to evade his order. When, in spite of Dutch
vigilance, Ball managed to purchase a quantity of spices on the island
of Wai, the Dutch landed a force on the island. But the natives rallied
to the support of the English and drove off the Dutch with heavy loss.
The upshot of it all was that two English merchants were left on the
island while a representative of the chiefs went to Bantam, where
Jourdain was Agent, to ask for help against the Dutch. Jourdain,
however, had not the strength at his disposal to challenge the Dutch
to a fight, and he was aware that negotiations for a settlement were in
progress in Europe. Nevertheless he was resolved to do what he could,
since he believed that the Dutch had no claim to Wai: its chiefs, he
was informed, had never made any agreement with them.[1] In January
1616, therefore, he sent a squadron of five ships under Samuel Castleton to the Bandas.

As soon as the Dutch at Neira heard of Castleton's arrival at Wai
they despatched a strong fleet to drive him off. Faced by overwhelm-
ingly superior numbers, he weakly accepted the terms dictated to him
by the Dutch commander, Jan Dirkszoon Lam. He gave an assurance
that no English assistance would be given to the natives of Wai on
the understanding that when the Dutch invaded the island they would
not interfere with the English factors there. If the Dutch conquered
the island the English factors would leave. To have attempted to put
up a fight would have been madness, but Sir William Foster claims
with justice that he could have withdrawn under protest, leaving the
Dutch with the embarrassment of dealing with the year-old English
factory on an island to which they had no valid claim.[2] Castleton's
squadron, leaving behind a pinnace for the evacuation of the factory
should the need arise, went on to seek for spices in the Moluccas. But
wherever the Dutch were in control the natives were prevented from
trading with them. Only at Tidore, where the Spanish still maintained
a fortress, were they able to barter rice for spices.

Meanwhile Richard Hunt, the chief English factor at Wai, was
determined not to leave the natives in the lurch. He therefore per-

[1] On this point, however, see Heeres, *Corpus Diplomaticum*, i, p. 35.
[2] *Op. cit.*, p. 264.

suaded them and the inhabitants of the neighbouring island of Run to make a formal surrender of their islands to the East India Company and to hoist the English colours over their defences. His fond hope that this would deter the Dutch from attacking proved false. They quickly made themselves masters of Wai. Most of the inhabitants fled in panic to Run. Hunt also eluded the infuriated Dutch and escaped to Macassar, whence he made his way to Bantam. For the time being they left Run alone, and Jourdain, as soon as he heard what had happened, sent a fresh expedition under Nathaniel Courthope to help the natives to defend the island. He was instructed to offer English protection to the people of Lonthor and Rosengijn also.

Courthope with his two ships, the *Swan* and the *Defence*, arrived at Run in December 1616. Although Wai was in Dutch hands, the ceremony of ceding both islands was re-enacted after he had received assurances from the chiefs that they had never made any agreement with the Dutch. Then guns were landed and preparations made for defence. Agreements were also made with Rosengijn and a town on Lonthor for the surrender of their lands to the British Crown. The Dutch, however, were just as determined as Courthope. They attacked and overpowered the *Swan*, killing in the fight one of the senior officers of the expedition. Courthope then prepared to make a desperate resistance. He fortified the little island of Nailaka overlooking his anchorage and prepared to beach the *Defence* in a sheltered place. Unfortunately during the operation she began to drift away and eventually a mutinous section of her crew sailed her off and surrendered her to the Dutch.

At this juncture the Dutch governor-general Laurens Reael arrived in Neira. Realizing the full seriousness of the situation, he decided to try negotiation before proceeding to sterner measures. His proposals were not unlike those previously accepted by Castleton at Wai: if the English would leave the Dutch a free hand to deal with the island their ships would be restored and they could depart with all the spices they had collected. But Courthope replied that he would neither turn traitor to his king and country nor would he betray the natives. His own counter-proposal was that if Reael would leave the matter of the disputed territory to be settled at Bantam or in Europe he would agree to depart. The governor-general in his turn rejected these terms and negotiations were broken off. Reael decided that he must await reinforcements before attacking Run; Courthope held on grimly at Nailaka and sent an urgent appeal for help to Bantam. But Jourdain was no longer in command there; he had gone home. Hence nothing effective was done to relieve the threatened post. In November 1617 Reael wrote to the English president at Bantam ordering the evacuation of Run and threatening that any English ship found in the Moluccas would be attacked. He received a defiant reply to the effect that the island would be defended to the last and he would be held responsible for any bloodshed that might occur.

In 1618 relations between the two parties became steadily worse. The Dutch were genuinely worried by the situation in the Spice Islands; they feared lest as a result of English encouragement the natives would fall upon and destroy their weak garrisons there. By this time they had spread themselves so widely that their strength was dangerously dispersed. In June of that year Jan Pieterszoon Coen became governor-general of the Netherlands Indies and at once began to infuse a new vigour into the administration. As early as 1614 he had submitted a statement on policy to the directors.[1] He recommended a programme of vast territorial expansion and colonization at the expense of the Spaniards and Portuguese, and the annihilation of the shipping of other European competitors. English competition he considered to be the greatest danger: in the Moluccas they ruined the piece-goods trade and got away with much spice. The Bandas, he thought, must be either peopled with colonists from other parts or completely conquered by arms. Moreover, to concentrate and direct their full strength the Dutch must have a rendezvous. In his instructions, which were signed by the Heeren XVII and confirmed by Maurice, he was enjoined to expel all foreigners, whether allies or enemies, from places where the Dutch traded—by force, if necessary. Their ships must be searched, and if spice were found on them it must be removed.

In the following November John Jourdain arrived in Bantam as the English president. His appointment indicated the adoption of a more vigorous policy by the English Company. While in England he had attended the Company's committee and pressed for force sufficient not only to hold Bantam but to trade with the Moluccas and Bandas. He affirmed his belief that uncompromising resistance to the Dutch monopolizing efforts would not lead to war, since the Dutch would hesitate before taking extreme measures. He underestimated Jan Pieterszoon Coen.

He was sent out with a fleet of six vessels under the command of Sir Thomas Dale and was given authority over all the Company's

---

[1] 'Discoers aen de E. Heeren Bewinthebberen, touscherende den Nederlantsche Indischen Staet.'

factories, except Surat and its dependencies. Off the coast of Sumatra the fleet's flagship, the *Sun*, was wrecked. On arrival at Bantam they were greeted with serious news. Two ships sent to relieve Courthope at Run had been captured by the Dutch, while in Bantam they had assaulted Englishmen in the streets. But the Dutch situation in Java was by no means happy. Their relations with Ranamanggala[1] of Bantam had been so strained that Coen had threatened to withdraw the factory. He had gone to Jacatra with the intention of making the Dutch factory there his rendezvous. But when, against the strict orders of the pangéran, he had begun to fortify it a state of war had developed. At about the same time the Dutch factory at Japara had been captured by the forces of the Sunan Agung of Mataram, whose ambition was to restore the empire of Majapahit, and he came to the conclusion that a coalition of Javanese states was forming against the Dutch. And as most of his ships were guarding the Spice Islands against an expected attack by the English in reprisal for the action against their ships at Run, Dale's arrival and junction with another English fleet under Martin Pring, which was already off Bantam, placed him in a position of serious inferiority at sea.

The trouble began on 14 December 1618, when the *Zwarte Leeuw*, on arriving at Bantam from Patani, was seized by Dale to be held as surety for the satisfaction of the English claims against the Dutch. Unfortunately she was accidentally set on fire and burnt out, and Coen in reprisal attacked and destroyed the English factory at Jacatra. Dale thereupon sailed to Jacatra and an indecisive engagement took place between the two fleets. Coen, however, managed to extricate his fleet and sailed away to Amboina to collect reinforcements and concentrate his forces. He was prepared to sacrifice the beleaguered fort at Jacatra in order to save his ships. And Dale, although the main objective of his expedition was to protect English trade in the Spice Islands, weakly decided against following Coen and taking relief to the gallant Courthope. Instead he remained at Jacatra to assist the pangéran against the Dutch fort. It was a bad miscalculation of the situation; for when the Dutch Council had agreed to articles of surrender under which the Dutch personnel were to be transported in English ships to the Coromandel Coast, Ranamanggala of Bantam suddenly appeared at Jacatra with an army and demanded that the fort and all the prisoners should be handed over to him. And, to cut a long story short, Dale, unwilling to go back on the agreement he had made with the Dutch, sailed away to Bantam; the Bantam army drove off the

[1] He was the chief minister and, as the king was a minor, was the effective head of the state.

pangéran's besieging force, but then found itself quite unable to capture the fort, which managed to hold out until the end of May 1619, when it was relieved by Coen, who returned from Amboina with a powerful fleet.

Coen's bold gamble succeeded beyond his highest expectations, for he found on returning that the whole situation had changed in his favour. In the first place the English had quarrelled with Ranamang-gala and had decided, temporarily at least, to leave Bantam. Dale and Pring, whose ships were in bad condition, had left for the Coromandel Coast to effect repairs and collect more ships with which to fight Coen. Jourdain himself, with two ships, had left to take much-needed help to the factories at Jambi, Patani, Ayut'ia and elsewhere. Coen learnt of these happenings when, having taken initial steps to establish the new city of Batavia on the site of Jacatra as the capital of the Dutch eastern empire, he went on to Bantam to challenge Dale and Jourdain. He at once detached three ships in pursuit of Jourdain. In the middle of July they found him at anchor off Patani and at once attacked. The result was a foregone conclusion; Jourdain was caught in a trap, and although he put up a stubborn fight his casualties were so heavy that he was compelled to negotiate for surrender. While the discussion was in progress under a flag of truce he unwisely appeared on deck and was at once killed by a shot from one of the Dutch ships. The Dutch claimed that his death was accidental, but the English account asserted that 'the Flemmings espying him most treacherously and cruelly shot at him with a musket'. Modern Dutch historical research confirms this view, for Terpstra in his history of the Dutch factory at Patani writes: 'Careful comparison of the evidence has convinced me that the English view is more acceptable than the Dutch.'[1]

This was not the only English disaster. In the following month the Dutch captured the *Star* in the Sunda Straits; and a few weeks later they surprised and captured no less than four English ships at the pepper port of Tiku on the west coast of Sumatra. Dale died at Masu-lipatam in August 1619. Not till December of that year was his squadron, under Pring, ready to return to the Archipelago. In March at Tiku it was joined by three ships from Surat. On 8 April, in the Sunda Straits, while on their way to Bantam the united squadrons met a ship coming from England bringing news of the signature of an Anglo-Dutch treaty whereby the two companies were to share the trade of the Archipelago and jointly bear the costs of defence. Four days later, on arrival at Bantam, they found that Coen had already

---

[1] *Op. cit.*, p. 215.

received notification of the agreement from Holland, so that instead of meeting as enemies they now had to co-operate as allies.

This short-lived attempt to end a rivalry which had deteriorated into a savage undeclared war was by no means so unrealistic as it might seem at first sight. The initiative had been taken by the Dutch late in the year 1618 because the directors of the V.O.C., with the end of the Truce of Antwerp in sight, felt it to be essential to come to terms with the English. The East India Company, however, was hostile, and the negotiations, which began in December 1618, threatened to be broken off several times before agreement was reached on 17 July 1619. Foster tells us that it was concluded only under pressure from James I,[1] but according to Stapel[2] the king's attitude was very reserved. Its main provisions were (a) that grievances on both sides were to be forgiven and forgotten, prisoners to be freed and captured ships restored; (b) that each company was to buy half of the total pepper available, and the English were to have a third share of the spice trade of the Moluccas, Amboina and the Bandas; (c) that a Council of Defence was to be established consisting of four members from each side and was to have at its disposal a defence fleet composed of ten ships from each party; (d) that each party was to keep its own forts and strongholds, and during the first two to three years was not to build new ones; and (e) the capital of the two companies was to remain separate and each was to keep its own accounts.

Coen's reaction on learning the terms of the treaty was characteristic. He wrote home that he wondered whether the directors had had good advice in so hastily assuming so hard a bridle and surrendering so many of their rightful conquests. They were, he said, nourishing a serpent in their bosom. What he found most difficult to understand was why a third of the cloves, nutmeg and mace should have been conceded to the English when they had no claim to a particle of the beach in the Moluccas, Amboina or the Bandas. There can be no doubt that, however one may view the difficulties which arose in the working of the other clauses of the treaty, the operation of this one was deliberately sabotaged by Coen. In 1608 the Heeren XVII had written: 'Banda and the Moluccas are the principal target at which we shoot'. They were now to be the principal rock upon which the unsteady bark of Anglo-Dutch co-operation foundered.

News of the treaty did not reach Robert Hayes, the English chief factor at Nailaka, until late in November 1620. A month earlier his

---

[1] *Op. cit.*, p. 276.
[2] *Geschiedenis van Nederlandsch-Indië*, iii, p. 142.

predecessor, the heroic Nathaniel Courthope, had been waylaid and killed by the Dutch while returning from a visit to Lonthor. The news of the agreement brought hostilities to an end, but left the situation otherwise unchanged. Meanwhile at Batavia Coen and his council had taken the fateful decision to complete the conquest of the Bandas which had been held up after their capture of Wai in 1616. Coen justified the decision to the directors on the plea that the Bandanese were delivering their produce to the Spaniards on Tidore. He invited the English to participate in the expedition, but according to the Dutch account they excused themselves on the grounds that they had no ships available.

In January 1621 Coen himself left in command of a fleet of twelve ships to carry out the task. The conquest of Lonthor was his first objective. While completing his preparations for a landing he offered the islanders peace if they would hand over all their nutmeg and mace exclusively to the Dutch under the terms of the original agreement. He also informed Robert Hayes of his intentions, and when the latter urged that he should await the arrival of English ships he bluntly refused. The islanders put up what resistance they could, but were eventually, on 11 March 1621, forced to capitulate. Soon afterwards the inhabitants of Run, fearing a Dutch attack, made their submission also. The Dutch occupied the island, forced the English there to leave, but left the English post on Nailaka alone. A few days later an English vessel under Captain Humphrey Fitzherbert arrived in the islands, and on 19 March the solemn farce was enacted of proclaiming the Anglo-Dutch treaty. The Dutch, however, began to consolidate their conquest by building a new fort, Hollandia Castle, on Lonthor.

The effect of all this upon the minds of the Bandanese was a conviction that they had been betrayed by the English, and a serious revolt began on Lonthor aided by partisans from other islands. Coen then proceeded to carry out his full plan of removing all the inhabitants and restocking the rebellious islands with other settlers. It was carried out with appalling frightfulness. Hundreds of people were rounded up on Lonthor and sent into slavery in Java, their kampongs and boats being systematically destroyed. Forty-seven orangkayas, held as hostages, were tortured and executed when the rebels, who had taken to the mountains, repulsed a Dutch attack. Thousands died of starvation in the mountains rather than surrender. Some 300 got away in praus to south Ceram. The inhabitants of Run, on learning of the atrocities in Lonthor, tried to flee en masse, but were rounded up and all the grown men killed to the number of 160. The cultivated lands in the islands were then parcelled out to Company's servants to work with slave labour. 'Coen acted in this whole business,' writes Colenbrander[1], 'which is a stain on his memory, with an inhuman ruthlessness which shocked even the Company's servants.' And when his former colleague, Aert Gysels, heard of it he wrote: 'We must realize that they fought for the freedom of their land just as we expended our lives and goods for so many years in defence of ours.' The directors themselves were moved to write to Coen that they wished he could have carried out his task with greater moderation.[2]

Having scored a bull's-eye on his chosen target, Coen next turned his attention to Amboina and the Moluccas. He forced the chiefs of Amboina to make a new treaty recognizing Dutch authority. Ceram, whose chiefs showed some reluctance to follow suit, was then treated to a dose of the same medicine as the Bandas. With the Moluccas, however, the difficulties were greater, since the Spaniards still held Tidore and Coen could not spare adequate forces to deal with them. Moreover, he had to return to Batavia before attempting a final settlement.

Meanwhile the arrangements for Anglo-Dutch co-operation in other spheres had completely broken down. The Council of Defence, provided for under the treaty, had been set up at Batavia. The Dutch quarrel with Ranamanggala of Bantam showed no signs of abating, and their blockade of the place became so intense that the English, unable to trade there, transferred their headquarters to Batavia. There they found their position an impossible one. The Dutch insisted that their authority was supreme there by right of conquest and that all Englishmen were amenable to Dutch tribunals. The Truce of Antwerp expired in 1621 and Coen planned expeditions against Manila and the Portuguese ports in India and at Mozambique. The English were dragged into these, and when they could not afford their share of the expenses and their quota of ships the effort to co-operate petered out. By the time that Coen left for home at the end of his first term as governor-general early in 1623 the decision had been taken to leave Batavia and to withdraw their factors from all the Dutch settlements. Before they could begin to carry out this decision an event took place which made a deeper and more lasting impression upon the relations of the two peoples than any other incident of this unhappy period. It became known as the 'Massacre of Amboina'.

[1] *Koloniale Geschiedenis*, ii, p. 117.
[2] Stapel, *op. cit.*, iii, p. 151.

On leaving Amboina in 1622 to return to Batavia Coen had reminded the governor, Herman van Speult, not to allow the English to reduce his authority. The English, under the treaty of 1619, traded there under the protection of the Dutch fort Victoria Castle. Relations with the Dutch were good until suddenly, on 23 February 1623, the members of the English factory—eighteen Englishmen, eleven Japanese, and one Portuguese—were arrested by the Dutch on a charge of conspiring to seize the fortress. Confessions were wrung from all of them under torture, and after a 'trial' ten Englishmen, including the chief factor Gabriel Towerson, ten Japanese and the Portuguese were beheaded. Stapel is of opinion that although the penalty was very heavy the fact that there was a conspiracy cannot be denied.[1] But as all the evidence was obtained under torture it was worthless, and the only conclusion to be safely reached is that the Dutch either acted in a state of panic, as in the case of Pieter Eberfelt's judicial murder at Batavia in 1721, which Stapel himself condemns,[2] or deliberately in order to force the English to quit the Spice Islands. The hurried nature of the proceedings and the flimsy excuses made for not referring the matter to Batavia before carrying out the executions arouse one's deepest suspicions.

Attempts to deal with the difficulties which had arisen under the treaty had been made in England, and in January 1623 a fresh agreement had been made. But the Amboina outrage now removed all hope of further co-operation. The English withdrew their factory from Batavia early in 1624 and tried to settle on an island in the Sunda Straits; but it was so unhealthy that they were soon too weak to defend themselves against plundering bands from Sumatra. In May 1625 they had to obtain Dutch help to return to Batavia, where Coen's successor, de Carpentier, housed them in a disused school building. In 1627 when Coen returned to Java they decided to transfer to Bantam, and the sultan, still on bad terms with the Dutch, willingly took them under his protection. There they remained until the Dutch conquered the place in 1682. Under the agreement of 1623 Pulo Run had been recognized as English property, but the Dutch clung on to it, and the East India Company was in no position to maintain a factory there. At the end of the First Dutch War in 1654 the Dutch agreed to restore it and pay a sum of £85,000 in compensation for the losses inflicted upon the East India Company. But the Company was still unable to take possession of the island. Charles II took the matter up

---

[1] *Op. cit.*, iii, p. 161.
[2] *Geschiedenis van Nederlandsch-Indië*, 1930, p. 133.

in 1662, and again the Dutch agreed to hand over the island. In 1665 the East India Company did actually occupy it, only to lose it a few months later as a result of the outbreak of the Second Dutch War. It was finally ceded to the Dutch by the Treaty of Breda, which ended that war in 1667.

It is interesting to note that during the years in which the English were competing with the Dutch for the trade of the Spice Islands the East India Company was able to pay higher dividends than the V.O.C. The reason was that the Dutch had to devote too much of their profit to the expense of building forts, maintaining large garrisons and equipping fighting squadrons. They were firmly convinced that the spice monopoly was a matter of vital national importance, and so, in the words of an acute critic,[1] 'applied their greatest effort of empire-building to an object that was only temporarily worth attaining'. For with the expansion of world trade the spice trade became less and less important, and the misapplication of Dutch energy in the East had its effect upon the decline of their national power in the second half of the seventeenth century.

But from the point of view of South-East Asia the Dutch triumph over the English is to be seen as the first decisive step towards the formation of a new empire, commercial at the outset like Śrivijaya and Malacca, but gradually becoming predominantly territorial; yet not in the true line of succession to either, since the centre of control lay thousands of miles away.

[1] J. A. Williamson, *The Ocean in British History*, p. 103.

CHAPTER 16

MATARAM AND THE EXPANSION OF THE V.O.C., 1623–84

JAN PIETERSZOON COEN was the founder of the Dutch empire of the East Indies; but its development after his death was hardly along the lines he had striven to lay down. According to his plans, Batavia was to be the centre of a great commercial empire based upon complete control of the sea. He did not envisage any wide extension of territorial power and was not interested in the political affairs of the interior of Java. The territories which, in his view, the V.O.C. should have in actual possession were small islands such as Amboina and the Bandas. The remainder of the empire should consist of strongly fortified trading settlements closely linked and protected by invincible sea-power.

Nor would it be confined to Indonesia: its forts and trading stations should be far-flung over the whole of the East. He was especially anxious to conquer Manila and Macao so as to drive the Spaniards and Portuguese from the Philippines and the China coast. And he wanted plenty of Dutch colonists; they were to direct slave labour in cultivating estates in the Spice Islands and elsewhere, to assist in defending the newly accquired possessions and to engage in the inter-Asiatic trade. This trade he believed to be capable of yielding far greater profits than the traffic between Europe and Asia, each of which had very limited requirements of the other's goods. His ideas were vague and imaginative rather than practical, and utterly ruthless. In the days when he was Director-General of Commerce at Batavia his plans for the Spice Islands shocked his predecessor as governor-general, Laurens Reael, who thought that their execution would involve such cruelty to the native people as would involve the ruin of the V.O.C.

His warlike measures vastly increased the Company's expenses; and although its methods of accountancy and the loss of some of its account-books made the presentation of an accurate statement of profit and loss for the early period impossible, his own estimate for the years 1613–20 showed a deficit of 8,000 guilders, and on occasion the directors had to borrow money in order to maintain an average dividend of 10 per cent. Nevertheless he was convinced that if the commercial system could be reformed in accordance with his suggestions enormous profits could be realized with the export of further capital from Holland. And after his death the development of the Company's inter-Asiatic trade, upon which he pinned his faith, certainly did yield a very satisfactory return, although the directors rejected his colonization proposal, which was the chief ingredient in his recipe.

Coen's short second term of office as governor-general (1627–9) provided an object lesson in the dangers to which a commercial empire with no territorial power was exposed. Sunan Agung of Mataram, as we have seen, had gone far towards realizing his ambition to revive the power of Majapahit. Of the Javanese powers only Balambangan in the east of the island, and the rich and powerful sultanate of Bantam in the west, refused to pay homage. After the conquest of Surabaya Bantam became Agung's next objective. He pushed his control westwards over the area south of Batavia, which had become a sort of no-man's-land through depopulation when the kingdom of Pajajaran had been destroyed. But his best approach was by sea, and it was barred by the Dutch. Batavia had in 1622 begun to send him formal embassies with presents, but it had refused his demands for assistance against Surabaya. In 1626 therefore he refused to receive the usual Dutch missions and prepared to attack Batavia.

It was at this juncture that Coen returned. Batavia still maintained its close blockade of the trade of Bantam which had been imposed during his previous governor-generalship, and it was against the raiding bands of his nearer neighbour that he had at first to strengthen the city's defences. On Christmas Eve 1627 a Bantam force actually got inside the citadel in a surprise attack, but was driven out. Eight months later Mataram also staged a surprise attack, by sea, but after a desperate resistance this also was beaten off. In 1629 Agung laid siege to the city with the biggest force he could muster. But so large an army could not be adequately supplied with food by overland transport and the Dutch reduced it to starvation by their attacks upon its supply ships. After five weeks the grand army of the susuhunan had to beat a disorderly retreat, leaving its track strewn with the bodies of men and animals who had died of starvation and exhaustion. During the siege Coen contracted cholera and died within a few hours. This second attack of Mataram upon Bavatia alarmed the Sultan of Bantam, who realized that if the city fell his state would be the next to be attacked. He therefore offered terms of peace which Coen accepted and the ten years' blockade was lifted.

The severe defeat inflicted on Sunan Agung's forces by the Dutch did not lead to any better relations, although Hendrik Brouwer, who became governor-general in 1632, made an attempt to reach an understanding with him. But there was little fighting, for the susuhunan left the west alone and concentrated his attention on the east. He was a fervent Muslim, and one of his most far-reaching acts was to develop relations with the Muslim powers of Arabia, as a result of which a new wave of Islamic missionary activity began in Indonesia. Pilgrims from Mecca sought to revive and intensify the faith of the peoples, who, though nominally Muslims, still clung to most of their old traditional customs and observances. Agung proclaimed a holy war against the two regions, Balambangan and the island of Bali, which up till then still held out against conversion to Islam. In 1639 he conquered Balambangan and deported much of its population. Bali, however, resisted his attacks with exemplary courage and maintained its independence.

The Dutch, freed from the threat of Mataram, entered upon a period of spectacular success and expansion. The great advance began under Antonie van Diemen, 1636-45. He had been Coen's choice as his successor in 1629, but the Council had decided otherwise and had appointed Jacques Specx acting governor-general. The directors at home after lengthy consideration appointed one of their number, Hendrick Brouwer. In comparison with Coen and Van Diemen, both Specx and Brouwer were mediocrities; but when Stapel describes their period as one in which little energy was shown for expansion in new regions[1] he is surely confining his attention too much to the Archipelago, for the early thirties saw much expansive activity on the Indo-Chinese mainland, in Arakan, Burma, Tenasserim, Siam, and Cochin China. It was in one sense a development of Coen's policy of annihilating native as well as foreign European shipping in the Indies. The Dutch Coromandel Coast factories, the 'left arm of the Moluccas', were striving to capture the export trade in Indian textiles from Indian and Arab merchants. And in order to achieve this it was found necessary to establish factories at all places outside India which imported these goods.

Thus in 1634, in an intensive effort to gain complete control over the trade of the Bay of Bengal, the Dutch reopened their factory in Arakan, planted one for the first time in Burma and sent a prospecting expedition to Tenasserim, then in Siamese hands. The re-establishment of the Arakan factory was also closely connected with the

[1] *Geschiedenis van Nederlandsch-Indië* (second ed.), 1943, p. 85.

permanent blockade of Malacca, which began in 1633 and lasted until the city fell in 1641. Arakan exported rice, and Batavia, faced by the hostility of Sunan Agung and his repeated prohibitions of the import of rice from his dominions by the Dutch, was anxiously looking round for new sources of supply. Throughout the factory's history, therefore, by far the greater part of its trade was carried on directly with Batavia.[1]

The ventures to Burma and Tenasserim, on the other hand, were undertaken and directed by Pulicat. In all three places the Dutch entered as competitors with Indian merchants; but although they carried on successfully for about half a century, they never ousted the Indians. Wherever there was relatively fair competition, the Asian—Arab, Persian, Indian or Chinese—could always maintain his position. Only where the Dutchman could resort to force, as in the Spice Islands, could he gain the advantage over the Asian trader; even then he could not drive him out of the field, but had to arrange a modus vivendi. With the more powerful monarchies of the mainland the Dutch were rarely in a position to dictate terms, and the Asian trader was too well established to be ousted.

The early thirties also saw developments in Dutch relations with Siam and Annam. Dutch ships were sent to assist King Prasat T'ong of Siam against the Cambodians and Portuguese on the one hand and rebellious Patani on the other. Prince Frederick Henry of Orange sent a congratulatory letter to the king in 1632, and in 1634 van Vliet was established as Dutch Agent in a solid brick headquarters at Ayut'ia. It was the beginning of a long period of Dutch ascendancy in Siamese trade. Like Arakan, Siam at this period assumed a new importance in Dutch eyes because of the food question. 'This station', wrote Joost Schouten in 1636 in his *Description of Siam*, 'supplies Batavia with great quantities of provisions.' From Ayut'ia a factory was planted in Cambodia in 1637, and in 1641 van Wuysthoff went from the latter up the difficult Mekong river to open relations with the Laos kingdom of Vien Chang (Vientiane). Settled commercial relations with Annam began in 1633 with the establishment of a factory at Qui-nam, but because of the factory planted four years later in Tongking they were never happy and were soon broken off. Both the Trinh of Hanoi and the Nguyen of Hué welcomed European merchants, but as they were at war with each other it was practically impossible to carry on trade with both.

[1] D. G. E. Hall, 'Studies in Dutch Relations with Arakan', JBRS, xxvi, pt. i, pp. 1–31.

Thus it can be seen that the period of Specx and Brouwer, though unable to show the spectacular advances made under Coen and van Diemen, has an interest all of its own. It has been passed over lightly by Dutch historians largely because the ventures described above had comparatively little success. The factory at Mrohaung in Arakan had a chequered existence and was finally withdrawn before the end of the century. In Burma, after several threats to withdraw, the factories were wound up in 1679. In Siam during the second part of the century King Narai attempted to escape from the grip of the Dutch by calling in the French; and although Louis XIV's attempt to secure a predominant influence there collapsed with the fall of Constant Phaulkon in 1688, the Dutch never managed to get back on the old footing. Their factory in Tongking lasted until 1700 but can never have been a commercial success.

Van Diemen has been called 'statesman, warrior, admiral and merchant in one'. As a builder of their empire of the Indies he ranks next to Coen in the estimation of the Dutch. He owed much to Coen, for soon after his first arrival at Batavia an order came from the directors that he was to be sent home because he was a bankrupt who had got into the Company's service under a false name. But Coen set aside the order and gave the young man rapid promotion. The most pressing problem when he entered upon his term of office in 1636 was that of the spice trade. The efforts constantly made by the Dutch to tighten their monopoly hit the peoples of Amboina and the Moluccas, and there was unrest and 'smuggling'. Sultan Hamja of Ternate was the ally of the V.O.C., but his *kimelaha* (deputy ruler) in south Ceram was hand-in-glove with the Sultan of Macassar and promoted the large clandestine trade of which Macassar was the centre. A Dutch attempt in 1635 to invade south Ceram failed badly and caused so much unrest throughout the islands that in 1637 van Diemen went with a fleet of seventeen ships to deal with the situation. He put down the rebellion in Ceram and restored peace in the islands, but as soon as his back was turned the old troubles broke out afresh.

In 1638, therefore, he returned to Amboina and made a new agreement with Sultan Hamja, who came to meet him in person. On his way back from his first visit he visited Macassar, where he brought to an end the long state of war which had existed since 1616 between the V.O.C. and the ruler by an agreement wherein the latter recognized the Company's rights in the Spice Islands and conceded to it the right to capture and destroy any Macassar ships found in their vicinity. Firmer action he hesitated to take, since his ships and soldiers were needed elsewhere. On his second visit to Amboina in 1638 he sent a punitive expedition against Buton, off the south-east coast of Celebes, which was deeply involved in the clandestine spice trade. These various measures brought some improvement to the situation but fell far short of a solution. While Macassar remained unsubdued and a prosperous centre of English, French, Portuguese and Danish spice merchants the spice monopoly remained an unrealized dream. But van Diemen's hands were tied by his commitments in Ceylon and before Malacca, while the susuhunan of Mataram, Agung, was again creating serious difficulties by forbidding the sale of rice to the Dutch and obstructing their trade on the north coast of Java.

Ceylon and Malacca were still important centres of Portuguese power. In Ceylon the King of Kandy, Raja Singa, was anxious to obtain Dutch help against their stranglehold on all his ports. In answer to a request made by him in 1636 to the governor of the Dutch Coromandel factories van Diemen had instituted a blockade of Goa. In 1638 a Dutch fleet under Adam Westerwoldt came to the help of Raja Singa, who was now at open war with the Portuguese, and took the Portuguese fort at Batticalo. In return Raja Singa made a treaty granting the Dutch the cinnamon monopoly. During the next few years the Dutch captured further Portuguese settlements and planted strong garrisons at Gale and Negombo. They were well on their way towards the complete domination of the island when Portugal, as a result of her successful revolt against Spain in 1640, made a ten-year truce with the Netherlands which left Colombo still in Portuguese hands.

Before the new agreement took effect in the East, Malacca fell at last in 1641. Right to the end it put up a magnificent resistance. Matalieff had failed to take it in 1606 and van der Haghen in 1615. On several occasions the Dutch made approaches to Acheh, the old enemy of the Portuguese, but nothing came of them. Malacca remained a thorn in the side of the Dutch, supporting both Mataram and Macassar against them. From 1633 onwards they instituted a close blockade of the port, which seriously interrupted its trade and supplies. In August 1640, with the help of the Sultan of Johore, a descendant of the last Sultan of Malacca driven out by Albuquerque, the Dutch began a regular siege of the city. It held out with incredible valour until the middle of January 1641, when the besiegers finally stormed the ruins and brought resistance to an end. Its fall revolutionized the situation in the Archipelago. Malacca quickly lost its importance. Many Portuguese families moved to Batavia. Mataram lost one of its best customers for rice; and with the Javanese merchants transferring their trade to Batavia, Agung had to revoke his prohibition of the export of rice to the Dutch, though he remained as hostile as ever. The Dutch were now unquestionably the strongest power in the Archipelago and their efforts to maintain the spice monopoly were greatly strengthened. Van Diemen was anxious to settle matters with Agung, who intrigued with the English, murdered Dutch hostages and finally fomented an attempt to seize the fortress at Batavia. But the directors were opposed to any strong action, and relations remained unsatisfactory and undecided until after both van Diemen and Agung passed from the scene in 1645.

Van Diemen's term of office saw other notable developments in the history of Dutch eastern enterprise in regions outside South-East Asia. When in 1641 Japan expelled all Westerners the Dutch alone were allowed to continue their commercial activities. They had to leave the main islands and confine themselves to the little island of Deshima off the port of Nagasaki, where they lived and worked under rigorous conditions and the closest supervision. Van Diemen sought compensation for this in a more determined pursuit of Chinese trade. In 1642 by the conquest of the Spanish fort at Quelang the Dutch gained possession of the whole island of Formosa, an important distribution centre in the sugar trade from China. They soon had a flourishing trade going there; but when the Manchus brought the Ming dynasty to an end and Ming leaders were flying in various directions, one of them, Kuo Hsing Yeh ('Coxinga'), established himself in Formosa in 1661, and soon afterwards forced the Dutch to abandon their factory.

Van Diemen's name is associated with a number of important voyages of discovery. He sent out navigators in search of the fabulous island of 'Rica Doro', which was said to be somewhere east of Japan. Two expeditions—one in 1639 under Matthijs Hendricksz. Quast and Abel Janszoon Tasman, and the other in 1643 under Maarten Gerritsz. de Vries—resulted in the discovery of the Kurile Islands and the east coast of Sakhalin, but there was no gold island to be found; and Tasman made far more valuable contributions to geographical knowledge in quite another direction.

Quite early on in their quest of the spice trade the Dutch had discovered that there was a better approach to the Archipelago than the one used by the Portuguese. The latter had adopted from the Arabs the practice of monsoon sailing whereby they proceeded up the coast of East Africa into the monsoon belt and approached the Archipelago by crossing the Indian Ocean north of the Equator and passing into the Straits of Malacca. Such a route hinged upon a strategic centre on the west coast of India. The Dutch, however, unhampered by such considerations, after passing the Cape used the westerly winds of the 'roaring forties' of the southern hemisphere, which gave them a much quicker passage across the Indian Ocean and made the Sunda Straits their natural approach to the Archipelago. Ships sailing too far along the southerly course had discovered what is now known as Australia, and not a few had been wrecked upon its inhospitable western shore.

In 1642 and again in 1644 van Diemen sent out Tasman and Frans Jacobsz. Visscher to determine its connection, if any, with the *Terra Australis Incognita* of the geographers. On their first voyage, after touching at Mauritius they passed round Australia from the west and made their first landing on the island named by Tasman van Diemen's Land, but subsequently, by the English, Tasmania. They then went on to discover New Zealand, which they thought to be a part of the great southern continent, and returned to Batavia by the north of New Guinea. Their second voyage was undertaken to discover whether there was a channel between New Guinea and Australia and whether the Gulf of Carpentaria was the opening of a channel which passed right through Australia. Although they failed to discover the strait which the Spaniards Torres and Prado had successfully navigated as early as 1607,[1] they mapped out the Gulf of Carpentaria correctly. But their voyage was the last important Dutch effort of exploration.

Van Diemen could point to no new openings for trade as a result of their efforts. The people they encountered on the north coast of Australia were 'without rice or any considerable fruits, very poor, and in many places evil-natured'. With his death in 1645 the V.O.C. lost interest not only in further discovery but also in the lands their intrepid mariners had placed on the map.

If Coen was the founder of Batavia, van Diemen was in many ways the creator of the city that was soon to be dubbed the 'Queen of the East'. He completed its castle, built a town hall and a Latin school and did much to expand and beautify the original settlement. Cultivation and industry were developed around it, chiefly by the Chinese whom Coen had encouraged to settle. A new church was built, houses in the Dutch style lined the banks of the canals, and the whole place began to look almost like a Dutch city transplanted from Europe. It became the home, and indeed the grave, of an increasing number of Dutchmen, for it was excessively unhealthy, and one of van Diemen's

---

[1] Both wrote accounts of their discovery but they were never published. Torres's manuscript only came to light in the middle of the eighteenth century.

more important contributions to the city's amenities was an orphanage founded in 1639.

Van Diemen's immediate successors, Cornelis van der Lijn (1645-50) and Carel Reijniersz. (1650-3), made no outstanding personal contributions to the development of the Dutch empire; but their period was far from one of stagnation. Amangkurat I (1645-77), Agung's son and successor, made peace with van der Lijn, and conceded to the V.O.C. freedom of trade in his dominions. The Company in return undertook to send an annual embassy to Mataram and to permit the susuhunan's Javanese subjects to trade everywhere save in the Moluccas. New agreements were also made with Raja Singa in Ceylon and with the tin-producing states of the Malay Peninsula which improved the Dutch position in both regions. In 1650 the directors issued a new comprehensive set of regulations (*Generale Instructie*) for the administration of the Indies. These emphasized the Company's position as a commercial body whose operations must be conducted according to the twin principles of the exclusion of competitors and of 'buy cheap, sell dear'. In order that the spice trade should be more effectively brought under control it laid down that the production of cloves should be confined to Amboina and the neighbouring islands and that of nutmeg and mace to the Bandas; overproduction and smuggling must be prevented by destroying trees elsewhere. In the same year for strategic reasons a decision was taken to colonize the Cape of Good Hope, and in 1652 Jan van Riebeeck planted there the one and only colony in the real sense that the V.O.C. ever possessed.

The policy of destroying the surplus spice trees which invited smuggling had actually been put into practice by Arnold de Vlaming van Oudshoorn in 1649, when he led what was known as a *hongitocht* to cut down trees in west Ceram, where the clandestine trade with Macassar still continued. A *hongi* was a fleet of cora-coras or large praus propelled by oars. This inhumane method of enforcing the monopoly was systematically employed until the production of cloves was practically eliminated in the Moluccas. In 1650 a serious revolt broke out in these unhappy islands which was not completely repressed until 1656. The Dutch arrested the Sultan of Ternate, Mandar Shah, and deported him to Batavia; and he was only reinstated when he had made a formal agreement permitting them to cut down clove trees wherever they liked in his dominions. As the price of compliance he was granted an annual allowance. His people were forced to plant rice and sago in place of cloves, and as their islands could not produce enough food they had to buy additional rice, at a higher price than they could afford, from the Dutch. Ruin spread over the once-prosperous islands, and an alarming increase of piracy naturally resulted.

Johan Maetsuycker's term of office as governor-general (1653–78) ranks with those of Coen and van Diemen as a period of notable advance in the affairs of the V.O.C.   Under van Diemen, as legal expert of the Council of the Indies, he had composed the Statutes of Batavia, which gave the Dutch empire its first code of law and remained until the beginning of the nineteenth century the chief authority in legal matters. Later, as Governor of Ceylon, he had cultivated good relations with Raja Singa and paved the way for the final elimination of Portuguese power there. One of his early achievements as governor-general was the accomplishment of this aim. Not only was Colombo taken (1656) and the Dutch headquarters established there, but van Goens, who was sent in 1657 to chase the Portuguese out of Ceylon and the Coromandel and Malabar coasts of India, carried out his task with such success that when the peace of August 1661 between the Netherlands and Portugal brought his conquest to an end at the beginning of 1663, the Portuguese had not only lost all their possessions in Ceylon but were left with only Goa and Diu in India. In that same year the Spaniards evacuated Tidore and the Dutch were left complete masters of the Moluccas.

Under Maetsuycker the Dutch achieved a great measure of control over the pepper ports of Sumatra. Firm action had to be taken against the Sultan of Palembang, who in 1658 treacherously attacked the Dutch factory, murdering the factors and the crews of two ships lying at anchor before it. A punitive expedition forced him to permit the construction of a Dutch fort close to his town and to grant the Dutch the exclusive right to purchase his pepper. Measures were also taken against Acheh, whose power had notably declined after the death of Iskander Muda in 1636. By the Painan Contract of 1662 the leading Minangkabau chiefs, in revolt against Achinese suzerainty, came under the protection of the V.O.C.; and when four years later Achinese agents stirred up trouble for the Dutch on the west coast, an expedition under Abraham Verspreet put an end to Achinese influence throughout the whole region.

After breaking all resistance in the Moluccas in 1656 the obvious next step was to put an end to the power of Macassar. But Hassan Udin had strongly fortified his city and was well supplied with arms by the Europeans who traded there; and moreover Maetsuycker shrank from a task which was certain to entail a heavy expenditure such as would be frowned on by the directors. For some years the renewed war with the Portuguese in Ceylon and south India prevented him from risking a large expedition against Hassan Udin. In 1660, however, a force under Johan van Dam captured one of Macassar's forts, and in consequence the sultan accepted terms by which he promised to stop all sailings to the Spice Islands, abstain from interference with the Company's allies, Buton and Menado, and expel the Portuguese from his dominions. But he failed to carry out his treaty obligations and reverted to his former attitude of hostility. In 1666, therefore, Maetsuycker entrusted Cornelis Janszoon Speelman with the task of settling accounts with him. Speelman enlisted the support of Aru Palakka, a Buginese chief of Boni, whose family had been murdered by Hassan Udin. The expedition began by destroying a large Macassar force which was operating against Buton. Speelman next sailed to the Moluccas, where he forced the ruler of Tidore to recognize Dutch overlordship and abandon his age-long feud with Ternate. Then, with further reinforcements from Ternate, he returned to Celebes and began the hard task of bringing Macassar to its knees. It took four months of desperate fighting to force Hassan Udin to submit. On 18 November 1667 he signed the Treaty of Bongaya, by which he accepted Dutch overlordship, dismantled his forts, granted the Dutch a monopoly of trade and agreed to expel all non-Dutch Europeans. He had also to pay a huge indemnity and permit the Dutch to occupy his principal fortress, which they named Fort Rotterdam after Speelman's birthplace. Four months later he tried once again to evade the peace terms. This time the Dutch took possession of his city, pensioned him off and placed south Celebes under a Dutch governor with his headquarters at Fort Rotterdam. Indonesian independence in the east of the Archipelago was now virtually stamped out.

Up to Maetsuycker's time there had been no deviation from Coen's policy of confining the Dutch empire to a chain of forts and trading posts and of eschewing territorial dominion save in the case of very small islands such as Amboina and the Bandas. A change, however, begins to be discernible with Maetsuycker; though it can scarcely have been realized by anyone at the time. In the first place the V.O.C. became the controlling power in Ceylon; and although the Raja of Kandy still continued to function as a ruler, the island had in fact become largely a Dutch territorial possession. Shortly before Maetsuycker's death events took place in the kingdom of Mataram which led to Dutch interference, and thereby set up a chain of consequences culminating in the establishment of their supremacy over the whole island. There was no conscious change of programme, no ambition on the part of the directors to transform their commercial empire into a territorial one. Yet such a transformation was inevitable, as in the case of the English in India at a later date, if they were to maintain and consolidate the position they had won for themselves in defeating their European rivals. The alternative was decline and in all probability extinction. Hence although it was clearly recognized that non-intervention in the mutual quarrels of the Indonesian rulers was essential, and Batavia was willing to recognize any de facto ruler so long as he was willing to fulfil the obligations of his state towards the V.O.C., the very condition upon which this policy was based was bound, sooner or later, to force its abandonment.

The trouble in Mataram which caused Dutch interference began in 1674 when Trunojoyo, a Madurese prince who claimed descent from the old royal family of Majapahit, led a formidable rebellion against Agung's successor, Amangkurat I, with whom the Dutch had been on good terms since the treaty of 1646. Amangkurat I, or Sunan Tegalwangi, to use the name by which he was commonly known, was a monster of cruelty whose atrocities were on so extravagant a scale as to be scarcely credible. In carrying out the reorganization of the administration of his empire his measures to crush local independence stirred up much discontent. The situation was complicated by the presence of a large number of refugees from Macassar who had settled on the east coast of Java and become pirates. With these and his own Madurese followers, who were angry at Javanese treatment of their island, Trunojoyo quickly overran East and part of central Java and established himself at Kediri. And the susuhunan, quite unable from the start to take effective measures against the rebels, called on Batavia for help.

Maetsuycker was not bound by the treaty of 1646 to give military help unless Mataram's enemies were also those of the Dutch. He realized, however, that the rebels contained strong anti-Dutch elements, and, moreover, that the Sultan of Bantam hoped to turn the confusion in Mataram to his own advantage by seizing its western provinces and thus encircling Batavia. He decided, therefore, to send help, but to cut down Dutch intervention to the absolute minimum. Speelman, whom he placed in charge of the naval force sent in 1676 against Trunojoyo's Macassar pirates, had quite different views. He wanted to pursue a strong policy which would restore Amangkurat's authority, while placing him in a position of dependence upon the

Dutch, and enable a decisive blow to be delivered against the plans of Abulfatah Agung of Bantam. Meanwhile Trunojoyo, profiting by the Dutch half-measures, stormed and sacked the kraton of Mataram, and Amangkurat, fleeing to place himself under Dutch protection, died at Tegalwangi, leaving his successor, Adipati Anom, completely dependent upon the Dutch so far as any hope of his restoration was concerned. In October 1677, in return for recognition as the legal sunan, he granted the Dutch vast commercial concessions together with the cession of much territory south of Batavia and the port and district of Semarang. He also promised to repay all their war expenses and handed over a number of coastal towns to be held as a pledge.

Maetsuycker was far from happy about the treaty which was negotiated by Speelman; but he died soon afterwards and was succeeded by the more warlike Rijklof van Goens, who made Speelman his right-hand man in the Council of the Indies and at once adopted a vigorous policy. Anthony Hurdt, in command of a strong force of Dutch troops, captured Kediri, and Adipati Anom was crowned as Amangkurat II with the ancient crown of Majapahit, which was handed over by the Dutch commander. Trunojoyo escaped but was followed up by two native forces, a Buginese and an Amboinese, in the service of the Dutch. He was finally run to earth in the jungle-covered mountains of East Java by the Amboinese and handed over to Amangkurat II at his new capital of Kartasura, where a few days later the susuhunan slew him with his own hands. Gradually the other rebels were hunted down and destroyed by Dutch and Mataram forces; but peace was only finally restored in 1682. 'He whom all obey' was now, for all practical purposes, a Dutch vassal maintained on his throne by a body-guard of Dutch troops.

The Mataram struggle was rendered all the more difficult for Batavia by the situation at Bantam. Abulfatah, who had come to the throne with the title of Sultan Agung in 1651, was a powerful ruler who sought to restore to his kingdom the important position she had earlier occupied in commerce. He had resumed hostile relations with the Dutch in 1656, but their close blockade of his capital had caused him to make peace in 1659. As soon as the blockade was lifted he made efforts to promote commercial prosperity, and with French and English factories operating there Bantam became once more a serious rival to Batavia. The treaty of 1677 between Batavia and Mataram roused him to make an attempt to prevent Amangkurat II from drifting into too close association with the Dutch, and in particular he laid claim to suzerainty over Cheribon, whose territory lay to the east of that of Batavia, and threatened the Dutch with war if they interfered.

But a family quarrel played into the hands of the Dutch. Agung's eldest son returned in 1676 from a pilgrimage to Mecca, which earned him the title of Sultan Haji, to find that during his absence his younger brother, who was married to a daughter of the chief minister, was to be invested as heir-apparent. This drove Haji to cultivate secret relations with the Dutch. In May 1680, when Agung was about to resort to arms to enforce his claim over Cheribon, a palace revolution forced him to abdicate in favour of Haji. The new ruler at once began negotiations with Batavia for a treaty of friendship. This caused a revulsion of feeling against him in certain districts; Agung was able to regain power and a civil war began between father and son. In 1683 Haji captured his father and handed him over to the Dutch, who kept him a prisoner until his death in 1692.

Haji's success was due entirely to the support he received from a strong contingent of Dutch troops and was achieved only after a very severe struggle. Hence in 1684 he had to make a treaty in which he practically signed away the independence of his state. Besides surrendering all claim to Cheribon he promised to pay the war-costs of the Dutch forces amounting to 600,000 dollars, granted the Dutch the exclusive right to the import and export trade of his kingdom, and agreed to expel all non-Dutch Europeans. He was relieved of the obligation to pay his debt so long as he honoured the monopoly conferred upon the Dutch. They in their turn made sure of his obedience by building a strong fortress at Bantam. The English, who had already lost their footing at Macassar, were now forced to leave Bantam. They retired to Bencoolen on the west coast of Sumatra, where they were to remain until 1824.

The Dutch were now unquestioned masters of the Archipelago. But they had won their supremacy at great cost and at a time when they were fighting with their backs to the wall in Europe against Louis XIV and Charles II. Their trade had passed through periods of serious interruption, and on a number of occasions during Maetsuycker's term of office the V.O.C. had been unable to pay its annual dividend. It was still, however, able to show a high average profit and to send rich cargoes of spices to Europe. But it was now changing from a commercial to a territorial power, and the time was soon to come when, with increased costs of administration and decreased trade, its steady decline was to set in.

CHAPTER 17

THE ZENITH AND DECLINE OF THE V.O.C., 1684-1799

IN 1684, when Governor-General Speelman died and was succeeded by the scholarly and unwarlike Johannes Camphuys (1684–91), the Dutch Company had become the most powerful political force in Java. The sultans of the two most important states, Mataram and Bantam, had been placed on their thrones by its troops and owed it vast sums of money by way of war costs. With both rulers the Dutch had concluded agreements by which, so long as they faithfully carried out the terms of the commercial treaties dictated to them, the question of repayment would not be raised. Quite apart from the indirect control which was thereby implied, the Dutch now possessed a belt of territory stretching across the island from Batavia southward to the opposite coast, thus completely separating the territories of the two states.

From the point of view of all the parties concerned, this was a highly unsatisfactory situation, though the Dutch higher command seems to have been slow to realize its implications. Dutch policy for some considerable period, so far from proceeding according to any overall plan, tended to wait upon events and to issue in positive action only when forced to by circumstances. Louis XIV's growing threat to their homeland in Europe made them hesitant about assuming new military or territorial responsibilities abroad. Such things involved much extra expense and no compensating increase in revenue.

Nevertheless the expansion of the Company's power and the methods it used in building up its trade monopoly created a situation which rendered further advance in Java inevitable, no matter how hard those in charge of its affairs, both at home and on the spot, might strive to limit its commitments. The treatment received by Mataram and Bantam at the hands of the Dutch 'infidels' caused many Mahommedans to take up arms in defence of their religion, and for a time a pirate fleet under a fanatical Malay of Sumatra, who assumed the name of Ibn Iskander ('Son of Alexander the Great'), terrorized the Java Sea until in 1686 a Dutch squadron under Krijn de Ronde destroyed it.

The threat of a widespread Mahommedan movement against them caused the Dutch no little uneasiness, especially as some of the Bantam

chiefs were involved, while the Susuhunan Amangkurat II of Mataram also allowed himself to be drawn into the intrigues. At the same
time trouble broke out in the lowlands to the south of Batavia and in
the mountains of the Preanger, where the Dutch had hesitated to
enforce their control over the districts ceded to them by Mataram in
the treaty concluded in 1678 by Speelman. These districts had become
the refuge of many lawless characters, one of whom, Surapati, once a
Balinese slave at Batavia, had found a happy hunting-ground there
at the head of a band of his compatriots. During the struggle against
Bantam he and his men had taken service with the Dutch, but as a
result of an insult offered him by a Dutch officer he and his followers
had fled to the Galungung mountains, where they were joined by
several hundreds of bad-hats. While the Dutch were busy with Ibn

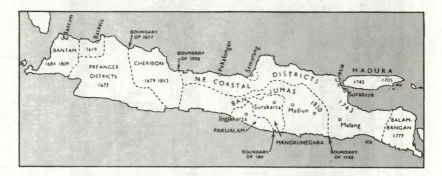

DUTCH EXPANSION IN JAVA

Iskander, Surapati and his 'patriots' were terrorizing the whole
countryside south of Batavia. A Dutch detachment was sent to hunt
him down, but he escaped to Kartasura, where he was favourably
received by the susuhunan.

Camphuys sent an embassy to demand his surrender. He appointed
as its leader Major Tack, who had distinguished himself in the fighting
against Trunadjaya in Bantam and shocked Javanese opinion at the
capture of Kediri in 1678 by trying on the sacred crown of Majapahit
before handing it over to Amangkurat II. Soon after his arrival at
Kartasura he intervened in an affray between some Javanese and
Surapati's Balinese and was killed together with a large number of his
escort. Although Batavia realized that the incident had been staged
with the object of getting rid of the detested Dutchman, Camphuys
held his hand. He had discovered signs of disloyalty among the Company's native troops. The susuhunan soon found his Balinese guests
an unwelcome encumbrance, and Surapati, escaping to Pasuruan in

BATAVIA IN THE SEVENTEENTH CENTURY

East Java, began to carve out a kingdom for himself and to make serious inroads into the territory owning allegiance to Mataram. But both Camphuys and his successor, Willem van Outhoorn (1691–1704), turned a deaf ear to the appeals of Amangkurat II for help.

While the affairs of central and East Java were thus in the melting-pot Amangkurat II died in 1703 and was succeeded by his son Amangkurat III, called by the Dutch Sunan Mas. He was a bloodthirsty tyrant whose quarrels with his uncle, Pangéran Puger, caused the latter to flee to Semarang and crave Dutch protection. Joan van Hoorn, who succeeded his father-in-law Van Outhoorn as governor-general in 1704, learnt that Sunan Mas was in league with Surapati against the Company and that a number of Mataram chieftains were in favour of raising Puger to the throne. He thereupon recognized him as susuhunan and lent him a Dutch force.

So began what is known to the Dutch historians as the First Javanese War of Succession. With his Dutch force Puger easily occupied Kartasura and was installed as Pakubuwono I. He had, however, to pay heavily for Dutch support. In 1705 he concluded a treaty which ceded them further territory at the expense of his kingdom up to the river Losari in the north and the river Donan in the south. He formally waived all claims to Cheribon and the Preanger besides the eastern half of the island of Madura. Moreover, he granted the Company full control over the trade of his kingdom and accepted a strong Dutch garrison in his capital, Kartasura.

Meanwhile the Dutch had driven Sunan Mas out of his kingdom to seek a refuge at the Court of Surapati. In 1706 a strong Dutch force landed at Surabaya and captured Surapati's frontier fortress of Bangil. He himself died of wounds sustained in attempting to defend it. In the following year, after heavy fighting against Sunan Mas and the sons of Surapati, the Dutch won a complete victory. Sunan Mas surrendered and with his family was sent into exile in Ceylon.

The Company was now master of Java, but it had yet to crush out the last embers of resistance. In 1712 Surapati's partisans made further trouble and were not finally liquidated until 1719. In that same year the Company's vassal, Pakubuwono I of Mataram, died and what is known as the Second Javanese War of Succession broke out. Pakubuwono's son Amangkurat IV's succession to the throne was contested by his own brothers, who rose in rebellion. It took the Dutch four years of hard fighting before the rebel leaders were all rounded up and sent away into exile, some to Ceylon and the remainder to the Cape of Good Hope. Like the empire of Majapahit,

Mataram had fallen through internal dissensions rather than as a result of outside pressure. Contrary to the accusations of Machiavellian policy levelled against them by their critics from Raffles onwards, the Dutch had intervened unwillingly in the case of Mataram. The ceaseless civil wars affected their trade adversely and might have had serious political consequences if they had not adopted a firm line. The extension of their control over the whole island was the inevitable result of their assumption of the rôle of a territorial power. A century later the British were to find themselves in a similar position in relation to India.

At the beginning of the eighteenth century the V.O.C. stood at the zenith of its power. To the outside observer it appeared to be rich and prosperous, with its annual fleets returning to Europe laden with merchandise and its annual dividends of between 20 and 40 per cent. Actually its financial condition was wretched. The long, expensive wars, the increase of territory, and the consequent increase in the numbers of officials involved it in immense expenditure at a time when its trade was actually decreasing.

The policy of 'sell dear, buy cheap' brought its own nemesis, for it reduced the Javanese to a condition of such poverty that he could not afford to buy the European goods or the fine Indian textiles brought to him by the Dutch. He learnt to supply his needs otherwise, by growing his own cotton and weaving it in traditional fashion, or by clandestine trade with Portuguese and English smugglers, who gave him better prices for his produce than the Dutch. On more than one occasion Governor-General van Hoorn (1704-9) had to report home that the goods sent out to Java had had to be sold at a loss.

The directors at home, with a blind eye to the defects of their own policy, attributed their losses to smuggling and the private trade, which was the common practice of their officials, whose salaries were below subsistence level for Europeans in the East. But the heavy penalties they imposed for these practices completely failed to achieve their object. In 1722, for instance, Governor-General Zwaardekroon had no less than twenty-six Company's servants beheaded in one day for theft and smuggling. And nine years later Governor-General Durven, Director-General Hasselaar and two members of the Council of India were dismissed for failing to deal adequately with the prevailing corruption. But the malpractices went on unchecked.

With a mounting deficit the directors pursued a policy of absolute secrecy regarding the Company's accounts, and in order to maintain its credit in the money-market paid out annual dividends of from 20 to 40 per cent, although to do so they had to float further loans. By the year 1700 the Company's debt already stood at 12 million guilders, and in order to fight its wars it was forced to apply to the States-General for help in the form of money and ships. Thus its outward appearance of riches and power concealed a state of deterioration and corruption. The most disturbing fact was the actual decline in its trade at a time when the expansion of its territory entailed a marked increase in the number of its officials.

The Batavia authorities, in suggesting methods to deal with the decline of trade, revived Coen's proposal to open the trade of the Indies to private enterprise and confine the Company's shipping to voyages between the East and Europe. But the directors refused to abandon the strict monopoly system and ordered it to be supplemented by the introduction of the method of 'contingencies and forced deliveries'. Contingencies were a form of tribute in kind levied on districts under the Company's direct control, while forced deliveries were in products which cultivators were forced to grow and deliver at a fixed price, always much to the advantage of the purchaser. The directors took no heed of the fact that such methods increased the poverty of the people and were a direct incentive to smuggling.

Governor-General Zwaardekroon sought to improve the situation by introducing new products into Java. He put into operation a better method of preparing indigo for the European market, which stimulated its production. His efforts also to improve cotton cultivation and to encourage the planting of sappan wood, which yields a red dyestuff, met with success. But the most important development of this period was the introduction of coffee planting, which proved an immediate success and freed the Dutch from their dependence upon the Mokka trade at a time when the Turks were placing difficulties in the way of their export of coffee. The first plantations grew up in the districts around Batavia and Cheribon, and Zwaardekroon's contracts for deliveries of coffee at the equivalent of fivepence a pound caused the Javanese to expand their cultivation of the crop to such an extent that production threatened to outstrip demand. Thereupon, against the advice of the governor-general, the directors insisted on the price being lowered by 75 per cent, and the growers in desperation cut down large numbers of their trees. The government therefore applied the system of forced deliveries to the community and raised the price somewhat.

The subsequent manipulation of the coffee trade by the Company during the eighteenth century is a sorry tale of measures taken to ensure a high price in the European market and a mere pittance for the producer, who was at the mercy of a government which changed its policy from time to time in such an arbitrary fashion as to make it impossible for him to cultivate on economic lines. Moreover, as the Dutch worked through the local chiefs, who in equally arbitrary fashion fixed their own share of the proceeds, the cultivator's position was worse than that of a slave. Furnivall sums up the final position thus: "The net result was that for every pikol of 126 pounds shipped, the cultivator had to supply 240 to 270 pounds and was paid the equivalent of 14 pounds.'[1]

During the third and fourth decades of the eighteenth century Dutch rule in Java passed through a period of turbulence. Before the end of the Second Javanese War of Succession there occurred the ugly incident known as Peter Erberfeld's 'conspiracy'. Erberfeld was a well-established free burgher of Batavia who developed a grievance against the government over a claim it enforced unfairly to some property left him by his father. In December 1721 he was accused of plotting with the Surapati party and a number of discontented chiefs to raise an insurrection with the aim of murdering all the Europeans in the city. Although the evidence was obtained under torture, nervous tension was stimulated to such a pitch that he and such of his supposed accomplices as were within reach were put to death. The authorities even went so far as to pull down his house, expose his head on the ruins and set up a stone inscription enjoining that the place should remain desolate for ever. Historians seem to be generally agreed that the evidence upon which he was condemned was worthless and that he was more sinned against than sinning.[2]

A few years later mass hysteria was responsible for a far worse crime which had serious consequences. There were Chinese settlers in Indonesia long before the coming of the Portuguese. Jan Pieterszoon Coen had a high opinion of their industry and diligence and encouraged them to settle at Batavia. By the year 1700 there were some 10,000 of them living in or in the neighbourhood of the city. They were craftsmen, tea-traders and sugar cultivators for the most part. They were useful to the Dutch as intermediaries in their trade with the Javanese. They were also a mainstay of the smuggling trade, while some of them had become so wealthy and powerful as to constitute a potential danger to Dutch rule. But the real problem in the early years of the eighteenth century arose from the fact that the tea-junks plying

---

[1] J. S. Furnivall, *Netherlands India*, p. 40.
[2] De Haan, *Priangan*, i, p. 210.

regularly from China brought increasing numbers without means of existence who became roving beggars and a menace to law and order.

As early as 1706 the Dutch issued stiff regulations aimed at preventing the entry of such undesirables. When this method proved of no avail the Batavia authorities rounded up numbers of wandering beggars and transported them to Ceylon, the Banda Islands and the Cape of Good Hope. Only those with a government pass might remain in Java. These measures also failed: deeds of violence by wandering bands of Chinese became frequent, and the officials entrusted with the issue of passes used them as a means of graft. The bad situation became suddenly critical when in July 1740 Governor-General Valkenier and the Council of the Indies decided on sterner measures. All Chinese unable to prove that they were suitably employed were to be deported to work in the cinnamon gardens in Ceylon. The regulation was carried out with gross unfairness: greedy officials seized Chinese long resident in Java in order to squeeze money out of them under threat of deportation. And when a baseless rumour went round that the deportees were thrown overboard as soon as their ships were out of sight of Java, large numbers of Chinese fled from Batavia and organized armed resistance.

The Dutch authorities discovered that those still remaining in the city were in league with the rebels and were preparing to defend themselves. A chance fire which broke out in a Chinese house was taken as a sign that those within the city and those without were to make a concerted attack. Thereupon the infuriated population, supported by soldiers, seamen, slaves and Javanese, fell upon the Chinese, and for a whole week massacre and plunder went on unchecked. Governor-General Valkenier lost his head so completely as to order the massacre of all Chinese prisoners and did nothing to prevent the Company's troops from participating in the bloodbath.

When the work of vengeance was over and order was restored, the government offered a general amnesty to all Chinese who surrendered their weapons within one month. The large numbers who availed themselves of this offer were housed in a special quarter that was built beyond the city limits. Many, however, trekked away and formed a formidable force which wreaked vengeance on Europeans at Rembang, Joana and elsewhere, and finally laid siege to Semarang. The situation became serious for the Dutch when the susuhunan, Paku Buwono II, openly declared for the rebels, seized the Dutch garrison at Kartasura and murdered its officers. Semarang, however, was saved by the timely arrival of Dutch reinforcements, and the Madurese, who had suffered much at the hands of Mataram, threw in their lot with the Dutch.

Then Paku Buwono II, suddenly realizing that he was backing the wrong horse, made his peace with the Dutch. His action nearly cost him his throne, for many of his chiefs, in their fanatical hatred of the Dutch, joined with the Chinese in driving him out of his capital and proclaimed as their ruler a grandson of the exiled Sunan Mas. He was saved, however, by quarrels which broke out between the Chinese and their Javanese allies. The Dutch recaptured Kartasura and reinstated him as ruler of Mataram.

But it was a sadly depleted Mataram over which he was allowed to rule. By a new treaty, which he was forced to conclude with Batavia in 1743, he had to cede the whole of the north coast of Java together with all his claims to the island of Madura. Moreover, he abandoned Kartasura as his capital city and built a new kraton in the Solo district to which he gave the name of Surakarta. The Dutch created a new North Coast Province with Semarang as its capital. Their Madurese allies, however, had come into the struggle in the hope of gaining their independence. They refused to accept the settlement and were only reduced to obedience after much fighting.

Governor-General Valkenier's handling of the Chinese question met with stiff opposition from a section of the Council of the Indies headed by van Imhoff. After a dramatic quarrel, in the course of which Valkenier had the members of the opposition arrested and sent home, he himself was put on trial at Batavia by order of the directors, and van Imhoff appointed governor-general in his stead.

This able and energetic man realized that exceptional measures were needed to arrest the economic decline of the Company. He persuaded the directors to open the inland trade and the sea trade between Indonesia and India to free burghers and natives subject to certain restrictions. For instance, Batavia must be the beginning and the end of each trading voyage. Inter-commerce between other ports was forbidden. The scheme failed to realize his expectations, partly because of this restriction. In any case it came a century too late, when private trading and smuggling in Indonesia had already passed beyond Dutch control. Also in the hope of reducing smuggling van Imhoff established in 1745 the Opium Society, with sole rights of trading in that article in the Dutch empire. Here also his efforts met with little success.

More success, on the other hand, attended his measures to extend land cultivation in the Batavian hinterland, especially in the parts affected by the Chinese depredations. Waste land was sold to private farmers with seignorial rights over the native settlers, but with the obligation to sell their produce to the government at fixed prices. He himself purchased land in the lovely Bogor region, where he built himself the stately mansion named Buitenzorg ('Carefree'), which at his death was taken over by his successors in turn until it ultimately became the official country residence of the governor-general. With his encouragement Dutch farmer families migrated from the homeland to take up lands in Java. He also improved the lot of the native cultivator by fixing the annual amount of coffee to be delivered to the Company, thereby aiming at preventing the destruction of redundant coffee when there was overproduction. His reforms were introduced as the result of journeys of inspection made to various parts of Java, where he met regents and other local officials and took measures to save the villager from the oppression of his immediate masters. His valuable report on his travels, full of interesting details of places and peoples, could not be published owing to the policy of secrecy sedulously maintained by the directors.

Van Imhoff's fertile brain produced scheme after scheme of reform in such rapid succession that he attempted far too much, and little that he did took root. The overall plan which he would have liked to carry out would have been to reduce drastically the Company's commitments in the way of trading stations outside Indonesia and Ceylon, and to concentrate upon its growing responsibilities as a territorial power. His ill-starred attempt to open direct trade with Mexico in order to import badly-needed silver for coinage shows how far his imagination could lead him to disregard hard facts such as the existing treaty stipulations preventing such enterprises.

His greatest failing was a lack of statesmanlike insight in his dealings with native potentates. While on a visit to the susuhunan, Paku Buwono II, at Surakarta his tactless intervention in a quarrel between that ruler and his brother Mangku Bumi caused the latter to rise in revolt, and a long struggle, the Third Javanese War of Succession, 1749–57, once more involved the Company in expensive military action. During its first year the death of the susuhunan changed its character from a dynastic squabble into a war of liberation from Dutch rule; for Paku Buwono II on his deathbed agreed with Van Hohendorff, the governor of the North Coast Province, to cede his kingdom to the Dutch, and his successor, Paku Buwono III, received his crown at the hands of the Company, not by virtue of birthright. This caused the majority of the Mataram chiefs to throw in their lot with Mangku Bumi, whom they proclaimed susuhunan. The Dutch therefore had to fight the most destructive of all their Javanese wars in order to maintain their candidate on the throne. And while they had their hands full in Mataram a serious rebellion broke out in the sultanate of Bantam which also involved them in heavy military sacrifices before it was crushed.

In the Mataram struggle, after two years of varying fortunes, Mangku Bumi defeated and killed the Dutch commander De Clercq in a battle at the Bogowonto river in 1751 and proceeded to occupy a large part of the North Coast Province, from which he threatened to advance deep into the Company's territory. After a great effort, however, he was driven out of the province, and luckily for the Company found himself involved in a fight for leadership with his nephew Mas Said which paralysed his efforts against the Dutch. Van Imhoff had died in 1750, and his successor, Jacob Mossel, decided to partition Mataram. In 1755 a treaty was made with Mangku Bumi by which he accepted Paku Buwono III as ruler of the eastern half of the kingdom. He himself received the western half with Jogjakarta as his capital and the title of Sultan Amangku Buwono. It took two years of fierce fighting to subdue Mas Said. At the Peace of Salatiga (1757) he recognized the suzerainty of the Company and received as its vassal a portion of Mataram now known as the Mangku-Negorose territory.

The trouble in Bantam arose out of a dynastic dispute, and again van Imhoff's intervention on the wrong side had serious results. The old sultan who had ruled since 1733, came so much under the influence of one of his wives, Ratu Fatima, of Arab race, that she persuaded him to nominate her son-in-law, his nephew, as heir-apparent in place of the rightful heir, Pangéran Gusti. Van Imhoff lent his support to the scheme, and in 1748, when the Sultan showed signs of madness, Ratu Fatima brought about his deposition in favour of her candidate, with herself as regent. When Pangeran Gusti attempted to assert his rights he was deported by the Dutch to Ceylon, and the old sultan was taken to Amboina, where he soon died. A general revolt at once broke out under the leadership of a priest, Kjahi Tapa, and a chieftain, Ratu Bagus. The Dutch troops sent in support of Fatima were defeated, and the rebels sought the help of the English at Bencoolen.

Such was the situation when van Imhoff died in 1750. Jacob Mossel, on succeeding him, decided to reverse his policy. He won

over the leading Bantam chiefs by banishing Fatima and her candidate, placed the brother of the dead sultan on the throne, brought
back Pangéran Gusti from Ceylon, and recognized him as heir-
apparent. The new sultan made a treaty in 1752 with the Company
by which he recognized its overlordship and ceded it control over the
Lampongs. The rebellion, however, continued. Ratu Bagus took the
title of sultan, while Kjahi Tapa, taking advantage of the Dutch preoccupation with the Mataram war, plundered Dutch territory and
even made an abortive attack on Batavia. For a time the Dutch troops
were closely besieged in Bantam by the rebels. It took much hard
fighting before the two rebel leaders gave up the struggle. In 1753
the new sultan abdicated in favour of Pangéran Gusti, who confirmed
the treaty with the Company, and quiet was restored. The Dutch
were now masters of the whole of Java, save for the territory in the
extreme east of the island, where the Balinese supporters of Surapati
still caused trouble. Not until 1772 were the Dutch able to put an
end to their activities.

The Dutch were now complete masters of Java. They had long
been more or less the dominant power over the rest of the Archipelago.
Of the larger islands only Bali and Lombok remained free from their
influence. Their products had little economic importance, while the
warlike character of their people and the doggedness with which time
and again in history they had resisted outside interference were a
strong deterrent to the Dutch. The remarkable success with which the
Balinese clung to their traditional religion with its Hindu associations
when all the great powers in the island world adopted Islam tells its
own tale.

In Sumatra they had broken the Achinese control over the pepper
trade before the end of the seventeenth century. The result was that
with the exception of Acheh, which stoutly maintained its independence, most of the coastal states were vassals of Batavia. But there
was little or no interference with native life, for the Dutch were
strongly averse to territorial expansion on the island; and in any case
the authority of the coastal sultans did not spread far inland. The
pepper monopoly could not be rigorously maintained, partly for geographical reasons, and also because of the factory established at Bencoolen by the English after their expulsion from Bantam. In more backward Borneo Dutch relations were mainly with the sultanate of Band-
jermasin, which attained some importance as a centre of the smuggling
trade after the Dutch conquest of Macassar in 1667. To end this
situation Batavia sent a special envoy in 1756 who concluded a new

trade agreement under which control passed into Dutch hands. The eighteenth century saw the rise of a Chinese mining colony to work at the rich gold deposits of the Sambas sultanate. The immigrants were organized in *kongsis*, and ultimately came to form semi-independent communities.

If the Dutch made little impact upon the life of Sumatra and Borneo, their rigid regulation of spice production and trade in the islands of the 'Great East' ruined alike the prosperity and the native culture of the region. The production of clove and nutmeg was limited to the Banda Islands and Amboina. Unlicensed trees grown elsewhere were destroyed by large fleets of prows under the command of Dutch officers which made annual voyages (*hongitochten*) to suspected areas. Ternate and Tidore, once prosperous centres of the clove cultivation and of inter-island shipping, became poverty-stricken and backward. Their hereditary ruling families received annual pensions for their compliance. But conditions in the 'privileged' areas were, if anything, worse than in those in which spice production was prohibited. The natives worked for a pittance, were forced to buy all their foodstuffs from the Dutch at exorbitant prices, and had to cut down their spice trees whenever the Company decided to restrict the supply. To make matters worse, the policy of monopoly and restriction brought its own nemesis, for it forced the English and the French to experiment with the planting of clove and nutmeg in their own tropical territories, and with enough success to keep the price at a reasonable level when the European demand began to expand towards the end of the eighteenth century.

One of the worst results of the harsh measures taken by the Dutch in building up and maintaining their trade monopoly was an immense increase in piracy. Among the Malays piracy had for many centuries been regarded as an honourable occupation, while to the Indonesian Mahommedans war against the infidel was a religious duty. The destruction of much of the native shipping trade and the extreme poverty to which many coastal districts of *nusantara* were reduced caused larger numbers than ever to swell the great pirate fleets which swarmed in the seas of the Archipelago. The defeat of the sea power of Macassar in particular opened the way for the rise of the Buginese state of Boni. Its intrepid and intelligent people began to prey upon the coasts of Java, Sumatra and the Malay Peninsula in increasing numbers from the latter part of the seventeenth century onwards. Throughout the eighteenth century they were the open enemies of the Dutch East India Company. They joined in the intervening wars waged by the sultans of the west coast of Borneo, overran the sultanate of Johore and even threatened Malacca. And as Dutch control of the seas declined during the latter half of the century immense pirate fleets made regular annual voyages from well-established bases in various parts of the Archipelago—at Tobelo on the north-east coast of Halmahera, in the islands off the coast of New Guinea, and in the Sulu Islands. The Illanos of the Sulu Islands were the most dreaded of all. Their large fleets of heavily armed galleys would fearlessly attack the strongest warships of the Company, while at the end of the century they planted a fortified base at the southern tip of Sumatra from which they preyed upon the Sunda Straits and carried their slave raids far and wide.

The restoration of peace in Java after the Third War of Succession and the Bantam rebellion brought some improvement in conditions there. The Company was at pains to maintain good relations with the vassal sultans of Surakarta and Jogjakarta, and refused to be drawn into the frontier disputes which constantly arose between the two. The cultivation of coffee and sugar was encouraged, and roads were built to improve the traffic in these articles. The salaries of officials were raised in the hope of reducing corruption and there was some attempt to raise the efficiency of the armed forces. But the increasing financial exhaustion of the Company and the steadily mounting deficit in its accounts prevented any thorough-going reforms.

Outside Java Dutch decline was more obvious. The growth of English power in India from the days of Clive onwards became a serious menace to their position there, especially in Bengal, from which Batavia imported not only vast quantities of textiles but also supplies of opium, the secret monopoly of which brought the Company's servants immense gains. Their blundering attempt at armed intervention in 1759 against Clive brought them a humiliating defeat as a result of which their Bengal trade came under English supervision.[1] In Ceylon their quarrels with the King of Kandy over the cinnamon trade resulted in open war. This, however, ended in 1766 in a treaty favourable to them. Elsewhere, in Sumatra, Borneo and the Spice Islands, it was a sad story of commercial stagnation and decline. To make matters worse, at the moment when only a great national effort could have saved the Company, the quarrel which broke out in 1780 between the Patriots and the Princely party in Holland prevented anything from being done.

In the same year also the 'Fourth English War', as it is called by

[1] *Cambridge History of India*, vol. v, pp. 153–5.

Dutch historians, broke out, and, as they bitterly remark, gave the Company its deathblow. Their government listened to the blandishments of the New Englander, John Adams, and agreed to recognize American independence. Lord North's government got wind of the agreement and declared war on Holland. In both the East and the West Indies her colonies were defenceless. Her losses of merchantmen were immense. Negapatam and other trading stations in India fell into British hands, as also all the Dutch stations on the west coast of Sumatra. Only through the help of a French naval squadron under the brilliant Suffren were the Dutch able to save Ceylon and the Cape from falling into British hands. They lost almost all their homeward-bound ships from the East. No trading ships dared leave the Dutch ports in Europe. Trade was at a standstill. Their godowns at Batavia were packed with unexportable goods, which they were glad to sell to neutrals at sacrifice prices.

The Treaty of Paris, which was signed in 1784, broke the Dutch monopoly system. Under it British shipping was granted free trade throughout the Indian seas. The way was open once more for the British to challenge the Dutch supremacy over the trade of Indonesia. Only two years later a significant step in that direction was taken when Francis Light founded a British settlement at Penang, off the coast of Kedah.

The loss of control by the Dutch over their eastern empire during the war of 1780–4 had further consequences. The Bugis seized the opportunity to threaten Malacca, and only the timely arrival of a Dutch squadron under van Braam saved the city. When in 1783 the Dutch brought about their expulsion from Johore they caused trouble to Dutch interests on the west coast of Borneo and at Banjermasin in the south of the island. This, combined with the foundation of Penang, led the Dutch in 1787 to enforce their control in that region, but not for long. Shortly afterwards trouble began to brew in central Java between the sultanates of Surakarta and Jogjakarta, and in the weakened state of Dutch power might have had serious consequences; happily Dutch pressure on the sunan in 1790 brought about a settlement.

The temporary restoration of Dutch naval power by van Braam's squadron came through the intervention of the home government in the Company's affairs. A committee sent out subsequently to investigate the state of defence of the Dutch eastern empire found the situation alarming. Equally alarming was the unchecked and rapidly mounting deficit in its accounts. In 1789 this stood at 74 million guilders. Two years later it had increased to 96 million guilders, the Company's credit was lost and it could negotiate no further loans in the open market. The States-General must now act. The great question was whether the Company's life could be saved by reform or whether the home government should dissolve it and take over all its responsibilities.

William V, who was reinstated as Stadhouder as a result of the counter-revolution of 1787, was anxious to save the Company. Notwithstanding the failure of previous commissions for reforming it, he appointed in 1791 a high commission composed of Nederburgh, the Company's advocate, and Frijkenius, the officer in charge of its maritime affairs, to proceed to the Indies, where it was to act with Governor-General Alting and van Stockum, the Director-General of Trade at Batavia. Nederburgh and Frijkenius did not arrive in Batavia until 1793. There they joined hands with the ruling clique and proceeded to stifle the demands for reform—for a time.

At the beginning of 1795, however, the troops of General Pichegru overran Holland, overthrew the Stadhouderate and established in its place the Batavian Republic under French protectorate. William V fled to England and issued the 'Kew Letters' by which he ordered the Dutch East Indies officials to place the Company's possessions in British hands as a safeguard against seizure by the French. The British, he explained, had given a solemn pledge to return them to the Netherlands when peace was restored. Under this arrangement the British in 1796 took over control of the Cape of Good Hope and Ceylon. All the Dutch posts in India and on the west coast of Sumatra, as well as Malacca, fell into British hands. In the Moluccas they took Amboina and the Bandas but failed to get Ternate.

The Government of Batavia under Nederburgh's influence was opposed to the policy laid down in the Kew Letters. It was equally opposed to the demands for a more democratic government, which began to arise from groups of free burghers and Company's employees in Java. While, therefore, Nederburgh and Governor-General van Overstraten sternly repressed the Liberal movement, they also prepared to resist any British attempt to occupy the island. But none was made, although the alliance between the Batavian Republic and revolutionary France brought once more a state of war between Britain and the Dutch. For the time being British hands were too full elsewhere.

The change of government at The Hague, however, brought a clear change of policy there towards the eastern empire. The College of

Directors was abolished. In its place a 'Committee for the Affairs of the East Indian Trade and Settlements' was established under close government supervision. In 1798 the decision was taken to wind up the Company itself; its debts and possessions were to be taken over by the State. The decree took effect on 31 December 1799 when the Company's charter expired and was not renewed. Its debt then stood at 134 million guilders.

CHAPTER 18

THE MALAY POWERS FROM THE FALL OF MALACCA (1511) TO THE END OF THE EIGHTEENTH CENTURY

TOMÉ PIRES, who came to Malacca in the year after its conquest by Albuquerque, describes conditions there and throughout the Peninsula in the sixth book of his *Suma Oriental*. He says that from Malacca up to Kedah are the tin lands, all of them previously subject to its sultan. In describing them he mentions Sungei Jugra, Selangor, Klang, Bernam, Mimjam, Bruas and a village called Perak. To the south are Muar and Singapore, the latter of which, he says, consists of only a few villages of Cellates, and is 'nothing much'. On the east coast, he says, Pahang and its tributary state Trengganu are in the land of Siam; but Pahang is also in the empire of Malacca and constantly at war with the Siamese.

When Sultan Mahmud lost the battle for Malacca he and his son fled across country to Pahang, whence he sent an emissary to China beseeching aid against the Portuguese. The Ming emperor, however, pleaded that with a war against the Tartars on his hands he was in no position to fight the Portuguese. Mahmud therefore had to search for a site for a new capital where he could re-establish his sway over the Peninsula and be reasonably safe from the Portuguese. His first settlement was at Sayong Pinang on the upper reaches of a tributary of the Johore river. This turned out to be too far from the sea, and in 1521 he removed to the island of Bintang, south-east of Singapore. Here, however, he was repeatedly attacked by the Portuguese. In 1523 and 1524 he beat them off with heavy loss, and even sent a force to lay siege to Malacca.

But in 1526 the Portuguese counter-attacked, destroyed his capital and gave the island to the Raja of Lingga. Mahmud himself fled to Kampar in Sumatra, where he died in 1528. His younger son Ala'ud-din succeeded him and planted his capital on the Johore river. There for a time he was a serious thorn in the flesh of the Portuguese, until at last in 1536 Dom Estavão da Gama led an expedition which forced him to make peace and take up his residence at Muar.

In the meantime his elder brother Muzaffar Shah had made his way up to Perak, where he founded the dynasty which still reigns there. For a time Perak, Johore and Pahang were content to remain on friendly terms with the Portuguese. They were watching with considerable alarm the rapidly rising power of Acheh, on the north-western tip of Sumatra, which under Sultan Ali Mughayat Shah had gained control over the pepper ports of Pedir and Pasai and was carrying on a rich trade with Gujerat and China. Under his son Ala'ud-din Ri'ayat Shah (1530–68) Acheh became the tough rival of Portuguese Malacca and for many years made repeated efforts to capture the city. Her ambitious policy threatened not only Malacca but also the Malay states of Sumatra and the Peninsula. The Portuguese drove off a surprise attack in 1537. Two years later the Achinese fleet captured Deli in Sumatra. In reply Johore, together with Perak and the Sumatran state of Siak, inflicted a crushing defeat upon the upstart power.

The Achinese setback was only a temporary one. By 1547 they had recovered sufficiently to launch another attack on Malacca. It came perilously near to success, and their Malay rivals were tempted to try their hand at the game. The combined fleet of Johore, Perak and Pahang sailed into the Muar estuary and waited to see what the outcome of the struggle with the Achinese would be. When the Portuguese at last beat off the Sumatran flotilla the Malay fleet sailed away. In 1551 it returned and for three months laid siege to Malacca. An attempt to storm the city was repelled with such determination that it was not repeated. In the end the Portuguese forced the besieging fleet to give up the enterprise by sending a fleet to harry the home harbours of the allies.

Acheh's bid for dominance over the Malay world assumed formidable proportions before the death of the second of the great sultans, Ala'ud-din Ri'ayat Shah, in 1568. He built up a league of states against the Portuguese, obtained gunners, guns and ammunition from Turkey, and amassed a bigger fighting force than ever before. Before striking at Malacca he dealt a staggering blow to his rival, the Sultan of Johore.

In 1564 his armada sacked Johore Lama and took away Sultan Ala'ud-din a captive to Sumatra. For some years after this a bitter feud raged between Johore and Acheh, and Johore swung over to the Portuguese side. So much so that in 1568, when Acheh's great attack was made on Malacca, the Portuguese sought Johore's aid. This was granted, but when the Johore fleet of sixty vessels arrived the Portuguese had already beaten off the Achinese. By way of retaliation an

Achinese fleet sailed up the Johore river and burnt a number of villages.

The ding-dong struggle between Acheh and Malacca continued until 1575, when, for a reason never explained, the Achinese fleet, after threatening Malacca, turned north and conquered Perak, killing its sultan, a kinsman of the Johore house, and carrying away his widow and children to Acheh. This caused some extraordinary changes in the Malay situation. The captive Crown Prince of Perak married an Achinese princess and in 1579 succeeded his father-in-law as Sultan Ala'ud-din Mansur Shah. He in turn married his daughter to Sultan Ali Jalla Abdul-Jalil Ri'ayat Shah of Johore and sent his younger brother to rule Perak as vassal raja.

The Johore marriage, however, did not improve the relations between the two states. In 1582 the Portuguese helped the Johore sultan to beat off an Achinese attack. In 1585 Mansur Shah appears to have been murdered by the admiral of his fleet. Four years later the murderer became Sultan Ala'ud-din Ri'ayat Shah (1589–1604). It was in his reign that the Dutch, French and English first visited Acheh. For a space there was a lull in the Acheh-Johore struggle. In 1584 the Portuguese had quarrelled with their ally over matters arising out of their trade monopoly. As a result in 1586, and again in 1587, Johore besieged Malacca and blockaded it by land and sea. She also made an alliance with Acheh. But it was of very short duration, for when the Portuguese made a great counter-attack, sending an expedition up the Johore river which destroyed Johore Lama and carried away immense booty, Acheh sent formal congratulations to Malacca.

Thus the triangular struggle continued. The feud between the two Malay empires was in the last resort of greater moment to them than their desire to drive out the Portuguese. By the end of the century Johore had recovered sufficiently to threaten Acheh so seriously that Ala'ud-din Ri'ayat Shah sent an embassy to Malacca to ask for help. And the Portuguese, with the Dutch and English trespassing in their preserves, decided that the wise course would be to bury the hatchet provided the sultan would kill Dutch 'pirates' and hand over his strongest fort. But the fortunes of war changed suddenly, as so often before, and the alliance did not take place. Then the sultan, having in 1599 killed Cornelis de Houtman and taken his brother Frederick prisoner, became alarmed at his dangerous isolation. And since he feared an alliance between the Portuguese and Johore more than the vengeance of the Dutch, he decided to turn the Dutch hostility against the Portuguese to his own advantage. Hence he released his Dutch prisoners and sent envoys to Holland. He even sent an expedition to besiege Johore's new capital at Batu Sawar, but without success.

The arrival of the Dutch and the English presented Johore, as well as Acheh, with new opportunities. Johore also saw in the Dutch a potential ally against her old enemy Portugal and began to listen to Dutch proposals for a joint attack upon Malacca, seemingly regardless of the fact that the Dutch had no intention whatever of restoring the city to Malay rule. In 1606 they joined in an attack on Malacca. But it failed, and for a time the sultan's confidence in the Dutch weakened so that he wavered.

In the following year a new ruler, Iskandar Shah, seized the throne of Acheh and began to pursue an expansionist policy with great vigour. Taking advantage of the decline of Portuguese power he extended his control not only over further coastal regions of Sumatra but also over the mainland states of Pahang (1618), Kedah (1619) and, most important of all because of its tin, Perak (1620). In 1613, and again in 1615, the Achinese sacked Johore because its sultan was negotiating with Malacca. In 1616, therefore, the Sultan of Johore deemed it prudent to join Iskandar Shah in a big attack on Malacca. Again it failed: the Portuguese with their backs to the wall proved themselves very tough fighters, still able to maintain possession of the famous emporium.

Nevertheless the expansion of the power of Acheh was indeed spectacular. In writing to James I of England Iskandar claimed overlordship over Johore itself. This was mere wishful thinking, but his control over both sides of the Straits of Malacca was extending to such a degree that he looked like gaining supremacy over all the native states of the Peninsula and the north-western parts of the Archipelago. On the other hand, his deportations of thousands of people from the states he conquered stirred up a deep hatred of the Achinese yoke and a movement to get rid of it. In 1629 the united forces of Malacca, Johore and Patani inflicted a crushing defeat on the Achinese fleet near Malacca. Thereafter the power of Acheh began to decline as rapidly as it had arisen. Iskandar died in 1636. He was succeeded by an adopted son Iskandar II. He died in 1641, the year in which the Dutch captured Malacca. Then for sixty years Acheh was ruled by queens. The pressure of the Dutch and their support of Johore caused Acheh to lose all her territories on the Peninsula except Perak.

Johore's great hope had been to recover Malacca through alliance with the Dutch. Her sultan styled himself King of Johore and Malacca.

The Dutch, however, refused to recognize his claim to the city. Nevertheless such was his hatred of the Portuguese that Sultan Abdul Jalil made a treaty with the Dutch in 1637 by which he undertook to co-operate with them in an attack upon the city, and in the final struggle in 1640–1 assisted them with a fleet of forty sail. He had already added Pahang to his dominions when Acheh's control over it lapsed. Now, free from any further threat from either the Portuguese or Acheh, he proceeded to build a new capital at Makam Tauhid, near the present Kota Tinggi. He was still the titular head of a great empire which included most of the Malay states of the Peninsula, the Riau Archipelago and Bengkalis, Kampar and Siak in Sumatra. Only when it was too late did he begin to realize that whereas the Portuguese had chastised with whips, the Dutch were to chastise with scorpions.

No sooner had they taken Malacca than the Dutch began to seek to control the tin-producing states. Tin was their main interest in the Peninsula; it was of prime importance to them in their commercial dealings with both India and the Chinese. In 1639 they had made a contract with Acheh permitting them to purchase tin in Perak. In 1641 the first Dutch Governor of Malacca presented the Sultan of Perak with a demand that he should stop all dealings with foreigners and in future sell all his tin to the V.O.C. When he refused to do so, Dutch cruisers blockaded the entrance to the Perak river. When, however, he still managed to evade their persistent attempts to establish a monopoly over his export trade the Dutch in 1650 extorted from his suzerain, the Queen of Acheh, a treaty whereby the Company was to share the Perak tin trade equally with her and to the exclusion of all other traders.

The subsequent history of Dutch relations with Acheh and Perak over the tin question may be briefly told. The 1650 agreement satisfied no one. It was detrimental to the large trade carried on between Acheh and Surat, through which quantities of Indian textiles came to Sumatra and the Peninsula. As a result the Dutch factory at Surat was attacked and plundered. Moreover, in 1651, with the connivance of Acheh, the Dutch factory at Perak also was attacked and plundered and nine of its officials killed. And they were too busy elsewhere to send a punitive expedition. In 1653 Sultan Muzaffar of Perak promised to restore the 1650 agreement, pay compensation for the loss of the Dutch factory, and execute the chiefs responsible for the murders. But he made no attempt to carry out his undertaking.

In 1655 the Dutch approached the sultan through Acheh, and in the presence of Achinese ambassadors he signed a further agreement to the same effect. Again, however, he failed to carry it out, and when the Achinese put new difficulties in the way of the Dutch it became obvious that as their rivals for the Perak trade they were double-crossing them. The Dutch therefore blockaded both ports, Perak and Acheh. In 1657 the Achinese replied by destroying the Dutch factories in their subject ports of Priaman, Tiku and Salido in Sumatra. Batavia thereupon sent a naval force to attack these ports and tightened the blockade of Perak and Acheh. Again Acheh climbed down. In 1659 an Achinese embassy was received at Batavia by Governor-General Joan Maetsuycker, and a treaty was signed which provided for the payment of compensation through a reduction in the price of the tin bought by the Dutch in Perak and a division of the trade whereby the Achinese were to take one-third and the V.O.C. two-thirds of Perak's tin export.[1]

This treaty, however, had no more value than its predecessors, since at this time the woman who exercised the sultan's powers at Acheh was merely the head of a confederation of chiefs, over whom, the Dutch were to discover, she had little or no real control. As we have seen, Johore and Pahang had already successfully asserted their independence of Acheh. Now Perak, annoyed by Acheh's action in concluding the treaty, threatened to transfer her allegiance to Johore. As things turned out, however, the Dutch tin trade with Perak improved considerably, for the reason that Acheh's decline became so marked that few of her vessels visited the port.

In their dealings with other tin states the Dutch had mixed success. In 1642 they made an agreement with Kedah for the delivery of half its product. In 1643 Junk Ceylon, and in 1645 Bangeri, promised the Dutch the whole of their product. Kedah, however, evaded her agreement, and the Dutch in retaliation resorted to blockade. The Malays indeed would appear to have been annoyed that a treaty should have been considered anything more than a diplomatic gesture. When the Dutch found themselves unable to maintain an effective blockade owing to Kedah's distance from Malacca and her easy communications with the Coromandel Coast, they tried to enlist Siamese support. In 1664 they made a treaty with Siam which granted them free trade with the Malay states under her suzerainty. But her overlordship over Kedah meant little or nothing in practice, and all the Dutch efforts to coerce the little state failed. With other states under Siamese

---

[1] Winstedt, *History of Malaya*, p. 132, says the tin was to be divided equally between the V.O.C. and Acheh, but Stapel's statement in *Geschiedenis van Nederlandsch Indië*, iii, p. 358, is the more acceptable.

control, notably Ligor and Selangor, they had better success, and ultimately made monopolistic agreements.

The decline of Acheh entailed the loss of her control not only over the states of the Peninsula but also over the Minangkabau pepper ports of west Sumatra. With these the Dutch long sought to make individual agreements by which they were to forsake their allegiance to Acheh and come under the Company's protection. In 1663 they were at last successful with an agreement known as the Painan Contract, which was signed by a number of West Coast sultans granting the V.O.C. an absolute monopoly over the pepper trade, together with freedom from tolls, in return for protection. It resulted in much fighting and led the Dutch to withdraw their factories from Acheh and Perak. But it brought the west coast of Sumatra practically under Dutch supervision.

The Dutch conquest of Malacca and the decline of Acheh offered Abdul Jalil a good opportunity to strengthen the position of Johore. In 1644 his younger brother married the Queen of Patani. Fear of the Dutch gave him Jambi and Acheh as allies, while the weakness of Acheh enabled him to extend his power over Siak and Indragiri on the east coast of Sumatra. For a time his capital became an important centre of trade, and he a rich man. But in 1666, owing to a broken contract of marriage between his heir and a daughter of the Pangéran of Jambi, resulting from the intrigues of an ambitious *laksamana* of Johore, who married his own daughter to the prince, the two states drifted into a chronic condition of warfare. In 1673 Jambi sacked Batu Sawar, Abdul Jalil's capital, and the old sultan fled to Pahang, where he died three years later at the age of ninety.

His nephew and successor Ibrahim settled at Riau, whence he carried on the struggle. But his empire was already falling apart. Unable to gain a decisive success, he called to his aid a Bugis mercenary leader Daing Mangika, who in 1679 sacked Jambi in retribution for her treatment of Johore six years earlier. The war, however, continued, and in 1682 Ibrahim wrote to Governor-General Cornelis Speelman suggesting a revival of the old alliance originally made in 1603, when an embassy had been sent to Prince Maurice at The Hague. Speelman replied by asking for the monopoly of the trade of Johore and Pahang.

Before anything came of the negotiations Ibrahim died in 1683, leaving a young son Mahmud to succeed him under the regency of his mother and Paduka Raja, the *laksamana* who had brought on the war with Jambi. The Governor of Malacca at once sent an envoy to ask for a monopoly of Siak's newly discovered tin. The regency, unable to control the Minangkabaus of that district, signed a treaty granting it in return for a Dutch undertaking to mediate between Johore and Jambi. The treaty, however, proved futile, and when in 1688 Paduka Raja was driven out and replaced by a new chief minister, who took the young sultan away from Riau back to Kota Tinggi on the mainland, a new one was made in 1689. This confirmed the provisions of the earlier one, granted the Dutch toll-free trade in Johore until the sultan came of age, and added a prohibition to Indian traders to settle in the Johore dominions. Winstedt asserts that this treaty also was futile.[1] F. W. Stapel on the other hand describes it as 'very profitable', and is of opinion that it greatly strengthened the Dutch position at Siak at the end of the seventeenth century.[2]

Mahmud turned out to be a pervert and sadist whose cruelties caused his murder in 1699. He was the last of the old Malacca royal line to rule in Johore. He was succeeded by the chief minister, Bendahara Sri Maharaja Tun Habib Abdul Jalil. But family feuds caused him to leave affairs of state in the hands of his brother the Raja Muda, and the latter's tyranny led to so much dissension that in 1717 the Minangkabau ruler of Siak, Raja Kechil, surprised Johore Lama and seized the throne. Abdul Jalil was reduced once more to the position of bendahara. In the *Malay Annals* the new ruler is known under the title Abdul Jalil Rahmat Shah.

Raja Kechil ruled the Johore dominions from Riau. In 1718 the deposed sultan intrigued with Daing Parani, a Bugis chief who had served Raja Kechil in Sumatra and was disappointed in his expectations of receiving the office of Yam-tuan Muda of Johore. The plot failed, and the fugitive Abdul Jalil was put to death while attempting to flee to Pahang. In 1722, however, Daing Parani and his Bugis followers drove out Raja Kechil and placed a son of Abdul Jalil on the throne. The new sultan was forced to appoint Daing Parani's eldest brother Yam-tuan Muda, or Under-king, of Riau and reign as the puppet of the Bugis. From then onwards the Bugis were the real rulers of Johore.

Malayan history throughout the eighteenth century is the story of Bugis ascendancy. The dominant people in Celebes in the seventeenth century, they become known to history first as mercenaries fighting for the Dutch. The Aru Palacca of Boni led a contingent of Bugis volunteers in Speelman's campaign against Macassar in 1666–7. They were of much assistance to the Dutch in the conquest of Mataram.

[1] *Op. cit.*, p. 146.   [2] *Op. cit.*, iii, p. 460.

Their native country was in the south-west limb of the island, where they were organized in a number of small states, which from time to time formed confederations. They were a maritime people and ranked among the most advanced in Indonesia. The Bongais Treaty of 1667, which ended the independence of Macassar, and the ruin of the Moluccas caused them to roam far and wide. Their pirate fleets swarmed all over the Archipelago, and before the end of the century had begun to attack the coasts of Java, Sumatra and the Peninsula. As early as 1681 there were large Bugis settlements on the Klang and Selangor estuaries.

Daing Parani, who secured Bugis ascendancy over Johore in 1722, was one of five famous brothers who had left Celebes to seek their fortunes in Borneo, the Riau Archipelago and the Peninsula. Riau now became the centre of their influence. From it they established control over the tin states of Kedah and Perak. A dynastic struggle in Kedah led to their being invited to assist a new sultan against his rebellious brother. For this they received a huge cash payment, and Daing Parani married the sultan's sister. In 1724 their enemy the Minangkabau Raja Kechil of Siak, whom they had driven out of Riau, led a force to Kedah against them, and for two years the Minangkabau and the Bugis fought for the possession of the state. The war had disastrous effects upon Kedah's trade. Daing Parani was killed, but in the end the Bugis drove Raja Kechil back to Siak.

Then the struggle spread to Perak and Selangor. Daing Parani's brother Daing Merewah, the Under-king of Riau, led an invasion of Perak, where Minangkabau warriors and Kedah chiefs were seeking to gain control over the country. This also was successful, and Bugis dominance established over a third state. Selangor was raided by a son of Raja Kechil and a renegade Bugis chieftain. This situation was dealt with by another of the famous brothers, Daing Chelak, who had succeeded Daing Merewah as Under-king of Riau. He and his puppet, Sultan Sulaiman, expelled the raiders. His son Raja Luma was then created sultan of Selangor, the first in its history. Two years later in 1742 he led another invasion of Perak to re-establish Bugis control against further Minangkabau interference.

This immense upsurge of Bugis activity and influence alarmed the Dutch. Their long efforts to monopolize the tin of Malaya were now in danger of coming to grief before the competition of Bugis traders under the protection of the fighting fleets of Riau. In 1745, therefore, they began to rebuild their fort at the Dindings. By that time there were signs that the Malays themselves were looking round for help to get rid of Bugis control. Sultan Sulaiman made a treaty with van Imhoff by which in return for a promise of Dutch assistance he ceded Siak besides granting them once again the tin monopoly in his dominions. So strong was Malay hostility at Riau that Daing Kemboja, who had become the power behind the throne at Riau, found it safer to transfer his headquarters to Linggi.

For some time the Dutch made no move to take over Siak. In 1753, however, a palace revolution there placed on the throne a ruler who began a commercial war against them. In 1755, therefore, they expelled him. Then they made a fresh treaty with Sultan Sulaiman by which they promised him help in recovering his lost possessions from the Bugis. He in his turn appointed a regent to look after Dutch interests at Siak and conferred on the Company the tin monopoly in Selangor, Klang and Linggi. Dutch ships also were to trade free of tolls throughout his kingdom.

There was now open war between the Dutch and the Bugis. In 1756 the Bugis attacked Malacca. In retaliation the Dutch, together with the forces of Trengganu, attacked the Bugis stronghold at Linggi. The fighting at both places was long and bitter, but in the end the Bugis were defeated. As a safeguard Sultan Sulaiman ceded Rembau and Linggi to the Dutch, and on 1 January 1758 the three Bugis leaders, Daing Kemboja of Linggi, Raja Tua of Klang, and Raja Adil of Rembau, signed a treaty of peace with the Dutch and confirmed the sultan's grant of the tin monopoly.

The empire of Johore was now a thing of the past. Selangor was an independent state under a Bugis sultan. The smaller inland states were under Minangkabaus or Bugis. Pahang was under Minangkabau chiefs. Anarchy reigned in Johore itself. And Siak was about to be lost, and just before his death in 1759 its vassal ruler, Sultan Muhammad, massacred the Dutch garrison on the island of Guntung. In 1761, therefore, the Dutch sent a punitive expedition which installed their own nominee as sultan. To complete the picture, in 1759, shortly before the death of Sultan Sulaiman, the Bugis leader Raja Haji, nephew of Daing Kemboja, staged a coup d'état at Riau and reinstated his uncle as under-king of the Johore dominions. In the next year, when Sulaiman himself died, the Bugis murdered his successor, and Daing Kemboja, as the guardian of his infant grandson born in that same year, thus remained the de facto ruler of the state.

Under Daing Kemboja's rule the imperial sway of Johore saw a temporary revival, mainly through the military prowess of Raja Haji and partly through his skill in maintaining good relations with the

Dutch. Raja Haji forced the rulers of Jambi and Indragiri to pay homage to Johore, thereby reviving her influence in Sumatra. Then he sailed north to deal with Perak and Kedah. The Sultan of Perak made the necessary acknowledgements, but the Sultan of Kedah resisted. For so doing he was deposed and expelled.

In 1771 Francis Light, later to be the founder of Penang, had urged the Madras authorities to guarantee the sultan's independence and accept his offer of a seaport in return. But when the East India Company learnt that the sultan wanted military help against a possible attack by the Bugis Sultan of Selangor, Raja Haji's brother, the negotiations broke down. The excuse was that such a move would cause trouble with the Dutch. How completely irrelevant this was becomes clear when one realizes that the decay of Dutch power was the main cause of the Bugis threat to the sultan's independence. So the way was left open for Raja Haji and his Selangor brother to gain control over Kedah and an ample share of the revenue drawn by its sultan from its extensive trade with Bengal, Surat and Sumatra.

In 1777, when Daing Kemboja died, Raja Haji went to Riau and wrested the chief authority from the dead leader's son, his cousin, although the latter had received Dutch recognition as his father's successor. For some time he maintained friendly relations with the Dutch, but in 1782 they quarrelled and the Bugis began to raid Dutch positions in the Malacca Straits. In 1783 a Dutch attempt to capture Riau failed through mismanagement. Thereupon Raja Haji, gathering together his utmost strength, besieged Malacca. He had caught the Dutch on the wrong foot; they were fully engaged in their disastrous 'Fourth English War' (1780–4) and could not muster adequate naval strength to defend their eastern empire. But Malacca stood firm. In June 1784 van Braam with a fleet of six ships, sent out from Holland in an attempt to restore their fortunes, suddenly attacked the besieging force and completely destroyed it, killing Raja Haji in the process.

In August van Braam followed up this success by driving its Bugis sultan out of Selangor. Then in October he expelled the Bugis from Riau and dictated a treaty whereby the sultan, the bendahara and the temenggong acknowledged that the port and kingdom were Dutch property and that they must entertain a Dutch Resident and garrison. In June 1785 the first Resident entered into occupation.

The war, however, had only finished its first phase. In that same year the Bugis Sultan of Selangor, Ibrahim, returned, and the Dutch garrison, unable to hold out against his attacks, evacuated their fort and fled to Malacca. He was soon blockaded by a Dutch fleet. In the vain hope of English assistance, he defied the beleaguering force for a year, but had finally to accept Dutch authority.

The Dutch hold on Riau was next challenged. Sultan Mahmud had sought the assistance of the dreaded Ilanuns of Borneo. In May 1787 they arrived and drove out not only the Dutch but also the sultan himself and his Malay chiefs. The fugitive sultan sought help first of the Dutch and next of Captain Francis Light, who in the previous year had taken possession of Penang for the English East India Company. When these overtures failed he formed a coalition composed of Trengganu, Kedah, Rembau, Siak, Solok, Lingga, Indragiri, Siantan and Johore, which had the declared aim of driving both the Dutch and the English from Malayan waters. But after some ineffectual attacks on the Dutch fort at the Dindings and the coast of Penang the grandiose coalition dissolved. The Dutch recovered Riau, the Ilanuns returned home, the Bugis migrated to Selangor, Siantan and Borneo, and the Malays, stimulated by Mahmud, turned to piracy.

Such remained the situation until in 1795 the French revolutionary armies overran Holland, and as a result of the Kew Letters, issued by the exiled Dutch government, the English began to occupy the Dutch possessions in the East. When that happened the Dutch had just concluded an agreement by which they had undertaken to restore the fugitive sultan. It was the English, however, who reinstated Mahmud and incidentally removed the Dutch garrison from Riau. In so doing they restored also the Bugis to power.

This revolution in Riau was to have consequences of no little interest, for the Bugis leader Raja Ali, by driving out the Malay under-king Enku Muda, started a feud which not only caused much trouble in the Malay world for a good many years but also presented Raffles in 1819 with the perfect opportunity for creating a sultan from whom to purchase the island of Singapore. For Raja Ali resisted all Mahmud's attempts to drive him out of Riau so stubbornly that at length in 1803 the sultan accepted him as under-king and gave him his younger son Tengku Abdur-Rahman to bring up. Then three years later, having failed to persuade the disappointed Engku Muda to accept it, he conferred the office of temenggong upon the Malay chief's nephew. At the same time he entrusted his elder son Tengku Hussein to Engku Muda to bring up, and in due course marry to his daughter. The new temenggong was the one who in 1819 was to enter into the famous deal with Raffles; while Tengku Hussein, cheated of his succession to the throne at his father's death by Raja

Ali's successor as under-king, was the sultan created by Raffles to give legal semblance to that deal.

The feud between Raja Ali and Engku Muda had its repercussions in other Malay states also. In 1800 the Bugis Sultan Ibrahim of Selangor intervened in support of his relative. Soon afterwards the Perak chiefs, unaware that the Bugis had the upper hand at Riau, sent an ill-timed offer of their throne to Sultan Mahmud. This brought down on them the full force of Sulaiman's wrath. In 1804 he conquered Perak, driving out the reigning sultan and holding the state for two years. In 1806, however, a new sultan of the old line succeeded, and when Sulaiman made a further attack to regain control the defence was too strong for him. Nevertheless he continued for many years, as Winstedt puts it, 'to fish in the troubled waters of the Perak river'.[1]

By the end of the eighteenth century, save in Selangor, the Bugis' ambitions had received, or were about to receive, a series of decisive checks, mainly through the intervention of outside powers. One further one remains to be recorded. Behind Malacca ever since the fifteenth century Malays from the Minangkabau region of Sumatra had been coming across to form new settlements. By the time of the Dutch conquest of Malacca in 1641 there were Minangkabau colonies at Naning, Rembau, Sungai Ujong and Klang. In the latter half of the century the Dutch had some trouble with them. In the early part of the eighteenth century the Bugis became the dominant factor in Malacca's hinterland and kept the Minangkabau power in check. Van Braam's conquest of Selangor and the expulsion of the Bugis from Riau by the Dutch left the way open for the formation of a loose coalition of the small Minangkabau states with a ruling dynasty at its head. Its founder, Raja Melewar (1773–95), claimed descent from the royal house of Minangkabau in Sumatra, which itself claimed descent from the Sailendras of Srivijaya fame. He seems to have been recognized by the Dutch Governor of Malacca, and by carefully eschewing rivalry with any of the powerful chiefs he gradually built up a compact wedge of Minangkabau states. At his death in 1795, the year in which the British took over Malacca and readmitted the Bugis to Riau, what is now the state of Negri Sembilan had become an independent unit.[1]

With the coming of the nineteenth century Malaya stood on the threshold of a new era. The ambitions of the Bugis had been thwarted. Dutch power was temporarily in abeyance while Napoleon dominated Europe. The Malay empire of Johore was at its last gasp. Meanwhile Siam, after her disastrous defeat by the Burmese in 1767, had made a

[1] *History of Malaya*, p. 163.

wonderful recovery, and under the new Chakri dynasty was beginning to revive her ancient claims over the Malay states. Finally the
British, having planted their flag on the island of Penang in 1786 and
occupied Malacca in 1795, were engaged in a mighty struggle with
France, and consequently were determined to deny their rival the
strategic advantages in the Indian Ocean which the occupation of the
Netherlands Indies would confer on her. Moreover, in 1805 the young
Stamford Raffles was to arrive in Penang. And although some ten
years later he was to be prevented from realizing his dream of substituting British for Dutch control over the Archipelago, he was nevertheless by the occupation of Singapore to do something of decisive
importance to the future of Malaya.

CHAPTER 19

SIAM AND THE EUROPEAN POWERS IN THE SEVENTEENTH CENTURY

NARESUEN, the 'Black Prince' of Siam, who turned the tables on the Burmese and restored the independence of his country, holds one of the most honoured places in her history. After the failure of his attack on Toungoo in 1600 he concentrated his attention upon the Shan states, all of which had become independent when Nanda Bayin was finally defeated in 1599. But, as we have seen, the Nyaungyan Prince, with Ava as his base, was soon engaged upon the task of reconquering them, and while campaigning against him in 1605 Naresuen died of a carbuncle.

His brother, the 'White King', succeeded him with the title of Ekat'otsarat. He was unwarlike and so the Siamese effort in the Shan states was abandoned and Burma recovered them. Ekat'otsarat was interested in financial reform and trade, and during his brief reign of five years the Dutch trading connection with Siam was established. In 1602 they opened a factory at Patani and in 1608 at Ayut'ia. Both places were important centres for Chinese and Japanese trade. The Japanese had been the first foreign traders to settle in Siam as soon as Naresuen's victories over the Burmese made a resumption of peaceful trade possible. Many of them were converts of the Jesuit missionaries in Japan and came to Siam when the religious policy of the Shogun Iyeyasu made their position unsafe in their own country. At Ayut'ia they were granted a settlement of their own by Ekat'otsarat, who enlisted a large force of them in his bodyguard under the command of their headman, Yamada. Siam also exchanged complimentary missions with the great shogun.

At both Patani and Ayut'ia the Dutch had to face the opposition of the Portuguese and the Japanese, but they were welcomed at both places by the rulers, and in 1609 a Siamese embassy from Ayut'ia was received at The Hague by Maurice of Nassau. It was the first recorded visit of Siamese to Europe. In 1610 Ekat'otsarat was succeeded by his son Int'araja, who is referred to in Siamese history as Songt'am, 'the Just'. His accession was the signal for a Japanese rising which

SIAMESE DANCING

for a time threatened to bring disaster to the kingdom. They rose because the minister who was their patron was executed on account of the part he had played in a conspiracy which had caused the death of the Maha Uparat in the previous reign. They sacked Ayut'ia and then made off to P'etchaburi, which they fortified and prepared to hold. At the same time the King of Luang Prabang invaded Siam on the pretext of coming to expel the Japanese. Songt'am, however, was equal to the emergency. He reduced P'etchaburi and then turned and inflicted a decisive defeat on the invaders. The Japanese seem to have made terms with the king, for they were retained in the royal body-guard and Yamada himself was given a Siamese title of honour.

Peace was restored in 1612, the year in which the *Globe* appeared at Ayut'ia bringing a complimentary letter from King James I of England. Notwithstanding Dutch opposition, Songt'am permitted the East India Company to establish a factory at his capital. In the following year Anaukpetlun of Burma captured Syriam and put an end to the stormy career of Philip de Brito. He then proceeded to strike at the parts of Bayinnaung's empire held by Siam. Binnya Dala handed over Martaban to him without a blow, but further south there was some severe fighting during the course of the year 1614. The Burmese, as we have seen, recovered Moulmein and Tavoy, but failed to capture Tenasserim, which was defended by Portuguese auxiliaries in the service of Siam.

In the following year the war was switched to Chiengmai, which the Burmese took. After three more years of struggle, during which the Siamese failed to regain the place, a truce was negotiated in 1618 which left the Burmese in possession of their gains. The cessation of the war was probably due to an event which took place in Cambodia in that year. Taking advantage of the Siamese preoccupation with the Chiengmai question, the Cambodians declared their independence and drove out the Siamese garrison, which Naresuen had placed in their capital in 1594. In 1622 a Siamese attempt to restore their control over Lovek failed. During the rest of his reign Songt'am repeatedly sought to enlist Dutch and English support against Cambodia, but both were unwilling to commit themselves to such a dubious adventure and Cambodia retained her independence. Although he had acted with firmness in face of the Japanese revolt and the Luang Prabang invasion, Songt'am disliked war. He had been a monk when called to the throne and was fond of study and devoted to religious exercises.

Relations between the English and the Dutch in Siam became steadily worse. The sea fight at Patani in 1619, in which John Jourdain lost his life, has been chronicled elsewhere. At Ayut'ia the Dutch had the advantage over the English as a result of the agreement they made with Songt'am in 1617 for the purchase of hides. In 1622 the English factories at both Patani and Ayut'ia were closed down, and for thirty-seven years they had no regular trade with Siam. The Dutch also closed their factory at Patani; trade there did not fulfil the great expectations cherished by both companies when they first settled there. At Ayut'ia, however, with the departure of the English they became stronger than ever.

When Songt'am died, while still a young man, in 1628, he was succeeded by his son Jett'a. He was a puppet in the hands of P'ya Sri Worawong, a cousin of Songt'am, who had had a stormy career and seized power with the help of the Japanese leader Yamada. In 1630 the ambitious minister seized the throne for himself and assumed the title of Prasat T'ong, the King of the Golden Palace. His nickname among the people was 'the bottled spider'. At the moment of his usurpation Yamada turned against him and essayed the role of king-maker. He succeeded, however, in outwitting the Japanese leader, who was promptly poisoned. Then after a bloody struggle in 1632 culminating in a massacre of the Japanese in Ayut'ia the survivors were expelled from the kingdom. The trouble with the Japanese played into the hands of the Dutch, who established even closer relations with the usurper and promised him their support against his enemies. In 1632 Prince Frederick Henry of the Netherlands sent a letter congratulating Prasat T'ong on his accession to the throne, and in 1634 the Dutch were permitted to build 'a stone lodge, with fit packhouses, pleasant apartments and a commodious landing-place' on the river-bank at Ayut'ia.[1]

But although Joost Schouten, who was the Dutch Agent at the time of Prasat T'ong's usurpation, described him in 1636 as 'ruling with great reputation and honour', his successor, Jeremias van Vliet, paints a very different picture of his rule.[2] The explanation is that relations between the Dutch and the 'bottled spider' passed through some critical phases. The Siamese became uneasy at the prosperity and power of the Dutch as a result of the elimination of their rivals. The reign was, moreover, one of murders and revolts, and the king on more than one occasion quarrelled with the Dutch over their failure to give

---

[1] Joost Schouten: *A True Description of the Mighty Kingdoms of Japan and Siam*, Roger Manley's translation, London, 1663, pp. 151–2.

[2] Jeremias van Vliet, *Révolutions arrivées au Siam en 1647*, Paris, 1663, and *Description of the Kingdom of Siam*, van Ravenswaay's translation in *Journal of the Siam Society*, vol. vii, pt. i.

him the help they had promised. Early on, the Queen of Patani refused to recognize his seizure of the throne and described him as a
'rascal, murderer and traitor'. In 1632, and again in 1634, the royal
army failed badly in attacks upon Patani. On the first occasion the
Dutch sent no help; on the second it came too late, though through
no fault of theirs. In 1636, when a further attack was planned, a
reconciliation was effected through Dutch mediation. But in that
year a further quarrel arose over the Siamese deliveries of rice
and an attack was made on two Dutch factors at Ayut'ia, who
were arrested and sentenced to be trampled to death by elephants.
Their lives were only saved by heavy bribes to the king and chief
ministers.

After this incident there was a long period of better relations. The
goodwill of the king was sedulously cultivated by the Dutch authorities, both at Batavia and The Hague. The growing strength of Batavia
and the conquest of Malacca in 1641 were not without their effects
upon the Dutch attitude towards the king. Thus when in 1649 the
Court of Ayut'ia failed to satisfy certain claims put forward by the
Dutch, van Vliet threatened to call in the Dutch fleet to attack the
city. This caused a serious crisis. The factory was besieged and all
its inmates arrested and threatened with death. Five years later, when
another crisis blew up over the Dutch refusal to assist Prasat T'ong
against rebellious Singora, van Vliet's successor, Westerwolt threatened to close the factory and leave the country. On this occasion a
Dutch naval demonstration was staged in the Gulf of Siam with appreciable effect. Prasat T'ong climbed down and there was no further
trouble.

When Prasat T'ong died in 1656 there was an uneasy period of a
few months during which two short-lived kings came to the throne
and were murdered. They were followed by Narai, a younger son of
Prasat T'ong, whose long reign of thirty-one years (1657–88) is of
unusual interest in the history of European rivalry in South-East Asia.
Apart from a recurrence of the perennial struggle with Burma for
Chiengmai, King Narai's policy was mainly concerned with efforts to
free himself from the economic control which the Dutch had been
gradually fastening upon his country during his father's reign. And
by inviting the assistance of Louis XIV of France he created a situation
which not only made his country for a time of no little importance in
the calculations of the European naval powers but developed to a
degree of dramatic intensity only equalled by the Paknam incident of
1893.

The renewal of the struggle for Chiengmai resulted from the confusion wrought in Burma and the Shan states through the flight of Yung Li, the last Ming emperor, from Yunnan to Bhamo in 1658.[1] Chiengmai, in terror of a Chinese invasion, felt impelled to seek Siamese aid. But when in 1660 Narai led a large force northwards better news from Ava caused Chiengmai to change its mind and the king was forced to retire. In 1661 the unsuccessful Mon revolt at Martaban led to a Burmese invasion of Siam by the Ataran river and the Three Pagodas Pass towards Kanburi, and during the lull in the Chinese invasions of Burma, caused by the energetic mopping-up operations of the Manchus in Yunnan, it looked as if the full-scale struggles of the latter half of the previous century between the two powers were about to be revived. But the Siamese easily drove out the invading force; and although they followed up their victory by raiding deeply into Burma in 1662, their real interest was in Chiengmai. Early in that year they had captured the city, and King Pye of Ava, threatened by the Manchus, was powerless to intervene. The Siamese were, however, quite unable to hold on to the place. In 1664 the people of Chiengmai rose in revolt and drove them out, and a Burmese prince was again installed as a vassal of Ava. It was to remain under Burmese control until 1727.

In 1659 the English factors of the East India Company's Cambodian factory, established at Lovek in 1654, were forced by an Annamite invasion to flee the country. They took refuge at Ayut'ia, where they were so warmly welcomed by Narai that in 1661 the Company reopened its factory there. In April of the following year Bishop Lambert de la Motte of the French Société des Missions Etrangères landed at Mergui en route for Annam. The society had been founded in Paris in 1659 with the object of undertaking missionary work, independently of the Jesuits, in China, Annam and Tongking. Louis XIV backed the scheme. It was bitterly opposed not only by the Jesuits, who had been in the field since the pioneer days of St. Francis Xavier in the middle of the sixteenth century, but also by Spain and Portugal,[2] who realized that it was intended as a means of spreading French influence in the Far East. The Pope, in an effort to disarm the opposition of the Archbishop of Goa, who claimed authority over all missionaries working in the East, conferred upon the bishops sent out

---

[1] *Infra*, pp. 379–81

[2] The Portuguese still guarded their old privileges granted by papal bulls during the sixteenth century. Under these, missionaries going to the East must embark at Lisbon and must have the permission of the King of Portugal. On arrival in the East they came under the jurisdiction of the Archbishop of Goa.

to organize the work on a territorial basis obsolete titles of bishoprics in existence in Asia Minor before its conversion to Islam, together with the rank of Vicar-Apostolic. Lambert de la Motte, for instance, was Bishop of Beritus.

His original intention had been to proceed to western China by the Irrawaddy and the old overland route from Bhamo. But owing to the news of Chinese incursions into Burma, which he received at Masuli-patam before crossing the Bay of Bengal, he decided to go to Ayut'ia, where he hoped to obtain a passage to Annam. After leaving Ayut'ia, however, his ship was wrecked and he had to return to the Siamese capital, where in January 1664 he was joined by a second missionary prelate, Pallu, Bishop of Heliopolis, and four priests. News of the outbreak of a very severe persecution of Catholics in Annam caused the two bishops to remain in Siam; and finding the king well disposed, they decided to make Ayut'ia the headquarters of their mission. They were permitted to build a church and a seminary there, and before long their priests began to penetrate into various parts of the country.

The favour shown by Narai to the English and the French aroused the hostility of the Dutch, who demanded additional commercial privileges. When these were rejected, a Dutch fleet blockaded the mouth of the Menam, and Narai, unable to resist this form of pressure, had to climb down. In August 1664 he signed a treaty granting the Dutch the monopoly of the trade in hides, the practical monopoly of sea-borne trade between Ayut'ia and China, and certain extra-territorial rights of jurisdiction. The Dutch had won the first round; but their victory made the king all the more anxious to shake off their control. He would have liked to obtain the support of the English East India Company, and the English factory at Bantam wrote to London urging that something should be done. The Ayut'ia factory, however, was under the jurisdiction of Fort St. George, on the Coro-mandel Coast, which was most unwilling to interfere in Siamese affairs. Moreover, while Sir Edward Winter remained in control at Fort St. George the Company's interests in Siam were so badly mis-managed that the factory was ruined and English trade in the country fell into the hands of interlopers.

Meanwhile the French missionaries at Ayut'ia were sending home exaggerated accounts of their success which led the Court of Versailles to entertain the fond hope that the conversion of Siam to Christianity was within sight. In 1673 Mgr. Pallu, who had been on a visit to Europe, returned to Siam with a personal letter from Louis XIV to the king. It was accorded so splendid a reception that the two bishops,

Pallu and Lambert, began to press the king to send a diplomatic mission to Versailles. Narai does not seem up to this point to have seriously contemplated attempting to obtain a French alliance against the Dutch, but Louis XIV's letter certainly turned his mind in that direction. France and Holland, however, were at war in Europe and for some years the plan hung fire—if indeed there was anything so definite as a plan in any other minds than those of the French missionaries. During these years a new actor appeared on the scene whose influence carried the king completely into the French camp.

In 1674 the English factory was reopened. The initiative came from Bantam, whose interest in Siam had never relaxed. From the start things went badly with the factory, and in 1678 Richard Burnaby was deputed by the Bantam Council to investigate the cause of the trouble. With him went a Greek, Constant Phaulkon, who had been in the East India Company's service at Bantam, and having won a large reward for saving the magazine there had resigned in order to try his fortune in Siam. Phaulkon was the son of an innkeeper on the island of Cephallonia; he had run away from home to become a cabin-boy on an English merchant ship. His real name was Constantin Hiérachy, but at the suggestion of George White, whom he apparently accompanied to India in 1670, he changed it to its French equivalent, by which he became known to history. White went on to Siam, where he became a pilot on the Menam river. In 1675 his younger brother Samuel followed him there and became the captain of a Siamese ship trading between Mergui and Masulipatam. On arrival in Ayut'ia Burnaby persuaded George White to enter the service of the East India Company, and for a time the two of them employed Phaulkon in private trading ventures. Then in 1680 they hit upon a plan whereby the Greek was to enter the Siamese service and use his position to further the interests of the English Company against the Dutch. He was accepted by P'ya Kosa T'ibodi, the Siamese Minister of the Treasury, as an interpreter, and showed such high ability that he was soon promoted to the post of Superintendent of Foreign Trade.

The chief object of the plan, however, was never achieved. Burnaby quarrelled so badly with his colleague Potts, who heartily disliked Phaulkon, that he was recalled to Bantam in 1682, while George White resigned in disgust and went home to London, where he set up in business on his own account. Potts, left in charge of the factory, plunged into a bitter quarrel with Phaulkon over a debt he owed to the Company. The latter, therefore, finding it impossible to maintain good relations with the English factory, allowed his favour to be wooed by a young French commercial agent, Boureau-Delandes, who appeared at Ayut'ia early in 1682 with a special recommendation from Louis XIV transmitted to King Narai by Bishop Pallu. The young Frenchman, who was a son-in-law of François Martin, the founder of Pondicherry (1674), set himself to win over Phaulkon to the French interest. He was considerably aided by an incident which occurred in December 1682. The English factory was burnt out and Potts was foolish enough to hint that the Greek adventurer had engineered the fire. Even then, however, Phaulkon seems to have wavered for a long time before committing himself finally, and there can be no doubt that had he received any encouragement from the English he would have preferred them to the French.[1] But his closest associates were Burnaby, who after dismissal by the Company had returned to Ayut'ia as a private trader, and Samuel White. And William Strangh, who was sent to Ayut'ia in 1683 by Surat[2] to decide whether or not to close the factory there, would neither co-operate with the friend of Burnaby and White nor submit to the conditions of trade imposed upon the factory; so in January 1684 it was closed and its personnel left for Surat.

During this period Phaulkon's influence at Court had increased to such a degree that he had become the controlling factor in its foreign policy. Narai was as anxious as ever to bring in another power as a counterpoise to the influence of the Dutch. The English were obviously unable to fill the role effectively, and the fact that their king, unlike Louis XIV, completely ignored his existence was a source of keen disappointment. He would have preferred not to commit himself wholly to a French alliance, but there seemed to be no alternative. In 1680, therefore, he had deputed an embassy to the Court of Versailles, but the French ship conveying it was lost off the coast of Madagascar. The news of this disaster reached Siam in September 1683. Narai therefore decided to send two minor officials to France with the request that a French ambassador should be sent to Ayut'ia with powers to conclude a treaty. It is a fact of some significance, however, that the ship, which left in January 1684 with the envoys on board, was bound for England and carried despatches from Phaulkon to George White and the East India Company and a consignment of presents for judicious distribution. Thus before they proceeded to France the envoys made a brief stay in London, and Father Vachet,

---

[1] The question is carefully analysed by E. W. Hutchinson in *Adventurers in Siam in the Seventeenth Century*, pp. 68–91.

[2] The Bantam factory had been closed in 1682 as a result of Dutch action against the sultan.

their compère, was personally received by Charles II. The East India Company, however, was so firmly opposed to Phaulkon, who was regarded as the chief cause of the failure of the Ayut'ia factory, that White's efforts on his behalf were in vain. Moreover, the envoys were accredited only to the Court of Versailles, and for obvious reasons Vachet was in a hurry to get them safely across the Straits of Dover.

They were accorded a magnificent reception in France, though behind the scenes Vachet found himself up against an unexpected situation. The king had come completely under the influence of Madame de Maintenon and the Jesuits, and the Société des Missions Etrangères no longer held the place it had once had in the royal favour. Moreover, the high hopes of Narai's personal conversion to the Catholic faith, with which Pallu had earlier stimulated Louis XIV's interest in Siam, had given way to disillusionment. Vachet, however, held a trump card in his hand in that he was able to tell Père de la Chaise, the king's Jesuit confessor, that Phaulkon had been converted to the Catholic Church by a Jesuit. This, in fact, had been one of the chief reasons for Phaulkon's hesitancy in committing himself whole-heartedly to the French interest. He was a patron of the Jesuits and disliked the influence exerted on King Narai's mind by the missionaries of the Société des Missions Etrangères, their rivals. Vachet's description of Phaulkon as the dominating personality in the Siamese government and the staunch friend of the Jesuits completely won over Père de la Chaise, and as a result Louis XIV decided to send the Chevalier de Chaumont as his accredited ambassador to the Court of Ayut'ia together with a large suite of priests and Jesuits and with the avowed object of converting King Narai to Christianity.

The embassy, conveyed in two French men-of-war, arrived at Ayut'ia in October 1685 and was received with the utmost pomp by the king. De Chaumont, a Huguenot converted to Catholicism, was a religious fanatic whose one aim was the conversion of King Narai; he had no interest in the negotiation of commercial concessions and little, indeed, in the question uppermost in the minds of Narai and Phaulkon —a political alliance against the Dutch. Phaulkon, however, who acted as interpreter at all royal audiences, carefully parried all de Chaumont's clumsy attempts to raise the question of the king's conversion and behind the ambassador's back made secret arrangements with the Jesuit Père Tachard to lay before Louis XIV a plan for the conversion of the kingdom by the Jesuits. His suggestion was that a large number of them should be sent to Siam dressed as laymen and he would then secure for them appointments to the governorships of provinces, cities and fortresses. To ensure the success of the scheme it would be necessary, he said, to have two good colonies of French soldiers in the country. He cleverly manœuvred de Chaumont into making a public affirmation of a French alliance. In return he negotiated a draft agreement containing trading concessions, privileges for missionaries and the promise of the cession of Singora, near to Patani on the east coast of the Malay Peninsula, as a French garrison town, the ostensible object of which was to deter the Dutch from any offensive action against Siam. De Chaumont left for France in December 1685, taking with him Kosa Pan, a high official of the Court of Ayut'ia, as ambassador to Versailles charged with the task of negotiating the arrangements for the despatch of French troops to Singora.

De Chaumont, with Kosa Pan and Tachard, arrived in France in June 1686. Again a double set of negotiations was carried on, with Kosa Pan completely ignorant of the extremely shady arrangements that were being made behind his back by Tachard. Louis XIV's advisers were of opinion that Singora, in spite of its strategic position, was too far away from the capital. They decided to raise the price of Louis XIV's support for Phaulkon's scheme as high as possible. De Seignelay, Colbert's son, went so far as to question Kosa Pan regarding the feasibility of ceding Mergui as a depot for shipbuilding and repairs, but his arguments against the proposal were so strong that no more was said about it to him. And he was kept completely in the dark as to the real destination of the troops for whose despatch to Siam he had been sent to negotiate. Had he known that the arrangement made with Tachard was for the occupation of Bangkok, a move which was calculated to strangle the independence of his country, he would have broken off negotiations at once. The upshot of it all was that on 1 March 1687 a squadron of six warships left Brest for Siam with 636 soldiers under the command of Marshal Desfarges. With them went Kosa Pan, two French plenipotentiaries, Claude Cébéret de Boullay, a director of the Compagnie des Indes, and Simon de la Loubère,[1] together with Père Tachard and a number of Jesuits. Tachard was entrusted with the task of persuading Phaulkon to agree to the substitution of Bangkok for Singora. He was also to arrange for a French governor and garrison to be posted to Mergui, which, he was informed, was as vital for French trade with the Coromandel Coast in particular and India in general as Bangkok was for the control of trade with the

---

[1] His *Du Royaume de Siam*, 2 vols., Paris, 1691, is the best account of Siam at this time.

Gulf of Siam and the China coast. In return for his compliance Phaulkon was to be created a Count of France and a Knight of the Order of St. Michael. In case of opposition Desfarges was instructed to seize Bangkok by force.

Phaulkon's dilemma when the mission arrived in Siam in September 1687 may well be imagined. French garrisons at Bangkok and Mergui would be highly unpopular with the Siamese and might easily endanger his hold over King Narai. Refusal, on the other hand, might

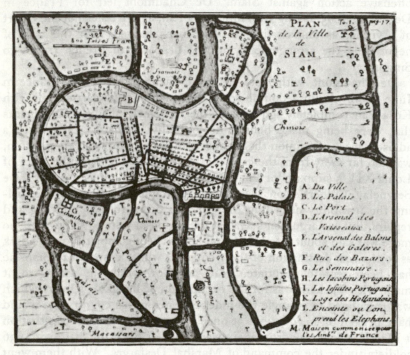

A. Du Ville
B. Le Palais.
C. Le Port.
D. L'Arsenal des Vaisseaux
E. L'Arsenal des Balons et des Galeres.
F. Rue des Bazars.
G. Le Seminaire.
H. Les Jacobins Portugais
I. Les Jesuites Portugais
K. Loge des Hollandois.
L. Enceinte ou l'on prend les Elephans.
M. Maison commencee pour les Amb.ʳˢ de France

SEVENTEENTH CENTURY AYUT'IA

ruin the co-operation with Louis XIV upon which his scheme for the conversion of Siam depended. He decided to throw caution to the winds and commit himself wholeheartedly to the French plan; but in order to overcome the scruples of his royal master he insisted that Desfarges and his troops must become mercenaries of Siam under his personal control and must take the oath of allegiance to the king. In due course, therefore, Desfarges and the main body of his troops occupied Bangkok, which they proceeded to fortify strongly, and Dubruant was sent as governor to Mergui with a garrison of 120 men. In due course also the two plenipotentiaries negotiated a treaty granting the French extra-territorial jurisdiction over all subjects of Louis XIV in Siam, permission to build suitable trading posts and, significantly, the cession of all the islands within a ten-mile radius of Mergui.

Before following the course of this extraordinary French adventure further it is necessary to turn back and take note of its repercussions in the English camp. Siam's possession of Mergui had resulted in the development of a very profitable trade with the Coromandel Coast. Before Phaulkon's time this was entirely in the hands of Mohammedan shippers belonging to the kingdom of Golconda. Phaulkon's policy was to develop this trade by using ships flying the Siamese flag and captained by English 'interlopers'. The ships were built at Mergui, and the place soon had quite a colony of English seafaring men in Phaulkon's employment. The Indian traders naturally resented this intrusion into their domain and English skippers complained of ill-treatment at Golconda ports. In 1681 Samuel White's ship was wrecked through the refusal of the port officer at Masulipatam to supply him with cables. In 1683 Phaulkon appointed Burnaby Governor of Mergui and White its shabander. Their task was to superintend the building and commissioning of ships at what had now become a very busy port. White, in his new capacity, was anxious to exploit his grievance against Golconda in such a way as to make a fortune rapidly and get away home with it. In 1684, therefore, he instituted a war of reprisals against Indian shipping in the Bay of Bengal. It was not long before this began to cause the English factory at Fort St. George, Madras, considerable inconvenience, and very naturally Phaulkon was held to blame for the acts of piracy committed by the ships based on Mergui. Madras therefore began to contemplate strong action against Siam.

The rift became wider through a quarrel which arose in 1685 between Elihu Yale and Phaulkon over a contract for the supply of some jewellery ordered for King Narai through Thomas Ivatt, the agent for Siam at Madras. Yale had sent in what can only be characterized as an outrageously heavy bill which Phaulkon had refused to pay. Yale's brother Thomas and two other factors had taken the jewels to Ayut'ia with the intention of reopening the English factory. They had arrived in time to be present at the reception of de Chaumont's embassy. When soon afterwards Phaulkon ordered them to take the jewels back to Madras fuel was added to a fire that was already becoming dangerously strong. And although as soon as he discovered the effect upon Madras of the piracies organized at Mergui he withdrew his sanction for them, Samuel White and his associates found easy excuses for going on with them, and thereby made war between the East India Company and Siam inevitable.

James II on coming to the throne in 1685 had sent an autograph letter to Phaulkon thanking him for the presents he had sent in 1684 for distribution by George White. In July 1686, however, before the letter arrived at its destination, the king held a council at Windsor Castle at which the decision was taken to issue a proclamation forbidding British subjects from serving in the ships of foreign rulers in the East. By this time the Fort St. George authorities had already begun a war of reprisals against the Mergui pirates and were looking for a base on the east coast of the Bay of Bengal from which to conduct operations. Their first plan was to seize the island of Negrais at the entrance to the western arm of the Irrawaddy delta, but the expedition was a fiasco. It left Madras in October, after the changeover from the S.W. to the N.E. monsoon had begun, and was forced by contrary winds to return. A few weeks later, at the beginning of 1687, news came of James II's proclamation and it was decided to send a couple of warships, the *Curtana* and the *James*, to Mergui to order all the English to leave and to seize all the shipping there pending settlement of a claim for £65,000 damages by King Narai. Meanwhile in November 1686 Phaulkon, who had become alarmed at the irresponsible behaviour of White at Mergui, had written to Père de la Chaise offering to hand over Mergui to the French. Needless to say, he was quite unaware of the fact that the occupation of the port had already become a prime object of French policy in the East.

The two English warships carrying James II's proclamation arrived at Mergui in June 1687 at the very moment when White, fearing an English attack on the place, was making final preparations to escape homewards in his ship the *Resolution*. White, finding himself trapped, decided that his only possible course was to comply with the orders sent from Madras, and he and all the English in the town signified their intention to leave the Siamese service. Anthony Weltden, the commander of the expedition, who had been instructed to keep up a blockade of Mergui until late in October, when the change of monsoon would permit him to return to Madras, took White's submission at its face value, and with the most surprising unpreparedness against a possible Siamese attack he and the English on shore gave themselves up to a series of lavish entertainments. On the night of the 14th, during an orgy on shore, the Siamese batteries began to fire on the ships, sinking the *James*, while on shore their troops fell upon the

English and massacred them. White and Weltden were among the few survivors to get away, and with their two ships, the *Resolution* and the *Curtana*, they ran for shelter among the islands of the Archipelago, where they lay waiting for the change of monsoon. White then persuaded Weltden to allow him to sail for England in the *Resolution*, while Weltden returned to Madras.

While this little drama was in progress the French squadron under the command of Marshal Desfarges was on its way to Siam. On learning of its departure from Brest the East India Company had represented to James II how serious would be the position of its shipping in the Bay of Bengal were the French to possess Mergui on its eastern side in addition to Pondicherry on the Coromandel Coast. The king had therefore sent secret instructions to Governor Elihu Yale of Madras to seize Mergui before it fell into French hands. These arrived in August 1687, and Yale, in the belief that Weltden with his two ships was still blockading the port, at once despatched a frigate to reinforce him, hoping that he would thus be able to force it to surrender. Sailing unsuspectingly into the harbour on 22 September in chase of one of the Siamese commerce raiders under an English captain, the frigate's commander found himself neatly trapped and had to surrender to Dubruant, who had already taken over control there.

By this time Siam was officially at war with the East India Company. The declaration was published in August 1687 and was the direct consequence of Weltden's action at Mergui in the previous June and July. It had, however, strangely little effect, for Phaulkon in handing over Bangkok and Mergui to the French had fatally weakened his own position in the government, and the Company after its failure at Mergui was content to play a waiting game. That also had been the policy of the Dutch throughout the period of King Narai's flirtation with France. As his relations with the Court of Versailles had become closer Phaulkon had gradually adopted a more uncompromising attitude towards Dutch trade. Consequently in 1686 the position of the Dutch factory had become so difficult that it was closed and Phaulkon was told to deal directly with Batavia. When Desfarges's expedition arrived in 1687 there were rumours of a Dutch declaration of war on Siam, but nothing came of them. The astute Dutch waited for the inevitable reaction which the presence of a foreign garrison within striking distance of the capital must have upon the feelings of the Siamese.

In any case the forces at the disposal of Desfarges were too small and too widely dispersed to be of any use in case of serious trouble.

To make matters worse, Phaulkon in supporting the demands of the Jesuits quarrelled hopelessly with Bishop Laneau, the head of the Missions Etrangères at Ayut'ia, and a serious rift appeared in the French camp. Then in March 1688 King Narai became so seriously ill at Lopburi that he was unable to conduct business. This gave an opportunity for an anti-foreign conspiracy led by Pra P'etraja, the general in charge of the royal elephants, to gain control over the palace. Too late Phaulkon summoned Desfarges to his aid; thousands of armed Siamese were rallying to the cause of the conspirators. Pra P'etraja was appointed regent, and in the middle of May he arrested Phaulkon. The French, threatened by overwhelming numbers of Siamese troops, were thrown upon the defensive and could do nothing to save their ally. On July 5 he was publicly executed. In the next month the king died and Pra P'etraja was raised to the throne.

All that Desfarges could now hope to do was to secure the best terms possible for the evacuation of his small force and the safety of the French residents at the capital. His fortified area at Bangkok was besieged by a force large enough and well enough equipped to have exterminated it; but the Siamese had a wholesome fear of the sort of resistance they might meet, and preferred to negotiate. In September an agreement was reached by which the French troops were to be evacuated to Pondicherry while their missionaries and traders were to retain their privileges. The Bangkok garrison departed towards the end of November, leaving behind the two sons of Desfarges and the Catholic bishop as hostages. At Mergui Dubruant, hemmed in by hostile forces, fought his way out with severe losses and took the remnant of his garrison to Pondicherry. Notwithstanding the agreement made with Desfarges, the French missionaries and other residents were treated with great severity, and many of them lost their lives.

Late in 1689 Desfarges made an unsuccessful attempt to restore French influence in Siam by seizing the island of Puket, better known as Junk Ceylon, the European corruption of its Malay name Ujung Selang. His foolish act caused a renewal of the severities against the remnant of the French at Ayut'ia, and many of them, including the bishop, were killed. To stop further slaughter Père Tachard went to Ayut'ia, proclaiming that he came to conclude peace on behalf of Louis XIV, while Desfarges withdrew once more to Pondicherry and eventually sailed for home. Nothing came of Tachard's negotiations, and at the end of 1690 he left for Pondicherry. But the persecution of Christians stopped, the French were released and the missionaries

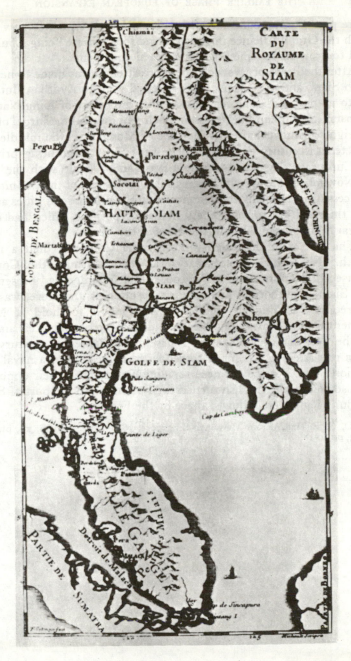

LA LOUBÈRE'S MAP OF SIAM, 1691

were permitted to continue with their work. France was now at war with the Grand Alliance in Europe, and for the time being Louis XIV had to drop his scheme for the conversion of Siam.

After the Peace of Ryswick one more attempt was made to negotiate with Siam, and once again Père Tachard went to Ayut'ia. But it was all to no purpose. The reaction against the policy of King Narai and Constant Phaulkon had caused such a powerful upsurge of anti-foreign sentiment that until the days of Mongkut in the middle of the nineteenth century Siam was to be very chary of granting privileges to Europeans. A new agreement was indeed made with the Dutch in November 1688 by which they recovered some of their commercial concessions, especially those concerning the purchase of hides and tin, but they had lost for ever the dominating position which had caused Narai to throw himself into the arms of the French.

The war with the English East India Company died a natural death. No formal peace treaty was made because the Company refused to drop its claim to £65,000 which Weltden had presented to the Siamese authorities at Mergui. No attempt, therefore, was made to reopen the English factory at Ayut'ia. A foothold at Mergui rather than the conversion of Siam had all along been the real ambition of the French Foreign Office. Early in the eighteenth century more than one attempt was made to reopen the question of a naval repair station there, but the Siamese remained adamant in their opposition. Consequently the English turned their attention to the port of Syriam in Burma and were followed there by the French.[1]

[1] D. G. E. Hall, 'From Mergui to Singapore, 1686–1819', in JSS, xli, pt. i, July 1953, pp. 1–18.

CHAPTER 20

BURMA UNDER THE RESTORED TOUNGOO DYNASTY,
1600–1752

WHEN the united kingdom of Burma fell apart in 1599 the condition
of the old Mon kingdom of Peġu was indeed wretched. Not only was
the capital city in ruins but the whole countryside was laid waste by
the invading armies of Arakan, Toungoo and Siam. Syriam was in
Arakanese hands, and thither came Philip de Brito y Nicote, a Portuguese in the service of King Min Razagyi, to take charge of the custom-
house and control the Portuguese living there under their own laws.
With him went two Jesuit missionaries, Pimenta and Boves, both of
whom wrote accounts of their experiences, translations of which were
published by Samuel Purchas in his *Pilgrimes*.[1] Boves wrote: 'I also
went thither with Philip Brito, and in fifteen days arrived at Syriam,
the chief port in Pegu. It is a lamentable spectacle to see the banks of
the rivers set with infinite fruit-bearing trees, now overwhelmed with
ruins of gilded temples and noble edifices; the ways and fields full of
skulls and bones of wretched Peguans, killed or famished or cast into
the river, in such numbers that the multitude of carcasses prohibits
the way and passage of any ship.'[2]

De Brito formed an ambitious plan to gain control over Syriam and
hold it under the authority of the Viceroy of Goa. Together with a
Portuguese officer, Salvador Ribeyro, he erected a fort and expelled
the Arakanese governor. Then, leaving Ribeyro to hold the place, he
went to Goa to obtain official recognition and help. He received a
daughter of the viceroy in marriage and returned as captain-general
with six ships containing reinforcements and stores. During his
absence Salvador Ribeyro had beaten off successive Arakanese and
Burmese attacks and had cultivated such good relations with the Mon
chiefs that they offered to accept de Brito as king. The latter on
arrival accepted the offer on behalf of his sovereign, and Ribeyro then
retired into the background and soon left the country. His wisdom
in handling a difficult situation during his chief's absence gives the

[1] Both accounts are in vol. ii of the 1625 edition of the work.
[2] *Op. cit.*, ii, p. 1748.

impression that had he remained in control the adventure might have had a far better chance of success than it had under the impulsive leadership of the over-ambitious de Brito. At first, however, success followed success. A large Arakanese flotilla under the command of the heir-apparent was defeated and the prince himself captured and held to ransom. A further Arakanese attack in league with the Toungoo Min was beaten off, and in 1604 both rulers came to terms with de Brito.

The strongest of the Mon chiefs, Binnya Dala, who held Martaban as the vassal of Ayut'ia, made a marriage alliance by which de Brito's son by a former wife married his daughter. For some years the Portuguese adventurer was the unchallenged lord of much of the Mon country, though Bassein and the western part of the delta remained independent. As yet, however, no full-scale Burmese attack had been launched against him. It was certain to come as soon as the Burmese found a leader capable of uniting them. But the Nyaungyan Prince, a younger brother of Nanda Bayin, who was ruling at Ava when the kingdom broke up, and took up the task of restoring the fortunes of his family, died in 1605 while striving to bring the rebellious Shan states of the north and east into subjection. And for some years afterwards his son and successor, Maha Dhamma Raja, better known by his later title of Anaukpetlun, was too busily engaged in the north to devote attention to the south. De Brito should have concentrated upon conciliating and uniting the Mons. Instead, however, he alienated them by plundering pagodas and pressing ahead with deeply resented measures for the mass conversion of Buddhists to Christianity. In 1608, having established his authority over the north, Anaukpetlun captured Prome. Two years later he forced his cousin, the ruler of Toungoo, to acknowledge his overlordship. De Brito chose to regard this as an act of treachery, and in league with Binnya Dala of Martaban he attacked Toungoo, captured the prince, plundered and burnt the palace, and then retired. Thereupon Anaukpetlun, after the most careful preparations, laid siege to Syriam early in 1613. De Brito was caught unprepared, but the Burmese king had no heavy guns capable of battering the fortifications. After a siege of a little over a month, however, a Mon chief in de Brito's service opened one of the gates and the Burmese captured the city. De Brito was impaled on an eminence above the fort and most of his officers were done to death. The remainder of his Portuguese followers were sent upcountry to be settled in a number of villages between the Chindwin and the Mu, where for centuries afterwards their descendants formed a Catholic community with its own priests. They were enrolled in the royal guard as musketeers and gunners.

Anaukpetlun next turned against the provinces of his grandfather's kingdom which had been occupied by Siam. The warlike Pra Naret had died in 1605 and had been succeeded by his unwarlike brother Ekat'otsarat, who in turn had died in 1610. The latter's son Int'araja (1610-28) sent an army to oppose the Burmese invasion of Tenasserim and managed to halt it after Martaban and Ye had submitted without a blow. In 1615, however, Anaukpetlun turned eastwards and struck at Chiengmai, which he captured. There his campaigns against Siam stopped, and after placing one of his sons in charge of the kingdom, which he reorganized as a Burmese province, he returned home. He wisely refrained from attempting to reassert Burmese claims to Luang Prabang, but the fact that on his return from Chiengmai he made Pegu his headquarters and was intent upon restoring it as the capital of his dominions shows that he hoped for an opportunity of renewing the old struggle for the possession of Ayut'ia which had brought so much humiliation to his dynasty. Hostilities continued for some years, but they were mainly over the question of Chiengmai. According to the Siamese account, both sides tried to enlist the support of Goa but failed. Anaukpetlun certainly sent an envoy to Goa, but his object seems to have been to explain away what had taken place at Syriam and to offer help against Arakan, which a Goa fleet had unsuccessfully attacked in 1615. But when a Goanese envoy in due course appeared at Pegu the king refused to receive him. No reason was given for this *volte-face*, and one can only assume that the king had discovered that the Portuguese were not in a position to exact vengeance for his treatment of de Brito.

Among the captives taken by the Burmese at Chiengmai was Thomas Samuel of the East India Company's Ayut'ia factory. He was taken to Pegu and died there. News of this reached Lucas Antheunis at Masulipatam in 1617 through Indian merchants trading with Burma. He sent over two of his assistants, Henry Forrest and John Staveley, on an Indian ship to claim the East India Company's goods in Samuel's hands at the time of his death. Anaukpetlun promised to hand over the goods if the Company would open trade with his country, and retained at Pegu the two young men as hostages when he realized that it had no such intention. Eventually, however, after long delay he restored the goods and sent the two factors back to Masulipatam with a small present and a letter inviting the Company to trade. His overture led to nothing. The Company was too deeply committed elsewhere under the Anglo-Dutch treaty of 1619 to open new factories in countries where the chances of profitable trade were highly doubtful; and as a result of its unsuccessful struggle with Jan Pieterszoon Coen it was soon to begin drawing in its horns and closing a number of its factories. Moreover, Forrest and Staveley reported so adversely on trading conditions at Pegu that the Masulipatam factory was for many years opposed to the planting of a factory in Burma, and it was not until after Fort St. George was founded at Madras in 1639 that the country came to be seriously considered as a field for English commercial enterprise.

In 1628 Anaukpetlun completed the transfer of his household from Ava to Pegu and began to plan an attack upon Ayut'ia. In the next year, however, he was murdered and the throne seized by one of his brothers, Thalun, who carried out a complete reversal of his policy. The Siamese project was abandoned and in 1635 the capital was transferred from Pegu back to Ava. Immediately after his accession a considerable Mon insurrection had broken out, and when it was suppressed another mass exodus of Mons into Siamese territory had resulted. The idea of a united kingdom of Mons and Burmese which Tabinshwehti and Bayinnaung seem to have cherished no longer existed. The Burmese treated the Mons as a subject race, and as Pegu had become useless as a port through silting the choice was between Syriam and Ava. From the economic point of view Syriam would have been a better capital, and by going there the government would have maintained contact with the outside world. But no king after Anaukpetlun appreciated the value of overseas intercourse, and Upper Burma was essentially the Burmese homeland. So the dynasty surrendered to traditionalism and isolationism, and its increasing intransigence and xenophobia made Western trade with Burma on any satisfactory scale, and even ordinary diplomatic relations, impossible.

Thalun's policy was peaceable and conservative; he aimed at restoring order and social organization. His reign, therefore, is chiefly interesting for his administrative work. His minister Kaingsa compiled the *Manusarashwemin*, the first law-book in the Burmese language. Thalun also reconstructed the administration of the Kyauksè irrigated area and the system whereby lands were held there by regiments of the royal army. His Revenue Inquest of 1638 was his biggest achievement. It entailed the compilation of a Domesday survey of the whole kingdom, which were it in existence today would be an invaluable historical record. Unfortunately, like most of the palm-leaf and parabaik records not only of this dynasty but also of its successor, none of it has survived, and the little that is known of it comes from the references to it in the compilations of a similar nature made during Bodawpaya's reign in 1799 and 1802.

During Thalun's reign in 1635 the Dutch planted their first factory in Burma. It was at Syriam, but their factors, Dirck Steur and Wiert Jansen Popta, had to follow the Court up to Ava, where in September of that year the king received them and treated them to 'sundry spectacles of dancing, leaping and fighting'. Their trade in Burma was managed from Pulicat, and they had come with the object of elbowing out the Indian and Portuguese merchants who ran the country's foreign trade. Mon merchants and ships had carried on a substantial amount of trade to foreign parts, and among the records of Lancaster's first voyage on behalf of the East India Company there is a brief word-list of the 'Pegu language' which seems to have been picked up at Acheh. Hardly any Burmese, however, engaged in foreign trade, which was left almost entirely in the hands of foreigners. And there are no further signs of Mon activity. When the Dutch tried to employ their well-tried methods for obtaining a monopoly Thalun protected the Indian merchants against unfair competition and wrote to the Governor of Pulicat telling him to abstain from hostile measures against the Portuguese, who, he complained, were being prevented from carrying on their accustomed trade with Burma. The Dutch were so disappointed in the trade that in 1645 they seriously thought of closing their factories, and only held on to them for fear lest the English would step into their shoes.

The English, on the other hand, who planted their first factory in Burma at Syriam in 1647, went there partly because of rumours of fabulous Dutch profits there. Before their factors arrived in Ava Thalun had died (1648) and his son Pindale (1648–61) had succeeded. They found the Dutch so well established that there was little hope of success; and when the First Anglo-Dutch War broke out in 1652 and the Dutch literally cleared the Bay of Bengal of English shipping their factories in Burma were doomed. They were withdrawn in 1657.[1]

Pindale, a weak king, had to face an unprecedented situation which arose out of the war in China when the Manchus drove out the Mings. Yung-li, the last of the Mings, had in 1644 fled to Yunnan, where for a long time he defied the Manchus. His heavy demands upon Hsenwi and Maingmaw for men and supplies led Pindale to send a force to their assistance; and with some success, since in 1650 the

---

[1] The story is told in D. G. E. Hall, *Early English Intercourse with Burma*, pp. 47–84.

English factors in Burma reported to Madras that the Burmese had defeated 'their plundering neighbours and the country was like to be settled and in a peaceful condition'.[1] In 1658 Yung-Li was driven out of Yunnan and fled by the old Burma Road to Bhamo with 700 followers. They were disarmed and permitted to reside at Sagaing. This caused a spate of raids by bands of Ming supporters who endeavoured to rescue their leader. A Burmese army was defeated at Wetwin, and for three years Upper Burma was ravaged up to the walls of Ava and as far south as Pagan. In 1661 the Dutch factors at the capital reported that the confusion was so great that all trade had stopped.[2]

Worse was to follow. Mon levies summoned to the defence of Ava deserted and there was a revolt at Martaban.[3] Then, fearing Burmese reprisals, thousands of Mons fled into Siam. A Burmese force pursuing them was defeated by the Siamese at Kanburi, beyond the Three Pagodas Pass, and the Siamese followed up their victory by raiding deep into Lower Burma. The Dutch at Syriam reported that they were taking special measures to protect their factory there. Pindale seemed incapable of dealing with the situation. In 1661, therefore, he was dethroned and his brother Pye placed upon the throne. The disorder gradually subsided, but not through any action the new king was able to take. The Siamese turned their attention to Chiengmai, which they recovered, and Pye was too weak to attempt a reassertion of Burmese authority there. The people of Chiengmai, however, drove out the Siamese garrison and the Burmese returned. The Manchus showed such energy in bringing Yunnan under control that the Chinese raiders, unable to use it as a base of operations, disintegrated. Then in 1662 the Manchu Viceroy of Yunnan marched into Burma and demanded the surrender of Yung-li. Pye had no alternative but to hand over his embarrassing guest, who was taken to Yunnanfu and publicly strangled with a bow-string in the market-place.

Burma had now entered upon a long period of stagnation. Pye died in 1672, and his son Narawara, who succeeded him, died within a year. A number of influential people at the Court thereupon took possession of the palace and placed the youngest son of the Prince of

[1] Foster, *English Factories in India*, 1650–4, p. 19.
[2] D. G. E. Hall, 'The Daghregister of Batavia and Dutch Relations with Burma', *JBRS.*, xxix, pt. ii, p. 149   See also Pieter van Dam.
[3] Phayre (*op. cit.*, p. 139) and Wood (*op. cit.*, p. 193) place this incident in 1662 after the accession of Pye to the throne of Ava. Harvey, however, assigns it to the year 1661 before Pindale's deposition, and the references to it in the correspondence of the Dutch factors at Syriam seem to confirm his date (Hall, *op. cit. sup.*, p. 150).

Prome on the throne. Opposition within the royal family was crushed by a considerable number of secret executions. Minrekyawdin, or Sri Pawara Maha Dhamma Raja, reigned for nearly twenty-six years (1673-98). He was little more than a figurehead; real power was in the hands of a small coterie of ministers. Both internal and external peace was maintained, but there was no leadership and consequently no vigour. Outlying districts were lost because when encroachments such as the occupation of the Kabaw valley by the Raja of Manipur took place there was no one capable of expelling the intruders.

The narrow tradition-ridden policy of the Court had particularly bad effects upon foreign trade. The Dutch finally lost their patience and in 1679 closed their factories. They had been particularly anxious to plant one at Bhamo, which was once again beginning to attract large caravans of Chinese traders now that firm rule was restored in Yunnan. The idea of opening up trade with western China through Burma had great attractions for them, and when the Court of Ava flatly prohibited their project they decided that the trade of Burma *per se* was not worth pursuing any further. The Dutch withdrawal inclined the English East India Company to make another attempt at trading with the country. Madras and the other Coromandel Coast factories, which felt themselves threatened by the sweeping raids of Sivaji and his Marathas, were arming and needed saltpetre and lead, which Burma produced, for making munitions. It was Sir Streynsham Master, the Governor of Fort St. George, therefore, who in 1680 started the ball rolling by sending an envoy to Ava.

There was another cogent reason for the move. The French had opened a factory at Ayut'ia in 1680 and were hand in glove with the Greek adventurer Constant Phaulkon, who was coming to be the dominating personality in King Narai's government. The representatives of the East India Company there were coming up against the increasing hostility of Phaulkon and the English interlopers, who swarmed at Mergui. Hence although the Company far preferred Siam, whose attitude towards foreign trade was altogether more enlightened than that of the Court of Ava, its unhappy position there made it willing to try its luck once more in Burma. And it was prodded on by James Duke of York, who was persuaded by a Dutchman named Spar, previously head of the Dutch factory at Ava, that it was worth while making a further attempt to exploit the overland trade route to western China. The directors were extremely hesitant about embarking on such a scheme and were relieved when the evasive answers made by the Burmese ministers to all the Company's proposals caused the negotiations to peter out. The Burmese would under no circumstances permit the export of saltpetre or lead. And Fort St. George discovered that it could obtain all the supplies of other products of Burma it needed through the operations of Indian, Armenian and other private traders living under its jurisdiction at Madras.

Meanwhile the development of Louis XIV's Siamese project and the piratical operations of the English private traders at Mergui had brought on not only a severance of relations with Siam but a war of reprisals, and late in 1686 the Fort St. George Council made an abortive attempt to seize the island of Negrais, just inside the mouth of the western arm of the Irrawaddy delta, with the intention of using it as a naval station from which to threaten Mergui.[1] In the following year in the course of a struggle to gain control of Mergui Captain Anthony Weltden did actually visit the island, but the Company, which had become involved in a quarrel with Aurungzeb, could spare no forces with which to plant a settlement there. And although the French managed to hold Mergui for a short time, their whole adventure in Siam crashed in 1688 and the immediate need for strong action by the Company on the eastern coast of the Bay of Bengal passed away.

Instead, therefore, the Fort St. George authorities turned their attention to the port of Syriam, from which valuable cargoes of teakwood were coming regularly to Madras. The development of French naval power in the eastern seas, and the lessons learnt from their brief occupation of Mergui, pointed to the need for a repair station somewhere on the eastern side of the Bay. The Coromandel Coast had no good harbour where repairs could safely be executed, especially during the period beginning in October with the changeover from the southwest to the north-east monsoon. In any case it was impossible to keep a fleet off the Coromandel Coast during the stormy weather of October and November, so that the factories there and shipping in the Bay might be at the mercy of an enemy fleet if one appeared while they were denuded of naval protection. A naval repair station on the opposite side of the bay would be of great value; and although the full strategic significance of the question was not realized until the beginning of the great naval struggle with France for the mastery of the Indian Ocean during the War of the Austrian Succession (1740–8), it is significant that soon after its failure to seize Mergui in 1687 Fort St. George began to consider the possibility of establishing a dockyard at Syriam. Thus in 1689 the frigate *Diamond* was sent there for repairs.

---

[1] Hall, *Early English Intercourse*, pp. 129–37.

This initial experiment had no immediate results, probably because the directors at home had set their faces against any project for reviving the English factory there. In 1692, however, the Burmese authorities at Martaban seized a small sloop belonging to an Armenian resident at Madras and imprisoned her crew; and as she was carrying a consignment of goods belonging to Nathaniel Higginson, the Governor of Fort St. George, he decided to send an envoy to Ava to negotiate the release of the captive merchant and his property. Higginson guessed that if he could promise the reopening of official trade between the Company and Burma all would be plain sailing. But he was not in a position even to send an accredited Company's servant, much less make any offer which would involve the Company officially. His agent, Edward Fleetwood, who made the journey to Ava in 1695, was a private merchant of Madras whose expenses were paid personally by Higginson. But he did his best to pass off the mission as an official one and instructed Fleetwood to ask for 'free liberty of repairing and building of ships' at Syriam. As he had expected, the Burmese ministers let Fleetwood know quite plainly that if the Company would reopen the Syriam factory all his requests would be granted; but if not it was useless to negotiate.

Eventually a method of procedure was agreed upon which satisfied them. Fort St. George was to appoint a Chief who was to take charge of an English dockyard at Syriam and be the responsible person in charge of all the English merchants trading in Burma. As, however, the Company could not be brought into the venture, Higginson, after failing to form a private syndicate to take it over, appointed Thomas Bowyear, a 'freeman inhabitant' of Madras, to reside at the English dockyard at Syriam and superintend work there, and all Englishmen trading to Burma were required to 'pay due respect and obedience' to him. In practice the English Chief did not normally reside in Burma; he went out with the Madras skippers in September each year and returned with them in March. The arrangement was an unsatisfactory one: the Company had no control over the Chief, and his control could be flouted by the private traders at Syriam. The refusal of the captain and supercargo of an English ship which put into Syriam for repairs in 1720 to recognize the authority of the Chief, Captain George Heron, resulted in a brawl in which two of the ship's company lost their lives.

Madras thereupon replaced the Chief by a Resident, who had to pay down a large sum to the Madras Council as security money and was given regular contracts for the construction and repair of ships

on behalf of the Company. This experiment also was far from successful. Some of the Residents were unsatisfactory; one actually absconded. There were serious complaints about both the workmanship
and the cost of the ships built at Syriam, and in 1741 the Fort St.
George Council decided to transfer its building orders to the Parsi
yards at Bombay. The dockyard, however, remained in use as a repair
depot until it was destroyed by rebellious Mons in 1743.

Meanwhile the French had followed the English example by opening a dockyard at Syriam. Dupleix, who had arrived at Pondicherry
in 1720, was soon awake to the importance of the Burmese ports in
the naval strategy of the Bay of Bengal. In 1727 he suggested the
planting of a dockyard at Syriam, and two years later it began work.
It was well managed by experienced shipwrights and built some
excellent teak ships. Plans for considerable extensions were under
consideration when the great Mon rebellion broke out in 1740 and
forced it to close down.

Minrekyawdin died in 1698 and was followed by the last three
kings of the dynasty: Sané (1698–1714), Taninganwe (1714–33), and
Mahadammayaza Dipati (1733–52). Like him they were nonentities
who rarely, if ever, left the capital and were practically palace prisoners.
Even the fact that under them Burma pursued a policy of peace reflects
no credit on their rule, since it was dictated by weakness alone. How
much power the Court of Ava exercised over the feudal lords who
administered the various parts of the country it is difficult to say. Its
control over Lower Burma probably did not extend beyond the
Irrawaddy highway, the city of Pegu and the port of Syriam.

The delta had never recovered from its appalling state of devastation
at the end of the sixteenth century. But the Mons had never lost their
desire for independence and were bound one day to make another
bid at restoring the kingdom of Pegu, should the opportunity occur.
It came in due course when the little mountain state of Manipur
began a series of raids upon Upper Burma which the enfeebled rulers
of Ava were quite unable to check. In the sixteenth century Bayinnaung had forced Manipur to recognize his suzerainty, but later it
reasserted its independence, and, as we have seen, in the reign of
Minrekyawdin succeeded in encroaching upon the Kabaw valley
running alongside the Upper Chindwin. Under Gharib Newaz
(1714–54) its expert horsemen became the terror of Upper Burma.
They destroyed villages and pagodas and got away with their loot
before they could be intercepted. On more than one occasion they
defeated Burmese armies sent to hold the frontier. They had recently

KAUNGHMUDAW PAGODA NEAR SAGAING

been converted to Hinduism, and their Brahmans incited them on with
the promise that they would obtain blessedness by bathing in the
Irrawaddy at Sagaing. In 1738 they camped near Sagaing, stormed
the stockade built to defend the famous Kaunghmudaw Pagoda
erected by Thalun, massacred its garrison and burnt every house and
monastery up to the walls of Ava. Plunder was their object, not conquest, and there was no leader in Burma strong enough to take the
situation in hand.

The degradation of the monarchy caused the disintegration of the
kingdom. It began in 1740 when a colony of Gwè Shans at Okpo,
near Madaya in Upper Burma, discontented at the exorbitant taxes
demanded on their areca palms, rose in rebellion under a leader named
Gonna-ein. They united with a band of Mon deportees and drove the
Burmese out of their district. Almost simultaneously Lower Burma
rose in revolt. The Burmese governor of the province of Pegu aspired
to overthrow the government and marched on Syriam. But his troops
mutinied and killed him, and when the king sent a force to restore
order the Mons rose en masse, defeated it, seized Syriam and Martaban
and massacred all the Burmese they could lay hands on. They then
proceeded to invest a king of their own, Smim Htaw Buddhaketi, in

Pegu. He was the son of a Governor of Pagan who had failed in an attempt to seize Ava in 1714 and had fled to the hill country east of Pegu. Smim Htaw Buddhaketi was a monk when he was called to occupy the throne. He proved an ineffectual leader, but such was the weakness of Ava that his forces quickly occupied Lower Burma up to Prome and Toungoo and began raiding far up the Irrawaddy until they threatened the capital itself.

The Burmese resistance to this new threat was seriously hampered by the Manipuri raids, which continued until 1749. They could rarely take the initiative and attack the delta because of the danger of leaving the homeland unprotected. Not until they found a leader capable of solving that problem were they in a position to turn the tables on the Mons; and by that time Ava had fallen. The Governor of Prome did indeed lead a raid in 1743 which gave him temporary possession of Syriam, but his followers then proceeded to get so drunk that a Mon counter-attack soon cleared them out, and by a rapid follow-up of their victory the Mons captured Prome. Thereafter the initiative lay with them. During their occupation of Syriam the Burmese burnt the Armenian, French and Portuguese churches there and destroyed all the factories of foreign merchants save the English, which was defended by a small force of sepoys sent over from Madras. The victorious Mons, however, annoyed at the strict neutrality maintained by Jonathan Smart, the Resident, in face of their repeated requests for help, compelled him to surrender and burnt the factory to the ground. He and his small company were permitted to return to Madras.

In that same year Father Gallizia, who had been consecrated by the pope as the first Bishop of Burma, arrived at Syriam with a small band of assistant clergy bound for Ava. Unable to proceed to his destination he went to Pegu, where he was permitted to reside. Not long afterwards six ships belonging to the Ostend Company put into Syriam harbour bearing the staff and effects of their former factory at Banki-bazar in Bengal, from which they had been expelled. The Mon government at Pegu sent Bishop Gallizia to ascertain their intentions, and when he learnt that their leader, de Schonamille, sought permission to open a factory at Syriam he prevailed upon him to go to Pegu to lay his request before the king. De Schonamille very unwisely took with him a considerable armed escort, which roused the suspicions of the Mons to such a degree that a plot was formed to murder the whole party. Gallizia, hearing of the plot, warned de Schonamille, who made a desperate effort to escape. But he and all his following, together with the bishop and two priests, were surrounded and massacred. Four survivors only escaped to the ships, which managed to make good their escape from Syriam.

Smim Htaw Buddhaketi was popular with the people, who appreciated his kindly disposition; but his ministers became weary of his incapacity as a leader. Matters came to a crisis in 1747 when a Mon attack up the Irrawaddy towards Ava was repulsed with heavy loss. The king thereupon left Pegu and settled at Sittaung, where after some deliberation he announced his intention to retire from his uncongenial post. Then with a strong guard he made his escape to Chiengmai. His chief minister, Binnya Dala, was chosen king in his place and announced that he intended to revive the empire of Bayinnaung. For such a project he had neither the resources nor the ability; and although he appointed as commander-in-chief Talaban, a soldier with a great reputation among the Mons, the only result was an intensification of the raiding activities which had gone on unceasingly since the achievement of independence. The Burmese, however, could put up no effectual resistance, and soon the raiders were penetrating beyond Ava, apparently with the aim of linking up with the Shans of the upper Irrawaddy. At last in 1751, having assembled a large army equipped with arms procured from European traders at Syriam, Talaban made a full-scale invasion of Upper Burma which culminated in April 1752 in the capture of Ava and the deposition of the last king of the Toungoo dynasty.

The campaign had been carried through all too easily, and the Mons were deceived into thinking that in taking the capital they had conquered the country. Hence, instead of concentrating upon stamping out all possible centres of resistance, the heir-apparent, who had accompanied Talaban upon the expedition, returned to Pegu with the main body of the troops, leaving the commander-in-chief to exact the allegiance of the chiefs of the Ava kingdom with inadequate forces at his disposal. Before starting back the prince heard the disturbing news that the Mon detachment sent to receive the allegiance of the town of Moksobomyo ('the town of the hunter chief'), some sixty miles north of Ava, had been cut to pieces by the inhabitants. But as he mistakenly supposed that trouble was brewing with Siam, which had recently exchanged friendly missions with the deposed King of Ava, he preferred to treat the incident as trivial and left with the parting injunction to Talaban to make an example of the place. Little did he realize that the Moksobomyo incident was the prelude to a Burmese national uprising that was to clear the Mons out of Upper Burma and destroy their kingdom utterly.

CHAPTER 21

THE RISE AND FALL OF THE KINGDOM OF MROHAUNG IN ARAKAN

ARAKAN stretches for some 350 miles along the eastern shore of the Bay of Bengal to the south of the Chittagong division of East Bengal. It is separated from Burma by a long, deep range of mountains, the Arakan Yoma, through which there are only two serviceable passes, the An connecting with Minbu on the west bank of the Irrawaddy, and the Taungup connecting with Prome. The Arakanese call them-selves Rakhaing and their country Rakhaingpyi. According to Sir Arthur Phayre,[1] the word is a corruption of the Pali *rakkhaso* (Skt. *rakshasa*) meaning 'ogre' (Burmese *bilu*) or guardian of the mansion of Indra on Mount Meru. Sir Henry Yule[2] identifies the Argyre or Silverland of Ptolemy with Arakan. But Arakan produced no silver and the previously accepted views of Ptolemy's data concerning the Indo-Chinese peninsula are now open to question.[3]

The Arakanese of today are basically Burmese, though with an un-mistakable Indian admixture. Although mainly Buddhist, they have been influenced by long centuries of contact with Muslim India. Their language is Burmese with some dialectical differences and an older form of pronunciation, especially noticeable in their retention of the 'r' sound, which the Burmese have changed to 'y'. The Bengalis refer to them by the name *Magh*, a word adopted by seventeenth-century European writers and written 'Mugg'. The name is also applied to a class of people belonging to Chittagong who are Buddhists but speak Bengali and are not Mongoloid. Much that is fanciful has been written about its possible etymology,[4] but the question is as yet unsolved.

Buddhism would seem to have reached Arakan long before its arrival in the interior of Burma, and the famous Mahamuni image, brought

---

[1] *History of Burma*, 1883, p. 41.

[2] Originally in his contribution to *Proceedings of the Royal Geographical Society*, November 1882.

[3] See G. E. Gerini, *Researches on Ptolemy's Geography of Eastern Asia*, pp. 37–40, for the stock view.

[4] See Phayre's note in *op. cit.*, pp. 47–8, and the article s.v. Mugg in *Hobson-Jobson*.

from Arakan by the Burmese in 1785, and now to be seen in the
Arakan Pagoda at Mandalay, may date from the early Christian era.
Inscriptions mention a Candra dynasty, which may have been founded
as early as the middle of the fourth century A.D.[1] Its capital was called
by the Indian name of Vaisali, and thirteen kings of the dynasty are
said to have reigned there for a total period of 230 years. The Arakanese chronicles claim that the kingdom was founded in the year
2666 B.C., and contain lists of kings beginning with that date.[2]

The Burmese do not seem to have settled in Arakan until possibly
as late as the tenth century A.D. Hence earlier dynasties are thought
to have been Indian, ruling over a population similar to that of Bengal.
All the capitals known to history have been in the north near modern
Akyab. It was a district subject to chronic raids from hill tribes—
Shans, Burmese, and Bengalis—and there were long periods when
settled government can hardly have existed. But the spirit of independence was always strong, and in the business of raiding the Arakanese could usually give as much as they received. Their main
activity was by sea into Bengal, and they developed great skill in sea
and riverine warfare. By the middle of the sixteenth century they
were the terror of the Ganges delta.

North Arakan was conquered by Anawrahta of Pagan (1044–77), but
was not incorporated in his kingdom. It remained a semi-independent
feudatory state under its hereditary kings. When Pagan fell in 1287
Arakan asserted its independence under the famous Minhti, whose
reign, according to the chronicles, lasted for the fabulously long period
of ninety-five years (1279–1374). His reign is also notable for the
defeat of a great Bengali raid. After his death Arakan was for a considerable time one of the theatres of war in the great struggle between
Ava and the Mon kingdom of Pegu. Both sides sought to gain control
over it. First the Burmese, then the Mons, placed their nominees on
its throne.

When in 1404 the Burmese regained control King Narameikhla[3]
fled to Bengal, where he was hospitably received by King Ahmed
Shah of Gaur. During his exile he distinguished himself while assisting his host to repel an invasion, and when in 1426 Ahmed Shah died

---

[1] E. H. Johnson, 'Some Sanskrit Inscriptions of Arakan', *Bulletin of the School of
Oriental and African Studies*, xi, 2, pp. 357–85.

[2] Phayre, *op. cit.*, pp. 293–304, gives the whole list. Harvey, *History of Burma*,
pp. 369–72, gives it only from A.D. 146. For the legends concerning the foundation of
the kingdom see Phayre, *op. cit.*, pp. 42–4. Phayre served in Arakan as senior assistant
to the commissioner from 1837 to 1846 and during that period published valuable
studies of its early history and antiquities.

[3] Phayre, *op. cit.*, p. 79, calls him Meng Soamun and gives the date as 1406.

and was succeeded by Nazir Shah the new ruler provided him with a force for the recovery of his kingdom under the command of a general called in the Arakanese Chronicle Wali Shah. This man, however, turned traitor, and in league with a disloyal Arakanese chieftain imprisoned Narameikhla. The king managed to escape, and in 1430 regained his throne with the aid of a second force supplied by Nazir Shah.

He thereupon built himself a new capital named Mrauk-u in Arakanese, but usually known by its Burmese name of Mrohaung. The date of its foundation is given as 1433. King Narameikhla held his kingdom as the vassal of Gaur, and in token of this he and his immediate successor, though Buddhists, added Mahommedan titles to their Arakanese ones and issued medallions bearing the Kalima, the Mahommedan confession of faith.

In 1434 Narameikhla was succeeded by his brother Min Khari, also known as Ali Khan, who declared his independence of Gaur. His son Basawpyu, who succeeded him in 1459, took advantage of the weakness of Barbek Shah of Gaur to seize Chittagong. He and his successors continued to use Mahommedan titles, no longer as a sign of vassaldom but as a token of their sovereignty over Chittagong, which was recognized as lying beyond the geographical borders of Arakan. Chittagong had for centuries been a bone of contention between Arakan and Bengal and had often changed hands. It was now to remain in Arakanese hands until 1666, when the Mughals recovered it permanently for India.

Basawpyu was murdered in 1482 and his country entered upon a half-century of disorder and dynastic weakness. No less than eight kings came to the throne; most of them were assassinated. Then in 1531 a capable young king, Minbin, came to the throne and Arakan entered upon a new era. It was in his reign that the first European ships made their appearance, as raiders, and that the Portuguese freebooters (*feringhi*) began to settle at Chittagong. It was in his reign also that Tabinshwehti revived Burmese power, conquered the Mon kingdom of Pegu, and threatened the independence of Arakan. With great foresight Minbin strengthened the defences of his capital with massive earthworks and dug a deep moat, which was filled with tidal water from the river. Hence in 1544, when the inevitable Burmese attack came, although Minbin could not defeat the invaders in the open, the defensive works of Mrohaung proved an obstacle against which even the great Tabinshwehti could not prevail when he appeared before them in 1546. While the siege was on the Raja of

Tipperah raided Chittagong and Ramu with his wild tribesmen. But again victory was on the side of the Arakanese.

When Minbin died in 1553 he had a force of Portuguese mercenaries. His sea-power, based on Chittagong, was the terror of the Ganges region, and his country was on the threshold of the greatest period of her history. But her somewhat spectacular rise was hardly due to the genius of her rulers. It coincides with a period of weakness in Bengal, when, before the gradual extension eastwards of the Mughal power, the native governments of that region were tottering. The possession of Chittagong was the key to the situation; for Minbin leased to the *feringhi* who took service under his flag the port of Dianga on the sea-coast south of the mouth of the river Kurnaphuli, some twenty miles south of the modern city of Chittagong. The place soon attracted a large European and Eurasian population which drove a thriving trade with the ports of Bengal. But piracy and slave-raiding were the chief occupations of the *feringhi*, who gathered there in increasing numbers and before long became as great a source of embarrassment to the King of Arakan as to the Viceroy of Goa.

Matters came to a crisis during the reign of Min Razagri (1593–1612). He was the king who employed Philip de Brito in his attack on Nanda Bayin of Pegu, thereby opening the way for the *feringhi* leader to make himself master of Syriam. When de Brito defeated the Arakanese flotilla sent to dislodge him from the Mon port and captured the crown prince, Min Razagri decided that he must break the power of the Portuguese at Dianga. For that port also was coveted by de Brito; he planned to use it as a base for the conquest of Arakan. In 1607, therefore, the king sent an expedition which attacked Dianga by land and massacred its inhabitants without mercy. Six hundred Portuguese are said to have fallen.[1]

Among those who escaped was the egregious Sebastian Gonzales Tibão. He had been engaged in the salt trade. Now with other refugees he took to piracy, and in 1609 made himself 'king' of Sandwip Island by exterminating the Afghan pirates who had made their nest there. At Sandwip he received a refugee Arakanese prince who, as Governor of Chittagong, had quarrelled with his brother, King Razagri. Tibão married the prince's sister and when he died suddenly, probably from poison, seized all his treasure. Soon afterwards the Mughal Governor of Bengal began an attack upon the district of

[1] That is the number given by the king in a letter to the Dutch at Masulipatam in 1608. De Jonge, *Opkomst van het Nederlandsch Gezag in Oost-Indië* (1595–1610), iii, p. 291.

Noakhali, east of the Ganges mouth, which had submitted to Arakan. This threw Tibão and Min Razagri into one another's arms. But while his ally was conducting an unsuccessful land campaign Tibão took possession of the Arakanese fleet by luring its leaders to a conference and murdering them. Then he raided up the Lemro river to the very walls of Mrohaung, capturing the royal barge as a trophy.

When in 1612 Min Razagri died his successor, Minhkamaung (1612–22), decided that the power of Tibão and his ruffians must be finally broken. His first effort failed because the Raja of Tippera raided at the crucial moment and he had to withdraw his forces. Tibão, aware of his precarious position, with hostile Bengal on one side and revengeful Arakan on the other, appealed to Goa, urging the viceroy to avenge the massacre of Dianga. He suggested a joint attack on Arakan and offered to pay annual tribute to the Portuguese crown for his island 'kingdom'. The viceroy sent a fleet of fourteen galliots, which arrived off the coast of Arakan at the end of the wet monsoon in 1615. Mrohaung was attacked, but partly through faulty arrangements for co-operation and partly through the help given to the Arakanese by a Dutch ship lying in the harbour the Portuguese failed to effect a landing and sailed away. Two years later Minhkamaung captured Sandwip, wiped out the *feringhi* settlement and destroyed its fortifications. Tibão is said to have escaped, but is heard of no more.

The *feringhi* had now shot their bolt. Philip de Brito's escapade at Syriam had already come to its sorry end in 1613. So they made their peace with the king and settled down once more to assist him in his efforts to gain control over the south-eastern parts of Bengal—'the conquest of the middle land', as the Arakanese Chronicle euphemistically calls it. There was no conquest in the real sense, though for a time Arakan held the districts of Noakhali and Backergunge and some of the Sunderbunds delta. What chiefly took place was slave-raiding, and it was on so extended a scale that Dacca itself was threatened and in 1625 even captured and held for a short time. This kind of thing could never have occurred had it not been for the crisis in the Mughal empire resulting from Shah Jahan's rebellion in 1612 against his father Jehangir. Year after year the *feringhi* armada returned to Dianga bringing thousands of Bengali slaves. Before long not a house was left inhabited on either side of the rivers between Chittagong and Dacca.

Min Razagri's attempt to rid himself of the Portuguese coincided with the first Dutch trading voyage to Arakan. In 1605 they had planted factories at Masulipatam and Petapoli on the Coromandel Coast. From these two centres they began to explore the possibility of establishing trading relations with Bengal and Arakan. An invitation from Razagri led to the despatch of two merchants, Pieter Willemsz.[1] and Jan Gerritsz. Ruyll, to Mrohaung in 1607, the year of the Dianga massacre. The king, like so many other rulers in South-East Asia, received them with delight, offered them customs-free trade in his dominions, and expressed the hope that they would assist him 'to drive the Portuguese out'.

He asked particularly for their help against Philip de Brito at Syriam. 'So would he give us to wit the aforesaid Castle in Pegu, the island of Sundiva, Chittagong, Dianga, or any other places in Bengal, as he had given the same previously to the Portuguese,' wrote Pieter Willemsz. in his report.[2] And he went on to represent that if the opportunity were not seized the Portuguese would 'determine it so well for themselves that it would be to the great detriment of the Company'. But the Dutch wanted trade, not war, even against the Portuguese, in this region, for, with their hands full with the struggle to gain control over the spice-bearing areas, they were unwilling even to contemplate an expedition against Syriam.

The envoys returned to Masulipatam in May 1608. In September 1610 van Wesick, the Dutch chief of the Coromandel factories, decided to make a trial venture with an established factory at Mrohaung. Jacob Dirckszoon Cortenhoof went to take charge of it. The king, however, wanted military help rather than trade and pressed hard for it. He wanted the Dutch to build a fort at Dianga. In 1615, as we have already seen, they played an important part in warding off the attack of the Portuguese fleet on Mrohaung.[3] They had, however, no desire to become involved in Minhkamaung's wars, and especially in his projected operations against Tibão, because, as they put it, 'of the small profits, which could be made there, and the great expenses the Company must first be put to, in order to establish the king again in his kingdom, which at present is much in trouble'.[4] The factory was accordingly withdrawn in 1617.

[1] Later he left the Dutch service and joined the English East India Company, returning to the East in 1611 as one of the leaders of the Seventh Voyage. To the English he was known as Peter Floris. An English translation of extracts from his Journal, written in 1613, was published by Samuel Purchas in his *Pilgrimes*. The complete Journal was published by the Hakluyt Society in 1934.

[2] De Jonge, *op. cit.*, iii, 287–91. The castle in Pegu is Syriam, or San Jago, as the Portuguese appear to have called it. Sundiva = Sandwip.

[3] Professor Gehl has stated that the Portuguese attack on Mrohaung in 1615 was made 'to expel the Dutch' (*Camb. Hist. India*, v, 34).

[4] J. E. Heeres, *Corpus Diplomaticum Neerlando-Indicum*, i, 412.

But Arakan remained on the programme, and from 1623 Dutch ships were going there to buy the Bengali slaves captured by the marauding *feringhi*, and the surplus rice that the country produced as a result of the abundant slave labour available for cultivating the fields.[1] Early in 1625 the Dutch planted another factory at Mrohaung, with Paulus Cramer Heyn as its Chief. It came about through an expedition under Anthonij Caen which had been despatched from Batavia in September of the previous year[2] to attack Portuguese vessels. He was instructed to call at Mrohaung and discuss with King Thirithudamma (1622–38) the possibility of co-operation against 'our common enemy', and to conclude an agreement for the export of rice and slaves. Little came of the negotiations, although the king sent an envoy to Batavia in 1627, and as the slave trade did not go well Jan Pieterszoon Coen issued orders for the factory to be closed for the second time.

Trade, however, continued. The free burghers of Batavia were allowed to have a share in it, and envoys passed frequently between Batavia and Mrohaung. The Dutch, having completely depopulated the Banda Islands and given over the land there to Company's servants to cultivate with slave labour, were anxious to buy all the slaves that Arakan could spare from the proceeds of the *feringhi* raids. So the factory was soon reopened; again only for a short time. In 1631 Cornelis van Houten, the chief factor, reported that trade had been brought to a standstill by a terrible famine and pestilence. He was accordingly withdrawn and the trade again thrown open to private merchants.

Meanwhile Dianga and the *feringhi* had once more come into the limelight. In 1630 Thirithudamma appointed a new Viceroy of Chittagong, who took so violent a dislike to the *feringhi* that he sent an alarmist report to Mrohaung alleging a Portuguese plot to admit the forces of the Mughal Viceroy of Dacca into Chittagong. His intention was to persuade Thirithudamma to administer to Dianga a further dose of the medicine given in 1607. As the *feringhi* fleet was away upon its annual slaving expedition, the inhabitants, who got wind of the scheme, deputed two envoys to hurry to the capital to persuade the king that the rumour was without foundation. They were a *feringhi* captain, Gonzales Tibão, a relative of the erstwhile 'king' of Sandwip, and Fra Sebastião Manrique, an Augustinian friar of Oporto, who had

---

[1] F. W. Stapel, *Geschiedenis van Nederlandsch-Indië*, iii, p. 213.
[2] Stapel, *loc. cit.*, gives the date as 1625, but the entry in the *Daghregister* shows that Caen left Batavia on 3 September 1624. D. G. E. Hall, 'Dutch Relations with King Thirithudamma of Arakan', JBRS, xxvi 1931, pt. i, p. 3.

recently arrived in Dianga as its vicar under the jurisdiction of the archbishopric of Goa. Years later, after his return home to Portugal, Manrique told the story of his travels in detailed memoirs, which are of exceptional interest and value.[1]

The mission was successful. The king called off a large expedition he was preparing for the punishment of Dianga. He also gave permission for the construction of a Catholic church in the suburb of Daingri-pet, on the western side of the capital, where the Portuguese mercenaries of the royal guard lived. The outspoken friar, who did not fear to adjure the king to abandon his false religious beliefs and become a Christian, was treated as an honoured guest. He was shown the loot taken from Pegu in 1599 and was greatly impressed by the white elephant. Nanda Bayin's daughter, who had been carried off to Mrohaung and married to King Razagri, received him and related the story of her sufferings with deep emotion. Early in 1631, after a stay of six months, Manrique returned to Dianga.

In the following year Shah Jahan, now the Great Mughal, decided to wipe out the Portuguese settlement at Hugli. He suspected it of being implicated in the intolerable slave-raids of the Dianga freebooters. His religious fervour also had been deeply stirred by the abduction in 1629 by the *feringhi* of the wife of a high official near Dacca and her subsequent conversion to Catholicism by Fra Manrique. The town put up a desperate resistance, but without timely help could not possibly hold out. Some of the defenders cut their way out, boarded their ships and got away to Saugar Island, just outside the river mouth, where they proceeded to establish themselves. At the same time they sent a Jesuit, Father Cabral, to ask King Thirithudamma for help. News of the siege, however, had already reached him long before Cabral's arrival, and he had ordered the *feringhi* armada of Dianga to make a surprise attack upon the Mughal fleet in the Hugli river. The armada was held up by bad weather, and when at last it was able to sail it arrived too late to save the city. It managed, however, to follow up the Mughal fleet and destroy it. Then it fell back on Saugar to await reinforcements.

In launching this attack the king appears to have had a double object. He aimed at preventing the Mughals from attempting the capture of Chittagong; he naturally expected this to be their next objective after taking Hugli. He hoped also that a decisive victory

[1] See the Hakluyt Society's edition of the *Travels of Fray Sebastien Manrique, 1629–1643*, edited by Lt.-Col. C. E. Luard, 2 vols., 1927. Manrique's adventures at Dianga and Mrohaung are also the subject of Maurice Collis's *Land of the Great Image*.

MROHAUNG IN THE SEVENTEENTH CENTURY

over the Mughal fleet would enable him to persuade the Viceroy of Goa to join forces with him in an invasion of Bengal. The viceroy was indeed willing to discuss matters, and in 1633 deputed Gaspar de Mesquita to proceed to Mrohaung for this purpose, with Fra Manrique as his adviser. The negotiations, however, came to nothing. The king's grandiose scheme for the conquest of Bengal had to be dropped.

The Goanese envoy sailed away, but Manrique had to remain behind. The king liked him. Moreover, he knew too many state secrets to be allowed to return at once to Dianga. Not until two years later, in 1635, was he permitted to depart. His book tells of further strange adventures while at Mrohaung. He gives also a vivid description of Thirithudamma's coronation, which was not celebrated until 1635 because of a prophecy that he would die within a year of it. Before it took place barbarous propitiatory sacrifices were made to avert this fate. But three years later his chief queen procured his murder and placed her lover on the throne. He was King Narapatigyi (1638–45).

Manrique makes no mention of Thirithudamma's relations with the Dutch. In 1633 he had sent two envoys to Batavia to invite them to reopen their factory. They were engaged upon the blockade of Malacca and needed the food supplies that could be obtained from Arakan. Two Dutch ships, therefore, with cargoes of goods for sale escorted the Arakanese envoys home, and in 1635 Adam van der Mandere reopened the factory. At first trade went well. But soon difficulties arose. The king wanted a military alliance, and when he heard that Mughal ambassadors had been received at Batavia he sent an angry letter to warn the governor-general that the Mughals were his enemies. Moreover, van der Mandere's relations with the king were bad. The king established a royal monopoly over rice, and when van der Mandere objected to the price and attempted to buy his supplies in the open market serious trouble resulted.

Van der Mandere's conduct was considered undignified by Governor-General Anthony van Diemen and his books were found to have been carelessly kept. He was accordingly transferred elsewhere, and van Diemen directed that in future 'men of good bearing and not slovens' should be appointed to Mrohaung. The next Chief, Arent Jansen van den Helm, got on extremely well with the usurper Narapatigyi as a result of lavish presents of wine and spirits, which the latter much appreciated.[1] But in 1643 the king's health broke down and he lost

---

[1] A *firman* granted to van den Helm by 'Narabidrij' in August 1643 is printed in Heeres, *Corpus*, i, p. 414.

control over affairs. Then an incident occurred which caused the Dutch to close the factory once more. A frigate belonging to a Dutch free burgher, bound for Chittagong with a valuable cargo of piece-goods, was decoyed into Mrohaung harbour, its cargo confiscated and its captain and crew imprisoned. When efforts for their release failed and several of them died in prison the Dutch broke off relations. For eight years the factory was empty, and the Dutch subjected Arakanese shipping to severe reprisals.

Narapatigyi's nephew Thado, who succeeded him in 1645, was a nonentity and reigned for only seven years. But his son Sandathu-damma, who came to the throne in 1652 and reigned for thirty-two years, became famous as one of the best of the Arakanese monarchs. Although he was quite young at the time of his accession,[1] it soon became known at Batavia that he had a more enlightened attitude towards trade than his predecessors. And as the directors of the V.O.C. were urging Batavia to reopen trade with Arakan, a Dutch envoy, Joan Goessens, left in October 1652 with a long list of stipu-lations for negotiations with the new king. Agreement seems to have been easily reached, and the terms, embodied in the form of a treaty, were accepted by both parties in 1653.[2] Its main provisions were to the effect that the Dutch were to enjoy customs-free trade under royal licence and be exempt from the necessity of buying and selling through the king's agents. Goessens was much impressed by the riches and splendour of the Court. There can be no doubt of the prosperity of the kingdom at this time.

The Dutch factory, thus reopened in 1653, carried on successfully until 1665, when it was again closed, this time for a political reason. Shah Shuja, the second son of the Great Mughal Shah Jahan, had been appointed Viceroy of Bengal in 1639. In 1657, when the emperor fell so seriously ill that there were premature rumours of his death, a struggle for power began between his sons. It was won by Aurang-zeb, who deposed his father in 1658 and became emperor himself. Shah Shuja refused to accept this arrangement but was defeated by Aurangzeb's general Mir Jumla, and after failing to hold Bengal fled from Dacca to Chittagong, together with his family and a bodyguard of some 500 faithful followers. Sandathudamma granted him permission to continue his journey to Mrohaung on condition that his followers

---

[1] The Dutch estimate of thirteen or fourteen in the *Daghregister* is surely wrong. Walther Schouten, who saw him in 1661, estimated his age at about twenty-eight.
[2] A full account of the negotiations is in the *Daghregister* for 1653, pp. 98–103. Valentijn prints the terms of the treaty in his *Oud en Nieuw Oost-Indiën*, v, i, pp. 140–6.

surrendered their arms. He arrived there on 26 August 1660 and was favourably received by the king, who assigned him a residence near the city on the right bank of the Wathi Creek at the foot of Bah-budaung Hill. He asked for ships to convey him and his people to Mecca and was promised that they would be supplied.

But the promise remained unfulfilled and the fugitive prince soon found his situation intolerable. Repeated demands for his surrender came from Mir Jumla, and Sandathudamma, expecting trouble, posted his fleet off Dianga and sent up reinforcements. A state of alarm developed and a rumour spread that Mir Jumla had taken Dianga. Moreover, the king asked for one of Shah Shuja's daughters in marriage and his request was indignantly rejected. Thus were bad relations fomented; deliberately, suggests Phayre, in order that Sandathudamma might have a specious cause for quarrel, since he was only too conscious of the contempt in which the haughty Mughal held him and was greedy to get possession of the rich hoard of treasure the other had brought with him.

Shah Shuja, realizing his peril, made a desperate attempt to escape from the country. But his plans miscarried, and when the populace set upon his followers the latter ran amok and set fire to a large part of the city before they were rounded up and massacred. That was in December 1660. It was given out that he had attempted to seize the palace. The king, it was said, had only been dissuaded by his mother from having him killed. She argued that killing princes was a dangerous sport for which his own subjects might acquire a taste. But on 7 February 1661 Shah Shuja's residence was attacked and there was another massacre. Shah Shuja was never seen again. It was rumoured that he had fled to the hills with his sons but had been caught and put to death. Not until months afterwards did Gerrit van Voorburg, the Chief of the Dutch factory, discover what had happened. His report is summarized in the *Daghregister* thus:

'The prince Chasousa, of whom in the previous Arakan advices of 22 February last it was said that he was a fugitive, and had not been found either alive or dead, is believed, though with no certainty, to have perished in the first fury, but his body was made unrecognizable by the grandees in order the better to be able to deck their persons with the costly jewels which he wore. His three sons together with his wives and daughters have been taken; the wives and daughters have been brought into the king's palace, and the sons, after being imprisoned for some time, have been released and permitted to live in a little house. Every day the gold and silver, which the

Arakanese have taken, are brought into the king's treasury to be melted down.'[1]

As soon as the Viceroy of Bengal heard, through the Dutch factory at Dacca, of Shah Shuja's murder he commandeered a Dutch ship to carry an envoy to Mrohaung with a peremptory demand for the surrender of his children. It was refused, and the king protested to Batavia against the use of a Dutch ship by a Mughal envoy. As the threat of war increased, so did the Dutch position as neutrals become correspondingly more uncomfortable. In July 1663 a desperate attempt to rescue the three captive princes failed. Thereupon the king burnt his boats by having them beheaded and slaughtering a large number of Bengalis and Moslems at the capital. Early in the next year the *feringhi* fleet sailed up the river towards Dacca, put to flight a Mughal flotilla of 260 vessels, destroying more than half of them, and carried away hundreds of people into slavery.

The time was now past when that sort of thing could go on with impunity. Shayista Khan, Aurangzeb's maternal uncle, had just been appointed Viceroy of Bengal and was determined to burn out the pirate nest at Dianga. He called on the Dutch for assistance and threatened them with expulsion from all their Bengal factories if they refused. At the same time the King of Arakan, who was preparing yet another great raid on Bengal, ordered them to lend their ships for service with his armada. Luckily for them, a storm shattered his fleet before it sailed, and while he was repairing the damage the Dutch ships got away. When at last it did sail it carried out an even more devastating raid than the previous one.

In July 1665 the Council of the Indies at Batavia held a special meeting at which secret orders were passed for the abandonment of the Mrohaung factory. The king was cleverly hoodwinked, and on a dark night in November the factors hurriedly loaded everything that could be carried away on four ships and decamped. At the mouth of the river they were overtaken by a special messenger bearing a letter from the king for delivery to the governor-general. Why, he asked, were the Dutch so much afraid of the Viceroy of Bengal? It would be easier for him to build the Tower of Babel than conquer Arakan.

But the *feringhi* navy was to raid Bengal no more. Shayista Khan, who had built and equipped a new fleet, had already seized Sandwip Island as a base for an attack upon Dianga. What would have happened had the *feringhis* decided to fight it out it is hard to say, for they were more than a match for the Bengal navy. But at the crucial moment

[1] Hall, 'Studies in Dutch Relations with Arakan', iii, JBRS, xxvi (1936), pt. i, p. 24.

they quarrelled with the Arakanese, and when Shayista Khan seized the opportunity to invite them to change sides most of them did so. Then early in 1666 he assailed Dianga by land and sea. In February he defeated the Arakanese fleet in a fierce fight. Dianga surrendered, and the whole of the Chittagong district down to the River Naaf was annexed to the Mughal empire.

Shorn of its powerful fleet the Arakan kingdom declined rapidly after 1666. Some years later the Dutch returned and reopened their factory, but we know little about it. The *Daghregister* for 1682 contains a letter from Governor-General Cornelis Speelman to King Sandathudamma announcing that owing to the lack of trade the factory was to be 'reduced'. A resident factor would no longer remain there after the business of collecting outstanding debts had been completed. He hoped, however, to send one or two ships annually for the purchase of rice.[1]

When Sandathudamma died in 1684 the country became a prey to internal disorder. As Harvey puts it: 'the profits of piracy had gone but the piratical instinct remained, rendering government impossible.'[2] Many of Shah Shuja's followers had been taken into the royal service as Archers of the Guard. Their numbers were maintained by a constant supply of recruits from north India. In 1685 they murdered Thirithuriya, Sandathudamma's son and successor, plundered the treasury, and placed his brother Waradhammaraza on the throne. When he was unable to give them their promised pay they mutinied and set the palace on fire. Then they roamed about the country doing as they pleased. After some time they came to terms with the king, and he returned to his capital. But in 1692 they deposed him and placed his brother Muni Thudhamma Raza on the throne, only to murder him some two years later and place another brother on the throne.

So things went on until 1710. In that year an Arakanese chieftain Maha Danda Bo, with the support of a band of devoted men, overcame the Archers and deported them to Ramree Island, where their descendants still live, speaking Arakanese and retaining their Mahommedan religion. Maha Danda Bo became king Sandawizaya and reigned until 1731. But he spent little of his time on constructive work and much of it in raiding his neighbours. He made war on the Raja of Tippera and collected booty and prisoners. He took advantage

---

[1] Vol. ii of 1682, pp. 1127–8. Pieter van Dam, in his *Beschryvinge van de Oostindische Compagnie*, makes no mention of Arakan after the Shah Shuja episode.
[2] *Op. cit.*, p. 148.

of the weakness of the Toungoo dynasty's hold on central Burma to cross the mountains and raid Prome and Malun. The decline of the Mughal power after the death of Aurangzeb in 1707 tempted him to push his authority towards the north and raid Sandwip Island. But nothing came of all these efforts, and when he was murdered in 1731 the country relapsed into chaos.

Fourteen more kings came to the throne before King Bodawpaya's armies entered the kingdom and deposed the last king Thamada in 1785. Long before that event Arakanese chieftains were fleeing to the Court of Ava and urging Burmese intervention. When at last it came it brought such evils that half the population of Arakan fled into the Chittagong district and a situation was created that again challenged the security of Bengal, this time with consequences of far greater moment. For it was one of the main causes of the first Anglo-Burmese war of 1824-6.

CHAPTER 22

THE BEGINNINGS OF THE KONBAUNG DYNASTY IN BURMA, 1752–82

WHEN he returned to Pegu the Yuva Raja left Talaban with inadequate forces to deal with a rebellion on a big scale. This was precisely what the Moksobomyo rebel leader's successful resistance created within a surprisingly short time. Calling himself Aungzeya, 'the Victorious', and 'inspired by the good Nats who observe religion', as the *Mahayazawin* puts it, he found himself the leader of a national movement. In May 1752 he defeated an attack upon his stronghold led by Talaban in person. In the following month he went over to the offensive and attacked a Mon stockade set up to cut off his supplies. Its garrison abandoned it in a panic, leaving all their equipment behind. He was now a *minlaung* or claimant to the throne, styling himself Alaungpaya, or 'embryo Buddha', and provided with a pedigree connecting him with Mohnyinthado, who had reigned at Ava from 1427 to 1440. Everywhere he went he exacted the oath of allegiance. Moksobomyo, 'the town of the hunter chief', became Shwebo, 'the town of the golden leader', and there he began to build a palace in the approved traditional style.

But the Mons were not easily driven out of Upper Burma, and they were joined by the Gwe Shans of Madaya-Okpo. It was a war of stockades and in its course the patriot forces suffered many setbacks. Not until December 1753 was Alaungpaya able to encircle Ava, but by that time he had formed a considerable flotilla, mainly of boats captured from the enemy. The Mons, after failing to capture his main stockade, lost heart. There was no sign of reinforcements from Pegu, and they feared that the Burmese and Shan inhabitants of the city would join hands with the besiegers outside. Accordingly they abandoned it by night with the greatest secrecy and made their escape downstream before the Burmese realized what was happening.

Alaungpaya was not in a position to pursue the retreating Mons or stage an attack upon the south. He had first to make sure of the allegiance of the Shan sawbwas of the north. While he was engaged upon this task King Binnya Dala of Pegu launched an attack in great force upon the Ava region. Had it been delivered earlier, while the

Mons still held the city, it might easily have tipped the scale against Alaungpaya. But the Yuva Raja, the commander-in-chief of the Mon forces, was an incompetent leader; and although he defeated a Burmese army at Talokmyo and ravaged the country as far as Kyauk-myaung, close to Shwebo, a counter-attack delived by Alaungpaya from Shwebo, and a sortie on the part of the beleaguered garrison in Ava, inflicted such losses that in May 1754 the whole invading force began a hasty retreat which did not stop before Prome was reached. Meanwhile discontent in the Mon kingdom had come to a head in a plot aiming at the restoration of the captive Mahadammayaza Dipati, who was at Pegu. When it was discovered, and the deposed king, three of his sons and many others implicated were done to death, the delta Burmese rose in revolt and rushed the town of Prome, which they proceeded to hold, even though it was invested by the Mon forces retreating from Ava.

But the siege was not pressed with vigour, and early in 1755 Alaungpaya, having collected a great force for the conquest of the Pegu kingdom, relieved its Burmese defenders without difficulty. The Mons, however, had constructed a strongly defended earthwork just to the south of the town, and there was much heavy fighting before this was finally stormed. This success enabled him to claim the allegiance of central Burma, and he spent some weeks at Prome engaged upon the task of pacification. Then he pushed on southwards to meet the Mons at Lunhse in the Henzada district. The decisive victory which he gained inspired him to rename the place Myanaung, 'Speedy Victory'. Here amidst scenes of festival and rejoicing he received the submission of Toungoo, Henzada, Myaungmya, Bassein and even the Arakanese district of Sandoway. Finally, pushing on through Danubyu, he drove the Mons out of Dagon at the beginning of May and celebrated the close of his campaign with a festival at the Shwe Dagon Pagoda. He planned to make the place the chief port of his kingdom and began work on the foundation of a new city, which he optimistically named Rangoon, 'the End of Strife'.

The strife, however, was by no means ended. The capital, Pegu, still maintained its independence, and Syriam, its port, the head-quarters of European trade, where the main Mon force was concentrated, close to Rangoon, was far too strongly defended for him to risk an attack upon it. Moreover, the Mons were aided by a brilliant Frenchman, the Sieur de Bruno, whom Dupleix had sent some years earlier to Pegu as his agent.

At the end of the War of the Austrian Succession, while Dupleix as Governor of Pondicherry was busy with schemes for extending French influence at the expense of his British rivals, the Court of Pegu was looking for a European ally from whom it might obtain the fire-arms which would give it a decisive advantage over the Burmese. After the closing of the European dockyards at Syriam during the early stages of the struggle for independence, while the British were repre-sented by a few private traders who counted for little, French interests had been left in the hands of an Italian priest, Père Vittoni, who was a *persona grata* with the Mons. At his suggestion a Mon mission was sent in 1750 to sound Dupleix regarding assistance. Hence it came about that a few weeks after one agent, Bussy, left Pondicherry to establish French influence in the Deccan, another, Bruno, departed for Burma on a similar mission. He arrived at Pegu in July 1751 and had no difficulty in negotiating a treaty by which, in return for com-mercial concessions, the Mons were to receive substantial French aid. On his return to Pondicherry he convinced Dupleix that a dazzling opportunity awaited the French in Burma if he was prepared for armed intervention in the Mon-Burmese struggle. With 500 or 600 well-equipped French troops, he said, it would be a simple matter to gain control over the Mon kingdom. Dupleix at once wrote home commending the plan and asking for the necessary reinforcements to put it into execution.

Meanwhile the British at Madras had become highly suspicious of French designs upon Burma. Even before Bruno's mission Thomas Saunders, the Governor of Fort St. George, had reported home a rumour that the French intended to seize the island of Negrais[1] and had urged the East India Company to forestall them by planting a settlement there. The directors gave their full approval to the plan. Their reply was despatched in December 1751, long before news of Bruno's mission to Pegu could have reached London. Before Saunders received this despatch he had word, through English private traders at Syriam, of Bruno's treaty with the Mon government, and at once took action on his own authority. He sent a small expedition under Thomas Taylor to survey the island and commissioned Robert West-garth, a private trader at Syriam, to negotiate with the Court of Pegu for its cession to the East India Company.

Taylor found the local officials extremely hostile, and after a cursory survey went on to Pegu to join forces with Westgarth. They found the Mon government resolutely opposed to any settlement on the island. While they were there, in November 1752, Bruno returned as

---

[1] D. G. E. Hall, 'The Tragedy of Negrais', JBRS, xxi (1931), pt. iii, p. 63.

Dupleix's resident agent; and since it became only too obvious that his influence with the Mons was supreme, negotiations were broken off and Taylor returned to Madras. After leaving Negrais he had sent off a very unfavourable report on the island, which had caused Saunders to have doubts as to the wisdom of going on with the scheme, notwithstanding the enthusiastic sanction accorded to it in the directors' despatch. But when Taylor arrived in Madras with the story of Bruno's ascendancy at Pegu, Saunders cast all doubts aside and sent a strong expedition which took possession of the island on 26 April 1753. Had he known that the directors of the French Company had already turned down Dupleix's proposal, he might have acted differently. In a letter dated 2 January 1753 they had advised Dupleix that the shipbuilding concessions at Syriam granted in the treaty of 1751 were adequate; anything involving military commitments would be certain to provoke a further contest with the British.

Taylor had reported that the island was very unhealthy and would be useless as a trading station. His estimate proved only too true; it was flooded during the rainy season and malaria-ridden. No attempt was ever made to develop it as a naval station. But although disease took a terrible toll of its staff, both European and Asian, and all its supplies of food and labour had to be brought across from Madras, there could be no thought of abandoning the settlement while Bruno remained at Pegu.

The rise of Alaungpaya, on the other hand, caused both Dupleix and the Mons to have second thoughts regarding their alliance. The former sent a present of arms to Alaungpaya. The latter asked the English East India Company for military aid and offered to cede Negrais. These were manœuvres, but the Mons certainly needed far more help than Pondicherry could afford. When, late in 1754, Dupleix was recalled to France, the hope of any real French help to the Mons faded out, though Bruno remained at Pegu. At almost the same time Thomas Taylor returned to Madras from Negrais completely convinced that Alaungpaya's success was assured, and that the Company should cultivate good relations with him. And a few months later, when the Burmese king, in the course of his rapid thrust down the Irrawaddy, sent envoys to Negrais asking for arms, Henry Brooke, the Company's agent there, wrote to Fort St. George urging that all possible assistance should be given to him. But Madras could no more afford to satisfy Alaungpaya's demands for arms than could Pondicherry those of the Mons, and for the simple reason that a new Anglo-French struggle in India was imminent.

Alaungpaya's final victory, however, was by no means assured when his campaign came to a halt at Dagon just before the onset of the wet monsoon of 1755. He had totally inadequate siege equipment with which to assault such strongly defended cities as Syriam and Pegu. Serious trouble had broken out in the north. The Manipuris were raiding again, the Shans were restive, and there was some fear that a member of the old Toungoo royal family who had taken refuge in Siam was planning to recover the throne of his fathers. Alaungpaya had perforce to return to deal with these threats, knowing full well that as soon as his back was turned the Mon army at Syriam would strive to defeat his holding force at Rangoon.

This indeed happened, but the Mon attacks were made with so little determination that they failed dismally, although the Mon heir-apparent and Bruno, who directed them, received a certain amount of unwilling assistance from a number of English ships that had come to Syriam for trade. One of them happened to be a Company's vessel, the *Arcot*, whose entirely unauthorized action caused grave concern to the Fort St. George authorities, for when Alaungpaya heard of it he at once suspected the good faith of the Negrais factory, which had agreed to negotiate with him.[1] Hence, when Captain George Baker, who had been deputed by Henry Brooke to negotiate an agreement, appeared at Shwebo, he found the king in no mood to come to terms. The handsome present of cannon which Baker brought with him, and the promise to supply him with all the military stores the Negrais settlement could spare, somewhat mollified the king's anger, but the utmost concession he would make was that negotiations might be resumed when he returned to Rangoon to direct operations aganst Syriam.

Alaungpaya tackled the problems which had brought him back to his homeland with characteristic vigour. A punitive expedition, the first of many, against Manipur wrought fearful havoc. A strong detachment went to the Shan states and received tokens of submission. The Viceroy of Yunnan accorded the king official recognition. Then with a large force, which included Shan and Chin levies, he returned to the Mon country. At Rangoon Ensign John Dyer and Dr. William Anderson met him and concluded an agreement whereby in return for military stores he recognized the Negrais settlement and gave permission for a factory to be established at Bassein. The terms were recorded in a royal letter on gold-leaf, directed to the King of England. It was beneath Alaungpaya's dignity to deal with a Governor

---

[1] 'Account of the English Proceedings at Dagoon, 1755', in Dalrymple's *Oriental Repertory*, vol. i, pp. 177–200.

of Madras representing a mere trading company. The missive was delivered through Mr. Secretary Pitt, Britain's great war minister, early in 1758. By that time the East India Company had thoroughly repented of its rash action in seizing Negrais. Orders had already been sent out for complete withdrawal from Burma.

In February 1756 the siege of Syriam began in earnest. Everything now depended upon whether Bruno's urgent appeals would move Pondicherry to send the necessary help. Had the relief expedition which was at last despatched only arrived in time the city could have been saved. The first two ships bringing it arrived just two days too late, when Alaungpaya had captured the place by a surprise attack. The third ship, sent from Pondicherry, was delayed by bad weather, and on arrival at the river-mouth learnt of the fall of the city in time to turn homewards. The other two, ignorant of what had happened, were decoyed up the river by a false message which Alaungpaya forced the captive Bruno to write before executing him. They were neatly run aground by their Burmese pilots and forced to surrender. The guns, muskets and ammunition they were bringing for the Mons were a godsend to Alaungpaya: even more so the 200 fighting men he impressed into his service.

He could now tackle the defences of Pegu. The city, however, put up a dogged resistance and was not finally taken until May 1757. During its long siege Alaungpaya was insatiable in his demands on Negrais for munitions and threatened to treat the settlement in the same manner as Syriam if they were not met. But with the elimination of French influence in Burma the Negrais settlement had lost its *raison d'être*, and with the Seven Years War in progress it had become urgent for the British to concentrate upon the French threat in India. As early as March 1757 the directors of the Company had issued orders for the liquidation of the Burma venture. Some months, of course, elapsed before they were received in Madras. When they did arrive Fort St. George was not in a position to carry them out, for Lally's operations in the Carnatic absorbed its whole attention. Indeed, throughout the whole of 1758 the British were on the defensive in that region, and from December of that year until the following February Madras itself was besieged by the French.

In the meantime Alaungpaya, having completed the conquest of the Mons, sent peremptory orders for the Chief of Negrais to attend on him at Prome while on his way back to his capital. But Captain Thomas Newton deemed it unwise to go in person and deputed Ensign Thomas Lester instead. Lester describes in detail his interviews with the king in a journal which is one of the most interesting of the many documents which have survived from this period of British contact with Burma.[1] He found Alaungpaya somewhat piqued that George II had failed to reply to the gold-leaf letter he had despatched in the previous year. But his victory had put him in a very good humour, and he agreed to make a 'treaty' recognizing the British position at Negrais and Bassein in return for an annual present of munitions and a promise of military aid against his enemies. The 'treaty', was, of course, valueless, since the Burmese king could not bind himself in such a way; he could only issue orders, and in any case they were not binding on his successor. Aitchison significantly omitted the document from his collection of the East India Company's *Treaties, Sanads and Engagements.*[2] Nevertheless under its second clause, which granted the British a site 'on the bank of the Persaim River, opposite to the Pagoda Hill, and the Old Town of Persaim', a factory was actually constructed at Bassein in 1757 and became an agency for the purchase of teak timber.

With Madras unable to carry out the directors' order to evacuate the Negrais settlement, the task devolved upon the Governor of Fort William, Calcutta. The main operation of bringing away Captain Thomas Newton and the garrison was performed in April 1759. But at both Negrais and Bassein the collected timber and stores were more than the ships could carry away. Lieutenant Hope and a small guard were accordingly left behind in charge of them. During the cold season of 1758-9 Alaungpaya was absent on a campaign in Manipur. His absence was the signal for a desperate effort on the part of the Mons to throw off the Burmese yoke. They massacred the Burmese in several districts, defeated the Burmese viceroy and drove him into Henzada. Alaungpaya had to abandon his campaign and hurry to Rangoon. When he arrived there, however, the local forces had mastered the rebels. An Armenian in the royal service whispered to the king a rumour that the Chief of Negrais had helped the Mon rebels. A few months later Burmese troops surprised the settlement, massacred its personnel, and destroyed its buildings.

The cause of this treacherous act was at the time thought to have been the king's fury at what he must have taken to be a second case of British perfidy. But it was not the reason given by the king himself to an English survivor of the massacre at a subsequent interview. He said it was because the King of England had not replied to his letter,

---

[1] Dalrymple, *op. cit.*, vol. i, pp. 201-22.
[2] His comments on the 'treaty' are in vol. i, p. 325.

and that he had come to the conclusion that 'the English and the Company looked on him and his people as fools'.[1] One must bear in mind that the rumour cannot have reached Alaungpaya later than May 1759, and the massacre did not take place until the following October. It is not without significance also that the Bassein factory was unharmed. The story itself was a *canard* deliberately invented by the Armenians, who took every possible opportunity at this time to bedevil the British because of a pathological jealousy of their increasing influence in India and elsewhere in the East. The evidence goes to show that Alaungpaya was all along determined to evict the British from Negrais. He wanted them closer under his control. To achieve his aim by means of a massacre, however, was not his intention. It was deliberately planned and carried out by the French officer in charge of the troops sent to seize the settlement, presumably as an act of revenge for the defeats sustained by his country at British hands.[2]

Alaungpaya's expedition against Manipur, from which he had been recalled by the Mon rising, inflicted upon that country one of the worst disasters in its history. Thousands of people were deported and settled in the Sagaing and Amarapura districts of Upper Burma. From this time the astrologers at the Court of Ava were Manipuri Brahmans, while Manipuris formed a cavalry regiment in the Burmese army.

The last exploit of Alaungpaya's stormy career was an invasion of Siam. The destruction of the Mon kingdom had caused a further great exodus of its inhabitants to Siam, and the border districts in consequence were in a state of constant disorder. In reviving the old struggle with Ayut'ia Alaungpaya's motives were strikingly similar to those which had inspired Bayinnaung in the sixteenth century. He hoped to regain control over Chiengmai. He seems also to have planned to repopulate the delta districts by large-scale deportations from Siam.

The Siamese were expecting his invasion and had massed to defend the westward approaches to their capital. The Burmese, however, took them by surprise by an attack from the south. Alaungpaya's force went by way of Tavoy to Tenasserim, crossed over to the Gulf of Siam, and then marched northwards to Ayut'ia, which it encircled in April 1760. During the following month the king was desperately wounded by the bursting of a siege-gun while he was directing the fire of a battery. The siege was at once abandoned and the army began a hurried retreat homewards. The king died at Taikkala just before

[1] Hall, *op.cit.*, p. 116.   [2] *Ibid.*, p. 119.

reaching the Salween. His body was borne back to Shwebo and buried there in the presence of a vast concourse of his mourning subjects. He had been a great leader who had restored the self-respect of the Burmese after the disasters they had suffered at the hands of the Manipuris, the Shans and the Mons. He had also given them a taste for military glory which for over half a century was to make them the terror of their neighbours.

Naungdawgyi, Alaungpaya's son and successor, had a short and troubled reign, full of rebellions. The most serious was led by one of his father's generals, Minkaung Nawrahta, who seized Ava and planned to restore the Toungoo dynasty. While the siege was in progress Captain Walter Alves arrived from India to seek permission to remove the East India Company's effects at Bassein, and to request the surrender of a number of English prisoners. The new king was most anxious for the Company to resume trading operations in his country and sent Alves back to Calcutta to ask Fort William to reconsider the decision to withdraw. But it was to no purpose; the Governor of Bengal was under firm orders from home to liquidate the Burma venture. When Alves returned to Burma in the following year his requests were granted. With his departure relations between the Company and the Court of Ava ceased for a long term of years.

Naungdawgyi's brother and successor, Hsinbyushin (1763–76), transferred his capital from Shwebo back to Ava. The troubles during his predecessor's reign taught him that it was essential for the capital in Upper Burma to be near to the vital Kyaukse district. And although he revived his father's project of conquering Siam, neither Pegu nor Rangoon in the disaffected Mon country was considered suitable as a capital. His plan was to exploit the northern approach to Ayut'ia by subduing the Laos country and using it as a base of operations. Hence in 1764 the war began with campaigns which resulted in the conquest of Chiengmai and Vien Chang (Vientiane). Early in 1766 Ayut'ia was besieged. It made a long and stubborn resistance. When at last it fell, in March 1767, the Burmese reduced it to a heap of ruins. Even the royal records were burnt. Thousands of captives and vast booty were deported. 'The King of Hanthawaddy [i.e. Bayinnaung] waged war like a monarch,' comments the Siamese chronicler, 'but the King of Ava like a robber.'

But again the Burmese were unable to hold Siam in subjection. Their incursion into the Laos country caused such a ferment among the states bordering on Yunnan that the Chinese were forced to intervene, and between 1766 and 1769 Burma had to defend herself against a series of Chinese invasions. This diversion weakened her hold upon Siam and enabled the Siamese under a leader P'ya Taksin ('Paya Tak' in the Burmese chronicles) to stage a rapid recovery, and while Burma was straining every nerve to repel the Chinese he began systematically to exterminate their garrisons, and by the end of 1768 had regained Ayut'ia.

The Shan states had been disturbed for some years before 1764. The Gwe Shans of Okpo-Madaya, the prime movers in the revolt of 1740 which had brought the downfall of the Toungoo dynasty, had caused so much trouble by raiding the northern states that in 1758-9 Alaungpaya himself had sent a punitive expedition against them. The survivors settled in Mongmit, Hsenwi and Menglien, a trans-Salween state, whence they carried their raids across the Chinese border. The Chinese began to suspect that the Burmese were at the bottom of the trouble, especially when in 1764 a Burmese army marching against the Laos states passed through Kengtung, which was at loggerheads with Kenghung, a tributary of China. So much uneasiness was caused by the Burmese invasion of Chiengmai and Vien Chang that when in 1765 they sent a general to collect tribute from some minor Salween states these complained to China. There was nothing unusual in the Burmese demand. For centuries these states, though under Chinese protection, had been accustomed to pay tribute to the more powerful kingdoms near their borders. Hsinbyushin's ambitious policy, however, filled them with alarm.

The war began in 1766 with a punitive expedition directed by the Yunnan viceroy against Kengtung, the largest and most easterly of the Shan states subject to Burma. With Burmese help the sawbwa drove out the Chinese. This disaster caused the Viceroy of Yunnan such loss of face that he committed suicide. Imperial China therefore decided that Burma must be taught a severe lesson. Late in the same year, in obedience to orders from Peking, a new viceroy, Yang Yingchu, led an invading force over the well-worn trade route through Bhamo, only to be held up by Burmese frontier forces at Kaungton on the Irrawaddy, south of the town. The arrival of reinforcements from Ava enabled the defenders to take the offensive, and the Chinese were pushed back over their frontier. A larger Burmese force marched through Mohnyin and Mogaung to Waingmaw, south of Myitkyina, and thence to the Nammyin Creek, where it defeated a Chinese detachment. Both Burmese forces thereupon entered Chinese territory.

These embarrassing failures led to another change in the Yunnan viceroyalty. Ming Jui, a son-in-law of the emperor, now took Yang

Ying-chu's place. His plan was to launch a double attack on Burma as soon as the rainy season of 1767 ended. While one force was to attack through Bhamo, the main attack, directed by Ming Jui in person, was to proceed by a more southerly route, passing through Hsenwi and Hsipaw, which the Manchu force had used a century earlier when chasing the last Ming emperor Yung-li. This nearly succeeded. After defeating two Burmese armies Ming Jui got to Singaung, within thirty miles of Ava, and the situation became critical (February 1768). But although large Burmese forces were tied up in Siam, a third army managed to cut Ming Jui's communications through the Shan states. And when he turned to deal with the threat he got into such difficulties that he lost the main body of his army in trying to cut his way out of the trap that closed round him. The other Chinese army, which should have come to his assistance, wasted precious time trying to reduce the Kaungton stockade, and finally gave up the task and retreated homewards. A frightful example was made of its commander for his part in the general debacle. Ming Jui could have escaped, but rather than face his emperor he cut off his pigtail, sent it to him, and then committed suicide.

In 1769 the Chinese made a final attempt to wipe out these disasters. This time their army made a third attempt to reach Ava by the Bhamo route. Once more it was held up by the Kaungton stockade. Unable to take it, the Chinese built a great fortified camp at Shwenyaungbin. When the Burmese stormed this and drove them out they asked for terms, and a peace treaty was signed on the spot in December 1769. Under its terms, which were never ratified by King Hsinbyushin, the Chinese were to withdraw, trade was to be restored, and decennial missions were to be exchanged. The king was furious when he heard that the Chinese were to be allowed to return home, and the victorious commanders dared not return to face his wrath. To appease it they led off their forces to attack Manipur. There they won a decisive victory which caused the raja to flee to Assam. Then, having placed a Burmese nominee on the throne, they deported thousands more Manipuris to Burma.

The Kaungton Treaty was a statesmanlike measure. Once more the large caravans with hundreds of pack animals began to traverse the 'Old Burma Road', while Sino-Burmese relations gained a new cordiality which lasted until the end of the dynasty, and beyond. Burma took immense pride in this fine achievement: it stimulated her expansive ardour to a dangerous level. The remainder of Hsinbyushin's reign, however, provided little glory and much evidence of the need

for a new policy. The war with Siam, which only ceased with Hsinbyushin's death in 1776, saw nothing but disasters for the Burmese.
Paya Tak drove them out of the Laos country, recovered Chiengmai
and reunited Siam. In 1773 there was another sudden Mon rising,
which showed how precarious was the Burmese hold on the south
country. Rangoon was burnt, together with a number of ships that
were being built there by French shipwrights. When the Burmese
recovered their strength and put down the rebellion thousands again
fled into Siam, where they were well received. A Burmese force
which pursued them along the Three Pagodas route was surrounded
and captured by the Siamese. In the following year Hsinbyushin
made a state progress down the Irrawaddy to Rangoon. There he
put to death Binnya Dala, the captive Mon king, who had been taken
in 1757 when Pegu fell.

When Hsinbyushin died in 1776 his chief commander, Maha
Thihathura, had just suffered a disastrous defeat in Siam. His son
Singu, who succeeded him, decided to bring the war to an end and
ordered the Burmese forces to evacuate Siamese territory. He was an
inefficient young man who was bored with palace routine and spent
his time making pilgrimages to pagodas. In 1782, while he was absent
on one of these expeditions, a palace intrigue brought to the throne a
younger brother of Hsinbyushin, the Badun Min, better known as
Bodawpaya, 'the great-grandfather king', the epithet applied to him
in the *Konbaungset Chronicle*, compiled in the reign of his great-grandson Mindon Min.

CHAPTER 23

ANNAM AND TONGKING, 1620–1820

(a) The struggle of Trinh and Nguyen, 1620–1777

THE rivalry between the Trinh and the Nguyen led to over half a century of warfare in the seventeenth century. The wearisome indecisive struggle went on from 1620 to 1674. On paper the Trinh should have won comfortably. According to the accounts of the Christian missionaries, they could muster 100,000 men, 500 elephants and 500 large junks; and the numbers do not seem to have been exaggerated. War was the sole occupation of the mandarins, and the social system of the country was organized upon a military basis. But the Nguyen army, though much smaller, was better equipped with arms procured through the Portuguese. The Nguyen fought defensive wars and could count on the loyal support of their people. North of Hué they built two great walls to block access from the north, and for a long period these proved a serious obstacle to the Trinh forces. Moreover, the presence of the small Mac principality in the north, weak though it was, was felt as a constant threat to Tongking.

The war began over the withholding of the revenues of Than-hoa and Quang-nam from the capital by Nguyen Phuc-Nguyen (1613–35), better known to contemporary European writers as Sai Vuong. In 1630, after a long period on the defensive, he took the offensive and occupied southern Bochinh, now the district of Ha-tinh. This remained for many years the great bone of contention between the two sides. It was temporarily recovered by the Tongkingers from Cong Thuong Vuong (1635–48), Sai Vuong's successor, but lost again in 1648 after their serious defeat at the wall of Truong-duc, the more southerly of the two great defence-works north of Hué. In 1655 they made another attempt to recover it which brought so strong a reaction on the part of the Nguyen that in the following year the situation became serious for the Trinh. But the Nguyen could not gain a decisive victory and the struggle continued for year after year with no advantage to either side.

In 1659 Trinh Tac, who had succeeded Trinh Trang two years earlier, inflicted a double defeat on the Nguyen; but he in his turn was unable to follow this success up with a knock-out blow. In 1661 while attempting to deal one he was held up at the Dong-hri wall and disastrously defeated. This brought a lull in the fighting for some years, since the Nguyen were quite unable to strike back. In 1672 Trinh Can again took the offensive and a tremendous struggle took place along the walls. But in the following year, finding Nguyen resistance unconquerable, he called off the invasion, and the senseless struggle ended. For upwards of a century peace reigned between the north and the south. The Trinh concentrated upon developing their authority in Tongking, while the Nguyen devoted their attention to southwards expansion at the expense of the Chams and Cambodians and to the spread of Annamite influence.

The Portuguese had established regular trading connections with both Annam and Tongking before the end of the sixteenth century. They maintained no factories there, but used their settlement at Macao in China as their base. They went to Tongking to buy raw silk for the Japanese market, where the demand was so great that this commodity had become one of the chief objects of trade in the Far East. Fai-fo, close to Quang-nam, was the commercial port of the Nguyen dominions. It was a market rather than a city. When the Portuguese began to trade there the Chinese and Japanese, who had long frequented the place, formed the bulk of its population, living each in their separate quarter under their own magistrats. The foreign trade of Annam and Tongking was almost entirely in the hands of foreigners, who were given easy access by the rulers in each case. The natives themselves engaged only in the coastal trade.

During the sixteenth century the Dominicans, who were making energetic though unsuccessful efforts to spread their faith in Cambodia, made sporadic appearances in Annam, but without result. In the seventeenth century the Jesuits, expelled from Japan, began to look to Indo-China as a new field for their activities. The practice had been for Jesuits from Goa or Malacca to be trained for the Japanese field at the Society's college at Macao. In 1614, in consequence of the change of policy in Japan, several Jesuits found themselves immobilized at Macao. They gladly accepted the suggestion of a Portuguese merchant from Fai-fo that they should go there instead. Early in the next year they commenced operations there under the leadership of Francesco Busomi, a Neapolitan, who remained in the country until 1639 under the tolerant patronage of Sai Vuong.

By 1625 the mission to Cochin China, the Portuguese name for the Nguyen territories, promised so well that it was decided to open another in Tongking. This was the work of the celebrated Alexander of Rhodes, who went there in 1627; but after a promising start he was expelled by Trinh Trang in 1630.

For some 200 years, until after the suppression of the Society in Europe, the Jesuits continued to work in the Vietnamese lands, often up against bitter persecution, often secretly, living at Macao and accompanying Portuguese trading ships disguised as merchants. The Trinh at Hanoi were their declared enemies, but the Nguyen, anxious to obtain Portuguese support in their struggle for independence, were less intolerant, though fundamentally hostile to the Christian faith. Hien Vuong, who was annoyed because he had not received the hoped-for support from Europeans in the campaigns of 1655–61 against the Trinh, stopped missionary work and killed many native Christians. During the latter part of the century there were massacres of native Christians, churches were burnt and missionaries imprisoned.

The early missionaries invented *quoc-ngu*, the Romanization of the Vietnamese written language now in general use. Portuguese, the commercial language used by Europeans of all kinds in their inter-course with the Vietnamese people, provided *quoc-ngu* with its basic values. One of the earliest works to use it was Alexander of Rhodes's Vietnamese Catechism printed in Rome in the middle of the century.

It was through Alexander of Rhodes that the French entered the Indo-Chinese mission field. His efforts to persuade the Pope to give the Far Eastern Christians an independent organization of their own brought him up against such determined Portuguese opposition that he turned to France for support. There he stimulated such enthusiasm that the Société des Missions Etrangères was formed, as we have noted in a previous chapter,[1] and in 1662 established its base of operations at Ayut'ia. From there missionaries were sent to Cambodia, Annam and Tongking. Notwithstanding the opposition of both the Jesuits and the Portuguese, they made headway while Lambert de la Motte and Pallu lived to direct their endeavours. But they did so only by posing as merchants in the employment of the Compagnie des Indes Orientaux. When in 1682 the Dutch forced all their European competitors to leave Bantam, and shortly afterwards Rome forbade missionaries to engage in trade, a severe blow was dealt to French influence in the Vietnamese lands. The failure of French intervention in Siam was another cause of decline, and in 1693 the oriental vicarate passed to the Spanish Dominicans at Manila.

[1] *Supra*, p. 362.

Still, the Société continued to operate in the Far East, though in the eighteenth century suffering from serious lack of men and resources. The quarrels between the various missionary societies became so intense that in 1738 Pope Clement XII sent out a commission of enquiry. As a result the decision was taken to assign separate territorial spheres to each. Under this arrangement the Jesuits received Tongking and the northern provinces of Annam, while to the French society was assigned the region from Hué southwards. But once again the native rulers struck at the missionaries. The Trinh instituted periodical persecutions and many missionaries lost their lives. The Nguyen were less severe; and although in 1750 nearly all the missionaries were rounded up and deported, a few, who possessed expert mathematical or scientific knowledge, were retained as government servants.

The Portuguese trade between Macao and Vietnam was challenged in the seventeenth century by the Dutch. As soon as the latter were established at Patani and Ligor, the Nguyen, always on the look-out for foreign aid, invited them to come and trade. At first, however, the main Dutch efforts in the Far East were made to secure direct trade with China and Japan. Their first factory in the south was planted in 1636 at Qui-nam. In the next year they founded another in Tongking at Hien-nam, and later a third at Ke-cho. Their connection with Tongking, however, and the fear that they would listen to the appeals for help made by the Trinh, led to trouble with the Nguyen. In 1641, as the result of the harsh treatment given to the crews of two ships which were wrecked near the Pulo Cham islands, they abandoned their factory and for some years carried on a war of reprisals. An attempt to come to terms was made after Hien Vuong succeeded his father in 1648. A treaty was signed in 1651 and a new factory opened at Fai-fo. But again quarrels broke out, and in 1654 the factory was closed, this time finally.

The English made a disastrous attempt to open trade with the Nguyen territories in 1613. Richard Cocks, the chief of the factory at Hirado in Japan founded by John Saris, sent a junk to Fai-fo with a letter and presents from James I to the Hué ruler. But as soon as the agent, Walter Carwarden, and his interpreter landed they were murdered by Annamites. A few years later the Hirado factory sent a trading expedition to Tongking, but it also was a failure. For many years Dutch hostility checked every attempt to open trade. In 1672, however, Bantam took the initiative and sent William Gyfford to open a factory in Tongking. Gyfford was received by Le Gia-Ton and permitted to settle at Hien-nam. But the factory never achieved any success, and after being moved successively to Ke-cho and finally to Hanoi was closed in 1697. A letter written in 1680 complains of bad debts which could not be collected because there was no direct approach to the king and the mandarins took what they wanted without payment. There were the usual difficulties arising from Dutch opposition and Portuguese intrigues, but the chiefs seem to have been incapable and there were dissensions among the factors. And the expulsion of the English from Bantam in 1682 was a blow from which the factory never recovered. The chief cause of failure, however, lay in the attitude of the ruling class, and it is significant that the Dutch also failed to make their factory pay for the same reason and abandoned it in 1700.

In 1695 Nathaniel Higginson, the Governor of Madras, sent Thomas Bowyear to Fai-fo on what may be described as a reconnoitring expedition. Like Edward Fleetwood, who was sent to Ava in the same year, Bowyear was a private merchant and had no power to conclude an agreement on behalf of the East India Company. His proposals were received with the same scepticism as the Court of Ava displayed towards Fleetwood's. He was told that if the Company would establish a factory suitable conditions of trade would then be discussed, and he was entrusted with a letter couched in similar terms from Minh Vuong to Higginson. His mission led to nothing, and soon after his return to Madras he was sent to assume control over the dockyard at Syriam that was opened as a result of Fleetwood's mission.

During the century of peace which ensued after the Tongkingese defeat by the Annamites in 1673 both ruling families continued to hold undisputed sway in their respective territories. In the north the Trinh continued to make and unmake kings at will. Their rule was firm and ensured peace and stability everywhere. They had inherited an administrative system which functioned adequately and was well in advance of any other native administration in South-East Asia. But they did much to improve it. Trinh Cuong (1709–29) commenced a cadastral survey of land and renovated the taxation registers, thereby reforming the collection of revenue from the products of the soil and the mines. He reduced the power of the mandarins by forbidding them to create villages under their own exclusive feudal jurisdiction. He also improved the procedure of the courts and reduced the severity of the penal code. His successor, Trinh Giang (1729–40), carried through further financial reforms by regulating the salt trade and the exploitation of the mines. He sought to reduce Chinese influence by taxing Chinese settlers at a higher rate than the Vietnamese and pro-hibiting the sale of Chinese books. He also had editions of the Viet-namese canonical and classical works and of the Annals printed.

In the south the Nguyen, unlike the Trinh, had to create a largely new administrative system in order to unify their diverse territories. As might be expected, it was very similar to the one which had grown up under the Le dynasty. For instance, the census system and the method of assessing the land tax established by Sai Vuong (1613–35) were imitations of those introduced by Le Thanh-Ton in 1465. In fixing the land tax account had to be taken of the area of the fields, which was officially measured, the nature of the crops and the value of the lands. Hien Vuong (1648–87) set up a bureau of agriculture which classified cultivated lands and encouraged the cultivation of virgin soil. Under Sai Vuong's census system the population was divided into eight categories and personal tax fixed according to category. Those inscribed in the first two categories owed military service. Great attention was devoted to the army, which was organized on a terri-torial basis. Its basic unit was the *thuyen*, which was a platoon of thirty to fifty men drawn from the same village or neighbouring ones. From two to five *thuyen* went to make up a *doi*, or company. *Doi* in turn would be grouped into a *co*, or regiment; though, more rarely, the latter might consist of from six to ten *thuyen* without the inter-position of the *doi*. The largest group was the *dinh*, or provincial army.

In the middle of the eighteenth century, after expanding their control over the south down to the Mekong delta, the Nguyen organized their territory into twelve provinces (*dinh*), with a governor (*tran-thu*), treasurer (*cai-bo*) and judge (*ki-luc*) at the head of each. From about 1632 the provincial mandarinate was recruited by examinations based upon the Chinese model. In 1675 Hien Vuong strove to improve upon this by introducing a sort of practical examination on the current situation.

From time to time the Nguyen made attempts to secure recog-nition from China as independent rulers. On every occasion, how-ever, the imperial reply was that tribute could not be accepted, nor investiture accorded, while a legitimate Vietnamese dynasty was in existence.

After the defeat of the Chams by Le Thanh-Ton in the second half of the fifteenth century, a few Cham districts, as we have seen, still maintained their independence. These were gradually absorbed by the Nguyen during the seventeenth century. They were formed into the two *dinh* of Tran-bien and Thai-khang. A Cham kinglet still

continued to exist. In 1692, no doubt as a protest against the rigour
with which the Vietnamese were imposing their culture upon the
south, the Cham king, Ba Tranh, rebelled. He was defeated and
put to death together with all his ministers. The territories he had
ruled became the *dinh* of Thuan-thanh, later renamed Binh-thuan,
and were placed under a Cham prince as provincial governor. But
Vietnamese influence increased and the Chams were harshly treated.

The Vietnamese expansion at the expense of Cambodia followed
much the same pattern as in the case of Champa. Exiles, deserters
and other vagabonds infiltrated into the country. In time their numbers enabled them to form colonies, the inevitable prelude to annexation. Thus in 1658 the provincial governor of Tran-bien occupied
the colony of Moi-xui under the pretext that the King of Cambodia
had violated the Vietnamese frontier. When King Ang Chan resorted
to arms he was defeated and captured and sent in a cage to Hué.
There, on paying homage as a vassal, he was liberated and escorted
back to his capital. His two brothers, however, refused to accept the
situation, chased the Vietnamese out of the disputed territory and set
themselves up as joint kings. In 1673 the inevitable succession dispute
gave the Vietnamese an opportunity to intervene effectively and install
two tributary rulers, one as king at Udong and the other as second
king at Saigon.

The Saigon area, the Water Chen-la of the ancient Khmer kingdom,
was a tempting field for Vietnamese expansion. It had a population
of only about 40,000 families, so that there were vast empty spaces.
Ang Non, the ruler of Saigon, attempted to seize the Cambodian throne
in 1679, but his cousin Ang Sor called in Siamese aid and defeated
him. At the moment when he arrived as a fugitive in Annam a large
fleet of junks carrying 3,000 Chinese fugitives arrived at Tourane.
They were partisans of the defeated Mings under the command of two
officers, Yang and Ch'en, who asked permission to settle under
Vietnamese authority. Anxious to give them as wide a berth as
possible, Hieng Vuong passed them on to Ang Non, who led them
into his old appanage and settled them there. Ch'en and his followers
established themselves at Bien-hoa, which they made into a prosperous
agricultural centre; Yang went to Mi-tho on the eastern branch of the
Mekong, where his followers adopted the more adventurous rôle of
river pirates. With their help Ang Non made another bid for the
throne in 1682, but failed after some initial success. Some years later,
finding himself unable to control them, he called in Vietnamese help.
The Nguyen forces defeated the freebooters and killed Yang. They

were then placed under the jurisdiction of the Bien-hoa chief, Ch'en. The Vietnamese then forced King Ang Sor to acknowledge Nguyen overlordship. After this expedition the Water Chen-la passed under Nguyen sway, and when Ang Non died his son Ang Em had to admit a Vietnamese governor and his dominions were formed into two *dinhs*.

This was not the end of Vietnamese expansion at the expense of Cambodia. A third Chinese refugee leader, Mac Cuu, settled in what is now the Ha-tien region on the Gulf of Siam. Colonists flocked to his district and several prosperous villages were founded, notably Kampot. In 1714 another succession dispute broke out at Lovek, and Siam seized the opportunity to gain control. The Chinese settlement at Ha-tien was attacked and Mac Cuu fled to Hué. Minh Vuong (1691-1725) invested him with the governorship of Ha-tien, and a further spate of Vietnamese invasions of Cambodia gave the Nguyen two more provinces, Dinh-tuong and Long-ho. When Mac Cuu died in 1735, his son Mac Thien Tu was confirmed in his place by Hué, and under his competent rule Ha-tien prospered. In 1739 Cambodia attempted to reassert its domination over the place, but Mac Thien Tu drove out the invading forces. This gave the Vietnamese a further pretext for intervention, and in 1749 Cambodia purchased peace only by abandoning all the territory south of Gia-dinh up to the arm of the Mekong which passes Mi-tho.

The Burmese threat to Siam which developed under Alaungpaya (1752-60) gave the Nguyen a fair field for demanding more territory from Cambodia, and the provinces of Bassac and Prea-pateny were yielded. But the tide of Vietnamese expansion had now reached its high-water mark. Ayut'ia was captured and destroyed by the Burmese in 1767; but almost immediately afterwards, under the impact of a series of Chinese invasions, the conquerors lost their grip on Siam, while that country found a leader in P'ya Taksin, under whom it speedily revived its strength. A misguided attempt by Mac Thien Tu in 1769 to place a pretender on the Siamese throne brought P'ya Taksin into his dominions, and soon the Siamese king, having reduced Ha-tien to ruins, was essaying the rôle of kingmaker at Phnom Penh. The Vietnamese thereupon invaded Cambodia and defeated the Siamese. But although they replaced Ang Tong, the vassal of the Nguyen, on the throne, he was unable to maintain himself there, and in 1773 retired in favour of Ang Non, the Siamese nominee. And Mac Thien Tu made his peace with P'ya Taksin, who withdrew the Siamese garrison from Ha-tien. Everything was now set for a fresh trial of strength between

Siam and the Nguyen for the control of Cambodia, and Ang Non began to prepare to meet another Vietnamese invasion. But sudden disaster had overwhelmed the Nguyen lands and it was to be some years before the Vietnamese were again in a position to challenge Siamese influence in Cambodia.

In 1765 when Vo Vuong died a Court intrigue raised up as his successor a boy of twelve who was the son of a concubine. Power was seized ·by a greedy minister, Truong-Phuc-Loan, who proclaimed himself regent. He proved unequal to the task, and in 1773 in the district of Tay-son a revolt began under three brothers, Nguyen Van-Nhac, Nguyen Van-Lu and Nguyen Van-Hué, which speedily attained formidable strength. The rebel leaders, who, though bearing the family name of Nguyen, were unconnected with the ruling dynasty, seized the city of Qui-nhon and defeated the government troops sent against them.

In the following year the situation was made worse by a Tong-kingese invasion launched by the Trinh, and early in 1775, while the Nguyen army was engaged with the rebels, the Tongkingese seized Hué. Trinh Sum, when launching the invasion, proclaimed that his intention was to help the Nguyen, but beyond occupying Hué and the old Cham province of Quang-nam his forces could make no further progress. For a time, indeed, they were thrown on to the defensive, since Van-Nhac, having inflicted another defeat on the Nguyen army, made an all-out bid to gain possession of Hué. In this he failed, but he next turned his attention to the south, where his brother Van-Lu was engaged in a struggle for the possession of Saigon. Early in 1776 Van-Lu had captured the city, only to be driven out by Mac Thien Tu of Ha-tien, who came forward as the champion of the Nguyen cause and was joined there by the surviving members of the family. In 1777 the Tay-son leaders recaptured Saigon and hunted down the Nguyen, killing three of them. The sole survivor, Nguyen Phuc-Anh, generally known as Nguyen Anh, a boy of fifteen, got away to the island of Pulo Panjang, helped by a French Catholic priest, Pigneau de Behaine, who was later to play an important part in his restoration. For the time being, however, the Nguyen cause appeared to be lost. Everywhere except in the Hué region the Tay-son brothers were dominant, and Van-Nhac had even proclaimed himself 'emperor'.

The story of Nguyen Anh's long struggle to recover his inheritance and of his relations with Pigneau de Behaine belongs to a later section. The present one must end with a brief reference to the attempts of the European powers to re-establish commercial relations with the

Vietnamese lands in the eighteenth century. The English had left Tongking in 1697, the Dutch in 1700. The French were still represented by missionaries operating as traders. There were no European factories in Cochin China, but the Portuguese of Macao continued to send cargoes of porcelain, tea and tutenag and to receive in return sugar, raw silk and eaglewood, while the Jesuits remained active participants in this traffic. During the long period of peace between the two rival houses the princes no longer needed European help and hence made no effort to attract the European trader.

The English, ever on the look-out for places where Chinese goods might be purchased, planted a settlement in 1702 on the island of Pulo Condore, lying off the western mouth of the Mekong. The French East India Company had in 1686 commissioned its agent in Siam to look for a factory site on the route to China, and he had reported that, since all the commerce of China, Tongking, Macao, Manila and Cochin China must pass close to the island, Pulo Condore possessed the combined advantages of the Straits of Malacca and Sunda. By settling there in 1702 the English apparently forestalled a French move to occupy the island. But three years later their factory came to an early and sudden end. The Macassar troops of the garrison, annoyed at being kept there beyond the term of their contract, mutinied and slaughtered all the Europeans there save two, who made their escape in a small boat to Johore. The French East India Company in 1723 sent an agent to examine the island. He submitted a very adverse report, and as it was known that the English had no intention of returning there the Company dropped the scheme.

Nevertheless the French were anxious for a settlement in the China Sea, since their factors at Canton found their position almost unendurable. In 1744 Dupleix's nephew Friel, one of the Canton merchants, visited Vo Vuong at Hué and was encouraged to open trade there. He went to Pondicherry to obtain Dupleix's support, but the war with the English East India Company, that broke out as a result of the participation of Great Britain in the War of the Austrian Succession, held up the project. In 1748, however, Dupleix sent an agent to Cochin China. At almost the same time Pierre Poivre discussed a similar plan with the Minister of Marine at Paris and was sent out to put it into operation. He arrived in Tourane in 1749 and went on to Hué, where he was well received by Vo Vuong, but lost the major part of his cargo either by sheer theft or through purchases without payment. His report caused the French East India Company to abandon the idea of opening trade with the Nguyen lands. Dupleix, however, still cherished the plan; and although the agent he sent there in 1752, a missionary of the Missions Etrangères, was arrested and expelled by Vo Vuong, he sent yet another, but in vain. His own recall to France and the outbreak of the Seven Years War caused the scheme to be put back once more into cold storage.

When the war ended, Choiseul tried to revive interest in it 'pour compenser les pertes subies', as Maybon puts it,[1] but failed to enlist support. Then in 1774 Vergennes, who became Minister of Foreign Affairs on the accession of Louis XVI, turned his attention to the scheme. It was talked of as a way of freeing France from the supremacy achieved by England in colonial wars by enabling her to intercept English trade with China in time of war. As a result a ship was sent in 1778 from Chandernagore to examine the situation. The report that its commander brought back to Chevalier, the energetic commandant at Chandernagore, led him to write home that the situation in Cochin China offered a splendid career there for the French nation if intervention on behalf of the legitimate prince, Nguyen Anh, were undertaken. He suggested that the policy 'so happily pursued earlier' by Dupleix in India should be applied in Indo-China.

At almost the same time the much-harassed Warren Hastings in Calcutta was being urged to adopt the same plan. Late in 1777 an English ship, the *Rumbold*, returning from China to India, put in at Tourane and took on board two members of the Nguyen family who were anxious to rejoin Nguyen Anh at Saigon. Unable to make the entrance to the Saigon river, however, the master took his passengers on to Calcutta, where they were received by Warren Hastings. They were provided with a passage back to their country and were accompanied by an English agent, Charles Chapman, who was sent to examine the prospects of opening trade there. Chapman had an adventurous voyage. He found the whole country in the hands of the Tay-son brothers. He had an interview with Van-Nhac, who was anxious to use his two ships in fighting Nguyen Anh, and only with difficulty saved one from seizure. He returned to Calcutta in 1779 with an optimistic report. He strongly advised intervention with the object of restoring Nguyen Anh, and stressed that if the English were forced to abandon Canton and it became necessary to look for a place where Chinese goods could be purchased they could be had in Cochin China cheaper than at Canton. He pointed to the strategic value of the Bay of Tourane, which, he said, offered a splendid shelter to ships and would be a useful base from which they could operate

---

[1] Ch. Maybon, *Histoire d'Annam moderne*, p. 170.

against enemies. Finally, he warned Hastings that France intended to gain influence in the country.

Neither France nor the East India Company could attend to these suggestions; they were too deeply committed elsewhere at the time. But the matter did not rest there. For, as we have seen, a French priest, Pigneau de Behaine, had already been of service to the fugitive Nguyen Anh, and out of their chance meeting a friendship was forged which was to have immensely important results not only for the prince but also, in the long run, for France.

(b) The establishment of the Nguyen empire of Cochin China, Annam and Tongking, 1777–1820

The French missionary Pierre-Joseph-Georges Pigneau, who helped the young Nguyen Anh to escape to Pulo Panjang after the second capture of Saigon by the Tay-son rebels in 1777, was born in 1741 at Behaine in the commune of Origny-en-Thierache, in what later became the département of the Aisne. He was trained as a missionary in the Séminaire des Missions-Etrangères and left France in 1765 for work in Cochin China. There he joined the college at Hon-dat in Ha-tien, which had been set up by refugee missionaries forced by the Burmese invasions to leave Siam. It was a wretched little collection of bamboo huts with some forty Annamite, Chinese and Siamese pupils. And it was not left long in peace, for in 1768 P'ya Taksin complained to Mac Thien Tu, the son of the founder of the Ha-tien principality, that it had afforded shelter to a refugee Siamese prince, and the missionaries were all thrown into gaol for three months.

In the next year Chinese and Cambodian pirates attacked the settlement, massacred a number of the students, and burned down all the buildings. Pigneau managed to escape with some of his pupils and made his way via Malacca to Pondicherry. In 1770 he set up another seminary at Virampatnam close by, and while there was nominated Bishop of Adran. Four years later, having been consecrated Apostolic Vicar of Cochin China, he went to Macao to collect personnel for staffing the Ha-tien mission, which he proposed to re-establish.

In 1775 he arrived in Ha-tien. He was hospitably received by Mac Thien Tu and permitted to resume his work. Exactly how he came to meet the fugitive Nguyen Anh the Annamite sources do not reveal, and European writers do not agree. The young prince appears to have been in hiding in a forest close to Pigneau's seminary at Can-cao

during September and October 1777 before getting away to Pulo
Panjang. At the same time Mac Thien Tu, the champion of the Nguyen
cause, deciding that all was lost, fled from Ha-tien, ultimately at the
invitation of P'ya Taksin making his way to the Siamese Court.

At the very moment when he thus abandoned hope of the Nguyen
cause, Nguyen Anh, learning that the main body of the Tay-son army
had left the Saigon region, quietly slipped across to the mainland,
rejoined his supporters and regained possession of the city. This
success was largely due to the efforts of a devoted supporter, Do Thanh-
Nhon, who had raised a new army for the Nguyen cause after the
disaster at Saigon. During the year 1778 Do Thanh-Nhon again
proved his worth by clearing the rebel troops out of the province of
Gia-dinh and destroying their fleet. The situation began to look so
hopeful that Nguyen Anh despatched a mission to Siam to propose a
treaty of friendship.

Events in Cambodia, however, brought this move unexpectedly to a
halt. In 1779 the mandarins, under the leadership of Mu, Governor
of Bassac, rebelled against the Siamese puppet Ang Non and appealed
to Nguyen Anh for help. Do Thanh-Nhon, who was sent in response
to this request, assisted Mu to win a decisive victory, as a result of
which Ang Non was executed and Ang Eng, the infant son of his old
rival Ang Tong, placed on the throne, with Mu as regent. Do
Thanh-Nhon then returned to Saigon loaded with honours and began
to concentrate all his efforts upon the improvement of the Nguyen
navy.

Siam naturally could not allow the new set-up at Phnom Penh to go
unchallenged. In November 1780 three armies were sent to invade
Cambodia. In April 1781, however, just when, having won some
initial successes, they were about to meet a force sent by Nguyen Anh,
news came of P'ya Taksin's madness, and the invasion was called
off.

At this juncture Nguyen Anh ruined his chances of success for many
years to come by having Do Thanh-Nhon murdered. The cause of
this senseless crime is obscure. The most likely suggestion is that
the distinguished general put his young master too much in the shade.
It was a most impolitic act; Do Thanh-Nhon was the one military
commander in the Nguyen service whom the Tay-son brothers really
feared. The eldest is said to have 'leapt for joy' when he heard the
news. The dead man's supporters at once rebelled, and the Nguyen
cause was so badly weakened that a few months later the Tay-son
brothers again captured Saigon. Pigneau de Behaine escaped into

Cambodia. Nguyen Anh, after beating a fighting retreat into Ha-tien, took refuge on the island of Phu-quoc. His supporters, however, continued to carry on guerrilla warfare against the Tay-son.

In October 1782 fortune turned once again; the royal troops led by Nguyen Man, Nguyen Anh's younger brother, succeeded in driving the rebels out of Saigon. Nguyen Anh returned to the city, as also did Pigneau. But the situation was very precarious, and it was obvious to both that when the inevitable counter-attack came there was no hope of holding it.

It came early in 1783, and the Nguyen forces were defeated with frightful losses. Prince Man was killed. Nguyen Anh again got away to the island of Phu-quoc, but his hiding-place was discovered, and he only just managed to escape the pursuing forces and take refuge on the island of Koh-rong in the Bay of Kompongsom. Again his sanctuary was discovered. Fortune, however, still favoured him, for when his island was completely encircled by the Tay-son fleet a typhoon suddenly blew up, and in the darkness and confusion he got away to another island.

Pigneau fled first of all to his seminary, but the approach of rebel forces caused him to take refuge in Siam. He arrived at Chantabun in August 1783, and almost immediately afterwards received an invitation to rejoin Nguyen Anh. The Annamite Chronicle says that they had an interview, at which the prince asked the bishop to obtain French help to enable him to crush the Tay-son; whereupon the bishop asked for a pledge and the prince gave him his son Canh, who was just four years old. The real story, however, is not so simple, and the details are difficult to piece together, for Pigneau had to observe the greatest discretion in the matter. As a missionary he was expected to avoid any participation in the politics of the country to which he was posted, and there were already those who were expressing dissatisfaction with his conduct. Moreover, before anything was decided, Nguyen Anh went early in 1784 to seek Siamese aid. Siam was favourable and provided a contingent with which he returned to the contest. His campaign, however, failed, and he turned again to the the question of French aid. The upshot was that in December 1784 Pigneau and Prince Canh left the Nguyen headquarters on Pulo Panjang on the first stage of a journey that was to take them ultimately to Versailles. Soon afterwards, in April 1785, Nguyen Anh and his suite left Pulo Panjang in five junks for Siam. His object seems to have been to await there the results of Pigneau's mission.

Pigneau and his young protégé arrived at Pondicherry in February

1785 to find Coutenceau des Algrains, the acting governor, uncompromisingly hostile to intervention in Cochin China, 'comme étant contraire aux intérêts de la nation, à la saine politique, très difficile et très inutile'. In any case Pondicherry could take no such action without instructions from home. Pigneau therefore asked for a passage to France, and after a long delay Governor de Cossigny granted his request. In July 1786 he and Prince Canh left Pondicherry on board the merchantman *Malabar*.

Their arrival in France in February 1787 caused no little excitement in the salons of Paris and Versailles. The world of fashion made a pet of the young prince. Pigneau was received by Louis XVI and submitted to the ministers his plan for an expedition to establish Nguyen Anh on the throne of Annam. It was turned down, chiefly on the score of expense. France was tottering on the brink of the national bankruptcy which was to bring on the Revolution. But the project was seized on by a number of important people, at the head of whom was Pierre Poivre, who had been to Hué in 1749 and had had a long connection with Far Eastern affairs. Even with his enthusiastic support, however, Pigneau could obtain no more than paper promises. On 28 November 1787, in the name of Nguyen Anh, he concluded a treaty of alliance between France and Cochin China. Ships, men and arms were promised. In return France was to receive Pulo Condore and territory in the Bay of Tourane. If French aid was vital to Nguyen Anh, then his one ray of hope was the nomination of Pigneau de Behaine as French Commissioner in Indo-China.

In December 1787 Pigneau and his charge left for Pondicherry. They arrived there in May of the following year. Again there was a long hold-up. De Conway, the governor, would not afford any help and raised every possible obstacle to prevent the indomitable bishop from collecting munitions and volunteers for the enterprise. But with money he had raised in France from various sources, and help received in Pondicherry, he managed to despatch four shiploads of stores and several hundreds of volunteers. They arrived in September 1788 at an opportune moment, when Nguyen Anh had at long last recaptured Saigon and needed to consolidate his position. The help thus afforded turned the scale in his favour.

After Nguyen Anh went to Siam in April 1785 important developments had taken place in the Vietnam lands. Having made themselves masters of Cochin China, the Tay-son brothers turned their attention to Hué, which had been in Tongkingese hands for a good number of years. In July 1786 they took the city. Their success emboldened them to strike northwards against Tongking itself, where the Trinh still held sway and controlled the puppet Le emperor. With remarkable speed they occupied Quang-tri and Quang-binh, defeated the army sent against them by Trinh Khai, and seized Hanoi. They then set about partitioning the empire, Van-Hué taking Tongking and upper Annam, Van-Nhac the centre with Hué as his capital, and Van-Lu Cochin China. Actually the Trinh were not yet disposed of, and the war against them continued until late in 1788. When at last all opposition was stamped out, Van-Hué proclaimed himself emperor at Hanoi, and the last *roi-fainéant*, Le Man Hoang De, escaped to China.

Nguyen Anh remained in Siam until August 1787. With a contingent of Annamite troops he served with distinction in the Siamese war against Bodawpaya of Burma. When the Tay-son brothers embarked on their campaigns to gain possession of Tongking their garrison in Cochin China was weakened by the withdrawal of troops from Gia-dinh. King Rama I offered Nguyen Anh help to regain the province. In August 1787 he secretly left Siam for Cochin China. At first he hoped to detach the Governor of Gia-dinh from the Tay-son cause, but the plan failed. Then he seized Mi-tho, which he made his base of operations, and began to build up his strength for the reconquest of his patrimony. His early operations were directed against Saigon. There was much stiff fighting before the city fell on 7 September 1788. The timely arrival of the help sent from Pondicherry by Pigneau de Behaine enabled him systematically to reduce Cochin China to obedience. When Pigneau himself arrived, on 24 July 1789, its conquest had just been completed.

The help afforded by the French volunteers was of immense value to the Nguyen cause. Some of them performed notable service in helping to train and organize the army and navy. Thus Jean Marie Dayot took command of the navy and welded it into a strong fighting force, which showed its worth by destroying the Tay-son fleet at Quinhon in 1792. Olivier du Puymanel took charge of the training of recruits for the army and of the planning and construction of fortifications. The 'great master' himself became Nguyen Anh's chief minister and conducted his foreign correspondence.

For many years, however, the final outcome of the struggle lay in the balance. Not until 1792 was Nguyen Anh strong enough to attack the north. In that year Van-Hué, who had secured recognition of China as Emperor of Annam, died and was succeeded by his son Quang-Toan. The greatest obstacle was the fortress of Qui-nhon. Up to 1799 it seemed impregnable, but in that year it capitulated to an army

under the command of Prince Canh. Shortly afterwards Pigneau de
Behaine died there of dysentery at the age of fifty-eight. By that time
victory was assured, though much hard fighting was still to come.
For the Tay-son recaptured the city, and it did not finally come into
Nguyen hands until 1801, when the last great Tay-son counter-
attack was broken there.

Thereafter events moved rapidly. In June of that year Hué fell,
and Nguyen Anh was crowned there as King of Annam. He then
addressed himself to the task of overrunning Tongking. On 22 July
1802 Hanoi was taken and the work of conquest was complete. Just
before that final triumph, on 1 June 1802, Nguyen Anh proclaimed
himself Emperor of Vietnam at Hué and assumed the title of Gia-
Long. An embassy was despatched to China asking for formal investiture. This was granted in 1803 by the Emperor Kia-k'ing. He
stipulated that tribute must be sent every two years and homage
performed every four years. These conditions were faithfully observed by Gia-Long throughout his reign.

Nguyen Anh had fought almost unceasingly for a quarter of a
century. But the struggle had now raised his family to a position it
had never previously occupied. For by the conquest of Tongking he
had 'added the kingdom of the suzerain to the fief of the vassal, and
realized to the full a project that none of his predecessors had ever
dared to contemplate'.[1] By the ceremony enacted at Hué on 1 June
1802 he founded the dynasty which has continued to occupy the
throne until today.

The new state of Vietnam which thus came into existence comprised three main regions, each with its administrative headquarters.
The old patrimony of the Nguyen formed the central part of the
empire. It comprised nine provinces, five of which were directly
governed by the sovereign. Its capital Hué was also the capital of the
empire. Tongking, with the administrative seat of its imperial
governor-general at Bac-thanh, had thirteen provinces, and in the
delta the old officials of the Le administration were continued in
office. Away in the extreme south Gia-dinh, the administrative centre
of the four provinces of Cochin China, was also the seat of an imperial
governor-general (*Tong-tran*).

Under the emperor the central administration was divided among
six ministries: Public Affairs, Finance, Rites, War, Justice, and
Works. Each was under a president, assisted by two vice-presidents
and two or three councillors. The heads of the administration together

[1] Maybon, *op. cit.*, pp. 349–50.

formed the *Noi-cac* or Supreme Council. A governor-general in charge of a number of provinces was assisted by a treasurer-general and a Chief of the Judicial Service. Throughout the empire the provinces were classified into *tran*, i.e. first class, and *dinh*, i.e. second class. They were divided into *phu* (prefectures) under *tri-phu*, and these in turn subdivided into *huyen* and *chau*. These last two have been described by French administrators as roughly equivalent to the *arrondissement* and *commune* respectively.

The task of re-establishing settled administration after so long a period of civil war was an immense one, but like Henry VII of England Gia-Long was no innovator. He used the old familiar administrative framework and methods that were hallowed by long tradition. In such a society once disorder was stamped out the power of self-adjustment was considerable, but the supreme authority had to be ever on the alert to see that the proper persons performed their functions in the proper manner. The confusion which reigned everywhere has been vividly described by Maybon. 'The wheels of administration were warped or no longer existed; the cadres of officials were empty, the hierarchy destroyed; taxes were not being collected, lists of communal property had disappeared, proprietary titles were lost, fields abandoned; roads, bridges and public granaries had not been maintained; work in the mines had ceased. The administration of justice had been interrupted, every province was a prey to pirates, violation of law went unpunished, while even the law itself had become uncertain.'[1]

With so complicated a task of reconstruction on his hands it is not surprising that Gia-Long should have sought peaceable relations with his neigbours. Perhaps his biggest external problem was Cambodia. Bereft of her former provinces, through Annamite conquest and colonization, in what had come to be known to Europeans as Cochin China, she was only a pale shadow of her former self, and since the middle of the seventeenth century had recognized the overlordship of the Nguyen of Hué. Early in the eighteenth century Siam had begun to compete with Hué for control over her, while both sides were constantly looking for opportunities to filch slices of her territory. True, Siam's ambitions of eastward expansion had been brought to a temporary halt by the Burmese destruction of Ayut'ia in 1767. But her rapid revival under P'ya Taksin had brought her back into Cambodia just at the moment when Nguyen influence there was paralysed by the Tay-son rebellion.

---

[1] *Ibid.*, p. 350.

The eclipse of Nguyen power seemed to offer Siam a wonderful opportunity to work her will in Cambodia; but things did not go as well for her as might have been expected. Nguyen Anh's survival, and his temporary reoccupation of Saigon in 1777, enabled the mandarin Mu of Bassac to replace the Siamese puppet Ang Nhon by his nephew Ang Eng. And P'ya Taksin's attempt at intervention against this arrangement was frustrated by the revolution which caused his death and the accession of General Chakri to the Siamese throne. Still, at almost the same time as Nguyen Anh lost Saigon the youthful Ang Eng's supporters lost control over the situation and Cambodia fell a prey to disorder. Then, while Siam was prevented from intervening by King Bodawpaya's revival of the Burmese efforts to conquer her, the Tay-son seized the opportunity to invade and occupy a large part of the much-sinned-against land.

This latest development played into the hands of Siam. The boy-king Ang Eng, who had been placed on the throne by the pro-Nguyen faction, was now removed to Bangkok for safety and grew to manhood at the Court of Siam. In 1794 he was crowned at Bangkok and sent back to his own country with the support of a Siamese army under the command of the mandarin Ben, Governor of Battambang, previously a Cambodian province, which now, together with the neighbouring province of Siemreap, once the heart of the empire of Angkor, came under Siamese rule.

In 1796 Ang Eng died, leaving a young son, Ang Chan, who had been born in 1791. No successor, however, was appointed to the throne until 1802, the year in which Gia-Long completed the unification of the Vietnam lands. Then the eleven-year-old boy was granted formal investiture by Siam, presumably in order to steal a march upon Hué.

The new situation in Vietnam could not fail to have its effects upon Cambodia. The young king's advisers were naturally most anxious to prevent their country from again becoming a battleground between Siam and Vietnam. They therefore did their utmost to remain on good terms with both, and in the characteristic fashion of small states in that region paid tribute and homage to both. In 1803 Gia-Long received at Hanoi a complimentary mission from Cambodia and sent presents in return. Two years later Ang Chan asked to be permitted to pay homage annually to the sovereign of Vietnam, and his request was granted.

In 1806 he went to Bangkok for his coronation. This did not prevent him from sending a mission to Hué in the following year bearing tribute and requesting investiture as a vassal of Gia-Long. The emperor at once responded by sending him an embassy bearing the book of investiture together with a seal of gilded silver surmounted by a lion. This evoked a further mission in 1808 from Cambodia with thanks for the investiture thus accorded. Hardly a year went by without a mission between the two Courts. So things might have continued had it not been for the inevitable family squabble which offered the ever-watchful Siam the longed-for opportunity to intervene.

Ang Chan's brother Ang Snguon wanted to be nominated Second King and receive part of the kingdom. When this was refused he rebelled in 1812, and Rama II of Siam sent an army to support him. Ang Chan thereupon fled to Saigon. In the following year Gia-Long sent so large a force to reinstate him that the Siamese prudently retired, taking Ang Snguon with them. He settled in Siam and died there in 1822. As a guarantee against further disturbances a Vietnamese garrison was installed in the citadel at Phnom Penh.

Neither side allowed this incident to affect the strictly correct diplomatic relations they had maintained with each other from the moment when, having obtained possession of Tongking, Gia-Long sent a mission in 1802 to announce the fact to Bangkok. A Siamese mission was at once despatched to offer him formal congratulations, and thereafter frequent embassies were exchanged throughout the rest of his reign. Relations were never cordial, for Siam never abandoned her hope of regaining control over Cambodia. But she would not risk a clash with a monarch who had given such ample demonstration of his ability to wage war.

Of the French volunteers who had given such valuable assistance to Nguyen Anh in his long struggle, four only remained in his service after 1802. They were Philippe Vannier, Jean-Baptiste Chaigneau, de Forsans, and the doctor Despiau. All were given high rank as mandarins and special privileges. The Treaty of Amiens was signed in the year in which Nguyen Anh became the Emperor Gia-Long, and Napoleon Bonaparte was urged by the now aged Charpentier de Cossigny, once commandant at Pondicherry, to re-establish diplomatic relations with Cochin China. Little came of the move, since the resumption of the European war and the activities of the British navy prevented France from doing anything effective in so distant a quarter of the globe.

After the downfall of Napoleon, however, Louis XVIII's minister the Duc de Richelieu was anxious to revive French commerce in the

China Sea, and in 1817 French merchantmen based on Bordeaux began to trade with the ports of Vietnam. On one of them Chaigneau returned to France to discuss with Richelieu proposals for opening official relations with Vietnam. Richelieu conferred on him the title of consul and empowered him to negotiate a commercial treaty. When, however, he arrived back in Hué he learnt that Gia-Long had died in February 1820. Minh-Mang, his son and successor, held a very different view of Europeans from his father's. Hence the projected treaty never materialized. In 1825 Chaigneau and Vannier, the last of Pigneau de Behaine's volunteers, left Vietnam to end their days in France.

CHAPTER 24

THE RAPE OF CAMBODIA

At the beginning of the seventeenth century, after the successive crises of the Siamese capture of Lovek and Spanish intervention from the Philippines, a much feebler Cambodia became a prey once more to exhausting dynastic struggles. Siam, having helped Soryopor to the throne in 1603, became his suzerain power; he in return proclaimed himself Siam's vassal and adopted Siamese court ceremonial. The inevitable Khmer reaction occurred, and in 1618 Soryopor was forced to abdicate in favour of his son, who declared his independence of Siam and restored the traditional Khmer court dress and usages. He was Chey Chettha II, and to emphasize the new policy he founded a new capital at Udong, just to the south of Lovek. Siam sought to restore her influence: in 1623 she launched two separate land invasions. Both came to grief, the king himself defeating one which was advancing towards the Tonle Sap Lake, and his brother, Prince Outey, the other in the province of Banteay Meas. In the following year a further Siamese attack by sea also failed.

The Siamese threat caused Chey Chettha to turn to the Court of Hué for help. The Nguyen 'Lords of the South', though nominally under the Le emperors at Hanoi, were in fact independent and anxious to expand southwards, though between 1620 and 1674 prevented from doing so by their struggle with the Trinh 'Lords of the North'. Chey Chettha II was thus laying up future trouble for his country when he married a Vietnamese princess and allied with Hué against Siam. Indeed, Hué's price for its support was the right to plant Vietnamese colonies in the Cambodian province of Prey Kor, later Saigon. When this was granted, Vietnamese settlement was officially encouraged, with a Vietnamese general at Saigon to superintend it. Chey Chettha died in 1628. His eldest son, Ponhea To, was too young to assume power; accordingly his uncle, Prince Outey, became regent. The king had come straight from a monastery to the throne and was without any experience of statecraft. He failed in an attempt to recover the former Cambodian province of Korat from Siam. Worse still, during a visit to the Angkor Wat he had a love affair with one of his uncle's wives, whom he had been promised in marriage when she and he were children. He persuaded her to go and live with him at the royal palace. But Outey stirred up the populace to massacre their Chinese guards, and, when the lovers attempted to flee, they were caught and shot.

To's younger brother Nou was then (1630) made king, and reigned for ten years under Outey's tutelage. When he died in 1640, Outey raised his own son, Ang Non, to the throne. But a third son of Chey Chettha II, Chan, with the help of Cham and Malay mercenaries managed to seize the palace in 1642 and carried out a veritable blood-bath. Outey himself, various members of the royal family and even the ministers appointed by Outey, perished horribly. The king escaped, but was caught and beheaded. Chan then had himself consecrated as king. His reign was notable for his attack upon the Dutch factory and shipping at Phnom Penh. They had opened a factory at Kompong Luong near Udong in 1623, largely in order to deny Cambodian trade to their rivals, the Portuguese. There had been quarrels about the seizure of vessels by both sides, but Outey had favoured the Dutch and done business with them. After his murder Chan wrote to the governor-general at Batavia expressing his desire to maintain good relations with the Company, and the governor-general went so far in replying as to congratulate him on his victory over the usurper. But Chan had a Malay wife, and in order to retain the support of the Muslim Chams and Malays, who had helped him to the throne, he accepted Islam as his faith and changed his name to Ibrahim. The Muslim traders in Cambodia, who were competitors of the Dutch, persuaded the king to break with them. Hence in 1643 the massacre and destruction of their ships. As a reprisal Batavia sent a fleet of five ships to blockade Phnom Penh and demanded reparation. The Khmers, however, put up a spirited resistance, and ultimately in 1652 the Dutch made peace.

In the end the crimes by which Chan had mounted the throne brought retribution upon him. Two sons of Outey had escaped the massacre. In 1658 they essayed a revolt against him. Failing in it, they fled to Hué, where they sought the aid of the Vietnamese widow of Chey Chettha II. Through her intercession Hien Vuong gave them forces with which they defeated and captured Chan in 1658. He was deported to Quang-Tinh in the northern part of the Nguyen dominions and died not long afterwards. Outey's son So now ascended the throne with the title Batom Reachea. Hué's price for its assistance was a treaty whereby Cambodia was to pay tribute and grant the Vietnamese settlers in her dominions full possession of their lands and equality of rights with the Khmers.

Batom Reachea's accession in 1660 was the signal for a revolt by the Chams and Malays who now lost the special privileges they had received from Chan. It was suppressed, and they together with his sons and ministers took refuge in Siam. In 1672 Batom Reachea was assassinated by a nephew who seized the throne and made the dead king's widow his chief queen. She, however, stirred up Chan's Malay partisans to murder him. Ang Chei, Batom Reachea's son, was the next to sit upon the throne, in 1673, but lost his life campaigning against his brother Ang Tan, who had secured a Vietnamese force with which to try his luck at becoming king. He, however, died of disease immediately after his victory and Prince Ang Non in command of his Vietnamese force proceeded to establish control over the capital; but not for long, for a few months later another brother of Ang Chei, Ang Sor, arrived with a Khmer army, defeated the Vietnamese, drove out Ang Non, and was consecrated king as Chey Chettha.

Chey Chettha IV was nineteen years old when he came to the throne in 1674. For many years he had to deal with repeated attempts by his cousin, Ang Non, to oust him from the throne. He was also under severe pressure from Hué to admit more Vietnamese colonists into his territories. The Cambodian provinces of Baria and Daung-Nay were already partly occupied by Vietnamese settlers. In 1680, as we have seen above (p. 421), some 3,000 Ming partisans in 50 storm-battered junks, all that was left of a fleet of 200, arrived at Tourane demanding asylum, and were sent on to settle in the Baria and Daung-Nay provinces under the auspices of the pretender Ang Non. They were discontented, however, with the lands assigned to them, and one of their leaders, Yang Yen-ti, led his men off to the My-tho district. The others settled peaceably at Bien-hoa, which became a prosperous agricultural centre. Chan's men were exceedingly turbulent, and in 1682 the aspiring Ang Non recruited a force among them with which he made another bid for the throne. The Khmer army fled before him, abandoning the provinces later to be known by the Vietnamese names of Bassak and Tra-Vinh. Oudong, however, did not fall. Siamese forces were sent to its assistance, and in 1684 the king was able to take the offensive and drive out the invaders. Ang Non nevertheless returned to the fray and fortified himself at Srey-Santhor. Siamese help enabled him to do so, for as Adhémar Leclère writes, Siam's policy was to keep the civil war alive, not to assist Cambodia to her feet.[1] From his Srey-Santhor base he made an attempt to capture Phnom Penh, but failed.

According to Khmer sources, in 1688 the Chinese leader Yang was

[1] *Histoire du Cambodge*, p. 357.

killed by his lieutenant Houang Tsin, who then proceeded to build a fort, defy Cambodia's authority and hold Khmer commerce to ransom. Ang Non lent his assistance to the revolt. Hence, when it was defeated by Ang Sor, who thereupon refused further tribute to Hué, the Chua Ngai, who had succeeded in 1687 with the title Phuc Tran, sent an army of 20,000 men, which first of all defeated and killed Houang Tsin, and subsequently went on to capture Oudong. But it had to beat a general retreat, since Ang Non's force, which was co-operating with it, was defeated. In the next year with Vietnamese help and a force of Chinese mercenaries Ang Non made a further attempt to seize the throne. Although he took Phnom Penh, he was unable to gain a decisive victory. Chey Chettha brought the struggle to an end by concluding an agreement with Hué accepting Vietnamese suzerainty and permitting Ang Non to reside in freedom at Srei Santor. When the latter died in 1691 his son Ang Em had to admit a Vietnamese governor. In 1698 Hué appointed a High Commissioner for Lower Cambodia and created two provinces, Bien-hoa and Gia-dinh, which were then systematically colonized by Vietnamese chosen by lot. Villages were founded, and registers of people and rice-fields compiled.

Chey Chettha now turned his attention to legal reform. When the Siamese had conquered Lovek in 1594, a holocaust of Cambodian records had taken place. Subsequently search was made in the monasteries and many copies of old legal writings were discovered. Chey Chettha appointed a commission of six to collate and revise them. The result of its labours was the promulgation in succession of twelve volumes, in two of which, the *Kram Chor*, the 'Law against Criminals', and the *Kram Sopheathipdey*, the 'Law of the Great Judges', their revisions, according to Adhémar Leclère,[1] showed in the abolition of the death penalty and a general reduction in the severity of the penal code. In 1695 Chey Chettha abdicated and placed a nephew, Prince Outey, on the throne. The latter, however, died after a reign of only six months, and Chey Chettha was again consecrated king. His second reign was a short one; he abdicated a second time in 1699. The relentless pressure southwards of the Vietnamese preyed on his mind. During his first reign they had overrun the small surviving Cham state south of Cap Varella. In 1692 its royal family with 5,000 refugees had appeared on the Cambodian frontier imploring protection, and had been permitted to settle on land near to Lovek. Their own country was absorbed into the dominions of Hué. In 1699 a Cambodian mandarin, Em, with substantial Vietnamese aid invaded up the Mekong to Kom-

---

[1] *Histoire du Cambodge*, pp. 363–4.

pong Chhnang. There he was stopped by the royal army which was led by two princes, a son of Thommo Reachea and Ang Em, a son of the former rebel Ang Non. The Vietnamese thereupon scattered into the provinces of Prey Kor (Saigon), Kampeay Srekatrey (Bien Hoa) and Baria, which the rebel mandarin had promised Hué in return for its help. It was this situation which led to Chey Chettha's second abdication. He handed over the crown to Prince Ang Em, who had distinguished himself in dealing with the invasion. The new king, however, is said to have proved incapable, and in 1701 he was deposed and Chey Chettha ascended the throne for the third time. This time he had to face another rebellion supported by the Vietnamese. He and his whole court left the capital and fled to Pursat. There he managed to rally the royal army and counter-attacked with complete success. Again he abdicated, in 1702, and placed his twelve-year-old son on the throne with himself as regent. Two years later he deposed the boy and resumed the crown himself. His fourth reign lasted only until 1706 when he again abdicated, for the last time. His successive abdications and resumptions of the crown had the worst possible effects upon the royal prestige and power. The princes he had raised to the throne and then deposed became rivals whose efforts to gain power weakened the country and led to more foreign intervention. Ex-king Ang Em, for instance, who was a son of the famous rebel Ang Non, cherished his father's ambitions and hostility to the ruling family at Oudong. Thus, when Chey Chettha's deposed son, Thommo Reachea II, was again raised to the throne, and Ang Em needed a pretext for rebellion, he found it ready-made in a revolt by members of the exiled royal family of Laos, whom Chey Chettha had granted asylum in the province of Bati. Their revolt was against the provincial administration and they appealed to Ang Em for help. He enlisted some of the primitive peoples of the provinces of Angkor and Kompong Thom as well as a Vietnamese force and blockaded the capital. After a resistance of some three months, the king and his younger brother, Ang Tong, escaped through the lines of the besiegers and got away to Siam. Ang Em then (1710) became king for the second time.

Siam now took a hand in the game. An appreciable Siamese force was sent to Cambodia in support of a demand for Ang Em's abdication. But with Vietnamese aid he was able to defy Siam. Again in 1714 and 1722 further Siamese expeditions were sent with the object of reinstating Thommo-Reachea; but Ang Em held his ground. The Nguyen of Hué reaped the advantage from this situation to extend their control over all the Cambodian coastal lands in the Gulf of Siam. We have seen above[1]

¹ Pp. 421–2.

how some years earlier another refugee Ming leader, Mac Cuu, had settled with his followers at Peam (later Hatien). The Siamese invasion of 1714 caused him to flee to Hué. There he was invested by the Nguyen with authority over the Cambodian lands on the Gulf of Siam, though no formal cession by their rightful owner had taken place. On returning to his appanage Mac Cuu annihilated a Siamese expedition sent against him. In the north, however, in 1722 a Siamese invasion force defeated Ang Em's Vietnamese troops and threatened Oudong. To save himself Ang Em now offered tribute to Siam. It was accepted and the Siamese army retired taking with it ex-king Thommo Reachea and his brother Ang Tong. For this volte-face Ang earned the contemptuous epithet of 'the Siamese king'. He deemed it wise to abdicate in favour of his son, Ang Chey, who became Satha II.

Cambodia was now in complete disorder with one king and three ex-kings (Chey Chettha IV, living until 1725, Thommo Reachea and Ang Em) bidding for the support of either Siam or Hué indiscriminately. In 1731 the enraged Khmer population of Banam region fell upon the Vietnamese there and massacred them. Hué then intervened under the pretext of restoring order. The Cambodians put up a strong resistance, but finally King Satha, who had fled from his capital, gave in and made a formal surrender of the provinces of Me Sa (My-tho) and Long Hor (Vinh-long) to Hué. It was merely a formal recognition of a *fait accompli*. He then transferred his capital to Lovek: Oudong was too easily accessible to an enemy from the south.

In 1738 Satha lost his throne. Suspecting a plot against himself involving the chief queen and other members of the royal family, he was about to seize the suspects when they forestalled him by rebelling. They called in the Siamese and invited Thommo Reachea to return. They banked on the fact that by the Khmer people the Siamese were regarded as a much lesser evil than the Vietnamese. A Siamese army entered from Korat in the north and a small sea expedition landed troops at Kampot. The operations were successful. Satha fled to Vietnam. The restored Thommo Reachea at once took the lead in a national movement to expel the Vietnamese. Many took refuge on the island of Hong Peam Misa in the Mekong, over which Hué proceeded to extend its authority. Baffled here, Thommo Reachea directed an attack against Mac Cuu's appanage. He himself had died in 1735 and his son, Mac Thien Tu, had taken over with the sanction and assistance of Hué. Against him Thommo Reachea again failed.

Thommo Reachea died in 1747. His eldest son, who succeeded him, was at once murdered by an ambitious younger brother. The ministers, however, rejected the candidature of the murderer, choosing his brother, Ang Tong, as king. He, however, was forced to flee by an incursion of refugee princes from Cochin-China led by ex-king Satha. Ang Tong and his high officials fled to Siam while the rebel princes established themselves at Oudong. Their Vietnamese followers then proceeded to behave as if the country had been annexed to Hué. Vietnamese generals took over the administration, levying taxes, removing provincial governors and introducing Vietnamese methods of administration. The Cambodians driven to desperation rose as one man against them and drove them out. The Kralahom Ok, Minister of Transport, led the resistance, and also took the lead in reorganizing the country after the Vietnamese expulsion. He then choose a son of the murdered Thommo Reachea III as king with the title of Chey Chettha (V). The refugee king Ang Tong was passed over. Chey Chettha died after a troubled reign of six years and Ang Tong succeeded him. His short reign was disastrous. The quarrels and atrocities at the palace rose to a new height, while the king himself was helpless in face of Vietnamese pressure. Further Cambodian provinces fell into Vietnamese hands, Treang, Bantei Meas, Bati and Preykrabas; while in 1757 the king had to make a formal cession of Phsar (Sadec) and Meât Chrouk (Chaudoc). In 1758 he was driven from the throne by a grandson, Prah Outey, who had gradually eliminated all his rivals in a whole series of palace murders. Outey on his part sought investiture of Hué, and as the price for it ceded two more provinces, Srok Trang (Soctrang) and Preah Trapeang (Travinh). The whole of what later became the French colony of Cochin-China had now been lost to Vietnam by Cambodia.

The remainder of this grim story up to the establishment of the French protectorate over Cambodia in the eighteen-sixties is told in the chapters devoted to Vietnamese and Siamese history. Our knowledge of it comes basically from the Cambodian Chronicle together with the Vietnamese Annals and T'ai chronicles. They are concerned solely with dynastic events: the people are out of the picture. On either side of the beleaguered kingdom were the two harpies, Vietnam and Siam, snatching away its territories, and each vying with the other in seeking to dominate what was left. Siam's efforts, however, were seriously hampered by the Burmese conquest of Ayut'ia in 1767, the subsequent struggle to re-unify the country, and by a fresh spate of Burmese attacks. The Nguyen power also collapsed before the Tayson rebellion in 1773 and the Tongkingese occupation of Hué in 1775. For the next quarter of a century the Nguyen were engaged in a struggle to regain their inheritance and, with that secured, to extend their control over the heartland of Vietnam in the north. When Nguyen Anh finally triumphed in 1802, and, as the Emperor Gia Long, united all the Vietnamese lands—for the first time in their history—Vietnam was to become a stronger competitor than ever for control over the rump of Cambodia. But a reviving Siam under the Chakri dynasty was also a power to be reckoned with. Thus, when the rivalry between them broke out afresh, as it did in the reign of Minh Mang of Hué, it was more severe than before. The Vietnamese were militarily the stronger, but were hated by the Cambodians, who, with no love for the Siamese either, yet co-operated with them against the common enemy. By 1845 it was a drawn fight, and under an agreement placing Cambodia under the joint protection of both competitors, she escaped absorption by either. France perhaps saved the situation for the Khmers by making Cambodia a protected kingdom. It thus retained its individuality. History seldom teaches so clear-cut a lesson as in Cambodia's case since 1600; its influence upon Cambodian policy since the recovery of independence in 1954 has been significant.

CHAPTER 25

THE KINGDOM OF LAOS, 1591–1836

WHILE the empire built up by Bayinnaung's military prowess was in a state of disintegration and his son Nanda Bayin was deeply involved in his struggle with Naresuen of Ayut'ia[1] the kingdom of Laos, far away on the upper Mekong, had regained its independence under Nokèo Koumane. He was proclaimed king at Vientiane in 1591, and in the following year his forces overcame the resistance of Luang Prabang and reunited the realm. The little state of Tran Ninh also, with its capital Chieng Khouang close to the Plain of Jars, recognized the revived strength of the Laos kingdom by sending the traditional tokens of allegiance. Incidentally, sandwiched as it was between two states more powerful than itself, Laos and Annam, it paid tribute to both. It is perhaps significant that while its acknowledgement of the suzerainty of Vientiane was accorded every three years, Annam received it annually.

Nokèo Koumane reigned for only five years. His successor was a cousin by marriage, Vongsa, who took the title of T'ammikarat and reigned until 1622. His reign had an unhappy end. His son Oupagnouvarat became so popular and began to assume so much control over the government that his jealous father drove him into rebellion. The army supported the young prince, who overcame his father and put him to death. A year later he himself disappeared and the country was plunged into a series of dynastic struggles lasting until 1637. During this period five kings reigned, but the dynastic annals are so obscure that little is known of them.

The competition for the throne reached its climax in 1637, when Souligna-Vongsa, one of five warring claimants, defeated his rivals and seized power. He proved himself the strong man that the faction-torn country needed. During his long reign of fifty-five years not only was internal peace restored but excellent relations were cultivated with all the neighbouring states. His firm and just rule gave his kingdom a reputation for strength which was sufficient to deter any would-be aggressor from risking an attack upon it. He was thus able to negotiate

[1] *Supra*, chap. 15, b.

444

a series of agreements with his neighbours by which the frontiers of his kingdom were exactly defined.

A vivid account of a visit to Vientiane during his reign has come to us from the pen of the Dutchman van Wuysthof, who went there in 1641 from the Dutch factory at Phnom Penh with two assistants. Governor-General van Diemen at Batavia was anxious to tap the resources of the 'land of gumlac and benzoin'. The difficult and dangerous journey up the Mekong took from 20 July to 3 November. The merchants were well received by the king at the That-Luong Pagoda and treated to a gala exhibition of dancing, jousting and boat-racing which delighted them. The delivery of huge supplies of gumlac and benzoin was promised. Van Wuysthof, profoundly impressed, departed on 24 December, leaving his two assistants to follow later with a Laos envoy and presents for van Diemen.

In view of the briefness of his stay it is difficult to know how much value to attach to his statements about Laotian affairs, particularly since his account of Souligna-Vongsa's accession is at complete variance with the information given in the indigenous records. Regarding the government of the country, he mentions three great ministers as sharing the highest authority with the king. The first was commander-in-chief of the army and commandant of the city of Vientiane. Van Wuysthof calls him 'Tevinia-Assen', which seems to indicate Tian-T'ala, the king's son-in-law, who was indeed the chief minister. The second was the governor of Nakhone and was viceroy over the southern part of the kingdom stretching down to the Cambodian frontier. The third was the minister of the palace who dealt with foreign envoys. There was also a supreme tribunal, composed of five members of the royal family, which dealt with civil and criminal matters.

Van Wuysthof was the first European ever to visit Vientiane. His notions of the geography of the kingdom were inaccurate and his ignorance of Buddhism profound; but his journal seems to paint a faithful picture of the prosperity of the kingdom as well as of the number and beauty of its pagodas and other religious buildings. It appears as a Buddhist arcadia, attracting pilgrims from far and wide.

One other European, the Piedmontese Jesuit Father Giovanni-Maria Leria, arrived in Vientiane in the year after van Wuysthof's visit. He tried without success to obtain permission to open a Christian mission in the country. Against the stiff opposition of the Buddhist clergy he managed to stay there for five years. His memoirs were used by another Jesuit, Father Merini, as the basis for his *Relation nouvelle et curieuse des royaumes de Tonquin et de Laos*, published in Paris in 1666. Nothing came of this sudden intrusion by Europeans into the unknown regions of the upper Mekong. The river itself, with its rapids, narrows and shifting sandbanks, was a sufficient deterrent to the establishment of European trade, and Buddhism to the penetration of Christian missions. Not until 1861, apparently, was the next European prospector, Henri Mouhot, to set foot in the secluded kingdom, and he travelled to Luang Prabang by bullock-waggon.

Only one war disturbed the profound peace maintained by the firm hand of Souligna-Vongsa. In 1651 the King of Tran Ninh refused his request for the hand of his daughter Nang Ken Chan in marriage. After the request had been made several times with the same result Souligna-Vongsa sent a detachment of troops, but it was repulsed. Hence in 1652 a stronger expedition was sent, which captured the capital, Chieng Khouang, and compelled the king to yield. This unhappy incident caused a long and disastrous feud between the two states which lasted into the nineteenth century. Apart from this the reign of the greatest of the Laotian sovereigns was mainly distinguished by notable achievements in the traditional culture of the country. Music, architecture, sculpture, painting, gold and silver work, basket work and weaving all flourished.

But even a king such as Souligna-Vongsa could not ensure the continuance of stability after his death. His only son, the crown prince, seduced the wife of the chief of the corps of royal pages, a crime punishable by death. When the royal tribunal condemned the young man to death his father refused to interfere with the course of justice. The result was that when the king himself died in 1694 his direct heirs, his grandsons King-Kitsarat and Int'a-Som, were too young to rule, and the aged chief minister Tian-T'ala seized the throne. Six years later, in 1700, he was dethroned and murdered by Nan-T'arat, the Governor of Nakhone, who himself became king.

News of this coup reached the ears of a prince of the royal house who had spent the whole of his life as an exile at Hué, and since 1696 had been agitating for Vietnamese aid for an invasion of the Laos kingdom. He was Sai-Ong-Hué, the son of Souligna-Vongsa's eldest brother Som-P'ou, who had been defeated in the struggle for the throne in 1637. In 1700 with a Vietnamese force, and strongly reinforced by partisans collected at Tran Ninh, he swooped down on Vientiane, captured the city, put to death the usurper Nan-T'arat, and proclaimed himself king.

When Tian-T'ala was dethroned in 1700 the two grandsons of Souligna-Vongsa, King-Kitsarat and Int'a-Som, had fled to Luang Prabang. Sai-Ong-Hué, on gaining the throne from Nan-T'arat, sent his half-brother T'ao-Nong to take possession of Luang Prabang in his name. The two young princes, unable to resist, thereupon fled to the Sip-Song-Panas, where their cousin Khamone-Noi, who ruled there, took them into his safe keeping. In 1707 with an army of 6,000 men, raised by Khamone-Noi, they drove T'ao-Nong out of Luang Prabang. King-Kitsarat was then proclaimed king and sent an ultimatum to Sai-Ong-Hué that in future the Laos provinces north of Chieng Khane would form a separate independent kingdom. And Sai-Ong-Hué, preoccupied with the task of making good his rule over the southern provinces, was in no position to dispute the arrangement.

The once-powerful kingdom of Souligna-Vongsa was no more. From 1707 Luang Prabang and Vientiane were the capitals of two separate and mutually hostile states. Each was decisively weakened by the fact that the other was constantly looking for an opportunity of restoring the former unity, and with this aim was seeking the aid of neighbours such as Burma, Siam or Annam, all of whom at one time or another during the next century or so adopted expansionist policies.

Vientiane under Sai-Ong-Hué (1707–35) was in difficulties from the start. Tran Ninh refused homage. An army was thereupon sent to occupy Chieng Khouang. The king fled and his younger brother was raised to the throne. But as soon as the troops of Vientiane were recalled the deposed king recovered his throne. He then decided to do the politic thing and make formal submission to Sai-Ong-Hué. With Bassak and the provinces in the far south Sai-Ong-Hué was less successful. Chao-Soi-Sisamout, who ruled there from 1713 to 1747, had close relations with Siam and Cambodia, and Sai-Ong-Hué, with his attention fixed upon the dynastic troubles in Luang Prabang, left him in virtual independence.

In 1735 Sai-Ong-Hué was succeeded peaceably by his son Ong-Long. His reign of twenty-five years saw great convulsions in Burma, Siam and Luang Prabang, but he managed to pursue a policy of 'safety first' with success. When Alaungpaya, the Burmese conqueror, having crushed the independent Mon kingdom of Pegu, struck eastwards in an attempt to revive the policy of Bayinnaung, Ong-Long saved his kingdom from invasion by assisting the Burmese expedition which brought Luang Prabang to its knees.

He had trouble, however, with Tran Ninh. It was the old story of a refusal of tribute followed by an invasion by the army of Vientiane. This time, however, Annam intervened to order the disputants to cease fighting. Ong-Long therefore withdrew his forces and invited King Chom-P'ou of Tran Ninh to negotiate. Chom-P'ou, suspecting a trap, waited three years before going to meet his overlord. When he did at last go he was kidnapped and kept a prisoner at Vientiane. Again in 1760 Annam intervened; Ong-Long was ordered to liberate his prisoner, and did so. For the rest of his reign Chom-P'ou paid his tribute regularly and went personally every third year to render homage.

Ong-Long died just before the Burmese raised the siege of Ayut'ia owing to Alaungpaya's fatal wound. His son Ong-Boun continued his father's policy of supporting Burma. At first all went well. King Hsinbyushin crushed the attempt of Luang Prabang to rebel and in 1767 destroyed Ayut'ia. But his own kingdom was invaded by the Chinese, and he lost his hold not only on Siam but also on Chiengmai and Luang Prabang. Vientiane was now in dire peril. In 1771 she was attacked by Luang Prabang. Luckily for her Hsinbyushin had by this time disposed of the Chinese invaders by the Peace of Kaungton (1770) and was able to send a strong force which defeated Luang Prabang.

But P'ya Taksin's movement to restore the power of Siam and drive the Burmese out of the Laos states met with increasing success, notwithstanding the efforts of Hsinbyushin to recover the ground lost during his struggle with the Chinese. When, therefore, in 1774 Int'a-Som of Luang Prabang allied with P'ya Taksin, Vientiane's only safe course would have been to have abandoned her Burmese alliance and to have made terms with Siam. Ong-Boun, however, chose the foolish alternative of defiance, and in consequence lost everything. In 1778 Siam seized on a convenient pretext to invade Vientiane. After a few months' siege General Chulalok captured the city and proceeded to place the country under military occupation. Ong-Boun escaped and made his way into exile.

Among the loot taken in Vientiane was the fabulous 'Emerald Buddha', carved from green jasper, today one of the sights of Bangkok. Said to have been discovered at Chiengrai in 1436, it had been housed successively in Chiengmai and Luang Prabang before being carried to Vientiane in 1564. In 1779 it came to shed lustre upon P'ya Taksin's capital, Dhonburi. In due course, when the old royal palace was built at Bangkok, its present temple was constructed for it in the palace precincts. That was not the only loot taken away from the ravaged city. According to Wood,[1] the Siamese on this occasion rivalled the Burmese in 'frightfulness'.

In 1782, when P'ya Taksin disappeared from the scene and General Chakri seized the throne of Siam, the fugitive Ong-Boun made formal submission. He was then permitted to return to Vientiane, and his eldest son Chao-Nan was invested with the government of the kingdom as the vassal of Siam. In 1791 dynastic troubles in Luang Prabang tempted the young man to interfere. He won a brilliant success, took the city by assault, and annexed the Houa P'an cantons. His overlord Rama I, however, highly disapproved of his conduct. On his return home, therefore, he was deposed and replaced by his younger brother Chao-In (1792-1805).

Chao-In remained throughout his reign a loyal vassal. He assisted the Siamese to expel the Burmese from Chiengsen. His brother, the Oupahat Chao-Anou, distinguished himself in the fighting and received the congratulations of the Court of Bangkok. When, therefore, Chao-In died in 1805, Chao-Anou was at once recognized as king by Siam.

Chao-Anou was a man of outstanding ability, but his vaulting ambition brought to his country the worst disaster of its whole history. The military prowess he had displayed in Chiengsen endeared him to the Siamese, but his great aim was to free his country from subordination to Bangkok. For many years he cleverly concealed this while he strengthened his position and beautified his capital. In 1819 he put down a revolt of the Khas in the Bassac region and obtained for his son Chao-Ngo the governorship of the province. He then instigated Chao-Ngo to fortify Ubon under the pretext that it was a measure designed for the defence of Siam. He sent tokens of allegiance to the Emperor Gia-Long of Annam, and in 1820 offered Luang Prabang a secret alliance against Siam. At his splendid new temple of Sisaket, founded in 1824, he held twice a year a grand assembly of all his feudatories to pay him homage.

In 1825 he journeyed to Bangkok to attend the funeral rites of Rama II. There he made a formal request for the repatriation of the Laos families deported to Siam during the struggles of the previous century. The refusal of so unreasonable a request was a foregone conclusion; it was made merely for the sake of obtaining a useful pretext for the highly dangerous step of renouncing his allegiance to his overlord. In the following year Captain Henry Burney went to Bangkok to

[1] *History of Siam*, p. 268.

GATEWAY AND ANCIENT CITY WALL AT KORAT

negotiate a treaty. While he was there an entirely baseless rumour reached Vientiane that the negotiations had broken down and a British fleet was about to threaten Bangkok. Anou at once decided that now was the time to wring his independence from Siam at the point of the sword.

His sudden attack caught the Siamese entirely unprepared. Three armies simultaneously began a march on Bangkok: one under Chao-Ngo from Ubon, a second under the Oupahat Tissa from Roi-Et, and the third under Anou himself from Vientiane. Anou managed to get as far as Korat by the simple device of proclaiming that he was marching to assist the King of Siam against a British attack. His advance guards even threatened Saraburi, only three days' march from the capital.

But the Siamese resistance soon began to stiffen and his donkey's gallop was over. His advanced guards were driven back to Korat, and the Siamese used the breathing space thus acquired to raise a large army, which was placed under the command of General P'ya Bodin. When this force advanced on Korat it met with no resistance: Anou was found to be in full retreat northwards. His decision seems to have been taken as a result of the suprise and defeat of one of his marauding detachments by a small Siamese force in the Samrit plain.

P'ya Bodin, with the initiative in his hands, carried out a systematic campaign which involved first the storming of Ubon and the capture of Chao-Ngo, and finally in 1827 the decisive battle of Nong-Boua-Lamp'on, where, after a desperate fight lasting seven days, the Siamese army forced the crossing of the Mekong. That was the end of the struggle. Anou fled into the dense jungles, sending out vain appeals for help to Chiengmai, Luang Prabang and Chieng Khouang. The Siamese made a complete holocaust of Vientiane. They then proceeded methodically to devastate the whole kingdom, driving off the population to repeople areas of their own country similarly treated by the Burmese in the preceding period.

That was the end of the kingdom of Vientiane. In 1828 Anou, chased across the Annamite Chain by the Siamese, appeared at Hué, and the Emperor Minh-Mang promised to help him regain his kingdom. But most of the troops with which he set out on his return journey deserted on the way. And as soon as he arrived in his ruined capital the approach of a Siamese force caused him once more to betake himself to flight, this time into the territory of Tran Ninh. King Chao-Noi therefore had to choose between offending either Siam or Annam; and since Siamese forces were actually threatening his country, and he himself had inherited the traditional hatred of his family for the rulers of Vientiane, he captured the fugitive and handed him over to Siam.

Anou died in Bangkok in 1835 after four years' captivity. Pallegoix says that he was exposed in an iron cage and eventually died of the ill-treatment he received. But there are other conflicting stories, and the matter remains an unsolved mystery. On Chao-Noi of Chieng Khouang the vengeance of Annam fell speedily and relentlessly. Summoned to Hué to explain his conduct, he sought to appease the anger of Minh-Mang by sending an envoy with rich presents. But it was to no avail. A Vietnamese force seized him and took him off to Hué, where he was publicly executed. His kingdom, Tran Ninh, became a prefecture of the empire of Annam.

The story of the Luang Prabang kingdom from 1707 onwards may be more briefly told. Its early years were troubled by dynastic squabbles, through the attempts of Int'a-Som to oust from the throne first his brother King-Kitsarat (1707–26) and then his cousin Khamone-Noi (1726–7). Khamone-Noi, an interesting personality whose adventurous wanderings are still the subject of much story-telling, had a passion for hunting. During one of his absences on a hunting expedition Int'a-Som, whom he had carelessly allowed to live in complete freedom at the capital, notwithstanding one attempt already to seize the throne, staged a palace revolution and made himself king. Khamone-Noi, on learning what happened, went off to seek his fortune in Chiengmai, which ten years earlier had rebelled against Burma. There he gained control over the kingdom, routed a Burmese army sent against him in 1728, and was crowned as king.

Int'a-Som had a long reign which lasted until 1776. Internally it was one of complete tranquillity. Externally, however, he was faced by serious dangers. His isolation led him to enter into diplomatic relations with China. The chronicles of his reign attach much importance to the two embassies he sent to Peking in 1729 and 1734. In 1750 Annam claimed tribute, and when it was refused sent a detachment of troops to collect it. These, however, were driven out of the country, and there the matter ended. Internal troubles in Annam, caused by the fact that the kings of the Le dynasty had lost all control over affairs of state, have been taken to account for this display of weakness.

But the greatest danger came from the revival of the Burmese power under Alaungpaya (1752-60) and his successors. Luang Prabang, as we have seen, was reduced to submission in 1753 and had to furnish a large body of hostages, including Int'a-Som's son Tiao-Vong. When Alaungpaya died Int'a-Som attempted unsuccessfully to regain his independence. But the Chinese invasions of Burma and P'ya Taksin's victories in Siam brought a more favourable situation, and he not only renounced Burmese overlordship but in 1771 ventured to attack Vientiane, Burma's ally. A Burmese force defeated him at the battle of Muong Kassy and relieved the beleaguered city, but returned home without doing anything towards restoring Burmese suzerainty over Luang Prabang.

Int'a-Som was therefore emboldened to throw in his lot with P'ya Taksin, and in 1774 entered into a defensive alliance with him against the Burmese. He had unwittingly taken a step too far, for when in 1778 the Siamese captured Vientiane and wiped out its independence they demanded of his son Sotika-Koumane (1776-81) the acceptance of conditions such as reduced Luang Prabang also to a position of dependence.

In 1781 Sotika-Koumane's younger brother, Tiao-Vong, forced him to abdicate in his favour. Six years later the new king died prematurely without issue, and for four years the country was distracted by a succession struggle between the remaining brothers. This, as we have seen above, tempted Chao-Nan of Vientiane to intervene. One of the squabbling brothers, Anourout, Int'a-Som's second son, organized the resistance to the invader, but failed to save the city. On its fall he escaped to Bangkok, where for two years (1791–3) he lived as a state prisoner.

Meanwhile King Chao-Nan, having carried out a large-scale massacre in Luang Prabang, deported many households of people and returned home. He would have pushed his conquest farther, but feared to incur the wrath of his suzerain. By attacking at all, however, he had gone too far, and in consequence was deposed and ordered to live in Bangkok. Shortly after his arrival there the fugitive Anourout was released at the request of imperial China and returned to rule over Luang Prabang. There he busied himself with repairing the ruins of the city and carrying out works of Buddhist merit. In 1817 he abdicated in favour of his son Mant'a-T'ourat.

The new king, who was no longer young, having been born in 1775, was content to follow in his father's footsteps and reign quietly. He was far too cautious to be drawn into the anti-Siamese alliance proposed by Anou of Vientiane. The Siamese triumph over Anou, however, and the downfall of Vientiane caused him to attempt some redirection of his policy. Hence in 1831, and again in 1833, he sent missions to Hué offering the homage and traditional tribute of gold and silver flowers which his grandfather had so brusquely refused in 1750.

But it was to no purpose. The Siamese yoke was firmly fixed on his shoulders, and Minh-Mang of Hué discreetly pigeonholed the letters borne by his envoys. Years later, however, they were a godsend to the French when they were seeking a pretext to extend their control from Annam to the Laos lands across the Mekong.

When Mant'a-T'ourat died in 1836 a Siamese minister attended his cremation and publicly proclaimed Siam's rights of sovereignty. His son and designated successor, Souka-Seum, was then living as a hostage at Bangkok. He was significantly kept waiting three years before receiving official investiture from the King of Siam and permission to return to his country.

CHAPTER 26

SIAM FROM 1688 TO 1851

P'RA P'ETRAJA, the usurper who saved his country from French domination, had a troubled reign of fifteen years.[1] There were constant internal disorders and various parts of the kingdom were involved. They began with a dangerous attempt in 1690 by an impostor, pretending to be a brother of King Narai, to seize Ayut'ia. He gained much support in the districts of Nakhon Nayok, Lopburi and Saraburi; but during his attack on the city the elephant he was riding was shot down and he himself wounded and captured. His followers then dispersed. His defeat caused such panic in the rebellious districts that there was a mass movement from them into Burma. In the next year two provincial governors rebelled, one at Korat in the north and the other at Nakhon Srit'ammarat in the Malay Peninsula. The Korat rising was dealt with first. After much trouble the city was subdued by the novel method of flying kites, to which flaming torches were attached, over it and setting fire to the roofs of the houses. The rebel governor escaped and fled to join the Nakhon Srit'ammarat rebels. These were attacked in 1692, and, again with much difficulty, subdued. The Governor of Korat was killed in the early stages of the fighting. The Governor of Nakhon Srit'ammarat, a Malay and an old friend of the admiral commanding the royal fleet, when further resistance became impossible, killed his wife and family and escaped in a boat with fifty followers by the connivance of his friend. The admiral paid for this with his life, and his head was set over the city gate.

Korat provided yet another insurrection in 1699, this time led by a magician, who with only twenty-eight followers at first completely terrorized the governor and people with his magic powers. After some time he was persuaded to transfer to Lopburi, whither he went with a force of about 3,000 men. When threatened by the royal forces they surrendered their leader and his original twenty-eight followers and the movement collapsed.

[1] There is some conflict of opinion about the date of his death, which the *P'ongsawadan* gives as 1697. See Wood, *History of Siam*, p. 223, n.2.

In 1700 a serious succession dispute broke out in the Laos kingdom which ultimately led to its division into two mutually hostile parts ruled respectively by Luang Prabang and Vien Chang. The Nguyen of Hué helped one candidate to the throne of Vien Chang on condition that he should recognize their overlordship. According to the Siamese, they also sent him help, in return for which a princess was presented and became the wife of the Uparat.[1] From this time onwards Vietnam and Siam became competitors for the control of the Laos country.

The Uparat, who succeeded his father as king in 1703, is known to Siamese history as P'rachao Süa, 'King Tiger'. He was a cruel and depraved tyrant about whose excesses many stories have been preserved. His reign contains nothing worthy of record.

The next reign, that of T'ai Sra (1709-33), P'rachao Süa's eldest son, is notable for a big effort to combat the growing influence of Hué in Cambodia. In 1714 King Prea Srey Thomea, called by the Siamese Sri T'ammaraja, was driven out of his capital by his uncle Keo Fa with the assistance of Vietnamese and Laotian troops. The king and his younger brother fled to Ayut'ia. In 1715, and again in 1716, Siamese forces sent to restore them were defeated. In 1717 two large Siamese expeditionary forces attacked Cambodia. One, supported by a large fleet, operated against the coastal districts; the other marched overland against Udong, Keo Fa's capital. The southern force met with disaster—one of the greatest disasters in Siamese history, says Wood,[2] who blames it to the incompetence and cowardice of the commander. The fleet, he says, fell into a panic owing to the loss of a few ships and put out to sea, leaving the land force to be mopped up by the Cambodians. According to the Annamite account, however, the expedition, after capturing Ha-tien, was destroyed by a storm.[3] The northern force, after defeating the Cambodians in a number of engagements, threatened the capital. Thereupon Keo Fa offered his allegiance to Siam and was left in possession of the kingdom. Apparently he hoped in this way to obtain Siamese help against Hué, whose expansionist policy at the expense of his country was costing it dear. But Siam appears to have made no attempt to assist him, and the Nguyen proceeded to make themselves masters of further Cambodian provinces.

When T'ai Sra died in 1733 a struggle for the throne broke out between his younger brother, the Uparat, and his second son, Prince

---

[1] Compare Le Boulanger, *Histoire du Laos Français*, pp. 130-5, and Wood, *op. cit.*, pp. 222-3.
[2] *Op. cit.*, p. 228.
[3] Maybon, *op. cit.*, p. 124.

Ap'ai. It was won by the Uparat, who took the title of Maha T'amma-raja II, but is usually referred to as King Boromokot. He took a fearful revenge on his opponents, but afterwards ruled so peaceably that his reign, which lasted until 1758, is described in the Siamese histories as a golden age. While he was on the throne dramatic developments were in progress in Burma. The Mon rising of 1740 caused the Burmese governors of Martaban and Tavoy to flee to Ayut'ia. As a result friendly relations were established with Ava, and in 1744, for the first time in over a century, a Burmese embassy was deputed to Ayut'ia. Boromokot had refused to give a daughter in marriage to the Mon king, Smim Htaw—'Saming T'oh' in the Siamese rendering—and the Burmese hoped for help in subduing the rebels. But although a Siamese return mission went to Ava in 1746, Boromokot maintained strict neutrality. In the following year when 'Saming T'oh' lost his throne he fled to Chiengmai. There, according to Wood,[1] he recruited an army with which he made an unsuccessful attempt to regain his throne. Then in 1750 he made his way to Ayut'ia. But Boromokot would not help him and eventually put him on a Chinese junk bound for China. He landed on the coast of Annam and made his way back to Chiengmai. In 1756 with a small band of supporters he offered his services to Alaungpaya, who put him into safe custody until his death two years later.

Boromokot was a peace-loving sovereign and a great patron of Buddhism. In 1753 the King of Kandy[2] invited him to send a deputation of Buddhist monks to purify Sinhalese Buddhism. A commission of fifteen under the leadership of a monk named Upali was sent to Ceylon. The success of the mission is attested by the fact that the sect which it founded, known as the Upaliwong or Sayamwong, became the largest in Ceylon.

Before he died in 1758 Boromokot made his second son, Prince Ut'ump'on, Uparat in preference to the elder one. But the new king found his position so difficult that he retired to a monastery in favour of his brother, who ascended the throne as Boromoraja (1758–67). He was the last king to reign at Ayut'ia. In the year after his accession Alaungpaya invaded Siam and besieged the capital. The ostensible reason for the attack was the Siamese refusal to surrender Mon rebels who had taken refuge in their country, but Alaungpaya was looking

[1] Op. cit., p. 235.
[2] King Kirti Soi was an Indian, but he was a great supporter of the religion of his kingdom. Finding the Buddhist hierarchy decadent, he sent deputations to both Burma and Siam asking for monks through whom he might stimulate a religious revival.

for an excuse to revive the glories of Bayinnaung's reign. The Siamese assert that even had the Burmese monarch not been mortally wounded he would have given up the siege, since he was not prepared for a long campaign and had decided to return home before the onset of the wet monsoon of 1760. His death merely postponed the next invasion for a few years.

As we have seen in a previous chapter,[1] as soon as Hsinbyushin succeeded Naungdawgyi in 1763 he began to prepare for another assault upon Ayut'ia. And even before his main army began to approach its objective by way of Chiengmai, another force, sent to capture Mergui and Tenasserim, made such good progress that it occupied all the Siamese states in the Malay Peninsula and its advance was only checked at P'etchaburi by General P'ya Taksin,[2] who was later to achieve renown as the saviour of Siam. When the full-scale campaign began, late in 1765, Siam was invaded by three Burmese armies, one from Chiengmai, a second by the Three Pagodas route and the third from the south. Gradually they closed in round the capital. The siege began in February 1766. The onset of the rainy season brought no respite, for the Burmese were well supplied with boats with which to carry on the fight when the surrounding country was flooded. At the end of the rains Burmese reinforcements poured in, but the Siamese, who were refused an honourable surrender, held out desperately until April 1767. Before the end came, P'ya Taksin, who had come to loggerheads with the incompetent king, cut his way out with 500 followers and escaped to Rayong on the Gulf of Siam, where he proceeded to raise a new army. The Burmese destroyed everything they could lay hands on, except what could be carried away as plunder. The palace and principal buildings were burnt along with thousands of private houses. The ruined city was never rebuilt. When Siam recovered from the disaster a new capital arose at Bangkok.

When Ayut'ia fell Burma was already involved in serious trouble with China. Early in 1768 Ming Jui's invasion threatened Ava and the situation became critical. Siam was therefore presented with a wonderful opportunity for recovery, provided the right leader was available. During the final assault on the city King Boromoraja had disappeared and was never heard of again.

Several members of the royal family had survived the disaster, but there was no P'ra Naret among them. It was P'ya Taksin who, though

---

[1] Chap. 22.
[2] Called 'Paya Tak' by the Burmese.

half Chinese, became the leader of the resistance movement against Burmese domination. Immediately after the fall of the city he had begun to extend his control over the districts neighbouring Rayong In June 1767 he captured Chantabun. This success caused thousands of followers to join him. In October he sailed up the Menam and took T'anaburi (Bangkok), executing the Siamese governor placed over it by the Burmese. Finally he boldly attacked the camp of the main Burmese occupation force at Three Bo Trees, close to Ayut'ia, and won a complete victory.

This success led him to assume the royal power. At first his idea was to make Ayut'ia his capital, but to do so would have involved greater resources than he had at his command as yet. His coronation, therefore, was celebrated at T'anaburi. Siam, however, had fallen apart. The peninsular provinces were under the Governor of Nakhon Srit'ammarat, who had proclaimed his independence and assumed the title of King Musica. Korat and the eastern provinces were controlled by a son of King Boromokot, who also pretended to royal power. So, too, did the Governor of P'itsanulok, who called himself King Ruang, while in the extreme north of his province a Buddhist monk, Ruan, had established a theocratic state called the kingdom of Fang. Moreover, at Ratburi on the Mekhlong river the Burmese had a strong force and a fleet of boats.

When the Chinese retreat from the Ava region began in 1768, Hsinbyushin ordered the Burmese Governor of Tavoy to link up with the Ratburi force in an attack upon Bangkok. The plan failed completely; P'ya Taksin drove out the Governor of Tavoy's force and captured Ratburi. The whole of the Burmese fleet stationed there fell into his hands. He followed up this victory in May 1768 with an attack on P'itsanulok. This time, however, he was unsuccessful. Thereupon King Ruang staged a formal coronation and declared himself King of Siam. But he died immediately afterwards, and the monk-king of Fang seized his territory.

At the close of the wet monsoon Taksin marched into the Korat region, where Prince T'ep P'ip'it was assisted by a Burmese force. Here again he won a decisive victory. The Burmese commander was killed in battle, and the prince, while fleeing towards Vien Chang, was captured and executed.

There was still much to be done before Siam was unified, but at this juncture affairs in Cambodia demanded attention. A fugitive king, Rama T'ibodi, better known as Ang Non, driven out by his brother Ang Tong with the assistance of Cochin-Chinese troops, fled

RUINS OF PHRA MONGKHONBOPIT, AYUT'IA

to Bangkok. P'ya Taksin demanded tribute of the usurper, and when this was refused sent his Korat force to occupy Siemreap and Battambang, as a first step towards restoring the exiled king. He himself was at the time busy with preparations to reduce King Musica of Nakhon Srit'ammarat, and hence for the time being had to leave events in Cambodia to take their course. The operations against Nakhon Srit'ammarat were speedily brought to a successful conclusion, but when P'ya Taksin returned to his capital in March 1769 his armies had been defeated and forced to leave Cambodia.

It was useless to attempt at once to reassert Siamese suzerainty there; the Burmese were threatening from Chiengmai and the monk-king of Fang had still to be dealt with. He decided to strike at Chiengmai first. But his attack failed, and while he was away in the north Mac Thien-Tu of Ha-tien attacked Chantabun and Trat in September 1769. An attack of plague in the invading force, however, saved the situation and enabled P'ya Taksin to regain the initiative. He himself led a large army to punish this incursion, while at the same time sending an expedition to deal with the monk-king. The expedition against P'itsanulok made short work of the kingdom of Fang. The city itself was easily occupied, and when the monk-king's stockaded capital of Sawangburi was attacked he fled away to the north and was never heard of again. P'ya Taksin's expedition was directed first against Ha-tien, which he took. Then he proceeded up to Phnom Penh, drove out Ang Tong and replaced him with Ang Non. In 1772, however, with Vietnamese help Ang Tong defeated the Siamese army and recovered his capital. But, as we have seen above,[1] he failed to maintain himself there and the Siamese nominee in 1773 was once more installed as king. And before the Nguyen could attempt to reimpose control over the distracted kingdom they themselves were overwhelmed by disaster at home. Siam, now rapidly regaining its strength, remained the controlling power in Cambodia.

As soon as peace was made with the Chinese in 1770, Hsinbyushin of Burma had begun to prepare fresh aggressive moves against his eastern neighbours. In 1771 Vien Chang was besieged by the forces of Luang Prabang and implored his help. At the approach of the Burmese army the siege was abandoned and a way was thus opened for further interference in northern Siam. In 1772 and 1773 attempts were made to capture P'ijai, but Siamese resistance caused both to fail completely. The Mon rebellion of 1773 held up the Burmese plans for a full-scale invasion of Siam for a time, and P'ya Taksin used the

1 Page 422.

SIAMESE SHADOW PUPPET

breathing-space thus afforded him by marching northwards to deprive the Burmese of their Chiengmai base. In January 1775 he took the city and immediately hurried south to undertake the defence of the homeland. Various Burmese incursions across the border in pursuit of Mon fugitives had been repulsed during 1774. In February 1775 a new attack was in progress, and a Burmese force had driven back the Siamese frontier guard to Kanburi and established itself at Ratburi. P'ya Taksin's reappearance on the scene, however, soon restored the situation. In April he captured Ratburi, taking a large haul of prisoners, while another Burmese force, which was raiding to the northwards, only just made good its escape. Late in the same year the Burmese, who had made Chiengsen their base after losing Chiengmai, made an attempt to recover the latter city, but a Siamese relieving force drove them off.

At the end of the year the long-prepared full-scale invasion began under Maha Thihathura. In January 1776 he defeated a large Siamese army near Sukhot'ai and captured the city. He then besieged P'itsanulok and beat off P'ya Taksin's attempts to relieve it. Before its fall the Siamese cut their way out, and the Burmese, suffering from shortage of supplies, were soon forced on to the defensive. They had to abandon the place and retreat homewards harried by the Siamese, who·inflicted defeat after defeat upon them. The remnant of their army crossed the border in August 1776. In the previous June Hsinbyushin had died. His son Singu, as we have seen, was opposed to further adventures in Siam. But before calling a halt to the war he made one further attempt to retake Chiengmai. It nearly succeeded; but in September 1776 the Siamese drove off the besiegers. By this time the city was so impoverished that its governor and most of its inhabitants left it and settled at Lampang. It remained practically deserted for some twenty years.

P'ya Taksin had now reunited Siam and driven out the Burmese, but his reign had been one long uninterrupted series of campaigns, and the strain began to tell on him. He showed signs of mental disorder. Most of the victories in the Chiengmai struggle and the operations against Maha Thihathura had been won by General Chakri, and as the king's insanity developed he became more and more the director of the national effort. In 1778 an opportunity came to assert Siamese overlordship over the two Laos kingdoms of Luang Prabang and Vienchang. An incursion by the latter into Siamese territory led to its conquest and at the same time the King of Luang Prabang was forced to accept Siamese suzerainty.

Soon afterwards the arrangements made by P'ya Taksin earlier in his reign for the government of Cambodia broke down and an attempt was made by the Cochin-Chinese to regain power by setting up the infant son of the ex-king Ang Tong as king. In 1781 a Siamese army led by General Chakri went to restore Siamese suzerainty and place Prince In P'itok on the throne. Before he could carry out his mission, however, Chakri had to hurry homewards. A serious rebellion had broken out at Ayut'ia. The rebels declared their intention to kill the insane king and place Chakri on the throne. An ambitious palace official, P'ya Sank'aburi, had thereupon placed himself at their head, entered Bangkok, taken possession of the king and forced him to retire to a monastery. His object was to take advantage of Chakri's absence to secure his own recognition as king.

Chakri received news of these events from the Governor of Korat, P'ya Suriya, whom he ordered to repair at once to the capital and restore order. He himself arrived there in April 1782 to find the rebellion quelled and the would-be king a prisoner in P'ya Suriya's hands. Chakri was at once hailed with joy by the populace and urged to assume the crown. The chief difficulty lay in the continued existence of P'ya Taksin. The mad monarch was still only forty-eight years old, and after so glorious a reign might be expected to become a source of serious internal disturbance. Accordingly in the general purge of rebel leaders which ensued the restorer of Siamese independence was himself liquidated and General Chakri was elevated to the throne with the title of Rama T'ibodi.

King Rama I (1782–1809) was the founder of the present reigning dynasty at Bangkok. His reign was to see another great struggle with Burma. In the month before he ascended the throne of Siam a palace revolution at Ava brought to the Burmese throne Bodawpaya, the ablest of the sons of the great Alaungpaya. A man of boundless ambition, he aimed at forcing all the neighbouring states to yield to his sway, and in 1785 the wearisome struggle between the two states broke out once more and was to last for many years. But the Siam of Rama I's time was no longer the state that had been reduced to chaos by Hsinbyushin's devastating armies. It was a victorious power governed by a tried leader of men, and the Burmese armies suffered such disasters that the struggle gradually deteriorated into chronic frontier raiding. The new King of Siam was too wise and too wary to attempt a major invasion of Burma in reply to Bodawpaya's disastrous expedition of 1785. He was anxious to turn his attention to the consolidation of his kingdom and the reorganization of its

THE ROYAL BALLET, PHNOM PENH, CAMBODIA

administration. He did indeed seek to regain the Tenasserim provinces of Mergui and Tavoy upon which his country had real claims. But after holding them for a brief period he had finally to abandon them to Burma in 1792. And although Chiengmai and Kengtung in the north and the island of Puket (Junk Ceylon) in the south remained bones of contention between the two kingdoms, such operations as took place were chiefly of the nature of raids by local leaders.

Rama I was the founder of modern Bangkok. P'ya Taksin's capital had been at Dhonburi, on the west bank of the river Menam. Rama I built himself a palace on the opposite side of the river at Bangkok proper and surrounded it with a double line of fortifications, and there under the shelter of the outer wall the present city began to arise. Much was done to settle not only the administration of the provinces but also the development of the central government along traditional lines. Long before he died his kingdom had so far recovered from the devastation caused by the Burmese invasions and the subsequent struggles of P'ya Taksin to assert his authority that at the beginning of the nineteenth century Siam was more powerful than ever before. And the time was soon to come when she would again pursue an expansionist policy aiming at extending her control over the Laos kingdoms of Luang Prabang and Vientiane in the north, the ancient Khmer kingdom of Cambodia to the east, and the Malay states in the south.

Rama I was offered an opportunity by the Tay-son rebellion, and the long eclipse of the power of the Nguyen, to strengthen Siamese influence in Cambodia. His early efforts were severely hampered by Bodawpaya's attacks on his own country. But the pro-Nguyen boy-king Ang Eng was a refugee at his Court. In 1794 he crowned him king at Bangkok, and in the following year sent him back to Udong, the capital of Cambodia, with a Siamese army under the command of Ben, the pro-Siamese governor of the frontier provinces of Battam-bang and Siemreap (Angkor). For some years Siam was undisputed master of Cambodia. She took advantage of her position to gain control of the three Cambodian provinces to the north of Battambang —Mongkolbaurey, Sisophon, and Korat. She 'silently' annexed them in 1795, writes Adhémard Leclère.[1] In 1795 also Battambang and Siemreap (Angkor), under the semi-independent Ben, were trans-ferred from Cambodia to Siam; presumably they were the price with which Ang Eng purchased his restoration.

The foundation of the empire of Vietnam by Gia-Long in 1802 gave Siam once more a competitor for the control of Cambodia. The Cam-bodian ministers were resolved to give the Vietnamese no excuse for turning their country once more into a battleground. They therefore sedulously sent homage and tribute to both Bangkok and Hué, and Rama I wisely accepted this curtailment of his authority.

This delicately poised situation lasted only until 1812. In that year Rama II (1809-24) intervened in support of a rebel brother of the then king Ang Chan, who fled to Saigon. A strong Vietnamese force reinstated him in the following year, and the Siamese prudently retired with their candidate, who lived out the rest of his days at Bangkok. A Vietnamese garrison took over the citadel at Phnom Penh, and for the time being Siamese influence there was in a state of eclipse. But the Bangkok government remained ever on the alert for an opportunity to regain control. Meanwhile it compensated itself by sending an army in 1814 to Korat which proceeded to occupy all the territory between the frontier of the province of Prohm-Tep and the Dangrek mountains, and in addition the provinces of Mlou-prey and Tonlé-Repou, which were too far distant from Udong to be effectively under the control of the central government. There was no opposition,

---

[1] *Histoire du Cambodge*, p. 402.

and the Siamese army then proceeded to cross the Mekong and occupy Stung Treng. By this operation Siam gained possession of a thick slice of territory in the north of Cambodia and drove a wedge between that kingdom and the kingdom of Vientiane, which a few years later it was to absorb (1828).

Save for this Cambodian adventure Rama II's reign was free from any major conflict. The Burmese war went on, but it was chiefly a matter of raiding and counter-raiding, and it affected only the Malay Peninsula. In 1810 the Burmese captured the island of Puket (Junk Ceylon) and besieged Jump'orn, but they were expelled without difficulty. Another Burmese attack was expected in 1819, but it did not materialize. Their main energies were now concentrated upon gaining control over Assam, and Siam had nothing more to fear from them.

One result of this scare was the deposition of the Sultan of Kedah, who was discovered to have been in correspondence with the Burmese. Siam had never forgiven him for having ceded Penang in 1786 and Province Wellesley in 1800 to the British. In 1821 Siamese forces invaded his state and he fled to Penang. This was the beginning of a period of more or less intensive Siamese pressure upon the Malay states which alarmed the British and resulted in a good deal of activity on both sides. The story, however, is more conveniently dealt with in connection with the history of Malaya.[1]

Ever since the failure of the attempt of Louis XIV to gain control over the old kingdom of Ayut'ia in the seventeenth century the Siamese had become inordinately suspicious of Europeans, and every possible restriction was placed on their trade. During the first half of the nineteenth century this attitude was firmly maintained. But one may discern the faint beginnings of change in Rama II's reign. In 1818 he received a Portuguese envoy, Carlos Manuel Silveira, and consented to make a commercial agreement whereby Silveira supervised Portuguese trade in Siam. Wood describes his position as that of Portuguese consul;[2] but as it was not until the reign of Mongkut (1851–68) that any appointment of such a sort by a foreign power was permitted, the definition cannot be accepted. Moreover, he was given the Siamese title of 'luang' and seems to have carried on his work entirely under Siamese authority. The East India Company was at the same time seeking the removal of the restrictions upon the trade of British subjects in Siam. Letters to this effect and presents were sent to Bangkok by the Government of India in 1818 and 1819, but

[1] See chap. 29, a.   [2] *History of Siam*, p. 276.

without avail. In 1821, therefore, Governor Phillips of Penang sent a Singapore merchant named Morgan to Bangkok in a private capacity, but with the object of collecting information and sounding the Siamese ministers with regard to the possibility of alleviating conditions. But the Government of India had also decided to move officially in the matter, and in the same year John Crawfurd, whose mission is dealt with in a later chapter,[1] made his abortive attempt to break the impasse. Nevertheless British trade did begin to expand. The Siamese, like the Burmese earlier on, were unwilling to commit themselves to an agreement in black and white, but they were willing to permit individual traders to settle in their country. An English trader, John Hunter, who took up residence in Siam at this time is said to have been the first of his kind to live there.

Rama II died in July 1824 shortly after the opening of the first Anglo-Burmese war. Prince Maha Mongkut, his eldest son by a royal mother, had been expected to succeed him. He was a Buddhist monk at the time of his father's death. A strong party at Court, however, placed the dead king's eldest son, though not by a royal mother, on the throne, and he became Rama III. Mongkut was to succeed him in 1851 and was one of the most remarkable personalities that ever occupied the Siamese throne.

Rama III's reign has been described as a 'somewhat unprogressive' one.[2] He represented the old-fashioned traditionalist attitude, which was becoming dangerously out of date. Britain at first hoped that Siam would join her in the war with Burma, but Rama III's government remained suspiciously aloof, conscious of its clash of interests with the British in Malaya. This showed itself strongly in the reception accorded to Captain Henry Burney, the second ambassador to be sent to Bangkok by the East India Company. He did, however, manage to conclude a treaty in 1826, which is discussed in its proper context of Malayan affairs in a later chapter.[3] There had been some thought of offering to cede the conquered Burmese province of Tenasserim to Siam, but the Siamese attitude on all matters was too intransigent, and the subject was not even introduced into the negotiations. When Burney went to Siam the Government of India was considering the question of resurrecting the old Mon kingdom of Pegu in Lower Burma. As it was known that there were thousands of refugee Mons living in Siam, he was instructed to search for any members of the old Mon royal family who might be among them, or any possible candidates for the throne from among the Mons holding high official posts

[1] Chap. 29, b.   [2] Wood, *op. cit.*, p. 277.   [3] Chap. 29, b.

in the Siamese service. His report on this subject has considerable interest, but he could find no traces of any members of the royal family, nor any suitable candidate outside it.

In 1833 the United States of America sent an envoy to Bangkok who managed to make a treaty regulating the treatment of American citizens who might visit Siam. Both Burney and Roberts, the American envoy, tried hard to persuade the king to agree to the establishment of consuls, but to no purpose.

It was in Rama III's reign that the Laos kingdom of Vientiane was extinguished and its capital destroyed.[1] That was in 1828. This success emboldened him to make an effort to restore Siamese control over Cambodia. Accordingly, without any declaration of war, P'ya Bodin, the conqueror of Vientiane, was sent in 1831 to lead an invasion, which at the outset was completely successful. The Cambodian army was defeated at Kompong-chhnang, King Ang Chan fled to Vinh-long, and the Siamese occupied in rapid succession Phnom Penh, Oudong and Chaudoc. Then fortune turned against the Siamese. The eastern provinces rapidly armed against them; bands of partisans cut off and destroyed the detachments Bodin sent out to secure allegiance; and in attempting to capture Vinh-long he lost his whole flotilla of war-boats. The Emperor Minh-Mang sent 15,000 Vietnamese troops who drove out the Siamese pell-mell and replaced Ang Chan on his throne. When in December 1834 Ang Chan died unexpectedly of dysentery the Vietnamese Resident, Ong Kham-Mang, by order of his emperor, summoned the Cambodian magnates to elect his successor, since his only son had died a few hours after birth. Siam was not even informed. And as under Ong Kham-Mang's direction a young princess, Ang Mey, was elected queen it was obvious that Minh-Mang intended to absorb what was left of Cambodia into his empire. Indeed, he proceeded to reorganize the administration completely, dividing the kingdom into thirty-three provinces, all with new names attached to Cochin China. His aim was, as Leclère puts it, to *décambodgienniser* the country.[2]

The resentment which this policy inevitably caused played into the hands of Siam. After seven years of suffering the Cambodians revolted, massacred every Vietnamese they could lay hands on, and the magnates, meeting in secret, set up a provisional governing committee which appealed to Siam for help and offered the crown to Prince Ang-Duong, who was living under Siamese protection. The aged General

[1] The subject is dealt with in chap. 25.
[2] *Histoire du Cambodge*, p. 422.

Bodin was thereupon in 1841 sent a second time to re-establish Siamese influence.

It was easy to install Ang-Duong as king. But the Vietnamese were a tough enemy and there were four years of hard fighting before a settlement was reached. They had built more than fifty forts with which to hold down the country. These were all captured by the peasantry, but the king and his mentor Bodin could not drive out the Vietnamese army. In 1845, therefore, a compromise solution was agreed to: Cambodia was to be under the joint protection of both Siam and Vietnam. Two years later Ang-Duong was consecrated and invested with his royal regalia in the name of the sovereigns of Vietnam and Siam by the deputies of those two rulers. Such a solution depended for its success largely upon the personality of the Cambodian king, for neither Siam nor Vietnam abandoned their designs upon his country. Luckily he was a man of wisdom and piety who was resolved to give neither side the much-hoped-for opportunity for further adventures at the expense of his impoverished and unhappy land. He distrusted the Siamese, regarding them as his enemies; he hated the Vietnamese. Therefore it was to Bangkok that he sent his eldest son Ang Votey—later King Norodom, 1860–1904—for his education.

Shortly before Rama III's death both Britain and the United States made further efforts to obtain more reasonable terms for their merchants. The British were disappointed with the results of the Burney treaty; they complained of royal monopolies, especially in sugar, and the prohibition of the teak trade. Sir James Brooke of Sarawak was the British plenipotentiary, and he arrived in Bangkok in August 1850. The king was anxious for good relations with Britain, but was too ill to take part in the negotiations. Brooke's attempts to negotiate a satisfactory treaty, however, failed. The reasons for this sound strangely irrelevant. On the way up the Menam one of his ships grounded on the bar at Paknam, and he had to ask for assistance to refloat. Further, rumours were circulated of his own lack of success in Borneo. Most important of all, his letters were two years out of date and were signed only by Lord Palmerston, not by Queen Victoria herself. But such things counted in dealing with monarchies such as the Siamese of that time.

Brooke was followed by the American Ballestier, who arrived in a United States sloop of war with a commission from his government to represent the grievances complained of by American citizens and obtain a new and more favourable treaty. He failed even more abjectly than Brooke. He was refused an audience of the king and had to leave without presenting the president's letter. He was a merchant who, as Bowring puts it, 'had not been fortunate in his commercial operations at Singapore',[1] and the Bangkok ministers deemed it beneath their dignity to have any dealings with him. Both Brooke and Ballestier advised their governments that in their opinion only a warlike demonstration would move the Siamese. But Rama III died in April 1851 and Siam entered upon a new era.

[1] Sir John Bowring, *The Kingdom and People of Siam*, vol. ii, p. 211.

PART III

THE PERIOD OF EUROPEAN TERRITORIAL EXPANSION

CHAPTER 27

INDONESIA FROM THE FALL OF THE V.O.C. TO THE RECALL OF RAFFLES, 1799–1816

THE disappearance of the 'Kompenie' made at first little difference to the management of affairs in Indonesia. No matter how loudly the Batavian Republic might echo the French revolutionary doctrine that liberty and equality were the inalienable rights of men, it was not prepared to do anything calculated to destroy the value of its East Indian empire to the home country. The security of that empire, it was firmly convinced, depended upon keeping its peoples in strict subordination. Hence while Dirk van Hogendorp, an ex-governor of the North-East Coast Province of Java and a determined opponent of Nederburgh, pleaded for the separation of trade from government and the abolition of forced deliveries and of the economic servitude known as *hierendiensten*, Nederburgh's theory, that the native peoples were naturally lazy and compulsory labour was therefore essential for their own welfare as well as for Dutch commercial profits, was assured of the stronger support.

The government took refuge in yet another committee, to which both men were appointed. It met in 1802 and was charged with the task of drafting a 'charter for the Asiatic Settlements', which would provide for 'the greatest possible welfare of the inhabitants of the Indies, the greatest possible advantages for Dutch commerce, and the greatest possible profits for the finances of the Dutch state'. Its nature may easily be gauged from the fact that the draft accepted by the committee was penned by Nederburgh. But it was never carried into effect. The Napoleonic wars, which had temporarily ceased with the Treaty of Amiens in 1802, were renewed in 1803 and put an end to all trade between the Batavian Republic and the colonies. And although the Charter, issued in 1804, was replaced by a slightly more liberal Administrative Act, passed in 1806, the replacement of the Batavian Republic by the kingdom of Holland under Louis Bonaparte rendered that also a dead letter. Louis Bonaparte's one object was to strengthen the defence of Java against the British, and at the suggestion of his imperial brother he deputed Marshal Herman Willem Daendels with dictatorial powers to carry out the task.

Meanwhile affairs in Indonesia had passed through critical phases. Van Overstraten, who remained in office as governor-general after the fall of the Company, was mainly concerned with the maintenance of Java's independence against the threat of a British invasion. In 1800 an English naval squadron actually blockaded Batavia, but failed to effect a landing. British preoccupation, first with Napoleon's Egyptian expedition and afterwards with the internal situation in India, prevented the organization of a force strong enough to deal with Java, but the remaining Dutch warships at the disposal of Batavia were all destroyed.

The Peace of Amiens in 1802 brought some relief, for all the Dutch possessions previously taken over by Britain were restored, with the sole exceptions of Ceylon and the Cape. The situation, indeed, was better than might have been expected, for freed from the strict control of the Board of Directors Batavia had been able to sell its products in the open market for good prices. Owing to the slave revolt in Haiti, West Indian coffee production was ruined and neutral shipping, notably American and Danish, flocked to Batavia. The demand for coffee was actually greater than Java could supply. Moreover, relations with the native princes remained good. The Sultan of Bantam rallied to the support of Batavia when the English attacked in 1800. Surakarta and Jogjakarta also remained on good terms with the Dutch. There was indeed serious trouble in Cheribon through the succession to the throne of an illegitimate son of the sultan, who died in 1797. But Dutch authority was not threatened, since the hatred of the population vented itself upon the Chinese middlemen employed by the sultan. Order was ultimately restored by the Dutch governor of the North-East Coast Province, who re-established the legitimate line.

When the European war was resumed in 1803 the British rapidly reconquered most of the territories they had surrendered. During the peace interval a Dutch squadron under Hartsinck was sent to Java; but it arrived in bad condition and inadequately manned. In 1806 it was destroyed in the roadstead of Batavia by a powerful English fleet under Admiral Pellew, but no attempt was made to conquer the island. The one aim of the Dutch authorities at Batavia was to avoid giving any support to the French and thereby force the British to invade Java. The accession of Louis Bonaparte to the Netherlands throne was regarded by them with dismay. They wished for no change in the position of semi-independence, which had brought them prosperity and a full treasury. But now Daendels was appointed to reorganize the administration and strengthen the military defences of Java in the French interest.

The new governor-general had begun his career as an advocate at Hattum, where he had headed the Patriots in their struggle against the Princely Party. When the stadhoudership was restored, he had fled to France and taken service in the French army. In 1793 he served under Dumouriez as commandant of the Batavian Legion in the abortive attack on the republic. He returned with the French in 1795 and proved such a mainstay of French power that Napoleon conferred on him the rank of marshal. He was a great admirer of Napoleon, and under his influence had developed from a revolutionary demagogue into a full-blooded supporter of military dictatorship. He arrived in Java on 1 January 1808 after a long and adventurous voyage via Lisbon and Morocco.

Invested with special powers which made him supreme over the Council of the Indies, Daendels took full advantage of the fact that all communications with the homeland were cut to behave in a thoroughly independent manner. With tremendous energy he set about the task of strengthening Java's defences. The army was increased and improved, and, since it was impossible to obtain reinforcements from Europe, new regiments of native troops were enrolled and trained. Stern discipline was enforced, but at the same time better measures for the welfare of the troops were introduced than had ever been known under the Company's rule. Barracks and hospitals were built, a gun foundry was opened at Semarang and an arms factory at Surabaya. Surabaya itself was fortified, while Batavia was strengthened by the construction of new forts at Weltevreden and Meester-Cornelis. To improve military communications a great mailroad was constructed from Anjer to Panarukan, a distance of 1,000 kilometres. The overland journey from east to west was thereby reduced from a matter of forty to six and a half days, but the work had to be carried out by forced labour and entailed immense loss of life. Possessed of no warships owing to the destruction of Hartsinck's squadron in 1806, Daendels built a fleet of small fast vessels based on Meeuwenbaai and Merakbaai in the Sunda Straits, and in the east at Surabaya. This eastern base was further strengthened by a second fort, Fort Lodewijk, which was erected on an island in the Madura Straits.

Early on Daendels attempted a thoroughgoing reform of the administration of Java. His aim was naturally to introduce the most complete and rigid centralization, and in order to carry it out he had no compunction whatever in riding roughshod over everything that stood in his way. Thus he abolished the governorship of the North-East Coast Province and divided the land into five divisions and thirty-eight regencies, all of which were brought directly under the control of Batavia. The whole island was parcelled out into nine divisions under landdrosts standing directly under the central government, and the native chiefs, known as regents, previously semi-autonomous native rulers, were declared to be officials of the Dutch government, given military rank and paid salaries. The change, designed to safeguard them in their relations with European officials, had the effect of reducing both their incomes and their status in the eyes of their people. The Residents in the native states, who had previously received their instructions from the governor of the North-East Coast Province, now came directly under the control of Batavia, with their title changed to that of minister.

Daendels' instructions, besides laying special emphasis upon his military mission, entrusted him with the task of examining the possibility of abolishing the compulsory cultivation of coffee and forced deliveries, and of improving conditions of life among the native peoples. How much serious attention he gave to these matters is doubtful, for he seems to have unquestioningly accepted the stock Dutch verdict on the Javanese as lazy. Instead of abolishing the compulsory cultivation of coffee he increased it to such an extent that the number of coffee trees rose from 27 to 72 million, while the price for the forced deliveries was reduced. But he did his utmost to suppress illegal emoluments, and to see that all payments were made direct to the cultivators. Inspectors were therefore appointed to check abuses, and the coffee cultivator was freed from all other forms of *hierendiensten*. He also improved the lot of the *blandong* people, whose forced labour in the teak forests was little better than slavery, by an issue of rice and salt. But his belief was that the best means of ameliorating the condition of the Javanese was to stamp hard enough on corruption.

That the organization and práctice of the judiciary of Batavia had long needed complete overhaul was recognized by the Charter of 1804. In particular a proper system of justice for the native according to his *adat* (i.e. customary usage) had never existed under the Company. This shameful situation Daendels sought to end by establishing courts in every regency and division (*landdrostambt*) wherein justice would be dispensed according to *adatrecht*. These were separate from the Councils of Justice established at Batavia, Semarang and Surabaya which dealt with cases involving foreigners—i.e. Europeans, Chinese, Arabs and any who were not natives of Java. In these justice was in accordance with Dutch-Indian law. In the lower native courts native officials and priests sat on the bench. The prefecture courts were presided over by the landdrost with a Dutch official as secretary and a number of native assistants. A system of appeal also from the lower courts to the Councils of Justice was instituted. Daendels' method of segregation in matters of justice took root and was further developed by his successors. But he was in office for too short a time to do more than lay its foundations. He had in practice little respect for legal processes, even such summary ones as were conducted under martial law.

Both in his lifetime and ever since opinion has been sharply divided on the question of the quality of Daendels' work in Java. So powerful were the accusations levelled against him that in 1814 he published an apologia entitled *Staat der Nederlandsche Oostindische bezittingen onder het bestuur van den G. G. H. W. Daendels*, together with two immense volumes of documents. Through no fault of his, just when he was doing his utmost to stimulate coffee production, the British blockade was tightened to such an extent that the bottom fell out of the market and he had millions of guilders' worth of unsaleable goods on his hands. Unfortunately his administration cost more to run than any previous one. The expense of his military and naval preparations alone was staggering. But he had also given substantial increases of pay to government officials as one means of reducing corruption. His first issue of paper money failed because the government had no credit with which to back it. Hence he resorted to the expedient of selling land to private persons. On the plea that all land not in the possession of the native princes was government domain, he sold not only large estates of land but also the rights over the cultivators previously enjoyed by the government.

One of his most spectacular deals was the sale of the Prabalingga lands for a million rix-dollars (= 2½ million guilders) to the *Kapitein-Chinees* Han Ti Ko under an agreement whereby the capital sum was payable in instalments. But his need of ready money caused him to issue so many paper notes on the strength of this deal that before long his 'Prabalingga paper' was worth only a fraction of its face value, and many people refused to accept it. In his frantic search for means of acquiring an adequate revenue he floated forced loans, farmed out opium dens and introduced a state rice monopoly, whereby all rice had to be delivered to the government, which sold it at a profit to the public. He even compelled the banks to hand over their coin to the treasury in return for paper.

His greatest weakness showed itself in his dealings with the native princes. His dictatorial and tactless methods alienated them to such a degree that when the inevitable British attack came they 'emulated each other in disloyalty' to the Dutch régime. His demands for labour brought strife with the Sultan of Bantam. When some of the sultan's Dutch guards were murdered together with their commandant, Daendels personally led an army which stormed and plundered the city. He shot the chief minister, banished the sultan to Amboina and declared his state royal domain of the King of Holland. He issued new regulations for 'ceremonial and etiquette' under which Dutch officials were forbidden to pay the traditional marks of honour to the ruling princes and must wear hats in their presence. This sort of treatment did more to undermine their loyalty than almost anything else. His high-handed treatment of Amangku Buwono II, Sultan of Jogjakarta, threw that ruler into the arms of the British. A quarrel between the sultan and the Susuhunan of Surakarta caused the former to increase his army beyond what Daendels considered reasonable. He therefore found an excuse to invade the suitan's dominions and depose him in favour of the heir-apparent, who was appointed prince-regent. But the deposed sultan had so much secret support that as soon as Daendels was recalled to Europe he resumed his old position and entered into correspondence with the British.

Daendels sacrificed everything to the defence of Java. Of the Dutch stations in other parts of the Archipelago, those difficult to defend or unprofitable, such as Banjarmasin in Borneo, were abandoned. Others, such as Palembang in Sumatra and Macassar in Celebes, had their garrisons reduced to a minimum. For the spice-bearing Moluccas he showed more concern, and Amboina was reinforced by the French colonel Filz and 1,500 men. But the garrison lacked money and provisions, and when the British attacked in 1810 the native troops were disloyal and Filz had to surrender. He had done his best under impossible conditions, but on his return to Batavia the Iron Marshal had him court-martialled and shot. Mutiny among the native troops was also the cause of the fall of Ternate to the British. Then speedily all the remaining Dutch posts outside Java fell.

It was now Java's turn; but before Lord Minto's great expeditionary force appeared off Batavia in 1811, the Tuwan Besar Guntur ('great thundering lord'), as the Javanese dubbed him, had been recalled. So many complaints against him had been made by high officials to King

Louis that he appointed General Jan Willem Janssens in his stead.[1] Janssens had been governor of Cape Colony when it fell for the second time to the British. He was now faced with a second hopeless task.

In August 1810 the English East India Company's Board of Control issued instructions to Lord Minto, the Governor-General of India, that 'the enemy' was to be expelled from Java. There was no thought in their minds of the permanent occupation of the Dutch empire: their one object was to counter Napoleon's designs for the encirclement of India. The work of Daendels in Java was the direct cause of the expedition launched against the island in 1811. Dutch historical writers[2] have represented this step as the result of the persuasive powers of the young Thomas Stamford Raffles, a junior official at Penang, who was employed by Minto to prepare the way for the enterprise by establishing relations with discontented native princes throughout the Archipelago.

Raffles was thirty years old at the time of the Java expedition. At the age of fourteen he had entered the East India Company's office in London as a clerk. His immense industry earned him rapid promotion, and in 1805 he was sent to Penang as assistant secretary with a salary of £1,500 a year. Penang had just been raised to the status of a presidency with a governor and council and was expected to become a great trading centre for the East Indian islands. On the outward voyage he made an intensive study of the Malay language, and soon after his arrival in Penang his proficiency in it was considered remarkable by people who met him. Through personal contacts with Malays and the study of their culture and history he became an expert in what was then to the Britisher a little-known oriental field.

Lord Minto's attention was first drawn to Raffles by his fellow-countryman Dr. John Leyden, also an accomplished student of Malay, and in 1810 Raffles himself took leave from his duties in Penang and paid a visit to Calcutta, where he met the governor-general in person and discussed with him the situation in the Archipelago. His knowledge and enthusiasm so impressed Minto that before the end of the year he was appointed 'Agent to the Governor-General with the Malay States'. Then, with his headquarters at Malacca, he began to make his

[1] On his return to Europe Daendels served with Napoleon's ill-fated Russian expedition of 1812. After Napoleon's fall he offered his services to King William I of the United Netherlands, who sent him as governor of the Dutch settlements on the west coast of Africa. There he died in 1818.
[2] See F. W. Stapel: *Geschiedenis van Nederlandsch-Indië*, 1930, p. 221. But Vlekke's interpretation of the events leading to the conquest of Java is more acceptable (*Nusantara*, pp. 238–9). See also Coupland. *Raffles of Singapore*, p. 26.

plans for the annexation of Java to the East India Company's eastern empire.

Minto's objective was to give the *coup de grâce* to French influence in the East, not to increase the British empire, and his plans envisaged taking over the administration of Java with Dutch co-operation wherever possible. Leyden and Raffles, however, were at one in their belief that Dutch rule in the East was utterly pernicious, and that British 'justice, humanity and moderation' should be used to give a better life to the native peoples whom they had so long oppressed. Raffles's original idea, therefore, was that the Indonesian princes could be prevailed upon voluntarily to accept the superintendence of the Government of India, which would exercise its control in the form of a protectorate of much the same kind as was to be introduced later in Malaya. It was in this spirit that he set about the task of working upon the minds of the native rulers in the Dutch empire.

Janssens assumed the management of affairs in Java in the full knowledge that the British were preparing an invasion. He found the population restless and discontented, and the princes so embittered by Daendels' behaviour that their support could not be relied upon. The financial situation at Batavia was so desperate that he could barely find the necessary money for the ordinary expenses of government, let alone any consideration of further defensive preparations. To make matters worse, Jumel, the commander of the few French troops he had with him, was totally unfit for his post.

At the beginning of August 1811 the British fleet of about 100 ships carrying an expeditionary force of some 12,000 men appeared before Batavia. The city was occupied without a blow, since the incompetent Jumel had taken up a defensive position at Meester Cornelis. Janssens then took over the command, rejected Lord Minto's call to surrender, and for sixteen days put up a splendid resistance before being forced to beat a retreat in the direction of Buitenzorg. The retreat, however, soon degenerated into a disorderly flight; and despairing of making an effective stand in the west, Janssens made his way eastwards with all speed to organize the defence of central Java.

On 1 September he arrived at Semarang, where he took up a good position on a hill to the south of the city and awaited reinforcements from the Javanese rulers. In this, however, he was disappointed: the preliminary work carried out by Raffles had completely undermined the loyalty of the princes. When the British landed at Semarang, therefore, he was in a very difficult position. His troops panicked and killed many of their Dutch officers. He himself with a small force escaped to Tuntang, where he was forced to ask for an armistice. By the capitulation, signed at Semarang on 17 September, he agreed to surrender Java and all its dependent posts, including Palembang, Timor and Macassar, to the British. It was further stipulated that all officials who were willing to transfer to the British service might remain in office.

Meanwhile Lord Minto had issued a proclamation setting forth the principles upon which the new government was to be based. The Bengal system of administration was to be established. The Dutch legal system was to remain in force, but torture was to be abolished. The paper money issued under Dutch rule would be recognized, but not that issued by Daendels after the annexation of the kingdom of the Netherlands by France. The native peoples were promised an amelioration of their condition, and in particular the abolition of contingencies and forced deliveries.

Raffles, who had accompanied the expedition, was appointed Lieutenant-Governor of Java and its dependencies, Madura, Palembang, Banjarmasin and Macassar. He was to work with the assistance of an advisory council composed of the commander-in-chief Gillespie and the Dutchmen Cranssen and Muntinghe. The last-named, with a fine record of service under Daendels, proved the most influential member of this group; his ability and wide knowledge of the Indies were made full use of by Raffles, who was soon on such friendly terms with his Dutch colleagues that Gillespie, already irritated at having to serve under so young a Company's servant, became uneasy and hostile. On 19 October Lord Minto left for Bengal. 'While we are in Java', he said to Raffles, 'let us do all the good we can.' Rarely in the East India Company's history had a man of Raffles's age been called to a position of such heavy responsibility. Owing to the distance of Java from Bengal, his position was one of virtual independence.

The new lieutenant-governor's first efforts had perforce to be directed to the establishment of relations with the princes. His agents had supported a rebel chief, Pangéran Ahmed, against the puppet Sultan Mahommed set up by Daendels when he made his spectacular incursion into Bantam. He now decided to support Mahommed, and accordingly arrested Ahmed and banished him to Banda. Mahommed, however, was regarded by many of his subjects as illegal and found himself unable to quell the chronic unrest in his territories. In 1813, therefore, he surrendered his powers to Batavia in return for a large annuity and the retention of the courtesy title of sultan. Such was

killed many of their Dutch officers. He himself, with a small force,
escaped to Bantam, where he was forced to eat, for an emigrant, fly

A RONGGENG OR DANCING GIRL
(Raffles: *History of Java*)

the end of the kingdom of Bantam. The Sultan of Cheribon received similar treatment. He had caused the Dutch serious trouble on account of his appalling misrule. Daendels had reduced him to the rank of a regent. But his dominions remained in a state of unrest and Raffles's action provided the only logical solution of the problem.

In Jogjakarta the deposed Sultan Sepuh resumed office from his son, the prince-regent, as soon as the British arrived. John Crawfurd, who became Resident at his Court, soon reported that both he and the Susuhunan of Surakarta were disloyal. In December 1811 Raffles went to Semarang to deal with the affairs of the two states. There he was met by the chief minister of the susuhunan; Sepuh, however, sent only a letter couched in such terms as to arouse serious suspicions regarding his intentions. Raffles went personally to Surakarta to settle relations with the susuhunan. The affairs of Jogjakarta he placed in the hands of the experienced Muntinghe. With the susu-hunan Raffles made an agreement whereby he received back the territories seized by Daendels, but subject to certain special con-ditions. He was to recognize British overlordship on the same terms as he had previously made with the Dutch, to accept the central government's jurisdiction over all non-Javanese inhabitants of his realm and its supervision of his correspondence.

With Sepuh Muntinghe made a similar arrangement. The terms were better than Sepuh might have expected, having regard to his arrogant attitude. He was foolish enough to think that such mild treatment was a sign of weakness. He began to increase his armed forces and fortify his capital. Raffles therefore resorted to stern measures. With an army of 1,200 men under Gillespie he entered Jogjakarta, deposed and banished Sepuh, and placed the former prince-regent on the throne as Amangku Buwono III. Sepuh's treasury, containing Spanish dollars to the value of 2 million guilders, was confiscated as war booty for the troops.

In the captured kraton Raffles discovered evidence of intrigues with the susuhunan against British rule. He therefore marched on Surak-arta and forced that prince to make a new agreement whereby he lost the districts previously restored to him and had to reduce his army to the strength of a mere bodyguard. He had also to agree to vest the appointment and dismissal of his chief minister in the hands of the central government. In all the native states contingencies and forced deliveries were abolished, while tolls and the farming of opium were taken over by the government in return for a cash compensation.

In asserting his authority over the dependent states such as Palembang, Madura, Bali, Banjermasin and western Borneo, with all of which he had intrigued against the Dutch before the invasion of Java, Raffles had to deal with one very ugly incident for which the Dutch have laid much of the responsibility at his door. The Sultan of Palembang, on learning of the British landing at Batavia, surprised the Dutch garrison in his city and murdered them all, together with the women and children. In the previous year Raffles had indeed written urging him to 'expel and annihilate all Hollanders'. When Raffles's commissioner, ignorant of what had taken place, arrived to demand the surrender of the Dutch fortress at Palembang the sultan blandly announced that he had driven out the Dutch before the capitulation of Janssens and was therefore independent. He refused to make a treaty recognizing British overlordship. Raffles thereupon announced publicly his intention to punish the sultan for the massacre. In April 1812 Gillespie, at the head of an expeditionary force, captured the city. The sultan escaped, and his brother Ahmed Najam was placed on the throne in his stead. As compensation for the massacre the new ruler had to cede the tin-bearing islands of Banka and Billiton in return for a cash payment.

Only when he had firmly established British authority was Raffles free to apply himself to the task of administrative reform. A close study of his measures shows that they were a blend of British-Indian methods and of proposals already made by Dirk van Hogendorp on the basis of the Bengal system. He divided Java up into sixteen *landdrostampts*, entitled Residencies, among which both Surakarta and Jogjakarta were included. The Resident performed administrative and judicial functions and in addition acted as collector of government revenue.

The greatest innovation was the introduction of a general tax on land. Raffles's aim was to substitute this for all compulsory services, contingencies and forced deliveries. He declared the government the sole owner of the soil. The Javanese inhabitants therefore became government tenants paying rent for the land they cultivated. The rent was levied not on individuals but on desas, and was to be assessed according to the productivity of the soil. The most productive land was to pay half its yield, the worst a quarter only. The average was estimated at two-fifths. The cultivator had the free disposal of the remainder of his produce, which was in most cases rice. He might pay his dues in either rice or money. If the latter, he could make it to the desa headman, who paid it into the divisional office. If in rice, he had to convey it at his own expense to the Residency headquarters. Thus the local chief's opportunities for graft were reduced, since he no longer had a personal interest in the yield of the crops and lost much of his power of demanding forced services. As a government servant he was to receive a fixed salary.

But such a revolution in the lives of the great majority of the people could not be carried out by a stroke of the pen. It was not until late in 1813 that preparations were far enough advanced for a start to be made in practice. And it was found to be too difficult, or too inconvenient, to introduce it into the important coffee-producing districts of the Preanger, where the system of compulsory cultivation and deliveries was deeply rooted. At the time Napoleon had his back to the wall in Europe, and the restoration of peace was calculated to cause a boom in Java coffee. In view of the scarcity of money, therefore, it looks as if the hope of selling the coffee at a huge profit was the real determining factor in this case; for Java did not pay its way, and Raffles well knew that there was no hope of persuading the British government to hold on to the island if he could not prove it to be an economic proposition. In the teak-bearing districts also the old compulsory services remained in force.

It was not long before Raffles realized that his new methods brought neither the revenue increase nor the improvement in the position of the cultivator that he had hoped for. In the system of desa assessment the headman still possessed too much power in the apportionment of lands among the inhabitants. Raffles therefore went over to the method of individual assessment. But the relations inside the desa were very complex, and without a detailed cadastral survey it was quite impossible to work out individual assessments fairly. His attempt to introduce such a survey failed through lack of time and qualified staff. For instance, in Surabaya only 50 out of 2,700 villages could be surveyed. Hence the revenue demand in most cases had to be fixed according to the arbitrary estimates of the Residents. In practice also the abolition of all compulsory services proved unworkable, and the previously existing arrangements for the maintenance of roads and bridges by the people continued.

On the question of slavery Raffles, as a disciple of Wilberforce, had strong views. The institution, however, was too firmly established for him to attempt its complete abolition. Hence he had to take what practical steps he could towards alleviating the lot of slaves and increasing their chances of liberation. He began in 1812 by imposing a tax on the keeping of slaves, and by issuing an order whereby the importation of new slaves into Java and its dependencies was forbidden as from the beginning of January 1813. Shortly afterwards he passed a regulation prohibiting the slave trade throughout the Archipelago. In 1815 he deprived the police of the power to hold an unwilling slave under arrest at the request of the owner. One longstanding evil of native origin, the *pandelingschap*, whereby a debtor with his wife and children could be seized by his creditor for an unpaid debt and made to work for him without pay, was wholly forbidden. Finally, in the year of his recall home, he founded the Java Benevolent Institution to carry on propaganda against slavery. The net result of his campaign was that, although slavery still existed, there was a great reduction in the number of slaves.

In his energetic overhaul of the whole range of the existing administration Raffles reported that Daendels' reorganization of the judicial system was 'complicated and confused'. Much of it, however, had never been carried out. In order to simplify procedure he abolished the old Supreme Court and Court of Aldermen and provided the three large ports of Batavia, Semarang and Surabaya with a Court of Justice, a Court of Requests and a Police Court. These courts administered Dutch colonial law in civil cases, and in criminal cases used British procedure with a jury. In all legal processes torture was abolished. In the matter of native jurisdiction he abolished the courts set up by Daendels and substituted for them sixteen Land Courts, one for each Residency. For criminal cases involving the death penalty he instituted a Court of Circuit (*Rechtbank van Ommegang*), which conducted the case at the place of the crime.

Finance had been one of the weakest features of Daendels' administration. In his own day Raffles was charged with financial inefficiency, and the directors of the East India Company accused him of rendering the occupation of Java 'a source of financial embarrassment to the British government'. He believed that the introduction of the land-rent system would provide a surplus which would cover expenditure. Revenue did indeed increase, but expenditure also increased, and every year saw a deficit. He started off with one appalling handicap: he had to carry out Lord Minto's promise to redeem the paper money still in circulation from the Dutch period at the rate of 20 per cent discount. The burden this imposed on the treasury prevented him from carrying out his proposal to abolish the oppressive toll-gates and free internal trade. The establishment of a state monopoly in salt together with an import duty of 10 per cent. on all imports into Java failed to cover the deficit. Hence he had to adopt Daendels' expedient of selling government land to private persons. But it brought little profit, partly because the land was sold in very large plots to purchasers with inadequate capital at their disposal. Moreover, there was so much discontent with the landlords created by Daendels' sales that he had to redeem much of the land sold to them. The land sales, however, were merely a temporary expedient for dealing with an immediate need. His land-revenue system must be judged by its long-term results. It was retained by the Dutch when Java was restored to them, and ultimately justified Raffles's own expectations. As Furnivall, himself an expert in land-revenue matters, puts it, Raffles's calculations were not wrong but merely too optimistic.[1]

The range of Raffles's activities was too great for an adequate survey to be attempted in a work of this kind. The literature that has accumulated on the subject, in Dutch as well as in English, is considerable,[2] and to this the reader is referred for further light on what is only touched on here. General Gillespie, who repeatedly disagreed with him, left for Bengal at the end of 1813, and soon afterwards began a series of spiteful attacks upon him which caused the directors of the East India Company to conduct an inquiry into his administration. Although he was cleared of all the charges, both the directors and Lord Moira, Minto's successor as Governor-General of India, were so dissatisfied with his work that early in 1816 he was removed from office and returned home.

He had dreamed of making Batavia the centre of a new British empire of the islands. But soon after the introduction of his land-rent system Napoleon fell and the Netherlands regained independence. Lord Castlereagh's announced aim, long before the meeting of the Congress of Vienna, was to create a strong kingdom of the Netherlands as part of his plan to render impossible any further movement of French aggression in Europe. Hence he turned a deaf ear to suggestions that Britain should retain the Dutch eastern empire, and by the Convention of London, signed in August 1814, Britain promised to restore it to the Netherlands. But the Dutch hopes of receiving it back were temporarily shattered by Napoleon's escape from Elba,

---

[1] *Netherlands India*, p. 77.
[2] See especially Lady Raffles, *Memoir of the Life and Public Services of Sir Thomas Stamford Raffles* (1930); T. S. Raffles, *Substance of a Minute recorded on 11 February 1814 and other documents* (1814). Biographies by Demetrius Charles Boulger (1897), H. E. Egerton (1900), J. A. Bethune Cook (1918) and Sir Reginald Coupland (1926). F. W. Stapel, *Het Engelsche Tusschenbestuur* in vol. v of his *Geschiedenis van Neder-landsch Indië* (1940); M. L. Van Deventer, *Het Nederlandsch gezag over Java en onder-hoorigheden sedert 1811* (1891); H. D. Levyssohn Norman, *De Britische heerschappij over Java en Onderhoorigheden 1811–1816* (1857).

and Raffles seized the opportunity to send home a comprehensive exposition of Java's importance to Britain. The directors, however, faced by the undeniable fact that he had so far failed to make ends meet in Java, were in no mood to oppose Castlereagh's decision, and after the final defeat of Napoleon at Waterloo arrangements were made to hand over the Netherlands Indies. Before that took place, in August 1816, Raffles had left Java, and it fell to his successor, John Fendall, to carry out the promise made two years earlier.

Some idea of the importance of Raffles's work in Java may be gained from the fact that on regaining control the Dutch accepted most of his administrative and judicial reforms, though with certain changes. But in the long run it was the spirit in which he had laboured that had the most lasting effect, for it touched the imagination of the more liberal-minded Dutchmen and inspired them with his philanthropic ideals. He had set the welfare of the native peoples as the supreme end of government. Moreover, although he was in Java for slightly less than five full years, he was able to accumulate a knowledge of its people, languages, institutions and history which was beyond praise, especially when one takes into account the fact that at the time they were badly neglected by the Dutch themselves. It was he indeed who ordered the first survey of the magnificent Borobodur and drew attention to the need to preserve the ancient monuments that aroused his admiration when he toured the island. He was not only a very active president of the Batavian Society of Arts and Science but he gave powerful support to the researches of scholars such as Thomas Horsfield, the American naturalist; John Crawfurd, the author of many distinguished contributions to oriental knowledge;[1] and Colin Mackenzie, who in the course of investigating land ownership collected scientific material and studied Javanese antiquities. Raffles's own *History of Java*, first published in 1817, was the first comprehensive work on its subject. 'In scientific acumen', writes F. W. Stapel, 'Raffles stands head and shoulders above earlier Dutch governors.'[2]

---

[1] His *History of the Indian Archipelago* was published in 1820. In 1856 he expanded it to form his still valuable *Descriptive Dictionary of the Indian Archipelago and Adjacent Countries*.

[2] *Geschiedenis van Nederlandsch Indië* (1930 edition), p. 232.

CHAPTER 28

BRITISH BEGINNINGS IN MALAYA: BACKGROUND TO SINGAPORE

THE acquisition of Penang in 1786 by the English East India Company was dictated by motives of naval strategy. Commercial considerations were, of course, involved, but they bore small relation to the trade of the Malay Peninsula, and the Company had no intention whatever of expanding its political control over Malaya. Pitt's India Act of 1784 had firmly laid down the doctrine of non-intervention, and Warren Hastings' successor, Lord Cornwallis, was determined to observe it to the utmost of his ability. Moreover, since the abandonment of the factory at Patani in 1623 the Company had lost interest in Malaya. Great things had been expected of the Patani factory when it was founded by the *Globe* in 1612.[1] It was regarded as one of the key places for trade in the East, along with Surat, the Coromandel Coast and Bantam. Its function was envisaged as the headquarters of the Company's trade in Siam, Cambodia, Cochin China, Borneo and Japan. When Dutch competition forced its abandonment no further effort was made to establish a trading post in the Peninsula, save for a small, short-lived agency planted at Kedah in 1669 for the purchase of tin.

Ever since about the year 1687 strategic considerations rendered it increasingly necessary for the British to have a naval station on the eastern side of the Bay of Bengal. Up till then the west coast of India had been the chief centre of British power, and Bombay the sole important naval station. But in 1687, with the sudden appearance in the Indian Ocean of a powerful French fleet bound for Siam, and the subsequent French seizure of control over Mergui for use as a naval repair depot,[2] a new phase in the naval strategy of the East India Company may be said to have begun. For Madras at once realized the danger to the British factories on the Coromandel Coast that such a depot constituted. And although Louis XIV's Siamese adventure

---

[1] *Supra*, pp. 300, 359. The most comprehensive account of European trade at Patani is H. Terpstra's *De Factorij der Oostindische Companie te Patani*, Verbandelingen van het Koningklijk Instituut, 's-Gravenhage, 1938.
[2] *Supra*, pp. 367–8.

came to a sudden and sorry end, it provided the British with an object lesson, too little heeded at first, but later to become increasingly important when the Anglo-French struggle for the upper hand in India was found to depend very largely upon the question of naval control over the Bay of Bengal.

In this contest the east coast of India, and especially the Coromandel Coast, became the centre of gravity. Now not only was there no good roadstead for ships on the Coromandel Coast, but with the changeover from the south-west to the north-east monsoon in October they all became positively dangerous owing to the violent hurricanes which blew up during that month and November. Hence a fleet must retire to a safe port early in October—not later than the 12th, said naval experts. During the south-east monsoon, which begins to show itself early in May, the Coromandel Coast was quite safe for ships, though at times the continuous high surf would prevent communication with the shore. This might be very inconvenient for ships undergoing repairs; for there was no dockyard available, and repairs had to be undertaken in an open roadstead. Seriously disabled ships, therefore, which could not be repaired while riding at anchor, must make their way to Bombay.

During the eighteenth century, with naval battles generally being fought in the Bay of Bengal during the period of the south-west monsoon, the need for a repair depot on its eastern coast became a matter of urgency. For after the break imposed by the storms of October and November the side which could have a squadron in the Bay the earliest—and the Coromandel Coast was safe from January onwards—scored an immense advantage in attacking the other's settlements and sea-borne commerce. For the British this became a particularly acute problem from 1740 onwards, when the development of the excellent harbour at Mauritius by Labourdonnais gave the French a decided advantage, which Dupleix was quick to seize during the War of the Austrian Succession.[1] British experience showed that a fleet could not leave the Coromandel Coast to refit at Bombay and be at its station again before the beginning of April. In this way three valuable months were lost, when an enemy fleet which had refitted at a more convenient depot could dominate the Bay.

During the hostilities between the English East India Company and Siam resulting from the depredations carried out by the Mergui freebooters in the sixteen-eighties, the Madras Council had considered the island of Negrais, just south of the mouth of the Bassein river, as a

[1] Dodwell, *Dupleix and Clive*; see also *Cambridge History of India*, v, pp. 119–23.

possible naval repair station and a base from which to deal with enemy activities on the eastern side of the bay. But the attempt to occupy the island miscarried, and the decision was taken to seize Mergui itself. After the 'Mergui massacre' of 1687 it was decided to give the Mon port of Syriam a trial, and in September 1689 the frigate *Diamond* was sent there for repairs. This was, as we have seen above,[1] the beginning of a long association with the port as a repair depot.

The French also, at Dupleix's instigation, opened a dockyard at Syriam, and between 1730 and 1740 both nations were building ships there. Then came the Mon revolt, which offered Dupleix a tempting opportunity to intervene, once his hands were freed by the conclusion of the Peace of Aix-la-Chapelle in Europe. So we have the sorry story of the British settlement at Negrais and the abortive French attempt to save the Mon kingdom from disaster. Alaungpaya, the conqueror of the Mons, destroyed both Syriam and the Negrais settlement, and the East India Company cut its losses in Burma and concentrated on defeating the French in India, for these events occurred during the Seven Years War.

British experience in that war underlined the need for a repair depot in at least a more convenient place than Bombay. In October 1758, after a campaign on the Coromandel Coast against d'Aché's squadron, the British admiral Pocock had to take his squadron off to Bombay for refitting and was absent until the end of April 1759. During his absence a French squadron appeared in the bay and Lally, attacking Madras by land, was able to besiege the city for sixty-six days. Luckily for the British, six Company's ships arrived from Europe on 16 February and Lally at once abandoned the siege. It is not surprising, therefore, that when the war ended in 1763 the directors of the Company sent orders for a search to be made for a suitable port on the eastern side of the bay.

Under these circumstances one might at first wonder why no suggestion is heard of a possible return to Burma. Alaungpaya, it will be remembered, had died in 1760, and his successor, Naungdawgyi, had tried to persuade the Calcutta authorities to reopen trade with his country. The French indeed did go back after a discreet interval. The prisoners taken from their ships decoyed up the river when Syriam fell performed useful service to the Court of Ava, and some rose to positions of responsibility. Through one of them, Pierre Milard, who became Captain of the Royal Guard, good relations were established with Pondicherry, and in 1768 a French envoy named Lefèvre

[1] Chapter 20.

obtained from King Hsinbyushin permission to open a dockyard at Rangoon. Little is known of the history of this venture, but it produced a number of excellent teak ships, one of which, the *Lauriston* of 1,500 tons, took part with some success in the French naval operations in Indian waters during the War of American Independence.

British attention, however, was now directed to quite a different quarter. New factors resulting from the commercial revolution which occurred in the Indian Ocean in the mid-eighteenth century began to exercise a predominant influence. These were the rapid expansion of trade between India and China on the one hand, and on the other the weakening of Dutch control over the trade of Malaya and Indonesia. The revolution was the work of British private captains and merchants, who, while the East India Company was engaged in defeating the French and laying the foundations of its territorial dominion in India, gained control over her 'country' trade and played a vital part in developing her commercial relations with China.

The expansion of India's trade with the Far East arose out of the difficulties experienced by the European East India Companies in finding means of financing their purchases of Chinese goods without exporting silver from Europe. The 'country' traders helped to solve their problem by exporting raw cotton from Bombay to China, by taking Indian wares—notably Coromandel Coast piece-goods and Bengal opium—to Malaya and Indonesia, where they exchanged them for dollars or other commodities in demand at Canton and Macao, and, in the end, by smuggling opium into China.[1] Under these circumstances the clear need in the second half of the eighteenth century was for a harbour which would combine the advantages of a repair station with those of a trading centre for the Malay Archipelago, and at the same time would lie on a main sea route to China.

When the Dutch forced the English East India Company to withdraw from Bantam in 1682, it planted a settlement at Bencoolen on the west coast of Sumatra. Unfortunately this proved to be too far away from the principal trade routes, and British ships in need had normally to seek the shelter of Batavia. The exorbitant charges of the Dutch there were the source of bitter complaints. Nor, as it turned out, could their friendship be relied on. Thus the expanding trade with China could be threatened by their control over the straits of Malacca and Sunda.

---

[1] Holden Furber, *John Company at Work* (1948), chap. 5, The 'Country' Trade of India.

All kinds of projects for combating this difficulty came under consideration from time to time. One, which attracted the attention of both the English and French East India Companies towards the end of the seventeenth century, was to occupy the island known as Pulo Condore lying off the western mouth of the Mekong. When the British tried the experiment in 1702, however, it proved a failure.[1]

Another, which was fathered by the Madras authorities during the Seven Years War, was to look for a site either in the Sulu Islands or in the islands immediately to the north of Borneo. The idea arose out of Commodore Wilson's discovery in 1757–8 of what came to be known as the eastern or 'outer' passage to China. On a voyage to China in the *Pitt* he had arrived at Batavia in 1757 too late to go to China by the usual course through the South China Sea. He had therefore sailed eastwards with a north-west wind through the Moluccas, and thence by the coast of New Guinea in order to pick up the north-east wind in the Pacific. With this he had then kept well to the eastwards of the Philippines and passed between Luzon and Formosa, eventually reaching Canton in a shorter time than by the usual route. His report on the islands he had seen or heard of induced the Madras Secret Committee to send Alexander Dalrymple in the *Cuddalore* to establish relations with the Bugis Sultan of Sulu and seek for an establishment somewhere in his dominions. He was also to report on the harbour used by traders in the Nicobars.

Dalrymple left Madras in 1759. On 28 January 1761 he concluded a treaty of friendship and commerce with the Sultan of Sulu, under which the Company was granted permission to purchase ground for a trading station on condition that it would assist the Sultan if he were attacked. In the following November he made a separate agreement with the Dato Bendahara, who was the principal merchant in Sulu, whereby he was to bring a cargo of Indian goods, in exchange for which he was to obtain a cargo of Sulu goods for sale in China. He expected to make a profit of 400 per cent on his original outlay. It seems doubtful if the venture realized the hopes placed in it, but his second voyage, made in 1762 in order to carry it through, enabled him to make up his mind as to the most suitable site to become the Company's headquarters for trade in the Malay Archipelago. This was the island of Balambangan in the Sulu Sea, just thirteen miles distant from the most northerly point of Borneo.

In September 1762 he made a treaty with the Sultan of Sulu for the cession of the island, and shortly afterwards went there and hoisted

---

[1] See above, chap. 23, a.

the Union Jack. In that same year Manila was captured from the Spaniards by Cornish and Draper's expedition coming from Madras. Dalrymple, who was present at the capture of the city, found that the legitimate Sultan of Sulu, Alimud Din, was a prisoner there, and that the sultan, Bantila, with whom he had been dealing was a usurper. The legitimate sultan was so delighted at being set at liberty by the British that he gladly confirmed all Bantila's concessions. Dalrymple, to whom fell the task of restoring him to his throne, was able to negotiate with him a new treaty containing still larger cessions of territory. But it was some time before he could take any steps towards realizing them in practice, for under the Treaty of Paris (1763), which ended the Seven Years War, Manila was to be restored to Spain, and in 1764 he was appointed provisional deputy governor for the purpose of superintending the transfer. After carrying out this task he paid a visit to Canton before returning to Madras.

To his great disappointment Madras accorded a cold reception to his proposals. He accordingly returned to England in 1765, hoping to persuade the directors of the East India Company to ratify his treaty and establish a settlement on Balambangan. They, however, wanted a site in a much less remote region. They were particularly interested in Acheh in Sumatra, and missions had been sent there in 1762 and 1764. But the sultan was unswervingly hostile to any plan for a European fort to be erected in his country. Attempts to find a suitable site were made in the Sunda Straits and to the south of them. But the search was fruitless.

The failure of all these attempts made the directors more amenable to Dalrymple's arguments. Moreover, in 1767 he published a pamphlet, 'An Account of Discoveries in the South Pacific Ocean before 1764', which probably helped his cause. Soon afterwards he applied for the command of the expedition fitted out in 1768 by the Admiralty to observe the transit of the planet Venus, but was turned down by Lord Hawke in favour of Captain James Cook. Then it was that the directors decided to plant a settlement on the island of Balambangan and offered him the management of it.

Dalrymple, who, according to Sir John Laughton,[1] held a higher opinion of the value of his services than other people, now ruined his chances of leading the expedition by quarrelling violently with the directors regarding his powers, and further by publishing his version of the controversy in pamphlet form.[2] He had been turned down by

---

[1] DNB, s.v. Alexander Dalrymple.
[2] 'An Account of what passed between the East India Company Directors and Alexander Dalrymple', 1769.

Lord Hawke for demanding a Royal Navy commission. Now he insisted that the absolute management of the venture should be vested in him without control. The quarrel culminated in March 1771 with his dismissal on the grounds that he had failed to pay due deference and obedience to the Court of Directors.[1]

The plan for a settlement, however, was actually carried through; in December 1773 the *Britannia*, under the command of Captain John Herbert, arrived at Balambangan to establish a settlement there. Herbert's mismanagement of the business entrusted to him was scandalous, but it was not the cause of the ignominious end of the settlement a little more than a year after its foundation. The island was found to be in the heart of a pirate-infested region, and in February 1775 the settlement was surprised and completely wiped out by Sulu pirates. Herbert and a few survivors got away to Brunei. They persuaded the sultan of that state to cede the island of Labuan to the East India Company, and in April 1775 actually took possession of it. In the following November, however, they were withdrawn under orders from the directors.

The Balambangan scheme was to be revived later under very different circumstances. But even if it had succeeded it would not have solved the naval problem of the defence of British interests in the Indian Ocean. It would have assisted the China trade and provided an entrepot for the trade of the Malay world. There were, however, those who hoped to find a place which would satisfy all three requirements. In 1769 Francis Light came forward as an exponent of this school of thought. He suggested that the island of Bintang, south of Singapore, was from this point of view the best place for a settlement.

Light was a merchant captain in the service of the firm of Jourdain, Sullivan and De Souza of Madras, which carried on trade with the ports in the Straits of Malacca. Like so many of the 'country captains' of his time, he was an ex-naval officer. He had an intimate knowledge of the various Malay states, and the pressure he brought to bear upon the East India Company did at last attract its attention to the region in which he was interested. In 1771 the directors instructed Madras to inquire into the nature of the trade that private firms were carrying on with Acheh, Kedah and other places nearby, and consider making a further approach to the Sultan of Acheh.

---

[1] The Balambangan story has been told by Johannes Willi of Gais in *The Early Relations of England with Borneo to 1805* (Langensalza, H. Beyer und Söhne, 1922), a dissertation submitted to the University of Berne for the doctor's degree.

Madras was naturally sceptical of the prospects of doing anything in Acheh, but when, in 1771, Light was in Kedah he found the sultan very anxious to secure European help against the neighbouring state of Selangor, whose forces had invaded his territory. At Light's suggestion he wrote a letter to the Governor of Madras, but received a noncommittal reply. Light therefore wrote to his firm asking them to let Fort St. George know that in return for help the sultan was willing to cede the port of Kedah to the Company. Then, finding that this drew no response from the Fort St. George authorities, and fearing lest the Dutch might get wind of the proposal, he wrote on 17 January 1772 direct to Warren Hastings urging immediate acceptance of the offer.

When at last, as a result of all this pressure, Madras did act, it sent accredited agents to both Acheh and Kedah. Both missions failed. The Sultan of Acheh refused to discuss the proposals submitted to him by Charles Desvoeux. The Sultan of Kedah, on the other hand, was only too anxious to co-operate in return for a guarantee of assistance in case of an attack by Selangor. Light negotiated an agreement in such terms, and knowing well that the Company would refuse to accept anything involving military commitments, yet at the same time convinced the mere promise of help would be sufficient to deter any would-be aggressor, skilfully persuaded the Madras agent, the Hon. Edward Monckton, to initial it. But the Madras Council flatly refused to confirm the agreement, offering as their excuse a baseless rumour that the Sultan of Selangor, in anticipation of trouble, had called upon the Dutch for help. And although Monckton went on to sound the rulers of Trengganu and Riau, it was to no purpose, since 'the stuttering boy', as the disappointed Sultan of Kedah dubbed him, could not bind the Company to the one condition without which no Malay ruler would grant the facilities sought.

For twelve years Light's project languished. It was, of course, shortly after the failure of the missions of Desvoeux and Monckton that the ill-starred attempt to settle on Balambangan was made. Then followed the War of American Independence with the consequent revival of the Anglo-French struggle, not to mention the fourth Anglo-Dutch war of 1780-4. Warren Hastings was far too harassed with other matters to pay attention to the project; and although Light saw him personally in Calcutta in 1780, and this time urged the occupation of Junk Ceylon, where he had settled as a private trader on his own account, neither troops nor money could be spared.

The renewed war with France was soon to furnish Hastings with fresh object lessons, if indeed he needed any, of the dangers to which the Coromandel Coast was exposed when French naval operations were directed by a leader as redoubtable as de Suffren. Between February and September 1782 the French admiral fought a series of four indecisive engagements with Sir Edward Hughes. Then he took his fleet off to Acheh Roads to refit. Hughes remained off the Coromandel Coast in case his opponent should decide on yet another attack. He stayed too long. In the middle of October his squadron was so severely damaged by a hurricane that he had to make his way to Bombay to refit. Before he could return in the following year, de Suffren had driven British commerce out of the Bay of Bengal and nearly succeeded in blockading Calcutta.

Another interesting incident occurred in 1783. The French *Arrogant* and the British *Victorious* fought a duel, after which the former put into Mergui to refit, while her rival had to go all the way to Bombay. Thus does Mergui return to the picture. It had been wrested from Siam by Alaungpaya in 1759. But its importance was slight now that it was no longer the gateway from the Indian Ocean to Siam. The capture of the French settlements during the war had led to the abandonment of the French dockyard at Rangoon. Mauritius therefore developed a close connection with Mergui. This was to cause the British further trouble during the struggle with revolutionary France which began in 1793.

As soon as the Peace of Versailles was concluded in 1783, Hastings himself began to take positive action. In 1784 a further agent, Kinloch, was sent to Acheh, while another, Forrest, went to Riau. Several other sites also came under review—the Andamans, the Nicobars, Trincomalee in Ceylon, and the Hugli. In 1785 the directors appointed a committee to examine the New Harbour in the Hugli. After sitting for three years they reported that not only was the site unsuitable for a naval base but also there was not one anywhere on the Indian side of the Bay of Bengal.

Meanwhile both the missions sent to the other side of the bay in 1784 had failed. The Sultan of Acheh, when approached about the base previously used by the French, was as hostile as ever. The Sultan of Riau was under effective Dutch control. For the Dutch, thoroughly alarmed by their naval weakness in the 'Fourth English War', were engaged upon a series of efforts to restore their supremacy in Indonesian waters. Forrest therefore found himself forestalled at Riau by van Braam's squadron.

It was at this juncture that Light came forward with his suggestion of Penang. The acting Governor-General of India, Sir John Macpherson, had his eye on Junk Ceylon, but Light persuaded him that Penang was preferable. It was closer to the Straits of Malacca and only a week's sail from the Coromandel Coast. Macpherson recommended the scheme to the directors and suggested the appointment of Light as superintendent of the proposed settlement. The directors agreed, but made it quite clear that they did not regard the occupation of the island as a solution of the naval question. To them it was a move towards breaking the Dutch monopoly, a means of helping Malay rulers to resist 'Dutch attempts to enslave them', and of securing the greater safety of the China shipping. Naval opinion for another ten years considered the Andamans preferable as a base. In 1786 the island was occupied by agreement with the Sultan of Kedah.[1]

It was during the war with revolutionary France that naval opinion changed in favour of Penang. The French invasion of the Netherlands, and the consequent issue of the 'Kew Letters' of February 1795, led to the British occupation of a large number of Dutch forts and factories, including Malacca, Amboina, Banda and the stations on the west coast of Sumatra. Penang and Bencoolen were used as bases for the naval expeditions carrying out these operations. And when in 1797 it was decided to send an expedition commanded by Arthur Wellesley to destroy Spanish shipping at Manila in the Philippines, Penang was its rendezvous. Wellesley himself sent a highly favourable report on the place to the Government of India. Every possible effort was made to divert the trade of captured Malacca to Penang, and in 1800, in order to develop its harbour, the territory opposite on the nainland was purchased from the Sultan of Kedah and became Province Wellesley. The height of the boom period in the hopes cherished for the port was reached in 1805, when it was raised to the status of a fourth Indian presidency.

Then came gradual disillusion. Raffles, who arrived there as assistant secretary in September 1805, was not long in realizing that it lay too far to the west of the Archipelago to become a great trading centre for the islands: the pirate-infested waters of the Straits were too grave a deterrent to native shipping. Moreover, so far as the Dutch empire was concerned, Penang was 'outside the gates'. Malacca lay in the narrowest part of the Straits, and in 1808, when he visited the city, he was shocked by the efforts that were being made to destroy it as an emporium in favour of Penang. As a naval base also Penang ultimately justified the scepticism expressed by the directors in 1786. Dockyards could not be built there and the local timber was unsuitable

[1] *Infra*, chap. 29, a.

for shipbuilding. In 1810 Malacca was the centre from which, as agent-general for Lord Minto, Raffles organized the conquest of Java, and in the following year the rendezvous of the expedition which carried out the operation. In 1812 the plan for making Penang a naval station was finally abandoned.

By that time Raffles, as Lieutenant-Governor of Java and its dependencies, was already planning the permanent substitution of British for Dutch rule throughout the Malay Archipelago, and the whole situation had become revolutionized. When later his dream was shattered by the decision of the home government to restore the Netherlands Indies to the new kingdom of the United Netherlands, and the disappointed empire-builder was relegated to Bencoolen, the new scheme that began to take shape in his fertile brain envisaged once more the acquisition of a station that should be 'inside the gates' of the Dutch empire.

There were now several schemes in the air. If we may go back a few years, the Treaty of Amiens of 1802 had provided for the restoration to the Dutch of all the powers and privileges they had possessed before the year 1795. But the British possession of the Moluccas had proved of great value to the China trade. Hence in 1803, when faced with the necessity of handing them back, Lord Wellesley, the Governor-General of India, decided to reoccupy the island of Balambangan. It had a good harbour for sheltering and provisioning a fleet in the eastern seas, and he thought it might be a useful place from which to keep a watch upon the Dutch in the Moluccas and the Spanish in the Philippines.

Accordingly R. J. Farquhar, the British Resident at Amboina, on receiving instructions to restore that island to the Dutch, was told to take charge of an expedition to resettle Balambangan. This he accomplished at the end of September 1803. Then on 7 December he went on to Penang to become its lieutenant-governor, leaving behind a commissioner in charge of the settlement. In the course of the next year Balambangan was placed under the jurisdiction of Penang, and Farquhar drew up an outline scheme for the complete reorganization of British trade in the Malay Archipelago. It involved the fortification of Balambangan and the formation of a network of treaties with all the rulers of the Archipelago.

In 1805, however, the settlement was abandoned. The Court of Directors had vetoed Wellesley's plan to reoccupy the island as soon as the information reached them. The renewal of war with France and the Batavian Republic involved the reoccupation of the Dutch islands and settlements, and troops and ships could not be spared for such a venture. Farquhar protested against the abandonment of the island and commented bitterly upon the Company's indifference to the problem of piracy. But the attention of the Board of Directors was concentrated upon India, and every question was examined purely in the light of its bearing upon the British position there. Men such as Raffles and Farquhar, with a South-East Asian, as distinct from an Indian, outlook, laboured under a severe handicap.

Thus when the decision was made to restore the Dutch empire not only Raffles but Farquhar as well was on the look-out for a station 'inside the gates'. In 1818 while Resident at Malacca, Farquhar cast his eye on the west coast of Borneo. The Dutch, however, got wind of his intentions and forestalled him at Pontianak, the only feasible place for his purpose. He also visited Riau and advised the Bugis under-king to summon British help immediately if the Dutch attacked.

In that same year Raffles paid a visit to Calcutta and won over the governor-general, the Marquess of Hastings, to his project for establishing 'a station beyond Malacca, such as may command the southern entrance to those Straits'. Riau was the place that both had in mind. But in case the Dutch were to forestall him, as they had Warren Hastings's agent Forrest in 1784, Raffles was instructed to 'open a negotiation with the Chief of Johore' for a site in his dominions. Furthermore, before dealing with the southern end of the Straits he was to make one more effort to persuade Acheh to permit the Company to plant a settlement.

On arrival at Penang Raffles learnt that the Dutch had beaten him to Riau. Bannerman, the governor, was violently opposed to the whole scheme. Raffles therefore decided that no time must be lost in carrying out the plan for a station to the south of the Straits: the Acheh negotiations must wait. He accordingly sailed southwards, picking up on his way Colonel Farquhar, who, having surrendered Malacca to the Dutch, had been instructed by Calcutta to postpone his departure on furlough and join with Raffles in his mission.

Farquhar's suggestion was to try the Carimon Islands at the extreme southern end of the Straits. But they were found unsuitable. So also was Siak on the coast of Sumatra. So they sailed for Johore, and on the way, 'either by accident or design', says Swettenham,[1] landed on the island of Singapore on 28 January 1819. Raffles at once decided that here was the ideal site for his purpose. The Malay chief there was the Dato Temenggong of Johore. He was willing to permit the

[1] *British Malaya*, p. 66.

British to plant a settlement on the island, and two days later a 'Preliminary Agreement' was signed by both parties. It was clear, however, that this could only have force of law if confirmed by the Sultan of Johore. The question was, who was the Sultan of Johore?

It will be recalled that at the end of the eighteenth century the empire of Johore had split into three main divisions.[1] The sultan had become the puppet of the Bugis Raja Muda, the Governor of Riau, and his effectual rule was limited to the Riau-Lingga Archipelago. The sultan's continental dominions were divided between two great officers of state, the Temenggong of Johore and the Bendahara of Pahang. In 1803 Sultan Mahmud II had installed the Bugis Raja Ali as Raja Muda, or under-king, and entrusted him with the guardianship of his younger son, Tengku Abdur-Rahman. The elder son, Hussein, who was his destined successor, he had entrusted to Engku Muda to bring up. The young man had married a sister of the temenggong and a daughter of the bendahara, and, as Winstedt puts it, Mahmud had, by marrying him to relatives of the two greatest Malay chiefs in the empire, clearly planned to enable him as emperor to maintain the balance of power against the Bugis.[2]

While Hussein was away in Pahang in 1812 for the celebration of his marriage with the bendahara's daughter, however, Sultan Mahmud died, and Raja Ja'far, who had succeeded Raja Ali as under-king, persuaded Tengku Abdur-Rahman to accept the throne. When Hussein returned home he was unable to recover his rights. And the Dutch, in obtaining control over Riau in 1818, ignored him and made their treaty with Abdur-Rahman. Raffles ascertained that the provisions of the treaty applied only to Riau, and concluded that the Dutch could lay no claim to Singapore. He chose, therefore, to regard Hussein as the rightful sovereign and invited him to be installed at Singapore as Sultan of Johore.

Hussein had no difficulty in leaving Riau, where he had been living in poverty, and on 6 February 1819 was proclaimed sultan at Singapore. On the same day he and the temenggong signed a treaty confirming the 'Preliminary Agreement' made on 30 January. In return for granting the East India Company liberty to plant factories in his dominions, he was to receive an annual allowance of 5,000 dollars and the temenggong one of 3,000.

Thus did Raffles acquire Singapore for Britain. He installed Farquhar as its first governor and wrote home: 'What Malta is in the West, that may Singapore become in the East.'

[1] *Supra*, chap. 18.   [2] *History of Malaya*, p. 168.

CHAPTER 29

THE STRAITS SETTLEMENTS AND BORNEO, 1786–1867

(a) From the acquisition of Penang to the Anglo-Dutch treaty of 1824

WHEN Francis Light took possession of the island of Penang on 11 August 1786 and renamed it Prince of Wales Island he and Sir John Macpherson, the acting Governor-General of India, were under no illusions regarding the fact that the young Sultan of Kedah made the grant almost entirely for the sake of obtaining assistance to maintain his independence.[1] This had been made perfectly clear in a letter written in the previous year by the sultan to the Government of India, wherein he explained the terms upon which he was willing to permit the British to settle on the island. In accepting the grant the Government of India sent the sultan assurances so worded as to induce him to believe that it also accepted the obligation involved. Light himself certainly hoped, possibly believed, that the sultan could count on the assistance of the Company should the kind of occasion arise that was envisaged, namely an attack by Siam. Soon after taking over he assured the sultan that while the British were there they would assist him if distressed.

Nevertheless in January 1787 the Government of India decided not to make a defensive alliance with Kedah. And although for the rest of his life Light continued to urge that the Company was in honour bound to grant the sultan's request, and the sultan himself became so angry that in 1791 he made an abortive attempt to expel the British from Penang, the Company firmly maintained its attitude. The matter assumed real importance in 1821, when Siamese forces invaded Kedah, drove out the sultan, and indulged in an orgy of frightfulness against his subjects. The Company refused to assist him; and notwithstanding the series of definite refusals by the Company from 1787 onwards to commit itself to a defensive agreement, the sultan contended that it had broken its word to him.

---

[1] The matter is dealt with at length in Sir Frank Swettenham, *British Malaya*, pp. 36–54; L. A. Mills, *British Malaya, 1824-1867*, pp. 33–42; and Sir Richard Winstedt, *A History of Malaya*, pp. 174–83.

The most striking thing is that his contention was supported by a number of British officials, among whom were John Anderson, Robert Fullerton and Raffles himself, besides the great majority of non-official Europeans in Malaya. From the point of view of strict legality the sultan was undoubtedly wrong, but there can be equally no doubt that in occupying Penang the Company assumed a moral responsibility towards Kedah which it shamefully refused to recognize, and thereby, to quote Swettenham's words, 'sullied the British name and weakened its influence with the Malays for many years'. To a practical man such as Light the Company's attitude was beyond comprehension. 'Two companies of sepoys,' he wrote to the governor-general, 'with four six-pounder field pieces, a supply of small arms and ammunition, will effectually defend this country against the Siamese.' His own belief was that neither Siam nor Burma would attack Kedah so long as they thought that Britain would support the sultan. The history of Siamese relations with the Malay sultanates in the nineteenth century goes far to show that his confidence was justified.

The original agreement under which Penang was occupied by the British did not take the form of a treaty. When in 1791, after Light had defeated the sultan's weak effort to retake the island, he signed a treaty ceding it in return for a pension of 6,000 dollars a year, the document contained no provision for the protection of Kedah by the East India Company. In 1800 a second treaty was made by which the sultan ceded a strip of land on the opposite mainland, and his pension was raised to 10,000 dollars a year. Again there was no mention of a defensive alliance. The Company merely bound itself to refuse shelter to rebels or traitors from Kedah and to protect the coast from 'enemies, robbers or pirates' that might attack it by sea. The omission, however, did not mean that the sultan had abandoned his claim to protection. He had defined his position in his original letter of 1785 laying down the conditions upon which he was prepared to permit the occupation of the island.

The question of whether Kedah in 1786 was an independent state and had the power to cede territory to the East India Company has also been the subject of much debate. The fact that Siam could allege ancient claims to overlordship over the whole of the Pensinsula and the states therein is of no consequence. China could make similar claims to the whole of South-East Asia, including Siam herself. Burma in 1786 actually claimed the allegiance of Siam by virtue of conquest as recent as 1767 and was attempting to vindicate her claims by force of arms. Kedah sent the Bunga Mas, the ornamental plants with leaves and flowers of gold and silver, every three years to the Siamese capital. She might also be called on for contributions of men and money. But such obligations must not be judged by European ideas of international law. They were common practice throughout Indo-China; weaker states would undertake them towards stronger neighbours as a form of insurance against interference; often, as in the case of Cambodia in her relations with Siam and Vietnam, with more than one superior simultaneously. Exactly what the Bunga Mas signified cannot be precisely defined, but Siam herself in sending it triennially to Peking would have flouted the notion that she thereby demonstrated that she was not an independent state. So much depended upon circumstances. In 1786 Siam had long before expelled her Burmese conquerors, but was still in no position to pursue a forward policy in Malaya. Kedah was thus to all practical purposes independent. But Siam was recovering rapidly and was soon to make a powerful effort to assert her pretensions over the states of Malaya.

Under Francis Light as its first superintendent until his death in 1794 the new settlement flourished. Immigrants flowed in steadily, and the system of free trade, which was in force up to 1802, enabled it rapidly to become a valuable distribution centre, where the products of India and Britain were exchanged for Straits produce such as rice, tin, spices, rattans, gold dust, ivory, ebony and pepper. In 1789 the total value of its imports and exports amounted to 853,592 Spanish dollars and five years later was nearly double this figure. Light was anxious to introduce the growth of spices. His attempts to grow cloves, nutmeg and cinnamon failed, but with his encouragement and financial support a Chinese introduced pepper plants from Acheh, and the experiment was ultimately crowned with success. Penang's chief weakness lay in the fact that it could not produce enough food for its increasing population. Its dangerous dependence upon Kedah for supplies was one of the reasons for the acquisition of territory on the mainland in 1800. The hope was that sufficient rice could be grown in Province Wellesley, as the new territory was named, to make it independent of foreign imports.

Light had had no previous experience of administration. He alienated land unconditionally and himself appropriated large estates. No land was reserved for public purposes and there was no land revenue. Owing to the heavy mortality rate much land came upon the market, only to be bought up by the firm of Light's friend, James Scott, which had almost a monopoly of the import and export trade and of banking. Not until 1807 did Penang have legally established courts or a code of law. The Government of India in 1788, and again in 1794, issued a few general rules laying down the mode of trial in criminal cases and the nature of the punishments. Light had to preserve order by imprisonment and other common punishments. He could not deal with murder or offences by British subjects. Each nationality on the island had its own system of law, and petty civil cases were tried by the captains of the different communities, Chinese, Malay or Tamil. More important ones were dealt with by the superintendent's European assistants. Not a single magistrate was a trained lawyer until John Dickens, a Calcutta barrister, was sent to the settlement in 1800. He stated that the only law in force was the law of nature; a later commentator more appropriately described it as a rough-and-ready application of the dictates of common sense. In 1807, after over twenty years of chaos, the directors obtained the sanction of the British Parliament to establish a Recorder's Court at Penang. Along with it British civil and criminal law was introduced, subject to the proviso that in its procedure the court must consult native religions and usages in so far as they were compatible with the spirit of English law.

From 1786 until 1805 Penang was a dependency of Bengal. During the early part of this period the Company was unable to make up its mind whether the island was suitable for a naval base. The capture of Malacca in 1795 raised expectations that its trade would be transferred to Penang. Its use in 1797 as a rendezvous for the force intended for an expedition against Manila, and Arthur Wellesley's glowing recommendation, caused opinion as to its prospects to swing over from cautious hesitation to extravagant optimism. At last the much-sought-for site for a naval base had been found. Hence the acquisition of Province Wellesley in 1800 to give control over both sides of the harbour and make Penang as far as possible independent of external food supplies.

In 1805, when hopes for the future of the island were at their highest, but when there were no public buildings save temporary structures, no schools, no proper legal system, and the settlement was far from paying its way, it was raised to the rank of a fourth Indian presidency with more than fifty officials, among whom were covenanted civil servants from India. Naturally the extravagant hopes soon began to give way to disappointment and disillusion. The harbour was excellent, but it was found to be quite unsuitable for a naval base. Dockyards could not be constructed there, and Burma was the nearest source of good timber. Then its commerce did not develop according to expectation. It was badly placed for trade with the Archipelago; it was too far to the west for native vessels to run the gauntlet of the pirate-infested waters of the Straits when nearer harbours were available. As these disadvantages became clearer so did official alarm at the cost of its upkeep increase. For it had far too many officials and an average deficit of £80,000. Some pruning took place in 1826 when Malacca and Singapore were transferred from Bengal to Penang, and the presidency of the Straits Settlements was formed. Four years later, however, the presidency was abolished. The Straits Settlements became a Residency under the Governor and Council of Bengal. Then in 1832 their capital was transferred to the rapidly developing Singapore.

The history of Malacca under British rule during the Napoleonic period has yet to be written. In the year before the outbreak of the French Revolution an Anglo-Dutch treaty was signed which provided that should a European war break out either party might occupy the colonies of the other as a defence against a common enemy. It was in accordance with this agreement that the exiled Stadhouder, William V, signed the 'Kew Letters' in February 1795 authorizing the Dutch colonies to admit British forces, to prevent them from falling into French hands. The consequent British occupation of Malacca was unopposed by the Dutch. The Dutch governor and troops left, but the council was retained in order that the administration might be continued in accordance with Dutch methods. Already Malacca's population had declined to 1,500 compared with Penang's level of 20,000 reached in that year.

Not only was everything possible done to attract trade from Malacca to Penang, but in British hands the opportunity was seized of demolishing the splendid old fort A Famosa lest one day the British might have to attack the city. Even more vandalism might have been committed had not Raffles gone on a holiday there from Penang in 1808 and written a report which, as Winstedt puts it, saved Malacca. Incidentally he vastly overestimated its strategic value when he advised the Company that it should be retained 'until we are actually obliged to give it up'. Malacca was to have been restored to the Dutch under the Treaty of Amiens (1802), but the war with Napoleon started up again before it was handed over, and it was not until 1818 that the Dutch received it back.

Raffles's visit to Malacca in 1808 had more important consequences than the salvaging of an ancient city, for his report aroused the interest of Lord Minto, the Governor-General of India, in its writer and led to his appointment in 1810 as Governor-General's Agent to the Malay States. His task was to soften up Java's resistance to the projected British invasion by establishing relations with native rulers. Thus was the way prepared for his remarkable career and its greatest achievement, the foundation of Singapore.

The difficulties which beset the new settlement in 1819 were formidable. Not only might serious Dutch opposition be expected, but there were many on Raffles's own side who were more than capable of selling the pass. Some of his old colleagues in Penang were so jealous of his meteoric rise that they had done their utmost to prevent him from carrying out his scheme to plant a settlement south of the Straits. Colonel Bannerman, the Governor of Penang, who had tried hard to persuade him to abandon the scheme, was so consumed with jealousy, both of Raffles and of what he rightly suspected was to prove a successful rival to Penang, that when, in fear of a Dutch attack, Colonel Farquhar, the Resident of Singapore, appealed to him for reinforcements he refused them. He even went so far as to urge Farquhar to abandon the place, and to advise Lord Hastings to restore it to the Dutch, who, he averred, were its lawful owners.[1]

The Dutch, as might have been expected, protested in the strongest possible terms against Raffles's action. But their arguments regarding the validity of their claims did not convince the governor-general, though he was extremely annoyed with Raffles for involving him in a quarrel with them. And their bluff, together with Bannerman's obvious jealousy, made him only the more decided that an immediate withdrawal could not be countenanced. He delivered the Governor and Council of Penang so crushing a rebuke that they despatched the required reinforcements at once to Farquhar. And he also saved the exasperated directors from allowing their feelings about Raffles's *fait accompli* to get the upper hand to such an extent as to give an order which they would have deeply repented afterwards.

For it soon became obvious that Singapore had a great future. Never again would the Dutch be able to build up a monopoly such as they had once exercised; Singapore as a free-trade port would break the spell. No longer would it be possible for them to close the Straits in the event of war and threaten the China trade. By June 1819 the population numbered over 5,000, and a year later it was considerably above 10,000.[2] And right from the start the Chinese formed the great

---

[1] L. A. Mills, *British Malaya, 1824–1867*, p. 60.
[2] T. Braddell, in *Statistics of the British Possessions in the Straits of Malacca* (1861), thinks these figures, which represent Raffles's own rough calculation, an exaggeration.

majority. Trade increased at an amazing rate; in 1823 the value of imports and exports totalled well over 13 million dollars. More convincing even, from the point of view of a government perhaps a little too much concerned with immediate questions of profit and loss, was the fact that by August 1820 Singapore's revenue was already adequate to cover the costs of its administration. Hence it may be said with all truth that Singapore won its own victory. The storm with the Dutch blew itself out. The directors changed their minds about the validity of the Dutch claims. And in 1824 both sides decided to put an end to their constant friction in the East by making a treaty that would fairly and squarely draw a dividing line between their respective spheres of influence.

Under its first Resident, Colonel Farquhar, Singapore was administered subject to the general supervision of Raffles as Lieutenant-Governor of Bencoolen. He paid his second visit there from October 1822 to June 1823 and worked like a Trojan to lay the foundations of its future prosperity. The most pressing problem was that, with too few officials and a painfully inadequate police force, lawlessness was rife. He issued a regulation appointing twelve magistrates from among the principal British merchants and drew up a provisional code of law based upon English law, but with special provision for native customs regarding such matters as religion, marriage and inheritance. He drafted regulations for a land registry, for the management of the port, for the prevention of the slave trade, for the police force, for the suppression of gaming-houses and cockpits and for an institution which was to teach the languages of China, Siam and the Malay Archipelago and serve as a means to the 'improvement of the moral and intellectual condition of the peoples of those countries'. He also busied himself with 'remodelling and laying out my new city', as he put it. The wisdom of some of his efforts as a town-planner has been called in question, and John Crawfurd, whom he appointed to succeed Farquhar in 1823, successfully challenged the legality of his regulations for the maintenance of law and order. But the problem was so urgent that any stop-gap arrangement was better than nothing, until such time as the directors could provide a proper legal system. And that was not until 1826.

Before leaving in 1823 he arranged for Sultan Hussein to receive a pension of 1,500 dollars a month and the temenggong 800 dollars, in return for which they surrendered the monopolies and dues they had previously imposed on trade and placed Singapore entirely under British control. The provisions of the Anglo-Dutch treaty of 1824 rendered it necessary to revise this arrangement, for both men had claims to territories placed finally within the Dutch sphere of influence. Hence in August of that year Crawfurd made a treaty whereby the sultan and temenggong alienated the island of Singapore for ever to the East India Company. In return the sultan received a lump sum of 33,200 dollars and a pension of 1,300 dollars a month for life, and the temenggong a lump sum of 26,800 dollars and 700 dollars a month for life. They promised further to enter into no alliance with any foreign power without the consent of the East India Company, and to admit British commerce freely into all the ports of Johore on most-favoured-nation terms.

The Anglo-Dutch treaty concluded in London on 17 March 1824 represents primarily an effort on the part of the British government to secure the friendship of the kingdom of the United Netherlands in European affairs by putting an end once and for all to the rivalry and hostility of the two nations in the East. As such it was the natural consequence of the Convention of 1814, whereby the Dutch empire in Indonesia had been restored to the new kingdom. Under its territorial provisions the Netherlands ceded to Britain all her factories in India, withdrew her objections to the occupation of Singapore, ceded Malacca, and engaged never to form any establishment on the Malay Peninsula or conclude any treaty with any of its rulers. The British ceded to the Netherlands Bencoolen and all the East India Company's possessions in Sumatra, and pledged themselves never to form any settlement on the island or make any treaty with any of its rulers. They gave the same undertaking with regard to the Carimon Islands, the Riau-Lingga Archipelago or 'any other islands south of the Straits of Singapore'. None of the ceded territories was to be transferred at any time to any other power, and if either of the parties should ever abandon the ceded possessions the right of occupation should at once pass to the other. For the future it was agreed that the officials on both sides were to be warned 'not to form any new settlement on any of the islands in the Eastern Seas without previous authority from their respective governments in Europe'. There was thus a clear recognition of two quite separate spheres of influence, and of the principle that each side must refrain from interference in the other's sphere.

The commercial clauses of the treaty provided that the Netherlands should make no attempt to establish a commercial monopoly in the Archipelago and should never discriminate unfairly against British trade. Both sides agreed to grant each other most-favoured-nation treatment in India, Ceylon and the Archipelago, and general rules regarding the amount of customs duty were laid down. Moreover, they were to make no treaties with any native ruler in the Eastern Seas aiming at excluding the trade of the other party from his ports. Britain, however, agreed to exclude the Moluccas from the scope of these provisions and recognized the Dutch right to the spice monopoly in the islands. The concession was of little importance since Europe now had other sources of supply and the trade had lost much of its old value. Finally both powers bound themselves to co-operate effectually in repressing piracy.

The territorial clauses of the treaty were of the utmost importance in removing one of the greatest causes of friction. But for many years afterwards there were constant complaints that the Dutch were evading the commercial clauses and were hampering British trade with the Archipelago wherever possible. In a material sense the Dutch were the greater gainers by the treaty, for when it was made Sumatra and many other islands in the Archipelago were as yet unoccupied by them. But British policy was wise in forgoing the opportunity to build a vast empire in the Archipelago, and in gaining thereby the guarantee that the Dutch would refrain from all interference in the Peninsula. On a point of detail Britain lost nothing by giving up the moribund station of Bencoolen and gained little by taking over the strategically worthless Malacca. The Straits were now dominated by Penang at one end and Singapore at the other. And the commercial development of both ports left Malacca with only a small fraction of her previous trade. Her harbour was rapidly silting, and she became little more than a collecting centre of Straits produce for Penang and Singapore. Still, the exclusion of the Dutch from Malacca was a great advantage; it had been their centre for extending control over the Peninsula.

Winstedt's quip[1] that the history of Singapore is written mainly in statistics is an apt commentary upon the policy of its governors, certainly up to the middle of the century. Their great concern was to increase its commercial importance. It throve on the policy of free trade laid down with almost religious fervour by Raffles. In its early years it attracted to itself much of the commerce of the Netherlands Indies and developed important trading connections with China, Siam, Indo-China and the Philippines. It was essentially an entrepot with world-wide connections and depended hardly at all upon the trade of the undeveloped Malay Peninsula.

[1] *Malaya and its History*, p. 60.

With the treaty of 1824 the ghost of the former empire of Johore was finally laid. The Lingga or Riau Sultan, as he was called, ruled over its island possessions lying within the Dutch sphere, but could do nothing to enforce his claims to Johore and Pahang. Hussein, known as the Singapore Sultan from the fact that he lived there, exercised no authority whatever. The temenggong ruled Johore and the bendahara Pahang, and neither would allow him to interfere. The temenggong died in 1825 and was succeeded by his able son Tun Ibrahim. Hussein died ten years later, after having moved his residence to Malacca. His son Ali was too young to succeed and for twenty years the title was held in suspense. This led to a duel of claims between the young man and Ibrahim which caused the British administration no little embarrassment. It was settled in 1855 by an arrangement ceding full sovereignty over Johore to Ibrahim. Ali received the sultan's title, a small strip of land between the Kesang and Muar rivers and a pension. The title died with him in 1877, the land and pensions passing to his heirs and successors in perpetuity.

Immediately after the occupation of Singapore Raffles had negotiated a treaty with the Sultan of Acheh. Nothing came of it, for the central government in the state had broken down and the country was passing through one of its recurrent periods of lawlessness. Actually a flourishing trade grew up between Acheh and Penang which was in no way connected with the treaty but was due to the fact that the various vassal rajas of Acheh in asserting their independence gladly threw open their ports to British trade. Under the Anglo-Dutch treaty of 1824 Britain agreed to abrogate Raffles's treaty on the grounds that it had been designed to exclude Dutch trade from Acheh. In return the Dutch guaranteed to respect the independence of Acheh. The Penang Council decided that it was unnecessary to negotiate a further agreement with Acheh.

(b) The Straits Settlements from 1824 to 1867

The period from the conclusion of the Anglo-Dutch treaty of 1824 to the beginnings of the Residential system in Malaya has been somewhat inappropriately described as 'a half-century of inactivity'.[1] Until in 1925 L. A. Mills published his careful study entitled *British Malaya, 1824–1867* it tended to be neglected, presumably because after the heroic period of Raffles the developments and personalities of the

[1] Rupert Emerson, *Malaysia, A Study in Direct and Indirect Rule*, New York, 1937, p. 91.

ensuing period seemed somewhat flat until the resumption of a forward policy in the eighteen-seventies revived interest again. And, after all, to the people of the period itself Malayan affairs seemed such very small beer compared with the great events which were taking place in India, or even with the struggles to open China to British commerce. Nevertheless one has only to glance through the many volumes of records relating to the period to realize that even if there was little or no spectacular achievement there was plenty of activity, and of a sort which the historian is wise not to neglect.

Even if by 'inactivity' is meant the pursuit of a non-intervention policy in native affairs, the term is misleading. If, however, it is intended merely to indicate that the period was one in which Britain made no further important territorial advances, then the same is true of the Dutch; but even less than the British could they be described as inactive at the time. It seems to be one of those words which occasionally slip out from the pens of American writers and unconsciously betray their conception of British imperialism.

It was a period during which Singapore grew with astonishing rapidity, Penang developed at a more modest rate, and Malacca stagnated. But in addition to such things there were two outstanding problems, Siamese activities and piracy, which forced the East India Company, much against its will, to pursue an active policy. Its constantly reiterated instructions to its servants forbade them to intervene in the affairs of the Malay states. Increase of territory was absolutely forbidden; political alliances with the sultans were frowned on; in fact the Company was resolutely opposed to anything which might in any way increase its responsibilities in Malaya. It was ignorant of, or ignored, the fact that the Malay states were in a state of chronic unrest, external and internal, and had become completely incapable of putting their house in order. Intervention, therefore, could not be avoided. There was indeed constant intervention, notwithstanding all the rules to the contrary and all the thunders of Calcutta and East India House.

The situation that was mainly responsible for this was that Siam at the beginning of the nineteenth century had so far recovered from the Burmese invasions that she was reviving her ancient claims to dominion over the whole Peninsula. Ever since her failure to prevent the rise of the sultanate of Malacca they had been kept in cold storage. But under the Chakri dynasty she was more powerful than at any other time in her history, and the Governors of Penang feared that much of the Peninsula would fall under her yoke. Under Bodawpaya Burma also had ambitions to expand southwards at the expense of Siam into the Peninsula. But from about 1816 her efforts were concentrated on Assam and its neighbours and no longer constituted a serious threat to the growing power of Siam. Still, she continued to intrigue with the Malay rulers against Bangkok, and even in 1819 threatened to invade Siam.

Bangkok, therefore, did not lack excuses for interference in Malaya. Had the East India Company not been so obtuse as to refuse to follow Francis Light's advice regarding Kedah, it might have saved its servants a great deal of trouble at a later date. For in 1818 Bangkok ordered the Sultan of Kedah to invade Perak, his neighbour, and force its sultan to send the Bunga Mas. Siam's claims to Perak were without any foundation and there was no cause of quarrel between the two Malay states. Then in 1821 the Sultan of Kedah was ordered to go to Bangkok to answer a number of charges, including one of intriguing with Burma. When he refused to obey, a Siamese army made a sudden attack upon his state, conquered it and laid it waste with frightful barbarities. The sultan took refuge in Penang. Thousands of refugees poured into Province Wellesley, followed by the Siamese. But as soon as a company of sepoys was sent to the scene of trouble the Siamese fled headlong back into Kedah. The Raja of Ligor, who was in command of the Siamese force, demanded the surrender of the sultan, but the Governor of Penang flatly refused to take such a step. The sultan, finding that the Company turned a deaf ear to his request for help in recovering his throne, got into touch with the Burmese and preparations were made for a joint attack on Siam by Burma, Selangor and other Malay states. This so disturbed the British authorities at Penang that they reported the matter to the Raja of Ligor and nothing came of the intrigue.

The Siamese conquest of Kedah caused much apprehension at Penang regarding its food supply. All attempts to make the settlement self-sufficing had failed and it still imported most of its food from Kedah. For some time also Penang had been attempting to obtain more favourable trading conditions with Siam. It had an important trade in tin with Perak, Patani and Junk Ceylon, all dependencies of Siam, and difficulties had arisen in the case of Junk Ceylon, whence its principal supply came. Hence Calcutta was persuaded to send a full-dress mission to Bangkok to discuss all the outstanding questions. For this task John Crawfurd was chosen. He had already served under Raffles in Java and was later to become Farquhar's successor at Singapore. He had joined the Bengal Medical Service in 1803 and had become a recognized authority on Malayan affairs.

Crawfurd went to Bangkok in 1822 with instructions not only to negotiate but also to collect as much information as possible about the country. His attempts to obtain the restoration of the Sultan of Kedah and the removal of restrictions upon British trade completely failed, but indirectly he secured some sort of recognition of the British possession of Penang. His reports were of the greatest value, as also the book which he subsequently published in London entitled *A Journal of an Embassy from the Governor-General of India to the Courts of Siam and Cochin-China* (1828).[1] He was able to show that Siamese power was far weaker than the Penang government had believed, and that there was nothing to be feared from the Siamese in Kedah. Had the Company opposed by force the invasion of Kedah in 1821, he said, the Siamese would have withdrawn.

In 1824 the Anglo-Burmese war began, and the Government of India instructed the Penang authorities to approach Siam as a possible ally. Penang sent a couple of envoys to try to persuade the Raja of Ligor to send a force against Burma. They failed, but Lieutenant Low in his report on the mission explained that the raja was not a semi-independent ruler, as had been thought, but a Siamese official. He warned Penang that Siam aimed at gaining control not only over Perak but over Selangor as well. When his report came into the hands of Robert Fullerton, the energetic and capable new Governor of Penang, he urged Calcutta to restore the Raja of Kedah and extend British protection to all the threatened Malay states against Siam. But the Government of India refused to be swayed by his arguments.

Meanwhile Perak had regained its independence in 1822 with the aid of Sultan Ibrahim of Selangor. Early in 1825 Fullerton learned that the Raja of Ligor was about to send a fleet to conquer Selangor and Perak. He accordingly warned the raja that the British, as the inheritors of the previous Dutch treaty-rights with the two states, might resist an attack upon them. His threat went unheeded. Hence in May 1825, on receiving news that the raja's fleet of 300 galleys was about to set out from the Trang river, he sent gunboats to watch the river mouth. The ruse was completely successful; the expedition was called off.

Fullerton's envoy to Ligor was Captain Burney, a nephew of Fanny Burney, Madame d'Arblay. He had been military secretary to the Governor of Penang from 1818 to 1824 and had earned the praise of

---

[1] Another book on the mission from the pen of its naturalist, George Finlayson, was published in London in 1826, entitled *The Mission to Siam and Hué, The Capital of Cochin-China, in the years 1821-22.*

the Government of India for the valuable information he had collected about the politics and geography of the Malay Peninsula. His mission to Ligor paved the way for a second approach directly to Bangkok, which Fullerton was strongly advocating, and a visit that he paid to Calcutta after his return from Ligor convinced the governor-general that he was the best man to go to the Siamese capital should a decision be taken to follow up Fullerton's suggestion.

Before anything was finally decided Burney was sent again to Ligor, where he found that the raja was now preparing to send a land force to 'help' the Sultan of Perak against Sultan Ibrahim. Burney resorted to the same kind of bluff as Fullerton had previously used. He warned the raja that such a move would involve a quarrel with the British and persuaded him to sign a preliminary treaty promising not to attack Perak or Selangor in return for a British guarantee not to interfere in Kedah. This was signed on 31 July 1825 on the understanding that Burney would submit it personally to the Government of India, and if it were approved would return with it to Ligor and go with the raja to Bangkok, where it would serve as a basis for the negotiation of a settlement of issues between the Company and Siam. Burney was fully aware that his action in negotiating such a treaty was completely out of step with the doctrine of non-intervention. Accordingly he wrote to the Penang Council explaining that the policy he had pursued could not be avoided and its inconveniencies would be slight 'compared with the greater evil of permitting Siam to overrun the territories of our Selangor neighbours, to turn the inhabitants of them into pirates, and to disturb for many years all native trade'. Furthermore, it would not entail war with Siam. In negotiating the treaty he gained a further valuable point by persuading the Raja of Ligor to leave the Sultan of Perak free to decide whether or not to send the Bunga Mas to Bangkok.

Governor Fullerton was delighted with Burney's treaty and at once sent John Anderson to settle the disputes that had arisen between Perak and Selangor so as to leave no way open for Ligor to break his promise. In both states Anderson was received with enthusiasm and concluded treaties whereby each guaranteed not to interfere with the other and agreed to the Bernam river as their common boundary. The Raja of Ligor, however, made one more attempt to deal with Perak. Under the pretence of sending an embassy to the sultan he despatched a small armed force, which was a clear infraction of the treaty. Fullerton ordered its recall, but the raja made an evasive reply, and while the matter was still undecided news came from Calcutta that Burney was to go as British envoy to Bangkok.

The Government of India fully approved the measures taken by Burney and Fullerton. It even went so far as to ratify Burney's preliminary treaty with Ligor. But it had no great hopes of the outcome of his mission to Bangkok. It chief object in sending him was to reassure the Siamese government that the British successes in the war with Burma, and the conquest of Tenasserim, were in no way a threat to Siam, and that the East India Company had no intention of extending its sway over the Malay Peninsula. Fullerton, who had been authorized to add his own instructions to those of Calcutta, ordered him to deal energetically with all the questions concerning the independence of the states in the area that came later under British control.

Burney arrived in Bangkok at the end of 1825 and remained there until June 1826. Siamese fears of a possible British attack were so great that everything he did was regarded with the utmost suspicion. But his patience and firmness achieved more than Crawfurd had succeeded in doing. He had to permit the ministers to draft the treaty they were at last persuaded to concede in Siamese, and they introduced into it a vagueness which stood out so prominently in the English translation that the sceptical Fullerton refused to take any of the concessions at their face value. The commercial clauses granted British trade slightly more favourable terms than Crawfurd had managed to obtain, but were so systematically violated afterwards by the Siamese as to justify Fullerton's criticisms. Both sides guaranteed Perak against attack, recognized the sultan's right to govern his country according to his own will, and agreed that he should not be prevented from sending the Bunga Mas to Bangkok if he desired to do so. Burney failed completely to persuade the ministers to withdraw the Siamese garrison from Kedah and permit the sultan to return. And he had to give in to their demand that the British should prevent him from attacking Kedah and remove him from Penang to some place where he would be unable to be a nuisance to Siam. This raised a storm of protest in Penang, but the Government of India ratified it and the sultan was removed to Malacca.

There was almost as strong feeling against the agreement he finally reached regarding Trengganu and Kelantan after months of wrangling. It read: 'Siam shall not go and obstruct or interrupt commerce in the states of Tringano and Calantan; English merchants and subjects shall have trade and intercourse in future with the same facility and freedom as they have heretofore had; and the English shall not go and molest attack or disturb those states upon any pretence whatever.'[1] The fact

---

[1] Article XII of the treaty.

that nothing was said about the Bunga Mas led the critics to declare that it amounted to an admission of their dependence upon Siam. Burney, however, contended that it gave the British the right to prevent Siam from interfering in those states, and thus made them the protectors of their independence. Fullerton remained unconvinced, but the Government of India accepted Burney's interpretation.

After Burney's return to Penang it soon became obvious that the Siamese did not intend to honour the agreement regarding Perak. In September 1826, therefore, Governor Fullerton sent Captain James Low with forty sepoys and a small warship to assure the sultan that he need not send the Bunga Mas if he had no desire to do so, and might rely on British aid to maintain his independence. The sultan, who was threatened by a pro-Siamese faction at Court and detachments of Siamese troops in his country, was only too glad to take a firm line provided the British guarantee were made in the form of a treaty. To this proposal Low readily agreed, and on 18 October 1826 signed a treaty of alliance with the sultan. It provided that in return for British assistance against anyone threatening his independence the sultan would have no communication with Siam, Ligor, Selangor or any other Malay state on political affairs, and would refrain from sending the Bunga Mas or any other form of tribute to Siam.

This treaty, coupled with the fact that on Low's advice the sultan had dismissed all his pro-Siamese officials, settled the Perak question. The Siamese troops left the state and the sultan regained his independence. But Low had, in his fervour for checkmating Siam, blithely disregarded not only his instructions but also the express orders of the Company regarding non-intervention. The grateful sultan offered to cede Pulo Dinding, Pangkor and other islands off the Perak coast. And before the Government of India's comments on Low's actions arrived in Penang he had placed the sultan farther in debt to the British by destroying a pirate nest on the Kurau river from which raids were being made upon Penang harbour. The pirate chief, Nakhoda Udin, who was captured, was as a Siamese subject sent to the Raja of Ligor for trial. It turned out that he was a henchman of the raja's engaged upon the task of destroying the authority of the Sultan of Perak, and the enraged raja cajoled Burney into accepting a version of the story, which when reported to Calcutta led the Government of India to suspend Low from all political employment.

Fullerton, however, had no difficulty in proving that nothing less drastic than Low's action could have saved Perak's independence, and, moreover, that Udin really was a pirate. He neatly spiked Burney's guns by using the latter's own report and map to demonstrate that Kurau was in the territory of Perak. The Government of India therefore revoked its censure on Low; and although it continued for some time to condemn his treaty as unauthorized, and never formally ratified it, no attempt was made to negotiate a substitute. In time, therefore, it came to be regarded as actually binding, and on no less than three occasions—in 1844, 1853, and 1874—when appeals were made under it by Perak for British assistance, both Calcutta and London recognized its validity.

After this incident the Siamese abandoned their attempts to gain control over the Malay states on the west coast and transferred their attentions to Kelantan and Trengganu on the east coast. But it was not until much later, in 1862, that matters really came to a head there. Over Kedah British assistance was frequently called on by the Siamese because of the frequent attacks on them by supporters of the exiled sultan and the alarming development of piracy, which they could not check. The worst revolt was in 1831 and was planned in Penang right under the noses of the British authorities. Governor Ibbetson by his energetic blockade of the Kedah coast gave valuable help to the Siamese in crushing the revolt, which might otherwise have been successful.

Again in 1836 and 1838 Penang co-operated with the Siamese in the ungrateful task of preventing Malays from recovering control over a Malay state. But this series of revolts made the Siamese weary of their resistance to the claims of the sultan, and when finally he was persuaded by the British to offer his submission to Siam, and his son went to Bangkok with a letter from the Straits Government warning the Siamese that they could expect no further help should another revolt occur, the Siamese government accepted the situation and in 1842 reinstated him.

In the following year, with a perversity which forcibly illustrates what has been described as the process of hara-kiri prevalent among the Malay states after the fall of the Johore empire, he seized the district of Krian from his neighbour Perak. The Sultan of Perak would have fought, and appealed for British help under the Low treaty. But the Government of the Straits Settlements persuaded him to hold his hand, and eventually in 1848 compelled Kedah to restore the occupied territory.

Meanwhile Kelantan and Trengganu were struggling against the slow but persistent pressure of Siamese efforts at control. Kelantan was stated in 1836 to have 'almost succumbed to the Siamese yoke'.

Trengganu for some time offered a successful resistance to the devious and obscure manœuvres which characterized Siamese policy. Then in 1858 there broke out in Pahang one of those family quarrels which have so often changed the history of states in South-East Asia. The Bendahara of Pahang died and his two sons fought for the inheritance. Colonel Cavanagh, the Governor of the Straits Settlements, offered mediation, since the Singapore merchants were complaining of stoppage of trade, but his offer was rejected, and finally in the middle of 1861 the elder drove the younger son out. He made his way to Bangkok, where he found another refugee pretender, a Sultan of Lingga, banished by the Dutch; but by virtue of the fact that he was a descendant of the Abdur-Rahman who had been recognized by them in 1818, and repudiated by Raffles when he proclaimed his brother Hussein sultan in 1819 at Singapore, he insisted that he was the rightful ruler of Pahang and Johore.

Colonel Cavanagh received information that strongly pointed to a Siamese plan to obtain control over both Pahang and Trengganu, using the two exiles as their tools. The ex-Sultan of Lingga was to be substituted for the Sultan of Trengganu, who had refused to toe the line. Wan Ahmad, the claimant to Pahang, was to be assisted to make another attempt against his brother. In July 1862 the ex-Sultan of Lingga was taken to Trengganu in a Siamese warship accompanied by Wan Ahmad and a fleet of praus. Sir Robert Schomburgk, the British minister in Bangkok, was assured that the ex-sultan was on a purely personal visit to his mother. But the evidence against this bland assertion began to mount up, especially when Wan Ahmad, at the instigation of the ex-sultan, invaded Pahang. Before strong pressure applied through Schomburgk by Cavanagh, backed up by the Government of India, the Siamese promised to remove the ex-sultan, but did nothing towards carrying their promise into effect. It soon became obvious that they were waiting for the change of monsoon in the middle of November, which would render the east coast of Malaya dangerous and so give them an excuse for not sending a ship to bring away the ex-sultan. He and Wan Ahmad would thus have the period until the following April in which to carry through their plans.

Cavanagh therefore yielded to the heavy pressure brought to bear on him by the Singapore Chamber of Commerce and sent a warship to threaten Trengganu with bombardment unless the ex-Sultan of Lingga were handed over and the sultan promised to give no further assistance to Wan Ahmad. When his ultimatum was rejected the British warship shelled the sultan's fort. But the show of force miscarried: the ex-sultan fled inland; and although the coast was blockaded for some weeks, it was without effect. Ultimately in March 1863 the Siamese removed the ex-sultan after protesting to the British government that the bombardment was a violation of their territorial rights. But Siam made no further overt attempts to bring Trengganu under her control. As for the Pahang civil war, it petered out; and when the bendahara died a few years later, his brother Wan Ahmad succeeded him and the British government raised no objection.

Cavanagh's action in bombarding the fort at Trengganu caused something like an uproar in Britain. In 1860 he had intervened in the Menangkabau states of Sungei Ujong and Rembau to protect Chinese miners, and again in Perak in 1862 to force a settlement in the case of the trouble that had arisen over the Chinese miners in the Larut area. After two debates in the House of Commons he was given strict orders against any further intervention. Small wonder that people with interests in Malaya were agitating for the transfer of the Straits Settlements from the India Office to the Colonial Office. They felt that Malayan affairs were neglected. For many years men on the spot who realized the need for a stronger policy in relation to the native states pursued it not only at their own risk, but with odds against them so far as their own government was concerned. The fact was that the Government of India was not interested in Malaya.

The agitation for transfer was mainly the work of Singapore, and it drew its impulse from the feeling that British interests were being foolishly sacrificed so long as the keystone of her commercial supremacy in Eastern Asia was treated as 'a third-rate Residency in an isolated quarter of the Indian Empire'.[1] In face of the growing strength of the Dutch in Indonesia and the appearance of France as an imperialist power in Indo-China, control by the Government of India and the India Office, with the consequent fettering of the hands of the Singapore government in its relations with the Malay states, became an intolerable grievance. But the immediate cause of the agitation which led to the actual transfer in 1867 lay in the misguided attempts of the Indian government to interfere with the policy of free trade, which was the cardinal point in Raffles's plans for the development of Singapore and the chief cause of its miraculous success.[2]

[1] L. A. Mills, *op. cit.*, pp. 263-4.
[2] Mills, *op. cit.*, chap. xiv, gives a detailed analysis of the factors involved.

(c) Borneo to 1839

Borneo, the largest island in the Malay Archipelago, and the third largest in the world, occupies a place in history quite disproportionate to its immense area. Its interior is still largely covered by dense forest, imperfectly known and scantily populated. The home of the Dyak, it has received as colonists during the many centuries before the arrival of the European Malays, Javanese, Bugis and Sulus, whose largely unchronicled activities resulted in the formation of a ring of states around its coasts. Traces have been discovered in both Kutei on the east coast and Sambas on the west of early states with Indianized courts. Śrivijaya's influence and sway were probably acknowledged by west coast ports participating in the trade between Indonesia and China concerning which records begin to appear in the fifth century A.D. Some of the Bornean states must have paid tribute to the Javanese empire of Majapahit during its hey-day in the fourteenth century. It is only with the arrival of Islam, however, that a relatively clear picture of the political set-up of the island begins to emerge. The Muslim sultanate of Brunei, from which the island takes its name, was founded at the end of the fifteenth century. During the following one Muslim dynasties appeared at Sambas, Sukadana and Landak on the west coast, and at Banjermasin on the south. Brunei was a rich and powerful state when visited in 1521 by Antonio Pigafetta, the historian of Magellan's voyage, who wrote the earliest first-hand account of Borneo. Banjermasin and Sukadana tended to come under the political dominance of the north Javanese powers Demak and Surabaya during their brief periods of greatness after the disappearance of Majapahit. Sambas had close ties with Johore on the Peninsula.

The Portuguese at Malacca developed commercial relations with Brunei. After the foundation of Manila the Spaniards, in rivalry with the Portuguese, sought to play the part of kingmaker there, but without success. The Dutch became interested in Banjermasin because of its pepper production, but their attempts to obtain control over the trade led to bloodshed and reprisals. Monopoly contracts were signed by the sultan in 1635 and again in 1664, but both were broken, and in 1669 the Dutch withdrew from the south coast. Only by planting permanent garrisons there could deliveries be enforced, and the trade was not worth the expenditure involved. On the west coast the Dutch planted factories at Sambas and Sukadana, but local opposition soon led to their liquidation. In 1608 through their control over Bantam they were drawn into a war waged by Bantam's vassal Landak against

Sukadana, and after its successful conclusion gained a sort of theoretical suzerainty over the west coast states which recognized Bantam's suzerainty. But this meant little in practice.

The Dutch failure was mainly due to the Chinese, who had a well-established trade with the ports of Borneo, buying up not only the pepper, gold and diamonds sought by European traders but a whole range of other products such as camphor, rattans, wax, resin, timber and the popular table-delicacies *agar-agar*, *tripang*, sharks'-fins and edible birds'-nests. The Dutch could frighten local rulers into signing empty contracts, but the Chinese paid higher prices and got the goods. The English East India Company merchants also tried—and failed—to develop trade with the Borneo ports, at which spices were to be obtained, after the Dutch had driven them out of the Moluccas and Bandas. Then, during the eighteenth century their main interest switched to the China trade and tea, and Borneo acquired a new value for them as a possible site for a commercial entrepôt on the way to China. Hence Alexander Dalrymple's plan to establish a settlement on the island of Balambangan, which, as we have seen above,[1] came to a sorry end in February 1775.

The Dutch during the eighteenth century made further efforts to gain control over the trade of Borneo. In 1747 they made a new pepper contract with Banjermasin, this time providing for the erection of a fort at Tibanio to ensure deliveries. A dynastic upheaval in 1785 enabled them to gain a stronger hold by placing their candidate upon the throne, and two years later he recognized the Dutch East India Company as his sovereign lord. On the west coast during the seventeen-seventies they utilized Bantam's dormant sovereign rights to enable them to plant a factory at Pontianak, and in 1786 with the aid of the sultan they established their influence over Sukadana and the Bugis settlement of Mampawa. But all these advances came to nothing as a result of their setback in the war of 1780-4 with Britain. Batavia decided that the west coast settlements were 'useless and intolerable nuisances', and in 1791 they were abandoned.

There was a similar withdrawal from Banjermasin in 1797 in consequence of which one small fort at Tatas on the south coast was the sole remaining Dutch settlement on the island. In 1809 even this was evacuated when Marshal Daendels concentrated upon the defence of Java after the Dutch naval defeats off its coast in 1806 and 1807, followed by the British capture of the Moluccas in 1808. The sultan, fearing that he might now be unable to defend his kingdom against

[1] *Supra*, pp. 493–6.

attacks by his neighbours, applied to Penang for British protection. His application was supported by Raffles, and after the surrender of Java Alexander Hare with the approval of the Calcutta government was commissioned to plant a British settlement at Banjermasin. Raffles, of course, had his eye on the possibility that were Java to be handed back to the Dutch Britain might retain her hold upon Borneo.

In a treaty signed on 1 October 1812 the sultan ceded to the East India Company the former Dutch forts of Tatas and Tabanio together with the Dyak provinces of south Borneo and the districts subject to them on the south and east coasts. Among a number of potential commercial concessions he granted the pepper monopoly. The Company in its turn was to station a force of light armed vessels off his capital adequate for its defence against his enemies. It also released him from all obligations to the Dutch. In its provisions, and in their precise value, which was slight, the treaty was very similar to those the sultan had made earlier with the Dutch.

Hare as President of Banjermasin obtained for himself personally 1,400 square miles of land south of the capital, and proceeded to live the life of an oriental potentate, complete with harem. He was the moving spirit behind the move to secure British protection for Banjermasin, and his sole aim had been to further his own schemes of personal aggrandisement. The settlement proved a fiasco, and Raffles's reputation was injured by his misplaced trust in a plausible rogue. The scandalous story of the labour force, recruited with official backing in Java to work in Hare's rice-fields and pepper gardens has been told by Graham Irwin in his able study of nineteenth-century Borneo.[1] Equally scandalous was the administration of the settlement, and in 1816 the East India Company, faced with a deficit of £60,000 on its running costs, decided to abandon it and ship the settlers back to Java. Before the withdrawal was effected, Raffles's successor at Batavia, John Fendall, had to make it quite clear to the Dutch that in view of Daendels's formal abandonment of all Dutch possessions in south Borneo in 1809 and the treaty freely negotiated with the sultan in October 1812, their claim to Banjermasin *as of right* could not be recognized. When therefore, a few days after the departure from the place of the British commissioners sent to superintend the withdrawal, a Dutch warship arrived with an officer gazetted as 'commissioner for the purpose of taking over the establishment at Banjermasin', Anglo-Dutch relations in Batavia were not improved.

---

[1] *Nineteenth-Century Borneo; A Study in Diplomatic Rivalry*, 's-Gravenhage, 1955, pp. 19–21, 35–41.

The disappearance of the Dutch fleet from the eastern seas had been followed by an upsurge of piracy, and while Raffles had been stationed at Malacca in 1810 as Governor-General's Agent to the Malay States the menace to British shipping had forced him to turn his attention to the piratical activities of the rulers of Sarawak and Sambas. With the decline of the power of the sultanate of Sukadana, Sambas and Pontianak had become rivals for the control of the west coast of Borneo. Pontianak was willing to carry on peaceable trade, and hence was favoured by Europeans. In 1812 Raffles attempted to put an end to the power of Sambas, but the expedition was a disastrous failure. He planned therefore to back Pontianak's ambitions. He wanted no further settlement in Borneo: his efforts were to be directed solely to the promotion of legitimate trade and the suppression of piracy. Accordingly in 1813 he established a Commercial Agent at Pontianak; next he captured and crippled Sambas; then he declared a blockade of all the ports of Borneo except Brunei, Banjermasin and Pontianak, and at the same time sent Captain R. C. Garnham to tour the west coast as 'Special Commissioner to the Borneo Ports and Macassar' with the object of encouraging trade and warning the local rulers against indulging in piracy. Within a short time the Sultan of Sambas had accepted a British protectorate and the other leading states had recognized British suzerainty.

Obviously, however, these moves were not inspired merely by a desire to safeguard trade. There was a deeper motive. Raffles himself described them as part of a 'grand design' which envisaged the 'permanent political ascendancy' of British authority in South-East Asian waters and the exclusion of Dutch power. This, however, was certainly not in accord with the wishes of his masters. In the first place Lord Minto's successor at Calcutta, Lord Moira, called a halt to Raffles's plans for Borneo: they were too expensive and involved waste of troops, and he made it quite clear that he was opposed to any design for 'advancing policies inimical to Dutch interests' during their 'temporary absence'.[1] So all the plans for blockading Borneo had to be called off. The Directors of the East India Company also were equally firm in their opposition to a policy of aggrandisement in Borneo: 'trade, not territory' east of the Straits of Malacca was, they emphasized, their guiding principle, and it was in complete accord with the British government's unwavering determination, as displayed in the Convention of London of 13 August 1814 to restore the Dutch 'colonies, factories and establishments' at the end of the war with Napoleon. The case of

[1] Irwin, op. cit., pp. 30–1.

Sambas must have afforded Raffles especial humiliation, since the sultan, with whom he had made his treaty, died at the very moment when the blockade policy had to be dropped, and he had to recognize as the new sultan Pangeran Anom, the pirate leader, who had been the cause of the action he had taken in 1813.

The Dutch, on returning to Banjermasin, concluded a treaty in double-quick time with the sultan whereby, in return for a promise of aid against all native and foreign enemies, he granted them a vast amount of territory 'in full ownership and sovereignty', extensive commercial concessions and a degree of control over his affairs that in effect established their indirect rule over his state. The protests of the 'white raja of Moluko', Alexander Hare, at this invasion of his kingdom were in vain: Calcutta told the Batavia authorities that they regarded him as a delinquent; and although the India Board represented to Lord Castlereagh that Hare's forcible dispossession of his property by the Dutch was inequitable, since the sultan was a free agent when he alienated the land to Hare, the British Treasury turned a deaf ear to all his memorials.

The establishment of Dutch sovereignty over Banjermasin in January 1817 was soon followed by invitations from Pontianak and Sambas for their assistance. Accordingly in 1818 a Dutch expedition sailed from Batavia to show the flag on the west coast of Borneo, and the formalities bringing the two states under Netherlands sovereignty were concluded. The expedition, arriving unexpectedly at Sambas, surprised the sultan in the act of leading a piratical raid against Pontianak, and he had somewhat quickly to cancel his plans.

The energy with which Batavia went ahead with the restoration of Dutch influence in Borneo and elsewhere, where for over a generation British merchants had traded without hindrance, aroused Penang's fears regarding a reintroduction of the former Dutch monopoly system, and both London and Calcutta became alarmed lest a threat to the East India Company's cherished trade to China might arise. In June 1818 Governor Bannerman, under pressure from the Penang merchants, sent Major John Farquhar, the Resident of Malacca, to negotiate commercial treaties with Riouw, Lingga, Pontianak and Siak. Farquhar found the Dutch already at Pontianak, but was able to conclude treaties with the rulers of the other three places.

By this time Governor-General Lord Hastings—who as Lord Moira had countermanded Raffles's plans for Borneo in 1814—was changing his mind about the Dutch, and Raffles himself from Bencoolen was bombarding the East India Company in London with suggestions for the protection of British interests against Dutch expansionism. He demanded that a line should be drawn against Dutch aggression, and insisted that they had no claims on Borneo. Hastings was shocked by the Dutch occupation of Banjermasin and Pontianak, and in particular by their complete disregard of Marshal Daendels's formal annullment of their former treaty with Banjermasin. Such was the climate of opinion in which Raffles was able to carry out his Singapore exploit early in 1819. This, of course, had no direct connection with the Borneo question, but, as Graham Irwin has shown, in the angry exchanges between The Hague and London, which followed that event, Lord Castlereagh laid down two principles as of vital importance in relation to Dutch claims anywhere in the Archipelago. The British Government, he wrote, 'cannot acquiesce in a practical exclusion, or in a mere permissive toleration, of British commerce throughout the immense extent of the Eastern Archipelago; nor can they consent so far to expose the direct commerce of this country with China to all the obvious dangers which would result, especially in time of war, from all the military and naval keys of the Straits of Malacca being exclusively in the hands of the Netherlands Government'.[1]

The Netherlands government at The Hague expressed itself unable to concur. Nevertheless it was anxious to come to a permanent settlement with Britain, and so it was that in the middle of 1820 the discussions began which ultimately led to the Anglo-Dutch Treaty of 1824.[2] On the subject of Borneo Britain made it clear that she would be prepared to recognize the treaties made with Bornean states by the Dutch since 1817 provided that they contained no article excluding British trade. A Dutch attempt to assert a claim to supremacy over the whole island caused such a sharp British reaction that the Dutch representative issued an emphatic disavowal of any such pretension. Also, the question of where Borneo stood in relation to the imaginary line delimiting the two respective areas of aspiration which the Dutch wished to draw caused such a divergence of view between the two sides that it had to be dropped. It was finally agreed that Borneo should not be mentioned, and that the demarcation line should not extend beyond the Singapore Straits. Thus, when Article Twelve of the treaty recognizing the British possession of Singapore went on to prohibit the British from setting up any establishments on, or concluding any treaties with the rulers of, any of the remaining islands belonging to the ancient kingdom of Johore 'or any of the other islands south of the Straits of Singapore', both sides understood it as referring only to the

[1] Irwin, *op. cit.*, pp. 56–7.   [2] *Supra*, pp. 509–11.

immediate area of Singapore. Neither Borneo nor any of the other un-occupied territories of the vast island world were included within its scope.

While the talks were in progress the Dutch were busy strengthening their hold on Borneo. They installed residents at Banjermasin, Pontianak and Sambas, and induced the more important rulers of the west and south coasts to recognize Netherlands suzerainty. Then, in 1825, their progress was cut short by the outbreak of the Java war, which seriously aggravated a financial situation already giving cause for much alarm. Once again as in Daendels's time the most drastic reductions had to be made in their Borneo establishments. By 1830 on the west coast only a Resident at Pontianak, an Assistant-Resident at Sambas and a couple of customs inspectors at Tajan, and on the south coast only the Resident at Banjermasin and a single European clerk, were left to represent their authority.

During the next ten years, with their main attention focused upon the development of the Culture System in Java, they showed practically no interest in their Borneo establishments, and none whatever in the vast northern part of the island, which, as Dr Irwin points out, 'lay open to colonization by other European powers'.[1] Thus they could not be bothered to take appropriate action in 1831, when their west coast Resident urged that a treaty should be negotiated with the sultan of Brunei to forestall such a possibility in his dominions, or again in 1838, when their Assistant-Resident at Sambas drew attention to the fact that British ships were using Sarawak to 'smuggle' goods into the interior of Sambas. Indeed, in February 1839 he was instructed that nothing need be done about British trade in Sarawak. That was exactly six months before the arrival there of James Brooke.

(d) Piracy and the work of Raja James Brooke

By Article V of the Anglo-Dutch treaty of 1824 the two powers bound themselves 'to concur effectually in repressing' piracy. How great had become the need for concerted action against this appalling evil may be realized merely by glancing through the indices to the many volumes of the Straits Settlements records. It is one of the most prominent subjects of correspondence. In the Malay world it was an evil so old, so widespread and with so many facets that even when the European powers in the nineteenth century decided that it must be

[1] *Op. cit.*, p. 68.

stamped out it baffled all their efforts for many years. For it was an honourable profession which was connived at, promoted, or even directly engaged in by the highest potentates in that strange Malay world of Raja Brooke's memoirs and Ioseph Conrad's early novels. And nowhere else in the world is geography so favourable to piracy.

There can be no doubt, however, that the particular phase that was acute in the eighteenth century and 'a great and blighting curse' in the nineteenth arose mainly out of the disorganization of the native commerce in the Archipelago by the impact of the Portuguese and the Dutch in the sixteenth and seventeenth centuries. And by comparison with the Portuguese filibustering methods of enriching themselves, the systematic and carefully calculated methods by which the Dutch built up their trading monopoly caused so much ruin to the native peoples and disintegration to their governments as to have constituted the biggest single factor in the situation. Thus it was that, with the weakening of the control of the V.O.C. itself over its island empire during the eighteenth century, the way was open for piracy to increase to what must have been unexampled proportions. And it is ridiculous to attempt to explain it away by the argument that it was only in the eighteenth century that European writers began to make a clear distinction between a pirate and an honest trader.[1]

In the eighteenth century the Bugis, who gained so great an ascendancy in the Malay states and were described by Francis Light as 'the best merchants among the eastern islands', were also the terror of the Archipelago as pirates. It was the Dutch treatment of Macassar in 1667 and the ruin of the Moluccas which started them on their career as freebooters. And it was a passing phase; for in the nineteenth century no more is heard of them as pirates.

Even more formidable were the Moros or Illanos of the Sulu Archipelago. In the nineteenth century they were referred to as the Balanini, from the island group which was their home. Like the Lanuns, or 'Pirates of the Lagoon', who came from the great bay of that name in the south of the island of Mindanao, they used praus of 40 to 100 tons with crews of 40 to 60. These were, in fact, the regular native war-boats in use all over South-East Asia. The Lanuns and Balanini sent out fleets of several hundreds of them every year. The smaller junks and the native trading praus were their prey; they seldom attacked European ships or even the larger Chinese junks. Sulu was their commercial headquarters. By far their worst raids, for slaves and booty, were upon the Philippines; and although the Spanish

[1] Vlekke, *Nusantara*, pp. 198–9.

sent many punitive expeditions which destroyed their strongholds and burnt their villages, they could never bring them under effective control.

For their operations against the Malay Archipelago the Lanun fleets sailed first to Tampassuk on the coast of north-west Borneo, where they divided into squadrons, each with its own special beat. Every year the 'pirates' wind' brought them to the Straits of Malacca to lie in wait for praus bound for Singapore. The Riau-Lingga Archipelago was a regular hunting-ground for them, and whole islands were depopulated by their slave raids. They visited Penang and the Kedah coast as late as 1835. They wrought incalculable havoc and damage.

The most bitter enemies of the Lanun and Balanini were the Malay pirates of the Riau-Lingga Archipelago, the Carimons, and other islands near the southern entrance of the Straits of Malacca. Pulo Galang was their principal market for the sale of captured goods and slaves. The Lingga Sultan was suspected of encouraging them; his chief officers equipped pirate fleets, as also did the sultans of Sumatra and the Peninsula. Pirate praus would seem to have been fitted out even at Singapore. The Malay praus, however, were much smaller than the large Lanun and Balanini war-boats and carried fewer men. Compared with the operations of their rivals, Malay piracy was on a much smaller scale.

In the early part of the nineteenth century the north-west coast of Borneo was one of the most notorious pirate centres. The actual piracy was carried on by the Sea-Dyaks, the *Orang Laut*, but they were employed and directed by the Malay chieftains and individual Arabs who had settled among them. They and the Lanuns, whose strongholds were north of Brunei, were the pirates against whom the efforts of Raja James Brooke came chiefly to be directed.

As in the case of the Moorish corsairs of the Mediterranean in the sixteenth and seventeenth centuries, it was the lack of concerted action against them by the European naval powers that enabled piracy to survive as long and as successfully as it did. The co-operation provided for in the Anglo-Dutch treaty of 1824 never materialized. The British for long had inadequate naval forces at their disposal because the East India Company after 1833, when it ceased to be a trading concern, was unwilling to incur expense on the Straits Settlements, from which it received no revenue. The Dutch, who had far more warships in the Archipelago than the British, did more than any other nation to suppress piracy, but they confined their efforts to their own area. The Spanish in the same way concentrated upon protecting the

Philippines against the Lanuns. In 1848 they expelled the Balanini from their islands. In 1851 they captured Sulu and forced the Lanuns to transfer their trading centre elsewhere. But it was only later, when they gradually brought the Sulu Archipelago and Mindanao under their control, that the Lanun raids on the Philippines came to an end.

The development of Singapore brought so much native trade there that it increased the prosperity of the pirate profession. From 1819 to 1830 the Straits Settlements had only a few gunboats and schooners, which were quite inadequate to cope with the evil. The Bugis merchants of Singapore complained of their inadequate protection in 1831 and threatened to abandon their voyages. So difficult was the situation that in 1832 the Chinese of Singapore were permitted to fit out four ships of their own for service against pirates. In 1835 petitions for better protection were made to the British parliament and the Government of India by the European and Chinese merchants of Singapore and the Bengal Chamber of Commerce. As a result H.M.S. *Andromache* was sent out to the Straits of Malacca, while her captain and the Governor of the Straits Settlements were appointed joint commissioners for the suppression of piracy. In 1836 two more warships and three gunboats were sent to Singapore, and as a result of their efforts severe blows were dealt at Malay pirate centres. In particular the Galang centre was destroyed. In 1837 the Government of India stationed a permanent force of two Royal Navy ships and five gunboats in the Straits. But more important still was the arrival of the small steamship *Diana* there in that year. It was steam power alone that could cope adequately with the galley, which could out-manœuvre the sailing ship by using its oars.

For some years there was a notable decrease of piracy near the Straits Settlements. But in 1843 a great recrudescence of Malay and Lanun activities occurred. In the meantime, however, a new personality had arrived on the scene in 1839, and under his inspiring leadership the operations against piracy took on a vigour which in a few years reduced it to insignificance. James Brooke was the son of a member of the Bengal Civil Service and had himself served in the East India Company's army in the Assam operations during the first Anglo-Burmese war. A serious wound in an engagement near Rangpur caused him to return to England in 1826, and soon afterwards he left the Company's service. In 1830 he sailed to China, and while passing through the Malay Archipelago he was so deeply impressed with its beauty and the devastation wrought by piracy and internecine warfare that when his father died, leaving him a large property, he invested in a yacht, the *Royalist* of 140 tons burden, trained a picked crew, and in 1839 arrived in Borneo with the immediate object of carrying on exploration and scientific research.

He found the district of Sarawak in revolt against the Sultan of Brunei, whose uncle, Pangéran Muda Hashim, had just failed to suppress the rebellious Dyaks. Muda Hashim and Brooke became firm friends, and in the following year Muda Hashim offered him the governorship of Sarawak in return for his proffered help in dealing with the rebels. Brooke not only crushed the rebellion but won the allegiance of the Malays and Dyaks, who had long suffered under the misrule of Brunei. After some delay, due to the opposition of the existing governor, he received his appointment in September 1841, and in the following year it was confirmed by the sultan.

While engaged with conspicuous success upon the task of introducing just and humane government into the territory entrusted to him he was busy trying to interest the British government in Brunei. With the growth of steamship traffic to China the need had arisen for a coaling station between Singapore and Hong Kong, which had been acquired in 1841. In those days ships consumed such large quantities of coal that its storage took up valuable cargo space, and it was essential to have coaling stations at not too great a distance from each other so as to reduce the amount that it was necessary to carry. Brunei itself and the island of Labuan both possessed seams of excellent coal, and Brooke learnt that the Dutch were casting longing eyes upon them. In 1844 Sultan Omar offered to cede Labuan to Britain, and Brooke suggested that not only should the offer be accepted but also a British Resident should be appointed to Brunei as adviser to the sultan. The idea that was germinating in his mind was something along the lines of the Residential system that was later introduced into Malaya. And it is of no small significance that Sir Hugh Low, who in 1877 became Resident of Perak and was the real creator of the Residency system in Malaya, served his apprenticeship under Brooke in Sarawak.

Meanwhile in 1846 matters came to a crisis in Brunei. The sultan, under the influence of the piratical faction of the Malay nobles, who saw in Brooke's measures against piracy the end of their profitable enterprise, had Pangéran Muda Hashim and all his supporters murdered. He attempted to procure Brooke's murder also and to kidnap Admiral Cochrane, whose squadron had in the previous year dealt Borneo piracy its heaviest blow by the capture of the Lanun stronghold of Marudu. The Lanun leader, Sharif Osman, who had been killed in the fight, was the ally of Pangéran Usop, the sultan's favourite. Usop himself had in 1845 led an attack on Muda Hashim, but had been captured and put to death.

The measures against piracy which brought matters to a head in this way had begun with the decisive defeat of the raids of the Sea-Dyaks on Sarawak. The sultan's governors of the Sea-Dyaks were four Arab sharifs, who were pirate chiefs and slavers. They planned a big attack on Brooke in 1843 and were supported by Usop and Makuta, the ex-Governor of Sarawak, whose misrule had caused the rebellion into which Brooke had run in 1839. Their plot, however, misfired, because before it could be carried out Captain Keppel arrived in H.M.S. *Dido* to investigate attacks that had been made on Singapore praus off the Borneo coast, and Brooke at once advised an attack on the Serebas and the Sekarran, the two tribes into which the Sea-Dyaks were divided. Thereupon the *Dido*, with Brooke's flotilla of Sarawak Malays, set about destroying the strongholds of the Serebas. Before the fight could be carried into the Sekarran country the *Dido* had to proceed to China. But she returned in 1844 and dealt with the Sekarran in the same way as she had with the Serebas. Then in the following year, as we have seen, Admiral Cochrane's squadron dealt the Lanun a staggering blow by destroying their fortified settlement at Marudu.

The triumph of the piratical party at Brunei in 1846 was short-lived. Brooke and Cochrane appeared at the entrance to the river on which Brunei town stands, the sultan refused to negotiate, and after a short sharp fight the town was captured and the sultan fled inland. He was allowed to return, since the piratical party which had forced his hand was now powerless and he was willing to co-operate with the British for the suppression of piracy and slaving. Hence, leaving Captain Mundy behind to negotiate, Admiral Cochrane departed for China. On his way his squadron destroyed the two important Lanun settlements of Tampassuk and Pandassan. At the same time Mundy, in H.M.S. *Iris*, completed the work of stamping out the Lanun power in north-west Borneo by the systematic destruction of the settlement that Haji Saman, one of the leaders of the piratical party at Brunei, had established in the Mambakut river. As a result every Lanun settlement in north-west Borneo was abandoned, and the refugees made their way round to the north-east coast to establish a new centre at Tunku.

On being restored to his throne Sultan Omar ceded Sarawak in full sovereignty to Raja Brooke. Almost at the same time a despatch from

Lord Palmerston authorized the acceptance of the sultan's offer to cede Labuan and the conclusion of a commercial treaty, but rejected the proposal for establishing a British Resident at Brunei. The treaties that were signed in 1846 as a result of the ensuing negotiations pledged the sultan to suppress piracy and slavery, granted British commerce most-favoured-nation treatment, and provided that there should be no alienation of territory by the sultan without British consent. Brooke then returned to Britain in triumph. He was knighted and appointed Governor of Labuan and commissioner and consul-general to the sultan and independent chiefs of Borneo.

Right from the start the Dutch had watched Brooke's actions in north-west Borneo with growing apprehension. In the years 1845-6 in a series of notes to the British Government they put forward the surprising contention that the British operations in Brunei, and in particular the acquisition of Labuan, constituted a breach of the treaty of 1824. The correspondence became somewhat heated, since Britain not only refuted the Dutch claim by pointing out that the treaty guaranteed the Netherlands' rights south of the Malacca Straits, and that Sarawak and Brunei were situated on a higher degree of latitude than Singapore, but reminded the Dutch of their own continual violations of the commercial provisions of the treaty. On the subject of Borneo the Dutch put forward an argument which went much farther than mere questions of latitude; they claimed that wherever there was a Dutch post on an island in the Archipelago the British might not plant an establishment anywhere on the same island, even in an independent state.

The Lanuns had been driven away from the north-west coast of Borneo, but Sea-Dyak piracy once more lifted its head in 1847. The reason was that once again Brooke had inadequate forces at his command, and the China squadron, which had given such effective help in the previous period, was too small to carry out all the duties required of it. At the very time when Malay and Lanun piracy was being suppressed Chinese piracy began to rise to formidable proportions, and from about 1840 to 1860 the native trade of the Straits Settlements suffered from the attacks of their large well-armed junks, which even attacked European vessels. Not until 1849 could Brooke again secure the help of a British warship.

Early in 1849, at the request of the Sultan of Brunei, Brooke and his Malays, with the boats of the H.C. steamer *Nemesis*,[1] raided the

---

[1] H.C. ('Honourable Company's') was used to distinguish the East India Company's ships from those of the Royal Navy.

Sea-Dyak country, but were too weak to inflict a decisive blow. Soon afterwards, however, Admiral Collier, in command of the China squadron, managed to send two Royal Navy warships and two Company's steamers, and with these Sea-Dyak piracy was ruthlessly stamped out. The decisive action took place at Batang Maru, where a pirate fleet of over a hundred war-boats was ambushed and destroyed. Then over a wide area Serebas and Sekarran villages were burnt and the country ravaged. Out of 4,000 pirates, their total loss was estimated at no more than 800. It would have been at least three times that number had not Brooke deliberately allowed large numbers to escape. The Serebas and the Sekarran made their submission, the chiefs who were opposed to piracy regained power, and in order that a firm hand might be kept on the Sea-Dyaks, to prevent the piratical party from organizing their forays once more, the Sultan of Brunei ceded their land to Brooke in return for half its surplus revenue.

The effect of this victory on the trade of the Straits Settlements was marked. For not only was the native trade freed, but also Singapore developed a new trading connection of great value with Sarawak and Brunei. Brooke, however, found himself the object of a furious press attack in Singapore and London for his action against the Sea-Dyaks. It began in the *Straits Times* in 1849 and was taken up by the London *Daily News*. Ultimately David Hume, the Peace Society, the Aborigines Protection Society, Sydney Herbert and Gladstone himself were drawn into the fray against Brooke, and *The Times*, Lord Palmerston, Lord Grey, Keppel and Mundy in his defence. In 1854, however, he was completely cleared by a royal commission. What had happened was that Brooke's former agent, Henry Wise, had put up a needy journalist, Robert Wood, to print a flagrantly false account of the Batang Maru operation in the *Straits Times*, which was copied by the *Daily News*. Wise had also managed to obtain the confidence of David Hume, who welcomed the opportunity of gaining notoriety by attacking the much-lionized hero. Brooke had broken with Wise in 1848 for fraudulent dealings in connection with the latter's Eastern Archipelago Company, founded in 1847. The campaign, therefore, was inspired by Wise's desire for revenge on Brooke because of his refusal, in his own words, 'to shut my eyes, say nothing, and see what God will send me'. In 1853 Brooke successfully prosecuted the Eastern Archipelago Company for fraud. As a result its charter was cancelled and the company dissolved.

One lamentable result of this attack on Brooke was that the belief became current in Sarawak that in case of further trouble he would receive no support from the British Navy. Hence in 1857 the Chinese secret society there stimulated a revolt. Kuching, the capital of Sarawak, was burnt and many Europeans and natives butchered before it was suppressed. Two years later some discontented Malay chiefs attempted a rising. It is significant that throughout these troubles the Sea-Dyaks remained staunchly loyal to the man who had cured them of piracy.

Besides contesting through diplomatic channels Raja Brooke's right to establish himself at Sarawak, the Dutch began to take special measures to place their sovereign rights in Borneo—and the rest of their 'Outer Possessions' also—wherever possible, beyond doubt. They had indeed cut to the bone all expenditure upon activities in Borneo, but in November 1843 the authorities at The Hague authorized the adoption of tentative measures aimed at extending their power there. A few months later the disastrously unsuccessful attempt of a British private merchant, Erskine Murray, to open up trade with the Sultan of Kutei, brought the east coast to Batavia's notice. Accordingly, a small naval expedition was despatched there in March 1844, and new contracts made with the sultans of Kutei and Pasir. Treaties were also negotiated with the rulers of Bulungan, Gunong Tabur and Sambaliung whereby, among other things, they undertook to forbid non-Dutch Europeans to establish themselves in their territories. How much such agreements were worth in fact was demonstrated shortly afterwards, when Captain Sir Edward Belcher in the H.M.S. *Semarang*, going to the rescue of a British merchantman wrecked off Gunong Tabur, took the opportunity to negotiate treaties with its ruler and the sultan of Bulungan. The British government, however, did not confirm them.

All these threats of foreign interference in their own preserves, as incidents of such a kind were in Dutch eyes, made it obvious to Governor-General Rochussen, when he took over in 1845, that more effective control must be established over Borneo. The measures he took towards that end, however, were totally inadequate, since without effective occupation, which he was not in a position to carry out, they were seen to be mere paper schemes. His appointment of a 'Governor of Borneo and Dependencies' with his capital at Sintang three hundred miles up the River Kapuas in western Borneo, and his efforts to extend Dutch influence over the east coast through contracts negotiated with its rulers by an 'administrator' (*gezaghebber*) stationed at Kutei, were of course intended primarily to impress foreign powers. But the chief foreign power, Britain, rejected with contempt the Dutch attempts to twist the meaning of the Treaty of 1824 to their own advantage, and reserved the right to found colonies in Borneo, should she so desire. Then also Sintang was found to be useless as a capital, and the plan for a unified administration had to be abandoned. Moreover, the political situation in Europe during 1848, the 'year of revolutions', convinced the statesmen at The Hague that friendly relations with Britain were essential. So the British treaty of 1847 with Brunei was silently swallowed, and in 1850 it was decided to acquiesce in Britain's actions on the north coast.

Once more the Dutch reorganized their Borneo administration, this time into a Western Division and a Southern and Eastern Division. Then within these more restricted limits they began gradually, and more effectively, to strengthen their hold. Dutch private enterprise was granted free access to the mineral wealth of the Archipelago except Java and Banka, and although it achieved little before 1880, the way was opened for bigger steps later. From 1850 onwards also force was resorted to in order to bring under direct rule parts of Dutch Borneo hitherto unsubdued. The Chinese gold-mining kongsis of the Western Division, which had always flouted external authority, were reduced to submission, and in 1854 formed into a new Dutch province. And some years later, when a Dutch attempt to place their candidate upon the throne of Banjermasin led to a general revolt, the conquest of the state was put in hand. It took several years, even after the Dutch gained the upper hand in 1862; but military actions supplied an excellent pretext for establishing direct rule.

While the Dutch were strengthening their hold on western and southern Borneo, British interest in the island was waning. The Labuan settlement, which had resulted from Brooke's negotiations with the sultan of Brunei in 1846, was conceived as a coaling depot for ships on the Far East run, a centre for action against piracy and an entrepôt for the north-west coastal trade. It proved a dismal failure. The coal-mining companies were badly run, and coal from Britain could undercut their prices in Singapore. It played practically no part in the suppression of piracy which was carried out by the Dutch, Spanish and British naval forces; indeed, British warships found Kuching a more convenient base, and Labuan had no gunboat of its own until 1877. Its trade remained negligible, since few European ships visited it on account of its inadequate wharves and warehouses. But it was retained: for some reason or other the Colonial Office was persuaded that it might one day become useful in connection with the expanding British trade with China. On the other hand, the rigours of official economy made such inroads upon its administrative staff that by 1888 only an acting-governor and a gaoler were left to run the place on the spot. Finally in 1890 it was placed under the administration of the British North Borneo Company.

During his later years as ruler of Sarawak Brooke was much occupied with the question of the status of his principality. In 1852 he approached the British Foreign Office regarding his recognition as an independent ruler. This, however, seemed hardly compatible with his obligation to make certain money payments, tributary in nature, to the sultan of Brunei, and, moreover, the Foreign Office held that as a British subject he could not acquire independent sovereignty without the consent of the Crown. The Chinese insurrection of 1857 made him regard the matter of recognition as one of real urgency: he felt that he needed the protection of a European power. At one moment of panic he even toyed with the idea of seeking Dutch suzerainty. Further approaches to the Foreign Office in the course of the year 1858 again brought no result. Both the British government and the electorate were convinced that Britain already had too many colonial commitments, and should cut down rather than increase her responsibilities in this field. Besides, the failure of Labuan did not inspire confidence in Sarawak, and it was realized that Brooke's financial difficulties were one impelling reason for his search for a suzerain.

In 1859, when he was again toying with the idea of surrendering Sarawak to the Dutch, Miss Angela Burdett-Coutts, the well-known philanthropist, came to his aid. But in the following year he actually approached Napoleon III of France and the government of Belgium in turn. Nothing came of all these moves, and indeed his nephew and heir-designate, Captain James Brooke Brooke, who took charge of the Sarawak internal administration in 1858, was thoroughly opposed to cession. In 1863, through the personal intervention of the prime minister, Lord Palmerston, a British consul was appointed to Kuching, and in his official documents 'Sir James Brooke, Raja of Sarawak' was named, with the implication that he was an independent ruler. Nevertheless the Foreign Office doctrine continued to be that no such recognition had in fact been given.

James Brooke left Kuching for permanent retirement in England on 24 September 1863, the twenty-second anniversary of his assumption of the title of raja. He had been a poor administrator and incompetent at finance, writes Sir Steven Runciman,[1] but he had profoundly

[1] *The White Rajas*, Cambridge, 1960, p. 156.

changed for the better the lives of the Land Dyaks and other peoples who had come under his aegis. He died in June 1868 leaving to his successor 'a disorganized and impoverished state'.[1]

[1] *Ibid., loc. cit.*

CHAPTER 30

THE RESTORED DUTCH RÉGIME IN INDONESIA AND THE CULTURE SYSTEM, 1816–48

AFTER Napoleon's defeat at Leipzig in 1813 the Dutch had joined in the general revolt against him. Van Hogendorp's younger brother[1] organized a provisional government and recalled William VI of Orange, the son of the old Stadhouder, from England. As sovereign prince under the new Fundamental Law adopted in 1814, he was given extensive powers, which included not only the management of the state's finances but also 'exclusive control' over the colonies. In the following year, when by the union of Belgium and Holland the kingdom of the United Netherlands was formed under the provisions of the Treaty of Vienna, William's rank was raised to that of king.

By the Convention of London, accepted by both sides on 13 August 1814, provision was made for the restitution by Britain of all the former colonies of the Dutch East India Company 'conquered from Holland since 1803', save the Cape Colony. Ceylon was excluded from this agreement, since it had already been ceded to Britain in 1802 by the Peace of Amiens. The tin-bearing island of Banka off the east coast of Sumatra, which had been conquered in 1812, was exchanged for Cochin on the Malabar Coast of India. The remark was once made that Britain acquired her empire in the nineteenth century in a fit of absentmindedness. In much the same vein is Stapel's suggestion that the reason why there was no opposition in Britain to the restitution of Java was because the British had no idea of its value and beauty.[2]

To take over the government of the Dutch islands the king appointed three commissioners-general: Cornelis Theodorus Elout, Baron van der Capellen, a statesman of high reputation, and A. A. Buyskes, previously lieutenant governor-general under Daendels. Elout, the chairman, was a liberal of the orthodox school of the day—i.e. a humanitarian and a follower of Adam Smith. When the others returned home van der Capellen was to remain behind as governor-general. In January 1815 the king furnished the commissioners with

---

[1] Gijsbert Karel. The colonial reformer was Dirk.
[2] In his single-volume *Geschiedenis van Nederlandsch Indië*, 1943 edition, p. 225.

a *Regerings-reglement*—i.e. constitutional regulation—modelled on the charter of 1803 and based on the principle of freedom of cultivation and trade. A month later he issued a decree throwing open the trade of the Netherlands Indies.

Napoleon's return from Elba and the Waterloo campaign delayed the departure of the commissioners, and when they arrived in Java, in April 1816, John Fendall, Raffles's successor, had received no instructions to hand over. Not until 19 August did the official ceremony of rendition take place. There were further difficulties and delays in the case of the other possessions, especially those in or about Sumatra, for in March 1818 Raffles returned to the scene as Lieutenant-Governor of Bencoolen and began to work with might and main against the restoration of Dutch power there. Calcutta, however, supported the Dutch against him, and after the surrender of Malacca in September 1818 all their old stations were handed over speedily except Padang, which Raffles managed to retain until May 1819.

The new government found its task a heavy one. The Dutch had lost much of their old prestige. The home country was too poor to give adequate financial support, and the commissioners had no fleet at their disposal and only a very small army. Overseas trade was mainly in British and American hands. Moreover, under the liberal system introduced by Raffles the cultivation of export crops, which had been the chief aim of the old Dutch administration, had fallen into decay.

The financial question was perhaps the most pressing one. Under both Daendels and Raffles the colony had failed to pay its way. Elout found that the British 'taxation system', as opposed to the Dutch 'trade system', was much more profitable for the individual than for the state. As a liberal he was predisposed to favour free peasant cultivation. So, he found, was Muntinghe, when the question was referred to the Council of the Indies. Hence, after a prolonged tour of inspection, the decision was taken to retain Raffles's land-rent system, using the *desa* method of assessment. The system was to be gradually improved by measuring up and valuing the land, and in order to help the taxpayer to keep out of the hands of the moneylender he was to be free to pay his tax in either money or kind.

These principles were embodied in Land-rent Ordinances published in 1818 and 1819. They determined the framework of the system of territorial administration which was laid down by the commissioners-general in a *Regerings-reglement* issued in December

1818. This retained Raffles's framework of Residencies, Districts, Divisions and Villages, with the District renamed 'Regency' and the Division 'District'. But whereas Raffles's system had tended towards direct rule, with the Regent and his native staff subordinate to the Resident, the new arrangements reverted to the method of 'supervision', the old dual system, whereby the Regent, though shorn of many of his attributes as a hereditary noble, was in charge of a separate branch of the administration.[1] And his subordination to the Resident tended once again to become feudal rather than administrative. He was to be treated as a 'younger brother'—i.e. a vassal ruler in the accepted meaning of a term that was current throughout South-East Asia. These arrangements applied only to Java. Elsewhere, in what the Dutch called the 'Outer Provinces', the native peoples remained under the rule of their own chieftains, who themselves were under the supervision of the Dutch provincial governors.

The system of justice underwent a more thoroughgoing revision, though here again much of Raffles's system was retained. The old dual system of different law and separate courts for Europeans and natives was revived and strengthened, and where Raffles had appointed a single judge or magistrate, sitting alone with either a jury or assessors, the old method of a bench of judges, each with a vote, was restored. For natives the Residency Courts and Circuit Courts of the Raffles régime were retained. The former was renamed *Landraad* and consisted of a bench of native judges under the presidency of a Dutch official. For Europeans the Courts of Justice established by Raffles at the ports of Batavia, Semarang and Surabaya were retained, while others were set up at Amboina, Macassar, Malacca and, in 1825, Padang. That of Batavia became a High Court with general appellate jurisdiction for the whole of the Netherlands Indies.

The commissioners-general made all manner of regulations for the protection of the native. Native officials were to be remunerated by the method of fixed salaries instead of by assignments of land worked for them by serf labour. They might not engage in trade or industry, nor might *desa* headmen hire out the labour of their villages under any pretext whatever. The slave-trade was forbidden, and Raffles's regulations regarding slavery were confirmed. Unfortunately, however, the safeguards were more honoured in precept than in practice. And, like Raffles, the restored Dutch régime found it necessary to retain the forced coffee culture in the Preanger, and the *blandong*

---

[1] See Furnivall's analysis of the principles applied by the *Regerings-reglement* of 1818 in *Netherlands India*, pp. 87–92.

people's serfdom in the teak forests. Worse still, in 1830, with the introduction of the Culture System, the principle of free peasant cultivation was abandoned completely.

By the beginning of 1819 nearly all the Dutch possessions outside Java had been handed over and the work of the commissioners-general was finished. Elout and Buyskes therefore returned home, leaving van der Capellen behind as governor-general. He was the least progressive of the three, and as early as 1820 gave the native chiefs greater powers over their people, in direct contravention of the policy laid down by the *Regerings-reglement*. He disliked the fact that an increasing number of Europeans was taking up planting in Java. He refused to allow them to settle in the Preanger, for fear of their competition with the government's system of coffee culture, which he was extending considerably. And because those who already owned estates there paid higher rates for their Javanese labour than the government, he forced them to sell their coffee to the government at the same price as the Javanese himself.

He was on stronger ground in excluding Europeans and Chinese from all trade in the Preanger. By advancing money to the cultivators they could buy their crops at much lower prices. This practice, besides impoverishing the cultivator, hit the government, for he was unable to pay his taxes in full and tended to sell to private capitalists coffee that was really government property.

In 1822, while on a tour of Java, van der Capellen found that Europeans unable to obtain land from the government could rent it in the native states under agreements known as 'contracts of land-tenancy', which gave the tenant not only the use of the land but also power to exercise the lord's rights over the cultivators attached to it. In the following year he decreed that all such contracts were to become null and void as from 1 January 1824. His action aroused great indignation. Most of the contracts were long-term ones, in respect of which the native chiefs had received large advances, which they would now have to repay. And since they had already spent the money, they could only discharge their debts by further pressing the already depressed cultivator. This bred much discontent and a spirit of resentment against the government, especially in the Jogjakarta area.

To make matters worse, the post-war boom, which had raised the prices of coffee and sugar and brought an increasing number of ships to Javanese ports, gave way to a slump, and hence revenue, which had shown a surplus up to 1822, began to show an annual deficit thereafter. Incidentally, it is interesting to note that land-revenue continued to increase; it was a fall in revenue from other sources that caused the deficit.

Part of the trouble lay in the fact that the new administration was far more costly than that of Raffles and spent money too freely on roads and other public works. And it so happened that just when a policy of retrenchment was urgently needed van der Capellen had to deal with a number of outbreaks of unrest in the Moluccas, Borneo, Celebes, Palembang and on the west coast of Sumatra, all of which were a drain upon his diminishing financial resources.

From the point of view of most Dutchmen the chief source of grievance was the fact that overseas trade was mainly in foreign hands. Dutch trade was specially favoured by the preferential system of customs duties adopted in 1817; but the superiority of English piece-goods over those produced in the Netherlands enabled British merchants to retain their dominating position. In the hope of dealing a blow at British competition Muntinghe suggested that the Dutch merchants should pool their resources by setting up a big national company with the king at its head. William jumped at the idea, and in 1825 the Nederlandsche Handelmaatschappij came into existence with a capital initially fixed at 37 million guilders, a guaranteed dividend of $4\frac{1}{2}$ per cent, and the king himself as a principal shareholder. It was a far more ambitious project than Muntinghe had envisaged. In its early years at least it proved just as incapable as the private merchants of combating British competition.

Van der Capellen's efforts to help the native peoples led him to attempt to reduce the evil effects of the spice monopoly upon the Moluccas. He paid the islands a visit in 1824 and announced the abolition of the hated *hongi-tochten*, by means of which the number of spice trees had been kept down to the level required for restricting supply and maintaining prices. He hoped to persuade the home government to abolish the monopoly altogether, but failed to do so.

Van der Capellen also failed to make ends meet. Hence in 1825 it was decided to remove him from office on the score of the inefficiency of his financial administration. King William felt that a special effort was needed to cope with the continued annual deficit, and to this end conferred on his successor, Du Bus de Gisignies, the rank of commissioner-general with special powers to carry through such reforms as he might consider necessary. Van der Capellen should have returned home in 1825, but his departure was delayed by the outbreak of a serious rebellion in central Java.

The Java War of 1825-30 arose from a variety of causes. Discontent had risen to a high pitch in the native states, and particularly in Jogjakarta, where the consequences of van der Capellen's cancellation of contracts for land-lease had hit all classes of people. Another strong grievance was over the tolls levied at the boundaries between native and government territory, and the vexatious exactions of the Chinese to whom they were farmed. The general unrest came to a head under the leadership of a prince of the royal house of Jogjakarta, Dipo Negoro, who had personal reasons for hating the Dutch.

Pangéran Anta Wiria, better known as Dipo Negoro, was the eldest son of Amangku Buwono III, who had been placed on the throne by Raffles when in 1810 his father, Sultan Sepu, had been banished to Penang. Amangku Buwono III had died in 1814, and in accordance with Javanese *adat* law had been succeeded by a younger son Djarot because his mother was a queen of higher rank than Dipo Negoro's. But Raffles, in order to pacify the elder brother, who was a man of outstanding influence, had promised him the eventual succession in the event of Djarot's previous death. When, however, Djarot (Amangku Buwono IV) died in 1822, the Dutch government passed over Dipo Negoro's claim and recognized the dead sultan's two-year-old son as Amangku Buwono V. They would appear to have been genuinely ignorant of Raffles's promise, for they appointed Dipo Negoro and another member of the royal house, Mangku Bumi, as joint guardians of the young sultan.

Not long afterwards Dipo Negoro fell foul of the Dutch Resident over an incident which occurred as a result of van de Capellen's abolition of land-lease contracts. But what finally caused him to raise the standard of revolt was the decision of the government to make a road over some of his property where a sacred tomb was situated. He was a religious fanatic, given to solitary meditation in sacred caves, and felt himself deeply injured when the Dutch refused to recognize him as religious head of Java. As the chosen of Allah to drive out the 'kaffirs' he aroused widespread sympathy among the common people, who saw in him the prince-liberator of ancient legend.

The revolt began when Dipo Negoro, his co-guardian Mangku Bumi and other discontents 'went to the mountains'. When he suddenly appeared before Jogjakarta with a powerful force the population rose in his support, the Dutch carried away the young sultan, and there was a massacre of Europeans and Chinese toll-farmers. The Dutch were caught on the wrong foot, for a large part of their army was away on an expedition to Palembang and Boni. General de Kock was sent to central Java with so small a force that he could do little to prevent the spread of the conflagration. He did, however, by negotiation persuade the Susuhunan of Surakarta from making common cause with Dipo Negoro.

There were no pitched battles; Dipo Negoro and his nephew showed themselves adepts in guerrilla tactics, and even after de Kock was reinforced, continued to maintain the upper hand. In vain did the Dutch restore to the throne Sultan Sepuh, whom Raffles had deposed. He could gain no support and died in 1828.

Gradually, however, de Kock learnt how to deal with the revolt. He began to establish a system of strong-points (*bentengstelsel*) in territory recovered from the rebels. These were linked up by good roads on which flying columns operated. Du Bus de Gisignies disliked the high cost of the system, but de Kock was adamant in defending it, and it produced decisive results. In 1828, notwithstanding his assumption of the rank of sultan, Dipo Negoro was losing ground rapidly, the devastation was appalling, and there were frightful outbreaks of cholera. In 1829 Mangku Bumi and Sentot, Dipo Negoro's principal lieutenants, finding their position hopeless, deserted to the Dutch. In the next year Dipo Negoro offered to negotiate. At the conference he refused to give up the title of sultan and protector of Islam in Java, and after much delay de Kock broke the impasse by arresting him. He was banished to Menado in the north of Celebes, and later removed to Macassar, where he died in 1855.

To prevent a recurrence of trouble the Dutch annexed much territory—Banjumas, Bagelen, Madiun and Kediri—from Jogjakarta and Surakarta. Compensation was paid to both rulers for the loss of territory, but the susuhunan, indignant at the shabby treatment he had received in return for his loyalty, left his kraton and went into retreat. The Dutch, fearful of another outbreak, banished him to Amboina. His successor, Pakubuwono VII, without ado signed the treaty offered him by Batavia, and there was no further trouble.

The Java War prevented any real restoration of the financial situation by Du Bus de Gisignies. It had cost 20 million florins and had been financed entirely by loans. He did manage to effect some much-needed reduction in the cost of administration and the number of Residencies; and the establishment of the Java Bank and a new currency was calculated to bring good results in the long run. He also withdrew the prohibition of the land-lease contracts which had caused so much unrest. But at the moment when the financial situation in Java was working up to a crisis Belgium revolted against Holland, and the home government was threatened with bankruptcy.

This final development, however, was unforeseen when King William, aware that some quite new approach must be made to the problem of the Java finances, had appointed Johannes van den Bosch to succeed Du Bus de Gisignies as governor-general and, acting on his advice, had in 1829 issued a *Regerings-reglement* which was to usher in a change of profound importance in economic policy. Van den Bosch was a self-made man who had risen from the ranks of the army in Java, reclaimed a derelict estate near Batavia, quarrelled with Daendels and been deported to Europe in 1810, spent two years as a prisoner-of-war in England, risen to be Chief of the General Staff in the kingdom of the United Netherlands, and then retired to study political economy.

In his writings he was a great critic of the 'perverted Liberalism' of Daendels and Raffles. He was a practical reformer rather than a philosopher, and as the founder of the Benevolent Society did much to relieve the appalling urban poverty in his own country by settling self-supporting colonies in the less cultivated districts of Friesland and Drente. In 1827 he was sent on a special mission to restore prosperity in the Dutch West Indies, and a year later returned with a report in which he showed how to make them yield a large annual profit to the mother country. This so impressed William that he appointed him as the successor to Du Bus de Gisignies in order that he might try out in the East Indies the ideas he had expounded.

The new governor-general landed in Java in January 1830 and proceeded at once to carry into effect a project that became known as the 'Culture System' (*Cultuur-stelsel*). In many ways it was the old system of forced deliveries and contingencies with a new look. The Javanese peasant was held to be too ignorant to make the best of his land; he must therefore be compelled to devote a portion of it to the cultivation of export crops as directed by the government, and the latter would take the product in lieu of land-rent in cash. The supplies thus raised were to be handled by Dutch merchants, shipped in Dutch vessels, and sold in the Netherlands, which would by this means become once more a world market for tropical produce. At the same time home industry was to be stimulated by being given a closed market in the colonies.

The principles of the system in its application to the cultivator were outlined thus by van den Bosch:[1]

[1] Quoted from the *Indisch Staatsblad* by Colenbrander, *Koloniale Geschiedenis*, iii, pp. 37–8.

1. Agreements are made with the people for setting apart a portion of their rice-fields for the cultivation of products suitable for the European market.

2. The portion set apart shall amount to one-fifth of the cultivated ground of each *desa*.

3. The cultivation of products suitable for the European market must not entail more labour than the cultivation of rice.

4. The land set apart is free of land-rent.

5. The cultivated product is delivered to the district, and whenever its assessed value is greater than the land-rent that has been remitted the difference is credited to the people.

6. Crop failure, when not due to lack of zeal or industry, is the government's liability.

7. The native works under the direction of his chiefs. Supervision by European officials is limited to the control of the working of the fields, the harvesting and transport of crops on time, and the finding of a suitable place.

8. The labour must be distributed in such a manner that a part of the people is responsible for bringing the crop to maturity, another part for harvesting it, a third for its transport, and a fourth for work in the factory, but the last only if there are insufficient free labourers available.

9. Where the system still encounters difficulties in its practical application, freedom from land-rent shall be firmly maintained, and the people shall be considered to have discharged their obligation when they have brought the product to maturity; the harvesting and finishing shall then be the subject of separate agreements.

The system was introduced under favourable circumstances, for the Java War had brought much new territory under Dutch rule. Van den Bosch began with indigo and sugar. The Residents held conferences of heads of *desas* and elders and explained the system. Contracts were made with Chinese and Europeans to receive the produce for delivery to the government at fixed prices. The experiment was a success, and accordingly van den Bosch added coffee, tea, tobacco, pepper, cinnamon, cotton and cochineal to the list of products to be cultivated for the government. There was opposition to the scheme from the highest to the lowest, but the enormous cost of the Belgian war provided an unanswerable argument for its continuance. In 1832, therefore, van den Bosch was invested with dictatorial powers, and his system became 'the lifebelt on which the Netherlands kept afloat'. This unfortunately changed its character; it had come into being as an expedient for saving Java from bankruptcy. It now became one for saving Holland, and, in time, for enriching her at Java's expense.

From 1832 onwards the element of compulsion was increased. Each Residency must deliver export produce to the value of two guilders a head of its population. From January 1833 all coffee produced in addition to the government quota must be sold to the government at a fixed price. This was in direct contravention of the original promise that after the cultivator had satisfied the requirement to cultivate an agreed government product on one-fifth of his land he was free to do what he liked with the rest and could dispose of its produce how he liked. Moreover, although van den Bosch's third principle laid down that the cultivation of government products must not entail more labour than the cultivation of rice, in practice, since the cultures were in several cases new to the Javanese, they cost him more time and trouble than rice cultivation, and in any case the cultivation of coffee, sugar and indigo demanded more labour than rice.

The government in its need for money turned a blind eye to such things as these; in fact all the safeguards provided in the original scheme were thrown overboard. The European and native officials who superintended the system received a percentage of the products of their districts; hence they were anxious to raise the proceeds as high as possible and used means forbidden by government decrees and promises to the people. For instance, often more than one-fifth of the acreage of a *desa* was set apart for government cultures, and the best land was chosen for the purpose. Worse still, the cultivator must cultivate government land before starting on his own. Food production therefore diminished because the Javanese had insufficient time to cultivate their own *sawahs*. For although van den Bosch laid down that a maximum of sixty-six days a year was necessary for labour on land set apart for government cultures, at least ninety days were required by coffee cultivation; and since the *hierendiensten* (forced labour) remained in force for the upkeep of roads and bridges, in some districts the cultivator had to work more than 200 days a year for the government. During the years 1848–50 there was widespread famine in central Java for this reason. Stapel suggests that the worst abuse lay in the fact that, in spite of the clear prohibition contained in the fourth and ninth principles, land-rent was collected almost without exception.

The financial results of the new system right from the start fulfilled expectations to the utmost. As early as 1833 a profit of 3 million guilders was paid to the Netherlands. It came to be known as the *batig saldo*, the surplus, and it has been estimated that in all the home country's exchequer benefited to the extent of some 900 million guilders. It was used for the repayment of the national debt and the construction of the Dutch railways. The Culture System also revived the fortunes of the Nederlandsche Handelmaatschappij, which obtained the sole right to ship the government products to Holland. The Government of the Netherlands Indies shared in this prosperity, for under an arrangement known as the 'Consignment System' a portion of its proceeds had to be made over to the treasury at Batavia.

'The Culture System', writes Furnivall,[1] 'was succeeded by a Liberal reaction, and the writers of this school depicted it in its darkest colours; since then it has never been critically re-examined.' This fact has been too often overlooked by Dutch historians. 'The Indies gained nothing; but the consequences were prejudicial,' seems to reflect the general view. It is about as true as the statement that George III lost the American colonies. The population of Java increased under the Culture System from 6 millions to $9\frac{1}{2}$ millions. The rice export figures show that its cultivation must have increased. There was a rise in the revenue from salt and bazaar dues, and a large increase in the import of cotton textiles. The introduction of many new export crops, and the experimentation carried out by the Department of Agriculture, especially in tea cultivation, was of undoubted benefit to Java.

One must beware of generalizations. In some areas, notably East Java, where the officials paid as much attention to rice as to sugar, there was prosperity. In others, where they attended only to the cultivation of export crops and neglected rice, there was famine. There were good officials who thought in terms of the welfare of the people; unfortunately there were too many who allowed their commission on export crops, or their good repute with the government to dominate their outlook. From the point of view of Indonesia as a whole, during the period of the full application of the system, roughly from 1830 to 1860, two very serious charges may be levelled at Dutch rule. The Outer Possessions were neglected: the Dutch concentrated on Java more than ever, and in the middle of the century showed little concern for the other islands. They also failed to tackle systematically the vast problem of piracy.

It was the series of rice famines between 1843 and 1848 that first brought people up against the fact that something was seriously

[1] *Netherlands India*, p. 135.

wrong. The trouble began in Cheribon, a rice-growing area, which under the Culture System was forced to produce coffee, sugar, indigo, tea and cinnamon. In 1843 rice was included among the export crops, and the tax on rice-land was collected in kind. This caused a serious famine and a large exodus of people. Other areas in central Java experienced even worse conditions in the succession of famines which followed. These caused an agitation against the system which little by little grew in intensity. Governor-General Rochussen was forced to reduce the cultures in the affected areas and did his utmost to see that van den Bosch's original instruction, that due attention should be paid to rice cultivation, was carried out.

But of far greater effect in the long run was the fundamental constitutional change that took place in Holland in 1848 under the influence of the revolutionary movements which shook all Europe during that year. A constitutional revision took away from the king the sole responsibility for the colonies and vested it in the States-General. This enabled the growing opposition to come to a head under the leadership of Baron van Hoëvell in the Second Chamber. Liberal opinion was that the system had been out of date by 1840. There was a long road to be travelled yet before it was finally abolished, and, some would say, before anything really effective was done to mitigate its evils. But the chorus of voices demanding that the interests of the native peoples should be the first care of the government was rising; and notwithstanding a succession of reactionary governments at The Hague, the Colonial Opposition began to work out a constructive Liberal policy. This was in due course to sweep away a system which, as the antithesis of private enterprise, the Liberal panacea, was to their way of thinking 'rooted in unrighteousness'.

CHAPTER 31

THE BRITISH FORWARD MOVEMENT IN MALAYA AND BORNEO

THOSE people who had agitated for the transfer of the responsibility for the Straits Settlements from the India Office to the Colonial Office must have been disappointed at the immediate results of the change, for during the term of the first Colonial Office governor, Sir Harry Ord, from 1867 to 1873, the policy of non-intervention was maintained even more rigidly than before. Ord himself was the unwilling instrument of the home government in this matter and complained later that he had been unduly hampered in his dealings with the Malay rulers. For he was a helpless spectator of the growing disorder and disintegration to which most of the Malay states were a prey, and was only too well aware of the strong feeling among the mercantile communities in the Straits Settlements that the interior of the Peninsula was rich in natural resources and, given peace and order, was capable of far greater trade than then existed.

Besides the internecine feuds among the Malay chiefs themselves, there was the growing problem of the mass invasion of Chinese miners in the tin areas from the middle of the century. Mining camps with thousands of miners had sprung up at Larut in Perak, Kuala Lumpur and Klang in Selangor, and Sungei Ujong in the Negri Sembilan, the loose confederation of nine Minangkabau states. Larut had been governed from 1850 by a chief, Long Ja'far, who had persuaded thousands of Chinese to come to the tin mines there. They were divided between two great hostile societies, the Ghi Hins and the Hai Sans, and under his son Ngah Ibrahim's rule their faction fights had become intolerable. Moreover, there was serious danger of Penang becoming involved, since the headquarters of both societies were there, and it was through Penang that they imported arms and supplies. Piracy became rampant on the Perak coast, and there were clan fights in the streets of Penang itself. To make matters worse, the sultan died in 1871 and a quarrel broke out regarding the succession. And when Sir Harry Ord, in the hope of securing a cessation of the hostilities, suggested summoning a meeting of the chiefs to settle the matter they refused to come, and he was powerless to interfere further.

The normal state of Selangor has been described by Sir Frank Swettenham as one of 'robbery, battle and murder'. In Ord's time a bloodthirsty struggle was in progress between Raja Mahdi, a member of the ruling family, and the sultan's progressive son-in-law, a brother of the Sultan of Kedah, whom he had created viceroy. In 1871 an act of piracy by Chinese from Kuala Selangor against a junk trading under British colours brought the intervention of H.M.S. *Rinaldo*. Other Malay states joined in the faction fight, and the disorder became so serious that the tin supplies of the Malacca and Singapore merchants were threatened. Again Ord's attempt to negotiate a settlement failed. When the Singapore Chamber of Commerce complained about the impossibility of trading in the Peninsula, the Secretary of State instructed him to tell them that no interference was possible except to suppress piracy or repel aggression against British persons or territory.

In 1873 he received a petition from 248 Chinese, who included every leading Chinese merchant in the Straits Settlements, asking for protection for their legitimate trade, and in reporting the matter to Lord Kimberley, the Secretary of State for the Colonies in the Gladstone administration, he used almost their exact words: 'In fact the present state of affairs in the Malay Peninsula is . . . that the richest part of it is in the hands of the lawless and turbulent and, with the exception of Johore, it is only in those states dependent in a certain degree on Siam that order is preserved.'

In 1863 Britain began what has been called a 'serious diplomatic battle'[1] with the Dutch concerning their alleged violations of the treaty of 1824 by extending their possessions in Sumatra. The Singapore Chamber of Commerce had complained that in bringing under control certain east-coast ports which were open to British trade the Dutch had told the rajas that the engagements entered into by their predecessors were no longer in force. In the course of the exchanges it transpired that the Dutch were willing to meet the British demands in return for a free hand to deal with Acheh, whose piracies had caused trouble to both sides for half a century.

The matter became all the more important to the Dutch when they learnt that in 1869 the Sultan of Acheh had unsuccessfully applied to Turkey for help against them. In that year, also, with the opening of the Suez Canal the position of Acheh at the northern tip of Sumatra became of far greater strategic importance than ever before. In 1871 a bargain was struck by which, in return for the cession of the Dutch

[1] Rupert Emerson, *Malaysia*, p. 380.

possessions on the Gold Coast in West Africa, the Dutch were given a free hand in Sumatra, on the understanding that the British trade in the Archipelago was to be treated on exactly the same basis as Dutch.

The Sumatra Treaty, as it was called, was signed on 2 November 1871 and inaugurated a new forward movement by the Dutch in Indonesia. In 1873 they began a long war of conquest in Acheh. In September of the same year Lord Kimberley inaugurated a change of policy in Malayan affairs which involved the open abandonment of non-intervention. In his instructions to Ord's successor as Governor of the Straits Settlements, General Sir Andrew Clarke, he told him to use his influence with the native princes to rescue 'their fertile and productive countries from the ruin that must befall them if the present disorders continue unchecked'. The change was not in any way due to the adoption of a forward policy by the Dutch, though it coincided so closely with it in point of time. It was due entirely to local conditions. But, as Rupert Emerson puts it,[1] both the Dutch and the British advances to establish greater control in their respective spheres of interest 'were symptomatic of the new imperialist spirit which was beginning to be felt at the time', and was likewise manifest in the renewal of the French advance in Indo-China at exactly the same time.

A further paragraph in Sir Andrew Clarke's instructions contained a definite suggestion regarding a line of approach to the problem. After requesting him to ascertain the actual condition of affairs in each state and report on possible steps to be taken to restore order and protect trade, Lord Kimberley went on: 'I should wish you especially to consider whether it would be advisable to appoint a British Officer to reside in any of the States. Such an appointment could, of course, only be made with the full consent of the Native Government, and the expenses connected with it would have to be defrayed by the Government of the Straits Settlements.' A request for a British officer to teach him how to rule the country had already been made to Sir Harry Ord by Abdullah, one of the claimants to the sultanate of Perak. He was induced to repeat it to Sir Andrew Clarke. It was in Perak, therefore, that the first steps were taken.

Clarke was a man of action; he did not send in proposals and wait for instructions. His first enquiries showed that the problem of the Chinese immigrants was more than the Malay rulers could tackle. Accordingly he sent his officer in charge of Chinese affairs, W. A.

[1] *Op. cit.*, p. 112.

Pickering, to Penang to persuade the heads of the warring Larut factions to accept his arbitration. When they agreed, he called a joint meeting of Perak chiefs to be held on the island of Pangkor, off the mouth of the Perak river, in January 1874. There he proceeded to recognize Abdullah, the legitimate claimant, as sultan, notwithstanding the fact that he commanded little support in the country, and to negotiate the famous Pangkor Engagement by which he accepted a British Resident.

This important document, which ushered in the new order, provided for British intervention to protect Perak and assist its rulers. Two clauses established the basic principles of the Residential system. Clause 6 laid down 'that the Sultan receive and provide a suitable residence for a British Officer, to be called Resident, who shall be accredited to his Court, and whose advice must be asked and acted upon in all questions other than those touching Malay religion and custom'. Clause 10 provided 'That the collection and control of all revenues and the general administration of the Country be regulated under the advice of these Residents'.

The heads of the Chinese factions were also present at the meeting and signed a bond undertaking, under a heavy penalty, to disarm completely and keep the peace. The Mantri of Larut, who had been appointed by Abdullah, with the subsequent approval of Sir Harry Ord, was confirmed in his appointment and provided with an Assistant Resident. Having acted, Sir Andrew Clarke reported his proceedings to Lord Carnarvon, the new Secretary of State for the Colonies in Disraeli's recently formed administration. Needless to say, he had gone a considerable distance beyond anything envisaged by Lord Kimberley in starting the ball rolling. But the arrangements set down on paper had yet to become established in practice.

Selangor was next dealt with. The 'immediate excuse', says Sir Richard Winstedt, 'was a particularly atrocious piracy at Kuala Langat against a Malacca boat, resulting in the murder of eight British subjects by pirates in the employment of a son of the sultan'. In February 1874 Sir Charles Shadwell, the Admiral of the China Fleet, was invited to join Sir Andrew Clarke in a naval demonstration, as a result of which the sultan consented to the trial of the accused men, though attempting to dismiss the affair as 'boys' play', and to receive a Resident. In this case Clarke's first action was to leave young Frank Swettenham as informal adviser. There was no formal agreement like the Pangkor Engagement, but Swettenham's tact and understanding so won the heart of the sultan that he wrote to the governor: 'I should be very glad if my friend would set my country to right and collect all its taxes'. An official Resident, J. G. Davidson, was therefore appointed with Swettenham as his Assistant Resident.

The third state to come into the new system was Sungei Ujong, the most important member of the Minangkabau Negri Sembilan confederation lying behind Malacca. Illegal tax-gatherers were pestering Chinese miners on the Linggi river, and in April 1874 Clarke intervened and persuaded the Chiefs of Sungei Ujong and Linggi to sign a bond to abandon the practice and keep the peace in return for British protection. The Dato Klana Putra of Sungei Ujong thereupon asked for a British officer, and Captain Tatham was appointed Assistant Resident in his state. Civil war resulted, since the Dato' Bandar, who had drawn his revenues from oppressing the Chinese miners, naturally objected to the new arrangement. A small British force, therefore, had to be sent to deal with the trouble, and after some guerrilla skirmishing the region was brought under control.

In the following year firm action had also to be taken in Perak, where on 2 November J. W. W. Birch, its first Resident, was murdered. Sir Andrew Clarke had left Singapore in the previous May to become a member of the Governor-General's Council in India. His successor, Sir William Jervois, was anxious to move somewhat faster in dealing with the old privileges and rights of the chiefs, which were the main obstacle to any improvement in the condition of the people, and Birch, when he should have shown tact and caution, had proceeded to ride roughshod over them in his zeal for cleaning up what from the point of view of a European administrator was an Augean stable of abuses.

He travelled all over the state with boundless energy enquiring into cases of oppression, particularly the institution of debtor-slavery, which was intrinsically bad in any case, but in Perak was exploited in such a way by Abdullah and his chiefs as to be a foul and intolerable evil. The measures he took against it and for the proper collection of taxes led to a conspiracy on the part of the offended chiefs to get rid of him. But lest it should be thought that Birch's own attitude and actions were the cause of his undoing, it must be clearly stated that the conspiracy was rather against the Pangkor Engagement itself than against the agent chosen to carry it out. The chiefs who entered the Engagement, it has been well said,[1] either did not fully realize what was involved or, if they did, had no serious intention of honouring the contract.

[1] The Lieutenant-Governor of Penang, quoted by Emerson, op. cit., p. 125.

The rising was suppressed by a strong expedition which hunted down the murderers and their abettors. For a time there was danger of a general Malay rising and it took several years to restore law and order. Three chiefs were hanged; three others, including Sultan Abdullah himself, were banished. Governor Jervois, who had advocated annexation, or, failing that, the conversion of the Residents into Queen's Commissioners, governing the states in the name of the sultans, was censured by Lord Carnavon for giving the Residents powers greater than the Colonial Office had sanctioned. The result was an acrimonious struggle between the governor and the Secretary of State over the functions of Residents. The governor's position was that the system was unworkable if Residents were to be mere advisers; and although Lord Carnavon refused to alter his theory concerning the fundamental principles of indirect rule, in practice the Residents became more and more the actual rulers in their states.

In 1878, when a Resident was held to have exceeded his powers in a particular case, the governor laid down the rule that if a Resident disregarded the principle by which he was an adviser only and exercised the functions of a ruler he would be held responsible for any trouble arising therefrom. This was approved by the Secretary of State, and there the matter ended so far as the home government was concerned. For after the Perak War there was no further trouble. The Malays gave in, the rebellious chiefs had been removed, and the Residents were able to go ahead with the task of reconstruction under much more favourable conditions.

In Selangor the new system got under way without any difficulty, since the viceroy and Davidson were old friends. A government treasury was set up with a proper system of accounts, a police force was organized, and the Kapitan China loyally maintained order in the mining community of the Kuala Lumpur area. In Sungei Ujong the Dato' Klana seems to have been only too anxious to do everything according to British methods. Moreover, the introduction of British administration brought prosperity such as had not been known previously. The abolition of slavery and of the many vexatious imposts that had fettered trade, the maintenance of order by a reliable police force, and the substitution of fixed allowances for the sultans and other chiefs in place of arbitrary exactions, not to mention the beginnings of education and the introduction of modern public health measures, did much to improve the lot of the ordinary people.

Perak after so disastrous a beginning was transformed into a peaceful and flourishing state by Mr. (later Sir) Hugh Low, whose methods during his long tenure of the Residency (1877-89) provided the model for the administration of all the other protected states. 'How much of his policy was original,' writes Winstedt,[1] 'how much was due to the governor and how much to Downing Street has not yet been explored.' His method was never to dictate but to gain the co-operation of the chiefs by establishing close friendly relations with them.[2] The difficulties which he had to face on taking office were immense, since although the rebellious chiefs had been removed there were others who could stimulate quite effective passive resistance. Moreover, he himself was a stranger to Malaya when he went to Perak. His previous service had been in Borneo.

One original cause of trouble had been the loss by the chiefs of their feudal dues without compensation. Low sought to remedy this injustice by giving them adminstrative posts and a percentage of the government revenue collected in their districts. Another measure which greatly improved relations was the establishment of a State Council on the model of the Indian councils created by the Act of 1861. The sultan was its president; the Resident, the major Malay chiefs and two or three leading Chinese businessmen were members. The business was conducted in Malay, and the Council discussed all important matters. Its work was mainly legislative and it passed all the state legislation. The annual estimates of revenue and expenditure were laid before it. All death sentences had to be referred to it for confirmation or modification. The appointments and salaries of all Malay chiefs and headmen were subject to its decision. It served its purpose so well that similar councils with identical procedure were instituted in other states.

The greatest innovation was the institution of courts of justice presided over by European magistrates, often with the assistance of Malay magistrates. The Penal Code of the Straits, which was adapted from the Indian Penal Code, was administered, together with codes of criminal and civil procedure drafted according to Indian and colonial patterns. Each state was divided into districts under European and Malay magistrates. The districts in turn were subdivided into *Mukim* and villages with Malay headmen. As a measure of economy police duties were given to headmen. This enabled the police force to be reduced and many village police stations to be closed. It signified the abandonment of a policy of intimidation for one of co-operation.

---

[1] *Malaya and its History*, p. 69.
[2] Swettenham makes the following penetrating comment on Low's methods: 'To gain their co-operation it is necessary to show them at least as much consideration as if they were Europeans, and infinitely more patience' (*op. cit.*, p. 253).

Debtor slavery was still the great evil when Low became Resident; it was not abolished until 1 January 1884. In the other states it was more easily got rid of. The establishment of the state finances on a satisfactory basis also presented great difficulties. The state was saddled with a debt of £160,000 in 1877. Low's achievement in paying this off in six years was a notable one. The rapid increase of Perak's population was a further tribute to his work. The official estimate was 80,000 in 1879 and 195,000 in 1889. The census in 1891 showed a population of 214,254.

In Larut Captain Speedy had practically a free hand. There were almost no Malays in the neighbourhood, hence, although he consulted the Mantri, who was the local chief, in every matter of importance, he made his own decisions and acted accordingly. His measures included the creation of a police force, the establishment of a magistrate's court, a treasury, a customs service and a Land and Survey Office. Larut prospered; the Chinese were only too glad to settle down to work, and the community was unaffected by the disturbances which shook the rest of Perak. In 1884 the first railway to be built in Malaya connected Taipeng, the Larut mining centre, with Sa-petang on the Larut river, a distance of eight miles. Incidentally Selangor immediately followed it up, constructing one from its mining centre, Kuala Lumpur, to Klang, a matter of twenty-two miles.

As all the protected states depended upon their tin mines for a revenue, everything possible had to be done to provide them with means of transport. Pending adequate provision of roads, use was made of many navigable streams by clearing them of the accumulation of forest trees which had fallen across them in the course of the ages. But every possible effort was put into road construction and all surplus revenue devoted to it.

Until practically the end of the century the economic development of the Peninsula was almost exclusively in Chinese hands. Their capitalists did much to develop the protected states. Tin-mining was their chief occupation, and their primitive methods were most effective. The lack of labourers was a great difficulty and led to negotiations with the Government of India for the recruitment of Indian coolies. In 1884 agreement was reached which permitted recruitment for the protected states. Efforts were made to induce European miners and planters to open up the country, but at first these met with little response. A French company began to mine tin in the Kinta district of Perak in 1882, and later extended its operations elsewhere. Other European companies followed, but the great obstacle to European enterprise in these early years before federation seems to have been the inadequacy of the labour supply.

The earliest Residents spent most of their time touring the country and from time to time reporting to the Governor of the Straits Settlements. They built up the administration of their states with little interference from above and with merely routine references to the governor. At first the Resident was quite alone. Then he recruited a clerk or two, an N.C.O. in charge of his police, a Eurasian apothecary for the first hospital to be established, and a Malay warder to look after prisoners. So writes Swettenham, who was closely associated with the evolution of the Residential system from its inception.[1] Owing to lack of communications it was very difficult for Singapore to control and co-ordinate the work of its servants in the three states. From 1876 to 1882 the governor had a Secretary for Malay Affairs who periodically visited the states to audit accounts and to secure uniformity of method, but after 1882 there was no one in the Singapore secretariat with enough personal knowledge of the Malay states for this procedure to be continued.

During the first ten years of the system Residents kept daily journals as a method of supplying information to the governor, but as their work increased no time was left for continuing the practice. Their annual budgets had to be regularly submitted for the approval of the governor. Besides furnishing this and his annual report, says Swettenham, 'the correspondence of the Resident with Singapore was mainly occupied with the appointment, promotions, salaries, and complaints of Government officers'. There was only one way for a governor who was interested in the Malay states to exercise any influence over their administration, and that was by visiting them and studying conditions on the spot. Until 1903, when the main trunk railway line came into operation with its terminus in Province Wellesley, the difficulties of correspondence between the states and Singapore, as well as with each other, forced each Resident largely to follow his own line. Sir Frederick Weld (1878–87), who spent much time travelling in the states, came to the conclusion that the large authority the Residents had gradually acquired could be safely left in their hands. There was to come a time, however, when the lack of co-ordination resulting from the abolition of the Secretaryship for Native Affairs was to bring such differences between states as to lead to federation.

In 1888 the number of protected states was augmented by the addition of Pahang, a very large but underdeveloped state with a

[1] *British Malaya*, pp. 245–71.

population of only 50,000 Malays and a few hundred Chinese. Mis-government was so rife there that in 1887 Weld had persuaded the sultan to make a treaty under which he received a British consular agent. In the following year, however, the murder of a Chinese British subject led to further pressure from Singapore, as a result of which the sultan, very unwillingly, requested the appointment of a Resident. The application of the new system caused some of the chiefs to rebel and resulted in long and expensive operations which ended only with their being hunted out into the Siamese states of Kelantan and Trengganu, where the survivors were captured and deported to Siam. Young Hugh Clifford, who later rose to positions of great distinction and produced valuable studies of the work and experiences of the pioneers who opened up Malaya and Indo-China, took a prominent part in these operations.

Similar pressure to that brought to bear on Pahang was exerted in the case of the Minangkabau states, with the result that by a treaty made in August 1895 all nine agreed to form the confederation of Negri Sembilan under British protection, and to follow the advice of a British Resident in all matters of administration save those touching the Mahommedan religion. This new turn of policy came largely as the result of a careful review of the Residential system made by Sir Frederick Weld in 1880. The alternatives, he said, were to retire or to annex. The former was out of the question, since immigration and the investment of foreign capital were taking place in the confidence that British control would remain. Annexation he was opposed to on the grounds that a colonial system of government was inappropriate to the states in their existing condition. Hence he recommended the extension of the Residential system to further states and the open recognition of the real functions of Residents.

Weld made it clear that annexation was not the proper solution of the problems of Malaya. But it was Swettenham who made it equally clear that the Residential system could not be left to develop indefinitely without co-ordination. In 1893 he submitted a scheme for federation to Governor Sir Cecil Clementi Smith. This went up to the Colonial Office, with the result that Smith's successor, Sir Charles Mitchell, was asked to report on the proposals. After two years' consideration Mitchell in 1895 recommended that, subject to the approval of the Malay rulers concerned, the scheme should be adopted.

He argued that the four protected states were drifting seriously apart in matters of justice, taxation and land settlement, and that in the absence of some centralizing power administrative uniformity was impossible. A governor, he pointed out, dealing with four separate Residents either left them to their own devices or was overwhelmed with work. He therefore recommended that a Resident-General should be appointed as chief executive officer to supervise the administration of the states, but to act only through the individual Residents; that while legislation should be left in the hands of the State Councils there should be occasional meetings of an assembly of chiefs and Residents with a competence entirely advisory. Instead of appointing officers to separate states there should be a common civil service acting under the departmental heads of the federal government. Each state, however, should remain financially autonomous.

Frank Swettenham, then Resident of Perak, had the task of persuading the rulers to accept the plan and was instructed by the Secretary of State to explain that in so doing they would in no way diminish their own powers and privileges, nor curtail the rights of self-government which they enjoyed. On this 'fictitious basis', as it has been described, Swettenham easily performed his task, and the Treaty of Federation was concluded whereby Perak, Selangor, Pahang and Negri Sembilan were united to form the Federated Malay States. Its glaring inconsistencies from the point of view of constitutional theory are obvious. There was no differentiation between the respective powers of the states and of the Federation as in the normal federative enactment. It provided against the curtailment of the powers of the ruler but placed a Resident-General in control of 'matters of administration other than those touching the Muhammedan religion', though the actual word 'control' is carefully omitted. It expressly stated that the new arrangement did not alter the existing relations between the individual states and the British empire, but in fact they were made into an administrative union.

But notwithstanding the discrepancies between theory and fact the sultans were satisfied. They retained their offices with added guarantees, larger incomes and enhanced pomp and ceremony. And the British built up at Kuala Lumpur a large and efficient central administration, in the approved modern style, in which the sultans had little or no say. Yet against the claims of the rapidly increasing Chinese population the theory that they were Malay states under sovereign Malay rulers was a most convenient device for refusing to take action likely to be resented by the Malays.

Sir Frank Swettenham became the first Resident-General when the Federation was inaugurated on 1 July 1896. His administration soon blossomed out with a Legal Adviser, a Secretary for Chinese Affairs, a Financial Commissioner, a Judicial Commissioner, a Commissioner of Police and a Director of Public Works. As time went on other departments were added. The Resident-General himself, though subordinated to both the Governor of the Straits Settlements in his function as High Commissioner of the Federation and the Secretary of State for the Colonies, managed in practice to maintain great freedom of action. And since the treaty placed no limits on his competence, save in the matter of the Mahommedan religion, the real substance of legislative power was in his hands.

The first of the promised conferences of Malay rulers was held at Kuala Kangsar, in Perak, in 1897. Never before in Malay history had such an assembly met, and as the proceedings were in Malay the Malay members took a full share in the debates. A number of important subjects for legislation came up for discussion, and as they were unanimously agreed to, they were passed on to the State Councils for legislative enactment in identical terms. Thus Kuala Lumpur became the legislative as well as the administrative centre, and the position of the State Councils, which had been so vital a feature of the old Residency system, necessarily deteriorated before the inevitable growth of centralization.

The second conference of Malay rulers, held at Kuala Lumpur in 1903, brought up the question of Malay participation in the government, and the Sultan of Perak regretted that no way had been found of handing over to Malays any considerable portion of the administration. He also made a dignified and fair-minded protest against overcentralization which drew attention to the growing need for reforms in the federal structure. The departmentalization of the government and the urge for uniformity could have only one result, the tightening of central control. For the Judicial Commissioner framed the procedure of the state courts, the Financial Commissioner reorganized the whole financial system, the Public Works Departments in all the states were fused into one under the Director at Kuala Lumpur, railway construction came under the Federal Director of Railways, forest conservation was systematized under the central Forest Department, and agriculture and education under federal directors.

The increase in efficiency was marked and the records of prosperity impressive. The population of the four states rose from 424,218 in 1891 to 678,595 in 1901. The revenue increased from just under 8½ million dollars in 1895 to just under 24 million dollars in 1905 and there was an appreciable surplus of revenue over expenditure. In 1874 the states did not boast of a single post office. In 1904 their postal services dealt with 10 million covers, issued money orders for more than 1¼ million dollars, had in their savings banks deposits of 275,000 dollars, and maintained over 2,000 miles of telegraph wires. There were hospitals treating many thousands of patients and schools attended by 13,000 children. There were over 2,400 miles of good roads and 340 miles of railway built out of current revenue. 'It may be questioned', wrote Sir Frank Swettenham with justifiable pride, 'whether it is possible to find, in the history of British administration overseas, a parallel to this record.'[1]

But the opponents of centralization argued that British pledges to the sultans had been ignored and that there was a tendency to forget that the powers exercised by the government were derived entirely from their gift. There was an uncomfortable feeling that the Resident-General was not under any effective control. And, moreover, the rapid increase of the commercial, mining and planting communities had led to a desire on their part to obtain representation in the government. Hence in 1909 an Agreement for the Constitution of a Federal Council was laid before the rulers and accepted by them.

The new body was to be under the presidency of the High Commissioner. Its membership comprised the Resident-General and the four Residents, the four sultans and four unofficial members to be nominated by the High Commissioner with the approval of the king. The High Commissioner was also empowered, if he thought it desirable, to add to the Council one or more heads of departments, but if he made an official addition in this way he must add another unofficial member. The Council was given the task of dealing with the draft estimates of revenue and expenditure of each state. It was a legislative body, but its legislative powers are referred to only incidentally and indirectly in the document. There is a statement in the preamble about the proper enactment of all laws intended to have force throughout the Federation, or in more than one state, and the provision in the body of the document that laws passed by the State Councils were to continue to have full force and effect, save where repugnant to laws passed by the Federal Council. The exclusive jurisdiction of the State Councils over questions concerning the Mahommedan religion and certain matters involving Malay customs was confirmed, with the addition of the words 'and any other questions which in the opinion of the High Commissioner affect the rights and

[1] *Op. cit.*, p. 301.

prerogatives of any of the above-named Rulers or which for other reasons he considers should properly be dealt with only by the State Councils'.

There has been much comment on the legal inconsistencies of the document, about the propriety of the governor of a Crown Colony acting as president of a council controlling the affairs of a federation of protected states under their own rulers, and about the fact that the nominated members of the Council were to be appointed subject to the approval of the Crown and not of the rulers of the states. But the practical effect of the measure was further to decrease the importance of the sultans and of the State Councils. On the Federal Council the sultans were reduced to the same level as any ordinary member. They could not preside over it; they had no veto; the Council legislated whether they were present or not, and the bills passed were signed by the High Commissioner and not by them. As for the State Councils, their new position has been summarized thus: 'The Federal Council apportioned the combined revenue of the four states as it saw fit and later informed the State Councils of its decisions. The legislative function of State Councils ended, since all laws of any importance were henceforth passed by the Federal Council.'[1]

The High Commissioner, Sir John Anderson, who introduced these changes, which had an effect so different from what he had intended, followed them up by changing the title of the Resident-General to Chief Secretary, hoping thereby to reduce the independence of the holder of the post. But this measure also misfired. Of the four non-officials there were three British and one Chinese. In 1913 the Legal Adviser and a further unofficial member were added and in 1920 the Treasurer and another official member. Ultimately before the reform of the Council in 1927 there were eight non-official members: five Europeans, two Chinese, and a Malay chief.

The main factor which was instrumental in producing the change in the position of the Malay rulers was the economic revolution which during the first twenty years of the twentieth century brought Malaya right into the forefront of world commercial development, and her states face to face with conditions that their rulers with their mediaeval outlook were unable to grasp. Malaria control, agricultural chemistry, modern educational policy, the world price of tin and rubber, and suchlike questions became the main concern of the government, and they could no longer be dealt with by the old method of a Resident using his persuasive powers upon sultans and chiefs. Everywhere

[1] L. A. Mills, *British Rule in Eastern Asia*, p. 50.

throughout the world it was an era of greater, rather than less, centralization.

During the last ten years of the nineteenth century tin mining was beginning to pass from the primitive form of open-cast extraction to that of large-scale excavation by modern Western machinery. The world demand for tin became so great and the price so high that a vast amount of foreign capital, mainly British and Chinese, was invested in the industry, and a huge immigration of labour, mainly from China, was stimulated. Malaya's exports, which had risen to 26,000 tons in 1889, were 51,733 tons in 1904 and just under 70,000 tons in 1929. By the beginning of the century Malaya's output of tin was over 50 per cent of the total world output.

Her tin industry, however, was now rivalled by rubber, the production of which was stimulated by the invention of the motor-car using rubber tyres and the universal popularity of the bicycle. Rubber had been introduced to Malaya as early as 1877, when the Royal Botanic Gardens at Kew had sent two cases of seedlings to the Botanic Gardens at Singapore for experimental purposes. But although government nurseries were established and seedlings offered to planters little headway was made, and by 1897 only 345 acres were under rubber. By 1905 the acreage under rubber had risen to 50,000, and 200 tons were exported. That was a mere drop in the ocean compared with the 62,145 tons of jungle rubber produced elsewhere in the world. Then came a period of rapid development, stimulated by Brazilian speculators, who forced up the price so that immense profits were made by existing plantations, and there was a rush to float new rubber companies in London. That was during the great boom of 1910–12. Land was easily available, and by 1914 the Malayan plantation could deliver rubber in New York at a price lower than that of jungle rubber from South America.

In 1920 Malaya exported 196,000 tons of rubber, or 53 per cent of total world production. In the plantations the need for labour was met by the recruitment of thousands of immigrant coolies—Indian in this case. In the newly developed areas the Malay was in a minority. His country was dominated by British and Chinese entrepreneurs, capitalists and businessmen. Its labour force was composed mainly of Chinese and Indians, who were ultimately to form a majority of the population, while the bulk of the Malays remained small rice farmers growing in addition some rubber and coconuts as cash crops. The racial character of the Peninsula had been changed within one generation, and the Malays, unable to adapt themselves to the sudden change, found themselves both politically and economically 'pushed out of their own house on to the doorstep'.[1]

The greater part of the tin mines and rubber plantations were in the four federated states. In 1913 their total exports had risen to the value of 154,974,195 Straits dollars and their government revenues to 44,332,711. In the general rush of development and the consequent increase of prosperity political issues dropped into the background. Not until after the First World War did the old issues concerning centralization, bureaucracy and the position of the Malay sultans return again to the forefront.

Against this background it is significant that when in 1909 the four northern states of Kedah, Perlis, Kelantan and Trengganu came under British control, under the terms of the Anglo-Siamese Treaty of that year, their rulers all refused to join the Federation. Actually, in taking them over Britain confined her power to the right to advise, thereby conferring on them a large degree of internal independence. They enjoyed privileges—notably that of financial autonomy—that contrasted strongly with the subjection to Kuala Lumpur that was the lot of the federated states.

Johore also would have no part in a federation. Ever since the foundation of Singapore in 1819 it had been closely associated with the British. Not until 1914 did it have a General Adviser, but in 1895 its sultan, Abubakar, gave it a written constitution that was drafted by British lawyers. This, with its one amendment introduced in 1914, became the pattern of what in Malay opinion should have been the constitution of all protected states. In its original form it had a Council of Ministers, all of whom must be Malays professing the faith of Islam, and a Council of State, membership of which was limited to Johore subjects irrespective of race or religion. In 1914 membership was thrown open, and British officials could sit on it without taking the oath of allegiance to the sultan. The Council of Ministers was a purely consultative body; the Council of State enjoyed the functions of a legislative council. In 1912 a third body, an Executive Council, was added. It was modelled on the executive councils in British colonial administration.

All the Unfederated States had Advisers whose functions were different from those of Residents. The Adviser had the right to be consulted by the ruler on all questions, but did not issue any orders. He could insist that the ruler should follow his advice, but usually

[1] L. A. Mills and Associates, *The New World of Southeast Asia*, Minneapolis and London, 1949, p. 177.

made an effort to persuade him to accept his view and used his power as little as possible, even giving way if the matter were not one of prime importance.

There were thus up to the Second World War three types of constitution in Malaya:

The Straits Settlements, a British Colony, comprising Singapore Island, Penang and Province Wellesley, and the territory of Malacca, including Naning:

The Federated Malay States of Perak, Selangor, Negri Sembilan and Pahang and:

The Unfederated Malay States of Kedah, Perlis, Kelantan, Trengganu and Johore.

The second Raja Brooke, Charles Johnson, who succeeded his uncle in 1868, was the younger brother of Captain James Brooke Brooke, who had originally been designated heir apparent, but was subsequently disinherited for insubordination. He inherited a principality stretching from Cape Datu on the Sambas border in the south to Cape Kidurong just north of the mouth of the River Bintulu in the north. This was much larger than the original territory created by the sultan of Brunei. In 1853 the Rajang basin had been acquired, and in 1861 the land between the Rajang and the Bintulu, the sultan being compensated for loss of territory by a payment of 4,500 Straits dollars annually. The expansion had been dictated by economic considerations. The additional territories produced most of the sago exported from Kuching to Singapore, and the local Brunei chiefs, by oppressing the native traders handling the commodity, were threatening a trade of vital importance to Sarawak's prosperity. Charles Brooke in 1868 asked for a further hundred miles of coastline. The sultan objected, and had the support of the British Foreign Office, which saw itself as the protector of Brunei against the 'restless aspirations' of Sarawak.

But it soon appeared that foreign competition was likely to be more dangerous than Brooke to the integrity of Brunei. Already in 1865 the sultan had leased most of North Borneo to an American speculator, who had sold his rights to the 'American Trading Company of Borneo'. But the small trading settlement planted by the latter on Kimanis Bay had soon petered out. Then, in the early eighteen-seventies, there was an Italian plan to establish a penal colony in Gaya Bay, but this also came to nothing. The situation was next complicated by the decision of the Spanish government of the Philippines finally to crush the power of its old enemy the sultan of Sulu. In 1873 Spain began the blockade of the Sulu ports in preparation for their conquest. The trade of Sulu was mainly in the hands of British and German firms in Singapore, and their respective home governments began to threaten joint action to restore freedom of trade. Their threats combined with the success of enterprising blockade-runners, ultimately forced Madrid in 1877 to grant free access to the Sulu Archipelago. In the following year the sultan was forced to capitulate, and Spanish sovereignty was proclaimed over all his dominions. This involved Borneo, since the sultans of Sulu were hereditary suzerains of the whole of the north-east coast of Borneo from Bulungan to Maruda Bay, and of the north-west coast as far south as Pandasan. Spain therefore now claimed suzerainty over an enormous area of northern Borneo.

In the meantime, however, a Labuan Trading Company had received the permission of the sultan of Sulu to establish a depot at Sandikan on the north-east coast with the object of smuggling arms, opium, tobacco and other things into Sulu. Thereupon a certain Joseph Torrey, representing the now-no-longer-operating American Trading Company had laid claims to the area, thereby arousing the interest of Baron von Overbeck, the Austro-Hungarian consul at Hong Kong. He, having failed to interest his own government in Vienna in the commercial prospects of north Borneo, proceeded to purchase Torrey's rights and went into partnership with Alfred Dent, a son of his previous employer in Hong Kong. In December 1877 the two of them obtained from the sultan and the pangeran temenggong of Brunei the cession of all the territory between Kimanis Bay on the north-west coast and the Sebuku River on the east coast. In return the sultan was to receive 12,000 Straits dollars annually and the temenggong 3,000. The sultan, be it noted, was actually giving away territory over which he did not exercise any effective authority whatever, and, indeed, as von Overbeck soon discovered, not only was the whole of the north-east coast claimed by the sultan of Sulu, but his was the only authority recognized by the local chiefs. Hence it is not surprising that within a matter of weeks (22 January 1878) the enterprising baron had negotiated a further agreement with the sultan of Sulu whereby, in return for an annual payment of 5,000 Straits dollars, he received the cession of all the lands between the Sebuku and Pandasan rivers, and recognition as 'supreme and independent ruler' over them. He and his partner Dent thus acquired ownership of some 30,000 square miles of territory with about 850 miles of coastline. They began immediately to establish administrative posts at various places, and to search for the requisite capital to go ahead with their enterprise. Von Overbeck failed a second time to gain the support of the Austrian government, and finally sold out his share to Dent, who with his associates in London floated a 'British North Borneo Provisional Association Limited', and sought official recognition of the British Government for their undertaking.

They certainly needed it. Spain, the Dutch and the raja of Sarawak all regarded with concern their intrusion into Bornean affairs. In September 1878 a Spanish warship arrived off their new settlement at Sandakan and announced to the resident, W. B. Pryor, that in accordance with the Spanish treaty of the previous July with the sultan of Sulu the whole of north-east Borneo, from Maruda Bay to the Dutch border, belonged to Spain. Pryor, however, presented a determined front to both arguments and threats, and eventually the Spaniards sailed away to leave the respective home governments to argue the matter out. The dispute was finally settled by a protocol of 7 March 1885 in which Spain abandoned all territorial claims in Borneo in return for the recognition by Britain and Germany of her sovereignty over the whole Sulu Archipelago. Incidentally, in August 1899 this passed into the possession of the United States of America.

Exactly twelve months after the Sandakan incident the Dutch made their first move. A Dutch gunboat appeared at Batu Tinagat, forty miles within the new company's territory from the Sebuku River. At the time Pryer could do nothing, but later he managed to lodge a protest with a visiting Dutch commander. The Dutch government at The Hague then took upon itself to warn London that anything of the nature of a British protectorate over the area would be contrary to the spirit of the treaty of 1824; whereat London at once replied—quite correctly —that the treaty had never applied to Borneo. It soon appeared, however, that Dutch opposition to Dent's enterprise was much weaker than it had been to Raja Brooke's. The Dutch Liberals, who were in power, were aware that by accepting the British treaty of 1847 with Brunei the Netherlands was in no position to oppose this new extension of British influence. When, therefore, Dent's association, which had powerful backing in Britain, managed to persuade the British Government to grant it a royal charter (1 November 1881), the Netherlands Government, as Graham Irwin puts it, 'accepted the *fait accompli*'.[1] It had been shown the document some months earlier, but all its objections had been summarily rejected.

Dutch concern now came to centre upon their frontier in eastern Borneo. In 1884 an agreement was reached for the establishment of a

---

[1] *Op. cit.*, p. 205.

joint frontier commission. It began its work in July 1889, and an Anglo-Dutch frontier convention was signed in 1891. The line, however, could not be drawn in detail because of the complete ignorance of both sides about the geography of the interior. Not until 1912 was the work completed by an Anglo-Dutch survey team. These dates form an intriguing commentary upon the urgency of the matter.

Raja Brooke II's opposition to the cessions of territory was, unlike the Dutch, well based. He claimed that they were contrary to the treaty of 1847 with Brunei, which had forbidden the sultan to cede territory to 'any other nation or the subjects or citizens thereof without the consent of her Britannic Majesty'. Von Overbeck, he pointed out, was a foreign subject, and the cessions were made without the British Government's knowledge. But the British Government refused to withdraw its support from Dent's proposals. In its view the real danger was lest another foreign power—Spain, Germany or the Netherlands—might annex North Borneo; and Gladstone, who assumed office in 1880 while the discussions were in progress, believed that under the circumstances, with the cession of the territories already a *fait accompli*, the grant of a royal charter would be the only means of ensuring that the Government could exercise a restraining influence over the company. The charter itself, indeed, imposed a number of restrictions upon the company's freedom of action. For instance, it might not alienate its territories without the consent of the British Government, and its relations with foreign governments were to be subject to the British Government's control. Moreover, it was under obligation to abolish slavery in its dominions, preserve native religion and custom, and administer justice with due regard to native law.

The British North Borneo Company, as is well known, was the first of a new series of chartered companies created during the eighteen-eighties for the commercial exploitation of vast tracts of territory, mainly in Africa. The grant of the charter made it impossible for the British Government any longer to maintain its ban on Sarawak's acquisition of more territory. Hence, in 1882 Raja Charles Brooke obtained the cession of the large area forming the basin of the Baram River. The Brunei sultanate was now so weak that intense rivalry grew up between Sarawak and the North Borneo Company for control over the rest of its territories. And with the French under Jules Ferry's leadership pushing ahead in Tongking, and the Germans acquiring the Caroline Islands and north-eastern New Guinea, there was the further fear that the distracted state of Brunei might tempt the interference of the one or the other. So in 1886 the decision was taken to extend

British protection to North Borneo and Sarawak, and in 1888 protectorate agreements were negotiated with them and with the sultan of Brunei. It was a guarantee of stability and security which all welcomed, the sultan not least, since he could now put up a more effective resistance to the greedy concession-hunting of which he had been the unwilling victim.

CHAPTER 32

THE DUTCH FORWARD MOVEMENT IN INDONESIA

UNDER Article 59 of the Dutch constitutional revision of 1848, while the king was recognized as the supreme authority over the colonies the stipulation was added that a colonial constitution must be established by law, and that the chambers of the Dutch Parliament were to have specific rights of legislation over colonial currency and finance and such other matters as might be necessary. Article 60 laid down that the king must report annually on colonial affairs. These important changes in the relationship between the mother country and the colonies had at first very little effect upon conditions in the Indies. The Colonial Department was in the grip of officials with a conservative outlook, and the chambers for some time had too little knowledge of colonial affairs to exert any effective influence. But the *Regerings-reglement*, or Constitutional Regulation, which was passed in 1854 and came into effect in 1856, made one significant change in the colonial government by entrusting the chief power in the Indies to the governor-general and Council. This abolished the rule introduced in 1836, whereby the Council had been reduced to the position of a mere advisory body. Moreover, the Regulation looked forward to the ultimate abandonment of the Culture System and showed clearly that state cultivation was no longer to be fostered by the government. The governor-general was instructed to see that the cultures did not interfere with the production of adequate means of subsistence, and that the oppression connected with them was removed.

Still, the movement for reform moved incredibly slowly. Baron van Hoëvell, a past president of the Batavia Society of Arts and Sciences and the founder of the newspaper *Tijdschrift van Nederlandsch Indië*, who had stoutly opposed corruption in giving contracts in Java, was a member of the Second Chamber from 1849 to 1862. There he not only championed the cause of the Javanese people but helped to form what came to be known as the 'Colonial Opposition'. But for a long time the Conservatives dominated the home government and there was painfully little progress in actual reform.

In 1860 the struggle against the Culture System received new life as a result of two publications. One was a novel, *Max Havelaar*, written by Edward Douwes Dekker under the pseudonym of 'Multatuli'. In it Dekker tells the story of his career as an insubordinate official in West Java who had been dismissed, according to his account, for defending the Javanese against the oppression practised against them under the Culture System. Quite apart from its propaganda value, it is a work of high literary value, one of the most striking contributions to Dutch prose literature in the nineteenth century. It stirred up wide support for the Liberal campaign against government control over cultures in Java. Its effect was enhanced by the pamphlets of Isaac Fransen van der Putte, and especially one entitled *The Regulation of Sugar Contracts in Java*. He had been employed by a sugar factory dealing with the product of cultures and had afterwards, as a tobacco planter in the extreme east of Java, become acquainted with free cultivation. He showed in his writings so intimate a knowledge of conditions there that in 1863 the Liberal leader Thorbecke appointed him Minister of Colonies in his Cabinet.

During van der Putte's term of office (1863–6) things began to move in the direction of free enterprise, the Liberal specific to end economic oppression. His own view was that direct taxation should take the place of deliveries under forced culture, and that private enterprise should have free access to land and labour. What he and his supporters did not advocate was the abolition of the infamous *batig saldo*. Moreover, the cultures that were abolished during this period—pepper in 1862, cloves and nutmeg in 1863, indigo, tea, cinnamon and cochineal in 1865, and tobacco in 1866—were no longer profitable. The forced culture of sugar and coffee, the chief source of Dutch profits, was retained. Some serious abuses, however, were removed. The percentage system, for instance, whereby European officials received commission on the proceeds of the forced cultures, was abolished, and it was forbidden for more than one-fifth of the cultivator's land to be used for government crops. A big step forward was made by the passage of the *Comptabiliteitswet* (Accounts Law) of 1864, which provided that from 1867 onwards the budget for the Indies must be passed annually by the home parliament. Another useful measure was the abolition in 1865 of compulsory labour in the forest districts.

De Waal's Sugar Law of 1870 represents the culminating point of the struggle against the Culture System. It provided that the government was to withdraw from sugar cultivation in twelve annual stages beginning in 1878, and permitted the free sale of sugar in Java. Again one notes the exceptional caution shown by the Dutch in this matter, and the striking fact that coffee, which brought by far the greatest profit from the system, remained a forced culture until 1 January 1917. The same almost incredible slowness was shown in the case of the various profitable monopolies which inflicted so much hardship on the people. The revenue from the sale of these in the eighteen-forties was over 15 million guilders. A beginning was made by Governor-General van Twist (1851–6) by the abolition of the much-detested farming of bazaars, and fishery auctions. But the opium and pawn-shop farms, which were the most profitable, continued. By 1927 the gross revenue from the monopolies of opium, salt and pawnshops amounted to no less than 82.6 million guilders. It is obvious, therefore, that Dutch Liberalism differed very considerably from its contemporary Gladstonian Liberalism in Britain.

The Dutch outlook, in fact, in the matter of colonies was completely different from the British. Even the Liberals regarded them as a business concern, and their advocacy of private enterprise in place of government-controlled cultures was largely inspired by the desire of the individual Dutchman to have a greater share in the concern. More and more privately owned or run estates were coming into existence, and the private capitalists were demanding the removal of all restrictions to their activities. Van Twist, who was anxious to open up Java to private capital, allowed them to make collective contracts with the villages for labour. But the practice gave rise to such abuses, through advances of money to village headmen, that it had to be abolished in 1863. The truth was that the Liberals had two largely contradictory objects—to free the native from oppression and to make the Indies safe for the individual capitalist.

De Waal's Agrarian Law of 1870 ushered in the great age of private enterprise. It aimed at giving greater freedom and security to private enterprise by enabling capitalists to obtain from the government heritable leases for periods up to seventy-five years, and to hire land from native owners on short-term agreements subject to certain conditions. This opened the door for an immense expansion of private enterprise, and the export figures for plantation products are illuminating, as the following table shows:

COMPARATIVE VALUE OF STATE AND PRIVATE EXPORTS IN MILLIONS
OF GUILDERS[1]

	State	Private
1856	64.4	34.3
1870	46.5	61.2
1875	41.4	130.7
1885	16.3	168.7

Even more important by comparison with what happened in French
Indo-China and British Burma was the clause which prohibited the
selling of land belonging to Indonesians to non-Indonesians. The
immediate reason was that there was such a rush on the part of
Europeans to cultivate culture products for the home market that
there was a danger that land needed for the production of food stuffs
for the native population would be used for other purposes.

In 1869 the Suez Canal was opened. The development of large-
scale cultivation combined with the increasing use of steamships to
produce a constant expansion of trade. It was in this period that the
Netherlands Steam Navigation Company (1870) and the Rotterdam
Lloyd (1875) were founded.

The development of Java between 1830 and 1870 is in striking contrast to the neglect of the Outer Possessions that characterizes the
same period. The Java War followed by the struggle with Belgium
prevented an energetic policy from being carried out. It was only with
the greatest difficulty that General Cochius was able to muster
adequate strength to bring the Padri wars to an end in 1837 with the
siege and capture of Bondjol. Then the home government sent instructions that in the future there was to be as little interference as
possible with the powers of the native chiefs outside Java. The native
populations were thus left the victims of despotic or quarrelsome
chiefs, who lost respect for a government which failed to intervene.

Worse still from the Dutch point of view were the activities of Raja
James Brooke in Sarawak and Brunei and the acquisition of the island
of Labuan by Britain. Governor-General Rochussen (1845–51) feared
lest this might open the door for other powers to occupy parts of the
Archipelago. He proposed, therefore, that Dutch power should be
effectively established over the whole of Indonesia. For financial
reasons alone the home government could not permit so ambitious a

[1] Taken from Furnivall, *Netherlands India*, p. 169.

scheme. It was willing to sanction a display of military powers where the circumstances warranted it, but the Batavian authorities pointed out that punitive expeditions were useless unless followed up by continuous occupation.

Nevertheless the establishment of British power in north-west Borneo did stir the Dutch to adopt a more energetic policy. The age of steam led to a search for coalfields, with rewarding results. Mines were opened in south-west Borneo near Banjermasin and in the east of the island at Kutei, and when the working of the Banjermasin mine led to a quarrel with the sultan and a war (1859–63) his dominions were annexed. The Dutch were taking no chances in that region. In 1854 and 1855 they intervened to stop the disorders in the sultanates of Sambas and Pontianak caused by the feuds between the Chinese gold-mining kongsis. Moreover, the discovery of rich tin deposits in the island of Billiton led to its occupation in 1851 and the exploitation of its tin by the Billiton Tin Company.

Elsewhere there was enough activity to make it clear that the Dutch were becoming more and more aware of the need to maintain a dominant position in the Archipelago, if only to prevent outside interference. They were worried by the proud, independent attitude of the rulers of Bali, whose internecine war and slave trade went on unchecked. Dutch expeditions to the island in 1846 and 1849 encountered fierce resistance. In consequence of the latter they annexed some territory, and the chiefs of the remainder made formal recognition of Holland's suzerainty. The Bugis rulers in Celebes also gave much trouble, and there was heavy fighting in 1858 and 1859 against Boni before Dutch authority was made more or less dominant over the south-west parts of the island, mainly through the loyalty of the dynasty of the Aru Palaccas. But more trouble was to come later.

It was on Sumatra, however, that Dutch attention came to be chiefly focused as time went by. Piracy and the slave-trade were rife in Acheh, Palembang, Bencoolen and the Lampongs. From 1856 onwards the Dutch began a series of moves designed to bring more and more of the island under control. In that year the Lampongs districts were subdued. Two years later the Batak districts received similar treatment, and in 1868 Bencoolen. Palembang had been brought under direct Dutch rule in 1825, but like Bencoolen had become a prey to disorder. So Dutch control had to be tightened there. Siak gave the Dutch a severe shock in 1856 when its sultan, at loggerheads with his brother, the vice-sultan, called in the help of an Englishman named Wilson, who enlisted a force of Bugis in Singapore, defeated the vice-sultan and took control over the state. The Dutch had to send a warship to enforce his expulsion. Then in 1858 they made a treaty with the sultan whereby his state and its dependencies—Deli, Serdang, Langkat and Assahan—came under their sovereignty. The acquisition of this territory to the north of Siak was an immense step forward for Dutch power on the east coast of Sumatra. Soon European enterprise was to make a start there with tobacco-planting, which was to make that region one of the richest districts in the Netherlands Indies.

But the Siak Treaty brought strained relations with Acheh, which claimed the state as one of its dependencies. The weak spot there was that Acheh was not strong enough to control effectively the places over which she made such claims, though they had at one time recognized her overlordship. The way in which the Dutch enforced their control over these places affected adversely the trade that had long been carried on by the merchants of Singapore and Malacca, and their loud complaints forced the British government to take action. Its protest at The Hague led to the negotiations which produced the epoch-making treaty of 1871, dealt with in the previous chapter. With its signature a new period of Dutch expansion in Indonesia begins. It was happily one in which, with the passage of van der Putte's Tariff Law abolishing differential rates of customs duties between Dutch and foreign trade, better relations grew up between Holland and Britain.

Acheh, the sworn enemy of the Portuguese in the sixteenth century, had become under Sultan Iskander early in the seventeenth century a powerful state ruling much of Sumatra. After his death the kingdom declined. In the nineteenth century it was divided into several states under practically independent chiefs. The sultan's capital was at the present town of Kutaraja; his main revenues came from port dues. The Treaty of London (1824) had given the Dutch the task of safeguarding the seas around Acheh against piracy, but they argued with cogency that as the Achinese were the chief pirates there they could not carry out their task satisfactorily without occupying the principal ports of the country. Under the treaty they could not do so because they had undertaken to respect the sovereignty of the state. The number of piratical attacks on shipping—off Sumatra's west coast in particular—was legion, and British, Dutch, American and Italian ships were plundered.

Matters came to a head through the attempts of the sultan to obtain foreign aid against the Dutch. His application to the Porte failed because Turkey at the time needed European help against the threat of Russia. After the treaty of 1871 the Government of Batavia made an attempt to settle matters with Acheh by negotiation. The sultan sent an embassy for talks with the Dutch Resident on the island of Riau. On its return journey the mission stopped at Singapore, where the envoys entered into secret discussions with the American and Italian consuls. The Italian consul turned down their proposals, but the American consul-general, Mr. Studer, drafted with the envoys the preliminaries of a commercial treaty. The Dutch consul-general sent to Batavia what later turned out to be a false report that Studer had asked for warships to be despatched to the Sumatran coast to protect American interests. This led to a sharp passage of arms between The Hague and the American Secretary of State. It led also to a final attempt on the part of Batavia to obtain an agreement with the sultan, and, when the latter's attitude proved uncompromising, to a declaration of war.

The war proved to be one of the longest and toughest in Dutch colonial history. It also attracted more public interest in Holland than any previous colonial struggle. It began in April 1873 with the despatch of a small Dutch expeditionary force, which was too weak for its task and had to withdraw. In December of the same year a larger one under General van Swieten landed in Acheh and in a few weeks captured the sultan's kraton. When, shortly afterwards, he died operations were suspended in the hope that his successor would sign a treaty accepting Dutch sovereignty subject to a guarantee of his autonomy in internal affairs. Instead, however, the Dutch found themselves faced by a general revolt, in which the local chiefs and the religious leaders everywhere took the lead. Guerrilla fighting became the order of the day, and the Dutch found themselves faced by a seemingly insoluble problem. When they won a few successes and tried to negotiate, the fighting would break out afresh. Their troops were decimated by cholera, and the hands of their commanders were tied by orders from above to limit military operations as far as possible.

Between 1878 and 1881 General Karel van der Heyden forced so many chiefs to submit that Batavia jumped to the conclusion that the resistance was broken. It began, therefore, to set up civil government. The decision was a disastrous one; the fighting flared up again with all its old vigour, and the religious leaders proclaimed a holy war against the infidel.

The Dutch had once again to pour into the country a very large force and undertake immensely costly operations. As a measure of economy it was decided to concentrate the forces in a strong defensive position, and a line of strong-points connected by a railway was established, stretching across from the east to the west coast in the form of a ring covering Kutaraja. The system was completed in March 1885 and the Dutch troops were withdrawn behind it, not without suffering severe casualties. But the hope that this would enable the Dutch to negotiate from strength a plan for the restoration of the sultanate proved vain, since the chiefs looked upon the new defensive system as a sign of weakness.

Meanwhile the years were slipping by and Dutch policy changed with each new governor of Kutaraja. Governor Demmeni tried pacification by lifting the naval blockade of the coastal regions; but this only made matters worse. His successor, van Teijn (1886-91), reversed this policy and coerced many of the chiefs into submission. Pompe van Meerdervoort, who next held office for a few months (1891-2), reverted to the policy of leniency; the Achinese response, however, convinced Batavia that only by force could a solution be achieved. But how could force be employed with effect?

Colonel Deykerhoff, who took office in January 1892, believed that the best method was to win over a powerful chief and provide him with the supplies necessary to enable him to conquer the recalcitrant. In 1893 Tuku Uma, a chief who had submitted, was taken into the pay of the government and allowed to form a well-armed legion of 250 men. His operations were successful, and the Dutch forces occupied the reconquered districts and established a new line. Then suddenly in March 1896 he with his legion went over to the enemy.

The Dutch now realized that nothing short of an all-out effort of conquest would suffice. Two books of a very different size and nature, which achieved a wide circulation at this time, helped to put an end to hesitancy. The first, *De Atjehers*, written by the famous Arabic scholar Dr. Snouck Hurgronje, appeared in 1893. It was in the form of a report put together by him as a result of a visit to Acheh in 1891-2. Quite apart from its influence upon the conflict through its advocacy of strong measures, the book has immense intrinsic value as a description of native customs and institutions. It is a classical work of cultural anthropology.

The other book was a brochure written by Major Joannes Benedictus van Heutsz, who had been van Teijn's chief of staff. In it he explained the methods which he advocated for the complete conquest of the country, without using more troops than were already in occupation of the 'concentrated system'.

But before a forward move could be made the damage caused by Tuku Uma's treachery had to be repaired. The whole populace, both within and without the *Geconcentreerde Linie*, as it was called, had gone over to his side. General Vetter, who took command in April 1896, commenced a series of large-scale operations with a greatly augmented army which by March of the following year gave him control over the area terrorized by Tuku Uma and forced the latter to flee to Daya on the west coast. Van Heutsz played a distinguished part in these operations, and it was finally decided to put him in charge of the whole campaign. In March 1898 he was appointed Governor of Acheh, with Snouck Hurgronje as his adviser for native affairs.

Heutsz completely revolutionized the morale of the Dutch troops. His first operations resulted in the conquest of the district of Pidië, the very heart of the rebellion, where the claimant to the sultanate, Tuku Uma, and Panglima Polem, another leader, had joined forces. By the beginning of 1899 the Dutch dominated Acheh proper and the rebellious chiefs were being chased into the outer territories of the Gayo and Alas lands. Early in the year Tuku Uma, a fugitive since the conquest of Pidië, was ambushed on the west coast and killed. During that year and the following one all resistance was crushed and large-scale operations were abandoned. Lightly armed flying columns were then organized alike for the maintenance of internal peace and the harassing of the chiefs who still held out. Repeated expeditions of this sort had to be sent to the Gayo lands, where the claimant to the sultanate had taken refuge. In January 1903 he made his submission, and at about the same time the great Panglima Polem surrendered.

The final operations were then handed over by van Heutsz to Lieutenant-Colonel van Daalen. In June 1904, when van Heutsz left Acheh to become governor-general, most of the more important chiefs had submitted, but the opposition had still not been stamped out. Insurrections—some of them serious—continued until 1908, and were only brought to an end by the exile of the claimant to the sultanate and a number of other chiefs to Amboina. Even then it was necessary to maintain military government for another ten years.

The outbreak of the war had caused something like a sensation in the Islamic world, and, followed as it was by the victories of the Mahdi of Kordofan in the Sudan, played its part in stimulating a revival of Muslim fanaticism in Africa and Arabia. Thousands of Indonesian pilgrims went to Mecca annually, and Snouck Hurgronje found a large colony of 'Djawahs' in the holy city when he visited it in 1885. Hence one essential element in the pacification of Acheh was for the Dutch to cultivate good relations with Mecca. This they did by encouraging the pilgrimages which brought such profits to the Meccans, and by appointing an Indonesian vice-consul as the representative of Batavia there.

The Dutch forward movement in the latter part of the nineteenth century did not confine itself to the task of conquering northern Sumatra, heavy though it proved to be. Notwithstanding the opposition of the home authorities to any expansion of territory there, much was done to open up the Outer Possessions. Governor-General Lansberge (1875–81) gave much attention to the Moluccas and the Lesser Sunda Islands, where piracy, wrecking and the slave trade were still rife. Much also was done to consolidate the Dutch hold on the rest of Sumatra outside the Acheh territories. They were constantly apprehensive of attempts by foreign powers to establish settlements in their preserves, and kept an eagle eye on the small islands fringing Sumatra. In the interior, to the south of Lake Toba, the work of the Rhenish Missionary Society in converting the Battak region of Silindung caused strife with the Padri sect, and in 1878 Si Singa Mangaraja, a local chieftain who threatened the Christians, was driven out by the Dutch and a new Residency, Tapanuli, formed.

Bali, which had taught the Dutch expensive lessons on the subject of interference with its independence, caused Batavia much heart-burning from time to time owing to its cruel oppression of the Sasaks of Lombok, who were Mahommedans. A general rebellion broke out in 1891, and after fruitless attempts at mediation a Dutch expedition in 1894 established control over Lombok. This marked the final abandonment of the policy of non-intervention. Van Heutsz in 1898 had introduced a new system in Acheh, known as the 'Short Declaration', whereby a chief who recognized the authority of Batavia was confirmed in his rule. In the period up to 1911 this was used so extensively that some 300 self-governing states came under Dutch control. It was during this period that the remainder of Bali was brought to heel.

The extension of Dutch rule in these territories resulted in an immense amount of survey and development work. The Topographical Service laid out roads and mapped previously uncharted regions. Experts carried out researches into the manner of life, the customs and religion of the various peoples, as well as into the nature of the soil and of the vegetable and animal life. The expeditions of A. W. Nieuwenhuis to the interior of Borneo (1893–8) and the researches of the Swiss scholars Paul and Fritz Sarasin in Celebes (1893–1903), under the auspices of the Royal Netherlands Geographical Society, opened the way for trade and industry and made valuable contributions to knowledge.

From 1870 onwards the economic development of the Netherlands Indies was impressive. Much land previously cultivated for the state was handed over to private planters; there was a rush to produce sugar, and many new factories were built. Tobacco-growing also expanded rapidly. Coffee held its own, and copra, palm-oil, fibres, pepper, cassava, kapok, tea and cocoa provided important exports to world markets. Save for the sugar factories there was little large-scale industry. The most important native industries to survive the competition of European manufactured goods were pottery, spinning, and weaving.

Construction on the first railways—from Semarang to Surakarta and from Batavia to Buitenzorg—was begun in the 'sixties, but the two lines were not completed until 1873. The planters everywhere clamoured for railways, and in 1875 a state railway to open up the sugar area from Surabaya to Malang was begun. At about the same time the strategic line in Acheh was constructed. In 1883 the prosperous Deli Tobacco Company began to build a railway on the east coast of Sumatra, and in 1887 a state railway was constructed between the Ombilin coalfield and Padang. Between 1890 and 1900 much greater progress was made and the total length rose from 1,600 to 3,500 kilometres.

The first inland telegraph service was opened in 1856, and the inland postal service commenced operations in 1866. In the next period the greatest progress was made with the development of telephonic communications. The first telephone company was founded in 1882, to be followed in the next few years by no less than thirty-four more. The state thereupon intervened in 1898 and took over the whole service.

The opening of the Suez Canal and the freeing of the sugar trade wrought a revolution in the Dutch shipping trade. The Dutch sailing ships had to face the competition of steamships, mostly flying the English flag. Even the Netherlands-Indies Steamship Company was linked up with the British-India Steam Navigation Company and all its repair work executed at Singapore. The Dutch therefore had to set about building an entirely new fleet; and although the Nederland Steamship Company was founded in 1870, it had for many years to buy its steamers from abroad and engage foreigners to run them.

Until 1891, when the last contract of the Netherlands-Indies Company expired, it enjoyed a practical monopoly of the inter-island traffic. Then the contract was transferred to the Koninklijk Paketvaart Maatschappij, which had been founded in 1888.

The growth of steamship traffic called for a vast improvement in harbour facilities. In 1873 a beginning was made on building a new harbour for Batavia at Tanjong Priok. This was completed in 1893. By that time similar work was going ahead at Surabaya, Macassar, Belawan, Emmahaven (for Padang) and Sabang.

In 1883 the first concession for the exploitation of petroleum was made to the Royal Netherlands Company. Oil had then been discovered in paying quantities in Sumatra, Java, and Borneo. But it was not until the next century that the great advances were made. The development of coal-mining, however, made great progress during the second half of the nineteenth century in western Sumatra, south Borneo and the Palembang area. Efforts to persuade private capital to exploit the tin that was found in great quantities in Banka, Billiton and Singkep met with little response, notwithstanding the rich profits made by the largely government-owned Billiton Company, which was founded in 1852. The Singkep Company was founded in 1889, but achieved little during its early years.

The results of all this progress, expressed in terms of imports and exports, show the export trade more than doubled in value between 1870 and 1900, and the import trade quadrupled. The total value of exports rose from 107·57 million guilders in 1870 to 258·23 million in 1900; that of imports rose from 44·45 million guilders to 176·07 million over the same period. The great feature in the expansion of imports lay in the fact that it was mainly accounted for by such goods as fertilizers, iron, steel, machinery and tools, which all tended to enhance Indonesia's productive capacity.

CHAPTER 33

THE REIGN OF BODAWPAYA AND THE FIRST
ANGLO-BURMESE WAR, 1782–1826

THE king known to history as Bodawpaya used a great variety of titles during his own reign. The one which came to be most commonly applied was Mintayagyi Paya, 'Lord of the Great Law'. He was the third son of Alaungpaya and possibly the ablest statesman of his line. But Michael Symes, who was twice deputed to his Court as the representative of the Government of India, described him as 'a child in his ideas, a tyrant in his principles, and a madman in his actions'. His long reign, which lasted until 1819, had a decisive influence upon his country's history.

It began with a blood-bath, in which he made a clean sweep of all possible rivals in the royal family. But a brother who escaped the ceremonial massacre plotted with Maha Thihathura, one of Hsinbyushin's most distinguished generals, to overthrow him. This caused a second blood-bath, in which they, with every member of their families and all their servants, were done to death. Late in the same year 1782 a pretender, Nga Myat Pon, who claimed descent from the Toungoo dynasty, scaled the palace walls with 200 desperate men. He and his band were overcome and killed by the palace guard. Then the district of Paungga near Sagaing, where they had hatched their plot, was punished by the destruction of every living thing— human beings, animals, fruit trees and standing crops—save for a few people who were made pagoda slaves.

To atone for so much bloodshed the king built a new pagoda at Sagaing. He also abandoned the palace at Ava, fearing that it had come under an evil spell. A new royal city was laid out at Amarapura, about six miles north-east of Ava, and thither the Court was transferred with due ceremonial in May 1783. In the following September Mons of the Bassein province made a surprise attack on Rangoon, which they captured and held for a time, intending to revive their old monarchy. A Burmese counter-attack was successful, and the city was retaken after desperate fighting—only just in time, for it soon became obvious that a much wider movement had been nipped in the bud.

584

One of Bodawpaya's earliest acts after restoring order in his turbulent kingdom was to institute a general revenue inquest. The register that was compiled by his commissioners, after taking the evidence of myothugyis and village headmen throughout the land, has been called the Burmese Domesday Book. It provided the king with a record of his country's taxable capacity, and the first use to which he put it was for an extraordinary payment towards the repair and regilding of pagodas and monasteries of royal foundation. Not since Thalun's reign (1629–48) had such a survey been made, and, unfortunately for students of history, none of its original records survives. Bodawpaya followed up his survey of 1784 with a further one in 1803. Many of the records on palm-leaf and *parabaik*[1] thus collected are still extant and afford first-hand evidence, of a sort too rarely encountered in South-East Asia, of social and economic conditions.

Bodawpaya's next big enterprise was the conquest of Arakan. There had been no let-up in the long anarchy which had prevailed ever since the murder of Sandawizaya in 1731. Village fought against village, and everywhere dacoity was rife. From time to time refugee leaders appeared at the Court of Ava seeking help. In 1784 Bodawpaya decided that the time was ripe for annexation: the country would be an easy prey. Nevertheless he made careful preparations. In October Arakan was attacked by three land columns and a powerful flotilla of war vessels. By the end of December the conquest was complete and King Thamada a fugitive in the jungle. A month later he was captured, and in February 1785 he, his family and no less than 20,000 of his people were deported to Burma, together with the famous Mahamuni image, now in the Arakan Pagoda at Mandalay. Arakan became a province under a viceroy supported by a Burmese garrison. Its subjugation was the most far-reaching event of Bodawpaya's reign; it brought the frontier of Burma up to that of British India and ushered in a new period of Anglo-Burmese relations with immense conse quences.

Bodawpaya's easy success in faction-torn Arakan seems to have gone to his head, for before the year 1785 was out he launched a full-scale invasion of Siam. The chronicles of his reign are full of the white-elephant myth. He was publicly proclaimed as Arimittiya, the coming Buddha, and it may be that for a short time he really believed himself destined to be a world conqueror. If so, the illusion was soon rudely shattered. His grandiose plan to overwhelm Siam by four simultaneous attacks came to grief mainly through his own

---

[1] A very stout local-made paper.

incompetence as a commander. For though completely lacking in military training or experience, he personally led the main attack over the Three Pagodas Pass, and through his ignorance of even the elementary principles of logistics suffered disaster so overwhelming that he himself barely escaped capture.

Two of his attacking forces—one marching overland from Tavoy and the other going by sea to occupy the island of Junk Ceylon—aimed at cutting off the Siamese provinces in the Malay Peninsula. In expelling them the Siamese reasserted control over Patani, Kedah, Kelantan and Trengganu. It was during this campaign in 1786 that the Sultan of Kedah, hoping for British support against Siam, handed over the island of Penang to the East India Company.

The fourth Burmese force, operating in the Chiengmai region, won some initial successes, occupied Chiengsen and Chiengrai, but got no further. For many years there was backwards-and-forwards fighting throughout this area. Chiengmai was the main Burmese objective. They staged two fairly large-scale offensives—one in 1787 and the other in 1797—but both failed. Finally in 1802 the Siamese, based on Chiengmai, cleared their Laos provinces of the Burmese. But by that time the state of Chiengsen was so depopulated that it never recovered. In the south the Siamese made great efforts to regain the Tavoy and Mergui regions, but failed. Their raids into the area continued until after the British occupation of Tenasserim in 1824.

The effect of all this upon the king was to increase his religious mania. He persecuted heretics, and even decreed the death penalty for such things as drinking intoxicants, smoking opium and killing an ox or a buffalo. When the Buddhist clergy attempted to moderate some of the worst of his excesses he announced plans to reform the Order and confiscated monastic lands. He built dozens of pagodas, and at Mingun, on the west bank of the Irrawaddy some miles to the north of his capital, he began to erect an enormous pagoda which, if finished, would have been 500 feet high. For seven years thousands of Arakanese and other deportees worked on its construction under his personal supervision. His wars and his buildings made him insatiable in his demands for man-power. The drain on Upper Burma, as well as on the Mon country, was so serious that, as Harvey puts it, 'the framework of society cracked'. No proper arrangements were made for the supply of food and necessaries to his armed forces or his labour gangs. Thousands died of starvation, there was wholesale desertion, whole villages fled to the jungle to escape enrolment, and dacoity became widespread.

It was in Arakan that the most serious consequences of this extravagant and cruel policy showed themselves. There the inordinate demands for forced labour and conscript service drove the tough and unruly Arakanese into open revolt. In 1794 a general rising broke out and the rebels were assisted by armed bands from the Chittagong district, where some thousands of refugees had already settled. Against the strong reinforcements sent from Burma the rebellion collapsed, and again large numbers of refugees poured into British territory. They were closely pursued by a large Burmese force, which crossed the river Naaf and established a base on the British side of the frontier. Colonel Erskine was sent by Calcutta to deal with the incursion. The Burmese commander offered to retire peaceably if three refugee leaders were apprehended and handed over. Erskine had too small a force to take strong measures. He promised, therefore, to arrest the three wanted men; and if on investigation the charges against them were deemed to be true, to surrender them. This was done and the Burmese returned to their own territory with their prey.

This disturbing incident caused the British-Indian government to awake to the fact that the Arakan frontier constituted a serious potential danger. Sir John Shore, the governor-general, accordingly took the precautionary step of addressing a letter to the Court of Ava with a detailed analysis of the situation as it appeared to him. After waiting in vain for several months for a reply he decided that the matter was one of sufficient urgency for him to break the long diplomatic impasse that had lasted ever since the withdrawal of the Bassein factory in 1762. He feared that unless some approach were made to the Burma government the French, who were again at war with Britain, would seek to use Burmese ports as bases against British shipping in the Bay of Bengal.

This was indeed what had happened during the War of American Independence.[1] And although the French dockyard at Rangoon had had to be abandoned, Admiral de Suffren and Charles Castlenau de Bussy, who had been sent out in 1782 in a vain attempt to restore French fortunes in south India, had made a determined effort to persuade Versailles that Burma offered a more inviting field than India for an expansionist policy and was the best place from which to attack the British in India. In 1783 de Bussy had sent an envoy to conclude a commercial treaty with Burma. Nothing had actually come of these

---

[1] On this subject see Sonnerat, *Voyage aux Indes Orientales et à la Chine* (1782), vol. ii, p. 43; Henri Cordier, *Historique abrégé des rélations de la Grande Bretagne avec la Birmanie* (1894), p. 8; and Edmond Gaudart, *Catalogue des Manuscrits des Anciennes Archives de l'Inde Française*, vol. i, Pondichéry, 1690-1789'.

RECEPTION OF BRITISH ENVOY AT THE PALACE AT AMARAPURA

moves, but the French in Mauritius had used Mergui as a repair depot since its transfer from Siamese to Burmese hands.

Shore's envoy, Captain Michael Symes, who went to Burma in 1795, was charged with the task of removing the causes of misunderstanding over the Arakan frontier incident, and of persuading the Court of Ava to close its ports to French warships. In particular he was to negotiate a commercial treaty under which a Company's agent would be permitted to reside at Rangoon to supervise British trade. Symes was treated with a mixture of studied rudeness and friendly hospitality. He was given clearly to understand that it was beneath the dignity of the Court of Ava to treat on terms of equality with the representative of a mere governor-general.

He took back with him a royal letter, in which the king informed the Calcutta authorities that it was understood that in future Arakanese refugees settled in Chittagong who crossed over the border to commit crimes in Burmese territory were, on written application, to be surrendered. Permission was granted for the Company 'to depute a person to reside in Rangoon, to superintend mercantile affairs, maintain a friendly intercourse, and forward letters to the Presence'. But the king flatly refused to close his harbours to French vessels. Symes published the account of his mission in a delightful book which was the first full-scale account of Burma ever to appear in a European language.[1]

In October 1796 Captain Hiram Cox arrived in Rangoon to take up his duties as British Resident in accordance with the agreement made by Symes. Before leaving Calcutta he had had a sharp tussle with his government regarding his status. He had refused to accept the Burmese definition of it as set down in the royal letter and contended that a Resident was equal to an envoy or minister of the second class, and far above an agent or consul.[2] The Government of India, however, had told him plainly that he was not an ambassador and had specifically warned him not to attempt to procure any relaxation of ceremonial 'as practised towards Captain Symes'.

Nevertheless he went to Burma determined to uphold his own interpretation of his status, and, what was more, to refuse to repeat what he termed 'the humiliating concessions' to Court etiquette made by Symes. He thereby played into the hands of suspicious officials, who, in his own words, regarded his appointment as 'an attempt to

---

[1] *An Account of an Embassy to the Kingdom of Ava sent by the Governor-General of India in the year 1795*, London, 1800.
[2] *Bengal Political Consultations*, 2 March 1798, no. 5.

smuggle the wooden horse of Troy into their Dominions'. After a long and increasingly unhappy sojourn at Amarapura,[1] whither he had gone in a vain endeavour to persuade the Court to accord him the kind of recognition he sought, he announced his intention to leave the country, only to find on returning to Rangoon that a royal order for his arrest had been publicly proclaimed. His defiance of the local officials caused them to declare a state of emergency, and in a moment of despair he sent an urgent message to Calcutta asking for the despatch of an armed frigate to rescue him, since his life was in danger.

The Government of India on receiving this news proceeded with the utmost caution. It was convinced that his conduct had been provocative. An order was therefore sent recalling him, and he was strictly charged to avoid all unconciliatory language or anything that might lead the Court of Ava to suspect that hostile action might be taken against it. At the same time the king was requested to facilitate Cox's departure; the letter to him, though guardedly phrased, was apologetic in tone. But long before the arrival of these missives the excitement at Rangoon had died down, and by the time of Cox's departure in April 1798 his relations with the local authorities had become most friendly.

On returning to Calcutta he warned the Government of India that if the Arakan frontier question were not dealt with according to their wishes the Burmese threatened to invade Bengal, and that the king was actually planning intervention in Assam. He attributed his failure partly to the fact that he had incurred the hostility of the party at Court that was behind these schemes, since he had warned them that pursuit of such a policy would force the British to intervene.

But the chief cause of his troubles, he claimed, lay in the fact that Captain Symes had grossly misled the Government of India regarding the Burmese. 'It appeared to me that he had wandered in a maze of error from the beginning to the end of his negociation, and if some glimmerings of light occasionally reached him, that it had been quench'd by false shame, which forbid his revealing it', he wrote in a most intemperate attack upon his predecessor. Shore was only too well aware of the extent to which Cox had been personally responsible for the difficulties he had encountered, but Lord Wellesley, who had become governor-general when Cox arrived back in Calcutta, had expressed his entire satisfaction with his conduct. He felt it to be unwise, however, to court further insults by sending another Resident

---

[1] Captain Hiram Cox, *Journal of a Residence in the Burmhan Empire*, London, 1821.

to Rangoon. His attention was concentrated upon the flirtation of Tipu Sultan of Mysore with Mauritius and Paris. He fondly hoped, therefore, that a policy of inaction in regard to the Arakan frontier might prove the safest way of avoiding complications.

While the governor-general was away in Madras superintending preparations to invade Mysore trouble again flared up in Arakan. An influential Arakanese chieftain, when ordered to comply with a Burmese demand for a large contingent for service against Siam, fled to Chittagong. His flight started another mass exodus. Once more a Burmese pursuit force crossed the frontier and stockaded itself on British territory. The magistrate at Chittagong attempted negotiations, but they broke down. Next he sent a small force of sepoys to attack the Burmese position, but they were repulsed. Then suddenly the Burmese decamped and returned to their side of the border. Wellesley, with his hands full in India, sent Captain Thomas Hill to parley with the Burmese Viceroy of Arakan at Mrohaung. That was in June 1799. Meanwhile the plight of the refugees was so desperate that Captain Hiram Cox was deputed to Chittagong to superintend relief measures and settle the immigrants in the neighbourhood of the Bagholi river, where land was available for cultivation. Cox's Bazar, named after him, remains today a memorial of his labours, and of his death while engaged upon them.

Hill found that the viceroy would consider no other settlement of the problem than the total expulsion of the immigrants from British territory. When he broke off negotiations the viceroy sent a delegate to Calcutta in March 1800 to present the demand to the governor-general. Wellesley in reply pointed out the impossibility of carrying out the request, but promised to close the frontier to all further immigrants from Burmese territory. He was playing for time; for although Tipu Sultan had been disposed of in the shambles of Seringapatam, his attention was now absorbed by the growing anarchy in the Maratha dominions. He began, however, to contemplate a further embassy to the Golden Feet, and commissioned Major William Francklin, an orientalist of some repute, to study the Burma files and suggest a new method of approach to the Court of Ava.

Francklin's report, submitted in July 1801, advised that the discontented Arakanese leaders likely to disturb the peace of the frontier should be removed to the interior of Bengal, and that an offer of subsidiary alliance should be made to Burma by an ambassador provided with an escort of such magnificence as would demonstrate to the Court of Ava the full dignity and power of the Government of India.

Wellesley, however, pigeon-holed the report and seems to have deliberately returned to the policy of procrastination.

He had reckoned without the Burmese. In January 1802, while he was on a visit to Cawnpore, a letter was forwarded to him from the Viceroy of Arakan demanding in the king's name the expulsion of all the Arakanese from Chittagong, and threatening armed invasion should the demand be rejected. Wellesley at once ordered the frontier guards to be strongly reinforced, and called on Symes, who had just returned from a long furlough in England and was in Cawnpore with his regiment, to undertake a second mission to Amarapura. Why he chose Symes in preference to Francklin the records do not say. Why he chose Symes at all, after the strictures passed upon his first mission by Hiram Cox, is a matter for surmise. All that is known is that after a personal interview he announced the appointment of Symes with the intriguing remark that his 'abilities, personal experience, and complete knowledge of the affairs of the Government of Ava' qualified him 'in a peculiar degree' for the task with which he was charged. Events were to show that he could not have made a more appropriate choice.

Symes arrived in Burma at the end of May 1802 with the embarrassingly large escort suggested by Francklin, and a draft treaty of subsidiary alliance in his portfolio. His immediate task was to seek some clarification of the Arakan viceroy's threat to invade Bengal, and to give the Court of Ava an opportunity to disclaim responsibility for it. He was also to explain why the Government of India could not agree to the demand for the total expulsion of the refugees. Regarding the subsidiary alliance proposal, a special set of additional instructions of a highly confidential nature informed him that there was reason to believe that King Bodawpaya seriously contemplated abdication, and that in such an event the Toungoo Prince might be expected to attempt to deprive his brother, the heir-apparent, of the succession. He was therefore to offer military support to the heir-apparent against such a contingency. On this last point it may be remarked here that Symes's enquiries showed that the rumour of the king's intended abdication was baseless, and he was far too discreet to pursue the line laid down in his instructions.

On arrival at the capital he was kept for a matter of months waiting for recognition. He learnt that the king had only with difficulty been persuaded from sending him ignominiously back to Calcutta. His instructions permitted him to wind up his mission and leave the country should his further stay there appear to be useless. But he decided that such action would render war inevitable, and that the utmost patience and forbearance must be his best weapons. It turned out that before paying any attention to him the king proposed to stage the pantomime of receiving a bogus French mission, specially rigged up for the occasion. Symes's dignified restraint, however, won him the support of the heir-apparent and the most influential people at Court, and their advice ultimately prevailed. The French 'mission' was received without ceremony and hastily dismissed. Then Symes was accorded a full-dress reception, at which the king departed from the usual procedure by making a short speech. He paid Symes a personal compliment and remarked that, having seen his face again, he would 'forget every cause of umbrage'.

Symes returned to Calcutta with an official letter, the contents of which he summed up thus: 'The King was displeased at the conduct of Capt. Cox . . . but he is now pleased to be reconciled.' It contained no reference to the Viceroy of Arakan's threat of war: that matter was disposed of by a 'verbal communication' made to Symes in the king's name assuring him that the viceroy had not been instructed to demand the fugitives in such terms as he had used, and renouncing for ever the claim for their wholesale expulsion. Symes's advice to his government was that 'a paramount influence in the government and administration of Ava, obtain it how we may, is now become indispensably necessary to the interest and security of the British possessions in the East'.

The king's letter permitted the re-establishment of a British Resident at Rangoon, and Lieutenant John Canning, who had accompanied Symes to Ava, was deputed to go there in that capacity. But so as to avoid involving the Government of India, should things go wrong, he was sent as Symes's private agent and not as an official delegate of the East India Company. He arrived at the end of May 1803. The Viceroy of Hanthawaddy, who had been a good friend to Symes, had been recalled to the capital, and his deputy made things so difficult for Canning that in the following November the latter returned to Calcutta.

The expedient of maintaining a Resident in Rangoon was thereupon abandoned as useless. The Arakan frontier, however, remained at peace for some years. The firmer control exercised by the British authorities was mainly responsible for this. Moreover, the Burmese kept their word: there were no further demands or threats. The Burma question receded into the background. The evidence of both Symes and Canning showed that French influence and activities there were negligible. In 1809, when Lord Minto instituted a blockade of Mauritius and Bourbon before proceeding to conquer them, Canning was again deputed to Burma, this time to reassure the Court of Ava regarding British policy. He was received with the greatest cordiality. He discovered that for some years there had been a complete cessation of relations between the islands and Burmese ports. From the signs of depopulation and misery that he saw on his way to and from the capital he came to the conclusion that Burmese power was in rapid decline. Nevertheless he warned his government that King Bodawpaya cherished as one of his aims the ultimate conquest of Chittagong and eastern Bengal.

Had the Calcutta authorities but paid serious attention to his warning much trouble might have been saved. But the Arakan frontier region was one of dense jungle intersected by innumerable creeks, and a breeding-place for the most malignant forms of malaria. Hence at an early date the additional forces stationed there in 1802 were withdrawn and the policy of neglect resumed. After years of deceptive calm the inevitable nemesis came in 1811. A new leader, Chin Byan,[1] scion of an important myothugyi family of northern Arakan, secretly collected a powerful force on British territory and made a surprise attack on Mrohaung, which he captured. From the ancient capital he sent an urgent appeal for help to Calcutta, offering in return to hold the kingdom under British suzerainty.

The Government of India flatly refused his offer and in September 1811 sent Captain Canning once more to Burma, this time to assure the Court of Ava that the British authorities had in no way instigated or aided the rising. Canning was confronted by the Burmese with evidence which they considered proof positive of British aid to the rebels. It certainly pointed to serious negligence on the part of the local officers at Chittagong. To make matters worse, while Canning was at Amarapura assuring the ministers that effective measures would be taken to prevent any further movement of refugees across the frontier the Burmese forces in Arakan proceeded to crush the rebellion, and Chin Byan, with a large body of his followers, escaped back into British territory with the greatest ease.

Once more Burmese pursuit parties crossed the frontier, and the Viceroy of Arakan threatened to invade Chittagong with a force of 80,000 men if the fugitives were not handed over, together with Dr. McRae, the civil surgeon at Chittagong, whom he accused of aiding Chin Byan to make his original incursion. The British rushed reinforcements to the centre of disturbance and made frantic efforts to

[1] B. R. Pearn, 'King-bering', JBRS, vol. xxiii, 1933.

capture the elusive rebel leader. But he evaded all his pursuers, and with the approach of the wet monsoon of 1812 the Burmese retired to their own territory and the British gave up the chase.

No sooner had they done so than Chin Byan occupied one of the frontier posts from which the Company's troops had just been withdrawn, and, using it as his headquarters, made an attack upon Maungdaw. This time the Magistrate of Chittagong sent a timely warning to the Burmese, who routed the invaders. As refugees came seeping back into British territory the Company's forces arrested many of them. But through the connivance of the local population Chin Byan and most of his lieutenants escaped and were soon plundering the countryside for food.

This sort of thing continued throughout the years 1812, 1813 and 1814. Late in 1812 the British crippled Chin Byan's ability to wage large-scale operations by capturing his whole fleet of 150 war boats. But they could neither stop him nor capture him. And the Burmese, though able to defeat all his incursions, failed equally to lay their hands upon him. Nevertheless, before the double pressure of the Burmese and the Company's troops the rebellion was obviously petering out by the end of 1814. When, therefore, in January 1815 Chin Byan died the movement collapsed completely.

It had wrought irreparable harm to Anglo-Burmese relations. The Burmese, unable to realize the extent to which the hands of the British were tied by commitments elsewhere, in Java, the Maratha country and Nepal, developed an unfortunate contempt for their power, which one determined patriot leader had so long so impudently defied. After Captain Canning's return from Amarapura in 1812 no further attempts were made to establish settled diplomatic relations between Fort William and the Court of Ava. Both sides became increasingly suspicious of each other. The seeds of the first Anglo-Burmese war had already been sown; but Bodawpaya was far too shrewd to provoke war with the British, and until the Marathas had been finally dealt with the Government of India was not in a position to adopt a strong line with Burma. In 1819, however, Bodawpaya died and the last disorderly elements in central India were crushed.

By that time Burmese policy had created in Assam a situation essentially the same as in Arakan. The Ahom monarchy had been sinking into decline since the seventeenth century. In the later years of the eighteenth century the rebellion of the persecuted sect of the Moamarias, who denied Brahman supremacy, and the incapacity of the imbecile Gaurinath Singh (1780–94) brought so intolerable a state of disorder that British help was sought. But Captain Welch, sent there in 1792 by Lord Cornwallis, reported that nothing effective could be done short of complete annexation. That was out of the question, and he was accordingly withdrawn.

Conditions, however, showed no sign of improving, and in 1798, as we have seen, Captain Hiram Cox reported that King Bodawpaya was contemplating intervention. But he held his hand for a considerable time, possibly because Cox had warned him that such action on his part would be strongly resented by the British. Shortly after the close of the Chin Byan affair the Bar Phukan, who had fled from Assam, appeared at Calcutta to solicit British aid against the Burha Gohain. When Fort William turned down his request he appealed to Bodawpaya. This time the Burmese king decided to act. In March 1817 a Burmese army marched to Jorhat and placed his nominee on the throne. As soon as the Burmese left, however, their candidate was deposed. In 1819 they returned, reinstated the original raja, Chandrakanta Singh, and again went home. Again as soon as their backs were turned disorder broke loose, and Chandrakanta, unable to maintain himself, fled to British territory.

The situation in Burma had now radically changed. Bodawpaya's weak and amiable grandson Bagyidaw had succeeded to the throne, and under the influence of the brilliant and ambitious general Maha Bandula he had no scruples about a forward policy in Assam. So a Burmese army returned there once again, this time to stay, and Bandula assumed control over the country. When this happened two Assamese pretenders, Chandrakanta Singh and Purandar Singh, both refugees in British territory, were engaged upon collecting troops and arms in order to drive out the Burmese, and the British magistrate at Rangpur was vainly urging Calcutta to assist one or the other. Both invasions failed, and, as in the case of Arakan, Burmese troops chasing refugees crossed the frontier into British India. That was early in 1822. In July of that year Maha Bandula sent an envoy to Calcutta to demand the surrender of the Assamese leaders, who were sheltering in British territory.

Assam, however, was not the only state suffering from this fresh outbreak of Burmese pugnacity. The failure of the Raja of Manipur to attend Bagyidaw's coronation was used as an excuse to dethrone him and devastate his country. He and thousands of his people fled into the neighbouring state of Cachar. The Raja of Cachar, with his state plundered by hordes of desperate refugees and threatened by the Burmese, thereupon fled to British territory and besought aid of the

Government of India. Fort William, bearing in mind that with the passes of Cachar in their possession a Burmese attack upon eastern Bengal would be greatly facilitated, decided that the time had come to make a firm stand. Hence a British protectorate was declared over both Cachar and its northern neighbour, the little hill state of Jaintia, which was also threatened by the Burmese.

Bagyidaw's accession to the throne was also the signal for an outbreak of further trouble on the Arakan frontier. Burmese troops began to cross into the Ramu region and seize the East India Company's elephant hunters on the pretext that they were trespassing on Burmese territory. These and other incidents caused the British to strengthen their frontier post at Tek Naaf and station an outpost on the island of Shahpuri at the river mouth. The Burmese replied by seizing the island in September 1823. A British force reoccupied it, but an effort to set up a boundary commission failed and further outrages occurred.

Meanwhile fighting had already begun in Cachar. Notwithstanding a warning from David Scott, the British frontier officer, that the state would be defended by the British, the Burmese staged a full-scale invasion. Greatly outnumbered, the British forces there could barely hold their own, but their fighting retreat was enough to cause the Burmese to call off the operation and retire into Manipur. That was in February 1824. In the previous month Maha Bandula had assumed command in Arakan and begun operations preparatory to an attack on Chittagong. Lord Amherst, the governor-general, now realized that the Burmese were bent on war. Hence on 5 March 1824 Fort William declared war on Burma. The truth was that Bandula, ever since taking control in Assam, had been directing the frontier moves from the Brahmaputra to the Naaf as a co-ordinated plan for the conquest of Bengal.

The British plan of campaign was to draw away Bandula's forces from the Indian frontier by concentrating upon a large-scale seaborne invasion of Lower Burma, while conducting subsidiary operations for the conquest of Assam, Manipur, Arakan and the Tenasserim coastal strip. The main drive was to proceed up the Irrawaddy in the direction of the capital. The expeditionary force, secretly assembled at a rendezvous in the Andaman Islands, achieved a complete strategic surprise when on 10 May it passed up the river to occupy Rangoon without a blow. Meanwhile, completely unaware of what was afoot, Bandula had crossed the Naaf and gained a success against a detachment of Company's troops, causing something like panic in Calcutta.

That was as far as he was to go, for the news of the British capture of Rangoon caused him to halt his offensive and hurry off southwards.

But the campaign, which had begun so well for the British, soon began to show serious defects of planning. Sir Archibald Campbell's force was so badly supplied with transport that it was tied down to Rangoon, unable to press through to Upper Burma before the wet monsoon rendered a campaign up the Irrawaddy impossible. It had been rashly assumed that the Mons of the delta region could be relied upon to supply not only the necessary transport but plentiful fresh food as well. But the Mons, fearing Burmese vengeance, did not stir a finger to help. Thus for six months during the height of the rains the invaders were held up at Rangoon, while dysentery and fever wrought such havoc that out of the original force of 11,000 men only some hundreds were fit for operations.

The Court of Ava's initial plan seems to have been to contain the British in Rangoon by building a ring of stockades placed at strategic points between Kemmendine and the Pazundaung river, in the hope of forcing them to abandon the campaign. But when two successive commanders, the Thonba Wungyi and the Kyi Wungyi, had failed before British attacks on their stockades it was realized that an all-out effort was needed. Bandula was then thrown in with a force of 60,000 men and a considerable artillery train. Against him the British could muster less than 4,000 men, supported by gunboats on the Rangoon river and the Pazundaung creek.

On 1 December 1824 Bandula attacked and was decisively repulsed. A few days later his main position at Kokine was stormed and his army began to disintegrate. With 7,000 picked men he retired on Danubyu. By this time reinforcements were rapidly arriving for Sir Archibald Campbell, and he was able to organize a field force with Prome as its objective. On 1 April 1825 Bandula was killed while trying to make a stand at Danubyu and his army fled in disorder. The British then occupied Prome and went into cantonments for the rainy season.

Meanwhile, in the other theatres of war much progress had been achieved. During the hold-up in Rangoon forces were detached which occupied Syriam, Martaban, Ye, Tavoy and Mergui. Soon it was possible to send supplies of fresh food to the beleaguered army in Rangoon. Early in 1825 the Arakanese capital of Mrohaung was taken and the systematic occupation of the country carried out. But the hope that an attack on the Burmese capital could be launched across the Arakan Yoma had to be abandoned owing to the lack of a practicable route across the mountains.

Captain Canning had made the interesting suggestion that Amarapura might be reached by a column marching through Manipur to the Chindwin valley. But when the Burmese had been driven out of Cachar, which they had again invaded, the attempt to follow them up through Manipur was abandoned because of the difficulties of the country and the heavy rains. Instead the exiled raja was provided with troops and some British officers, and with their aid gradually recovered his principality. Other forces drove the Burmese out of Assam with little difficulty.

Bandula's death and the British occupation of Prome caused the utmost consternation at Amarapura. Feverish efforts were made to raise fresh armies. In 1825, at the end of the rains, under cover of armistice proposals the Burmese tried to launch a surprise attack on Prome. But the ruse was discovered, and after some heavy fighting the Burmese army was again defeated. The way to the capital now lay open; the last serious resistance had been quelled. Moreover, Sir Archibald Campbell now had adequate river transport, and rapid progress was made upstream.

At Malun peace talks were resumed. But the British peace terms —the cession of Arakan, Tenasserim, Assam and Manipur, together with the payment of an indemnity in rupees equal to a million sterling —so staggered the Burmese commissioners that they tried every possible means to persuade the British to reduce their demands, and especially to delete the clauses relating to Arakan and the indemnity. But the British were adamant, and the advance on the capital was resumed. Not until the British army arrived at Yandabo, only a few days' march from the capital, did the Burmese finally accept the terms. On 24 February 1826 the Treaty of Yandabo was ratified and the British advance came to a halt. In addition to the large cessions of territory and the crippling indemnity—for Burma had no coinage and the royal revenue came mainly in kind—the Court of Ava had to promise to refrain from all interference in the states on the northeastern frontier of British India, to receive a British Resident at Amarapura, and to depute a Burmese envoy to reside in Calcutta. It was also stipulated that immediate negotiations were to begin for a separate treaty to regulate commercial relations.

The war, strategically so well conceived, operationally so mismanaged in its early stages, had been won at a very heavy cost in men and treasure. No less than 15,000 out of the 40,000 men serving in the British expeditionary forces died, the vast majority from fever and dysentery. But it had also exposed the weakness of Burma after three-quarters of a century of expansionist efforts which had completely exhausted her. Not even the genius of Bandula, had he survived, could have saved her.

Burmese history was now to take an entirely new turn. She still kept her three chief ports of Bassein, Rangoon and Martaban. But she had lost her two large coastal provinces to the expanding British empire in India with its sea-power now dominating the Indian Ocean. Could she adjust herself to this strange situation, or must the traditionalism, pride and ignorance of the Court of Ava provoke the British to further intervention?

CHAPTER 34

BURMA FROM THE TREATY OF YANDABO TO THE CREATION OF THE PROVINCE OF BRITISH BURMA, 1826–62

BURMA'S defeat in her war with the British had far-reaching consequences. Her territorial losses were great, but even greater was the blow to her national pride. Her military power, once the terror of all her neighbours, was broken beyond recovery. The British, having wrested from her Tenasserim and Arakan, not to mention her more recently acquired territories in Assam and Manipur, were in 1852 to take from her the rich province of Pegu, and finally in 1885 to bring the Alaungpaya dynasty to an end and annex all that remained of its dominions.

Yet such was not the intention at the outset; no Macchiavellian policy of expansion was involved. British official records show only too clearly that just as they had striven to avoid war before 1824, so after Yandabo they continued to search for ways and means of establishing peaceable relations. What they failed to realize was that once they had a foothold in the country the sheer force of circumstances was bound ultimately to bring about complete annexation, no matter how unwilling they were to extend their territorial commitments. The only way of avoiding it would have been to hand back all the conquered territories that could reasonably be considered to belong to the kingdom of Burma; but while this would have been an easy matter in the case of Tenasserim, the safety of India's north-east frontier demanded the retention of Arakan. The Company hoped that peace could be established on a basis of direct relations and, notwithstanding the failures of the pre-war period in this respect, stipulated in the Treaty of Yandabo that a British Resident must be entertained in the Burmese capital and a Burmese ambassador in Calcutta.

Such a stipulation assumed that the shock of defeat would have a salutary effect upon the Court of Ava and lead it to mend its ways. Quite the reverse happened. King Bagyidaw became subject to recurring fits of melancholia, which ultimately led to insanity. The cruel loss of face that it had suffered made the Court not less but more arrogant. There was the same elementary ignorance of the outside world, the same refusal to learn. Above all, Burmese pride continued to revolt against the humiliation of having to carry on diplomatic relations with a mere viceroy. Hence the ministers found excuse after excuse for failing to open an embassy in Calcutta, and no amount of persuasion could prevail upon them to carry out this item of the treaty.

There was considerable delay in appointing a British Resident to the Court of Ava. He should have been put upon a proper footing before the British army left Yandabo. Instead, however, the expedient was adopted of sending an envoy to negotiate the separate commercial treaty provided for at Yandabo and report on the feasibility of establishing a permanent Residency. The envoy chosen was Raffles's old colleague John Crawfurd, who had been Resident at Singapore from 1823 to 1826, and thereafter had spent six months as Civil Commissioner at Rangoon.

He arrived at the capital on 30 September 1826 to find that the Court had already begun to recover from its first fright, and that all the old arts of subterfuge and evasion were once more to be employed to render his business nugatory. He was a distinguished scholar but a bad negotiator. Hence while, as in the case of his previous mission to Bangkok, the treaty he negotiated was practically worthless, the book he wrote on his experiences was extremely valuable. It takes its place with the works of Symes and Yule as one of the best accounts of the old kingdom of Burma.[1]

Crawfurd's reception by the king took place on an ordinary *kodaw* —i.e. 'beg-pardon'—day, when his vassals assembled to make customary offerings. The official presents from the governor-general were described as a token of his submission to the Golden Feet and his desire for pardon for past offences. Over the extremely simple and innocuous draft commercial treaty which Crawfurd presented to the ministers they haggled for weeks, seeking to barter commercial concessions against the cancellation of the unpaid portion of the indemnity and the restoration of the ceded territories. Of the original twenty-two articles, four only appeared in the final treaty that was signed on 24 November 1826.

In the discussions the ministers brought up a whole list of matters arising out of the fact that the Treaty of Yandabo had been clumsily drafted with regard to frontier lines. There were genuine problems

[1] *Journal of an Embassy from the Governor General of India to the Court of Ava in the year 1827*, London, 1829.

to be settled. But Crawfurd, with his rigid ideas of diplomatic correctness, had become weary of Burmese methods. He pleaded that his instructions did not permit him to deal with political matters arising out of the treaty. On his return to Calcutta, however, the Government of India did not take the same narrow view of the scope of his powers and criticized him for not having made a better attempt to establish political relations on a proper footing before leaving the country.

His advice—that it was inexpedient to appoint a permanent Resident —led the Government of India to shelve the matter for the time being. He argued that an officer no less than 1,200 miles distant by water from Calcutta would be an object of perpetual jealousy to a government 'indescribably ignorant and suspicious', and his position would be 'little better than honourable confinement'. He thought that relations with Ava could be carried on by a political officer stationed at Moulmein, the capital of the new British province of Tenasserim.

But the fate of Tenasserim was in the balance. The original idea had been to offer it to Siam. But the Siamese attitude towards the various matters at issue in their relations with the British had caused that idea to be dropped. Now the directors, finding that its revenues were quite inadequate to meet the cost of its establishment, were anxious that its possible retrocession to Burma should be considered. There were other matters also which could only be properly dealt with by a duly accredited representative at Amarapura. For instance, when a Burmese mission appeared in Calcutta to go into the questions which Crawfurd had refused to discuss—the unpaid half of the indemnity and the frontiers of Arakan and Manipur—it was found to have no power to settle the points at issue but must refer everything back to Ava.

The boundary questions caused no little friction. The Burmese claimed the Kabaw valley between the river Chindwin and the Manipur mountains, which had been occupied by Gambhir Singh when he had driven them out of his country during the war. An Anglo-Burmese boundary commission failed to agree, and Pemberton, the British expert on the north-east frontier regions of India, declared that the map used by the Burmese commissioners was a fake. When a further meeting to check up the map was arranged the Burmese did not turn up, and the Government of India proceeded to give its decision in favour of the Raja of Manipur. When, a year later, the commission did meet again and the Burmese found that the British had planted boundary flags on the right bank of the Chindwin their protests were so strong that the government postponed further action until the matter could be thoroughly investigated in the Burmese records at the capital.

By the end of the year 1829 it had become quite clear that matters of this sort could not be dealt with by a political agent in Moulmein, but only by the Resident provided for in the Treaty of Yandabo. For this task the Government of India chose Major Henry Burney, who had already won its high praise for his tactful handling of the Raja of Ligor and the Court of Bangkok. He arrived at Amarapura in April 1830, charged with the duty of dealing with all outstanding matters—the indemnity, the frontier questions, the retrocession suggestion, and trade. And, as every previous attempt to place relations between Ava and Calcutta on a satisfactory footing had failed, the situation with which he had to cope was enough to daunt the most sanguine man.[1]

In matters of Court etiquette his attitude was firm but reasonable. He made it quite clear, however, that he would not be received on a *kodaw* day. He won his point. Before long he had established such cordial relations with the ministers of the Hlutdaw, the supreme council of the realm, that they would come to the Residency to dine with him. King Bagyidaw himself went so far as to have frequent private conversations with him. In February 1831 their relations were so friendly that the king conferred on him the rank of Wundauk.[2]

On the main matters in dispute discussions took place in both Ava and Calcutta. The Burmese attempts to scale down the amount of the indemnity failed, and the final instalment was handed over in October 1832. A Burmese deputation went to India and waited upon the governor-general to appeal against the Kabaw valley decision. In 1832 Burney was recalled to Calcutta to join in the discussions. His study of the records of the Court of Ava had led him to the conclusion that the Burmese case was a sound one, notwithstanding Pemberton's opposition. In March 1833 the Government of India accepted his argument and the valley was restored to Burma, although it had been occupied by the Manipuris since the end of the war.

On the subject of Tenasserim he could not persuade the ministers to offer reasonable terms for its retrocession. They were aware that

---

[1] For a detailed study of Burney's mission based on the India Office records see W. S. Desai, *History of the British Residency in Burma, 1826–1840*, University of Rangoon, 1939.

[2] Minister of the Second Class, next in rank to Wungyi. See *Handbook of Oriental History* (C. H. Philips, editor), Royal Historical Society, London, 1951, pp. 120–1, s.v. Ministers of State (B).

financially it was a dead loss to the East India Company, and mistakenly supposed that they had only to wait long enough for the Company to hand it back as a free gift. Even the warning that the Siamese might be willing to make a good offer for the territory failed to shake their resolution. Burney failed also to persuade them to appoint a resident minister in Calcutta. The argument that it was contrary to Burmese custom was final in their eyes, and nothing he could tell them about diplomatic practice elsewhere availed.

To make matters worse, before the end of 1831 King Bagyidaw began to display symptoms of the insanity that was later to incapacitate him. Power therefore tended to get more and more into the hands of the chief queen and her brother, the Minthagyi, both of low origin, who dominated the Council of Regency. Under the strain of his difficult task Burney's health broke down. In a letter written in 1834 he indicated clearly the impossible situation with which he was faced: 'When any important event or discussion arises here, the consideration that there exists no certain means of communicating with your own Government, which possesses less knowledge of the real character and customs of this than of any other Indian Court, greatly enhances, in such a climate and situation, near a crazy King, and an ignorant and trembling set of Ministers, the mental anxiety which preys upon the health of a public servant holding a responsible office.' He was granted furlough.

In July 1835, when he returned to Burma, though his reception by the ministers was flattering to a degree, the king's malady had become so severe that he could no longer bear to meet the representative of the power that had caused him such acute humiliation. Matters came to a climax early in 1837, when the king's brother, the Tharrawaddy Prince, convinced that the Minthagyi aimed at seizing the throne, fled to Shwebo and raised the standard of rebellion. He was a friend of Burney's and hoped for his support. Burney had to explain that the rules of his government forbade him to interfere.

His one wish now was to retire from the capital and leave the opposing sides to fight it out. But the panic-stricken ministers refused to let him go. He then undertook the role of mediator and negotiated the surrender of the capital on condition that there should be no bloodshed. On obtaining possession of Amarapura Tharrawaddy broke his promise, and Burney had again to intervene to stop the executions. But five ministers had been done to death, and the wife and daughters of the Minthagyi horribly tortured, before his protests availed. 'These hat-wearing people cannot bear to see or hear of women being beaten or maltreated,' was Tharrawaddy's contemptuous comment, and he never forgave Burney for interfering with his royal right to break a promise.

During the war of 1824-6 Tharrawaddy had been in favour of an early termination of hostilities, and he regarded the hard terms of the Treaty of Yandabo as due to his brother's refusal to take his advice. On coming to the throne, therefore, he announced his repudiation of the treaty, and Burney learnt with consternation that there was a party at Court which advocated the recovery of the lost provinces by force of arms. His position had become intolerable; he was completely cold-shouldered by the king. In June 1837, therefore, on a plea of ill-health, he removed the Residency to Rangoon. He had become afraid that if it remained at Amarapura some outrage would occur which would endanger peace. He advised Calcutta that it should not be re-established at the capital until the king undertook to recognize the Treaty of Yandabo. He reported that Tharrawaddy was buying arms and calling up more men to the colours than were necessary in peacetime. He recommended, therefore, that some form of coercive military action should be undertaken.

Lord Auckland, the governor-general, refused to consider such a course of action. He was far from satisfied with Burney's conduct in leaving Amarapura. Burney was accordingly recalled and a successor, Colonel Richard Benson, appointed with instructions to re-establish the Residency at the capital. When he arrived there his official position was ignored, and he was assigned a residence on a sandbank which was flooded to a depth of several feet by the overflow of the Irrawaddy during the wet monsoon. He complained to Calcutta that his treatment was 'such as no English gentleman, or, more extensively, no British subject, ought to be exposed to'.

In March 1839, on a plea of ill-health, he retired to Rangoon, leaving his assistant, Captain William McLeod, in charge at Amarapura. When the monsoon broke and the ministers refused to find him more suitable quarters he also left for Rangoon, in July 1839. By that time the breakdown of every Resident's health at his capital had become one of Tharrawaddy's stock jokes. Early in the following year the Government of India withdrew the Residency and severed diplomatic relations with the Court of Ava.

Was war now inevitable? Benson, like Burney, warned Calcutta that nothing short of invasion would bring the Burmese government to its senses. But the Afghan War made it impossible to take a firm line with the Court of Ava. On the other hand, the British disasters in that war were seized on by the war party at Tharrawaddy's Court as arguments in favour of a more energetic policy. Two rebellions— one in Lower Burma in 1838, and the other in the Shan country in 1840—gave the king an excuse to get rid of all the people he had intended to put out of the way in 1837 when Burney had intervened to save their lives. The ex-queen was trampled to death by elephants, and her brother, the Minthagyi, even more barbarously executed. A significant outbreak of dacoity in the Salween neighbourhood gave rise to wild rumours of a Burmese plan to invade Tenasserim. A royal visit to Rangoon in 1841, which was of the nature of a military demonstration, caused so much apprehension that the British garrisons in Arakan and Tenasserim were reinforced.

Nothing came of these incidents. Tharrawaddy was playing with fire, but was shrewd enough not to push things too far. Blundell, the Commissioner of Tenasserim, warned the Government of India that the dacoities in the Salween area were officially instigated in order to spread alarm on the British side of the frontier; and that no matter how forcibly he might stamp them out, action of a far more comprehensive kind was really called for. But the Government of India, having brought the Afghan War to an end, had its attention fixed on Sind and the Sikhs and was unwilling to risk adventures in Burma.

How long the uneasy peace would have continued had Tharrawaddy continued to direct affairs is a matter for surmise. But like his brother he became insane. His madness showed itself in fits of ungovernable rage, during which he committed abominable cruelties. These became so serious that in 1845 his sons put him under restraint. The struggle for power which then ensued was won by Pagan Min, who killed off those of his brothers whom he considered dangerous, together with every member of their households.

In 1846 Tharrawaddy died and Pagan Min became king. His tyranny and atrocities were far worse than those of Thibaw and Supayalat which so shocked a later generation of Britishers. His first chief ministers, Maung Baing Zat and Maung Bhein, carried out a systematic spoliation of his richer subjects by procuring their deaths on trumped-up charges. During their two years of power more than 6,000 people are said to have been put out of the way, and the public fury at last rose to such a pitch that to save himself the king handed over his favourites to be tortured to death. He rarely attended to business, and local officers could do much as they pleased so long as the due amount of revenue was paid regularly to the capital. Local officers like Gaung Gyi of Tharrawaddy, later a famous dacoit leader against the British régime, were as independent as mediaeval marcher lords in Europe.

It was this breakdown of central control which was finally instrumental in bringing on the long-threatened war with the East India Company. After the withdrawal of the Residency in 1840, Calcutta began to be plagued with complaints about the ill-treatment of British subjects at Rangoon. Some were frivolous, others exaggerated, but Maung Ok, the Governor of Pegu appointed by Pagan Min at the beginning of his reign, gained a bad name for extortion. In July and August 1851 two particularly bad cases of this occurred, in which, by allowing frivolous charges of murder and embezzlement to be brought against two British sea-captains, Sheppard of the *Monarch* and Lewis of the *Champion*, and members of their crews, he collected from them sums totalling just short of 1,000 rupees. His acts were not mere clumsy attempts to enrich himself: his aim was publicly to degrade Britishers.

It was a singularly inopportune moment to stage an anti-British demonstration. When claims for damages were submitted by the injured parties to the Government of India Lord Dalhousie was governor-general and had recently defeated the Sikhs. Compared with all the provocations of the earlier period the affair was trifling, but he knew that the Court of Ava would most certainly reject a demand for reparation made in the ordinary way, and he felt that if this kind of thing were permitted to continue it might seriously affect British prestige in the East. 'The Government of India', he wrote in a minute, 'could never, consistently with its own safety, permit itself to stand for a single day in an attitude of inferiority towards a native power, and least of all towards the Court of Ava.' Hence he decided to serve the claim in such a way as he believed would make it impossible for the Burmese government to reject it. He sent Commodore Lambert, the deputy commander-in-chief of the East India Company's naval forces, in H.M.S. *Fox*, together with two Company's warships, the *Proserpine* and the *Tenasserim*, to Rangoon with a demand addressed to the king not only for compensation but also for the removal of Maung Ok.

The Government of Burma promised redress and promptly recalled Maung Ok. The appearance of British warships in Rangoon harbour, however, caused a state of alarm. Large detachments of troops were sent to Bassein and Martaban, and Maung Ok's successor brought with him a considerable force. Unfortunately he belonged to the violently anti-British party at the capital and came with the intention of adopting an uncompromising attitude, regardless of consequences. When Commodore Lambert sent an official deputation to wait on him to discuss the claim to compensation it was refused admission in a grossly insulting manner, and the governor sent a written protest to the commodore complaining that a party of drunken officers had rudely attempted to interrupt his siesta.

The 'combustible commodore', as Dalhousie later described Lambert, at once declared a blockade of the port and proceeded to take reprisals on Burmese shipping. When the shore batteries fired a few shots he silenced them with a broadside from the *Fox*. Then, having destroyed every Burmese war-boat within reach, he returned to Calcutta. 'So all that fat is in the fire,' commented the governor-general, and preparations for war were at once set on foot. 'We can't afford to be shown to the door anywhere in the East,' he wrote to a friend.

His next step was to despatch a strong expeditionary force to Rangoon. It bore with it an ultimatum demanding compensation, this time to the tune of ten lakhs of rupees,[1] the estimated cost of the war preparations. His letters show that he still hoped against hope that the Court of Ava would consent to negotiate. But on 1 April 1852 the ultimatum expired without a sign from the Golden Feet. A few days later Rangoon and Martaban were occupied. Richard Cobden in a famous pamphlet[2] strongly censured the Government of India for sending a commodore of the Royal Navy to negotiate in the first place, and then for raising the sum demanded as compensation to a hundred times the original amount. Dalhousie admitted his error in the choice of an emissary, but contended that Lambert was not the cause of the war. In his view war had long been inevitable. Actually he had disapproved of Lambert's action and reprimanded him.

The war which followed was in complete contrast to the previous one.[3] Dalhousie tackled with masterly zeal the problems of organization, transport and co-operation created by the employment of two separate naval and military services—those of the Crown and those of the Company. His measures for safeguarding the health of the expeditionary force were so effective that the mortality from sickness

---

[1] Then worth £100,000.
[2] 'How wars are got up in India', *Political Writings of Cobden*, London, 1867, vol. ii, pp. 25–106.
[3] The best concise account of the war is in Sir William Lee-Warner's *Life of the Marquess of Dalhousie*, London, 1904, chap. xii. For the settlement after the war see D. G. E. Hall (ed.), *The Dalhousie-Phayre Correspondence, 1852–1856*, London, 1932.

was actually lower than the peacetime average in India. Materials were prepared ahead for the rapid construction of barracks. Plentiful supplies of fresh food were collected at Amherst, hospitals built there, and a regular service of fast steamers kept them in close touch with the expeditionary force. His biggest difficulty lay in the personality of the commander-in-chief, General Godwin, a septuagenarian, who disagreed with the whole plan of campaign and was notorious for his jealousy of the Navy, on whose co-operation he was entirely dependent.

The initial plan of campaign was to seize Rangoon, Martaban and Bassein before the onset of the wet monsoon, and thus force Pagan Min to negotiate. There was no intention to annex more territory. But as the rains dragged on their weary course and the Court of Ava made no move Dalhousie realized that the Burmese also were playing a waiting game. In July 1852 he went personally to Rangoon to confer with General Godwin and Commodore Lambert. Godwin wanted to dictate terms in Amarapura itself and was loudly supported by the London press. Dalhousie, however, preferred a more limited objective. It was useless to hold the three captured ports without a hinterland. Hence he suggested to London the feasibility of annexing the old kingdom of Pegu. This would strengthen the British position in Burma by linking up Arakan and Tenasserim, and reduce the Court of Ava to impotence. The brilliantly reasoned minute in which he conveyed this proposal to the home government won its complete assent.

When, in November 1852, its reply arrived Godwin had occupied Prome, after sweeping aside the main Burmese army under the amiable but incompetent son of the great Bandula, who prudently surrendered rather than face the fate of a defeated commander at the hands of his own government. During the next few weeks the remainder of the province of Pegu was systematically occupied against slight resistance. The home government, in sanctioning the annexation, stipulated that the Court of Ava must be made to sign a treaty recognizing the fact. Dalhousie, on the other hand, was convinced that a King of Burma would never sign away territory unless his capital were directly threatened; and as he considered a march on Amarapura would serve no useful purpose, the only thing to do was to proclaim the annexation of Pegu and present the Court of Ava with a *fait accompli*. On 20 December 1852 the proclamation was read with due ceremonial at Rangoon by Major Arthur Purves Phayre, whom Dalhousie had chosen to be the first Commissioner of Pegu.

Still no sign came from the Golden Feet. Dalhousie therefore began most reluctantly to make plans for a march on the capital. Actually, however, all unknown to him, a revolution was in progress in Upper Burma. The Mindon Prince, half-brother to the king, was the leader of a party at Court which had opposed the war from the start. The news of the British advance to Prome made him a popular idol, who, it was hoped, would restore the situation. The king therefore tried to get rid of him, but on 17 December 1752 Mindon and his brother, the Kanaung Prince, fled to Shwebo, as Tharrawaddy had done in 1837, and raised the standard of revolt. After confused fighting lasting for some weeks the Magwe Mingyi, Pagan's chief minister, suddenly declared for Mindon on 18 February 1853, took possession of Amarapura and deposed the king. Mindon thereupon left Shwebo and was crowned at the capital amidst general rejoicing.

The new king was a sincere Buddhist who hated bloodshed. He permitted Pagan Min to retire into honourable captivity. He survived until 1881. He also signalized his accession by releasing all the Europeans imprisoned at the capital and sending two of them, the Italian priests Father Domingo Tarolly and Father Abbona, post haste down the Irrawaddy to meet the British commander-in-chief with the announcement that a peace delegation would be despatched as soon as possible. They found him not at Prome, as they had expected, but fifty miles higher up the river at Myédé. In the absence of any word from Amarapura, it had been decided to annex yet another slice of Burmese territory, which included a rich belt of teak forest. The envoys were sent back to Mindon with a copy of the proclamation of annexation and an invitation to accept the inevitable.

Mindon Min could not believe that the British seriously intended to keep Pegu. At the end of March 1853 the Burmese peace delegation, headed by the Magwe Mingyi, met the British commissioners, Phayre, Godwin and Lambert, and begged them to give back the territory they had taken. They pleaded that the new king was an entirely different kind of man from his predecessor and was only too anxious to be on friendly terms with Britain. As a forlorn hope Dalhousie authorized the commissioners to offer to give up the additional territory that had been occupied north of Prome in return for a treaty recognizing the British possession of Pegu. But as he had prophesied earlier, when the treaty question was first mooted in London Mindon would on no account sign a treaty yielding Burmese territory to a foreign power. So in May 1853 the negotiations were broken off and the Myédé boundary was retained.

At first the alarmists prophesied a renewal of the war. The Kan-aung Min, who had become heir-apparent, was in favour of it. But Mindon, who had more political sagacity than any of his advisers, vetoed any hostile move and sent a reassuring letter to Phayre telling him that frontier officials had been ordered to prevent any further hostilities. Lord Dalhousie accordingly announced the official termina-tion of hostilities. 'All that is known of his character and past history', he wrote of Mindon, 'mark him among Burmese rulers as a prince of rare sagacity, humanity and forbearance, and stamp his present declarations with the seal of sincerity.'

But the army in Pegu had to remain on a war footing. Rebellion flared up everywhere in the annexed territory. Local myothugyis, the heads of the old district administration, became the leaders of a stubborn resistance movement which seriously hindered attempts to establish civil government, while Burmese officials from across the border raided frontier villages. Myat Tun and Gaung Gyi, the two most daring leaders, put up a magnificent fight which wrung admira-tion from Dalhousie himself. It took three years to bring the province under control.

Meanwhile both Dalhousie and his able lieutenant Phayre had come to the conclusion that positive action must be taken to prevent a drift back into war. On both sides of the frontier the air was full of alarmist rumours. It remained to be seen also whether Mindon could maintain himself on the throne. If the diplomatic impasse could not be broken it was urgent to find some informal means of direct contact with the new king so that trustworthy intelligence could be purveyed by each side to the other and mutual confidence built up. Among the Europ-eans released by Mindon was a burly bearded Scottish trader named Thomas Spears, with a Burmese wife and a good reputation in Amarapura. Phayre interviewed him at Rangoon and was so impressed with his matter-of-fact good sense that he suggested to Dalhousie that Spears should be appointed unofficial news-writer at the Burmese capital. Dalhousie at first fought shy of the proposal. Spears in such a position, he felt, might be liable to outrage and thus involve the Government of India in unwelcome responsibilities. Other possible candidates were considered and turned down. Late in 1853, on his second visit to Rangoon, Dalhousie met Spears and decided to try the experiment, provided it met with Mindon's full approval.

Happily Mindon knew Spears well personally and welcomed his appointment. His task was simply to keep Phayre, as Commissioner of Pegu and Governor-General's Agent, informed of conditions at the capital. But his position demanded almost superhuman tact, for not only did Mindon give him absolute liberty to write completely uncensored despatches but he constantly sought to use him as his official channel of communication with the British. There were occasions when the wary Dalhousie had to warn Phayre that Spears was merely a news-writer without any official standing. Nevertheless both Mindon and Phayre came to rely absolutely upon his good judgment and common sense. Mindon discussed with him every matter affecting British relations before taking action, and Phayre apprised him of everything of importance from the British side for the information of the king. And although the king never acquiesced in the loss of Pegu, frontier peace was gradually established and friendly relations promoted between Rangoon and the Court of Ava. This excellent arrangement lasted without interruption until 1861, when Spears went home on furlough.

In March 1854 Dalhousie was able to write home to his friend Sir George Couper: 'There is perfect quiescence, and the King is actually withdrawing from the frontier his whole troops.'

During that year relations improved so well that Mindon sent a goodwill mission to Calcutta headed by the Dalla Wun. Its real object was to persuade the governor-general to consider the retrocession of Pegu, which Mindon felt he could reasonably expect after the practical demonstration he had given of his peaceable intentions. And although Lord Dalhousie's uncompromising refusal was deeply disappointing, the report taken back by the Burmese delegation of their courteous treatment at Calcutta so impressed Mindon that he at once invited the Government of India to depute a return mission to his capital. Photography was coming into vogue, and the king was much interested in the collection of photographs the envoy and his suite brought back with them.

The return mission, headed by Phayre, to the Court of Ava in 1855 achieved fame through the splendid volume from the pen of its secretary, Colonel (later Sir) Henry Yule, who not only reported its proceedings fully but also included in his scope a vast amount of information of every kind about Burma and the Burmese.[1] From the point of view of the East India Company, which constantly harped on the subject of a treaty, the mission was a failure. For, notwithstanding long private talks with the king, Phayre was unable to persuade him to sign even a general treaty of friendship, making no

[1] *A Narrative of the Mission sent by the Governor-General of India to the Court of Ava in 1855*, London, 1858.

allusion whatever to any loss of territory. On the other hand, as a step towards better Anglo-Burmese understanding the mission was an outstanding success. Never before in Burmese history had so genuinely friendly a welcome been bestowed upon the envoys of a foreign power.

Much of the credit for this must go to Phayre himself, who spoke Burmese fluently, had an intimate knowledge of the literature, religion and history[1] of the Burmese, and a great reputation with them for courtesy and kindliness. But an equal share must be given to Mindon. The Crimean War was in progress, and the Armenian community at Amarapura was busily engaged in spreading rumours that a great Russian invasion of India was imminent and British rule there was 'finished'. Shady French adventurers also, such as 'General d'Orgoni', were capping this by playing up British weakness in the Crimea and representing that it was only the French army that was saving them from defeat. But the king's shrewdness was proof against such assaults; he was convinced that the only safe policy was to cultivate good relations with the British. And he found the sound common sense of Thomas Spears an unerring guide.

Lord Dalhousie was more than satisfied with the results of the mission. In his minute summing them up he wrote: 'From its first entrance into Burmese waters until its return to our frontier the Mission was treated with the highest distinction and with the utmost hospitality and liberality ... and I desire to record my firm conviction that peace with Burma is to the full as secure as any written treaty could have made it.' The good understanding born of these friendly exchanges survived the even greater strain of the Indian Mutiny of 1857-8. When the British garrison in Lower Burma was depleted through India's need for reinforcements Mindon was urged by his advisers to invade Pegu. 'We do not strike a friend when he is in distress,' he is reported to have said.

The India Office records contain a vast mass of material on his reign, and it shows quite clearly that his position was never an easy one. The traditionalist elements at his Court constantly worked against him, and in the face of the plots and disorders that were rife throughout his reign his hands were weakened by the crippling loss his kingdom had sustained in the war. He needed peace for the task of setting his own house in order, and of coming to terms with the new order that the European impact was forcing upon Asia. Like his contemporary, Mongkut of Siam, he felt the challenge of the West, but in his

[1] His *History of Burma*, London, 1883, is a remarkable piece of pioneer work.

land-locked kingdom, now more than ever isolated from the out-side world, his handicap in the effort to meet it was immeasurably greater.

When Arakan and Tenasserim were annexed in 1826 they were separately administered under the direct supervision of the Government of India. In Arakan's case the arrangement did not last very long, for it was found to be more convenient to transfer it to the Bengal administration. From 1828 it was under the charge of a superintendent, who worked under the supervision of the Commissioner of Chittagong. Tenasserim remained directly under the Government of India until 1834. But its connection with India was slight, since its European administrators up to 1843 came from Penang. Thus while Indian administrative methods were speedily introduced in Arakan, in Tenasserim's case, partly because for some time the question of retrocession was in the air, Burmese officials and administrative methods were largely retained.[1]

It was the age of Liberalism, when men such as Sir Stamford Raffles, Sir Thomas Munro, Mountstuart Elphinstone and Lord William Cavendish-Bentinck, who was Governor-General of India from 1828 to 1835, accepted the ideals of economic freedom, equality before the law, and the general welfare of the governed as the guiding principles of government. A. D. Maingy, the first Civil Commissioner of Tenasserim, was an enthusiast for these things; and although he found that Liberalism and Burmese custom did not always agree, and that where they clashed the latter tended to prevail, he was able to introduce administrative methods which contributed to the welfare of the people. And whatever may be said in criticism of the new administration, the fact remains that in both Arakan and Tenasserim official oppression and extortion became illegal, banditry was suppressed far more energetically than before, while security of life and property became established features of the governmental system.

Under the Burmese system, while the heads of the provincial government were appointed by the king, actual administration was largely in the hands of hereditary local magnates such as the myothugyis. Thus in Tenasserim at first the system of administration was akin to the indirect rule of the Dutch in Java, with Europeans supervising a native administration functioning on traditional lines. In 1834, however, the judicial and revenue administration came under Bengal, and in consequence standardization on Indian lines was

[1] The early administrative history of Tenasserim is treated in detail in J. S. Furnivall's 'The Fashioning of Leviathan' in JBRS, vol. xxix, 1939.

increasingly applied. Still, a surprising amount of the older Burmese practice managed sturdily to survive.

When Pegu was annexed in 1852 it became a separate commissioner-ship under the governor-general. Phayre framed its administration on the Tenasserim model. The province was divided into five districts under deputy commissioners. These in turn were sub-divided into townships under myo-oks. Each township comprised a number of 'circles' under taikthugyis, who supervised the subordinate officials in the villages. As, however, most of the British officers appointed to administrative posts had held commissions in the Bengal and Madras armies and spoke little or no Burmese, the administration tended to develop more and more along the approved Indian lines.

The method of three separate commissioner's divisions was costly and inconvenient. Hence in 1862 they were amalgamated to form the province of British Burma, of which Rangoon was the capital and Phayre the first Chief Commissioner. This naturally resulted in greater uniformity of administration. It was also the beginning of the gradual reorganization of the government into departments. But, significantly enough, the circle under the taikthugyi remained the real unit of local government, as it had done under Burmese rule. Indirect rule thus continued to be the general practice, and the life of the ordinary villager went on much as it had done under Burmese rule.

Tenasserim and Arakan at the time of their annexation in 1826 were of slight economic value. In the seventeenth century Arakan had driven a considerable export trade in rice. The instability of the government in the eighteenth century had caused this to decline. Under Burmese rule quite half of its population had emigrated, and in any case the Burmese government did not permit the export of rice. British rule brought more settled conditions and the removal of the restrictions on export; hence the proximity of the Indian market caused a revival of rice-planting. Akyab, the administrative head-quarters, soon became a flourishing commercial centre.

Tenasserim had a very sparse population living mainly on sub-sistence agriculture. Its valuable teak forests were thrown open to licensed private enterprise, and for a time Moulmein became a thriving port with saw-mills and shipbuilding yards. But the rapid develop-ment of Rangoon after 1852 soon brought about the eclipse of Moul-mein. Lord Dalhousie's work as the creator of modern Rangoon shows up by comparison with Raffles's at Singapore as a compre-hensive and efficient professional job against a slapdash amateur one.

In his plans Rangoon's future was envisaged as not only a great port but also 'one of the most beautiful cities and stations within the whole bounds of India'. But his most sanguine hopes for the city's development must have fallen far short of reality when Rangoon became the world's greatest rice port as a result of expansion of cultivation in the Irrawaddy delta region that was to be one of the most spectacular developments in the recent economic history of Asia.

CHAPTER 35

THE LAST DAYS OF THE KONBAUNG DYNASTY
AT MANDALAY, 1862–85

MINDON, who was a son of Tharrawaddy, had been twelve years of age when Arakan and Tenasserim were annexed in 1826. He was raised to the throne just after Pegu and a deep strip of territory to the north of the Burmese province had gone the same way. His kingdom was still a large one stretching many miles up the Irrawaddy and its great tributary, the Chindwin. It contained what was *par excellence* the Burmese homeland, together with a fringe of mountainous areas occupied by other peoples, principally Shans, Chins and Kachins. Of these the Shans were far the most important, and the thick wedge of their feudatory states paying allegiance to Burma stretched far across the river Salween to the borders of Yunnan, and in the case of Kengtung reached to the upper Mekong. But Mindon was painfully aware of his weakness. He was cut off from the sea; not a vestige of the old military strength of Burma remained, and he himself was a man of peace, not a soldier. He realized, therefore, that it was essential for him to remain on good terms with the British, and he did so.

His greatest personal interest was in Buddhism. Though not a profound scholar of Buddhist learning, he was deeply imbued with its doctrines and had a more genuinely religious outlook than any other ruler of his house. In 1857 he chose a new site for a royal city on the plain lying to the south-west of Mandalay Hill and transferred his capital there from Amarapura. He strove to make it a principal centre of the Buddhist culture, reviving and conserving the best traditions of the past. In and around it he built large teak monasteries richly adorned with wood carvings displaying pure Burmese art at its best. Among the many religious buildings with which he adorned his new capital perhaps the most interesting and significant was the complex of pagodas known as the Kuthodaw ('great work of royal merit'), where, around a central pagoda, are grouped 733 smaller ones containing upright marble slabs, each engraved with verses of the Pali scriptures, and together forming a complete copy of the Tripitaka, the 'three baskets' of the Buddhist 'bible': the Sutta, the Vinaya, and the

Abhidammapitaka. In the central pagoda was enshrined the Pali Commentary inscribed on leaves of gold and silver. To the Burmese Mandalay was Shwemyo, 'the golden city'; its official Pali name was Yadanabon, 'cluster of gems'. The royal city containing the palace was a walled square with each side a mile and a quarter long, and with mud-mortar-built machicolated walls twenty-six feet high, surmounted by wooden look-out towers of traditional Burmese design. The walls were pierced by twelve gates, three on each side, and surrounded by a wide moat.

Thomas Spears continued to act as British Correspondent to the Court of Ava until 1861, when he left for a long visit to Europe.[1] In the following year Colonel Phayre, the new Chief Commissioner of British Burma, came to Mandalay to negotiate a commercial treaty. British policy now aimed at developing trade with western China along the old Burma Road running into Yunnan from Bhamo. The idea of discovering a practicable overland route to China had been revived. Symes, in reporting his first mission to Ava in 1795, had mentioned that Burma carried on an extensive cotton trade with Yunnan. Hiram Cox had followed this up by making careful enquiries, on the results of which he wrote a fairly detailed report, which Major Francklin published in 1811 in a collection of papers on Burma.[2]

The acquisition of Tenasserim in 1826 led to great efforts to stimulate the trade of Moulmein, and attempts were made to discover its overland connexions. Crawfurd's estimate, in his report of his mission to Ava in 1827, that Burmese exports amounted to an annual value of £228,000 brought to the fore the feasibility of finding a way there from Moulmein. It also aroused the interest of the Government of India in the ancient land route from Bengal to China, and the Calcutta authorities published a map showing possible routes to Yunnanfu. Numerous surveys were made and a vast amount of information piled up.

In 1831 Captain Sprye suggested the Salween route to China from Moulmein via Kenghung, and in 1837 Captain McLeod followed up his suggestion by making the journey with six elephants, thus becoming the first European to penetrate China by the Salween route. Another doughty explorer of this period was Dr. David Richardson, who made three visits to Chiengmai from Moulmein and was apparently the first Britisher to visit that city since the unfortunate

Samuel in 1615. Other gallant adventurers explored routes from India to Upper Burma. In 1830, for instance, Lieutenant Pemberton, the author of an invaluable *Report on the Eastern Frontier of British India*,[1] crossed the mountains from Manipur by the Akui route to Kindat and made his way down the Chindwin to Ava. Five years later Captain Hannay travelled from Bengal to Bhamo by the route across northern Burma. But after Tharrawaddy came to the throne in 1837 all hopes of developing this route were quenched for a generation, and all attempts to develop the overland trade of Moulmein in the direction of Chiengmai or Yunnan failed.

The journals of these explorers were studied by Colonel Henry Yule in connection with Phayre's mission to the Court of Mindon Min in 1855. One of the objects hoped for from the mission was the signature of a treaty permitting trans-Burma trade with China. But the king was not to be persuaded to agree to any plan which might provide excuses for further British interference. Moreover, Yule found that Burma's trade with Yunnan was declining, and soon afterwards it came to a complete standstill through the Panthay rebellion. Sprye, on the other hand, continued to recommend his route from Moulmein to Kenghung and thence on to Szumao, though without avail, since it passed through thinly populated, malarious areas, and in any case Lord Dalhousie's plan to develop Rangoon as a port in preference to Moulmein, together with the obvious advantages of the Irrawaddy over the Salween, caused attention to be focused more and more upon overcoming the opposition of the Court of Ava.

In 1860 the Manchester Chamber of Commerce, in the belief that western China would prove a good market for Lancashire cotton goods, asked the British government to take practical measures to open the Moulmein–Yunnan route. Almost at the same time an English army surgeon, Dr. Clement Williams, while stationed at Thayetmyo, had been studying Burmese accounts of the old trade between China and Upper Burma, and found the theme so fascinating that he went to Mandalay on furlough to find out more about it. Thenceforward he became an enthusiast for the Bhamo route.

In response to all this pressure the Government of India sent Phayre on a mission to Mandalay in 1862. The union of the three divisions of Arakan, Tenasserim and Pegu in that year to form the province of British Burma had made a deep impression on Mindon Min's mind. He realized that the time had come for a clarification of his relations with the British. He regarded Phayre as an old friend.

[1] Published in Calcutta in 1835.

Williams also he liked. Hence he was prevailed upon to sign a commercial treaty. It was based upon the principle of reciprocity. Britain undertook to abolish within a year the customs duties on goods coming down the Irrawaddy from Upper Burma. Mindon agreed to make reciprocal concessions, if he felt inclined, within a rather longer period. Rice was to be imported into Upper Burma free of duty. Traders from British territory were to be permitted to operate along the whole course of the Irrawaddy in Upper Burma in return for a guarantee of similar privileges to traders from Upper Burma along the British section of the river. The most important clause, however, was one which permitted a British Agent to reside in Mandalay to remove any misunderstandings that might arise.

Both Mindon and Phayre would have preferred to maintain the unofficial method of communication so ably conducted by Spears. But there was no suitable man. Hence the appointment of an official Agent was resorted to as the best arrangement under the circumstances, and Clement Williams was seconded from the army to become High Commissioner's Agent at the Court of Ava. His first object on assuming his duties in 1862 was to persuade the king to allow him to survey the upper part of the Irrawaddy. In this he was successful and started off in January 1863. At Bhamo his inquiries convinced him that the trade route was practicable. He was unable, however, to make a journey to the Chinese border because an insurrection occurred at Mandalay and Mindon recalled him. But he forwarded a Memorandum to the Government of India[1] and began an intensive canvass for his scheme in British mercantile circles. 'Burmah proper is no longer a barrier,' he wrote, 'but a gangway, open to the use of whoever will avail themselves of it.'[2]

This was mere wishful thinking. The obstacles forming the barrier had only been slightly dislodged. Most of the ministers were against the king in this matter, and all attempts to carry out further surveys failed before the difficulties raised by local officials. Trade also was badly hampered by the system under which nearly every staple article of produce was a royal monopoly, and as such could be sold only through royal brokers or by special permission of the local authorities. And the Court of Ava found ways and means of postponing indefinitely its part of the agreement regarding the abolition of customs duties.

The king, unfortunately, was up against practically insuperable

---

[1] The gist of it is given in his book *Through Burmah to Western China*, London, 1868.
[2] *Ibid.*, p. 6.

QUEEN'S GOLDEN MONASTERY, MANDALAY

difficulties, insurrections were rife, and at any moment a palace revolution might deprive him of his throne. He almost alone at his Court realized that before the insistent pressure of European expansion the old isolationism must lead to disaster. But unlike his contemporary, Mongkut of Siam, whose country had not been defeated and carved up by a European power, any move he made towards relaxing the rigid traditionalism of his government was bound to look in the eyes of his ministers like selling the pass.

In 1866 an attempted revolution came so near to success that the king was badly shaken. On 2 August, when he was at the Summer Palace a few miles out of Mandalay, two of his sons, with armed followers, rushed into the temporary Hlutdaw building, where a meeting was in progress, and killed the crown prince, who was presiding, one of the Wungyis and the two princes who stood next in the succession. Mindon escaped on foot to Mandalay, where he was besieged in the royal palace all night by the insurgents until his guards managed to drive them off. Major Sladen, the British Agent, was in the Summer Palace when the outbreak occurred, but managed to escape. The situation remained so tense that the king suggested that Sladen should evacuate all the Europeans to Rangoon, and he took them down on a merchant steamer that was moored off Mandalay city.

Later in the same year Phayre went to Mandalay with the object of negotiating a new commercial treaty, but the king pleaded that the country was still too unsettled and impoverished for him to forgo any of his monopolies or reduce the frontier duties. In March 1867 Phayre retired, and was succeeded as High Commissioner by Colonel Albert Fytche, a descendant of the Elizabethan prospector and a cousin of Alfred Tennyson, the poet laureate. He had far less ability and insight into the Burmese character than Phayre, but a great deal more self-assurance. And his first act was to resume the negotiations that Phayre had had to break off. The situation had now changed; the king wanted steamers and arms to guard against further trouble, and naturally turned to Britain for them.

Fytche took his wife up with him, and both were received very graciously.[1] The treaty that he concluded was on paper a great advance on the 1862 one. The king promised to abandon all his monopolies save those on rubies, earth-oil and timber, and to reduce all the frontier customs duties to 5 per cent *ad valorem*. He also granted certain rights of extra-territoriality, whereby the British Agent received full jurisdiction over civil cases between British subjects at

_____
[1] Phayre remained a bachelor all his life.

the capital, while those between British subjects and Burmese sub-jects were to be tried by a mixed court composed of the Agent and a Burmese officer of high rank. It was further arranged that British officers were to sit as observers in Burmese customs-houses and Burmese officers in British customs-houses.

The king made further concessions that were not embodied in the treaty.[1] A British Agent was to reside at Bhamo, British steamers were to be permitted to navigate the Irrawaddy beyond Mandalay, and British explorers to survey the route from Bhamo into western China. When this agreement was negotiated Doudart de Lagrée and Francis Garnier had already made their epoch-making journey up the Mekong, the Suez Canal was nearing completion, as also the first American trans-continental railway to the Pacific. The keenest competition for the China trade was developing between Britain, France and the United States, and the agitation in Britain and at Rangoon for the opening of an overland route to western China had become very powerful.

In November 1868 Captain Strover assumed the duties of British Agent at Bhamo. Before his arrival, however, Major Sladen, the Political Agent at Mandalay, had brushed aside all the difficulties raised by the Burmese frontier officials and made his way via Bhamo to Momein (Tengyueh). The Panthay rebellion prevented him from going further, but Fytche wrote to the Viceroy of India in a spirit of unrestrained optimism that Burma promised 'to furnish a highway to China,' and after alluding to the threat of American competition in the Pacific he urged that Britain 'should be in a position to substitute a western ingress to China'. The enthusiasts went further; they now advocated the construction of a railway through Burma to Shanghai. It is not without significance that Sladen's expedition had been partly financed by the Rangoon Chamber of Commerce, which from now onwards pressed for stronger measures in dealing with the Court of Ava. There were even those in the British service who advocated that Britain should take over the direction of its foreign relations.

Lord Lawrence, however, viewed Sladen's exploit with disfavour; he was strongly opposed to any further expansion likely to involve difficulties with Burma. His successor, Lord Mayo, warned Fytche that the scheme he had in mind was a generation too early. Hopes were damped also by Strover's disappointing reports of British trade at Bhamo consequent upon the opening of steamer traffic there.

[1] A detailed account of the negotiations is given in Albert Fytche, *Burma Past and Present*, vol. ii, appendix C, pp. 252–85.

They revived in 1874 when Lord Salisbury, the Secretary of State for India in Disraeli's newly-formed administration, in response to a petition from the British Associated Chambers of Commerce, ordered a fresh survey to be undertaken along either Sprye's route or some other. The Government of India thereupon decided in favour of the Bhamo route. The plan was for a double expedition. Colonel Horace Browne, with the geographer Ney Elias and Dr. John Anderson, was to start from Bhamo, and Augustus Margary from Shanghai. Margary completed his journey and arrived at Bhamo on 17 January 1875, before Browne's departure. He therefore started back a day ahead of the Bhamo party in order to make arrangements for them. But on 21 February at Manwyine, halfway to Tengyueh, he was murdered by Chinese tribesmen, incensed by the report that the object of the expedition was to arrange for a railway to be built through China. The threat of a still larger Chinese attack caused Browne's party to return to Bhamo, and the expedition was called off.

This was the last attempt made during the period of the Burmese kingship to penetrate China by the Bhamo route. The British agents sent from Hankow to Yunnan to investigate the Margary murder reported that the route was unsuitable for railway construction. Thibaw's accession in 1878, the subsequent withdrawal of the British Agent from Bhamo, and the closing of the Mandalay Residency rendered it impossible for the time being to search for a better route through Upper Burma, and attention was accordingly transferred to the Moulmein route.

Mindon Min was regarded by both Burmese and British as a man of the highest character. He holds a special place in the history of Burmese Buddhism as a reformer. Like Bodawpaya he held the orthodox view that the Buddhist Order's concern was solely with religion. He tightened up discipline and at the same time took measures to ensure the Order's loyalty to the throne, its protector and patron. He made liberal offerings to monks at the capital, and excused the cultivators of religious lands from payment of *thathameda* tax. He consulted the clerical authorities on all matters of religion. The *sayadaws* (abbots) were invited to address the king directly on civil matters. Village headmen and other local officials were appointed on the recommendation of the heads of local monasteries. The king went so far as to order the crucifixion of U Po, a layman, for denying that there were any genuine Buddhist monks. Unlike Bodawpaya, his relations with the Buddhist church were excellent. His officials worked harmoniously with the Thathanabaing, the head of the Order. The

Mahadanwun supervised monastic discipline. The Thudamma Council tried monks for offences against the state; those found guilty were unfrocked and handed over to the civil power. In 1865 U Nyeya, the Thathanabaing, died, and owing to a difference of opinion between the king and the chief queen his place was left vacant. Mindon himself then discharged the duties of the office. The cause of the trouble was the breach between the puritanical Shwegyin Gaing and the Thudamma sayadaws. It was never healed, and, much later on, held up for many years the appointment of a Thathanabaing by the British.

Mindon's policy, imitated by Prime Minister U Nu in recent times, was to make his court and capital the centre of Buddhist light and learning in the world. He surrounded Mandalay with large monasteries containing the finest contemporary specimens of Burmese art. In 1871 he achieved the dearest wish of his life by convoking there the Fifth Buddhist Council in the history of the religion. In 1860, in preparation for it, a complete revision of the Pali scriptures was begun. At the meeting itself, in the presence of some 2,400 monks, the texts of the Tripitaka and of the Pali Commentary, thus revised, were solemnly recited, and afterwards inscribed in Burmese characters at the Kuthodaw (Royal Merit) Pagoda, the 'Bidagat Thonbon'[1] (Three Baskets of the Law) on 733 upright marble slabs, the Commentary on the central pagoda on gold and silver leaves. One of the king's aims was, of course, the uniting of all Burmese Buddhists in allegiance to himself. The decision was taken by the Council to erect a new *hti*, 'umbrella', on the summit of the Shwe Dagon Pagoda at Rangoon. The British authorities, realizing that it was intended as a nationalist demonstration, sanctioned the ceremony, subject to the one condition that the king himself should not be present. It was carried out by his envoys amidst the greatest rejoicings. The *hti*, studded with jewels estimated then to be worth £62,000, still surmounts the majestic stupa.

Mindon's relations with the British, notwithstanding many disappointments, were always correct. He had hoped to induce Britain to restore Pegu, but patiently bowed to the inevitable. After the rebellion of 1866 he was particularly disappointed at the obstacles raised by the British in the way of his importation of arms. He felt that they ought to have adopted a more sympathetic attitude in face of his serious internal difficulties. Hence with great astuteness he cultivated relations with other European states, notably France and Italy, as a counterpoise to British power. In 1872, partly as a result of the friendly letters he received from Queen Victoria, he sent the

[1] The Burmese rendering of the Pali 'Tripitaka'.

Kinwun Mingyi, his chief minister, on a visit to England. The
Mingyi was the first member of the Hlutdaw Council ever to visit
England, but his visit did little to improve Anglo-Burmese relations.
For one thing, he was deeply disappointed because at his official

THE SHWE DAGON PAGODA, RANGOON

community in Rangoon, which was annoyed at the failure of the
various efforts to ... ... a state of constant
agitation against the king's commercial methods. Notwithstanding
the promise in the treaty of 1867 to abolish monopolies, the royal
control was never relaxed over articles of export such as cotton, wheat

Kinwun Mingyi, his chief minister, on a visit to England. The Mingyi was the first member of the Hlutdaw Council ever to visit England, but his visit did little to improve Anglo-Burmese relations. For one thing he was deeply disappointed because at his official reception by Queen Victoria he was introduced by the Secretary of State for India instead of by the Foreign Secretary. For another, the British government was somewhat piqued by the fact that on his way to London he had negotiated treaties with France and Italy. French technicians had long been employed at Mandalay. They had helped to construct the palace-city, superintended the minting of Mindon's new coinage, and ran his arms factory.

The French without delay sent out the Comte de Rochechouart to obtain ratification of the draft commercial treaty signed in Paris. On his way to Mandalay in 1873 he crossed India. At Agra, where he met the viceroy, he gave the firmest assurances that France had no designs on Burma. But the negotiations did not result in a treaty, for Burma wanted a full alliance providing for the import of arms, while the French wanted to take over the ruby mines of Mogok, hitherto one of the most rigid royal monopolies. Agreement, however, was reached on three secret articles. By the first France promised her good offices to settle disputes to which Burma was a party; the second provided that France would supply officers to train the Burmese army, and the third that Frenchmen in Burma were to be subject to the Burmese courts of law. These exceeded the envoy's instructions and were accordingly disavowed by the French Foreign Minister.

With Italy a harmless commercial treaty was concluded in 1872. This diplomatic activity is chiefly accounted for by Mindon's ardent desire to demonstrate Burma's independence. The British government's decision in 1871 that its relations with the Court of Ava were to be conducted through the Viceroy of India injured his pride. He resented being treated like the ruler of a native state in India. With a little more imagination and insight on the British side, Anglo-Burmese relations could have been so much happier, and the marked deterioration which set in some years before Mindon's death need never have occurred.

The atmosphere was not improved by the attitude of the business community in Rangoon, which was annoyed at the failure of the various efforts to open trade with China, and in a state of constant agitation against the king's commercial methods. Notwithstanding the promise in the treaty of 1867 to abolish monopolies, the royal control was never relaxed over articles of export such as cotton, wheat, palm-sugar, pickled tea, cutch and ivory, and the exporter had to pay substantially above the open market rates for these commodities. A further source of annoyance was the practice of the king's agents in buying rice directly in the delta instead of through the big brokers, and in making purchases of piece-goods in Calcutta when the Rangoon prices were too high.

But the real turning-point, after which it became impossible to restore proper relations, came as a result of Sir Douglas Forsyth's mission to Mandalay in 1875. In fixing the frontier between British and Burmese territory at the end of the Second Anglo-Burmese War Lord Dalhousie had agreed to respect the claim to independence put forward by the chiefs of the Red Karens, whose tribes inhabited the hill tracts known as Western Karenni. They were, however, slave-raiders who made a business of collecting Burmese and Shan slaves for sale in Siam. There was constant friction between Rangoon and Mandalay owing to the fact that Burmese local officials instigated them to commit depredations into British territory.

In 1873 Mindon sent troops to occupy Western Karenni, and since Lord Dalhousie had promised to protect the tribes from aggression from the north a British objection was lodged at Mandalay. Mindon replied by claiming suzerainty over the area. The matter was settled in 1875 by the Forsyth Mission, which negotiated an agreement whereby the independence of the Red Karens was recognized by both sides. On his return from Mandalay Forsyth protested against having to take off his shoes and sit on the floor at royal audiences. The 'Shoe Question', as it was called, had long been a grievance with British envoys, but the requirements of Burmese etiquette in the matter had been so much reduced as to impose no hardship on Europeans, and, in Burmese eyes, no indignity. Unfortunately, however, a time had come in British history when a new pride in empire was being instilled, and with it a national arrogance which in matters of this sort could make mountains out of molehills.

Later in that same year Burmese envoys went to the grand durbar at Calcutta in honour of the Prince of Wales, later Edward VII, on the occasion of his official tour of India. At the ceremony they were, as a matter of course, accommodated with chairs and wore their shoes. Then, in an attempt to force Mindon's hand, the Government of India issued instructions that in future the British Resident at Mandalay was not to take off his shoes on going into the royal presence. Before such an ultimatum Mindon could not give way. Henceforward the British Resident could no longer be received in audience. The loss of direct personal contact with the king was disastrous for both sides.

During Mindon's reign the first steps were taken towards modernizing Burmese administration by the substitution of fixed salaries for higher officials instead of the traditional practice of assigning them feudal appanages for their maintenance. To raise the necessary revenue for financing this new measure Mindon introduced the *Thathameda* tax on the household, with an assessment variable from year to year, in which such factors as a failure of monsoon rains or damage by fire were taken into consideration. It was a notable advance on previous practice, but Mindon was himself too ignorant of other systems of administration to carry out any far-reaching reforms in this direction; and, unlike Mongkut of Siam, he knew no European language and did not employ English tutors for his children. Nevertheless, his efforts at modernization were far from negligible. His commercial treaties with British India led to a striking increase in trade between Upper and Lower Burma. The Irrawaddy trade increased from 71 lakhs of rupees in 1858–9 to 377 lakhs in 1877–8. He established a telegraph system based on the Morse Code adapted to the Burmese alphabet, and ran a state-maintained fleet of river steamers on the Irrawaddy. He built factories equipped with European machinery for lac, cutch, sugar, and cotton and silk piece-goods. He was the first king of Burma to issue a coinage. His handsome peacock rupee took the place of the small lump of silver, used as currency in both his kingdom and Mongkut's, and called in both the tical, one-hundredth of the Indian viss of 3·65 lb.

Mindon died in 1878 without having settled the succession to the throne. In 1867 he had told Albert Fytche, when negotiating the commercial treaty of that year, that since the murder of the Heir Apparent in the previous year he had not declared his successor because he wished to avoid the danger of exciting a premature ambition in one of his sons. According to Fytche,[1] he went on to say that in any case on his death 'there would be great dissensions among the different claimants to the throne, and that disturbance would be caused even in British territory so that the English Government would have to interfere, whether it wished to do so or not'. The British Resident frequently urged him to name a successor. The most popular candidate was the Nyaungyan Prince. When the king was dying he summoned this prince to the palace, presumably with the intention of nominating him as his successor. But the prince, learning that there was a plot

[1] Albert Fytche, *Burma Past and Present*, 1878, vol. i, p. 234.

afoot to place the Thibaw Prince on the throne, and fearing a trap, took sanctuary with his younger brother at the British Residency. The Kinwun Mingyi sent a formal demand for their surrender, but, most unwisely, it would seem, the Resident sent them away to Calcutta, where they became British pensioners.

The dying king then suggested that three of the royal princes should be nominated as joint rulers, but the Kinwun Mingyi and his colleagues would not consent to a measure which they felt would certainly cause a civil war. At this juncture they fell in with the plot to make Thibaw king. He was a complete nonentity, and the Wungyis planned to establish a form of ministerial control such as they were dimly aware existed in the case of constitutional monarchies. Even the British Resident allowed himself to indulge in the fond hope that in this way the beginnings of constitutional reform might be introduced.

The Kinwun Mingyi's trump card was to have been to depose Thibaw should he prove troublesome. But he had failed completely to reckon with the Princess Supayalat, whom the conspirators had arranged for Thibaw to take as his principal wife. As soon as she became queen she prevailed upon her husband to imprison, and ultimately, in February 1879, massacre, about eighty members of the royal family, on the grounds that there was imminent danger of a rebellion. The Kinwun Mingyi and his colleagues made no real attempt to prevent this atrocious deed; they seem to have believed that it would simplify their task of gaining control over the government. Hence, when the now completely disillusioned Resident, Shaw, sent in a strong protest the Kinwun Mingyi replied that the king, as an independent sovereign, had a right to take such measures as were necessary to prevent disturbances in his own country, and that there were very good precedents for his action. Nevertheless Shaw's threat to haul down the British flag and break off all relations caused something like a panic at the Court, and troops were hastily mobilized for fear of a British march on Mandalay.

It was not long before the ministerial party discovered that far from reducing Thibaw to impotence they themselves were reduced to that position by the strong-willed queen and the ruthless men who were behind her. For she proceeded to place her minions, notably the Taingda Mingyi, in key positions in the palace. The Kinwun Mingyi remained the senior member of the government, for the king dared not risk a revolt by dismissing him, but the Taingda Mingyi and the palace clique surrounding the queen wielded all the power. Supayalat's influence over the weak Thibaw was so complete that she actually prevented him from taking the regulation number of wives considered necessary for the royal dignity.

In some ways the most tragic aspect of the situation was the impotence of the British Resident because of the Government of India's stupid ruling on the subject of footwear. Shaw died of rheumatic fever in June 1879 and was succeeded by Colonel Horace Browne, who spoke Burmese well and had had long experience of the country. The comment he made in his journal shortly after his arrival at the capital gives a good idea of what had been lost. He wrote: 'As the old King was his own Minister of Foreign Affairs, and no negotiations were ever concluded except at personal interviews with him, this sudden change [i.e. the footwear ruling] put an absolute stop to all important business. . . . The frequent visits of former Residents to the palace, and their unconstrained intercourse with the King and his entourage, formed the best, and, indeed, the only means of ascertaining exactly what was going on outside our rampart of mat walls.'

Unfortunately for Anglo-Burmese relations the bellicose Lord Lytton was Viceroy of India at the time of Thibaw's accession. He instructed Shaw to let the wungyis know that British recognition and support would depend upon the extent to which the king adopted a new policy towards Britain, granting the British Resident free access to him and greater influence over the policy of the Court of Ava. Thibaw, however, by-passed Calcutta and wrote directly to Queen Victoria and Lord Salisbury, the Foreign Secretary. On receiving news of the massacre of February 1879 Lytton urged the British Government in London to send an ultimatum to Mandalay. One's impression is that he was deliberately seeking to create a situation that would lead to war. But Britain was already fighting, somewhat ingloriously, two wars— one against Afghanistan, and the other against the Zulu warlord Cetewayo. And trouble with the Boers was brewing in South Africa. War with Burma therefore was not to be risked. It would be easy to take Mandalay, said the military experts, but many thousands more men, than were at present available, would be required for the subsequent pacification. In the light of this advice the British Cabinet enjoined upon the Government of India a policy of 'extreme forbearance', and told Lord Lytton firmly that British policy aimed at cultivating more friendly relations with Thibaw's government. But much concern was felt for the safety of the British Residency, and an armed steamboat was kept at the frontier, ready to rush aid in case of trouble.

THE GOLDEN PALACE, MANDALAY

There was a general exodus of Britishers from Mandalay, and at the end of August 1879 Colonel Browne was allowed to hand over charge to his assistant, Mr. St. Barbe, and return to British Burma. In the following month Sir Louis Cavagnari, the British Resident at Kabul, was murdered, and the Government of India, in a panic, fearing that Thibaw might be tempted to imitate the Afghans, hurriedly withdrew St. Barbe and his whole staff.

The Court of Ava, sobered by the seriousness of this step, deputed an ambassador to the Viceroy appealing for the resumption of friendly relationships. The British frontier authorities, however, held him up for clarification of his powers. He was told that only if he were empowered to negotiate a new treaty providing for the return of the British Resident to Mandalay with adequate powers, i.e. of access to the king, would the Viceroy consent to receive him. For six months he remained at Thayetmyo as the guest of the British while Calcutta and Mandalay debated his powers. At last, when it became obvious that the Court of Ava would not offer terms acceptable to Lord Lytton, the envoy returned to Mandalay. Again the Viceroy was seeking to provoke a showdown; the British Government in London on the other hand expressed its strong disapproval of his action, and sharply criticized the handling of the affair.

In April 1880 Mr. Gladstone and the Liberal Party came into power, and Lord Ripon was their choice as Viceroy in place of Lord Lytton. In London, in Calcutta and in Rangoon a more positive policy was now pursued for the improvement of relations with Mandalay. Annexation was ruled out, and on the two main subjects, which had caused estrangement in Mindon's day, the arms question and the shoe question, Lord Ripon's sympathies were with the Burmese. He told the Secretary of State for India that on the shoe question a compromise, acceptable to both sides, should be sought, and the Secretary of State replied that he would gladly act on his advice. When in the following year the Rangoon commercial community demanded strong measures on the grounds that the Court of Ava had deliberately broken the commercial treaty of 1867, Lord Ripon added his refusal to that already given by Sir Charles Bernard, the British High Commissioner for Burma. He told a deputation that he had no belief in a war to extend trade, and wrote to the Secretary of State that if the Burmese had broken faith over monopolies, so had the British over arms. This was true. Article VIII of the 1867 treaty gave the Burmese Government the right 'to purchase arms, ammunition and war materials in British territory, subject in each case to the consent and approval of the British Chief Commissioner'; but Fytche, in negotiating the treaty, had let it be understood that consent, when asked, would not be refused. Later on, however, as relations with Mindon deteriorated, the British authorities had become obstructionist in the matter.

Hopes of settlement ran high when at the end of April 1882 a Burmese embassy arrived in Simla for talks. The immediate cause of the move was the recurrence of trouble in the Kabaw valley. After the surrender of the valley to Burma in 1834 no precise demarcation of the boundary line with Manipur had been made. Thibaw's accession had been followed by a series of frontier disturbances provoked by the Burmese. Ripon's government accordingly in 1881 suggested a joint boundary commission, but the Court of Ava rejected the proposal. So a British commission proceeded unilaterally to mark out the boundary. Matters came to a head when the Burmese were found to be in occupation of a village claimed by Manipur. The Court of Ava thereupon deputed the Panjit Wun to go to discuss matters with the Government of India.

He brought with him a draft treaty covering a much wider field than the boundary dispute, and Lord Hartington, the Secretary of State in

London, welcomed this as a sign of a change in Burmese policy. He wanted to settle the shoe question and agreed with Ripon's advice that the king should have all the arms he wanted. The envoy was given a very friendly reception by the Simla authorities, who showed every desire to meet the Burmese demands. But at the end of August, without any reason given, the delegation was abruptly recalled to Mandalay. The reason for the move is abundantly clear in the record of the discussions. The Burmese had introduced into the discussions a demand for the recognition of their right to maintain direct relations with the British Government over the head of Calcutta, and to carry on communications with European powers. This was diametrically opposed to Calcutta's view of Burma's special relationship with British India. To both sides it was a question of fundamental importance: to the British for reasons of imperial security; to the Burmese because of their overmastering desire for the substance rather than the shadow of independence.

The Viceroy tried to compromise by offering two treaties, one in the Queen's name and the other a business treaty with the Government of India dealing largely with commercial matters. After the mission's return to Burma the Court of Ava sent two draft treaties to the Chief Commissioner in Rangoon for transmission to the Viceroy, one with the Queen and the other with the Government of India. In both they had inserted clauses they must have known were unacceptable: such items as the denunciation of the Treaty of Yandabo, much higher import duties and other severe restrictions upon British trade. It was clearly an act of defiance if the Burmese Government knew what it was doing; and in the light of subsequent events one cannot escape the conclusion that it acted deliberately. Lord Ripon intimated to the Court of Ava that his government could not accept them. There were no further negotiations between Mandalay and Calcutta. The first sign of the breakdown was that Burma's attitude towards Manipur over the boundary question became so provocative that the Government of India sent reinforcements to the Raja and authorized him to resist any Burmese action by force of arms. The disturbances ceased at once.

Meanwhile Upper Burma was in a state little short of chaos. Dacoity was rife, the Kachins rebelled, Chinese guerrillas burnt Bhamo, and most of the feudatory Shan sawbwas threw off their allegiance to Ava. There were movements to dethrone Thibaw. The Myingun Prince, who was a strong candidate for the throne, was at Pondicherry. He was invited to lead a rebellion, but the French interned him. In 1884, when a movement in his favour was suspected, the slaughters at

Mandalay caused the British and Chinese mercantile communities at Rangoon to demand either a change of government at Mandalay or annexation; and Dr. Marks, the most prominent Anglican divine there thundered from his pulpit against Thibaw's misdeeds. But Sir Charles Bernard, the Chief Commissioner, was opposed to annexation. He thought that the Nyaungyan Prince would prove an acceptable ruler, and recommended intervention on his behalf. The Government of India, however, refused to move: it argued that internal misgovernment did not justify intervention. In 1885 the prince died, and with him the hope of establishing a satisfactory king at Mandalay.

Thibaw's sudden withdrawal from the Calcutta negotiations proved to be the result of a desperate decision to resume the negotiations with France that had been broken off during his father's reign. In May 1883 he sent a mission to Europe ostensibly to gather information about the industrial arts and sciences, but in reality to seek alliances. It went straight to Paris, and the British Government learnt that the old question of the import of arms had again been raised. For a state as negligible militarily, and as important strategically to British India as Burma was, it was the height of folly, for France at the time was engaged upon the conquest of Tongking, and was suspected of cherishing even wider territorial ambitions in the Indo-Chinese peninsula. Britain warned France that although Burma was an independent country, it came within the British sphere of influence, and no interference from any other European power would be tolerated. Jules Ferry, the French premier, was accordingly asked to guarantee that in the event of a Franco-Burmese treaty being concluded, no facilities would be granted for the purchase of arms. He gave full assurances.

The Burmese mission, however, remained in Paris, and as the months passed by British suspicions mounted. Again and again the British ambassador sought from Ferry a clarification of the situation. After a long period of fencing Ferry at last admitted that the Burmese wanted nothing less than a full political alliance, together with facilities for the purchase of arms. He promised, however, that no such alliance would be concluded.

In the following January (i.e. 1884), since the Burmese mission was still in Paris, the British ambassador again saw Ferry. He said that the Burmese were causing such difficulties for the Government of India that should Britain be compelled to use force to bring the Court of Ava to a due regard for its obligations it would be most unfortunate if a treaty between Burma and France were the cause of such action. Ferry replied that a purely commercial treaty had just been agreed to, but it contained no political or military commitments. A French consul, he said, was to be stationed at Mandalay, but his exact powers had not yet been settled. He assured the ambassador that the treaty was a very harmless affair. The announcement in no way allayed British suspicions.

In Rangoon the mercantile community had long been agitating for annexation, and it was supported by chambers of commerce in Britain. On the other hand Sir Charles Bernard, the Chief Commissioner, remained opposed to so drastic a step, even when late in 1884 he was literally besieged by demands for strong action. He sent a firm despatch to the Government of India saying that the accounts of Thibaw's misrule were much exaggerated and British merchants had no reason to complain. Burma, he wrote, had not transgressed her frontiers, or invaded her allies, or maltreated British subjects, or broken treaties, or continued massacres, or rejected British protests, or refused redress; there was no justification for annexation.

But a few months later, in May 1885, Frederic Haas arrived in Mandalay to assume his duties as French consul. It soon became clear that very extensive concessions, damaging to British interests, had been agreed to with the Court of Ava, and that even more were in the air. In July the Secretary of State for India cabled to the Viceroy that under the terms of the treaty the French were to establish a bank at Mandalay and to finance the construction of a railway from Mandalay to Toungoo in British Burma. Haas, on his part, was urging Thibaw to improve his relations with the British and receive a British Resident. Then, under the cloak of better relations, he should negotiate treaties with France, Germany and Italy proclaiming his kingdom to be neutral territory. His advice, however, was rejected.

Meanwhile rumour had become very active. The French, it was said, were negotiating to take over the management of the royal monopolies, control the postal system, run river steamers in competition with the Irrawaddy Flotilla Company, obtain a lease of the ruby mines, and open up overland trade with Tongking. If the reports were true, such concessions would give France a dominating position in the economy of Upper Burma. Sir Charles Bernard was sceptical about them. 'But,' he wrote to the Viceroy, 'I believe this much, namely, that French agents are trying to establish themselves strongly at Mandalay with a view to joining hands at some future time with the French possessions on the upper reaches of the Red River.'

In August the Government of India passed a resolution declaring that 'the establishment by France of exclusive or dominant influence in

Upper Burma would involve such serious consequences to our Burmese possessions and to India that it should be prevented even at the risk of hostilities'. At the same time the text of a secret letter, handed by Ferry to the Burmese envoy when the commercial treaty had been signed in Paris in the previous January, leaked out from Mandalay. It contained a guarded promise that, as soon as peace and order should be restored in Tongking, arms and military stores of all kinds would be delivered to Burma through that country. Ferry, however, was no longer in power; a revulsion of feeling against his rash external policy had forced his resignation in the previous March. France was up against great difficulties in Tongking, and had wars with China and Madagascar on her hands.

Lord Salisbury on 7 August confronted the French ambassador, M. Waddington, with a copy of Ferry's letter, and told him plainly that Britain would not agree to the proposed French concessions in Burma. The ambassador disclaimed any knowledge of the matter, and promised to make enquiries. Over a month later, when no communication on the subject had been received, the French Government was pressed by Britain to clarify the situation. Its reply, communicated through M. Waddington at the end of September, was to the effect that it knew absolutely nothing about any such agreements. But by this time another Burmese envoy had arrived in Paris, and soon the French and British press carried the text of an alleged secret treaty between France and Thibaw's government. The French Minister for Foreign Affairs, when challenged, denied its existence. At the same time, early in October, Haas was withdrawn from Mandalay 'pour raison de santé'. France had left Thibaw in the lurch: she would not risk a showdown with Britain. But worse was to follow, for when Britain now pressed for a clear assurance that France recognized Burma as within the British sphere of influence, she hedged. In British eyes, therefore, a showdown with Thibaw had become essential, and his government's handling of the Bombay Burmah case provided the opportunity.

The Bombay Burmah Trading Corporation, with its chief office and timber mills in Rangoon, had for many years worked the Ningyan teak forests, north of Toungoo and somewhat beyond the British-Burma frontier, under a contract with the Mandalay government. Early in his reign, under severe financial stress, Thibaw had adopted the expedient of squeezing the corporation for higher payments. New contracts, involving substantially higher payments, were made in 1880, 1882 and 1883, and inevitably caused a certain amount of confusion. This made it easy for the Court of Ava to trump up a case against the corporation. It was accused of extracting more than twice the number of logs paid for, of bribing the local officials, and of failing to pay its Burmese foresters their due amount. The Toungoo Forest Office was willing for its records to be examined and to produce the aquittances signed by its employees.

The case came before the Hlutdaw, which, on the information that a French syndicate was being formed to take over the forests if the corporation were evicted, proceeded to give an *ex parte* judgement that it had defrauded the king of the equivalent in English money of £73,333 and the foresters of £33,333. The corporation was accordingly fined double the amount of the first sum and ordered to pay the second to the foresters. In default the corporation's timber in the Ningyan forests was to be seized. The case was a false one; its object was not to secure justice, and no real attempt was made to sift the evidence.

The Hlutdaw's decision was published in August 1885. The British government at once asked the Court of Ava to submit the matter to arbitration. No reply was received from Mandalay until the middle of October, when, still hoping for French support, the Burmese government summarily rejected the proposal. For some years the Military Department at Calcutta had had a plan ready for the invasion of Upper Burma should the need arise. The governor-general, Lord Dufferin, therefore was in a position to deliver an ultimatum to the Court of Ava. It was received on 30 October and was due to expire on 10 November. The Court of Ava was caught completely unprepared. The king sent a blustering reply, refusing to reopen the case against the corporation, but stating that if the British government wished to reappoint an agent he might 'come and go as in former times'. To the demand in the ultimatum that he must place the external relations of his government under the control of the Government of India, as in the case of Afghanistan, he made the uncompromising reply that 'friendly relations with France, Italy and other states have been, are being, and will be maintained'.

This was taken as a rejection of the British terms, and the army was ordered to march on Mandalay. Operations began on 14 November, and a fortnight later, after an almost bloodless campaign, Mandalay was occupied and Thibaw surrendered. Burma neither threatened nor was prepared for war, and it has been argued that French difficulties in Tongking presented Britain with a heaven-sent opportunity to clinch matters with Thibaw. But in view of the French rivalry with Britain for supremacy in the Indo-Chinese peninsula, which was soon

VERANDAH, MANDALAY PALACE

to develop to a further stage, involving the valleys of the upper Mekong and the Menam, the British action, in Furnivall's judgement, 'can best be justified as removing at an opportune moment a potential cause of a European war'. The refusal to reopen the Bombay Burmah Corporation case was, in all the circumstances, a sufficient *casus belli*, but the challenging assertion that friendly relations with France, Italy and other states 'have been, are being, and will be maintained', could be met by no other reply than a showdown.

With the king gone the fate of his kingdom remained to be settled. A provisional government headed by a Council of State composed of thirteen ministers was first set up under General Prendergast, the commander-in-chief of the army of occupation. The Government of India would have preferred to place the country under a protectorate, with an approved member of the royal family on the throne. But there was no suitable candidate. Hence on 1 January 1886 a proclamation was issued annexing the territories formerly governed by King Thibaw to the British dominions. After a further consultation, in February 1886 it was decided that the annexed territory should be directly administered. Burma therefore was united as a province of British India, with Sir Charles Bernard as its Chief Commissioner.

The British decision to stage a showdown with King Thibaw brought up the question of Burma's relations with China. On 26 October 1885 the Viceroy of India asked the British Chargé d'Affaires in Peking if a British march on Mandalay would lead China to protest. In reply he was told that traditionally Burma was regarded as tributary to China, and a large tribute-bearing mission had come to China in 1875. These missions, the reply continued, were decennial, but there was no record of Thibaw having sent one. Four days later, when the British ultimatum was issued to Thibaw, the Chinese minister in London offered to recommend to his government that as the suzerain power it should take the necessary action to cause Burma to rescind the order concerning the Bombay-Burmah Trading Company, and apologize to Britain. Sir Halliday Macartney, the Adviser to the Chinese Legation in London, went further, saying that the Emperor had already issued orders to this effect to the Yunnan officials. Then on 1 November came a telegram from Sir Robert Hart in Peking declaring that Burma was a tributary state and that China's position as sovereign would compel her to interfere.

China's claims seem to have taken the British Government completely by surprise. Faced by this sudden outburst it nevertheless decided that the Chinese offer was now too late, that Britain should go ahead with her action against Burma, and afterwards discuss matters with China. Lord Salisbury accordingly announced that in dealing with Thibaw Britain would give China's rights 'the most complete recognition'. This failed to satisfy Sir Robert Hart, who took upon himself the task of conducting negotiations on behalf of China. He suggested an agreement whereby in the first place Burma was 'to send tribute as before' and China was to respect whatever treaty Britain should make with Burma. Furthermore, a point on the Burma-China frontier should be opened to British trade on the same footing as the Treaty Ports. The British Foreign Office, however, was opposed to considering any convention with China until the military issues in Burma were settled; Lord Salisbury had become suspicious that Hart's definition of Sino-Burmese relations would not stand up to scrutiny. On 20 November, while the march to Mandalay was in progress, he telegraphed Hart saying there was no record of Burma having paid tribute to China: the last Sino-Burmese treaty had been concluded on 31 December 1769, and had merely stipulated the exchange of affectionate letters every ten years. Hart's reply, threatening Chinese intervention if tribute were discontinued, and suggesting that a position should be 'invented' whereby China as sovereign authorized Britain to govern a tributary state, was too fantastic to be treated seriously; he was told that when the war was over Her Majesty's Government would discuss future arrangements regarding Burma. After the occupation of Mandalay the British Chargé d'Affaires at Peking was instructed to inform the Chinese Government that Britain intended to annex Upper Burma on 1 January 1886.

Sir Charles Bernard, the British High Commissioner, was convinced that Burma was not tributary to China. Presumably he must have read the authoritative paper by Henry Burney in the sixth volume of the *Journal of the Asiatic Society of Bengal*, 'Some Account of the Wars between Burmah and China', in which, on the basis of official Burmese documents at the Court of Ava, he had carefully analysed Burma's relations with China and demolished the Chinese claims to suzerainty and tribute. The matter was referred to the Burmese ministers of the Hlutdaw in their advisory capacity to the new administration. Their reply in an official memorandum signed on 1 January 1886 pointed out that Burma had 'never at any time, or on any account whatsoever, paid anything in the shape of tribute to China'. And they went on to explain that by the Treaty of Kaungton,[1] which brought the last war with China to an end, the Burmese being victors, it had been agreed that once every ten years missions with letters of friendship should be exchanged. This, said the ministers, was in order to establish peace.

Lord Salisbury, however, was anxious to avoid hurting Chinese feelings; he told the Chinese Minister in London that his government was willing to continue the interchange of missions as provided for in the Sino-Burmese treaty of 1769, and also to negotiate concerning the frontier. In Peking, on the other hand, the Tsungli Yamen insisted that the Burmese presents were tributary. When the British Chargé d'Affaires produced a copy of the treaty taken from the Burmese *Mahayazawin*, they vehemently denied its existence. The India Office then entered the fray with a careful, factual refutation of the Chinese position; it expressed regret that the Foreign Office had been in such a hurry to accept the inaccurate statements of Hart and Macartney and said it was opposed to the despatch of any missions to Peking. But the Chinese remained obdurate, and Britain wanted a settlement, particularly of the frontier questions which had now begun to assume an urgency such as they had never done before annexation. Hence, when at last in July 1886 an Anglo-Chinese convention was signed, Britain conceded the point regarding decennial missions. But the wording of the clause was extremely guarded. It ran: 'Inasmuch as it has been the practice in Burma to send ten-yearly Missions with articles of local produce, England agrees that the highest authority in

---

[1] *Supra*, p. 413.

Burma shall send the customary ten-yearly Missions.' The intention was to commit Burma to nothing she had not already been committed to in the past. But the Burmese and the British Burma officials were unanimously against the commitment, and rightly so, for it reflected a fundamental misconception concerning Burma's position *vis-à-vis* China and concerning Burma's view of her place in the world. The clause was never carried out. China's breach of the Convention of 1894, provided an easy way out for Britain. Had it not done so, one wonders how in practice such an unrealistic commitment could have been carried out, so strong was the opposition to it in Burma.

CHAPTER 36

VIETNAM AND THE BEGINNINGS OF FRENCH EXPANSION IN INDO-CHINA, 1820–70

PRINCE CANH, the eldest son of the Emperor Gia-Long, who had accompanied Pigneau de Behaine to the Court of Versailles, died in 1801. His brother, Minh-Mang, who succeeded to the throne in 1820, hated the 'barbarians from the West'. He refused to conclude a commercial treaty with France, or even to receive the letter on the subject which Louis XVIII sent him in 1825. Three French attempts to renew commercial relations with his country were made during his reign: by Bougainville in 1825, by de Kergariou in 1827, and by Admiral Laplace in 1831. All were unceremoniously rejected. In 1826 he refused to receive a French consul and broke official relations with France.

When he died Gia-Long had enjoined upon his successor that there was to be no persecution of the three religions established in his empire—Confucianism, Buddhism, and Christianity. Minh-Mang, however, was a strict Confucian and an admirer of Chinese culture. He revived the eighteenth-century Nguyen policy of persecuting Christianity. There was much opposition among the mandarins to this reversal of his father's policy. Many of them had been friends of the Great Master, as they called Pigneau, and Le Van-Duyet, the Governor of Cochin China, once Grand Eunuch in Gia-Long's palace, was courageous enough to write a letter of protest to the emperor. 'We still have between our teeth', he wrote, 'the rice which the missionaries gave us when we were starving.' His firm stand was successful; the emperor held his hand so far as the six southern provinces were concerned. But Le Van-Duyet died in 1833, and in the following year an edict was issued for a general persecution of Christians. Le Van-Duyet's tomb was even desecrated at Minh-Mang's orders. This outrage provoked a revolt at Gia-dinh. It was cruelly repressed and several missionaries were actually put to death.

Towards the end of his life Minh-Mang seems to have changed his mind regarding the European question and to have sought ways and means of establishing contacts with European states. In November

1839 war had broken out between Britain and China, and it may be that the British occupation of Chusan and their attack on the Taku forts at the mouth of the Pei river made him realize that his rigid isolationist attitude might have dangerous consequences. But he died in January 1841, and his successor, Thieu-Tri (1841–7), revived the policy of persecution with even greater rigour. He was a man of less intelligence than his father and failed to realize that the British acquisition of Hong Kong in the very month of his accession, and the opening up of five Chinese ports to European trade, had introduced a new era in the Far East. The French were no longer willing to submit to the treatment meted out to their missionaries and traders by Minh-Mang.

Thus in February 1843, when five missionaries were awaiting death in a Hué prison, a corvette, the *Héroine*, under Commandant Lévêque, suddenly appeared before Tourane, in the name of Admiral Cécile, the commander of the French naval division in the China Sea, demanded, and obtained, their release. And in the same year the *Alcmène* delivered yet another condemned missionary. These actions were symptomatic of a new attitude on the part of the European nations and the United States of America that was causing a growing demand for extra-territorial rights. In 1844, for instance, the U.S.A. obtained such rights for its residents in China under the Treaty of Wanghsia, and in the same year by the Treaty of Whampoa France secured from China toleration for Catholics.

In 1845 Admiral Cécile again intervened at Tourane, this time to force the release of Mgr. Lefèvre, the Bishop Apostolic of the western part of Cochin China. Again the emperor gave way, under threat of the bombardment of the city. The bishop was taken to Singapore, where he managed to persuade the master of a Cochin-Chinese ship to smuggle him back into the country. The Straits Settlements Records contain an interesting document[1] giving an account of the sequel to this rash adventure 'pour l'honneur de son pays', as one French account describes it.[2]

Governor Butterworth, in a letter of 13 March 1847, reported to the Government of India that trading vessels coming from Cochin China had brought notice of new stringent regulations against foreigners there, and that he told the mandarin in charge of them that 'the English sovereign would be displeased', if they were put in force against British subjects. 'The mandarin', he continued, 'at once gave me to understand that the regulations originated in the visit to Turon

[1] Governor's Letters to Bengal, R. 14, 13 March 1847.
[2] Guy Chastel, *Un Siècle d'Epopée Française en Indochine*, p. 63.

Bay of the American ship *Constitution*, when that vessel fired upon the town and destroyed several of the inhabitants, because the demand of her commander to have a French missionary bishop, then in prison, given up to him, was not complied with. And that the restrictions in question must be viewed as a bit of policy on the part of the king, who was anxious to show his subjects that the insult offered to him had not been passed over with impunity. In proof of this he gave me a letter from the Chief Mandarin in charge of the Marine Department . . . intimating that he had sent, and wished to hand over to me, the very bishop above referred to, who had again made his way to Cochin China, after being released from prison by a French ship sent for the purpose.'

The governor then went on to say that Bishop Lefèvre had called to see him, 'as he had done about one year since, on his release from the Cochin Chinese prison as previously mentioned', and that he had forbidden him 'from any further movement towards Cochin China, more especially as the unfortunate Naquodah,[1] who took the bishop back to that country on the last occasion, had his head chopped off, and every other Cochin Chinese on board was sent into confinement with hard labour'. 'But', he commented, 'these Jesuits are little scrupulous about the means so long as they effect the end in view, and I must add that they are not sparing of themselves.' He was, however, of opinion that on this occasion the bishop would not find a boat to convey him back to Cochin China.

In that year 1847 France attempted to force Thieu-Tri to climb down by staging another naval demonstration at Tourane. Commandant Lapierre, with the *Gloire* and the *Victorieuse*, came with a demand in the name of the French government for guarantees for the safety of French nationals. Thieu-Tri kept him waiting a month for an answer. During that time he assembled a large body of troops at Tourane on the pretext of paying honour to the envoys of France. He invited the officers of the two ships to an entertainment, where they were to be assassinated. Their vessels were then to be completely destroyed by burning. When the invitation was refused the Vietnamese vessels in the port attacked the two ships and tried to set them on fire. In the fight which ensued the French ships destroyed a large number of junks and other vessels and then sailed away.

It was under Thieu-Tri's son and successor, Tu-Duc (1848–83), that matters came finally to a head. A pious and learned Confucian, he was even more devoted than his predecessors to the ideal of sealing

---

[1] Ship's master.

up his country against all European influence. At first, however, he hesitated before carrying out the policy of violence urged upon him by his mother and the *literati* but frowned on by two of his most influential servants, the Governors of Tongking and Cochin China. Finally he decided to take the plunge and issued edicts for the dispersal of all Christian communities, the destruction of their villages, and the redistribution of their lands. Men were to be separated from women, and each person was to be branded on the left cheek with the characters 'Ta Dao' (infidel) and on the right with the name of the district to which he or she was banished. Many thousands died of the treatment they received.

At the same time he turned on the European missionaries. In 1851-2 two French priests were put to death. M. de Montigny, the French consul to the governments of Siam and Cambodia, was thereupon ordered to proceed to Hué and lodge a very strong .protest. When this was rejected another French warship, the *Catinat*, bombarded the forts at Tourane.

This stiffer attitude towards Europeans coincided with a similar move in China, where Britain, France and the United States were making a concerted effort to obtain a revision of treaties. It was the period when Commissioner Yeh Ming-shen of Canton was flouting every attempt at negotiation and encouraging acts of violence against Europeans. There can be no doubt that Tu-Duc took his cue from China and was too simple-minded to realize that the consequences for his country would be far more serious than those of the blustering Yeh's exhortations to exterminate the English devils for China. In 1856 a French Catholic missionary was tortured and killed for alleged complicity in a rebellious society in Kwangsi province. Minh-Mang's victims had been executed on a similar charge, one may note in passing. In 1857 Tu-Duc had the Spanish Bishop of Tongking, Mgr. Diaz, put to death.

It was a piece of crass stupidity. France under the Third Empire was looking for a pretext for seizing territory in Annam. She already had a strong naval squadron in Chinese waters which, as a result of the murder of her missionary in 1856, was co-operating with the British against Commissioner Yeh of Canton. Spain had a base nearby in the Philippines and was anxious to join with France in dealing with Annam.

In 1857 for the second time de Montigny was sent to Hué. He presented three demands to Tu-Duc: (1) a guarantee of religious liberty for Christians, (2) permission to establish a French commercial agency at Hué, and (3) sanction for the appointment of a French consul there. His terms were sullenly rejected. In any case his mission was sent merely to justify action that France had already decided on. As soon as Canton had been seized by the Anglo-French task force early in 1858 and the Treaty of Tientsin wrung out of China in June of that year, a Franco-Spanish force under Admiral Rigault de Genouilly made its way to Tourane. It arrived there on 31 August 1858. The forts were soon put out of action and a small occupation force was landed.

Then difficulties began to pile up. The Annamites in evacuating Tourane had stripped it of everything. Supplies were unobtainable. Sickness began to take serious toll of the garrison. It was too weak to attack Hué. After considering the feasibility of a demonstration in Tongking the admiral decided to seize Saigon, the granary of Annam. Tourane accordingly was evacuated, and in February 1859 Saigon was captured.

Further large-scale operations were then held up by the resumption of hostilities in China, which culminated in the occupation of Peking by an Anglo-French army in October 1860. Meanwhile in November 1859 Rigault de Genouilly was replaced by Admiral Page who had received instructions to negotiate with Tu-Duc. The original demands were now increased. There were to be French consuls in three parts of the Vietnamese empire and a chargé d'affaires at Hué. Tu-Duc tried delaying tactics, whereupon Page proceeded to Tourane and destroyed some more forts. He had, however, to go on to assist the French forces in China, leaving a Franco-Spanish garrison of less than 1,000 men at Saigon. For nearly a year (March 1860–February 1861) the small garrison had to hold out unaided against a besieging force of 12,000 Vietnamese.

The China war ended in January 1861, and at once Admiral Charner, with a strong naval squadron and 3,000 troops, left for Saigon. On 25 February, at the battle of Chi-hoa, he defeated the besiegers and relieved the city. This was followed in April by the capture of Mi-tho. Then followed the occupation of Gia-dinh, Thu-dau-mot and part of the provinces of Bien-hoa and Go-cong. In November 1861 Admiral Bonard took over from Charner and in a few months had made himself master of the whole of Lower Cochin China, together with Pulo Condore and all the small islands at the entrances to the Mekong delta.

In May 1862 Tu-Duc sent two envoys to ask for terms. The emperor, they explained, was involved in difficulties in Tongking and wished to end the struggle in the south. In the following month a draft treaty was signed at Saigon by which Tu-Duc ceded to France three eastern provinces of Cochin China and agreed to pay a heavy indemnity in instalments over ten years. He promised the free exercise of the Catholic religion in his dominions and to open the ports of Tourane, Balat and Kuang-An to French trade.

There was considerable delay in obtaining the ratification of the treaty by the Emperor Napoleon III, since the ship carrying the delegates to France was held up by a severe storm. In the meantime Bonard committed the error of replacing the French Residents, appointed by his predecessor to supervise the native administration in each province, by Vietnamese mandarins. The result was a crop of rebellions everywhere in December 1862. Hence, when the treaty signed by Napoleon III arrived from Paris Tu-Duc at first refused to add his own ratification, and Bonard, who had taken the documents to Hué for its final confirmation, only secured it by threatening to send French aid to the rebels in Tongking.

When the next admiral-governor, Lagrandière, took over the new colony in 1863 the situation was perilous in the extreme. One rebel leader terrorized the province of Bien-hoa; another held the Cambodian frontier. Moreover, Tu-Duc, before ratifying the treaty, had already sent the mandarin who negotiated it, Phan Thanh-Gian, to Paris to plead for the restoration of the ceded territory in return for an increased indemnity. In France herself there was growing opposition to the policy of colonial expansion, while the supporters of the Mexican adventure wanted Indo-China to be abandoned in favour of their pet scheme. Even Napoleon III himself cherished grave doubts of the wisdom of the Far Eastern project. He was won over to it by the unyielding attitude of the Ministre de la Marine, Comte de Chasseloup-Laubat, who threatened to resign if Cochin China were relinquished, and by the clumsy attempts of Tu-Duc to evade the commitments he had undertaken.

While Rear-Admiral Lagrandière was engaged on the task of restoring order in his three provinces and settling their administration a further important advance in French influence in Indo-China occurred. King Norodom of Cambodia, who had come to the throne in 1860, had run into serious difficulties in 1861, when his youngest brother, Si Votha, revolted and forced him to take refuge at Battambang. For many years, as we have seen, Cambodia had maintained an uneasy existence between her two more powerful neighbours, Siam and Vietnam. Her kings had attempted to maintain some semblance of independence by paying homage and tribute to both sides. But there were constant dynastic squabbles which invited intervention.

On this occasion the refugee king made his way to Bangkok, seeking for armed support with which to regain his throne. His application was supported by Mgr. Miche, Vicar Apostolic of Cambodia, who wrote to the French consul at Bangkok to approach the Siamese government in the matter. The Siamese government sent Norodom back to Kampot in a steamer, and in March 1862 he re-entered his capital. Mgr. Miche's *démarche* was frowned on by the French authorities. Their great aim now was for France to assume the rôle of 'protector' of Cambodia. Luckily Siam did not supply armed forces. The situation in Cambodia permitted Norodom to return peaceably. The rebels were badly led, and the king's second brother soon had the situation well in hand. A French gunboat also, which Admiral Charner despatched to Phnom Penh to protect French missionaries there, had helped in bringing about the discomfiture of the rebels, for they took its appearance to indicate French support for the royal cause.

Interest in the Cambodian situation had been shown by Charner as early as March 1861, when he sent one of his officers to tell Norodom that France had decided permanently to occupy Cochin China and was anxious to help Cambodia to maintain her freedom. The king in reply had told the envoy that his kingdom owed its continued existence to the Siamese, who had saved it from Vietnamese dominance. Notwithstanding the king's assurances that in his relations with Siam he was a free man, it appeared that the latter kept a tight hold over him by maintaining a Resident at his capital.

In September 1862 Bonard himself paid Norodom a visit and suggested that through conquering Cochin China France considered that she now had a right to the tribute he had previously paid to Hué. France, it seemed, was much more concerned with pressing her claims than with safeguarding the independence of Cambodia. In April 1863 Bonard took a decisive step towards the establishment of French influence there by sending a naval lieutenant, Doudart de Lagrée, as Resident. He instructed him to make a geographical survey of the country and to establish close contacts with the king. The new Resident reported to Saigon that the King of Siam was more powerful in Oudong than the King of Cambodia himself.

This news caused Bonard's successor, Lagrandière, to decide that any further delay would give Siam time still further to strengthen her hold on Cambodia. Accordingly in July 1863 he paid a personal visit to Norodom at Oudong and offered him French protection in order to safeguard his independence against Siam. The king hesitated. He welcomed the offer of French help, for his position was still perilous in the extreme. He distrusted his brother Ang Sor, who had defeated the rebels during his absence. He also feared lest the agitator Po Kombo, who was giving the French trouble on his frontier, might attempt to seize the crown from him. But how would he stand if he threw over both Siam and Vietnam for France, and the French were then to evacuate Cochin China? Lagrandière, however, overcame his scruples on this point and he was persuaded to sign a treaty placing his kingdom under French protection.

The treaty was at once despatched to Paris for Napoleon III's signature. Then the inevitable difficulties arose. The French Minister of Foreign Affairs hesitated to advise ratification; Siam, supported by Britain, had raised the objection that, since Cambodia was her vassal state, communications between Norodom and the French could only be made through her as the intermediary. And while the matter was undecided the Siamese Resident at Oudong prevailed upon the weak king to sign a document not merely recognizing his vassalage to Siam but asserting that his true title should be 'Viceroy of Cambodia'. In return the King of Siam announced that he proposed to go himself to superintend Norodom's coronation and receive his homage. As much of the regalia, including the sacred sword, which was used in the ceremony, had been left in Siamese safe-keeping by Norodom when he returned home after his flight to Bangkok, the position was indeed delicate. But Lagrandière declared that the action proposed by the King of Siam constituted a new claim to sovereignty which had no justification. King Mongkut therefore compromised by insisting that Norodom should go personally to Bangkok to receive his crown.

Norodom decided on 3 March 1864 as the date of his departure for Bangkok. Doudart de Lagrée, on hearing of this decision, threatened to take possession of the capital by force and sent off in haste to Saigon for reinforcements. And when, in spite of this, Norodom started on his way French marines occupied the royal palace at Oudong and hoisted the tricolour. The distracted King changed his mind and returned. He found the treaty establishing a French protectorate over his kingdom awaiting him on his return, duly signed by the Emperor Napoleon. There was nothing to be done but accept the inevitable, and on 17 April 1864 the ratifications were completed.

King Mongkut, pressed by the French government to restore the insignia to Cambodia, agreed to do so on condition that Norodom should be crowned by the representatives of Siam and France. Admiral Lagrandière accepted the condition, and on 3 June 1864 the ceremony took place. Doudart de Lagrée, however, refused to allow the Siamese delegate to place the crown on the king's head, and on the following day the Siamese departed home, but not before he had made a formal statement of his king's claims to suzerainty over Cambodia and to the possession of her two westerly provinces of Battambang and Angkor. A few months later Norodom paid a state visit to Saigon, where he was received by Admiral Lagrandière. Then in April 1865 he went to Kampot to fulfil a promise he had made to pay homage to Mongkut. Such is Maspero's explanation of the incident.[1] Leclère, however, says that he went there in response to an invitation from Mongkut to a conference.[2] Doudart de Lagrée, having failed to persuade him to reject the invitation, accompanied him. The King of Siam did not turn up.

Meanwhile negotiations were in progress between Paris and Bangkok on the vexed question of the status of Cambodia. They ended in 1867 in a treaty whereby, in return for the surrender by Siam of all rights to suzerainty over the kingdom, France, on behalf of Cambodia, abandoned all claims to the provinces of Battambang and Angkor, usually known in modern times as Siemreap, which, according to the French interpretation of Cambodian history, Siam had held 'irregularly' since 1795. Norodom, who had not been consulted, protested in vain. The French at the time considered it a good bargain.

In 1866 the priest-pretender, who had for long disturbed the border between Cambodia and Cochin China, had gained enough support to make a bid for the throne. The name he took, Pu Kombo, was that of a prince of the Cambodian royal family who had died a few hours after birth. His imposture attracted wide support. He collected a large harem, put to death the Governors of Kratié and Sambor when they refused allegiance, and fortified himself at the village of Choeutéal-phlos in the province of Kanhchor. In June 1866 he defeated a royal army at Ba-phnom, but was himself subsequently defeated. Then for many months he played hide-and-seek with both the Cambodian and French forces sent against him. Every time they defeated him he disappeared, only to reappear a few weeks later and carry on a fresh struggle, until at last in December 1867 he

[1] *L'Indochine*, vol. i, p. 148.
[2] *Histoire du Cambodge*, p. 456.

was caught and killed by the inhabitants of Kompong-thom, where he had taken refuge.

While this quite serious resistance movement was in progress in Cambodia the French had their hands full with the same kind of unrest in Cochin China. Armed bands came over from the regions of Go-cong and the Plaine des Joncs into French territory and terrorized the population. The Court of Hué attempted to allay French suspicions of its complicity by appointing Phan Thanh-Gian, the ambassador to Napoleon III in 1862, as viceroy of the three provinces of western Cochin China. But there was no improvement in the situation, and in June 1866 Admiral Lagrandière decided to take possession of them. Within a week, 17–24 June, his troops occupied in succession Vinh-long, Chau-doc and Ha-tien. 'The population received us without fear and without repugnance', records Georges Maspero.[1] The viceroy committed suicide.

The French were now well set for building up a new empire in Indo-China. The next big move, undertaken while they were settling the administration of the territories under their control, was to explore the course of the river Mekong. Hardly anything was known of it save that it flowed down from Tibet. Possession of its delta was a challenge to the French to rival the British, who occupied the delta of the Irrawaddy, in a race for the trade of western China. Phayre's mission to the Court of Mindon Min in 1855 had had as one of its aims that of persuading the king to permit trans-Burma trade with China. The development of a short cut to China by an overland route to Yunnan had interested the Dutch in the seventeenth century. But van Wuysthoff's report on the Mekong, and Burma's refusal of trading facilities at Bhamo, had killed the project. The British had become interested in the idea at the time of the First Burmese War, and surveys had been made from Assam in the north and Moulmein in the south, though without success.[2]

Mindon was at first positively opposed to the scheme. But the immense pressure exerted by the textile industry in Britain from about 1860[3] led to further efforts by Phayre and his successor, Major-General Albert Fytche, which resulted in the establishment of a British Agent at Bhamo in 1868 and further attempts to find a suitable trade route into China. The agitation that finally moved the French authorities

[1] Op. cit., i, p. 149.
[2] J. L. Christian, Modern Burma, pp. 212–25.
[3] See on this point Clement Williams, Through Burma to Western China, being notes of a Journey in 1863 to establish the practicability of a trade route between the Irawaddi and the Yang-tse-kian, London, 1868.

in Saigon to send a surveying expedition up the Mekong in 1866 was largely the work of a young naval officer, Francis Garnier, who had served on Admiral Charner's staff in the China war and afterwards at the relief of Saigon, and in 1863 became district officer in charge of Cholen, a suburb of Saigon. He was inspired by two equally powerful emotions; a passionate desire to explore the unknown and a burning hatred of Britain as a colonizing power—the colossus with rotten feet, as he described her. 'Shake her and she will fall.'[1] As he was considered too young to be entrusted with command of the expedition, it was vested in Doudart de Lagrée.

The expedition, composed of ten Frenchmen and a number of native interpreters, left Saigon on 5 June. On leaving Cambodian territory it was held up by the need for Siamese passes and money, and spent the time studying the ruins of Angkor, with which Doudart de Lagrée had become familiar during his service at Oudong. Their existence had been discovered by a Catholic missionary in 1570, but although the word 'Onco' appears in a number of seventeenth-century maps it was the French naturalist and photographer Henri Mouhot who for the first time drew the attention of the West to their importance in an account of his travels published in the *Tour du Monde* in 1863.[2] His account of them, however, was that of an amateur enthusiast. It was Doudart de Lagrée's mission which gave the earliest exact data, and this was published in Francis Garnier's book in 1873.

After leaving Angkor the expedition proceeded slowly upstream to the ruins of the city of Vientiane, which were found to be completely overgrown with jungle. Then on to Luang Prabang and the nearby village of Ban Naphao, where Mouhot had died five years earlier and was buried. King Tiantha Koumane treated the members of the mission well, but warned them against pushing on into Yunnan because of the disorders there caused by the Panthay rebellion. He had paid no tribute to China since the revolt had begun in 1855 on the grounds that the roads were impassable, and on that account alone was anxious that the French travellers should not demonstrate the thinness of his pretext.

But at this stage no warnings could relieve Garnier of the obsession that he describes as 'la monomanie du Mekong', and he persuaded Doudart de Lagrée to push on into Chinese territory. There his

---

[1] Sir Hugh Clifford, *Further India*, p. 135. Clifford gives a picturesque account of his subsequent expedition. His own account of it is entitled *Voyage d'Exploration en Indo-Chine, effectué pendant les années 1866, 1867 et 1868, etc.*, 2 vols., Paris, 1873.

[2] A year later he published, in English, *Travels in the Central Parts of Indo-China (Siam), Cambodia and Laos during 1858–60*, 2 vols., London, 1864.

leader died, worn out by the fatigues and deprivations of the journey. And when the expedition, now directed by Garnier himself, arrived at Talifu the Chinese authorities courteously but firmly refused to allow it to proceed further. Garnier had, willy-nilly, to renounce his ambition of exploring the sources of the Mekong. It was obvious, too, that the river was utterly useless as a trade route connecting Saigon with Yunnan. That dream was shattered.

A new one, however, began to form, which was to have a notable influence upon the policy of the Third Republic. Garnier and his companions made their way across the Yunnan plateau and down to the Yang-tse, where they procured boats and quickly made their way down to Hankow. They had left Talifu on 4 March 1868. They arrived at Hankow on 27 May. In Yunnan they acquired from Chinese mandarins and French missionaries most valuable information concerning the waterways which linked that province with the Red River of Tongking. French interest, therefore, in the approach to western China was transferred from the Mekong to Tongking. And the Franco-Prussian War of 1870–1 forms a convenient dividing line between two quite distinct phases in French expansion in the Far East.

CHAPTER 37

THE SECOND STAGE OF FRENCH EXPANSION IN INDO-CHINA, 1870–1900

IN May 1868, when he was at Hankow on his return journey from Yunnan-fu, Francis Garnier met a French merchant Jean Dupuis. The discoveries made by the Doudart de Lagrée-Garnier mission interested Dupuis in the possibility of opening up a trade route into Yunnan by means of the Red River (Song-Koi), and he seems almost immediately to have set out for Yunnan. During 1868–9 he was in the province, but, as in Garnier's case, the disturbed state of the country consequent upon the Panthay rebellion (1855–73) prevented him from going beyond Yunnan-fu. In February 1871 he left Yunnan-fu for Hanoi in order to carry out a contract to supply the Chinese army in Yunnan with arms and ammunition. Proceeding southwards, he struck the Song-koi at Mang-hao, and from there managed to navigate it to the sea.

In the following year, notwithstanding much opposition from the Tongking mandarins and the difficulties of the route, he delivered his cargo of military stores to the Yunnan government. Then he purchased a cargo of tin and copper at Yunnan-sen for sale in Hanoi and undertook to bring back a return one of salt from that city. Salt, however, was a monopoly of the mandarins, and they refused to let him have any. Thereupon Dupuis and his followers, a mixed collection of Chinese and Filipinos, proceeded to occupy a part of the city by force and appealed to Saigon for help. The Court of Hué also appealed to Saigon; it claimed that the presence of Dupuis in Tongking was contrary to existing treaty arrangements with France and requested Admiral Dupré, the Governor of Cochin China, to put a stop to his activities.

Tongking was at the time in a deplorable state. After the T'ai P'ing rebellion (1850–64), which had caused devastation over vast areas of China, especially in the south, where anti-Manchu sentiment was strongest, bands of rebels had escaped over the border into northern Tongking and were making a living by terrorizing the local population. The Emperor Tu-Duc, quite unable to cope with them, had called on the Viceroy of Canton for help, and the latter had sent regular troops, who, instead of carrying out their task, had joined with the insurgents in the game of pillage. All these robber bands, whether regulars or irregulars, came to be known to the French as the Black Flags. Admiral Dupré saw in this state of affairs an admirable opportunity for intervention, and Dupuis's grievance as a heaven-sent excuse. He asked his government for a free hand, but was told to avoid armed intervention. Nevertheless he sent the impulsive Francis Garnier to Hanoi with a small force of 188 French and 24 Cochin Chinese troops, and instructions to arbitrate between Dupuis and the mandarins.

Garnier arrived on 5 November 1873. His attempt at arbitration lasted only a few days. Finding the mandarins obdurate, he issued a proclamation declaring the Song-koi open to general commerce. This unwarranted action goaded them into making military preparations, to which Garnier replied on 20 November by seizing the citadel by assault. His reckless audacity succeeded so well that with the additional volunteers he enrolled he was able to gain possession of five strongholds, including Hai-phong and Ninh-binh, and to control the administration of Lower Tongking. The Court of Hué was now ready to negotiate, but the mandarins of Hanoi called on the Black Flags for assistance. They appeared before the city on 21 December 1873, and Garnier was killed while heading a sortie against them. He had impetuously rushed so far ahead of his men that he was ambushed and killed before they could reach him.

Had he lived the French conquest of Tongking would have begun ten years earlier than it did, for he went there determined to force France's hand. Her prestige had become dangerously low in Asia as a result of her overwhelming defeat in the Prussian war of 1870-1, and men such as Garnier believed that the best way to revive it was to restart the movement of expansion that had been interrupted by her debacle in Europe.

The French government, however, was bound to disavow such a rash act of war as the seizure of the citadel at Hanoi, and as soon as he heard of it Admiral Dupré despatched an inspector of native affairs named Philastre to order Garnier to refrain from further acts of aggression and to negotiate a settlement with the Court of Hué. Philastre had been a personal friend of Garnier's, but he had an immense admiration for Chinese culture and had been so profoundly shocked by his friend's coup that he had written to him: 'Le mal est irréparable et pour vous et pour le but que l'on se propose en

France. Vous vous êtes donc laissé séduire, tromper, et mener par ce Dupuis?'[1]

Philastre reached Hanoi on 3 January 1874, and at once ordered the evacuation of all the forts held by the French. He realized to the full the heavy blow this would deal to French prestige, but 'justice above all things' was his motto. Dupuis's vessels were sequestrated. Then Philastre proceeded to negotiate a treaty with Tu-Duc. On 15 March 1874 it was signed at Saigon by Admiral Dupré. Tu-Duc recognized French sovereignty over Cochin China. He agreed to receive a French Resident at Hué, to open the ports of Qui-nonh, Tourane and Hanoi to French trade, and conceded to France the right to appoint a consul at each with an escort for his protection. The navigation of the Red River was declared free up to Yunnan. Once again Tu-Duc promised freedom to Christians. In return for all these favours France released him from his obligations with regard to the unpaid balance of the indemnity and agreed to supply him with gunboats, arms and instructors to enable him to deal more effectively with the Black Flags. A supplementary treaty of commerce was also concluded which granted French vessels and trade more favourable terms than those of other nationalities and provided for the appointment of French officers to key positions in the Vietnamese customs service.

On paper the concessions were considerable, but in his zeal for justice Philastre had overlooked the fact that in Vietnamese eyes his actions were taken to be a sign of weakness on the part of France. Hence as soon as the French forces had left Tongking Tu-Duc renewed the persecutions of Christians, subjected the new French consuls to the greatest indignities, and punished all who had been French partisans during the Garnier adventure. Moreover, as a counterpoise to the French threat he moved closer to China, renewing his declaration of allegiance to the emperor and seeking a fresh investiture as his vassal.

Meanwhile, with the final defeat of the Panthay rebellion in Yunnan, fresh hordes of refugees, chased out by Chinese armies, were swelling the numbers of the insurgents in neighbouring states. Their depredations affected the Laos states just as much as Tongking. There were Black Flags, Yellow Flags and Red Flags, besides professional pirates. Between them they rendered null and void the clause of the 1874 treaty declaring the freedom of the navigation of the Red River.

[1] The letter is quoted in full in C. B. Norman's *Tonkin or France in the East*, London, 1884, pp. 142–3. For a concise account of this period see Georges Maspero (ed.) *L' Indochine*, Paris et Bruxelles, 1930, vol. i, pp. 150–3 and vol. ii, pp. 1–15.

To add to the confusion, a revolt against the Nguyen emperor was stirred up by partisans of the old Le dynasty that had been brought to an end in 1804. Tu-Duc himself played the double game of encouraging banditry as a counterpoise to the French, and of asking for Chinese aid in suppressing it, fondly hoping that should France make a further move she would find herself embroiled with both.

The French were acutely conscious that any move to annex the remainder of the empire of Vietnam was calculated to arouse strong opposition on the part of China. They felt also that Peking would resent the clause in Philastre's treaty opening the Red River to European commerce as constituting an infringement of the Treaty of Tientsin (1858). The French ambassador at Peking was accordingly instructed to do his utmost to lull the suspicions of the Chinese government. But when news arrived of the murder of the Englishman Margary while attempting to explore a trade route from Burma across Yunnan, France decided to go all out for the recognition of the 1874 treaty. She jumped to the conclusion that Britain would use the murder as a means of forcing Peking to open Yunnan to British trade via Burma.

France's attitude towards China stiffened still further when in 1876 it was reported that, without any reference to her, Tu-Duc had despatched an embassy to Peking bearing the customary triennial tribute. Earlier, when the French ambassador had asked the Peking government to recall its troops from Tongking the latter had promised to do so, but in such terms as to show plainly that it regarded Vietnam as its vassal and entirely independent of France. The fact was that France, in spite of the declaration of Tu-Duc's independence in the Philastre treaty, was trying to stake the claim that the real effect of that document was to transfer the protectorate of Vietnam from Peking to Paris. Her representatives on the spot, however, were well aware that any move in this direction was bound to cause an open rupture with China.

But the Tongking situation had to be dealt with, and without assistance Tu-Duc was powerless to suppress the insurgents. He called on China for further assistance, and it was granted. Then in 1880 the Peking government publicly restated China's position. It announced that the insurgents in Tongking had been defeated by the armies she had sent to the aid of her vassal Tu-Duc, whose investiture as such had been granted by the Emperor of China. In response to this Tu-Duc sent an embassy to present his humble gratitude to the emperor.

De Freycinet was now Minister of Foreign Affairs in Paris. He was an advocate of the new expansionist policy that was producing an unparalleled movement of European economic imperialism and bringing vast territories into the colonial empires of the great powers. The choice, as he saw it, was between complete withdrawal from Tongking and further annexation. He was determined to revive French power in the East at the point of the bayonet. France was rapidly recovering from the knock-out blow she had received at the hands of Bismarck. In July 1881 both chambers of her Parliament voted the credits necessary for a renewal of military operations in Tongking.

In the next year the French attack was launched. Their difficulties in Tongking were increasing so rapidly that they had an excellent excuse for armed intervention. On the plea that the insurgent activities were menacing the safety of French subjects in Hanoi, Captain Henri Rivière was sent with an expeditionary force to operate against the bands of Black Flags infesting the Red River. His real object was to begin again the conquest of Tongking which Francis Garnier had essayed in the previous period.

Rivière seized Hanoi in April 1882 and Nam-dinh in March of the following year. But the redoubtable Black Flags in the pay of Tu-Duc again laid siege to Hanoi, and again the French leader was killed in a sortie against them. Jules Ferry, the chief exponent of the views of the 'colonial party', was now Prime Minister of France. He decided that not only must Tongking be conquered but the Court of Hué itself must be brought under French control. A strong expeditionary force was despatched to the East, General Bouet was sent to take command at Hanoi, and Admiral Courbet placed in charge of the fleet. Dr. Harmand, who had been one of Garnier's colleagues, was commissioned to organize the protectorate which was to be established over Annam and Tongking.

Bouet found Hanoi so closely invested by Black Flags that at first he could do little more than stand on the defensive until such time as Courbet's fleet should arrive with reinforcements. On 18 August 1883 Courbet appeared before the mouth of the Hué river and proceeded to attack the forts guarding it. The French gave no quarter, and the capture of the forts involved such fearful loss of life to the defenders that the Vietnamese Foreign Minister came personally under a flag of truce to negotiate. It transpired that Tu-Duc had died in the previous month, and his death had been followed by a dynastic crisis. Prince Ung-Chan, whom he had designated as his successor, had been deposed by the Council of Regency after a reign of only three days and replaced by Prince Hong-Dat, who had been raised to the throne as the Emperor Hiep-Hoa on 30 July.

An armistice was concluded, under which all forts and war vessels in the neighbourhood of Hué were to be surrendered to the French and a new treaty was to be drawn up immediately. A few days later, on 25 August, this document was signed by Hiep-Hoa and Harmand acting on behalf of France. Under its provisions Vietnam recognized the French protectorate and surrendered control over her external relations to France. French Residents with suitable garrisons were to be appointed to all the chief towns and were to have jurisdiction over the Vietnamese authorities everywhere. The French were to occupy the forts of the Hué river and all forts deemed necessary for the preservation of peace in Tongking. The customs service was to be placed under French administration. All Annamite troops serving in Tongking were to be immediately recalled, while France undertook the task of opening the Red River to commerce, suppressing rebellion and piracy, and repelling all foreign aggression. Vietnam ceded to France the province of Binh-thuan bordering on Cochin China, all her ships of war, and agreed to pay an indemnity to cover the cost of the French occupation. Pending its payment France was to retain all the proceeds of customs dues.

The first result of this action was a formal protest by China. She pointed out that no treaty with Vietnam was valid without the approval of the Peking government. The Quai d'Orsay, however, brushed this aside as a matter of no importance. Reinforcements were hurried to the East and General Bouet was told to act with vigour. China therefore replied with vigour by sending troops from Yunnan to the Vietnamese bases of Son-tay and Bac-ninh and placing orders for warships and ammunition in Europe and America. General Bouet thereupon advanced in the direction of Son Tay as far as Pallen, which he captured from its Chinese and Vietnamese defenders, but could go no further owing to the inundations caused by the enemy. He was up against regulars, but chose to regard them as insurgents, and hence beheaded all his prisoners.

While his operations were held up in this way Bouet suddenly and without warning left for France. The official announcement was that he had gone to report on the state of affairs in Tongking. Later it transpired that he had quarrelled with Harmand, the Civil Commissioner. The management of operations was taken over by Admiral Courbet, and in December 1883 he captured Son-tay from the Chinese. Soon reinforcements were pouring in, and three generals—

Millot, de Négrier, and Brière de Lisle—assumed charge of separate columns as the fighting moved further inland. Bac-ninh was taken in March 1884 and Thai-nguyen soon after. Then while one column cleared the Black River region another in June gained possession of Tuyen-quang.

In that same month a new treaty was signed with the Court of Hué which in some degree modified the harsh terms of the Harmand Treaty. For instance, the province of Binh-thuan, which had been annexed to Cochin China, was restored to Annam. Annam itself remained a protectorate, but France was given the right to occupy militarily any place in it. The administration of Tongking became a French responsibility: the emperor was left with nominal suzerainty only. But the northern Annamite provinces, which had been linked with Tongking by the Harmand treaty, were now restored to Annam.

Meanwhile, with a difficult struggle on their hands in Tongking and considerable unrest in Annam, the French became involved in an undeclared war with China. The capture of the important towns of Son-tay and Bac-ninh, garrisoned by Chinese troops, was regarded by China as an act of war. An attempt, however, to bring about a settlement was made by Li Hung Chang and the peace party at Peking. Commandant Fournier of the French navy, a personal friend of the Chinese statesman, met him in Peking for discussions. On 11 May 1884 they signed a draft convention. France was to guarantee China's southern frontier, and, in case of need, protect it; China in return was to withdraw her troops from Tongking.

The convention satisfied neither side. The Chinese Foreign Office wanted to maintain China's suzerainty over Vietnam and to close the Yunnan frontier to French trade. Worse still, a quarrel developed over the date on which the Chinese troops were to be evacuated, and Colonel Dugeune, the commander of the French troops in the Lang-son area, clashed with a Chinese force at Bac-le and sustained a serious defeat. War, therefore, was resumed. General de Négrier took the field against the Chinese in the Lang-son area, and after much hard fighting captured the place on 13 February 1885.

Admiral Courbet, after an unsuccessful attack on the port of Kelung on the northern coast of Formosa, steamed across to Foochow, where he destroyed the Chinese fleet, as it lay at anchor, and the new arsenal there. Then, returning to the blockade of Formosa, he made attack upon attack on the Kelung forts until at last, in March 1885, he captured them. Soon afterwards he occupied the Pescadores.

By this time both sides were utterly war-weary. The French,

engaged in exhausting guerrilla warfare with the Black Flags, had begun to register some progress. But on 28 March 1885 their forces at Lang-son suffered a terrible defeat at the hands of the Chinese. General de Négrier, while on a cavalry reconnaissance outside the town, was attacked and wounded. His second-in-command, Captain Erbinger, on taking over, decided to evacuate the place. His troops panicked, abandoned all their baggage and guns, and fled to the mountains.

The news of this disaster, telegraphed to Paris, caused such consternation that on 31 March, before the attack of Clemenceau, Jules Ferry's Cabinet fell. At almost the same moment negotiations which were already in progress between China and France resulted in the signing of a peace protocol. On 9 June, after the details of a settlement had been agreed between Li Hung Chang and M. Patenôtre, the French Minister at Peking, the Treaty of Tientsin was signed. Ironically enough, the agreement which it brought into effect was almost identical with the one reached a year earlier between Li and Fournier. France restored Formosa and the Pescadores to China.

Throughout the period since Tu-Duc's death in July 1883 one crisis after another had arisen at the Court of Hué. Hiep-Hoa, who had signed the Harmand Treaty at the point of the bayonet, was murdered by patriots in the following November. He was succeeded by Kien-Phuc, who reigned until July 1884, when he was deposed and replaced by Ham-Nghi. In July of the following year there was further trouble in the palace, and Ham-Nghi fled to the Laos. Thereupon the French intervened and placed their own candidate, Dong-Khanh, on the throne. With him they made a convention whereby they installed Residents in each province of Annam. In January 1886 the tightening-up process went a stage further; two *Résidents Particuliers* were appointed, one for Tongking and the other for Annam, to work under the Resident-General. In the following month a corps of Civil Residents common to both countries was created.

A similar tightening up process had been going on in Cambodia. Thomson, the Governor of Cochin China, made the abuses of the mandarinate the excuse for imposing on King Norodom a convention whereby he agreed to accept such reforms of the administration of his kingdom as the French might consider necessary. He was permitted to retain his Court ceremonies and other prerogatives but had to transfer the real government to the French *Résident Supérieur*, who could ignore the assembly of ministers if he chose. In addition each province of his realm received a Resident, whose task it was to supervise the hierarchy of native officers and councils forming its administration.

The agreement was signed in June 1884. It created a crop of fresh difficulties at a moment when the French had enough on their hands elsewhere. The population rose in revolt under a prince of the royal house, Si Vattha. They were already thoroughly discontented through the forcing upon the king of a number of previous conventions dealing with the traffic in arms, the suppression of the capitation tax on Vietnamese, and the collection of opium and alcohol dues. They were determined to prevent the establishment of the new officers. Armed bands broke over the frontier in places and the military escorts of Cochin-Chinese troops provided for the Residents were massacred. The rebellion, which began in January 1885, lasted for eighteen months and caused the French heavy losses. Then Si Vattha became a hunted man; but not until 1892, when he was at the end of his resources, did he surrender.

While this revolt was in progress the French hold on Cochin China went through a critical period. Drained of troops for service in Tongking, and with the Cambodian situation making large demands on those that were left, Cochin China was threatened with invasion by armed bands of insurgents who had assembled in the Annamite province of Binh-thuan. Then at an awkward moment, when the authorities had only 300 troops at their disposal in the city, a revolt broke out in Saigon also. When this was suppressed the governor called for native volunteers to make up a force for the invasion of Binh-thuan and Phu-yen. In response to this the Tong-doc Tran Ba-Loc, who was loyal to the French régime, left Saigon in July 1886 at the head of a force of partisans, stiffened by a handful of regulars, and treated the two provinces to a dose of such frightfulness that they were 'entirely pacified'. His merciless repression was long remembered. Everywhere indeed in the new French empire unrest and rebellion were constant factors for many years. Not until 1895 was Tongking completely 'pacified'; her discontented elements found a formidable leader in De-Tham, who proved a sore thorn in the flesh to the French.

The administrative arrangements were rounded off by decrees issued in October 1887. These placed the Protectorates of Annam and Tongking in the hands of the Minister of Marine and Colonies in Paris and brought together Cambodia, Cochin China, Annam and Tongking to form the *Union Indochinoise*. The higher administration of this was entrusted to a civilian governor-general and was divided into five departments under the *Commandant supérieur des troupes*, the *Commandant supérieur de la Marine*, the *Secrétaire général*, the *Chef du Service judiciaire*, and the *Directeur des Douanes et régies*, respectively. Under the direct authority of the governor-general Cochin China had a lieutenant-governor, Annam and Tongking combined a resident-general, and Cambodia a resident-general. Each of these units maintained an autonomous organization and had its separate budget.

CHAPTER 38

SIAM UNDER MONGKUT AND
CHULALONGKORN, 1851–1910

MONGKUT, who was the rightful heir to the throne when Rama II died in 1824, was a Buddhist monk when his elder brother, Pra Nang Klao, seized the throne and became Rama III. He was then twenty years old and quite inexperienced in matters of state. Though he had entered a monastery only for the short period that was customary for all young men, he now remained in the order and eventually became Sangkaret Bawaraniwate. In his early years as a monk he became famous for his knowledge of the Pali scriptures, and later for the reformed sect, the D'ammayutika, which he founded. Soon he began to widen the scope of his studies, learning Latin, mathematics and astronomy from the scholarly French missionary Bishop Pallegoix, and English from the American missionaries Caswell, Bradley and House. He became an enthusiast for the study of English, which became his second language; as a king he signed all state papers in roman characters, and his fluent, ungrammatical style makes his letters delicious reading. 'My gracious friend,' he wrote to Sir John Bowring, the British envoy, who came to negotiate a treaty in 1855, 'It give me today most rejoyful pleasure to learn your Excellency's arrival here. . . . Please allow our respects according to Siamese manners. Your Excellency's residence here was already prepared. We are longly already for acceptance of your Excellency.'[1]

These years of study gave Mongkut something which no previous King of Siam had had—a range of contacts beyond the almost prison-like isolation of life in the royal palace. As a monk his pilgrimages and preaching brought him into touch with all sorts and conditions of people, while from his European teachers and books—for he was a voracious reader—he gained information about foreign countries and international relations which was to prove of the utmost value to him and his country. It is perhaps not too much to say that Siam owed to Mongkut more than anyone else the fact that she preserved her

[1] A facsimile of the letter is in Bowring's *The Kingdom and People of Siam*, London, 1857, vol. i, attached to p. 1.

independence when by the end of the nineteenth century all the other states of South-East Asia had come under European control. For he almost alone among his people could see clearly that if China had failed to maintain her isolation against European pressure, Siam must come to terms with the external forces threatening her and begin to accommodate herself to the new world, in which Asian traditionalism appeared outworn and inefficient.

King Nang Klao had sons of his own and intended that the eldest should succeed him. But when he lay dying a meeting of the chief princes of the royal family and the highest officials of the realm invited Mongkut to accept the crown, and after some hesitation he agreed on condition that his brother, Prince Itsarate Rangsán, should be appointed Second King. Prince Itsarate, whose English was perfect, and whose home was built and furnished in European style, never took a prominent part in public affairs; but as an adviser to the government his influence was great. He had more advanced political ideas than his brother and a mind at least as acute.

The introduction of Western ideas and methods, even on a limited scale, caused a double conflict—one between the king and the ruling classes, and the other in the king's own mind, where Western progressive ideas clashed with oriental conservatism, leaving him a mass of contradictions. The picture of him portrayed by the excellent Mrs. Leonowens, the English governess he engaged in 1862 as tutor for the royal children, gives some idea of the contradictions, although the lady was gifted with more imagination than insight in her description of his domestic life.[1] The Siamese memory of him today is certainly not of a revengeful or cruel man, nor of one needlessly suspicious. Judged against the background of his own people, he emerges both morally and intellectually head and shoulders above the level of the Siamese aristocracy of his day. It is not too much to claim that among the benevolent despots of the world he ranks high.

Mongkut opened the door for European influence when in 1855 he concluded the Treaty of Friendship and Commerce with Britain. In their resentment at the treatment they had received both 'Raja' Brooke and the American envoys, who had failed with Pra Nang Klao, had foolishly advised that only warlike demonstrations would move the Siamese. An interesting sidelight on this is the fact that in the negotiations with Sir John Bowring one of the greatest obstacles in

[1] *An English Governess at the Court of Siam*, Boston, U.S.A., 1870. Margaret Landon's *Anna and the King of Siam*, which is based on it, is equally unfair to Mongkut. The fairest estimate of him is in Malcolm Smith's *A Physician at the Court of Siam*, London, 1946.

the way of agreement was Mongkut's fear that Siam's rival Vietnam would assume that he had been intimidated by the British into signing a treaty. Bowring's task was rendered easier by the simple fact that his plenary powers had been conferred on him by Queen Victoria, whose sign manual was affixed to his documents. But his greatest asset came from the fact that he liked and respected the Siamese and won the personal friendship of the king. The overriding fact was that Mongkut was particularly anxious for the friendship of Britain.

RAMA IV (KING MONGKUT) OF SIAM

The treaty, which contained more important concessions than Siam had ever granted to a foreign power, was negotiated in less than a month. It limited the duty payable on goods imported by British merchants to 3 per cent *ad valorem*, permitted the import of opium duty-free but subject to certain necessary restrictions, and laid down that exports were to be subject to duties according to an agreed schedule. British subjects were to be permitted to purchase or rent land near the capital, and no additional charge of any kind might be imposed on them, save with the sanction of both the supreme Siamese authorities—i.e. the First and Second Kings—and the British consul.

Bowring claimed that these provisions 'involved a total revolution in all the financial machinery of the Government'. They must, he thought, bring about a complete change in the whole system of taxation, seeing that they affected a large proportion of the existing sources of revenue and would uproot a great number of long-established privileges and monopolies held by the most influential nobles and the highest functionaries in the state. Both Mongkut and his successor, Chulalongkorn, carried out the treaty faithfully.

The other main concession was the establishment of the extra-territorial system for British subjects. The treaty laid down that a British consul was to reside at Bangkok and exercise civil and criminal jurisdiction over all British subjects in Siam, who were thus made independent of the Siamese courts and answerable to the consul alone. This was not a complete novelty in Siam's relations with European powers; the Dutch had extorted a similar concession, though not in identical terms, from King Narai in the seventeenth century. But by Bowring's time it had long fallen into desuetude. In the days of the great chartered companies of the seventeenth and eighteenth centuries rulers in South-East Asia had preferred that each community of foreign merchants—and this included the Chinese as well—should be under the control of a chief, with whom the ruler could deal directly in all matters concerning them. Mongkut's initial hesitation to accept the system lay mainly in his fear that he would be unable to control the consul, but he accepted Bowring's assurance that only men worthy of his confidence would be appointed.

The conclusion of this treaty was epoch-making. It speedily attracted the attention of other powers, and during the next few years a spate of similar treaties came into being. They were made with France and the United States in 1856, Denmark and the Hanseatic cities in 1858, Portugal in 1859, Holland in 1860, and with Prussia in 1862. In 1868 Sir John Bowring himself was commissioned to conclude treaties on behalf of Siam with Belgium, Italy, and Norway and Sweden. British trade reaped the greatest harvest from this revolutionary change in Siamese policy. Singapore and Hong Kong began to carry on a thriving trade with Siamese ports. The British Bombay-Burmah Corporation secured a preponderating share of the teak industry in the forests of northern Siam. British firms did most of the foreign business in Bangkok, and Britain soon came to have by far the largest capital investment in the country.

Important as these treaties were in introducing new commodities to Siam and providing new contacts, they probably contributed less to the modernization of the country than Mongkut's policy of employing Europeans to reorganize the government services. They came in as advisers and teachers, but, in the absence of Siamese officers with technical training or the right kind of administrative experience, many of them became heads of departments. In this matter Chulalongkorn went even farther than his father. Most of his foreign advisers were British, since their experience in India and Burma suited them for the conditions of work prevailing in Siam. But he also appointed Belgians and Danes. His General Adviser, who carried through most of his reforms, was Rolin-Jaequemins, a Belgian lawyer of repute, who had been Minister of the Interior at Brussels. One of his most efficient servants, a Dane, was head of the provincial gendarmerie. The Italian Major Gerini, who was in charge of the military cadet school, achieved distinction for his scholarly contributions to Siamese history and archaeology, and later for a pioneer study of the section of Ptolemy's *Geographia* relating to South-East Asia.

With France Mongkut's relations were at first quite cordial, and Napoleon III's envoy was given a splendid reception at Bangkok in 1856. French missionaries were given much freedom to build schools, seminaries and churches, though the king and his Court remained fervently Buddhist. But French trade failed to make much headway in face of British competition, and when France began to expand in Cochin China and her interests clashed with those of Siam in Cambodia Mongkut became decidedly uneasy. The treaty of 1867, whereby Siam surrendered her claims over Cambodia in return for France's recognition of her rights over the old Cambodian provinces of Battambang and Siemreap, and the French exploration of the middle and upper Mekong only served to increase his suspicions concerning the trend of Napoleon III's imperial ambitions, and to strengthen his desire for closer co-operation with Britain.

Mongkut's intense interest in science was the cause of his death in 1868. A total eclipse of the sun was due to occur on 18 August of that year, and as it was to be visible from peninsular Siam a French scientific expedition chose Sam Roi Yot, on the Gulf of Siam 140 miles south of Bangkok, as the spot from which to study it. Mongkut did all he could to make the expedition a success by clearing the jungle and erecting houses for his guests and himself. Sir Harry Ord, the Governor of the Straits Settlements, and his wife attended by special invitation of the king, who also invited all the Europeans in Bangkok to witness the eclipse. It was, he felt, a wonderful opportunity for demonstrating to his subjects the importance of scientific knowledge. Everything went well, the eclipse was seen under perfect conditions, and the king's joy was unbounded. But it was a malarial spot, and the king went down with fever as soon as he reached home. He died in the following month.

He had promoted the digging of canals, the construction of roads, shipbuilding, and especially the teaching of foreign languages. He had established a mint in the palace, and from 1861 minted flat coins in substitution for the rounded lumps of gold or silver previously in circulation. Was it a coincidence that Mindon of Burma had begun to mint coins in the previous year? He had patronized the printing press introduced by Christian missions, constructed buildings in a European style, and begun the reorganization of the army.

An immense amount still remained to be done. Siam was still in 1868 a backward oriental country, unready in general for such violent changes as the adoption of European models in the various public services must inevitably bring. The situation which faced Chulalongkorn has been summed up thus:

'There was no fixed code of laws; no system of general education; no proper control of revenue and finance; no postal or telegraph service. Debt slavery was not fully abolished; the opium laws were badly administered; there was no medical organization to look after the health of the city. There was no army on modern lines; there was no navy at all; there were no railways and almost no roads. The calendar was out of step with the rest of the world. The list could be extended.'[1]

Chulalongkorn was only sixteen years old when his father died and he became King Rama V. His education had begun under Mrs. Leonowens, who had never ceased to instil into him her views on the reforms necessary in his country. Later he had been placed under the absolute authority of an English tutor, Robert Morant, but owing to his father's death this discipline lasted only a year and a half. As he was a minor, the government was under a regency until 1873, and he seized the opportunity to travel and study on the spot methods of administration in Java and India. This tour made a deep impression on his mind. He returned home far more enlightened than almost any of his subjects, and at once began to put into operation a series of reforms which in the long run introduced radical changes into every

[1] Malcolm Smith, op. cit., pp. 85–6.

department of the national life. He realized forcibly that if his country were to preserve her independence she must, willy-nilly, put her house in order according to the prevailing European notions, or at least keep up the appearance of doing so.

His first essay in this direction was the dramatic announcement at his coronation in 1873 of the abolition of the practice of prostration in the royal presence. His father had done something towards increasing the monarch's accessibility by abolishing the ancient taboo against looking on the royal face or watching a royal procession. Rama III had left the palace only once a year for a ceremonial visit to the temples of the city. He had travelled by water, but the people had had to shut themselves in their houses out of sight, and the route to be traversed by the royal barge was cleared of all craft. Chulalongkorn often drove about in public and had informal conversations, but he made no attempt to rid himself of the traditional harem life, which tended to isolate him in a sacred city of women and children and servile officials, with its atmosphere poisoned by jealousy.

Like the abolition of prostration, his early reforms sprang from a realization that there were certain abuses which it was not to his interest to tolerate any longer. The ignorance of the aristocracy was one, and he forced them to send their children to the two schools with European curricula which he established at the palace. These produced a few men of outstanding attainments such as Prince Devawongse, the first Siamese Foreign Minister to speak European languages, and Prince Damrong, who as Minister of the Interior introduced European efficiency into his office and transformed the whole system of local administration.

Slavery was another intolerable abuse. Though not as harsh as the plantation system of America, and governed by the precepts of the Laws of Manu, its abolition was an obvious essential of the modernizing process. Mongkut had issued regulations to mitigate the lot of the slave, but Chulalongkorn in 1874 struck a powerful blow at its root by decreeing that thenceforward no one could be born a slave, and that the practice of selling oneself for debt was illegal. There was, however, still much to be done to root it out and check its persistence under other names. Gambling was its chief cause, and it was only the abolition of public gambling-houses and the placing of restrictions on moneylenders that rendered the decree effective. These reforms did not come until the present century.

Along with slavery disappeared the compulsory services of the *Prai* and *Sui* classes in the army and police, and in private labour for the profit of the Crown. In their case it was the reform of the military system and the introduction of modern forms of taxation that revolutionized their life. The long-term results of these measures have been most striking, especially by contrast with Siam's two neighbours, French Indo-China and British Burma. The Siamese peasantry became, in Graham's words, 'a sturdy and independent class free from the ancient thraldom, owning its own land, depositing money in the savings bank, in fact, acquiring a stake in the country.'[1]

The corruption and peculation prevalent among the officials gave Siam the reputation of being one of the worst-governed countries in the world. One of the most pressing needs was to put the country's finances in order. And it was not simply a case of bringing into the Treasury the money that was finding its way into the pockets of extortionate officials, but of controlling expenditure, setting up a proper system of audit and accounts, and reorganizing the Customs and the Inland Revenue. This problem was for long beyond the competence of the government, until in 1896 the services of a financial adviser were obtained from the British government, and after him those of a former Accountant-General of Burma.

Even then it was not until 1901 that the government's first budget was published. Before the fiscal system was modernized it was estimated that from five to six millions sterling were squeezed annually out of the people by tax-gatherers and monopolists, while of this amount only £1,200,000 ultimately reached the Treasury. A favourite money-making device was to collect land taxes without giving receipts, so that the tax could be forcibly collected several times over. Writing in 1902, J. G. D. Campbell was able to say that even Siam's worst enemies would admit that the improvement in the collection of taxes had been enormous, and as a result the people were 'immeasurably better off' than they had been ten years earlier.[2]

Provincial administration was an equally black spot. Under the old system provinces were largely autonomous; in practice so long as the provincial governors regularly remitted the due amount of revenue to the capital they were left alone. The great evils were the farming of dues, feudal privileges—especially in the matter of forced labour—and general inefficiency. The abuses of local justice were also, from a European point of view, flagrant. In 1892, therefore, the whole system of administration was centralized under the Ministry of the Interior, and the direct collection of practically all the taxes was

[1] W. A. Graham, Siam, I, p. 238.
[2] J. G. D. Campbell, Siam in the Twentieth Century, p. 180.

substituted for the old farming system. The reform of local administration was then carried out by Prince Damrong, who introduced the system developed by the British in Burma. The whole kingdom was divided into eighteen *monthons*, each with a resident High Commissioner at its head. These were subdivided into provinces, villages and hamlets. Each hamlet of about twenty families was placed under an elder, and the elders together elected the headman of the whole village.

The reorganization of the administration of justice was mainly due to the efforts of Rolin-Jaequemins, who called in the assistance of a number of Belgian lawyers to advise the judges. He was ably seconded by Prince Rabi as Minister of Justice. Rabi was one of hundreds of young men whom Chulalongkorn sent abroad to learn Western methods. He was educated in England and took his degree at Oxford. One of his achievements as minister was to establish a legal school for the training of Siamese lawyers, for the immediate result of the modernization of the legal system had been to throw the chief legal business into the hands of foreigners. A further result of the judicial reforms was the reform of the prison system and the modernization of the police force. For the last-named task officers were recruited from the Imperial Police Service of India and Burma.

Waterways were the main mode of transport in Siam, and rulers who gave their attention to the improvement of communications concentrated on cutting canals to link up rivers and creeks rather than on roads. Villages were built along the banks of waterways. Provincial towns were simply larger settlements on a maze of waterways with many houses on floating pontoons. When Chulalongkorn came to the throne, Bangkok had hardly any streets and was called the Venice of the East. The best roads were simply bullock-cart tracks usable in the dry season, or mountain tracks for pack animals. Under such conditions the railway age was late in arriving. Chulalongkorn first became aware of the importance of railways through the British efforts to survey routes from Burma to western China. But the first railway in Siam was not completed until 1893. It covered the sixteen miles between Bangkok and Paknam and was built by private enterprise, though with valuable financial help from the king.

France's encroachments upon Siam's eastern frontier in the eighteen-nineties caused so much alarm that the government decided to build a strategic railway from Bangkok to Korat. Chulalongkorn himself cut the first sod in 1892, and a Royal Railway Department was formed to control the work, which was under an English contractor

WAT BENCHAMA BOPHIT, BANGKOK

with experience of similar work in Ceylon and Malaya. Unfortunately the department was under a German who had unsuccessfully tendered for the contract, and he quarrelled so much with his English rival that ultimately in 1896 the government cancelled the contract and completed the work with its own engineers. The first section—from Bangkok to the old capital of Ayut'ia—was only completed in 1897. The remainder of the work was completed before the end of 1900, and in opening the railway Chulalongkorn proudly said that he counted the day one of the most auspicious in his life. A further section carrying the railway to Lopburi, seventy miles north of Bangkok, was opened in 1901. This northern line was gradually extended to Utaradit and Sawankalok in 1909. The first section of the future Peninsula Railway that was ultimately to link up with the Malayan Railways and connect Bangkok with Singapore was begun in 1900 and reached Petchaburi in 1903. The agreement for its extension to the frontier of British Malaya was made in 1909 with the Government of the Federated Malay States.

As in the case of Burma, Siam's education in the past was conducted entirely in the Buddhist monasteries. The missionaries were the first to introduce secular education of a more advanced type. In 1891 Prince Damrong was sent to study educational methods in Europe, and on his return a government Department of Education was set up. This later became the Ministry of Public Instruction. Its initial task was to improve primary education, and it did so by adapting the monastic school buildings to educational needs and providing apparatus. The task of developing secondary and higher education was more difficult owing to the absence of textbooks in the Siamese language. English was considered the best medium for higher education; hence the original provision for state secondary education was for a dual system of schools. One type was to give a course in Siamese for boys proceeding no further; the other was to provide a five-year course in English as a preliminary to the scientific study of a special subject.

In 1899 the Siamese government applied for the loan of a British civil servant to reorganize the educational system, and the Board of Education sent out Mr. J. G. D. Campbell to act as adviser to Prince Damrong for two years. So much effort, however, was being concentrated upon the other departments of state that the Education Department made little progress, and when Campbell left the Siamese service he reported that education was still in a very backward state. Secondary and higher education were almost non-existent outside

Bangkok, and even there school accommodation was inadequate and of a low standard, there was a dearth of qualified teachers, and systematic inspection was only in its earliest beginnings.

Notable advances were made by the establishment during the 'nineties of three government schools entirely controlled by English teachers. One of these was a school for girls, Sunandalaya. This and one of the boys' schools, King's College, were boarding schools for the children of the nobility. The other was a boys' day school for sons of middle-class parents. The curriculum was largely that of the similar class of school in England, and the object was to transplant the English public-school system into Bangkok. When these schools were founded a fairly large number of Siamese boys had received their education at leading English public schools, and among the new generation at the end of the century there were many enthusiasts who believed that the upper classes in their country needed a strong dose of the qualities, such as *esprit de corps*, manliness and honour, which the English system inculcated.

Siam had no university in Chulalongkorn's day, and only a very few Siamese proceeded to British universities. There were, however, departmental schools for training in specialist subjects, law and medical schools, a survey school, and military and naval cadet schools. But until much later Siam had no technical school and no institution for the systematic study of art. The great developments in education were to come after Chulalongkorn's death. His reign saw only the small-scale beginnings of things and the gropings after a policy. The monastic schools catered only for boys, and the hopelessly inadequate sums of money the Education Department had at its disposal crippled its efforts, notwithstanding the immense zeal which two Englishmen on its permanent staff, R. L. (later Sir Robert) Morant, Mrs. Leonowens's successor as tutor to the royal children, and W. G. Johnson, who reorganized primary education, displayed in combating enormous difficulties.

The recruitment of so large a corps of European advisers was indeed a step of the utmost importance, but it can hardly be said that the best use was made of their abilities and experience. Few Siamese officials gladly co-operated with them. There was what Campbell has called 'a universal horror' of anything of the nature of a permanent European Civil Service in the country.[1] It arose from the fear that such a step might lead to loss of independence. Hence the path of the European adviser was strewn with the subtle forms of obstruction,

[1] *Ibid.*, p. 172.

the technique of which the shrewd Siamese knows so well. But in the light of later developments, and against the background of deeply-ingrained traditionalism, one may assess the achievements of Chulalongkorn's reign as truly remarkable. And if one refuses to attribute to him personally the zeal for reform that his admirers have praised in somewhat exaggerated terms, the fact remains that the real progress that was made was possible only through the exercise of his absolute power.

CHAPTER 39

BRITAIN, FRANCE AND THE SIAMESE QUESTION

(a) Luang Prabang

THE French conquest of Cochin China wrought a profound change in Franco-Siamese relations. In the first place it brought Siam's eastwards expansion to a stop. France took the place of Vietnam as the competitor with Siam for dominance over Cambodia, and within the briefest possible time won the contest decisively. King Norodom, who had already accepted Siamese suzerainty, was literally forced by the French in 1863 to accept their protection—a position which, he was soon to find, was tantamount to complete control—and four years later Siam signed a treaty with France accepting the inevitable, though with Battambang and Siemreap as a quid pro quo. Siam's attempts to expand southwards and secure a dominant position in Malaya had likewise been stopped by British action to secure the independence of the threatened states. Unlike France in Indo-China, Britain was in no hurry to force her 'protection' on the Malay rulers. The contrast between them as empire-builders, one may venture to comment, was to become even clearer as French expansionist efforts in Indo-China progressed. 'Britain', it has been well said,[1] 'annexed areas where she had interests to protect, whereas France annexed areas where she *wished* to have interests to protect, and so had to shut out competition from the start.'

The French thesis regarding Siam was that her policy was expansionist, and that, finding her ambition thwarted on the east by France and on the west and south by Britain, she naturally began to concentrate her attention upon the Laos states in the north.[2] Auguste Pavie, who played so important a part in French expansion into these Laos states, seems to have been the first to have expressed this view; his belief was that Siam's advance, checked in one region, would be sure to break out elsewhere. It was a most plausible theory, and extremely convenient propaganda for French empire-builders. For

[1] E. V. G. Kiernan, *British Diplomacy in China, 1880 to 1885*. Cambridge, 1939.
[2] Le Boulanger: *Histoire du Laos Français*, 4th ed., Paris, 1931. This thesis has been uncritically accepted by Virginia Thompson in *Thailand, the New Siam*, pp. 183–92.

the time was to come when they would be at pains to show that the
Siamese suzerainty over the Laos state of Luang Prabang constituted
an unwarranted denial of the older and better claims of the empire of
Vietnam to its allegiance. The fundamental fallacy in such an argument lay in reading European diplomatic ideas into the relationships
between the states of the Indo-Chinese peninsula. But the French did
it consciously and deliberately, and with the single-minded aim of
exploiting to the full any situation that could be used to their advantage.

In 1827 the Siamese armies under P'ya Bodin had extinguished the
Laos kingdom of Vientiane for attempting to assert its independence.
When this occurred Vientiane's sister state of Luang Prabang, which
had acknowledged the suzerainty of Siam for half a century, became
restive, and in 1831, and again in 1832, offered homage to Hué in the
hope of gaining independence by playing off the one against the
other.[1] Nothing came of this effort, however, for Minh-Mang had too
much on his hands in Cochin China and Cambodia to risk serious
entanglements elsewhere.[2]

Souka Seum, who succeeded to the throne of Luang Prabang in
1836, had lived for ten years as a hostage at Bangkok and did not
receive Siamese recognition and permission to return until 1839.
Annamite sources contain a story that during the interval between his
father's death and his own return home a prince of Luang Prabang took
advantage of a rebellion against Minh-Mang in Tongking to ravage the
the provinces of Thai-nguyen, Cao-bang and Lang-son round about
1836–7, but was finally defeated and burnt alive in the woods in which
he took refuge. Souka Seum, who reigned until 1850, was a prudent
man who made no attempt to take advantage of Siam's concentration
upon Cambodia by pursuing a heroic policy. Throughout his reign
his kingdom maintained strict peace and well-being.

His brother, Tiantha Koumane, who succeeded him in 1851,
received the French explorer Henri Mouhot in 1861, and it was in the
little village of Ban Naphao, not far from his capital, that Mouhot died
of fever in October of that year.[3] During his reign also other European
explorers busied themselves with surveys of his country. There was a
Dutchman, Duyshart, who was employed by the Siamese government,
and whose papers, never published, were presumably utilized by

---

[1] See above, chap. 25.

[2] See above, chap. 26.

[3] Mouhot described Luang Prabang as a 'delicious little town' in a charming situation, with only about 8,000 inhabitants. His *Travels in the Central Parts of Indo-
China (Siam), Cambodia, and Laos during 1588-60* was published in London in 1864.
For shorter accounts of his work see Sir Hugh Clifford's *Further India*, pp. 208–11,
and Le Boulanger's *Histoire du Laos Français*, pp. 219–29.

James M'Carthy in the preparation of the detailed map of Siam published by the Royal Geographical Society in 1888. There was also the Doudart de Lagrée-Garnier expedition, which arrived at Luang Prabang in April 1867 on its way to Yunnan.

Garnier's anglophobia had been ablaze at reports that they had been forestalled by a party of English explorers, about forty in number, who had cut in above them from Burma; but near Chieng Kang, as the Frenchmen were pushing on determined to die rather than suffer themselves to be outdone, they met Duyshart journeying downstream, a solitary Dutchman with his native staff, and realized to their immense relief that his activities were the cause of the rumours which had so greatly disturbed their minds. The incident is interesting for the light it throws upon the French outlook in the matter of Indo-China. The term 'Anglo-French rivalry' has been too loosely used in this connection. The rivalry was mainly from the side of the French, who shivered at the thought of an imaginary Englishman already ahead of them in whichever direction they proposed to expand. Their actions again and again forced the British to react in defence of what they regarded as their legitimate interests, as in the case of the march to Mandalay in 1885.

During Tiantha Koumane's reign the Tran Ninh question came to a head again. The kingdom of Chieng-Khouang[1] had been extinguished in 1832 by Minh-Mang and its territories annexed to Vietnam. It was brought into strict servitude by the most brutal methods, and everything possible was done, even to forcing its people to wear Annamite dress, in order to crush out all traces of its long-prized individuality. This played into the hands of Siamese secret agents, who stirred up a revolt in which the Vietnamese governor was killed. After restoring order Vietnam won over Chao Pho, the eldest son of the previous king, Chao Noi[2], and in 1855 placed him in control of the administration of Chieng-Khouang, with the rank of 'imperial mandatory prince'. This caused Tiantha Koumane to take up the position that the old kingdom had been restored and must therefore resume payment of its ancient tribute to Luang Prabang. After lengthy negotiations, which were rendered easier for Tiantha Koumane by the fact that the Emperor Tu-Duc became deeply involved in trouble with the French, Chao Pho agreed to pay triennial tribute to Luang Prabang, while continuing to pay annual tribute to Vietnam.

[1] The kingdom itself is often referred to by the name of its capital, Chieng-Khouang, or, in many maps, Kiang Kwang.
[2] See chap. 25.

Tiantha Koumane's last years were rendered happy by the gracious act of King Mongkut in restoring the famous Prabang image of the Buddha to its historic home. It had been carried away from Luang Prabang to Vientiane in 1707, when the division of the old kingdom into two occurred. In 1778 it had been taken away from the latter place by the Siamese general Chulalok, but restored four years later. Then when P'ya Bodin destroyed Vientiane in 1828 it had been brought to Bangkok.

In 1864, five years before Tiantha Koumane's death, refugees began to pour out of western China into Tongking and the various Laos states. Tongking was the first to suffer when they began to organize themselves into armed bands known by the colours of their flags. The turn of Luang Prabang and Tran Ninh was to come early in the reign of Tiantha Koumane's successor, Oun Kham (1872–87).[1] Among the Thai peoples they were known by a word transliterated as 'Ho' or 'Haw' and meaning 'Chinese'. In 1871 a band of some 2,000 Hos, belonging to the Red Flag organization, was driven away from the Black River of Tongking by the Yellow Flags. They thereupon made their way across country into Tran Ninh and built themselves a fortified camp at Tung-Chieng-Kam, some three days' march from the capital. Having defeated the combined forces of Luang Prabang and Tran Ninh, supported by a Vietnamese contingent, they captured Chieng Kham and Chieng Khouang and devastated the country so thoroughly that they soon had to look elsewhere for booty.

They next threatened Luang Prabang, but suddenly turned southwards to Vientiane and Nongkai. Almost simultaneously in 1872 the Siamese government received frantic appeals for help from King Oun Kham and its own Governor of Nongkai. A Siamese army was accordingly sent to co-operate with the Luang Prabang forces. The campaign, successful at first, soon petered out when the Hos retired on their fortified strongholds. The Siamese therefore called off the campaign on receiving a vague recognition of the suzerainty of Bangkok and evacuated the survivors of the local population to Siam.

Luang Prabang was spared for the moment, but complete anarchy reigned on its northern and eastern borders, especially in Dinh-binh-phu and the Sip-song Chu-Thai running along the south-western side of the Black River. Oun Kham, who was powerless to deal with the growing disorder in his own territories, found himself forced to

---

[1] His reign begins officially only in 1872 when he received investiture from Siam. Tiantha Koumane had died in 1869.

rely more and more on Siamese support, especially when his friend
Cam-Sinh, the Chief of the Sip-song Chu-Thai, having driven off
the attacks of the Yellow Flags from his own territory, was drawn into
the guerrilla warfare which the exploits of Francis Garnier and Henri
Rivière had aroused in the delta region of Tongking.

The French advance in Tongking very naturally caused the Siamese
to tighten their hold on the Laos country. In 1883, the year in which
the French forced Vietnam to become a protectorate, a force of
Laotians and Siamese made a further attempt to storm the Ho strongholds in Tran Ninh and were so severely defeated that Chulalongkorn
decided to send a large army to occupy all the country to the north and
east of Luang Prabang right up to the basin of the Black River. This
arrived at its destination in October 1885, and its commander-in-chief,
Chao Mun Vai Voronat, appointed two Siamese commissioners to
superintend the administration of the kingdom at the side of the
ageing Oun Kham.[1]

The Siamese expedition had been prepared so secretly that the
Comte de Kergaradec, the French representative in Bangkok, only
learnt of it after its departure. Le Boulanger asserts that this step was
taken on the suggestion of Chulalongkorn's British advisers, because
Britain regarded French penetration into the Red River region with
jealousy owing to its obvious threat to their plans for commercial
penetration into Yunnan.[2] Graham, however, is much nearer the
point in drawing attention to the fact that the 'unofficial advocates' of
French colonial expansion were already beginning to advance the
theory that the territory held by Siam to the east of the river Mekong,
having at one time formed part of Annam, should be restored now
that Vietnam was a French protectorate.[3]

A young British journalist, Mr. (later Sir) James George Scott, who
had been with the French forces in Tongking and was shortly to join
the Burma Commission, took the matter much further in a book,
France and Tongking, which he published in 1885.[4] After stating that
'it was the encroachment of the French on the eastern borders that
decided the fate of Upper Burma', he showed that Siam was now
threatened by France. 'It cannot be too strongly urged', he wrote,
'that the whole French procedure in regard to Siam is as scientifically

---

[1] Then between seventy and seventy-five; the date of his birth was somewhere
between 1811 and 1816.
[2] *Op. cit.*, pp. 251–2.
[3] *Op. cit.*, i, p. 220.
[4] Quoted in G. E. Mitton (Lady Scott), *Scott of the Shan Hills*, London, 1936, pp.
47–8.

mapped out as a game of draughts. Every counter-move has been calculated and provided for, and we are no disinterested spectators, we do not want Siam and have no particular hankering for the Shan states but we do want to keep France out of them.' His advice was that a railway connecting Moulmein with Chiengmai, and Chiengmai with Bangkok, would supply all that was wanted. 'Siam would then be connected with us directly, and so much capital would be involved that she would cease to be the safe quarry she is now for sinister French designs. If anything is to be done it must be done at once. In a year or two Siam will be so surrounded she will be unable to stir.' They were strangely prophetic words, but no one heeded them then.

The Siamese action caused the Quai d'Orsay to issue a warning note to Bangkok and to invite the Hué government to formulate its claims on Luang Prabang. Siam in reply stated that her sole aims in sending an army there were to defend the region against the Hos. Hué claimed the region on the score of payment of tribute since the seventeenth century. France therefore asked Siam to agree to a joint commission to examine the boundaries of Luang Prabang on the spot. On 7 May 1886 a provisional agreement was concluded sanctioning the creation of a French vice-consulate at Luang Prabang—a method of approach to the question which, be it noted, implicitly recognized Siamese authority over the disputed principality.

The French choice for the new post was Auguste Pavie, who was to achieve a great reputation for his scholarly work of exploration in the Mekong valley. He had started his career with a commission in the Marines. In 1868 he had transferred to the Postal and Telegraphic Department of Cochin China. After the Franco-Prussian War he was stationed at Kampot, the Cambodian port on the Gulf of Siam, where he had attracted attention by his study of the old Khmer civilization. In 1880 he had been entrusted with the construction of a telegraph line from Phnom Penh to Bangkok. For the next five years he had busied himself with detailed surveys of Cambodia. The work of Mouhot, Garnier and others had inspired him with a great ambition to follow in their footsteps by exploring the Laos country. His immediate instructions were to explore routes connecting the upper Mekong valley with Tongking and hold himself in readiness to join the frontier commission, if and when it materialized.

The Bangkok government, only too painfully aware of the direction of French policy, kept Pavie waiting six months for his permit, in the hope that Vai Voronat would have time to complete his mission before the Frenchman's arrival.

Meanwhile the Siamese siege of the Ho stronghold of Tung-Chieng-Kam had failed in 1885. In the following year they staged a much stronger effort with reinforcements which achieved no little success. And soon after Pavie arrived in Luang Prabang in February 1887, Vai Voronat appeared in triumph to announce that the whole country had been cleared of the invaders, and with a map showing exactly the territories owing allegiance to King Oun Kham. There was obviously to be no joint frontier commission. Pavie therefore went ahead with preparations for exploring a practicable route from the Mekong into Tongking.

He left at the end of March 1887, but had not gone far before news reached him of an impending attack by armed bands on the capital itself. He at once sent a courier back to warn the Siamese commander-in-chief; but received the reply that while no importance need be attached to the rumour, he would be wise to return to Luang Prabang, as the season was unfavourable for the survey work he had in hand. Accordingly he retraced his steps, only to find on arrival at the capital that Vai Voronat and the Siamese chief commissioner had already left for Bangkok with the main body of the army, a number of Ho hostages and the eldest sons of the king and the Oupahat.

Vai Voronat's easy assumption that his task was completed was soon to be proved mere wishful thinking. For in carrying out the task of pacification he had foolishly alienated the most powerful chief of the T'ai cantons of the Black River region, Cam Sinh of Muong-Laï. The old chief was a firm friend of King Oun Kham and had entrusted him with the upbringing of two of his sons. But he was the enemy of both the French in Tongking and the Siamese. Vai Voronat had therefore completely failed to persuade him to recognize Siamese overlordship. He had then taken the drastic step of kidnapping some of the old chief's sons and carrying them off as hostages.

Now Cam Sinh employed in his service a band of Black Flags. They were commanded by his eldest son, Cam Oum, or Deo-van-Tri, as he was known by the Vietnamese. Early in June, with 600 followers, he appeared at the city of Luang Prabang to demand the release of his brothers. Finding that they were no longer there, he sacked the city. The king, his Siamese adviser and Pavie took refuge at Paklay, near the Siamese border, but Deo-van-Tri made no attempt at conquest.

On receipt of news of the disaster Chulalongkorn invited Oun Kham to Bangkok, where he was received with honour. Vai Voronat, who had received the title of P'ya Surrissak, was ordered to mobilize another army to restore order in the principality. The captive princes of Muong-Laï were liberated, and one of them was entrusted with a conciliatory message to his father. Late in the year the boundary commission, consisting of Pavie and two French officers together with three Siamese commissioners, was appointed.

Pavie now began to take matters very much into his own hands. Two French columns under Colonel Pernot and Commandant Oudri were engaged on the pacification of the upper region of Tongking bordering on the Sip-song Chu-Thai. Pavie therefore got into touch with Pernot, who was engaged in some stiff fighting with Deo-van-Tri and his Black Flags in the Muong-Laï region. They met in the middle of February 1888 and agreed on a plan of action which involved the annexation of the twelve T'ai cantons to the French empire. And to cut a long story short, Pavie returned to Luang Prabang at the end of March and announced to P'ya Surrissak, who was once more engaged upon the military occupation of the principality, that he intended to recommend the annexation of the T'ai cantons by France on the grounds that they were dependencies of Vietnam. He then made his way to Hanoi, where General Bégin entrusted to him the task of organizing the annexed territory.

In October of the same year he received the submission of the Black Flags, and in the following December P'ya Surrissak made formal surrender of the cantons on behalf of Siam. In January 1889 he was back in Luang Prabang to witness the reinstatement of the aged Oun Kham on his return from Bangkok. Then he began the investigation of France's claims to a further tract of territory, this time in 'Middle Laos'—the cantons of Camkeut and Cammon, once part of the kingdom of Vientiane. But Siamese forces were in control of them, and it was impossible for him to attempt again the methods which had been so successful in the Black River region. In June 1889, therefore, he wound up his first 'mission' and returned to France on furlough. There he strove to convert the Quai d'Orsay to the view that it should aim at extending the boundaries of its Indo-Chinese empire to the river Mekong.

(b) The Mekong Question

Pavie's second 'mission', which he began to organize as soon as he arrived back in France, was planned as a scientific expedition on the big scale not only to study the geography of the Laos country but also 'to investigate land and river routes, create trading depots, collect specimens, examine existing commercial procedure, and produce a definite statement on the nature and value of the products of the Mekong basin'. In close association with his project a Syndicat français du Haut-Laos was formed, which placed fifteen tons of merchandize at the disposal of the mission. The results of the mission's work as set forth in Pavie's monumental *Mission Pavie*[1] were of immense importance as contributions to knowledge. But the ultimate aim of the work was to pave the way for another big annexation of territory by France.

The mission began work in January 1890. The party was split into several groups working separately in Tran Ninh, Cammon and Stung Treng, and with the leader himself in Luang Prabang, where after six months all the members were to meet to co-ordinate their work. Late in the year he made his way down the Mekong to Saigon, and thence to Bangkok, where he hoped to continue the softening process by talks with the government. But the Siamese politely evaded his advances. They were alarmed at the way the French were striving to increase their influence among the Laos people, and at the agitation that was being worked up in France for 'the incontestable rights of Annam' to all the territory east of the Mekong.[2]

The Siamese suggestion, made at the time when Pavie wound up his first mission in the previous year, had been that the disputed territory should be regarded as neutral until the frontier could be properly delimited; and an agreement to this effect had been made. But both sides then began to accuse each other of infringing it. The French theory was that Siam was encroaching upon territory she had never previously occupied in order to compensate herself for what she had had to surrender in the Black River region. But it reflects too closely the outlook of the French themselves. Actually Siam's actions were capable of the simple explanation that they were entirely defensive. Pavie, however, before the end of the year 1890 was describing them as 'the Siamese invasion' and was urging Governor-General Piquet to instruct French frontier posts to do their best to stop them, while avoiding any clash. During the first half of 1891 he was engaged in the north upon a study of conditions in the Sip-song Pannas. There news reached him that Siam was summoning additional troops to the colours, laying in supplies of arms and constructing fortified posts. On the grounds that these constituted real preparations for war, he broke off his work to return to Paris, declining on his way an

---

[1] *Mission Pavie: Indochine 1879–1895*, 11 vols., Paris, 1898–1919.
[2] At this stage only the middle Mekong was in question.

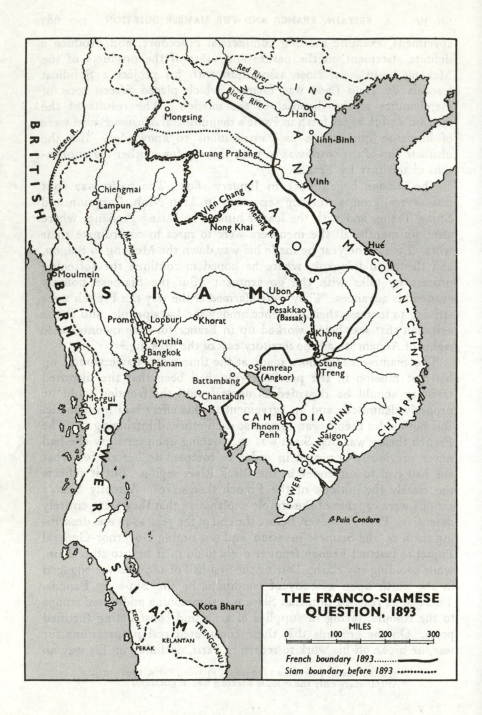

THE FRANCO-SIAMESE QUESTION, 1893

MILES

0   100   200   300

French boundary 1893..........

Siam boundary before 1893 ··········

offer by the Bangkok government to discuss the matter. Thus ended his second mission.

The annexation of Upper Burma by Britain at the beginning of the year 1886 involved the large block of Shan states which had paid allegiance to the Court of Ava ever since the sixteenth century. This brought the eastern frontier line under anxious consideration. Military opinion favoured the Salween as the eastern boundary of British Burma, but some of the states which had been subject to the Burmese monarchy stretched across that river, and the two most important trans-Salween states, Kengtung and Kiang Hung, claimed territory east of the Mekong; in fact Kiang Hung's richest part lay on the far side of the river.

But the further question arose: what would become of the trans-Salween territories if Britain declined responsibility for them? China and Siam, it was argued, might be invited to absorb them and thus place a buffer belt between British territory and Tongking. China, however, did not favour such a solution, and Siam, though favourable, was weak; and the fear was that if such a plan were carried out France might then be tempted to push her boundary up to the Salween. It was therefore decided that Britain must accept her full responsibilities, and measures were accordingly taken to secure the allegiance of all the states. The last to be brought under control was Kengtung; Scott was sent there in 1890 and at a durbar presented the sawbwa with his patent of appointment.

Britain had two anxieties in this matter: to avoid a frontier running with French Indo-China, and to reach an amicable agreement with Siam on all frontier questions. There were several delicate questions to be solved with regard to Siam. In 1889, therefore, Britain appointed the Ney Elias Commission to survey the Anglo-Siamese frontier and settle disputes with Siam. No Siamese officials were sent in reply to Britain's invitation for co-operation; but the commission completed its work and Siam accepted its decisions.[1] With France, however, difficulties cropped up.

In 1889 M. Waddington, the French ambassador in London, called on the prime minister, Lord Salisbury, with the suggestion that it would be to the advantage of both countries to declare Siam a buffer state between their respective empires. He thought that in the first instance the frontier between Cochin China and Siam should be fixed and a settlement made of the boundaries of Burma. Regarding

[1] A summary of the work of the commission is given by Sir Charles Crosthwaite in his *The Pacification of Burma*, London, 1912, pp. 219–21.

Luang Prabang, he said, his government proposed to draw a line from a point nearly due east of that place southwards to the Mekong, and below that point to make the river the dividing line between French and Siamese territory until it entered the territory of Cambodia. The boundaries of Siam should be defined up to the Chinese frontier on both the British and the French sides.

Salisbury's immediate reply was sympathetic on the subject of a buffer state. With regard to the other proposals, however, he said he had insufficient evidence on which to express an opinion, but would be grateful for exact details of the proposed frontier line between Cochin China and Siam. After consultation with the India Office Salisbury sent a considered reply to Waddington on 27 August. Britain, he indicated, would welcome measures which would establish a strong independent kingdom of Siam with well-defined boundaries; and he forwarded a map showing the India Office view of her boundaries. The western one was clearly demarcated up to the northern limit of British Burma before the annexation of Thibaw's kingdom. Those on the north and north-west were shown as approximate. He asked for the views of the French government on the subject of the east and north-east ones, saying that as soon as he received them he would be prepared to discuss with Waddington the next step for carrying his proposal into effect. He warned him, however, that Siam's territorial claims could only be settled in communication with her government.

Before we proceed to deal with the next phase of the story two points must be emphasized. In the first place Luang Prabang had been under Siamese suzerainty for a century at least, and in the French official maps in use up to the date of this exchange of views was marked as part of Siam.[1] In the second place the Convention of 7 May 1886, providing for the appointment of a vice-consul there, had implicitly acknowledged the sovereignty of Siam.

Waddington never replied to Salisbury's communication of 27 August 1889. The matter indeed was not taken up again until February 1892. During the interval Pavie was sent on his 'second mission', and there can be no doubt that France's sudden lapse into silence on the Siamese question was a result of the decision to despatch it. Before the next approach was made to the Foreign Office in February 1892, the Quai d'Orsay had taken certain significant steps. It had increased its agencies in Siam by opening semi-commercial,

---

[1] J. G. D. Campbell, *Siam in the Twentieth Century*, illustrates this point with a sketch-map (p. 293) and a coloured folding map (pp. 328–9).

semi-political bureaux at Utene, Bassac and Stung Treng; it had also appointed Pavie to be resident minister at Bangkok. The reason for these moves is not far to seek. Siam had learnt that France had made approaches to both London and Peking regarding the Mekong question. She had therefore begun to stiffen her attitude considerably and to play for British support. Hence the object of Pavie's new 'mission' was to apply the softening-up process at the centre. And it is no mere coincidence that on 16 February 1892, the day after the announcement of his appointment to Bangkok, Waddington broke the long silence between London and Paris on the Mekong question by suddenly coming forward with a new proposal.

His government, he explained, was concerned to avoid further difficulties with Britain in the matter, and thought that the best method would be for each power to bind itself not to extend its influence beyond the upper Mekong. The implications of this proposal were so unwarrantable that Lord Salisbury proffered the obvious objection that French influence did not extend to the upper Mekong. This evoked from Waddington what can only be described as a deliberately lame explanation of his proposal. It was, he said, of the nature of a prophylactic; he did not intend to imply that the actual sphere of influence of either France or Britain did indeed extend up to the Mekong.

Before the discussion could go further Salisbury's government fell and Gladstone returned to power. Lord Rosebery took over the management of foreign affairs. In due course Waddington in a personal conversation took up the matter of the French proposal. Lord Rosebery accordingly made a considered statement of the British position. It was contained in two notes delivered respectively in December 1892 and April 1893. He explained that through its annexation of the kingdom of Ava the British government had acquired rights in certain districts east of the Mekong. Thus Keng Cheng, a dependency of Kengtung, extended east of that river, as also did the district of Kiang Hung, the northern portion of Kengtung. He went on to say that Britain proposed to limit her frontier to the Mekong by transferring Kiang Hung to China and Keng Cheng to Siam. He warned Waddington that an engagement along the lines suggested by France would cause alarm and suspicion in Siam, and stated categorically that until France explained quite clearly her views regarding Siam's eastern and north-eastern frontiers Britain could not consider the conclusion of a formal agreement.

On this note negotiations broke down a second time, but not

before Waddington, in a conversation with Rosebery in March 1893, had let the cat out of the bag regarding the real nature of French intentions. His government, he said, did not admit that any part of Siam lay on the left bank of the Mekong, since all the country lying on that side belonged to Vietnam. Rosebery's attitude in face of this astounding volte-face was one of cautious diplomatic reserve. The Siamese have never ceased to deplore the weakness which he showed at this moment, when in their view a firmer stand would have saved so much subsequent trouble. There can be little doubt that his failure to pursue a more positive line actually encouraged France to go ahead alone. But the accusation made by French writers that Britain backed down after encouraging Siam to oppose France[1] is a complete travesty of the facts. Throughout this period Britain was urging the Siamese to do nothing likely to precipitate a rupture with France.

Meanwhile 'incidents' had been taking place on the spot, and were being played up as much as possible in France with the object of rousing public opinion in favour of a forward move. To this more disillusioned age they appear rather petty. Two that caused a violent storm in the Chamber of Deputies were the expulsion by the Siamese authorities of two French agents, Champenois and Esquilat, from Oudene without explanation, and the death of Massie, the French agent at Luang Prabang, after leaving the place in despair at the difficulties placed in his way by the Siamese representatives there. His death was due to natural causes; there was no suggestion of foul play. But the Colonial Party was looking for martyrs.

The agitation caused by these incidents led the French government in February 1893 to authorize the Governor-General of Indo-China to take energetic action on the Siamese frontier if immediate reparation were not obtained. In the following month, it will be remembered, Waddington told Lord Rosebery that in the French view all the territory on the left bank of the Mekong belonged by right to Vietnam. At the same time Pavie, under instructions from the Quai d'Orsay, made the same claim to the Foreign Office at Bangkok. The Siamese protested. They offered to refer any doubtful matters

---

[1] This view has been accepted uncritically by Virginia Thompson in *Thailand, the New Siam*, p. 162. She also (p. 187) gives a completely false picture of the negotiations between France and Britain. The French archives have only recently been opened to students and only a selection of them has been published, *Documents Diplomatiques, Affaires du Siam et du Haut Mékong*, Paris, 1893 and 1896. The British archives are open up to 1937, but no definitive study of the subject has yet been published. There is an unpublished Ph.D. thesis by B. S. N. Murti, *Anglo-French Relations with Siam, 1880–1904*, which was successfully submitted to the University of London in 1952 and is based on a detailed study of the extensive materials in the Public Record Office.

to arbitration. But Pavie demanded the immediate evacuation of all positions held by Siam in the disputed territory.

In April the French followed up their claim by organizing three columns to occupy, by force if necessary, the territory on the Lower Mekong which they claimed. One under Captain Thoreux seized Stung Treng on the Mekong inside the Siamese frontier, and shortly afterwards the island of Khone below the rapids. The second began an advance towards Muong-Phine, and the third went to the Cammon region.

Bangkok, faced by this critical situation, and with an army quite incapable of standing up to the French, continued to offer arbitration, while at the same time making frantic appeals for help to Britain. Lord Rosebery's reply, which he also communicated to the Quai d'Orsay, was eminently correct. He urged the Siamese to avoid anything that might provoke France to resort to war. But it was cold comfort to the harassed Prince Devawongse. And the inevitable frontier incidents occurred. There was an attack on the French position at Khone. The French commander, Thoreux, was taken prisoner and some Vietnamese soldiers killed. The Siamese tried to place the reponsibility for it upon the semi-barbarous tribes in the neighbourhood. Then they changed their tone and contended that Captain Thoreux had been in command of an aggressive expedition and his capture was justified. Lord Rosebery, however, supported the French demand for his surrender, and as an act of grace the Siamese handed him over.

The systematic advance of the French columns along the Mekong brought a whole series of incidents. It seems impossible to establish the truth about them; and since their propaganda value to France was high, one naturally distrusts the French version. The French were looking for trouble in order to turn it to their own ends. The most publicized incident was one in which, according to the French account, the Siamese murdered a French official, M. Grosgurin, while he was conducting one of their frontier garrisons from an abandoned post back to the Mekong. Subsequent investigation established the fact that the attack had been made by the French party on the Siamese. But long before this was known the French version of the affair caused the agitation in France against Siam to reach such a pitch that the government was able to take the drastic action which was the object of all this manoeuvring.

(c) Paknam and after

By April 1893 the tension in Bangkok had become so acute that a British gunboat, the *Swift*, was sent there to protect British lives and property in case of trouble. Two months later there were rumours that the French intended to send a naval squadron to close the port. It was feared that if such action were indeed to be taken there would be a mass outbreak of the lower classes of the Chinese population in the city. A further British warship, the *Pallas*, was accordingly despatched from Singapore. A full explanation of these moves was sent to the French government and assurances were given that the British government was doing its utmost to persuade Siam to come to a friendly agreement with France. The French government in return gave Britain an undertaking to report at once to her any movements of its fleet in the neighbourhood of Siam.

A French gunboat, the *Lutin*, was anchored in the Menam off the French legation. Early in July Pavie notified the Siamese government that two more French gunboats were being despatched and would arrive at Paknam on the 13th. He asked for pilots to bring them up to Bangkok. The Siamese government replied that under its treaty with France no warships of any foreign power could proceed further than Paknam without its consent. This was certainly the intention of the clause in the Franco-Siamese treaty of 1856 dealing with the subject, though it may be conceded that its wording was not so clear as in the Anglo-Siamese treaty of the previous year. Pavie, however, brushed aside the Siamese objection and informed them that the *Inconstant* would proceed up to Bangkok, even in face of opposition.

On receiving this information the Siamese began to close the mouth of the river, while Lord Rosebery reminded the French of their promise to keep his government informed of any movements of their fleet and made it clear that the additional British ships sent from Singapore would not go beyond Paknam. In response to this warning the French Foreign Minister, M. Develle, telegraphed Rosebery that the additional French ships would also remain outside the bar at Paknam, and on the morning of 13 July Pavie in Bangkok gave a similar assurance to Prince Devawongse.

On that same day the *Inconstant* and *Comète* arrived at Paknam to find the British warships lying at anchor there. Captain Macleod, the British commander, informed the French that they might expect instructions to wait outside the bar. The French commander, however, disregarded this advice, and after a twenty minutes' engagement with the Paknam fort, in which both sides suffered casualties, the two warships made their way up the river to Bangkok. The best account of the incident is given by Warrington Smyth in his *Five Years in Siam*.[1] He was an eye-witness. Captain Macleod in reporting the incident declared that the French commander actually received instructions to remain at Paknam before entering the river. Be that as it may, the Siamese committed the serious blunder of firing the first shots in the encounter. By disregarding Rosebery's reiterated advice they had played into the hands of the French. The two ships anchored off the French legation at Bangkok. At this critical moment Prince Devawongse rose to the occasion by congratulating their commander on his skill and daring in forcing an entrance. His admirable suavity and restraint probably saved the situation.

Pavie at once seized the opportunity to demand that the Siamese troops should be withdrawn from the Mekong and all hostilities suspended. Prince Devawongse agreed to the demand, but the French government at home was by no means satisfied. It instructed Pavie to deliver an ultimatum demanding that the whole of the territory on the left bank of the Mekong, including the principality of Luang Prabang, should be ceded to France, that an indemnity of three million francs[2] should be paid in respect of the casualties inflicted on the French ships, and that the officers responsible for the firing at Paknam and the murderers of Grosgurin should be punished. Failing this a blockade of the Menam would be established.

The ultimatum was delivered on 20 July. The Siamese government accepted the second and third demands but offered a compromise in place of the first. Pavie, however, refused to bargain and announced that he would leave Bangkok on the 26th if the demands were not met in toto. It was now Britain's turn to be alarmed. She had optimistically believed that the French dispute with Siam was concerned merely with the frontier on the lower Mekong. Now she saw that if France annexed all the territory covered by the first demand, not only was the question of the integrity of the Siamese dominions involved, but on the upper Mekong the French would come directly into contact with Burma and their claims would clash with British interests in that region.

The British ambassador in Paris was accordingly instructed to obtain from M. Develle a clear statement regarding France's aims. Develle

[1] New York, 1898.
[2] The exchange rate of the franc was then twenty-five to the £.

replied that since the terms of the ultimatum had been published to the world France could not, in the excited state of her own public opinion, climb down. He assured the ambassador, however, that when Siam had accepted the terms the way would be open for the establishment of a buffer state between the French and British empires. Notwithstanding its previous experience of the value of French promises regarding the Mekong question, the British government accepted the French assurance. Develle indeed promised that France would respect the independence of Siam. Lord Rosebery therefore went so far as to urge the Siamese to accept the French demands.

On 25 July, when the Siamese government had given no sign of acceptance, the French proceeded to blockade the Menam. Two days later Chulalongkorn, who had been in a state of collapse throughout the crisis and had left matters entirely to Prince Devawongse, accepted the terms of the ultimatum unconditionally. On 3 August the blockade was called off, but Chulalongkorn had to agree to further stipulations thrown in as guarantees. Pending the Siamese evacuation of the east bank of the Mekong France was to occupy Chantabun. Moreover, Siam was to withdraw her forces to a distance of twenty-five kilometres from the west bank, and in addition evacuate the provinces of Battambang and Siemreap (Angkor), which had once belonged to Cambodia.

Even then the state of tension was in no way relaxed. When negotiations began for a treaty in which all these concessions were to be embodied France attempted to insert a number of supplementary terms, ostensibly designed as additional guarantees, but, in Lord Rosebery's words, calculated to infringe materially the independence and integrity of Siam, which she had pledged herself to respect. Throughout the negotiations Britain constantly applied pressure on France to modify her demands. Chulalongkorn, however, had hoped for much more positive support and was bitterly disappointed at what he regarded as British neutrality. The Siamese government did its utmost to resist the French demands, and it was not until France had served a further ultimatum upon him that Chulalongkorn, acting on British advice, gave way and on 3 October accepted the treaty.

France had scored a diplomatic triumph over Britain, whose hands were tied by the fear that firmer action on her part would lead to a European war. From the moment when the Siamese fired their first salvo at Paknam the game was in France's hands, and in the opinion of shrewd observers Rosebery went as far as he could consistently with prudence. What Lord Curzon described as 'the fiery Chauvinism of the Colonial Jingoes of Tongking and Saigon'[1] had risen to a dangerous pitch. They were demanding control over Battambang and Siemreap, and further resistance by Siam might have resulted not only in their loss to France but also in a real threat to her independence. Had matters reached such a pass it is an interesting speculation what action Britain would have taken. As it was, Siam owed her salvation not a little to the consistency with which British diplomacy concentrated upon obtaining from France a guarantee of the independence of the basin of the Menam.

After the immediate crisis had passed, Britain's interest was in the creation of the promised buffer state on the upper Mekong. In August 1893 J. G. Scott was recalled from his special work in the Shan states and sent to take charge of the legation at Bangkok so that in due course he might represent Britain on the Buffer State Commission. His opposite number was to be Auguste Pavie. Since the previous year arrangements had been in progress between Britain, China and Siam for the rectification of Burma's eastern frontier. Kiang Hung and Möng Lem had been ceded to China on condition that they were not to be alienated to another country without British permission. When, however, France forced Siam to surrender her territory on the upper Mekong, China broke the treaty by ceding the trans-Mekong state of Kiang Hung to France.

Britain had been about to make a similar arrangement for the transfer to Siam of Keng Cheng with its capital Möng Sing. But now under the Franco-Siamese Treaty of 1893 France claimed the state as being on the left bank of the Mekong. It was in this area that the proposed buffer state was to be formed; Scott and Pavie accordingly arranged to meet at Möng Sing at the end of December 1894. The little state was under a Myosa. He received so many contradictory messages regarding both the actual and the future status of his principality that he finally decided that the way of safety was to hoist the French flag over his *haw*. But when members of the British delegation began to arrive first he took fright and fled. 'It was the wisest thing he could do,' commented Scott.[2] Scott, who arrived there on Christmas Day to find the French flag flying, promptly had it hauled down. On 1 January 1895, when Pavie turned up, the Union Jack was flying over the *haw*. The fat was then truly in the fire. The petty little affair almost flared up into a first-class international incident. The Buffer State Commission broke up and the negotiations

---

[1] J. G. D. Campbell, *op. cit.*, p. 311, fn. 1.
[2] Mitton, *Scott of the Shan Hills*, p. 211.

had to be transferred to Europe. The plan for a buffer state vanished into thin air. Scott and Pavie could not agree on its limits, and on the grounds that under any form of arrangement it would become a dangerous focus of intrigue Scott persuaded the British government to abandon the idea.

The Möng Sing incident and the failure of the Buffer State Commission caused a hysterical outburst in France against Britain very similar to the one that was three years later to be produced by the Fashoda affair. The two countries actually came to the brink of war. In the negotiations which began in June 1895 Britain traded her claims to territory east of the Mekong for a joint guarantee of the independence of the Menam valley. It was a good bargain, since she had never intended to hold on to the trans-Mekong territory. And Lord Salisbury's idea of defining Siam in terms of the Menam valley, though denounced by indignant journalists,[1] did result in an effective guarantee of the independence of the area which contained four-fifths of her population and was economically one of the richest regions in the Indo-Chinese peninsula. Moreover, France was fobbed off with territories which, though large, were economically worthless.

The Anglo-French agreement was signed in January 1896. Möng Sing went to France. Both states guaranteed the independence of the Menam valley and promised to seek no exclusive advantages in Siam. The agreement did not affect the Korat plateau, the old Cambodian provinces of Battambang and Siemreap, or the Malay Peninsula. Salisbury was careful to point out that these were as integral parts of Siam as the Menam valley, but from the point of view of an agreement with France concerning British interests were of no importance.[2]

It was only with the lapse of time that the soundness of this policy became evident. France indeed soon discovered how worthless were the Mekong territories she had acquired, compared with the Menam valley. Her Colonial Party actually proclaimed, loudly and publicly, that control over the Menam was essential to the economic success of French Indo-China. It was some years before the danger was really averted. There were constant quarrels between France and Siam, and the continued occupation of Chantabun, which was a heavy drain on French colonial finances without any compensating advantages, caused much heart-burning to both sides.

[1] *Ibid.*, p. 166. Scott's comment on the abandonment of Möng Sing was that Lord Salisbury, 'who was, without exception, the worst Foreign Secretary we ever had for matters east of Suez, . . . gave up the whole question.'

[2] Ninety per cent of Siam's foreign trade was in Britain's hands, and seven-eighths of this was with the Menam valley.

The most dangerous quarrel was over a badly-drafted clause in the treaty of 1893, under which Siam promised to hand over to the French legation at Bangkok all such Annamite, Khmer and Laotian subjects of France as were detained in the country, and allow any deported inhabitants of the Laos states to return home. The French consulate thereupon went ahead with the enrolment of as many 'French protégés' as possible, without any proper investigation of their cases. It then complained to the Siamese government that they were being prevented from receiving the protection of French jurisdiction. The matter caused no little embarrassment to the Siamese, since their navy was manned largely by Khmers. Had it not been for her fear of Britain's possible reaction to any attempt to sabotage the agreement of 1896, this question could easily have afforded France a useful pretext for extinguishing Siam's independence.

Anglo-French bickering over the question of trade with Yunnan gradually died a natural death. In 1897 an agreement permitted the construction of a railway from French Indo-China to Yunnan and provided for its ultimate connection with the Burma Railways. The French built a line linking Tongking with Yunnanfu (Kunming), but went no farther. The British abandoned their surveys beyond Bhamo and Lashio respectively. Between 1894 and 1900 Major H. R. Davies surveyed all possible railway routes into Yunnan and produced an extremely valuable book and map on the subject. He showed that the country to be traversed was exceptionally difficult and the profits of the enterprise doubtful, but advocated construction. By this time, however, it had become quite clear that the best approach to Yunnan was from Tongking. At the turn of the century also Britain had become too preoccupied with the Boer War on the one hand and German ambitions on the other to devote much attention to Indo-Chinese affairs. When, therefore, Lord Curzon as Governor-General of India dubbed the idea of linking up the Burma Railways with Yunnan 'midsummer madness' and vetoed the proposal it was summarily relegated to the limbo of lost illusions.

In April 1904 the conclusion of the Entente Cordiale wound up finally the Franco-British controversy over Siam and left both sides free thereafter to come to terms separately with Bangkok. In that same year France concluded a new treaty with Siam whereby the Laos frontier was modified to her advantage. Siam renounced her sovereignty over Luang Prabang and agreed to a joint commission to deal with the Cambodian frontier. In return France agreed to evacuate Chantabun and reduced her demands in connection with her 'protégés' and the neutral zone. This proved to be a turning-point in the relations between the two countries. In 1907 they made a further agreement whereby Siam surrendered the Cambodian provinces of Battambang and Siemreap. France in return handed back some of the territory surrendered by Siam in 1904 and abandoned all claims to jurisdiction over her Asian subjects.

British policy during the period from the annexation of Upper Burma in 1886 to the Entente Cordiale of 1904 was to avoid a common frontier between British India and French Indo-China. Siam accordingly was seen as a necessary buffer state, and Britain sought throughout to restrain France from making excessive demands on the Court of Bangkok. The Anglo-French Agreement of 1896 probably saved the heartland of Siam from falling into French hands. It was followed in 1897 by an Anglo-Siamese Convention whereby Siam agreed not to cede territory south of the 11th parallel of north latitude (i.e. in the Siamese Malay States) or grant special privileges in that region without British approval, and Britain promised to support Siam against any third power seeking to gain influence there. The explanation of this is to be found in the acute state of international rivalry in the Pacific at the time. Britain was particularly aware of the dangerous situation arising from the vagueness of Siam's actual authority over the states immediately to the north of the newly formed Federation of Malay States. Her first endeavours were to strengthen Siamese authority over these states. But she discovered that in the cases of Kelantan and Trengganu this was open to dispute; Siamese suzerainty was little if anything more than a mere formality. In 1899, however, an agreement over the frontier between Pahang and Trengganu was made with Bangkok over the head of the Sultan of Trengganu. In 1900 in the case of the grant by the Sultan of Kelantan of a concession to the Duff Development Company the British Foreign Office insisted that Siam's approval was essential, even though the Siamese Government itself admitted the Sultan's independent right to make such a grant. The result of these moves was the conclusion of an Anglo-Siamese agreement whereby Siam was to offer identical treaties with the rulers of Kelantan and Trengganu specifying that they were dependencies of Siam, would conduct their foreign relations through Siam, and would accept Siamese advisers, though subject to the stipulation that Siam would not normally interfere in their internal administration. They were further required to grant no concessions to foreigners without Siamese consent and to pay one-tenth of their revenues to Siam. Both states accepted, though in Trengganu's case

Siam made no attempt to assert her rights in practice. W. A. Graham, an Englishman in the Siamese service, was sent to Kota Bahru as Siamese Adviser. Both states were, in Rupert Emerson's words, 'in something of a state of nature'.[1]

Arrangements for the 'regularization and modernization'[2] of the relations of Kedah and Perlis with Siam had also to be undertaken. They were not completed until 1905. By this time, however, British policy had begun to change. The pressure of German interests for a share in Siam's economic development had its influence upon this, as well as apprehension lest a foreign power might be tempted to revive the Kra Canal project which had from time to time haunted the minds of politicians and prospectors since the eighteen-sixties. The terms of the new Anglo-Siamese treaty, concluded in March 1909 after long negotiations, indicate perhaps less a change of basic policy than of method. For the object was still the same, namely to exclude foreign influence from the Peninsula. By it Siam transferred to Britain all her rights over the four states of Kedah, Perlis, Kelantan and Trengganu and the adjacent islands. The British Government undertook to negotiate an individual treaty of protection with each state. Britain on her part agreed to the abolition of consular jurisdiction in Siam. The Federated Malay States loaned the sum of four million pounds for railway construction to link Siam's railway system with that of Malaya. In addition, in an exchange of notes, it was agreed that south of Ratburi (Rajaburi) in the Bight of Bangkok Siam would not cede or lease any territory to a foreign government, or permit the establishment of coaling stations or docks or the exclusive occupation of any harbours, which could be prejudicial to British strategic interests.[3]

The story of what Graham appositely terms 'the long-drawn-out series of diplomatic contortions' by which Siam fended off a ravenous enemy at the cost of sacrificing 90,000 square miles of territory is not a pleasant one. It belongs to the most intense period of European competition for colonial possessions and reflects some of its worst features. Siam, it has been said, 'gained morally by this physical loss'[4] in that she became a more compact and homogeneous country. She had certainly not shown her best qualities in exercising dominion over other peoples. The Anglo-French agreement of January 1896 did much to raise Siam's morale; it inaugurated a new period of reform largely influenced by British ideas.

[1] *Malaysia, A Study in Direct and Indirect Rule* (New York, 1937), p. 253.
[2] *Ibid.*, p. 229.   [3] *Ibid.*, pp. 231–2.   [4] Virginia Thompson, *op. cit.*, p. 163.

PART IV

NATIONALISM AND THE CHALLENGE TO EUROPEAN DOMINATION

CHAPTER 40

THE PHILIPPINES TO THE END OF SPANISH RULE

DURING the first half of the seventeenth century the Spanish hold upon the Philippines was strenuously challenged by the Dutch. Although they came into the island world of South-East Asia mainly in order to wrest control over the spice trade from the Portuguese, the Dutch were equally concerned to break the power of Spain. Quite apart from their general hostility to Spain as the enemy of their independence, they were impelled by two special considerations. In the first place the Spaniards from their Philippine bases could give vital assistance to the Portuguese in the Moluccas; in the second Manila's strategic position as an entrepôt for Far Eastern trade offered dazzling opportunities of which the Dutch were only too well aware. Hence their onslaught upon the Hispano-Portuguese power in the Moluccas was accompanied by a grim naval warfare waged year after year in Philippine waters. It began in 1600 with an attempt by Oliver van Noort to intercept the Acapulco galleon. When he failed to do so, he cruised about Manila Bay plundering Chinese and Filipino shipping. But at the battle of Mariveles the Spaniards inflicted so severe a check on him that he had to limp away with the loss of one of his ships.

The Spanish counter-attacks in the Moluccas, which culminated in the downfall of Sultan Zaide of Ternate in 1606, provoked a new Dutch offensive under Cornelis Matalief which inflicted much damage upon Spanish and Portuguese forts and sea patrols in Indonesian waters, and Matalief, on returning home, advised the States General to make an all-out attack upon the Philippines in alliance with the Moros. This was made in 1609, the year of the conclusion of the Twelve Years Truce between Spain and Holland; for there was no let-up in their warfare in the East. A powerful Dutch fleet under Admiral Wittert attacked first the port of Iloilo on Panay, but finding the opposition too determined went on to Manila Bay, which it blockaded for five months. The Spaniards, however, decisively defeated his fleet on 26 April 1610 in a stretch of water known as Playa Honda not far from Manila, and Wittert himself was killed. The indefatigable Governor-General Juan de Silva then followed up this success by an incursion into the Moluccas.

705

There, however, he found the enemy so well established on the island of Amboyna that he returned home to prepare for a much greater effort involving the co-operation of Goa. This offensive was launched early in 1616, but came to nothing. The Portuguese fleet was late in arriving at the rendezvous, and while awaiting them at Malacca de Silva died and his second-in-command thereupon took the armada back to Manila.

In the meantime the Dutch, convinced that while Manila could come to the help of the Portuguese in the Moluccas their own trade would be insecure, had undertaken a new effort to conquer the Philippines. Thus while de Silva's expedition was in Indonesian waters, Joris van Speilbergen with a Dutch squadron, that had sailed via the Magellan Straits, appeared before the entrance to Manila Bay at the end of February 1616. Had he attacked, the city must have fallen. But hearing of de Silva's expedition he sailed away to Ternate, only to find that the great offensive had misfired. In the following year, however, the Dutch returned to the attack; a second battle was fought at Playa Honda and again they sustained a severe defeat. They continued, however, to harass the Philippines. In 1618 and 1619 their squadrons entered Manila Bay and plundered shipping, and in 1620 they made another abortive attack upon the Manila-bound galleon from Acapulco. They could sail about almost at will, for after the sea-fight in 1617 the Spaniards could not muster another fleet capable of challenging them; and in 1619 the Anglo-Dutch treaty was signed which placed English ships also at the disposal of Jan Peterszoon Coen. In January 1621 an Anglo-Dutch fleet began the blockade of Manila, and kept it up until May of the following year, preventing any ships from leaving or entering the Bay. Again the Spaniards were unable to take effective action at sea. Their opponents, on the other hand, made no attempt to test the defences of Manila, but contented themselves with immobilizing the trade of the port.

In 1622 the Dutch planted a fort on the Pescadores Islands from which to intercept the trade of Manila with China and Japan. In 1624 they transferred to Formosa, and managed to divert to that island much of the Chinese trade that normally went to Manila. But the Spaniards could still struggle gamely. They won a third naval engagement with a Dutch squadron at Playa Honda, and in the lull which ensued sent an expedition to Formosa and established two forts there as a counterpoise to the Dutch. They also fought the Moros, who were receiving arms from the Dutch, and strengthened their forts in the Moluccas. They still possessed five there, but they were in such jeopardy from Dutch attack that Spaniards on the spot believed that without much stronger military support from home, they, and indeed the whole Spanish empire in the western Pacific, would fall into Dutch hands.

After a longish spell of commerce-raiding the Dutch went over to the offensive again in 1640, the year of the Portuguese breakaway from Spain under Braganza leadership. In 1641 Malacca fell, and in the following year the Dutch captured the Spanish strongholds on Formosa, thereby securing a valuable base for operations against the Philippines just to the north of Luzon. In July 1645 they bombarded the Spanish fort at Jolo, though without success. The year 1646 saw no less than five naval engagements in which the Spaniards with two reconditioned old galleons inflicted one reverse after another upon Dutch marauding squadrons. The fighting culminated in 1647 with an attack upon Manila Bay by Martin Gerretsen with a fleet of twelve ships. He bombarded the fort at Cavite, but was repulsed and killed and his flagship sunk in an intense artillery fight. The remainder of his force then made the island of Corregidor their base and plundered the towns of Bataan until, deterred by Spanish and Filipino resistance and the outbreak of an epidemic among them, they abandoned the enterprise and sailed away. In 1648 Spain and the United Provinces signed the Treaty of Munster, and Dutch attacks upon the Philippines ceased. Their raiding, however, continued; it only ceased when, on account of Coxinga's threat to attack Manila in 1662, the Spanish garrisons were withdrawn from Zamboanga and the Moros area, and at the same time from Ternate.

The Spanish success in retaining the Philippines, in spite of the long series of Dutch attempts to destroy their hold upon the islands, was of decisive importance in South-East Asian history. It had been one of the main recommendations of Jan Peterszoon Coen's political programme that Manila and Macao should be conquered and Hispano-Portuguese power overthrown in the western Pacific. The Dutch failure was due in large measure to the tenacity of the Spaniards in defence and counter-attack; but perhaps in even larger measure to the loyalty of the Filipinos to their Spanish masters. When one takes into account the appalling sacrifices the Filipinos were called upon to make, the fact that the Spaniards were able to command adequate support from them to repel both the Dutch and their allies the Moros bears striking testimony to the work of the Catholic missionaries.

By the middle of the seventeenth century the Spanish effort to subdue the Moros had reached a position of stalemate. The abandonment of Zamboanga in a moment of panic greatly stimulated Moro raids, especially upon the Christian communities in the islands just to the north of Mindanao. Hence, as soon as the Coxinga threat was lifted, the Jesuits began to agitate for the reoccupation of the fort, and in 1666, as a result of their pressure, the queen-regent sent instructions to that effect. But they were disregarded: the settlement had been very costly to maintain, and the Manila authorities had begun to cherish the hope that negotiation was worth a trial, since the Muslim Malays had come to have a real interest in trade with the Spanish-controlled regions. Moreover, what had once been semi-feudal confederacies of Magindanaus and Sulus were, long before the end of the century, becoming welded into centralized sultanates with claims to international status. In 1704 Manila was invited to arbitrate in a quarrel between the sultans of Magindanau and Sulu, and the opposing parties not only accepted a Jesuit priest as arbitrator, but his decision as well. Nevertheless, royal orders continued to be issued every so often for the reoccupation of Zamboanga until finally in 1718 the standard of Spain was unfurled once more over the fort of Our Lady of Pilar, and military expeditions again directed against the Moros.

The peace-by-negotiation policy was not, however, abandoned. In the seventeen-twenties a commercial treaty was made with the Sultan of Sulu which provided also that Christian captives should be released and Christianity tolerated in the sultan's dominions. And, prompted by the Jesuits, Philip V sent personal messages to the Moro chiefs offering them alliances with Spain. Neither force nor conciliation had any appreciable effect upon the situation. The Moros continued to raid and to be in effect the real masters of the Philippine seas.

Among the rulers approached by Philip V was Alimud Din, Sultan of Sulu, a learned and respected ruler, who had revised the Sulu code of laws and translated Arabic texts, including parts of the Koran, into the Sulu language. At the king's request in 1744 he agreed to permit a Jesuit to preach in his dominions, and a Spanish church and fort to be erected. Five years later, however, his brother Bantilan, disliking the pro-Spanish tendency of his policy, seized the throne. Alimud Din and his family escaped to Zamboanga and thence went on to Manila, where they were welcomed. He accepted Christian baptism, and sent his son and daughter to school in Manila, where he came to be known as Don Fernando de Alimud Din I, Catholic Sultan of Jolo. In 1751 he accompanied a Spanish expedition against Jolo, which aimed at restoring him; but, on the grounds that a letter, alleged to have been written by him to the Sultan of Mindanao, was treasonable, he was sent back to

Manila and imprisoned, though later he was accorded a measure of freedom and a monthly pension. As we have already seen,[1] he was still living in Manila at the time of the British capture of the city in 1762. The British restored him to his throne, but he soon abdicated in favour of his son Israel, who reigned until 1778, when he in his turn was deposed by a son of Bantilan.

The British occupation of Manila (October 1762–May 1764) was an incident in the Seven Years War. The British Government expected it to yield enormous plunder and do serious damage to Spanish commerce in the Pacific, but had not envisaged its retention after the war. They certainly aimed at ousting Spain from the China seas, in extending their own commerce there, but thought that the annexation of the island of Mindanao might best serve this purpose. The news of the capture of the city, however, did not reach Europe in time to affect the peace negotiations at Paris, and the East India Company were thus prevented from using it as a bargaining counter. Manila was handed back to Spain, and the huge ransom of four million dollars, promised by the Spanish authorities when the city surrendered, was repudiated by Madrid. In any case, the splendid resistance, led by the lieutenant-governor Don Simon de Anda, which prevented the British from extending their conquests beyond Manila, showed that the annexation of the Philippines was out of the question.

The effects of the occupation upon the Philippines, on the other hand, were far-reaching. World attention became focused on Manila for the first time; for a few months it was opened to foreign trade, and British and other foreign merchants came to examine its potentialities as a commercial centre. More important still, the ease with which the city had been captured broke for ever Spain's military prestige, and rebellions flared up everywhere. It is not surprising therefore that during the later years of the eighteenth century the Moro raids became worse than ever before. Every Christian town between Mindanao and Luzon suffered horribly. Attacks were even made upon the coasts of Luzon up to the very wharves of Manila. Thousands were massacred and enslaved, and it was estimated that an average of 500 Filipinos a year were sold in the slave markets of the Malay Archipelago. The Spaniards, notwithstanding a vast expenditure upon expeditions against the Moros, seemed to be helpless; actually, nothing availed until the advent of the steamship in the next century.

The systematic propagation of Christianity among the Filipino peoples gave to the religious orders who supplied the missionaries,

[1] *Supra*, p. 494.

the Augustinians, the Franciscans, the Jesuits, the Dominicans and
the Recollects—to name them in the order of their arrival in the
Philippines—a necessarily important place in the colony. As in all
Spanish colonies, Church and State were united. There were two sets
of authorities, civil and ecclesiastical, and their work necessarily
overlapped. Ideally they formed the interrelated parts of one whole.
The civil authority from the governor-general downwards had, in addition to their ordinary duties, the supreme one of assisting the propagation of Christianity. The ecclesiastical authorities, besides tending
to the spiritual needs of their flocks, were concerned with the maintenance and spread of Spanish sovereignty, and the cost of ecclesiastical
administration was borne by the State. The position was that the
Spanish Crown, having been entrusted by the papacy with the administration of the Church in the Indies, delegated to the regular clergy the
task of Christianizing the native peoples.

From this relationship two main sources of contention arose. In
the first place no satisfactory division between the civil and ecclesiastical authority could be made, and there were constant complaints
by the civil authority of ecclesiastical interference involving the usurpation of its powers. In the second place the regular clergy, i.e. the
members of religious orders, denied the right of the bishop to jurisdiction over them in their role as parish clergy, although it had been
firmly laid down by the Council of Trent that no priest should exercise
care over the souls of laymen without being subject to episcopal
authority.

The struggle for power went on without abate throughout the whole
Spanish period. On the churchmen's side it must be remembered that
they were generally more interested in welfare than their opponents,
and that in fact Spanish power in the Philippines depended more upon
them than upon the army. But there can be no doubt that, like the
Church in mediaeval Europe, the Church in the Philippines did tend to
overstep the mark in the exercise of its authority, and that the complaints, which were so frequent, were not entirely without foundation.

A few special examples must suffice. In 1606 the fiscal of Manila
reported to the king that ecclesiastics were interfering in local administration and making improper assessments upon the people. He asked
that the Audiencia should be instructed to investigate the situation.
In 1610 the governor-general himself reported an incident in which
the Dominicans had brought about the escape of a condemned prisoner
by threatening the alcalde with excommunication. A royal order
to the Dominican provincial, telling him to restrain his subordinates

from meddling in civil affairs, resulted from this complaint. In 1618 the Augustinians were the subject of a complaint; they were accused of charging excessive fees for masses, burials and other services, and of levying taxes for the erection of churches and convents without the sanction of the civil authority. The king in response issued a decree against this, but the governor-general reported that the archbishop of Manila thought the decree unnecessary. Hence, in 1622 another royal decree ordering the ecclesiastical authority to stop 'irregularities' was issued. Royal decrees, however, seem to have had no effect, and in local government matters the friars tended to be more readily obeyed than the *acalde-mayor*.

In trying to uphold the civil power two governors-general came to grief. In the first case, which occurred in the sixteen-forties, Governor-General Hurtado de Corcuera and Archbishop Hernando Guerrero came to loggerheads over a soldier, who had killed a girl and taken refuge in an Augustinian church. Corcuera had the soldier apprehended and executed, and the archbishop's protests resulted in his own imprisonment in Fort Santiago. On the expiry of the governor-general's term of office the *residencia* sentenced him to five years' imprisonment, and notwithstanding his distinguished services against the Moros the king refused to interfere with the court's decision. The second case was that of Governor-General Diego de Salcedo, who in 1668 was arrested by the Inquisition because when his opponent Archbishop Miguel Poblete died, he forebade the bells to be tolled or the body embalmed. But the real cause of trouble was said to have been that he had refused a military office to the nephew of the commissary of the Inquisition. On his way to Mexico to answer the charges he died; he was subsequently exonerated.

In 1680 a tremendous controversy broke out over a complaint to Governor-General Vargas on the part of the parish priest of Vigan that the acting head of the diocese of Nueva Segovia had interfered with the exercise of his functions, although he did not reside in the diocese. The matter was brought before the Audiencia, and when Archbishop Pardo challenged its right to hear the case, he was deported to Lingayen, and a number of his fellow Dominicans, who supported him, were banished to various other places. But the governor-general's successor in 1684 upheld the archbishop's claim, and Vargas and his associates were all excommunicated. Vargas himself was offered pardon if he would publicly perform a most humiliating penance. When he refused, he was confined to an island in the Pasig River. In 1689 he also died while on his way to Mexico, a prisoner. In 1719 Governor-General

Bustamente was murdered in the course of a quarrel with the ecclesiastical authority over the arrest of the archbishop, when he refused to hand over an accused man who had taken refuge in a church. The friars led a rabble which attacked the governor's palace, and in the ensuing mêlée he and his son were killed. In each of these cases the governor-general abandoned a strong position by an arbitrary act which put him in the wrong, or appeared to. Hence the sum effect of these struggles was the gradual enhancement of the Church's power at the expense of that of the civil authority, and Le Gentil's comment in 1781 that the religious orders in the Philippines were more absolute than the king himself, was only too true. This state of affairs was to bring its own nemesis in the nineteenth century, when the friars had lost their missionary ardour and found themselves faced with the growing opposition of the Filipino people.

The struggle over episcopal visitation had in the long run an even more profound effect upon Philippine history than the conflict between the lay and ecclesiastical authorities. Beginning as a conflict about episcopal jurisdiction over regular clergy exercising parochial functions, it developed into one between the regular and the secular clergy for possession of the parishes; and as the Spanish friars clung to their parochial rights, and sought to prevent them from passing into the hands of the Filipino secular priests, it became racial in character, and thus a main factor in the later nineteenth-century revolutionary movement.

The regular clergy, who undertook the task of Christianizing the Filipinos, were subject to the heads of their respective orders, known as 'provincials', but as parish priests they were nominally under episcopal jurisdiction, and they objected to this. Against them were ranged the ruling of the Council of Trent (1564), Canon Law, which laid down the episcopal right of 'visitation', and the decrees of the papacy. Bishop Salazar, who had had long experience in Mexico, where episcopal visitation was accepted by the friars, asserted his right to this type of jurisdiction in 1582, and was supported by the governor-general. He had, however, to abandon the plan in practice because of the opposition of the friar-missionaries. A second attempt was made in 1620 by Archbishop Serrano to enforce visitation; but, although he appealed to the king, he failed. Archbishop Poblete in 1654 made the third attempt to assert episcopal authority over the friar-curates, but had to abandon it because the Audiencia supported his opponents; and he could not fight the matter to the final issue because he had at his disposal only 59 seculars as against 254 friar-curates.

At the end of the century Archbishop Camacho seized the opportunity to raise the matter again, when the friars appealed to him for support against the Audiencia over its action in investigating the validity of their land-titles. He was willing to help them, he told them, if they would accept episcopal visitation. When they refused, he supported the investigator appointed by the Audiencia. The procurators of the religious orders in Madrid thereupon (1699) delivered a protest to the king in which they offered him the alternative of granting exemption from episcopal control or the withdrawal of all friars from curacies. As there were only 60 secular priests for some 800 parishes, they felt themselves to be on strong ground. Nevertheless, the king in May 1700 issued a decree supporting the archbishop, and in January 1705 the pope issued a bull confirming the powers claimed by Camacho. Yet the friars again won the day. Their hostility resulted in such turbulence that the governor-general and the Audiencia withdrew their support from the archbishop. His successor, Archbishop Cuestra, on taking office in 1707 renewed the struggle by insisting upon putting the papal bull into effect. But the reports of the resistance so alarmed the king that he ordered the archbishop to postpone all action until further notice.

The matter was revived once more in 1767, when Archbishop de Santa Justa ordered the regular clergy in the parishes to submit to visitation. He had the support of the governor-general on the strength of orders received from Madrid. The Pope also had issued two bulls ordering the friar-curates to accept visitation. Because of this the Dominicans in council decided to accept the archbishop's mandate. After long discussion a compromise was arrived at and embodied in a royal decree issued in December 1776. The friar-curates were to accept visitation but only by their own superiors. Episcopal visitation was to be limited to parishes served by secular clergy.

In 1768 the Jesuits were expelled from the Philippines—for reasons connected purely with European history—and as a result the secularization question came into the foreground. The parish vacancies caused by their departure were filled with secular priests. The seculars appointed were all Filipinos, and because of the shortage of candidates some of the new priests were inadequately trained and highly unsuitable. Governor-General Anda, however, thought he had found the key to the solution of the visitation problem, and on his advice the king in 1774 decreed that all parishes on becoming vacant were to be secularized. Once again the anger of the friars blazed forth, and with apparent reason because of the low quality of the appointees. The complaints reaching the king were so bitter that in 1776 he suspended further secularization. It was a sad blow to the cause of the Filipino clergy. In 1804 the pendulum swung still further against them, when a beginning was made to the restoration to the regular clergy of parishes previously taken from them. But a worse blow still fell in 1861 when, to compensate the Recollect friars for the loss of the missions in Mindanao restored to the Jesuits on their return to the Philippines in 1859, a number of wealthy parishes in the Manila neighbourhood in the hands of secular priests were transferred to them. The situation now was vastly different from what it had been in 1776: the Filipino seculars were now well educated and thoroughly competent, and they bitterly resented the slurs cast upon their race, intelligence and morality in the very unpleasant controversy which this grave blunder stirred up.

Their cause was championed by one of their number, the learned Father Pedro Pelaez, who became acting archbishop of Manila in April 1862. Only a month earlier he had addressed a strong remonstrance to Queen Isabella II asking for the revocation of the decree of the previous year ordering the transfer of the parishes. His plea was rejected, but he went on to lead a powerful campaign against racial discrimination. When he lost his life in the Manila earthquake of 3 June 1863, his pupil Father José Burgos continued the agitation. His *Manifesto to the Noble Spanish People*, published in June 1864, attacked with tremendous vigour the current assertions of the superiority of the white race, but it failed in its objective. In 1870 there were still only 181 out of 792 parishes administered by the Filipino clergy. In that year, however, the Spanish Archbishop of Manila, realizing that the growing resentment against the regular clergy was stirring up strong anti-Spanish feeling, wrote a serious warning to the Regent of Spain, saying that grave evil, involving the danger of revolution, might result from the secularization grievance. But once again Spain did nothing. When, indeed, in 1896 the nationalist explosion came, the secularization question was one of its strongest ingredients.

The galleon trade brought such prosperity to Manila before the end of the sixteenth century, and expanded so rapidly that before long the Seville and Cadiz merchants, who managed Spain's export trade to America, began to be worried lest the flood of oriental goods—notably Chinese textiles—would affect their own trade and the manufacturing industries upon which it drew. The export of a large quantity of silver from Spanish America to the orient instead of to Spain was a further source of worry to minds, dominated as they were by the bullionist theory. Accordingly, in 1593 Spain applied a closed-door policy to

Philippine commerce, and applied it with full rigour until 1815. Philippine commerce with Spanish America had to be carried on in government-owned galleons only and with Manila and Acapulco in Mexico as its sole terminals. In 1585 Philip II had tried to stop all Chinese trade with Manila, but the viceroy of Mexico had refused to take action. He then forbade the shipment of Chinese textiles from Mexico to Peru, and direct trade between Peru and the Philippines. When in 1593 the Manila–Acapulco run became the rule, it was laid down that exports from Manila to Mexico were to be restricted to a maximum value of 250,000 pesos, and imports to Manila from Mexico to 500,000 pesos, while the run was to be limited to two galleons of not more than 300 tons burden each. But the Manila merchants ignored the quota, and the colonial officials connived at the evasions. When royal decrees reaffirming the quota had no effect, and the Seville and Cadiz merchants were losing heavily, the king in 1635 sent Pedro de Quiroga to investigate. His severe measures, however, aroused so much opposition that the Manila merchants refused to freight the Acapulco galleon, and in the years 1636 and 1637 the galleon trade was at a standstill. Their protests eventually won the day: in 1640 a new royal decree fixed the quotas at the more realistic maxima of 300,000 and 600,000 pesos, with two galleons of not more than 500 tons burden each to carry the trade. In 1734 the quotas were raised to 500,000 and one million pesos, but the galleons reduced to one.

In the eighteenth century the galleons varied in burden from 300 to 2,000 tons and were armed with from forty to sixty guns each. Many of them were built in the Philippines, of excellent local unsplinterable hardwood and equipped with equally good local-made cordage and sail-cloth. Their Filipino builders were first-rate craftsmen, and their Filipino crews were among the best seamen of the Pacific. Their crews numbered between 60 and 100, and in addition they might carry up to 400 passengers. In the seventeenth century usually more than two made the annual voyage across the Pacific. In the 1730s, however, the number was reduced to two; but the cost was found to be too high, and the Manila authorities limited the number to one. To Mexico they carried Chinese silk fabrics, cotton and linen cloths, porcelain, spices, amber, musk and perfumes. From Mexico they brought anything from a million to three million silver pesos, vastly exceeding the legal limit. Losses were heavy through typhoons, overloading or the incompetence of navigating officers. Some fell into the hands of English freebooters; others during the Anglo-Spanish wars of the eighteenth century were captured by the British Navy. These losses, combined with the establishment of the Royal Company of the Philippines in 1785, and the smuggling trade with Mexico developed by British and American private venturers, caused the galleon trade monopoly to lose its value so much that in April 1815 it was abolished, and the trade of Mexico, California, Peru and Ecuador was opened to Philippine commerce.

The galleon trade had effects of great importance in Philippine history. It drew most Spaniards to the Manila area, and far too much attention was paid to it by the officials, to the neglect of agriculture and industry. More important still in the long run was the fact that it forged strong links between the Philippines and America. Manila was the gateway to trade with Spanish America, and the channel through which Mexican pesos flowed into eastern Asia. But by concentrating upon the American connection the Spaniards failed to develop Philippine trade with Asia: the economic ties of the Philippines were with America rather than Asia.

The events of the eighteenth century, and notably the shock of the British occupation of Manila, resulted in the beginnings of a new policy abandoning isolation. It began to show itself clearly during the governor-generalship of José de Basco y Vargas (1778-87), when for the first time a comprehensive plan to develop the natural resources of the Philippines was set in motion. Through the Economic Society of Friends of the Country, which he founded in 1781, he sought to foster all kinds of cultivation suitable to the country, indigo, cotton, tobacco, cinnamon, pepper, sugar on a big scale, silk, hemp, tea, coffee and the opium poppy. In the following year he established the government tobacco monopoly, by which tobacco was to be cultivated in certain areas under government supervision and sold at a fixed price to the government. Large tracts of land were taken into cultivation in this way, and the Philippines became the chief tobacco-producing country in the East. Governmental revenue was much increased, so much so that the profits of the monopoly helped to make the Philippines financially self-supporting during the nineteenth century. On the other hand the operation of the monopoly opened the way for much official corruption and oppression. Together with other government monopolies, notably that of wine, it caused much popular unrest.

Vargas aimed at making the Philippines economically independent of Mexico. For many years the idea of direct trade between Spain and Manila had been discussed. King Philip V (1700-1746) had actually formed a company for trade with Manila via the Cape of Good Hope, but the opposition of the Manila merchants caused the scheme to be dropped.

Charles III (1759–88) ordered the opening of direct trade, and in 1766 sent a royal frigate with a cargo of European goods round the Cape to Manila, and, even in face of the refusal of the Manila merchants to co-operate, maintained the practice annually until 1783. In 1785 he went a step further by establishing the Royal Company of the Philippines with himself as a principal shareholder. It was given monopolistic trade privileges with Manila, no tariffs were to be charged on the import of Philippine products into Europe, and a percentage of the company's net profits was to be invested in Philippine industry. After some successful early ventures, however, it failed, partly because of the opposition of the Manila merchants engaged in the galleon trade, but also through bad management. Yet its effects upon the Philippine economy were beneficial: it invested money in textile factories, in the production of pepper and spices and the manufacture of indigo, sugar and silk.

The royal decree of 6 September 1834, which abolished the Royal Company, opened the port of Manila to world trade. Spanish mercantilism, which had again clamped down its restrictions upon Philippine trade after the British occupation, remained as rigid as ever, but Mexico's declaration of independence in 1821, and subsequent secession, forced Spain's hand. Hostility to foreigners was intense. In 1800 they had been forbidden by royal edict to live in the Philippines. How little real effect the edict had is shown by the fact that within a very few years it had to be reissued more than once. In 1828 foreigners were forbidden to engage in retail trade, or visit the provinces for purposes of trade. As late as 1857 these anti-foreign laws were renewed. Foreigners were the enemies of God and Spain, the Filipinos were told, and the 'Cholera Massacre' of 1820 was a grim reminder of the way the Spaniards could work up mob frenzy against them. But in spite of the often-repeated decrees against them, foreigners did gradually work their way into the Philippine economy after the opening of Manila to foreign trade in 1834. Keen rivalry, indeed, developed between American and British merchants for trade supremacy there. The latter won, for with their far-flung banking connections and commercial bases at Hong Kong, Singapore and in India, they were in a more favourable position to push their trade in the Philippines. The opening of the islands to world commerce also stimulated developments in their agriculture, and their hemp and tobacco became famous in the markets of the world. And such things in turn stimulated road-building, the construction of harbour-facilities and port works, the development of a modern postal and telegraph service and of a modern banking system.

All this material progress brought into being, during the latter half of the nineteenth century, a new middle class of Filipino families, often with mixed Chinese or Spanish blood, prosperous, well-educated, becoming increasingly Westernized, and interested in sending its sons abroad to widen their outlook. It was through these people that the old isolationism, which had kept Filipino society largely *incommunicado* from the outside world, was broken down. And with the impact of modern ideas and nineteenth-century liberalism came the beginnings of the political awakening of the Filipino people.

For most of the Spanish period education in the Philippines was exclusively in the hands of the missionary friars and Jesuits, and aimed at propagating Christianity and Spanish culture through the medium of the Spanish language. On the lowest level there were parochial schools, the first of which was founded on the island of Cebu as early as 1565. On the secondary level there were a number of boys' colleges, in the founding of which the Jesuits took the lead, opening their first in Manila in 1589. They also took the lead in higher education when their college of San Ignacio received papal recognition as a university in 1681. It was followed by the Dominican foundation of Santo Tomas, recognized by Innocent X in 1645, which in 1870 became the University of the Philippines. Some colleges for girls were also established in connection with convents. But until the second half of the nineteenth century Spanish education was given only to a very small proportion of the people, and few Filipinos received secondary education.

The secession of Mexico, which brought the Philippines into direct relations with Spain, also brought to the Philippines many Spaniards imbued with the new liberal ideas that were stirring Europe. The ruling concept of education as the handmaid of religion came thus to be challenged, and at the same time a growing demand arose for its extension. Ever since 1770 the establishment of a system of public primary education had been spasmodically under consideration. Provision for it was at last made in 1863. The commission, upon whose report the new education code was based, had been decreed in 1839, appointed in 1855, and took six years over its deliberations. Spain was not in a hurry to provide the Filipinos with the means for their own emancipation.

The code laid down that at the headquarters of every *pueblo* there must be at least one primary school for boys and one for girls. Attendance was to be compulsory, and for the poor free. The parish priest was to be the local inspector, and the direction of the system was vested in Provincial Boards dominated by ecclesiastics and a Superior

Commission presided over by the Archbishop of Manila. Normal schools were to be set up for the training of teachers. The first, for men, was opened in Manila in 1865. The figures given in various sources for the numbers of schools and pupils vary, but it would appear that by the end of the Spanish régime the Philippines had some 2,150 public schools with a total enrolment of well over 200,000 pupils. As far back as 1843, long before the system came into operation, a Spanish investigator stated that in proportion there were more literates in the Philippines than in Spain herself. By the end of the nineteenth century they were ahead of any other country of South-East Asia in education, and particularly in female education, and there were said to be better schools there than Spain established anywhere in America. The spread of the Spanish language and the Latin alphabet linked the Filipinos closer to Europe than to Asia. Thus culturally as well as economically the Philippines stood apart in South-East Asia. Nowhere else had Western culture and Christianity made so powerful an impact. Nowhere else also had a modern-type nationalist movement shown itself as a powerful and cohesive force.

Opposition by force to Spanish rule never ceased in the Philippines. The Moros of Mindanao and the Sulu archipelago from the start had rejected Spanish domination outright and vigorously retaliated against all attempts to conquer them. In the middle of the seventeenth century they forced the Spaniards so much on to the defensive that they had to leave their settlements in Formosa in the lurch in order to concentrate on the danger from Mindanao. Not until late in the nineteenth century, when the steamship and modern arms forced the brave people of Sulu to acknowledge defeat, was the pacification of the Moros completed. In July 1878 the sultan capitulated and accepted Spanish suzerainty.

Elsewhere also in the territories occupied by Spain attempts were made again and again to cast off her yoke. More than one hundred were of appreciable size. In the seventeenth century discontent with the hardships caused by the long struggle with the Dutch was a main source of trouble, but there was no general outbreak and Spanish power was never seriously threatened. They were usually local disturbances due to forced labour, the appalling slowness of government in paying for services or goods, and other crushing burdens. Some, like the Bohol revolt in 1621, the Leyte rising which followed it, and in particular the uprising of 1660–1 in Pangasinan and Ilokos were anti-Spanish in character and aimed at the restoration of what the Church called 'paganism'. They were watched with sympathy in other parts of the islands, but regional jealousies were such as to enable the Spaniards to crush each revolt with the help of 'friendly Indians'. Only a handful of Spanish soldiers was used. In Bohol in 1744 there was an unusual type of revolt, which began over the refusal of a parish curate to bury a body in consecrated ground. Three thousand rebels under Francisco Dagahoy, the brother of the deceased man, murdered priests, fled to the hills and defeated every attempt to dislodge them. Dagahoy established an independent régime which lasted until 1829, long after his death. His followers increased in number to some 20,000, and when, after very hard fighting, the patriots were overcome and accepted pardon, there were 19,420 survivors.

Discontent with the occupation—of disputed legality—of Filipino lands by the religious orders caused a whole series of agrarian uprisings in 1745–6 in the provinces of Bulacan, Batangas, Laguna, Cavite and Risal, around Manila. They were so serious that Philip VI appointed an investigator into the charges brought against the ecclesiastics. They refused, however, to submit their land-titles to a secular judge and although they were adjudged to have usurped the lands, and the decision was upheld on appeal by both the Audiencia and the Council of the Indies in Madrid, they refused to hand them over and eventually won their case.

The British occupation of Manila (1762–4) triggered off a number of rebellions because of the ease with which the Spaniards had been defeated. The most important was led by Diego Silang in the Ilokos region. He began by asking for the abolition of tribute, because of the Spanish failure to defend the country, and offered to lead Iloko troops against the British. When his demands were refused, he made Vigan the capital of an independent government which maintained itself against all attacks for nearly a year. Silang was assassinated, but his heroic wife, the 'Ilokano Joan of Arc', held out for some months until hunted down and captured by a flying brigade of loyal Filipinos. There were about a dozen other risings at the time, but the vigorous action of Governor-General Anda, helped by militant friars and loyal Filipinos, caused their failure in every case. Although many of the leaders of the revolts of the seventeenth and eighteenth centuries are today acclaimed as national heroes, their revolts were purely local in character, and it has been well said that 'it took two hundred and fifty years of the *pax hispanica* before a Philippine national consciousness could become articulate'.[1]

The nineteenth century saw a growing spirit of unrest in the Philippines. There were risings due to the abuses of the monopoly system

[1] J. L. Phelan, *Hispanization of the Philippines*, 1959, p. 151.

and also to the rapacity of the religious orders. But developments elsewhere, in Spain and Spanish America, now began to have their influence. The Sarrat rebellion of 1815, for instance, was caused by the decree of Ferdinand VII suppressing the liberal Spanish Constitution of 1812. The dramatic Novales Mutiny of 1823, which almost resulted in the seizure of Manila by rebellious Filipino troops, arose out of racial discrimination in the army. Racial discrimination in ecclesiastical matters caused the revolt of 1841–2, which itself led to the mutiny of the Tagalog Regiment in 1843. All these revolts, like those of the earlier period, failed, and for the same reasons. National cohesion was completely lacking, and none of the revolutionary leaders was a national figure. But they were of great significance, for they were the sign of an unquenchable spirit of independence, which deeply resented Spanish pride and intolerance and the rapacity of the religious orders.

National sentiment existed, but it was inchoate and very slow in expressing itself effectively. The geography of the islands, of course, was a great hindrance to its development as a conscious force. But by the middle of the century all the ingredients for a national movement were there. The Filipinos possessed a common racial origin, a common cultural heritage, to which Spain had contributed much, and a common hatred of the Spanish yoke. Spanish policy had helped to unite them by giving the islands for the first time a centralized government, and by spreading Christianity and Spanish civilization. The opening of the Philippines to world trade, and the rise of an enlightened middle class of Filipinos, were powerful factors in preparing the way for a nationalist movement, and it was this new middle class which provided the movement with its leaders.

The movement was sparked off by the Spanish revolution of 1868 when Queen Isabella II was dethroned, reactionary laws were repealed, the religious orders abolished, and universal suffrage and a free press established. The Philippines felt its impact, for colonial officials with democratic ideas were sent to the islands and the administration was transformed in the direction of greater autonomy. Newspapers and books with European liberal ideas circulated openly, and a liberal governor-general, De la Torre, abolished the censorship, fostered free discussion, and introduced an entirely new spirit of humanity into the relations of government and people.

The immediate effect of all this was a tremendous agitation among both priests and laymen for Filipinization. But General Prim, the moving spirit in the provisional government, set up after the queen's flight, was assassinated in December 1870, and soon afterwards a reactionary governor-general was sent to replace De la Torre. The Filipino nationalist priests were forbidden to say mass, and De la Torre's policy was completely reversed. The mutiny of some 200 Filipino soldiers at Cavite in January 1872, speedily repressed, was magnified into an attempt at revolution, and numbers of laymen and priests, who had supported the liberal régime, were arrested for treason, and after a farcical trial given heavy prison sentences. Some were executed, among them three blameless Filipino priests, Fathers Burgos, Gomez and Zamora, who thereupon became the martyrs of the nationalist cause.

The judicial murder of the three priests was followed by the deportation of various Filipino leaders to penal colonies, and by such a persecution of intellectuals that many fled abroad to Hong Kong, Singapore and Japan, and in particular to London, Paris and Madrid itself. There they carried on a publicity campaign known as the 'Propaganda Movement' with such moderate demands as equality of Spaniards and Filipinos before the law, the assimilation of the Philippines as a Spanish province with representation in the Spanish cortes, the Filipinization of the parishes, and liberty of speech, the press, meeting and petition. Their aims were reform, not revolution. They themselves were loyalists. The chief Propagandists were the brilliant young Dr José Rizal, Marcelo del Pilar and Graciano López Jaena. Rizal, the soul of the movement, was born in 1861 and educated at the Jesuit college at Manila. He showed marked ability as a poet, writer and sculptor. Sent to complete his education in Spain, he there took his diploma as a doctor of medicine. He then travelled in Europe, and in 1887, in Berlin, published his novel *Noli Me Tangere*, in which he described Filipino sufferings under Spanish rule. Four years later its sequel, *El Filibusterismo*, in which he attacked the religious orders, was published in Ghent. These two novels did for the Filipino opposition to Spain what *Max Havelaar* did for the opponents of the Culture System in Java, or *Uncle Tom's Cabin* for the anti-slavery movement in the United States.

Rizal produced a vast amount of published work on a wide variety of subjects, much of it consisting of articles contributed to the organ of the Propaganda Movement *La Solidaridad*, a fortnightly journal founded by Jaena in Barcelona in 1889, and later transferred to Madrid, where Del Pilar became its editor until in 1895 it failed for lack of funds. In 1887 Rizal returned to Manila, but finding that his presence in the Philippines endangered his family he left and returned to Europe to continue his writing and propaganda. In June 1892, because of the eviction of his father and sisters from their home on the Dominican estate of Calamba, he insisted on returning to Manila. There he tried to found the *Liga Filipina*, a peaceful association for the social and political betterment of his people, but his arrest a few days after its formal inauguration, and his deportation to Dapitan in Mindanao, brought its existence, and his own political career, to an end. He was not a revolutionary in the ordinary sense, but the Spanish government chose to treat him as one.

The propaganda movement also came to an end; support for it dried up, its leaders died in poverty and *La Solidaridad* went out of circulation. Spain was moved by their denunciations to announce reforms, but they were ludicrously inadequate. The way was thus open for the real revolutionaries to take the lead. In July 1892 a secret society, the Katipunan, was founded in Manila. It had two aims: to win independence by force and to unite all Filipinos into a nation-state. Its founder was Andres Bonifacio, of humble origin, orphaned at fourteen and self-educated. With him was associated Emilio Jacinto, also of humble origin but with a university education. The society was directed by a Supreme Council, which worked through local councils in each province and city; but real power was in the hands of a secret junta of three. The leaders got into contact with Rizal at Dapitan in July 1896, but he warned them that their plan to start a revolution was premature: much more preparation was needed. Matters were taken out of their hands, however, by the discovery of the Katipunan and its revolutionary plan, and when during August 1896 the government tried to apprehend Bonifacio and his associates, sporadic fighting began. Then almost simultaneously nationwide rebellion blazed up. It was met by a reign of terror, in which among others José Rizal was tried on charges of rebellion, sedition and illicit association, and on 30 December 1896 was shot. His death added fury to the revolution, but the initial movement, involving the capture of Manila, had collapsed, and Bonifacio had gone to take refuge in the hills of Montalban in northern Luzon. And against a new governor-general, Polovieja, who arrived with reinforcements in December, the main rebellion in the Cavite region, led by Aguinaldo, also failed, notwithstanding desperate resistance.

Bonifacio had set up a revolutionary government at Tejeros. Aguinaldo's brave stand, however, in the Cavite fighting showed him to be a better military leader, and in March 1897 a revolutionary assembly at Tejeros elected him President of the Philippine Republic. The deposed leader tried to set up a breakaway government at Limbon, but he and his brothers were caught and sentenced to death by a military court appointed by Aguinaldo.

Aguinaldo's revolutionaries, however, could not prevail against the much better equipped Spanish forces, and in July 1897 he himself took refuge in Bulacan. The way now seemed open for a settlement by negotiation, and with the warlike Polovieja removed from the scene by illness, his successor, Fernando Primo de Rivera, tried diplomacy. Aguinaldo was induced to reduce his demands very considerably, but even these the Spanish authorities could not accept. Finally in December 1897 the so-called Pact of Biacnabato was agreed upon, by which the revolution was to stop and its leaders go into voluntary exile in Hong Kong. Spain in her turn was to pay them the sum of 800,000 pesetas by instalments upon the surrender of their arms. The government was also to grant an indemnity of a further 900,000 pesetas to the families who had suffered from the war.

The pact was soon broken. Aguinaldo and his associates received the first instalment of their money, 400,000 pesetas, in Hong Kong, and proceeded to use it for the purchase of new arms. Primo de Rivera distributed a little money in cash to war sufferers, but the full sums promised were never paid. And nothing was done about the reforms, which had been the subject of the negotiations, although not formally stated in the terms of the 'pact'. It was a case of bad faith on both sides. In February 1898 new risings began, and shortly afterwards a new revolutionary government under General Francisco Makabulos established itself in central Luzon. Such was the situation when on 1 May of that year the Spanish fleet was sunk in Manila Bay by Commodore Dewey's American fleet.

CHAPTER 41

THE RESURGENCE OF SOUTH-EAST ASIA

AT the beginning of the twentieth century new factors of far-reaching significance may be discerned in the historical development of South-East Asia. Asia as a whole was becoming aware of itself as never before. A fermentation was in process that in many ways bears a striking resemblance to the European Renascence of the fifteenth and sixteenth centuries. Only in South-East Asia's case, unlike Europe's, the attack upon traditionalism, the introduction of new ways of thinking and new techniques, and the break-up of the older regimented, feudal social order came as a result of the imposition of alien political and economic domination. By the end of the nineteenth century all her states save Siam had come under European control, and Siam's own political independence, threatened in 1893 by France, was still in jeopardy.

The threat of European dominance had made itself felt from 1511, when Albuquerque conquered Malacca. But the European states of the sixteenth and seventeenth centuries were in no position to establish territorial sway over immense regions so remote from their shores. Nor did they covet it at first. They planted 'factories'. They sought to monopolize commerce, not to exercise political power with all its responsibilities. Their control was maintained by powerful fleets and forts with garrisons. And when, like the Dutch towards the end of the seventeenth century, they gained political control they did not administer territories directly, but through native rulers. There was hardly any interference with native institutions, though in some places considerable interference with economic activities.

The Portuguese were pledged to a crusade against the infidel, but against both Islam and Theravada Buddhism their missionaries had strikingly little success. The Dutch and English made no attempt before the nineteenth century to interfere with the established religions. The French, on the other hand, in the latter half of the seventeenth century launched a grandiose scheme of Catholic missionary enterprise, using Ayut'ia as their base. But Louis XIV's pet project to convert the Far East foundered on the rock of its deeper political implications. It aroused intense anti-European xenophobia in Siam which was not relaxed until the days of Maha Mongkut. The other states of the mainland also—notably Burma, Annam, and Tongking—developed this same tendency to an increasing degree. They showed the greatest suspicion towards all types of European activity.

The nineteenth century brought a new phase in the European impact, with a far more dangerous threat to the jealously guarded independence of the South-East Asian states. It was a period of rapid Western political and territorial advance, when Britain, France and Holland acquired colonial empires in South-East Asia. The whole situation changed. The great companies of commerce, the directors of European enterprise in the earlier period, disappeared from the scene. Government officials took the place of merchants, territorial revenues of trading profits, and at home control by ministers of state was substituted for that of boards of directors.

There was extensive exploration of natural resources; foreign capital, not all of it European, was invested on an ever-increasing scale; economic development, particularly that of interiors, was rapid—breathlessly so in some cases. The effects upon native life were revolutionary. Producers became dependent upon external markets and the heartbreaking problem of agricultural indebtedness came to assume gigantic proportions. Foreign immigration, notably of Chinese and Indians, on an immense scale caused deep resentments and acute problems. For some time the indigenous peoples of the 'colonial' territories looked on helplessly as their economic subjection became more and more complete. Their growing realization of their plight gave impetus to the movements for national independence which characterized the first half of the twentieth century.

The response of the West to the nationalist challenge was not unsympathetic. As early as the year 1900 the Dutch publicly proclaimed their adoption of the 'New Course', whereby government *of* the Indies was to be *for* the Indies. The French defined their function as a *mission civilisatrice*. The British, in response to political developments in India, promised to train the native peoples for self-government according to Western democratic methods, and to introduce it by gradual stages. All three powers expanded and liberalized their colonial administration by adopting methods of social welfare similar to those they were developing at home. All three fostered the spread of European education. Save in the case of British Malaya, however, where there was no strong national movement until after the

Second World War, the new policy failed signally to arrest the growing discontent with Western domination.

The national movements which attained such a pitch of intensity in Burma, Indo-China and Indonesia were powerfully influenced by developments elsewhere in Asia. The Boxer Rising of 1899 in China, the emergence of Japan and her spectacular defeat of Russia in 1905, the Chinese revolution of 1911 and the establishment of the Kuomintang Party by Sun Yat-Sen, the increasing dominance of the Swaraj Party in the Indian National Congress, the rise of Mohandas Karamchand Gandhi and the launching of his non-co-operation movement against British rule in India, aroused their enthusiasm with the sight of Asia casting off her chains.

The upsurge of nationalism, however, was at this time by no means confined to Asia. The peace conference at Versailles at the end of the First World War had taken the lid off a boiling cauldron of nationalist claims in Europe itself. In remaking the map of Europe the nation-state was accepted as the guiding principle, though with the rather flimsy safeguard of a League of Nations to restrain what the more penetrating thinkers ominously described as its 'giant egotism'. Nationalism, and the rights of small nations in particular, became the main topic of discussion, and the increasing numbers of Burmese, Vietnamese and Indonesians who reached the higher grades of European education in their own countries or proceeded to famous centres of learning in Europe inevitably imbibed the heady wine of Western political thought.

From their study of Western history they learnt of Britain's constitutional struggles, the American War of Independence, and the French Revolution. They read John Stuart Mill's *Essay on Liberty*; they caught the thrill of Shakespeare's ardent patriotism when they read:

> *This England never did, nor never shall*
> *Lie at the proud foot of a conqueror,*

and the flame of freedom scorched their souls. They were the people who became most acutely sensitive to the racial discrimination practised by their Western rulers, for they suffered most from it. It was from their numbers, therefore, that the political agitators, and eventually the national leaders, were recruited. Thus the nationalist movements acquired both means of expression and technique through Western education.

Nationalism, however, was not born of the revolt against European

domination. Its cultural roots go as far back in South-East Asia as in
Europe. Notwithstanding the strength of the influences coming from
India on the one side and China on the other, the more advanced
peoples who absorbed them showed marked individuality very early
in their history. The great cultures which flowered so richly, especially
in art and architecture, during the Middle Ages—Mon, Khmer, Cham,
Javanese, and Burmese—not only reflect that individuality but even in
their earliest expression are quite distinct from Indian. And even in
the case of Vietnam, where it may be contended with reason that
Chinese was the parent culture, the differences are significant, for the
Vietnamese struggle for political independence, which came to a
successful issue in the tenth century, was also a reaction against the
intense sinization systematically enforced by China.

Long before the arrival of the European the peoples mentioned
above were producing their own vernacular literatures. Some—
notably Burmese, Mon, Javanese, and Balinese—exhibit a great
variety of forms and literary qualities of a high order. In Bali's case it
is of interest to note that Stutterheim claims that just as in Europe
through the stimulus of the Greek and Roman classics the various
peoples developed their own national cultures, so out of Hinduism
the Balinese created 'a proper, purely national culture'. The same can
be said with equal truth of the Burmese, Mon, Khmer, Cham, and
T'ai peoples.

It is perhaps questionable how far the great mediaeval states such
as Pagan, Angkor, Ayut'ia or Majapahit represented national ideas or
aspirations. The dynastic factor played a prominent part in their
history. But in the struggle of the Burmese against Shan domination,
of the Mons for independence against Burmese rule, and in the wars
between Burma and Siam in the sixteenth and eighteenth centuries,
national sentiment was evoked and played its part. Naresuen and P'ya
Taksin, for instance, were in a real sense national leaders. The struggle
between the Chams and the Vietnamese in its later stages seems
pretty certainly also to assume a nationalist character. Nationalism
as a political sentiment does seem to show itself in these cases; but
the subject still awaits systematic investigation, and its discussion here
must be considered exploratory only.

There can be no doubt that much of the opposition the European
powers had to meet in their territorial expansion during the nineteenth century had a strong nationalist content. Not a few of the
rebel leaders of that period are revered today as pioneers in the
struggle for freedom. A recent study of Dipo Negoro is worth

examination in this connection. At the beginning of the twentieth century the great majority of people in Burma and Indo-China had been born in the days before the final extinction of independence, and memories remained green of a time before European rule. All the nationalist movements gained some of their driving force from an awareness of a historic past before the European intrusion. It was a sedulously cultivated awareness, as was only to be expected, of a glorified past bearing little resemblance to sober history. And the situation was not without its irony, for it was the European archaeologist and historian who discovered the real achievements of the past and rescued the historic monuments from decay and, in not a few cases, oblivion.

In each country the nationalist movement pursued a largely independent course. There was practically no liaison between the leaders in one country and those in another. Their ties were much closer with left-wing movements in the European countries under whose sway they lived. Moreover, the methods of the British, Dutch and French in dealing with their respective areas differed considerably. Hence it is difficult to draw comparisons between the different movements and dangerous to generalize. Among the peoples themselves there was much divergence of opinion regarding aims and methods. Some were for gradualness, others for revolution. There were sincere patriots who were anxious not to break the political ties with the West. Few indeed advocated the reinstatement of the obsolete or obsolescent monarchies. And, unlike in India, there were extremely few opponents of Western techniques and scientific methods. Traditionalism, however, showed its influence in Buddhist and Islamic revivalism, and in Burma the Young Men's Buddhist Associations and in Indonesia Sarekat Islam played important roles. Buddhism became closely identified with national sentiment in both Burma and Siam, and the patriotism of those who belonged to other religions was impugned. Partly for this reason Communism failed to appeal to the great majority of people. Only in French Indo-China did the Communists gain control over the Vietnamese nationalist movement, and then only because of French intransigence.

CHAPTER 42

BRITISH BURMA, 1886–1942

BRITAIN'S greatest mistake in dealing with Burma was to attach the country to the Indian empire. It was the natural thing to do, seeing that each stage of the conquest was organized and carried out by the Government of India. But its inevitable result was the standardization of Burma's administration according to the Indian model. In Malaya the mistake was avoided because the British forward move there came after the transfer of the Straits Settlements to the Colonial Office. Even as late as 1886 it could have been avoided if, when the whole country came under British rule, the fact had been adequately recognized that its culture, history and outlook gave it an individuality which it was the duty of the conquerors to preserve with all possible care. But as few people knew anything about these things administrative convenience was the overruling consideration.

It used to be said that three generations in Ireland makes an Irishman. It would be equally true of Burma. Moreover, the earliest British administrators found that the only effective way of getting anything done was to do it according to the Burmese method. The Burman judged everything according to the extent to which it conformed to Burmese custom, and the reply, 'It is not our custom', given by the Court of Ava to a proposal made by a British envoy, was final. It was useless to argue further. Hence in Tenasserim after its annexation in 1826, and in Pegu after 1852, although the administrative layout conformed to the Indian model, administrative practice tended to conform to Burmese traditional methods. And although in theory the Bengal method of direct rule was employed, in practice indirect rule not unlike the Dutch system in Java prevailed. The life of the ordinary villager went on much as it had under Burmese rule, and very few Burmans lived in towns.

Various factors combined to bring a fundamental change in this state of affairs. In the first place the process of standardization according to the Indian model received considerable impetus from the efforts that had to be made to quell disorder after the annexation of 1886. In the long run, however, the effects of this might not have been decisive, and the traditional Burmese methods might in time have reasserted themselves, had it not been for the development of increasing specialization in functions and the additional responsibilities which governments of the modern Western type began to undertake during the succeeding period. The old policy of *laissez-faire* was abandoned and new forms of governmental interference, aiming at improved efficiency or social welfare, were invented. And along with them, as a result of immensely improved communications, came greater and ever greater central control—the control of the Rangoon Secretariat over district administration, and the control of the Government of India over provincial administration.

The immediate problem after the annexation was that of disorder. The Burmese army disregarded the order to surrender and melted away into the jungle villages with its arms to carry on guerrilla warfare over a wide area. The *thugyis*, who had been the backbone of the Burmese system of district administration, became the leaders of the resistance movement, and at the head of marauding bands roamed far and wide to prevent the establishment of settled government. No less than five princes of the royal family, each claiming the throne, held out in different regions. And a serious rebellion broke out in Lower Burma. The abolition of the kingship, worthless as Thibaw had proved himself to be, evoked a nation-wide reaction against foreign rule. It took five years of hard campaigning to subdue the country, and at the peak period of the resistance an army of 32,000 troops and 8,500 military police was fully engaged.

For purposes of civil administration Upper Burma, excluding the Shan States and the extensive hill tracts inhabited by non-Burmese peoples, was divided into fourteen districts, each under a Deputy or Assistant Commissioner. So far as revenue and civil justice were concerned, the original intention of Sir Charles Bernard was for these to work through indigenous agencies according to local methods. But Bernard's successor, Sir Charles Crosthwaite, who came with firmly fixed ideas of Indian administration, brought with him a ready-drafted scheme for making the village, as in India, the basic social and political unit. His theory was that the circle headman of the older administration, known as *myothugyis* or *taikthugyis*, had, in the words of a recent study,[1] 'overshadowed and usurped the rightful power of the village headman'. His plan, therefore, was to break up the circle into villages and strengthen the village as an administrative unit, primarily in order to use it for the restoration of law and order. For his

[1] F. S. V. Donnison, *Public Administration in Burma*, London and New York, 1953.

immediate intention was to hold the village community responsible for crimes committed within its tract.

The new policy was set in motion by the Upper Burma Village Regulation of 1887 and the Burma Village Act of 1889, which applied it throughout the country. These two measures imposed statutory duties concerning the maintenance of order and the collection of revenue upon the headman and villages. As a result of their enforcement the *myothugyis* and *taikthugyis* were gradually eliminated. The largest indigenous social and political unit of the previous period was thus destroyed and a stereotyped direct administration imposed, with the village tracts placed under the charge of a civil servant, the *myo-ok* or township officer.

Mr. J. S. Furnivall, who during his long experience as an administrator in Burma not only had a close view of the working of the new system but also made a careful study of the existing indigenous materials relating to the *myothugyi* system,[1] has summed up the effects of the change in a recent work.[2] In the first place, he writes, the villages had duties imposed upon them without any compensating rights. In the second place, in order to equalize headmen's charges so as to combine adequate emoluments with efficient administration (from the point of view of supervision by the *myo-oks*), a comprehensive scheme of amalgamation was carried through after 1909. The merging of villages which this involved led to a reduction in the number of headmen by over 2,000 and made the 'village' a mere artificial administrative unit. In the third place, with the disappearance of the *myothugyi* the habit of referring serious disputes between adjacent villages to his arbitration 'so as to arrive at a compromise according to known custom' tended to die out and 'the mechanical logic of the law courts' was substituted. His general conclusion is that 'the popular self-government of Burmese times was replaced by a foreign legal system'.

It seems doubtful whether the semi-feudal power of the *myothugyi* can be rightly termed 'popular self-government', though it must be admitted that the *myothugyi* was bound by local custom; he did not give arbitrary decisions. But whether the old Burmese institution was capable of carrying out the new duties necessarily imposed by twentieth-century conditions may also be doubted. The great evil of

---

[1] The main records are a mass of several thousand documents known as *Sittans*. Furnivall printed a large collection of these in a volume which was apparently never published. It was used by Ma Mya Sein for the researches upon which she based her *Administration of Burma*, Rangoon, 1938.

[2] *Colonial Policy and Practice*, pp. 74–6.

the new system was that the *myo-ok* as a civil servant was subject to frequent transfer and rarely stayed long enough in one place to learn all that was necessary for good administration, whereas the *myothugyi* was a local man whose ancestors had held the office before him.

Burma's artificial connection with India had other unfortunate results. Her first two Chief Commissioners, Sir Arthur Phayre and Sir Albert Fytche, had spent most of their previous careers in the country; they spoke the language, understood its religion and customs, and Phayre wrote the first standard history of Burma in English. After Fytche's retirement in 1871, however, the office of Chief Commissioner, and thereafter of Lieutenant-Governor, was held by men who had been trained in India and looked forward to returning there on promotion. They never learnt the language and had only a smattering of knowledge of the country.

Moreover, the Indian connection imposed upon British administrators in Burma a negative attitude towards the religion of the country. Now Buddhism was the established religion of the country, supported and maintained by every king since Anawrahta of Pagan (1044–77). Hence the abolition of the monarchy raised the important question of the position of the Buddhist organization under the new régime. The men with long service in Burma, especially Colonel (later Sir Edward) Sladen, who had known Mindon intimately, urged that the new government should support the ecclesiastical authority in the same way as the Burmese kings had done. Responsible Burmese leaders added their pressure and the Thathanabaing, the head of the Buddhist hierarchy under Thibaw, headed a deputation to Sir Frederick Roberts, the British commander-in-chief, offering to preach submission to British rule, if the jurisdiction of the ecclesiastical commission, the Thudhamma Council, as it had operated under the kings, were confirmed.

But the provincial government could not undertake such a task: it was bound by the Queen's proclamation of 1858 after the Indian Mutiny ordering all British authorities in India to 'abstain from all interference with the religious belief or worship of any of our subjects on pain of our highest displeasure'. Two of the Thathanabaing's requests, the safeguarding of ecclesiastical endowments and the sponsoring of the system of examinations in the Pali scriptures, were readily granted; but the difficulty arose over his extra-legal disciplinary powers. The British position was that the ecclesiastical courts must not override the established civil or criminal law. They were, however, most anxious to go as far as they could in supporting his authority. In practice, therefore, the appellate courts upheld his jurisdiction, when it was appealed against; the rule was laid down that 'so long as he does nothing contrary to law, it is not for the courts to question the correctness of either his orders or proceedings in ecclesiastical matters'. Sir Charles Bernard, the Chief Commissioner, in an effort to use the Thathanabaing's moral influence, built a rest-house for him at the Shwe Dagon Pagoda. But the sect-ridden Sangha of Lower Burma flouted his authority and exposed thereby the weakness of the British position. This became even clearer in 1895 when he died. The provincial government could not itself select a successor, and because of a serious split in the Upper Burma Sangha no one could be appointed. When this healed, in 1903, an assembly of monks at Mandalay chose a new Thathanabaing, and the Lieutenant-Governor of Burma granted him a *sanad*, defining his authority, and an official seal. It was an inadequate substitute for the royal ecclesiastical commissioners of the past, but the support of the civil courts in practice gave much authority to the Buddhist hierarchy.

Nevertheless, there was a decline in monastic discipline. It began to manifest itself for the first time as a serious problem at the end of the First World War. By this time a younger generation of monks had become politically-minded. One of their number, U Ottama, who had absorbed left-wing Congress ideas during a stay in India, began in 1921 to lead agitation against British rule. Nationalism within the Order resulted in the organization of the Sangha Sametggi in 1922 with the professed aim of promoting the advancement of religion and education on national lines. Its members ranged far and wide throughout the land preaching non-co-operation, non-payment of taxes and the use of the boycott. They took their cue from Ireland. Young men began to assume the yellow robe as a cloak for political activities. The senior monks condemned such activities, and in 1921 the Thathanabaing forbade monks to participate in politics, but without effect. The Burma Government therefore took further measures to strengthen his authority, and in particular revived the office of mahadanwun to carry out his decisions in matters of discipline. But, unlike in Thailand, there was no registration of monks, and in practice therefore no power to unfrock. In 1935 the effort to boost the Thathanabaing's powers received a knock-out blow when the Rangoon High Court, by the unanimous decision of five judges, two of whom were Burmans, laid down the ruling that the Buddhist hierarchy had no special legal status, any more than other religions not established by the state. This disaster could have been overcome by legislation, and in 1937 the Burmese democratically-elected parliament received full powers to deal with the situation. But in the welter of political strife among the factions contending for power nothing was done. In 1938 the Thathanabaing died and no successor was appointed.[1]

The decline of the Order's hold on education has been adduced as one reason for the activities of the pongyi agitators: they were trying to revive their influence as teachers of the people. The monastic schools had for many centuries played a fundamental part in Burmese life. Through their efforts the literacy rate among males was very high. Hence Sir Arthur Phayre, the first Chief Commissioner of British Burma had aimed at using them as the basis of the educational structure of government-aided schools that he began to build in 1866. His plan was to introduce secular subjects into the monastic schools, with government providing books, equipment and money for buildings. It failed, because very few monasteries would accept government aid or admit secular subjects into the curriculum. Therefore Albert Fytche, Phayre's successor, encouraged the opening of lay vernacular schools. Even with pupils leaving the monastic schools for the lay schools with their wider curriculum the monks remained unwilling to co-operate. After the annexation of Upper Burma the Thathanabaing forbade secular education in monastic schools. Only a handful of liberal pongyis defied him. The government's policy was to give grants-in-aid to such monastic schools as would co-operate, and not to encourage lay schools in places where monastic education was efficient. But, notwithstanding repeated efforts to integrate the monastic schools in the governmental educational system, 'so as not to deprive the pongyis of their greatest sphere of usefulness', as a Lieut.-Governor put it in 1912, more and more pupils were attracted to the lay schools. The monastic schools gained a reputation for inefficiency; and the demands of government and business offices for clerks with a knowledge of English caused attention to be diverted more and more to Anglo-Vernacular schools. Government Anglo-Vernacular schools had been founded in the seventies. They and the grant-aided mission schools provided by the Roman Catholics, the Society for the Propagation of the Gospel, and in increasing numbers by the American Baptist Mission, prepared their best pupils for the matriculation examination of Calcutta University. Thus the eclipse of monastic education may be seen as a result of British rule, though not of British policy. It came about through the refusal of the Sangha to co-operate; and the chief ingredient in its attitude was its opposition to what may be termed modernity.

The other main feature of monastic education, Pali studies, flourished during the British period. The opposition of the Mandalay monks held

---

[1] The matter, it must be noted, was no longer a British responsibility.

up for some years the British effort to revive the *patamabyan* examinations in the Pali scriptures previously conducted under royal auspices. But in 1895 the government decided to go ahead with them, and did so with increasing success. The committee in charge of the examinations sponsored the publication of a complete printed edition of the Tripitaka, and the number of candidates, mainly monks, grew until in the nineteen-thirties they were rarely less than 3,500, notwithstanding persistent opposition by the Sangha Sametggi using terrorist tactics. In 1941 the government of separated Burma considered a scheme for the establishment of a Pali university, but the Japanese occupation prevented its implementation. U Nu's government was later to revive the plan after independence.

To return to the general development of education in Burma under British rule, the whole system was overhauled in 1880 and provincial examinations instituted. By this time the Calcutta University Matriculation had become the final aim of most secondary schools. The Rangoon Anglo-Vernacular High School, founded in 1873, went further; it developed a higher department, which became Rangoon Government College, and in 1884 began to prepare students for the external degrees of Calcutta University. But departmental policy was to encourage voluntary schools rather than found government ones. In 1900 there were sixteen missionary secondary schools and a small Baptist college in Rangoon for the higher education of Karens. The Education Department maintained five normal schools for the training of teachers, and in addition to the Rangoon Government High School and College, a number of technical schools for surveying, elementary engineering, forestry and midwifery. Throughout the country there were 17,000 vernacular schools, 341 of them for the education of girls.

In the twentieth century the increasing demand for secondary education in English caused the serious neglect of monastic schools and concentration upon the multiplication of secondary schools. This inevitably brought the question of higher education to the forefront, and the first big separation issue arose through the demand that Burma should have its own independent university. This brought the University of Rangoon into existence in 1920 as a teaching and residential institution, blending the work of the two existing institutions of higher education, Government College and the Baptist College, which became its constituent colleges.

The university began its life at a moment of high political tension over the question of dyarchy, and the refusal of the Education Department to countenance an institution after the Calcutta model, granting external degrees and encouraging local affiliated intermediate colleges, combined with a simultaneous quarrel over anglo-vernacular education to bring about a nation-wide boycott of government and missionary educational institutions. An attempt was made by a Council of National Education to create a complete educational system free from government control. National education was to be the key to unlock the door to national independence and self-government.

It was a most impressive movement, but after the introduction of dyarchy and the transfer of education to the control of a Burmese minister it lost its vitality. Efforts at conciliation succeeded, especially when in 1924 a University Amendment Act was passed giving Burmans greater control. The boycott was called off and the more efficient C.N.E. schools qualified for government grants. The university also was given enough money to expand its scope to include medicine, engineering and forestry, as well as to establish a large modern teachers' training department, complete with practice schools. It gave immense stimulus to education and culture throughout the country.[1] Its graduates notably improved the standards of the services to which they were appointed.

But political pressure, often attempted before 1937, became far more effective with the establishment of the new constitution for Burma in that year, and inevitably the high standards that had been built up against great difficulties in the earlier period began to deteriorate. The Students' Union also became a happy hunting-ground for the less responsible type of political agitator, and discipline was undermined. The forcing of a new constitution upon the university in 1939 was inspired by not a single honest educational object. The intention was to use it to produce political agitators against the British. Unfortunately, however, far too much attention has been directed to this aspect of the question, so that the real value of the work done by the university during this period has tended to be obscured.

After the suppression of what had been a national uprising after the deposition of King Thibaw, Burmese nationalism remained quiescent for a long period. It began to manifest itself early in the twentieth century in the cultural sphere under leaders sprung from the new Western-educated *élite*. A Buddhist revival began among the laity. It

---

[1] Donnison's complaint (*op. cit.*, p. 70) that 'the courses of study provided were often unrealistic and imperfectly related to the needs of the country', merely reflects the pathetically wrong-headed attitude of the European community towards university education for Asians. Its real crime to them lay in the fact that it *was* university education and not a superior form of technical education 'related to the needs of the country'.

was to some extent inspired by the decline of the monastic schools. It expressed itself in the formation of Buddhist associations. The first appeared in 1904 at Rangoon College. Two years later the Young Men's Buddhist Association came into being. Officially it was non-political, but in the years 1916–18 it carried on an agitation against 'Footwear' at pagodas and other sacred places, that was directed against Europeans and had clear political undertones. National sentiment was boosted by glorification of the past in the teaching of history in schools and in the popularization of the study of the chronicle writings. The *Konbaungset* was printed and published in Mandalay in 1905, and the *Hmannan Yazawin*, or *Glass Palace Chronicle*, in 1908. The academic Burma Research Society, founded in 1910 largely through the efforts of U May Oung, a distinguished lawyer, and J. S. Furnivall, then a British civil servant, brought Burmese and Western scholars together in common efforts for the advancement of knowledge. No one, however realized the force of the national sentiment that lay apparently dormant until the First World War ended and the question of Burma's future political progress came to the fore.

The promotion of the Chief Commissioner in 1897 to the rank of Lieutenant-Governor assisted by a Legislative Council of nine nominated members, including five non-officials, was the prelude to, though not the cause of, a considerable expansion in the functions of government and a multiplication of new departments concerned with social welfare. There was also the gradual introduction of a judicial system based upon the British principle of the separation of powers. It began with the establishment of a Chief Court for Lower Burma in 1900 and was followed in 1905 by the creation of a separate judicial service to relieve local executive officers of all their civil and some of their criminal cases. At first, for reasons of economy, the change was not applied to Upper Burma, where Divisional Commissioners sat as sessions judges and Deputy Commissioners tried civil cases in the remoter districts. Moreover, the view was rightly held by many people that the separation of powers below High Court level was not in the interests of good government, and that, at least so far as the Deputy Commissioner was concerned, it was better to concentrate rather than disperse his authority.[1]

The increase of specialist departments, which began in 1899 with the creation of a separate department to take over the management of prisons from the Inspector-General of Civil Hospitals, came partly from a new campaign for 'efficiency' inspired by Big Business and

[1] F. S. V. Donnison, *op. cit.*, pp. 40–1, has some useful observations on this subject.

partly from concern for social justice, which had been growing throughout the nineteenth century among the more progressive sections of the
British people and was to have so powerful an influence on policy in the
twentieth. The Dutch felt this humanitarian impulse at the same time
and proclaimed the 'New Course' in Indonesia. In Burma it was
hurried on partly because the great increase of crime and general lawlessness, which were the ordinary Burman's protest against the new
conditions introduced by alien rule, made it necessary to free the hands
of the general administrative officers for concentration upon the
campaign against the criminal.

In 1900 a Commissioner of Settlements and Land Records was
appointed for the more efficient handling of land revenue matters.
From 1900 also a closer control over education was instituted and a
considerable extension of state education began. In 1904 the Co-
operative Credit Department was set up. In 1905 a Chief Conservator
of Forests was appointed and in 1906 a Director of Agriculture.
Agricultural, Veterinary and Fishery departments came into being,
while in 1908 a Sanitary Commissioner was appointed and a Public
Health Department began to function as an organization distinct from
its parent, the Medical Department. In Rangoon a large new secretariat
came into existence to link up all these departments, and bureaucratic
government became the order of the day.

Gladstonian Liberalism sought to foster the political education of the
people of India by the gradual introduction of local self-government.
As early as 1874, at the instance of the Government of India, nominated
Municipal Committees were established in a few Burmese towns. In
1882 the electoral principle was introduced. Little progress, however,
was made in self-government. The fact that urban populations were
composed of different communities—Burmese, Chinese, and various
types of Indian—made common action difficult. Local opinion also was
against any line of action which might increase taxation, and was often
not in sympathy with the sort of amenities that such communities
existed to provide. Hence only in Rangoon, with its relatively large
European element and educated Asian community, was the system
reasonably successful.

The rural District Committees, first established in 1884 at the
instance also of the Government of India, failed rather badly as an
experiment in self-government. The local officer had to retain a tight
hold over them, and as the great evil of frequent transfer prevented him
from gaining a thorough knowledge of his district the general result
was inefficiency, and corruption among the subordinate officials.

In 1909 the Minto-Morley reforms in the government of India increased the size of the Burma Legislative Council to a membership of thirty with a non-official majority. It could ask questions, move resolutions and take votes, but no resolution had binding force on the government. Notwithstanding Morley's own strongly expressed desire that the reforms should not lead either directly or indirectly to the introduction of the parliamentary system into India, it seems obvious now that in 1909 Britain did in effect cross the Rubicon, although the principle of popular election was not introduced. This became clear when, under the stress of the First World War, Britain in order to hold India, made promises of political advancement, with responsible self-government as the ultimate aim.

The Montagu-Chelmsford Report, however, upon which the Government of India Act of 1919 was based, recommended that Burma's case should be reserved for special consideration, since her people were of a different race, at a different stage of political development, and with altogether different problems. The storm of protest which suddenly arose in Burma when the nature of the alternative proposals for her political development became known took everybody by surprise. Burmese national sentiment flared up to fever pitch. It expressed itself in the form of a universal strike of the pupils of government and missionary educational institutions, in December 1920. In their stead 'national schools' sprang up everywhere under the direction of a Council for National Education. For the hundreds of students who walked out of the newly opened University of Rangoon a 'National College' was established in monastic buildings on the slopes leading up to the majestic Shwe Dagon Pagoda. U Ottama and bodies of young monks of the Sangha Sametggi went around the countryside preaching revolution. A new political General Council of Burmese Associations, the G.C.B.A., took the place of the General Council of the Young Men's Buddhist Association, and advocated the non-co-operation techniques of the Indian *swaraj* movement. Its extremist wing took the Sinn Fein movement in Ireland as its pattern.

In 1921, therefore, parliament decided to extend to Burma the dyarchical form of constitution introduced into the other Indian provinces by the Government of India Act of 1919.

A Burma Reforms Committee under the presidency of Sir Frederick Whyte was appointed to work out the details of the new arrangement on the spot; and although the extremists among the Burmese politicians condemned dyarchy as inadequate, Burma became a governor's province in 1923, and subject to the exclusion of the Shan states, Karenni and the Tribal Hills the first steps were taken towards 'the progressive realization of responsible self-government'.

The main features of the new scheme were as follows: the Legislative Council was increased to 103 members, of whom 79 were to be elected on a democratic franchise, 2 were *ex officio* and 22 nominated; the government was entrusted to the governor with an Executive Council of two Members in charge of Reserved Subjects, and two Ministers, responsible to the legislature, in charge of Transferred Subjects. The reserved subjects comprised defence, law and order, finance and revenue. The transferred departments included education, public health, forests and excise. The transference of the important Forest Department placed Burma ahead of all the other provinces except Bombay. The franchise was granted to householders without sex disqualification and with eighteen as the minimum age limit.

Why was so wide a franchise qualification introduced, with an age limit below that in any European democracy? Mr. Furnivall's comments on it sum up succinctly the various attempts that have been made to explain so surprising a step.[1] 'The official explanation was that no qualifications of age, property or education could be devised; simplicity welcomed it as evidence of faith in liberal ideals; cynics ascribed it to petulance, "making the best of a bad job" or to astuteness—if the people do not like bureaucracy, let them have democracy in full measure to disillusion them. The kindest explanation is that the government trusted, as it believed, the well-merited affection of the "conservative element" against the disaffection of a few pernicious agitators.'

In addition Burma was given five seats in the new Indian legislature at New Delhi which dealt with what were known as 'central subjects'. A great increase in self-governing local bodies was also provided for, and the majority of members of both municipal committees and rural district committees were to be elected. Moreover, the wide range of responsibilities entrusted to these bodies, including the maintenance of roads other than main roads, public health, sanitation, the maintenance of hospitals, the health of cattle, the provision and regulation of slaughter-houses, the establishment and control of markets, the operation of ferries and the creation of school boards, gave Burma a very real degree of self-government in local affairs as well as at the centre. The administration of justice was not affected, though at almost the same time a High Court was created to replace the Chief Court of Lower Burma and the Judicial Commissioner in Mandalay,

[1] *Op. cit.*, p. 160.

while the separate judicial service was extended in such a way that divisional commissioners no longer held Sessions.

Dyarchy began its fourteen years' span in Burma in an atmosphere of agitation that went right down to village level. The G.C.B.A. had been responsible for the organization of *Wunthanu Athins*, 'own race' associations, in 1921–2 in many rural areas. Their ostensible function was to combat corruption and crime, but their real one was to secure the boycott of the lawful administration and the non-payment of taxes. There were also *Bu Athins*, secret societies, with horrific membership oaths using terrorist methods. The G.C.B.A. under the leadership of U Chit Hlaing was for some time allied with the extremist pongyis of the Sangha Sametggi. It declared a boycott of all elections under the new constitution; but this caused a split in its ranks and the dissidents formed the People's Party, or Twenty-One Party, so-called from the number of members who signed its first programme. Led by U Ba Pe, it declared for qualified co-operation 'so long as the speedy attainment of Home Rule is not prejudiced thereby'. It was, of course, highly critical of the administration. At the elections to the first Legislative Council it won the largest number of seats. There was also a small Independent Party led by Sir J. A. Maung Gyi which was anxious to make the constitution work. But the electorate was apathetic or intimidated: less than seven per cent of the voters went to the polls. And personal rivalries among the elected nationalist representatives weakened their powers of effective combination so as to control the government. Office offered rewards, and there was no difficulty in obtaining candidates for the ministerial posts, even from the opposition. The earliest demands from the Burmese members were for improved education to fit Burmans for self-government, rapid Burmanization of the public sevices, the promotion of indigenous economic development, the end of foreign 'exploitation', and the provision of more agricultural credit and of more money for the 'nation-building' departments. There was notable progress in education and public health, but the impulse came from the 'experts' specially recruited by the administration. And no attempt was made to deal with the pressing economic and racial problems. And while the legislators had to learn how to exert their powers without jamming the governmental machine, the boycotters were seeking to learn how to bring its authority into contempt. But here again there was dissension inside the G.C.B.A. and between that body and the pongyi agitators over the no-tax campaign and other revolutionary methods. Thus when in 1924 the government took a firm line, gaoling U Ottama and sending military police to the disaffected districts, disillusionment with the efficacy of the boycott method spread. At the second election to the Legislative Council over sixteen per cent of the electorate participated; but again the divisions among the opposition groups weakened the nationalist cause in the Chamber, and caused the ministerial posts to go to conservatives who had little support among the main body of elected members, and pursued a policy of compromise. No constructive legislation was passed for this would have stirred up controversy. In 1927 a Burma Agrarian Bill was introduced from the government side. It sought to combat the evils of agricultural indebtedness and land alienation by establishing reasonable safeguards for the cultivator. But it aroused the opposition of the landlord class and was abandoned. It was said that in India under dyarchy while the Indians went on talking the government continued to govern as before. In Burma's case it was manœuvring and intriguing that stultified the nationalist effort.

Nevertheless dyarchy was a real step forward in the political education of both sides. There was, however, what has been described as 'an unsettling air of impermanence'[1] about it, for under the Government of Burma Act of 1921 it was laid down that after ten years a Statutory Commission should be appointed to consider the possibility of a further instalment of reforms. Early on a demand went up for its appointment sooner than the stipulated date, and for full responsible government and separation from India. The desire for separation was natural, for the increasing Indian immigration and economic competition made the Burman fear that his country might one day become a vassal state of an Indian commonwealth governed by Indians.

In 1928 the 'Simon Commission' came to review the working of the reforms introduced in 1923. It reported in favour of separation and a number of constitutional advances. Then suddenly Burmese opinion veered on the separation issue. A loudly-vocal section led by Dr. Ba Maw, a young aspirant to political leadership, proclaimed that if Burma were separated from India her rate of constitutional progress might be slower than India's. The fact that the government and Big Business gave unqualified support to separation aroused the deepest suspicions. Actually one of the chief reasons for the support given in official circles to separation was that India's share of the Burma revenues was considered too large. The central taxes, such as income-tax and customs revenue, were capable of much greater expansion than provincial revenues.

While a special Burma Round Table Conference sat in London

[1] Donnison, *op. cit.*, p. 55.

between November 1931 and January 1932 to discuss the main lines
of a constitution for a Burma separated from India, the agitation in
Burma came to a head with the formation of a strong Anti-Separation
League, which advocated joining the proposed Indian federation with
the option of secession. At a general election held in November 1932
the League won a complete victory. Hardly a single Burmese anti-
separationist was in favour of permanent union with India. Hence
when Britain made it clear that she was not prepared to give Burma
the option of contracting out of the Indian government at will, the
League executed a complete *volte-face*, and the Government of India
Act of 1935 provided for the separation of the two countries to take
effect on 1 April 1937.

The new constitution of separated Burma, outlined in Part XIV and
Schedules X to XV of the Government of India Act, 'was given body
in the Government of Burma Act, 1935, and spirit in the Instrument
of Instructions from His Majesty to the Government'.[1] The Burma
government came directly under the British Parliament, the Secretary
of State for India became Secretary of State for India and Burma, and
a separate Burma Office was created under an Under-Secretary for
Burma. The governor became solely responsible for defence, external
and internal, monetary policy, currency and coinage, foreign affairs
and the Excluded Areas of the Shan states, Karenni and the Tribal
Hills. In all other matters, save certain emergency powers entrusted
to his special responsibility, he was bound to act on the advice of
his ministers. General administration was entrusted to a cabinet of
ministers, limited to ten, under the leadership of a prime minister
and responsible to the legislature.

The legislature was bicameral. The upper house was a Senate
of thirty-six members, half of whom were elected by the House of
Representatives and half nominated by the governor. The House of
Representatives contained 132 members, of whom 92 were elected by
territorial constituencies and the remainder represented communal and
other special interests such as the University of Rangoon, commerce
and labour. The franchise was made even wider by including most
males over twenty-one and all females over that age who could pass a
simple literacy test.

The governor's reserve powers were greater in theory than in
practice. The Instrument of Instructions counselled him 'so to exercise
his powers as not to enable his Ministers to rely on his special responsibilities in order to relieve themselves of responsibilities which

[1] Donnison, *op. cit.*, p. 73.

are properly their own'. And wherever possible he was to consult them even in matters left to his special responsibility. It was hoped that his 'special responsibility powers', which included the prevention of grave menace to internal peace, the protection of minorities, and the prevention of unfair discrimination against British subject or their goods, would as far as possible be held in abeyance.

The Burmese Cabinet and parliament now had almost complete control over internal affairs. The first general election was keenly contested. Dr. Ba Maw was the first prime minister, and he and his colleagues gained office by promising to tackle the serious problems of agrarian distress, corruption and village administration. Their early efforts were not very effective. But the new system had no chance to settle down and learn its job, for the peace of the world was already threatened by Nazi Germany and the Japanese penetration into China. And internally political life was vitiated by the personal rivalries of aspirants to power, with the consequent development of splinter parties. Mr. Donnison, who served in Burma under the new system, writes that 'the first reaction of the new Ministers to the increased power conferred on them by the new Act, was to become bolder, less scrupulous, and more cynical, interfering with the administration as a matter of course and even at times tampering with the courts'.

At the time of the annexation in 1886, when the question of the Sino-Burmese frontier came under discussion, the Chinese Minister in London, supported by Sir Robert Hart and Sir Halliday Macartney, suggested the cession of Bhamo to China. When this was rejected, Macartney claimed that the country north of Bhamo on the left bank of the Irrawaddy was Chinese; hence, he said, Britain must not go 'beyond the Irrawaddy'. This absurd claim, ridiculed by Sir George Scott, underlined the need for a frontier settlement, and the Anglo-Chinese Convention of 1886, by which China recognized the British conquest of Upper Burma, provided for the establishment of a frontier commission to delimit the boundaries. Two regions were involved, The Kachin area north of Myitkyina between India, Tibet and Yunnan, which came to be known as the Triangle, and the block of Shan states that had previously paid tribute to the Court of Ava. Their boundaries with China had never been precisely defined, and there was much ignorance about them on both sides. Warry, the British Political Officer at Bhamo, from enquiries made in the Kachin area reported in May 1888 that the Chinese had never exercised, or claimed suzerainty over the Kachins. Surveys of the territory north of Bhamo revealed a situation which caused the British Foreign Office to decide in 1891 that the

Kachins must be brought under control. But, although considerable progress was made in consolidating British authority in northern Burma, nothing was done regarding the frontier.

With regard to the Shan States the Chinese had become aware that in deference to military opinion Britain had at first been unwilling to assume responsibility for the trans-Salween states.[1] They had therefore come to regret that they had not taken advantage of this situation. Further negotiations began in September 1892, and ultimately after long delay a new Convention was signed on 1 March 1894, providing for a joint commission to demarcate the boundary southwards from latitude 25' 31" north, i.e. the Shan States' frontier with China. The boundary northwards of that point, namely, the Kachin area, was to be left alone for the time being until the features and condition of the country were better known. In addition, Britain renounced her suzerain rights over the two trans-Mekong states of Mong Lem and Keng Hung to China, but with the strict proviso that China must not cede either of them to any other nation without British consent.[2] She also made two small cessions of territory on the Chinese frontier, Sima, a fortified pass south of Myitkyina, and the Kokang Circle of the Shan State of North Hsenwi. The Chinese on their part opened the narrow Namwan wedge of territory to the transport of British troops between Bhamo and Namkhan.

This agreement was wrecked by the action of the French, who had staged the 'Paknam Incident' on 13 July 1893 and subsequently occupied all Siam's territories east of the Mekong. China ceded Keng Hung to France and, in due course, after the Möng Sing incident of 1 January 1895, Keng Cheng, which Britain had proposed to cede to Siam,[3] also went to France. China's breach of the Convention entailed the negotiation of a new agreement between her and Britain. It was embodied in the Anglo-Chinese Treaty of June 1897. The terms were stiffer. Kokang was returned to Hsenwi, Sima was returned to Burma, and the Namwan tract was made over to Britain in perpetual lease for the annual rent of one thousand rupees. The long-delayed implementation of the decision to set up a joint boundary commission was at last carried out, and work began in the same year. Good progress was made until 1900, when disagreement over the Wa States boundary line led the British Commissioner, Sir George Scott, to break off the discussions. Two lines were drawn named after the respective commissioners on both sides, the Liu-Chen line and the Scott line. The disputed area

[1] *Supra*, p. 689.   [2] *Supra*, p. 697.
[3] The story of these events is told above in Chapter 39, pp. 697–8.

between them included the 'Wild Wa' states of Kanghso, Mankuei and Motel. It was for many years treated as a no-man's-land. In 1934–5, however, the Burma Corporation, which worked the great silver-lead mine in the Northern Shan States, sent prospectors into the area to examine the Lufang silver mines, once worked by the Chinese. They were driven out by Wa tribesmen and Chinese 'bandits', who proceeded to invade British territory, and had to be dealt with by military action.

By this time the Kuomintang were carrying on an agitation for the 'recovery' of territories China claimed once to have held in northern Burma. Sir Alexander Cadogan, the British Ambassador in Peking, thereupon proposed the establishment of a new Anglo-Chinese commission under the chairmanship of a League of Nations appointee. China agreed, and the League appointed the Swiss Colonel Frédéric Iselin as chairman. In October 1935 the commission started work. Trouble with the Was was effectively dealt with by a powerful military escort, and the commission compiled the first reliable map of the area ever to be made. Its final report was signed on 24 April 1937. It awarded three-fifths of the disputed area to China and the remaining two-fifths to Britain. The Japanese invasion of China, which began a fortnight later, prevented a formal settlement. Both sides, however, accepted the commission's findings, and on 18 June 1941 the settlement was formalized by an exchange of notes between the British Foreign Office and Chiang Kai-shek's government in Chungking.

The Kuomintang agitation had begun in 1931, when Ch'en Yu-k'o became Chief of the Bureau of Propaganda of the Yunnan Provincial KMT Executive Committee. In the following year he published *Yunnan Pien-ti Wen-ti Yan-chin*, which was translated into French by J. Siguret and published in Peking in 1937 under the title *Territoires et Populations des Confins du Yunnan*. Its extreme claims to tribute and territory caused Britain some uneasiness regarding the Triangle, where she had ever since 1891 been taking action to prevent Kachin outrages. Between 1905 and 1910 Chinese activities in Tibet had caused the Indian Government to feel that its back door was threatened. They had ceased when India announced that she was prepared to use force to prevent any further advance towards her frontiers. But the feeling persisted that China might seek to annex the Kachin lands from the Tibetan side. In 1911 the Government of India started the systematic survey of the Tibetan borderlands which resulted in the Simla Conference of October 1913. Sir A. H. McMahon met the Chinese and Tibetan representatives, and on 27 April 1914 the Chinese representative initialled an agreed map. Afterwards, however, China made a number of protests, and when in July Britain and Tibet signed an agreement, the Chinese delegate withheld his signature. In the Kachin country the British established military police posts from Namkhan northwards along the Irrawaddy-Salween watershed. Hence, in response to Ch'en Yu-k'o's agitation, Sir Hugh Stephenson, Governor of Burma, on 8 January 1934 announced the extension of British-Indian control over the Triangle. And there the matter rested until after the Pacific War of 1941–5.

CHAPTER 43

THE DUTCH 'NEW COURSE' AND NATIONALISM IN INDONESIA, 1900-42

By 1900 Dutch opinion on colonial affairs had come to regard liberalism as out of date. It was obvious that the supporters of private enterprise cared little about the interests of the Indonesians, and that the immense power that private capital had come to wield was in the hands of a few great corporations able to take common action in defence of their interests—the 'over-mighty subjects', in truth, of modern times. Dr. Abraham Kuyper, who became prime minister in 1901, was the writer of a pamphlet published in 1880, *Ons Program*, in which he argued that the government must adopt a policy of moral responsibility for native welfare. This idea he incorporated in the 'Speech from the Throne' of that year. Thus was launched what became known as the 'Ethical Policy'.

The first Socialists had by this time entered the Dutch parliament and were loudly proclaiming the doctrine of 'Government of the Indies for the Indies', with their eyes open to the ultimate aim of self-government. But a far deeper impression was made by the Liberal C. Th. van Deventer, who not only drafted a new programme for his party, advocating welfare, decentralization and the greater employment of Indonesians in the administration, but in 1899 caused a sensation by his article *Een Eereschuld* ('A debt of honour'), in which he argued that all the money drawn from the Indies under the *batig saldo* since 1867, when parliament assumed responsibility for the finances of the Indies, should be repaid.

So once more, after a tremendous outpouring of noble sentiment, a programme of 'decentralization' and native welfare was set in motion, with the same almost incredible hesitation that had marked the abandonment of the Culture System. 'Decentralization' was the new gospel. It envisaged the delegation of powers from The Hague to Batavia, from the governor-general to departments and local officers, and from European to Indonesian officers. It also meant the establishment of autonomous organs managing their own affairs in co-operation with the government. In practice, however, the Decentralization Law of 1903 and the decrees of 1904-5 creating local councils composed of Indonesians, Europeans and Chinese went nothing like as far as the decentralization scheme which Governor-General Mijer had submitted to the home government as far back as 1867. And up to the outbreak of the First World War, which cut off Batavia's communications with The Hague, the governor-general remained completely under the control of the home government.

In 1905 the Deputy Director of the Civil Service, de Graaff, raised the question of the substitution of Indonesians for Europeans and the unification of the two services, in connection with his proposal for a reform of Java's territorial organization which would give local officers greater power. But for the time being it was side-tracked. In 1914, he submitted a wider scheme embracing the reorganization of the whole of the Indies into twelve governments, each with a degree of financial autonomy. This also was shelved, but his plan to give Indonesian officers greater powers—the word actually used was *ontvoogding*, 'emancipation'—was generally approved. Nothing, however, was done until 1921, when it was laid down that certain concessions might be made to regents in recognition of special merit. But the first regent to be 'emancipated' declared that it made no difference whatever to his position, and for another ten years, in the words of Raden Djajadiningrat, 'the European administration remained just as before'.[1]

Meanwhile the promoters of the 'ethical policy' had turned to the village as the lever for the improvement of native welfare. Beginning with de Graaff's Village Regulation of 1906, which provided for a Village Government, comprising the headman and village officers, and a Village Gathering competent to regulate village institutions and provide for its requirements, measures were taken to improve agricultural production and veterinary care, to establish village schools, provide sound credit and promote public health. The most elaborate village administration was built up. But it was an instrument for such excessive interference from above that there was hardly any village autonomy left, and the general effect was to turn villages against Dutch rule. The Dutch method has been described by Mr. Furnivall as 'let me help you, let me show you how to do it, *let me do it for you*'.[2]

The first signs of an awakening national self-consciousness began to show themselves in Java early in the century. Such external

---

[1] *Indonesische Genootschap*, 1929, p. 83, quoted by J. S. Furnivall in *Netherlands India*, p. 269.
[2] *Op. cit.*, p. 389.

influences as the Boxer Rising in China, the Filipino revolt against Spain, and the rise of Japan undoubtedly played their part, for they had a marked effect on the minds of little groups of *literati* in the various countries of South-East Asia, who were worried by the inferior status accorded to them under Western domination. It was significant that in 1899 Japan claimed, and received, equal rights with Europeans

RADEN ADJENG KARTINI

in the Netherlands Indies. But in each country the nationalist movement took on a special character of its own.

In Indonesia the predominance of Java, with two-thirds of the total population crowded into one-fifteenth of the total area, was a marked feature of its early stages. Cultural factors here were active, an increased awareness of the value of Javanese culture with its roots deeply in the far-distant past, and a demand for the spread of education, regarding which the Dutch had shown themselves woefully negligent before the twentieth century. A new chapter in the native movement opened with the emergence in 1900 of the gifted Raden Adjeng

Kartini, daughter of the Regent of Japara, as a champion of education for women. Her letters,[1] published in 1911, stimulated the release of a native spiritual energy which led to the foundation of Kartini schools for girls. Both she and Dr. Waidin Sudira Usada, a retired medical officer, who began a campaign for the advancement of Java in 1906, looked to the spread of Western education as the means of salvation.

In 1908 Usada founded the first nationalist association, Budi Utomo ('High Endeavour'), with a membership mainly of intellectuals and Javanese officials. It aimed at organizing schools on a national basis and took its inspiration from the Indian poet Rabindranath Tagore, and to some extent from Mahatma Gandhi. It was followed in 1911 by an association of a very different character, Sarekat Islam, which was an offshoot of an Islamic revival among Sumatrans and Javanese, resulting from an intensification of Christian missionary enterprise. Sarekat Islam made its first appearance, however, as a combination of Javanese *batik* traders against Chinese exploitation. Its four original aims were announced as the promotion of Indonesian commercial enterprise, mutual economic support, the intellectual and material well-being of Indonesians and the true religion of Islam. It rapidly became a popular movement, and within a quarter of a century had a membership of two millions. 'Islam was the bond and symbol of common action against other nationalities', writes Colenbrander.[2] At its first congress, held at Surabaya in January 1913, its leader, Omar Said Tjokro Aminoto, asserted forcibly that it was not directed against Dutch rule, and that it would pursue its aims in a constitutional manner. Its first nation-wide congress was held in 1916, when representatives of 80 local societies with a membership of 360,000 attended and passed a resolution demanding self-government on the basis of union with the Netherlands.

Meanwhile Socialism had made its appearance not only among Indonesians but also among the Indos, or Dutch Eurasians. The Russian Revolution of 1917 had immediate effects upon the situation in Java. Hendrik Sneevliet formed the Indian Social Democratic Club with revolutionary aims, and Semaun, one of its members, strove to win over Sarekat Islam to Communism. At the National Congress of October 1917 at Batavia Tjokro Aminoto changed his tone to one of hostility to the government, though he still recommended

---

[1] The Dutch edition is entitled *Door duisternis tot licht. Gedachten over en voor het Javaansche volk.* There is an English edition entitled *Letters of a Javanese Princess by Raden Adjeng Kartini,* New York, 1920. She died in 1904 aged twenty-five.
[2] *Koloniale Geschiedenis,* iii, p. 129.

constitutional action. There was strong disappointment at the postponement of the establishment of the long-promised Volksraad, and with the limitation imposed by the Dutch upon franchise regulations. War was declared on 'sinful capitalism'. But Semaun, who had organized an energetic Communist section (Section B) closely in touch with Moscow, failed to gain control of the movement and broke away to form the Perserikatan Komunist India (P.K.I.), which joined the Third International of Moscow. An outbreak of passive resistance in the Preanger in July 1919, coming after an ugly incident in central Celebes in which the Dutch controller and some officials lost their lives, led to an enquiry, which showed that secret societies belonging to Section B were involved, and it was thereupon dissolved by the government.

The struggle was now between the P.K.I. and Sarekat Islam, and the religious question was the main issue. P.K.I.'s second congress in 1920 decided that Communism was just as much opposed to Pan-Islamism as it was to Western domination. Communism, however, was not a mass movement, and the Communists, though exceptionally energetic and intelligent, were few in number. Hence their tactics were to attempt to steal their influence from the leaders of Sarekat Islam and to win over the trade unions. And Tan Malaka, a Communist leader exiled for inciting a strike of government pawnshop employees, went to Moscow and tried to persuade the Comintern to accept Pan-Islamism.

When the sixth national congress of Sarekat Islam met in October 1921 at Surabaya, Tjokro Aminoto was under arrest because of his connection with underground activities, and Abdul Muis and Hadji Agus Salim, who presided in his place, carried a motion forbidding members of the Sarekat to belong to any other party. This forced the Communists out of the movement. But for five years Sarekat Islam fought a losing fight against the relatively small group of Communists who went ahead organizing Sarekats of their own, supporting strikes and making preparations for revolutionary action in parts of northern and western Java. In 1922, under the influence of young Indonesian graduates from Europe, who were discontented with their status in the government services, Sarekat Islam established relations with the Indian National Congress and adopted the policy of non-co-operation.

The years 1923–6 saw a series of revolutionary attempts. The post-war depression, with its crop of industrial disputes, presented the extremists with excellent opportunities for bringing about the maximum dislocation of political and economic life in the hope that it would enable them to seize power. Moscow at the time regarded Java as a strategic centre of the highest importance. Through agents in Singapore contact was made between the P.K.I. and the Chinese Communist Party. For the time being the Communists became the most vital force in the Indonesian movement, and lawlessness and intimidation were the order of the day. Against this Sarekat Islam became increasingly hostile and turned more and more to religion as a means of combating Communism.

The P.K.I., with a large following among the trade unions, organized a railway strike in May 1923 which caused the government to amend the penal code by providing heavy penalties for action likely to dislocate economic life. But the policy of repression only encouraged the spread of revolutionary views. In 1925 a strike in the metal industry was forcibly suppressed. In the following year, encouraged by vague promises of assistance from Zinoviev and Bucharin, the Communist leaders tried to start a revolution in West Java and Sumatra. The operations were described as carefully planned and widespread. Nevertheless they were easily suppressed, and before the measures of severe repression taken by the Dutch the whole revolutionary movement collapsed. The Communist Party was banned, Communist meetings prohibited and about 1,300 members of the party interned in New Guinea. Communism was not entirely suppressed, but its leadership of the Indonesian movement was ended and a new phase in the history of that movement began.

The failure of the revolutionary movement left Sarekat Islam as the main organ of nationalism, though by this time a multiplicity of parties had arisen—some local, such as Sarekat-Ambon, Perserikatan-Minahasa and the Sumatranen-Bond; others based upon the division of political parties in Holland; and still others, such as the Indo-European League and various Chinese societies, representing special communal interests. Sarekat Islam now began to pay more attention to education and economic conditions. It put great energy into the foundation of 'wild' schools and co-operative institutions. This kind of work, however, did not satisfy the aspirations of the discontented students of the Indonesian Club in Holland. Through their influence, and under the leadership of Djipto Mangun Kusuma, the leader of the Bandung Study Group, and of Sukarno, a popular young demagogue of incorruptible character, a new political party, Perserikatan National Indonesia, came into being in 1927. It sought to rally all the existing nationalist organizations behind a big non-co-operation movement on the Gandhi model. But when Sukarno began to show revolutionary tendencies he and two of his helpers were jailed in December 1929, and once more the extremist attempt to capture the nationalist movement failed; as a political force it came to an end for the time being. New leaders interested in social service and social justice came forward. Ki Hadjar Dewantoro ('teacher of all the gods'),[1] to use the pseudonym he adopted as a public man, went ahead with the planning and development of national education, while Dr. Sutomo, who as a young medical student had been associated with Dr. Sudira Usada in founding Budi Utomo, directed the energies of the National Party into various types of constructive activity, and in particular the struggle to free the peasantry from the tyranny of the usurer.

Much of the trouble of these post-war years was the result of disappointment at Dutch unwillingness to effect any real transfer of power. During the First World War, in response to insistent nationalist demands for a greater share in the government, a scheme for a Volksraad was passed by the Netherlands Parliament in 1916, and what has been called an experiment in self-government[2] held its first meeting in May 1918. Half of its members were elected by local and city councils, and half were appointed by the governor-general. It was in no real sense a representative body, it had a European majority, and its powers were limited to the offering of advice, which the governor-general could not accept without authorization from The Hague. At its first meeting the disappointed deputies rejected a proposal to address a loyal cable to the queen in token of gratitude. And although under the Constitution (*Staatsinrichting*) of 1925 its numbers were raised from forty-eight to sixty-one and it was given an elective majority, Indonesians received only thirty seats and its financial and legislative powers remained very slight, if indeed they can be dignified by the name of 'powers'.

The reformed Volksraad must be seen in relation to the general scheme of decentralization introduced by the Constitution of 1925. A new system of provincial government was devised above the residencies. As a first step Java's twenty-two residencies were in 1929 combined so as to form three provinces, and each under a governor assisted by a partly elected council with a non-European majority. Regency councils also were created, and these, together with the existing town councils, formed the electorates for both the Volksraad

---

[1] Raden Mas Suwardi Suryaningrat; he belonged to the princely house of Paku Alam.

[2] Vlekke, *Nusantara*, p. 346.

and the provincial councils. Outside Java, in areas where the political development of the population was considered too backward for any form of self-government, 'governments' without representative councils were established instead of provinces. The new system was a long time in taking shape and was only completed shortly before the Japanese invasion. It represented the utmost concessions the Dutch were prepared to make before the coming of the deluge.

Dutch policy, like Conservative policy in Ireland in the 'nineties, was to 'kill home rule by kindness'. The energy and enthusiasm in the cause of economic and social welfare shown by Dutch administrators was quite outstanding. Their comparative lack of success was due chiefly to the phenomenal rise in the population of Java and the opposition of private interests in both Holland and Indonesia. But the effects of the great depression of the early nineteen-thirties led them to encourage native industry; and when the revival of trade and industry began, a spirit of greater co-operation began also to show itself between Dutch and Indonesians.

But though the political atmosphere was less heated, the Indonesian movement continued to cherish its two aims of economic self-suffic-iency and political self-government with unabated fervour. In 1936 the Volksraad passed a motion asking the Netherlands government to call an imperial conference to discuss the method by which self-government should come into effect, and to fix a time-limit. It was characteristic of Dutch policy that no real response to this request was made until July 1941, when Queen Wilhelmina and her government were refugees in London. Under such a chastening experience it was only natural that she should promise to hold such a conference immediately after the war. But without undue scepticism the doubt may be expressed whether in 1941 the Dutch government had the serious intention of ever granting Indonesia real self-government.

Like the French in Indo-China, the Dutch were not enthusiasts for native education beyond the elementary stage. Fear of stimulating popular discontent made them slow in providing secondary and higher education. The pressure exerted by Sarekat Islam practically forced them to improve the Dutch-vernacular schools and thereby create a demand for more advanced education. In response to this M.U.L.O. (More Extended Lower Instruction) Schools were founded, and in 1919 General Middle Schools, which provided courses in Western languages, mathematics, science and oriental literature leading up to university entrance. But the rate of progress in the provision of schools of this type was too slow for the nationalists, who tried to fill in the gaps by establishing 'wild' schools literally by the thousand. The inefficiency of most of these, coupled with the fact that many of them were used for the purpose of spreading political discontent, compelled the government to take them more and more under its control. Hence, when provincial councils were created, education was not one of the subjects transferred to them.

From 1907 onwards immense efforts were put into the foundation of village schools. The practice was for the village, or group of villages, to build the school, often with materials provided free of cost by the government, and to contribute ninety guilders annually towards its upkeep. The government provided the teachers and textbooks. Parents were expected to pay a few cents a month, but were usually exempted, since pressure had to be brought on many of them to send their children. By 1930 there were more than 1½ million at these schools. But they were so closely controlled that they were organs of the central government rather than of the village communities. Perhaps the most paternal feature of the whole system was its extremely efficient provision of reading matter not only for the children but for popular consumption as a whole.

The extremely tardy development of higher education must be understood in the light of the few opportunities that existed outside government service for Indonesians with specialist qualifications. In their early years few Indonesians qualified for entrance to the Bandung Technical College opened in 1919, the Law College in 1924, the Medical College in 1926, and the government institutions teaching agriculture and forestry. In 1941, when the University of Batavia (now the University of Indonesia) was formed, its enrolment of Indonesian students was small. The instruction given at these institutions maintained the very best traditions of Dutch scholarship, but from a British point of view it was instruction rather than education. There were no hostels for students coming from a long distance, and no community life such as similar British institutions fostered.

Notwithstanding the great strides taken by the Dutch to extend education in Indonesia under the 'New Course', the annual budget allotment, compared with the Philippines, was very small. Moreover, the provision of education failed to keep pace with the rise of population, and the number of illiterates was actually greater in 1940 than it had been at the beginning of the century.

CHAPTER 44

FRENCH ADMINISTRATION AND NATIONALISM IN INDO-CHINA

THE fashioning of what has been appropriately described as 'the neat hierarchy of French colonial administration modelled on the Napoleonic pattern'[1] was largely the work of Paul Doumer, who held the office of governor-general from 1897 to 1902. He unified the corps of civilian services, reconstituted the administration of Tongking, and organized the government of the newly-acquired Laos territories. In Tongking he wiped out the last vestiges of autonomy by abolishing the offices of viceroy, Tong-doc and Tuan-phu, and transforming what was theoretically a protectorate into what became for all practical purposes a directly administered colony. The Laos territories became an 'autonomous protectorate' under a *résident supérieur* responsible to the governor-general. From Doumer's regime, writes Georges Lamarre,[2] dates *l'Indochine actuelle*.

Two of Doumer's pre-war successors strove to liberalize the administration by native collaboration. Paul Beau (1902–7) re-established the Tong-doc and Tuan-phu in Tongking and set up an indigenous consultative chamber there. He also created provincial councils and schools for the training of native officials. Albert Sarraut (1911–14) went further in the same direction by introducing the method of 'association', whereby more natives were recruited into the subordinate services and public instruction was reorganized so as to increase the supply of native candidates for government service and improve its quality. He also established further consultative chambers of natives in the protectorates similar to the Tongking one. But the rigid structure built by Doumer survived all attempts to check excessive centralization. In any case colonial self-government was never the aim of French policy; assimilation rather than association was its keynote.

Theoretically the governor-general had quasi-absolute powers; but he was under the close supervision of the Directorate of Control

[1] Charles A. Micaud in *The New World of Southeast Asia*, p. 227.
[2] In Georges Maspero (ed.) *L'Indochine*, ii, p. 18.

in the Ministry of Colonies, which periodically sent out Inspectors of Colonies to investigate his administration. And as he was not a professional colonial administrator but usually a politician unacquainted with the internal problems of the territories he was called upon to govern, his function was to pass on the dictates of his superiors to the experienced permanent officials who served under him.

The governor-general was assisted by a Grand Council of Economic and Financial Interests. This was composed of high-ranking French and Indo-Chinese officials together with representatives of the Colonial Council of Cochin China and of the Chambers of Commerce and Agriculture. It was a purely advisory body and could deal only with matters brought before it by the governor-general; but the general budget of the colony and those of its various divisions had to be submitted to it. The bulk of the legislation for Indo-China was enacted by the French parliament or took the form of decrees issued by the Ministry of Colonies.

Technically Cochin China was the only one of the five divisions to rank as a colony and to be under direct control. Annam, Cambodia, Laos and Tongking were all protectorates. Cochin China's government was in the hands of a governor, assisted by a Privy Council and a Colonial Council. The former approximated to an Executive Council, the latter to a Legislative Council, in a British colony. The colony of Cochin China was divided into major districts named provinces with a French administrative officer at the head of each. Notwithstanding the policy of 'association' enunciated by Albert Sarraut, the percentage of native subordinate officials in the French service was much lower than in the case of the Dutch and British regimes in South-East Asia. In Burma, for instance, while in 1900 Europeans occupied nearly all the posts in the 'covenanted' civil service, the vast majority of the administrative posts were outside this in the 'provincial' services, and with a very few exceptions were filled by Burmese or Indians. After the introduction of dyarchy in 1923, Burmese and Indians were recruited in increasing numbers into the highest grade of the administrative and police services.

In Annam, Cambodia and Laos the kings and their Courts, together with their hierarchy of mandarins, continued to exist alongside the French administration. The real control, however, in each protectorate was in the hands of a *résident supérieur*, assisted by a Privy Council and a Protectorate Council with composition and powers similar to those of their counterparts in Cochin China. Each protectorate was divided into provinces under Residents, who were Frenchmen. In a protectorate, however, the exercise of power was less direct than in Cochin China. The actual administration was carried out by the native officials under the guidance of their French opposite numbers, who never intervened directly unless it became absolutely necessary. The mandarins therefore were in no sense figureheads, but French control was absolute. *Mutatis mutandis* the system was not unlike the Dutch method of indirect rule in Indonesia. But in both cases the distinction between direct and indirect rule was a legal rather than a practical one.

The façade of native administration was imposing; it was also useful in making foreign rule somewhat less unpalatable. The Consultative Native Assembly, which assisted the *résident supérieur*, is an excellent example of the system of camouflage used by the French. Most of its members were elected, but by a narrow group of officials and others of trusted loyalty. Even then it could not debate political subjects, while on other matters it could express its views only if the *résident supérieur* agreed to a debate. The budget estimates of the protectorate were laid before it, but merely as a matter of form.

In Cochin China the chief aim of French educational policy was at first simply to train interpreters. Franco-vernacular schools were accordingly opened in the larger centres. When it was found that they were channels to promotion the sons of notables flocked to them. A scheme drawn up in 1879 to promote the official policy of 'assimilation' provided for secular elementary schools to be established in every canton and village; but it made little progress, while left to themselves the village schools of the traditional type were gradually disappearing and leaving an unfilled gap. In the protectorates the native systems continued to function and Western education made very slow progress. A few Franco-vernacular schools were established at provincial capitals for training native subordinates; their standards were very low. As in the case of the other colonial territories in South-East Asia, Vietnamese nationalism seems to have been the special product of the Franco-vernacular schools. In 1900 it was complained that in Cochin China the curves of crime and of European education rose concurrently.[1]

Paul Beau founded the modern educational system by creating in 1906 the *Conseil de Perfectionnement de l'Enseignement Indigène* to reorganize public instruction. It was to be based on the village

---

[1] J. S. Furnivall, *Educational Progress in Southeastern Asia*, p. 40, quoting Jules Harmand, *Domination et Colonisation*, 1910, p. 264.

elementary school teaching literacy by the use of either Chinese characters or *quoc-ngu*.[1] The best pupils were to go to Franco-vernacular primary[2] and secondary schools; the rest might proceed to a primary vernacular school at the headquarters of the canton, where French was optional, or in a few cases to a secondary vernacular school. This system was introduced first into Annam and Tongking, and later, in 1909–10, into Cochin China. But by 1913 there were only 12,103 pupils in the government primary schools; in Annam and Tongking private education was preferred. In Cambodia and Laos the monastic schools remained the sole purveyors of elementary education.

Cultural assimilation became still more the aim of French policy during the First World War. In 1915 the traditional competitive examinations for the mandarinate in Tongking were abolished. Sarraut, during his second term of office (1917–19), followed this up by introducing a scheme under which the state was to take over all primary instruction and make the study of French universal. This project, however, proved too expensive and had to be abandoned. Hence the division into vernacular and Franco-vernacular schools was restored in 1924; but so slow was the actual progress in providing state schools in the villages that in 1926 where there was no state school a village was allowed to provide its own.

Generally speaking, the French were not interested in vernacular education; they aimed at injecting larger and ever larger doses of French culture. There was a curious inconsistency about their policy in this matter, for a comparatively small coterie of French scholars carried out remarkable researches into the languages and literatures, the history and archaeology of the East, and made the École Francaise d'Extrême Orient, established at Hanoi in 1899, the finest centre of oriental studies in the world. No praise can be too high for the work it has done in discovering, caring for and restoring Indo-Chinese historical monuments, and in particular revealing to the world the glories of Khmer and Cham art and architecture.

The policy of assimilation had strangely different results from those it was intended to produce. It has been said that the bitterest opponents of the French were those who knew the language best. When Paul Beau, as a concession to nationalism, founded the University of

---

[1] The system of romanization invented by Catholic missionaries in the seventeenth century.

[2] The term 'primary' in this connection represents the stage above 'elementary' and must not be interpreted according to its present meaning in the English system of education.

Hanoi in 1907, there was such an outburst of nationalistic assertiveness among the students that in the following year it was closed, and not reopened until Sarraut's second term as governor-general.

The nationalist movement in Indo-China was almost entirely confined to the Vietnamese.[1] They were the most numerous of all the peoples of the area, and by 1945 constituted about 75 per cent of a population roughly estimated at 25 millions. They had a tradition of nationalism dating from their long struggle for independence against China. Though their civilization remained predominently Chinese in character, after independence was achieved in 939, it was no less their own, and in their expansion southwards into the territories previously held by the Chams and the Khmers—i.e. central and southern Annam and Cochin China—they substituted it for the Indianized culture they found in those areas. They held themselves to be superior to the other peoples of Indo-China and their culture to be at least as good as that of the West, save on the technical plane. Their *élite* were influenced by the writings of the contemporary Chinese reformers, notably Kang Yu Wei, who had submitted a plan of radical reform to the Chinese emperor in 1898, advocating the study of Western culture. They turned to the study of the French philosophical writers and flocked to the University of Hanoi when it first opened in 1907. But their introduction to the writings of Montesquieu and Rousseau bred in them feelings of frustration, that the rights of liberty and equality should be taught and denied at the same time.

Japan's victory over Russia in 1905 led to the development of a revolutionary movement of Vietnamese with headquarters at Tokyo. Its leader, Phan Boi Chau, was joined there by Prince Cuong De of the royal house of Hué. But in 1910 they were expelled, because Japan wanted French loans and to obtain them they had to agree to respect the French position in Asia. Chau then transferred to Canton, and under the influence of the Chinese revolution founded in 1912 a political group called 'The Association for the Restoration of Vietnam'. It was responsible for a number of outrages in Tongking, but was suppressed by the French. Phan Chau Trinh, an associate of Chau's in Tokyo, believed that modern science offered the key to Vietnamese freedom. Back in Vietnam he went ahead promoting the formation of study groups, which under the cloak of 'modernization' disseminated revolutionary propaganda. Both he and Chau were arrested, and ended their

[1] See Virginia Thompson's survey in Emerson, Mills and Thompson, *Government and Nationalism in Southeast Asia*, pp. 198–210; see also Philippe Devillers, *Histoire du Viet-Nam de 1940 à 1952*, chaps. ii and iii.

days under police supervision. French measures of repression, including the rounding-up of suspects and their imprisonment on Pulo Condore, and the closing of the University of Hanoi, brought what may be considered the first phase of the twentieth-century national movement to an end.

Sarraut's liberal policy during his first tenure of office (1911–14) helped to keep Indo-China relatively quiet during the First World War. But France had made generous promises which she was not prepared to redeem after the war. She also injured Vietnamese susceptibilities by forcibly recruiting nearly 100,000 of them for war service in Europe. They brought back subversive ideas when they returned home. Because of the reduction in the French armed forces, there was an attempted rebellion in 1916 with leaders drawn from the official class. The French learnt of the plan and disarmed the Vietnamese troops at Hué. The young emperor Duy Tan, a party to the conspiracy, made a dramatic effort to retrieve the situation, for which he and his father were exiled to the island of Réunion in the Indian Ocean.

The post-war period saw the rise of political parties taking their inspiration from developments in the outside world. The *élite* were stirred by the doctrine of self-determination proclaimed by President Wilson among his 'Fourteen Points' for the settlement of Europe. Some wished to imitate Gandhi's *swaraj* movement in India, while others imbibed the teachings of the Cantonese Communists. The constitutionalists were headed by the emperor Khai Dinh, who in 1922 went to Paris to try to persuade France to abandon coercion and seek Vietnamese co-operation in the administration of Annam and Tongking. He failed, but on returning home left his nine-year-old son, Vinh Thuy (later the emperor Bao Dai), to be educated in France. The Tongkingese Party, led by the journalist Pham Quynh, campaigned for such constitutional reforms as the establishment of an elected Consultative Assembly and the appointment of ministers responsible to the emperor. The French did indeed establish Consultative Assemblies in Annam and Tongking, but they were given no political power. Moreover, they frustrated an attempt to form a Vietnamese People's Progressive Party to advocate Pham Quynh's proposals.

In the French colony of Cochin China Bui Quang Chieu, after founding a Constitutionalist Party, went in 1923 to France to present proposals for reform, but ultimately had to return empty-handed. The French community in Cochin China was utterly opposed to any forward policy, and was supported by powerful financial groups in France.

The uncompromising rebuff of the moderates naturally opened the way for the rise of revolutionary groups who now stole the limelight from the constitutionalists. In 1925 the Revolutionary Party of Young Annam was founded. But the mutual jealousies of its leaders paralysed it, and when its Communist members seceded in 1929 it soon came to grief; for the secessionists informed the police against their former comrades and the party was suppressed. A Tongkingese party, the Viet Nam Quoc Dan Dang (Vietnam National Party) was formed clandestinely in 1927 through Kuomintang contacts. It consisted largely of journalists and teachers, who began by preparing booklets on current affairs for publication, but went on to advocate strong-arm methods. It had a very limited following, but hoped for foreign aid. It sought also to win over the Vietnamese battalions in the army. In January 1929 it made an unsuccessful attempt to assassinate Governor Pasquier, and in the following month killed Bazin, the head of the Labour Bureau. Its terrorist activities brought the police so hot on its trail that it was forced to launch a rebellion with inadequate precautions. This began with the abortive Yenbay mutiny of February 1930, and there were outbreaks of violence in many places. The French reacted with tremendous severity. Every kind of manifestation, even unarmed demonstrations, was broken up by force, and so many of its leaders were arrested that the party dissolved. The surviving leaders fled to Yunnan.

The struggle had become one for national independence, and the Communists now took the lead. In 1925 émigrés in Canton had founded the Association of Revolutionary Vietnamese Youth. Five years later this became the Communist Party of Indo-China. The leader of the movement called himself Nguyen Ai Quoc (Nguyen the Patriot). He was later to be known as Ho Chi Minh. Born in 1890, the son of a minor local official in northern Annam, he had gone to Europe in 1911 as a galley boy on a French merchant vessel, and for the next few years had travelled widely. At the end of the First World War he was in Paris sharing lodgings with Phan Chau Trinh, the ex-agitator, and helping him with his work as a photographer's assistant. There he formed an Association of Vietnamese Peoples, and on its behalf presented a memorandum to the Versailles Peace Conference. He edited *Le Paria* for the French Communist Party, and in 1923 was sent as a representative of the party to the Congress of the International Peasant Council at Moscow. In Russia he studied revolutionary technique. In 1925 he was in Canton as an interpreter on the staff of the Borodin mission, then associated with Dr. Sun Yat-sen. His Association of Revolutionary Vietnamese Youth was composed largely of young men at the Whampoa Military Academy, where Kuomintang officer cadets were trained under Russian supervision. When in 1927 the Borodin mission was expelled from China, Ho Chi Minh left with it.

In the following year the headquarters of the Association was transferred to Hong Kong; but with the removal of Ho's control all discipline in the movement vanished. An appeal to him for help brought him to Hong Kong in January 1930. He restored the authority of the Central Committee, changed the Association's name to the Vietnam Communist Party and transferred its headquarters to Haiphong. Nevertheless at this time his chief aim was that of winning Vietnamese national independence, and he was willing to co-operate with anti-French nationalists of all types. According to his book, *Le Procès de la Colonisation française* (Paris, 1926) national independence was to be accomplished through a democratic bourgeois régime: communism was to be introduced only at a later stage. His programme envisaged winning the support of both intellectuals and peasants. It included the reduction of fiscal burdens, the redistribution of land among the peasantry, and the abolition of the conscription of labourers and soldiers for service abroad.

At the time of the move to Haiphong in 1930 Tongking and north Annam were in turmoil. The Nationalist Party's premature attempt at revolution had been a complete failure, but there was grave peasant unrest occasioned by the Great Slump and the failure of two successive rice harvests. The communists sought to exploit the situation by organizing mass demonstrations, strikes and other disturbances. The French reacted with the same vigour as before; thousands were arrested and the communist organization was completely disrupted. In June 1931 Ho himself was arrested in Hong Kong and sentenced to deportation on a French ship. But the British Privy Council granted his appeal and he was released. He then disappeared for the time being.

With the suppression of the northern risings, Cochin China became the next centre of unrest. In 1932 two communist leaders, who had been studying abroad, returned home, Tran Van Giau from Moscow and Ta Thu Thau from France. They proceeded to found a French-language journal *La Lutte*, which gained considerable influence. The Communist Party functioned under the guise of rural friendly societies, but was watched closely by the French Security Service, which, as soon as war broke out in Europe in 1939, carried out mass arrests of suspects. An underground Stalinist section organized a peasants' revolt late in 1940, but was quickly suppressed.

In 1925 Prince Vinh Thuy was chosen by the French to succeed to the throne at Hué and took the regnal title of Bao Dai. He was the first of his line to have a European upbringing and education, and much was hoped of him when in 1932 he returned from France. He had studied the writings of the constitutionalist Pham Quinh, and was anxious to play his part in the conduct of affairs. In May 1933, accordingly, he appointed a new group of younger men as ministers. Among them, incidentally, was Ngo Dinh Diem, who as Minister of the Interior occupied a key position for carrying out a programme of reform. But Bao Dai found the opposition not only of the French, but also of the Vietnamese conservatives, too much for him; he lacked the force of character to put up a real fight.

Thus, with the failure of other parties and leaders, the national movement came under communist control; Ho Chi Minh's self-effacing, firm and intelligent leadership was ultimately to prevail. His movement, though driven underground, defied all attempts to extirpate it. In May 1941 Ho emerged from obscurity in Kwangsi Province in China, and together with a number of other political exiles founded, with the Chungking government's blessing, the Viet Nam Doc Lap Dong Minh Hoi (League for the Independence of Vietnam), better known as the Viet Minh, which was to become the spearhead of the nationalist movement, in the first place against the Japanese occupying forces in northern Vietnam. Thus while in the pre-war period the Vietnamese national movement was ineffective and weakened by personal rivalries and local jealousies, it was to find new life under the direction of a leader of inflexible will and tireless energy. The pity was that French intransigence was chiefly responsible for this state of affairs. The Vietnamese, with their deep attachment to property and the patriarchal family system were not natural recruits to communism.

CHAPTER 45

THE UNITED STATES AND FILIPINO NATIONALISM

THE blowing up of the American battleship *Maine*—presumably by accident—in Havana Bay on 15 February 1898 set off a far greater explosion, of anger against Spain as the suspected perpetrator, in the United States with the result that the two countries soon found themselves at war. Even Spain's expressed willingness to submit the matter to impartial examination on Washington's own terms was peremptorily swept aside. On the very day on which the United States Congress formally declared war, Commodore Dewey, then in Hong Kong harbour, received orders to lead his squadron into battle against the Spanish fleet at Manila. So on the morning of 1 May, before the eyes of the Manila populace on shore, he sailed into the Bay and destroyed or disabled the whole Spanish fleet without himself sustaining a single casualty.

Unable to land adequate forces to capture the city, Dewey then got into touch with Aguinaldo in Hong Kong and with the promise of independence for the Philippines as the prize for assistance against the Spaniards he brought the exiled leader home to head another nationalist revolt. Within a matter of weeks the whole of Luzon except Manila itself had come into insurgent hands, and on 12 June 1898 Filipino independence was solemnly proclaimed at Aguinaldo's headquarters at Kawit, Cavite, and he himself was again president of the revolutionary government. His forces, however, were not strong enough to capture Manila; the fall of the city had to await the arrival of reinforcements for Dewey from America. Its capitulation after a token resistance took place on 13 August 1898, when the Spanish governor-general surrendered to the American High Command by a prearranged ruse which kept the Filipino army out of the city. There then began a chain of events which led inexorably to the cession of the Philippines to the United States and the rejection of the Filipino claim to independence. The treaty bringing the Spanish-American war to an end was signed at Paris on 10 December 1898; Aguinaldo's envoy was denied entrance to the conference.

Opinion in Washington was so divided on the subject of annexation that the necessary two-thirds majority in the Senate for ratification of the treaty was obtained with only one vote to spare. The issue was clinched largely because two days before the vote was taken fighting broke out between the troops of Aguinaldo's republican army and the American occupying forces. Attempts had been made at peaceful negotiation, but the Filipinos were as determined to assert their independence against America as they had been against Spain. The headquarters of the Philippine Republic were set up at Malolos, and there a constitution was drawn up embodying ideas from a wide variety of existing constitutions. On 23 January 1899 it was formally promulgated and Aguinaldo ceremonially sworn in as president. For about a year its organized forces put up a determined and bitter resistance to the Americans throughout Luzon and in Panay. But Aguinaldo himself with the main army was gradually forced back into the mountains of northern Luzon, and by early 1900 the Filipino forces had become disorganized, and the rest of the struggle was carried on by guerrilla warfare. These operations petered out after the capture in March 1901 of Aguinaldo himself.

Controversy still rages over the promises made to Aguinaldo in order to obtain his co-operation against the Spaniards. Seen in its proper perspective America's move to acquire the Philippines was not an accidental, unpremeditated act. She had long been acquiring growing interests in the western Pacific. She wanted a base for ships engaged in the China trade, and American imperialists such as Theodore Roosevelt had already begun to think of Manila as a prize to be won through a war with Spain. Moreover, in an age when the partition of China looked to be a strong possibility, it was considered essential that in the event of the collapse of the decadent Spanish régime, the Philippines should not be permitted to fall into the hands of, say, Germany. When Dewey went into Manila Bay there was an even stronger German fleet near by, and when, after destroying the Spanish fleet, he blockaded Manila, the German commander created a tense situation by deliberately refusing to recognize the blockade. It seems probable that only the support of a British squadron at the critical moment prevented a second battle of Manila Bay. Thus any hope of Filipino independence under such conditions was a forlorn one.

While the American army was dealing with the patriots, Washington in 1899 sent out a five-man commission under President Schurman of Cornell University to enquire into the Philippine situation. It reported to President McKinley that to a man the Filipinos wanted independence, but were as yet incapable of self-government. It made a series of comprehensive recommendations. They included the creation of a Filipino legislature and the institution of civil government as soon as possible, immediate measures to develop the country's resources, the establishment of a system of provincial and municipal government, the setting-up of a complete system of public instruction with English as its medium, and the recruitment of specialists for the chief administrative posts.

The transition from military rule came on 4 July 1901 when a new five-man commission headed by Judge William H. Taft was installed at Manila, and proceeded with tremendous vigour to implement the Schurman recommendations. The Filipinos were given the specific assurance that their customs, habits and traditions would be fully taken into account, but that American principles of government were essential to the rule of law and to individual freedom. Throughout the country law and order had to be restored, and famine, plague, cholera and various epidemics fought. No less than 440 laws, establishing the new system of government, were adopted and put into effect. The new municipal and provincial codes provided for Filipino participation in local government, but the administrative decentralization, recommended by McKinley, was not in accord with the Spanish tradition of centralization, with which the Filipinos were familiar, and in the interests of efficiency it was found expedient to maintain American supervision, particularly over the new municipal governments, which were to be served by elective officials. A vast educational campaign was set in motion, with no less than six hundred teachers immediately recruited in America for service in the Philippines. Departments of Agriculture, Waters and Forests, and a Public Health Service, were created. In legal matters Spanish civil law tradition, long established, had necessarily to be retained, but an American-type Supreme Court was superimposed, and its first chief justice was a Filipino. Three Filipinos were also added to the Commission.

At first the Commission itself acted as both supreme executive and legislature, its president being in effect the civil governor of the colony. In July 1902, however, Congress passed the Philippine Organic Act, providing that after a census a popular assembly, of eighty members elected by single-member constituencies, was to come into being, and the Commission was then to become the upper house of a bi-cameral legislature. Executive power was to be in the hands of a governor-general, and as the Commission continued to be his cabinet, when the new system began to function in 1907, several members of the upper house of the legislature were also heads of executive departments. A further provision of the act, which was to have important effects upon Philippine political development, was that two Filipino delegates were to sit in the American Congress, though without votes.

Notwithstanding the extremely liberal policy pursued by the Americans, contrasting strongly with that of Spain, the nationalist agitation for independence became so intense that the government felt compelled to pass a Sedition Act forbidding the advocacy of independence and the use of the Philippine flag. The moderate Federal Party, aiming at ultimate federal union with America, gained hardly any support, and the first general election on an electoral roll restricted by qualifications of property and language—i.e. the ability to use either English or Spanish—resulted in a complete victory for the Nacionalista Party, which made independence its supreme objective. The election brought to the fore two dominating personalities, Sergio Osmena, who became the first speaker of the Assembly, and Manuel Quezon, the leader of the majority party. Both were mestizos, the former being of Chinese-Malayan mixture and the latter of Spanish-Malayan. Quezon, who became a delegate to Washington in 1909, devoted himself to the task of impressing upon Congress that the Filipinos were politically mature. Through his influence Filipinos gained a majority of seats on the Commission and a number of ministerial posts. He also played an important part in securing the passage of the Jones Law (1916), which accorded a substantial degree of autonomy to the Philippines.

The McKinley instructions in 1901 had laid down that preference should be given to Filipinos in appointments to public offices, but the tendency had been for more, rather than fewer, Americans to be appointed to the civil service, as time went on. In 1912, however, the Democrat victory brought President Woodrow Wilson to office, and in due course he appointed Francis Burton Harrison governor-general of the Philippines. The acceleration of progress towards self-government now became the order of the day, and Harrison went over to a policy of rapid Filipinization. The Jones Law, named after the deputy who sponsored it in the Chamber, announced in its preamble that it was America's intention to grant independence to the Philippines as soon as a stable government could be established there. It provided for a government modelled upon that of the United States, with executive power in the hands of a governor-general, legislative power in those of a bi-cameral legislature composed of a Senate and a Chamber of Deputies, and judicial power vested in a Supreme Court. In place of the Commission there was to be an elective Senate of twenty-four members, twenty-two elected by manhood suffrage and two appointed by the governor-general to represent non-Christian tribes. The Chamber of Deputies was to consist of eighty-four members elected on a similar franchise and nine appointed by the governor-general. Certain restrictions upon full autonomy were provided for in the act. The governor-general could veto acts of the legislature, and laws regarding public land, timber, mining, currency, coinage, immigration and tariffs must go to him for signature. The control of money was reserved to the President of the United States. The right to annul any law was reserved to Congress. In certain legal cases appeal lay to the Supreme Court in Washington.

The general effect of the act was to give the Filipinos complete control over their own internal affairs, notwithstanding the reservations listed above. True, it conferred greater powers upon the governor-general, and he was an American appointed by Washington. This was later discovered to be a serious defect from the Filipino point of view, but Harrison had no intention of using them arbitrarily. Legally, for instance, the cabinet was not responsible to the legislature but he permitted heads of departments, at the request of the legislature, to present reports to it. In 1918, at the request of Speaker Osmeña, he appointed an advisory Council of State composed of the members of the Cabinet and the presidents of both houses. Through this means the two leaders of the Nacionalista Party managed in effect to control the top executive appointments. Harrison pushed ahead with the development of education, drew up a programme of economic development, founded the Philippine National Bank to grant long-term loans for industrial development and a number of industrial projects under state control. But his economic administration was too extravagant for the means at his disposal, and his policy of rapid Filipinization stirred up much opposition. In 1921 the Wood-Forbes Commission of Enquiry, appointed by a Republican Congress, condemned his governmental methods as transgressing the Jones Law, and asserted that immediate independence would be a betrayal of the Filipino people. What they needed, it said was a period of apprenticeship.

Accordingly, Leonard Wood, on taking office in 1921 as governor-general, announced his intention of applying the Jones Law strictly. His use of the veto on legislative enactments soon brought him into violent conflict with the Filipino leaders, and in July 1923 all the Filipino secretaries of departments together with Quezon, the president of the Senate, and Manuel Roxas, the speaker of the House of Representatives, resigned from the Council of State. The political deadlock thus created lasted until Wood's sudden death in 1927. His successor, acting Governor-General Eugene A. Gilmore, revived the policy of

co-operation, and Henry L. Stimson, the next governor-general, introduced new machinery to ensure it. He revived the Council of State,
appointed his cabinet from the majority party in the legislature, and
arranged for cabinet members to speak in the legislature and answer
questions.

In June 1933, as a result of the Democratic victory in the American
elections, Frank Murphy became governor-general. He was a Catholic
and a sympathizer with Filipino aspirations, and with immense energy
he began to put into operation a policy aimed at counteracting the
disastrous effects upon the Philippines of the Great Depression of 1930.
By this time opinion in the United States was turning strongly in favour
of Filipino independence. The depression was not without its effects
upon this situation, for it had caused loud demands for restrictions on the
entrance into America of Philippine sugar and immigrants, and on the
employment of Filipinos on American ships. The farmers, the sugar
producers and the trade unions were behind this agitation, and their
hope was that, if independence were granted, the Philippines would no
longer enjoy free trade with America, and would be treated as a foreign
country. Partly for this reason, but also because it was the policy of the
Democratic majority in Congress to help the Philippines towards the
achievement of independence, Osmeña and Roxas, who had arrived in
Washington in December 1932 at the head of a Philippine independence
mission, were able to secure the passage through Congress of the Hare-
Hawes-Cutting Independence Act. But President Herbert Hoover
vetoed it. Congress replied by repassing the act over his head. The
Filipino legislature, however, rejected the measure as unsuitable. The
reasons given by Quezon as president of the Senate were that the provisions regarding commercial relations were to the disadvantage of the
Philippines, the clause limiting the entry of Filipinos into the United
States was injurious, and the retention of military and naval bases by the
United States in the Philippines constituted a violation of Filipino
national dignity.

Quezon then went himself to Washington and persuaded Congress to
approve a new independence measure, the Tydings-McDuffie Act,
which was signed by President Roosevelt on 24 March 1934 and subsequently accepted by the Philippine legislature. It differed surprisingly
little from the rejected measure, but mentioned only naval bases.
Moreover, Roosevelt gave the assurance that before full independence in
1946 the 'inequalities and imperfections' would all be ironed out.
Under its provisions a Commonwealth of the Philippines was to come
into being on 4 July 1936. Its constitution was to be drawn up by a

popularly-elected Convention of 200 members. It was to function for ten years, at the end of which, on 4 July 1946, the independent Republic of the Philippines was to be inaugurated, and the American forces withdrawn. Up to then foreign relations and national defence were to remain under American control, and the United States president was to retain power to approve or veto any constitutional amendment, or any acts affecting currency, coinage, imports or exports. The United States also reserved the right to intervene in the Philippines in order to preserve constitutional government.

The Constitutional Convention was speedily elected and a constitution closely resembling the American one was framed, and on 14 May 1935 ratified by a national plebiscite. On 15 November 1935 it was formally inaugurated at Manila. Frank Murphy, the governor-general, became America's first High Commissioner to the Philippines. Manuel Quezon was elected the new Commonwealth's first president with Osmeña as vice-president. Thus was the rift in the Nacionalista Party, caused by Quezon's rejection of the Hare-Hawes-Cutting Act, healed. No other party had any strength whatever, so that the new régime was essentially a one-party government.

The price, which the Philippines were called upon to pay for this new measure of freedom, was not so heavy as had at one time seemed probable. Filipino immigration into the United States was to be limited to fifty persons a year; no limitation was imposed upon American entry into the Philippines. Regarding the import of Philippine products into America, maximum quotas were laid down for the duty-free entry of raw sugar, refined sugar, copra and hempen cord. Then, beginning from 1941 all Philippine imports into the United States were to pay 5 per cent duty, with an additional 5 per cent annually until in 1946, on attaining independence, when the Philippines would be outside the American tariff barriers and their products would pay 25 per cent duty on entering America. American goods, on the other hand, were to enter the Philippines duty-free during this period.

The United States thus within a very short period of time introduced an advanced form of political democracy into the Philippines. It had serious defects. In effect power was conferred upon the property owners and the intelligentsia, and the men who exercised it came almost entirely from the landed gentry; for notwithstanding the most tremendous drive to establish schools, enrol pupils and train teachers, education of the masses could never keep pace with political progress. The landed classes, who wielded power, were not at all interested in democratization, but in preserving their own social and economic privileges. And as their co-operation was important to the American authorities, nothing was done to break up the big estates, save those of the friars, and even then it was not the cultivators who benefited. At one end of the scale there were vast estates and at the other a vast number of holdings of less than a hectare, i.e. just under 2½ acres. The number of owner-cultivators too small under the Spanish régime, declined further under the American, and the condition of the peasantry was the worst in the whole of South-East Asia. And as the representatives and allies of the landed interest were the people who replaced the American authorities, when the commonwealth came into being, nothing effective was done before the Japanese onslaught at the end of 1941 brought far worse troubles to the under-privileged.

The American Congress had in 1902 empowered the Philippine Government to classify and dispose of all public lands for the benefit of the people. In the following year an adaptation of the American 'homestead system' was introduced into the Philippines whereby every citizen could have the opportunity to acquire 24 hectares of public land. At the same time the purchase or lease of public lands by any corporation was limited to a maximum of 1,024 hectares. But the homestead policy proved a disappointment; the procedure was too complicated for the average peasant and the credit facilities inadequate. And, more important still, the Bureau of Lands connived at the manoeuvres of the land-grabbers, so that the legal restrictions against speculation in land and agricultural exploitation were evaded. It is a significant fact that while the number of cultivators increased by about 700,000, less than 35,000 homestead applicants received land titles. Anti-usury legislation failed to prevent the loss of the peasant's land for what began as a trifling loan, which he did not repay in time. Co-operative credit schemes also failed.

The purchase in 1904 by the American government for seven million dollars, of the friar lands, which Aguinaldo's régime had marked down for nationalization, offered a wonderful opportunity to create peasant-ownership on a big scale. The lands were to be sold on an instalment plan with preference given to the actual cultivators—who, by the way, had paid no rent since the outbreak of the revolution in 1896. But, partly because of the poor drafting of the legal provisions, and largely because of landlord pressure upon the Filipino administrators of the scheme, ownership actually went into the hands of a class of small or medium landlords, not those of the cultivators themselves.

Thus the evils of usury and of land-grabbing through the courts reduced the majority of owner-cultivators to share-cropping tenants, at the mercy of their landlords, or to wage-earners. The opening of the American market to Philippine produce favoured large-scale agricultural production, to the detriment, and consequent break-up, of the traditional economy. Large-scale sugar production played an important part in this process, and private corporations and large estate owners succeeded the Church and the friars in land-ownership. The new 'sugar-baron' became more powerful than the old 'rice-baron', and it is significant that the leading Filipino politicians came from the sugar provinces.[1]

The normal method was for the landlord to divide up his estate into small farms cultivated by share-croppers. The *kasama* system was the most widespread, especially in rice-growing. The landlord provided land, seed and capital, the tenant labour and working animals. The tenant took 50 per cent of the crop after his portion of the expenses of cultivation had been paid. In regions where there was competition for land occupancy the *inquilato*, or cash rent, system was common. Both were sources of injustice. The share-cropper had to pay usurious rates of interest on the advances made to him: for instance, a usual rate of interest was two cavans of paddy at harvest for every one loaned, and failure to pay doubled the debt at the next harvest. The cash tenant had no security: population pressure would force his rent up, and if he failed to pay, he could be expelled from his holding without compensation. A system of extra services and heavy fines added to the misery of all tenants.

The increasing demand, caused by expanding foreign trade and increase of population, led to a corresponding increase in the area cultivated, which rose from 1,267,000 hectares in 1903 to 4,017,000 hectares in 1935. But the bulk of the additional income thus created went to Government, the landlords and the urban areas; very little to the peasantry. During the Spanish period there had been many agrarian risings; and to Aguinaldo's peasant supporters 'independence' meant the abolition of the tenure system which tied them down to abject poverty. When, therefore, the Great Depression of 1930 knocked the bottom out of the world market for primary products, agrarian revolts began once more to break out; and just as the angry peasants of the earlier period believed that land reform would not come while the Spaniards remained, so in the nineteen-thirties they cherished the same feelings about the Americans.

The unrest among the depressed classes showed itself also in the rise of left-wing organizations. In June 1924 communism made its first

[1] E. H. Jacoby, *Agrarian Unrest in Southeast Asia*, p. 170.

appearance when at the invitation of the Soviet Government a delegation of Filipinos attended the International Conference of Labour at Moscow. On their return they organized the Society of Workers of the Philippines. Other left-wing groups, which made the tenant-landlord relationship and agrarian indebtedness main items in their agitation, were the Tanggulan, which caused a rising in 1931, and the Sakdal, which caused one in 1935. Communism easily made converts in the agricultural provinces of central Luzon, where the worst evils of landlordism were rampant. There was no political party in the legislature at Manila which represented the needy classes.

The spread of education was America's greatest achievement in the Philippines. It has been well said that whereas the church building and the missionary were the official instruments for the spread of Spanish culture, their equivalents for the spread of American culture were the schoolhouse and the teacher; and, it might be added, the social progress achieved by their means in a matter of decades exceeded that of over three centuries of Spanish rule. To carry the new education system into effect, thirty-seven divisions were organized, each under a superintendent, and 379 school districts, each under a supervising teacher. By 1922 there were over a million pupils in the public schools, and the expenditure on education was nearly one-half of the total governmental expenditure. Teacher training in the Philippines went ahead so fast that by 1927 the number of American teachers was only one per cent of the total of 26,200 public school teachers.

English was the medium of instruction from the primary grade upwards. By 1939 literacy had been raised from 20 to 49 per cent of the population over ten years of age, and nearly 27 per cent of the population spoke English. By that time there were 11,000 public schools with 1,750,000 pupils, of whom some 76,000 were in secondary schools. The private education system also developed rapidly, especially in the higher grades. In 1940 its elementary schools accounted for 71,000 pupils and its secondary schools 63,000. At the top of the scale, competing with the older established Spanish foundations, was the University of the Philippines, founded on the American model in 1908. In 1940 it had nearly 8,000 students, and the total number in state-supported institutions of higher education was something over 12,000. Against that, the private universities and institutions of higher education had a little over 36,000 students. Thus they played a very substantial part in higher education. The Filipino response to these wider educational opportunities was enthusiastic, and support for education increased with the increase in Filipino participation in government.

The demand was always ahead of the accommodation. Everywhere education was regarded as the key to independence and political progress.

When Manuel Quezon became the chief executive in the Philippine Government as a result of the victory of the Nacionalista Party in the elections of September 1935, he took as his motto 'less politics, more government'. Certainly the external and internal problems that were mounting up called for the utmost wisdom and resources he could command—and more. On account of the growing dangers in the international situation he was forced to devote his chief attention to national defence, and with General Douglas MacArthur as his adviser he built up the armed services through a system of compulsory military service. Rural discontent had risen to an alarming degree. To combat it his policy was to introduce a general minimum wage of one peso a day, an eight-hour day, a rent law and a law for the expropriation of large estates and their subdivision among the cultivators. The actual results, however, were meagre. For one thing, to have achieved success would have cost far more money than he had at his disposal, and, for another, he lacked a civil service sufficiently honest and independent to be able to counteract the means of sabotage used by the powerful landed interest against such a policy.

Actually, in terms of exports agriculture was making much progress. In addition the new Commonwealth enjoyed an unexpected gold boom, which caused the number of its mines to increase from six to 104, and raised the annual production to 80 million pesos in value. Nevertheless, there was a growing lack of confidence on the part of American investors, and Quezon, aware of the extent to which Philippine prosperity depended upon the customs union with the United States, became more and more uneasy about the situation that would arise when Philippine products had to compete on equal terms with other foreign imports in the American market. As a result of his representations at Washington a Joint Preparatory Committee on Philippine Affairs, composed of six Filipinos and six Americans, was appointed in 1937 to go into the matter, and in the following year recommended that the trade preferences, accorded by America to Philippine exports should terminate in 1960, not 1946. It was a *pis aller*. The alternative envisaged by Quezon —diversification of production, improvement of techniques and reduction of net costs—was a long-term policy, and, moreover, would entail the abandonment of the free enterprise to which both America and the Philippines were committed. Thus, with an economy tied to that of America, and with American military bases in their midst, real independence for the Philippines was a long way off; and in the wicked world of Mussolini and Hitler, of Japan's wanton invasion of China and of the violent overthrow of the Spanish Republic, the neutrality provided for in the Tydings-McDuffie Act was mere wishful thinking.

The Japanese attack on Pearl Harbour on 8 December 1941 (Philippine time) was followed within a matter of hours by the bombing of military objectives in the Philippines from bases on Formosa. On 10 December the invasion began, and a week or two later two Japanese armies, one from Lingayen in northern Luzon and the other from Atimonan and Mauban in the south, were converging upon Manila. The American and Filipino forces under General MacArthur retired before superior numbers to the Bataan Peninsula and the fortified island of Corregidor commanding the entrance to Manila Bay. To save Manila from destruction it was declared an open city, and on 2 January 1942 it fell to the Japanese. The magnificent defence of Bataan and Corregidor upset Japan's programme and gave America and the British Commonwealth desperately needed time to go ahead with their preparations. On 9 April the 36,000 surviving defenders of Bataan surrendered; on 6 May the 12,000 on Corregidor. President Quezon and Vice-President Osmena had earlier escaped to Australia by submarine. General MacArthur also, under orders from America, had got away to Mindanao in March and gone thence to Australia.

Many from the defeated American and Filipino forces fled to the mountains and began to organize guerrilla warfare on a big scale. Their numbers swelled to large proportions: post-war investigation showed that not less than 260,000 men had been actively engaged, with the support of probably an even larger number in the underground resistance. The Japanese promises, and the propagation of the Greater East Asia Co-prosperity Sphere, made no appeal to the mass of the Filipinos. The Japanese brutalities and atrocities, their systematic pillage of everything that could be carried away, the drug traffic carried on by the Japanese army and its gambling and prostitution rackets, the forced labour expected from the peasantry, and the general reduction of the workers to slavery, all these were far more powerful arguments than boastful propaganda.

In the Philippines under Japanese rule there was less disruption of the social system than in Burma and Indonesia. A large proportion of the Filipino officials continued to serve, since, after all, government had to function, and their excuse was that by collaboration they could the better protect the people from Japanese brutality. Political parties were suppressed. They were replaced by an organization called from the initial letters of its name Kalibapi, the 'Association for the Service of the New Philippines'. Every member of the administration had to belong to it. It received its orders from Tokyo. In June 1943 a convention of the Kalibapi, summoned under Japanese instructions, chose a Constitutional Commission to draft a new constitution for the 'independent republic' of the Philippines, which Japan proposed to establish. It was presided over by José P. Laurel, the most prominent member of the Filipino ruling classes to collaborate with Japan. In October 1943 the new republic was formally inaugurated, with Laurel as its president. He had absolute power of veto over the National Assembly, but was himself, of course, completely under Japanese control. In the following month he headed a Filipino delegation, which attended the 'Assembly of the Nations of East Asia' at Tokyo, and participated in the establishment of the Pacific Charter drawn up by Japan in anticipation of her ultimate victory.

But American submarines were decimating the Japanese mercantile marine, and there was famine throughout the Philippines. The underground and guerrillas became so effective that the Japanese were able ultimately to control only twelve out of the forty-eight provinces. The guerrillas established contact with General MacArthur in Australia, and received American supplies by submarine and parachute. The backbone of the resistance on Luzon was supplied by the Hukbalahaps led by Luis Taruc and Casto Alejandrino. The movement had originated in central Luzon as a part of the pre-war agrarian agitation against landlordism. Its name was composed of the initial letters of their Filipino designation 'The People's Army against Japan'. They gradually expanded their hold over much of Luzon, and by well-planned attacks upon Japanese patrols and depots were able to arm 30,000 men and deny possession of the harvests of much of the island to the Japanese. They sovietized their areas, redistributed land to the cultivators and created co-operatives. Their contribution towards the final defeat of Japan was substantial.

Meanwhile, Quezon's government-in-exile was at Washington preparing for the post-war reconstruction of the Philippines. It became one of the founder-members of the United Nations, and in June 1944 had the satisfaction of seeing the passage through Congress of the law authorizing the President of the United States to proclaim Philippine independence on 4 July 1946. When that law was passed the Americans were poised for the reconquest of the Philippines. The initial bombing began late in September. On 20 October four divisions of American troops began to disembark on Leyte from a fleet of 650 ships. General MacArthur commanded the expedition, and with him was Sergio Osmeña, who had become head of the exiled government upon the death of Quezon on 1 August 1944. The Japanese threw everything they could muster against the Leyte expedition, and it was in this connection that the decisive naval battles of 23–26 October were fought and Japan's sea power annihilated. Marshal Yamashita's attempt to keep the Americans out of Luzon was also frustrated when on 9 January 1945 they landed in strength in the Gulf of Lingayen. There was a frightful struggle for Manila, which lasted until 23 February and left the city a mass of ruins. Then came mopping-up operations throughout the archipelago. They lasted several months, and it was only on 3 September, the day after Japan's formal surrender to General MacArthur, that Yamashita himself surrendered with the remnant of his forces at Baguio.

During 1944 it looked as if collaboration was going to become a major issue in the Philippines after the war. General MacArthur declared that he would 'run to earth every disloyal Filipino'. The difficulties in attempting to carry out such a policy were found to be too great, however, and MacArthur's support for his pre-war friend Manuel Roxas, who had served with Laurel, as director of the wartime rice procurement agency, made it quite impossible to deal with the great collaborators. A People's Court was set up to try traitors, but none of the high-ups was convicted, and in January 1948 President Roxas proclaimed an amnesty for all, except those who had committed heinous offences such as murder, theft and rape. The worst type of collaboration had been that of the 'peso millionaires', who as middlemen had made vast profits through helping the Japanese to exploit the country's iron-ore, chromite, manganese, copper and wolframite for the supply of their munitions factories.

CHAPTER 46

THE ECONOMIC ASPECT OF EUROPEAN DOMINATION

Economic imperialism provided the main stimulus to the extension of European domination over the lands and islands of South-East Asia. Europe's insatiable hunger for markets and for tropical products went through a number of distinct phases between 1500 and 1900. The most acute one coincided with the revolution in human life begun by the railway, steamship and electric telegraph, and intensified by the motor car, aeroplane and wireless. European industry became more and more dependent upon products that South-East Asia could supply in abundance, such as oil, rubber and various metals, while Europe's growing population made ever greater demands on the rice, coffee, tea and sugar of the area.

After 1870 the process of opening up interiors was carried on with rapidly increasing momentum. It was the age of science, and before the advance of applied science all the barriers that had previously prevented European exploitation of interiors were rapidly broken down. Thus traditional systems of economic life which for centuries had resisted the European impact, and in which subsistence agriculture, cottage industries and barter were dominating features, disappeared with startling suddenness, to be succeeded by new conditions under which crops, financed by money advances, were grown for a world market, and the cultivator's home market was flooded with manufactured European goods to the detriment of his own native handicrafts. This happened on a vast scale in the rice-growing areas of South-East Asia and it had effects of fundamental importance in every country affected.

(a) British Burma

Before the British acquisition of the province of Pegu in 1852 Burma had never exported rice. Merchant vessels might take away with them no more than they required for food until their next port of call. Arakan, on the other hand, grew rice for export in the seventeenth century, and when it came into British hands in the nineteenth century the growing Indian demand caused its rice cultivation to flourish. The Irrawaddy delta region, however, was a land mainly of swamp and jungle which had never recovered from the effects of the Burmese policy towards the Mons in the late sixteenth century. Its sparse population grew paddy almost entirely for its own needs, and when these were met any surplus crops for which there was no demand might be left unreaped. Moreover, the immediate effect of the second Anglo-Burmese war of 1852 was a movement of population into Upper Burma.

The Indian Mutiny of 1857-8 seems to have caused the first upward tendency in the production of rice in the delta. Rangoon, rapidly developing its facilities as a port, could handle an increase of trade, and immigrants came down from Upper Burma to take up rice cultivation. The expansion of the acreage under rice in Lower Burma was striking. The figure for 1845 is 354,000 acres, while for 1860 it is 1,333,000. The American Civil War of 1861-5, which cut off Carolina's rice exports to Europe, caused Britain to look to Burma to make up the deficiency, and by 1870 the acreage figure had risen to 1,735,000. The opening of the Suez Canal in 1869 caused rice cultivation to go ahead at an even faster rate. During the next fifteen years no less than a million acres more came under rice, and the expansion continued without a break up to the great world slump in 1930, when the figure for both Upper and Lower Burma had risen to 12,370,000. It was the most spectacular development of her economic history. At the end of the century Burma exported 2½ million tons of rice; by 1940 her total production was 4.94 million tons.

There was a wild scramble for land. But the task of clearing it involved hiring labour, for it was in most cases overgrown with heavy jungle, and it took more than one harvest before the cost of cultivation was recovered by the cultivator. As there were hardly any Burmese with capital to spare, Indian money-lenders of the *chettyar* caste stepped into the breach and provided cultivators not only with all the money they needed at a conservative estimate, but up to the limit of the security. The European exporters also adopted the practice of giving out advances to ensure supplies. Under normal conditions in the early days the cultivator could keep his head above water. But he operated so near the danger level that a fall in world prices, the failure of the monsoon rains, his own illness, or the death of his cattle, might cause him to be sold up, and his land would pass to another; for such was the demand for land that it was easy to find another purchaser.

By 1895 land in the delta was constantly changing hands. At first one peasant proprietor would be supplanted by another. But speculation more and more took a hand in the business: traders and brokers interested in the export business bought land in order to control supplies of paddy; Indian and Chinese merchants in the towns bought it as an investment for their surplus money. Thus, as time went on, an increasing number of cultivators did not own their holdings, and peasant proprietorship began to break down. In 1930, when the great world depression broke in full force on Burma, although only 27 per cent of the occupied land was recorded as in the ownership of non-agricultural landlords, the difficulty of finding purchasers able to take over holdings at anything like the full value of the outstanding loans revealed the fact that practically half the cultivated land in Lower Burma belonged to non-agricultural absentee landlords. The total agricultural indebtedness was estimated at £40 million.

Worse still, from the point of view of the Burmese, was the fact that the demand for labour during the years of rapid expansion had attracted increasing numbers of Indian immigrants. With a much lower standard of living than the Burmese, they were able to undercut them in competition for land tenancy. Thus between 1915 and 1930 native owners lost no less than 1,300,000 acres of delta land through debt. At the same time the small Burmese rice-millers were being driven out of business by the multiplication of large steam-driven mills employing Indian coolie labour, the development of steam navigation on the rivers and creeks in place of the native craft was forcing many Burmese out of their traditional occupations, and cheap Indian labour was driving them from the wharves.

At the beginning of the twentieth century Indians were arriving in Burma at the rate of 250,000 a year. The number rose each year until in 1927 it reached the peak figure of 480,000. The majority came over only for seasonal occupations on the land and returned home afterwards, or stayed only a year or two. But enough remained for each decennial census to show a marked increase in the proportion of Indians to the total population. The fact that Burma was a province of the Indian empire made it well-nigh impossible for the government to take effective safeguarding measures such as the Dutch took in 1870 when they made it illegal for an Indonesian to alienate his land to a foreigner. The result, therefore, was a dangerous development of communal discord.

This flared up in 1930 in a frightful outbreak of anti-Indian riots in Rangoon, when the Burmese, having been used to break an Indian dockyard strike, objected to being dismissed and in three days' fighting killed 120 Indians and wounded 900. The agrarian unrest also showed itself at the end of the same year when a formidable rebellion broke out in the Tharrawaddy district under a leader called Saya San and spread rapidly over most of the delta. Saya San was the usual type of *minlaung* (pretender to the throne) that Burma has often produced in times of unrest; he sought to overthrow the British regime, but most of his adherents were concerned mainly with the recovery of their lands from Indian money-lenders and tenants.

Early in the eighteen-eighties the government became concerned for the defence of the peasant cultivator against the private money-lender. In 1882 and 1883 legislative Acts were passed to provide cultivators with loans at much lower rates of interest than those charged by the *chettis*. But the conditions imposed were too stringent, and the *chettis* knew far better than government officers how to manage the improvident Burmese.

Then early in the twentieth century the co-operative movement was inaugurated as a further measure for combating the evil. A co-operative department was established to foster the development of co-operative societies of cultivators financed by land banks. Thousands of these societies were formed in the first flush of enthusiasm for the movement. Most of them failed, and when the great depression began in 1930 the two most important land banks, the Burma Provincial Co-operative Bank of Mandalay and Dawson's Bank, with its head-quarters at Pyapon in the delta, ran into serious difficulties. The government therefore revived the co-operative movement, and in 1935 passed a measure making it possible for foreclosed land to be returned to its original owners on payment of its actual market value spread over a period of fifteen years. This was followed in 1936 by a Debt Conciliation Act, which established boards for scaling down debts and accumulated interest.

In 1937, when Burma was separated from India and given almost complete control over her internal affairs, one of the first acts of her new legislature was to pass, against strong *chettyar* opposition, a Burma Tenancy Bill for the protection of tenants. Settlement reports had long stressed the fact that throughout Lower Burma, and in some parts of Upper Burma, after subtracting rent, debt charges and cost of cultivation, most tenants had insufficient money left from the sale of their produce to maintain a livelihood. The Bill was based upon the findings of a committee set up to investigate the matter. But, according to Furnivall, the measure was 'not very wisely conceived',[1] and before

---

[1] *Colonial Policy and Practice*, pp. 193-4.

the still unsolved agrarian problem could be dealt with more effectively the Japanese invasion took place.

Before the spectacular development of rice production in Burma during the last quarter of the nineteenth century her chief article of export was teak. The annexation of Pegu in 1852 led to the first important steps for the preservation of her forests. This began with a survey by Dr. Dietrich Brandis of the valuable forests in the Tharrawaddy-Prome area and the Toungoo district. He laid the foundation of the Burma Forest Department. The annexation of Upper Burma in 1886 brought further forest areas within the scope of European exploitation and conservation. A Forest Service of three grades of officers came into being which ultimately disposed of a departmental personnel of 2,000. The commercial output between 1919 and 1924 averaged over 500,000 tons annually and only slightly less between 1925 and 1940. India took three-quarters of this. Besides teak the forests produced other hardwoods, notably *pyinkado* (iron wood), which was used for railway sleepers in Burma and India. There were also many minor forest products, such as bamboo, cutch, lac, firewood used in steamers, mills and railway engines, and charcoal in universal use for cooking. It was estimated that the Burma forests could yield 787,000 tons of paper pulp per annum, but before the Second World War little had been done in this connection. The forests provided as much as 20 per cent of the state revenue.

The absence of suitable coal operated against attempts to industrialize Burma. The petroleum wells of the Yenangyaung region had been worked for many generations by hereditary Burmese owners when Britain took over Upper Burma. The Burmah Oil Company, the parent of the Anglo-Iranian Company, was founded in 1886. At first it bought oil from the native drillers and confined itself to refining and distribution. Expansion began in the present century, when modern methods of drilling were introduced and large-scale production began. A line of oilfields was opened up from Indaw on the Upper Chindwin through Sabe and Singu to Yenangyaung, and in 1908 a pipeline of 275 miles was built from the oilfields on the Irrawaddy to Syriam, the site of the refineries. Production by 1940 had risen to 270 million imperial gallons, which was .5 per cent of world production. By that time other oil companies had joined in, but the B.O.C. controlled three-quarters of the industry. Practically its whole output was absorbed by India and Burma.

Other large-scale industrial undertakings developed by British capital and technical skill in Burma were the great lead-silver Bawdwin mine in the Northern Shan States, worked by the Burma Corporation; the Mawchi mine in Karenni, which produced half the tin and tungsten in Burma; and other tin and tungsten mines in Tenasserim.

Before the British conquest Burma's main communications were by her great rivers and innumerable creeks. These were the first to be developed by British enterprise, and the Irrawaddy Flotilla Company, founded in 1865, operated a fleet which in the present century included some of the largest shallow-draught steamers in the world. They served the Irrawaddy up to Bhamo, the Chindwin up to Homalin, and the chief delta towns. Roads came late. By 1918 there were only 2,000 miles of metalled roads in the country. Then came a big expansion, and twenty years later there were 6,000 miles of all-weather roads plus another 5,000 to 6,000 miles that could be used by motor traffic in dry weather. Railways came after the opening of the Suez Canal. They were built for the areas not served by water transport. Before the end of the nineteenth century Prome, Mandalay and Myitkyina were connected with Rangoon. Later lines were built through the Northern Shan States to Lashio and through the Southern Shan States to Shwenyaung, near Taunggyi. In all there were 2,060 miles in 1941.

Burma was developed by foreign capital. Indians, Chinese and Europeans owned all the large factories and industrial concerns, the greater part of Burma's public debt was foreign-held, and Indian *chettis* in 1930 had an investment of 750 million rupees in the delta rice-lands. In 1939 foreign investments totalled £155.25 million— three times as much as in 1914. The European corporations owned just over £47 million of this, the *chettis* £56 million, the Chinese £2.8 million, and the government and municipal obligations amounted to £45 million. The Burma Railways were built by the Government of India. Little of the capital cost had been repaid when Burma separated from India in 1937 and took over the debt to the extent of 344.5 million rupees.

(b) *French Indo-China*

French Indo-China contained two ancient centres of rice cultivation, the deltas of the Red River of Tongking and of the Mekong in Cochin China. French policy was rigidly protectionist. In French eyes the function of a colony was to supply the mother country with raw materials and products which did not compete with her own. The economy of French Indo-China therefore came to depend almost completely on the interests of France. Most of the population remained cultivators and were overcrowded in the two rice-producing areas. If native industries survived, it was largely because the majority of the people were too poor to buy French imported goods.

The Vietnamese were industrious farmers, good fishermen and skilful workers; the Cambodians tended to be indifferent and inactive; while the T'ai preferred hunting and fishing. The population problem in the crowded areas was very serious. Land in the hands of the peasantry was parcelled out in minute holdings. In Tongking the entire farming population cultivated only 40 per cent of the total rice area as smallholdings. Sixty per cent of the farmers owned less than one acre of land; 63 per cent of the tax-payers owned less than half an acre or were landless. In Cochin China holdings were larger but smallholdings only accounted for 45 per cent of the total cultivated area.

Before the French occupation inequalities in landed wealth were counterbalanced by the joint communal responsibilities of the villages, and people without rice-fields of their own could cultivate the communal lands. French administration favoured the establishment of large estates and European plantations. In Cochin China concentration of land in this way went so far that the landed class came to control over 80 per cent of the rice-fields, with 200,000 families employed in share-cropping. The share-cropper worked for a French landlord, who loaned him buffaloes, food and tools, and supplies of seeds and manure. The landlord usually demanded exorbitant interest on his capital, and the share-cropping tenant, discouraged and restless, often disappeared after having squandered his advance payments. The large estates were normally formed through the purchase of forfeited land or land on which loans at exorbitant interest rates had been made. By various methods encroachments upon communal land took place until far too little was left, and when with the great slump of 1930 many great land-owners became insolvent there was no redistribution of land to the needy population. French policy preferred the stabilization and consolidation of large estates to the redistribution of land.

The landlord-tenant relationship was feudal. The share-cropper paid his landlord 40 per cent of the crop, and in addition had to render onerous gifts and services. When a landlord furnished credit to a tenant it was usually at the rate of 50 per cent for a period of from eight months to one year. The system did not promote improved methods of cultivation, since the landlord came to rely more on the interest to be derived from his capital than on the productive capacity of his fields. Hence estates were usually divided into minute farms and leased to tenants for primitive, traditional cultivation.

Among the peasant proprietors the same problems of indebtedness were to be found as in Burma. Chinese middle-men monopolized the purchase of rice. Annamite and *chettyar* money-lenders were ready to lend money at rates of interest up to 120 per cent per annum. French legislation to limit the rates of interest failed. Beginning in Cochin China in 1913 mutual agricultural credit institutions were set up. But as they could lend only on land security their activities rarely reached the level of the tenants. They strengthened the landlord by helping him to lend to tenants and farmers at higher rates than those on which he borrowed the money.

A *Crédit Populaire* system was established in 1926 and reorganized in 1933 under the name *Crédit Mutuel Agricole*, but it did not operate in Cochin China. It made loans to agricultural co-operatives, whose activities included not only paddy but a great variety of products such as tung, castor oil, maize, tobacco, tea, sugar, coffee, mulberry, sticklac and palm sugar. They collected their members' crops and sold them, and attempted to educate them in the use of selected seeds, manure, etc. But in most cases the peasant was too poor to buy the fertilizers and other improvements recommended to him, and in any case the movement never got much beyond the experimental stage.

The general picture was that of an upper class with an agricultural proletariat densely packed into two areas in which too much labour was employed on the land. The evils of overpopulation and under-nourishment were aggravated by the improvements in sanitary and medical control, which caused a great increase of population—greater, in fact, than the increase in rice production. There was a constant reduction in the purchasing power of the peasant. Rice, the diet of almost the whole population, formed half the total exports of the country and was subject to the same risks—failure of the rains and fluctuation of the world price—as elsewhere.

The French attempts to attract people away from the deltas to work on inland plantations, notably rubber, failed, notwithstanding the better living conditions on them. The Vietnamese do not like moving away from the place where their ancestor cult is carried on. Moreover, the hinterland areas were malaria-ridden, there were difficulties of transport, and the government had no comprehensive development plan. The fundamental weakness of French economic administration is well shown by the contrast between Indo-China and Java in rubber production. In the former large plantations owned by Frenchmen and financed by the *Société Financière des Caoutchoucs* monopolized the whole production. In Java 50 per cent of the rubber was produced by natives on their own lands.

French economic expansion in Indo-China was financed by two methods: by money raised internally through taxation and by loans entirely subscribed in France. So successfully did the French resist the investment of non-French European capital in their close preserve that in 1938 they owned 95 per cent of the European capital invested in business enterprises and all the capital invested in government securities. There was, however, a large Chinese investment, which accounted for 80 million dollars (American) out of a total investment in business enterprises of 382 million dollars. Government securities added 82 million dollars to make a grand total of 464 million dollars.

No statistics exist for French investments in Indo-China before 1924. Mines first attracted French capital. The coal industry attracted 8–9 million francs by the beginning of the century. Tin mining began in 1901–2 with 2 million francs capital, zinc in 1906 with a similar amount. An Artificial Portland Cement Company was founded in 1899 with a capital of $1\frac{1}{2}$ million francs. Other ventures which attracted capital early in the century were the distillation of alcohol from rice, electrical works for urban consumption, the Yunnan Railway Company, which swallowed up 102 million piastres between 1901 and 1911, breweries, and tobacco and match factories. The big French metallurgical companies also had branches in the colony.

From 1910 onwards much capital was invested in timber extraction and rubber planting. At the end of the First World War a far more comprehensive programme was set in motion. The depreciation of the franc caused a great deal of French money to seek security in the piastre, and between 1924 and 1930 some 2,870 million francs were invested in the colony. The effect of the great slump, therefore, was very serious, and through failures or reductions in capital losses estimated at 1,255 million francs were incurred. When after 1936 the flow of capital investment was resumed it was far below the pre-slump level.

As time passed the economic ties between Indo-China and France grew progressively stronger. Between 1911 and 1920 an average of 19.6 per cent of Indo-China's exports went to France; in 1938 the amount was 53 per cent. Between 1911 and 1920 Indo-China's imports from France averaged 29.6 per cent of the total; between 1931 and 1938 they averaged 57.1 per cent. The French textile industry had a powerful influence over colonial policy; Indo-China's imports of French fabrics preponderated over those of other countries. The French metal industry also found a profitable market for its products in the colony. These two industries together accounted for two-thirds of French exports to Indo-China.

Before the competition of French manufactured articles native industries deteriorated. They might have disappeared had not the great mass of the people been too poor to buy the imported articles. Cotton and silk continued to be woven on primitive looms. Wood-working, stone-cutting, pottery and basketry also survived as native crafts, but on a reduced scale, since the peasant craftsmen could not afford to buy much raw material. France's economic aim for the native, it has been said, was to raise his standard of living to enable him to buy more French goods and to afford more employment to the French merchant marine.

(c) The Netherlands Indies

In 1900 in the Netherlands Indies production for the foreign market was almost wholly agricultural—rubber, tea, coffee, copra, quinine, tobacco, sugar—and almost wholly Dutch. The native contribution was negligible; it was carried on almost entirely for home consumption, and rice predominated over all other crops. Java's great problem, like that of the Red River and Mekong deltas, was over-population, but it affected the whole island, so that it could only be relieved by migration to other islands or the Malay Peninsula. The population of Java and Madura increased from 28.74 millions in 1900 to an estimated 49 millions in 1941, and in the latter year its annual rate of increase was in the region of 700,000. No other comparable area in the world supported so large a population with so great a rate of increase. There was a grim race between the increase of the population and the expansion of production.

In 1905 the Department of Agriculture, later a branch of the Department of Economic Affairs, was formed and was charged with the special task of devising measures for the permanent improvement of native agriculture. Native production, mainly of food crops, was multiplied by clearing new ground, by improvements in irrigation, improved technical methods and a vast increase in secondary crops. In 1918 the General Agricultural Experimental Station was established. The Department of Agriculture also began to develop special sections, notably one dealing with Agricultural Economy and another known as the Agricultural Information Service, whose expert *Landbouwconsulent*, its local officer, must be consulted with regard to the probable effect on native interests before land could be leased to Europeans.

But notwithstanding these excellent administrative measures the food margin dwindled and production failed to keep pace with population increase. Between 1929 and 1938 while population increased by 15 per cent the increase of cultivation was only 3.5 per cent, and the limit for expansion was already passed. Deforestation had reduced the forest area to 23 per cent, where 30 per cent was considered essential to protect the island's water supply, while signs of soil exhaustion through over-use were showing themselves. One difficulty lay in the fact that individual holdings were too small for efficient cultivation. The average at the beginning of the century was only 2½ acres per family, and it tended to diminish. This minute subdivision of the cultivated area was nothing so bad as in the congested areas of French Indo-China, but it meant that on the native lands agriculture was overmanned and underequipped.

By the Agrarian Law of 1870 the Dutch had prevented the formation of a landlord class such as was found elsewhere in South-East Asia, but the substitution of a cash economy forced the native population to live on credit. This was supplied mostly by Chinese pawnbrokers and Arab money-lenders at excessively high monthly rates of interest. In 1898 de Wolff van Westerrode was put on special duty to work out plans for state pawnshops and agricultural credit banks. State pawnshops were established in 1900, and four years later the beginnings of a popular credit system introduced in the form of 'paddy banks' and village cash banks. Civil servants were instructed to regard the formation of these banks as one of their foremost duties. By 1912 Java had 12,000 paddy banks and 1,161 village banks, and the village co-operatives were run by the headmen under official supervision.

But as elsewhere the co-operative movement languished. The private money-lender allowed rash borrowing and his working expenses were lower. The private money market continued at rates from 10 to 15 per cent monthly, while, to make matters worse, the earnings of the peasant through sale of his produce were reduced by the operations of middle-men, whose share of the market price averaged 50 per cent. The hard-pressed cultivator was often forced to lease his land to a European plantation company, and again the government had to step in to protect him by fixing minimum rentals and limiting the amount of village land that might be leased and the length of leases. Many migrated to work on the tobacco, sugar and tea plantations of Sumatra and the rubber plantations of Malaya, but when these were hit by the great depression in 1930 thousands of people returned to overcrowded Java.

RICE CULTIVATION IN JAVA

The effects of the great depression were not so severe on the Indonesians as on the Europeans, owing to the former's concentration on the cultivation of rice instead of export crops. But intense suffering was caused to those connected with the sugar industry. After the winding up of the Culture System sugar production had developed on estates composed of land rented from villagers. The slump caused the area under sugar to be reduced from 200,000 to 28,000 hectares,[1] ground rent fell from a total of 25 million guilders to one of 3.8 million, while wages dropped from just under 84 million guilders to 7.27 million. The industry never recovered. When production began again to expand, countries such as India, China and Japan, which had relied on Javanese supplies, had started to produce their own sugar. But the Dutch adopted a 'crisis policy' with all kinds of measures to stimulate native industry, stabilize the price of rice and promote native welfare. And Sarekat Islam, the main organ of the nationalist movement, threw its energies into the task of founding 'wild'[2] schools and 'wild' co-operative institutions. The general renascence of national life was reflected in a remarkable development of native agriculture. Judged by European standards the Javanese peasant's earnings remained pitiably low, since all the economic benefits introduced by the Dutch after 1900 were neutralized by the immense increase of the population. Furnivall's carefully considered opinion is that his standard of comfort was at least as high as in Burma outside the rice plains.

In Indonesia in 1900 the wholesale business and banking were mainly in Dutch hands, with the Chinese as middlemen and money-lenders. Natives were restricted to petty retail trade. The freedom accorded late in the day to European enterprise led to an increase in the numbers of non-Dutch settlers, especially after 1905. By 1930 these were 7,195 Japanese, 6,867 Germans, and 2,414 British settlers in Indonesia. Foreign (i.e. non-Dutch) capital was invested mainly in oil and rubber. British investment in tea plantations in about 1900 represented the first introduction of foreign capital on a large scale. From 1905 the British began to invest in rubber, and by 1912 half the rubber companies in Java were in British hands. The development of tobacco in the Deli region of Sumatra attracted British, Swiss and German capital. By 1913 the Dutch capital investment in east Sumatra was only 109 million guilders out of a total of 206 million. Dutch capital dominated the sugar industry. Just before the great slump the foreign capital invested in crops other than sugar was just over 40 per cent of the whole. At the time the total amount of foreign (including Dutch) capital invested in the Netherlands Indies was estimated at 5,000 million guilders. The deflation caused by the

---

[1] A hectare is just under 2½ acres (2.4711 acres).
[2] wild = based on voluntary effort, outside the government system.

great slump reduced this amount considerably, and in 1939 the total foreign capital was estimated at 2,875 million guilders. Of this amount about 75 per cent was Dutch, 13.5 per cent British, and 2.5 per cent American. In addition, foreign investors, mainly Dutch, held about 2,000 million guilders' worth of Indies government bonds.

The development of the Outer Possessions in the twentieth century was in marked contrast with their neglect until late in the nineteenth. Sumatra developed large rubber estates inland from Palembang and Jambi. After the conquest of Acheh the oil-wells of the north-east coast were exploited, and by 1940 Sumatra was yielding annually some 5 million tons of crude oil. The rich alluvial tin deposits in the islands of Banka and Billiton attracted an influx of Chinese labour and by 1940 were producing 44,000 tons of ore annually. Smelting was carried out on Banka, but most of the ore went to Singapore until the construction of the large Arnhem smelter in Holland. Bauxite was extracted on the island of Riau, and by 1938 275,000 tons were produced annually. British oil production in Brunei stimulated the Dutch to develop their section of Borneo. Samarinda provided one of the largest oilfields in Indonesia, and by 1940 was producing $12\frac{1}{2}$ million barrels annually for refining at Balikpapan. Gold, nickel, iron and petroleum were discovered in Celebes, but before the Second World War were not worked to any extent.

(d) Malaya

Malaya had no problems of population pressure. Her chief agrarian problem was that of the Malay continuing with subsistence farming and refusing to supply labour for the expanding rubber and tin industries. Only 15.5 per cent of the land had been taken under crop by 1940, and more than half of that was planted with rubber. The average Malay holding was only about $2\frac{1}{2}$ acres, but it was enough for the normal family, for the Malay did not rely solely on his rice; he grew much garden produce besides coconut and areca palms and fruit trees. He was also a fisherman and trapper.

At the beginning of the century, therefore, since the Malay was not interested in producing rice beyond his own needs, Malaya produced only one-third of the rice it needed. The remainder was purchased from Siam and Burma. After the First World War, and again after the great slump, as a result of government encouragement more rice was produced, but the ratio of local production to total consumption remained unchanged. The root of the evil was again agricultural indebtedness—in this case to Chinese and Indian money-lenders. The government's answer to the problem was, as elsewhere, to sponsor co-operatives. A small beginning was made in this direction in 1907, but the big effort to launch a co-operative movement was in 1922, when a Co-operative Societies Department was set up at Kuala Lumpur.

Malay individualism, however, was a great obstacle, as also a propensity for plunging into debt for a family celebration such as a wedding. The co-operative movement therefore languished. When after the great slump the government tried to induce the peasant to cultivate more rice by protecting him against the price-fixing methods of the Chinese millers, he was far too dependent upon credit from Indian or Chinese shopkeepers to respond. The danger that he would become a landless farm worker was real. He could not come to terms with the foreign industrial and capitalist system that had taken root in his country. 'If money comes into a Malay's hands', wrote C. F. Strickland in reporting on the Malayan co-operative movement in 1928, 'he spends it, regardless of the time when he will need it urgently.'[1]

The original object in founding rural co-operative societies in Malaya was to free the cultivator from his burden of debt. After the great slump it was felt that better methods of production and sale were necessary. New types of societies therefore were devised and achieved some success. They were general purposes societies, which promoted all kinds of co-operative effort, and 'better-living' societies, which sought to stir up a public opinion against extravagant expenditure and granted loans merely to tide the cultivator over the period between sowing and harvest.

At the beginning of the twentieth century labour in Malaya was predominantly Chinese and Indian. The Chinese came to work in the tin mines; then later, with the extension of rubber cultivation, Indian coolies came to work on the estates. A brief statement of the rise in their numbers will give some idea of the problem this has created. (See following page.)

There was a strong Chinese community in Malacca under Dutch rule. When Penang was founded by Francis Light in 1786 many Chinese were attracted there from Malacca. Singapore from its foundation in 1819 attracted large numbers of Chinese. They came from Dutch territory and also by direct immigration from China. By 1941 Penang and Singapore were predominantly Chinese. In the

[1] L. A. Mills, *British Rule in Eastern Asia*, p. 282.

	1911 *census*	1921 *census*	1931 *census*	1941 *census*
Malays	1,437,000	1,651,000	1,962,000	2,278,000
Chinese	916,000	1,174,000	1,709,000	2,379,000
Indians	267,000	471,000	624,000	744,000

Malay states the chief Chinese community before the nineteenth century was in Johore, where they went in order to be out of the way of the Dutch. The influx of Chinese into the mining areas began from about 1830 and became a flood from about 1850. Their secret societies supplied practically their sole social organization. It was the rivalry in the Larut area of Perak between the Cantonese Ghee Hins and the Hakka Hai Sans which led to the earliest British intervention to establish a protectorate over a Malay state.

Under the protectorate system the economic development of Malaya was mainly in Chinese hands. Europeans began to come into tin mining from 1882, but the Chinese remained for long the chief miners. They were also market gardeners, artisans, shopkeepers, contractors, financiers and revenue farmers. When rubber planting began they became in a few cases large-scale planters. Their importance was such that there were usually two Chinese representatives on each of the state councils in the Federation.

At first they regarded Malaya as a place in which to make money so as to return home as soon as possible. In the twentieth century, however, there was a growing number of Straits-born Chinese who regarded Malaya as their home. By the time of the Japanese invasion in the Second World War about one-third of the Chinese in Malaya had severed all connections with China save cultural ones. The immigrants brought political problems; there were underground organizations first of the Kuomintang and later of the Communist Party. When the Japanese invaded China in the 'thirties they were strong advocates of direct action. They formed boycotting groups which raided shops selling Japanese goods.

They established many schools, in which the written vernacular, the Kuo Yu, or National Language, replaced the literary language. Their teachers were nearly all China-born and taught Chinese nationalism in an extreme form which was hostile to the governments of Malaya. Their textbooks were imported from China and were full of subversive matter. The whole tone of the curriculum was unfavourable to the cultivation of a sense of Malayan nationality.

The British had first to deal with the activities of the secret societies, which from time to time caused serious disturbances. For a long time they lacked the precise information on which to take effective action. It was for this reason that the Chinese Protectorate was established in 1877 in the Straits settlements. From 1883 onwards its scope was gradually extended to look after the interests of Chinese labourers. In 1884 a Protector of Chinese was appointed, but as the first holder of the post regarded the secret societies as harmless 'friendly societies' performing the same useful functions as these organizations did in contemporary Britain, little headway was made for some time in coping with the Chinese problem.

In the matter of the labourers special laws had to be passed to deal with the appalling abuses of the 'contract' system and the ingenious devices of contractors and employers to 'squeeze' labourers. It was difficult, however, to enforce their provisions because of the Chinese preference for piece-work, in which there was scope for trickery in calculation. In 1937 some 80 per cent in the mines of the Federation were on piece-work. The payment of wages, housing and health were subject to government inspection. At the end of 1936 there were serious strikes because the drastic reductions in wages made during the depression had not been restored. The government intervened in the dispute and negotiated a settlement which provided for an increase of wages. In 1937 an Advisory Committee on Chinese Labour was set up for the whole of Malaya.

Up to 1930 no restrictions were placed upon Chinese immigration. But owing to the slump 167,903 unemployed labourers returned to China. The Secretariat for Chinese Affairs, the name given to the Chinese protectorates when they were later merged in 1934, repatriated no less than 13,000 destitute labourers. As, however, 242,149 fresh Chinese immigrants arrived in that year the policy of immigration restriction was adopted. During 1931, 1932 and 1933 control was maintained by a quota system, under which the monthly number of arrivals was gradually reduced to 1,000. In 1934, when conditions began to improve, the number was raised, but the old system of unrestricted immigration was not restored.

The problem of Indian immigration was not so serious as in Burma, but the numbers coming in—mainly for labour in the rubber plantations—rose steeply with the rubber boom of 1907, and as the Malay and Chinese population was also rising steeply the Indian population tended to remain at about 14 per cent of the whole. In 1907 the demand for Indian labour was so great that an Indian Immigration Fund was established to finance recruitment, and free passages from India were granted to all labourers who applied for them. This enabled the abuses of the older *kangany* system to be abolished. The *kangany* was a recruiting agent employed by Malayan planters to recruit labourers by advancing them their passage money and recovering it from them out of their wages on the estate. In 1922 the Government of India further regulated the system by passing an Emigration Act under which officials were stationed in India and Malaya to control immigration. The great slump caused assisted immigration to be suspended, but by 1934 the recovery enabled the system of controlled immigration to be re-established. Nationalist opinion in India, which had caused the Government of India to intervene in 1922, was still critical of the treatment of Indian immigrants, and in 1936 Srinivasa Sastri, who had already investigated the position of Indians in South Africa, was appointed by the Government of India to examine the condition of Indian labour in Malaya. He reported very favourably and advised that there was no justification for preventing Indian labour from going to Malaya. But he suggested that the *kangany* system should be discontinued, and in 1938 it was abolished.

Meanwhile great strides had been taken by the Labour and Health Departments at Kuala Lumpur in improving housing and health conditions on the estates. In the early days the death-rate from malaria had been very high, but Malaya was one of the first tropical dependencies to take advantage of the discoveries of Sir Ronald Ross and other pioneers of tropical medicine. In 1910 the Estate Health Branch of the Medical Department was established, and in ten years the annual death-rate among estate labourers was reduced from 62.9 per 1,000 to 18.57. In 1937 the death-rate among Indian labourers in Malaya was only 7.11 per 1,000. It is noteworthy that the European estates had a much better health record than the Asian-owned ones. As in the case of the great majority of Chinese, the chief problem in connection with the Indians in Malaya lay in their political affiliations with their mother country.

Out of all this immigration a serious problem was already taking shape during the period between the two world wars. The 1941 census showed that the Malays were outnumbered by the Chinese. Before the British period they had been in an overwhelming majority. Actually they outnumbered the Chinese in the Malay states, since it was Singapore with its 77 per cent Chinese population that tipped the scale. Excluding Singapore, the respective percentages were Malays 49 and Chinese 38, with Indians making up most of the remainder. But the Malay population itself was not wholly indigenous, since for many years there had been a modest but growing migration of Javanese and other Indonesians from the Netherlands East Indies.

Naturally the Malays regarded themselves as the people of the country and the rest as aliens. But there was little idea of Malaya as a political unit, since the ordinary Malay peasant's loyalty was to his sultan, and Malays from other states were foreigners to him. Moreover, the great majority of Chinese and Indians who came to Malaya regarded it as a place of temporary exile. Chiang Kai-shek's government did its best to inculcate that all Chinese living abroad were citizens of China, even if their families for several generations had been British citizens. The Indians also were deeply impregnated with their own nationalism. But in any case the Malays as Moslems, able to be raised to a high pitch of fanaticism, though normally easy-going, nourished a latent hostility against both races as heathen; there was practically no intermarriage, and harmony was maintained only through the close co-operation of the sultans and the British. Most of the Malays were head over heels in debt to the Chinese, but at the same time their leaders demanded that in the administration of the country no Chinese should be placed in authority over Malays. Had there been a strong Malay nationalist movement things must certainly have come to a head. But before the Japanese invasion the Malays were the most unpolitically-minded people in South-East Asia. That blissful state of mind, however, was not to survive the occupation period.

The history of Singapore since its early development as a free-trade entrepot and the centre of British trade in the area from Sumatra to New Guinea and from Java to China was one of growing prosperity and economic importance coupled with a shrinking trade area. Much of its China trade was transferred to Hong Kong after 1842. Its important trade with Indo-China was cut off by the French conquest, which resulted in the imposition of heavy duties in foreign trade and the establishment of direct steamship services between the colony and France. The somewhat belated establishment of Dutch steamship services between the principal ports of the Netherlands Indies and their overseas markets considerably changed Singapore's relations with that area. In the present century Port Swettenham began to draw much of the trade of the Federation.

But Singapore remained the collecting and distributing centre of the Malay Peninsula, central Sumatra and Borneo, and the immense extension of rubber cultivation in Malaya and Sumatra has more than compensated for the contraction of its trading area. Its trade with Java, Siam and Indo-China still remained important. The continuous improvement of its port facilities was one of the chief reasons for the maintenance of its position, as also the fact that it is extremely well placed on the principal trade route between Europe and the Far East. For instance, with oil becoming increasingly important it proved to be the most convenient centre for the distribution of the oil produced in Sumatra, Dutch Borneo and Sarawak. Its total trade reached the 2,000 million dollars[1] mark before the Second World War.

The economic development of Malaya was closely bound up with tin and rubber. Before 1900 tin mining had been carried on almost entirely by the Chinese. After 1900 the industry was revolutionized by British capital and direction, the installation of machinery and the application of scientific methods. Smelting was started as early as 1887 by the Straits Trading Company, and an American attempt at the end of the century to transfer all smelting to the United States and thereby gain complete control over Malayan tin production was frustrated by an export duty on tin ore. As a result Singapore became the biggest centre of tin smelting in the world, receiving ore for smelting from Siam, French Indo-China, Burma, Australia, China, and Central and South Africa.

Tin production rose steadily in Malaya until 1926, when the peak price of £284 7s 7d. a long ton was reached. Then overproduction brought the price down to £120. The difficulty lay partly in the fact that the United States had become the largest consumer of tin in the world and her demand tended to fluctuate violently. The Tin Producers Association, which represented the mines in the four richest areas—Malaya, Bolivia, the Netherlands East Indies, and Nigeria— worked out a restriction scheme, and in 1931 this came into force under the International Tin Committee. The weak point in the scheme was that it left out minor producers such as Siam, French Indo-China and the Congo, with the result that they had to be brought into the scheme on their own terms. From 1933 the demand

---

[1] Strait's dollar, then worth 2s. 4d.

began to increase, and to keep the price stable the International Tin Committee adopted the practice of manipulating a buffer stock of 15,000 tons. In 1938, the last normal year before the war, Malaya produced 29 per cent of the world's tin, her potential output being 100,000 tons a year.

The great development of Malaya as one of the chief world producers of rubber did not begin until 1905. Hence until the post-war slump in 1920 its cultivation was extended by Europeans, Chinese, and Malays. Malaya's export of 196,000 tons of rubber in 1920 was 53 per cent of the world total. Rubber production greatly increased Malaya's prosperity and was the chief cause of the fact that between 1901 and 1921 her population doubled—though, as we have seen, this was largely through immigration of non-Malays. To cope with the problems raised by this rapid expansion of cultivation the Department of Agriculture at Kuala Lumpur had to develop new branches for carrying out research and experimentation.

The slump of 1920 was due to overproduction, extravagance and the post-war depression in Europe. The price of rubber fell from 2s. per lb. in 1920 to 6d. in 1922. Britain thereupon set up the Stevenson Committee of Inquiry, which advised that a restriction scheme should be worked out with the co-operation of the Dutch and Ceylon. The Dutch, however, refused, because they were encouraging their Javanese smallholders to plant rubber. Malaya and Ceylon therefore, on the strength of the fact that they produced 70 per cent of the world production, decided to go on alone. This was a great mistake, as the tin producers were to discover later on. After six years' trial the scheme had to be abandoned owing to Dutch competition and the vast increase of native smallholders.

Then came the great depression, when the price dropped to $2\frac{1}{3}d.$ per lb. The situation during 1931–3 was far more serious than during 1920–2. The big estates were forced to reconsider the whole question of costs of production. Again also international co-operation had to be sought, and as a result of agreement in May 1934 between the producing countries the International Rubber Regulation Committee came into being to control research and restriction. In 1935 the price rose to 6d. per lb, and as a result of the improved methods they had been forced to adopt to tide over the crisis this yielded the big estates a profit. The armaments race and the immense development of the American motor-car industry then caused the price to rise; but again, as in the case of tin, it fluctuated too much according to conditions in the United States. The Rubber Regulation Committee then tried to stabilize the price at 9*d*. per lb., but had to abandon the effort because the demand in the manufacturing countries was found to be beyond its control. In 1938 Malaya had 3,302,170 acres under rubber and produced 41 per cent of the world supply. Of her acreage, 2,026,348 acres were owned by the big estates and 1,275,822 by small-holders, chiefly Malays. Her total production was 361,000 long tons, but the total export was 527,000 tons. This was because much of the rubber produced in Siam, Sumatra and Borneo was sent to Singapore, where it was graded and shipped overseas.

One lesson learnt from the great slump was the need to encourage additional cultures to rice and rubber. The oil palm was found to be an attractive alternative to rubber. But it had to be cultivated on large estates, for it had no interest for the smallholder. Although palm oil is more nutritious than coconut oil, the Malay refused to include it in his diet. Coconut production was mainly carried on in small holdings, but large estates for the production of copra began to develop. The production of oil was carried out mainly by power-driven mills along the western coast.

The British have never imposed any restrictions on foreign investment in Malaya. Before the Second World War American companies owned large rubber plantations, much Australian capital was invested in tin, and the Japanese controlled all the iron mines. The iron mines were in Johore and Trengganu and in 1938 produced ore worth £858,000. Western investments in Malaya reached a total of just over £40 millions in 1914. In 1930 they stood at £116.5 millions. British investments accounted for some 70 per cent of the whole. Chinese investments in 1937 totalled well over £41 millions.

The great criticism of economic imperialism, or 'colonialism', as it is now ineptly termed, was that the foreign capitalist drained profits away for the benefit of shareholders overseas instead of ploughing them back into the country. This theory, loudly asserted by political discontents, is plausible, but on close examination the facts are not capable of quite so simple an explanation. The imperial powers provided a vast amount of capital and technical skill, without which the development of the 'colonial' territories to their present economic importance could never have taken place. They revolutionized health conditions and delivered great masses of people from the decimating or enfeebling dominion of frightful diseases. Their research in tropical agriculture and their scientific investigation into other matters of fundamental importance laid the sure foundations on which prosperity and higher standards of life could be built up. Investigation of their fabulous profits, so far as it has gone, has tended to show that, as in all fables, imagination considerably outstripped reality, and that the critics of 'colonialism' have not taken into account the heavy losses that have occurred from time to time. And in most cases foreign investors contributed the major part of the state revenues. On the facts, as they are at present available, the sober historian dare not commit himself to the sweeping generalizations that are the weapons in political warfare.

It has been estimated that before the Second World War Europe's annual imports from the United States amounted to some 500 million dollars more than her exports in return, and that the greater part of the funds needed to balance this account was provided by the South-East Asian trade. The total foreign investment in South-East Asia, including the Philippines, was about 4,370 million dollars. The respective shares in the capital invested in business enterprises were as follows:

European (principally Dutch in Indonesia and French in Indo-China)	1,943 million dollars
British	860 ,, ,,
Chinese	640 ,, ,,
United States	330 ,, ,,
Japanese	60 ,, ,,

The undertakings in which these sums were invested provided Europe and America with important foodstuffs and vital raw materials for industry. Through the Straits of Malacca and Sunda ran trade routes of the highest importance to the great commercial powers. Singapore had fulfilled Raffles's expectations that it would become another Malta. The London Imperial Conference of 1921 decided to make it a first-class naval base, and in 1938 the work was completed at a cost of £20 million.

CHAPTER 47

SIAM IN TRANSITION, 1910–42

THE title of the chapter is borrowed from Professor K. P. Landon's book[1] dealing with the revolution of 1932, which, besides substituting a form of constitutional government for the old Chakri absolutism, considerably hastened the process of adjusting Siam to modern world conditions begun under Chulalongkorn. Chulalongkorn had thirty-four sons and forty-three daughters. In the early days of his reign the sons were sent to English public schools, universities or technical institutions. Quite a number showed exceptional ability. Some became specialists in law, agriculture or engineering. Others received training in the British, German, Russian and Danish armies, and the British navy. Their father wrote a little pamphlet of advice for their benefit during their sojourn abroad.

Prince Maha Vajiravudh, who succeeded his father in 1910, was one of those who had received this training, going to Cambridge University and serving for a time with the British army. As the nearest direct heir according to the Chakri rules of succession, the title of heir-apparent was conferred on him shortly before his return to Siam in 1902. During his long stay abroad he had almost lost contact with his family, and on his return he gathered about him as his associates a band of young men who were not members of the royal family. When he became king he discontinued his father's practice of seeking the advice of the more distinguished members of his family. His brothers and uncles were rarely consulted, and in order to counteract their influence he not only appointed his favourites to important positions in the government but also founded the 'Wild Tiger Scout Corps', in which volunteers from amongst the civil officials were enrolled on a quasi-military basis, under the personal leadership of the king as Chief Scout-General.

Vajiravudh was, however, unconquerably shy and lacking in real gifts of leadership. He was a lover of art and the theatre and wrote or translated plays in polished T'ai. But the appointment of his

[1] Kenneth Perry Landon, *Siam in Transition*, London, 1939. See also his contribution on Siam to L. A. Mills and Associates, *The New World of Southeast Asia*, pp. 246–72.

satellites to sinecures and the unparalleled corruption that resulted made his clique disliked and caused him much unpopularity. Throughout his reign there was subdued discontent in the country. There were even two attempts to dethrone him. The first, in 1912, was an assassination plot, nipped in the bud by his able brother, the Prince of Pitsanulok. It was due to discontent in the army and navy at the creation of the Wild Tiger Corps. The Bangkok troops were apparently ready to mutiny and march on the palace. But the censorship was so rigorous that even now the details are not known. Some sixty army officers were arrested. The second, in 1917, was also a military plot, caused by dislike of the king's pro-Allied sympathies on the part of the pro-German section of the army.

He has been somewhat unaccountably called democratic.[1] On the contrary, his attempts at tightening the royal absolutism were a contributing factor in bringing about the constitutional crisis of 1932. The Cabinet of ministers set up by Chulalongkorn rarely met. Ministers consulted the king individually and made individual decisions. There was thus no co-ordination. And the king's predilection for reviving old ceremonial, together with the increasing elaboration of state functions, betrayed an inordinate enjoyment of the pomp and circumstance of his office.

He had a great sense of the dramatic and he consciously fostered national pride. He realized the great value of the Boy Scout movement for such a purpose, and through his encouragement—one might almost say 'at his order'—the schools of Siam became Scout-minded and produced innumerable companies of 'Tiger's Whelps', as they were called, for they were affiliated to the 'Wild Tigers'. And as in the contemporaneous national movements in Burma and Indonesia, so in Siam religion was called in as the great unifying force. There is a curious parallel between Siam and Burma in this matter, for in both nationalist propaganda asserted that only a Buddhist could be a true patriot. Japan's victory over Russia in 1905 had a stimulating effect upon Siam's national sentiment, and it seems likely that in his efforts to carry the process of modernization further Vajiravudh was fully aware of the methods by which Japan had made herself strong enough to defeat a great European power.

Compared with his father, Vajiravudh accomplished few important administrative reforms. His social reforms, however, had far-reaching consequences. They were introduced largely in order to bring Siam into line with Western ideas and practices and thereby

[1] Virginia Thompson, *Thailand: The New Siam*, p. 49.

secure her acceptance into the comity of nations. This is the explanation of the recodification of law which was begun in Vajiravudh's reign, and particularly of the draft law of monogamy which, at the king's instance, was included in it. It did not spring from a single-minded desire to emancipate women. One of his deepest concerns was to obtain the abolition of the extra-territoriality rules affecting Europeans in his country, and he realized that to bring Siam's legal system into closer conformity with accepted European notions was an essential requirement of such a policy.

Some of his social reforms were undoubtedly due to ideas he had imbibed during his long period of education in England. His edict in 1916 ordering all his subjects to adopt patronymics may certainly be ascribed to this, as also his introduction of compulsory vaccination. It was also largely through his influence that women adopted European hair styles and the skirt in place of short hair *en brosse* and the *panung*, or waist-cloth with the end pulled between their legs and tucked in at the front. Other useful measures in the same spirit were the adoption of the Gregorian calendar, the introduction of compulsory elementary education (in 1921), the foundation of the Chulalongkorn University (in 1917), and the institution of the Red Cross Society. He was an enthusiast for football and athletics. Football in particular became, with his active support, immensely popular throughout the country, and he himself organized cup-ties. His own personal contribution to education was the foundation in Bangkok of the famous Vajiravudh School, a boarding school for boys modelled closely on the English public-school pattern and under a Siamese headmaster who was a product of Sanderson's Oundle.

Next to social reform foreign policy absorbed most of Vajiravudh's attention during his early years. When the First World War broke out in 1914 his personal sympathies were with the Allies. But anti-French sentiment was still very strong among the Siamese people, and there was a powerful pro-German section in the army. It was, however, certainly not to Siam's advantage that she should be a centre from which German intrigue radiated into the adjacent territories belonging to Britain and France. In July 1917 therefore, in consequence of Germany's contemptuous rejection of a Siamese protest against her methods of submarine warfare, Vajiravudh took the plunge and declared war. In the following year a small Siamese expeditionary force was sent to France. Siam gained much by joining the winning side. German shipping to the value of several millions sterling came into her hands as booty, and she was able to free her railway system from the control that Germany had managed to obtain over it in the pre-war period. Better still, she secured membership of the League of Nations, and in 1922 the United States made a fresh treaty abandoning all her extra-territorial rights in Siam.

Vajiravudh had always disliked the heavy work imposed upon him by having to attend to daily matters of government routine. He left much of the detailed work to his uncle, Prince Devawongse, who had been his father's closest companion and was for some thirty years Minister of Foreign Affairs. Dr. Malcolm Smith tells us that next to the king he was the most powerful man in the country.[1] He was a man of great intelligence and devotion to duty and performed notable services in the cause of Siam's independence and progress. After his death in 1923 the king relied mainly on Chao P'ya Yomarej, whose meteoric rise from an obscure post in the household of one of Chulalongkorn's brothers to become Minister of the Interior was the measure of his remarkable ability.

When Vajiravudh died in 1925 he left no son to succeed him. He had been a bachelor throughout most of his reign, to the great disappointment of his mother, Queen Saowapa, who died in 1919. When at last he did marry, in 1922, he failed to produce a male heir before his death and was succeeded by Prince Prajadhipok, his youngest brother. Prajadhipok had never expected or desired to become king. He was the seventy-sixth child of his father and his last son. His uncle, Prince Vajirayan, the Supreme Patriarch of the Buddhist Church, had tried to persuade him to devote his life to religion so as to qualify to become his successor, but after serving four months in 1917 as a novice he left the monastery in shattered health and abandoned the idea. He was a modest young man of liberal outlook and with a high sense of responsibility.

The most pressing problem facing him at his accession was the need for economy in public expenditure. Vajiravudh's extravagance had played havoc with the state finances. Prajadhipok therefore dismissed many of his brother's favourites, reduced the Civil List and Royal Household expenditure drastically, and cut down the Royal Corps of Pages from 3,000 to 300. These measures, combined with increased customs returns resulting from new commercial treaties and prosperous foreign trade, enabled the Treasury to balance its budgets without the necessity to negotiate foreign loans or raise taxation. He also set up a Supreme Council, composed of five of the most important princes, as an advisory body, and revived the Cabinet. In 1927, in order to obtain

[1] *Op. cit.*, p. 121.

advice from a wider circle of advisers, he created a large Privy Council, with a committee of forty to report to him on any matters he might submit to them.

The early years of his reign saw many interesting developments such as the establishment of a wireless service, the preparation of the Dom Muang airport for international air service, and the foundation of the Royal Institute of Literature, Architecture and Fine Arts, with its excellent National Library and Museum. The tical was linked with gold by a new Currency Act in 1928. Public Health laws were passed and the qualifications for the medical profession made more stringent. An Act for the Control of Commercial Undertakings of Public Utility was passed to increase governmental control over insurance and banking, and in 1930 Dr. Karl Zimmerman of Harvard University made an economic survey of the kingdom.

The great slump, the more acute effects of which began to be felt in that year, hit Siam in some ways less hard than other countries in South-East Asia. The bottom fell out of the rice market, and Britain's abandonment of the gold standard, which affected Siam's chief competitor in rice exports, Burma, forced Siam herself to abandon it in May 1932 after long hesitation. The consequent improvement in her export trade, especially to the silver controlled markets, ultimately benefited the cultivator and caused some criticism of the government for not acting earlier. But there was no serious unrest in the agricultural areas. The country lacked big industries; hence there was no large mass of unemployed. Foreign commerce was in foreign hands exclusively. The chief effects, therefore, of the depression were to strengthen the nationalist demand for the removal of foreign control over the country's economic life.

The government, however, got into serious financial difficulties. In March 1931 the Minister of Finance had to announce a budget deficit of 11 million ticals. As Siam failed in her attempts to raise foreign loans in Paris and New York, she was forced to introduce drastic economies involving salary cuts, which hit the junior official class very hard. They were already discontented because the road to middle-class promotion was blocked by the solid princely phalanx which monopolized all the key positions. Many of them had adopted democratic ideas through education in Europe and had become impatient with the working of the old-fashioned royal absolutism. At the same time, during the king's absence abroad for medical treatment in 1931 serious rivalry developed in the Supreme Council between the Minister of War, Prince Bovaradej, and the Minister of Commerce,

Prince Purachatra, over a question of economy. In October 1931 this produced a first-class political crisis which shook public confidence in that princely dominated institution.

This was not all the discontent, since there were those of the official class who had lost their jobs through Prajadhipok's drastic pruning of the Civil Service, and to them must be added a group of army officers resentful of the salary cuts and hostile to princely influence. In 1932 these discontented elements found a leader in Luang Pradist Manudharm, better known by his personal name of Pridi Banomyong, a brilliant young lawyer trained in Paris and Professor of Law at the Chulalongkorn University. He drafted a constitution and with military help took control over Bangkok and carried out a bloodless revolution on 24 June 1932.

The public took no part in the *coup* save as spectators. The king, who was away from the capital at the time, returned two days later and at once accepted the provisional constitution. By it he lost all his prerogatives save the right of pardon, the princes were excluded from ministerial posts and the army, and the People's Party, as Pridi and his supporters named themselves, took over the management of the government. They nominated a Senate of seventy members, which proceeded to appoint an Executive Council with power to promulgate laws and control ministers. The Senate was to be replaced by an elected Assembly after a lapse of six months, and there was to be universal suffrage after ten years.

The new government was therefore a party dictatorship. But Pridi and his lieutenants did not take over the actual government. They chose P'ya Manopakorn as President of the Executive Council. He had played no part in the revolution but had been a good President of the Court of Appeal. His appointment, like that of the President of the Senate, a previous Minister of Education, was an attempt to appease conservative opinion. From the point of view of the revolutionaries the arrangement was not a success. P'ya Manopakorn's policy was, on his own admission, a continuation of the pre-revolution regime's retrenchment policy. No one was satisfied, there was an atmosphere of alarm, and when the Communists and their Chinese supporters tried to cash in on the situation the government adopted a policy of repression.

The conservative influence in the government showed itself quite clearly in December 1932 when the new constitution, on which a special committee had been at work since the revolution, was promulgated. The committee had worked in close collaboration with the king, and the result was a document in which the royal powers were considerably greater than had originally been announced. Legislative competence, control over finance, and the power to interpret the constitution were vested in a unicameral Assembly of 156 members, of which, as a temporary measure, the king was to appoint half. Elections were to be held every four years. Candidates for seats must be Siamese of at least twenty-three years of age, resident in their constituencies, and able to fulfil certain educational requirements. The law of citizenship was redefined so as to include the right to vote among the privileges of the citizen. Ministers were to be responsible to the Assembly, but if a vote of confidence were moved the voting must not take place on the day of the discussion. The king secured three important powers. He could dissolve the Assembly without Cabinet approval, but a new election must be held within three months. He was given the right to veto legislation, but the Assembly could override his veto by a second vote. He could also enact emergency decrees so long as they were countersigned by the minister responsible.

The restrictions on the princes of the royal family were also relaxed. While they were prohibited from sitting as deputies or holding office as ministers, they were permitted to act as advisers and hold diplomatic posts. As a safeguard against party dictatorship a political party was forbidden to issue orders to any of its members with seats in the Assembly. In 1933 a further step was taken at the king's request. The People's Party was dissolved as a political party and became a social club. This was an astute piece of political engineering. The king had rejected a petition by a number of army officers and high officials to form a Nationalist Party and in consequence was able to bring pressure to bear on the People's Party. Apparently the petition had been presented solely with that intention.

P'ya Manopakorn now sought to free his government from the control of Pridi and his group. An unpublished scheme of national economy prepared by Pridi was declared to be Communistic, and by a well-prepared *coup* he was forced into exile. Then the government stole his thunder by announcing a national policy to exploit the national resources and promising assignments of vacant land to the unemployed. But P'ya Manopakorn went too far by securing a prorogation of the Assembly and assuming a more and more dictatorial attitude.

The rising alarm and the prime minister's preparation for another purge led four army leaders, with P'ya Bahol at their head, to offer their resignations. All had been colleagues of Pridi in the revolution of the previous year. When their resignations were accepted they planned another *coup d'état*, and on 20 June 1933 carried it through successfully. P'ya Manopakorn resigned and his place was taken by P'ya Bahol. A new Council composed of his followers was appointed and the Assembly recalled. The government publicly proclaimed that it was anti-Communist and would defend the constitution. The king, who had been conveniently absent from the capital for the *coup d'état*, returned and in the first radio speech ever made by a Siamese monarch to his people urged that peace and unity should be maintained.

In September Pridi, who had become the darling of the people, was permitted to return and was given an enthusiastic reception. A commission was appointed to investigate the charges of Communism that had been made against him, and in March 1934 its report completely cleared him. Meanwhile in October 1933 the government was faced by a serious military revolt led by the king's cousin, Prince Bovaradej. The rebel forces occupied the Dom Muang airport and demanded the resignation of P'ya Bahol and his associates. But the premier's popularity with the army ensured the loyalty of the troops guarding the capital, and when Luang P'ibun Songgram, in command of the government forces, recaptured Don Muang the rebel leaders fled to Saigon and the revolt collapsed.

Throughout the crisis the king had maintained a neutral attitude. It became known that he had been aware of what was brewing and that most of the royal princes had given moral and financial support to the rebels. He was never able to regain the confidence of his people, and in January 1934 went abroad on the plea that he must have specialist treatment for his eyesight, which was indeed causing him serious anxiety: The aristocracy also did not recover its position. On the other hand, the new middle-class movement became divided by the growing rivalry between P'ibun Songgram, who had risen to prominence by restoring order at the time of the military revolt, and Pridi. P'ibun was the leader of a group that was militarist and nationalist, while Pridi led a section in which the civilian element predominated. Only the strong personality of the prime minister, whom everybody liked for his humane temperament, held the government together.

In November 1933 a general election was held in order that the government might seek to counteract the influence of the rebel sympathizers by intensive propaganda. Less than a tenth of the electorate voted and comparatively few candidates offered themselves for election. Pridi's following apparently secured a majority of the seats. Pridi was all for a radical economic policy, but there were signs of unrest which caused much alarm, and P'ibun's campaign against what he called the Communistic element in the government caused much wariness of embarking on any fundamental changes. In September 1934 a crisis occurred when the Assembly threw out a measure for ratifying a rubber agreement with Britain. The Cabinet resigned, but P'ya Bahol's popularity was so great that he returned to office with a reconstructed ministry which won a vote of confidence with a secure majority.

Soon afterwards another crisis blew up which involved the king's abdication. He vetoed a Bill which sought to abolish the need for his signature to be appended to a death sentence, and when the Assembly objected he threatened to abdicate unless his conditions, involving the resignation of the Assembly and a new general election, were accepted. Attempts at a compromise failed and in March 1935 he announced his abdication. His nephew, Prince Ananda Mahidol, a ten-year-old schoolboy in Switzerland, was proclaimed king and a Regency Council of three members was appointed to act during his minority. Prajadhipok and his wife were in England when this crisis occurred, and he announced his intention of residing there in future with the title of Prince of Sukhodaya.

During the succeeding period P'ibun's influence continued to grow, especially after Pridi's departure on a foreign tour in the middle of 1935. The State Council was constantly weakened by quarrels between its members, and as more and more posts in the civil administration were given to army officers the government showed signs of a trend towards a military dictatorship which seriously alarmed the Assembly. P'ya Bahol's administration survived another general election in 1937; but the new Assembly was determined to assert its will, and in December 1938 passed against the government an amendment to its procedure to compel a more detailed explanation of the budget. This brought the resignation of the Council and P'ya Bahol announced his retirement.

The new government was headed by P'ibun, with Pridi as Minister of Finance. Its prevailing note was an intensified nationalism. Pridi's new Revenue Code, passed in March 1939, was an attempt to lighten the burden of the peasant and free him from dependence upon the money-lender. Much heavier taxation was levied on the commercial class, represented mainly by the Chinese and partly by European firms. It was followed by stringent regulations to check

Chinese immigration and reserve for Siamese nationals a number of occupations previously monopolized by Chinese. The government went so far as to close hundreds of Chinese schools, suppress Chinese newspapers, deport thousands of opium addicts and even arrest some of the leaders of the Chinese community. The reason given was that the terrorist activities of the Chinese secret societies constituted a menace to public order.

European interests were hit by these measures, since they employed Chinese labour in mining and forestry. Leases for the teak industry, which was under British management, were renewed on less favourable terms and more forest areas were reserved for Siamese enterprise. An attempt was made to take over local shipping by buying vessels to be operated by a state company and by legislation ruling that the capital of foreign shipping firms must be at least 70 per cent Siamese, all vessels must be registered as Siamese and their crews 75 per cent Siamese. State subsidies were given to private Siamese firms, technical, commercial and agricultural schools were founded, and many Siamese students sent abroad for technical training.

Other interesting manifestations of the new chauvinism were the change in the official name for the country from Siam to Thailand in June 1939. The Siamese had always proudly referred to their country as Muang Thai, 'the land of the free', and it was now decreed that foreigners also should use this name.[1] P'ibun also started a campaign to inculcate Western manners and social practices, and a series of pamphlets was issued to explain government policy in this connection. Both sexes were required to wear European shoes and hats in public, and a Westernized version of dress was prescribed. Efforts were also made to stop the practice of chewing betel. The education system was brought under the strictest control. All schools had to adopt the curricula, textbooks and examinations rigidly prescribed by the Ministry of Education, and all teachers had to be registered. The movement to equate Buddhism with patriotism was fostered, and there were many conversions from Christianity. It was made clear that non-Buddhists in government service were liable to lose their posts or their hopes of promotion. The rule was also laid down that no official might marry an alien without special permission.

In foreign affairs efforts were made to win concessions from the Western powers by threatening to co-operate with Japan. Much closer economic relations were formed with that country, and Japanese

[1] In September 1945 it was changed back to Siam, but in 1948 the name Thailand became again its official designation.

goods began to flood the Siamese market. Siamese irredentism was stirred up, particularly against French Indo-China, and demands were made for the restoration of the Cambodian and Laos territories, which France had forced Siam to yield in the earlier period.

The outbreak of the Second World War in 1939 and the consequent concentration of Britain and France upon the German menace enabled P'ibun with Japanese assistance—it was officially called 'mediation'—to regain much territory. After the Japanese landings in Indo-China a Thai-Japanese pact was signed in December 1940, and in the following March the French ceded the Cambodian provinces of Battambang and Siemreap, together with the Laotian territory to the west of the river Mekong.

Instead of playing off Japan against the Western Powers, P'ibun had now sold himself to the Japanese. He and a small group of high-placed officials adopted a policy of full co-operation with Japan, the natural result of which was the declaration of war by Siam against Britain and the United States on 25 January 1942.

CHAPTER 48

THE JAPANESE IMPACT

WHEN in November 1936 Germany and Japan signed the Anti-
Comintern Pact and in July of the following year Japan's second big
offensive began in China, another Russo-Japanese war seemed only
a matter of time. In the summer of 1938 there was open warfare near
the junction of the borders of Manchuria, Korea and Siberia, and a
state of severe tension in Soviet-Japanese relations. Both sides were
making huge concentrations of troops in Manchuria and Siberia.

Then in September 1938 came the Munich agreement. Its effects
upon Japanese policy were immediate. She decided that the weakness
displayed by Britain and France in face of the dictators indicated that
she could get away with a policy of expansion in South-East Asia.
Britain had the largest financial stake in China, and Japan was already
heartened by the extent to which her determined advance there had
resulted in British measures of appeasement. Her hope, therefore,
was that she could achieve her aims without full-scale hostilities. That
was why in the spring of 1939 she refused the invitation to join her
Anti-Comintern partners in a military pact.

Japan's southwards push began in the very month after Munich,
when she seized Canton and isolated Hong Kong from the mainland.
This was the prelude to the seizure of strategic points in the South
China Sea, Hainan Island off the coast of French Indo-China on 10
February 1939, and the Sinnan Islands, including Spratley, on 30
March. Thus she sought to overcome the serious disadvantage under
which she had laboured through having no naval base nearer Singapore
than Formosa. Hainan brought her within 1,300 miles of it. Spratley
Island took her 700 miles nearer still.

The big danger in the game that she was playing was from the
United States, where her actions had already aroused so much
apprehension that in the previous January the American fleet had been
transferred from the Atlantic to the Pacific. But Germany and
Russia signed their Non-Aggression Pact on 21 August, and within a
fortnight another great war began in Europe. Japan was worried by
the possible implications of the pact; but she calculated that while there

was danger of becoming involved in a war across the Atlantic America would do everything possible to avoid one in the Pacific. She decided, therefore, to commit herself fully to the South-East Asian gamble.

Her next move, in November 1939, was a big thrust into Kwangsi province to capture the city of Nanning and cut China's strategic road connection with French Indo-China. This left China with only the newly opened Burma Road and the Hanoi–Kunming railway for outlets to the sea, and Japan could threaten both from the air. French Indo-China now became her major objective. On 9 April 1940 Hitler's *blitzkrieg* began. Only just over a week later Arita, the Japanese Foreign Minister, made some significant references to the future of French Indo-China and the Netherlands Indies in the event of a German victory. These evoked a sharp reply from Cordell Hull, the American Secretary of State. But France and Holland fell, and their possessions in South-East Asia were left with quite inadequate defences against a possible Japanese attack.

In the same month that France fell, June 1940, Japan signed a treaty of friendship with P'ibun Songgram's government in Thailand. She was now well placed to bring that country under control by means of her technique of infiltration, pressure and menaces. Incidentally she had her eye on the new naval base which Thailand was building at Singora. But it was to French Indo-China that she now turned; the time had come to clinch matters.

In August 1940 the Konoye Cabinet demanded special concessions there. The Vichy régime, under pressure from Berlin, signed an agreement granting Japan permission to use Indo-China's ports, cities and airports for troop movements. In the following month a treaty was signed between Vichy and Tokyo which permitted Japanese forces to occupy the northern part of Indo-China as far south as Hanoi. In the same month Japan burnt her boats by forming a military alliance with the Axis. The treaty was worded in such a way as to warn America against interference in either Europe or the Pacific. In face of this American isolationism died a sudden death, and Washington began to prepare for the worst.

Japan's next concern was to reach a neutrality agreement with Russia and at the same time hold America off by negotiations. Meanwhile she played upon P'ibun Songgram's revisionist ambitions by permitting a mock Thai offensive on the Cambodian and Laos frontiers and then in January 1941 stepping in with an offer of 'mediation'. Vichy was forced to hand over the Cambodian provinces of Battambang and Siemreap and the Laos territory on the west bank of the

Mekong, which Siam had lost at the time of the Paknam incident in 1893. In April 1941 Japan's hoped-for Neutrality Pact with Russia was safely concluded. In that same month American, British, Dutch, Australian and New Zealand officers met in Singapore for staff conversations.

Then came a sudden check to Japan's plans for a southward drive; on 22 June 1941 Hitler began his surprise attack on Russia. Japan now hesitated, for a war on two fronts was something she was extremely anxious to avoid. It soon appeared, however, that luck was still on her side; for the overwhelming and rapid German successes against Russia made it obvious that she could resume her southwards course. During July her troops occupied the whole of French Indo-China. But by now America's attitude had hardened and her military preparations were a serious deterrent to a further step.

Japan therefore redoubled her efforts to lull the suspicions of the White House and the State Department. For some months negotiations were carried on amid growing tension. Both sides had become convinced that war was inevitable. On 6 December 1941 as a final despairing peace effort President Roosevelt sent a personal telegram to the Emperor of Japan. On the following day Japan made her surprise attack on Pearl Harbour and inflicted upon America one of the most disastrous defeats she has ever sustained. Her Pacific fleet was put out of action and Japan was free to go ahead with the conquest of South-East Asia.

She planned a short and decisive war. She was in a hurry, for she believed that a German victory in Europe was certain, and she wanted to reach her objectives before America could revive her power in the Pacific. After Pearl Harbour, therefore, her offensive went ahead with breathless speed. On the following day her troops landed in Thailand, and after a token resistance P'ibun's government capitulated and agreed to declare war on the Allies. Before the end of December the American bases of Guam and Wake and the British settlement of Hong Kong had fallen. Simultaneously with these moves the Japanese began the invasion of the Philippines. Only three days after Pearl Harbour two British capital ships, the *Prince of Wales* and the *Repulse*, on their way from Singapore to prevent a Japanese landing in north Malaya, were sunk by aeroplanes based on Indo-China. Japan now had overwhelming naval supremacy in the Pacific and East Asiatic waters.

The main Japanese army now moved down the Malay Peninsula towards Singapore, while another force of specially trained veteran troops invaded Burma. In all these spheres—the Philippines, Malaya, and Burma—the invaders possessed decisive ground and air superiority. While these campaigns were in progress other forces were landed in Bali and Sumatra in preparation for the invasion of Java. Singapore fell on 15 February 1942. The Burma invasion began in the third week of January with two thrusts from Siamese territory into Tenasserim. The British made their first stand on the Salween river around Moulmein. Thence they were driven westwards along the coast road through Thaton, and across the Sittang to Pegu. A second defeat there led to the evacuation of Rangoon on 7 March and a retreat on Prome.

By this time Java was in the throes of invasion, and on 9 March organized resistance ended there. Meanwhile the British forces in Burma were fighting a rearguard action up the Irrawaddy valley, while Chinese troops coming in by the Burma Road strove to co-operate with them by holding a line stretching across from Pyinmana to Allanmyo. In the Philippines the American and Filipino armies had been forced back to the Bataan peninsula, while others held out at Corregidor in Manila Bay. In both places they fought a grim battle against superior forces for some months.

In Burma the Japanese foiled the Anglo-Chinese attempt to establish a line by driving a wedge between them. The British thereupon fell back up the Chindwin valley towards Manipur. Stilwell, the American general commanding the Chinese, hoped to make a stand in northern Burma, but the Japanese prevented this by piercing the Shan hills and defeating the Chinese at Loilem. Stilwell's forces then disintegrated. He himself with a mixed band of Americans, British, Burmese and Chinese trekked off towards India, crossing the Chindwin at Homalin. The remainder pushed off along the Burma Road into China. By the end of April the whole of the Irrawaddy valley was in Japanese hands. By that time the war in the Philippines was in its last stages. Bataan had surrendered on 9 April. Corregidor was to surrender on 6 May. Five months after Pearl Harbour the Japanese had conquered most of their 'Greater East Asia co-prosperity sphere'.

Before her invasion of South-East Asia Japan had failed to stimulate any nationalist rising against the Western Powers. Indonesia was, for its economic resources, the region she most coveted. She had tried to persuade the Dutch, after the German conquest of Holland, to play the same part in Indonesia as the French in Indo-China. In September 1940 Ichizo Kobayashi, the Japanese Minister of

Commerce and Industry, had gone to Batavia to obtain full Dutch co-operation in the co-prosperity plan. His hope was that Britain would be forced to capitulate to Germany, and that he would then be able to 'persuade' the Dutch to accept a Japanese 'protectorate' over their Indonesian empire.

But Britain did not fall. Kobayashi therefore could not present his ultimatum, and Dr. H. J. van Mook proved a doughty antagonist in argument. When Kobayashi's successor, Kenkichi Yoshizava, arrived in January 1941 it soon became evident that the Dutch would not 'co-operate'. Japan's great object had been to prevent the destruction of Indonesia's oil industry and the carrying out of other scorched-earth practices which would deny her the supplies of raw materials she so much needed. Even when she knew she would have to fight for Java her first plan had been to by-pass the Dutch East Indies and occupy Australia. Apparently it was the stubbornness with which the Dutch prepared to defend their empire that caused her to change her plan.

The Indonesians had no desire to exchange Dutch for Japanese rule. The excessive demands made by Yoshizava in his talks with van Mook showed them the hollowness of the co-prosperity proposals. He asked for nothing less than unlimited Japanese immigration into all the islands outside Java, and complete freedom of action in the commerce and industrial development of Indonesia. Even the left-wing Gerindo group of the old Partai Indonesia proclaimed that the Greater East India idea had the one aim of depriving other peoples of their freedom through the same forms of domination as the Japanese had used in Manchuria, China and Indo-China. When the Dutch asked for 18,000 volunteers for Home and City Guards, 100,000 presented themselves.

Nowhere were the invading Japanese materially assisted by national movements. In Malaya there was no fifth column and no authenticated case of Malays firing on British troops. The stories to that effect arose from the fact that in their infiltration tactics the Japanese dressed as Malays. Only one battalion of the Malay Regiment was equipped and trained, and it fought with the utmost gallantry. Over a thousand Chinese helped in the defence of Singapore, but there was no equipment with which to arm them. As in Burma, the defence of the country was the responsibility of the British army, and very little had been done to recruit and train native forces.

The Burmese as a whole gave no support to the Japanese invasion. Some rebellious groups, organized by student nationalists of the

Thakin Party trained in Japan, provided the Japanese with guides and topographical intelligence. The criminal classes from the gaols ran wild, looted their own people and murdered Indian refugees. But the mass of the people looked on with dismay. The Burma Defence Force was loyal, but it contained only 472 Burmese against 3,197 Karens, Chins and Kachins. The non-Burmese peoples gave every assistance to the retreating British, and the Karens in particular suffered horribly for their loyalty.

The amazing Japanese success and the rapidity with which it was achieved did irreparable harm to Western prestige. 'Asia for the Asians' was the general theme of Japanese propaganda, and she sought the complete eradication of Western influence and culture. To the Buddhist countries of the mainland her propaganda made much play with the fact that she also was a Buddhist country, although the differences between their Theravada and her Zen Buddhism of the Northern school were irreconcilable. Her relations with the Mahommedan peoples were less easy. In Indonesia she loudly proclaimed a 'Three A Movement' with three slogans: 'Japan the Leader of Asia', 'Japan the Protector of Asia', and 'Japan the Light of Asia', but it had to be abandoned for lack of support. The Japanese in Asia, like the Germans in Europe, showed a genius for alienating any people over whom they established control. In Malaya they relied on stirring up Malay hostility against the Chinese, and with some success, but they failed to arouse Malay hatred against the British, notwithstanding the extent to which their defeat had shattered their prestige.

In Burma's case practically the whole British element in the administration, and much of the Indian, escaped to India. The Burmese members, together with those belonging to the non-Burmese indigenous races, remained behind at their posts, as indeed they had been expected to do. The Japanese retained the administration in operation with few changes. Their method of ensuring that their requirements were fulfilled was to appoint political commissars to work along with the civil administrators. Much of the work had to be carried on in English, since Burmese and Japanese were for the most part ignorant of each other's languages.

Much the same thing, *mutatis mutandis*, happened to the British administration in Malaya and the Dutch in Indonesia, save that in both cases the European members of the administrative corps were interned in prison camps. In all three cases the Europeans had to be replaced by generally inadequately trained, and often hostile, Burmese, Malays and Indonesians. And as the military dominated every form of activity and knew little or nothing of civil administration, misery and confusion resulted and an inevitable deterioration of economic conditions. Everywhere the Japanese attacked those parts of the administration where the European tradition was strongest.

The police came under the direction of the Kempeitai, and probably no one will ever know the full extent of the terrorism carried on against the native populations. Thousands of Chinese were massacred soon after the surrender of Singapore, especially those who had anything to do with the China Relief Fund. Rape was a real scourge in occupied Malaya. The Japanese, writes Victor Purcell, 'conducted rape on the grand scale'. The requisitions for forced labour were perhaps the worst form of tyranny. Thousands were used on the construction of the infamous 'death railway' connecting southern Burma with Bangkok through Kanburi. Thousands of Indonesians also were shipped to work for the Japanese forces in New Guinea and the northern Moluccas. The European and Eurasian prisoners of war were treated with unparalleled harshness. The immense European cemeteries situated near the Burma-Thailand railway are today grim reminders of the inefficiency and callous brutality which caused so many to be worked or starved to death.

There were resistance groups everywhere, for the dense jungle and mountainous areas lent themselves to this form of activity. They were often led by European officers, left behind by the retreating armies or parachuted in. In Malaya the Chinese Communists were the mainspring of the underground movement, though Kuomintang Chinese and Malays also played a part. As time went on they came to number nearly 7,000 men and women together with about 300 British, most of whom were dropped by parachute. The epic story of their struggle has been told by Lieutenant-Colonel Spencer Chapman, the T. E. Lawrence of the Malayan jungle.[1] They gradually disrupted rail traffic, and in 1945 were ready to paralyse the Japanese system of communications when the British army attacked.

In Burma a Karen resistance movement led by British officers was stamped out with appalling atrocities. But a large part of the Burmese Thakin Party, disgusted by the behaviour of the Japanese, also went underground, and by the end of 1943 were leading a small but well-organized resistance movement. In their case also the Communists were the leading spirits. In French Indo-China the Viet Minh League, under the leadership of Ho Chi Minh, became the spearhead of the resistance after the collapse of a number of nationalist risings.

[1] *The Jungle is Neutral.*.

In the last stage of the conflict they received American weapons and technical aid which enabled them to clear the Japanese out of several provinces of northern Tongking. In Cochin China Ho Chi Minh's guerrillas assisted the Resistance Committee which maintained touch with the Allies.

In Indonesia at the outset the nationalist leaders had, apparently by agreement, divided into two groups. One, headed by Sukarno and Hatta, co-operated with the Japanese as a means of furthering the nationalist cause. The other, headed by Sjahrir and Sjarifuddin, went underground to organize a resistance movement, in which they kept in touch with their comrades on the Japanese side.

In Thailand Pridi, who resigned his position as Minister of Finance when P'ibun capitulated to the Japanese, tried unsuccessfully to establish an independent government in the north. He was then made regent, and under cover of his privileged position organized an underground movement in secret touch with the Free Thai Movement in the United States and Britain. Allied forces working through his underground prepared airfields and imported arms ready for an attack on the Japanese, which never came off owing to the suddenness of their collapse in 1945. Members of the underground movement did much to help European prisoners of war working on the 'death railway'.

The Japanese success in overrunning territories had been greater than even they had bargained for. Tokyo therefore revised its plans to include the conquest of further territories than had originally been envisaged. In the central Pacific more island groups were added to the list, in the hope of preventing the American navy from establishing bases near to Asia. In Burma the Japanese began to build up their strength for an attack on India. The original plan for a movement by sea had to be abandoned—partly because of trouble with the Indian National Army, which had been recruited in Malaya and refused to move without clear assurances that India's future independence would be guaranteed.

To meet this the Allies had at first no co-ordinated plan. In the dry weather of 1942–3 a British attempt to seize northern Arakan failed disastrously. The Americans, anxious to relieve the pressure on Chungking, were all for reopening the land route to China and a drive to secure Myitkyina. The British were at first sceptical of the wisdom of a north Burma offensive, but finally agreed to the plan. The Americans thereupon began feverishly to construct the Ledo Road, and at the same time to supply Chungking with Lend-Lease materials by air over the Himalayan 'Hump'.

Meanwhile in the Pacific the Japanese rashness in over-extending their line of advance brought them into difficulties. At the Battle of Midway in June 1942 the American fleet sank the four aircraft-carriers accompanying a superior Japanese fleet and forced it to flee. This action has been taken as the turning of the tide in the Pacific war.[1] It was followed by a limited counter-offensive against northern New Guinea and the Solomons. In 1943 the Allies were preparing for a widespread offensive in the Pacific, with Japan itself as the ultimate goal. A co-ordinated plan also emerged for a campaign in Burma envisaging a drive by Stilwell's force for Myitkyina and a push across the Chindwin from Manipur by the main Allied army that was being built up in India.

In face of this threat the Japanese began to lose their confidence. They decided that everything must be done to win over the peoples of the occupied countries and enlist them to resist Allied attacks. Their method was to set up puppet régimes with the semblance of independence. On 1 August 1943 Burma became 'independent' under the presidency of the former premier Dr. Ba Maw, who took the title of 'Adipadi', the Pali equivalent of *Führer*. There was no talk of reviving the Constitution of 1937, and in any case real control was in the hands of Dr. Gotara Ogawa, formerly a Cabinet minister in Tokyo, who became 'Supreme Adviser' to the Burmese government. A similar régime was established in the Philippines on 15 October 1943 under Jose P. Laurel.

As Indonesia seemed unlikely to be threatened by an early Allied attack, the Japanese moved more slowly there. But the Indonesians were promised a share in their government, and in September 1943 a Central Advisory Council was established in Java under Sukarno, with Mohammed Hatta as his deputy. Advisory councils were also set up in the various residencies and cities. Sukarno's position, however, was less that of an adviser than of a mouthpiece for the interpretation and recommendation of Japanese policy to the general public.[2] At Singapore a Malayan Consultative Council was brought into being.

But these were all mere play-acting and failed to disguise the hollowness of Japanese promises and propaganda. Of all the occupied

---

[1] On this subject see *The Campaigns of the Pacific War*, Washington, 1946, *Battle Report, Pacific War*, published by the U.S. Navy, and the detailed operational histories under the direction of S. E. Morison.

[2] Dr. H. J. van Mook, *The Stakes of Democracy in South-East Asia*, London, 1950, p. 151. The book contains an illuminating chapter on the Japanese treatment of Indonesia.

countries Burma suffered worst at the hands of the Japanese. Many of her towns had been reduced to ashes by Japanese air-raids during the invasion. Her oil-wells, mines equipment and river transport were destroyed by the retreating British so as to be useless to the enemy. Allied air-raids kept her railways out of action. The Japanese systematically looted the country of machinery, scientific apparatus and even furniture. All her normal external markets were lost. The complete stoppage of her rice export through the failure of the Japanese to take it led to mere subsistence farming. The south suffered from a glut of rice while the north starved. Lower Burma was almost completely deprived of the cooking oil which only the dry zone could supply.

The inability of the Japanese to export Burma rice and import urgently needed consumer goods caused the greatest distress, which was further aggravated by the chaos and uncontrollable inflation caused by the Japanese currency policy. The peasantry lost a large proportion of their indispensable cattle through military requisition for food and an epidemic of rinderpest. Malaria control measures ceased and the people suffered heavily from the disease. There were epidemics of smallpox, cholera and bubonic plague, against which the Japanese had to take drastic preventive measures. Hence in 1944 the extremists, who had assisted the Japanese invasion and were in positions of political control, were secretly engaged in organizing a nation-wide Anti-Fascist People's Freedom League, which only awaited a favourable opportunity to come out openly against the oppressor.

In Malaya there was the same neglect of health measures with a consequent increase in malaria and other diseases, accompanied by a sharp rise in the death-rate. All this was particularly noticeable because the public health administration of Singapore and Malaya had been unsurpassed anywhere in Asia. The Japanese looted the hospitals of their modern up-to-date equipment and stores. The schools also were thoroughly looted and some of the native teachers executed. Famine and malnutrition in the towns were even worse than in Burma, since pre-war Malaya had imported two-thirds of its rice, and the Japanese failed to import enough from the rice-producing areas they controlled. There was also the same appalling shortage of consumer goods, and the same inflation through the uncontrolled issue of paper money. The great dredges in the European-run tin mines had been destroyed or put out of action during the British retreat in 1941–2, and there had been widespread destruction of buildings and machinery on the rubber estates.

Dr. van Mook has summed up the effects of Japanese misrule in Indonesia in a statement which for vigour and conciseness cannot be improved upon: 'Those who suffered most were the common people. Japanese economy was frightful, Japanese administration a farce. The country had been subdivided from the beginning into three almost watertight compartments: two, Java and Sumatra, under army commanders, and a third, the rest, under the navy. But as food and other commodities became scarce even the traffic between districts and islands was prohibited in order to facilitate pillaging by the military. The system of finance consisted of a number of printing presses, turning out crude government notes; inflation acquired disastrous proportions. Trade and export production were dead, because Indonesia was cut off from the world markets and Japan, her shipping going under the blows of allied submarines and aircraft, preferred to fetch the products she needed from Indo-China, a thousand miles nearer home. She remained interested only in oil, nickel and bauxite. Estates and factories rusted and decayed; plantations were uprooted to increase the food acreage; means of communication that broke down were no longer repaired; the import goods were gone or hoarded; clothing became almost unobtainable. This meant unemployment for hundreds of thousands; it meant poverty, poverty, poverty, for all but a few henchmen of the Japanese and a number of black marketeers.'[1]

So far as the war was concerned, the year 1943 was mainly one of Allied build-up, planning and try-outs. In the Pacific theatre plans were made for two lines of attack converging upon the Japanese homeland. They envisaged by-passing Japanese island bases where air control could be achieved. One route was via New Guinea to the Philippines and thence to the southern islands of Japan. The other was through the island groups of the central Pacific, the Gilberts and Marshalls to the Japanese strongholds in the Marianas. These in American hands were to be utilized as bases for widespread B-20 bombing attacks, which would include the Japanese cities in their scope.

In Burma Wingate's small 'Chindit' force of British, Burmese and Gurkhas marched across from Tonhe on the Chindwin to carry out a campaign of sabotage and destruction on the Mandalay–Myitkyina railway in co-operation with a planned push in that direction from the north by Stilwell's forces. Unfortunately this operation had to be cancelled, and the Chindit effort lost much of its purpose save as a

[1] *Op. cit.*, pp. 154-5.

magnificent demonstration of heroism. At the Quebec Conference in August 1943 a big step forward was taken by the formation of the South-East Asia Command, with Mountbatten as Supreme Commander and Stilwell as Deputy Chief. Operation Capital for the recovery of Burma from the north was then worked out. At the end of the year a second British attempt on northern Arakan was made, but was stopped by a Japanese counter-attack early in 1944.

China as a theatre of war was mainly inactive in 1943. America made great efforts, by diplomacy and military aid, to keep Chinese resistance alive. As the Burma Road was closed, supplies had to be flown in from India 'over the Hump'. The American airmen responsible for this perilous undertaking showed a gallantry beyond praise, although the trickle of supplies they managed to take to Chungking was inadequate to stimulate offensive action against the Japanese by Chiang Kai-shek. He was far more concerned with his struggle with the Communists in Yenan than with an energetic anti-Japanese policy. One rather overdue act of diplomatic 'encouragement' was the abandonment by Britain and the United States of their extra-territorial rights in China. Their example was followed in due course by other European states possessing such rights.

By the beginning of 1944 the Japanese had begun to realize something of the magnitude of the Allied preparations for a counter-offensive. In the central Pacific and New Guinea during that year they were fully extended trying unsuccessfully to stem the Allied advance. But in two other spheres they undertook major offensive operations in efforts to disrupt their opponents' plans. In both north and south China they struck hard to prevent the offensive that Stilwell was doing his utmost to persuade Chiang Kai-shek to launch, and to secure complete control over the main arterial Peiping–Hankow–Canton railway, which was their land link between Korea and Singapore.

Their offensive caused a quarrel between Stilwell and Chiang Kai-shek over the military reforms which the former urged were necessary in order to meet the threat and oppose the Japanese more effectively. Chiang protested to Washington, and in the middle of the Burma campaign 'Vinegar Joe' was relieved of his command. As the year progressed it became only too obvious that the Allies must ignore China in their strategic arrangements for crushing Japan. In November, however, Hurley, the United States ambassador at Chungking, made a somewhat *gauche* and completely abortive attempt to bring about a compromise between Chiang Kai-shek and the Communists.

The other sphere in which the Japanese launched a major offensive in 1944 was the Burma-India border. In March they began a very formidable movement into Manipur and Assam. It was not an all-out effort to conquer India. It came two years too late for that, when the Allies were gathering strength and Japan herself was fully extended in the Pacific. Her great gamble had depended for its ultimate success on Germany winning the war. But in 1944 Germany was losing the war. The Japanese movement against India therefore was undertaken merely to cause the postponement of the inevitable counter-attack from that quarter.

The first objective of the invaders was Imphal, the capture of which would afford them a stepping-off ground for a push into Bengal. They hoped also to isolate Stilwell when he was poised in the north for his drive southwards towards Myitkyina, and again render fruitless a further operation by Wingate's Chindits. When the attack began Stilwell's forces were moving towards the Hukawng valley, and a far more powerful Chindit force than the earlier one, this time airborne, was attempting to soften up Japanese resistance to their advance.

For some months the situation on the Indian frontier was critical, with the Japanese besieging Imphal and striking at Kohima in a desperate attempt to reach Dimapur Junction on the Assam Railway, along which most of Stilwell's supplies had to pass. It was a veritable bloodbath, but by the end of June the Japanese were firmly held and the road between Kohima and Imphal had been cleared.

This was the turn of the tide. Inside northern Burma Stilwell's group, with the co-operation of the Chindits, was relentlessly pressing towards Myitkyina, which fell at the end of August. But Wingate had been killed in an air accident at the beginning of the campaign, and after the capture of Myitkyina Stilwell was relieved of his command. By this time the Japanese defeat at Imphal had become a disaster and they were in disorderly flight, closely pursued by the Allied forces. Then, as the cold season drew on with the end of the wet monsoon in October, a third Arakan campaign began which cleared the Japanese from the Kaladan valley and the Mayu peninsula. This was followed in January 1945 by landings from the sea at Akyab and other places on the coast so that the essential forward airfields could be prepared in readiness for co-operation with the land invasion of Lower Burma.

Meanwhile equally decisive operations had been taking place in the two Pacific sectors. The Americans began an attack on Saipan in the Marianas on June 15, and in three weeks were in complete possession of the island. This was followed by the liberation of Guam and the conquest of Tinian. And in November the Japanese began to feel the impact of long-range bomber attacks from the Marianas. Moreover, the completion of the Allied conquest of New Guinea enabled American troops on 17 October to land in the Philippines. Their attack in this quarter began in the Gulf of Leyte in the central Philippines and had disastrous consequences for Japanese naval power. For they had to risk their battle fleet in a desperate attempt to break up the attack. Its repulse in a great naval battle was decisive. This action was the last stand of the Japanese navy as an organized force.

On 31 January 1945 the first convoy from Ledo across northern Burma arrived at Wanting, on the Burma-China border, and passed on its way along the Burma Road towards Chungking. The land route to China was open. After their defeat at Myitkyina the Japanese re-formed at Bhamo and for some weeks held off attacks until American-led, Chinese-manned tanks stormed the town. Then more American reinforcements poured into what had become known as the Northern Combat Area Command. A British division moved down the railway corridor, and the American Mars Task Force took the difficult route down the east of the Irrawaddy. Other forces began to comb out the Northern Shan States, and finally reached Lashio. The Japanese were retreating fast towards central Burma, where the decisive battle of 1945 was to be fought.

It was, however, from the Manipur hills and the Chindwin region that the real blow came. General Slim's Fourteenth Army carried out a masterly advance down the Chindwin to Mandalay and Meiktila in the early part of the year. Mandalay fell in March. At the beginning of April, when the Americans made their landing at Okinawa in the Liuchiu Islands and brought about the fall of the Koiso Cabinet at Tokyo, the Japanese main army in Burma was so heavily defeated at Meiktila that it began to disintegrate. Some melted into the Shan hills eastward. Others tried to get away southward across the Sittang. Their Twenty-eighth Army in Arakan began hurriedly moving out by the An and Taungup passes.

At this juncture the Burma National Army, organized and trained by the Japanese, and under the command of Aung San, went over to the Allies. Its Burmese leaders had carried on lengthy clandestine negotiations with Mountbatten, and its changeover, as the Allied army pushed rapidly down the Irrawaddy and Sittang valleys, was a carefully concerted move skilfully carried out.

The advance now became a race. Mountbatten's aim had all along been to capture Rangoon before the onset of the wet monsoon. And he achieved it. Prome was occupied before the Japanese Arakan army had extricated itself from the passes across the Yoma; its main escape route was thus sealed. Pegu was reached on 1 May, and on the following day Rangoon. The advance had been so swift that the plan for a sea-borne assault on Rangoon was rendered unnecessary. When the British advanced units arrived the Japanese had already evacuated the city.

One more major operation only had to be fought, the 'Battle of the Break-through', against 10,000 Japanese, whom General Koba collected in the Pegu Yoma from the remnants of the army moving out of Arakan and other forces on the west of the Prome–Rangoon road. It took place during the latter part of July, when the principal Allied powers were in session at Potsdam drafting their final answer to the requests for peace that Admiral Suzuki Kantaro, the new Japanese premier, had been proffering since the previous May. Thereafter it was only a matter of stamping out the resistance of outlying Japanese garrisons and chasing their forces through the mountains towards Siam.

The great gamble had failed. In May Germany had surrendered. The Americans were preparing to invade Japan. In Manchuria a million Japanese troops were awaiting a Russian declaration of war. Mountbatten's forces were preparing to land in Malaya and Sumatra. On 26 July the Allies at Potsdam published their terms for the Japanese surrender. When no answer was received the first atom bomb was dropped on Hiroshima on 6 August. Two days later Russia declared war on Japan. On 9 August an atom bomb was dropped on Nagasaki. On the following day Japan intimated her acceptance of the surrender terms.

CHAPTER 49

AFTER THE WAR, 1945–50

SOUTH-EAST ASIA before the Second World War was a little-known region to the majority of people in the West. It was completely overshadowed by India and China. The use of such terms as Further India or Indo-China to describe its mainland, and even of Indonesia or the Indian Archipelago for its island world, obscured its identity and minimized its importance. Now for a short time all that was changed. The limelight was focused upon the unfamiliar scene and broadcast announcers tried to master the strange, musical names. Burma, where the largest single land campaign was fought against the Japanese, became front-page news and figured in countless letters home. Thousands of Australian, British and Dutch families lost relatives in the labour gangs which slaved on the Burma–Thailand 'death railway'; still more over a far wider area of the world, including America and Africa, suffered bereavement through battle casualties. The post-war world, therefore, had become aware of South-East Asia as never before. And if this generalization is scarcely fair to Holland, a large proportion of whose national savings was invested in Indonesia, or to France, who regarded her Indo-Chinese empire as essential to the maintenance of her position in the world, the fact remains that their attention was concentrated solely on the countries they held.

So far as the peoples of the occupied territories were concerned, their experience of Japanese rule gave immense stimulus to their national movements. Moreover, they had witnessed a defeat of European forces by Asians which was so rapid, and at first so overwhelming, as to be almost incredible. And although the Asian victory had brought a vile tyranny such as the European had never practised, with plunder and famine instead of the much-advertised 'co-prosperity', nevertheless, with the possible exception of Malaya, it did not make them anxious for the restoration of white rule. In Indonesia, Burma and Vietnam it strengthened the desire for independence. In these countries, indeed, political passions ran so high that the hard facts of the economic situation were barely recognized.

For although their plight was desperate and measures to promote economic recovery should have been given priority over everything else, Indonesians, Burmese and Vietnamese were at one in their determination that European trade with their countries should never again be on the old footing, and in their belief that only through political independence could such an object be achieved.

(a) Malaya

Malaya's case was in many ways, but not all, exceptional. Before the war the Malays had been the least politically minded of all the peoples of South-East Asia. The British bureaucracy had been just and enlightened, and most of its members had tended to develop strong pro-Malay sympathies. During the occupation period, however, Malay national sentiment had become a reality; it was strongly anti-Chinese, and its rallying cry, 'Malaya for the Malays', transcended the particularism of the individual states. It showed itself in a most unpleasant form at the moment of Malaya's release from Japanese thraldom, when in many places Malays began to kill any Chinese on whom they could lay hands. The British military administration, which at first took over the management of the country, had to adopt stern measures to repress these outbreaks of fanaticism.

But these were not the only problems of law and order. Under the Japanese the Malay police force, which had been used against the guerrillas, had declined sadly in morale and efficiency. Firearms were easy to obtain, the Chinese secret societies had flourished, and for some time after the restoration of British rule there was an unparalleled outbreak of violent crime. Behind the scenes also the leaders of the Malayan People's Anti-Japanese Army, the M.P.A.J.A., most of whom were Communists, were making a determined bid for power. And although in December 1945 the British disbanded and disarmed them, giving each man a war gratuity of 350 dollars, their leaders resorted to the strike weapon, which they used with great effect in 1946, cashing in on the general discontent at high prices and the shortage of food.

The food problem was acute. Malaya was dependent upon supplies of imported rice, which at first were not available owing to the fall in production in Burma and the other rice-exporting countries. The government did what it could to stimulate local cultivation by means of subsidies, guaranteed prices and extensions of the irrigated areas. Rationing was imposed, and rice on the ration was sold at a price much lower than its cost. But the amount per person was much lower than had been consumed before the war. Native production, however, increased, and by 1948 was above the pre-war level.

Immense efforts were put into reconstruction. The public health services were quickly revived, hospitals were re-equipped, sanitation improved and anti-malarial measures reintroduced. They brought immediate results. In 1947, for instance, the infant mortality rate was the lowest on record. Schools were reopened. They were so overcrowded that they had to work by shifts, with one school occupying the buildings in the morning and another in the afternoon. The shortage of teachers and equipment was truly formidable, and in 1946 the number of children attending school was twice what it had been before the war.

In both Kuala Lumpur and Singapore the Education Departments went ahead with a vigorous policy of expansion which aimed at ultimately providing free primary education for all children. The creation of a common Malayan citizenship from among the diverse racial groups in the country, without which political advance towards self-government was recognized to be impossible, was the most urgent problem of the new era, and special attention was directed to the framing of an education policy which should contribute towards its solution. This involved finding some means of integrating the Chinese schools, the breeding-ground alike of Chinese nationalism and of Communism, into the general system of education. Another interesting step taken was that of making English the second language in all vernacular schools. A scheme was also worked out for combining Raffles College and the King Edward VII College of Medicine to form a university, and in October 1949 the University of Malaya commenced its first session.

Equal energy was directed to the furtherance of economic recovery. A vast programme of renovation was undertaken to put the railways, roads and harbours again into working order. The revival of the tin and rubber industries was of vital importance. The Chinese mines, dependent mainly on hand labour, got away to a quick start. But the British-owned mines, which accounted for two-thirds of the normal production, were up against serious problems. Their dredges had been destroyed or put out of action early in the war. Now a dredge cost nearly four times its pre-war price and took two years to build. Government compensation for war damage helped to the tune of 75 million dollars, but there was long delay in obtaining materials for repairs. Against a pre-war production of 80,651 tons only 8,432 tons were mined in 1946. But in the following year 36,079 tons were produced, and by 1950 the pre-war figure had been surpassed.

Rubber made a quicker recovery. The Japanese had cut down the trees on only $2\frac{1}{2}$ per cent of the total of 3,302,000 acres under cultivation. The Malays, who owned 40 per cent of the acreage, were able to start production at once. On the big European estates, however, an immense outlay on buildings and machinery was entailed, and there was an acute labour shortage. Nevertheless by 1948 the industry had recovered its pre-war status and was going ahead with trees giving a much higher yield. The Government of Britain made a large grant towards war compensation, and by 1950 rubber exports were three times their pre-war value. The total acreage under rubber was 3,359,251 and the production had risen to 692,585 tons against 372,000 tons in 1938. As tin and rubber together accounted for 86 per cent of Malaya's exports, their rapid increase was the most significant feature of her economic recovery. Moreover, she had become more important to Britain than ever before on account of her American dollar earnings. They rose from 519 millions in 1948 to 1,195 millions in 1950. But much of this increase, it must be remembered, was due to the enhanced prices of these two commodities resulting from the American rearmament programme.

During the reconstruction period much was also done to expand the production of palm-oil, copra, pineapples and tea. The forests too played their part in aiding recovery. There was a big local demand for timber for new building and repairs, while Britain's post-war housing programme caused her to make heavy purchases of Malayan light hardwoods as a substitute for softwoods from hard-currency areas.

Long before the Second World War responsible officials had been exercised in their minds concerning the constitutional development of Malaya. As early as 1880 Governor Sir Frederick Weld had made the pertinent remark that we were teaching the people of Malaya to govern under our guidance, but not to govern themselves. The experience of trying to repel the Japanese invasion with ten separate administrations in so small a country had demonstrated the inefficiency of such an arrangement at a time of crisis. The hope that other states which had accepted British protection would join the Federation had proved an illusion. In the Federation itself the problem of safeguarding the sovereignty of the sultans while developing a strong central government at Kuala Lumpur had caused strange anomalies between theory and practice.

After the First World War attempts were made to solve this intractable problem by 'decentralization'. But these were vitiated by the plain fact that from an administrative point of view what was needed was a form of union which would reduce the friction and expense of dealing with so large a number of separate administrations. Such an arrangement, however, was outside the range of practical politics. The particularism of the individual states was too strong. After interminable discussions of every aspect of the question throughout Sir Laurence Guillemard's term of office as Governor and High Commissioner, 1920–7, the Federal Council was reconstituted in 1927. The Malay rulers, who had never taken part in its discussions, withdrew from it. Their places were taken by the Principal Medical Officer, the Controller of Labour, the Director of Public Works and the Director of Education. Further unofficial members were added, and the new Council had a membership of thirteen officials and eleven unofficials. In future every Bill passed by the Council had to be signed by each of the four rulers before coming into force.

But this was not decentralization in any sense. With Guillemard's departure, says Rupert Emerson,[1] it was 'tucked away in a cubby hole'. 'There was so much money', writes Sir Richard Winstedt, 'that the Rulers felt no inclination to criticize.'[2] The great depression, however, caused decentralization to become a living issue once more. After further interminable discussions it was decided in 1936 that the post of Chief Secretary to the government was the greatest obstacle in the way, and it was accordingly abolished. The office of Federal Secretary was substituted, with precedence after that of the four Residents. His duties were those of liaison and co-ordination, while the machinery of the Federation was in future to be used merely to facilitate the transaction of business common to all four states. It was not a good arrangement, for instead of uniting the country, while safeguarding legitimate local interests, its tendency was to stimulate particularism at the expense of the common good. Moreover, it disregarded the feelings and interests of the 'immigrant races'. Victor Purcell's complaint, that the matter was dealt with as if 'the only political realities were the states, their Sultans, and the treaties with the King', has much justification, as also his charge that 'the ruling caste was emphatically "Malay-minded"'.[3]

It is against this background that the MacMichael plan for a post-war Malayan Union must be seen. During the war it seemed obvious

[1] *Malaysia*, p. 173.   [2] *Malaya and its History*, p. 90.
[3] *The Chinese in Southeast Asia*, p. 382.

to the planners of reconstruction that the great need was to promote a sense of security and common citizenship as a preparation for self-government within the British Commonwealth. The intention was excellent, but the way it was carried out caused an explosion of Malay national feeling as sudden and unexpected as the one with which a quarter of a century earlier Burma had greeted the announcement that she was to be excluded from the scope of the Indian constitutional reforms of 1921.

In the new Union all nine Malay states, together with Penang and Malacca, were to be combined to form one protectorate. Singapore was to remain a separate Crown colony. The sultan in each state would retain his throne and little else. He was to preside over a Malay Advisory Council, which would deal mainly with matters affecting the Mahommedan religion. Apart from that all power was to be concentrated in the central government at Kuala Lumpur, the State Councils would deal only with such matters as were delegated to them, and would be presided over in each case by a British Resident Councillor. MacMichael, who went to Malaya armed with special powers to investigate each sultan's conduct during the Japanese occupation and decide on his suitability to occupy his throne, was consequently able to negotiate treaties with all nine rulers, whereby they transferred their complete rights of legal sovereignty to Britain.

The other main provision of the plan related to citizenship of the Union. It was to be granted to (*a*) all persons born in the territory of the Union or in Singapore, and (*b*) immigrants who had lived there for ten out of the preceding fifteen years. Future immigrants could qualify for it after only five years' residence. Citizenship was to involve full equality of rights, including admission to the administrative services. There was to be no discrimination of race or creed.

The publication in January 1946 of a White Paper setting forth these proposals caused the storm to burst. Under the Prime Minister of Johore, Dato Onn bin Jaafar, the United Malay National Organization, U.M.N.O., sprang into being with branches everywhere. It was pledged to the task of 'warding off the devastating ignominy of race extinction'.[1] Malays wore mourning for a week and a mass non-co-operation movement was threatened. These efforts, however, had less practical effect than those of a group of ex-Malayan civil servants, including the nonagenarian Sir Frank Swettenham, who brought their influence to bear on the British government and stirred

[1] Dato Onn Bin Jaafar's words quoted by Purcell, *op. cit.*, p. 387.

up public opinion on behalf of the Malays[1] to such effect that the treaties and the scheme for a Malayan Union were alike dropped.

The British government then committed the mistake of going too far in the opposite direction. In April 1946 a Working Committee composed of representatives of the administration and U.M.N.O. was set up to draft new proposals. Later, another composed of Chinese and Indians was also set up, but only after the British government had given conditional approval of the Working Committee's proposals. In 1947 a revised constitution was drawn up on the basis of the recommendations of the two bodies. Legal sovereignty was handed back to the sultans, but they were to govern in accordance with British advice as previously. Singapore was to retain its separate status. Instead of a Union, all nine states, together with Penang and Malacca, were to form a Federation under a High Commissioner and Executive and Legislative Councils. In addition to the usual official members the Executive Council was to have unofficial members chosen from the various races in the country. The Legislative Council was to be composed of fifteen officials and sixty-one unofficial members, of whom thirty-one were to be Malays and the rest Europeans, Chinese, Indians and Eurasians. They were to be nominated by the High Commissioner at first, but as soon as possible election was to be introduced. The federal government was given very extensive powers, while those of the states were correspondingly limited.

The qualifications for Malayan citizenship were stiffened up appreciably. The people who automatically qualified for it in addition to Malays were Indians and Chinese British subjects of the second generation born in federal territory. Immigrants could become naturalized when they had lived in the Federation for at least fifteen years, if they intended to make it their permanent home.

The Malays were opposed even to this concession, since there was nothing to prevent the immigrants from retaining their original nationality while becoming citizens of Malaya. Chinese law, in fact, makes it impossible for a Chinese to divest himself of Chinese nationality. But the British government was convinced that a law permitting dual nationality was essential if the three races were to be welded together into a political unit. The main difficulty was that the Second World War had intensified national feeling. But the three races lived so closely intermingled that their co-operation must be assured if the ordinary amenities of life were to be preserved. Yet

---

[1] Winstedt in *Malaya and its History*, pp. 140-7, may be compared with Purcell, *op. cit.*, pp. 383 ff., on this subject.

one of those races was placed in a specially privileged position, for the new constitution, which came into effect on 1 February 1948, charged the High Commissioner with the responsibility of safeguarding the special position of the Malays. And in view of all the circumstances it is difficult to see what other arrangement could have been made.

The year in which the new Federation was inaugurated saw the outbreak of the Communist revolt. The Communists, who were comparatively few in numbers and almost exclusively Chinese, had received a setback to their attempt to paralyse economic recovery and discredit the government when in February 1946 firm measures were taken by the military. They thereupon went underground. Besides fomenting strikes they watched political developments with special interest, seeking to exploit any popular dissatisfaction.

The Chinese campaign against the proposals for federation in 1947 gave them a good oportunity for increasing their influence. For some months there were warnings of impending trouble. Then in June 1948 widespread outbreaks of violence occurred. European planters and tin miners and Chinese members of the Kuomintang party were murdered. This form of terrorism was intended to pave the way for revolt. The initial plan was to get a region under terrorist control and declare it an independent Communist area, then gradually to extend this over the whole country. Captured documents indicated that the declaration of a Communist Republic of Malaya was timed for 3 August 1948.

Once the government had recovered from its initial surprise its measures to deal with the threat showed the greatest energy and determination. But the Communists had laid their plans well. They had hidden large quantities of arms and their intelligence system was excellent. They split up into small groups making hit-and-run attacks and could make rings round the troops who were new to jungle war-fare and were unable to speak the vernaculars of the countryside. And the anti-Communist Chinese were in such fear of the terrorists that they paid large sums of protection money.

The recruitment of 26,000 Malay armed police and the systematic training of the troops in jungle warfare were among the measures that gradually brought the situation more or less under control by the middle of 1949. But the revolt was by no means broken, and the rapid collapse of the Kuomintang in northern China in 1948, and throughout the remainder of the country in 1949, put new heart into the Communist movement in Malaya.

Nevertheless it was a case of the revolt of a very few, never more than 7,000; and captured documents showed that the rebels had failed to win voluntary popular support and had been forced on to the defensive. On the other hand, the government's hope of victory within one year proved illusory. The Communists abandoned the more settled areas and went deeper into the jungle, whence at the time of writing they had still not been completely cleared, notwithstanding the introduction of the comprehensive Briggs Plan and the inspiring leadership of the High Commissioner, General Sir Gerald Templer.

(b) Burma

The Burmese had at first allowed themselves to hope that the nominal independence accorded them by the Japanese in 1943 might turn out to be the genuine article. They were soon disillusioned. Hence the return of the British was hailed with joy. But while they welcomed liberation from the Japanese tyranny, their experiences during the occupation period made them impatient of any form of foreign rule. At the end of the war Aung San, the commander of the Burma National Army, became the focus of nationalist aspirations, which found expression in the broad-based political organization known as the Anti-Fascist Peoples Freedom League, the A.F.P.F.L.

Aung San had sprung to fame as the organizer of a students' strike in the University of Rangoon in 1936. Thereafter he became the leader of the *Dobama Asiayone* ('We Burmans' Association), the extremist wing of the Burma Student Movement. The members of the association adopted the title Thakin ('lord'), the Burmese equivalent of the Indian 'Sahib', used as a term of respect for Europeans. Some of them were in contact with the Indian Communist Party and propagated Marxist doctrines in a small way. In 1940 some thirty of the Thakins, including Aung San, went to Japan at the invitation of the Japanese consul in Rangoon and received instruction in the role they were to play when the Japanese invaded Burma. They returned with the Japanese armies; and when Dr. Ba Maw became Adipadi, Aung San was appointed Minister of Defence, and his brother-in-law Than Tun Minister of Transport and Supply, in the Burmese Cabinet. There they were in an excellent position to organize the anti-Japanese swing of the Burma National Army. The movement was kept secret even from the Adipadi himself, who had planned for the army to detach itself from the Japanese as the British advanced down the Irrawaddy valley, but thereafter to maintain a neutral role, in the optimistic belief that he might somehow use it as a bargaining counter.

Ba Maw fled with the Japanese into Siam, leaving Aung San and the A.F.P.F.L. the most potent political force with which the British military government had to deal when it took over. The function of the military government, in which members of the administrative services who had been evacuated to India were incorporated, was to rally the personnel of the services that had remained in Burma during the occupation and re-establish administration on the old footing as soon as possible. This was carried out with such apparent success that in October 1945 civil government was officially restored. The changeover was made before effective measures to disarm the population had been taken. How unwise this was later events were amply to demonstrate.

British policy for Burma had been announced in a statement issued on 17 May 1945. This reaffirmed the intention to grant full self-government within the British Commonwealth. It envisaged a relatively short period of direct British rule in co-operation with the Burmese so that rehabilitation measures might be carried out which would in due course permit a general election to be held. Then the Constitution of 1937 would be re-established and the Burmese could begin to draw up a constitution on the basis of self-government. This would be embodied in legislation by the Imperial Parliament, and at the same time a treaty would be negotiated dealing with matters which would remain the responsibility of the British government after the grant of self-government.

Right from the start, however, the professed aim of Aung San and his party was complete independence. Dominion status did not appeal to them, for they had a deep distrust of British motives and feared that once British business interests regained their position in the nation's economy, self-government would prove illusory. They were by no means unaware of their need for British assistance, capital and expert knowledge, but they wanted to be in a position to keep it under firm control. When, therefore, the governor began to form his first ministry and offered the leaders of the A.F.P.F.L. places in it they demanded a majority of seats and the right for their representatives to accept guidance from the supreme council of the party. This was rejected, and they thereupon threw themselves into opposition.

Meanwhile Burma's progress towards recovery was held up by various difficulties. Much was done to restore road and rail transport and recondition the docks. But the much-needed relief supplies were very hard to obtain, and when the government cancelled the Japanese-issued currency the cultivators were everywhere without funds. The police were hampered by need of arms and adequate transport, and disorderly conditions militated against the revival of agriculture and local trade. The Communists were becoming active, and before long the government, instead of concentrating all its attention on the recovery programme, was forced to deal with the political issues. And Governor Dorman-Smith's manœuvres in encouraging the development of rival parties to the A.F.P.F.L. did not improve the situation.

In August 1946 General Sir Hubert Rance, who as military governor had earned the trust and goodwill of most of the Burmese, succeeded Dorman-Smith and came prepared to pursue the policy of conciliation, which was already beginning to yield good results in India. And although Aung San and his friends worked up a serious strike threat which affected the police and government officials, they were willing to enter into friendly negotiations with Sir Hubert. The result of these was that he accepted the demand for an A.F.P.F.L.-dominated Council of Ministers, and in October 1946 Aung San became its leader.

The first act of the A.F.P.F.L. on coming into power was to exclude Communists from their ranks. The maintenance of law and order, the achievement of economic stability, and the establishment of public confidence were now Aung San's responsibility, and he found that the sole aim of the Communists was revolution. This made it possible for Britain to view his demands with greater sympathy, and when in January 1947 he led a delegation to London to confer with Attlee's Labour Cabinet agreement was easily reached. There was to be a general election in the following April, and the British government bound itself to accept the verdict of the Burma electorate regarding the form of self-government. Meanwhile the ministers in the Burma Cabinet were to be given control over the armed forces and the budget.

This was a fair and reasonable agreement, honestly negotiated. It fell far short of the extravagant demands that Aung San had made as a revolutionary leader. But responsibility had caused his own understanding of the situation to develop rapidly, and he was immensely impressed with the British government's sincerity. Hence, although two of the members of his delegation—U Saw, a past premier with great ambitions, and Ba Sein, a mere demagogue—refused to be associated in the agreement, Aung San returned to Burma determined to carry it out.

The task before him was far from easy. The disorderly elements had got out of control, and the non-Burmese peoples—the Karens, Shans, Kachins, and Chins—were ready to fight rather than come under Burmese control. Britain had written into the agreement a proviso safeguarding their rights, but they were by no means re-assured. At the April general election the A.F.P.F.L. won a resounding victory, and Aung San, who more than any other Burmese leader had come to realize the need for a positive policy of conciliation towards the hill peoples, allowed them practically to write their own terms into the new constitution. The Karens alone, with the memory still

GENERAL AUNG SAN

fresh of their cruel treatment at the hands of the Burma Independence Army, remained unsatisfied. They stood out for a state of their own, disregarding the fact that with the majority of them living in the Irrawaddy and Tenasserim divisions, inextricably mixed with the Burmese, such a solution presented almost insuperable difficulties and was in any case of doubtful wisdom.

Aung San did his utmost to meet their more reasonable claims with statesmanlike patience and understanding, and had he lived would undoubtedly have succeeded in solving the problem. But on 19 July 1947 he and six of his colleagues in the Cabinet were murdered by hired assassins in the pay of the ambitious U Saw. It was a staggering blow which well explains the scepticism of many well-informed British regarding the efficacy of the method chosen for dealing with Burmese nationalist aspirations. No Burman at the time commanded such personal support or showed such gifts of leadership as Aung San, and what Burma needed more than anything else was effective leadership. The idea of a sovereign people making its will effective was entirely foreign to the political outlook of the country. Moreover, there is reason to believe that Aung San had determined to work out a settlement which would enable Burma to remain within the British Commonwealth. With him removed there was no leader left with sufficient influence to carry the country with him on such an issue. A.F.P.F.L. propaganda had always asserted with the utmost vehemence that nothing less than complete independence would satisfy Burma.

Sir Hubert Rance at once nominated Thakin Nu, vice-president of the A.F.P.F.L., as Aung San's successor. A deeply religious man who had never aspired to the position he was now called upon to occupy, he assumed the difficult task of holding his party together and saving the country from confusion. Under his leadership the Burma Constituent Assembly completed its work and on 24 September 1947 unanimously passed the new constitution. Its decision was for complete independence, and in mid-October Thakin Nu came to London to negotiate Burma's secession from the Commonwealth. The outcome was the signature on 17 October 1947 of a treaty recognizing the Republic of the Union of Burma as a fully independent state on a date to be fixed by parliament. A Burma Independence Bill was accordingly passed through parliament, and on 4 January 1948 Sir Hubert Rance formally handed over charge to the republic's first president, a Shan chieftain, the Sawbwa of Yawnghwe, Sao Shwe Thaik.

Britain made a generous financial settlement with the new state and provided a naval, military and air mission for training its armed forces. Thakin Nu on his part concluded a defence agreement whereby British forces were to have right of access to ports and airfields in Burma should she need their assistance. With an undemarcated Yunnan border, many Burmese felt it was running an unnecessary risk to assume full responsibility for defence before building up adequate armed forces.

The Nu-Attlee Agreement was violently opposed by the Communists as well as by the more irresponsible political elements which

INDEPENDENCE MONUMENT, RANGOON

the revolutionary movement had brought to birth. The A.F.P.F.L. had stirred up an agitation stronger than it could check. Disorder developed into rebellion, and the government lost control over much of the country. Rangoon itself was threatened, and when a number of Burmese battalions went over to the rebels its defence depended upon the Karen, Kachin and Chin contingents in the army. To make matters worse, in September 1948 U Tin Tut, by far the ablest and most experienced man in the government, was murdered, and with his removal the direction of affairs was left mainly in the hands of politicians whose training had been as agitators, with few oifts of statesmanship and great ignorance of administration.

PANDIT NEHRU AND U NU

The worst blow came through mismanagement of the Karen question. An attempt to disarm them caused them to rebel, and their revolt became far more dangerous than any other rebel movement. The year 1949, therefore, was a bad one. The government had effective control only in Rangoon and a few widely-scattered parts of the country. Road, rail and river communications were cut. The export of rice was less than half its pre-war amount, and national bankruptcy seemed inevitable.

The usual escape from such a state of affairs through a military dictatorship was not Burma's fate for the simple reason that her military forces were inadequate for such a purpose. Intervention by the Chinese Communists was feared, but they were too busy with their own problems; and effective Chinese military operations in Burma are not such an easy proposition as the alarmists are inclined to suggest. Burma therefore was left to work out her own salvation in her own way. Thakin Nu, through his transparent honesty and devotion to his task, gradually established confidence in the government. And as his team of young men gained experience and began to adopt a firmer front, so, little by little, their rule became more effective. By 1950 the critical corner had been turned. Since then, though serious difficulties remain, there have been indications of hopeful progress in a number of fields.

(c) French Indo-China

When in 1945 the defeat of Japan came within measurable distance many French officers in Indo-China hoped to be in a position to co-operate with Allied forces in liberating the country. The Japanese, however, forestalled such a move by staging a *coup d'état* on 10 March and taking over control from the French. They broadcast a statement that the colonial status of Indo-China had ended. Thereupon the Emperor of Annam, Bao Dai, and the Kings of Cambodia and Laos issued declarations of independence. Ho Chi Minh, the leader of the Viet Minh League, refused to recognize the emperor's declaration, and with seven provinces of Tongking under his control and an active resistance movement in Cochin China he was able to seize Hanoi as soon as the Japanese surrender was announced in August, while a national committee assumed power in Saigon.

In the previous month the Potsdam Conference had made quite different arrangements for the take-over from the Japanese. Chinese troops were to occupy the north down to the sixteenth parallel of latitude, and British troops the remainder. General Gracey, in command of the British contingent, arrived in Saigon on 13 September, and with his help the French authorities resumed control over that city and a number of others. But their writ ran no further, for the whole countryside was in the hands of nationalist guerrillas. Early in 1946 Admiral d'Argenlieu arrived as High Commissioner with General Leclerc as military commander, and the British forces were withdrawn.

In the Chinese sector above the sixteenth parallel it was quite a different story. The Chinese left Ho Chi Minh in control of the administration and refused admission to French troops. This situation continued until 28 February 1946, when a Franco-Chinese agreement

was signed under which, in return for concessions on the Yunnan–
Hanoi Railway and recognition of the special position of their nationals
in Indo-China, the Chinese agreed to withdraw their troops. Meanwhile in the previous month the French had come to terms with the
King of Cambodia whereby his kingdom was to exercise a degree of
autonomy, subject to the control of the French governor. Shortly
afterwards a similar arrangement was made with the King of Laos.

Early in March an agreement was concluded with the Vietnam government at Hanoi. France recognized the Republic of Vietnam as a free
state forming part of the Indo-Chinese Federation, which it was proposed to create, and of the French Union: a referendum was to be held
in Cochin China to decide whether it should join the republic. It was
also arranged that a further conference should be held to decide such
matters as the diplomatic relations of the republic, the future status of
Indo-China, and French cultural and economic interests in Vietnam.
This was held in April at Dalat in Cochin China, and it was at once
evident that the French interpretation of Vietnam's 'independence'
was markedly different from that of the nationalist government.

On 1 June Admiral d'Argenlieu announced the creation of an
autonomous republic of Cochin China as a provisional measure. This
evoked a storm of protest as constituting an infringement of the
agreement whereby Cochin China was to be free to decide its future
status by referendum. Thereafter things went from bad to worse.
In July a conference opened between France and Vietnam at Fontainebleau, and while it was in progress d'Argenlieu held a second
Dalat conference with representatives of Cambodia, Cochin China,
Laos and southern Annam. Vietnam was not invited to be represented.
The Vietnam delegates walked out of the Fontainebleau conference
in protest without any decision being taken, save for an agreement,
signed on 14 September, providing for a cessation of hostilities and
the settlement of a number of cultural and economic questions.

The agreement to cease hostilities was soon broken. There was
violent agitation. The Vietnamese leaders would consider nothing
less than full sovereignty and refused to budge an inch on the Cochin
China question. In November Dr. Nguyen Van Thinh committed
suicide as a protest against the 'unpatriotic' role he had found himself
forced to play as the French puppet ruler of Cochin China. Armed
uprisings brought French reprisals, and on 23 November they bombed
Haiphong, causing frightful casualties. On 19 December the Vietnamese staged a surprise attack on French garrisons in Tongking and
Annam, and full-scale war began.

France's plan for Indo-China was decided upon, in a series of
parliamentary debates in the summer of 1949, when Georges Bidault
was prime minister. The Left proposed that a federation should

BAO DAI AT THE HUÉ PALACE

precedent in North Africa, and it was the form of federation
therefore that was finally accepted by the French parliament provided
for federal bodies with purely advisory functions. The French parliament was to retain legislative power over all important matters.

France's plan for Indo-China was decided upon in a series of parliamentary debates in the summer of 1946, when Georges Bidault was prime minister. The Left proposed that a federation should gradually be formed by free negotiations with the representatives of the various states. They should be given equality of status and the right of secession. Bidault, however, insisted on the maintenance of

HO CHI MINH

French sovereignty; he argued that the recognition of dominion status after the model of the British Commonwealth would start a dangerous precedent for North Africa and Madagascar. The form of federation, therefore, that was finally accepted by the French parliament provided for federal bodies with purely advisory functions. The French parliament was to retain legislative power over all important matters.

On 24 March 1947 Ho Chi Minh made a firm statement of Vietnamese policy. If France would do to Vietnam, he said, what the United States had done to the Philippines and Britain to India the Vietnamese people would bring to France friendly co-operation. If not, they would continue to resist. To this the reply of d'Argenlieu's successor, Émile Bollaert, was: 'We shall remain. . . . The Constitution makes the French Union, of which Indo-China is an integral part, an institution of the Republic.'

The fact that Ho Chi Minh was a Communist was naturally a major obstacle to a settlement. Only ten of the 300 members of the Vietnamese National Assembly were known to be Communists, though the key positions in the administration were thought to be Communist-held. The movement, however, was primarily nationalist and depended for its main support on non-Communist nationalists. It has been the tragedy of Vietnam that its nationalist movement came under Communist direction. The suggestion has been made that in his anxiety to reach an agreement with France Ho Chi Minh was willing to forswear his Communism. But France would not enter into negotiations with him.

On 10 September 1947 France made a 'last appeal' to the rebels in Indo-China. She offered what she called a large degree of native control over native affairs, subject to Indo-China remaining in the French Union, with French control over military installations and the direction of foreign policy. An amnesty was to be proclaimed and prisoners exchanged. The appeal significantly made no reference to the question of recognizing Ho Chi Minh's government, or even of negotiating with it. Naturally, therefore, the Vietnam government rejected it. At the same time it appealed to the United Nations with the offer of peace on the basis of the unification of the three Vietnamese-speaking regions of Tongking, Annam and Cochin China into an independent state within the Indo-Chinese Federation and the French Union. France, however, successfully blocked the appeal.

The French made repeated overtures to Bao Dai to head a pro-French government in Vietnam. At first he refused to commit himself, but they went ahead with their preparations and on 20 May 1948 proclaimed the 'Central Provisional Vietnam Government' with Nguyen Van Xuan, the head of the French-sponsored state of Cochin China, as its president. Finally on 8 March 1949 Bao Dai was persuaded to become the head of a new French 'dominion' composed of Cochin China, Annam and Tongking, and officially took over on 30 December. It was, of course, yet another bogus version of 'independence'. Ho Chi Minh's position was in no way weakened, in spite of the fact that he had well over 100,000 of France's best troops fighting against him. He still held most of Tongking; elsewhere French troops occupied the cities and maintained some lines of communication. The economic life of the country was dislocated, and the strain on France herself was more than she could bear.

One of the first acts of the Communist government of China in the sphere of foreign affairs was, on 19 January 1950, to recognize the Viet Minh government of Ho Chi Minh as the sovereign power in Vietnam. Russia and her European satellites quickly followed suit. So the tragedy of Vietnam took a new turn, becoming merged into the 'cold war' between the American-led states and the Soviet bloc.

On 6 February 1950 Britain and the United States accorded formal recognition to Bao Dai. Both had at the outset sympathized with the Vietnam nationalist movement. Now France was to receive more and more American aid to continue the struggle, and Indo-China to become a vital outpost in the strategy of the Pentagon. Thus the general direction of policy slipped out of French hands into those of the State Department at Washington.

(d) Indonesia

Japan announced her willingness to accept the Potsdam terms on 10 August 1945. Two days earlier, at the invitation of Marshal Terauchi, the commander-in-chief of the Japanese armies in the southern regions, Sukarno, Hatta and a third Indonesian leader, Wediodiningrat, arrived in Saigon to discuss a declaration of Indonesian independence. It was arranged that a Commission for the Preparation of Independence should meet on 19 August in Batavia. The delegates returned to Java on 14 August. On the next day there were rumours that Japan had capitulated. The commission therefore got hurriedly to work, and on the 17th the proclamation of independence was issued. Not till five days later was Japan's capitulation officially announced by the Japanese commander in Java.

The original Allied arrangement had been for the American forces to occupy Indonesia. But this had to be abandoned, and instead the task was assigned to the British. The sudden collapse of Japan came so soon after this change of plan that it caught the British unprepared. So severe was the shortage of transport that no troops could be moved in until 29 September. Their task, when they began to arrive, was to disarm and repatriate 283,000 Japanese and protect 200,000 Dutch

PRESIDENT SUKARNO (WITH HADJI AGUS SALIM IN THE BACKGROUND)

and Allied prisoners of war and internees. To carry it out properly their numbers were at first far too few. It is not to be wondered at, therefore, that the British commander, General Christison, finding Sukarno's republican government in apparent control, requested its co-operation. And although his colleague, Vice-Admiral Patterson, stated clearly that the British did not recognize the Sukarno regime, his action was taken as tantamount to *de facto* recognition and many waverers of the pre-war administration decided to throw in their lot with the republic.

A few days later Dr. van Mook arrived in Batavia. He was prepared to open negotiations on the basis of Queen Wilhelmina's 1942 broadcast, but he announced that he would on no account parley with Sukarno as a collaborationist. On 14 November Sukarno was replaced as the head of the republican government by Sutan Sjahrir, a moderate, an intellectual, and one who had 'gone to the mountains' during the Japanese period. Informal discussions, therefore, were able to begin. A week before the change of government The Hague had announced its basic programme in vague terms that were already half a century out of date. Indonesia was to be a partner in a kingdom of the Netherlands so constructed that the national self-respect of all its participating peoples would be assured. Sukarno had summarily rejected this. Sjahrir in his turn announced on 4 December 1945 that his government's basic demand was for Dutch recognition of the Indonesian Republic.

Meanwhile the British and Dutch forces went steadily and carefully ahead with the occupation of the islands, while the republic on its side expanded its forces. There were frequent ugly scenes and clashes. Heavy fighting took place when the British landed at Surabaya, and shortly after taking over General Mallaby was murdered. Such was the state of disorder that Dutch women and children could not be evacuated from many of the inland concentration camps where the Japanese had herded them.

On 10 February 1946 the Dutch government made a detailed statement of its policy and offered to discuss it with authorized representatives of the republic. It proposed to set up a Commonwealth of Indonesia, composed of territories with varying degrees of self-government, and to create an Indonesian citizenship for all persons born there. Internal affairs were to be dealt with by a democratically elected parliament, in which Indonesians would have a substantial majority. The ministry would be in political harmony with parliament but would have a representative of the Crown at its head. The different regions of Indonesia would be linked together in a federal structure and the Commonwealth would become a partner in the Dutch Kingdom. The Netherlands would support Indonesia's application for membership of the United Nations Organization.

Soon afterwards Sjahrir headed a small Indonesian delegation which went to confer with the Dutch government at The Hague. Again he made it clear that the starting-point for negotiations must be the recognition of the republic as a sovereign state. On that basis Indonesia would be willing to enter into close relations with the Netherlands and would co-operate in all fields. Thereupon the Dutch government offered a compromise: it was willing to recognize the republic as a unit of the federative state to be created in conformity with the declaration of 10 February. In addition it offered to recognize the *de facto* rule of the republic over those parts of Java and Madura not already under the protection of Allied troops. As Sjahrir was unable to accept these terms, the conference broke up and he and his colleagues returned home.

In June 1946 a crisis occurred in the government of the republic. The Communists, under Tan Malaka, made an attempt to overthrow the Cabinet by kidnapping Sjahrir and several of his colleagues. The move, however, was defeated by the prompt action of Sukarno as president of the republic. He proclaimed a state of emergency and for some weeks exercised dictatorial powers. In the meantime, while negotiations were at a standstill, the Dutch had assumed control over Borneo and the Great East. In July a conference of representatives of these territories met at Malino, in Celebes, under Dr. van Mook and recommended the organization of the whole of Indonesia into a federation with four parts: Java, Sumatra, Borneo, and the Great East.

In August the Dutch government made another attempt to break the impasse by appointing three commissioners-general to go to Java and assist van Mook in new discussions with representatives of the republic. A conference between the two sides was held in October and November under the neutral presidency of the British special commissioner, Lord Killearn, at the hill station of Linggadjati, near Cheribon. After considerable pressure—notably British—from abroad, an agreement was reached on 15 November. The Dutch government recognized the government of the republic as exercising *de facto* authority over Java, Madura, and Sumatra. The two governments were to co-operate in establishing a sovereign democratic state on a federal basis to be called the United States of Indonesia. Of this Borneo and the Great East would form component parts. A constituent assembly was to come into being, composed of democratically elected representatives of the republic and the other component parts. The United States of Indonesia was in turn to form part of a Netherlands-Indonesian Union together with the Netherlands, Surinam and Curaçao. This would promote joint interests in foreign relations, defence, finance, and economic and cultural matters. The United States of Indonesia would apply for membership of UNO. Finally any dispute arising from the agreement was to be settled by arbitration.

There was considerable opposition to the agreement in both the Dutch parliament and the Central Indonesian National Committee, but in December 1946 it was passed by both, and on 25 March 1947 was signed at Batavia. It had been difficult enough to reach an agreement, but under the troubled conditions prevailing, and with frequent outbreaks of violence, it was supremely difficult to put it into practice. The Dutch were sincere in their intention to carry it out, but they did not believe that the republic seriously intended to do so. The important Masjumi Party, representing Moslem religious interests, was opposed to it and the republican government could not accept the

Dutch assumption that until the projected United States was actually established the Netherlands government was the sovereign power throughout Indonesia.

The Dutch accused the republic of not keeping its word, and on 27 May 1947 sent their demands in the form of an ultimatum. When a satisfactory reply was not forthcoming they proceeded to 'restore order' by 'police action'. Their troops occupied important areas of Java, Madura and Sumatra and cut off the republican forces into small isolated segments. While fighting was still in progress the United Nations Security Council, at the instance of India and Australia, issued a cease-fire order on 1 August, and shortly afterwards set up a Committee of Good Offices, composed of representatives of Australia, Belgium and the United States, to arbitrate in the dispute.

A conference took place in the United States warship *Renville* and resulted in another agreement, accepted by the disputants on 17 January 1948. There was to be a truce which provided for the establishment of a demilitarized zone. The United States of Indonesia was to be set up, but on different lines from the Linggadjati arrangements, for plebiscites were to be conducted to determine whether the various groups in the main islands wished to join the republic or some other part of the projected federation. Dutch sovereignty was to remain over Indonesia until it was transferred to the United States of Indonesia.

The *Renville* agreement, however, was no more successful than the one negotiated at Linggadjati. Both sides accused each other of violations of the truce, and the Indonesians accused the Dutch of establishing a blockade with the intention of forcing them to surrender. In July 1948 the Good Offices Committee, which had remained on the spot to supervise the implementation of the agreement, reported that the Indonesian complaints were substantially true. The Dutch then raised the Communist bogey. They asserted that the republic was in Communist hands. This led to an immediate purge by the republic of its Communist elements. Still the Dutch were not satisfied. In December 1948 negotiations broke down completely and they again resorted to 'police action'. They occupied the remainder of republican territory and clapped the leaders of its government in gaol.

This action caused serious agitation not only in the ranks of the United Nations but also throughout Asia. The Asian Conference, which met at New Delhi, asked the Security Council to intervene once more. In view of the pressure from many quarters the Security Council again took action. It ordered a cease-fire and called upon the Dutch to return the republican capital of Jogjakarta in central Java. The Dutch obeyed the order, and once again the seemingly interminable discussions began with the republican leaders. In May they agreed to permit the republic to be reconstituted as a part of the United States of Indonesia, and in July Jogjakarta was handed over.

By this time trouble had arisen in a new direction: the non-republican territories had begun to press for the establishment of the interim government provided for in the Linggadjati agreement. The state of East Indonesia took the lead, and the agitation showed that there was widespread suspicion of the republic, in which Javanese interests predominated. The suggestion was made that the federation should be completed, with or without the republic. This did not mean that these territories wanted the continuance of Dutch rule. It showed that the Indonesian question was not to be solved by dealing with the republic in the expectation that the rest of Indonesia would toe the line.

The attempt at a solution by force had failed. The Dutch felt deeply aggrieved at the extent to which their actions had turned world opinion against them. There was a strong revulsion of feeling in Holland in favour of a round-table settlement which would satisfy the aspirations of the Indonesian peoples. A conference accordingly opened at The Hague on 23 August 1949 to arrange for the transfer of sovereignty. The Netherlands government, the republic, and the member states outside the republic were all represented and had the assistance of the United Nations Committee for Indonesia. Dutch policy now was to grant independence, not grudgingly but, as Dr. van Mook puts it, 'with good grace and liberality'.

On 2 November agreement was reached; on 27 December the provisional government of the new national state was constituted. Mr. Sukarno became its president, with Mr. Mohammed Hatta as its prime minister. The United States of Indonesia was constituted as a sovereign federal republic of sixteen states enjoying equal partnership with Holland under the Netherlands Crown. A system of co-operation with Holland by consultation was worked out and embodied in the agreement, and the Netherlands government made generous offers of assistance to its new partner.

Judged in the best light, the Dutch plan was 'to achieve a sufficient measure of internal security and economic reconstruction *before* the United States of Indonesia was to be declared independent',[1] But

[1] Van Mook, *op. cit.*, p. 262.

nationalist sentiment takes little heed of such things when they are dictated by an external authority, and under post-war conditions in South-East Asia few people believed that once European authority was re-established its promises of future independence would be honoured.

(e) Siam

Siam, although Japan's ally and technically at war with the Allies, found her position little better than that of a conquered country. Her trade ceased, the Japanese confiscated whatever they required for their war effort, and completely failed to supply her with either the textiles or the machinery that she so badly needed. These facts, together with P'ibun's harsh treatment of officials who refused co-operation, aroused so much opposition to his regime that as soon as it became obvious that the Japanese were losing the war his government collapsed, in July 1944.

Pridi now became the real head of the government, but exercised his power through his friend Khuang Aphaiwong, who was prime minister until August 1945. At the end of the war the most urgent problem was that of the readjustment of relations with the victorious Allies. Khuang Aphaiwong fell foul of Pridi by attempting an independent line of his own. In September, therefore, he was dismissed and his place given to Seni Pramoj, who had been leader of the Free Thai Movement in the United States during the war and was now considered the most acceptable man for bringing about reconciliation with the Allies.

Pridi had already been paving the way towards the re-establishment of good relations. He had denounced Siam's declarations of war on the Allies, offered to return the territories annexed by P'ibun from French Indo-China, and suggested that disputed boundary questions should be referred to the United Nations. British commercial interests had suffered heavy losses in Siam, and there was naturally a demand for compensation. But unofficial American pressure was brought to bear, which caused her to relax her demands. The United States had never recognized the Siamese declaration of war and was consequently in a good position to advance her interests at the expense of Britain, who had done so. Britain's interests in Siam were much greater than America's but her claims for war damage brought constant American intervention in order to assure most-favoured-nation treatment to American trade. The post-war period therefore saw an immense growth of American influence in Siam. America had dollars to offer and wished to act the part of rich uncle. Britain, impoverished by her war efforts, was in no position to compete.

France would not resume friendly relations on any other terms than the retrocession of the territories yielded by Vichy in May 1941. The United States again acted as mediator. The matter was also discussed in the United Nations before final settlement was reached at Washington on 17 November 1946. In the following month the much-disputed territories were returned to Indo-China and a conciliation commission was appointed to examine the ethnic, geographic and economic questions involved. Its report showed clearly that Siam had no real claim to the territories, but recommended that suitable arrangements should be made for her to receive her due share of the superabundant supplies of fish from the Great Lake.

The signing of the Franco-Siamese agreement removed one great obstacle in the way of Siam's membership of the United Nations. France agreed to sponsor her application. But Russia now threatened to obstruct her election unless she annulled her law against Communism and resumed diplomatic relations. Siam's opportunism was again equal to the emergency: she accepted Russia's terms. Russia therefore held her hand and Siam was received into membership by the General Assembly of 1947.

Siam's chief internal post-war problem was the instability of her governments. Seni's government lasted until only just after the British-Siamese agreement of 1 January 1946. He had little administrative experience and no idea how to handle the various political forces in the country. Pridi therefore tried Khuang Aphaiwong again as prime minister. But he lasted only until the following March, when Pridi himself took over the post.

During his premiership the young King Ananda was found dead on 9 June 1946 with a bullet-wound in his forehead. His death was a mystery that has never been satisfactorily cleared up. The commission of enquiry could not decide as between suicide, accident or murder. He was succeeded by his younger brother, the present King Phumiphon Adundet, then being educated in Switzerland.

In the following August Pridi handed over the premiership to a former colleague, Thamrong Nawasawat, who held office until 8 November 1947, when a military *coup d'état* swept away Pridi's authority and placed P'ibun once more in power. At the end of the war he and a number of his colleagues had been arrested as war criminals. The court, however, decided that there was no law under which they could be tried, and they were accordingly released. P'ibun then began patiently and warily to build up his strength. The army was behind him, and he was regarded as the strong man who could give political stability. On both sides of Siam, in Burma on the one hand and Vietnam on the other, the Communist challenge to established authority was causing paralysis. Down in Malaya also the Communist threat was clearly to be seen.

When P'ibun decided that he could act without risk of serious external repercussions his one-day revolution was bloodless. He issued a new constitution, promised a general election in the near future, and installed Khuang Aphaiwong as interim prime minister. The election, held in January 1948, gave him the mandate he required for going ahead. He showed respect for world opinion by hiding his military dictatorship with the utmost care behind a ministry of all the talents. The chief difficulty was Pridi, who, it was suggested, might call in Chinese Communist or Viet Minh help in order to regain political power. But Siam became too hot for him. The new government decided that King Ananda had been murdered. Among others Pridi was accused of complicity and his arrest was ordered. He disappeared, however, and so effectively that in August 1948 no one knew his whereabouts.

P'ibun managed successfully to hold on to power. Shortly after winning the general election he took over the premiership himself. He revived his previous policy of modernism and launched a comprehensive scheme for the improvement of secondary education. But his chief efforts went towards strengthening Siam's military forces and building a new military city just outside the old town of Lopburi, where one may still see the ruins of King Narai's palace and Constant Phaulkon's mansion in close proximity to Mon-Khmer temples reminiscent of a time before the T'ai had set foot in that region.

In 1950, where this survey ends, he had survived several attempts to unseat him, and, compared with Burma, Vietnam and Malaya, Siam appeared like an oasis of calm, contentment and prosperity. Pridi was still in exile, and his sole chance of returning, it was thought, would be through a revolution supported by the Chinese minority or by an invasion from Communist China. Beneath the surface all was not so calm and contented. The large Chinese community, with its immense share in the country's commerce, had been deeply affected by the Communist victory in China, and to many Siamese it appeared to be more than ever a threat to the nation's security.

(f) The Philippines

In the Philippines, when the Japanese surrendered, the ruin and destruction everywhere were appalling, and famine and epidemics rampant. A vast amount of physical capital had been destroyed, and the leaping inflation caused by the 'mickey-mouse money' put into circulation by the Japanese had raised the cost of living to 800 per cent of the pre-war level. The American army did much to alleviate the immediate distress, re-establish order and reopen schools and communications. In the American plans for the invasion of Japan, that the atomic bomb rendered unnecessary, Luzon was a staging-base, and this meant that everything possible was done to restore its transport facilities, electric power, water supplies and sanitation, and to provide for the supply and accommodation of the troops. This itself made a substantial contribution towards rehabilitation. The army through its Civil Affairs Program provided food, clothing, housing and medical care where they were needed.

When the Commonwealth Government was re-established on 27 February 1945, this army relief work was rapidly cut down and the responsibility shifted to the United Nations Relief and Rehabilitation Administration (UNRRA). But UNRRA's emergency operations were inadequate to meet the full requirements of relief, and its policy was against using its resources to help an area whose government commanded enough foreign exchange to be able to pay for what it needed. The monetary policy of the Commonwealth, however, was controlled by the United States, who therefore had to come to its aid. This it did to the extent of 72 million dollars, a sum made up of remissions of certain taxes on Philippine imports into America, which were being held for future use in helping the Philippines to adjust their economy to the loss of American trade preferences. One of the most pressing problems was that of the Huks. MacArthur had dispersed them and gaoled Luis Taruc and Casto Alejandrino. The United States military police also had helped the Filipino constabulary and the landlords' private armies—known as 'civilian guards' and 'temporary police'—to restore order. But a well-armed group of Hucs had gone to the mountains, and with the departure of the American army they returned to central Luzon, 'the rice-bowl of the Philippines', and began to regain control.

At the first post-war general election, held on 23 April 1946, the peasantry of central Luzon supported the Democratic Alliance Party, and among those elected from the area were the Huk leaders Luis Taruc, who had been released, and Jesus Lava. They and five other successful

Democratic Alliance candidates were, however, refused admission to the House of Representatives on the grounds that they had used fraud and violence to secure election. Actually this was merely a specious excuse, as will be seen below. The consequence of this arbitrary act was serious: the Huk movement received an entirely new lease of life and was able to defy all attempts by government troops to suppress it.

The election saw the split of the old Nacionalista Party, with President Osmeña leading one wing and Manuel Roxas the other. Roxas had the support of MacArthur and a number of important Americans. He declared himself a liberal, and built up a party machine that was successful in carrying him and his followers to victory after an election campaign notable for its bitterness. He himself won the presidency by a very narrow margin of votes. His party, however, had a comfortable majority in both houses of Congress. His close associate Elpidio Quirino was elected vice-president, so that on 4 July 1946, when the independent Republic of the Philippines was inaugurated, they were the first heads of its administration.

Roxas's first concern after his election was with the economic arrangements for the new state. The American Congress had embodied these in two acts, both passed in 1946, the Philippine Trade Act, that came to be known as the 'Bell Act', and the Philippine Rehabilitation Act, subsequently known as the 'Tydings Act'. The Bell Act laid down that from 1946 to 1954 the Philippines were to have eight years of duty-free imports into America, subject to certain quotas. Then from 1954 to 1974 Philippine products entering America were to pay a graduated amount of duty beginning at 5 per cent of the American tariff and rising subsequently by 5 per cent annually until it reached the full amount of the American tariff in 1974. The quotas were as follows: raw sugar 952,000 tons, refined sugar 58,000 tons, hemp 6 million lb, rice 1,040,000 lb, cigars 200 million, tobacco 6 million lb, copra oil 200,000 tons and mother-of-pearl buttons 850,000 gross. From 1954 they were to be reduced by 5 per cent annually. There was to be no restriction upon the entry of American products into the Philippines. The Philippines were to pledge themselves not to levy export duties. They were to retain the exchange value of the peso at the rate of 2 pesos to one dollar, and not to suspend convertibility without the agreement of the United States President. They were also to accept a 'parity clause' providing that Americans in the Philippines were to have equal civil rights with Filipinos, i.e. in the exploitation of the natural resources of the country. Professor Frank Golay has dubbed these last three provisions 'obnoxious infringements of Philippine sovereignty'.[1] They caused much heart-burning in the Philippines.

The Tydings Act dealt with compensation for war damage. The United States War Damage Corporation had estimated the total damage in the Philippines, in terms of 1939 values, at 800 million dollars. The Tydings Law, which was before Congress at the time of the Philippine general election, provided for an outlay of 620 million dollars by the United States Treasury, of which 400 million dollars was earmarked for private compensation and 120 million dollars for the restoration of public property and essential services. The remaining 100 million dollars represented the value of the United States surplus property (excluding military weapons and munitions) that was to be transferred to the Philippine government. In addition, the act provided for extensive United States technical assistance to the Philippines. It made the stipulation, however, that war-damage payments in excess of 500 dollars were to be paid only after acceptance of the Bell Act by the Philippine Congress. It was a bitter pill for the Filipinos to swallow, though heavily sugar-coated. 'Diabolical' was the epithet applied by one Filipino speaker to the Bell Act. The free entry of American products seemed calculated to prevent the creation of national industries. Worse still, Filipino pride was hurt by the need to amend Article XIII of their constitution, which reserved the utilization of the natural resources of their country to Filipino citizens.

But the Filipino sugar interests were determined to secure the acceptance of the Bell Act; in their view the rehabilitation of the sugar industry depended upon their sugar having a tariff-free market in the United States. The amendment had to be passed by a three-quarters majority of their Congress, and Roxas's Liberal Party were only able to command enough votes by the ruse of refusing to allow ten of their opponents to take their seats, three Nacionalista Senators and the seven members of the Democratic Alliance, whose exclusion from the House of Representatives has already been mentioned. At the national plebiscite, held in March 1947 to confirm the amendment, only just over 40 per cent of the electorate voted; those who did, voted in its favour by an overwhelming majority.

Independence, it has been said, fell like a ripe fruit into the lap of the Filipinos; but their relief at the American departure was mixed with some regret, for the Americans left them unpleasant tasks to perform. The repression of the Huks was one of these. In the summer

[1] Frank H. Golay, *The Philippines, Public Policy and National Economic Development*, Ithaca, N.Y., 1961, p. 64.

of 1946 Luis Taruc attempted to negotiate a cease-fire with President Roxas. But the negotiations failed over the question of the surrender of arms by the rebels. Roxas then adopted a 'mailed-fist' policy far more ruthless than anything the Americans could have carried out. It was unsuccessful, as was also the attempt made at the same time to reduce the landlords' exactions from their tenants. In an earlier chapter we have seen that in the great majority of cases the tenant had to hand over more than half his crop to the landlord. He borrowed at rates varying from 200 to 500 per cent per annum. In 1946 the law of 70–30 was passed raising the tenant's share of his crop to 70 per cent and reducing the landlord's to 30 per cent. It was, however, utterly ineffective, for it was everywhere violated. The only effective law, it has been said, was the goodwill of the landlord. Besides, nothing was done to curb usury, and the tenant had no capital with which to purchase manure or up-to-date implements. Seventy-eight per cent of the cultivators used no manure. Until problems such as these were tackled honestly and intelligently, the Hukbalahap movement and communism could never be defeated. But while the Liberal Party was in power the appalling decline in public morality, which had become so marked under the Japanese, went farther than ever. The ill-health within the Filipino society caused by the open sore of peasant grievances was a major factor in building up a crisis, that became so acute by the middle of the year 1950, that, in Professor Golay's words, 'the continuity of the Philippine state was in question'.[1]

The independence accorded by the United States to the Philippines was in its early days quite unreal. The Americans retained missions of every sort in the country, missions for the distribution of war-damage compensation, for the working out of development plans, for the provisional upkeep of the information and security services, for the reform of education, and so on. What caused the greatest heart-burning to the Filipinos, however, was the Military Bases Agreement of March 1947, whereby America received a 99-year lease of twenty-three bases in the Philippines, with full legal jurisdiction over them. This included jurisdiction over Filipinos in the case of a large number of offences, and gave rise to controversy within a very short time.

As early as 1948 it was realized that the situation in the new republic was far from satisfactory. There were serious doubts about three matters of vital importance, the Philippine government's ability to deal with the Huks, its ability to build an economy capable of subsistence when American aid ceased, and its ability to purge itself of corruption.

[1] *Ibid.*, p. 59.

At the moment when they were being voiced in the American press Roxas suddenly died on 15 April and was succeeded by Vice-President Quirino. His early acts seemed to indicate a new determination to tackle the big problems. He set up a council of action for social progress, a council of labour, a bank of credit for agricultural co-operatives, and rural banks. He called off Roxas's unsuccessful campaign against the Huks and tried a new approach. He offered Taruc an amnesty if his troops would lay down their arms. Taruc accepted, and an accord was signed at Manila. Taruc himself then took the seat in the House of Representatives, which he had not been allowed to occupy in 1946. But once more things went wrong, and it was over the arms question. Taruc suddenly left Manila accusing the government of duplicity, and the struggle began again in a far more terrible form. Taruc announced his membership of the Communist Party, and Quirino began an all-out drive against the Huks. He appointed Ramon Magsaysay Minister of Defence and placed him in charge of the operations. Magsaysay's efforts met with remarkable success. In October 1950 the capture of practically all the central direction of the movement brought disaster to a big Huk operation with heavy casualties. The movement was disorganized, and for the time being had to go underground.

But the economic situation continued to deteriorate, prices of basic exports such as hemp and copra went down, there was an adverse balance of trade which constantly mounted, deficit budgets were the order of the day, the cost of living went up, and there was unemployment. Professor Golay, in examining the crises of the period from 1946 to 1950, strongly criticizes the administration's irresponsible policy.[1] He describes the period as one of 'economic and emotional binge'. 'By the end of 1949,' he writes, 'the government seemed willing to let the military go unpaid and the educational system wither for want of funds, and even to succumb to the Huk rebellion, rather than face up to minimum responsibility for governmental functions.'[2] The position of the Philippines in July 1946 for rehabilitation was favourable, he declares. The United States was committed to heavy war-damage payments, and the country's external security was guaranteed, so that there was no need for heavy expenditure on defence. Moreover, the economy was expanding. In 1949 production, which in 1946 had been only 40 per cent of the 1937 level, had recovered to 91 per cent, and the national income was rising. Why then this series of crises?

Much of the explanation lay in the refusal of the government to levy adequate taxes, he claims, and in its failure to collect even existing

---

[1] *Ibid.*, pp. 68–71. [2] *Ibid.*, p. 71.

taxes. Against a revenue of 100 million dollars in 1940, the 1945–6 figure was only 53 million, one-third of which came from cigarettes; and there was a six-fold inflation compared with 1940. The weakness of the administration is shown by the fact that the estimates for the war-profits tax assessed some 30,000 individuals and corporations as liable, whereas three months after the date for the receipt of the returns only 1,920 had come in, and of these 1,440 claimed no liability. The average government revenue for the five post-war years was 294 million pesos, the average expenditure 376 million. Government expenditure was only 6·8 per cent of the national income, but the tax revenue no more than 4·5 per cent. Among other causes of the crisis Professor Golay would include the restoration of the pre-war agricultural tenures and of the export economy of primary products, which bred a sense of frustration, the deterioration in public morality shown in the scandals in the handling of the disposal of surplus property, in the visas for Chinese immigrants and in corruption in import licensing, and the disastrous decline in faith in the integrity of the government.

So serious was the situation in 1950 that President Truman sent out an Economic Survey Mission under Daniel W. Bell. This reported that although something like 4 billion pesos had been invested in equipment, stocks and construction, this had involved no more than the necessary restoration and reconstruction. Production in 1950, it pointed out, was about the same as in 1937, but the population was 25 per cent larger, and there was a dangerous import surplus which was being financed by considerable drawing upon foreign exchange reserves. The mission formulated a new economic policy for the Philippine Government, and recommended the grant of United States aid to the tune of 250 million dollars to finance it.

The crisis in external payments was brought to an end by the imposition of exchange and import controls recommended by the Bell Mission. But the solution of that problem intensified the trouble in another quarter, for a traffic in import licences grew up which brought windfalls to the operators, while at the same time imports cost more though reduced in amount. And there were further scandals in the administration of exchange control. The changes, however, that were introduced into fiscal adminstration at the recommendation of the Bell Mission, did indeed go some way towards solving the problems which they were designed to combat; a new period of greater legislative and administrative responsibility dawned. But Filipino disillusionment increased.

The scandals in the administration brought a serious crisis in the

Liberal Party at the Presidential election of November 1949. Avelino, the president of the Senate, had been deposed for trafficking in American stocks. He tried to turn the tables on President Quirino by instituting impeachment procedure against him for abuse of power, violation of the constitution and malversation of funds. When the House of Representatives threw out the measure, Avelino created his own party and became a candidate for the presidency. The Nacionalista Party put up José P. Laurel as its candidate, and there was a three-cornered fight of unexampled spitefulness. Quirino won; his party machine decided the issue 'with armed men, money and few scruples', writes David Wurfel.[1] One-fifth of his votes came from fraudulent registration, fraudulent counting, and intimidation of voters.[2]

[1] David Wurfel, 'The Philippines' in G. McT. Kahin (ed.), *Governments and Politics of Southeast Asia*, 1959, p. 443.
[2] *Ibid., loc. cit.*

CHAPTER 50

INDEPENDENCE

(a) General questions

THE nineteen-fifties saw greater political changes in South-East Asia than any other previous decade in its history. When they dawned, the Philippines, Burma and Indonesia had just achieved independence. The states forming French Indo-China followed in 1954, when the kingdoms of Cambodia and Laos became independent in fact, and not merely in name, and Vietnam was divided at the 17th parallel of latitude into two independent states, the Democratic Republic of Vietnam in the north, and South Vietnam, initially under the one-time emperor of Annam, Bao Dai. In 1957 the Federation of Malaya achieved independence in the British Commonwealth by agreement with Britain, and in June 1959 Singapore, which had been excluded from the Federation, was granted internal self-government. Thus, whereas Thailand up to the Japanese invasion had been the only independent state, with the rest of South-East Asia under four Western imperial powers, now save for the British parts of Borneo, Portuguese Timor and Dutch Western New Guinea the imperial régimes had disappeared, and their places had been taken by independent states.

This new world of South-East Asia, created through the triumph of nationalism against foreign domination, was itself in a new setting. North-westwards of it were the newly independent states of India, Pakistan and Ceylon. Northwards of it lay Communist China, with a strength and an awareness of the outside world such as it had not shown since the early Ming period. In South-East Asia the Chinese question-mark was beginning to overshadow every other issue and complicate the internal affairs of the newly-independent states. With the coming of independence to India Mr. Nehru began to bid for the leadership of the emerging nations in South-East Asia, and much was said of their cultural ties with India. Nehru called an Asian Relations Conference in 1947 at New Delhi, a second one in January 1949 in support of Indonesian resistance to the Dutch, and a third early in 1954 to demand a cease-fire in French Indo-China. But the sentiment of independence was too strong for him, and the plans for a permanent organization, discussed at the first conference, came to nothing.

But if the South-East Asians did not want Indian domination, how-ever peaceful, still less did they want to bow the knee to China. Before World War II she had been separated from them by a screen of Euro-pean governments; and she was weak, and harried by Japan. With the coming of independence, however, a new China came into direct con-tact with them, exploiting the prestige that her progressive domestic policy gave her, and conducting a trade drive to impress them. At first their anti-colonial sentiment clouded their judgment of her in-tentions; and when Premier Chou En-lai in 1954 at a meeting with Nehru pledged himself to maintain the five principles of co-existence, showed sweet reasonableness at Bandung in 1955, and urged the over-seas Chinese to abide by the laws of the countries in which they lived and refrain from political activities, South-East Asian uneasiness re-garding Chinese policy was considerably reduced.

South-East Asian fears of China arose largely from three sources; (a) China's traditional claims to overlordship and her more recent claims to frontier territories, (b) communism and (c) the potential threat to independence of the ten million Chinese living in South-East Asian countries. From very early days, as we have seen, South-East Asian rulers have been encouraged to send missions to Peking and to seek recognition of the emperor. The Chinese records showed this relationship as one of overlord-vassal, but such was not the view of the rulers themselves, one of whose aims was the establishment of profitable trade with China. In modern times Chinese overlordship was really a myth which China of the Ch'ing period cultivated, along with her excessive cultural pride, in response to the great changes brought by the Western impact upon Asia. It may have influenced the outlook of the early Kuomintang leaders, but Communist China does not seem to have paid much attention to it so far. On the other hand China's historic concern has been over the security of her frontiers and the main-tenance of stable conditions beyond. Hence the possibility of her military intervention has caused acute apprehension in South-East Asia. There were at one time indications that she was toying with the idea of pressing the fantastic Kuomintang claims to territories beyond the Yunnan frontiers,[1] but actually realism was the prevailing note in carrying out the frontier settlement with Burma.

At the turn of the half-century communism was one of the most pressing questions in South-East Asia. Malaya was in the throes of a communist rebellion. In Burma a communist rebellion, small in itself,

[1] On this subject see J. Siguret, *Territoires et Populations des Confins du Yunnan*, 2 vols., Peking, 1937, 1940.

complicated a situation made dangerous by a far more serious Karen rebellion and an incursion of Kuomintang forces from Yunnan under the defeated General Li Mi. In French Indo-China the communist Viet Minh was leading the national resistance to the French. In Indonesia a communist outbreak at Madiun in September 1948 had been bloodily suppressed, but with the coming of independence communism had increased its influence in Java. In the Philippines the Huk leader Luis Taruc had declared himself a communist and was in control of large areas of Luzon's 'rice-bowl'. This upsurge of communist activity was inspired and encouraged by the Cominform, founded in October 1947. It was heralded by the Second Conference of the Communist Party of India, which met in Calcutta in February 1948, and was attended by representatives from Burma, Malaya, Indonesia, Indo-China and the Philippines.

Without massive aid all these revolts were bound ultimately to fail. Only in northern Vietnam did the communists gain control, with Chinese aid. Elsewhere their revolts failed. In March 1953 Stalin died, and a change came over communist strategy in Asia. In South-East Asia both Moscow and Peking switched over to a policy of outward acceptance of non-communist national régimes and of the illegality of the communist parties in Burma, Thailand and the Republic of South Vietnam. A new technique was devised, using embassies, peace movements, barter-trade-aid agreements, border problems and agitation for self-determination for the many discontented minority peoples, to further communist aims. South-East Asia was a key theatre of the cold war, and Communist China's aim was by subversion to secure governments willing to pursue policies which she approved. One noteworthy change in her tactics was to drop her propaganda line of concern for the welfare of the overseas Chinese, and to all appearances to throw their interests overboard in seeking to allay the fears of the local governments regarding her intentions.

The numbers of overseas Chinese in each country in the middle fifties in relation to its own population are shown in the table on p. 823. The figures themselves are significant, but less so than the fact that the Chinese occupied—and still do—key positions in the economies of these countries, with a measure of control over internal trade and industry quite disproportionate to their numbers. They had all along lived as a community apart, especially in the Islamic countries where intermarriage was rare, but also in the Buddhist countries, where religion imposed no bar to assimilation, and even in Vietnam with its Chinese-type civilization. Their economic importance and cultural

	Total population (in millions)	Chinese (in millions)	Chinese percentage of total
Burma	18	0·310	1·75
Thailand	19·5	3	15·0
Cambodia	4·5	0·3	7·0
North Vietnam	11·5	0·050	0·5
South Vietnam	9·5	0·950	10·0
Laos	2	0·005	0·25
Malaya	5·7	2·150	38·0
Singapore	1·120	0·860	77·0
Indonesia	80	2·0	2·5
Philippines	21	0·300	1·5
British Borneo and Sarawak	0·950	0·240	25·0
(Totals)	(173·77)	(10·165)	

unassimilability had led King Vajiravudh of Siam to call them 'the Jews of the East'. Their contempt for the culture of the 'southern barbarians' was increased by the Chinese Revolution of 1911; and when, after the Communist victory of 1949, China's position in the world became incomparably stronger than it had been previously, their national pride was deeply stirred. This upsurge of national sentiment among the overseas Chinese coincided with an equally strong nationalistic phase in the history of the South-East Asians, and at the end of World War II the conflict of nationalisms was extremely bitter. Hence, with the Communist victory in China every country of South-East Asia became uneasily aware of the presence of a potential Chinese 'fifth column' in its midst.

The international tension, which arose at the end of March 1954, when Mr. Dulles the American Secretary of State called for united action over Dien Bien Phu, only partially subsided when the Geneva Conference succeeded in bringing about a cease-fire in Vietnam. Mr. Dulles and Mr. (later Sir Anthony) Eden issued a statement on 13 April declaring that their respective governments were ready to examine, with other countries principally concerned, the possibility of establishing a system of collective defence 'to assure the peace, security and freedom of South-East Asia and the Western Pacific'. On the following day a similar communiqué was issued by Mr. Dulles and M. Bidault, the French Foreign Minister. So began the diplomatic negotiations which led to the signature, on 8 September 1954 at Manila, of the South-East

Asia Collective Defence Treaty. Its signatories were the United States, Britain, France, Australia, New Zealand, Pakistan, Thailand and the Philippines, and in accordance with its terms they joined together to form the South East Asia Treaty Organization (SEATO) for common action in defence of peace, and for economic co-operation and the development of the ability of its members to resist armed attack and counter subversion directed from outside.

When the Manila Treaty came officially into force on 19 February 1955, it was equipped with a Council of Foreign Ministers of its member states, which was to meet annually to decide on general policy, Council Representatives to carry on the day-to-day business of the Organization, and Military Advisers responsible for drafting plans to resist aggression in the area covered by the treaty. Bangkok was chosen as the Organization's headquarters, Prince Wan Waithayakon, the T'ai foreign minister, was the first chairman of its Council, and Nai Pote Sarasin, a former foreign minister and T'ai ambassador to the United States, became its first Secretary-General in July 1957. The Siamese wanted a permanent military force to be stationed in the treaty area. The Filipinos criticized the treaty for having no teeth, and would have liked SEATO to have military provisions similar to those of the North Atlantic Treaty Organization. But Mr. Dulles was opposed to both proposals on strategic grounds, believing that the most effective defence against aggression by China would lie in a highly mobile and very powerful strategic force, able to strike swiftly wherever necessary.

No other South-East Asian states would join the Organization. India, Burma and Indonesia expressed strong opposition to the scheme. Ceylon refused to attend the Manila conference, but announced the intention to keep an open mind on the subject. Moreover, while the United States with Britain and France had taken the initiative in the way described above, the prime ministers of Burma, Ceylon, India, Indonesia and Pakistan had got together at Colombo to discuss the situation. Of the so-named 'Colombo Powers' only Pakistan joined SEATO. The others believed that a military pact increased insecurity in South-East Asia, and that the best guarantee of peace lay in the pursuit of Nehru's policy of 'neutralism'. This was defined in the famous 'five principles of co-existence', which India and China had publicly agreed to on 29 April 1954 in the following terms:

1. Mutual respect for each other's territorial integrity and sovereignty;
2. mutual non-aggression;

3. mutual non-interference in each other's internal affairs;
4. equality and mutual benefit; and
5. peaceful co-existence.

The upshot of the Colombo meeting was a communique issued on 2 May 1954, in which a plan to hold a conference of Asian and African nations was outlined. At a further meeting at Bogor in Java late in December 1954 the Colombo Powers agreed to sponsor the plan, and twenty-five countries were invited to join the five sponsors in a conference on 18 April 1955 at Bandung.

Nothing like the Bandung Conference of Afro-Asian nations had ever previously happened in world history. It demonstrated to the world in no uncertain terms the desire of these countries to be heard in matters of international affairs, and especially on the subject of the vital questions of peace and co-operation. But, having said that, one is left asking what exactly was achieved. The plan was to hold further meetings, but none has been held, and no permanent organization was set up. The discussions had an air of unreality: the delegates have been described as talking loudly about questions for which they had no responsibility, and in more subdued tones about those, such as Kashmir, Vietnam and Korea, for which they bore some responsibility.[1] On such questions as co-operation with the West and communism they were sharply divided. No bloc, Afro-Asian, Asian or even South-East Asian, emerged from the meeting.

A spirit of goodwill did indeed manifest itself. In particular Premier Chou En-lai's conciliatory gestures, notably his signature of a general agreement with Indonesia regarding the citizenship of her overseas Chinese, and his bland assurances to the South-East Asian governments that they had no cause for alarm regarding China's intentions towards them, led to a noticeable reduction of tension. Many delegates expressed greater fear of 'colonialism' than of communism. Thus the terms 'Bandung policy' and 'Bandung spirit' came into use meaning non-aggression and the peaceful solution of disputes between members of the conference. And even Mr. Nehru thought that after Bandung it would be awkward for Peking to flout the Five Principles. China, of course, was playing her own game. She wanted to encourage neutralist sentiment, weaken pro-Western influences, gain support in the United Nations, and encourage the formation of governments likely to prepare the way for communist take-overs. Moreover, Chou En-lai had been

[1] A. Vandenbosch and Richard A. Butwell, *Southeast Asia among the World Powers*, p. 262.

genuinely surprised at the extent of the fear of China among the delegates at Bandung.

The 'Bandung spirit', however, soon began to evaporate. In any case South Vietnam, Thailand, Malaya and the Philippines were no more in favour of recognizing Peking after Bandung than before. And the Chinese conquest of Tibet and violations of the Indian frontier caused a thrill of dismay to run through South-East Asia. And, although a reasonable settlement of the Sino-Burman frontier was ultimately achieved, it took a long time, and Burmese suspicions were never satisfactorily removed.

The newly-independent states were faced with urgent problems arising from underdevelopment and poverty, lack of capital and technical skill, and the dependence of their key products upon world markets. The most immediate was the unresolved problem of agricultural indebtedness and underproduction, at its worst in the Philippines, but with parts of Vietnam a close second. Capital expenditure on a vast scale was called for, but the rate of domestic saving was far from adequate to provide for the necessary capital formation. Low *per capita* productivity and income were the greatest obstacle, but non-productive expenditure on such things as ornaments and festivities also played its part. Long-term investment was alien to most South-East Asians, but there was much hostility to foreign private investment for they felt that economic self-sufficiency was essential for the maintenance of independence. There is an interesting contrast in this connection between Burma and Malaya. Malaya's economic progress since the Japanese defeat has been much faster than Burma's, and her standard of living altogether higher. She has welcomed foreign investment, whereas Burmese governmental policy has severely restricted foreign interests and deterred the foreign investor.

There were of course certain basic development needs, such as transportation, irrigation, power, communications and public utilities, which could not be supplied by private investment. A modest approach to this problem was inaugurated at the meeting of British Commonwealth prime ministers at Colombo in January 1950. The 'Colombo Plan', as it was called, was a co-operative undertaking, with each member as a donor as well as a recipient, and it was open to non-members of the Commonwealth. In 1947 the United Nations Economic Commission for Asia and the Far East was founded. Its activities were similar to those of the Colombo Plan, but on a far greater scale. It dealt with agriculture, industrial development, flood control and water resources, trade and finance, technical training and assistance, research and statistics and inland transport. But its financial resources were limited by the amount of members' voluntary contributions, and the United States, by far the richest member of UNO, preferred bi-lateral government-to-government arrangements to multilateral ones through the United Nations.

The bilateral commitments of the United States were many times the amount of its contributions through the United Nations. They were an instrument of national policy, particularly with the cold war against the communist bloc. The conditions of American aid included specific political, economic or strategic *quid pro quo* commitments on the part of the beneficiary state, and the South-East Asia governments saw these as a possible source of American interference in their domestic affairs. The United States Congress indeed preferred to give military rather than economic aid: its policy was to build up a military bulwark against international communist aggression. The South-East Asians therefore would much have preferred bigger multilateral schemes to finance their economic and social development rather than American aid. Actually for projects suitable for financing by loans there was the International Bank for Reconstruction and Development. But its powers were limited, and so great were the capital needs of the underdeveloped countries that in 1955 the International Finance Corporation was established in affiliation with the Bank to make direct loans to private enterprises in such countries. Finally in 1958, after several years of hesitation, SUNFED, the Special United Nations Fund for Economic Development, came into being to make grants-in-aid and long-term low-interest loans for essential development projects such as hospitals, schools and roads, which were not capable of showing a commercial profit.

Help was also to come from another source. For when the period of unprecedented prosperity caused by the demand for tin, rubber and rice during the Korean War came to an end, the South-East Asian governments came under increasing pressure to trade with the communist bloc. At the same time that bloc repudiated Stalinism, played down the use of force, and adopted the policy of competing with the West in the provision of economic aid to backward countries.

(b) Vietnam, Cambodia and Laos

The recognition by the United States of Vietnam, Cambodia and Laos as 'independent states within the French Union' in February 1950 led to America shouldering more and more of the burden of carrying on the struggle with the Viet Minh. But, although France publicly declared that no powers were left in the hands of the French administration, there had in fact been no real transfer of power.[1] The French indeed insisted that American aid should not go direct to the associated states. The United States thus found herself in the uncomfortable position of subsidizing a French colonial war, and indeed of backing a certain loser, for Bao Dai, who had been brought back with the express purpose of rallying nationalist sentiment, was quite unable to compete with Ho Chi Minh. The nationalists preferred an independent government, even if communist-led, to one whose independence was a sham. As a result of the Pau Conference, which sat from 27 June to 29 November 1950, the Associate States made agreements with France which on paper provided them with the 'appurtenances of sovereignty',[2] but lack of trained personnel and technicians left them still in French hands. And the central organs of the Union, its Presidency, High Council and Assembly, remained in France and functioned in such a way as to prevent any power passing out of French control.

While the conference was in session, France sustained the greatest defeat she had ever suffered in colonial warfare. The communist victory in China enabled the Viet Minh to pass from guerrilla activities to a war of movement and to a series of attacks upon French garrisons in Tongking, which caused the French high command to make the disastrous decision to concentrate upon the defence of the Red River Delta and withdraw from the mountainous region to the north. On 3–7 October 1950, while carrying out the order to retreat southwards on Langson, the Cao Bang garrison was overwhelmed by the Viet Minh. It was a decisive defeat. Langson itself, commanding the main route into China, was next evacuated, and in such a hurry that vast stocks of food and war material were left behind. Then came a whole chain of further withdrawals which gave the Viet Minh possession of the Chinese frontier zone from the coastal town of Mong Cay to the Laotian frontier. Preparations were even made to evacuate Hanoi, but General Juin's arrival there checked the panic.

Morale revived still more with the appointment in December of General Jean de Lattre de Tassigny as High Commissioner. He had won glory in command of the French First Army which had liberated eastern France from the Germans. In the new year the French Expeditionary Corps won the battles of Vinh Yen and Dong Trieu, and pushed General Giap's forces back to their bases in Viet Bac. But French strategy remained defensive, and a new defence line to protect

[1] Donald Lancaster, *The Emancipation of French Indo-China*, 1961, pp. 205–6.
[2] *Ibid.*, p. 213.

the delta region was constructed from the Bay of Along to Vinh Yen covering the invasion route from China. But the loss of control over the China frontier meant that deliveries of arms and material from China were speeded up. Thus, while the French were dispersing their effectives in hundreds of scattered concrete strong points, the Viet Minh were building up a regular army capable of extended operations. For the time being, however, their attacks were beaten off, and in November 1951 'Le Roi Jean' took the first step in a new offensive plan by seizing Hoa Binh on the Black River, a communication centre vital to the Viet Minh. But this did not mean any real change in the strategy of static defence, which tied down vast numbers of men ineffectually, and left the China frontier open for the passage of aid on a huge scale to the Viet Minh as soon as armistice negotiations opened in the Korean war. Hence de Lattre's premature death in a Paris nursing-home in January 1952 had little effect upon French fortunes in the Tongking struggle. The forced evacuation of Hoa Binh, which followed soon after, would probably have happened in any case. On the other hand de Lattre had done much to help the formation of a Vietnamese national army, which had begun to take shape before his arrival, but was in urgent need of equipment. The increased aid that he secured from Washington for it, was not the least of his services to the anti-Viet Minh cause. Pressure from Washington during 1952 caused a rapid increase in its numbers, if not in its efficiency, for its conscripted, hastily-trained units were ineffective in operating against the Viet Minh in the south, still more as a means of relieving the French forces in Tongking.

During 1952 the Viet Minh forces under General Vo Nguyen Giap's direction were preparing for a winter offensive. It began in October with a sudden thrust to Lai Chau on the Black River. Then in November they occupied Dien Bien Phu and went on to cross the border of Laos. In March 1953 they launched an attack on Luang Prabang; it failed, but it was obvious that they intended to repeat the attempt later. Other forces threatened Annam, while progress was made with the encirclement of the delta region of Tongking. Through their command of the air French forces were able to check these moves, but the disputed territories usually remained under effective Viet Minh control, for the French Union forces were confined to camps and fortified positions.

There seemed no hope whatever of a French victory. In France, indeed, public opinion had turned against the bloody and expensive struggle, and in the highest quarters the possibility of 'an honourable way out' by negotiation was mooted. On the other hand by 1953 the

United States was paying 80 per cent of the cost of the French military effort, and there was growing American impatience at the defensive nature of French strategy. Such was the background to the 'Navarre Plan', which the French cabinet adopted on 24 July 1953. Its author, General Henri Navarre, had been appointed commander-in-chief in Indo-China in the previous May and commissioned to find the 'way out' so urgently desired by France and the United States.

The plan was for a build-up of military superiority, based upon massive deliveries of American aid, and aimed at containing the Viet Minh by defensive strategy until the offensive could be taken—in 1955 —with enough success to force the Viet Minh to negotiate. The military operations, which wrecked the scheme, arose out of France's engagement late in October 1953 to defend Laos against all attacks. General Giap took up the challenge and concentrated all the strength he could muster upon surrounding and destroying the powerful 'aero-terrestrial' base established by Navarre at Dien Bien Phu, close to the border of the Laotian province of Phong Saly. This he finally accomplished on 7 May 1954 after a dramatic struggle of some months watched intently by the whole world. He outgeneralled Navarre, causing him to disperse troops that could have rescued the beleaguered force, and using a huge army of coolies to bring up supplies in defiance of the intensive attacks of the French aviation.

There were divided counsels in France from cabinet-level downwards, and increasing pressure for an armistice. It was this fact and the decision on 25 January 1954 of the foreign ministers of the United States, Russia, Britain and France to invite Communist China to a conference on the Far East in the following April that led Giap to stake everything upon a spectacular victory.

The danger now became intense with massive American forces arriving off the coast of Indo-China, and Mr. Dulles hinting at the possible use of atomic bombs. Happily Britain's firm stand against allied intervention and in favour of a negotiated settlement carried the day. The Geneva Conference, which had assembled on 23 April, was able to conclude armistice agreements on 21 July covering Vietnam, Laos and Cambodia, and arranging for a cease-fire and the appointment of an International Armistice Control Commission composed of representatives of India, Canada and Poland. Vietnam was to be partitioned along the Ben Hai River at the 17th parallel of latitude close to the Dong Hoi wall, built in 1631 to defend the Nguyen domains from the 'lords of the North'. The north was to be under the 'Democratic Republic of Vietnam', i.e. the Viet Minh; the south was to be under the

Saigon government of which the ex-emperor was the head. It was only a provisional arrangement for general elections to unify Vietnam were to be held in both sectors in July 1956 under international control. Viet Minh forces were to withdraw from south and central Vietnam, Cambodia and Laos according to an agreed timetable; similarly French Union forces were to withdraw from north Vietnam, Cambodia and Laos, but France might maintain a limited number of instructors in Laos to train the national army, and retain the use of two military bases there.[1]

The Geneva Agreements provided a basis for the independence of what still continued to be called the 'associate states', South Vietnam, Cambodia and Laos. Subsequent negotiations held in Paris aimed at completing their economic and financial independence. France had never been willing to grant real independence: she had always kept her 'foot in the doorway', hoping for a resurgence of her domination.[2] Late in 1953, after Premier Laniel had made his offer to 'perfect' the independence of the Associated States, King Norodom Sihanouk of Cambodia had negotiated independence agreements, and the Kingdom of Laos had concluded a treaty of 'amity and association' by which France recognized her as a 'fully independent and sovereign state'. Moreover, on 28 April 1954, after the start of the Geneva Conference, France and Bao Dai had made a joint declaration of Vietnam's 'total independence'. But all such agreements and declarations could have easily been evaded had the situation turned in France's favour. The effect of her policy upon Vietnam was to drive the non-communist moderates from positions of influence in the national movement so that it became communist-dominated in the north, while in the south it sought independence outside the French Union. Laos, the most pro-French of the associated states, amended its constitution after the Geneva Conference to omit any reference to the French Union, although continuing to send representatives to the Assembly. Cambodia, on the other hand, under the strong nationalist leadership of Norodom, formally ended its association with France on 25 September 1955 by a constitutional amendment substituting 'Cambodia, an independent and sovereign state', for 'Cambodia, a self-governing state belonging to the French Union as an Associated State'.

The Geneva settlement was made over the heads of the Saigon authorities, who were strongly against partition. They were therefore able to evade the clause providing for general elections in July 1956.

[1] Lancaster, *op. cit.*, pp. 338–41, gives details of the armistice arrangements.
[2] A. Vandenbosch and R. Butwell, *op. cit.*, 1957, p. 118.

The systematic steps they took to free South Vietnam from French control cannot be treated in detail here. They entailed changing the title of the French commissioner-general to 'ambassador', denouncing the monetary and financial agreement with France and bringing the Vietnamese piastre into the dollar bloc, arrangements for the withdrawal of the French Expeditionary Corps and for channelling American aid directly to Saigon instead of through Paris, and finally the rejection of Bao Dai's authority and the proclamation on 26 October 1955 of the Republic of Vietnam after a referendum in which 'the final results surpassed even the most sanguine expectations, as the votes in some cases exceeded the number of names on the electoral roll'.[1]

Bao Dai had been ineffective as a national leader; in his place President Ngo Dinh Diem was built up as the saviour of the nation. He had been chosen as prime minister of the Saigon regime by Bao Dai because of his firm insistence on independence. But he was a Catholic and more French than Vietnamese in education and outlook. He had no support in the country, lacked administrative experience and showed little capacity as a leader. It was American support that kept him in power; the Americans saw him as an honest man and one whose anti-communism could be absolutely relied on. Thus he was able to defeat his rivals and establish a dictatorship. His rivals were formidable. The army under Major General Nguyen Van Hinh was independent, and Hinh himself had the backing of Bao Dai. Another general, Le Van Vien, was the head of the Binh Xuyen, a gangsterish organization controlling the police and the vice-rackets of Saigon. Then there were the two politico-religious sects, the syncretist Cao Dai and the reformed Buddhist Hoa Hao, with their private armies, controlling large areas of the country. To complete the picture, the Viet Minh in evacuating their forces to the north of the 17th parallel left behind large numbers of political cadres secretly working for the communist cause, while from Tongking hundreds of thousands of refugees poured southwards.

The story of Diem's struggle for control cannot be told here. Whether he or any other leader could have dammed up the communist south-wards flow without the all-out support of the United States is an idle speculation. The dominance of political and military considerations, however, severely hampered the work of economic and social reconstruction. The bulk of the population lived near starvation level, and the allied problems of landlordism and agrarian reform could not be seriously tackled by a government fearful lest its wealthy elite would turn against it. American economic aid could, and did, cover the annual

[1] Lancaster, op. cit., pp. 398–9.

budget deficits occasioned by refugee resettlement, a very large military establishment and the heavy cost of reconstructing the badly-disrupted communications system. But it was on a year-to-year basis, and the government had to look for ways of reducing its dependence upon foreign aid and of obtaining investment capital. A five-year plan of economic development was announced in 1957, but local industries did not receive prompt encouragement, and imports were too largely of consumer goods. Nevertheless there was economic development shown by a large increase in textile output, the development of coal-mining and a healthy programme of resettlement in the highland regions as well as of regrouping villages in 'agrovilles' to protect peasants from attack. Rural health measures, the provision of more schools and the establishment of a new university at Hué were further signs of progress.

A constitution for South Vietnam was promulgated on 26 October 1956, but on account of security conditions it remained largely inoperative and presidential rule by executive decree remained the order of the day. Autocratic government was accompanied by nepotism, favouritism, lack of delegation of authority, and graft. The administration remained inefficient and the morale of the civil service low. Viet Cong activity aimed at making things impossible for Diem, what with attacks on local leaders, intimidation of peasants and propaganda against 'the American imperialist regime of south Vietnam'. But by the later 1950s it was obvious that the government could not be overthrown by peaceful means. Hence in December 1960 the 'Front for the Liberation of the South' was formed in Hanoi, and preparations set on foot for military action 'when the time is proper'.[1]

The Viet Minh government in the north was in a much stronger position. It had been in control of its own house years before the Geneva Conference gave it legal status. It had fought a successful war, and as the real spearhead to the national resistance to alien domination it had much popular support, and could enforce a much stricter discipline—e.g. in rationing and land distribution—than could Ngo Dinh Diem. Nevertheless, it had its difficulties, and they were serious. The overpopulated Red River delta was now cut off from the rice-fields of Cochin-China, upon which it had relied for the additional food supplies to the tune of over 100,000 tons of rice annually, to make up for the deficiency in its own production. Much of its irrigation system had been ruined by the ravages of war. Vast damage had been done to mines and industrial plant, and there was a crippling shortage of trained

[1] Recent developments are examined by Ellen J. Hammer in 'South Viet Nam: The Limits of Political Action', *Pacific Affairs*, XXXV, no. 1, Spring 1962, pp. 24–36.

personnel for industry. As in the south, the transport system had broken down almost completely. On the deficiency of rice alone Ho Chi Minh's government could have fallen had it not been for a timely loan from Soviet Russia enabling it to buy rice purchased by Moscow in Burma. Its early plans had therefore perforce to be directed to increasing rice production. But it also aimed at progressive industrialization, and its close relations with Russia and China brought it long-term industrial credits.

The efforts of the Viet Minh to rescue North Vietnam from economic disaster made them very unpopular. The mass of the people were not communists and resented deeply the efforts to collectivize agriculture and the levy of forced labour for reconstruction. For the heavy hand of the government fell not only on the large landlords but also on the smallholders. An uprising in November 1956 in Nghe An showed how strong was the discontent, and the disturbances spread to other provinces. Repression, however, was swift and effective. Nevertheless, it was admitted that mistakes had been made, and civil rights and additional powers for the Assembly were written into the constitution. By mid-1956 two million acres had been redistributed among 2,200,000 families. In the next year it was claimed that self-sufficiency in rice production had been achieved. Thereafter collectivization became the main objective, and a three-year programme to achieve it was launched in 1958. Along with this the State Planning Board announced a comprehensive programme of industrial expansion 'to transform the economy along Socialist lines'. There was of course the same lack of capital and of technicians as in the south, and foreign aid was essential. In 1955 China promised $326 million and Russia $100 million to build factories, and supply technicians and equipment. French economic interests were liquidated, and North Vietnam's economy became firmly tied to the communist bloc.

Cambodia had become a constitutional kingdom under a constitution promulgated on 6 May 1947 by King Norodom Sihanouk. The central government consisted of a monarch with a Council of the Kingdom, a prime minister and cabinet, and a National Assembly elected every four years by direct suffrage. King Norodom's dramatic moves to free his country from French control brought him criticism as well as success. His self-imposed exile, his resignation of the crown in 1955 in favour of his father in order to fight a general election, and his subsequent changes of mind about his own position, looked to some like the exhibitionism of a politically immature young man. But as king he could not give the country the leadership it needed, and although undoubtedly erratic, he had a clear conception of his country's needs and especially of the realities of its precarious position in a world divided by the cold war. In external affairs he adopted the neutralist policy expounded by India's Mr. Nehru, and played off one side against the other in order to obtain economic help for Cambodia. With Communist China in 1956 he negotiated an agreement whereby China invested capital in Cambodian commercial undertakings. Next he secured an agreement with Russia for the supply of industrial equipment and technician-instructors. From the United States he received aid for irrigation, education, health and road-making projects, and towards the upkeep of his army, not to mention an emergency supply of rice when the Cambodian harvest failed.

In internal politics a socialist and genuine democrat, he was able to defeat the hopes of the local communists of gaining control. The 'Khmer Issaraks', who were closely linked with the Viet Minh and Pathet Lao movements, were reduced to impotence by the Geneva Agreements. At the subsequent general election the ex-king's Popular Socialist Community party won all the seats in the national assembly, and when the Issarak leader Son Ngoc Thanh resorted to revolt, he was decisively defeated. The International Commission for Supervision and Control, set up under the Geneva Agreement, saw Cambodia's post-settlement history as a 'success story', but Norodom himself was less happy about things, and was anxious for more to be done to safeguard his country's neutrality both from the expansive energies of the Vietnamese, and from Thailand, with whom there were boundary disputes. The Vietnamese were regarded as the greater threat: 300,000 of them lived in Cambodia, and 400,000 Cambodians in South Vietnam. North Vietnam at the Bandung Conference in 1955 gave bland assurances of readiness to establish relations on the basis of 'the five principles of co-existence', but Cambodian nationalism remained hostile to both Vietnamese states, and the Control Commission had to deal with constant disputes. Norodom's neutralism reflected the intense desire of his people for independence, and their remembrance of the long Thai-Vietnamese contest for control over his country.

The Kingdom of Laos, as we have seen in an earlier chapter,[1] had lost its identity long before the French acquired it in the eighteen-nineties. Vientiane, which had separated from Luang Prabang in 1707, had been conquered by Siam, and Luang Prabang had become a vassal of the Bangkok régime. France established a protectorate over Luang Prabang in 1893 and next proceeded successfully to claim the territories

[1] Chap. 25.

of Middle and Lower Laos from Siam. In April 1945, while still under the Japanese, King Sisavang Vong of Luang Prabang proclaimed his independence of France. After the Japanese collapse all the former Laotian territories were united by agreement with France, and the name of the kingdom was changed to Laos (27 August 1947). Luang Prabang remained the royal capital, but Vientiane, in a more central position, became the administrative capital. Both were quite small towns. Nearly all the Laotians lived in villages and supported themselves by subsistence agriculture. There were no railways, the roads were in a very bad state, and the navigation facilities on the river Mekong mediocre. Entirely land-locked, the kingdom was too far away from available sea-ports such as Saigon and Bangkok to have any appreciable foreign trade.

Like Cambodia, Laos received a constitution from its king on becoming an 'independent' member of the French Union. It was promulgated on 11 May 1947. On paper it introduced responsible government with a prime minister and cabinet responsible to a national assembly elected by universal suffrage every four years. The king himself was too old and infirm to carry out all his state duties; the Crown Prince Savang Vat'ana therefore acted on his behalf.

After the Geneva Agreement trouble at once arose over the position of the pro-communist Pathet Lao forces, which had co-operated closely with the Viet Minh in the anti-French struggle. They seized the provinces of Phong Saly and Sam Neua on the North Vietnam frontier, and in spite of the attempts of the Control Commission to negotiate a settlement, they refused to accept the authority of the Laotian government. They wanted the alignment of their country with its neighbours Communist China and North Vietnam. Their political wing, known as Neo Lao Haksat (Patriotic Party of Laos), was led by Prince Souphanou Vong, who had received communist indoctrination in China. There was much fighting until in 1956 a new prime minister, Prince Souvanna Phouma, negotiated a settlement with his half-brother by which Phong Saly and Sam Neua were to come under the jurisdiction of the central government and the Pathet Lao forces be integrated in the royal army.

The agreement was, however, extremely complex, and its implementation painfully slow because of the hostility and suspicions of both sides. There was also the fact that Laos had willy nilly become the battleground of forces beyond her control. On one side were the communist states China and North Vietnam, on the other anti-communist Thailand with the central organization of SEATO in Bangkok. Moreover, notwithstanding the neutral status laid down for Laos at Geneva,

American policy was seeking to build her up as an anti-communist bastion. American aid per head of the population was higher than to any other country in the world, and four-fifths of it went to the army and the police.

In May 1957 another crisis blew up when the Pathet Lao forces were reported to be getting outside aid. But in the following November things looked better when the National Assembly approved a new cabinet under Souvanna Phouma which included Souphanou Vong and one other Neo Lao Haksat representative. In May 1958 elections for new seats in an enlarged National Assembly resulted in greatly increased Neo Lao Haksat representation. This alarmed the right wing parties so much that a new group calling itself the Committee for the Defence of National Interests came forward demanding a cabinet able to check the increasing influence of the left wing. In July Souvanna Phouma resigned and the situation once more deteriorated. To cut short a very detailed story, a much worse crisis arose in 1959 involving an appeal to the United Nations by the Laotian cabinet, which alleged acts of aggression by North Vietnam. A subcommittee sent to the spot by the United Nations could find no evidence of violations of the frontier by North Vietnamese troops, and Secretary-General Dag Hammerskjold, who went on a personal visit to Laos in November, urged the adoption of a more neutral foreign policy and a reduction in military aid from the West.

In August 1960 a junior officer in the army carried out a *coup* against the right-wing American-dominated government which led to Prince Souvanna Phouma again becoming premier with a mandate to come to terms with the Pathet Lao movement and pursue a strictly neutral foreign policy. But the country was now plunged into civil war, in the course of which the right-wing General Phoumi Nosavan, a close connection of Field Marshal Sarit Thanarat, the military dictator of Thailand, with American moral support, captured Vientiane, drove out Souvanna Phouma and placed Prince Boun Oum, the extreme right-wing leader, in power. Neither side, however, could win an outright victory. The situation looked to be dangerous to world peace. Action was, however, taken jointly by Britain and Russia as co-chairmen of the original Geneva Conference, and eventually, after further crises, a settlement was arrived at in 1962 much along the lines of the original plan.

(c) Malaya and Singapore

The Federation of Malaya's progress to independence, not to mention its subsequent economic progress, was the most rapid of any of the dependent territories of the post-war world. Its first real general election was held in 1955, when its legislative council was accorded an elected majority. On 31 August 1957 it became fully independent. When in January 1952, with the appointment of Sir Gerald Templer as both commander-in-chief and high commissioner, the country came for all practical purposes under military rule, so serious was the 'emergency' that few people could have foreseen that in a little over three years a general election could be held, with independence so to speak just round the corner.

Actually, the real beginnings of improvement in the situation can be traced back to June 1950, when under the 'Briggs Plan' the half-million or so Chinese 'squatters', upon whom the guerrillas had depended for food, supplies and information, began to be resettled in new fenced villages provided with schools and community centres, piped water and electricity. Each householder was given a thirty-year lease of a small farm together with agricultural assistance. The ever-tightening pressure of the army upon the bandits was, of course, a factor of equal importance in their ultimate defeat, for the resettlement took several years to complete. By the end of 1953 there were 150 of these villages, each protected by its own home guards and with an elected village council. The total number finally built was 550.

As they lost support the communists became more selective in their targets, and it was the murder of the high commissioner, Sir Henry Gurney, in October 1951, together with an increase in planned outrages, that led to Templer's appointment. Opinion has been divided concerning the effectiveness of the measures he took to combat the rebellion. They included the creation of a Federal Regiment as a preliminary to the creation of a Malayan Army, compulsory service (which, incidentally, caused the disappearance abroad of many young Chinese), jungle forts to protect the aborigines, psychological warfare and—most disputed of all—the collective punishment of villages helping the rebels.[1] There can, however, be no doubt that his régime was a turning-point in the struggle; indeed, conditions improved so much by 1954 that Sir Donald MacGillivray, a civilian, succeeded him as high commissioner.

Two measures of some importance to the political future of Malaya were taken under Templer. The federal citizenship law was modified to enable more Chinese to qualify and the system of government appointments was changed to provide for the intake of one non-Malay for

[1] Victor Purcell, *Malaya, Communist or Free*, 1954, and *The Revolution in Southeast Asia*, 1962, pp. 101–2; Lennox A. Mills, *Malaya, a Political and Economic Appraisal*, 1958, pp. 62–7. Saul Rose, *Britain and South-East Asia*, 1962, p. 131.

every four Malays. But the biggest step forward was taken by the two major political parties themselves. In 1952 the United Malays National Organization (UMNO) and the Malayan Chinese Association (MCA) formed an 'Alliance' to contest the Kuala Lumpur municipal elections. Success encouraged it to aim higher. In 1954 under the leadership of Tungku Abdul Rahman, son of the Sultan of Kedah, a graduate of Cambridge University, who had served as a district officer in the Malayan Civil Service, the Alliance came forward with a demand for an elected majority in the legislative council. In London its deputation was rebuffed by the Secretary of State for the Colonies, Oliver Lyttleton. Their determined stand on their return to Malaya caused the British government to change its mind. An elected majority and a general election were conceded in 1955, and the high commissioner announced that the 'emergency' was no longer an obstacle to Malaya's advance towards self-government. In the general election the Alliance won 51 out of the 52 elected seats in the legislature and Tungku Abdul Rahman became chief minister. His demand for independence by 31 August 1957 was sympathetically received in London, where the policy of the government had now become that of making the transition to independence as smooth as possible. The victory of the Alliance also had its effect upon the 'emergency', for the communist leader Chin Peng made overtures for peace, and in December 1955 had a conference with the federal ministers together with representatives of Singapore. His terms were totally rejected; then for a time there was a position of stalemate. This was to be radically changed with the coming of independence in 1957. The new government, confident that the great mass of the people were with it, increased the penalties for helping communist guerrillas, and proposed to crush them within one year.

In 1951 the federal executive had been reorganized so as to include six of the unofficial members of the legislative council. Each member of the executive was to have charge of a department, and, although responsible to the high commissioner, was to be the spokesman for his department in the legislature. After the general election of 1955 the executive was composed of five officials and ten Malayan ministers, all members of the legislature. The ministers, of whom six were Malays, three Chinese and one Indian, were appointed by the high commissioner on the advice of the chief minister, and were responsible to the legislature. When in January 1956 at the Anglo-Malayan conference in London the British government accepted the demand for independence, interim arrangements were made pending its fulfilment. The high commissioner was instructed to accept the advice given him by the federal executive, except in case of special emergency, and arrangements were made for the Malayan ministers to take over additional functions from the official members.

The new constitution was drafted by a commission under Lord Reid, a Lord of Appeal in Ordinary, composed of two British members, an Australian, an Indian and a Pakistani. The draft, after some amendments, was adopted by the Malayan legislature, and on 31 August 1957 Malaya's independence was proclaimed. The new federal state had an elective monarchy, a conference of rulers, a cabinet responsible to a bicameral legislature and a judiciary independent of the executive as in Britain. The monarch—Yang di-Pertuan Agong—was to be chosen by the conference of rulers on the basis of seniority for a five-year term of office. He must act in accordance with the advice of the cabinet, and must also safeguard the special position of the Malays. The legislature consisted of a senate and a house of representatives. The senate contained thirty-eight members, twenty-two of whom were elected by the eleven state legislatures and sixteen were appointed by the Yang di-Pertuan Agong. Its members held office for six years, half of them retiring every three years. The house of representatives was composed of one hundred members elected by single-member constituencies. Its powers were similar to those of the British House of Commons. A chief justice and supreme court formed the judiciary together with such subordinate courts as parliament might establish. The supreme court's powers included those of interpreting the constitution and dealing with inter-state disputes. At the head of each state was its hereditary ruler, or, as in the cases of Penang and Malacca, its governor. The state had a democratically elected legislative assembly and an executive council appointed by the head of state on the advice of the chief minister and collectively responsible to the state legislature. In the division of powers between the federal and state governments the former was given predominance, and, where state law was inconsistent with federal law, the latter took precedence.

A recent commentator has posed the question why Malaya achieved independence so rapidly.[1] The British experience in India, Pakistan, Ceylon and Burma, he suggests, provided Britain with precedents and encouragement. The strength and solidarity of the Alliance showed that Malaya herself could best solve her communal problems. Moreover, mere military means could not remove the communist threat; Malayan nationalism was calculated to become a more effective weapon if its demands were granted. Less decisive but quite real factors were

[1] Saul Rose, *op. cit.*, pp. 133–4.

the Alliance's willingness for Malaya to remain in the British Commonwealth and to conclude a defence agreement permitting Britain to maintain military bases, including a Commonwealth strategic reserve, in the country. One may add that the personality of Tungku Abdul Rahman inspired confidence.

Britain gave military and economic assistance to independent Malaya, both directly and under the Colombo Plan. Membership of the Commonwealth also brought positive advantages. On the other hand, as an earner of surplus dollars through her exports of tin and rubber to the United States Malaya makes a useful contribution to the sterling area. Her decision to remain in it after independence was taken with eyes wide open to economic realities. She has been equally realistic regarding British economic predominance, which was restored when the Japanese departed. In consequence, the post-war development of Malaya's economy has been exceptionally rapid, and her standard of living is as high as anywhere else in Asia, much higher than anywhere else in South-East Asia of comparative size. Her economic revival has been in striking contrast to that of Burma, where foreign economic interests were jealously cut down to the absolute minimum.[1] The post-war period has also seen the forging of very close cultural links with Britain and the Commonwealth. For instance many hundreds of Malayan students and teachers have come to Britain for higher education and professional training, and even more have gone to Australia.

But Malayan independence was real. It was shown in her refusal to become a member of SEATO, and in the initiative Tungku Abdul Rahman has taken in seeking to organize better regional co-operation in South-East Asia, although his proposals, first, in 1959, for a South-East Asian Economic and Friendship Treaty, and next, in 1960, for an Association of South-East Asian states, have not received the support they deserved. On the other hand, his 'Malaysia' plan for expanding the Federation to include Singapore and the Bornean territories of North Borneo, Brunei and Sarawak received British official support in November 1961. It aimed at solving the Singapore problem, and at the same time maintaining the political ascendancy of the Malays.

When the proposals for a Malayan Union were drawn up in 1946, Singapore with its preponderatingly Chinese population would have tipped the scale against the Malays, had it been included. The 1947 census showed the Chinese as 45 per cent of the population of Malaya with Singapore and the Malays as only 43·3 per cent. Without Singapore the positions were reversed, with the Malays 49·5 per cent of the

[1] *Ibid.*, pp. 135-6.

population and the Chinese 38·4 per cent.[1] Another reason for Singapore's non-inclusion in the Union—and subsequent Federation—was that while Malaya depended on custom duties for three-fifths of her revenue, Singapore had grown up as a free port, and her success depended upon her free trade policy.

Singapore was accordingly given its own constitution with a governor, nominated executive council, and a legislative council with a majority of unofficial members, most of whom were elected. The Chinese electorate, however, were dissatisfied and boycotted the elections. Accordingly, the British government appointed a commission under Sir George Rendel in 1953 to make fresh constitutional proposals. Its recommendations came into effect in 1955. There was now a legislative assembly with 25 elected members out of a total of 32, and a council of ministers composed of three *ex officio* ministers responsible to the governor and six responsible to the assembly. The leader of the largest party became Chief Minister, but the government was a dyarchy, with the *ex officio* ministers responsible for finance, external affairs, defence and internal security.

This time more than fifty per cent of the electorate voted at the first general election under the new scheme, but no party was strong enough to form a government. Mr. David Marshall, the leader of the Labour Front, composed of the Socialist Party and a part of the Labour Party, managed with the help of the representatives of the UMNO-MCA Alliance to scrape up enough support to become Chief Minister. But he had a difficult task trying to hold his party together, and resigned in 1956 because in negotiations with the British government over his demand for internal self-government the latter laid down security arrangements which he would not accept. His successor, Lim Yew Hock, however, reached agreement with Britain in the following year over the security question, and Singapore received yet another constitution, this time conferring full self-government upon her. The governor was replaced by a Malayan Yang di-Pertuan Negara, or Head of State. There was to be an elected legislature of 51 members to which the Council of Ministers was to be collectively responsible. Citizenship was to go automatically to all born in Singapore. Others might register after a period of residence. The vexed question of security was solved by placing it in the hands of an Internal Security Council composed of the Chief Minister, two other ministers, the British Commissioner, two British representatives and one cabinet minister from Malaya. The first general

[1] The 1947 census gave the total population of Singapore as 930,000, of whom 75 per cent were Chinese. The 1957 census gave the total population as 1,445,929. Chinese accounted for 1,090,595, Malaysians 197,060, Indians and Pakistanis 124,084.

election took place in May 1959, and at midnight on 2–3 June 1959 the new state came officially into existence.

In the general election the People's Action Party won 43 out of the 51 seats, and its leader, Mr. Lee Kuan-yew became premier. The party was decidedly left-wing and contained a communist element. Lee himself was a moderate, and found himself increasingly doing battle with the communists. His aim was to bring to an end the separation of Singapore from Malaya, for it looked as if Singapore alone would never achieve real independence. He and the moderates in his party were quick to realize the responsibilities imposed upon them by the economic and strategic situation of Singapore, with its entrepôt trade shrinking and its population rising, its need for foreign investment, and its dependence upon the British naval base and the Harbour Board in order to earn the money to pay for the excellent social services to which its people had grown accustomed. If the British naval, military and air force installations were withdrawn from the island, the effect upon its economy and standard of life would be appreciable. For one thing it would put out of work some 40,000 well-paid workers. The PAP government, however, for all their anti-colonial ardour, did not challenge the British use of the island. When in 1963 Singapore entered the Federation of Malaysia, it was agreed that the bases were to remain under British control 'for the preservation of peace in South-East Asia'. They could not be used for SEATO purposes, save by Britain alone.

When in May 1961 Tungku Abdul Rahman declared in a speech in Singapore that Malaya could not stand alone and went on to suggest the need for an understanding with Singapore, North Borneo, Brunei and Sarawak, he was giving expression to a view that had been a frequent subject of discussion in Singapore political circles since that island-state had been excluded from the Malayan Union formed in 1946. Lee Kuan-yew at once welcomed the suggestion saying that, 'the relentless logic of geography, and the force of historic, ethnic and economic forces, must prevail'. The Singapore communists, on the other hand, wanted Singapore's separate status to continue: they hoped to make the place a communist stronghold in South-East Asia. As for the Borneans, they were hesitant, conscious of their political and economic backwardness, and afraid of the Chinese. North Borneo itself, which had been horribly devastated in the Japanese war, was concentrating upon restoring its economy; it had neither political parties nor an electoral system, and was still under a paternal administration. Sarawak had made rather more political progress, but had only held its first general election in December 1959, to local government bodies. And the 24

elected members of its legislature of 45 were chosen by the local government bodies, not by direct election. Brunei's sultan favoured merger
with Malaya, but the dominant party in his newly constituted legislature
was utterly opposed to it. There was the suspicion in Borneo that the
Tungku's Malaysia project masked a Malay takeover plan, and the
Borneans had no desire to exchange British colonial rule for Malay
dominance. Thus at the first meeting of their political leaders, at
Jesselton in July 1961, the project was pronounced 'totally unacceptable'. The formulators of British policy saw 'Greater Malaysia' as a
long-term objective, and the Governors of North Borneo and Sarawak
and the High Commissioner of Brunei advised that closer bonds should
be forged between the Borneo territories themselves before they joined
in a federation with Malaya and Singapore.

Soon after the Jesselton meeting, however, a meeting of the Malayo-
Borneo group of the Commonwealth Parliamentary Association was
held, and the opposition of the Bornean leaders began to relax; they
were persuaded to agree to the formation of a Malaysian Solidarity
Consultative Committee charged with the task of examining the Malaysia
plan in all its aspects. A further step forward was taken in August 1961
when the Tungku and Lee Kuan-yew reached agreement in principle,
and the way was opened for consultations between the Malayan and
British Governments. The upshot of these was the appointment of an
Anglo-Malayan Commission under Lord Cobbold, a former Governor
of the Bank of England, to ascertain the wishes of the Borneans. After
a two-months' tour of Sarawak and North Borneo in the early months
of 1962, the Commission reported unanimously in favour of merger. It
estimated the opposition in Sarawak at about 20 per cent of the electorate
and a little less in North Borneo. The British members, however, and
Lord Cobbold himself very emphatically, recommended a transitional
period of seven years before the Bornean states joined the others, so
as to enable them to gain more political experience. But the Malays
urged that there should be no delay; they feared lest it might offer an
opportunity to 'destructive elements' seeking to exploit racial and other
differences. They won their point when discussions began again in
London. Then the implementation of the safeguards suggested by the
Commission for the Bornean states and the date of the transfer of power
became the main items of the agenda.

On 31 July the Tungku and Mr. Macmillan signed an agreement that
the transfer of British sovereignty in North Borneo, Sarawak and
Singapore should be carried out by 31 August 1963 when the new
federal state of Malaysia was to come into being. It was agreed also

that an Inter-Governmental Committee under the Earl of Lansdowne should be appointed to work out the constitutional arrangements needed to safeguard the special interests of the Bornean states. These arose from the striking contrast between eastern and western Malaysia in political and economic development and in education. In the vital matter of education, for instance, the universities and other institutions of higher education and the research centres were all in the west. Then also in the Bornean states there was opposition to Islam as the state religion and to Malay as the sole official language. And there were demands for the recognition of the special position of the indigenous races of Borneo and for adequate protection against a flood of immigration, notably Chinese, into the Bornean states.

The Lansdowne Committee reported in February 1963 recommending that Sarawak and North Borneo be given nearly all their stipulated conditions for entry. These included a higher proportion of representation in the Malaysian Parliament than any Malay state or Singapore, control over immigration, the retention of English as an official language and a declaration that there should be no state religion in Borneo. These recommendations were subsequently embodied in the legislation passed by the British and Malayan Parliaments to establish the Malaysian Constitution. A distinguished journalist of many years experience in Malaya and Singapore[1] has drawn attention to the important part played by the Malayan Solidarity Consultative Committee in the decisions which shaped the pattern of the constitution and, moreover, in securing its acceptance by the peoples of the territories involved. It owed much, he says, to the efforts of Donald Stephens, the leader of the United National Kadazan Organization, representing North Borneo's largest ethnic group.

Lee Kuan-yew's party split on the issue of entry into Malaysia. The dissidents formed Barisan Socialis (the Socialist Front) and offered a serious challenge to the government in the Legislative Assembly. But Lee won a twelve-day debate in the chamber. Then, with characteristic aplomb, he defied his opponents in a referendum on the proposed terms of the merger. It was held in September 1961, 90 per cent of the electorate voted, and 71 per cent voted in favour of entry. It was a notable defeat for the communist cause.

The state of Brunei had sent observers only to the meetings of the Malaysia Solidarity Consultative Committee. Its dominant political party, Party Ra'ayat, led by Ahmad Azahari, agitated for a federation of the three Borneo states with ultimate independence as its objective,

[1] Harry Miller, *The Story of Malaysia* (London, 1965), pp. 224–5.

Azahari sought support in Manila and Djakarta. On 7 December 1962 his followers staged a revolt and he, from the safety of Manila, declared himself Prime Minister of the state of 'Kalimantan Utara' (Northern Borneo). A plan to kidnap the sultan was foiled, and at his request Britain sent troops from Singapore. The revolt was quickly suppressed; but the sultan accepted the omen and stayed out of Malaysia.

Azahari's revolt brought into the open the hostility of President Macapagal of the Philippines and President Sukarno of Indonesia to the Malaysia project. Azahari had received Indonesian support, and the technique of 'confrontation', successfully used against the Dutch in the case of West Irian, was put into operation against Tungku Abdul Rahman and the British Government. With the help of an underground Chinese communist organization in Sarawak Indonesian guerrillas started a campaign of terrorism in the area which brought British and Malayan forces into defensive operations against them. Sukarno's megalomania is suitably explained by the map of Majapahit which adorned his office. But he must also have feared the likely effects upon his people of the contrast between a prosperous and progressive Malaysia and their own shattered economy. Macapagal's attitude was partly inspired by pique at the British Government's rejection of his claim for the 'return' of the parts of North Borneo ceded by the Sultan of Sulu to the predecessors of the British North Borneo Company.[1]

The threat to the formation of Malaysia was a real one. Hence the Tungku, seeking a way out of the impasse, accepted an invitation to meet Sukarno in Tokyo, but failed to prevail upon him to abate his loudly proclaimed 'Crush Malaysia' policy. In August 1963 a further meeting was held at Manila with Sukarno and Macapagal. It was agreed to invite a United Nations team to examine the wishes of the Bornean peoples regarding Malaysia and to postpone its inauguration until it had completed its work. There was also agreement regarding the desirability of the association of Malaya, the Philippines and Indonesia in a body referred to as Maphilindo. Accordingly, in August 1963 a United Nations team, accompanied by Philippine, Indonesian and Malayan observers, toured the Borneo territories and checked on the validity of the elections of December 1962 in North Borneo and of June 1963 in Sarawak, in both of which the supporters of Malaysia had won large majorities.

On 13 September the United Nations team reported in favour of Malaysia. The Tungku decided at once to delay inauguration no longer, and risk any hostile reactions on the part of Sukarno and Macapagal.

---

[1] *Supra*, chap. 31.

So, three days later, on 16 September, Singapore, Sarawak and North Borneo (renamed Sabah) made formal declarations of independence and of membership of Malaysia. Then on the following day Tungku Abdul Rahman, now Prime Minister of Malaysia, formally proclaimed the formation of the new state as from 16 September 1963.

Indonesia and the Philippines publicly announced their repudiation of the findings of the UN Committee. They refused to recognize the new state, and on the day of its formation their ambassadors left Kuala Lumpur. Soon afterwards Malaysia's ambassadors were withdrawn from Manila and Djakarta. All trade except that of the smuggler had already ceased between Indonesia and Malaysia; the Maphilindo concept was forgotten. But 'confrontation', far from having the effect designed by Sukarno, helped to weld together the newly formed multiracial state and give it the internal strength it needed. The Malay world, once a prey to fragmentation, has probably gained much from this wider federation. Not very long after its formation Sukarno fell, and with him his misconceived attempt to 'crush Malaysia'.

(d) Indonesia

Indonesia began her career as an independent state with power in the hands of the leaders of the republic formed in 1945 at the time of the Japanese defeat. Under the constitutional arrangements then made there was to be a Consultative Assembly, a presidency and an elected Chamber of Representatives; but, as it was impossible to hold elections, the Independence Preparatory Committee laid down that all the powers were to be exercised by the president assisted by a Central National Committee. This consisted of 135 appointed members, and came to be referred to as KNIP from the initial letters of its Indonesian name. Its legislative powers, which were shared with the president, were in practice delegated to its Working Committee, which sat continuously. And it was to this body that the cabinet was responsible.

Until the coming of independence in 1949 there was close co-operation between the cabinet and the Working Committee, as also between President Sukarno and the vice-president, Mohammed Hatta. After independence, however, differences began to appear. Cabinets were unstable, there were seven between 1949 and 1958, and the president, taking advantage of the vagueness of the constitution regarding his position, tended to assume a role beyond the intentions of the constitution-makers, and in public speeches to appeal to the people above the heads of both cabinet and legislature. Moreover, relations between him and Hatta, whose work and political wisdom were invaluable, gradually deteriorated until breaking-point came in December 1956, and the vice-president resigned.

This sort of thing did not make for efficiency, and the welfare of the country suffered. Professor Kahin, a highly sympathetic student of Indonesian affairs, stresses Sukarno's view of himself as a revolutionary nationalist leader rather than a constitutional president, and makes penetrating comments upon his weaknesses as a head of state. He failed to understand regional sentiments, was unwilling to heed the advice of qualified leaders once his friends, and had little sense of economic realities, writes Kahin.[1] His attitude towards communism was also unsound, he says, for he was willing to use the support of the Indonesian Communist Party in order to combat the major Islamic party, the Masjumi, and he developed a tremendous admiration for Communist China. Incidentally, it was his hostility towards the Masjumi that brought the final rift with Hatta. Kahin also comments that in making the West Irian question one of personal prestige Sukarno neglected far more pressing matters, and tended to judge people and states by their attitude towards Indonesia's case.

Before the Round Table Conference met at the Hague to arrange for the transfer of sovereignty, the Dutch had organized the parts of Indonesia which they controlled into fifteen states, and the agreement was for the creation of a federal Republic of the United States of Indonesia, in which the Indonesian Republic would be one—though the most important—of sixteen component units. This arrangement lasted only a matter of months. By August 1950 it had been replaced by a unitary form of government. The argument was that for an archipelago nation the maintenance of unity was of supreme importance. But, as time went on, anti-Javanese sentiment and Jakarta's inadequacy in dealing with regional welfare and local autonomy caused the ever-present centrifugal tendencies to rise to dangerous heights. Java produced relatively little for foreign export, while some of the other regions contributed heavily to Indonesia's vital earnings of foreign exchange. There was also no little alarm in the rest of Indonesia at the increasing strength of the communist movement in Java.

From 1956 to 1958 crisis after crisis developed. Bloodless *coups* late in 1956 led to the establishment of army-led regional councils in Central, North and South Sumatra. In March 1957 similar things happened in East Indonesia and Kalimantan. The rebels maintained

[1] George McT. Kahin in *Major Governments of Asia*, pp. 539–40.

their power by diverting to their own use some of the export revenues of their respective areas. In suppressing the risings the central government surrendered much of its power to the army chief-of-staff and the regional military commanders, and as a result lost both prestige and authority. But the big showdown with the 'Revolutionary Government of the Republic of Indonesia', established at Padang in Central Sumatra in February 1958, showed that there was little support for a breakaway policy: national sentiment was against separation. Military measures, however, were no real solution: the problem of regional autonomy remained, and in bold terms it meant that the regions outside Java should have both more money and more power over its spending.[1] To deal satisfactorily with such a situation nothing less than a fundamental revision of the relations between the central government and the regions was called for. But, having declared itself so firmly against the Dutch-sponsored federation a few years earlier, Sukarno's government would not listen to any suggestions for a solution along federal lines.

Regionalism, however, was far from being the most urgent problem facing independent Indonesia. Economic conditions, resulting from the stresses of the Japanese occupation and the subsequent struggle against the Dutch, could not have been worse. The scorched-earth policy pursued against the Dutch had entailed a vast destruction of transport facilities, oil installations, plantation equipment and sugar centrals. Population increase and peasant poverty went hand in hand. In Java population pressure on the land caused peasant plots to decrease in size, and with the percentage of forest land already below the erosion danger-level only emigration on a large scale could prevent dire poverty. Elsewhere population growth was even faster than in Java, but, although there was plenty of land, there was severe lack of capital and, consequently, underemployment of labour. One result was that Indonesia did not produce enough food for her population: she had to import large quantities of rice, which took up foreign exchange she could better have used for purchasing industrial raw materials and capital goods. But so intense was national sentiment that measures seriously affecting her export-oriented economy were deliberately taken in order to displace Western, particularly Dutch, economic enterprise. She suffered from the start from a grave shortage of trained and experienced personnel. But this did not prevent her in December 1957 from taking over, for purely political reasons, Dutch assets and causing the departure of the Dutch technical and administrative staffs still in the

[1] Herbert Feith, 'Indonesia' in G. McT. Kahin (ed.), *Governments and Politics of Southeast Asia*, p. 226.

country. The effect was disastrous. Production declined, her exports suffered, her foreign reserves were hit, and the government's revenue, which depended largely upon export-import duties, was reduced. And the situation was made even worse by the smuggling which developed to Singapore, British Borneo and the Philippines on a scale large enough to affect the official volume of exports.

One of Indonesia's worst disabilities in her early days of independence sprang from the fact that under Dutch rule few Indonesians had served in positions of responsibility in the civil service or business. The dismissal or resignation of the great bulk of Dutch and Eurasian civil servants in, or soon after, 1950 meant that most of the Indonesians, who were promoted into the middle or upper ranks of the civil service, had had no training for the posts they came to occupy, while the lower grades came to be grossly overstaffed owing to various forms of political pressure. And, although salaries in all the services were much lower than they had been under the Dutch, the pay of the civil service and the army together accounted for some fifty per cent of governmental expenditure. Indonesia in Kahin's view had the weakest civil service of any contemporary major state.[1]

The West Irian question, which was used by Indonesia as a convenient excuse to get rid of the Dutch and Dutch interests, has been a dismal example of the way in which the real issues of national welfare are forgotten under the stress of artificially worked-up emotion. The Dutch argued that the recognition of Indonesian independence did not necessarily involve handing over all the territories of the former Netherlands Indies, that West New Guinea was not a part of Indonesia either geographically or racially, and with supreme tactlessness they pointed out that when the Indonesians could not keep order in their own house, they were unfit to take over the administration of a primitive people and an underdeveloped country. The Indonesians on the other hand saw Dutch New Guinea as a European colonial outpost on their doorstep, and asked the pertinent question why the Dutch were pressing the need for their experience and resources in the territory when in the past they had bothered so little about it. They also pointed out that the people of the Moluccas were of Papuan stock, and that their government's record for dealing with its own aborigines was not a bad one.

The agitation began in 1952 when Holland refused further negotiations on the subject. It was worked up to such proportions by Sukarno that he has been accused of exploiting the grievance in order to distract attention from internal troubles and the shortcomings of his own

[1] Kahin, *Major Governments of Asia*, p. 522.

administration. The losses both sides suffered from the affair were enormous, both in terms of economic recovery and for the bitterness it engendered. In October 1961 the Dutch offer to place West Irian under the supervision of the United Nations, and to pay an annual subsidy for its maintenance, was scornfully rejected. Nationalistic ardour was whipped up to the point of instituting operations to 'recover' it by force of arms, regardless of the serious dangers Indonesia herself would run, should they not achieve speedy and complete success. Following appeals by U Thant, the Acting Secretary-General of the United Nations, however, discussions began in America, and came to a successful conclusion on 15 August 1962, when both sides agreed that after a short period of United Nations administration, from 1 October 1962 to 1 May 1963, West New Guinea was to pass under Indonesian administration. Then later, in 1969, a Papuan self-determination plebiscite was to be held, and Indonesia and the Netherlands pledged themselves to abide by its results.

In 1949 the largest political parties were the Partai Nasional Indonesia (PNI) and the Madjelis Sjuro Muslimin Indonesia (Masjumi). The PNI was a continuation of the party founded in 1927 by Sukarno. It had two diametrically opposed wings, one composed of Sukarno's old associates, the 'old guard', extremely anti-Western and fiercely opposed to Sjahrir's policy of moderation, and the other made up of younger men willing to co-operate with the socialist leader and to pursue a positive policy of progress. The Masjumi was a federation of Muslim organizations, the 'Consultative Council of Indonesian Muslims', as its name indicates. It also was a combination of conservative and progressive elements. It dominated the first two cabinets. After the secession of the traditionalist Nahdat'ul Ulama in 1952, its leadership came into the hands of progressives, who, while pressing for Indonesia to become an Islamic state, were not opposed to co-operation with the West. It differed sharply with Sukarno on the subject of co-operation with communism. Of the smaller parties Sjahrir's Socialist Party at first exercised a good deal of influence, but he had little popular support; he believed firmly in a parliamentary executive, wanted to substitute serious work for revolutionary ardour, and to come to an agreement with the Dutch. It was greatly to the detriment of his country's interests that at the first general election, which was not held until September 1955, his group of able and honest men lost influence.

Four main parties emerged from the polls, the PNI and the Masjumi with equal representation, the Nadat'ul Ulama next and the Communist Party not far behind. The communist success was the most striking result, and a foreboding of possible danger ahead. The parties advocating the creation of a Muslim state held only forty per cent of the total seats of the Constituent Assembly. Unfortunately the way was not paved for better government or even for stability: cabinets were still too weak to deal resolutely with the great pressing problems. So there was disillusionment with the parliamentary system and a period of crisis, to which reference has been made above, set in. When the leadership of Ali Sastroamidjojo of the PNI, a coalition of the anti-communist parties, failed to come to grips with the situation, Sukarno offered 'guided democracy' in March 1957 as the solution. There was to be a new advisory National Council under his chairmanship, and an all-party cabinet including communists.

These proposals brought on a long dispute with the political parties, and were ultimately rejected in 1959 by the Constituent Assembly through the opposition of the Muslim parties. Whereupon by presidential decree of 5 July he dissolved the Constituent Assembly, abolished the Provisional Constitution, and restored the constitution of 1945, under which parliament could not overthrow the government. He then personally undertook the dual role of head of state and prime minister. He formed an inner cabinet of ten, and under it grouped twenty-five deputy ministers. Members of the armed forces formed one quarter of the membership of his government; all political activities were banned. In March 1960 he took two further steps by suspending parliament for opposition to his budget proposals and substituting for it a 'Mutual Co-operation' parliament composed of 130 members of political parties and 131 of the armed forces and certain functional groups. At its opening meeting on 16 August he announced the severance of relations with the Netherlands because of that country's 'persistent refusal' to transfer West Irian, and the dissolution of the Masjumi and Socialist parties.

If during the period reviewed in this section Indonesia's success in coping with her political and economic problems since independence has been somewhat doubtful, in the field of culture great progress has been made. A vast programme of popular education has been set in motion aiming at school attendance for all children between 8 and 14 by the year 1961 and at expanding secondary and university education correspondingly. Her achievement in this field has been unparalleled elsewhere in the world. And while obviously quality has been 'sacrificed to quantity, the overall advance has been tremendous; all the more so when it is borne in mind that this has included the imposition of Indonesian as the universal language of instruction, and that through the national language—unknown in many areas in 1950—real progress has been made in the great task of furthering national unity.

(e) The Union of Burma

The tide would have turned much faster in favour of the Burma government had it not been for the invasion of General Li Mi's defeated Kuomintang troops from Yunnan following upon the Communist victory in China. During 1950 they were infiltrating in civilian clothes into the Shan state of Kengtung. The Burma army drove them out but they returned in force, regrouped at Monghsat and in April 1951 launched an abortive offensive into Yunnan. When again attacked by the Burmese they took refuge in the frontier mountains. The diversion of Burmese troops against these invaders enabled the Communists, Karens and other rebels to regain lost ground.

During 1952 Li Mi was receiving considerable aid from Formosa through an American agency in Bangkok, and was building up his strength around the Monghsat airstrip. He was also in alliance with the Karen National Defence Organization. In January 1953 he attempted an offensive across the Salween, but it was repulsed, and the Burmese also captured some KNDO strongholds. At the same time the Burma army was keeping up its pressure upon the Communists and the rebellious elements of the People's Volunteer Army. But it did little more than hold its own. In April of that year Burma renounced further American aid and took the Kuomintang affair to the United Nations General Assembly. The upshot was an agreement by the Taiwan government to negotiate. At the end of the year, after long prevarication, a bogus evacuation was staged. The Burmese followed it up by carrying out 'Operation Bayinnaung', a major offensive, which resulted in the capture of the KMT headquarters early in 1954. A further evacuation was then ordered, but thousands of Li Mi's forces evaded it, and during the year more reinforcements from Formosa were flown in. In April and May 1955 the Burmese carried out another big military operation against them, but even then many remained at large operating, under central direction, along the Kengtung frontier, maintaining themselves by opium smuggling, passing counterfeit currency and levying blackmail on the hill villages.

The constitution of the Union of Burma contained three main features, the creation of a parliamentary democracy embodying the cabinet system and the rule of law; special treatment for certain non-Burman peoples involving separate constituent states for Shans,

Kachins and Karens and a special division for the Chins; and provision for the establishment of a socialist welfare-state. As we have seen in an earlier chapter, however, the outbreak of nation-wide rebellion on the part of the Communists, of Aung San's People's Volunteer Organization, defying disbandment, and of the Karens, severely handicapped the efforts of U Nu and the AFPFL to get the new state on to its legs. In June 1951 the internal situation had improved to the extent of making it possible to hold, region by region, its first general election. By that time also American aid had begun to flow in, and the outlines of a welfare programme were laid before the electorate by the AFPFL. It was based upon an economic survey prepared by the Knappen-Tippetts-Abbet Engineering Company of New York which turned out to be utterly unrealistic. The Korean war had stimulated a phenomenal rise in the prices of raw materials and foodstuffs, and Burma's foreign exchange reserves had soared. The KTA's preliminary report, presented in May 1952, created an atmosphere of false optimism, and at the Pyidawtha Conference held in the following August to usher in the welfare state hopes ran so high that its report makes sad reading in the light of subsequent events. Before the end of the year new Development Corporations for Rural, Industrial and Mineral Resources had begun to function, and were soon followed by a whole hierarchy of planning commissions.

Then in 1953 came the beginnings of disillusionment. With the Korean armistice the price of rice began to drop, and when in August the full KTA report was presented it had slumped. The plan, based upon the idea that rice exports would bring in an adequate revenue to finance a big industrialization programme, was seen to be unworkable. American economic aid also had stopped on account of the KMT trouble. Burma's foreign-exchange reserves began to dwindle. There was extravagance and corruption, while at the same time the continuance of insurgency held up the rehabilitation of mines, oil industry and timber trade. Even as late as 1957 the insurgents held half the total working force of 3,000 elephants belonging to the Department of Forests. But so strong was the belief that industrialization was the key to better living standards and an independent economy that revenues, which should have been applied to agriculture for the improvement of crops, methods of production and marketing, were spent on industrial schemes, often fantastic. Burma had to learn her lesson in economics the hard way. The most successful undertakings were the joint ventures in mining and oil established between the government and the former British companies; but civil disorder severely restricted their operations.

With seventy per cent of the labour force in agriculture the fortunes of the country were bound up with the land situation. Two and a half million acres of paddy land had gone out of cultivation under the Japanese, but the subsidy offered by the returning British administration on every acre brought back under cultivation had been immediately effective in raising output. The high price of rice in the world market and the insatiable demand for it were further incentives. Indian chettyar landlords, who had fled when the Japanese invaded, did not return, so the problem of financing the farmers, who had assumed possession of the lands they had previously held as tenants, had to be faced. Under the various nationalization schemes, which the Union government attempted to carry out after independence, there was actually little redistribution of land, and although the aim was to build up a system of co-operative farming, little progress was made in that direction, while the distribution of loans through government agency quickly led to bad debts on a huge scale.

All paddy for the market had to be sold at a fixed price to the State Agricultural Marketing Board, which in the boom years up to 1953, made huge profits on its rice exports. But when the slump began, and the SAMB was left with unsold rice on its hands, its inefficient handling of the rice, and bad storage in particular, gave Burma rice a bad name. Assistance was forthcoming from the Ford Foundation in the training of supervisors, and from the United Nations Food and Agriculture Organization in the improvement of mechanical equipment, milling, grading, storage and marketing. But the unsold, and unsaleable, rice was ultimately disposed of in barter deals with Japan, China, the Soviet Union and some of the communist countries of eastern Europe, and not altogether to Burma's advantage, so far as what she received in exchange was concerned.

The problem of the maintenance of national unity assumed increasing urgency as time went on. In his negotiations with the non-Burman peoples Aung San had yielded to practically all their demands for constitutional rights. The constitution even went so far as to allow the right of secession after ten years to the Shan and Karenni states. The Karens failed in their attempt to withdraw by force from the Union and establish an autonomous state, but guerrilla KNDO forces continued to hold out. The Shan sawbwas favoured secession, but realized its impracticability. Karenni insurgents demanded independence. The Arakanese in Arakan and the Mons in Tenasserim agitated for separate statehood within the Union, and in 1958 U Nu, having previously refused their demands, expressed a willingness to create Arakanese and

Mon states, and invited three Arakanese to join his cabinet. The Kachins could put a formidable army in the field, and became alarmed and despondent late in 1956 when U Nu agreed to hand over to China three Kachin villages, over which Britain had never claimed sovereignty, in return for China's recognition of the Kachin boundary drawn by the British in 1914.

In 1956 the AFPFL, which since the end of the Japanese war had completely dominated the Burmese political stage, won the general election with a reduced majority because of the strong opposition of the ultra-left National Unity Front. U Nu accordingly resigned the premiership in favour of his vice-premier U Ba Swe, and announced that as president of the AFPFL he would devote the next few months to the task of purging his party of corruption. In February 1957 he returned to office, having apparently been unable to achieve the purpose for which he had resigned. Then it became obvious that a rift was developing between him and his two deputies, Ba Swe and Kyaw Nyein. In June 1958 they and thirteen other ministers resigned, and the party split into two groups calling themselves respectively the 'Clean' and the 'Stable' AFPFL. U Nu at the head of the 'Clean' faction was kept in power only by the votes of the representatives of the minority peoples and of the National Unity Front. Surviving a vote of no confidence in parliament by a mere eight votes, he promised to hold a general election. Late in September of that year, however, he announced his resignation and said he had requested the commander-in-chief of the army, General Ne Win, to take over the government and pacify the country so that a general election might be held before the end of April 1959.

The split is explainable in terms of personal rivalries, but there was also real discontent with Nu's government for lack of firmness and administrative inefficiency. Army rule, on the other hand, showed standards of efficiency and integrity that Burma had not known since the coming of independence. There was a remarkable clean-up of crime and insurgency, as well as of much else. It was found to be impossible, however, to hold elections as early as April 1959; parliament, therefore, prolonged Ne Win's term of office. Presumably he could have taken matters into his own hands without resort to constitutional means, but the significant fact is that at this stage of his career he showed the greatest respect for the constitution.

As a result of his salvage operation a genuinely free and honest general election was held in February 1960. Its result was a walk-over for Nu's 'Clean' AFPFL, and in the following April he resumed office. This was not the sort of result the army leaders either expected or

desired. It was the support of the Buddhist Church and the dislike of
the average Burman for the vigorous methods of the army that won Nu
his victory, but it spelt the failure of democratic political institutions
in Burma. For the inefficiency and weakness, that had characterized
the latter part of Nu's previous administration, soon showed themselves
again, and national unity was once more in peril. As an observer on
the spot put it: 'the country was beginning to seethe, with the Karen
troubles still going on, and fresh outbreaks among Kachins and Shans'.[1]
It is against that background that the army *coup d'état* of 2 March 1962
has to be seen.

Recognizing that world peace was vital to Burma's security, U Nu
based his foreign policy upon support for the United Nations. He
believed also that in face of the growing hostility between the two great
power blocs, headed by Washington and Moscow respectively, the
path of safety lay in Nehru's neutralism and in the active cultivation
of good relations with Burma's neighbours. Hence his recognition of
the Chinese Republic in December 1949 and subsequent treaties of
friendship with Indonesia, India and Pakistan, and his goodwill visit
to Bangkok in December 1954 when he apologized for Burmese aggression against Siam in earlier centuries. Hence also his co-operation with
India, Pakistan, Ceylon and Indonesia at the Colombo meeting of their
prime ministers in April-May 1954 when together they sponsored the
historic Afro-Asian Bandung Conference, which met in April 1955.

In all this, and in the gathering together in Burma in 1954 of the
Sixth Buddhist Council, Nu's idealism played its part, but he also displayed ample realism in his relations with China, which from Chou
En-lai's visit to Burma in June 1954 onwards assumed increasing importance in Burma's foreign policy. Burma's 1,500 miles of boundary
with China, and the presence in the country of a large Chinese community constantly on the increase through infiltration, were potential
sources of danger no one could ignore. Peking, however, made no
trouble out of the KMT question so long as Burma took adequate
steps to deal with it, showed no interest in the Burmese communists,
and gave public assurances that China had no territorial ambitions. At
the Rangoon meeting in June 1954 Chou En-lai and Nu issued a joint
communique reaffirming their adherence to the Five Principles of Co-
existence.

There were, nevertheless, two disputed areas on the Sino-Burmese
frontier, in the Wa States in the north-east of the Shan State and in the
Kachin State north of Myitkyina, and the Chinese maps of the Kuomin-

[1] Bernard Fergussen, *Return to Burma*, p. 249.

tang period showed large parts of the Union as belonging to China. There was a long history of attempts to delimit the frontier after the British annexation of Upper Burma in 1886. In the Wa States region joint efforts at agreement had broken down in 1900 leaving two hundred miles of unmarked boundary. In 1934–5 an attempt on the part of the Burma Corporation to prospect in the area led to a local war and the consequent appointment of a new boundary commission under a neutral chairman, Colonel Iselin, which reached agreement in 1937. China, however, was at the time involved with the Japanese, and the final settlement made only in 1941 by exchange of notes. This Communist China refused to accept, and in 1951 circulated the Kuomintang map with its fantastic claims.

The Kachin area had been uncontrolled by either China or Burma. In 1906 Britain defined the border as the watershed between the N'mai Kha and Salween rivers, but the Chinese refused to accept this definition. In 1914, however, Britain despatched the MacMahon Mission to draw the boundary unilaterally. In 1932 the Kuomintang propaganda chief in Yunnan published a pamphlet agitating for the 'recovery' of the 'Triangle', the northern Kachin area between India and Yunnan.[1] To this the British government replied in 1934 by a formal announcement of its control over the area.

In their 1954 conversations Nu and Chou En-lai agreed to settle these boundary questions; but the matter dragged on, and in 1956 China caused no little concern in Burma by using the technique of intrusions by her troops in both areas. So in October of that year Nu went to Peking and as a result it was announced that China was prepared to accept the Iselin and MacMahon lines in return for the cession of the Kachin village tracts of Hpimaw, Gawhim and Kangfang, and a small readjustment of the frontier between Bhamo and Namkhan. There was very strong opposition from the Kachins, and the matter again hung fire. Finally in 1960 a treaty was signed in Peking. It was very much along the lines indicated by China in 1956.[2] It left the frontier for the most part following the identical line handed over to Burma by Britain in 1948. To obtain this result Burma neither joined the Communist bloc nor abandoned her policy of suppressing communist rebels. Moreover, she continued to watch the frontier situation anxiously.

[1] *Yunnan Pien-ti Wen-ti Yan-chin*, translated by J. Siguret in *Territoires et Populations des Confins du Yunnan*, Peiping, 1937.
[2] *Keesing's Contemporary Archives*, p. 1728–D.

(f) Thailand

Political instability during the post-war period, as we have seen in the previous chapter, had landed Thailand with a military dictatorship. Field Marshal P'ibun was maintained in control by an army group against the antagonism of the navy and marines, and while various political groups and leaders were struggling among themselves he was solidly building up his own power. It nearly toppled over in June 1951 when the navy and marines kidnapped him, but after three days of fighting the army and air force quelled the revolt. P'ibun's closest associates in running the government were General P'ao Sriyanon, the director-general of police and General Sarit Thanarat, commander of the Bangkok army. The triumvirate, however, had very shaky foundations, for both P'ao and Sarit were candidates for the succession and headed opposing cliques. To add to P'ibun's troubles, his opponents, the Democrat Party, led by Khuang Aphaiwong, whom he had supplanted in 1948, had while in office appointed a committee to draft a new 'permanent' constitution, which had begun to function in January 1949. Under it there was a bicameral parliament, the lower house of which was elected by universal adult suffrage, and the upper appointed by the king. This meant that P'ibun's group had no direct control over the composition of parliament, while the Democrat Party with a number of seats in both houses was in a position to embarrass the government, though unable to exert any real power. So in November 1951 P'ibun carried out another *coup d'état*, abolished the 1949 constitution, and announced the revival of the original constitution of 1932. This provided for a unicameral parliament in which half of the seats were filled by executive appointment. Of the 123 appointed members of the new house nearly all were army officers.

P'ibun's strongest card was his intense opposition to communism both at home and abroad, and his tough nationalistic line in dealing with the large Chinese community in Thailand. The Chinese in Thailand welcomed with immense enthusiasm the victory of the 'People's Liberation Army' in China in 1949. The Chinese Communist Party of Thailand became a power in the land, while communist influence increased in the Chinese labour unions, schools and press. Long before this Thai national sentiment had been aroused against the Chinese, but now severe decrees were issued excluding them from a long list of occupations, closing many of their schools and taking action against their newspapers. The annual registration fee for aliens, which in 1939 had been four baht, was by a law passed in 1952 raised to four hundred baht. Under the nationality law of Thailand anyone born in the country became a Thai national unless registered at birth with the consular representative of his father's nationality. In 1953, however, this was amended to exclude children whose parents were Chinese.

In November 1952 the police claimed the existence of a communist plot to overthrow the government, and carried out a long series of raids in Bangkok, arresting hundreds of Chinese, temporarily paralysing the activities of their associations and closing their schools. A sweeping Un-Thai-Activities Act was pushed through parliament forbidding communist activities under heavy penalties, and General P'ao asserted that if all the Chinese who had transgressed the act were to be arrested, their number would run to 100,000 or even 200,000. The anti-Chinese campaign, which continued with great acerbity throughout 1953, was partly inspired by the communist revolts that were taking place in Vietnam, Laos, Burma and Malaya, which had given the rulers of Thailand a real sense of insecurity. It may be suggested, however, that more enlightened measures could have been, but were not, adopted because anti-communism and anti-Sinicism were tools admirably suited for suppressing political opposition and useful arguments in justification of military dictatorship.

In foreign affairs P'ibun's anti-communist policy took the form of refusing to recognize the Peking régime, opposing China's entry into the United Nations, and without hesitation espousing the United Nations' cause in Korea in 1950. As the counterpart of this policy he built up ever closer co-operation with the United States, particularly in its antagonism towards Communist China. In 1954, when Dien Bien Phu was besieged and Mr. Dulles called for 'united action' to meet the communist threat in South-East Asia, Thailand responded with enthusiasm. She became an active participant in the formation of the South-East Asia Treaty Organization (SEATO) at Manila, and welcomed the decision to locate its headquarters at Bangkok.[1] P'ibun wanted stronger military guarantees than were incorporated in the pact, and in 1955 offered SEATO bases in his country.[2]

Close diplomatic relations between America and Thailand had begun in 1950 with a conference of senior American diplomats in the Far East at Bangkok and visits to Thailand by American economic and military survey missions. Agreements for economic and technical co-operation and for military assistance were signed between the two countries. In

[1] *Collective Defence in South East Asia*, Chatham House Report, London, 1956, p. 2.
[2] Russell H. Fifield, *The Diplomacy of Southeast Asia*, 1945–58, New York, 1958, pp. 271–2.

1951 America decided to grant Thailand military aid under the Mutual Security Act. Substantial American aid thus began to be allocated to Thailand: by 31 March 1955 the figure amounted to nearly 64 million dollars. Much of it was in military aid, but also through the Special Technical and Economic Mission in Bangkok, which undertook to examine the economic needs of the country: assistance was given to irrigation works, railway rehabilitation and extension, port improvements, road construction, electricity generation and many other projects. American technicians went to work in Thailand and to train various types of specialists there. Special help was given in malaria control and in improving rice culture. The list is impressive, but the programme has been criticized. It was said to be lacking in real co-ordination, and, worse still, to be a means whereby certain Thai politicians were enabled to divert other funds to their own uses.[1] Whatever be the truth of this, it can be fairly said that American aid benefited Thailand herself. It also helped to maintain her military dictatorship in power.

In 1955 P'ibun went on a tour of the United States and Britain. His return home ushered in a change of policy as dramatic as it was inexplicable. Political repression was lifted, democracy was to be allowed to bloom, political parties might be registered, politics might be freely discussed in the central park in Bangkok as in London's Hyde Park, the prime minister would give regular press conferences, there was to be a devolution of power from the centre to the local authorities, the Chinese were to have rights approaching as near as possible to those of Thai citizens, and naturalization was to be encouraged. What were P'ibun's motives? He may have been playing for popular support to strengthen his position *vis-à-vis* generals P'ao and Sarit. On the other hand, having seen democracy at work in the United States and Britain, he may have genuinely wanted to create the same sort of political conditions in his own country; and, so far as the Chinese were concerned, the Bandung Conference had convinced him that while Communist China did not contemplate military adventures in South-East Asia, she was likely to be a strong competitor for the loyalty of the Chinese in Thailand. The Thai delegation left Bandung with the distinct impression that general diplomatic recognition of the Peking régime and China's admission to the United Nations must soon come.

As soon as controls were relaxed no less than twenty-five political parties sprang into existence. Much the largest was the official Seri Manangkhasila, which included all the government's parliamentary

[1] James C. Ingram, *Economic Change in Thailand since 1850*, 1955, p. 223.

supporters. The leftist parties formed a Socialist Front and attacked the government's foreign policy. The 'Hyde Park' orators and the press attacked the government with tremendous aplomb. And although General P'ao spent many millions of baht upon Seri Manangkhasila Party propaganda, the government won only a bare majority at the general election of February 1957. Even then it was publicly accused of falsification of ballot papers. So strong were the expressions of public dissatisfaction that the government declared a national emergency, and the experiment in democracy came to a sorry end.

The new government formed by P'ibun after the election was weak from internal faction struggles, with antagonism between P'ao and Sarit gradually approaching breaking-point. Sarit had avoided playing any overt part in the general election, and afterwards managed to dissociate himself from the Seri Manangkhasila Party. When the state of national emergency was declared, he was appointed commander-in-chief of the army. He and his group held a stronger position in the cabinet than P'ao. In August 1957 they resigned as a body, and on the night of 16–17 September Sarit and the army carried out a bloodless *coup* which overthrew the government. P'ibun fled the country; P'ao was allowed to go into exile; parliament was dissolved and the constitution suspended. Nai Pote Sarasin, the Secretary-General of SEATO, was then placed in charge of a caretaker government. On 15 December a general election was held, but no party achieved an overall majority. Accordingly a coalition, known as the National Socialist Party, was formed out of the 123 nominated members, the 45 members of the Unionist Party, a centre party, and 40 of the members of the Seri Manangkhasila, who had been elected as independents. A new prime minister, General Thanom Kittikachorn, then took office and Nai Pote returned to his SEATO post.

A few months later, on 20 October 1958, yet another bloodless *coup d'état* took place, when Marshal Sarit, who had been for several months in the United States and England undergoing medical treatment, secretly returned home, sacked the prime minister and cabinet, and assumed power at the head of a military junta calling itself the 'Revolutionary Party'. All political parties were again abolished, and a large number of arrests made for alleged breaches of the Anti-Communism Law. Foreign observers on the spot, however, reported that there was no evidence of any communist danger, but that the real reason for the *coup* was that the government was faced with bankruptcy owing to the shrinkage of its foreign exchange reserves and a cut of nearly 24 million dollars in American aid for 1958. The impasse, it was suggested, had arisen because of the revival of anti-Chinese discrimination which had caused the Chinese community to lose confidence in the government. It controlled over 80 per cent of the country's non-agrarian capital.[1] The 'Revolutionary Party' proceeded to impose an 'interim' constitution providing for the appointment of a Constituent Assembly, which would both draft a permanent constitution and exercise legislative powers. Moreover, the prime minister might govern by decree and take any necessary emergency action. Marshal Sarit himself took over as prime minister on 9 February 1959.

The story of Thailand's attempts to achieve political stability makes disappointing reading. So far, constitutional democracy has failed there, public control over the government has proved ineffective, and politics have been dominated by the competition of various bureaucratic cliques for the spoils of government and for personal enrichment through corruption.

When, however, one turns to the social scene, the picture is brighter. The expansion of education since the war has been very rapid, and compulsory primary education was almost universal. The standards at all levels, however, tended to remain low. Population has grown rapidly, yet standards of living have been maintained. The economy remained based upon agriculture, but the evils of landlordism and agricultural indebtedness never developed in Thailand to the pitch found elsewhere among her neighbours, and with the high degree of internal peace, which had existed for well over a century, there was contentment verging upon spiritual lethargy. As an American observer put it: 'Thailand is a relatively well-to-do country. If much of its wealth consists in the opportunities provided by nature for the enjoyment of leisure and a good life, it is not out of harmony with the temperament of the people.'[2]

(g) The Philippines

The year 1950 saw the nadir of post-independence Filipino public administration after the corrupt elections of the previous year. It began with so grave a fiscal and balance-of-payments crisis that President Truman sent an Economic Survey Mission under Senator Daniel Bell, and emergency measures had to be taken to enable the government to meet its day-to-day monetary obligations. Yet it was estimated that from V-J Day up to January 1950 some two billion dollars' worth of

[1] *Manchester Guardian*, 3 November 1958.
[2] Thailand, Economic Survey Group, *Report on Economic Development Plans*, Bangkok, 1957, p. 11, quoted in 'Thailand' by David A. Wilson, in *Governments and Politics of Southeast Asia* (ed. Kahin), p. 62.

American aid had been given to the Philippines. The Hukbalahap threat also assumed new proportions in that year when the party changed its name to Hukbong Mapagpalaya ng Bayan (People's Liberation Army) and called for the total overthrow of the government.

President Quirino, however, displayed statesmanship and vigour in meeting the situation. He appointed Ramon Magsaysay Secretary of National Defence, and gave him full support in a campaign against the Huks, which achieved rapid success and transformed the internal situation. He also began at once to carry out the measures of reform recommended in the Bell Mission's report of October 1950, and there was a sharp reaction from the financial irresponsibility of the earlier post-war administrations. American policy played its part in the change, for the United States undertook an economic aid programme of 250 million dollars spread over five years, but 'strictly conditioned' by the Philippines carrying out the Bell Mission's recommendations. Accordingly a series of fiscal measures was passed which made the tax revenue of 1951–2 double that of 1949–50. A Central Bank was established with strict control over credit. An Agricultural Credit and Co-operative Financing Administration was created together with Farmers' Co-operative Marketing Associations. A minimum wage law was passed, and what was magniloquently termed a 'Magna Carta of Labour' permitting collective bargaining. And further American support in the form of a definitive defence commitment resulted from the collapse of the Kuomintang government in China; in August 1951 a Mutual Security Treaty was signed between the Philippines and the United States in Washington.

The effects of Quirino's economic measures must not be over-estimated. There was not the same drive to implement them as to pass them, and the graft and corruption remained unpurged. Little was done to tackle the problems of land reform and agricultural poverty, and the country's foreign exchange earnings continued to be inadequate. Moreover, Quirino's economic policy alienated the sugar planters, thereby weakening the Liberal Party. The elections of 1951 revealed how little support it had in the country. Magsaysay's security measures and the activities of the new National Movement for Free Elections ensured that they were honestly conducted; they resulted in heavy Liberal losses to the Nacionalista Party. When two years later Magsaysay broke with Quirino and was adopted as Nacionalista candidate for the presidency, he and the party won a complete victory all along the line.

Magsaysay took over amid a wave of enthusiasm for cleaning up the administration and raising its efficiency. He cleaned up the Bureau of

Customs and greatly reduced corruption in the allocation of foreign exchange. But without an adequate supply of capable lieutenants imbued with his zeal for reform there were limits to what he could effectively accomplish, and he soon began to run into difficulties on this score. He infused much more vigour into the enforcement of the measures passed by the Quirino government, but his own special efforts were in the field of agricultural reform. He established a National Rehabilitation and Resettlement Administration to encourage internal migration and land settlement, created a Court of Agrarian Relations, and appointed an Agricultural Tenancy Commission. But the landowners in his party were opposed to any measures likely to interfere too harshly with their own property rights, and the act which he promoted in the legislature for the distribution of agricultural estates to the cultivators was emasculated through their influence.

His policy was to stimulate expansion at the cost of unbalancing the budget, and his efforts to extend the agricultural co-operative movement and the system of rural banks resulted in a vast increase of agricultural credit. But the rapid expansion of credit to the government by the Central Bank led to price inflation and the deterioration of the balance of payments position. On the other hand there was considerable expansion, and it was rapid. During the years 1954–7 the index of production rose by 25 per cent. Magsaysay's own party with intense nationalistic ardour promoted a law to exclude all aliens, save United States citizens, from the retail trades, and the import and export controls were used to increase Filipino participation in the import trade and to protect domestic industries. There was growing anti-Americanism, and in the political controversy, which became acute in 1956 when the administration's honeymoon period was over, the opposition made political capital out of Magsaysay's good relations with the United States. There was great annoyance over the American bases in the Philippines, and it became bitter when the United States Attorney General expressed the view that his country held them in absolute ownership. Even a joint statement by Magsaysay and Vice-President Nixon recognizing Philippine sovereignty over them did little to allay the feelings aroused. Among other things it was claimed that American aid was a subtle form of colonialism aimed at prolonging Philippine economic dependence upon the United States and blocking industrial development.

The sudden death of Magsaysay in an aeroplane crash in March 1957 was a disaster for the Philippines. He left a very difficult economic situation for his successor, Vice-President Garcia, to cope with.

Garcia's method was to introduce an austerity programme of credit restriction and stringent exchange controls. When he had to relax it before a storm of protest, he went cap in hand first to Washington and later to Tokyo. In both cases credits were made available, but they were tied to specific projects: they were not available to ease the general exchange position of the Philippines. So once again the Philippines had resorted to the policy described by Professor Frank Golay as 'mendicancy and erratic belt-tightening'.[1] Nevertheless, there had been useful expansion in the Philippine economy, and evidence was not wanting that the Philippine policy makers were profiting by experience and gaining in competence.

Magsaysay had been a popular leader. Garcia, like Quirino before him, was comparatively unknown, and achieved and maintained power through his manipulation of the party organization and of patronage. But whereas Quirino and Garcia dealt with the political bosses, Magsaysay deliberately appealed to the masses. He felt himself called upon, as he put it, 'to restore the people's faith in the government'. And although an increase of corruption and political irresponsibility followed his death, he had demonstrated new political techniques to the electorate, and set a useful example.

One very interesting new departure under Magsaysay arose from the establishment of the South-East Asia Treaty Organization through the signature of the Manila Pact in 1954. Till then the Philippines had looked eastwards to America rather than westwards to Asia. Now its membership of the Organization made it more aware of its Asian setting. In the following year it participated in the Bandung Conference. Thus it began to build up significant contacts with Asia, and to show signs of a desire to pursue a policy in the field of international relations free of the guiding-strings of Washington.

[1] *Op. cit.*, p. 98.

SOUTH-EAST ASIA

Statute Miles

Scale 1:25,000,000

Kilometres

© John Bartholomew & Son Ltd., Edinburgh

APPENDIX

DYNASTIC LISTS, WITH GOVERNORS AND GOVERNORS-GENERAL

Burma and Arakan:

    A. Rulers of Pagan before 1044
    B. The Pagan dynasty, 1044–1287
    C. Myinsaing and Pinya, 1298–1364
    D. Sagaing, 1315–64
    E. Ava, 1364–1555
    F. The Toungoo dynasty, 1486–1752
    G. The Alaungpaya or Konbaung dynasty, 1752–1885
    H. Mon rulers of Hanthawaddy (Pegu)
    I. Arakan

Cambodia:

    A. Funan
    B. Chenla
    C. The Angkor monarchy
    D. The post-Angkor period

Champa:

    A. Linyi
    B. Champa

Indonesia and Malaya:

    A. Java, Pre-Muslim period
    B. Java, Muslim period
    C. Malacca
    D. Acheh (Achin)
    E. Governors-General of the Netherlands East Indies

Tai Dynasties:

    A. Sukhot'ai
    B. Ayut'ia
    C. Bangkok
    D. Muong Swa
    E. Lang Chang
    F. Vien Chang (Vientiane)
    G. Luang Prabang

APPENDIX

Vietnam:

- A. The Hong-Bang, 2879–258 B.C.
- B. The Thuc, 257–208 B.C.
- C. The Trieu, 207–111 B.C.
- D. The Earlier Li, A.D. 544–602
- E. The Ngo, 939–54
- F. The Dinh, 968–79
- G. The Earlier Le, 980–1009
- H. The Later Li, 1009–1225
- I. The Tran, 1225–1400
- J. The Ho, 1400–1407
- K. The restored Tran, 1407–18
- L. The Later Le, 1418–1804
- M. The Mac, 1527–1677
- N. The Trinh, 1539–1787
- O. The Tay-Son, 1778–1802
- P. The Nguyen
- Q. Governors and governors-general of French Indo-China

APPENDIX

DYNASTIC LISTS

BURMA AND ARAKAN

A. RULERS OF PAGAN BEFORE 1044
(According to the Burmese chronicles)

		date of accession
1. Pyusawti	. . . . . .	167
2. Timinyi, son of 1	. . . . .	242
3. Yimminpaik, son of 2	. . . .	299
4. Paikthili, son of 3	. . . .	324
5. Thinlikyaung, son of 4	. . .	344
6. Kyaungdurit, son of 5	. . . .	387
7. Thihtan, son of 6	. . . . .	412

(439–97 usurpers)

8. Tharamunhpya, grandson of 7	. . . .	494
9. Thaiktaing, son of 8	. . . .	516
10. Thinlikyaungnge, son of 9	. . . .	523
11. Thinlipaik, brother of 10	. . . .	532
12. Hkanlaung, brother of 10	. . . .	547
13. Hkanlat, brother of 10	. . . .	557
14. Htuntaik, son of 13	. . . .	569
15. Htunpyit, son of 14	. . . .	582
16. Htunchit, son of 15	. . . .	598
17. Popa Sawrahan, usurping priest	. . . :	613
18. Shwe Onthi, son-in-law of 17	. . . .	640
19. Peitthon, brother of 18	. . . .	652
20. Ngahkwe, son of 19	. . . .	710
21. Myinkywe, usurper	. . . .	716
22. Theinhka, of blood royal	. . . .	726
23. Theinsun, son of 22	. . . .	734
24. Shwelaung, son of 23	. . . .	744
25. Htunhtwin, son of 24	. . . .	753
26. Shwemauk, son of 25	. . . .	762
27. Munlat, brother of 26	. . . .	785
28. Sawhkinhnit, son of 27	. . . .	802

*date of
accession*

29. Hkelu, son of 28 829
30. Pyinbya, brother of 29 (founder of Pagan, 849) . . 846
31. Tannet, son of 30 878
32. Sale Ngahkwe, usurper 906
33. Nyaung-u Sawrahan, usurper 931
34. Kunhsaw Kyaunghpyu, son of 31 . . . 964
35. Kyiso, son of 33 986
36. Sokka-te, brother of 35 992

B. The Pagan Dynasty, 1044-1287

List compiled from the chronicles:

1. Anawrahta 1044
2. Sawlu, son of 1 1077
3. Kyanzittha, son of 1 1084
4. Alaungsithu, grandson of 3 1113
5. Narathu, son of 4 1167
6. Naratheinhka, son of 5 1170
7. Narapatisithu, brother of 6 1173
8. Nantaungmya (Htilominlo), son of 7 . . 1210
9. Kyaswa, son of 8 1234
10. Uzana, son of 9 1250
11. Narathihapate (Tarokpyemin), son of 10 . . 1254
12. Kyawswa, son of 11 1287
13. Sawhnit, son of 12 1298
14. Uzana, son of 13 1325

List compiled from the inscriptions by Professor G. H. Luce:

Kings of Pukam, 1044-1287

1. Aniruddha (Anawrahta) . . . . 1044?-1077?
2. Maṅ Lulaṅ (Sawlu) . . . . 1077?-1084
3. Thiluiṅ Maṅ (Kyanzittha) 1084-1113
4. Cañsū I (Alaungsithu) . . . . 1113-1165?
5. Imtaw Syaṅ (Narathu) . . . . 1165?-1174
6. Cañsū II (Narapatisithu) 1174-1211
7. Nātoṅmyā, (Nantaungmya) son of 6 . . 1211-1231?
8. Narasiṅgha Uccanā, (Naratheinhka) son of 7 . 1231?-1235
9. Klacwā (Kyaswa), brother of 8 . . . 1235-1249?
10. Uccanā, (Uzana) son of 8 . . . 1249?-1256?
11. Maṅ Yan, son of 10 1256
12. Tarukpliy (Narathihapate), brother of 11 . . 1256?-1287

C. Rulers of Myinsaing and Pinya, 1298–1364

			date of accession
1. Athinhkaya	⎫		
2. Yazathinkyan	⎬ The Three Shan Brothers	. .	1298
3. Thihathu	⎭		
3. Thihathu, at Pinya	.	. .	1312
4. Uzana, son of Kyawswa of Pagan	.	. .	1324
5. Ngashishin, half-brother of 4	.	. .	1343
6. Kyawswange, son of 5	.	. .	1350
7. Narathu, brother of 6	.	. .	1359
8. Uzana Pyaung, brother of 6	.	. .	1364
9. Thadominbya, descendant of 3 (founder of Ava)	.	.	1364

D. Rulers of Sagaing, 1315–64

1. Sawyun, son of Thihathu	.	. .	1315
2. Tarabyagyi, stepbrother of 1	.	. .	1323
3. Shwetaungtet, son of 2	.	. .	1336
4. Kyaswa, son of 1	.	. .	1340
5. Nawrahtaminye, brother of 4	.	. .	1350
6. Tarabyange, brother of 4	.	. .	1350
7. Minbyauk Thihapate, brother-in-law of 6	.	.	1352

E. Rulers of Ava, 1364–1555

1. Thadominbya (of Pinya)	.	. .	1364
2. Nga Nu, usurper	.	. .	1368
3. Minkyiswasawke	.	. .	1368
4. Tarabya, son of 3	.	. .	1401
5. Nga Nauk Hsan, usurper	.	. .	1401
6. Minhkaung, son of 3	.	. .	1401
7. Thihathu, son of 6	.	. .	1422
8. Minhlange, son of 7	.	. .	1426
9. Kalekyetaungnyo, son of 4	.	. .	1426
10. Mohnyinthado	.	. .	1427
11. Minrekyawswa, son of 10	.	. .	1440
12. Narapati, brother of 11	.	. .	1443
13. Thihathura, son of 12	.	. .	1469
14. Minhkaung, son of 13	.	. .	1481
15. Shwenankyawshin, son of 14	.	. .	1502
16. Thohanbwa, usurper	.	. .	1527
17. Hkonmaing, usurper	.	. .	1543
18. Mobye Narapati, son of 17	.	. .	1546
19. Sithukyawhtin, usurper	.	. .	1552

F. The Toungoo Dynasty, 1486–1752

date of accession

1. Minkyinyo 1486
2. Tabinshwehti, son of 1 1531
3. Bayinnaung, brother-in-law of 2 . . . 1551
4. Nandabayin, son of 3 1581

(Interregnum 1599–1605)

5. Anaukpetlun, grandson of 3 . . . 1605
6. Minredeippa, son of 5 1628
7. Thalun, brother of 5 1629
8. Pindale, son of 7 1648
9. Pye, brother of 8 1661
10. Narawara, son of 9 1672
11. Minrekyawdin, nephew of 9 . . . 1673
12. Sane, son of 11 1698
13. Taninganwe, son of 12 . . . 1714
14. Mahadammayaza Dipati, son of 13 . 1733–52

G. The Alaungpaya or Konbaung Dynasty, 1752–1885

Capitals at Shwebo (1752–65), Ava (1765–83), Amarapura (1783–1823), Ava (1823–37), Amarapura (1837–57) and Mandalay (1857–85)

1. Alaungpaya of Shwebo . . 1752
2. Naungdawgyi, son of 1 . . 1760
3. Hsinbyushin, brother of 2 . . 1763
4. Singu Min, son of 3 . . 1776
5. Maung Maung, son of 4 . . 1781
   (Reigned only seven days)
6. Bodawpaya, son of 1 . . 1781
7. Bagyidaw, grandson of 6 . . 1819
8. Tharrawaddy, brother of 7 . . 1838
9. Pagan Min, son of 8 . . 1846
10. Mindon Min, brother of 9 . . 1853
11. Thibaw, son of 10 . . 1878

H. Mon Rulers of Hanthawaddy (Pegu)

1. Thamala, legendary founder of Pegu . 825
2. Wimala, brother of 1 . . 837
3. Atha, nephew of 2 . . 854
4. Areindama 861
5. A monk 885

I. Rulers of Arakan

The chronicles list fifty-four kings of the Dinnyawadi first dynasty (2666 B.C.–825 B.C., and fifty-three kings of the second dynasty (825 B.C.–A.D. 746). These must be regarded as purely mythical. Then follow:

> Vesali dynasty, 12 kings, 878–1018
> First Pyinsa dynasty, 15 kings, 1018—1103
> Parin dynasty, 8 kings, 1103–67
> Krit dynasty, 4 kings, 1167–80
> Second Pyinsa dynasty, 16 kings, 1180–1237
> Launggyet dynasty, 17 kings, 1237–1433
> Mrohaung (Mrauk-u) dynasty, 1433–1785

The complete list is in A. P. Phayre, *History of Burma*, pp. 289–304. G. E. Harvey, *op cit.*, pp. 369–72, gives it from A.D. 146.

From the Sanskrit inscriptions of Arakan the late Professor E. H. Johnston[1] put together two lists of rulers. The historicity of the first cannot be checked, but it is probably a little nearer to fact than the lists of early rulers in the chronicles. It runs:

		duration of reign
1.	. . . . .	120 years
2.	. . . . .	120
3.	. . . . .	120
4.	Bahubalin	120
5.	Raghupati	120
6.	. . . . .	120
7.	Candrodaya . . .	27
8.	The Annaveta kings . .	5
9.	. . . . .	77
10.	Rimbhyappa (?) . . .	23
11.	Kuverami or Kuvera, a queen .	5
12.	Umavirya (?), husband of 11 .	20
13.	Jugna (?)	7
14.	Lanki	2

The second list is of a Candra dynsty. The coins of six of these rulers have been found. Johnson suggests that the dynasty began between A.D. 330 and 360. The chronicles show a Candra dynasty reigning between 788 and 1018. But save for its name and length, 230 years, it bears no resemblance to the other. Johnson's comment is: 'It would seem that the Chronicles derived ultimately from an authentic list, which has survived in a form corrupted beyond hope of restoration.'[2]

[1] 'Some Sanskrit Inscriptions of Arakan', BSOAS, xi, 2, pp. 357–85.
[2] loc. cit., p. 369.

The Candra Dynasty (Johnson's list)

		duration of reign
1. Dven Candra	.	55 years
2. Rajacandra	.	20
3. Kalacandra	.	9
4. Devacandra	.	22
5. Yajñacandra	.	7
6. Candrabandhu	.	6
7. Bhumicandra	.	7
8. Bhuticandra	.	24
9. Niticandra	.	55
10. Viryacandra	.	3
11. Priticandra	.	12
12. Prthvicandra	.	7
13. Dhrticandra	.	3

The Mrohaung Dynasty

	date of accession
1. Narameikhla, son of King Rajathu	1404
2. Ali Khan, brother of 1	1434
3. Basawpyu, son of 2	1459
4. Dawlya, son of 3	1482
5. Basawnyo, uncle of 4	1492
6. Yanaung, son of 4	1494
7. Salingathu, uncle of 6 on mother's side	1494
8. Minyaza, son of 7	1501
9. Kasabadi, son of 8	1523
10. Minsaw O, brother of 7	1525
11. Thatasa, son of 4	1525
12. Minbin, son of 8	1531
13. Dikha, son of 12	1553
14. Sawhla, son of 13	1555
15. Minsetya, brother of 14	1564
16. Minpalaung, son of 12	1571
17. Minyazagyi, son of 16	1593
18. Minhkamaung, son of 17	1612
19. Thirithudamma, son of 18	1622
20. Minsani, son of 19	1638
21. Narapatigyi, great-grandson of 11	1638
22. Thado, nephew of 21	1645
23. Sandathudamma, son of 22	1652

		date of accession
24.	Thirithuriya, son of 23	1684
25.	Waradhammaraza, brother of 24	1685
26.	Munithudhammaraza, brother of 25	1692
27.	Sandathuriyadhamma, brother of 26	1694
28.	Nawrahtazaw, son of 27	1696
29.	Mayokpiya, usurper	1696
30.	Kalamandat, usurper	1697
31.	Naradipati, son of 27	1698
32.	Sandawimala, grandson of 22	1700
33.	Sandathuriya, grandson of 23	1706
34.	Sandawizaya, usurper	1710
35.	Sandathuriya, son-in-law of 34	1731
36.	Naradipati, son of 35	1734
37.	Narapawara, usurper	1735
38.	Sandawizaya, cousin of 37	1737
39.	Katya, usurper	1737
40.	Madarit, brother of 38	1737
41.	Nara-apaya, uncle of 40	1742
42.	Thirithu, son of 41	1761
43.	Sandapavama, brother of 42	1761
44.	Apaya, brother-in-law of 43	1764
45.	Sandathumana, brother-in-law of 44	1773
46.	Sandawinala, usurper	1777
47.	Sandathaditha	1777
48.	Thamada	1782

CAMBODIA

A. FUNAN

1.	Kaundinya (Hun-t'ien)	latter part of first century A. D.
2.	Hun P'an-h'uang	second half of second century
3.	P'an-p'an, son of 2 (reigned three years)	early third century
4.	Fan Shih-man, general	c. 205–c. 225
5.	Fan Chin-sheng, son of 4	
6.	Fan Chan, usurper	
7.	Fan Ch'ang, son of 4	
8.	Fan Hsun, usurper	came to throne c. 240 reigning in 287
9.	Chu Chan-t'an	reigning in 357

10. Kaundinya II   died before 434
11. Che-li-pa-mo   embassies to China 434–5

12. (Kaundinya) Jayavarman   reigning in 484
                                                       died 514
13. Rudravarman   .   .   .   succeeded to throne 514
                                                reigning in 539

B. Chenla

date of accession

1. Bhavavarman I, grandson of Rudravarman of Funan   .   *c.* 550
2. Mahendravarman (Chitrasena), brother of 1   .   .   *c.* 600
3. Isanavarman I, son of 2   .   .   .   .   *c.* 611
4. Bhavavarman II, relationship unknown   .   .   . 635(?)
5. Jayavarman I, son of 4(?)   .   .   .   .   *c.* 650
6. Jayadevi, widow of 5   .   .   .   . reigning in 713

(a) Aninditapura

Baladitya
Nripatindravarman, grandson of Baladitya, latter half of seventh century
Pushkaraksha, son of above, marries heiress of Sambhupura

(b) Sambhupura

Sambhuvarman, son of Pushkaraksha, first half eighth century
Rajendravarman, son of above, died in last quarter of eighth century
Mahipativarman, son of above

C. The Angkor Monarchy

date of accession

1. Jayavarman II   .   .   .   .   .   . 802(?)
2. Jayavarman III, son of 1   850
3. Indravarman I, cousin of 2 877
4. Yasovarman I, son of 3   889
5. Harshavarman I, son of 4   900
6. Isanavarman II, brother of 5   .   .   .   . *c.* 922
7. Jayavarman IV, usurper   928
8. Harshavarman II, son of 7 942
9. Rajendravarman II, grandson of 3 944
10. Jayavarman V, son of 9   968
11. Udayadityavarman I, maternal nephew of 10   .   . 1001
12. [Jayaviravarman, 1002(?)–1011(?)]
13. Suryavarman I, usurper   1002

date of
accession

14. Udayadityavarman II, son of 13 1050
15. Harshavarman III, brother of 14 1066
16. Jayavarman VI, usurper 1080
17. Dharanindravarman I, brother of 16 . . 1107
18. Suryavarman II, maternal great-nephew of 17 . 1113
19. Dharanindravarman II, cousin of 18 . . 1150
20. Yasovarman II, son of 19 1160
21. Tribhuvanadityavarman, usurper . . . 1166
22. Jayavarman VII, son of 19 . . . 1181
23. Indravarman II, son of 22 . . . c. 1219
24. Jayavarman VIII, grandson(?) of 23 . . . 1243
25. Indravarman III, son-in-law of 24 . . . 1295
26. Indrajayavarman, a relative of 25 . . 1308
27. Jayavarman Paramesvara, a relative of 26 . . 1327–53(?)

L. P. Briggs's list of the remaining kings of Angkor:

28. Hou-eul-na . . . . reigning in 1371
29. Samtac Preah Phaya . . . died 1404 or 1405
30. Samtac Chao Phaya Phing-ya, Nippean Bat . . 1405–9
31. Lampong, or Lampang Paramaraja . . 1409–16
32. Sorijovong, Sorijong, or Lambang . . 1416–25
33. Barom Racha, or Gamkhat Ramadhipati . 1425–29
34. Phommo-Soccorach, or Dharmasoka . 1429–31
35. Ponha Yat, or Gam Yat . . . 1432–

Amended list according to O. W. Wolters, 'The Khmer King at Basan, 1371–73', *Asia Major*, vol. xii, part 1, pp. 88–9.

28. Nippean Bat (Nirvanapada) accession ?1362
Siamese interregnum in Angkor 1369–75
29. Kalamegha (*Huerh-na*) reigning at Basan 1371–3
30. Kambujadhiraja (Gamkat) recovered Angkor, missions to China 1377–83
31. Dharmasokaraja (*Pao-p'i-yeh*), missions to China 1387, 1388, died in sack of Angkor 1389
32. Ponhea Yat (*P'o-p'i-ya*), 1389–1404
33. Narayana Ramadhipati (*P'ing-ya*) 'Noreay', 1404–28
34. Sodaiya or Srey, at Angkor 1429–43, fled to Ayut'ia
35. Dharmarajadhiraja, at Phnom Penh, 1444–86, cremated at Phnom Sonthok
36. Srey Sukonthor, 1486–1512, eldest son of above
37. Kan, usurper, 1512–16
38. Ang Chan, 1516–66, youngest son of Dharmarajadhiraja

D. Rulers from 1566

date of accession

39.	Barom Reachea I, son of 38	1566
40.	Satha (Chettha I), son of 39	1576
41.	Reamea Chung Prei, usurper	1594
42.	Barom Reachea II, son of 40	1596
43.	Barom Reachea III, son of 39	1599
44.	Chau Ponhea Nhom, son of 40	1600
45.	Barom Reachea IV, son of 39	1603
46.	Chettha II, son of 45	1618
47.	Ponhea To, son of 46	1628
48.	Ponhea Nu, son of 46	1630
49.	Ang Non I, son of 45	1640
50.	Chan, son of 46	1642
51.	Batom Reachea, grandson of 46	1659
52.	Chettha III, son-in-law and nephew of 51	1672
53.	Ang Chei, son of 51	1673
54.	Ang Non, usurper	1674
55.	Chettha IV, son of 51	1675
56.	Outey I, nephew of 55, reigned 6 months	1695
57.	Chettha IV (second reign)	1695
58.	Ang Em, son-in-law of Chettha IV	1699
59.	Chettha IV (third reign)	1701
60.	Thommo Reachea, son of Chettha IV	1702
61.	Chettha IV (fourth reign)	1703
62.	Thommo Reachea (second reign)	1706
63.	Ang Em (second reign)	1710
64.	Satha II, son of 63	1722
65.	Thommo Reachea (third reign)	1738
66.	Ang Ton, son of 65	1747
67.	Chettha V, nephew of 66, grandson of 65	1749
68.	Ang Ton (second reign)	1755
69.	Preah Outey II, grandson of 68	1758
70.	Ang Non II, brother of 68	1775
71.	Ang Eng, son of 68	1779

(Interregnum 1796–1806)

72.	Ang Chan II, son of 71	1806
73.	Ang Mey, daughter of 72	1834
74.	Ang Duong, son of 72	1841 or 1845
75.	Norodom, son of 74	1859
76.	Sisovath, son of 74	1904
77.	Monivong, son of 76	1927
78.	Norodom Sihanouk, nephew of 77, great-grandson of 75	1941
79.	Norodom Suramarit, father of 78	1955

N.B.—Norodom Suramarit died in April 1960 and Norodom Sihanouk (No. 78) was appointed Chief of State.

CHAMPA

A. Linyi

K'iu-lien	192
Son	?
Fan Hsiung	270
Fan Yi	c. 284
Wen (previously chief minister)	336
Fan Fo embassies to China	372, 377
Fan Hu-ta, son of Fan Fo	?

B. Champa

According to G. Maspero, *Le Royaume de Champa*.

First Dynasty, A.D. 192–336

Sri Mara	192
X, son of Sri Mara	
Son and grandson of X	
Fan Hiong	reigning in 270
Fan Yi	end of reign 336

Second Dynasty, 336–420(?)

Fan Wen	336
Fan Fo	349
Bhadravarman I	reigning in 377
Gangaraja	
Manorathavarman	
Wen Ti	

Third Dynasty, 420(?)–529(?)

Seven rulers with title Fan	420(?)–510(?)
Devararman	reigning in 510
Vijayavarman	reigning in 526-7

Fourth Dynasty, 529(?)–757(?)

Rudravarman I	529(?)
Sambuvarman	reigning in 605
Kandharpadharma	629(?)
Bhasadharma	end of reign 645
Bhadresvaravarman	645
Daughter of Kandharpadharma	
Prakasadharma Vikrantavarman I	653
Vikrantavarman II	686(?)–731(?)
Rudravarman II	reigning in 749

Fifth Dynasty 758(?)–859(?)

*date of accession
unless
otherwise indicated*

Prithindravarman	758(?)
Satyavarman	between 774 and 784
Indravarman I	between 787 and 801
Harivarman I	between 803(?) and 817(?)
Vikrantavarman III	reigning in 854

Sixth Dynasty, 875(?)–991(?)

Indravarman II	between 875 and 889
Jaya Sinhavarman I	between 898 and 903
Jaya Saktivarman	.
Bhadravarman II	reigning in 910
Indravarman III	end of reign 959
Jaya Indravarman I	between 960 and 965
Paramesvaravarman I	end of reign 982
Indravarman IV	982
Lieou Ki-Tsong	986(?)

Seventh Dynasty, 991(?)–1044(?)

Harivarman II	991(?)
Yan Pu Ku Vijaya	between 999 and 1007
Harivarman III	reigning in 1010
Paramesvaravarman II	reigning in 1018
Vikrantavarman IV	end of reign 1030
Jayasinhavarman II	1044

Eighth Dynasty, 1044–74 (?)

Jaya Paramesvaravarman I	1044
Bhadravarman III . . .	reigning in 1061
Rudravarman III	1061

Ninth Dynasty, 1074 (?)–1139 (?)

Harivarman IV	1074 (?)
Jaya Indravarman II (first reign)	1080
Paramabhodisatva	1081
Jaya Indravarman II (second reign) . . .	1086
Harivarman V	between 1114 and 1129

Tenth Dynasty, 1139 (?)–45 (?)

Jaya Indravarman III	1139(?)

Eleventh Dynasty, 1145 (?)–1318

date of accession unless otherwise indicated

Rudravarman IV	reigning in 1145 (?)
Jaya Harivarman I	1147
Jaya Harivarman II	
Jaya Indravarman IV	1167 (?)

(Division into two kingdoms)

A. KINGDOM OF VIJAYA

Suryajayavarman	1190
Jaya Indravarman V	1191

B. KINGDOM OF PANRANG

Suryavarman	1190

(Kingdom reunited)

Suryavarman (of Panrang)	1192–1203

(A Khmer province 1203–20)

Jaya Paramesvaravarman II	1220
Jaya Indravarman VI	reigning in 1254
Indravarman V	1265 (?)
Jaya Sinhavarman II	end of reign 1307
Jaya Sinhavarman III	1307
Che Nang	1312–1318

Twelfth Dynasty, 1318–90

Che Anan	1318
Tra Hoa	1342
Che Bong Nga	end of reign 1390

Thirteenth Dynasty, 1390–1458

Ko Cheng	1390
Jaya Sinhavarman V	1400
Maha Vijaya	1441
Moho Kouei-lai	1446
Moho Kouei-yeou	1449

Fourteenth Dynasty, 1458–71

Moho P'an-lo-yue	1458
P'an-lo T'ou-ts'iuan	1460

INDONESIA AND MALAYA

A. Java, Pre-Muslim Period
(Compiled from Krom, *Hindoe-Javaansche Geschiedenis*)

(N.B.—The blanks indicate that no date is known).

I. West Java

	reigning in A.D.
Devavarman (?)	132
Purnavarman	*c.* 400
P'o-to-kia	424
Dvaravarman (?)	435
Jayabhupati	1030
Niskalavastu	
Deva Niskala	
Ratu Devata	1333–57
Sanghyang	1552

II. Middle Java

Simo (?)	674
Sanjaya, Raka Mataram	732
Pancapana, Raka Panangkaran	778
Raka Panunggalan	
Raka Varak	
Raka Garung	829 or 839
Raka Pikatan	864 (?)
Raka Kayuvangi	879–82
Raka Vatu Humalang	886
Balitung, Raka Vatukura	898–910
Daksa, Raka Hino	915
Tulodong, Raka Layang	919–21
Vava, Raka Pangkaya	924–28

III. East Java

Devasimha	
Gajayana	760
A . . . nana (?)	
Sindok, Raka of Hino	929–47

reigning
in A.D.

Sri Isanatunggavijaya, daughter of Sindok (married to Lokapala) . 947 (?)

Makutavamsavardhana, son of above . . . . .

Dharmavamsa Anantavikrama 991–1007

Airlangga 1019–49

Juru (? Janggala) 1060

Jayavarsa of Kediri 1104

Kamesvara I 1115–30

Jayabhaya 1135–57

Sarvvesvara 1160

Aryyesvara 1171

Kroñcaryyadipa, Gandra 1181

Kamesvara II 1185

Sarvvesvara II, Srngga 1190–1200

Kertajaya 1216–22

IV. Singosari and Majapahit, 1222–1451

date of
accession

1. Rajasa (Ken Angrok) 1222
2. Anusapati, stepson of 1 1227
3. Tohjaya, son of 1 1248
4. Vishnuvardhana, son of 2 1248
5. Kertanagara, son of 4 1268
6. Jayakatwang of Kediri, usurper . . . 1292
7. Kertarajasa Jayavardhana (Vijaya), nephew and son-in-law
   of 5 1293
8. Jayanagara, son of 7 1309
9. Tribhuvana, daughter of 7 1329
10. Rajasanagara (Hayam Wuruk), son of 9 . . 1350
11. Vikramavardhana, nephew and son-in-law of 10 . 1389
12. Suhita, daughter of 11 1429
13. Kertavijaya (Bhre Tumapel), son of 11 . . 1447–51

V. East Java Kings after 1451

Rajasavardhana, Bhre Pamotan 1451

(Interregnum 1453–6)

Hyang Purvavisesa, Bhre Vengker . . . 1456

Singhavikramavardhana, Bhre Pandan Solar . . 1466–78 (?)

Ranavijaya . . . . . reigning in 1486

Pateudra . . . . . reigning in 1516

B. Java, Muslim Period

I. Bantam

	date of accession
1. Susuhunan Gunung Jati (Faletahan)	1526
	(died *c.* 1570)
2. Maulana Hasanuddin (Pangeran Sebakinking) son of 1	*c.* 1550
3. Maulana Yusup (Pg. Pasarean), son of 2	1570
4. Maulana Muhamjad (Pg. Sedangrana), son of 3	1580
5. Sultan Abdul Kadir, son of 4	1596
6. Abdul Fatah, Sultan Agung, son of 5	1651
7. Abdul Kahar, Sultan Haji, son of 6	1682–7

II. Demak

1. Raden Patah Senapati Jimbun, son of 'Bravijaya', last king of Majapahit	(?)
2. Adipati Yunus, son of 1	1518
3. Pg. Sultan Tranggana, brother of 2	1521–46
4. Pg. Sultan Prawata, son of 3	(?)
5. Aria Pangiri (Adipati?), son of 4	(?)
6. Pangeran Mas ('king of Java'), son of 5	(?)

III. Rulers of Mataram

Sutavijaya Senopati	1582
Mas Djolang	1601
Tjakrakusuma Ngabdurrahman, Sultan Agung (1625 takes title of Susuhunan)	1613
Prabu Amangkurat I, Sunan Tegalwangi	1645
Amangkurat II	1677
Amangkurat III, Sunan Mas	1703
Pakubuwana I, Sunan Puger	1705
Amangkurat IV	1719
Pakubuwana II	1725
Pakubuwana III	1749

(Division of Mataram into Surkarta and Jogjakarta, 1755)

IV. Rulers of Surakarta

Pakubuwana III (of Mataram)	
Pakubuwana IV	1788
Pakubuwana V	1820
Pakubuwana VI	1823

date of
accession

Pakubuwana VII	. . . . .	1830
Pakubuwana VIII	. . . . .	1858
Pakubuwana IX	. . . . .	1861
Pakubuwana X	. . . . .	1893
Pakubuwana XI	. . . .	1939
Pakubuwana XII	. . . .	1944

V. Sultans of Jogjakarta

Abdurrahman Amangkubuwana I, Mangkubumi	. .	1755
Abdurrahman Amangkubuwana II, Sultan Sepuh	. .	1792
Abdurrahman Amangkubuwana III, Raja	. . .	1810
Abdurrahman Amangkubuwana IV, Seda Pesijar	. .	1814
Abdurrahman Amangkubuwana V, Menol	. .	1822
Abdurrahman Amangkubuwana VI Mangkubumi	.	1855
Abdurrahman Amangkubuwana VII	. . .	1877
Abdurrahman Amangkubuwana VIII	. . .	1921
Abdurrahman Amangkubuwana IX	. . .	1939

C. MALACCA

Paramesvara (Megat Iskandar Shah)	. . .	1403
Sri Maharaja, son of above	. . . .	1424
Raja Ibrahim, son of above	. . .	1444
Raja Kasim (Muzaffar Shah), half-brother of above	. .	1446
Mansur Shah, son of above	. . .	1459
Ala'ud-din Riayat Shah, son of above	. .	1477
Mahmud, younger brother of above	. .	1488–1511

D. ACHEH (ACHIN)

Ali Mughayat Shah	. . . .	1496
Salàh ud-din ibn Ali	. . . .	1528
Ala'ud-din al-Qahhar ibn Ali	. . .	1537
Husain	. . . . .	1568
Sultan Muda (a few days)	. . .	1575
Sultan Sri Alam	. . . .	1575
Zainal Abidin	. . . .	1576
Ala'ud-din of Perak (Mansur Shah)	. .	1577
Sultan Boyong	. . . .	1589 (?)
Ala'ud-din Riayat Shah	. . .	1596
Ali Riayat Shah	. . . .	1604

	date of *accession*
Iskandar Muda (Meukuta Alam)	1607
Iskandar Thani	1636
Safiyat ud-din Taj al-Alam bint Iskandar Muda (widow of Iskandar Thani)	1641
Naqiyat ud-din Nur al-Alam . . .	1675
Zaqiyat ud-din Inayat Shah . . .	1678
Kamalat Shah Zinat ud-din . . .	1688
Badr al-Alam Sharif Hashim Jamal ud-din . .	1699
Perkara Alam Sharif Lamtui . . .	1702
Jamal al-Alam Badr al-Munir . .	1703
Jauhar al-Alam Amin ud-din (a few days) .	1726
Shams al-Alam (a few days) .	1726
Ala'ud-din Ahmad Shah . .	1727
Ala'ud-din Shah Jahan . .	1735
Mahmud Shah (until 1781) .	1760
Badr ud-din (until 1765) . .	1764
Sulaiman Shah . .	1775
Ala'ud-din Muhammad . .	1781
Ala'ud-din Jauhar al-Alam I (under regent until 1802) .	1795
Sharif Saif al-Alam . . .	1815
Jauhar al-Alam II . .	1818
Muhammad Shah ibn Jauhar al-Alam I .	1824
Mansur Shah . . .	1838

(Dutch occupation 1874)

E. GOVERNORS-GENERAL OF THE NETHERLANDS EAST INDIES

1609	Pieter Both
1614	Gerard Reynst
1616	Laurens Reaal
1618	Jan Pieterzoon Coen
1623	Pieter de Carpentier
1627	Jan Pieterzoon Coen
1629	Jacques Specz (acting)
1632	Hendrik Brouwer
1636	Anthony van Diemen
1645	Cornelis van de Lijn
1650	Carel Reyniersz
1653	Joan Maetsuycker
1678	Rijklof van Goens
1681	Cornelis Speelman
1684	Johannes Camphuijs

1691 Willem van Outhoorn
1704 Johan van Hoorn
1709 Abraham van Riebeeck
1713 Christoffel van Swoll
1718 Henricus Zwaardecroon
1725 Matheus de Haan
1729 Dirk Durven
1732 Dirk van Cloon
1735 Abraham Patras
1737 Adriaan Valckenier
1741 Johannes Thedens
1743 Gustaaf W. van Imhoff
1750 Jacob Mossel
1761 P. A. van der Parra
1775 Jeremias van Riemsdijk
1777 Reinier de Klerk
1780 William A. Alting
1796 Pieter van Overstraten
1801 Johannes Siberg
1805 Albert H. Wiese
1808 Herman W. Daendals
1811 Jan Willem Janssens
1811 Thomas Stamford Raffles (Lieut.-Gov. of the English East India Company)
1816 John Fendall (Lieut.-Gov. of the English East India Company)
1816 Commissaries-General of William I of the Netherlands
1818 G. A. Baron van der Capellen
1826 L. P. J. Viscount du Bus de Ghisignies (Commissary-General)
1830 J. Count van den Bosch
1833 J. C. Baud
1836 D. J. de Eerens
1840 P. Merkus
1844 J. C. Reynst
1845 J. J. Rochussen
1851 A. J. Duymaer van Twist
1856 C. F. Pahud
1861 L. A. J. W. Baron Sloet van den Beele
1866 P. Mijer
1872 J. Loudon
1875 J. W. van Lansberge
1881 F. 's Jacob
1888 C. Pijnacker Hordijk
1893 C. H. J. van der Wijk
1899 W. Rooseboom

1904 J. B. van Heutsz
1909 A. F. van Idenburg
1916 J. P. Count of Limburg-Stirum
1921 D. Fock
1926 A. C. D. de Graeff
1931 B. C. de Jonge
1936 A. W. L. Tjarda van Starkenborgh-Stachouwer
1942 H. J. van Mook (to 1948) (Lieut-.Gov.-Gen.)

TAI DYNASTIES

A. Sukhot'ai

		date of accession
1.	Sri Int'arat'itya	1238
2.	Ban Müang, son of 1	(?)
3.	Rama Khamheng, brother of 2	c. 1275
4.	Lö T'ai, son of 3	c. 1317
5.	T'ammaraja Lüt'ai, son of 4	1347
6.	T'ammaraja II, son of 5	1370 (?)
7.	T'ammaraja III, son of 6	1406
8.	T'ammaraja IV, brother of 7	1419

(T'ammaraja IV and subsequent rulers were merely hereditary governors under Ayut'ia.)

B. Ayut'ia

		date of accession
1.	Rama T'ibodi	1350
2.	Ramesuen, son of 1	1369
3.	Boromoraja I, uncle of 2	1370
4.	T'ong Lan, son of 3	1388
2.	Ramesuen (second reign)	1388
5.	Ram Raja, son of 2	1395
6.	Int'araja, nephew of 3	1408
7.	Boromoraja II, son of 6	1424
8.	Boromo Trailokanat, son of 7	1448
9.	Boromoraja III, son of 8	1488
10.	Rama T'ibodi II, brother of 9	1491
11.	Boromoraja IV, son of 10	1529
12.	Ratsada, son of 11	1534
13.	P'rajai, half-brother of 11	1534
14.	Keo Fa, son of 13	1546
15.	Khun Worawongsa, usurper	1548
16.	Maha Chakrap'at, brother of 13	1549

date of accession

17. Mahin, son of 16	1569
18. Maha T'ammaraja, Chief of Sukhot'ai . . .	1569
19. Naresuen, son of 18	1590
20. Ekat'otsarot, brother of 19	1605
21. Int'araja II (Songt'am), son of 20	1610
22. Jett'a, son of 21	1628
23. At'ityawong, brother of 22	1630
24. Prasat T'ong, usurper	1630
25. Chao Fa Jai, son of 24	1656
26. Sri Sut'ammaraja, brother of 24 . . .	1656
27. Narai, brother of 25	1657
28. P'ra P'etraja, usurper	1688
29. P'rachao Sua, son of 28	1703
30. T'ai Sra, son of 29	1709
31. Maha T'ammaraja II (Boromokot), brother of 30 . .	1733
32. Ut'ump'on, son of 31	1758
33. Boromoraja V (Ekat'at), brother of 32 . .	1758–67

C. BANGKOK

1. P'ya Taksin, Chinese general in Siamese service . .	1767
2. Rama I (P'ra P'utt'a Yot Fa Chulalok), Siamese general .	1782
3. Rama II, son of 2	1809
4. Rama III (P'ra Nang Klao), son of 3 . . .	1824
5. Rama IV (Maha Mongkut), brother of 4 . . .	1851
6. Rama V (Chulalongkorn), son of 5	1868
7. Rama VI (Maha Vajiravudh), son of 6 . . .	1910
8. Prajadhipok, brother of 7	1925
9. Ananda Mahidol, nephew of 8 . . .	1935
10. Bumipol Adulet, brother of 9 . . .	1946

D. MUONG SWA

List of thirty-five rulers, undated, up to the year 1316, the date of the birth of Fa-Ngoun, founder of the kingdom of Lang Chang, taken from local chronicles (Le Boulanger, *Histoire du Laos Français*, pp. 39–40).

1. Phaya-Nan-Tha (of Ceylon?)
2. Phaya-Inthapatha (of Cambodia), who married his predecessor's widow
3. Thao-Phou-Tha-Saine, son of 2
4. Phaya-Ngou-Lueum, son of 3.
5. Thao-Phe-Si, son of 4
6. Ay-Saleukheuk, son of 5 .

7. Ay-Tiet-Hai, son of 6
8. Thao-Tiantha-Phanit, a betel-nut merchant who came from Vientiane
9. Khoun-Swa, a Kha chief
10. Khoun-Ngiba, son of 9
11. Khoun-Viligna, son of 10
12. Khoun-Kan-Hang, son of 11
13. Khoun-Lo, eldest son of a Tai prince
14. Khoun-Swa-Lao, son of 13
15. Khoun-Soung
16. Khoun-Khet
17. Khoun-Khoum
18. Khoun-Khip
19. Khoun-Khap
20. Khoun-Khoa
21. Khoun-Khane
22. Khoun-Phèng
23. Khoun-Phéng
24. Khoun-Pheung
25. Khoun-Phi
26. Khoun-Kham
27. Khoun-Houng
28. Thao-Thene, son of 27
29. Thao-Nhoung
30. Thao-Nheuk
31. Thao-Phin
32. Thao-Phat
33. Thao-Vang
34. Phaya-Lang-Thirat
35. Phaya-Souvanna-Kham-Phong, son of 34, father of Thao-Phi-Fa and grandfather of Fa-Ngoun

E. Lang Chang

(List compiled from Le Boulanger, *op cit.*)

		date of accession
1. Fa Ngoun	. . . . .	1353
2. Sam Sène T'ai, son of 1	. . . .	1373
3. Lan Kham Deng, son of 2	. . . .	1416
4. P'ommat'at, son of 3	. . . .	1428
5. Pak Houei Luong, son of 2	. . . .	1429
6. T'ao Sai, brother of 5	. . . .	1430
7. P'aya Khai, son of 3	. . . .	1430
8. Chieng Sai, son of 2	. . . .	1433
9. Son of 3, name unknown	. . . .	1434

date of accession

10. Kam Kheut, son of a palace slave 1435
11. Sai Tiakap'at, son of 2 1438
12. T'ène Kham, son of 11 1479
13. La Sène T'ai, brother of 12 . . . 1486
14. Som P'ou, son of 13 1496
15. Visoun, son of 11 1501
16. P'ot'isarat, son of 15 . . . 1520
17. Sett'at'irat, son of 16 . . . 1548
18. Sène Soulint'a (regent) 1571
19. Maha Oupahat, relationship uncertain . . 1575
18. Sène Soulint'a (king) . . . 1580
20. Nakhone Noi, son ot 18 . . . 1582

(Interregnum 1583–91)

21. Nokèo Koumane, son of 17 . . . 1591
22. T'ammikarat, cousin by marriage of 21 . . 1596
23. Oupagnouvarat, son of 22 . . . 1622
24. P'ot'isarat II, son of 18 . . . 1623
25. Mone Kèo, brother of 24 . . . 1627
26. Oupagnaovarat, son of 25 ⎫
27. Tone Kham, son of 26 ⎬ dates unknown
28. Visai, brother of 27 ⎭
29. Souligna Vongsa, son of 27 . . . 1637
30. Tian T'ala, son-in-law of 29 . . 1694
31. Nan T'arat, usurper . . . 1700
32. Saï Ong Hué, grandson of 29 . . 1700

In 1707 the kingdom was split up into two independent states with capitals at Vien Chang (Vientiane) and Luang Prabang.

F. VIEN CHANG (VIENTIANE)

1. Saï Ong Hué, of Lang Chang . . (1700)
2. Ong Long, son of 1 . . . 1735
3. Ong Boun, son of 2 . . . 1760

(Interregnum 1778–82)

4. Chao Nan, son of 3 . . . 1782
5. Chao In, brother of 4 . . . 1792
6. Chao Anou, brother of 5 . . 1805–28

G. LUANG PRABANG

1. King Kitsarat, son of 29 of Lang Chang . 1707
2. Khamone Noi, cousin and son in law of 1 . 1726

		date of accession
3.	Int'a Som, brother of 1	1727
4.	Sotika Koumane, son of 3	1776
5.	Tiao-Vong, brother of 4	1781
	(Interregnum 1787–91)	
6.	Anourout, son of 3	1791
7.	Mant'a T'ourat, son of 6	1817
8.	Souka Seum, son of 7	1836
9.	Tiantha, brother of 8	1851
10.	Oun Kham, brother of 9	1872
	(Interregnum 1887–94)	
11.	Zakarine, son of 10	1894
12.	Sisavang Vong, son of 11	1904

VIETNAM

A. The Legendary Dynasty of the Hong-Bang, 2879–258 B.C.

Kingdom called Van-Tang

Capital at Phong-chau

B. The Thuc Dynasty

Kingdom called Au-lac

Capital at Loa-thanh

	date of accession
Thuc An-Duong Vuong	257–208 B.C.

C. The Trieu Dynasty

Kingdom called Nam-viêt

Capital at Phien-ngu (Fan-yu)

Trieu Vo-Vuong (*or* Vo-De)	207 B.C.
Trieu Van-Vuong	136
Trieu Minh-Vuong	124
Trieu Ai-Vuong	112
Trieu Vuong Kiên-Duc	111

(Kingdom incorporated in China)

D. The Earlier Li Dynasty

Capital at Song-biên

Li Nam-Viêt De Bon (Li Bi)	A.D. 544
Trieu Viêt-Vuong Quang-Phuc, usurper	549–71

date of accession

Li Dao-Lang Vuong Thiên-Bao . . . 549–55
Li Hau-De Phat-Tu 571-602

(602 Viêtnam again under Chinese domination)

E. THE NGO DYNASTY
Kingdom called Dai-co-viêt

Ngo Vuong Quyen 939
Duong-Binh Vuong Tam-kha, usurper 945
Ngo Nam-Tan Vuong Xuong-Van 951–65
Ngo Thiên-Sach Vuong Xuong-Ngap 951–4

(965–8 period of anarchy)

F. THE DINH DYNASTY

Dinh Tiên-Hoang De 968
Dinh De-Toan 979

G. THE EARLIER LE DYNASTY

Le Dai-Hanh Hoang-De 980
Le Trung-Ton Hoang-De 1005

H. THE LATER LI DYNASTY

Li Thai-To (Cong-Uan) 1009
Li Thai-Ton (Phat Ma) 1028
Li Thanh-Ton 1054
Li Nhon-Ton 1072
Li Than-Ton 1127
Li Anh-Ton 1138
Li Cao-Ton 1175
Li Huê-Ton 1210
Li Chieu-Hoang 1224

I. THE TRAN DYNASTY

Tran Thai-Ton 1225
Tran Thanh-Ton 1258
Tran Nhon-Ton 1278
Tran Anh-Ton 1293

date of
accession

Tran Minh-Ton	1314
Tran Hiên-Ton	1329
Tran Du-Ton	1341
Duong Nhut-Le	1369
Tran Nghe-Ton	1370
Tran Duê-Ton	1372
Tran De-Hiên (*or* Phe-De)	1377
Tran Thuan-Ton	1388
Tran Thieu-De	1398

J. THE HO DYNASTY

Ho Qui-Li	1400
Ho Han-Thuong	1400–7

K. THE RESTORED TRAN DYNASTY

Tran De-Qui *or* Tran Gian-Dinh De	1407
Tran De Qui-Khoang	1409–13

L. THE LATER LE DYNASTY

Le Loi *or* Binh-Dinh Vuong	1418
Le Nga, usurper	1420
Tran Cao, usurper	1426
Le Thai-To *or* Cao Hoang-De	1428
Le Thai-Ton *or* Van Hoang-De	1433
Le Nhon-Ton *or* Tuyen Hoang-De	1442
Le Nghi-Dan, usurper	1459
Le Thanh-Ton *or* Thuan Hoang-De	1460
Le Hiên-Ton *or* Duê Hoang-De	1497
Le Tuc-Ton *or* Kham Hoang-De	1504
Le Ui-Muc De	1504
Le Tuong-Duc De	1509
Tran Cao	1516
Tran Thang ⎱ usurpers	1516
Le Bang ⎰	1518
Le Du	1518
Le Chieu-Ton *or* Than Hoang-De	1516–26
Le Hoang-De-Xuan (*or* Thung) *or* Cung Hoang-De	1522–7

(Interregnum of the Mac:

Mac Dang-Dung	1527
Mac Dang-Doanh	1530)

date of
accession

Le Trang-Ton *or* Du Hoang-De	.	.	.	.	1533
Le Trung-Ton *or* Vo Hoang-De	.	.	.	.	1548
Le Anh-Ton *or* Tuan Hoang-De	.	.	.	.	1556
Le The-Ton *or* Nghi Hoang-De	.	.	.	.	1573
Nguyen Duong-Minh, usurper	.	.	.	.	1597
Nguyen Minh-Tri, usurper	.	.	.	.	1597
Le Kinh-Ton *or* Huê Hoang-De	.	.	.	.	1599
Le Thanh-Ton *or* Uyen Hoang-De	.	.	.	.	1619
Le Chan-Ton *or* Thuan Hoang-De	.	.	.	.	1643
Le Than-Ton *or* Ugen Hoang-De	.	.	.	.	1649
Le Huyen-Ton *or* Muc Hoang-De	.	.	.	.	1662
Le Gia-Ton *or* Mi Hoang-De	.	.	.	.	1671
Le Hi-Ton *or* Chuong Hoang-De	.	.	.	.	1671
Le Du-Ton *or* Hoa Hoang-De	.	.	.	.	1705
Le De Duy-Phuong	.	.	.	.	1729
Le Thuan-Ton *or* Gian Hoang-De	.	.	.	.	1732
Le I-Ton *or* Huy Hoang-De	.	.	.	.	1735
Le Hiên-Ton *or* Vinh Hoang-De	.	.	.	.	1740
Le Man Hoang-De	.	.	.	.	1786–1804

M. The Mac Dynasty

Mac Dang-Dung	.	.	.	.	1527
Mac Dang-Doanh	.	.	.	.	1530
Mac Phuc-Hai	.	.	.	.	1540
Mac Phuc-Nguyen	.	.	.	.	1546
Mac Mau-Hop	.	.	.	.	1562
Mac Toan	.	.	.	.	1592
Mac Kinh-Chi	.	.	.	.	1592
Mac Kinh-Cung	.	.	.	.	1593
Mac Kinh-Khoan	.	.	.	.	1623
Mac Kinh-Hoan	.	.	.	.	1638–77

N. The Trinh Family of Tongking

Trinh Kiêm	.	.	.	.	1539
Trinh Coi	.	.	.	.	1569
Trinh Tong	.	.	.	.	1570
Trinh Trang	.	.	.	.	1623
Trinh Tac	.	.	.	.	1657
Trinh Con	.	.	.	.	1682
Trinh Cuong	.	.	.	.	1709
Trinh Giang	.	.	.	.	1729

date of
accession

Trinh Dinh	.	.	.	.	1740
Trinh Sam	.	.	.	.	1767
Trinh Can	.	.	.	.	1782
Trinh Khai	.	.	.	.	1782
Trinh Phung	.	.	.	.	1786–7

O. The Tay-Son Rulers

Nguyen Van Nhac, eldest of the three brothers .	1778–93
Nguyen Van-Hué, younger brother	1788–92
Nguyen Quang-Toan, son of Van-Hué .	1792–1802

P. The Nguyen of Hué

Nguyen Duc-Trung	.	(?)
Nguyen Van-Lang	.	died 1513
Nyuyen Hoang-Du	.	died 1518
Nguyen Kim .	.	died 1545
Nguyen Hoang	.	1558–1613
Nguyen Phuc-Nguyen	.	succeeded 1613
Nguyen Phuc-Lan	.	1635
Nguyen Phuc-Tan	.	1648
Nguyen Phuc-Tran	.	1687
Nguyen Phuc-Chu	.	1691
Nguyen Phuc-Chu	.	1725
Nguyen Phuc-Khoat	.	1738
Nguyen Phuc-Thuan	.	1765
Nguyen (Phuc)-Anh (becomes Emperor Gia-long of Annam)	.	1778
Gia-Long	.	1802
Minh-Mang	.	1820
Thieu-Tri	.	1841
Tu-Duc	.	1848
Nguyen Duc Duc	.	1883
Nguyen Hiêp-Hoa	.	1883
Kiên-Phuc	.	1884
Ham-Nghi	.	1885
Dong-Khanh	.	1886
Thanh-Thai	.	1889
Duy-Tan	.	1907
Khai-Dinh	.	1916
Bao Dai	.	1925

Q. GOVERNORS AND GOVERNORS-GENERAL OF FRENCH INDO-CHINA

Civil Governors

M. Le Myre de Vilers, July 1879–November 1882
M. Thomson, January 1883–July 1885
General Begin, July 1885–June 1886
M. Filippini, June 1886–October 1887
Noël Pardon, 23 October–2 November 1887, Lieut.-Gov. intérimaire
Piquet, 3 November–15 November 1887, Lieut.-Gov. intérimaire

Governors-General

Conetans, November 1887–April 1888
Richaud, April 1888–May 1889
Piquet, May 1889–April 1891
Bideau (intérimaire)
De Lanessan, April 1891–October 1894
Rodier (intérimaire)
Rousseau, December 1894–March 1895
Foures (intérimaire)
Paul Doumer, February 1897–March 1902
Paul Beau, October 1902–February 1907
Bonhoure (intérimaire)
Klobukowsky, September 1908–January 1910
Picquie (intérimaire)
Luce, February—November 1911
Albert Sarraut (1st term), November 1911–January 1914
Van Vollenhoven (intérimaire)
Roume, March 1915–May 1916
Charles (intérimaire)
Albert Sarraut (2nd term), January 1917–May 1919
Montguillot (intérimaire)
Maurice Long, February 1920–April 1922
Baudoin (intérimaire)
Merlin, August 1922–April 1925
Montguillot (intérimaire, second term)
Alexandre Varenne, November 1925–January 1928
Montguillot (intérimaire, third term)
Pierre Pasquier, August 1928
René Robin, February 1934
Jules Brevié, September 1936
General Georges Albert Julien Catroux, August 1939
Admiral Jean Decoux, July 1940

High Commissioners

Admiral Georges Thierry d'Argenlieu, 6 September 1945
Emile Bollaert, 27 March 1947
Leon Pignon, 20 October 1948
General Jean de Lattre de Tassigny, 6 December 1950
Jean Letourneau, 1 April 1952 (also Minister for the Associated States)

Commissioners General

Jean Letourneau, 22 April 1953 (also Minister for the Associated States)
Maurice Dejean, 28 July 1953
General Paul Ely, 10 June 1954

SELECT BIBLIOGRAPHY

SELECT BIBLIOGRAPHY

SELECT BIBLIOGRAPHY

I. Bibliographies

Asher, Adolf. *Bibliographical Essay on the Collection of Voyages and Travels, edited and published by Levinus Hulsius and his successors at Nuremberg and Francfort from anno 1598 to 1600*, Amsterdam, 1962.

Boudet, P., and Bourgeois, R. *Bibliographie de l'Indochine française, 1913-26*, Hanoi, 1929; *ibid. 1927-9*, Hanoi, 1932; *ibid. 1931-5*, Hanoi, 1943.

Brebion, A. *Bibliographie des voyages dans Indochine française du IXᵉ au XIXᵉ siècle*, Saigon, 1910.

Cheeseman, H. R. *Bibliography of Malaya*, London, 1959.

Coolhaas, W. Ph. *A Critical Survey of Studies on Dutch Colonial History.* Koninklijk Inst. voor Taal-, Land- en Volkenkunde. (Bibliographical Series 4.) 's-Gravenhage, 1960.

Cordier, Henri. *Bibliotheca Indosinica: Dictionnaire Bibliographique des ouvrages relatifs à la Péninsule Indochinoise.* 4 vols in 2. Paris, 1932.

Cotter, C. P. (*et al.*). *North Borneo, Brunei and Sarawak: a Bibliography of English Language, historical, administrative and ethnographic sources* [n.p., Honolulu, ?1963].

Embree, J. F., and Dotson, L. O. *Bibliography of the Peoples and Cultures of Mainland South-East Asia*, Yale Univ. Press, 1950.

Gaspardone, E. 'Bibliographie Annamite', *BEFEO*, xxxiv (1934), pp. 1-173.

Hay, S. N., and Case, M. H. *South-East Asian History. A Bibliographical Guide*, New York, 1962.

Hellman, F. S. *A Bibliography of British Malaya and British North Borneo*, Washington, 1943.

Hobbs, Cecil C. *South-East Asia: An Annotated Bibliography of Selected Reference Sources*, Washington, 1952.

Hobbs, Cecil C. (*et al.*). *Indochina: a Bibliography of Land and People*, Washington, 1950.

Irikura, James K. *South-East Asia: Selected annotated Bibliography of Japanese Publications*, New Haven, HRAF, 1956.

Kennedy, R. *Bibliography of Indonesian Peoples and Cultures*, Yale, South-East Asia Studies, HRAF, 1962.

Lafont, P. B. *Bibliographie du Laos*, Paris, École Française d'Extrême-Orient, 1964.

McKinstrey, John. *Bibliography of Laos and Ethnically Related Areas*, Los Angeles, 1961.

Maso, J. B., and Parish, H. C. *Thailand Bibliography* (Univ. of Florida, Bibliog. Series no. 4), Gainesville, 1958.

949

Philippines: *Selected Bibliography of the Philippines*, prepared by the Philippine Studies Program, Univ. of Chicago, HRAF, New Haven, 1958.

Trager, F. N. (*et al.*). *Annotated Bibliography of Burma*, HRAF, New Haven, 1956.

(*et al.*). *Japanese and Chinese Language Sources on Burma*, HRAF, New Haven, 1957.

Wainright, W. D., and Mathews, Noel. *A Guide to Western Manuscripts and Documents in the British Isles, relating to South and South-East Asia*, London, New York and Kuala Lumpur, 1965.

II. LOCAL CHRONICLES

Annales du Laos (Luang Prabang, Vientiane, Tran Ninh et Bassac), Hanoi, 1926.

Annales du Siam (traduction de Camille Notton), 4 vols. Vols i-iii, Paris, 1926–32; vol. iv, Bangkok, 1939.

Annales Impériales de l'Annam (ed. A. Des Michels), Paris, 1889–94.

Babad Tanah Djawi (in Javanese prose; original edition with notes by J. J. Meinsma), 's-Gravenhage, 1874 (many reprints).

Brown, C. C. (tr.). *Sějarah Mělayu or Malay Annals*: a translation of Raffles MS. 18, *JRASMB*, xxv, pts 2 and 3. Singapore, 1953.

Cense, A. A. *De Kronick van Banjarmasin*. Santpoort, 1928.

Cœdès, G. (tr.). *Documents sur l'histoire politique et religieuse du Laos Occidental* (including a translation of the Jinakālamālini, Chronicle of Chieng Mai). *BEFEO*, xxv (1925), pp. 1–189.

Damrong, Prince (ed.). *The Pongsawadan* (Royal Autograph Edition revised by King Mongkut, in Thai), Bangkok, 1907.

The Hmannan Yazawin (in Burmese), Mandalay, 1908.

The Konbaungset Chronicle (in Burmese), Mandalay, 1905.

Leyden, John. *Translations of Malay Annals* (with introd. by Sir Stamford Raffles), London, 1821.

Michels, Abel des (tr.). *Les Annales Impériales de l'Annam*, Paris, 1889.

The Nāgara—Kertāgama by Rakawi Prapañca of Majapahit, 1365 A.D. (ed. T. G. Th. Pigeaud, in *Java in the Fourteenth Century: A Study in Cultural History*. 5 vols), The Hague, 1960–3.

The Nagarakrtagama (tr. into Dutch by H. Kern, with notes by N. J. Krom), 's-Gravenhage, 1919.

Notton, C. (tr.). *Chronique de Xieng-Mai*, Paris, 1932.

Olthof, W. L. (tr.). *Babad Tanah Djawi in proza Javaansche Geschiedenis*, 's-Gravenhage, 1941.

Overbeck, H. (ed.). *Hikayat Hang Tuah*, München, 1922.

Pararaton: the Book of the Kings of Tumapel and Majapahit (ed. N. J. Krom), Batavia, 1920.

Pe Maung Tin and Luce, G. H. *The Glass Palace Chronicle of the Kings of*

Burma: a translation of the earlier parts of the Hmannan Yazawin, London, 1923, reprinted, Rangoon University Press, 1960.

Ratana Panyā: Jinakalamali (transcribed from a Siamese text and ed. A. P. Buddhadatta), Pali Text Society, London, 1962.

Shellabear, W. G. (ed.). *Sejarah Melayu* (in Malay), Singapore, 1960 (originally published 1909).

Hikayat Hang Tuah, Singapore, 1908–9.

Skinner, C. (ed. and tr.). *Amin, Entji' Sja'ir Perang Mengkasar* (the Rhymed Chronicle of the Macassar War), 's-Gravenhage, 1963.

Thipakon, chao phya: The Dynastic Chronicles, Bangkok Era, The Fourth Reign, B.E. 2394–2411 (A.D. 1851–68), tr. Chadin Flood (Kanjanavanit). 2 vols. Centre for East Asian Cultural Studies, Tokyo, 1965–6.

III. CONTEMPORARY ACCOUNTS

(COLLECTIONS OF DOCUMENTS, MEMOIRS)

Aitchison, C. U. (ed.). *A Collection of Treaties, Engagements and Sanads relating to India and Neighbouring Countries*. 14 vols. Calcutta, 1862–1939. Revised ed. 13 vols 1909; one further vol. 1939.

Albuquerque, Braz de. *The Commentaries of the Great Afonso Dalboquerque.* 4 vols. Hakluyt Soc., London, 1875–84.

*Anderson, John. *Political and Commercial Considerations Relative to the Malayan Peninsula and the British Settlements in the Straits of Malacca*, Prince of Wales Island, 1824. Facsimile reprint with introduction by J. S. Bastin in JRASMB, vol. xxv, pt. 4 (Dec. 1962), pp. 1–204.

Acheen and the Ports on the North and East Coasts of Sumatra, London, 1840.

Mission to the East Coast of Sumatra in 1823, Edinburgh, 1826.

†Anderson, John. *A Report on the Expedition to Western Yunnan, via Bhamo*, Calcutta, 1871.

Mandalay to Momein. A Narrative of the Two Expeditions to Western China of 1868 and 1875 under Colonel Edward B. Sladen and Colonel Horace Browne, London, 1876.

Anson, Sir A. E. H. *About Others and Myself, 1745–1920*, London, 1920.

Argensola, B. L. de. *Conquista de las Malucas*, Madrid, 1609.

Aymonier, E. *Textes Khmers*, Saigon, 1878.

Baird, J. G. A. (ed.). *Private Letters of the Marquess of Dalhousie*, London, 1910.

Baldinetti, G. 'La Relation sur le Tonkin du P. Baldinetti', *BEFEO*, iii (1903), pp. 71–8.

Bastin, John S. (ed.). *The British in West Sumatra (1685–1825): a selection of documents, mainly from the East India Company records preserved in*

---

* Agent to the Government of Prince of Wales Island.
† Superintendent of the Indian Museum, Calcutta.

the India Office Library, Commonwealth Relations Office, London, Kuala Lumpur and London, 1965.

Beeckman, Daniel. *A Voyage to and from the Island of Borneo in the East Indies*, London, 1718.

Benda, H. J. (ed.). *Japanese military administration in Indonesia: selected documents*, New Haven, Conn., 1965.

Berland, H. (tr.). 'Les Papiers du Dr. Crawfurd, envoyé spécial au Siam et en Cochinchine . . . en 1821', *Bull. Soc. Etudes Indochinoises*, n.s., 16 (1941), pp. 7–134.

Bijlsma, R. *De Archieven van de Compagnieën op Oost-Indië, 1594–1693*, The Hague, 1927.

Birdwood, G., and Foster, W. *The First Letter Book of the East India Company, 1600–1619*, London, 1893.

Blanc, R. P. le. *Histoire de la Révolution de Siam*, Lyon, 1692.

Bort, Balthasar. 'Report on Malacca' (trans. by Miss M. J. Bremner, ed. by C. O. Blagden), *JRASMB*, vol. 5, pt. 1, 1937, Singapore.

Bouchot, Jean. *Documents pour servir à l'histoire de Saigon, 1859 à 1868*, Saigon, 1927.

Bourges, de. *Relation du Voyage de Monseigneur L'Évêque de Béryte . . . jusqu'au Royaume de Siam*, Paris, 1666.

Bowditch, Nathaniel. *Early American–Philippine Trade: the Journal of Nathaniel Bowditch in Manila, 1796* (ed. T. R. and Mary McHale), Yale Univ. S.E. Asia Studies, 1962.

Bowring, Sir John. *The Kingdom and People of Siam, with a Narrative of the Mission to that Country in 1855*. 2 vols. London, 1857.

Brown, G. E. R. Grant. *Burma as I Saw It, 1889–1917*, with a chapter on recent events, New York, 1925.

Browne, Lieut.-Col. E. C. *The Coming of the Great Queen: A Narrative of the Acquisition of Burma*, London, 1888.

Burma. *Report of the Burma Provincial Banking Enquiry Committee*. 2 vols. Rangoon, 1930.

Report of the Committee of Enquiry into the Rice Trade, Rangoon, 1934.

Report of the Provincial Enquiry Committee on Vernacular and Vocational Education, Rangoon, 1936.

Report of Land and Agricultural Committee, pts 1, 2, and 3, Rangoon, 1938.

Report of the Bribery and Corruption Enquiry Committee, Rangoon, 1940.

Report of the Committee of Enquiry into the Village System, Rangoon, 1941.

Burnell, A. C., and Tiele, P. A. (eds). *The Voyage of John Huyghen van Linschoten to the East Indies*. 2 vols. Hakluyt Soc., Nos 70 and 71. London, 1885.

Burney, Henry. *The Burney Papers* (reprinted from the originals in the India Office). 15 vols. Bangkok, 1910–14.

Cabaton, Antoine (tr.). *Brève et Véridique Relation des Événements du Cambodge par le P. Gabriel Quiroga de San Antonio*, Paris, 1914.

Cadière, L. 'Documents Relatifs à l'Époque de Gia-Long', *BEFEO*, xii (1912), no. 7, pp. 1–82. Hanoi.

Cameron, J. *Our Tropical Possessions in Malayan India: Singapore, Penang, Province Wellesley, Malacca*, 1865. (Reprint, Oxford in Asia Historical Reprints, Kuala Lumpur, 1965.)

Careri, G. F. Gemelli. *A Voyage to the Philippines.* (Reprinted with chapters from the Travels of Fray Sebastian Manrique.) Manila, 1963.

Cavenagh, General Sir Orfeur. *Reminiscences of an Indian Official*, London, 1884.

Chapman, F. Spencer. *The Jungle is Neutral*, London, 1949.

Chaumont, de. *Relation de l'Ambassade de Mgr. Le Chevalier de Chaumont à la Cour du Roi de Siam*, Paris, 1687.

Chijs, J. A. van der. *Nederlandsch-Indische Plakaatboek, 1602–1811.* 17 vols. Batavia and The Hague, 1885–1900.

Choisy, F. T. de. *Journal du Voyage de Siam fait en 1685 et 1686*, Paris 1687.

Coast, John. *Railroad of Death*, London, 1946.

Cœdès, G. (ed.). 'Documents sur l'Histoire Politique et Religieuse du Laos Occidental', *BEFEO*, xxv (1925), nos 1–2, pp. 1–205. Hanoi.

Colenbrander, H. T. and Coolhaas, W. Ph. *Jan Pietersz Coen. Bescheiden Omtrent Zijn Bedrijf in Indië.* 7 vols in 8 parts. Vols i–v by Colenbrander, The Hague, 1919–23; vol. vi, *Biography*, The Hague, 1934; vol. vii, 2 pts, by Coolhaas.

Colesworthy Grant. *Rough Pencillings of a Rough Trip to Rangoon in 1846*, Calcutta, 1853.

Colquhoun, Archibald R. *Across Chrysê: being the Narrative of a Journey of Exploration through the South China Border Lands from Canton to Mandalay*, 2 vols. London, 1883.

Amongst the Shans, London, 1885.

Cook, James. *Voyages.* 2 vols. London, 1842.

Coolhaas, W. Ph. (ed.). *Generale Missiven van Gouverneurs-Generaal en Raden aan Heren XVII der Verenigde Oostindische Compagnie, Deel I, 1610–38*, 's-Gravenhage, 1960.

Cordier, H. 'Les Français en Birmanie au XVIIIe Siècle.' 'Notes et Documents', *T'oung pao*, i (1890), ii (1891). Leiden.

La Correspondence Générale de la Cochinchine, 1765–1791, Leiden, 1906.

Correspondence: *Correspondence of the Commissioner, Tenasserim Division, 1825–6 to 1842–3*, Rangoon, 1915.

Cortesão, Armando (ed.). *The Suma Oriental of Tomé Pires*, 2 vols. Hakluyt Soc. London, 1944.

Cowan, C. D. (ed.). 'Early Penang and the Rise of Singapore, 1805–1832' (documents from the manuscript records of the East India Company), *JRASMB*, xxiii, pt. 2 (March 1950). Singapore.

'Sir Frank Swettenham's Perak Journals, 1874–1876', *JRASMB*, xxiv, pt. 4 (Dec. 1951), pp. 1–148, Singapore, 1952.

Cox, Capt. Hiram. *Journal of a Residence in the Burmhan Empire*, London, 1821.

Crawfurd, John. *Journal of an Embassy . . . to the Court of Ava in the year 1827*, London, 1829.

    The Crawfurd Papers: A collection of official records relating to the mission of Dr. John Crawfurd sent to Siam by the Government of India in the year 1821, Bangkok, 1915.

    Journal of an Embassy from the Governor-General of India to the Courts of Siam and Cochin China, London, 1828.

Daendels, G. G. H. W. *Staat der Nederlandsche Oostindische Bezittingen onder het Bestuur van den G. G. H. W. Daendels.* 3 vols. The Hague, 1814.

Dagh-Register. *Dagh-Register Gehouden int Casteel Batavia vant Passerende Daer ter Plaetse also over Geheel Nederlandts India. 1624–82*, Batavia, 1887, etc.

Dalrymple, Alexander. *Oriental Repertory.* 2 vols. London, 1793, 1808.

    Oriental Repertory: A Reprint of Papers Relating to Burma, Rangoon, 1926.

Danvers, F. C. *Report . . . on the Portuguese Records Relating to the East Indies, contained in the Archive de Torre do Tombo, and the Public Libraries at Lisbon and Evora*, London, 1892.

Danvers, F. C., and Foster, W. *Letters received by the East India Company from its servants in the East, 1602–17.* 6 vols. London, 1896–1902.

Davies, H. R. *Report on the Burma-China Boundary between the Taiping and the Shweli*, Indian Army Intelligence Branch Report, Rangoon, 1894.

    Report on the Part of Yunnan between the Bhamo Frontier and the Salween, Indian Army Intelligence Branch Report, Rangoon, 1895.

Decoux, J. *A la barre de l'Indochine (1940–45)*, Paris, 1949.

Des Farges. *Relations des révolutions arrivées à Siam dans l'année, 1688*, Amsterdam, 1691.

Deventer, M. L. Van. *Daendels-Raffles* (tr. C. C. Batten), London, 1894.

    Het Nederlandsch Gezag over Java Sedert 1811 (vol. i, 1811–20), The Hague, 1891.

Deventer, S. van. *Bijdragen tot de Kennis van het Landelijk Stelsel op Java*, Zalt Bommel, 1865.

Douglas, W. O. *North from Malaya: Adventure on Five Fronts*, New York, 1953.

Duroiselle, C. and Blagden, C. O. *Epigraphia Birmanica.* 5 vols. Rangoon, 1919–36. Reprint, Government Press, Rangoon, 1960.

Earle, G. W. *The Eastern Seas: or Voyages and Discoveries in the Indian Archipelago in 1832–33–34*, London, 1837.

Ferrand, G. *Relations de Voyages et Textes Géographiques Arabes, Persans, et Turcs Relatives à l'Extrême-Orient du VIIIᵉ au XVIIIᵉ siècle.* 2 vols. Paris, 1913–14.

Finlayson, G. *The Mission to Siam and Hué*, London, 1826.

Forrest, T. *A Voyage from Calcutta to the Mergui Archipelago*, London, 1792.

Foster, Sir William (ed.). *The Journal of John Jourdain, 1608–1617.* Hakluyt Soc. Cambridge, 1905.

The English Factories in India, 1618–69. 13 vols. Oxford, 1906–27.

The Voyage of Thomas Best to the East Indies, 1612–14, Hakluyt Soc. London, 1934.

The Voyage of Sir Henry Middleton to the Moluccas, 1604–1606, Hakluyt Soc. London, 1943.

France, Livre Jaune: *Docs. dip. Affaires du Haut Mékong et du Siam, 1893–1902,* Paris, 1902.

France, Ministère des Affaires Étrangères. *Documents diplomatiques. Affaires du Tonkin.* 2 vols in 1. Pt. 1, 1874–82; pt. 2, 1882–3. Paris, 1883.

Docs. dip. Affaires du Tonkin, Convention de Tientsin du 11 Mai 1884; Incident de Lang Son, Paris, 1884.

Docs. dip. Affaires de Chine et du Tonkin, 1884–1885, Paris, 1885.

Docs. dip. Affaires du Haut Mékong, 25 Nov.–4 Déc. 1893, Paris, 1893.

Docs. dip. Affaires du Siam et du Haut Mékong, Paris, 1893, 1896.

Francklin, W. *Tracts, Political, Geographical and Commercial, on the Dominions of Ava and the North-Western parts of Hindostaun,* London, 1811.

Fytche, Albert. *Burma Past and Present: with Personal Reminiscences of the Country.* 2 vols. London, 1878.

Garnier, F. 'Voyage lointain aux Royaumes de Cambodge et Laowven par les Néerlandais et ce qui s'y est passé jusqu'en 1644' (M. P. Voelkel's translation of van Wusthof's Journal), *Bulletin de la Soc. de Géog,* Paris, 1871 (2), pp. 249–89.

Voyage d'Exploration en Indochine 1866–68. 2 vols. Paris, 1873.

Giles, Herbert A. *The Travels of Fa-hsien, 399–414, or Record of the Buddhist Kingdoms,* London, 1956.

Gobée, E. en Adriaanse, C. (eds). *Ambtelijke Adviezen van C. Snouck Hurgronje, 1889–1936.* 2 vols. 's-Gravenhage, 1957, 1959.

Gouger, H. *Personal Narrative of Two Years' Imprisonment in Burmah,* London, 1860.

Hakluyt, Richard. *The Principall Navigations . . . of the English Nation.* 3 vols. London, 1598–1600; Hakluyt Soc. ed. Glasgow, 1903–5.

Hall, D. G. E. (ed.). *The Dalhousie–Phayre Correspondence, 1852–6,* London, 1932.

(ed.). *Michael Symes, Journal of his Second Embassy to Ava in 1802,* London, 1955.

(ed.). 'R. B. Pemberton's Journey from Munipoor to Ava, and from thence across the Yooma Mountains to Arracan (14 July–1 October 1830)', *JBRS* (Dec. 1960), pp. 1–96.

Hallett, Holt S. *A Thousand Miles on an Elephant in the Shan States,* London, 1890.

Hamilton, Capt. Alexander. *A New Account of the East Indies.* 2 vols. Edinburgh, 1727.

Heeres, J. E. (ed.). De 'Consideratien van Van Imhoff' (*BKI*, Deel 66). 's-Gravenhage, 1912.

— and Stapel, F. W. (eds). 'Corpus Diplomaticum Neerlando-Indicum', *BKI*, 1907–55.

Hlutdaw Records. *Selections from the Records of the Hlutdaw*. 2 vols. Rangoon, 1889.

Hunter, W. *A Concise Account of the Kingdom of Pegu*, Calcutta and London, 1789.

Ibn Batuta. *The Travels of, in Asia and Africa, 1324–25*. Translated from the abridged Arabic MS. copies preserved in the Public Library of Cambridge; by the Rev. S. Lee. London, 1829.

Imhoff, G. W. van. *Consideratiën*, The Hague, 1763.

Indochine, Gouvernement General. *Contributions à l'Histoire des Mouvements Politiques de l'Indochine Française*. 7 vols of documents. Hanoi, 1933–4.

Institute of Asian Economic Affairs (ed.). *Union Catalogue of Documentary Materials on South-East Asia*. 5 vols. New York, 1965.

Jonge, J. K. J. de. *De Opkomst van het Nederlandsch Gezag in Oost-Indie*. 3 vols. 's-Gravenhage, 1862–5.

Jonge, J. K. J. de (Jr.). *De Opkomst van het Nederlandsch Gezag over Java*. 7 vols. The Hague, 1869–78.

Judson, Ann H. *An account of the American Baptist Mission to the Burman Empire. in a series of letters addressed to a Gentleman in London*, London, 1823.

Kartini, R. A. *Letters of a Javanese Princess*, New York, 1920. Reprint, Norton Library, N.Y., 1964.

Kaznacheev, A. I. *Inside a Soviet Embassy; experiences of a Russian Diplomat in Burma*, London, 1963.

Keppel, Capt. the Hon. Henry, R.N. *The Expedition of H.M.S. 'Dido' for the suppression of piracy, with extracts from the Journal of James Brooke, Esq., of Sarawak*, New York, 1846.

Laharpe, J. F. *Abrégé de l'Histoire Générale des Voyages*. 24 vols. Paris, 1816.

La Loubère, M. de. *Description du Royaume de Siam*. 2 vols. Paris, 1691. Amsterdam, 1714.

A new Historical Relation of the Kingdom of Siam, by M. de L. L. Envoy Extraordinary from the French King to the King of Siam in the years 1687 and 1688. 2 vols. London, 1693.

Lamb, Alastair. 'British Missions to Cochin China: 1778–1822', *JRASMB*, vol. xxxiv, pts 3 and 4, Kuala Lumpur, 1961.

Launay, Adrien. *Histoire de la Mission de Cochinchine 1658–1823*. Documents Historiques. 3 vols. Paris, 1923–5.

Histoire de la Mission du Tonkin. Documents Historiques. Paris, 1927.

Leonowens, Anna H. *The English Governess at the Siamese Court*, Boston, Mass., 1870; London, 1954.

Linschoten, J. H. van. *The Voyage of J. H. Linschoten to the East Indies*

(English tr. of 1598 ed. A. C. Burnell and P. A. Tiele). 2 vols. Hakluyt Soc., nos 70 and 71. London, 1885.

Loftus, A. J. *Notes of a Journey across the Isthmus of Kra . . . January–April 1883*, Singapore, 1883.

Luce, G. H. and Pe Maung Tin. *Inscriptions of Burma*. 3 portfolios of photo-gravures of rubbings. London, 1933–9.

Lyautey, L. G. H. *Lettres du Tonkin et de Madagascar (1893–9)*. 2 vols. Paris, 1920.

Ma Touan-Lin. *Ethnographie des peuples étrangers à la Chine;* traduit pour la première fois du Chinois avec un commentaire perpétuel par le Marquis d'Hervey de Saint-Denys, Geneva, 1883.

MacGregor, J. A. Translation of 'A Brief Account of the Kingdom of Pegu' by an anonymous Portuguese writer of the early seventeenth century. *JBRS*, xvi, pt. 2, Aug. 1926.

McMichael, Sir Harold. *Report of a Mission to Malaya*. G.B. Colonial Office, no. 194. London, 1946.

Maitre, E. 'Documents sur Pigneau de Behaine', *Rev. Indoch.*, 1913.

Major, R. H. *India in the Fifteenth Century*, Hakluyt Soc. London, 1857.

Malcom, Rev. H. *Travels in South-Eastern Asia*. 2 vols. London, 1839.

Manrique, Fray Sebastien. *Travels of, 1629–43*. (tr. Lieut.-Col. C. E. Luard). 2 vols. Hakluyt Soc. London, 1927.

Manshu (Book of the Southern Barbarians), trans. G. H. Luce, Southeast Asia Program Data Paper No. 44, Ithaca, N.Y., 1961.

Mantegazza, G. M. *La Birmania, Relazione Inedita del 1784 del Missionario Barnabita G. M. Mantegazza*. (Introduction by Renzo Carmignani; text in French.) Rome, 1950.

Marks, Dr. *Forty Years in Burma*, London, 1917.

Marshall, Lieut. John, R.N. *Narrative of the Naval Operations in Ava during the Burmese War in the years 1824, 1825 and 1826*, London, 1830.

Maxwell, W. G. and Gibson, W. S. (eds). *Treaties and Engagements affecting the Malay States and Borneo*, London, 1924.

Maybon, C. B. 'Quelques documents inédits concernant Pierre Poivre', *Études Asiatiques* (Hanoi, 1925), ii, pp. 143–57.

Mijer, P. *Verzameling van Instructien, Ordonnancien en Reglementen voor de Regering van Nederlandsch Indië*, Batavia, 1848.

Modelski, G. (ed.). *New Emerging Forces: Documents on the Ideology of Indonesian Foreign Policy*, Canberra, 1963.

Mongkut, King. 'English Correspondence of King Mongkut', *JSS*, vol. xxi, Bangkok, 1927.

Moreland, W. H. (ed.). *Peter Floris; His Voyage to the East Indies in the 'Globe', 1611–1615. A Contemporary Translation of his Journal*, Hakluyt Soc. London, 1934.

Relations of Golconda in the early seventeenth century, Hakluyt Soc. London, 1931.

Mouhot, H. *Voyages dans les Royaumes de Siam*, Paris, 1686.

Travels in the Central Parts of Indo-China (Siam), Cambodia and Laos during 1859–60. 2 vols. London, 1864.

Muller, Hendrik P. N. (ed.). *De Oost-Indische Compagnie in Cambodja en Laos* (verzameling van bescheiden van 1636 tot 1760). 's-Gravenhage, 1917.

Nan Chronicle, The, trans. by Prasoet Churatana, ed. by David J. Wyatt, Southeast Asia Program Data Paper No. 59, Ithaca, N.Y., 1966.

Neale, F. A. *Narrative of a Residence at the Capital of the Kingdom of Siam*, London, 1852.

Newbold, T. J. *Political and Statistical Account of the British Settlements in the Straits of Malacca.* 2 vols. London, 1939.

d'Orleans, Pierre. *Histoire de M. Constance, Premier Ministre du Roy de Siam*, Paris, 1690.

Pallegoix, Jean Baptiste. *Description du Royaume Thai ou Siam.* 2 vols. Paris, 1854.

Pallu, François. *Relation Abrégée des Missions et Voyages des Evesques Français, Envoyés aux Royaumes de la Chine, Cochinchine, Tonquin et Siam*, Paris, 1668.

Parkin, Ray. *Into the smother : a journal of the Burma-Siam Railway*, London, 1963.

Pavie, Auguste. *Mission Pavie.* 11 vols. Paris, 1898–1904.

Pemberton, Capt. R. Boileau. *Report on the Eastern Frontier of British India* (with a supplement by Dr. Bayfield on British Political Relations with Ava), Calcutta, 1835.

Penzer, N. M. (ed.). *The Travels of Marco Polo*, tr. John Frampton, London, 1929.

Phayre, A. P. 'Phayre's Private Journal of his Mission to Ava in 1855', *JBRS*, xxii (1932), pp. 68–89.

Pinkerton, John. *A General Collection of the best and most interesting Voyages and Travels in all Parts of the World.* 17 vols. London, 1808–14.

Pinto, Fernão Mendes. *Peregrinaçam de Fernão Mendes Pinto em que la conta de muytas e muyto estranhas cousas. . . .* Lisbon, 1614.
The Voyages and Adventures of Fernand Mendez Pinto. . . . Done into English by H[enry] C[ogan] Gent. London, 1653; reprinted 1663, 1692.
The Voyages and Adventures of Ferdinand Mendez Pinto during his Travels for the space of one and twenty years in the Kingdoms of Ethiopia, China, Tartaria, Cauchinchina, Calaminham, Siam, Pegu, Japan and a great part of the East Indies (reprint, slightly abridged, of Henry Cogan's translation). London and New York, 1891.

Polo, Marco. *The Book of Ser Marco Polo, the Venetian, concerning the Kingdoms and Marvels of the East* (Sir Henry Yule's translation revised by Henri Cordier). 2 vols. 1903.

Purchas, Samuel. *His Pilgrimes.* 4 vols. London, 1625; Glasgow, 1905–7.

Raffles, T. S. *Substance of a Minute Recorded by the Hon. T. S. Raffles on Feb. 11, 1814, on the introduction of an improved system of internal management and the establishment of a land rental on the Island of Java.* Privately printed, London, 1814.

Raskin, M. G. and Fall, B. B. (eds). *The Viet-Nam Reader; articles and documents on American foreign policy and the Viet-Nam crisis,* New York, 1965.

Realia. *Register op de Generale Resolutien van het Kasteel Batavia, 1632–1807.* 3 vols. 's-Gravenhage, 1882–6.

Richardson, Dr. 'Journal of a Mission from the Supreme Government of India to the Court of Siam', *JRAS Bengal,* viii (1839), pp. 1016–36; ix (1840), pp. 1–30, 219–50.

Rivière, Henri. *Correspondence Politique du Commandant Rivière au Tonkin, Avril 1882–Mai 1883,* Paris, 1933.

Rodger, George. *Red Moon Rising,* London, 1943.

Rouffaer, G. P., and Ijzerman, J. W. 'De Eerste Schipvaart der Nederlanders naar Oost Indië'. 3 vols. *Linschoten Vereeniging,* vii, xxv, xxxii. The Hague, 1915–19.

Sadka, Emily (ed.). 'Journal of Sir Hugh Low, 1877.' *JRASMB,* pt. 4, 1954.

Sangermano, Father Vincentius. *A Description of the Burmese Empire* (tr. from his MS. by William Tandy, D.D.), Rome, 1883; Rangoon, 1885.

Sayre, F. B. *Siam: Treaties with Foreign Powers 1920–1927,* Northwood, 1928.

Schouten, W. *Oost-Indische Voyagie* (original Dutch edn), Amsterdam, 1676. *Voyage aux Indes Orientales Commencé l'An 1658 et Fini l'An 1665.* 2 vols. Amsterdam, 1707; Rouen, 1725.

Scott, J. G. *France and Tongking: A Narrative of the Campaign of 1884 and the Occupation of Further India,* London, 1885.

Scott O'Connor, V. C. *The Silken East, a record of life and travel in Burma.* 2 vols. London, 1904.

Siam in the Dagh Register. *Dutch Papers from the Dagh Register, 1624–42,* Bangkok, 1915.

Siam. *Records of the Relations between Siam and Foreign Countries in the Seventeenth Century.* 5 vols. Bangkok, 1915–21.

Great Britain; Foreign Office; Correspondence Affecting the Affairs of Siam, London, 1894.

Sladen, Sir E. B. *Copy of Major Sladen's Report on the Bhamo Route* (Parliamentary Report, London, 1871). Original narrative, Rangoon, 1869.

'Expedition from Burma, via the Irrawaddy and Bhamo, to South-Western China', *Journal Royal Geog. Soc.,* xli, London, 1871.

Smith, Samuel J. *The Siam Repository, Containing a Summary of Asiatic Intelligence.* 6 vols. Bangkok, 1869–74.

Smyth, H. Warrington. *Five Years in Siam from 1891–1896.* 2 vols. London, 1898.

Notes on a Journey on the Upper Mekong, Siam, London, 1895.

Sonnerat. *Voyage aux Indes Orientales et à la Chine.* 2 vols. Paris, 1782; 4 vols. Paris, 1806.

A Voyage to the East Indies and China, 1774–1781. English tr. by Francis Magnus. Calcutta, 1788.

Stapel, F. W. (ed.). *Pieter van Dam's Deschryvinge over de Oostindische Compagnie,* The Hague, 1927- 39.

State Papers. *Calendars of State Papers, Colonial Series, East Indies, China and Japan,* London, 1862 onwards.

Symes, Michael. *An Account of an Embassy to the Kingdom of Ava,* London, 1800; Edinburgh, 1827.

Tachard, Guy. *Voyage de Siam des Pères Jésuites Envoyés par Le Roy aux Indes et à La Chine,* Amsterdam, 1687.

Second Voyage du Père Tachard et des Jésuites Envoyés par Le Roy au Royaume de Siam, Amsterdam, 1689.

Tcheou Ta-Kouan. 'Mémoires sur les Coutumes du Cambodge' (tr. by P. Pelliot), *BEFEO,* ii (1902). Hanoi. Reprint, Paris, 1951.

Templer, J. C. *The Private Letters of Sir James Brooke,* London, 1853.

Thomson, J. T. Translation from the *Hakayit Abdulla,* London, 1874.

Thorn, William. *Memoir of the Conquest of Java,* London, 1815.

Tiele, P. A. and Heeres, J. E. *Bouwstoffen voor de Geschiedenis van de Neder-landers in den Maleischen Archipel.* 3 vols. (supplement to de Jonge, *Opkomst.*), The Hague, 1886–95.

Travers, Thomas Otho. *The Journal of Thomas Otho Travers, 1813–1820* (ed. J. S. Bastin), Singapore, 1960.

Turpin, M. *History of the Kingdom of Siam and the Revolutions that have caused the overthrow of the Empire up to A.D. 1770,* Bangkok, 1908. (Original French edn, Paris, 1771.)

Vajiranana National Library. *Records of the Relations between Siam and Foreign Countries in the Seventeenth Century,* Bangkok, 1915.

Varthema, Ludovico di. *The Travels of.* Tr. J. W. Jones and ed. G. P. Badger. Hakluyt Soc. London, 1863.

Vaughan, W. *Adventures of Five Englishmen from Pulo Condore, a Factory of the New Company of the East Indies, who were shipwrecked in the little kingdom of Johore,* London, 1714.

Vliet, Jeremias van. *Révolutions arrivées au Royaume de Siam.* (English tr. L. F. van Ravenswaay, *Journal Siam Soc.,* vii, pt. 1.) Paris, 1673. Reprinted in vol. vii of *Selected Articles from the Journal of the Siam Society,* Bangkok, 1959.

Vollant des Verquains. *Histoire de la Révolution de Siam Arrivée en l'Année 1688,* Lille, 1691.

Wheeler, J. Talboys. *Journal of a Voyage up the Irrawaddy to Mandalay and Bhamo,* Rangoon, 1871.

Williams, Clement. *Through Burmah to Western China,* London, 1868.

Wilson, H. H. *Documents Illustrative of the Burmese War with an Introductory Sketch of the events of the War and an Appendix,* Calcutta, 1827.

Yule, Sir Henry. *A Narrative of the Mission sent by the Governor-General of India to the Court of Ava in 1855,* London, 1858.

IV. EARLY AND MEDIAEVAL PERIODS

Alip, Eufonio M. *The Philippines of Yesteryears: The Dawn of History in the Philippines*, Manila, 1964.

Aymonier, E. *Histoire de l'Ancien Cambodge*, Paris, 1920.

Bagchi, P. C. *Pre-Aryan and Pre-Dravidian in India*, Calcutta, 1929.

Berg, C. C. *De Evolutie der Javaanse Geschiedschrijving*, Mededelingen der Koninklijke Nederlandse Akademie van Wetenschappen, afd. Letterkunde (n.s.), vol. xiv, no. 2. Amsterdam, 1951.

'Kertanagara, de Miskende Empire-builder', *Orientatie* (July 1950), no. 34, pp. 3-32. Bandung.

'De Geschiedenis van Pril Majapahit, I Mysterie van der Vier Dochters van Krtanagara', *Indonesië*, iv (1950), pp. 481-520. Amsterdam.

'De Geschiedenis van Pril Majapahit, II Achtergrond en Oplossing der Pril-Majapahitse Conflicten', *Indonesië*, v (1951), pp. 193-233. Amsterdam.

'De Sadeng-Oorlog en de Mythe van Groot-Majapahit', *Indonesië*, v (1951), pp. 385-422. Amsterdam.

Herkomst, Vorm en Functie der Middeljavaanse Rijksdelingstheorie, Verhandelingen der Kon. Ned. Akad. van Wetenschappen, afd. Letterkunde (n.s.), vol. lix, no. 1. Amsterdam, 1953.

'Javanische Geschichtsschreibung', *Saeculum VII* (1956).

Het Rijk van de Vijfvoudige Buddha, Verhandelingen der Koninklijke Nederlandse Akademie van Wetenschappen, Amsterdam, 1962.

Bhattacharya, Kameleswar. *Les Religions Brahmaniques dans l'Ancien Cambodge d'après l'épigraphie et l'iconographie*, Paris, École Française d'Extrême-Orient, 1961.

Boisselier, J. *La Statuaire du Champa, recherches sur les cultes et l'iconographie*, Paris, École Française d'Extrême-Orient, 1963.

'La Statuaire Khmère et son évolution', *CEFEO*, Saigon, 1955.

Bosch, F. D. K. 'C. C. Berg and Ancient Javanese History', *Bijdragen tot de Taal-, Land- en Volkenkunde van Nederlandsch-Indië*, Vol. cxii (1956), pp. 1-24.

'"Local Genius" en oud-Javaansche Kunst', *Med. Inst.*, Amsterdam, 1952.

The Golden Germ, The Hague, 1960.

Selected Studies in Indonesian Archaeology, The Hague, 1961.

Braddell, Sir Roland. 'Ancient Times in the Malay Peninsula', *JRASMB*, xiii, pt. 2; xiv, pt. 3; xvii, pt. 1; xix, pt. 1; xx, xxii.

Briggs, Lawrence Palmer. *The Ancient Khmer Empire*. American Philosophical Society, Philadelphia, 1951.

Brown, J. Coggin. 'Relics of the Stone Age in Burma', *JBRS*, xxi (1931), pp. 33-51.

Brown, R. Grant. 'The Pre-Buddhist Religion of the Burmese', *Folk-lore*, xxxii (1921), pp. 77-100.

Casparis, J. G. de. *Inscripties uit de Çailendra-Tijd* (*Prasasti Indonesia, diterbitkan oleh Djawatan Purbukala Republik Indonesia*, i), Bandung, 1950.

Selected Inscriptions from the Seventh to the Ninth Century A.D., *Prasasti Indonesia*, ii, Bandung, 1956.

'Twintig jaar studie van de oudere geschiedenis van Indonesië (1931–51)', *Orientatie* (Jan. 1954), no. 46, Djakarta, 1954.

'Historical Writing on Indonesia (Early Period)' in D. G. E. Hall (ed.), *Historians of South-East Asia*, London, 1961.

Chijs, J. A. van der. *Proeve Eener Nederlandsch Indische Bibliographie (1659–1870)*, Batavia, 1875.

Christie, Anthony. *The Bronze Age in South-East Asia*, London, 1961.

Claeys, Jean Yves. 'L'Archéologie du Siam', *BEFEO*, xxxi (1931). Hanoi.

Introduction à l'Etude de l'Annam et du Champa, Hanoi, 1934.

Cœdès, G. 'Le Royaume de Çrivijaya', *BEFEO*, xviii (1918). Hanoi.

Le Royaume de Dvâravtî, Bangkok, 1929.

Recueil des Inscriptions du Siam, Bangkok, 1924–9. 2nd ed. 1961.

Inscriptions de Sukhodaya, Bangkok, 1924.

Inscriptions du Cambodge. 6 vols. Hanoi, 1937, 1942, 1951, 1953, 1956.

'Les Inscriptions Malaises de Çrivijaya', *BEFEO*, xxx (1930), pp. 29–80.

Les États Hindouisés d'Indochine et d'Indonésie, Paris, 1948. New and revised edn 1964.

Pour Mieux Comprendre Angkor, Paris, 1947. (English translation by E. F. Gardiner. *Angkor, An Introduction*, Oxford Univ. Press, 1963.)

'La Site Go-oceo, ancien port du Royaume de Funan', *Artibus Asiae*, vol. x, 1947.

Les Peuples de la Péninsule Indochinoise : Histoire—Civilisation, Paris, 1962. (English translation by H. M. Wright, *The Making of South-East Asia*, Berkeley and Los Angeles, 1966.)

Colani, M. *Mégalithes du Haut-Laos*, Paris, 1935.

'Recherches sur le Préhistorique Indochinois', *BEFEO*, xxx (1930), pp. 299–422.

Coomaraswamy, A. K. *History of Indian and Indonesian Art*, London, 1921.

Damais, L. Ch. 'Etudes javanaises: Les Tombes musulmanes datées de Tralaja', *BEFEO*, xlviii (1957), pp. 353 ff.

Études d'épigraphie indonésienne:

I. 'Méthode de reduction des dates javanaises en dates européennes' and

II. 'La Date des inscriptions en ère de Sanjaya', *BEFEO*, xlv (1951), pp. 1–63.

III. 'Liste des principales inscriptions datées de l'Indonésie', *BEFEO*, lxvi (1952), pp. 1–105.

IV. 'Discussion de la date des inscriptions', *BEFEO*, xlvii (1955), pp. 151–3.

'Epigrafische aantekeningen: I Lokapala—Kayuwangi', *TBG*, lxxxiii (1949), pp. 1–6.

Dupont, P. 'La Dislocation du Tchenla et la Formation du Cambodge Angkorien VIIᵉ-IXᵉ Siècle', *BEFEO*, xliii (1943-6), pp. 17-55.

'Les Débuts de la Royauté Angkorienne', *BEFEO*, xlvi (1952), pp. 119-76.

'La Statuaire Préangkorienne', *Artibus Asiae*, 1955.

L'Archéologie Mône de Dvāravatī, Paris, École Française d'Extrême-Orient, 1959.

Durioselle, C. 'The Art of Burma and Tantric Buddhism', *Annual Report of Archaeological Survey of Burma, 1915-16*, pp. 79-93.

Duyvendak, J. J. L. 'The True Dates of the Chinese Maritime Expeditions of the Early Fifteenth Century', *T'oung Pao*, xxxiv (1939). Leiden.

'Ma Huan Re-examined', *Verh. Kon. Akademie v. Wetensch. afd. Letterkunde*, n.s., 33, No. 3. Amsterdam, 1933.

Ferrand, G. 'Malaka, le Malaya et Malayur', *Journal Asiatique*, Mai-Juin et Juillet-Août, 1918.

'La Plus Ancienne Mention du Nom de l'Ile de Sumatra', *Journal Asiatique*, Mars-Avril, 1917.

'L'Empire Sumatrannais de Śrivijaya', *Journal Asiatique*, Juill-Sept., 1922.

Frédéric, Louis. *The Temples and Sculpture of Southeast Asia*, London, 1965.

Gerini, G. E. *Researches in Ptolemy's Geography*, London, 1909.

Giteau, M. *Sculptures Khmères: Reflets de la Civilisation d'Angkor*, Paris, 1965. (English edn, *Khmer Sculpture and the Angkor Civilisation*, London, 1965.)

Goloubew, V. 'L'Age du Bronze au Tonkin et dans le Nord-Annam', *BEFEO*, xxix (1929), pp. 1-46.

Art et Archéologie de l'Indochine, Hanoi, 1938.

L'Archéologie du Tonkin et les Fouilles de Dong-Son, Hanoi, 1937.

Goris, Roelof. *Prasasti Bali: I. Inscripties vóór Anak Wangçu, Inleiding, Transcripties, Inscripties in het Sanskrit. II. Vertalingen, Registers*. 2 vols, Bandung, 1954-5.

Grousset, R., Auboyer, J., and Buhot, J. *L'Asie Orientale des Origines au XVᵉ Siècle*, Paris, 1941.

Grousset, R. *Histoire de l'Extrême-Orient*. 2 vols. Paris, 1929.

Heekeren, H. R. van. *The Bronze-Iron Age of Indonesia*. Verhandelingen van het Koninklijk Instituut voor Taal-, Land-, en Volkenkunde. Deel 22. 's-Gravenhage, 1958.

The Stone Age of Indonesia, 's-Gravenhage, 1957.

Heine-Geldern, R. von. 'Urheimat und Früheste Wanderungen der Austronesier', *Anthropos*, xxvii (1932).

'Vorgeschichtliche Grundlagen des Kolonialindischen Kunst', *Wiener Beiträge zur Kunst- und Kultur-geschichte*, viii (1934).

'The Archaeology and Art of Sumatra', in M. Loeb, *Sumatra: its History and People*, Vienna, 1935.

'L'Art Prébouddhique de la Chine et de L'Asie du Sud-Est et son Influence en Oceanie', *RAA*, xi (1937), No. 4, pp. 177-206.

'Ein Betrag zur Chronologie des Neolithicums in Sudost-Asien', *Festschrift F. W. Schmidt*, 1938.

'Prehistoric Research in the Netherlands Indies', *Science and Scientists in the Netherlands Indies*, pp. 129–67 (1945).

Conceptions of State and Kingship in Southeast Asia, Southeast Asia Program Data Paper No. 18, Ithaca, N.Y., 1956 (Second printing 1963).

Hirth, F., and Rockhill, W. W. *Chau Ju-Kua, His work on the Chinese and Arab Trade in the Twelfth and Thirteenth Centuries*. Translated from Chinese. St. Petersburg, 1911.

Hocart, A. M. *Kingship*, London, 1927.

Hoop, T. à T. van der. *Megalithic Remains in South Sumatra*, Zutphen, 1932.

'Praehistorie', in F. W. Stapel (ed.), *Geschiedenis van Nederlandsch-Indië*, i (1938).

Hornell, J. 'The Origins and the Ethnological Significance of Indian Boat Designs', *Mem. Asiat. Soc. Bengal*, vii (1920).

Huber, E. 'La Fin de la Dynastie de Pagan', *BEFEO*, ix (1909).

Imbert, J. *Histoire des Institutions Khmères*, Phnom Penh, 1961.

Jack-Hinton, Collin (ed.). *Papers on Early South-East Asian History*, Singapore, 1964.

Janse, Olov R. T. *Archaeological Research in Indo-China: The District of Chiu-Chen during the Han Dynasty*. 2 vols. Cambridge, Mass., 1947, 1949.

Johnston, E. H. 'Some Sanskrit Inscriptions of Arakan', *BSOAS*, xi (1944), No. 2.

Kempers, Bernet. *The Bronzes at Nalanda and Hindu-Javanese Art*, Leiden, 1930.

Ancient Indonesian Art, Cambridge, Mass., 1959.

Krom, N. J. *Inleiding Tot de Hindoe-Javaansche Kunst*. 3 vols. 's-Graven-hage, 1923.

Barabudur, Archaeological Description. 2 vols. The Hague, 1927.

Hindoe-Javaansche Geschiedenis, '-Gravenhage, 1931.

Lamb, Alistair. *Chandi Bukit Batu Pahat—A Report on the Excavation of an Ancient Temple in Kedah*, Singapore, 1960.

LeMay, R. S. *A Concise History of Buddhist Art in Siam*, Cambridge, 1938.

Leuba, Jeanne. *Un Royaume Disparu: Les Chams et Leur Art*, Paris, 1923.

Lévy, Paul. *Recherches Préhistoriques dans la Région de Mlu Prei, Accompagnées de Comparaisons Archéologiques*, Hanoi, 1943.

Loewenstein, J. *Papers on the Malayan Metal Age*, Singapore, 1962. (*JRASMB*, vol. xxix, pt 2.)

Luce, G. H. 'Burma's Debt to Pagan', *JBRS*, xxiii, pp. 120–7.

MacDonald, A. W. 'A propos de Prajāpati', *JA*, 1952.

MacDonald, M. *Angkor*, London, 1958.

Majumdar, R. C. *Ancient Indian Colonies in the Far East*: i. *Champa*, Lahore, 1927. ii. *Suvarnadvipa*, Dacca, 1937–8.

Kambuja-Desa, Calcutta, 1944.

Malleret, Louis: *L'Archéologie du delta du Mekong*. Tome 1, *L'Exploration archéologique et les fouilles d'Oc-èo*, Paris, 1959; tome 2, *La Civilisation Matérielle d'Oc-èo*, (2 vols), 1960; tome 3, *La culture du Fou-nan* (2 vols), 1962; tome 4; *Le Cisbassac*, 1963. Paris, Publications de l'École Française d'Extrême-Orient, vol. 43.

Mansuy, H. *La Préhistoire en Indochine*, Paris, 1931.

Maspero, G. *Le Royaume de Champa*, Paris, 1928.

L'Empire Khmer, Phnom Penh, 1904.

Moens, J. L. 'Çrivijaya, Yāva en Ketāha' *Tijdschrift. Bat. Gen.*, lxxvii (1937), pp. 317–489. (Abbreviated English translation in *JRASMB*, 1939, pp. 1–108.)

Movius, H. J. (Jr.). 'The Lower Palaeolithic Cultures of Southern and Eastern Asia', *Trans. Am. Phil. Soc.* (n.s.) xxxviii, No. 4, pp. 329–420. Philadelphia, 1949.

Mus, P. 'Bârâbudur: Les Origines du Stûpa et la Transmigration', *BEFEO*, xxxii (1923), No. 1, pp. 269–439.

'Cultes Indiens et Indigènes au Champa', *BEFEO*, xxxiii (1933), pp. 367–410.

Naerssen, F. H. van. 'The Çailendra Interregnum', *India Antiqua*, 1947, Leiden.

'Twee koperen oorkonden van Balitung', *BKI*, xcv (1937), p. 445.

'Some Aspects of the Hindu-Javanese Kraton', *J. Oriental Soc. of Australia*, ii, No. 1 (1963).

O'Connor, S. J. 'An Ekamukhaliṅga from Peninsular Siam', *JSS*, liv (Part 1, January 1966), pp. 43–9.

'Satingphra: An Expanded Chronology', *JMBRAS*, xxxix (Part 1, 1966), pp. 137–44.

'Ritual Deposit Boxes in Southeast Asian Sanctuaries', *Artibus Asiae*, xxvii (1966), pp. 53–60.

'Note on a Mukhaliṅga from Western Borneo', *Artibus Asiae*, xxix (1967), pp. 93–6.

Parmentier, H. *L'Art Khmer Primitif*. 2 vols. Paris, 1927.

L'Art Khmer Classique. 2 vols. Paris, 1939.

'L'art Présumé du Fou-nan', *BEFEO*, xxxii (1932), pp. 183–90.

Patris, C. *Essai d'Histoire d'Annam*, Hué, 1923.

Pelliot, P. 'Le Founan', *BEFEO*, iii (1903), pp. 248–303.

'Deux Itinéraires de Chine en Inde à la Fin du VIIIᵉ Siècle', *BEFEO*, iv (1904), pp. 130–413.

Pigeaud, T. G. Th. *Java in the Fourteenth Century: A Study in Cultural History* (*The Nāgara-Kertāgama by Rakawi Prapānca of Majapahit, 1365 A.D.*) 5 vols. The Hague. Vols i, ii, iii, 1960; vol. iv, 1962; vol. v, 1963.

Pleyte, C. M. 'Bijdrage tot de Kennis van het Mahayana op Java', *Bijdragen van het Koningklijk Instituut*, lii, liv (1901 and 1902).

Poerbatjaraka, Raden, Ng. *De dood van Raden Wijaya, den eersten koning en stichter van Madjapahit*, Leiden, 1926.

Proceedings. *Proceedings of the Third Congress of Prehistorians of the Far East*, Singapore, 1938.

Przyluski, J. 'Kôl and Munda: a New Aspect of the Austro-Asiatic Problem', *JGIS*, iv, pt. 1 (Jan. 1937).

Quaritch Wales, H. G. *The Making of Greater India*, London, 1951. 2nd edn, rev. and enlarged, London, 1961.

Ray, Nihar-Ranjan. *Brahmanical Gods in Burma*, Rangoon, 1932.

Sanskrit Buddhism in Burma, Amsterdam, 1936.

Rémusat, G. de Coral. *L'Art Khmer, Les Grandes Étapes de son Évolution*, Paris, 1951.

Sastri, Nilakanta. *Śri Vijaya*, 1949.

Schnitger, F. M. *Forgotten Kingdoms of Sumatra*, Leiden, 1939. Reprint, Leiden, 1964.

Sivaramamurti, C. *Le Stupa du Barabudur*, Paris, 1961.

Solheim, W. G. *Archaeology of Central Philippines: A Study Chiefly of the Iron Age and Its Relationships*, Manila, 1964.

Stapel, F. W. (ed.). *Geschiedenis van Nederlandsch-Indië*, vols i and ii. Amsterdam.

Stein, Callenfels P. van. 'Bijdrage tot de Chronologie van het Neolithicum in Zuid Oost Azië', *Oudheidkundig Verslag*, 1926.

Stern, Philippe. *Le Temple Khmer: Formation et Développement du Temple-Montagne*, Saigon, 1937.

Le Bayon d'Angkor et l'Évolution de l'Art Khmer, Paris, 1927.

L'Art de Champa, ancien Annam, et son Évolution, Paris, 1942.

Les Monuments Khmers du Style du Bayon et Jayavarman VII, Paris, 1965.

'Le Temple-Montagne Khmer, le culte du linga et le Devarāja, *BEFEO*, xxxiv (1934), pp. 611–16.

'Diversité et rythme des fondations royales khmères', *BEFEO*, xliv (1954), pp. 649–85.

Stutterheim, W. F. *Rama-Legenden und Rama Reliefs in Indonesiën*. 2 vols. München, 1927.

Oudheden van Bali, Singaradja, 1930.

Cultural Geschiedenis van Indonesië, 3 vols, De Hindu's, vol. i. Groningen–Batavia, 1951.

Hinduisme in den Archipel, vol. ii. Groningen–Batavia, 1951.

De Islam en Zijn Komst in den Archipel, vol. iii. Groningen–Batavia, 1952.

Indian Influences on Old Balinese Art, London, 1935.

De Islam en Zijn Komst in den Archipel, Groningen–Batavia, 1935.

De Kraton van Majapahit, The Hague, 1948.

Het Hinduisme in den Archipel, Groningen–Djakarta, 1951.

'The Meaning of the Hindu-Javanese Candi', *J. Am. Or. Soc.*, vol. li, 1931.

Studies in Indonesian Archaeology, The Hague, 1956.

Takakusu, Junjiro. *A Record of the Buddhist Religion as Practised in India and the Malay Archipelago, by I-Tsing*, Oxford, 1896.

Terra, H. de, and Movius, H. J. (Jr.). 'Research on Early Man in Burma', *Trans. Am. Phil. Soc.* (n.s.), xxxii, no. 3, pp. 265 464. Philadelphia, 1943.

Tweedie, M. W. F. 'Prehistory in Malaya', *JRAS*, 1942, Part 1, pp. 1–13.

'The Stone Age in Malaya', *JRASMB*, xxvi, 1953, fasc. 2.

Verneuil. *L'Art de Java, Les Temples de la Période Classique Indo-Javanaise*, Paris, 1927.

Vogler, E. B. *De Monsterkop in de Hindoe-Javaanse Bouwkunst*, Leiden, 1949.

Wang Gungwu. 'The Nanhai Trade; A Study of the early history of Chinese Trade in the South China Sea'. *JRASMB*, vol. xxxi, pt. 2 (1958), pp. 1–135.

Wheatley, Paul. *The Golden Khersonese: Studies in the Historical Geography of the Malay Peninsula before A.D. 1500*, Kuala Lumpur, 1961.

Impressions of the Malay Peninsula in Ancient Times, Singapore, 1964.

Wolters, O. W. *Early Indonesian Commerce: a Study of the Origins of Srivijaya*, Ithaca, N.Y., 1967.

'The Khmer King at Basan (1371–73) and the Restoration of the Cambodian Chronology during the Fourteenth and Fifteenth Centuries', *Asia Major*, vol. xii, pt. 1 (1966), pp. 44–89.

The Fall of Srivijaya in Malay History, Asia Major Supplementum, London, 1968.

'Tambralinga', *Bull. School Orient. African Studies* (1958).

Zwaan, J. P. Kleiweg de. *De Oudste Mensheid van de Indische Archipel*, 1943.

V. BURMA

Andrus, J. R. *Burmese Economic Life*, Stanford, U.S.A., London, 1947.

Anstey, Vera. *The Economic Development of India* (includes Burma), New York, 1936.

Appleton, G. *Buddhism in Burma*, Calcutta, 1943.

Banerjee, A. C. *British Relations with Burma, 1826–1886*, Bombay, 1947.

Bayfield, G. T. *Historical Review of the Political Relations between the British Government in India and the Empire of Ava . . . to the end of the year 1834*. Revised by Lieut.-Col. Burney, British Resident, Calcutta, 1835.

Bigandet, P. *An Outline of the History of the Catholic Burmese Mission from 1720 to 1887*, Rangoon, 1887.

The Life or Legend of Gaudama, The Buddha of the Burmese, 2 vols in 1. London, 1911–12. (1st pub. Rangoon, 1866.)

Bourdounais, M. le Comte A Mahé de la. *Un Français en Birmanie*, Paris, 1891.

Burma. *Burma Gazetteer*, vol. A, reprint, 3 vols: *Salween District, Upper Chindwin District, Mergui District*, Rangoon, 1960–2.

Cady, John F. *A History of Modern Burma*, Ithaca, N.Y., 1958. 2nd printing, with Supplement, 1960.

Christian, J. Leroy. *Modern Burma A Survey of Political and Economic Developments*, California, 1942.

Burma and the Japanese Invader (revised edn of *Modern Burma*), Bombay, 1945.

Cochrane, W. *The Shans*, Rangoon, 1915.

Collis, Maurice. *The Land of the Great Image*, London, 1943.

Last and First in Burma, London, 1956.

Trials in Burma. London, 1938, 1953.

Cordier, Henri. *Historique abrégé des relations de la Grande-Bretagne avec la Birmanie*, Paris, 1894.

'Les Français en Birmanie', *T'oung Pao*, 1891.

'La France et L'Angleterre en Indochine et en Chine sous le Premier Empire', *T'oung Pao*, series 2 (1903), pp. 201–27.

Crosthwaite, Sir C. *The Pacification of Burma*, London, 1912.

Desai, W. S. *History of the British Residency in Burma, 1826–40*, Rangoon, 1939.

India and Burma, Bombay and Calcutta, 1954.

A Pageant of Burmese History, Bombay, 1961.

Donnison, F. S. V. *Public Administration in Burma*, London, 1953.

Ferrars, Max and Bertha. *Burma*, London, 1901.

Foucar, E. C. V. *Mandalay The Golden*, London, 1963.

They Reigned in Mandalay, London, 1946.

Furnivall, J. S. *Introduction to the Political Economy of Burma*, 2nd ed., Rangoon, 1938. 3rd ed., with new preface, 1957.

'The Fashioning of Leviathan: The Beginnings of British Rule in Burma', *JBRS*, xxix (1939).

Colonial Policy and Practice, a Comparative Study of Burma and Netherlands India, Cambridge, 1948.

The Governance of Modern Burma, New York, 1958. 2nd edn rev. and enlarged with an appreciation by F. N. Trager and with supplement on the Ne Win administration by J. S. Thompson, Vancouver, 1960.

Gazetteers. *British Burma Gazetteer*. 2 vols. Rangoon, 1880.

J. G. Scott and J. P. Hardiman. *Gazetteer of Upper Burma and the Shan States*. 5 vols. Rangoon, 1900.

Geary, Gratton. *Burma, after the Conquest, viewed in its Political, Social and Commercial Aspects, from Mandalay*, London, 1886.

Griswold, Alexander B. (*et al.*). *Burma, Korea, Tibet.* Art of the World Series (Methuen), London, 1964.

Hall, D. G. E. *Early English Intercourse with Burma, 1587–1743*, London, 1928. Reprinted 1968.

Europe and Burma. A study of European Relations with Burma from the Earliest Times to the Annexation of Thibaw's Kingdom, London, 1945.

'The Tragedy of Negrais', *JBRS*, xxi (1931), pp. 59–133.

'The Dagh Register of Batavia and Dutch Trade with Burma in the Seventeenth Century', *JBRS*, xxix (1939), pp. 139–56.

'Studies in Dutch Relations with Arakan in the Seventeenth Century', *JBRS*, xxvi (1936).

Burma, London, 1950.

Hall, H. Fielding. *The Soul of a People*, London, 1899.

A People at School, London, 1906, 1913.

Halliday, R. *The Talaings*, Rangoon, 1917.

Harvey, G. E. *History of Burma*, London, 1925.

British Rule in Burma, 1824–1942, London, 1946.

Hla Pe, U. *Narrative of the Japanese Occupation of Burma*, Ithaca, N.Y., 1961.

Htin Aung, U. *The Stricken Peacock: Anglo-Burmese Relations, 1752–1948*, The Hague, 1965.

Huber, E. 'Une Ambassade Chinoise en Birmanie en 1406', *BEFEO*, iv (1904), pp. 429–32.

'La Fin de la Dynastie de Pagan', *BEFEO*, ix (1909), pp. 633–80.

Ireland, Alleyne. *The Province of Burma*. 2 vols. Boston and New York, 1907.

Johnstone, W. C. *Burma's Foreign Policy; a Study in Neutralism*, Cambridge, Mass., 1963.

King, W. L. *A Thousand Lives away: Buddhism in Contemporary Burma*, Cambridge, Mass., 1964.

Laurie, W. F. B. *Our Burmese Wars and Relations with Burma*, London, 1880.

Leach, E. R. *Political Systems of Highland Burma*, London, 1954. Reprinted, 1964.

Lehman, F. C. *The Structure of Chin Society; a tribal people of Burma adapted to a non-Western Civilization*, Urbana, Univ. of Illinois, 1963.

Low, James. 'A History of Tenasserim', *JRAS*, iv (1837), pp. 304–32; v (1839), pp. 245–63.

Luce, G. H. 'Chinese Invasions of Burma in the Eighteenth Century', *JBRS*, xv (1925), pp. 115–28.

'Burma's Debt to Pagan', *JBRS*, xxiii (1933), pp. 120–7.

'A Century of Progress in Burmese History and Archaeology', *JBRS*, xxxii (1948).

'The Economic Life of the Early Burman', *JBRS*, xxx (1940).

'The Ancient Pyu', *JBRS*, xxvii (1937).

'Early Chinese Texts about Burma', *JBRS*, xiv (1924).

'Mons of the Pagan Dynasty', *JBRS*, xxxvi (1953).

'The Early Syām in Burma's History. *JSS*, xlvi (1958); *JSS*, xlvii (1959).

'Old Kyauksè and the Coming of the Burmans', *JBRS*, xlii (1959).

'Rice and Religion: a study of old Mon-Khmer evolution and culture, (with linguistic charts)', *JSS*, liii (1965), pp. 139–52.

'The Career of Htilaing Min (Kyanzittha), the Uniter of Burma, A.D. 1084–1113', *JRAS*, pts 1 and 2 (1966), pp. 53–68.

'Dvaravati and Old Burma', *JSS*, liii (1965), pp. 10–26.

Luce, G. H. and Pe Maung Tin. 'Burma down to the Fall of Pagan: An Outline' (pt. 1), *JBRS*, xxix (1939), pp. 264–82.

McKelvie, Roy. *The War in Burma*, London, 1948.

Marshall, H. I. *The Karen People of Burma*, Columbus, U.S.A., 1922.

Mason, Rev. F. *Burma, its People and National Products*, Rangoon, London, New York, 1860. 2 vols. Ed. enlarged by W. Theobald Hartford, 1882–3.

Maung Maung. *Burma in the Family of Nations*, Amsterdam, 1956.

Burma's Constitution, 2nd ed., rev. and enlarged. The Hague, 1961.

A Trial in Burma: the Assassination of Aung San, The Hague, 1962.

Maung Maung Pye. *Burma in the Crucible*, Rangoon, 1952.

Milne, Mrs. L., and Cockrane, Rev. W. W. *Shans at Home*, London, 1910.

Mitton, G. E. (Lady Scott). *Scott of the Shan Hills*, London, 1936.

Nai Thein. 'Intercourse between Siam and Burma as recorded in the "Royal Autograph Edition" of the History of Siam', *JBRS*, xxv (1935), pp. 49–108; xxviii (1938), pp. 109–76. (Reprinted in vols v and vi of *Selected Articles from the Journal of the Siam Society*, Bangkok, 1959.)

Nash, Manning. *The Golden Road to Modernity: Village Life in Contemporary Burma*, New York, London, Sydney, 1965.

Nisbet, John. *Burma under British Rule—and Before*. 2 vols. London, 1901.

Nu, Thakin. *Burma under the Japanese*, New York, 1954.

Parker, E. H. *Burma with Special Reference to her Relations with China*, Rangoon, 1893.

Précis of Chinese Imperial and Provincial Annals Relating to Burma, Rangoon, 1893.

Pearn, B. R. *A History of Rangoon*, Rangoon, 1939.

'King Bering', *JBRS*, xxiii (1933), pp. 55–85.

'Felix Carey and the English Baptist Mission in Burma', *JBRS*, xxviii (1938), pp. 1–91.

Judson of Burma, London, 1962.

Perrin, J. M. 'Les Relations entre La Birmanie et La Russe au XIXᵉ Siècle', *BEFEO*, xlix (1959), pp. 675–8.

Phayre, A. P. *History of Burma*, London, 1883.

Pye, Lucien W. *Politics, Personality and Nation Building; Burma's Search for Identity*, New Haven and London, 1962.

Ray, Nihar-Ranjan. *An Introduction to the Study of Theravada Buddhism in Burma*, Calcutta, 1946.

Ritchie, Anna J. *Lord Amherst and the British Advance Eastward to Burma*, Oxford, 1894.

Saimong Mangrai, Sao. *The Shan States and the British Annexation*, Ithaca, N.Y., 1965.

Scott, Sir J. G. *Burma: A Handbook of Practical Information*, London, 1921.

Burma, from the Earliest Times to the Present Day, London, 1924.

The Burman: His Life and Notions (by Shway Yoe, pseudonym), London, 1882. Reprinted by Norton, New York, 1963.

Scott, J. G., and Hardiman, J. P. *Gazetteer of Upper Burma and the Shan States*. 5 vols. Rangoon, 1900–1.

Sein, Daw Mya. *The Administration of Burma: Sir Charles Crosthwaite and the Consolidation of Burma*, Rangoon, 1938.

Sein, Win. *The Split Story*, Rangoon, 1959.

Sen, N. C. *A Peep into Burma Politics, 1917–42*, Allahabad, 1945.

Shakespear, Col. L. W. *History of Upper Assam, Upper Burmah and North-Eastern Frontier*, London, 1914.

Singhal, D. P. *The Annexation of Upper Burma*, Singapore, 1960.

Slim, Sir William. *Defeat into Victory*, London, 1956.

Smeaton, D. M. *The Loyal Karens of Burma*, London, 1887 and 1920.

Smith, Donald E. *Religion and Politics in Burma*, New Jersey, 1965.

Smith, Nicol. *Burma Road*, New York, 1940.

Snodgrass, Major J. J. *Narrative of the Burmese War*, London, 1827.

Stewart, J. A. 'Kyaukse Irrigation: a Sidelight on Burmese History', *JBRS*, xi (1921), pp. 1–4.

Tan Pei-Ying. *The Building of the Burma Road*, New York, 1945.

Temple, R. C. *The Thirty-Seven Nats*, London, 1906.

Than Tun. 'Religion in Burma, A.D. 1000–1300', *JBRS*, xlii (1959).

'History of Burma, A.D. 1300–1400', *JBRS*, xlii (1959).

Tin Hla Thaw. 'History of Burma, A.D. 1400–1500', *JBRS*, xlii, 2 (1959).

Tinker, Hugh. *The Foundations of Local Self-Government in India, Pakistan and Burma*, London, 1954.

The Union of Burma, London, 1957.

Trager, F. *Burma—from Kingdom to Republic*, New York, 1966.

Trager, Helen G. *Burma Through Alien Eyes: Missionary Views of the Burmese in the Nineteenth Century*, London, 1966.

Trant, T. A. *Two Years in Ava, from May 1824 to May 1826*, London, 1927.

Walinsky, L. J. *Economic Development in Burma, 1951–1960*, New York, 1962.

Wayland, Francis. *A Memoir of the Life and Labours of the Reverend Adoniram Judson*. 2 vols. London, 1853.

White, Sir H. T. *A Civil Servant in Burma*, London, 1913.

Burma, London, 1923.

White, Capt. W. *A Political History of the Extraordinary Events which led to the Burmese War*, London, 1827.

Wilson, H. H. *Narrative of the Burmese War in 1824–26 as originally compiled from official documents*, London, 1852.

Woodman, Dorothy. *The Making of Burma*, London, 1962.

VI. INDO-CHINA

(ANNAM, CAMBODIA, COCHIN CHINA, LAOS, TONGKING)

American Friends Service Committee. *Peace in Vietnam*, New York, 1966.

Anonymous. *Relations des Missions des Évêques Français aux Royaumes de Siam, de la Cochinchine, de Cambodge et du Tonking*, Paris, 1674.

Antonini, P. *L'Annam, Le Tonkin et l'Intervention de la France en Extrême-Orient* . . . Paris, *c.* 1889.

Aubaret, G. (tr.). *Histoire et Description de La Basse Cochinchine* (*Pays de Gia-Dinh*) . . . *d'après le Texte Original*, Paris, 1863.

Aurousseau, Leonard. 'La Première Conquête Chinoise des Pays Annamites; Origine du Peuple Annamite', *BEFEO*, xxiii (1923), pp. 137–264.

Aymonier, E. T. *Le Cambodge*. 3 vols. Paris, 1900–4.

Bazancourt, C. L. de. *Les Expéditions de Chine et de Cochinchine d'après les Documents Officiels*. 2 vols. Paris, 1861–2.

Berval, René de (*et al.*). *Kingdom of Laos*, Saigon, 1959 (original French publication, 1956).

Bezacier, L. *L'art Vietnamien*, Paris, 1955.

Blet, Henri. *L'Histoire de la Colonisation Française*. 3 vols. Grenoble and Paris, 1946, 1948, 1950.

Bouchot, Jean. *Documents pour Servir à l'Histoire de Saigon, 1859 à 1865*, Saigon, 1927.

Boudet, H. 'La Conquête de la Cochinchine par les Nguyên et le rôle des émigrés chinois', *BEFEO*, xlii (1942), pp. 115–32.

Boudet, Paul. 'Les Archives des Empereurs d'Annam et l'Histoire Annamite', *Bull. Amis du Vieux Hué*, xxix (1942), pp. 229–59.

Brodrick, A. H. *Little Vehicle: Cambodia and Laos*, London, 1949.

Buch, W. J. M. *De Oost-Indische Compagnie en Quinam; de Betrekkingen der Nederlanders met Annam in de XVII Eeuw*, Amsterdam, 1929.

'La Compagnie des Indes Néerlandaises et l'Indochine', *BEFEO*, xxxvi (1936), pp. 97–196; xxxvii (1937), pp. 121–237.

Buttinger, Joseph. *The Smaller Dragon: A Political History of Vietnam*, New York, 1958.

Vietnam: a dragon embattled. 2 vols. New York, 1967.

Cadière, L. 'Tableau Chronologique des Dynasties Annamites', *BEFEO*, v (1905), pp. 77–145.

'Le Mur de Dong-Hoi; Étude sur l'Établissement des Nguyen en Cochinchine', *BEFEO*, vi (1906), pp. 86–254.

Résumé de l'Histoire d'Annam, Quihnon, 1911.

'Les Européens au Service de Gia-Long'. *Bull. Amis Hué*, 1920–2–5–6.

Croyances et Pratiques Religieuses des Annamites, Hanoi, Saigon, Paris, 1944, 1955, 1957. 3 vols.

Cady, John F. *The Roots of French Imperialism in Eastern Asia*, Ithaca, N.Y., 1954.

Chaigneau, J. B. *Le Mémoire sur la Cochinchine de Jean-Baptiste Chaigneau*, Hanoi-Haiphong, 1923.

Chaigneau, M. Diuc. *Souvenirs de Hué*, Shanghai, 1941.

Chailley, J. *Paul Bert au Tonkin*, Paris, 1887.

Chapman, Charles. 'Relation d'un Voyage en Cochin-Chine en 1778', *Bull. de la Soc. des Études Indochinoises de Saigon* (n.s.), xxiii (1948), no. 2, pp. 15–75.

Chassigneaux, E. 'L'Indochine: Histoire des Colonies Françaises', in vol. v, pp. 311–599 of G. Hanotaux and A. Martineau (eds), *Histoire des Colonies Françaises et de l'Expansion de la France*, Paris, 1932.

Cheneau, H. *Du Protectorat Français en Annam, au Tonkin et au Cambodge*, Paris, 1904.

Chesneaux, Jean. *Contribution à l'Histoire de la Nation Vietnamienne*, Paris, 1955.

Cole, Allan B. *Conflict in Indo-China, and International Repercussions: A Documentary History, 1945–55*, Ithaca, N.Y., 1956.

Cunningham, A. *The French in Tonkin and South China*, Hong Kong, 1902.

Dang, Nghiem. *Politics and Public Administration*, Honolulu, 1966.

Dauphin-Meunier, A. *Histoire de Cambodge*. (Collection Que sais-je?) Paris, 1961.

Degeorge, J. B. *À la Conquête de Chau Laos*, Hong Kong, 1932.

Delvert, J. *Le Paysan Cambodgien*, Paris, 1961.

Deschanel, P. *La Question du Tonkin*, Paris, 1883.

Deveria, G. *Histoire des Relations de la Chine avec l'Annam-Vietnam du XVIe au XIXe siècle des Documents Chinois Traduits pour la Première Fois*, Paris, 1880.

Devillers, P. *Histoire du Viêt-Nam de 1940 à 1952*, Paris, 1952.

Deydier, H. *Introduction à La Connaissance du Laos*, Paris, 1952.

Diguet, E. *Annam et Indo-Chine Française*, Paris, 1908.

Dijk, L. C. D. van. *Neerland's Vroegste Betrekkingen met Borneo, den Solo-Archipel, Cambodja, Siam en Cochin-China*, Amsterdam, 1862.

Dommen, A. J. *Conflict in Laos: the Politics of Neutralization*, New York, Praeger, 1964.

Dupuis, Jean. *Les Origines de la Question du Tong-Kin*, Paris, 1896.
Le Tonkin de 1872 à 1886; Histoire et Politique, Paris, 1910.

Ennis, T. E. *French Policy and Developments in Indo-China*, Chicago, 1936.

Fall, B. B. *Le Viet-Minh, la République démocratique de Viet-Nam, 1945–60*, Paris, 1960.
The Two Viet-Nams; a Political and Military Analysis, New York, 1963.
Street Without Joy: Insurgency in Indochina, 1946–63, revised ed., London, 1966.

Faure, A. *Les Français en Cochinchine au XVIIIe siècle: Mgr. Pigneau de Behaine, évêque d'Adran*, Paris, 1891.

Ferry, Jules. *Le Tonkin et la Mère Patrie; Témoinages et Documents*, Paris, 1890.

Gaudel, A. *L'Indo-Chine Française en Face du Japon*, Paris, 1947.

Gautier, A. H. *Les Français au Tonkin, 1787–1883*, Paris, 1884.

Ghosh, Monomohan. *A History of Cambodia*, Saigon, 1960.

Giteau, M. *Histoire du Cambodge*, Paris, 1957.

Gosselin, C. *L'Empire d'Annam*, Paris, 1904.

Gourou, P. *The Future of Indochina*, Paris, 1947.

Gourou, Pierre. *Les Paysans du Delta Tonkinois*, Paris, 1936. (Revised English ed., *The Peasants of the Tonkin Delta; a study of human geography*, New Haven, HRAF, 1955.)

Grandjean, G. (ed. Malfère). *L'Épopée Jaune, Missionaires et Marins en Indo-Chine, 1765–1885*, 1938.

Groslier, Bernard P. *Angkor et le Cambodge au XVIe siècle d'après les sources portugaises et espagnoles*, Paris, 1958.

Recherches sur les Cambodgiens, Paris, 1921.

Indochina: Art in the Melting-Pot of Races. Art of the World Series (Methuen), London, 1962.

Groslier, Bernard P. *Indochina*, Cleveland, Ohio, 1966.

Groslier, Bernard P., and Arthaud, J. *Angkor, Art and Civilization*, London, 1957.

Halpern, J. M. *Economy and Society of Laos; a brief Survey*. Yale Univ. South-East Asia Studies, Monograph series no. 5, 1964.

Hammer, Ellen J. *The Struggle for Indochina*, Stanford, Calif., 1954.

Herz, M. F. *A Short History of Cambodia*, New York, 1958.

Hickey, G. C. *Village in Vietnam*, New Haven and London, 1964.

Hoang, Van-chi. *From Colonisation to Communism: A Case History of North Vietnam*, New York, 1963.

Honey, P. J. (ed.). *North Viet-nam Today*, New York, 1962.

Huard, P., and Durand, M. *Connaissance du Viêt-Nam*, Paris and Hanoi, 1954.

Isoart, Paul. *Le Phénomène National Viêtnamien: de l'indépendence unitaire à l'indépendence fractionnée*, Paris, 1961.

Lacouture, Jean. *Le Vietnam entre deux paix*, Paris, 1965 (English tr. by K. Kellan and J. Carmichael, *Vietnam between two Truces*. New York, 1966.)

Lacoutare, Jean, and Devillers, Philippe. *La fin d'une guerre*, Indochine, 1954; Paris, 1960.

Lanessan, L. de. *La Colonisation Française en Indo-Chine*, Paris, 1895.

Launay, A. *Histoire Ancienne et Moderne de l'Annam, Tong-King et Cochinchine*, Paris, 1884.

LeBar, F. M., and Suddard, A. (eds). *Laos*. New Haven, HRAF, 1960.

Le Boulanger, P. *Histoire du Laos Français*, Paris, 1931.

Leclère, A. *Histoire du Cambodge*, Paris, 1914.

Lehault, P. *La France et l'Angleterre en Asie*. Tome 1: *Indochine, les Derniers Jours de la Dynastie des Rois d'Ava*, Paris, 1892.

Lemire, C. *Établissement du Protectorat Français au Cambodge; Exposé Chronologique des Relations du Cambodge avec le Siam, l'Annam et la France*, Paris, 1879.

Le Thánh Khôi. *Le Viet-Nam, Histoire et Civilisation*, Paris, 1955.

Le-Van-Dinh. *Le Culte des Ancêtres en Droit Annamite*, Paris, 1934.

Levi, Sylvain (ed.). *Indochine*. 2 vols in 1. Paris, 1931.

Levy, Paul. 'Le Voyage de Van Wuysthoff au Laos (1641–1642) d'après son Journal (Inédit en Français)', *CEFEO*, no. 38 (1944).

'Les Royaumes Lao du Mekong', *CEFEO*, no. 25 (1940), pp. 11–17.

Levy, Roger. *L'Indochine et ses Traités, 1946*, Paris, 1947.

Lingat, R. *Les Régimes Matrimoniaux du Sud-Est de l'Asia*. Publications, EFEO, Paris, 1952.

Luro, E. *Le Pays d'Annam: Étude sur l'organisation politique et sociale des Annamites*, Paris, 1878, 2nd ed., 1897.

Madrolle, C. *Indochine du Nord*, Paris, 1932.

Indochine du Sud, Paris, 1936.

Mai-tho-Truyen. *Le Bouddhisme au Vietnam, Buddhism in Vietnam, Phat-giao Viet-Nam*. (Text in French, English and Vietnamese.) Saigon, 1962.

Malleret, L. 'Une Tentative ignorée d'établissement français en Indochine au XVIIIe siècle; les vues de l'Amiral d'Estaing', *CEFEO*, No. 29 (1941), pp. 10–16.

Maspero, G. (ed.). *Un Empire Colonial Français: l'Indochine*. 2 vols. Paris, 1929–30.

Maspero, H. 'Études d'Histoire d'Annam', *BEFEO*, xvi (1916), no. 1, pp. 1–55, and xviii (1918), no. 3, pp. 1–36.

Masson, André. *Histoire de l'Indochine*. (Collection Que sais-je?) Paris, 1950.

Histoire du Vietnam. (Collection Que sais-je?) Paris, 1960.

Maybon, C. B. *Histoire Moderne du Pays d'Annam (1592–1820)*, Paris, 1920.

Les Marchands Européens en Cochinchine et au Tonkin (1600–1775), Hanoi, 1916.

Maybon, C. B., and Russier, H. *Notions d'Histoire d'Annam*. 2 vols. Hanoi–Haiphong, 1909.

Meyniard, C. *Le Second Empire en Indo-Chine* (Siam, Cambodge, Annam). Paris, 1891.

Michels, A. *Les Annales Impériales de l'Annam Traduites entier . . . du texte Chinois*. 2 vols. Paris, 1889–92.

Migot, A. *Les Khmers, des origines d'Angkor au Cambodge d'aujourd'hui*, Paris, 1960.

Monet, P. *Français et Annamites*, Paris, 1925.

Moura, J. *Le Royaume du Cambodge*. 2 vols. Paris, 1883.

Mus, Paul. *Le Vietnam Chez Lui*, Paris, 1947.

Viet-Nam: Sociologie d'une guerre, Paris, 1952.

Naville, P. *La Guerre du Viet-Nam*, Paris, 1949.

Newman, B. *Report on Indo-China*, London, 1953.

Nguyen-Ai-Quoc (Ho Chi Minh). *Le Procès de la Colonisation Française*, Paris, 1926 (and Hanoi, 1962).

Nguyen-Huu-Khang. *La Commune Annamite; étude historique, juridique et économique*, Paris, 1946.

Nguyen-Kien. *Le Sud-Vietnam depuis Dien-Bien-Phu*, Paris, 1963.

Nguyen-Phut-Tan. *A Modern History of Viet-Nam (1802–1954)*, Saigon, 1964.

Nguyen-van-Huyen. *La Civilisation Annamite*, Hanoi, 1944.

Noir, L. S. *Les Français au Siam et au Cambodge*, Paris, 1894.

Norman, C. B. *Tonkin, or France in the East*, London, 1884.

Parmentier, H. *La Religion Ancienne de l'Annam*, Paris, 1906.

L'Art du Laos. Publications, EFEO, Paris, 1954.

Pasquier, P. *L'Annam d'autrefois, Essai sur la constitution de l'Annam avant l'intervention française*, Paris, 1930.

Patris, C. *Essai d'Histoire d'Annam*: Première Partie, 'l'Antiquité et le Haut Moyen Age'. Hué, 1923.

Pavie, A. *A la Conquête des Cœurs*, Paris, 1921.

Pelliot, P. 'Mémoire sur les coutumes de Cambodge'; *BEFEO*, ii (1902), pp. 123–77. (New and annotated ed., Paris, 1951.)

Petit, R. *La Monarchie Annamite*, Paris, 1931.

Priestley, H. I. *France Overseas, A Study of Modern Imperialism*, New York, 1938.

Reinach, L. de. *Le Laos*. 2nd ed.; Paris, 1911.

Renouvin, Pierre. *La Question d'Extrême-Orient, 1840–1894*, Paris, 1946.

Robequain, C. *The Economic Development of French Indo-China*, London, 1944.

Roberts, S. H. *History of French Colonial Policy 1870–1925*. 2 vols. London, 1929.

Rouger, C. E. *Histoire Militaire et Politique et l'Annam et du Tonkin depuis 1799*, Paris, 1906.

Sasorith, Katay D. *Le Laos*, Paris, 1953.

Schreiner, A. *Abrégé de l'Histoire d'Annam*. 2nd ed. Saigon, 1906.

Scott, J. G. *France and Tongking*, London, 1885.

Septans, A. *Les commencements de l'Indo-Chine française d'après les archives du Ministère de la Marine et des Colonies*, Paris, 1887.

Sisouk Na Champassak. *Storm over Laos : a contemporary history*, New York, 1961.

Smith, R. M. *Cambodia's Foreign Policy*, Ithaca, N.Y., 1965.

Steinberg, David J. (*et al.*). *Cambodia*, New Haven, HRAF, 1957.

Taboulet, G. *La Geste Française en Indochine : Histoire par les textes de la France en Indochine des origines à 1914*. 2 vols. Paris, 1955–6.

Teston, E., and Percheron, M. *L'Indochine Moderne*, Paris, 1932.

Thompson, V. *French Indochina*, London, 1937.

Tran-van-Giap. 'Le Bouddhisme en Annam, des Origines au XIIIᵉ siècle', *BEFEO*, xxxii (1932), pp. 191–272.

Villemerevil, A. B. de. 'Les Voyages des Européens des Côtes d'Annam à la Vallée du Mékong', *Bull. Soc. Geog. Rochefort*, ii (1880–1), pp. 117–29.

Walker, G. B. *Angkor Empire*, Calcutta, 1955.

VII. Malaya and Indonesia

Allen, G. C., and Donnithorne, A. G. *Western Enterprise in Indonesia and Malaya*, London, 1957.

Alting, J. H. Carpentier. *Grondslagen der Rechtsbedeeling in Nederlandsch Indië*, The Hague, 1926.

Angoulvant, G. *Les Indes Néerlandaises*. 2 vols. Paris, 1926.

Aziz, M. A. *Japan's Colonialism and Indonesia*, The Hague, 1955.

Baring-Gould, S., and Bampfylde, C. A. *A History of Sarawak under its Two White Rajahs*, London, 1909.

Bastin, John S. *The Native Policies of Sir Stamford Raffles in Java and Sumatra: an Economic Interpretation*, Oxford Univ. Press, 1957.

Essays on Indonesian and Malayan History, Singapore, 1961.

Bastin, John S., and Roolvink, R. (eds). *Malayan and Indonesian Studies; Essays presented to Sir Richard Winstedt*, Oxford Univ. Press, 1964.

Batten, C. C. *Translation of: Daendels–Raffles (by M. L. Deventer)*, London, 1894.

Baudet, H. (*et al.*). *Balans van beleid; terugblik op de laatste halve eeuw van Nederlandsche-Indië*, Assen, 1961.

Begbie, Capt. P. J. *The Malaysian Peninsula, embracing its History, Manners, Customs of the Inhabitants, Politics, Natural History . . . from its Earliest Times*, Madras, 1834.

Benda, Harry J. *The Crescent and the Rising Sun*, The Hague, 1958.

Bijllaardt, A. C. van den. *Onstaan en Ontwikkeling der Staatkundige Partijen in Nederlandsch Indië*, Batavia, 1933.

Blumberger, J. Th. P. *De Nationalistische Beweging in Nederlandsch Indië*, The Hague, 1931.

De Communistische Beweging in Nederlandsch Indië, Haarlem, 1928.

Boeke, J. H. *The Structure of the Netherlands Indies Economy*. Inst. of Pacific Relations, New York, 1942

The Evolution of the Netherlands Indies Economy, New York, 1946.

Boeke, J. H. (*et al.*). *Indonesian Economics; the concept of Dualism in Theory and Policy*, The Hague, 1961.

Bousquet, G. H. *A French View of the Netherlands Indies*, London and New York, 1940.

Boxer, C. R. 'The Third Dutch War in the East', *The Mariner's Mirror*, xvi (1930).

The Dutch Seaborne Empire, 1600–1800, London, 1965.

Brackman, A. C. *Indonesian Communism, a History*, New York (Praeger), 1963.

South-East Asia's Second Front: the power struggle in the Malay Archipelago, New York, 1966.

Braddell, Sir Roland. *The Law of the Straits Settlements: a Commentary*, Singapore, 1915, new ed., 1931.

Braddell, T., *Statistics of the British Possessions in the Straits of Malacca*, Penang, 1861.

Brakel, S. van. *De Hollandsche Handelscompagnieën der zeventiende eeuw*, The Hague, 1908.

Broek, J. O. M. *The Economic Development of the Netherlands Indies*, New York, 1942.

Brugmans, J. *Geschiedenis van het Onderwijs in Nederlandsch-Indië*, Groningen-Batavia, 1938.

Brugmans, I. J. (ed.). *Nederlandsch-Indië onder Japanese Bezetting*, Franeker, 1962.

Buckley, C. G. *An Anecdotal History of Old Times in Singapore*, London, 1903. Reprint by University of Malaya, Kuala Lumpur, 1965.

Cabaton, A. *Java and the Dutch East Indies*, London, 1911.

Cator, W. J. *The Economic Position of the Chinese in the Netherlands Indies*, Oxford, 1936.

Chai Hon-Chan. *The Development of British Malaya, 1896–1909*, Kuala Lumpur, 1964.

Chijs, J. A. van der. *De Vestiging van het Nederlandsch Gezag Over de Banda-Eilanden*, Batavia–The Hague, 1886.

De Geschiedenis der stichting van de V.O.C., Leiden, 1856.

Colenbrander, H. T. *Koloniale Geschiedenis*. 3 vols. 's-Gravenhage, 1925.

Cowan, C. D. *Nineteenth-Century Malaya; the Origins of British Political Control*, London, 1961.

Crawfurd, John. *History of the Indian Archipelago*. 3 vols. Edinburgh, 1820. *A Descriptive Dictionary of the Indian Islands and Adjacent Countries*. 2 vols. London, 1856.

Crofton, R. H. *A Pageant of Spice Islands*, London, 1936.

Das Gupta, Ashin. *Malabar in Asian Trade, 1740–1800*, Cambridge Univ. Press (in preparation, 1967 ?).

Day, Clive. *The Policy and Administration of the Dutch in Java*, New York, 1904. Oxford in Asia Historical Reprints, Kuala Lumpur, Oxford Univ. Press, 1966.

Deventer, M. L. van. *Geschiedenis der Nederlanders op Java*. 2 vols. Haarlem, 1886–7.

Het Nederlandsch Gezag over Java sedert 1811, The Hague, 1891.

Dijk, L. C. D. van. *Neerlands vroegste betrekking met Borneo*, Amsterdam, 1862.

Djajadiningrat, Pangeran A. A. Hoesein. *The Netherlands East Indies*, New York, 1941.

Dobby, E. H. G. *Agricultural Questions of Malaya*, Cambridge, 1949.

Dodd, E. E. *The New Malaya*, London, 1946.

Douwes Dekker, E. (Multatuli). *Max Havelaar*. 2 vols. The Hague, 1860. *Indonesia : Once More Free Labour*, Stanford, Calif., 1948.

Emerson, Rupert. *Malaysia : a study in Direct and Indirect Rule*, New York, 1937. (Reprinted as Univ. of Malaya Press paperback, Kuala Lumpur, 1964.)

Fatimi, S. Q. *Islam comes to Malaysia*, Singapore, Malaysian Sociological Research Institute, 1963.

Feith, Herbert. *The Decline of Constitutional Democracy in Indonesia*, Ithaca, New York, 1962.

Firth, Raymond. *Malay Fishermen : their Peasant Economy*, London, 1946.

Fitzgerald, C. P. *The Third China*, Vancouver, 1965.
Furnivall, J. S. *Netherlands India: a study of Plural Economy*, Cambridge, 1939, 1944.
  Colonial Policy and Practice, a Comparative Study of Burma and Netherlands India, Cambridge, 1948.
Geertz, Clifford. *The Development of the Javanese Economy*, Cambridge, Mass., 1956.
  Pedlars and Princes: social change and economic modernisation in two Indonesian towns, Chicago, 1963.
  Agricultural Involution: the process of ecological change in Indonesia, Berkeley, 1963.
  The Religion of Java. Glencoe, Ill., 1960.
Ginsburg, N., and Roberts, C. F. *Malaya*, Seattle, 1958.
Gonggrijp, G. *Schets Eener Economische Geschiedenis van Nederlandsch Indië*, Haarlem, 1949.
Goris, R. (*et al.*). *Bali, Studies in Life, Thought and Ritual*, The Hague, 1960.
Graaf, H. J. de. *De Regering van Panembahan Senapati Ingalaga*, 's-Gravenhage, 1954.
  De Regering van Sultan Agung, Vorst van Mataram, 1613–45, en die van zijn voorganger Panembahan Seda-ing-Krapjak, 1601–13, 's-Gravenhage, 1958.
  De Regering van Sunan Mangku-Rat I Tegal-Wangi, Vorst van Mataram, 1646–79, 's-Gravenhage, 1961.
  Geschiedenis van Indonesië, 's-Gravenhage, 1949.
  (ed.) *Nederlandsche-Indië onder Japanese Bezetting*, Franeker, 1960.
Gullick, J. M. *Indigenous Political Systems of Western Malaya*, London, 1958. Reprinted as paperback in London School of Economics Monographs on Social Anthropology, No. 17, 1965.
  A History of Selangor, 1742–1957, Singapore, 1960.
  Malaya, New York, London, 1963.
  Malayan Pioneers, Singapore, 1958.
  The Story of Early Kuala Lumpur, Singapore, 1956.
Haan, F. de. *Priangan*. 4 vols. Batavia, 1910–11.
  Oud Batavia, Bandung. 1935.
  Nederlanders over de zeeën, Utrecht, 1940.
Hall, D. G. E. 'From Mergui to Singapore, 1686–1819', *JSS*, xli, no. 1 (July 1953), pp. 1–18.
  'Problems of Indonesian Historiography' in *Pacific Affairs*, vol. xxxviii, 3 and 4, 1965–6.
Hanna, W. A. *Sequel to Colonialism: the 1957–60 Foundation for Malaysia*, New York, 1965.
  The Formation of Malaysia: new factor in world politics (based on a series of reports written for the American Universities Field Staff), 1964.
Helsdingen, W. H. van (*et al.*). *Mission Interrupted* (English translation by J. J. L. Duyvendak), Amsterdam, Elsevier, 1945.

Higgins, Benjamin. *Indonesia's Economic Stablization and Development*, New York, 1957.

Holt, Claire. *Art in Indonesia: Continuities and Change*, Ithaca, N.Y., 1967.

Hurgronje, C. S. *De Atjehers*. 2 vols. Leiden, 1893–4. (English ed. *The Archinese*. 2 vols. London, 1906.)

Irwin, Graham. *Nineteenth-Century Borneo, a Study in Diplomatic Rivalry*, 's-Gravenhage, 1955.

Jessy, Joginder Singh. *History of Malaya (1400–1959)*, Penang, 1961.

Johns, A. H. 'Malay Sufism'. *JRASMB*, Singapore, 1957.

Jones, S. W. *Public Administration in Malaya*, London and New York, 1953.

Josselin de Jong, P. E. de. *Minangkabau and Negri Sembilan; socio-political structure in Indonesia*, Djakarta, 1960.

Kaberry, Phyllis. *The Development of Self-Government in Malaya*. Roy. Inst. of Int. Affairs. London, 1946.

Kahin, G. McT. *Nationalism and Revolution in Indonesia*, Ithaca, N.Y., 1952.

Kat Angelino, A. D. A. de. *Colonial Policy*: abridged trans. of *Staatskundig Beleid en Bestuurszorg in Ned. Indië* by G. J. Renier. 2 vols. The Hague, 1931.

Kats, J. *Het Javaansch Tooneel: I Wajang Poerwa*, Weltevreden, 1923.

Kennedy, J. *A History of Malaya*, London, 1962.

Kennedy, R. *The Ageless Indies*, New York, 1942.

Kern, J. H. C. *Verspreide Geschriften*. 15 vols. The Hague, 1913–28.

Klavern, J. J. van. *The Dutch Colonial System in the East Indies*, The Hague, 1953.

Klerck, E. S. de. *History of the Netherlands East Indies*. 2 vols. Rotterdam, 1938.

De Atjeh Oorlog, The Hague, 1912.

Leeuw, W. J. A. de. *Het Painansch Contract*, Amsterdam, 1926.

Legge, J. D. *Indonesia*, New Jersey, 1964.

Leur, J. C. van. *Indonesian Trade and Society, Essays in Asian Social and Economic History*, The Hague, 1955.

Linehan, W. 'A History of Pahang', *JRASMB*, vol. xiv, pt. 2 (1936).

Louw, P. F. J., and Klerck, E. S. de. *De Java Oorlog van 1825 to 1830*. 6 vols. Batavia–The Hague, 1894–6.

Macfadyen, Sir Eric (ed.). *The History of Rubber Regulation, 1934–43*, London, 1944.

MacGregor, I. A. 'Notes on the Portuguese in Malaya', *JRASMB*, xxviii (May 1955), pp. 5–41.

(et al.). *Papers on Johne Lama and the Portuguese in Malaya, 1511–1641*, London, 1957.

McKie, Ronald. *Malaysia in Focus*, London, 1963.

The Emergence of Malaysia, New York, 1963.

McLarty, F. M. *Affairs of the Colony, Being a History concerning the Straits Settlements and the British Protected States of the Malay Peninsula*, Penang, 1893.

McVey, Ruth T. (ed.). *Indonesia*, Yale Univ., South-East Asia Studies, New Haven, HRAF Press, 1963.
  The Rise of Indonesian Communism, Ithaca, Cornell Univ. Press, 1965.
Makepeace, W., Brooke, G. E., and Braddell, R. St. J. *One Hundred Years of Singapore*, London, 1921.
Mansvelt, W. M. *Rechtsvorm en Geldelijk Beheer Bij de Oostindsche Compagnie*, Amsterdam, 1922.
  A Brief History of the Netherlands Trading Society, 1824–1924, The Hague, 1924.
Marks, Harry J. *The First Contest for Singapore, 1819–24*, 's-Gravenhage, 1959.
Marsden, W. *History of Sumatra*, London, 1811. (Reprinted Kuala Lumpur, 1966.)
Masselman, G. *The Cradle of Colonialism*, New Haven, 1963.
Meilink-Roelofsz, M. A. P. *Asian Trade and European Influence in the Indonesian Archipelago between 1500 and about 1630*, The Hague, 1962.
Miller, Harry. *Short History of Malaysia*, New York, 1966.
Mills, L. A. *British Rule in Eastern Asia*, London, 1942.
  British Malaya, 1824–1867, Singapore, 1925.
  Malaya, a Political and Economic Appraisal, London and Minneapolis, 1958.
Mills, L. A. *British Malaya, 1824–67*. (Edited for reprinting, with a bibliography by C. M. Turnbull and with a new introductory chapter on European influence in the Malay Peninsula, 1511–1786, by D. K. Bassett.) Singapore, 1961 (*JRASMB*, vol. xxxiii, pt. 3, 1960).
Mintz, Jeanne S. *Mohammed, Marx and Marhaen: the Roots of Indonesian Socialism*, New York, 1965.
Mollema, J. C. *De Eerst Schipvaart der Hollanders Naar Oost Indië, 1595–1597*, The Hague, 1935.
Molsbergen, E. C. Godée. *Geschiedkundige Atlas van Nederland*, 's-Gravenhage, 1938.
Mook, H. J. van. *De Organizatie van de Indische Regeering*, Batavia, 1932.
  The Stakes of Democracy in South-East Asia, London, 1950.
Moorhead, F. J. *A History of Malaya and her Neighbours*, vol. i, London, 1957; vol. ii, Kuala Lumpur, 1963.
Mooy, J. *Geschiedenis der Protestantsche Kerk in Nederlandsch Indië*, Batavia, 1923–31.
Morrison, Ian. *Malayan Postscript*, London, 1942.
Mundy, Capt. Rodney, R.N. *Narrative of Events in Borneo and the Celebes down to the occupation of Labuan, from the Journals of James Brook Esq., together with the operations of H.M.S. 'Iris'*. 2 vols. London, 1848.
Newbold, Capt. T. J. *Political and Statistical Account of the British Settlements in the Straits of Malacca, etc.* 2 vols. London, 1939.
Niel, Robert van. *The Emergence of the Modern Indonesian Elite*, The Hague, and Chicago, 1960.

Norman, H. D. Levyssohn. *De Britische Heerschappij over Java en Onder-hoorigheden (1811–1816)*, The Hague, 1857.

Palmier, L. *Indonesia and the Dutch*, London, 1961.

Indonesia, London, 1965.

Parkinson, C. Northcote. *British Intervention in Malaya, 1867–77*, Singapore, 1960.

Parmer, J. Norman. *Colonial Labor Policy and Administration: A History of Labor in the Rubber Plantation Industry in Malaya, 1910–41*, New York, 1960.

Pearson, H. F. *Singapore, a popular History, 1819–1960*, Singapore, 1961.

Peet, G. L. *Political Questions in Malaya*, London, 1949.

Percival, Lieut.-Gen. A. *The War In Malaya*, London, 1949.

Pierson, N. G. *Het Cultuurstelsel*, Amsterdam, 1868.

Pluvier, J. M. *Oversicht van de Ontwikkeling der Nationale Beweging in Indonesië*, The Hague, 1953.

Confrontations, A Study of Indonesian Politics, New York, 1965.

Purcell, Victor. *The Chinese in Malaya*, London, 1948.

Malaya: Communist or Free? Stanford, 1954.

Malaysia, London, 1965.

Raffles, Sir Stamford. *History of Java*. 3 vols. London, 1817, 1830. New ed. with introduction by J. S. Bastin. 2 vols. Oxford in Asia Historical Reprints, 1965.

Rengers, D. W. van Welderen. *The Failure of a Liberal Colonial Policy: Netherlands East Indies, 1816–30*, The Hague, 1947.

Reus, G. C. Klerk de. *Geschichtlicher Ueberblick der Administrativen, Recht-lichen und Finanziellen Entwicklung der Niederländischen Ostindischen Compagnie*, Batavia, 1894.

Robequain, C. *Malaya, Indonesia, Borneo and the Philippines, London, 1954*.

Robinson, J. B. Perry. *Transformation in Malaya*, London, 1956.

Runciman, The Hon. Sir Steven. *The White Rajahs, a History of Sarawak from 1841 to 1946*, Cambridge Univ. Press, 1960.

Rutter, Owen. *British North Borneo*, London, 1922.

Ryan, N. J. *Malaya through four centuries: An Anthology, 1500–1900*, London, 1959.

The Making of Modern Malaya; a history from the earliest times to the present, Kuala Lumpur, 1963.

St. John, H. R. *The Indian Archipelago. Its History and present state*. 2 vols. London, 1853.

Schrieke, B. J. (ed.). *The Effect of Western Influence on Native Civilization*, Weltevreden, 1929.

Indonesian Sociological Studies: selected writings, pt. 1, The Hague, 1955; pt. 2: *Ruler and Realm in Early Java*, The Hague, 1957.

Silcock, T. H. (ed.). *The Political Economy of Independent Malaya*, Berkeley, Los Angeles, Canberra, 1963.

(ed.). *Readings in Malayan Economics*, Singapore, 1961.

Smit, C. *De Liquidatie van een Imperium, Neederland en Indonesië, 1945-1962*, Amsterdam, 1962.

Smith, T. E. *Population Growth in Malaya: A Survey of Recent Trends*, London, 1951.

Soedjatmoko. *An Approach to Indonesian History: Towards an Open Future*, Ithaca, N.Y., 1960.

Soedjatmoko and others (eds). *An Introduction to Indonesian Historiography*, Ithaca, N.Y., 1965.

Soest, G. H. van. *Geschiedenis van het Kultuurstelsel*. 3 vols. Rotterdam, 1869-71.

Somer, J. M. *De Korte Verklaring*, Breda, 1934.

Song Ong Siang. *One Hundred Years of the Chinese in Singapore*, London, 1923.

Stapel, F. W. (ed.). *Geschiedenis van Nederlandsch-Indië*. 5 vols. Amsterdam, 1939.

(author). *Geschiedenis van Nederlandsch-Indië*, Amsterdam, 1930, 1943.

Swettenham, Sir Frank. *British Malaya*, London, 1948 (1st pub. 1906).
Footprints in Malaya, 1942.

Tarling, Nicholas. 'British Policy in the Malay Peninsula and Archipelago, 1824-71'. *JRASMB*. Singapore, 1957.
Anglo-Dutch Rivalry in the Malay World, Cambridge, 1962.
Piracy and Politics in the Malay World, Melbourne, 1963.

Teixeira, Manuel. *The Portuguese Missions in Malacca and Singapore, 1511-1958*. 3 vols. Lisbon, 1961-3.

Ter Haar, B. *Adat Law in Indonesia*, New York, 1948.

Terpstra, H. 'De Factorij der Oostindische Compagnie te Patani', *Verhandelingen van het Kon. Inst.*, i. 's-Gravenhage. 1938.
'De Nederlandsche Voorcompagnieen', in F. W. Stapel, *Geschiedenis van Nederlansch Indië*, Deel II, D. Amsterdam, 1938.
'Franschen en Engelschen', *ibid.*, Deel II, C. Amsterdam, 1938.

Thompson, V. *Postmortem on Malaya*, New York, 1943.

Tilman, R. O. *Bureaucratic Transition in Malaya*, Durham, N.C., 1964.

Tregonning, K. G. *Under Chartered Company Rule, North Borneo 1881-1946*, Singapore, 1958.
A History of Modern Malaya, Singapore, 1964.
Malaysia, Melbourne, 1964.
The British in Malaya, the first Forty Years, 1786-1826, Univ. of Arizona Press, 1965.
Papers on Malayan History (First International Conference of South-East Asian Historians), Singapore, 1962.
(ed.). *Malaysian Historical Sources*, Singapore, 1962.

Valentijn, F. *Oud en Nieuw Oost Indiën*, Dordrecht–Amsterdam, 1724-6.

Vandenbosch, A. *The Dutch East Indies*, California, 1944.

Van der Kroef, Justus M. *The Dialectic of Colonial Indonesian History*, Amsterdam, 1963.

Indonesia in the Modern World. 2 pts: Bandung, 1954 and 1956.

The Communist Party of Indonesia, Vancouver, 1965.

Verboeket, K. 'Geschiedenis van de Chineezen in Nederlandsch-Indië', *Kolonial Studien,* Nos 5 and 6 (1936).

Vermeulen, J. Th. *De Chineezen te Batavia en den Troebelen van 1740,* Leiden, 1938.

Veth, J. P. *Java, Geographisch, Ethnologisch, Historisch.* 4 vols. Haarlem, 1912.

Atchin en zijne betrekkingen tot Nederland, Leiden, 1873.

Vlekke, B. H. M. *Nusantara: A History of the East Indian Archipelago,* Cambridge, Mass., 1943. New Revised edition, The Hague and Bandung, 1959.

Vreede-de Stuers, Cora. *De Hindoe-Maatschappij in Beweging.* Sociologisch-Historisch Seminarium voor Zuidoost Azië, Universiteit van Amsterdam, 1962.

Wagner, Frits, A. *Indonesia, the Art of an Island Group.* Art of the World Series (Methuen), vol. ii. London, 1959.

Wang Gungwu (ed.). *Malaysia: A Survey,* London, 1964.

Wavell, Stewart. *The Naga King's Daughter,* London, 1964.

Wehl, David. *The Birth of Indonesia,* London, 1948.

Wertheim, W. F. *Effects of Western Civilisation on Indonesian Society,* Inst. of Pacific Relations, New York, 1950.

Indonesian Society in Transition: A Study of Social Change, New York and The Hague, 1956. 2nd rev. ed., 1959.

Wilde, de Neytzell, and Moll, J. Th. *The Netherlands Indies during the Depression.* Amsterdam, 1936.

Wilkinson, R. J. *History of the Peninsular Malays.* 3rd ed., Singapore, 1923.

'The Malacca Sultanate', *JRASMB,* xiii (1935), pt. 2.

Winstedt, Sir Richard. 'A History of Johore', *JRASMB,* x, pt. 3 (Dec. 1932).

The Malays: A Cultural History, London, 1950.

History of Malaya, Singapore, 1935. Rev. and enlarged ed., Singapore, 1962.

Malaya and its History, London, 1948; 6th ed., 1962.

The Malay Magician, being Shaman, Saiva and Sufi. Rev. and enlarged. London, 1961.

'A History of Johore', *JRASMB,* vol. x, pt. 3 (1932).

'A History of Selangor', *JRASMB,* vol. xii, pt. 3 (1934).

'Negri Sembilan, the History, Policy and Beliefs of the Nine States', *JRASMB,* vol. xii, pt. 3 (1934).

'Notes on the History of Kedah', *JRASMB,* vol. xiv, pt. 3 (1936).

Winstedt, Sir R., and Wilkinson, K. J. 'A History of Perak', *JRASMB,* vol. xii, pt. 1 (1934).

Wolf, C. *The Indonesian Story: the Birth, Growth and Structure of the Indonesian Republic,* New York, 1948.

Wong Lin Ken. *The Malayan Tin Industry to 1914, with special reference to the States of Perak, Selangor, Negri Sembilan and Pahang*. Univ. of Arizona Press, 1965.

Woodman, Dorothy. *The Republic of Indonesia*, London, 1955.

Wormser, C. W. (ed.). *Wat Indië Ontving en Schonk*, Wereldbibliotheek, Amsterdam, 1946.

Wright, A., and Reid, T. H. *The Malay Peninsula*, London, 1912.

Wright, A. (ed.). *Twentieth Century Impressions of Netherlands India: Its History, People, Commerce, Industries and Resources*, London, 1909.

Wright, H. R. C. *The Moluccan Spice Monopoly, 1770–1824*, Kuala Lumpur, 1961.

East-Indian Economic Problems of the Age of Cornwallis and Raffles, London, 1961.

Yao Tung. *History of Overseas Chinese in Malaya* (in Chinese), Chungking, 1943.

VIII. THAILAND

Anderson, J. *English Intercourse with Siam in the Seventeenth Century*, London, 1890.

Blanchard, Wendell (*et al.*). *Thailand; Its People, Its Society, Its Culture*, New Haven, HRAF, 1958.

Bouvet, Joachin. *Voiage de Siam du Père Bouvet* (with introduction, biography and bibliography of Bouvet by J. C. Gatty), Leiden, 1963.

Briggs, L. P. 'Treaty of March 23, 1907, between France and Siam and the Return of Battambang and Angkor to Cambodia', *FEQ*, v (1946), pp. 439–54.

'Dvaravati—Most Ancient Kingdom of Siam', *J. Am. Or. Soc.* (1945), pp. 98–107.

'Aubaret and the Treaty of July 15, 1867, between France and Siam', *FEQ*, vi (1947), pp. 212–38.

Busch, N. F. *Thailand: an Introduction to Modern Siam*, Princeton, N.J., 1959; 2nd ed., 1964.

Campbell, J. G. D. *Siam in the Twentieth Century: Being the Experiences and Impressions of a British Official*, London, 1902.

Cartwright, B. O. *English Trans. of Turpin's History of Siam*, Bangkok, 1909.

Chakrabongse, Prince Chula. *Lords of Life*, London, 1960.

Christian, J. L., and Nobutake Ike. 'Thailand in Japan's Foreign Relations', *Pacific Affairs*, xv (1942), pp. 195–221.

Collis, M. *Siamese White*, London, 1936.

Crosby, Sir Josiah. *Siam: the Crossroads*, London, 1945.

Damrong, Prince. 'Siamese History prior to the Founding of Ayuddhya', *JSS*, xiii, pt. 2 (1919), pp. 1–66.

Miscellaneous Articles written for the Journal of the Siam Society, Bangkok, 1962.

Deslandes, M. *Histoire de Monsieur Constance*, Amsterdam, 1756.

Dhani Nivat, Prince. 'The Reconstruction of Rama I, of the Chakri Dynasty', *JSS*, xliii (1955).

Drans, J., and Bernard, S. (eds). *Mémoire du Père de Bèze sur la vie de Constance Phaulkon, premier ministre du roi de Siam, Phra Narai, et sa triste fin*, Tokyo, 1947.

Duke, Pensri Suvarij. *Les Relations entre la France et la Thailande (Siam) au XIXe siècle, d'après les archives des affaires étrangères*, Bangkok, 1962.

Fistie, Pierre. *La Thailande* (Collection Que Sais-je?), Paris, 1963.

Fitzsimmons, Thomas. *Thailand*, New Haven, HRAF, 1957.

Gervaise, N. *Histoire Naturelle et Politique du Royaume de Siam*, Paris, 1688. (English tr. by H. S. O'Neil, Bangkok, 1929.)

Graham, W. A. *Siam*. 2 vols. London, 1924.

Guehler, U. 'The Travels of Ludovico di Varthema, and his Visit to Siam, Banghella and Pegu A.D. 1505', *JSS*, xxxvi, pt. 2 (1947), pp. 113–49.

Hoontrakul, Likhit. *The History of Siamese-Chinese Relations*, Bangkok, 1953.

Hutchinson, E. W. *Adventures in Siam in the Seventeenth Century*, London, 1940.

Ingram, James C. *Economic Change in Thailand since 1850*, Stanford, 1955.

Insor, D. *Thailand, a Political, Social and Economic Analysis*, New York and London, 1963.

Kruger, Rayne. *The Devil's Discus*, London, 1964.

Landon, K. P. *The Chinese in Thailand*, New York, 1941.

  Siam in Transition, Shanghai, 1939. (Pirated ed. *Thailand in Transition*, Bangkok, 1945.)

Lanier, L. *Étude Historique sur les Relations de la France et du Royaume de Siam de 1662 à 1703 d'après les Documents Inédits des Archives du Ministère de la Marine et des Colonies*, Versailles, 1883.

Launay, A. *Histoire de la Mission du Siam, 1662–1811*. 2 vols. Paris, 1920.

Le May, R. *A Concise History of Buddhist Art in Siam*, Cambridge, 1938.

  An Asian Arcady: The Land and Peoples of Northern Siam, Cambridge and New York, 1926.

LeMire, C. *La France et le Siam, nos Relations de 1662 à 1903*, Angers and Paris, 1903.

  Exposé Chronologique des Relations du Cambodge avec le Siam, l'Annam et la France, Paris, 1879.

Leonowens, Anna. *The English Governess at the Siamese Court*, Boston, Mass., 1870; London, 1954.

Loftus, A. J. *The Kingdom of Siam: Its Progress and Prospects*, London, 1891.

Luang Nathabanga. *Extraterritoriality in Siam*, Bangkok, 1924.

Notton, C. *Annales de Siam*. 4 vols. Paris, 1926–32, vol. iv, Bangkok, 1939.

Nuechterlein, D. E. *Thailand and the Struggle for South-East Asia*, Ithaca, N.Y., 1965.

Rajadhon, Phya Anuman. *Life and Ritual in Old Siam: Three Studies of Thai Life and Customs*. (Tr. and ed. W. Gedney.) New Haven, HRAF, 1961.

Reeve, W. D. *Public Administration in Siam*, London, 1952.

Riggs, F. W. *Thailand: the Modernization of a Bureaucratic Policy*, Honolulu, 1965.

Robert-Martignan, L. *La Monarchie Absolue Siamoise de 1350–1926*, Paris, 1939.

Sakae Miki. *The Exploits of Okya Senaphimocq; Yamada Nagamasa the Japanese General in Siam in the Seventeenth Century*, Tokyo, 1931.

Sayre, F. *The Passing of Extraterritoriality in Siam*, New York, 1929.

Seidenfaden, E. *The Thai Peoples*, Bangkok, 1958.

Siam Society. *Selected Articles from the JSS*, Bangkok, 1959 (including, vol. iii, *Early History and Ayudhya Period*; vol. iv, *Lopburi, Bangkok, Bhuket*; vols v and vi, *Relationships with Burma*; vol. vii, *Relationships with Portugal, Holland and the Vatican*; vol. viii, *Relationships with France, England and Denmark*.

Siffin, W. J. *Thai Bureaucracy: Institutional Change and Development*, Honolulu, 1966.

Skinner, G. W. *Chinese Society in Thailand: An Analytical History*. Ithaca, N.Y., 1957.

Smith, M. *A Physician at the Court of Siam*, London, 1946.

Smith, Samuel. *History of Siam, 1657–1767*, Bangkok, 1880–1.

Thompson, V. *Thailand, the New Siam*, New York, 1941.

Vella, Walter F. *Siam under Rama III, 1824–51*, New York, 1957.

The Impact of the West on the Government of Siam, Berkeley, Calif., 1955.

Wales, H. G. Quaritch. *Ancient Siamese Government and Administration*, London, 1934. (Reprint, New York, 1965.)

Siamese State Ceremonies: their History and Function, London, 1931.

Wells, K. E. *Thai Buddhism: Its Rites and Activities*, Bangkok, 1939.

History of Protestant Work in Thailand. 1828–1958, Bangkok, 1958.

Wilson, David A. *Politics in Thailand*, Ithaca, N.Y., 1962.

Wood, W. A. R. *History of Siam*, London, 1926.

Wyatt, D. K. 'Siam and Laos, 1767–1827', *Journal of South-East Asian History*, 4, no. 2 (Sept. 1963), pp. 13–32.

Young, John E. de. *Village Life in Modern Thailand*, Berkeley and Los Angeles, 1955.

Zimmermann, C. C. *Siam, Rural Economic Survey*, Bangkok, 1931.

IX. The Philippines

(a) works in spanish

Aduarte, Diego. *Historia de la provincia del Sancto Rosario de la Orden de Predicadores, en Philippinas, Japan, y China*, Manila, 1640.

Chirino, Pedro. *Relación de las islas Filipinas*, Rome, 1604.

Combes, F. (ed. W. E. Retana). *Historia de Mindanao y Joló*, Madrid, 1897.

Delgado, Juan, J. *Historia general sacro-profana, política y natural de las islas del poniente Llamadas Filipinas*, Manila, 1892.

Diaz, Casimiro. *Parrocho de Indios instruido*, Manila, 1745.

Hanke, L., and Carlo, A. Millares. *Cuerpo de documentos del siglo XVI sobre los derechos de España en las Indias y las Filipinas*, Mexico, 1943.

Juan de la Concepción. *Historia general de Filipinas*. 14 vols. Sampaloe, 1788–92.

Morga, Antonia de (ed. W. E. Retana). *Sucesos de las Islas Filipinas, Mexico, 1609*. Madrid, 1909.

Pastells, Pablo. *Labor Evangélica de los obreros de la Compañia de Jesús en las islas Filipinas por el Padre Francisco Colin de la misma compañia*. 3 vols. Barcelona, 1900–3.

Retana, W. E. *Archivo del Bibliofilo Filipina*. 5 vols. Madrid, 1895–1905.
Aparato bibliográfico de la Historia general de Filipinas. 3 vols. Madrid, 1906.
Vida y escritos del Dr. José Rizal, Madrid, 1907.

San Agustín, Gaspar de. *Conquistas de las Islas Filipinas*, Madrid, 1616.

Saniel, J. M. *Japan and the Philippines, 1868–1898*, Quezon City, 1962.

Vidal, D. José Monteroy. *Historia general de Filipinas desde el discubrimiento hasta nuestros días*. 3 vols. Madrid, 1889–95.
Historia de la pirateria malaya-mahometano en Mindanaó, Joló y Borneo, Madrid, 1888.

Zúñiga, J. Martinez de. *Historia de las islas Filipinas*, Sampaloe, 1803.

IX. THE PHILIPPINES

(b) WORKS IN ENGLISH (AND OTHER LANGUAGES)

Agoncillo, Teodora A. *Philippine History*, Manila, 1962.

Aguinaldo, E., and Pacis, V. A. *A Second Look at America*, New York, 1957.

Alip, Eufonio, M. *A Brief History of the Philippines*, Manila, 1963.

Benitez, Conrado. *History of the Philippines, Social, Political*, Boston, 1940.

Bernstein, David. *The Philippine Story*, New York, 1947.

Blair, E. H., and Robertson, J. A. (eds). *The Philippine Islands, 1493–1898*. 55 vols. Cleveland, U.S.A., 1905.

Boxer, C. R. 'Some Aspects of Spanish Historical Writing in the Philippines', in D. G. E. Hall (ed.), *Historians of South-East Asia*, London, 1961.

Buenafe, Manuel. *Wartime Philippines*, Manila, 1950.

Costa, H. de la. *The Jesuits in the Philippines, 1581–1768*, Cambridge, Mass., 1961.
The Trial of Rizal; W. E. Retana's transcription of the official Spanish documents, edited and translated with notes, Manila, 1961.
(ed.). *Readings in Philippine History, selected historical texts*, Manila, 1965.

Cunningham, Charles, H. *The Audiencia in the Spanish Colonies, as illustrated by the Audiencia of Manila*, Berkeley, Calif., 1919.

Eggan, Fred. (*et al.*). *Area Handbook on the Philippines*. 4 vols. New Haven, HRAF, 1956.

Forbes, W. Cameron. *The Philippine Islands*, Cambridge, Mass., 1945.

Golay, Frank H. *The Philippines: Public Policy and National Economic Development*, Cornell Univ. Press, Ithaca, N.Y., 1961.

Greindl, Léopold. *A la Recherche d'un État Indépendant: Leopold II et les Philippines, 1869–75*, Brussels, 1962.

Grunden, Gazel A., and Livezey, W. *The Philippines and the United States*, Norman, Univ. of Oklahoma Press, 1951.

Hayden, J. Ralston. *The Philippines: A Study in National Development*, New York, 1942.

Kalaw, T. M. *The Philippine Revolution*, Manila, 1925.

Keesing, F. M. *The Philippines: a nation in the making*, Shanghai, 1937.

Kirk, Grayson. *Philippine Independence*, New York, 1936.

Kolb, Albert. *Die Philippen*, Leipzig, 1942.

Liang, Dapen. *The Development of Philippine Political Parties*, Hong Kong, 1939.

McHale, T. R., and M. C. (eds). *Early American-Philippine Trade: the Journal of Nathaniel Bowditch in Manila, 1796*, Yale Univ. South-East. Asia Studies, 1962.

Majul, C. A. *The Political and Constitutional Ideas of the Philippine Revolution*, Quezon City, Philippines, 1957.

Malcom, G. A. *First Malayan Republic: The Story of the Philippines*, Boston, 1951.

Palma, Rafael. *The Pride of the Malay Race*, New York, 1949.

Phelan, J. L. *The Hispanization of the Philippines: Spanish Aims and Filipino Responses, 1565–1700*, Madison, U.S.A., 1959.

Quirino, Carlos. *Magsaysay of the Philippines*, Quezon City, 1958.

Rizal, José. *Noli Me Tangere* (English version), Manila, 1956.

Rizal, José. *The Lost Eden* (Noli-me-tangere). A new translation for the contemporary reader by León Ma. Guerrero, Indiana Univ. Press. 1961.

Schurz, W. L. *The Manilla Galleon*, New York, 1939. Reprint, 1959.

Smith, Robert A. *Philippine Freedom*, New York, 1958.

Spencer, J. E. *Land and People in the Philippines*, Berkeley, 1954.

Willoquet, Gaston. *Histoire des Philippines* (Collection Que Sais-je?), Paris, 1961.

Worcester, Dean C., and Hayden, R. *The Philippine Islands, Past and Present*, New York, 1930.

Zaide, Gregorio F. *Philippine Political and Cultural History*. 2 vols. Manila. Revised ed., 1957.

The Republic of the Philippines: History, Government and Civilization, Manila, 1963.

X. BIOGRAPHY

Boudet, P. *Un Voyageur Philosophe, Pierre Poivre en Annam (1749–50)*, Hanoi, 1941.

Boulger, D. C. *Sir Stamford Raffles*, London, 1897.

Boxer, C. R. *Three Historians of Portuguese Asia : Barros, Couto and Bocarro*, Hong Kong, 1948.

Butwell, R. A. *U Nu of Burma*, Stanford, California, 1963.

Cheng Hao-sheng. *Cheng Ho I Shih Hui Pien* (Life of Cheng Ho), Shanghai, 1948.

Clodd, H. P. *Malaya's First British Pioneer : The Life of Francis Light*, London, 1948.

Coen, Jan Pietersz. (Biography of.) Vol. vi of H. T. Colenbrander, and W. Ph. Coolhaas, *Jan Pietersz. Coen : Bescheiden omtrent zijn Bedrijf in Indië*, The Hague, 1934.

Collis, M. *Siamese White*, London, 1936, 1940.

The Grand Peregrination : being the Life and Adventures of Fernão Mendes Pinto, London, 1949.

Coupland, Sir Reginald. *Raffles of Singapore*, London, 1946.

Craig, Austin. *Lineage, Life, and Labours of José Rizal, Philippine Patriot*, Manila, 1913.

Dubois, P. H. (*et al.*). *Essays over Multatuli : 100 Jaar Max Havelaar*, Rotterdam, 1962.

Dupont de Nemours: 'Notice sur la vie de M. Poivre (avec une introduction et des notes par Louis Malleret)', *BSEI* (1932), no. 3, pp. 13–62.

Duyvendak, J. J. L. *Ma Huan Re-examined*, Amsterdam, 1933.

Egerton, H. E. *Sir Stamford Raffles*, London, 1900.

Faure, A. *Les Français en Cochinchine au XVIIIᵉ siècle : Mgr. Pigneau de Behaine évêque d'Adran*, Paris, 1891.

Freitas, J. A. de. *Subsidios para . . . a biographia de Fernão Mendes Pinto*, Coimbra, 1905.

Fernão Mendes Pinto, sua ultima viagem a China, 1554–1555 etc., Lisbon, 1905.

Gagelonia, Pedro A. *Man of the Century : Biography of José Rizal*, Manila, 1964.

Gaultier, M. *Gia-Long*, Saigon 1933.

Minh-Mang, Paris, 1935.

Gobius, J. F. *Nieuw Nederlandsch Biographisch Woordenboek*. 10 vols. Leiden, 1910.

Gruyter, J. de. *Het Leven en Werken van Ed. Douwes Dekker* (Multatuli). 2 vols. Amsterdam, 1920.

Hahn, Emily. *James Brooke of Sarawak*, London, 1953.

Raffles of Singapore, London, 1948.

Hall, Gordon L. *Golden Boats from Burma* (The Life of Ann Hasseltine Judson), Philadelphia, 1961.

Jackson, R. N. *Pickering, Protector of Chinese*, Kuala Lumpur, 1965.

Jacob, G. L. *The Rajah of Sarawak*. 2 vols. London, 1876.

Judson, E. *Adoniram Judson, D.D., His Life and Labours*, London, 1883.

Knowles, J. D. *Memoir of Mrs. Ann H. Judson . . . including a History of the American Baptist Mission in the Burman Empire*, London, 1829.

Lee-Warner, Sir W. *The Life of the Marquis of Dalhousie, K.T.* 2 vols. London, 1904.

Louvet, L. E. *Monseigneur d'Adran. Notice Biographique.* Saigon, 1896.

Lucena, J. *Historia da Vida do Padre Francisco de Xavier*, Lisbon, 1960.

Lyall, Sir A. *Life of the Marquess of Dufferin and Ava.* 2 vols. London, 1905.

Maung Maung (ed.). *Aung San of Burma*, The Hague, 1962.

Maung Maung Tin. *Life of Kinwun Mingyi*, Rangoon, 1936.

Moffat, Abbot Low. *Mongkut, the King of Siam*, Ithaca, N.Y., 1961.

Munier, P. *Gia-Long*, Hanoi, 1932.

D'Orleans, Père. *Histoire de M. Constance*, Paris, 1692.

Palma, Rafael. *Biografía de Rizal*, Manila, 1947.

Payne, R. *The White Rajas of Sarawak*, London, 1960.

Petit, E. *Francis Garnier, sa Vie, ses Voyages, ses Œuvres*, Paris, 1885.

Raffles, Lady. *Memoir of the Life and Public Service of Sir T. S. Raffles*, London, 1830.

Riley, J. H. *Ralph Fitch, England's Pioneer to India*, London, 1899.

Ritchie, A. I. *Lord Amherst and the British Advance Eastwards to Burma*, Oxford, 1909.

St. John, Sir Spenser. *The Life of James Brooke, Rajah of Sarawak.* 2 vols. Edinburgh and London, 1879; New York, 1899.

Saks, J. *Ed. Douwes Dekker: Zijn Jeugd en Indische Jaren*, Rotterdam, 1937.

Stapel, F. W. *Cornelis Jansz Speelman*, The Hague, 1936.
    Gouverneurs-Generaal van Nederlandsch-Indië, The Hague, 1941.

Stephens, H. M. *Albuquerque*, Oxford, 1912.

Vietnam Information Service. *Vietnam's President, Ho-Chi-Minh*, Paris, 1947.

Winstedt, Sir R. 'The Malay Founder of Mediaeval Malacca', *BSOAS*, xii (1948), pts 3 and 4. Univ. of London.

Wurzburg, C. E. *Raffles of the Eastern Isles*, London, 1954.

XI. General Works

Almond, G. A., and Coleman, J. S. (eds). *Politics of the Developing Areas*, Princeton, N.J., 1960.

Atlas of South-East Asia (with introduction by D. G. E. Hall), London, 1964.

Ba Shin *et al.* (ed.). *Essays offered to G. H. Luce in Honour of his Seventy-Fifth Birthday*, Ascona, 1966.

Barbosa, Duarte. *The Book of Duarte Barbosa, An Account of the Countries Bordering on the Indian Ocean and Their Inhabitants, A.D. 1518* (tr. M. L. Dames). 2 pts. Hakluyt Soc., 2nd ed., London, 1918, 1921.

Barros, J. de, and Couto, D. de. *Decadas da Asia.* 24 vols. Lisbon, 1718–88.

Beazley, Sir C. R. *The Dawn of Modern Geography.* 3 vols. London, 1897–1906.

Boxer, C. R. *The Dutch Seaborne Empire, 1600–1800*, London, 1965.
    Race Relations in the Portuguese Colonial Empire, 1415–1825, Oxford, 1963.

Brussels, Institut de Sociologie, Centre du Sud-Est Asiatique. *Aspects Actuels de la Situation Économique de L'Asie du Sud-Est*, Brussels, 1963.

Burling, R. *Hill Farms and Padi Fields—Life in Mainland South-East Asia*, New Jersey, 1965.

Buss, C. A. *Asia in the Modern World: A History of China, Japan, South and South-East Asia*, New York, 1964. (1st pub. 1955 as *The Far East*.)

Butwell, R. *South-East Asia Today, and Tomorrow*. Revised ed., New York, 1964.

Cady, John F. *South-East Asia: Its Historical Development*, New York, 1964. *Thailand, Burma, Laos and Cambodia*, New Jersey, 1966.

Cady, J. F., Barnett, P. G., and Jenkins, S. *The Development of Self-Rule and Independence in Burma, Malaya, and the Philippines*, New York, 1948.

Clifford, Sir Hugh. *Further India*, London, 1904.

Couto, D. de. *Da Asia*. 9 vols. Lisbon, 1778–88.

Cowan, C. D. (ed.). *The Economic Development of South-East Asia: Studies in Economic History and Political Economy*, London, 1964.

Danvers, F. C. *The Portuguese in India*. 2 vols. London, 1894. (Reprinted London, 1966.)

Daruvala, J. C. *Tensions of Economic Development in South-East Asia*, New York, 1963.

Dobby, E. H. G. *South-East Asia*, London, 1950. (8th ed., 1964.)

Dubois, Cora. *Social Forces in South-East Asia*. 2nd ed., Cambridge, Mass., 1959.

Eckel, P. E. *The Far East since 1500*, London, 1948.

Elegant, R. S. *The Dragon's Seed: Peking and the Overseas Chinese*, New York, 1959.

Elsbree, W. H. *Japan's Role in South-East Asian Nationalist Movements, 1940–1945*, Harvard, 1953.

Emerson, Rupert. *Representative Government in South-East Asia*, Cambridge, Mass., 1955.

Emerson, R., Mills, L. A., and Thompson, V. *Government and Nationalism in South-East Asia*, New York, 1942.

Faria Y. Sousa. *Asia Portugueza*. 3 vols. Lisbon, 1666–75.

Ferrand, G. *Instructions Nautiques et Routiers Arabes et Portugais des XVe et XVIe Siècles*. 3 vols. Paris, 1921–8.

Fifield, Russell H. *The Diplomacy of South-East Asia: 1945–58*, New York, 1958. *South-East Asia in United States Policy*, New York, 1963.

Fisher, C. A. *South-East Asia: a Social, Economic and Political Geography*, London and New York, 1964.

Fitzgerald, C. P. *The Third China, the Chinese Communities in South-East Asia*, Vancouver, 1963. *A Concise History of East Asia*, New York, 1966.

Foster, Sir W. *England's Quest of Eastern Trade*, Hakluyt Soc. London, 1933.

Furnivall, J. S. *Educational Progress in South-East Asia*, New York, 1943. *Progress and Welfare in South-East Asia*, New York, 1941.

Glamann, Kristof. *Dutch Asiatic Trade, 1620–1740*, Copenhagen and The Hague, 1958.

Grousset, R. *Histoire de l'Extrême-Orient.* 2 vols. Paris, 1929. *The Civilizations of the East.* 4 vols. London and New York, 1931–4. *De l'Inde au Cambodge et à Java*, Monaco, 1950.

Grousset, R., Auboyer, J., and Buhot, J. *L'Asie Orientale des origines au XVᵉ Siècle*, Paris, 1941.

Hall, D. G. E. 'South-East Asia and the Archipelago', in C. H. Philips (ed.), *A Handbook of Oriental History*, London, 1951
'Looking at South-East Asian History', *JAS*, Ann Arbor, Michigan, May 1960.
'On the Study of South-East Asian History', *Pacific Affairs.* Sept. 1960.
(ed.). *Historians of South-East Asia* (*Historical Writing on the Peoples of Asia*, vol. ii). London, 1961.
'International Conflicts in South-East Asia; an Historical Survey' (*Journal of the Oriental Society of Australia*, vol. iii, no. 2, Dec. 1965, pp. 27–38).

Hanna, W. A. *Eight Nation Makers: South-East Asia's Charismatic Statesmen*, New York, 1964.

Harlow, V. *The Founding of the Second British Empire*, London, 1952.

Harrison, Brian. *South-East Asia, a Short History*, London, 1954, 1963.

Heine-Geldern, R. von. *Conceptions of State and Kingship in South-East Asia.* Cornell University Data Paper, South-East Asia Program, 1956.

Henderson, W. (ed.). *South-East Asia; problems of U.S. Policy*, Cambridge, Mass., 1963.

Hsueh, S. S. (ed.). *Public Administration in South and South-East Asia*, Brussels, 1962.

Jacoby, E. H. *Agrarian Unrest in South-East Asia.* 2nd ed. rev. and enlarged New York, 1961.

Jayne, K. G. *Vasco da Gama and His Successors*, London, 1910.

Kahin, G. McT. (ed.). *Governments and Politics of South-East Asia*, Ithaca, N.Y., 1959. 2nd ed., 1964.
Major Governments of Asia, Ithaca, N.Y., 1958.

Kunstadter, P. (ed.). *South-East Asian Tribes, Minorities, and Nations.* 2 vols. Princeton, N.J., 1966.

Landon, K. P. *South-East Asia, Crossroad of Religions*, Chicago, 1949.

Lasker, Bruno. *Peoples of South-East Asia*, New York, 1944.

Launay, Adrien. *Mémorial de la Société des Missions Étrangères.* 2 vols. Paris, 1912–16.
Histoire Générale de la Société des Missions Étrangères depuis sa fondation jusqu'à nos jours. 3 vols. Paris, 1894 and 1920.

LeBar, Frank M. (*et al.*). *Ethnic Groups of Mainland South-East Asia*, New Haven, HRAF, 1964.

Le May, R. *The Culture of South-East Asia : The Heritage of India*, London, 1954.

Leroy-Beaulieu, P. *De la Colonisation chez Les Peuples Modernes*. 6th ed., Paris, 1908.

Mills, L. A. (ed.). *The New World of South-East Asia*, Minneapolis and London, 1949.

Mills, L. A. *South-East Asia : Illusion and Reality in Politics and Economics*, Minneapolis, 1964.

Morse, H. B. *Chronicles of the East India Company trading to China*. Vol. ii. London, 1926.

Panikkar, K. M. *Asia and Western Dominance*, London, 1953.

Parkinson, C. Northcote. *The Trade Winds*, London, 1948.
  Trade in the Eastern Seas, 1793–1813, New York, 1937.
  War in the Eastern Seas, 1793–1815, New York, 1954.

Pearn, B. R. *An Introduction to the History of South-East Asia*, Kuala Lumpur, 1963.

Pelzer, K. J. *Pioneer Settlement in the Asiatic Tropics*, New York, 1945.

Prestage, E. *The Portuguese Pioneers*, London, 1933.

Proceedings. International Congress of Orientalists, New Delhi, 1964.

Purcell, Victor. *The Chinese in South-East Asia*, London, 1951. 2nd rev. ed., Oxford Univ. Press, 1965.
  The Revolution in South-East Asia, London, 1962.
  South and East Asia since 1800, Cambridge, 1965.

Ribadeneyra, M. de. *Historia de las Islas Archipelago y Reynos de la Gran China, Tartaria, Cochin-Chine, Malacca, Siam, Camboxa y Japon*, Barcelona, 1591.

Rose, Saul. *Socialism in Southern Asia*, London, 1959.
  Britain and South-East Asia, London, 1962.

Sarkisyanz, E. *Südostasien seit 1945*, München, 1961.

Siguret, J. *Territoires et Populations des Confins du Yunnan*. 2 vols. Peking, 1937, 1940.

Silcock, T. H. *The Commonwealth Economy in South-East Asia*, Durham, N.C., 1959.

Soemarman. *Population Growth and Development in South-East Asia*, Center for International Affairs, Harvard, 1961.

Sottas, J. *Histoire de la Compagnie royale des Indes Orientales*, Paris, 1905.

Stamp, L. Dudley. *Asia : a regional and economic geography*. 9th ed., London, 1957.

Tarling, Nicholas. *A Concise History of South-East Asia*, New York, 1966.

Thayer, P. W. (ed.). *South-East Asia in the Coming World*, Baltimore, 1953.

Thompson, V. *Labour in South-East Asia*, Oxford, 1947.

Thompson, V., and Adolff, R. *The Left Wing in South-East Asia*, New York, 1950.
  Minority Problems in South-East Asia, Stanford, Calif., 1955.

Cultural Institutions and Educational Policy in South-East Asia. A Report. New York, 1948.

Thomson, J. O. *History of Ancient Geography*, Cambridge, 1948.

Trager, Frank N. (ed.). *Marxism in South-East Asia*, Stanford, Calif., 1958.

Vandenbosch, A., and Butwell, R. *South-East Asia among the World Powers*, Kentucky, 1957.

Vogel, J. Ph. *The Contribution of the University of Leiden to Oriental Research*, Leiden, 1954.

Von der Mehden, Fred R. *Religion and Nationalism in South-East Asia (Burma, Indonesia, The Philippines)*, Madison, Wisc., 1963.

Wales, H. G. Quaritch. *Ancient South-East Asian Warfare*, London, 1952.

Wickizer, V. D., and Bennett, M. K. *The Rice Economy of Monsoon Asia*, San Francisco, 1941.

Williamson, J. A. *The Ocean in English History*, Oxford, 1941.

Wint, Guy (ed.). *Asia: a Handbook*, London, 1965.

Wong Shion-fi. *General History of South-East Asia* (in Chinese), Shanghai, 1920.

Wyatt, Woodrow. *Southwards from China, a survey of South-East Asia since 1945*, London, 1952.

Yule, H., and Burnell, A. C. (ed. William Crooke). *Hobson-Jobson: Glossary of Colloquial Anglo-Indian Words and Phrases . . .* , London, 1903.

INDEX